**IF FOUND, please notify and arrange return to owner**. This text is an important study guide for the owner's career and/or exam preparation.

Name: ______________________________

Address: ______________________________

City, State, ZIP: ______________________________

Telephone: (____) ______________ E-mail: ______________

Gleim Publications, Inc., offers five university-level study systems:

*Auditing & Systems Exam Questions and Explanations with Exam Prep Software*
*Business Law/Legal Studies Exam Questions and Explanations with Exam Prep Software*
*Federal Tax Exam Questions and Explanations with Exam Prep Software*
*Financial Accounting Exam Questions and Explanations with Exam Prep Software*
*Cost/Managerial Accounting Exam Questions and Explanations with Exam Prep Software*

The following is a list of Gleim examination review systems:

*CIA Review: Part I, Internal Audit Role in Governance, Risk, and Control*
*CIA Review: Part II, Conducting the Internal Audit Engagement*
*CIA Review: Part III, Business Analysis and Information Technology*
*CIA Review: Part IV, Business Management Skills*

*CMA Review: Part 1, Business Analysis*
*CMA Review: Part 2, Management Accounting and Reporting*
*CMA Review: Part 3, Strategic Management*
*CMA Review: Part 4, Business Applications*

*CPA Review: Financial*
*CPA Review: Auditing*
*CPA Review: Business*
*CPA Review: Regulation*

*EA Review: Part 1, Individuals*
*EA Review: Part 2, Sole Proprietorships and Partnerships*
*EA Review: Part 3, Corporations, Fiduciaries, Estate and Gift Tax, and Trusts*
*EA Review: Part 4, IRS Administration and Other Topics*

Order forms are provided at the back of this book or contact us at www.gleim.com or (800) 87-GLEIM.

All orders must be prepaid. Shipping and handling charges will be added to all orders. Library and company orders may be purchased on account. Add applicable sales tax to shipments within Florida. All payments must be in U.S. funds and payable on a U.S. bank. Please write or call for prices and availability of all foreign country shipments. Orders will usually be shipped the day your request is received. Allow 10 days for delivery in the United States. Please contact us if you do not receive your shipment within 2 weeks.

Gleim Publications, Inc. guarantees the immediate refund of all resalable texts and unopened software and audios purchased directly from Gleim Publications, Inc. if they are returned within 30 days. Shipping and handling charges are nonrefundable. Returns of books purchased from bookstores and other resellers should be made to the respective bookstore or reseller.

**Groundwood Paper and Highlighters** — All Gleim books are printed on high quality groundwood paper. We recommend you use a non-bleed-through (dry) highlighter (e.g., the Avery *Glidestick*™ -- ask for it at your local office supply store) when highlighting page items within these books.

## REVIEWERS AND CONTRIBUTORS

Garrett Gleim, B.S., University of Pennsylvania, is one of our vice presidents. Mr. Gleim coordinated the production staff, reviewed the manuscript, and provided production assistance throughout the project.

John F. Rebstock, CIA, B.S., Fisher School of Accounting, University of Florida, specializes in ensuring that our answer explanations and Knowledge Transfer Outlines are user-friendly. Mr. Rebstock reviewed portions of the manuscript.

## A PERSONAL THANKS

This manual would not have been possible without the extraordinary effort and dedication of Julie Cutlip, Teresa Soard, Polly Werner, and Heather Williams, who typed the entire manuscript and all revisions; and drafted, scanned, and laid out the diagrams and illustrations in this book.

The authors appreciate the proofreading and production assistance of Justin Ash, Clint Berg, Katharine Cicatelli, Richard Dellifraine, Emily Gorovsky, Seth Kaye, Jean Marzullo, Shane Rapp, Cara Richardson, and Sonia Santana.

The authors also appreciate the critical reading assistance of Scott Grubbs, Thomas McDuffie, and Erica Malinowski.

Finally, we appreciate the encouragement, support, and tolerance of our families throughout this project.

Twelfth Edition

# AUDITING & SYSTEMS

## Exam Questions and Explanations

by

**Irvin N. Gleim, Ph.D., CPA, CIA, CMA, CFM**

and

**William A. Hillison, Ph.D., CPA, CMA**

with the assistance of
Grady M. Irwin, J.D.

**ABOUT THE AUTHORS**

Irvin N. Gleim is Professor Emeritus in the Fisher School of Accounting at the University of Florida and is a member of the American Accounting Association, Academy of Legal Studies in Business, American Institute of Certified Public Accountants, Association of Government Accountants, Florida Institute of Certified Public Accountants, the Institute of Internal Auditors, and the Institute of Management Accountants. He has had articles published in the *Journal of Accountancy, The Accounting Review,* and *The American Business Law Journal* and is author/coauthor of numerous accounting and aviation books and CPE courses.

William A. Hillison is Professor of Accounting at Florida State University, where he holds the Andersen Chair. His primary teaching duties include graduate and undergraduate auditing and systems courses. He is a member of the Florida Institute of Certified Public Accountants, American Accounting Association, and Institute of Management Accountants. He has had articles published in many journals including the *Journal of Accounting Research*; the *Journal of Accounting Literature*; the *Journal of Accounting Education*; *Cost and Management*; *The Internal Auditor*; *Advances in Accounting*; the *Journal of Accountancy*; the *CPA Journal*; the *Journal of Accounting, Auditing, and Finance*; ABACUS; and *The Journal of Forecasting*.

**Gleim Publications, Inc.**
P.O. Box 12848
University Station
Gainesville, Florida 32604
(800) 87-GLEIM or (800) 874-5346
(352) 375-0772
FAX: (352) 375-6940
Internet: www.gleim.com
E-mail: admin@gleim.com

ISSN: 1092-4159
ISBN: 1-58194-429-2

This is the first printing of the twelfth edition of ***Auditing & Systems Exam Questions and Explanations***. Please e-mail update@gleim.com with AUD EQE 12-1 as the subject or text. You will receive our current update as a reply. Updates are available until the next edition is published.

EXAMPLE:

| | |
|---|---|
| To: | update@gleim.com |
| From: | your e-mail address |
| Subject: | AUD EQE 12-1 |


First Printing: July 2005



## ACKNOWLEDGMENTS

Material from Uniform Certified Public Accountant Examination questions and unofficial answers, Copyright © 1972-2002 by the American Institute of Certified Public Accountants, Inc., is reprinted and/or adapted with permission.

The authors also appreciate and thank the Information Systems Audit and Control Association for permission to use sample CISA questions from *Study Guide - Certified Information Systems Auditor*.

The authors also appreciate and thank the Institute for Certification of Computing Professionals for permission to use sample CDP questions from the CDP *Instruction Manual*.

The authors also appreciate and thank The Institute of Internal Auditors, Inc. for permission to use The Institute's Certified Internal Auditor Examination questions, Copyright © 1978-1997 by The Institute of Internal Auditors, Inc.

The authors also appreciate and thank the Institute of Certified Management Accountants for permission to use problem materials from past CMA examinations, Copyright © 1977-1996 by the Institute of Management Accountants.

The authors appreciate questions contributed by the following individuals: Lynn Bailey, David Bradley, John Brooks, George Fiebelkorn, D. Finkbiner, Jim Heian, Kenneth Macur, Deborah Pavelka, D. Payne, Ken Plucinski, Nathan Schmukler, C.J. Skender, James Swearingen, and Don Wells.

---

# PREFACE FOR ACCOUNTING STUDENTS

The purpose of this study manual is to help you learn and understand auditing and systems concepts and their application. In turn, these skills will enable you to perform better on your undergraduate examinations, as well as look ahead to the CDP, CIA, CISA, CMA, CFM, and CPA examinations.

One of the major benefits of this study manual is comprehensive coverage of auditing and systems topics. Accordingly, when you use this study manual to help prepare for auditing courses and examinations, you are assured of covering virtually all topics that could reasonably be expected to be studied in typical college or university auditing courses.

The question-and-answer format is designed and presented to facilitate effective study. Students should be careful not to misuse this text by referring to the answers before independently answering each question. Accordingly, we have provided two removable bookmarks at the back of this book to use to cover the answers while considering the questions.

The majority of the questions in this book are from past CDP, CIA, CISA, CMA, and CPA examinations. In addition, hundreds of publisher-written questions test areas covered in current textbooks but not directly tested on accounting certification examinations.

All of the questions in *Auditing & Systems Exam Questions and Explanations* have been modified, if necessary, to accommodate changes in professional pronouncements, to clarify questions, and/or to emphasize an auditing or systems concept or its application.

Note that this study manual should not be relied upon exclusively to prepare for the professional examinations. You should primarily use review manuals specifically developed for each examination. The Gleim *CIA Review*, *CMA/CFM Review*, *CPA Review*, and *EA Review* are up-to-date and comprehensively cover all material necessary for successful completion of these examinations.

Thank you for your interest in this study manual. We deeply appreciate the many letters and suggestions received from accounting and auditing students and educators during the past years, as well as from CDP, CIA, CISA, CMA, CPA, and EA candidates. Please send us your suggestions, comments, and corrections concerning this edition. The last two pages of this book have been designed to help you note corrections and suggestions throughout your study process.

To continue providing our customers with first-rate service, we request that questions about our books and software be sent to us via <u>mail</u>, <u>e-mail</u>, or <u>fax</u>. The appropriate staff member will give each question thorough consideration and a prompt response. Questions concerning orders, prices, shipments, or payments will be handled via telephone by our competent and courteous customer service staff.

Please read the Introduction carefully. It is short but nonetheless very important.

Good Luck on Your Exams,

*Irvin N. Gleim*
*William A. Hillison*

July 2005

# PREFACE FOR ACCOUNTING PRACTITIONERS

The first purpose of this study manual is to permit you to assess your technical proficiency concerning auditing standards, ethics, and special skills such as systems and statistical sampling. The second purpose is to facilitate your review and update of auditing standards and techniques with our compendium of objective questions. The third purpose is to provide CPE credit for your self-assessment and review/update study effort in conjunction with the Gleim CPE program.

This approach to CPE is both motivating and intense. You should be continually challenged to answer each question correctly. When you answer a question incorrectly or have difficulty, you should pursue a complete understanding by reading the answer explanation and consulting reference sources as necessary.

Most of the questions were taken from various professional examinations, but many have been revised, adapted, etc., to provide broader, up-to-date coverage of the auditing and systems body of technical knowledge. While some are from the CPA exam, many are from other exams, such as CISA, CDP, CMA, and CIA. Thus, you have an opportunity to consider the appropriateness of pursuing these other accounting certifications. In addition, hundreds of publisher questions cover material not directly tested on the accounting certification examinations.

To continue providing our customers with first rate service, we request that questions about our books and software be sent to us via <u>mail</u>, <u>e-mail</u>, or <u>fax</u>. The appropriate staff member will give each question thorough consideration and a prompt response. Questions concerning orders, prices, shipments, or payments will be handled via telephone by our competent and courteous customer service staff.

Finally, we ask for any supplemental comments, reactions, suggestions, etc., that you may have as you complete our CPE program. The last two pages of this study book have been designed to help you note corrections and suggestions throughout your study process. Please attach it to the Course Evaluation form included with your CPE program.

Thank you for your interest, and we look forward to hearing from you. If you would like information on other CPE programs available from Gleim, please call us for a free brochure or visit our website at www.gleim.com/CPE.

Best Wishes in Your CPE Endeavors,

*Irvin N. Gleim*
*William A. Hillison*

July 2005

P.S. Please check out our new Online CPE, which offers the following advantages:

- You will know your results INSTANTLY.
- Print out your certificate from the Internet IMMEDIATELY.
- Corporate packages also available.

Visit www.gleim.com/CPE

# TABLE OF CONTENTS



**ACRONYMS:** All acronyms used in this book are listed in the index. See pages 17-22 for definitions of and cross-references to APB, AR, ARB, AS, AT, AU, BL, CS, FASAB, FASB, PFP, PR, QC, SAS, SFAS, SOX, and TS pronouncements.

# INTRODUCTION



The format and content of this study manual are innovative in the accounting text market. The first purpose is to provide auditing students with a well-organized, comprehensive compendium of objective questions covering the topics taught in typical auditing and information systems undergraduate courses. The second purpose is to provide accounting professionals with a comprehensive presentation of objective questions for self-diagnostic use and/or review of auditing standards and procedures.

The Gleim exam question and explanation books really work! You can pretest yourself before class to see if you are strong or weak in the assigned area. You can retest after class to see if you really understand the material. The questions in these books cover **all** topics in your related courses, so you will encounter few questions on your exams for which you will not be well prepared.

The titles and organization of Study Units 1 through 9 are based on the current auditing and information systems textbooks listed in Appendix A. Appendix A contains the table of contents of each of the listed books with cross-references to study units and subunits in this book. Some textbooks may have been inadvertently omitted. If you are using a textbook that is not included in our list, please fax, mail, or e-mail us the table of contents so that we may provide you with a cross-reference. In your correspondence to us, please include your name, address, school, professor, and course name.

## OUR USE OF SUBUNITS

Each study unit of this book is divided into subunits to assist your study program. Subunits permit broad and perhaps overwhelming topics to be divided into more manageable components.

Choosing subunits and arranging questions within them was difficult. Thus, topics and questions may overlap somewhat. The number of questions offers comprehensive coverage but does not present an insurmountable task. We define each subunit narrowly enough to cover a single topic but broadly enough to prevent questions from being repetitious.

Within each subunit, the multiple-choice questions are presented in a sequence moving from the general to the specific, elementary to advanced, etc., to provide an effective learning sequence. Duplicate questions and redundant explanations have been kept to a minimum.

## SOURCES OF OBJECTIVE QUESTIONS

Past CIA, CISA, CMA, and CPA examinations and sample questions are the primary sources of questions included in this study manual.

Gleim Publications will continue to prepare questions (coded in this text as *Publisher*) based upon the content of auditing and information systems textbooks, SASs, SFASs, etc. These *Publisher* questions were developed to review topics not adequately covered by questions from the other sources. We will continue to develop challenging, current questions to provide you with complete review materials. Also, professionals and professors from schools around the country have contributed questions. See the Acknowledgments on page iv for a list of their names. We invite professors and students to submit questions for future editions.

## IDENTIFICATION OF THE SOURCE OF EACH QUESTION

The source of each question appears in the first line of its answer explanation, in the column to the right of the question. Summary of source codes:

| | |
|---|---|
| *CDP* | *CDP* Instruction Manual |
| *CIA* | Certified Internal Auditor Examination |
| *CISA* | Study Guide -- CISA |
| *CMA* | Certified Management Accountant Examination |
| *CPA* | Uniform Certified Public Accountant Examination |
| *Publisher* | Your authors |
| *Individual name* | Name of professional or professor who contributed the question |

If you, your professor, or your classmates wish to submit questions, we will consider using them in future editions. Please send questions you develop, complete with answers and explanations, to the following e-mail address: accounting@gleim.com. Alternatively, you can mail questions to:

Gleim Publications, Inc.
EQE Question Bank
P.O. Box 12848, University Station
Gainesville, FL 32604

Writing and analyzing multiple-choice questions is an excellent way to prepare yourself for your exams. We will make every effort to consider, edit, and use questions you submit. However, we ask that you send us only serious, complete, carefully considered efforts.

## UNIQUENESS OF OBJECTIVE QUESTIONS

The major advantage of objective questions is their ability to cover a large number of topics with little time and effort when compared to essay questions and/or computational problems.

A multiple-choice question is actually a series of statements of which all but one are incorrect given the facts of the question. The advantage of multiple-choice questions over true-false questions is that they require more analysis and result in a lower score for those with little or no knowledge. Random guessing on questions with four answer choices results in an expected grade of 25%, whereas random guessing on a true/false test results in an expected grade of 50%.

Students and practitioners both like multiple-choice questions. Because they present alternative answers from which only one needs to be selected, students find them relatively easy to answer. Professors also like objective questions because they are easy to grade and because much more material can be tested in the same period of time. Most professors will also ask students to complete essay or computational questions.

## ANSWER EXPLANATIONS ALONGSIDE THE QUESTIONS

Our format presents objective questions and their answer explanations side by side. The answer explanations are to the right of each question. The example below is from the CPA exam.

Proper segregation of duties reduces the opportunities for persons to be in positions to both

A. Journalize entries and prepare financial statements.

B. Record cash receipts and cash disbursements.

C. Establish internal controls and authorize transactions.

D. Perpetrate and conceal errors and fraud.

Answer (D) is correct. (*CPA, adapted*)

**REQUIRED:** The effects of the segregation of duties and responsibilities.

**DISCUSSION:** Proper segregation of duties and responsibilities reduces the opportunity for an individual to both perpetrate and conceal an error or fraud in the normal course of his/her duties. Hence, different people should be assigned the responsibilities for authorizing transactions, recordkeeping, and asset custody.

Answer (A) is incorrect because accountants typically journalize entries and prepare financial statements. Answer (B) is incorrect because accountants may record both cash receipts and cash disbursements as long as they do not have custody of the cash. Answer (C) is incorrect because management establishes internal controls and ultimately has the responsibility to authorize transactions.

The format in this study manual is designed to facilitate your study of objective questions, their answers, and the answer explanations. The intent is to save you time and effort by eliminating the need to turn pages back and forth from questions to answers.

Be careful, however. Do not misuse this format by consulting the answers before you have answered the questions. Misuse of the readily available answers will give you a false sense of security and result in poor performance on examinations and decreased benefit from your studies. The best way to use this study manual is to cover the answer explanations with the bookmark provided for this purpose in the back of the book (or a sheet of paper) as you read and answer each question. As a crucial part of the learning process, you must honestly commit yourself to an answer before looking at the answer explanation. Whether you are right or wrong, your memory of the correct answer will be reinforced by this process.

## OVERVIEW OF ACCOUNTING CERTIFICATION PROGRAMS

The CPA (Certified Public Accountant) exam is the grandparent of all the professional accounting exams. Its origin was in the 1896 public accounting legislation of New York. In 1917, the American Institute of CPAs (AICPA) began to prepare and grade a uniform CPA exam. It is currently used to measure the technical competence of those applying to be licensed as CPAs in all 50 states, Guam, Puerto Rico, the Virgin Islands, and the District of Columbia. More than 100,000 candidates sit annually for the examination, which traditionally has been given in May and November. In April 2004, the CPA exam switched to a computerized format. It is available as often as six days per week for two of every three months. The new exam places greater emphasis on auditing and other attestation services, the assessment of such skills as research and communications, general business knowledge, and information technology.

The CIA (Certified Internal Auditor), CMA (Certified Management Accountant), and CFM (Corporate Financial Management) examinations are relatively new certification programs compared with the CPA exam. The CMA exam was first administered in 1972, and the first CIA exam was in 1974. The CFM exam was first offered in December 1996. Why were these certification programs implemented? Generally, the requirements of the CPA designation instituted by the boards of accountancy, especially the necessity for public accounting experience, led to the development of the CIA, CMA, and CFM programs. The IRS Enrolled Agent (EA) certification is available for tax specialists.

Certification is important to professional accountants because it provides

1. Participation in a recognized professional group
2. An improved professional training program arising out of the certification program
3. Recognition among peers for attaining the professional designation
4. An extra credential for the employment market/career ladder
5. The personal satisfaction of attaining a recognized degree of competency

These reasons hold particularly true in the accounting field due to wide recognition of the CPA designation. Accountants and accounting students are often asked whether they are CPAs. Thus, there is considerable pressure for accountants to become *certified*.

A new development is multiple certifications, which is important for the same reasons as initial certification. Accounting students and recent graduates should plan for career progression and expanded opportunities by obtaining multiple certifications. The table of selected CIA, CMA, CFM, and CPA exam data on the following page provides an overview. Additional information about the IRS enrolled agent (EA) exam is available at www.gleim.com.

## RATIONALE FOR ACCOUNTING CERTIFICATION PROGRAMS

The primary purpose of professional exams is to measure the technical competence of candidates. Competence includes technical knowledge, ability to apply such knowledge with good judgment, and comprehension of professional responsibility. Additionally, the nature of these exams (low pass rate, broad and rigorous coverage, etc.) has several very important effects.

1. Candidates are forced to learn all of the material that should have been presented and learned in a good accounting educational program.
2. Candidates must integrate the topics and concepts that are presented in individual courses in accounting education programs.
3. The content of each exam provides direction to accounting education programs; i.e., what is tested will be taught to accounting students.

## EXAMINATION CONTENT

The content of these examinations is specified by their governing boards with lists of topics to be tested. In the Gleim review manuals – *CIA Review, CMA/CFM Review, CPA Review, and EA Review* – the material tested is divided into subtopics called study units. A study unit is a more manageable undertaking than an overall part of each exam. The listings of topics on pages 6 through 9 provide an overview of the content of these exams.

### CIA, CMA/CFM, CPA EXAMINATION SUMMARY

| | CIA | CMA/CFM | CPA |
|---|---|---|---|
| **Sponsoring Organization** | Institute of Internal Auditors<br>247 Maitland Avenue<br>Altamonte Springs, FL 32701<br>(407) 937-1100<br>www.theiia.org | Institute of Management Accountants<br>10 Paragon Drive<br>Montvale, NJ 07645-1718<br>(201) 573-9000<br>(800) 638-4427<br>www.imanet.org | American Institute of Certified Public Accountants<br>Harborside Financial Center<br>201 Plaza Three<br>Jersey City, NJ 07311-3881<br>(201) 938-3750<br>www.aicpa.org |
| **Passing Score** | 75% | 70% | 75% |
| **Average Pass Rate by Exam Part** | 35%-40% | 55% | 40%-45% |
| **Cost** | $380 (50% student discount) | $460 (50% student discount; requires IMA membership) | $500-$800 (varies by state) |
| **Year Examination Was First Administered** | 1974 | 1972 | 1917 |
| **Major Exam Sections and Length** | I. Internal Audit Role in Governance, Risk, and Control (3-1/2 hours)<br>II. Conducting the Internal Audit Engagement (3-1/2 hours)<br>III. Business Analysis and Information Technology (3-1/2 hours)<br>IV. Business Management Skills (3-1/2 hours) | 1. Business Analysis (3 hours)<br>2. Management Accounting and Reporting (4 hours)<br>2. CFM. Corporate Financial Management (3 hours)<br>3. Strategic Management (3 hours)<br>4. Business Applications (3 hours) | 1. Business Environment & Concepts (2-1/2 hours)<br>2. Auditing & Attestation (4-1/2 hours)<br>3. Regulation (3 hours)<br>4. Financial Accounting & Reporting (4 hours) |
| **Length of Exam** | 14 hours | 13 hours CMA and 12 hours CFM | 14 hours |
| **When Administered** | Mid-May and Mid-Nov | On Demand | Jan-Feb Apr-May<br>July-Aug Oct-Nov |
| **Candidates Sitting for Exam:** | Total number of candidates sitting for two examinations; many are repeaters. | | |
| 1990 | 4,363 | 4,839 | 143,572 |
| 1991 | 4,547 | 6,404 | 140,042 |
| 1992 | 4,961 | 7,464 | 136,541 |
| 1993 | 5,103 | 7,879 | 140,100 |
| 1994 | 4,557 | 8,259 | 131,000 |
| 1995 | 4,649 | 8,675 | 126,000 |
| 1996 | 4,646 | 8,679 | 122,232 |
| 1997 | 5,169 | *5,456 | 121,437 |
| 1998 | 7,972 | *5,276 | 116,906 |
| 1999 | 11,724 | *4,950 | 126,770 |
| 2000 | 15,912 | *4,823 | 115,423 |
| 2001 | 19,451 | *5,791 | 106,079 |
| 2002 | 26,147 | *5,100 | 108,900 |
| 2003 | 31,539 | *5,200 | 108,700 |
| 2004 | 30,634 | *6,644 | **100,000 |

*Does not include double-counting which occurred in previous years.
**Exam parts, not candidates for three calendar quarters, which is about a 50% drop from 2000 and 2003 levels.

Other professional accounting-related designations include CBA (Certified Bank Auditor), CDP (Certificate in Data Processing), CFA (Chartered Financial Analyst), CFE (Certified Fraud Examiner), CISA (Certified Information Systems Auditor), Enrolled Agent (one enrolled to practice before the IRS).

**LISTING OF *CIA REVIEW* STUDY UNITS**

**Part I: Internal Audit's Role in Governance, Risk, and Control**

1. Introduction to Internal Auditing
2. Charter, Independence, and Objectivity
3. Standards and Proficiency
4. Internal Audit Roles and Responsibilities
5. Control I
6. Control II
7. Planning and Supervising the Engagement
8. Managing the Internal Audit Activity I
9. Managing the Internal Audit Activity II
10. Engagement Procedures

**Part II: Conducting the Internal Audit Engagement**

1. Engagement Information
2. Working Papers
3. Communicating Results and Monitoring Progress
4. Specific Engagements
5. Information Technology I
6. Information Technology II
7. Statistics and Sampling
8. Other Engagement Tools
9. Ethics
10. Fraud

**Part III: Business Analysis and Information Technology**

1. Business Performance
2. Managing Resources and Pricing
3. Financial Accounting -- Basic Concepts
4. Financial Accounting -- Assets, Liabilities, and Equity
5. Financial Accounting -- Special Topics
6. Finance
7. Managerial Accounting
8. Regulatory, Legal, and Economic Issues
9. Information Technology I
10. Information Technology II

**Part IV: Business Management Skills***

1. Structural Analysis and Strategies
2. Industry and Market Analysis
3. Environments and Strategic Decisions
4. Global Business Issues
5. Motivation and Communications
6. Organizational Structure and Effectiveness
7. Managing Groups
8. Influence and Leadership
9. Time Management
10. Conflict and Negotiation

*Persons who have passed the CPA or CMA exams (and many other professional exams) are not required to take Part IV of the CIA exam.

The explosive growth in the number of candidates sitting for the CIA exam (see previous page) is certainly the result of a combination of factors including the Sarbanes-Oxley legislation and the Enron/WorldCom scandals.

Each of the four parts consists of 80 multiple-choice questions and is 3 1/2 hours in length (8:30 - 12:00 and 1:30 - 5:00).

The first two parts of the CIA exam focus on the theory and practice of internal auditing. The body of knowledge of internal auditing and the auditing skills to be tested consist of

1. The typical undergraduate auditing class (as represented by auditing texts, e.g., Arens and Loebbecke, Taylor and Glezen, etc.)
2. Internal auditing textbooks (e.g., Sawyer and Dittenhofer, *Sawyer's Internal Auditing*, and Ratliff, Wallace, Sumners, McFarland, and Loebbecke, *Internal Auditing: Principles and Techniques*)
3. Various IIA (Institute of Internal Auditors) pronouncements (e.g., The IIA *Code of Ethics*, Standards for the International Professional Practice of Internal Auditing, and Practice Advisories)
4. Reasoning ability, communications, problem-solving, and relations with auditees in an audit context (i.e., the questions may cover audit topics, but test audit skills)

The remaining 50% of the exam, parts III and IV, assures that internal auditors are conversant with topics, methods, and techniques ranging from individual and organizational behavior to economics.

Management cannot personally observe the functioning of all officers, employees, and specialized functions (finance, marketing, operations, etc.). Each has a unique perspective. Only internal auditing is in a position to take a total organizational perspective.

**Listing of *CMA/CFM REVIEW* Study Units**

**Part 1: Business Analysis***

1. Microeconomics
2. Macroeconomics
3. International Business Environment
4. Risk Assessment and Internal Control
5. Internal Auditing
6. Decision Making Under Uncertainty
7. Linear Programming
8. Other Quantitative Methods
9. The Accounting Standard-Setting Environment
10. Financial Statement Analysis

**Part 2CMA: Management Accounting and Reporting**

1. Cost and Managerial Accounting Terminology
2. Process Costing and Overhead
3. Other Product Costing Topics
4. Cost Behavior
5. Budgeting
6. Quality, the Balanced Scorecard, and Control
7. Standard Costs and Variance Analysis
8. Responsibility Accounting
9. Information Systems I
10. Information Systems II
11. Conceptual Framework
12. Financial Statements
13. Current Assets and Investments
14. Long-Lived Assets
15. Liabilities
16. Liabilities -- Special Issues
17. Equity
18. Other Income Items
19. Other Reporting Issues
20. SEC Requirements and Audit Committees

*Persons who have passed the CPA exam are not required to take Part 1 of the CMA exam.
**CMAs in good standing need only pass this part to earn the CFM designation.

**Part 2CFM: Corporate Financial Management****

1. The Accounting Standard-Setting Environment
2. Working Capital Policy and Management
3. Long-Term Capital Financing
4. Financial Markets and Interest Rates
5. Investment Banking and Commercial Banking
6. Financial Statement Analysis
7. Business Combinations and Restructurings
8. Risk Management
9. External Financial Environment
10. Employee Benefit Plans and Deferred Taxes

**Part 3: Strategic Management**

1. Strategic Planning
2. Manufacturing Paradigms and Process Performance
3. Working Capital Finance
4. Capital Structure Finance
5. Risk and Return
6. Decision Analysis
7. Cost-Volume-Profit Analysis
8. Capital Budgeting
9. The Strategic Role of Marketing
10. Marketing Basics

**Part 4: Business Applications**

1. Organizational Theory
2. Organizational Theory and Decentralization
3. Motivation and the Directing Process
4. Motivation and Managing
5. Communication
6. Behavioral Issues
7. Ethics as Tested on the CMA Exam
8. CMA Part 1 Review
9. CMA Part 2 Review
10. CMA Part 3 Review

The CMA and CFM exams have broader coverage than the CPA exam in several areas. For example:

1. CMA topics like risk management, finance, management, and marketing are covered lightly, if at all, on the CPA exam.
2. The CMA exam tests internal auditing to a greater degree than does the CPA exam.
3. The CMA exam tests business ethics, but not business law.

CMA questions are generally more analysis-oriented than CPA questions. On the CPA exam, the typical requirement is the solution of an accounting problem, e.g., consolidated worksheet, funds statement, etc.

The CMA exam is given in a computer-based format. Parts 1, 2, and 3 consist of multiple-choice questions that test all levels of cognitive skills. Part 4 consists of approximately 6 essay questions that test knowledge and skills with respect to all material covered in Parts 1, 2, and 3, plus organization management and communication, behavioral issues, and ethical considerations.

**LISTING OF *CPA REVIEW* STUDY UNITS**

***Business Environment and Concepts***

1. Proprietorships and General Partnerships
2. Noncorporate Limited Liability Entities
3. Corporations: Formation, Powers, and Financing
4. Corporations: Governance and Fundamental Changes
5. Economic Concepts I
6. Economic Concepts II
7. Working Capital Policy and Management
8. Long-Term Capital Financing
9. Financial Statement Analysis
10. Risk Management
11. IT and Business Information Systems
12. IT Controls
13. Hardware, Software, and Data
14. Processing Modes, Databases, and Networks
15. E-Commerce
16. Planning and Budgeting
17. Business Performance
18. Cost Behavior and Definitions
19. Product Costing and Related Topics
20. Standard Costs and Variance Analysis

***Financial Accounting and Reporting***

1. Concepts and Standards
2. Financial Statements
3. Income Statement Items
4. Financial Statement Disclosure
5. Cash and Investments
6. Receivables
7. Inventories
8. Property, Plant, and Equipment
9. Intangibles and Other Assets
10. Payables and Taxes
11. Employee Benefits
12. Long-Term Liabilities
13. Leases and Contingencies
14. Equity
15. Business Combinations
16. Foreign Currency Issues and Other Topics
17. Governmental Concepts
18. Fund Accounting and Reporting
19. Not-for-Profit Concepts
20. Not-for-Profit Accounting and Reporting

***Regulation***

1. AICPA Ethics
2. CPAs and the Law
3. Agency
4. Contracts
5. Debtor-Creditor Relationships
6. Government Regulation of Business
7. Negotiable Instruments, Bank Transactions, and Related Topics
8. Sales
9. Secured Transactions
10. Real Property and Insurance
11. Gross Income
12. Deductions
13. Tax Computations and Tax Procedures
14. Property Transactions
15. Corporate Taxable Income
16. Corporate Tax Computations
17. Corporate Tax Special Topics
18. S Corporations
19. Partnerships
20. Estates and Trusts

***Auditing and Attestation***

1. Engagement Responsibilities
2. Risk Assessment
3. Strategic Planning Issues
4. Internal Control Concepts and Information Technology
5. Internal Control -- Sales-Receivables-Cash Receipts Cycle
6. Internal Control -- Purchases-Payables-Cash Disbursements Cycle
7. Internal Control -- Payroll and Other Cycles
8. Tests of Controls
9. Internal Control Communications
10. Evidence -- Objectives and Nature
11. Evidence -- The Sales-Receivables-Cash Cycle
12. Evidence -- The Purchases-Payables-Inventory Cycle
13. Evidence -- Other Assets, Liabilities, and Equities
14. Evidence -- Key Considerations
15. Evidence -- Sampling
16. Reports -- Standard, Qualified, Adverse, and Disclaimer
17. Reports -- Other Modifications
18. Review, Compilation, and Special Reports
19. Related Reporting Topics
20. Governmental Audits

Computer Administered CPA Exam (effective April 2004)

The CPA exam is now an on-demand test administered at hundreds of Prometric testing centers throughout the United States. The quality, integrity, and prestige of the CPA exam increased and the exam became easier for candidates to prepare for and pass. Computerization of the CPA exam is a win-win development. Every aspect of the exam is explained and analyzed in *CPA Review: A System for Success*. Faculty and student organizations should order this book in bulk for distribution.

**LISTING OF *EA REVIEW* STUDY UNITS**

**Part 1: Individuals**

1. Gross Income
2. Deductions
3. Above-the-Line Deductions and Losses
4. Itemized Deductions
5. Filing Requirements
6. Tax Credits
7. Basis
8. Adjustments to Asset Basis and Capital Gains and Losses
9. Business Property, Related Parties, and Installment Sales
10. Nonrecognition Property Transactions

**Part 2: Sole Proprietorships and Partnerships**

1. Accounting Methods and Periods
2. Income and Property Transactions
3. Business Expenses
4. Other Deductions
5. Basis
6. Depreciation
7. Credits, Losses, and Additional Taxes
8. Contributions to a Partnership
9. Partnership Operations
10. Disposition of a Partner's Interest

**Part 3: Corporations, Fiduciaries, Estate and Gift Tax, and Trusts**

1. Corporations
2. Corporate Formation
3. Corporate Income and Losses
4. Corporate Deductions
5. Distributions
6. Corporate Liquidations and Redemptions
7. S Corporations
8. Decedent, Estate, and Trust Income Tax Returns
9. Estate Tax
10. Gift Tax

**Part 4: IRS Administration and Other Topics***

1. Practice Before the IRS
2. Income Tax Preparers and Penalties
3. Representation
4. The Collection Process
5. Examination of Returns and the Appeals Process
6. Tax Authority
7. Record Keeping and Electronic Filing
8. Exempt Organizations
9. Individual Retirement Arrangements
10. Retirement Plans for Small Businesses

Enrolled agents are individuals who have demonstrated special competence in tax matters and professional ethics and have been enrolled to practice before the IRS as taxpayers' agents or legal representatives. Practice before the IRS includes all matters connected with presentations to the IRS relating to a client's rights, privileges, and liabilities under laws or regulations administered by the IRS. Such presentations include

1. Preparing and filing documents;
2. Communicating with the IRS; and
3. Representing a client at conferences, hearings, and meetings.

The 11-hour IRS Special Enrollment Examination (SEE) covers federal taxation and tax accounting and the use of tax return forms for individuals, partnerships, corporations, trusts, estates, and gifts. It also covers ethical considerations and procedural requirements.

The exam consists of four parts (3 hours each for parts 1, 2, and 3; 2 hours for part 4), which take 2 days to complete. Parts 1 and 2 are given on the morning (9:00 a.m. - Noon) and afternoon (1:30 - 4:30 p.m.) of the first day. Parts 3 and 4 are given on the morning (9:00 a.m. - Noon) and afternoon (1:30 - 3:30 p.m.) of the second day. The questions on the examination are directed toward the tasks that enrolled agents must perform to complete and file forms and tax returns and to represent taxpayers before the Internal Revenue Service. The examination includes true/false questions and multiple-choice questions and covers the following tax topics:

Part 1 – Individuals
Part 2 – Sole Proprietorships and Partnerships
Part 3 – Corporations, Fiduciaries, Estate and Gift Tax, and Trusts
Part 4 – IRS Administration and Other Topics*

*NOTE: We have shortened the title of Part 4 for your convenience. The full title is "Ethics, Recordkeeping Procedures, Appeal Procedures, Exempt Organizations, Retirement Plans, Practitioner Penalty Provisions, Research Materials, and Collection Procedures."

## CERTIFIED INFORMATION SYSTEMS AUDITOR PROGRAM

The Certified Information Systems Auditor™ (CISA®) program, administered by the Information Systems Audit and Control Association® (ISACA™), is designed to assess and certify individuals in information systems auditing, control, and security. To earn the CISA designation, candidates must successfully complete the CISA examination; adhere to ISACA's Code of Professional Ethics; and submit evidence of a minimum of 5 years of professional information systems (IS) auditing, control, or security work experience, subject to the following substitutions/waivers:

- A maximum of 1 year of IS experience OR 1 year of financial or operating auditing experience can be substituted for 1 year of IS auditing, control, or security experience.
- An A.A. or B.A. (the equivalent of 60 to 120 college semester credit hours) can be substituted for 1 or 2 years, respectively, of IS auditing, control, or security experience.
- Two years of experience as a full-time university instructor in a related field can be substituted for 1 year of IS auditing, control, or security experience.

Candidates must have gained experience within the 10-year period preceding the date of the application for certification or within 5 years from the date of initially passing the examination. Experience is verified independently.

The CISA examination is offered every June in more than 200 locations around the world. Candidates may take the exam in Dutch, English, French, German, Hebrew, Italian, Japanese, Korean, Mandarin Chinese, or Spanish. The CISA examination is now also offered in December in select locations in English, Japanese, Korean, and Spanish. The examination consists of 200 multiple-choice questions in 4 hours. Candidates may take the CISA exam prior to meeting the experience requirements.

Following is a summary of the content areas on the examination, with recommended percentages of questions for each subject.

**Process Area**

- The IS Audit Process (10%)

**Content Areas**

- Management, Planning, and Organization of IS (11%)
- Technical Infrastructure and Operational Practices (13%)
- Protection of Information Assets (25%)
- Disaster Recovery and Business Continuity (10%)
- Business Application System Development, Acquisition, Implementation, and Maintenance (16%)
- Business Process Evaluation and Risk Management (15%)

To assist candidates with the development of a successful study plan, ISACA offers a comprehensive study guide, question/answer/explanations manuals, and review courses.

### Contact Information

For additional information regarding the CISA certification, program please contact ISACA at:

Certification Coordinator
Information Systems Audit & Control Association
3701 Algonquin Road, Suite 1010
Rolling Meadows, Illinois 60008-3124 USA

Telephone: +1.847.253.1545
Fax: +1.847.253.1443
E-mail: certification@isaca.org
Website: www.isaca.org

## WHEN TO SIT FOR THE EXAMS

Sit for all examinations as soon as you can. The CIA, CMA, and CFM exams can be taken in your last undergraduate quarter or semester, and are offered with a 50% reduction in fees to full-time students. In many states, you may also take the CPA exam in your last quarter or semester. The EA exam does not have an educational requirement. If you are graduating in May, consider taking the CIA exam in May and the CPA, CMA, CFM, and EA exams by the end of the year. Your preparation program for all of these exams is very synergistic and not appreciably more work than preparing for just the CPA exam.

## EXAMINATION PASS RATES

The pass rates on the CIA and CMA exams are about the same and are somewhat higher than the pass rate on the CPA exam. Nationally, the pass rate on the CPA exam averages about 40%-45% on each of the four parts. The pass rates on the CIA and CMA exams range from 35%-65% per part (see the tables below).

Many schools and CPA review courses advertise the quality of their programs by reporting pass rates. Obviously, the best rates are emphasized. Thus, the reported percentage may be that for first-time candidates, all candidates, candidates passing a specific section of the examination, candidates completing the examination, or even candidates successfully completing the exam after a specified number of sittings.

| CIA Exam Pass Rates | | | | | | |
|---|---|---|---|---|---|---|
| | 5/02 | 11/02 | 5/03 | 11/03 | 5/04 | 11/04 |
| *Part I* | 38.1 | 33.2 | 41.3 | 33.1 | 39.8 | 34.3 |
| *Part II* | 41.0 | 34.2 | 45.0 | 33.9 | 42.2 | 34.6 |
| *Part III* | 39.0 | 45.4 | 42.7 | 33.6 | 42.7 | 32.8 |
| *Part IV* | 32.6 | 27.6 | 37.4 | 29.9 | 45.6 | 39.9 |

| CMA Exam Pass Rates (revised exam, smal numbers) | |
|---|---|
| *Part 1* | 68% |
| *Part 2* | 48% |
| *Part 3* | 50% |
| *Part 4* | 64% |

## IRS Special Enrollment Examination Pass Statistics

For those who sit for all four parts of the EA exam in recent years, about 20% pass all four parts; 15%-20% pass one, two, or three parts; and about 50% fail all four parts. The vast majority of candidates attempting to pass remaining parts are successful.

Remember, if you do not pass all four parts on your first sitting, you must pass the remaining parts within the following 3-year period or you will lose credit for the parts previously passed.

### Reasons for the Low Pass Rates

Although a very high percentage of serious candidates successfully complete each of the examinations, the 35%-55% CPA, CIA, and CMA pass rates warrant an explanation. First, the pass rates are low (relative to bar and medical exams) because these examinations reflect the high standards of the accounting profession, which contribute greatly to the profession's reputation and also attract persons with both competence and aspiration.

Second, the pass rates are low because most accounting educational programs are at the undergraduate rather than graduate level. Undergraduate students are generally less career-oriented than graduate students. Undergraduates may look on their program as a number of individual courses required for graduation rather than as an integrated program to prepare them for professional practice.

Third, the pass rates are low because accounting programs and curricula at most colleges and universities are not given the budgetary priority they deserve. Accounting faculties are often understaffed for the number of accounting majors, the number and nature of accounting courses (problem-oriented vs. descriptive), etc., relative to other faculties. However, you cannot use this as an excuse or reason for not achieving your personal goals. You must do your best to improve your control systems and study resources.

## COST TO OBTAIN AND MAINTAIN PROFESSIONAL CERTIFICATION

The cost to take the CIA exam for members of The Institute of Internal Auditors (The IIA) is a $60 registration fee plus a $70-per-part examination fee, which totals $340 (assuming you pass all parts the first time you take them). Full-time students save 50%. Nonmembers pay a $75 registration fee plus a $95-per-part examination fee. Nonmembers must also include a $50 processing fee when they submit their CPE report every 2 years. Membership in The IIA is not required. Membership dues vary from $30 to $115. See The IIA website at www.theiia.org for more information.

The cost to take the CMA/CFM exam is $115 for each of the parts and a $75 credentialing fee plus Institute of Management Accountants (IMA) membership dues, which vary from $35 for students to $175 for regular members. Membership in the IMA is required. Students may take each part of the examination once at a reduced fee of $57.50 per part and do NOT pay a credentialing fee. See the IMA website at www.imanet.org for more information.

The cost of the CPA exam varies by state. The table on page 14 lists the URL for each state board. Most states require an annual fee to maintain the CPA certificate and/or license. See www.cpa-exam.org for more information.

For the IRS EA exam, the fee for applicants taking all four parts of the 2004 examination was $55. For applicants taking fewer than four parts, the examination fee was $45. These fees are nonrefundable, but a credit may be granted toward the next year's examination fee under some circumstances, e.g., illness or death in the family, as explained in the instructions for Form 2587, the application form to be filed with the IRS. See the IRS website at www.irs.gov/taxpros/agents/ for more information.

## WHERE TO TAKE THE CPA EXAM

If you are not going to practice public accounting, you may wish to become certified in a state that

1. Issues a CPA certificate separate from a license to practice
2. Does **not** require experience to receive a CPA certificate
3. Does **not** require continuing professional education of CPA certificate holders
4. Does **not** require residency to sit for the CPA exam

You may also be concerned with the 150-hour requirement to sit for the CPA exam. Consult your state board contact information on page 14.

## STEPS TO BECOME A CPA

1. Decide when you are going to take the CPA exam (the sooner, the better!).
2. Determine the state board to which you will apply to sit for the CPA exam. Read "Where to Take the CPA Exam" above.
3. Obtain, complete, and submit your application form, including transcripts, etc.
4. Commit to thorough, systematic preparation for the exam as described in *CPA Review: A System for Success*, also available on our website at **www.gleim.com/accounting/cpa/systemforsuccess.php**
5. Work systematically through each study unit in the four Gleim *CPA Review* books (*Business*, *Auditing*, *Regulation*, and *Financial*).
6. Use Gleim's ***CPA Test Prep*** software: over 6,000 CPA questions, all updated to current tax law, FASB Statements, etc.
7. Sit for and PASS the CPA exam while you are in control, as described in Study Units 6 and 7 of *CPA Review: A System for Success.* Gleim will make it easy. Call (800) 87-GLEIM for more information.

## STATE BOARDS OF ACCOUNTANCY

All 50 states (and the District of Columbia, Guam, Puerto Rico, and the Virgin Islands) have an administrative agency that administers the laws and rules which regulate the practice of public accounting in each state. Each of these 54 jurisdictions contracts with the AICPA to use the AICPA's Uniform CPA Examination.

While the 54 jurisdictions agree on using the same examination, the rules and procedures for applying to take the exam and becoming licensed to practice public accounting vary considerably. Accordingly, you should call or write to your state board for a CPA exam application form. With the form, you will receive that board's rules, regulations, and directions to you as a CPA candidate.

The following page contains a list of the state boards, their addresses, phone numbers, and information relevant to most CPA candidates. Please visit our website at www.gleim.com for the most current information regarding CPA requirements by state. If you have any questions, please check with your state board for final verification.

## STATE BOARDS OF ACCOUNTANCY CONTACT INFORMATION

**NOTE: Each State Board is currently updating requirements to accommodate the 2004 changes in the CPA exam. Contact your State Board for complete up-to-date information.**

| STATE BOARD • ADDRESS | | Telephone # | Website |
|---|---|---|---|
| AK | P.O. Box 110806 • Juneau, AK 99811-0806 | (907) 465-3811 | www.dced.state.ak.us/occ/pcpa.htm |
| AL | P.O. Box 300375 • Montgomery, AL 36130-0375 | (334) 242-5700 | www.asbpa.state.al.us |
| AR | 101 East Capitol, Suite 430 • Little Rock, AR 72201 | (501) 682-1520 | www.state.ar.us/asbpa |
| AZ | 100 N. 15th Avenue, Room 165 • Phoenix, AZ 85007 | (602) 364-0900 | www.accountancy.state.az.us/ |
| CA | 2000 Evergreen St., Suite 250 • Sacramento, CA 95815-3832 | (916) 263-3680 | www.dca.ca.gov/cba |
| CO | 1560 Broadway, Suite 1340 • Denver, CO 80202 | (303) 894-7800 | www.dora.state.co.us/accountants |
| CT | 30 Trinity Street • Hartford, CT 06115 | (860) 509-6179 | www.sots.state.ct.us/SBOA/SBOAindex.html |
| DC | 941 N. Capital St., NE Rm 7200 • Washington, DC 20002 | (202) 442-4461 | www.dcra.dc.gov/information/build_pla/occupational/accountancy/index.shtm |
| DE | Cannon Building, Suite 203, 861 Silver Lake Blvd. • Dover, DE 19904 | (302) 744-4500 | www.professionallicensing.state.de.us |
| FL | 240 NW 76th Drive, Suite A • Gainesville, FL 32607 | (352) 333-2500 | www.state.fl.us/dbpr/cpa/index.shtml |
| GA | 237 Coliseum Drive • Macon, GA 31217-3858 | (478) 207-1400 | www.sos.state.ga.us/plb/accountancy/ |
| GU | Suite 508, GCIC Building 414 W. Soledad Ave. • Hagatna, GU 96910-5014 | (671) 477-1050 | www.guam.net/gov/gba/ |
| HI | P.O. Box 3469 • Honolulu, HI 96801-3469 | (808) 586-2696 | www.state.hi.us/dcca/pvl/areas_accountancy.html |
| IA | 1920 SE Hulsizer Avenue • Ankeny, IA 50021-3961 | (515) 281-4126 | www.state.ia.us/iacc |
| ID | P.O. Box 83720 • Boise, ID 83720-0002 | (208) 334-2490 | www.state.id.us/boa |
| IL | 505 E. Green, Room 216 Champaign, IL 61820-5723 | (217) 333-1565 | www.illinois-cpa-exam.com |
| IN | 302 West Washington St., E034 • Indianapolis, IN 46204-2246 | (317) 232-5987 | www.state.in.us/pla/bandc/accountancy/ |
| KS | 900 SW Jackson St., Suite 556 • Topeka, KS 66612-1239 | (785) 296-2162 | www.ksboa.org |
| KY | 332 W. Broadway, Suite 310 • Louisville, KY 40202-2115 | (502) 595-3037 | cpa.state.ky.us |
| LA | 601 Poydras St., Suite 1770 • New Orleans, LA 70139 | (504) 566-1244 | www.cpaboard.state.la.us |
| MA | 239 Causeway St., Suite 450 • Boston, MA 02114 | (617) 727-1806 | www.state.ma.us/reg/boards/pa |
| MD | 500 N. Calvert Street, 3rd Floor • Baltimore, MD 21202-3651 | (410) 230-6322 | www.dllr.state.md.us/license/occprof/account.html |
| ME | 35 State House Station • Augusta, ME 04333 | (207) 624-8603 | www.state.me.us/pfr/olr/categories/cat01.htm |
| MI | P.O. Box 30018 • Lansing, MI 48909-7518 | (517) 241-9249 | www.michigan.gov/cis/0,1607,7-154-10557_12992_13878-40080--,00.html |
| MN | 85 East 7th Place, Suite 125 • St. Paul, MN 55101 | (612) 296-7938 | www.boa.state.mn.us |
| MO | P.O. Box 613 • Jefferson City, MO 65102 | (573) 751-0012 | www.ded.mo.gov/regulatorylicensing/professionalregistration/account/ |
| MS | 5 Old River Place, Suite 104 • Jackson, MS 39202-3449 | (601) 354-7320 | www.msbpa.state.ms.us |
| MT | P.O. Box 200513 • Helena, MT 59620-0513 | (406) 841-2389 | www.discoveringmontana.com/dli/pac |
| NC | P.O. Box 12827 • Raleigh, NC 27605-2827 | (919) 733-4222 | www.cpaboard.state.nc.us/ |
| ND | 2701 S. Columbia Rd. • Grand Forks, ND 58201-6029 | (800) 532-5904 | www.state.nd.us/ndsba |
| NE | P.O. Box 94725 • Lincoln, NE 68509-4725 | (402) 471-3595 | www.nol.org/home/BPA |
| NH | 6 Chenell Drive, Suite 220 • Concord, NH 03301 | (603) 271-3286 | www.nh.gov/accountancy/ |
| NJ | P.O. Box 45000 • Newark, NJ 07101 | (973) 504-6380 | www.state.nj.us/lps/ca/nonmed.htm |
| NM | 1650 University NE, Suite 400-A • Albuquerque, NM 87102 | (505) 841-9108 | www.rld.state.nm.us/b&c/accountancy/index.htm |
| NV | 200 South Virginia St., Suite 670 • Reno, NV 89501-2408 | (775) 786-0231 | www.nvaccountancy.com |
| NY | 89 Washington Avenue, 2nd Floor East Mezzanine • Albany, NY 12234-1000 | (518) 474-3817 ext. 160 | www.op.nysed.gov/cpa.htm |
| OH | 77 South High St., 18th Floor • Columbus, OH 43215-6128 | (614) 466-4135 | www.acc.ohio.gov |
| OK | 4545 Lincoln Blvd., Suite 165 • Oklahoma City, OK 73105-3413 | (405) 521-2397 | www.youroklahoma.com/oab |
| OR | 3218 Pringle Road SE, Suite 110 • Salem, OR 97302-6307 | (503) 378-4181 | www.boahost.com/index.lasso |
| PA | 124 Pine Street, 1st Floor • Harrisburg, PA 17101-2649 | (717) 783-1404 | www.dos.state.pa.us/bpoa/accbd/mainpage.htm |
| PR | Box 9023271, Old San Juan Station • San Juan, PR 00902-3271 | (787) 722-4816 | www.estado.gobierno.pr/contador.htm |
| RI | 233 Richmond St., Suite 236 • Providence, RI 02903-4236 | (401) 222-3185 | www.dbr.state.ri.us/account.html |
| SC | P.O. Box 11329 • Columbia, SC 29211-1329 | (803) 896-4770 | www.llr.state.sc.us/POL/accountancy/INDEX.ASP |
| SD | 301 E. 14th St., Suite 200 • Sioux Falls, SD 57104 | (605) 367-5770 | www.state.sd.us/dcr/accountancy |
| TN | 500 James Robertson Pkwy., 2nd Floor • Nashville, TN 37243-1141 | (615) 741-2550 | www.state.tn.us/commerce/boards/tnsba/index.html |
| TX | 333 Guadalupe Tower III, Suite 900 • Austin, TX 78701-3900 | (512) 305-7800 | www.tsbpa.state.tx.us |
| UT | P.O. Box 146741 • Salt Lake City, UT 84114-6741 | (801) 530-6396 | www.dopl.utah.gov |
| VA | 3600 West Broad Street, Suite 696 • Richmond, VA 23230-4916 | (804) 367-8505 | www.boa.state.va.us |
| VI | Office of Boards and Commissions Golden Rock Shopping Center • Christiansted, St. Croix, VI 00820 | (340) 773-4305 | www.dlca.gov.vi |
| VT | 26 Terrace St, Drawer 09 • Montpelier, VT 05609-1106 | (802) 828-2191 | www.vtprofessionals.org/opr1/accountants |
| WA | P.O. Box 9131 • Olympia, WA 98507-9131 | (360) 753-2585 | www.cpaboard.wa.gov |
| WI | P.O. Box 8935 • Madison, WI 53708-8935 | (608) 266-5511 | www.drl.state.wi.us |
| WV | 122 Capitol Street, Suite 100 • Charleston, WV 25301 | (304) 558-3557 | www.state.wv.us/wvboa/ |
| WY | 2020 Carey Avenue • Cheyenne, WY 82002-0610 | (307) 777-7551 | cpaboard.state.wy.us |

CPA Examination Services, a division of the National Association of State Boards of Accountancy, processes the CPA exam applications in many states, and issues Notices To Schedule (NTS) to all CPA candidates. Call (800) 877-EXAM

## USING EXAM QUESTION AND EXPLANATION BOOKS TO IMPROVE GRADES

Use the other Gleim exam question books to ensure your understanding of each topic you study in your accounting and business law courses. Access the largest bank of exam questions (including thousands from past certification exams) that is widely used by professors. Get immediate feedback on your study effort while you take your "practice" tests.

### *AUDITING & SYSTEMS EXAM QUESTIONS AND EXPLANATIONS* (Twelfth Edition)

**Introduction**
1. External Auditing Standards and Professional Responsibilities
2. Audit Planning and Risk Assessment
3. Internal Control
4. Audit Evidence and Procedures
5. Information Systems
6. Statistical Sampling
7. Audit Reports
8. Special Reports and Other Reporting Issues
9. Internal Auditing

### *FINANCIAL ACCOUNTING EXAM QUESTIONS AND EXPLANATIONS* (Twelfth Edition)

**Introduction**
1. Conceptual Framework
2. The Accounting Process
3. Comprehensive Income and the Statement of Income
4. Present Value and Future Value
5. Current Assets, Cash, Accounts Receivable, and Short-Term Notes Receivable
6. Inventory
7. Property, Plant, and Equipment
8. Depreciation and Depletion
9. Intangible Assets and Research and Development Costs
10. Investments in Debt Securities, Equity Securities, and Derivatives
11. Current Liabilities, Compensated Absences, and Contingencies
12. Long-Term Liabilities
13. Pensions, Other Postretirement Benefits, and Postemployment Benefits
14. Leases
15. Corporate Equity
16. EPS and Share-Based Payment
17. Accounting for Income Taxes
18. Accounting Changes and Error Corrections
19. Statement of Cash Flows
20. Accounting for Changing Prices
21. Financial Statement Disclosures
22. Long-Term Construction-Type Contracts, Installment Sales, and Consignments
23. Financial Statement Analysis Based on Percentage Relationships
24. GAAP Accounting for Partnerships
25. Business Combinations, Consolidations, and Branch Accounting
26. Interim Financial Reporting
27. Foreign Currency Translation and Transactions
28. Accounting for State and Local Government Entities
29. Not-for-Profit Organizations
30. Specialized Accounting Issues

### *COST/MANAGERIAL ACCOUNTING EXAM QUESTIONS AND EXPLANATIONS* (Seventh Edition)

**Introduction**

**Part I: Cost Accounting**
1. Overview and Terminology
2. Activity-Based Costing
3. Job-Order Costing
4. Process Costing
5. Quality
6. Cost Allocation: Support Costs and Joint Costs
7. Absorption and Variable Costing
8. Cost-Volume-Profit Analysis

**Part II: Planning and Control**

9. Budgeting
10. Standard Costs and Variances
11. Responsibility Accounting, Performance Measurement, and Transfer Pricing

**Part III: Nonroutine Decisions and Quantitative Methods**

12. Nonroutine Decisions
13. Capital Budgeting
14. Inventory Management: Traditional and Modern Approaches
15. Probability and Statistics
16. Regression Analysis
17. Linear Programming
18. Other Quantitative Approaches

## FEDERAL TAX EXAM QUESTIONS AND EXPLANATIONS (Fifteenth Edition)

**Individual**
1. Gross Income
2. Exclusions from Gross Income
3. Business Expenses and Losses
4. Limitations on Losses
5. Other Deductions for AGI
6. Deductions from AGI
7. Individual Tax Computations
8. Credits

**Property**
9. Basis
10. Depreciation, Amortization, and Depletion
11. Capital Gains and Losses
12. Sale of Business Property
13. Nontaxable Property Transactions

**Other Entities**
14. Partnerships: Formation and Operation
15. Partnerships: Distributions, Sales, and Exchanges
16. Corporate Formations and Operations
17. Advanced Corporate Topics
18. Income Taxation of Estates, Trusts, and Tax-Exempt Organizations

**Other Topics**
19. Accounting Methods
20. Employment Taxes and Withholding
21. Wealth Transfer Taxes
22. Preparer Rules
23. Federal Tax Process and Procedure

## BUSINESS LAW/LEGAL STUDIES EXAM QUESTIONS AND EXPLANATIONS (Sixth Edition)

**Introduction**
1. The American Legal System
2. The American Court System
3. Civil Litigation and Procedure
4. Constitutional Law
5. Administrative Law
6. Criminal Law and Procedure
7. Tort Law
8. Contracts: The Agreement
9. Contracts: Consideration
10. Contracts: Capacity, Legality, Mutuality, and Statute of Frauds
11. Contracts: Interpretation, Conditions, Discharge, and Remedies
12. Contracts: Third-Party Rights and Duties
13. Sale of Goods: The Sales Contract, Interpretation, and Risk of Loss
14. Sale of Goods: Performance, Remedies, and Warranties
15. Negotiable Instruments: Types, Negotiation, and Holder in Due Course
16. Negotiable Instruments: Liability, Bank Transactions, and EFTs
17. Negotiable Instruments: Documents of Title and Letters of Credit
18. Secured Transactions
19. Suretyship
20. Bankruptcy
21. Personal Property and Bailments
22. Computers and the Law
23. Real Property: Interests and Rights
24. Real Property: Transactions
25. Mortgages
26. Creditor Law and Liens
27. Landlord and Tenant
28. Wills, Estate Administration, and Trusts
29. Agency
30. Partnerships and Other Entities
31. Corporations: Nature, Formation, and Financing
32. Corporations: Operations and Management
33. Federal Securities Regulation
34. Insurance
35. Environmental Law
36. Antitrust
37. Consumer Protection
38. Employment Regulation
39. International Business Law
40. Accountants' Legal Responsibilities

## INCREASE YOUR COMPETITIVENESS!

After graduation, you will be competing with graduates from schools across the country in the job market. Make sure you measure up to the standards your counterparts at other schools measure up to (which will be tested on the CPA and other certification exams).

Gleim's ***Exam Questions and Explanations Test Prep*** software is a powerful knowledge transfer tool for students and professors. The software allows students to test themselves interactively with all of the multiple-choice questions from the corresponding *Exam Questions and Explanations* book. Professors use the same software to generate quizzes and exams.

## CITATION TO AUTHORITATIVE PRONOUNCEMENTS

This book cites authoritative pronouncements using the abbreviations in the following list. The internal auditing abbreviations and acronyms are listed in Study Unit 9, Internal Auditing.

| | |
|---|---|
| APB | APB Opinions were issued by the AICPA Accounting Principles Board from 1959 to 1973. A total of 31 opinions were issued. |
| AR | Statements on Standards for Accounting and Review Services (SSARS) are a series of AICPA pronouncements setting standards for engagements in connection with unaudited financial statements or other unaudited financial information of nonpublic entities. |
| ARB | Accounting Research Bulletins were issued by the Committee on Accounting Procedure until 1959. A total of 51 ARBs were issued. |
| AS | Auditing standards are issued by the PCAOB applicable to "issuers" (public companies). |
| AT | Statements on Standards for Attestation Engagements (SSAEs) are issued by the ASB, the Accounting and Review Services Committee, and the Management Consulting Services Executive Committee. |
| AU | SASs are codified in the professional standards volumes using the AU prefix. |
| BL | Bylaws of the AICPA are abbreviated as BL. |
| CS | Statements on Standards for Consulting Services are codified using the CS prefix. |
| FASAB | The Federal Accounting Standards Advisory Board promulgates officially established accounting principles for federal governmental entities. |
| FASB | The Financial Accounting Standards Board issues Statements of Financial Accounting Standards and Interpretations. |
| PFP | Statements on Responsibilities in Personal Financial Planning Practice are codified using the PFP prefix. |
| PR | Standards for Performing and Reporting on Peer Reviews are codified under the PR prefix. They apply to the parties involved in practice-monitoring programs. |
| QC | Statements on Quality Control Standards are codified using the QC prefix. These AICPA pronouncements set standards for quality control by CPA firms. |
| SAS | Statements on Auditing Standards issued by the AICPA Auditing Standards Board (ASB) are codified using the SAS prefix. The 10 standards and the SASs are generally accepted auditing standards. Conduct Rule 202 requires compliance with them. |
| SFAS | Statements of Financial Accounting Standards are issued by the Financial Accounting Standards Board (FASB), which was established in 1973. Many SFASs supersede prior SFASs, APB Opinions, and Accounting Research Bulletins. |
| SOX | Sarbanes-Oxley Act of 2002. |
| TS | Statements on Standards for Tax Services (SSTS) set enforceable standards for responsibilities to the taxpayer (client), the public, and government. |

When a pronouncement is cited in the text, the pronouncement number follows the abbreviations. For example, AU 110 refers to Auditing Standards, Section 110.

The first time an authoritative pronouncement is cited, the abbreviation and number are followed by the pronouncement title, e.g., AU 339, *Audit Documentation*. In subsequent citations within a related series of questions, the title is usually omitted.

The next two sideheadings give two-way cross-references:

- Study units in this book referenced to authoritative pronouncements
- Authoritative pronouncements referenced to study units in this book

## COVERAGE OF AUTHORITATIVE PRONOUNCEMENTS

The listing below and on the following page indicates coverage by study unit in this book

**Study Unit 1 External Auditing Standards and Professional Responsibilities**

110 Responsibilities and Functions of the Independent Auditor
150 Generally Accepted Auditing Standards
161 The Relationship of Generally Accepted Auditing Standards to Quality Control Standards
201 Nature of the General Standards
210 Training and Proficiency of the Independent Auditor
220 Independence
230 Due Professional Care in the Performance of Work
310 Appointment of the Independent Auditor
311 Planning and Supervision
312 Audit Risk and Materiality in Conducting an Audit
313 Substantive Tests Prior to the Balance Sheet Date
315 Communications between Predecessor and Successor Auditors
316 Consideration of Fraud in a Financial Statement Audit
317 Illegal Acts by Clients
319 Consideration of Internal Control in a Financial Statement Audit
380 Communication with Audit Committees
410 Adherence to Generally Accepted Accounting Principles
411 The Meaning of *Present Fairly in Conformity with Generally Accepted Accounting Principles* in the Independent Auditor's Report
431 Adequacy of Disclosure in Financial Statements
504 Association with Financial Statements
AT 101 Attest Engagements
AT 601 Compliance Attestation
AR 100 Compilation and Review of Financial Statements
PR 100 Standards for Performing and Reporting on Peer Reviews
Statements on Standards for Consulting Services
Statements on Quality Control Standards
Statements on Standards for Tax Services
AICPA Code of Professional Conduct
Assurance Services
Statements on Responsibilities in Personal Financial Planning Practice
AS No. 2 An Audit of Internal Control over Financial Reporting Performed in Conjunction with an Audit of the Financial Statements

**Study Unit 2 Audit Planning and Risk Assessment**

310 Appointment of the Independent Auditor
311 Planning and Supervision
312 Audit Risk and Materiality in Conducting an Audit
315 Consideration of Fraud in a Financial Statement Audit
316 Training and Proficiency of the Independent Auditor
317 Illegal Acts by Clients
319 Consideration of Internal Control in a Financial Statement Audit
326 Evidential Matter
329 Analytical Procedures
331 Inventories
333 Management Representations
339 Audit Documentation
350 Audit Sampling
508 Reports on Audited Financial Statements
Conduct Rule 201
AS No. 2 An Audit of Internal Control over Financial Reporting Performed in Conjunction with an Audit of the Financial Statements
AS No. 3 Audit Documentation

**Study Unit 3 Internal Control**

313 Substantive Tests Prior to the Balance Sheet Date
316 Consideration of Fraud in a Financial Statement Audit
317 Illegal Acts by Clients
319 Consideration of Internal Control in a Financial Statement Audit
322 The Auditor's Consideration of the Internal Audit Function in an Audit of Financial Statements
328 Auditing Fair Value Measurements and Disclosures
325 The Communication of Internal Control Related Matters Noted in and Audit
326 Evidential Matter
331 Inventories
350 Audit Sampling
380 Communication with Audit Committees
532 Restricting the Use of an Auditor's Report
AS No. 2 An Audit of Internal Control over Financial Reporting Performed in Conjunction with an Audit of the Financial Statements

**Study Unit 4 Audit Evidence and Procedures**

311 Planning and Supervision
312 Audit Risk and Materiality in Conducting an Audit
313 Substantive Tests Prior to the Balance Sheet Date
316 Consideration of Fraud in a Financial Statement Audit
317 Illegal Acts by Clients
319 Consideration of Internal Control in a Financial Statement Audit
326 Evidential Matter
328 Auditing Fair Value Measurements and Disclosures
329 Analytical Procedures
330 The Confirmation Process
331 Inventories
332 Auditing Derivative Instruments, Hedging Activities, and Investments in Securities
333 Management Representations
334 Related Parties
336 Using the Work of a Specialist
337 Inquiry of a Client's Lawyer Concerning Litigation, Claims, and Assessments
339 Audit Documentation
341 The Auditor's Consideration of an Entity's Ability to Continue as a Going Concern
342 Auditing Accounting Estimates
390 Consideration of Omitted Procedures after the Report Date
508 Reports on Audited Financial Statements
530 Dating of the Independent Auditor's Report
560 Subsequent Events
561 Subsequent Discovery of Facts Existing at the Date of the Auditor's Report
901 Public Warehouses -- Internal Controls and Auditing Procedures for Goods Held
AR 100 Compilation and Review of Financial Statements
AS No. 2 An Audit of Internal Control over Financial Reporting Performed in Conjunction with an Audit of the Financial Statements
AS No. 3 Audit Documentation

**Study Unit 5 Information Systems**

319 Consideration of Internal Control in a Financial Statement Audit
AS No. 2 An Audit of Internal Control over Financial Reporting Performed in Conjunction with an Audit of the Financial Statements

**Study Unit 6 Statistical Sampling**

350 Audit Sampling

**Study Unit 7 Audit Reports**

110 Responsibilities and Functions of the Independent Auditor
150 Generally Accepted Auditing Standards
310 Appointment of the Independent Auditor
316 Consideration of Fraud in a Financial Statement Audit
317 Illegal Acts by Clients
331 Inventories
333 Management Representations
334 Related Parties
336 Using the Work of a Specialist
337 Inquiry of a Client's Lawyer Concerning Litigation, Claims, and Assessments
341 The Auditor's Consideration of an Entity's Ability to Continue as a Going Concern
380 Communication with Audit Committees
410 Adherence to Generally Accepted Accounting Principles
411 The Meaning of *Present Fairly in Conformity with Generally Accepted Accounting Principles* in the Independent Auditor's Report
420 Consistency of Application of Generally Accepted Accounting Principles
431 Adequacy of Disclosure in Financial Statements
504 Association with Financial Statements
508 Reports on Audited Financial Statements
530 Dating of the Independent Auditor's Report
534 Reporting on Financial Statements Prepared for Use in Other Countries
543 Part of Audit Made by Other Independent Auditors
544 Lack of Conformity with Generally Accepted Accounting Principles
551 Reporting on Information Accompanying the Basic Financial Statements in Auditor-Submitted Documents
552 Reporting on Condensed Financial Statements and Selected Financial Data
558 Required Supplementary Information
560 Subsequent Events
561 Subsequent Discovery of Facts Existing at the Date of the Auditor's Report
623 Special Reports
625 Reports on the Application of Accounting Principles
634 Letters for Underwriters and Certain Other Requesting Parties
711 Filings under Federal Securities Statutes
AT 101 Attest Engagements
AT 601 Compliance Attestation
AT 701 Management's Discussion and Analysis
AR 100 Compilation and Review of Financial Statements
Conduct Rule 203
Conduct Rule 301
AS No. 1 References in Auditors' Reports to the Standards of the Public Company Accounting Oversight Board
AS No. 2 An Audit of Internal Control over Financial Reporting Performed in Conjunction with an Audit of the Financial Statements

**Study Unit 8 Special Reports and Other Reporting Issues**

150 Generally Accepted Auditing Standards
324 Service Organizations
504 Association with Financial Statements
532 Restricting the Use of an Auditor's Report
543 Part of Audit Made by Other Independent Auditors
550 Other Information in Documents Containing Audited Financial Statements
551 Reporting on Information Accompanying the Basic Financial Statements in Auditor-Submitted Documents
552 Reporting on Condensed Financial Statements and Selected Financial Data
558 Required Supplementary Information
623 Special Reports
625 Reports on the Application of Accounting Principles
634 Letters for Underwriters and Certain Other Requesting Parties
711 Filings under Federal Securities Statutes
722 Interim Financial Information
801 Compliance Auditing Considerations in Audits of Governmental Entities and Recipients of Governmental Financial Assistance
AT 101 Attest Engagements
AT 201 Agreed-Upon Procedures Engagements
AT 301 Financial Forecasts and Projections
AT 401 Reporting on Pro Forma Financial Information
AT 501 Reporting on an Entity's Internal Control over Financial Reporting
AT 601 Compliance Attestation
AT 701 Management's Discussion and Analysis
AR 100 Compilation and Review of Financial Statements
AR 200 Reporting on Comparative Financial Statements
AR 300 Compilation Reports on Financial Statements Included in Certain Prescribed Forms
AR 400 Communications between Predecessor and Successor Accountants
AR 600 Reporting on Personal Financial Statements Included in Written Personal Financial Plans
AS No. 2 An Audit of Internal Control over Financial Reporting Performed in Conjunction with an Audit of the Financial Statements

**Study Unit 9 Internal Auditing**

The IIA Code of Ethics
International Standards for the Professional Practice of Internal Auditing (Standards)
Practice Advisories

## PRONOUNCEMENT CROSS-REFERENCE

The following is a directory listing the subunits in this study manual that cover the professional standards. The subunit number(s) follow(s) the pronouncement title. Most pronouncements are covered by at least two multiple-choice questions.

| Sec. No. | Statements on Auditing Standards |
|---|---|
| 110 | Responsibilities and Functions of the Independent Auditor - 1.1, 1.2, 1.7, SU 7 |
| 150 | Generally Accepted Auditing Standards - 1.2, 7.1, 7.2, 7.5, 8.1 |
| 161 | The Relationship of Generally Accepted Auditing Standards to Quality Control Standards - 1.10 |
| 201 | Nature of the General Standards - 1.2, 1.3 |
| 210 | Training and Proficiency of the Independent Auditor - 1.3 |
| 220 | Independence - 1.3 |
| 230 | Due Professional Care in the Performance of Work - 1.3 |
| 310 | Appointment of the Independent Auditor - 1.4, 2.1, 7.7 |
| 311 | Planning and Supervision - 1.10, 2.1, 2.2, 2.5, SU 4 |
| 312 | Audit Risk and Materiality in Conducting an Audit - 1.4, 2.3, SU 4 |
| 313 | Substantive Tests Prior to the Balance Sheet Date - 1.4, 3.4, SU 4 |
| 315 | Communications between Predecessor and Successor Auditors - 1.3, 2.1, 2.2, 2.4, 2.5 |
| 316 | Consideration of Fraud in a Financial Statement Audit - 1.7, 1.9, 2.4, SU 4, 7.6 |
| 317 | Illegal Acts by Clients - 1.5, 2.4, 3.2, 4.12, 7.5, 7.7 |
| 319 | Consideration of Internal Control in a Financial Statement Audit - 1.1, 1.4, 1.6, 2.2, 2.3, 2.5, 3.1 - 3.5, 3.7, 3.11, 3.13, 3.14, 4.1, 4.12, 5.13 |
| 322 | The Auditor's Consideration of the Internal Audit Function in an Audit of Financial Statements - 3.4, 3.13 |
| 324 | Service Organizations - 8.5 |
| 325 | The Communication of Internal Control Related Matters Noted in an Audit - 3.2, 3.7, 3.12 |
| 326 | Evidential Matter - 2.2, 3.9, SU 4 |
| 328 | Auditing Fair Value Measurements and Disclosures - 3.9, 4.1 |
| 329 | Analytical Procedures - 2.5, 4.2, 4.11 |
| 330 | The Confirmation Process - 4.1, 4.3 |
| 331 | Inventories - 2.2, 3.10, 4.1, 4.4, 4.6, 4.14, 6.2, 7.5 |
| 332 | Auditing Derivative Instruments, Hedging Activities, and Investments in Securities - 4.8, 4.9 |
| 333 | Management Representations - 2.4, 4.1, 4.12, 7.7 |
| 334 | Related Parties - 4.16, 7.4, 7.5, 7.10 |
| 336 | Using the Work of a Specialist - 4.14, 7.5, 7.12 |
| 337 | Inquiry of a Client's Lawyer Concerning Litigation, Claims, and Assessments - 4.13, 7.5, 7.7 |
| 339 | Audit Documentation - 2.5 |
| 341 | The Auditor's Consideration of an Entity's Ability to Continue as a Going Concern - 4.2, 7.4, 7.5, 7.11 |
| 342 | Auditing Accounting Estimates - 4.1 |
| 350 | Audit Sampling - 2.3, 3.5, SU 6 |
| 380 | Communication with Audit Committees - 1.3, 3.12 |
| 390 | Consideration of Omitted Procedures after the Report Date - 4.15 |
| 410 | Adherence to Generally Accepted Accounting Principles - 1.4, 7.2 |
| 411 | The Meaning of Present Fairly in Conformity with Generally Accepted Accounting Principles in the Independent Auditor's Report - 1.4, 7.1, 7.2, 7.4, 7.5 |
| 420 | Consistency of Application of Generally Accepted Accounting Principles - 7.3 , 7.4, 7.11 |
| 431 | Adequacy of Disclosure in Financial Statements - 1.7, 7.4, 7.6 |
| 504 | Association with Financial Statements - 1.3, 1.8, 7.1, 7.5, 7.6, 7.9, 8.3, 8.4 |
| 508 | Reports on Audited Financial Statements - 2.4, 4.16, SU 7 |
| 530 | Dating of the Independent Auditor's Report - 4.15, 7.8, 7.9, 7.11 |
| 532 | Restricting the Use of an Auditor's Report - 3.12, 8.1, 8.2 |
| 534 | Reporting on Financial Statements Prepared for Use in Other Countries - 7.2 |
| 543 | Part of Audit Made by Other Independent Auditors - 7.5, 7.9, 7.12, 8.3, 8.5 |
| 544 | Lack of Conformity with Generally Accepted Accounting Principles - 7.2, 7.5 |
| 550 | Other Information in Documents Containing Audited Financial Statements - 8.2 |
| 551 | Reporting on Information Accompanying the Basic Financial Statements in Auditor-Submitted Documents - 7.4, 8.2 |
| 552 | Reporting on Condensed Financial Statements and Selected Financial Data - 7.12, 8.2 |
| 558 | Required Supplementary Information - 7.7, 8.2 |
| 560 | Subsequent Events - 4.9, 4.15, 7.4, 7.5, 7.8, 7.11 |
| 561 | Subsequent Discovery of Facts Existing at the Date of the Auditor's Report - 4.15, 7.11 |
| 623 | Special Reports - 7.2, 7.7, 8.1, 8.4 |
| 625 | Reports on the Application of Accounting Principles - 7.2, 8.1 |
| 634 | Letters for Underwriters and Certain Other Requesting Parties - 7.5, 7.9, 8.4, 8.7 |

| Sec. No. | Statements on Auditing Standards |
|---|---|
| 711 | Filings under Federal Securities Statutes - 7.11, 8.2, 8.7 |
| 722 | Interim Financial Information - 4.2, 8.1, 8.3, 8.4, 8.7 |
| 801 | Compliance Auditing Considerations in Audits of Governmental Entities and Recipients of Governmental Financial Assistance - 8.8 |
| 901 | Public Warehouses -- Internal Controls and Auditing Procedures for Goods Held - 4.6 |

Statements on Standards for Attestation Engagements

| | |
|---|---|
| AT 101 | Attest Engagements - 1.13, 7.9, 8.1, 8.9 |
| AT 201 | Agreed-Upon Procedures Engagements - 8.1 |
| AT 301 | Financial Forecasts and Projections- 1.5, 7.5, 8.1, 8.6 |
| AT 401 | Reporting on Pro Forma Financial Information - 8.6 |
| AT 501 | Reporting on an Entity's Internal Control over Financial Reporting - 8.1, 8.5 |
| AT 601 | Compliance Attestation - 1.13, 8.9 |
| AT 701 | Management's Discussion and Analysis - 8.10 |

Statements on Standards for Accounting and Review Services

| | |
|---|---|
| AR 100 | Compilation and Review of Financial Statements - 1.8, 1.9, 4.2, 7.6, 8.4, 8.5, 8.7 |
| AR 200 | Reporting on Comparative Financial Statements - 8.4 |
| AR 300 | Compilation Reports on Financial Statements Included in Certain Prescribed Forms - 8.4 |
| AR 400 | Communications between Predecessor and Successor Accountants - 8.4 |
| AR 600 | Reporting on Personal Financial Statements Included in Written Personal Financial Plans - 8.4 |

Statements on Standards for Consulting Services

| | |
|---|---|
| CS 100 | Consulting Services: Definitions and Standards - 1.12 |

Statements on Standards for Tax Services

| | |
|---|---|
| TS 100 | Tax Return Positions - 1.6, 1.11 |
| TS 200 | Answers to Questions on Returns - 1.11 |
| TS 300 | Certain Procedural Aspects of Preparing Returns - 1.11 |
| TS 400 | Use of Estimates - 1.11 |
| TS 500 | Departure from a Position Previously concluded in an Administrative Proceeding or Court Decision - 1.11 |
| TS 600 | Knowledge of Error: Return Preparation - 1.11 |
| TS 700 | Knowledge of Error: Administrative Proceedings - 1.11 |
| TS 800 | Form and Content of Advice to Clients - 1.11 |

Statements on Quality Control Standards

| | |
|---|---|
| QC 20 | System of Quality Control for a CPA Firm's Accounting and Auditing Practice - 1.3, 1.10 |
| QC 30 | Monitoring a CPA Firm's Accounting and Auditing Practice - 1.10 |
| QC 40 | The Personnel Management Element of a Firm's System of Quality Control -- Competencies Required by a Practitioner-in-Charge of an Attest Engagement - 1.10 |

Standards for Performing and Reporting on Peer Reviews

| | |
|---|---|
| PR 100 | Standards for Performing and Reporting on Peer Reviews - 1.10 |

Statements on Responsibilities in Personal Financial Planning Practice

| | |
|---|---|
| PFP 100 - 500 | Basic Personal Financial Planning Engagement Functions and Responsibilities - 1.15 |

Code of Professional Conduct

Conduct Rule 101 - 1.3, 1.5, 1.6
Conduct Rule 102 - 1.5, 1.6, 1.8
Conduct Rule 201 - 1.2, 1.5, 2.1
Conduct Rule 202 - 1.2, 1.5
Conduct Rule 203 - 1.4, 1.5, 1.8, 7.2
Conduct Rule 301 - 1.7, 7.4
Conduct Rule 302 - 1.6, 1.8
Conduct Rule 501 - 1.5, 1.8
Conduct Rule 502 - 1.5, 1.8
Conduct Rule 503 - 1.5, 1.8
Conduct Rule 505 - 1.5

Public Company Accounting Oversight Board

| | |
|---|---|
| AS No. 1 | References in Auditors' Reports to the Standards of the Public Company Accounting Oversight Board - 7.5 |
| AS No. 2 | An Audit of Internal Control over Financial Reporting Performed in Conjunction with an Audit of the Financial Statements - 1.1, 1.4, 1.6, 2.2, 2.3, 2.5, 3.1 - 3.5, 3.7, 3.11, 3.13, 3.14, 4.1, 4.12, 5.13 |
| AS No. 3 | Audit Documentation - 2.5 |

## RECENT SASs AND THEIR AU NUMBERS

| | | |
|---|---|---|
| SAS 85 | Management Representations [1] | 333 |
| SAS 86 | Amendment to SAS No. 72 | 634 |
| SAS 87 | Restricting the Use of an Auditor's Report | 532 |
| SAS 88 | Service Organizations and Reporting on Consistency [2] | |
| SAS 89 | Audit Adjustments [3] | |
| SAS 90 | Audit Committee Communications [4] | |
| SAS 91 | Federal GAAP Hierarchy [5] | |
| SAS 92 | Auditing Derivative Instruments, Hedging Activities, and Investments in Securities [6] | 332 |
| SAS 93 | Omnibus Statement on Auditing Standards - 2000 [7] | |
| SAS 94 | The Effect of Information Technology on the Auditor's Consideration of Internal Control in a Financial Statement Audit | 319 |
| SAS 95 | Generally Accepted Auditing Standards | 150 |
| SAS 96 | Audit Documentation | 339 |
| SAS 97 | Amendment to SAS No. 50, Reports on the Application of Accounting Principles | 625 |
| SAS 98 | Omnibus - 2002 [8] | |
| SAS 99 | Consideration of Fraud in a Financial Statement Audit [9] | |
| SAS 100 | Interim Financial Information [10] | |
| SAS 101 | Auditing Fair Value Measurements and Disclosures | 320 |

[1] Supersedes old AU 333 and also slightly amends AU 508
[2] Amends AU 324 and AU 420
[3] Amends AU 310, AU 333, and AU 380
[4] Amends AU 380 and AU 722
[5] Amends AU 411
[6] Supersedes old AU 332
[7] Withdraws AU 622 and amends AU 315, AU 411, and AU 508
[8] Amends AU 150, 161, 312, 324, 508, 558, 551, 560, 561, 530
[9] Supersedes old AU 316 and amends AU 230 and AU 333
[10] Supersedes old AU 722

# STUDY UNIT ONE

# EXTERNAL AUDITING STANDARDS AND PROFESSIONAL RESPONSIBILITIES



The first subunit in this study unit provides an overview of the nature of independent, external auditing. The next three subunits concern the 10 standards applicable to audits. Subunit 1.3 covers the three general standards, which are not addressed elsewhere in the book. The three standards of field work and the four standards of reporting are dealt with in a single subunit (1.4) because these standards and their applications are covered further in

Study Unit 2 – Audit Planning and Risk Assessment
Study Unit 3 – Internal Control
Study Unit 4 – Audit Evidence and Procedures
Study Unit 7 – Audit Reports

Subunits 1.5 through 1.8 concern the AICPA *Code of Professional Conduct*, and Subunit 1.9 covers the legal liability of CPAs. Subunit 1.10 addresses the quality control and peer review standards applicable to CPA firms (GAAS apply to individuals) that help them to comply with GAAS. Subunit 1.11 contains questions on the AICPA Statements on Standards for Tax Services. Subunit 1.12 covers the AICPA Statement on Standards for Consulting Services. Subunit 1.13 deals with AT 101, *Attest Engagements*, and addresses the 11 attestation standards. These standards are an extension of the 10 standards applicable to audits. They apply to attest services rendered by a CPA in the practice of public accounting. These services also include compliance attestation (AT 601). A new category of services, assurance services, is the subject of Subunit 1.14. Subunit 1.15 addresses personal financial planning (codified in PFP 100-500). Questions relating to the Sarbanes-Oxley Act of 2002 and the Public Company Accounting Oversight Board (PCAOB) are included in a number of subunits, although this act mostly concerns audits of public companies.

## QUESTIONS

### 1.1 Introduction to Auditing

**1.** The primary reason for an audit by an independent, external audit firm is to

A. Satisfy governmental regulatory requirements.

B. Guarantee that there are no misstatements in the financial statements and ensure that any fraud will be discovered.

C. Relieve management of responsibility for the financial statements.

D. Provide increased assurance to users as to the fairness of the financial statements.

Answer (D) is correct. *(CMA, adapted)*

**REQUIRED:** The primary reason for an independent, external audit.

**DISCUSSION:** The objective of an audit is to express an opinion as to whether an entity's financial statements present fairly, in all material respects, its financial position, results of operations, and cash flows in conformity with generally accepted accounting principles (GAAP). An audit performed by an independent, external audit firm provides assurance of the objectivity of the auditor's opinion.

Answer (A) is incorrect because, although governmental regulation has increased [e.g., the requirement of the Foreign Corrupt Practices Act (FCPA) that certain companies maintain adequate internal control], the primary objective of the audit continues to be an opinion on the fairness of the financial statements. Answer (B) is incorrect because the auditor is neither a guarantor nor an insurer. Answer (C) is incorrect because, according to both AU 110, *Responsibilities and Functions of the Independent Auditor*, and the FCPA, management is responsible for the financial statements.

**2.** Independent CPAs perform audits on the financial statements of public companies. This type of auditing can best be described as

A. An activity whose purpose is to search for fraud.

B. A discipline that attests to financial information presented by management.

C. A professional activity that measures and communicates financial and business data.

D. A regulatory function that prevents the issuance of improper financial information.

Answer (B) is correct. *(Publisher)*

**REQUIRED:** The statement that best describes independent auditing.

**DISCUSSION:** The objective of the audit is to express an opinion on (attest to) the fairness of presentation and conformity with GAAP of management's financial statements.

Answer (A) is incorrect because the auditor plans and performs the audit to provide reasonable assurance of detecting material misstatements, whether caused by error or fraud. However, (s)he need not search for all instances of fraud, and the ultimate objective is to determine whether the statements are fairly presented. Answer (C) is incorrect because the accounting, not auditing, process is a professional activity that measures and communicates financial and business data. Answer (D) is incorrect because an auditor lacks regulatory authority.

**3.** Users of a public company's financial statements demand independent audits because

A. Users demand assurance that fraud does not exist.

B. Management may not be objective in reporting.

C. Users expect auditors to correct management errors.

D. Management relies on the auditor to improve internal control.

Answer (B) is correct. *(Publisher)*

**REQUIRED:** The reason for an independent audit.

**DISCUSSION:** Management and financial statement users may have an adversarial relationship because their interests in the firm are different. The independent auditor provides assurance that the financial statements are not biased for or against any interest.

Answer (A) is incorrect because the independent auditor is ultimately concerned with the fair presentation of the financial statements in conformity with GAAP, not just with the detection of fraud. However, the audit should be planned and performed to provide reasonable assurance that material misstatements are detected. Answer (C) is incorrect because management is responsible for error correction. Answer (D) is incorrect because poorly designed internal control is not necessarily inconsistent with a fair presentation of the financial statements. However, the Public Company Accounting Oversight Board (PCAOB), AS No. 2 requires an auditor's opinion on internal control in conjunction with the opinion on the financial statements.

**4.** An audit of the financial statements of Camden Corporation is being conducted by an external auditor. The external auditor is expected to

A. Express an opinion as to the fairness of Camden's financial statements.

B. Express an opinion as to the attractiveness of Camden for investment purposes and critique the wisdom and legality of its business decisions.

C. Certify the correctness of Camden's financial statements.

D. Make a 100% examination of Camden's records.

Answer (A) is correct. *(CMA, adapted)*

**REQUIRED:** The responsibility of an external auditor for an audit of financial statements.

**DISCUSSION:** The fourth standard of reporting requires the auditor to express an opinion regarding the financial statements taken as a whole or to make an assertion to the effect that an opinion cannot be expressed. The opinion concerns the fairness, in all material respects, with which the financial position, results of operations, and cash flows reported in the financial statements have been presented in conformity with GAAP.

Answer (B) is incorrect because the external auditor does not interpret the financial statement data for investment purposes or evaluate management decisions. Answer (C) is incorrect because the external audit normally cannot be so thorough as to permit a guarantee of correctness. Answer (D) is incorrect because a 100% examination is seldom, if ever, feasible.

**5.** Brandnew Company is going public, and its stock will be listed on a stock exchange. Audited financial statements are required to be filed with the Securities and Exchange Commission (SEC). Who is expected to be the primary user of the audited financial statements?

A. The stock exchange.

B. Brandnew Company's investors.

C. The SEC.

D. Brandnew Company's board of directors.

Answer (B) is correct. *(Publisher)*

**REQUIRED:** The primary user of audited financial statements of a publicly held corporation.

**DISCUSSION:** An audit's primary objective is to provide assurance to current and potential creditors and investors and other users of financial statements that the financial statements present fairly, in all material respects, the financial position, results of operations, and cash flows of the company.

Answer (A) is incorrect because a stock exchange can require disclosures suitable for its purposes. Investors may not have this power. Answer (C) is incorrect because the SEC can require whatever disclosures are desired. Answer (D) is incorrect because the board of directors can require whatever disclosures are desired.

**6.** The Committee of Sponsoring Organizations (COSO) of the Treadway Commission issued a document in 1992 that has been embraced by numerous organizations, including the AICPA and the GAO. That document is titled

A. The Yellow Book.

B. Internal Control--Integrated Framework.

C. Statements on Auditing Standards.

D. *Code of Professional Conduct.*

Answer (B) is correct. *(Publisher)*

**REQUIRED:** The document issued by the COSO.

**DISCUSSION:** Many professional and regulatory bodies have recognized the COSO's internal control framework by incorporating its terms, definitions, and concepts into their policies, procedures, pronouncements, and other literature.

Answer (A) is incorrect because the Yellow Book, or *Government Auditing Standards,* is issued by the GAO. Answer (C) is incorrect because Statements on Auditing Standards are issued by the Auditing Standards Board of the AICPA. Answer (D) is incorrect because the *Code of Professional Conduct* has been adopted by the members of the AICPA.

**7.** When Congress passed the Sarbanes-Oxley Act of 2002, it imposed greater regulation on public companies and their auditors and required increased accountability. Which of the following is not a provision of the act?

A. Executives must certify the appropriateness of the financial statements.

B. The act provides criminal penalties for fraud.

C. Auditors may not provide specific nonaudit services for their audit clients.

D. Audit firms must be rotated on a periodic basis.

Answer (D) is correct. *(Publisher)*

**REQUIRED:** The provision not included in the Sarbanes-Oxley Act.

**DISCUSSION:** The act requires rotation of the lead audit or coordinating partner and the reviewing partner on audits of public clients every 5 years. It also requires certain other partners to be rotated every 7 years. However, the act does not require the rotation of audit firms.

Answer (A) is incorrect because the CEO and CFO of a public company must provide a statement to accompany the audit report. This statement certifies the appropriateness of the financial statements and disclosures. However, a violation of this requirement must be knowing and intentional. Answer (B) is incorrect because Title VIII, *Corporate and Criminal Fraud Accountability Act of 2002*, creates a new crime for securities fraud with penalties of fines and up to 10 years in prison, extends the statute of limitations on securities fraud claims, and makes it a felony to create or destroy documents to impede a federal investigation. Answer (C) is incorrect because the act makes it unlawful for a registered public accounting firm to perform certain nonaudit services for audit clients, for example, bookkeeping, systems design, management functions, or any other service the Public Company Accounting Oversight Board (PCAOB) determines by regulation to be impermissible.

**8.** Who establishes generally accepted auditing standards?

A. American Institute of Certified Public Accountants.

B. Financial Accounting Standards Board.

C. State Boards of Accountancy.

D. Securities and Exchange Commission.

Answer (A) is correct. *(Publisher)*

**REQUIRED:** The organization that promulgates generally accepted auditing standards (GAAS).

**DISCUSSION:** AICPA Conduct Rule 202, *Compliance with Standards*, requires adherence to standards promulgated by bodies designated by the AICPA Council. The Auditing Standards Board (ASB) is the body designated to issue auditing standards. They are in the form of Statements on Auditing Standards (SASs), which are codified within the framework of the 10 standards. The Public Company Accounting Oversight Board (PCAOB) was created by the Sarbanes-Oxley Act of 2002. It establishes by rule auditing, quality control, ethics, independence, and other standards relating to the preparation of audit reports for public entities. The PCAOB is required to cooperate with the AICPA and other groups in setting auditing standards and may adopt their proposals. Nevertheless, the PCAOB is authorized to amend, modify, repeal, or reject any such standards.

Answer (B) is incorrect because the FASB issues Statements on Financial Accounting Standards and other financial accounting pronouncements and interpretations. Answer (C) is incorrect because Boards of Accountancy in the states and territories regulate the practice of accounting. They typically grant CPA certificates and licenses. Answer (D) is incorrect because the SEC issues Financial Reporting Releases and Accounting and Auditing Enforcement Releases.

**9.** The authoritative body designated by the AICPA to promulgate standards concerning an accountant's association with unaudited financial statements of a nonpublic entity is the

A. Financial Accounting Standards Board.

B. General Accounting Office.

C. Accounting and Review Services Committee.

D. Auditing Standards Board.

Answer (C) is correct. *(CPA, adapted)*

**REQUIRED:** The body that promulgates standards for an accountant's association with unaudited statements.

**DISCUSSION:** The Accounting and Review Services Committee is the AICPA's senior technical committee authorized to issue pronouncements in connection with the unaudited financial statements or other unaudited financial information of a nonpublic entity (one not required to file financial statements with an agency regulating issuance of the entity's securities).

Answer (A) is incorrect because the FASB is charged with establishing GAAP. Answer (B) is incorrect because the GAO is the federal agency that issues *Government Auditing Standards* (the Yellow Book). Answer (D) is incorrect because the ASB is the AICPA senior technical committee responsible for issuing auditing and attest standards and procedures.

**10.** CPAs within each state have formed state societies or associations of CPAs. Which of the following statements about these associations is false?

A. Most associations have their own codes of professional ethics that closely parallel the AICPA *Code of Professional Conduct*.

B. The state societies are independent of the AICPA.

C. All CPAs in the state must be members of the state association or society.

D. Members of state associations may also be members of the AICPA.

Answer (C) is correct. *(Publisher)*

**REQUIRED:** The false statement concerning state associations or societies of CPAs.

**DISCUSSION:** Membership in state societies as well as the AICPA is voluntary. State societies typically function through small, full-time staffs or committees composed of their members. They promote the interests of the membership through communication and continuing education programs.

Answer (A) is incorrect because many state societies have adopted codes of ethics that are similar to the AICPA *Code of Professional Conduct*. Answer (B) is incorrect because the state societies are independent of the AICPA, although they cooperate in promoting the mutual interests of CPAs. Answer (D) is incorrect because members of state societies may also belong to the AICPA.

## 1.2 Nature of Generally Accepted Auditing Standards

**11.** Which of the following best describes what is meant by generally accepted auditing standards (GAAS)?

A. Pronouncements issued by the Auditing Standards Board (ASB).

B. Rules acknowledged by the accounting profession because of their universal application.

C. Procedures to be used to gather evidence to support financial statements.

D. Measures of the quality of the auditor's performance.

Answer (D) is correct. *(CPA, adapted)*

**REQUIRED:** The best description of GAAS.

**DISCUSSION:** According to AU 150, *Generally Accepted Auditing Standards*, "standards provide a measure of audit quality and the objectives to be achieved in an audit." The 10 standards include three general standards, three standards of field work, and four standards of reporting. Standards in the form of Statements on Auditing Standards (SASs) are issued by the ASB. An auditor must exercise professional judgment in applying the 10 standards and the SASs.

Answer (A) is incorrect because the ASB also issues pronouncements that are not included in GAAS. Moreover, the 10 standards were adopted by the membership of the AICPA. However, the PCAOB has ultimate authority with respect to standards for audits of public clients. Answer (B) is incorrect because adherence to good practice is not universal. Answer (C) is incorrect because "procedures are acts that the auditor performs during the course of an audit to comply with auditing standards" (AU 150).

**12.** Generally accepted auditing standards (GAAS) are

A. Sufficiently established so that independent auditors generally agree on their interpretation.

B. Generally accepted based upon a pronouncement of the Financial Accounting Standards Board.

C. Generally accepted by the business community.

D. Binding on members of the AICPA.

Answer (D) is correct. *(CPA, adapted)*

**REQUIRED:** The true statement about GAAS.

**DISCUSSION:** The 10 standards are binding on AICPA members as a result of adoption by the AICPA membership. Moreover, SASs issued by the ASB must be followed by an AICPA member who performs an audit. Conduct Rule 202, *Compliance with Standards*, requires members to comply with standards issued by bodies (e.g., the ASB) designated by the AICPA Council. They are also considered standards of the profession by state boards of accountancy and the courts, so they are also binding on non-AICPA members.

Answer (A) is incorrect because, although the 10 standards were adopted by the AICPA membership, the SASs, which are now issued by the ASB and are codified within the framework of the 10 standards, are often controversial. Answer (B) is incorrect because auditing standards are issued by the AICPA, not the FASB. Answer (C) is incorrect because adoption by the accounting profession and the PCAOB determines whether an auditing standard is binding, not acceptance by the business community.

**13.** Which of the following statements best describes the primary purpose of Statements on Auditing Standards (SASs)?

A. They are guides intended to set forth auditing procedures applicable to a variety of situations.

B. They are procedural outlines intended to narrow the areas of inconsistency and divergence of auditor opinion.

C. They are authoritative statements, enforced through the *Code of Professional Conduct*, and are intended to limit the degree of auditor judgment.

D. They are generally accepted auditing standards.

Answer (D) is correct. *(CPA, adapted)*

**REQUIRED:** The primary purpose of SASs.

**DISCUSSION:** SASs are codified within the framework of the 10 standards and are deemed to have the status of GAAS. Conduct Rule 202 requires members who perform professional services to "comply with standards promulgated by bodies designated by Council." This rule therefore does not distinguish between the 10 standards and the SASs.

Answer (A) is incorrect because SASs are intended to establish auditing standards rather than auditing procedures. Answer (B) is incorrect because SASs narrow areas of inconsistency in auditing, but they are standards and are therefore broader than procedural outlines. Answer (C) is incorrect because compliance with SASs is enforced by the AICPA through the *Code of Professional Conduct*. However, the intention is not to limit the auditor's judgment but to provide guidelines for its exercise.

**14.** Through legal precedent, the generally accepted auditing standards established by the AICPA apply

A. Only to CPAs who belong to local CPA societies.

B. To all CPAs.

C. Only to those CPAs who choose to have quality reviews.

D. Only to CPAs conducting audits subject to AICPA jurisdiction.

Answer (B) is correct. *(Publisher)*

**REQUIRED:** The legally determined applicability of GAAS.

**DISCUSSION:** GAAS apply to all CPAs, whether or not they are members of the AICPA. GAAS are deemed to be standards of the profession (explicitly or implicitly) by state boards of accountancy, which issue, renew, suspend, or revoke licenses and otherwise regulate CPAs in all states. Furthermore, the courts in both civil and criminal cases involving independent accountants also treat GAAS as standards of the profession.

Answer (A) is incorrect because GAAS are binding on all CPAs who perform independent, external audits. Answer (C) is incorrect because GAAS are binding on all CPAs who perform independent, external audits. Answer (D) is incorrect because AICPA jurisdiction concerns only membership in the AICPA. The right to perform the attest function is controlled by state boards of accountancy, all of which require compliance with GAAS.

**15.** In deciding to undertake an audit engagement, the CPA would most likely consider which generally accepted auditing standard(s)?

A. The four reporting standards.

B. The three field work standards.

C. The second field work standard requiring consideration of internal control.

D. The three general standards.

Answer (D) is correct. *(Publisher)*

**REQUIRED:** The GAAS most likely to be considered in choosing to accept an audit engagement.

**DISCUSSION:** The three general standards require the auditor to (1) have adequate technical training and proficiency as an auditor, (2) have an independent mental attitude, and (3) use due professional care in planning and performing the audit and preparing the report. An auditor who cannot meet any one of these requirements should not accept the audit engagement. Conduct Rule 201, *General Standards*, requires an AICPA member to "undertake only those professional services that the member or the member's firm can reasonably expect to be completed with professional competence."

Answer (A) is incorrect because the standards of reporting apply to communicating the results of an engagement. Answer (B) is incorrect because the standards of field work apply to the conduct of the engagement. Answer (C) is incorrect because the second standard of field work requires understanding of internal control.

**16.** What is the nature of the generally accepted auditing standards classified as standards of field work?

A. They require persons performing the audit to be competent.

B. They identify the criteria for the content of the auditor's report on financial statements.

C. They identify the criteria for audit planning and evidence gathering.

D. They state the need to maintain an independence in mental attitude in all matters relating to the audit.

Answer (C) is correct. *(Publisher)*

**REQUIRED:** The nature of the standards of field work.

**DISCUSSION:** The three standards classified as standards of field work relate to (1) planning the audit and supervising assistants, (2) obtaining a sufficient understanding of internal control, and (3) gathering sufficient competent evidence.

Answer (A) is incorrect because the competence of persons performing the audit relate to the general standards. Answer (B) is incorrect because criteria for the content of the auditor's report concern the standards of reporting. Answer (D) is incorrect because independence relates to the second general standard.

**17.** Which statement is not one of the generally accepted auditing standards of reporting?

A. The report must state whether the financial statements are presented in accordance with GAAP.

B. The report must state whether the audit was conducted in accordance with GAAS.

C. Informative disclosures in the financial statements are to be regarded as reasonably adequate unless otherwise stated in the report.

D. The report must contain either an expression of opinion regarding the financial statements taken as a whole or an assertion to the effect that an opinion cannot be expressed.

Answer (B) is correct. *(Publisher)*

**REQUIRED:** The statement that is not one of the generally accepted auditing standards of reporting.

**DISCUSSION:** The scope paragraph of the auditor's standard report states that the audit has been conducted in accordance with GAAS, but that statement is not specifically required by a standard of reporting. The fourth reporting standard does state that, when an auditor's name is associated with financial statements, the report should contain a clear-cut indication of the character of the auditor's work, if any (AU 150).

Answer (A) is incorrect because the first standard of reporting requires that the report state whether the financial statements are presented in accordance with GAAP. Answer (C) is incorrect because the third standard of reporting concerns informative disclosures. Answer (D) is incorrect because the fourth standard of reporting concerns the expression of an opinion.

**18.** Auditing Interpretations are issued by the Audit Issues Task Force of the Auditing Standards Board (ASB) to provide timely guidance on the application of pronouncements of the ASB. They are

A. Less authoritative than pronouncements of the ASB.

B. Equally as authoritative as pronouncements of the ASB.

C. More authoritative than pronouncements of the ASB.

D. Nonauthoritative opinions that are expressed without consulting the ASB.

Answer (A) is correct. *(CPA, adapted)*

**REQUIRED:** The authoritative weight of Auditing Interpretations.

**DISCUSSION:** Auditing Interpretations of the SASs are numbered in the AU 9000 series and immediately follow the related sections in the codification of professional standards. They are interpretive publications that are not as authoritative as ASB pronouncements. However, members should be prepared to explain how they complied with the relevant SASs if they do not apply the interpretive guidance. Other interpretive publications include appendixes to the SASs, guidance in AICPA Audit and Accounting Guides, and AICPA auditing Statements of Position.

Answer (B) is incorrect because interpretations are less authoritative than pronouncements of the ASB. Answer (C) is incorrect because interpretations are less authoritative than pronouncements of the ASB. Answer (D) is incorrect because interpretations provide timely guidance on the application of pronouncements, are considered authoritative, and are reviewed by the ASB.

## 1.3 GAAS – General Standards

**19.** An individual just beginning an auditing career must obtain professional experience primarily to achieve

A. A positive employment evaluation.

B. Seasoned judgment.

C. A favorable peer review.

D. A specialty designation by the AICPA.

Answer (B) is correct. *(CPA, adapted)*

**REQUIRED:** The purpose of requiring professional experience in the auditing profession.

**DISCUSSION:** AU 210, *Training and Proficiency of the Independent Auditor,* states that a junior assistant just beginning an auditing career must obtain professional experience with proper supervision and review by a more experienced supervisor. An auditor charged with the final responsibility for an engagement must be capable of exercising the seasoned judgment developed through professional experience.

Answer (A) is incorrect because a positive employment evaluation is possible before significant professional experience has been obtained. Answer (C) is incorrect because a peer review is an external evaluation of a public accounting firm's practice. Answer (D) is incorrect because, although the AICPA may provide for specialty designations, professional experience will continue to be necessary for the development of the professional proficiency of all independent auditors.

**20.** Within the context of quality control, the primary purpose of continuing professional education (CPE) and training activities is to provide a CPA firm with reasonable assurance that personnel within the firm have

A. Technical training that assures proficiency as an auditor.

B. Professional education that is required to perform with due professional care.

C. The ability to fulfill assigned responsibilities and the qualifications for advancement.

D. Knowledge required to perform a peer review.

Answer (C) is correct. *(CPA, adapted)*

**REQUIRED:** The primary purpose of CPE and training activities relative to a CPA firm's quality control.

**DISCUSSION:** According to QC 20, the firm should adopt policies and procedures to obtain reasonable assurance that "personnel participate in general and industry-specific CPE and other professional development activities that enable them to fulfill responsibilities assigned, and satisfy applicable CPE requirements of the AICPA and regulatory agencies." Furthermore, personnel chosen for advancement should "have the qualifications necessary for fulfillment of the responsibilities they will be called on to assume."

Answer (A) is incorrect because technical training does not assure proficiency as an auditor. Professional experience complements formal education to develop seasoned judgment. Answer (B) is incorrect because professional education alone does not assure performance with due professional care. Answer (D) is incorrect because CPE is important to all personnel, not just to peer reviewers.

**21.** The first general standard requires that an audit of financial statements be performed by a person or persons having

A. Seasoned judgment in varying degrees of supervision and review.

B. Adequate technical training and proficiency.

C. Knowledge of the standards of field work and reporting.

D. Independence with respect to the financial statements and supplementary disclosures.

Answer (B) is correct. *(CPA, adapted)*

**REQUIRED:** The subject of the first general standard.

**DISCUSSION:** The first general standard requires adequate technical training and proficiency as an auditor. AU 210 states that this requirement can be met through education and experience.

Answer (A) is incorrect because the first standard of field work requires that the audit to be planned and that assistants be properly supervised. Answer (C) is incorrect because, although the auditor should have knowledge of the field work and reporting standards, the first general standard does not state this requirement. Answer (D) is incorrect because the second general standard requires the auditor to be independent.

**22.** Competence as an independent auditor includes all of the following except

A. Having the technical qualifications to perform an engagement.

B. Possessing the ability to supervise and evaluate the quality of staff work.

C. Warranting the infallibility of the work performed.

D. Doing additional research or consulting others.

Answer (C) is correct. *(CPA, adapted)*

**REQUIRED:** The statement not consistent with professional standards of competency.

**DISCUSSION:** The auditor is not a guarantor. The auditor's responsibility is to express (or disclaim) an opinion on whether the financial statements, taken as a whole, are presented fairly. The audit is planned and performed to provide reasonable, but not absolute, assurance that the financial statements are not materially misstated.

Answer (A) is incorrect because adequate technical training and proficiency as an auditor are required by the first general standard. Answer (B) is incorrect because due professional care requires that the auditor with final responsibility for the engagement be "responsible for the assignment of tasks to, and the supervision of, assistants" (AU 230). Answer (D) is incorrect because, according to an Interpretation of Conduct Rule 201, the need for additional research or consultation with others is a normal part of the performance of professional service.

**23.** According to the standards of the profession, which of the following activities may be required in exercising due professional care?

| | Consulting with Experts | Obtaining Specialty Accreditation |
|---|---|---|
| A. | Yes | Yes |
| B. | Yes | No |
| C. | No | Yes |
| D. | No | No |

Answer (B) is correct. *(CPA, adapted)*

**REQUIRED:** The activity(ies) that may be required in exercising due professional care.

**DISCUSSION:** A CPA should undertake only those services that (s)he reasonably expects to complete with professional competence and should exercise due professional care in performing those services. According to an Interpretation of Conduct Rule 201, additional research or consultation with others may be necessary to gain sufficient competence to complete a service in accordance with professional standards. However, professional standards do not require specialty accreditation, although many CPAs choose to specialize in specific services.

**24.** GAAS require the auditor to be independent in mental attitude. An auditor is independent if (s)he is

A. Intelligent.

B. Independent in fact and in appearance.

C. Consistent and independent in fact.

D. Logical and intellectually honest.

Answer (B) is correct. *(Publisher)*
**REQUIRED:** The true statement about auditor independence.
**DISCUSSION:** Auditors must be independent in both fact and appearance. This crucially important quality gives credibility to the auditor's opinion. If an auditor does not maintain the appearance of independence, however unbiased (s)he may be in fact, the public will be reluctant to believe that (s)he is unbiased (AU 220).
Answer (A) is incorrect because intelligence is not a dimension of auditor independence. Answer (C) is incorrect because consistency is not a dimension of auditor independence. Answer (D) is incorrect because logic is not a dimension of auditor independence.

**25.** Beth Babett, CPA, is associated with a client's financial statements but is not independent with respect to that client. If she is requested to perform an audit on the financial statements, she should

A. Recommend that the engagement be downgraded to a review.

B. Disclaim an opinion.

C. List the procedures performed in the audit report.

D. Express a piecemeal opinion.

Answer (B) is correct. *(Publisher)*
**REQUIRED:** The action taken by a CPA who lacks independence in connection with an audit.
**DISCUSSION:** The CPA may perform audit procedures according to an agreement with the client. However, a CPA who lacks independence is precluded from expressing an opinion on financial statements because any procedures (s)he performs are not in accordance with GAAS. Hence, the CPA should disclaim an opinion on the financial statements and state specifically that (s)he is not independent (AU 504).
Answer (A) is incorrect because a review engagement is an attest service that requires the CPA to be independent. Answer (C) is incorrect because the public might be misled into believing that the CPA has performed an audit and is expressing an opinion on the statements if audit procedures are listed. Answer (D) is incorrect because a piecemeal opinion (expressing an opinion on only part of the financial statements) is not acceptable if the CPA has disclaimed an opinion or expressed an adverse opinion on the statements taken as a whole.

**26.** The Sarbanes-Oxley Act limits the nonaudit services that an audit firm can provide to public company audit clients. Which of the following services is still an allowable service that an auditor may provide to a public client?

A. Internal audit services.

B. Legal services.

C. Management consulting services.

D. Tax compliance services.

Answer (D) is correct. *(Publisher)*
**REQUIRED:** The type of service that an audit firm may provide to an audit client.
**DISCUSSION:** The Sarbanes-Oxley Act prohibits audit firms from providing consulting, legal, and internal auditing services to public audit clients.
Answer (A) is incorrect because audit firms may provide conventional tax planning and compliance services to public audit clients. However, the audit committee must preapprove nonaudit services to be provided by the auditor. Answer (B) is incorrect because audit firms may provide conventional tax planning and compliance services to public audit clients. However, the audit committee must preapprove nonaudit services to be provided by the auditor. Answer (C) is incorrect because audit firms may provide conventional tax planning and compliance services to public audit clients. However, the audit committee must preapprove nonaudit services to be provided by the auditor.

**27.** The Sarbanes-Oxley Act has strengthened auditor independence by requiring that management

A. Engage auditors to report in accordance with the Foreign Corrupt Practices Act.

B. Report the nature of disagreements with former auditors.

C. Select auditors through audit committees.

D. Hire a different CPA firm from the one that performs the audit to perform the company's tax work.

Answer (C) is correct. *(CPA, adapted)*
**REQUIRED:** The Sarbanes-Oxley requirement that strengthened auditor independence.
**DISCUSSION:** The Sarbanes-Oxley Act requires that the audit committee of a public company hire and pay the external auditors. Such affiliation inhibits management from changing auditors to gain acceptance of a questionable accounting method. Also, a potential successor auditor must inquire of the predecessor auditor before accepting an engagement.
Answer (A) is incorrect because the SEC does not require an audit report in accordance with the FCPA. Answer (B) is incorrect because reporting the nature of disagreements with auditors has been a long-time SEC requirement. Answer (D) is incorrect because the Sarbanes-Oxley Act does not restrict who may perform a company's tax work. Other types of engagements, such as the outsourcing of the internal audit function and certain consulting services, are limited.

**28.** Audit committees have been identified as a major factor in promoting independence in both internal and external auditors. Which of the following is the most important limitation on the effectiveness of audit committees?

A. Audit committees are composed of independent directors. However, those directors may have close personal and professional friendships with management.

B. Audit committee members are compensated by the organization and thus favor a shareholder's view.

C. Audit committees devote most of their efforts to external audit concerns and do not pay much attention to internal auditing and the overall control environment.

D. Audit committee members do not normally have degrees in the accounting or auditing fields.

Answer (A) is correct. *(CIA, adapted)*

**REQUIRED:** The most important limitation on the effectiveness of audit committees.

**DISCUSSION:** The audit committee is a subcommittee made up of outside directors who are independent of corporate management. The Sarbanes-Oxley Act of 2002 requires members of audit committees of public companies to be independent. The Act precludes audit committee members from accepting any consulting, advisory, or other compensatory fee from the issuer; or being an affiliated person of the issuer or any subsidiary thereof. The purpose of the audit committee is to help keep external and internal auditors independent of management and to assure that the directors are exercising due care. However, if independence is impaired by personal and professional friendships, the effectiveness of the audit committee may be limited.

Answer (B) is incorrect because the compensation audit committee members receive is usually minimal. They should be independent and therefore not limited to a shareholder's perspective. Answer (C) is incorrect because, although audit committees are concerned with external audits, they also devote attention to the internal auditing function. Answer (D) is incorrect because not all audit committee members need degrees or experience in accounting or auditing for the committee to function effectively. However, the Sarbanes-Oxley Act of 2002 requires at least 1 member of the audit committee of a public company to be a financial expert.

**29.** The auditor should not initiate discussion with the audit committee concerning

A. The extent to which the work of internal auditors will influence the scope of the audit.

B. Details of the procedures that the auditor intends to apply.

C. The extent to which change in the company's organization will influence the scope of the audit.

D. Details of potential problems that the auditor believes might cause a qualified opinion.

Answer (B) is correct. *(CPA, adapted)*

**REQUIRED:** The subject not appropriate for discussion.

**DISCUSSION:** The auditor should not discuss with the audit committee the specific procedures to be applied during the audit. The auditor exercises professional judgment in determining appropriate procedures. To remain independent (s)he must not subordinate this judgment to others. Also, audit testing is done on a sample basis, and the client should not have knowledge of how samples are selected.

Answer (A) is incorrect because, according to AU 380, *Communication with Audit Committees*, certain communications with those responsible for oversight of the financial reporting process are required. For example, the auditor should communicate the responsibility assumed under GAAS, including the extent to which the work of internal auditors will influence the scope of the audit. Answer (C) is incorrect because the audit scope is a legitimate subject for discussion with the audit committee. Answer (D) is incorrect because potential problems should be discussed with the audit committee.

**30.** The exercise of due professional care requires that an auditor with final responsibility for an engagement

A. Examine all available corroborating evidence.

B. Be responsible for the assignment of tasks to, and supervision of, assistants.

C. Attain the proper balance of professional experience and formal education.

D. Design the audit to detect all instances of illegal acts having direct and material effects on financial statement amounts.

Answer (B) is correct. *(CPA, adapted)*

**REQUIRED:** The meaning of due professional care.

**DISCUSSION:** According to AU 230, *Due Professional Care in the Performance of Work*, "Due professional care imposes a responsibility upon each professional within an independent auditor's organization to observe the standards of field work and reporting." The first standard of field work requires proper supervision of assistants (AU 150). Thus, AU 230 states, "The auditor with final responsibility is responsible for the assignment of tasks to, and the supervision of, assistants."

Answer (A) is incorrect because cost-benefit considerations ordinarily require the auditor to examine evidence on a test basis. Answer (C) is incorrect because the first general standard requires the audit to be performed by persons having adequate technical training and proficiency as auditors. The attainment of proficiency begins with formal education and extends into the auditor's subsequent experience (AU 210). Answer (D) is incorrect because the auditor is required to plan and perform the audit to obtain reasonable, not absolute, assurance of detecting illegal acts having direct and material effects.

## 1.4 GAAS – Field Work and Reporting Standards

**31.** The 10 standards consist of general standards, standards of field work, and standards of reporting. The standards of field work include which one of the following?

A. The audit is to be performed by a person or persons having adequate technical training and proficiency.

B. In all matters relating to the assignment, an independence in mental attitude is essential.

C. The work is to be adequately planned, and assistants, if any, are to be properly supervised.

D. Due professional care is to be exercised in the planning and performance of the audit and preparation of the audit report.

Answer (C) is correct. *(CMA, adapted)*

**REQUIRED:** The standard of field work.

**DISCUSSION:** The first standard of field work states that the work is to be adequately planned and that assistants, if any, are to be properly supervised. The second and third standards of field work require obtaining a sufficient understanding of internal control and sufficient competent evidential matter, respectively.

Answer (A) is incorrect because the first general standard provides that the audit is to be performed by a person or persons having adequate technical training and proficiency. Answer (B) is incorrect because the second general standard states that, in all matters relating to the assignment, an independence in mental attitude is essential. Answer (D) is incorrect because the third general standard provides that due professional care is to be exercised in the planning and performance of the audit and preparation of the audit report.

**32.** Early appointment of the auditor enables preliminary work to be performed by the auditor that benefits the client because it permits the audit to be performed in

A. A more efficient manner.

B. A more thorough manner.

C. Accordance with quality control standards.

D. Accordance with generally accepted auditing standards.

Answer (A) is correct. *(CPA, adapted)*

**REQUIRED:** The benefit of early appointment of the auditor.

**DISCUSSION:** AU 310, *Appointment of the Independent Auditor*, indicates that an early appointment of the auditor is advantageous to both the auditor and the client. Early appointment aids the auditor in planning the work, especially work to be done before the end of the year. The client benefits from more efficient scheduling of the audit and an early completion of the work after the end of the fiscal year.

Answer (B) is incorrect because thoroughness is directly related to the requirement to collect sufficient competent evidential matter, not to the date of appointment. Answer (C) is incorrect because adherence to quality control standards is necessary regardless of the date of appointment. Answer (D) is incorrect because adherence to GAAS is necessary regardless of the date of appointment.

**33.** With respect to the auditor's planning of a year-end audit, which of the following statements is always true?

A. An engagement should not be accepted after the fiscal year-end.

B. An inventory count must be observed at the balance sheet date.

C. The client's audit committee should not be told of the specific audit procedures that were performed.

D. It is an acceptable practice to carry out part of the audit at interim dates.

Answer (D) is correct. *(CPA, adapted)*

**REQUIRED:** The statement about the year-end audit that is always true.

**DISCUSSION:** Much of the audit work, including obtaining a sufficient understanding of internal control, assessing control risk, and the application of substantive tests to transactions, may be conducted prior to the balance sheet date (AU 313).

Answer (A) is incorrect because an engagement may be accepted after year-end. Answer (B) is incorrect because, if observation at year-end is not feasible, the auditor may observe inventory at another date. Answer (C) is incorrect because the audit committee (usually consisting of outside directors) may sometimes be told of specific audit procedures already performed, e.g., how a major defalcation was discovered. However, specific procedures should not be discussed with the client prior to the audit.

**34.** Which of the following elements underlies the application of generally accepted auditing standards, particularly the standards of field work and reporting?

A. Relevant internal controls.

B. Corroborating evidence.

C. Quality control.

D. Materiality and audit risk.

Answer (D) is correct. *(CPA, adapted)*

**REQUIRED:** The element(s) affecting the application of GAAS.

**DISCUSSION:** Materiality and audit risk affect the application of GAAS, especially the field work and reporting standards, and as a result are reflected in the auditor's standard report. The auditor must make judgments about materiality and audit risk in determining the nature, timing, and extent of procedures to apply and in evaluating the results (AU 312).

Answer (A) is incorrect because the second standard of field work concerns internal control. Answer (B) is incorrect because the third standard of field work concerns evidence. Answer (C) is incorrect because quality control is covered by a separate series of pronouncements, Statements on Quality Control Standards.

**35.** The 10 standards include standards of reporting. Which of the following is not a reporting standard?

A. The report shall identify those circumstances in which GAAP have not been consistently observed in the current period in relation to the preceding period.

B. Informative disclosures in the financial statements are to be regarded as reasonably adequate unless otherwise stated in the report.

C. Sufficient competent evidential matter is to be obtained through inspection, observation, inquiries, and confirmations to afford a reasonable basis for an opinion regarding the financial statements under audit.

D. The report shall state whether the financial statements are presented in accordance with GAAP.

Answer (C) is correct. *(Publisher)*

**REQUIRED:** The standard that is not a reporting standard.

**DISCUSSION:** The standard requiring the auditor to collect sufficient competent evidential matter is the third standard of field work, not a standard of reporting.

Answer (A) is incorrect because the second standard of reporting states that the report shall identify those circumstances in which GAAP have not been consistently observed in the current period in relation to the preceding period. Answer (B) is incorrect because the third standard of reporting states that informative disclosures in the financial statements are to be regarded as reasonably adequate unless otherwise stated in the report. Answer (D) is incorrect because the first standard of reporting states that the report shall state whether the financial statements are presented in accordance with GAAP.

**36.** The first standard of reporting requires that "the report shall state whether the financial statements are presented in accordance with generally accepted accounting principles." This standard should be construed to require

A. A statement of fact by the auditor.

B. An opinion by the auditor.

C. An implied measure of fairness.

D. An objective measure of compliance.

Answer (B) is correct. *(CPA, adapted)*

**REQUIRED:** The interpretation of the first reporting standard.

**DISCUSSION:** AU 410, *Adherence to GAAP*, states, "The first reporting standard is construed not to require a statement of fact by the auditor but an opinion as to whether the financial statements are presented in conformity with such principles." The opinion is based on the auditor's judgment as to whether the principles selected and applied have general acceptance and are appropriate in the circumstances.

Answer (A) is incorrect because AU 410 construes the first reporting standard not to require a statement of fact by the auditor. Answer (C) is incorrect because the auditor's judgment about the fairness of the presentation of financial statements is applied within the framework of GAAP, not as an implied measure. Answer (D) is incorrect because, if an objective measure of compliance were available, the auditor could state a fact, not express an opinion.

**37.** Several sources of GAAP consulted by an auditor are in conflict as to the application of an accounting principle. Which of the following should the auditor consider the most authoritative?

A. FASB Technical Bulletins.

B. AICPA Accounting Interpretations.

C. FASB Statements of Financial Accounting Concepts.

D. AICPA Issues Papers.

Answer (A) is correct. *(CPA, adapted)*

**REQUIRED:** The most authoritative source of GAAP.

**DISCUSSION:** The FASB establishes the GAAP hierarchy. FASB Technical Bulletins are in the second tier. The first tier of GAAP for nongovernmental entities consists of officially established accounting principles, which are principles contemplated by Conduct Rule 203. The next three tiers consist of other sources of established accounting principles. The fifth tier consists of other accounting literature.

Answer (B) is incorrect because AICPA Accounting Interpretations are in the fourth tier. Answer (C) is incorrect because FASB Statements of Financial Accounting Concepts are in the fifth tier. Answer (D) is incorrect because AICPA Issues Papers are in the fifth tier.

**38.** An auditor should obtain sufficient knowledge of an entity's information system relevant to financial reporting to understand the

A. Safeguards used to limit access to computer facilities.

B. Process used to prepare significant accounting estimates.

C. Procedures used to assure proper authorization of transactions.

D. Policies used to detect the concealment of fraud.

Answer (B) is correct. *(CPA, adapted)*

**REQUIRED:** The purpose of obtaining sufficient knowledge of an entity's information system relevant to financial reporting.

**DISCUSSION:** The auditor should obtain sufficient knowledge of the information system relevant to financial reporting to understand (1) the classes of significant transactions, (2) the ways those transactions are initiated, (3) the accounting records and supporting documents for those transactions, (4) the accounting processing involved, and (5) the financial reporting process used to prepare the entity's financial statements, including significant accounting estimates and disclosures (AU 319).

Answer (A) is incorrect because safeguards used to limit access to computer facilities involve policies and procedures outside the information system relevant to financial reporting. Answer (C) is incorrect because procedures used to assure proper authorization of transactions involve policies and procedures outside the information system relevant to financial reporting. Answer (D) is incorrect because policies used to detect the concealment of fraud involve policies and procedures outside the information system relevant to financial reporting.

**39.** Under the AICPA *Code of Professional Conduct*, a CPA may express an unqualified opinion on financial statements that contain a departure from promulgated GAAP if (s)he can demonstrate that because of unusual circumstances the financial statements would be misleading if the departure were not made. Which of the following is an example of unusual circumstances that could justify such a departure?

A. The evolution of a new form of business.

B. An unusual degree of materiality.

C. Conflicting industry practices.

D. A theoretical disagreement with a standard promulgated by the FASB.

Answer (A) is correct. *(Publisher)*

**REQUIRED:** The circumstance that could justify a departure from promulgated GAAP.

**DISCUSSION:** According to an Interpretation of Conduct Rule 203, examples of unusual circumstances that would permit a departure from promulgated GAAP (SFASs and their Interpretations, ARBs, and APBs) are new legislation or the evolution of a new form of business transaction. What constitutes unusual circumstances is normally a matter of professional judgment.

Answer (B) is incorrect because an unusual degree of materiality is an event that is not so unusual as to justify departure from promulgated GAAP. Answer (C) is incorrect because the existence of conflicting industry practices is an example of an event cited in an Interpretation of Conduct Rule 203 that is not so unusual as to justify departure from promulgated GAAP. Answer (D) is incorrect because the client's or CPA's theoretical disagreement with a standard does not justify a departure from the standards.

## 1.5 Nature of the *Code of Professional Conduct*

**40.** Which of the following statements best explains why the CPA profession has found it essential to promulgate ethical standards and to establish means for ensuring their observance?

A. Vigorous enforcement of an established code of ethics is the best way to prevent unscrupulous acts.

B. Ethical standards that emphasize excellence in performance over material rewards establish a reputation for competence and character.

C. A distinguishing mark of a profession is its acceptance of responsibility to the public.

D. A requirement for a profession is to establish ethical standards that stress primarily a responsibility to clients and colleagues.

Answer (C) is correct. *(CPA, adapted)*

**REQUIRED:** The reason for ethical standards.

**DISCUSSION:** Article II of the AICPA *Code of Professional Conduct* states, "Members should accept the obligation to act in a way that will serve the public interest, honor the public trust, and demonstrate commitment to professionalism." According to the accompanying explanation, "A distinguishing mark of a profession is acceptance of its responsibility to the public. The accounting profession's public consists of clients, credit grantors, governments, employers, investors, the business and financial community, and others who rely on the objectivity and integrity of CPAs to maintain the orderly functioning of commerce."

Answer (A) is incorrect because vigorous enforcement is significant but secondary to the creation of an environment in the profession that fosters voluntary adherence to ethical principles. Answer (B) is incorrect because excellence in performance is but one of the effects of accepting responsibility to the public. Answer (D) is incorrect because the responsibility of CPAs is to a public that is not limited to clients and colleagues but includes all those who rely on their objectivity and integrity.

**41.** The AICPA *Code of Professional Conduct* contains both general ethical principles that are aspirational in character and also a

A. List of violations that would cause the automatic suspension of a member's license.

B. Set of specific, mandatory rules describing minimum levels of conduct a member must maintain.

C. Description of a member's procedures for responding to an inquiry from a trial board.

D. List of specific acts discreditable to the profession.

Answer (B) is correct. *(CPA, adapted)*

**REQUIRED:** The content of the *Code of Professional Conduct.*

**DISCUSSION:** The AICPA Code contains two sections: Principles and Rules. The principles are goal-oriented. The rules provide more specific guidance. The principles "call for an unswerving commitment to honorable behavior," but are not mandatory. Members who fail to comply with the rules, however, may face disciplinary action.

Answer (A) is incorrect because the bylaws (BL 730), not the Code, list violations resulting in an automatic suspension. Answer (C) is incorrect because the bylaws (BL 740R) describe trial board procedures. Answer (D) is incorrect because Conduct Rule 501, *Acts Discreditable*, simply states that discreditable acts are prohibited. However, the related interpretations specify certain types of discreditable acts.

**42.** Which AICPA Conduct Rule applies only to members in the practice of public accounting?

A. *General Standards* (201).

B. *Accounting Principles* (203).

C. *Independence* (101).

D. *Compliance with Standards* (202).

Answer (C) is correct. *(Publisher)*

**REQUIRED:** The AICPA Conduct Rule that applies only to members in public accounting.

**DISCUSSION:** Conduct Rule 101 states, "A member in public practice shall be independent in the performance of professional services as required by standards promulgated by bodies designated by Council." The scope of services comprehended by this rule is broader than the expression of opinions on financial statements. Hence, it applies to such professional services as reviews, reports on prospective financial information, and reports on other attestation engagements.

Answer (A) is incorrect because Conduct Rule 201 applies to all members, whether or not in public practice. Answer (B) is incorrect because Conduct Rule 203 applies to all members, whether or not in public practice. Answer (D) is incorrect because Conduct Rule 202 applies to all members, whether or not in public practice.

**43.** The AICPA *Code of Professional Conduct* does not include enforceable Conduct Rules on which of the following?

A. Independence and integrity and objectivity.

B. Professional competence and due professional care.

C. Accounting principles.

D. Responsibilities to colleagues.

Answer (D) is correct. *(Publisher)*

**REQUIRED:** The subject on which the Code provides no enforceable Conduct Rules.

**DISCUSSION:** At one time the Code included two rules concerning colleagues, but they were deleted after threats of antitrust actions against the profession by both the Federal Trade Commission and the U.S. Justice Department. The principles express the profession's recognition of its responsibilities to colleagues as well as to the public and clients, but adherence to them is not mandatory.

Answer (A) is incorrect because independence and integrity and objectivity are covered by Conduct Rules 101 and 102, respectively. Answer (B) is incorrect because professional competence and due professional care are two of the general standards listed in Conduct Rule 201. Answer (C) is incorrect because Conduct Rule 203 covers accounting principles.

**44.** Conduct Rule 201, *General Standards*, does not require a member to

A. Complete all engagements with professional competence.

B. Plan and supervise adequately the performance of professional services.

C. Obtain sufficient relevant data to afford a reasonable basis for all conclusions.

D. Provide assurance about prospective financial statements.

Answer (D) is correct. *(Publisher)*

**REQUIRED:** The subject not encompassed by Rule 201.

**DISCUSSION:** The section on prospective financial statements was deleted from Conduct Rule 201 because guidance has been provided by the ASB in AT 301, *Financial Forecasts and Projections.*

Answer (A) is incorrect because Conduct Rule 201 requires compliance with the following standards: professional competence, due professional care, planning and supervision, and sufficient relevant data. A member should undertake only those professional services that can reasonably be expected to be completed with professional competence. Answer (B) is incorrect because Conduct Rule 201 requires that the performance of professional services be adequately planned and supervised. Answer (C) is incorrect because Conduct Rule 201 requires that a member obtain sufficient relevant data to afford a reasonable basis for all conclusions or recommendations related to any professional services performed.

**45.** CPAs are required to complete engagements competently. Competence embraces all of the following except

A. An unbiased mental attitude.

B. The technical qualifications of the CPA's staff.

C. The capacity to exercise judgment.

D. The ability to research subject matter and consult with others.

Answer (A) is correct. *(Publisher)*

**REQUIRED:** The item not associated with competence.

**DISCUSSION:** Conduct Rule 101 requires the CPA to maintain an unbiased mental attitude. "A member in public practice shall be independent in the performance of professional services as required by standards promulgated by bodies designated by Council."

Answer (B) is incorrect because, according to an AICPA Interpretation of Conduct Rule 201, "Competence relates both to knowledge of the profession's standards, techniques, and the technical subject matter involved, and to the ability to exercise sound judgment in applying such knowledge in the performance of professional services." Answer (C) is incorrect because competence includes the ability to exercise sound judgment in applying knowledge in the performance of services. Answer (D) is incorrect because, in some cases, "additional research or consultation with others does not ordinarily represent a lack of competence, but rather is a normal part of the performance of professional services."

**46.** When management refuses to disclose material illegal acts that were identified by the independent auditor, the independent auditor may be charged with violating the AICPA *Code of Professional Conduct* for

A. Disclaiming an opinion.

B. Withdrawing from the engagement.

C. Failing to uncover the illegal activities during prior audits.

D. Reporting these activities to the audit committee.

Answer (A) is correct. *(CPA, adapted)*

**REQUIRED:** The inappropriate auditor action relative to disclosure of illegal activities.

**DISCUSSION:** When the auditor concludes that an illegal act is material and that the act has not been appropriately disclosed or accounted for, a normal disclaimer of opinion is not suitable. The auditor should disclose the problem in a report that includes either a qualified or an adverse opinion or withdraw from the engagement. Moreover, the auditor may, in some circumstances, have a duty of disclosure outside the entity, e.g., in a report on Form 8-K or in a response to a subpoena. The Private Securities Litigation Reform Act of 1995 may also be applicable to reporting on illegal acts.

Answer (B) is incorrect because, under AU 317, *Illegal Acts by Clients*, withdrawal may be warranted in certain cases. Answer (C) is incorrect because audits in compliance with GAAS cannot assure detection of all illegal acts. Answer (D) is incorrect because the auditor may notify the client's audit committee of illegal acts.

**47.** The AICPA *Code of Professional Conduct*

A. Prohibits encroachment on the practice of another CPA.

B. Prohibits offers of employment to employees of another CPA without notice.

C. Encourages but does not require CPAs to cooperate with each other.

D. Encourages but does not require CPAs to refrain from advertising or engaging in other forms of solicitation.

Answer (C) is correct. *(Publisher)*

**REQUIRED:** The true statement concerning the *Code of Professional Conduct.*

**DISCUSSION:** The nonbinding Principles state that members "have a continuing responsibility to cooperate with each other to improve the art of accounting, maintain the public's confidence, and carry out the profession's special responsibilities for self-governance."

Answer (A) is incorrect because no Conduct Rules currently govern responsibilities to colleagues. Answer (B) is incorrect because no Conduct Rules currently govern responsibilities to colleagues. Answer (D) is incorrect because CPAs are not encouraged or required to refrain from solicitation unless it is false, misleading, or deceptive.

**48.** Which of the following is required for a CPA firm to designate itself as "Members of the American Institute of Certified Public Accountants" on its letterhead?

A. All CPA owners must be members.

B. The owners whose names appear in the firm name must be members.

C. At least one of the owners must be a member.

D. The firm must be a dues-paying member.

Answer (A) is correct. *(CPA, adapted)*

**REQUIRED:** The requirement for a CPA firm to use the designation, "Members of the AICPA."

**DISCUSSION:** Conduct Rule 505, *Form of Organization and Name*, states that a firm may not use the quoted designation unless all of its CPA owners are members of the Institute.

Answer (B) is incorrect because all CPA owners, not just certain owners, must be AICPA members. Answer (C) is incorrect because all CPA owners, not just certain owners, must be AICPA members. Answer (D) is incorrect because the CPA owners, not the firm, must be members of the AICPA.

**49.** According to The Institute of Internal Auditors' Practice Advisory 1220-1, *Due Professional Care*, "Due care implies reasonable care and competence, not infallibility or extraordinary performance." This statement makes which of the following unnecessary?

A. The conduct of examinations and verifications to a reasonable extent.

B. The conduct of detailed reviews of all transactions.

C. The reasonable assurance that compliance does exist.

D. The consideration of the possibility of material fraud.

Answer (B) is correct. *(CIA, adapted)*

**REQUIRED:** The item stating what is unnecessary under the due care standard.

**DISCUSSION:** PA 1220-1 states, "Due care requires the internal auditor to conduct examinations and verifications to a reasonable extent but does not require detailed reviews of all transactions."

Answer (A) is incorrect because due care requires the internal auditor to conduct examinations and verifications to a reasonable extent. Answer (C) is incorrect because the internal auditor cannot give absolute assurance that noncompliance or irregularities do not exist. Answer (D) is incorrect because the possibility of material fraud or noncompliance should be considered.

**50.** Anyone inquiring about the professional reputation and standing of a CPA firm may contact the AICPA Division for CPA Firms and expect to receive

A. Copies of complaints against the CPA firm that are currently being adjudicated by the AICPA Joint Trial Board.

B. Copies of peer review reports on the CPA firm after the reports have been accepted.

C. Information regarding prima facie violations of the *Code of Professional Conduct* or AICPA bylaws not deemed of sufficient gravity to warrant further formal action.

D. Information regarding pending investigations of individuals within the CPA firm.

Answer (B) is correct. *(CPA, adapted)*

**REQUIRED:** The information obtainable from the Division for CPA Firms.

**DISCUSSION:** Anyone inquiring about the professional reputation and standing of a CPA firm may contact the Division for CPA Firms and receive information on the firm's enrollment in an AICPA-approved practice monitoring program and, if the firm is enrolled in either the SEC Practice Section or Partnering for CPA Practice Success/The Alliance for CPA Firms (PCPS), copies of the firm's most recent peer review report after the report has been accepted by the relevant report acceptance body. The Division will provide copies of accepted peer review reports and information submitted by member firms on applications for membership and annual updates. There is no charge for this service.

Neither the Division for CPA Firms nor the Professional Ethics Division may respond to inquiries about complaints against CPA firms currently being adjudicated, violations not deemed of sufficient gravity to warrant further formal action, or pending investigations of individuals within the CPA firm. However, the Professional Ethics Division may respond to inquiries about disciplinary action taken by the Joint Trial Board or one of its sub-boards and published in a membership periodical of the AICPA.

## 1.6 Code – Independence, Integrity, and Objectivity

**51.** An auditor strives to achieve independence in appearance to

A. Maintain public confidence in the profession.

B. Become independent in fact.

C. Comply with the generally accepted auditing standards of field work.

D. Maintain an unbiased mental attitude.

Answer (A) is correct. *(CPA, adapted)*

**REQUIRED:** The reason the auditor strives to achieve independence in appearance.

**DISCUSSION:** Third parties depend on the CPA's report because (s)he is viewed as possessing the necessary impartiality. Public confidence would be impaired if such objectivity even appeared to be lacking. The auditor must guard against the presumption of a loss of independence in addition to maintaining independence in fact.

Answer (B) is incorrect because an auditor must be independent both in fact (an unbiased mental attitude) and in appearance. Answer (C) is incorrect because independence relates to the general standards, not to the standards of field work. Answer (D) is incorrect because an auditor must be independent both in fact (an unbiased mental attitude) and in appearance.

**52.** Which of the following most completely describes how independence has been defined by the CPA profession?

A. Performing an audit from the viewpoint of the public.

B. Avoiding the appearance of significant interests in the affairs of an audit client.

C. Possessing the ability to act with integrity and objectivity.

D. Accepting responsibility to act professionally and in accordance with a professional code of ethics.

Answer (C) is correct. *(CPA, adapted)*

**REQUIRED:** The best description of the accounting profession's definition of independence.

**DISCUSSION:** Integrity, objectivity and independence are overlapping concepts. Integrity requires honesty and candor within the limits of confidentiality. It also requires observation of the principles of objectivity and independence. Objectivity is impartiality, intellectual honesty, and freedom from conflicts of interest. Independence precludes relationships that may appear to impair objectivity in rendering attestation services. Members in public practice should therefore be independent in appearance and in fact.

Answer (A) is incorrect because, although his/her performance of the attest function serves the public interest, an auditor's adoption of any viewpoint other than strict impartiality is inconsistent with professional standards. Answer (B) is incorrect because the auditor must be independent in fact as well as in appearance. Answer (D) is incorrect because one who accepts responsibility for acting in accordance with a set of professional standards is not necessarily required to be independent.

**53.** The concept of materiality is least important to an auditor when considering the

A. Effects of a direct financial interest in the client upon the auditor's independence.

B. Decision whether to use positive or negative confirmations of accounts receivable.

C. Adequacy of disclosure of a client's illegal act.

D. Discovery of weaknesses in a client's internal control.

Answer (A) is correct. *(CPA, adapted)*

**REQUIRED:** The item with respect to which materiality is least important.

**DISCUSSION:** According to Interpretation 101-1, independence is impaired if, during the period of the professional engagement, a covered member had or was committed to acquire any direct or material indirect financial interest in a client. Whether this direct interest is material is irrelevant. The test of materiality is applied, however, if the financial interest is indirect.

Answer (B) is incorrect because negative confirmations may be used when the combined assessed level of inherent and control risk is low, many small balances are involved, and the auditor has no reason to believe that the recipients are unlikely to give them consideration. Answer (C) is incorrect because, in considering the effect of an illegal act, an auditor should evaluate its qualitative and quantitative materiality. Answer (D) is incorrect because an auditor who is considering internal control must make materiality judgments.

**54.** Jaye B. Honest, CPA, was offered the engagement to audit Wicket Corporation for the year ended June 30, 20X1. She had served as a director of Wicket Corporation until June 30, 20X0, and her spouse currently owns 10 of the 10,000 outstanding shares of Wicket Corporation. Under the AICPA *Code of Professional Conduct*, she should

A. Accept the engagement.

B. Let a partner from the same office accept and conduct the engagement.

C. Refuse the engagement because she had served as a director.

D. Refuse the engagement because of her spouse's stock ownership.

Answer (D) is correct. *(Publisher)*

**REQUIRED:** The effect of a spouse's ownership of stock and the CPA's former position as a director.

**DISCUSSION:** According to Interpretation 101-1, independence is impaired if, during the period of the professional engagement, a covered member had or was committed to acquire any direct or material indirect financial interest in a client. With some exceptions, the immediate family (spouse, spousal equivalent, or dependent) of a covered member is subject to Conduct Rule 101 and its interpretations and rulings. Thus, the CPA should refuse the engagement to audit the company because her spouse's stock ownership is a direct interest that is ascribed to her. Materiality is not an issue.

Answer (A) is incorrect because she is not independent and should not accept the engagement. Answer (B) is incorrect because the term "covered member" includes a partner in the office in which the lead attest engagement partner primarily practices in connection with the engagement. Answer (C) is incorrect because, if she has not served as a director during the period covered by the financial statements or during the period of the professional engagement, independence is not impaired by reason of prior association with the client as a director.

**55.** Dickins & Co., CPAs, offers to maintain on its computer certain routine accounting records for its audit client, Lake. If Lake accepts the offer and Dickins & Co. continues to function as independent auditor, Dickins & Co. is most likely to violate the rules relating to auditor's independence of which organization(s)?

| | SEC | AICPA |
|---|---|---|
| A. | Yes | No |
| B. | Yes | Yes |
| C. | No | Yes |
| D. | No | No |

Answer (A) is correct. *(Publisher)*

**REQUIRED:** The SEC and the AICPA positions on the independence of a CPA firm that provides computerized accounting services to its client.

**DISCUSSION:** Under federal law (Sarbanes-Oxley Act of 2002) as enforced by the SEC, performing nonaudit services for the audit client impairs the independence of the audit firm. The AICPA view, however, is that the firm may retain its independence while performing various bookkeeping and other nonattest services. Thus, certain "other services" may be allowed in some cases under the AICPA's *Code of Professional Conduct* but are prohibited by the SEC for public company audit clients. For example, in addition to bookkeeping services, federal law expressly prohibits the following nonaudit services: (1) financial information systems design and implementation; (2) appraisal or valuation services, fairness opinions, or contribution-in-kind reports; (3) actuarial services; (4) internal audit outsourcing services; (5) management functions or human resources; (6) broker or dealer, investment adviser, or investment banking services; and (7) legal services and expert services unrelated to the audit. Dickins & Co. has violated SEC rules, but not necessarily AICPA rules.

**56.** A CPA who has a direct financial interest in a nonclient having a material investment in the CPA's audit client

A. Lacks independence only if the CPA's investment in the nonclient is material.

B. Lacks independence only if the CPA can exercise significant influence over the nonclient.

C. Lacks independence.

D. Does not lack independence.

Answer (C) is correct. *(Publisher)*

**REQUIRED:** The effect of a direct financial interest in an entity having a material investment in an audit client.

**DISCUSSION:** If the investment by the nonclient in the client is material, any direct or material indirect financial interest a covered member has in the nonclient will impair independence. Thus, whenever the CPA has a direct financial interest, materiality is not an issue and the CPA lacks independence.

Answer (A) is incorrect because an immaterial direct interest impairs independence when the nonclient investor has a material interest in the client investee. Answer (B) is incorrect because the ability to exert significant influence is relevant only when the nonclient investor's interest in the client investee is immaterial. Answer (D) is incorrect because independence is impaired.

**57.** A CPA purchased stock in an audit client corporation and placed it in an educational trust for the CPA's minor child. The trust securities were not material to the CPA but were material to the child's personal net worth. Is the independence of the CPA considered to be impaired with respect to the client?

A. Yes, because the stock is considered a direct financial interest and, consequently, materiality is not a factor.

B. Yes, because the stock is considered an indirect financial interest that is material to the CPA's child.

C. No, because the CPA is not considered to have a direct financial interest in the client.

D. No, because the CPA is not considered to have a material indirect financial interest in the client.

Answer (A) is correct. *(CPA, adapted)*

**REQUIRED:** The effect of a CPA's purchase of the client's stock and placing it in a trust for a minor child.

**DISCUSSION:** Interpretation 101-1 states that independence is impaired if, during the period of the professional engagement, a covered member had or was committed to acquire any direct or material indirect financial interest in the client. With some exceptions, the immediate family (spouse, spousal equivalent, or dependent) of a covered member is subject to Conduct Rule 101 and its interpretations and rulings. Assuming the minor child is a dependent, his/her direct financial interest impairs the CPA's independence regardless of materiality. The same result would follow if the CPA were a trustee of the trust, even if (s)he had no other relationship to the beneficiary, provided that (1) the covered member trustee had investment authority, (2) the trust owned more than 10% of the client, or (3) the value of the trust's holdings exceeded 10% of its assets.

Answer (B) is incorrect because a dependent person's interest is ascribed to the CPA. The CPA therefore has the same direct interest as the child. Answer (C) is incorrect because the CPA is deemed to have a direct interest. Answer (D) is incorrect because materiality is irrelevant if the CPA is deemed to have a direct interest.

**58.** Under the ethical standards of the profession, which of the following situations involving nondependent members of an auditor's family is most likely to impair the independence of an individual participating in an audit engagement?

A. A parent's immaterial investment in a client.

B. A first cousin's loan from a client.

C. A spouse's employment with a client.

D. A sibling's loan to a director of a client.

Answer (C) is correct. *(CPA, adapted)*

**REQUIRED:** The situation involving a nondependent family member that most likely impairs auditor independence.

**DISCUSSION:** The immediate family (spouse, spousal equivalent, or a dependent) of a covered member (such as an individual on the attest engagement team or who is able to influence the engagement) is subject to Conduct Rule 101. Under that Rule, independence is impaired if, during the period covered by the financial statements or during the engagement, a firm partner or professional employee (including an immediate family member of such an individual) was also associated with the client as an officer, director, employee, promoter, underwriter, voting trustee, or member of management. However, independence is not impaired solely because of an immediate family member's employment by the client in a nonkey position.

Answer (A) is incorrect because independence is impaired if a close relative (parent, sibling, or nondependent child) holds a financial interest in the client that (1) is material to the close relative and is known to the covered member or (2) permits the close relative to exert significant influence over the client. A parent's immaterial financial interest does not impair the auditor's independence. Answer (B) is incorrect because a first cousin is not a member of the immediate family (unless dependent) or a close relative (parent, sibling, or nondependent child). Hence, the first cousin's position and financial interests are not attributed to the auditor. Answer (D) is incorrect because a loan by the auditor's sibling (a close relative) to a director of a client does not impair the auditor's independence. A loan to a director is not a financial interest in the client. However, a loan to a director by an immediate family member would be ascribed to the auditor.

**59.** Under Conduct Rule 101, *Independence*, which of the following must be independent in the performance of an audit?

A. Only the partners of the audit firm.

B. Only individuals on the attest engagement team.

C. All individuals on the attest engagement team, except those performing routine clerical functions.

D. All professional employees of the audit firm.

Answer (C) is correct. *(Publisher)*

**REQUIRED:** The personnel to whom Conduct Rule 101 applies.

**DISCUSSION:** Interpretation 101-1 states circumstances in which the independence of covered members is impaired. A covered member includes an individual on the attest engagement team. The attest engagement team consists of individuals participating in the engagement but excludes specialists and individuals who perform only routine clerical functions.

A covered member is an individual on the attest engagement team, an individual able to influence the engagement, a partner or manager providing the client with at least 10 hours of nonattest services, a partner in the same office as the lead engagement partner, the firm (including its benefit plans), or an entity that can be controlled by the foregoing. Moreover, partners and professional employees who own more than 5% of the client or who are associated with the client in certain capacities (director, officer, employee, promoter, underwriter, voting trustee, or trustee of a pension or profit-sharing trust) are also subject to Conduct Rule 101. In addition, a covered member's immediate family and close relatives may have relationships that impair the independence of a covered member.

**60.** The appearance of independence of a CPA, or that CPA's firm, is most likely to be impaired if the CPA

A. Provides appraisal, valuation, or actuarial services for an attest client.

B. Joins a trade association, which is an attest client, and serves in a nonmanagement capacity.

C. Accepts a token gift from an attest client.

D. Serves as an executor and trustee of the estate of an individual who owned the majority of the stock of a closely held client corporation.

Answer (D) is correct. *(CPA, adapted)*

**REQUIRED:** The basis for the impairment of the appearance of independence.

**DISCUSSION:** According to Interpretation 101-1, independence is impaired with regard to the client if, during the period of the professional engagement, a covered member was a trustee of any trust or executor or administrator of any estate if such trust or estate had or was committed to acquire any direct or material indirect financial interest in the client, and the value of the estate's holdings in the client exceeded 10% of the estate's assets. An Ethics Ruling states that mere designation as trustee or executor does not impair independence but that actual service does.

Answer (A) is incorrect because an Interpretation of Conduct Rule 101 describes the requirements that a member who performs other nonattest services for an attest client must meet to be considered independent. A member who provides appraisal, valuation, or actuarial services for a nonpublic attest client should not perform any of the general activities that impair independence. Accordingly, the member may perform such services as preparing separate valuations of assets or liabilities included in client financial statements to test their reasonableness. The member might also perform a valuation of the client's business, provided all matters of judgment are approved by the client, and the client is in a position to have an informed judgment about the valuation. However, these types of services may not be performed for public audit clients.
Answer (B) is incorrect because independence is not impaired, provided the CPA does not participate in management.
Answer (C) is incorrect because a token gift will not impair independence. However, a CPA who accepts more than a token gift, even with the knowledge of the member's firm, will appear to lack independence.

**61.** Under the AICPA *Code of Professional Conduct*, a covered member is most likely not permitted to

A. Have any direct financial interest in a client during the period covered by the financial statements.

B. Perform bookkeeping services for an audit client.

C. Perform tax preparation services for an audit client.

D. Have any joint closely held investment with a principal shareholder of an audit client during the period of the audit engagement.

Answer (D) is correct. *(D. Wells)*

**REQUIRED:** The situation impairing independence.

**DISCUSSION:** According to Interpretation 101-1, during the period of the professional engagement, a covered member may not have "a joint closely held investment that was material to the covered member." A joint closely held investment is an investment in an entity or property by the member and (1) the client, (2) its officers or directors, or (3) an owner with the ability to exercise significant influence over the client that enables the member and the other party(ies) to control the entity or property.

Answer (A) is incorrect because a covered member may have a direct financial interest in a client during the period covered by the financial statements if that interest is disposed of prior to beginning the professional engagement. Answer (B) is incorrect because the member may perform such bookkeeping services as preparing financial statements from the trial balance, posting client-approved entries to the trial balance, proposing journal entries, providing data-processing services, posting coded transactions to the general ledger, and recording transactions if the client has approved the account classifications. However, auditors of public companies may not perform bookkeeping and related services. Answer (C) is incorrect because tax preparation services do not impair independence. For a public client, tax preparation services are permitted if preapproved by the audit committee.

**62.** According to the profession's ethical standards, an auditor is considered independent in which of the following instances?

A. The auditor's checking account, which is fully insured by a federal agency, is held at a client financial institution.

B. The auditor is also an attorney who serves the client as its general counsel.

C. A professional employee of the auditor is the treasurer of a charitable organization that is a client.

D. The client owes the auditor fees for two consecutive annual audits.

Answer (A) is correct. *(CPA, adapted)*

**REQUIRED:** The instance in which an auditor is considered independent.

**DISCUSSION:** If an individual is a covered member, independence is not considered to be impaired (1) provided that the checking (or savings, CD, or money market) account is fully insured by the appropriate state or federal government deposit insurance agencies or by another insurer, or (2) the uninsured amounts in the aggregate were not material to the net worth of the covered member. A firm's depository relationship does not impair its independence provided that the likelihood of the financial institution's experiencing financial difficulties is remote.

Answer (B) is incorrect because, under an Interpretation of Conduct Rule 101, a member may perform other nonattest services. However, certain general activities in the performance of these other services are deemed to impair independence, for example, serving the client as its stock transfer or escrow agent, registrar, general counsel, or the equivalent. Such service constitutes acting in a management capacity. Answer (C) is incorrect because a treasurer is an officer who performs management functions. Answer (D) is incorrect because independence is impaired if billed or unbilled fees, or a note receivable arising from such fees, for professional services rendered more than 1 year prior to the report date remain unpaid when the current year's report is issued.

**63.** In which of the following instances is the independence of the CPA most likely not considered to be impaired? The CPA has been retained as the auditor of a

A. Charitable organization in which the spouse of the CPA serves as treasurer.

B. Municipality in which the CPA owns $25,000 of the $2,500,000 indebtedness of the municipality.

C. Credit union of which the CPA is a member.

D. Company in which the CPA's investment club owns a 10% interest.

Answer (C) is correct. *(CPA, adapted)*

**REQUIRED:** The situation that does not impair the CPA's independence.

**DISCUSSION:** According to an Ethics Ruling, membership in a credit union will not impair independence if (1) the member or his/her partners or employees individually qualify for the membership other than as a result of the services rendered; (2) the member has no significant influence over credit union policies; (3) any loans to the member meet the requirements of Interpretation 101-5; and (4) any deposits are fully insured or, if uninsured, the amounts are not material

Answer (A) is incorrect because the employment of the spouse is ascribed to the CPA. The treasurer is an officer and is therefore considered to be a member of management. Answer (B) is incorrect because independence is impaired if a covered member has any loan to or from the client unless the loan is a "grandfathered loan" or an "other permitted loan" under Interpretation 101-5. Answer (D) is incorrect because ownership of stock in a client through an investment club is a direct financial interest. It impairs independence regardless of materiality.

**64.** Which of the following legal situations is considered to impair the auditor's independence?

A. Intention by current management to commence litigation against the auditor alleging deficiencies in audit work, although the auditor believes there is only a remote possibility that such a claim will be filed.

B. Actual litigation by the auditor against the client for an amount not material to the auditor or the client's financial statements arising out of billing disputes.

C. Actual litigation by the auditor against the current management alleging management fraud or deceit.

D. Probable litigation by the client against the auditor for an amount not material to the auditor or to the financial statements of the client arising out of disputes as to billings for tax services.

Answer (C) is correct. *(CPA, adapted)*

**REQUIRED:** The actual or intended litigation that impairs the auditor's independence.

**DISCUSSION:** According to an AICPA Interpretation, the following are guidelines for determining when actual or threatened litigation impairs independence: (1) litigation alleging deficient audit work has begun; (2) litigation alleging fraud or deceit by current management has begun; and (3) management has expressed an intention to commence litigation alleging deficient audit work, and the auditor concludes that it is probable that such a claim will be filed.

Answer (A) is incorrect because independence is impaired if the auditor concludes that it is probable that such a claim will be filed. Answer (B) is incorrect because, if the litigation is related to an engagement not requiring independence, such as tax or consulting services, impairment does not necessarily result unless the amount in controversy is material to one of the litigants. Answer (D) is incorrect because, if the litigation is related to an engagement not requiring independence, such as tax or consulting services, impairment does not necessarily result unless the amount in controversy is material to one of the litigants.

**65.** In which of the following circumstances will a CPA who audits XM Corporation lack independence?

A. The CPA is a director of, but does not control, YN Corporation, which has a loan from XM.

B. The CPA and XM's president each owns 25% of FOB Corporation, a closely held company.

C. The CPA has an automobile loan from XM, a financial institution. The loan is collateralized by the automobile.

D. The CPA reduced XM's usual audit fee by 40% prior to the audit because XM's financial condition was unfavorable.

Answer (B) is correct. *(CPA, adapted)*

**REQUIRED:** The circumstance in which a CPA will lack independence.

**DISCUSSION:** According to Interpretation 101-1, independence is impaired with regard to a client if, during the period of the professional engagement, "a covered member had a joint closely held investment that was material to the covered member."

Answer (A) is incorrect because the CPA will lack independence only if (s)he controls YN and the loan was not a permitted type. However, according to an Ethics Ruling, a member who does not control such an entity, but is an officer, director, or principal shareholder, must consider the conflict of interest. If the member believes the service can be performed with objectivity and the relationship is disclosed to appropriate parties who consent to the service, the service may be performed. Answer (C) is incorrect because an automobile loan from a financial institution client is permitted if it is collateralized by the automobile. The only new loans permitted from a financial institution client for which independence is required are (1) automobile loans and leases collateralized by the automobile, (2) loans fully collateralized by the cash surrender value of an insurance policy, (3) loans fully collateralized by cash deposits at the same financial institution (e.g., passbook loans), and (4) credit cards and cash advances if the aggregate outstanding balance on the current statement is reduced to $5,000 or less by the payment due date. The loans must have been made under normal lending procedures, terms, and requirements and must, at all times, be kept current as to all terms. Answer (D) is incorrect because the only ethical prohibition regarding fees is that contingent fees not be charged for certain services (Conduct Rule 302). Otherwise, fees may vary with many factors as long as they are related to services rendered and not to the findings or the results of findings. Hence, a fee may be charged on an ability-to-pay basis.

**66.** AICPA Interpretation 101-1 prohibits loans to a covered member from a client financial institution except for certain permitted loans made under normal lending procedures, terms, and requirements. When making the comparison between the terms of the member's loan and those of other borrowers, which item(s) should be considered in the determination of normal lending procedures?

A. Repayment terms.

B. Interest rate, including points.

C. Closing costs.

D. All of the answers are correct.

Answer (D) is correct. *(Publisher)*

**REQUIRED:** The item(s) considered to determine whether normal lending procedures have been followed.

**DISCUSSION:** Covered members are permitted to obtain certain loans from client financial institutions for which independence is required if the loans are made under normal conditions. The procedures, terms, and requirements should be reasonably comparable with those of similar loans committed to other borrowers in the same period. Among the items to be considered in determining whether the loan was made under normal lending procedures are (1) the amount in relation to the collateral and the credit standing of the borrower, (2) repayment terms, (3) interest rate (including points), (4) closing costs, and (5) general availability of such loans to the public.

Answer (A) is incorrect because the items to be considered include repayment terms. Answer (B) is incorrect because the items to be considered include interest rate, including points. Answer (C) is incorrect because the items to be considered include closing costs.

**67.** A CPA audits the financial statements of a local bank. According to the AICPA *Code of Professional Conduct*, the appearance of independence ordinarily is not impaired if the CPA

A. Serves on the bank's committee that approves loans.

B. Owns several shares of the bank's common stock.

C. Obtains a home mortgage from the bank.

D. Uses the bank's time-sharing computer service to solve client-related problems.

Answer (D) is correct. *(CPA, adapted)*

**REQUIRED:** The situation in which the CPA retains the appearance of independence.

**DISCUSSION:** Using the bank's time-sharing computer services to solve client-related problems is considered a normal incident of an audit, and the CPA's independence is not impaired.

Answer (A) is incorrect because a CPA's independence is impaired if (s)he serves in any capacity equivalent to that of a member of management or of a decision-making employee. Answer (B) is incorrect because even an immaterial direct financial interest impairs independence. Answer (C) is incorrect because a home mortgage ordinarily impairs independence. However, a loan of a certain type (home mortgages, other secured loans, and unsecured loans not material to the member's net worth) may be grandfathered and therefore not impair independence. Such a loan is grandfathered if (1) the loan is under the financial institution's normal lending procedures, terms, and requirements; (2) it is kept current and the terms do not change; and (3) it was obtained before the lender became a client requiring independence or in certain other cases.

**68.** Jordan is the executive partner of Cain & Jordan, CPAs. One of its clients is a large nonprofit charitable organization. The organization has asked Jordan to be on its board of directors, which consists of a large number of the community's leaders. For Jordan to be considered independent, which of the following requirements must be met?

| | Board Participation Purely Honorary | Audit Participation by Jordan Prohibited |
|---|---|---|
| A. | Yes | Yes |
| B. | No | Yes |
| C. | No | No |
| D. | Yes | No |

Answer (D) is correct. *(Publisher)*

**REQUIRED:** The best description of the effect of a CPA's position as a board member of a charitable organization.

**DISCUSSION:** According to an AICPA Interpretation, the member will be independent as long as the position is purely honorary, it is identified as such in all letterheads and externally circulated materials in which (s)he is named as a director or trustee, the member restricts participation to use of his/her name, and (s)he does not vote or participate in management functions. Jordan may directly participate in the audit even though (s)he serves as an honorary director.

**69.** An audit independence issue might be raised by the auditor's participation in engagements involving other nonattest services. Which of the following statements is most consistent with the profession's attitude toward this issue?

A. Information obtained as a result of a consulting engagement is confidential to that engagement and should not influence performance of the attest function.

B. The decision as to loss of independence must be made by the client based upon the facts of the particular case.

C. The auditor should not make management decisions for an audit client.

D. The auditor who is asked to review management decisions is also competent to make these decisions and can do so without loss of independence.

Answer (C) is correct. *(CPA, adapted)*

**REQUIRED:** The statement most consistent with the profession's attitude toward independence relative to consulting services.

**DISCUSSION:** Under Interpretation 101-3, a member must evaluate the effect on his/her independence of performing other services. The member should take care not to "perform management functions or make management decisions for the attest client, the responsibility for which remains with the client's board of directors and management."

Answer (A) is incorrect because the auditor should use all information available in assessing the fairness of the financial statements. Answer (B) is incorrect because the auditor, not the client, must determine whether (s)he has been put in a position in which independence might be questioned. Answer (D) is incorrect because the auditor may review management decisions and make suggestions, but (s)he may not actually make those decisions without losing independence.

**70.** A CPA who performs primary actuarial services for a nonpublic client normally is precluded from expressing an opinion on the financial statements of that client if the

A. Fees for the actuarial services have not been paid.

B. Actuarial services are a major determinant of the pension expense.

C. CPA prepared an actuarial report using assumptions determined by the CPA and not approved by the client.

D. Actuarial assumptions used are not in accordance with GAAS.

Answer (C) is correct. *(CPA, adapted)*

**REQUIRED:** The situation in which a CPA could not provide actuarial and auditing services to a nonpublic client.

**DISCUSSION:** Under Interpretation 101-3, a member must evaluate the effect on his/her independence of performing other services. The member should take care not to "perform management functions or make management decisions for the attest client, the responsibility for which remains with the client's board of directors and management." An example given in the Interpretation of another attest service that impairs independence is the preparation of an appraisal, valuation, or actuarial report using assumptions determined by the member and not approved by the client.

Answer (A) is incorrect because, unless the fees have been unpaid for over a year at the date of the current year's report and thus might be deemed to be a loan to the client, the CPA may accept the audit engagement. Answer (B) is incorrect because, even if the results of the actuarial services are incorporated into the financial statements, the auditor's independence is not impaired as long as the nonpublic client performs management functions and makes management decisions. However, the auditor is precluded from performing actuarial services for a public client. Answer (D) is incorrect because the assumptions should be in accordance with GAAP, not GAAS.

**71.** Which of the following does not impair a CPA's independence?

A. The CPA performs the duties of a transfer agent or a registrar for a client.

B. The CPA participates as the treasurer of a charitable organization who is a client.

C. The client is in bankruptcy and has not paid fees related to the previous year's audit.

D. The CPA is a university faculty member who audits the student senate fund.

Answer (C) is correct. *(Publisher)*

**REQUIRED:** The situation that does not impair a CPA's independence.

**DISCUSSION:** An Ethics Ruling states that independence will be impaired if, when the current year's report is issued, billed or unbilled fees, or a note receivable arising from such fees, remain unpaid for any professional services provided more than 1 year prior to the report date. These unpaid fees are tantamount to a loan. However, this ruling does not apply to fees owed by a client in bankruptcy.

Answer (A) is incorrect because serving as the attest client's stock transfer or escrow agent, general counsel, or its equivalent is deemed to impair independence. Answer (B) is incorrect because a CPA's independence is impaired by connection with the client as an officer or in another capacity equivalent to that of management. Answer (D) is incorrect because the CPA cannot become independent of his/her employer (the university), which administers the student senate fund.

**72.** Burrow & Co., CPAs, have provided annual audit and tax compliance services to Mare Corp. for several years. Mare has been unable to pay Burrow in full for services Burrow rendered 19 months ago. Burrow is ready to begin field work for the current year's audit. Under the ethical standards of the profession, which of the following arrangements will permit Burrow to begin the field work on Mare's audit?

A. Mare sets up a two-year payment plan with Burrow to settle the unpaid fee balance.

B. Mare commits to pay the past due fee in full before the audit report is issued.

C. Mare gives Burrow an 18-month note payable for the full amount of the past due fees before Burrow begins the audit.

D. Mare engages another firm to perform the field work, and Burrow is limited to reviewing the working papers and issuing the audit report.

Answer (B) is correct. *(CPA, adapted)*

**REQUIRED:** The arrangement allowing the CPAs to conduct an audit of a client that has not paid for prior services.

**DISCUSSION:** The AICPA has ruled that audit fees that are long past due take on the characteristics of a loan under Conduct Rule 101. An Ethics Ruling considers independence to be impaired if billed or unbilled fees, or a note arising from the fees, for client services rendered more than 1 year prior to the current year's report date remain unpaid when the current year's report is issued. However, this Ruling does not apply if the client is in bankruptcy. Moreover, long overdue fees do not preclude the CPA from performing services not requiring independence. Accordingly, payment in full prior to issuance of the report will satisfy the requirements of the Ruling.

Answer (A) is incorrect because, under a two-year plan, some fees would still be unpaid at the date the report is issued. Answer (C) is incorrect because the note arising from the fees would still be unpaid at the date the report is issued. Answer (D) is incorrect because reporting on the audit requires independence, which is impaired as a result of the overdue fees.

**73.** Under the ethical standards of the profession, which of the following investments in a client is not considered to be a direct financial interest?

A. An investment held through a nonclient regulated mutual fund.

B. An investment held through a nonclient investment club.

C. An investment held in a blind trust.

D. An investment held by the trustee of a trust.

Answer (A) is correct. *(CPA, adapted)*

**REQUIRED:** The investment in a client that is not a direct financial interest.

**DISCUSSION:** An Ethics Ruling states that shares of a regulated mutual investment fund that holds securities of a member's clients "represent indirect financial interests of the member in securities of his or her clients." Independence is impaired only if (1) the indirect interest is material or (2) the member has significant influence over the fund.

Answer (B) is incorrect because an Ethics Ruling states that ownership of stock in a client through an investment club is a direct financial interest. Answer (C) is incorrect because, under an Ethics Ruling, transfer of a direct financial interest (the investment in the client) to a blind trust does not prevent the interest from impairing the member's independence. Answer (D) is incorrect because an Interpretation states that a covered member's independence is impaired by service as a trustee of a trust that has a direct financial interest in a client. A trustee of a trust holds the legal title to trust property. Hence, a trustee is deemed to hold any investment in the client held by the trust.

**74.** In which of the following situations is a CPA's independence considered to be impaired?

I. The CPA maintains a checking account that is fully insured by a government deposit insurance agency at an audit-client financial institution.

II. The CPA has a direct financial interest in an audit client, but the interest is maintained in a blind trust.

III. The CPA owns a commercial building and leases it to an audit client. The lease meets all the criteria of a capital lease, and the rental income is material to the CPA.

A. I and II.

B. II and III.

C. I and III.

D. I, II, and III.

Answer (B) is correct. *(CPA, adapted)*

**REQUIRED:** The situations in which independence is impaired.

**DISCUSSION:** Under an Ethics Ruling, when a member or member's firm leases property to or from a client, independence is not impaired if the lease meets the criteria of an operating lease, the terms and conditions of the agreement compare with those of similar leases and all amounts are paid in accordance with the lease. However, if the lease meets all the criteria of a capital lease and does not qualify as a grandfathered or permitted loan under Interpretation 101-5, it will impair the member's independence. The reason is that a capital lease is considered a loan to or from the client. Moreover, independence is impaired if a member has any direct financial interest in the client. An Ethics Ruling states that independence is impaired whether or not the financial interest is in a blind trust.

No impairment occurs if the member's depository relationship is fully insured or if aggregate uninsured amounts are not material to the member's net worth.

**75.** According to the profession's ethical standards, a CPA is considered independent in which of the following instances?

A. The CPA agrees to indemnify the client against losses from client acts.

B. The CPA has a material direct financial interest in a client but transfers the interest into a blind trust.

C. The CPA owns an office building, and the mortgage on the building is guaranteed by a client.

D. The CPA belongs to a country club client in which membership requires the acquisition of a pro rata share of equity.

Answer (D) is correct. *(CPA, adapted)*

**REQUIRED:** The circumstances in which a CPA is considered independent.

**DISCUSSION:** If membership is essentially social, independence is not impaired because the equity (or debt) ownership is not a direct financial interest. But the CPA should not serve on the governing board or participate in management.

Answer (A) is incorrect because this agreement violates Interpretation 101-1. Answer (B) is incorrect because independence is impaired if a member has any direct financial interest in the client. An Ethics Ruling states that independence is impaired whether or not the financial interest is in a blind trust. Answer (C) is incorrect because independence is impaired if the CPA has a loan from the client. A loan includes a guarantee of a loan.

**76.** Within the meaning of the Securities Act of 1933 and the Securities Exchange Act of 1934, an accountant deemed to be independent with regard to a specific entity must

I. Confirm in writing its independence from the audit client.
II. Have no relationships with the audit client.
III. Discuss its independence with the audit committee.

A. I and II only.
B. I and III only.
C. II and III only.
D. I, II, and III.

Answer (B) is correct. *(Publisher)*
**REQUIRED:** The requirements regarding independence discussions with the auditee.
**DISCUSSION:** An auditor who wishes to be deemed independent within the meaning of the Securities Act of 1933 and the Securities Exchange Act of 1934 must make an annual written disclosure to the audit committee of all relationships between the auditor and its related entities and the company and its related entities that may reasonably bear on independence. The auditor must confirm its independence in the letter and must discuss its independence with the audit committee.
The standards do not require that auditors of public companies have no relationships with audit clients.

**77.** The AICPA *Code of Professional Conduct* states, in part, that a CPA should maintain integrity and objectivity. Objectivity in the Code refers to a CPA's ability to

A. Be impartial, intellectually honest, and free of conflicts of interest.
B. Distinguish independently between accounting practices that are acceptable and those that are not.
C. Be unyielding in all matters dealing with auditing procedures.
D. Choose independently between alternate accounting principles and auditing standards.

Answer (A) is correct. *(Publisher)*
**REQUIRED:** The definition of objectivity in the *Code of Professional Conduct*.
**DISCUSSION:** According to the Principles, "Objectivity is a state of mind, a quality that lends itself to a member's services. It is a distinguishing feature of the profession. The principle of objectivity imposes the obligation to be impartial, intellectually honest, and free of conflicts of interest."
Answer (B) is incorrect because the CPA uses both judgment and GAAP to evaluate whether a client's accounting practices are acceptable. Answer (C) is incorrect because the CPA is expected to use professional judgment, which may include flexibility, in applying audit procedures. Answer (D) is incorrect because auditing standards are concerned with the quality of the auditor's performance, whereas adherence to accounting principles by management is a prerequisite for fairly stated financial statements.

**78.** A CPA most likely does not violate Conduct Rule 102, *Integrity and Objectivity*, if the CPA

A. Performs expert witness services for a client.
B. Subordinates his/her judgment to that of client personnel when performing consulting services.
C. Knowingly makes materially misleading entries in an entity's financial records.
D. Accepts the judgment of a client instead of his/her own when performing tax services.

Answer (A) is correct. *(Publisher)*
**REQUIRED:** The situation in which the CPA most likely does not violate Conduct Rule 102.
**DISCUSSION:** According to an Ethics Ruling, a CPA who serves as an expert witness is not an advocate as contemplated by Interpretation 102-6. Rather, an expert witness is someone with "specialized knowledge, training, and experience who should arrive at and present positions objectively." However, if expert services unrelated to the audit are provided to an audit client that is a public company covered by the Securities Exchange Act of 1934, the CPA will lack independence (Sarbanes-Oxley Act of 2002).
Answer (B) is incorrect because, in the performance of any professional service, a member shall not subordinate his/her judgment to others, including the client (Conduct Rule 102). Answer (C) is incorrect because, under an Interpretation of Conduct Rule 102, a member is deemed to have knowingly misrepresented facts in violation of the rule when (s)he knowingly makes or permits or directs another to make, materially false and misleading entries in an entity's financial statements or records. Answer (D) is incorrect because, in the performance of any professional service, a member shall not subordinate his/her judgment to others, including the client (Conduct Rule 102).

## 1.7 Code – Responsibilities to Clients

**79.** Which of the following statements best describes the distinction between the auditor's responsibilities and management's responsibilities?

A. Management has responsibility for maintaining and adopting sound accounting policies, and the auditor has responsibility for internal control.

B. Management has responsibility for the basic data underlying financial statements, and the auditor has responsibility for drafting the financial statements.

C. The auditor's responsibility is confined to the audited portion of the financial statements, and management's responsibility is confined to the unaudited portions.

D. The auditor's responsibility is confined to expressing an opinion, but the financial statements remain the responsibility of management.

Answer (D) is correct. *(Publisher)*

**REQUIRED:** The statement that best distinguishes between the auditor's and management's responsibilities concerning audited financial statements.

**DISCUSSION:** AU 110, *Responsibilities and Functions of the Independent Auditor*, states that the auditor is responsible for the opinion on financial statements, whereas management is responsible for the representations made in the financial statements.

Answer (A) is incorrect because management has responsibility for establishing and maintaining internal control. Answer (B) is incorrect because management is responsible for preparing the financial statements. Answer (C) is incorrect because the auditor expresses an opinion on the financial statements taken as a whole, and management is responsible for all the assertions in the financial statements.

**80.** Which of the following statements concerning an accountant's disclosure of confidential client data is ordinarily true?

A. Disclosure may be made to any state agency without subpoena.

B. Disclosure may be made to any party on consent of the client.

C. Disclosure may be made to comply with an IRS audit request.

D. Disclosure may be made to comply with generally accepted accounting principles.

Answer (B) is correct. *(CPA, adapted)*

**REQUIRED:** The condition allowing disclosure of confidential client data.

**DISCUSSION:** Under Conduct Rule 301, an accountant may disclose any confidential client information with the specific consent of the client.

Answer (A) is incorrect because disclosure may be made to a state agency only pursuant to a subpoena or summons or with the client's consent. Answer (C) is incorrect because, without consent, an accountant may disclose confidential information to the IRS only pursuant to a subpoena or summons. Answer (D) is incorrect because compliance with GAAP is a responsibility of clients who issue financial statements, not the accountants who report on them.

**81.** Thorp, CPA, was engaged to audit Ivor Co.'s financial statements. During the audit, Thorp discovered that Ivor's inventory contained stolen goods. Ivor was indicted and Thorp was subpoenaed to testify at the criminal trial in state court. Ivor claimed accountant-client privilege to prevent Thorp from testifying. Which of the following statements is most likely true regarding Ivor's claim?

A. Ivor can claim an accountant-client privilege only in jurisdictions that have enacted a statute creating such a privilege.

B. Ivor could claim an accountant-client privilege if a criminal tax case were brought in federal court.

C. The accountant-client privilege can be claimed only in civil suits.

D. The accountant-client privilege can be claimed only to limit testimony to audit subject matter.

Answer (A) is correct. *(CPA, adapted)*

**REQUIRED:** The statement most likely true concerning accountant-client privilege.

**DISCUSSION:** Although communication between lawyers and clients is privileged, no common-law concept extends this privilege to the accountant-client relationship. A minority of states have enacted statutes recognizing as privileged the confidential communication between an accountant and a client.

Answer (B) is incorrect because federal law does not recognize a broad privilege for accountant-client communications. However, the Internal Revenue Service Restructuring and Reform Act of 1998 extends a confidentiality privilege to most tax advice provided to a current or prospective client by any individual qualified under federal law to practice before the IRS. The federal law does not extend to criminal tax matters, private civil matters, disclosures to other federal regulatory bodies, or state and local tax matters. The privilege is available only in matters brought before the IRS or in proceedings in federal court in which the U.S. is a party and applies only to advice on legal issues. Answer (C) is incorrect because, in jurisdictions where the privilege exists, it also applies to criminal actions. Answer (D) is incorrect because, in jurisdictions where the privilege exists, it is not limited to audit matters.

**82.** An external auditor is not permitted to discuss confidential client information except with the specific consent of the client. This ethical proscription

A. Is unenforceable.

B. Will prevent the auditor from engaging another auditing firm to conduct a peer review.

C. Will not preclude the auditor from complying with a validly issued court subpoena.

D. Is often used by a client to blunt the auditor's efforts to modify the standard auditor's report.

Answer (C) is correct. *(CMA, adapted)*

**REQUIRED:** The effect of prohibiting disclosure of confidential client information.

**DISCUSSION:** Conduct Rule 301 does not prohibit a CPA from disclosing confidential client information

1. In compliance with a validly issued and enforceable subpoena or summons,
2. In the proper discharge of his/her professional obligations under Conduct Rules 202, *Compliance with Standards*, and 203, *Accounting Principles*,
3. In a review of the CPA's professional practice under AICPA or state CPA society or board of accountancy authorization, or
4. During the initiation of a complaint with, or in response to any inquiry made by, the professional ethics division, trial board of the AICPA, or an investigative or disciplinary body of a state society or board of accountancy.

Answer (A) is incorrect because conduct rules are enforceable through the AICPA and state CPA societies. Answer (B) is incorrect because an exception is made for peer reviews. Answer (D) is incorrect because the CPA is not independent if the client can dictate the content of the report. However, the auditor cannot ordinarily disclose, without the client's specific consent, information not required to be disclosed in financial statements to comply with GAAP (AU 431).

**83.** AICPA Conduct Rule 301, *Confidential Client Information*, is violated when a member in public practice

A. Provides client profit and loss percentages to a trade association without the client's consent.

B. Uses outside computer services to process tax returns.

C. Performs consulting services for similar clients.

D. Advises potential consulting services clients about previous problems on similar engagements.

Answer (A) is correct. *(Publisher)*

**REQUIRED:** The activity violating Conduct Rule 301.

**DISCUSSION:** An Ethics Ruling states that, prior to disclosing confidential client profit and loss percentages to a trade association, the CPA must have specific client consent.

Answer (B) is incorrect because, according to an Ethics Ruling, using outside computer services to process tax returns is permissible as long as client confidentiality is maintained. Many CPAs use outside computer services for processing tax returns. Answer (C) is incorrect because most CPAs perform consulting services for clients in the same or related industries. Answer (D) is incorrect because, according to an Ethics Ruling, CPAs must make full disclosure about any reservations concerning the usefulness of potential consulting services, especially those based on past experience with similar engagements. However, client confidentiality must be preserved or waived.

**84.** To which of the following parties may a CPA partnership provide its audit documentation, without being lawfully subpoenaed or without the client's consent?

A. The IRS.

B. The FASB.

C. Any surviving partner(s) on the death of a partner.

D. A CPA before purchasing a partnership interest in the firm.

Answer (C) is correct. *(CPA, adapted)*

**REQUIRED:** The party who may receive audit documentation from a CPA without a subpoena or client consent.

**DISCUSSION:** Audit documentation may be disclosed to another partner of the accounting firm without the client's consent because such information has not been communicated to outsiders. A partner of the CPA has a fiduciary obligation to the client not to disclose confidential information without consent.

Answer (A) is incorrect because the partnership may not provide the IRS with confidential client information without client permission, a subpoena, or a summons. Answer (B) is incorrect because the CPA or his/her firm may not disclose confidential information to the FASB without client consent. Answer (D) is incorrect because a CPA may not provide audit documentation to a prospective purchaser. However, an exception is made for a review of the practice in conjunction with a prospective purchase, sale, or merger.

**85.** A publicly held company that disagrees with the independent auditor on a significant matter affecting its financial statements has several courses of action. Which of the following courses of action is inappropriate?

A. Appeal to the FASB to review the significant matter.

B. Modify the financial statements by expressing in the notes its viewpoint with regard to the significant matter.

C. Ask the auditor to refer in the auditor's report to a client note that discusses the client point of view with regard to the significant matter.

D. Engage another independent auditor.

Answer (A) is correct. *(CPA, adapted)*

**REQUIRED:** The inappropriate action by a public company when a disagreement arises with its auditor.

**DISCUSSION:** The disagreement would not be considered by the FASB. The board does not provide services for the settlement of disputes between clients and CPAs.

Answer (B) is incorrect because the viewpoint may be communicated in the notes. Answer (C) is incorrect because the viewpoint may be communicated in the notes. Answer (D) is incorrect because one alternative of the client is to engage a new auditor. However, the SEC requires public companies to disclose the reason for an auditor change by filing Form 8-K, and the AICPA requires predecessor-successor communication.

**86.** An auditor has withdrawn from an audit engagement of a publicly held company after finding fraud that may materially affect the financial statements. The auditor should set forth the reasons and findings in correspondence to the

A. Securities and Exchange Commission.

B. Client's legal counsel.

C. Stock exchanges on which the company's stock is traded.

D. Audit committee.

Answer (D) is correct. *(CPA, adapted)*

**REQUIRED:** The party or parties to be notified when an auditor withdraws after finding fraud.

**DISCUSSION:** When an audit indicates the presence of errors or fraud that require a modification of the opinion, and the client refuses to accept the auditor's report as modified, the auditor should withdraw and communicate the reasons for withdrawal to the audit committee of the board of directors (AU 317). Withdrawal may or may not be appropriate in other circumstances, depending on the diligence and cooperation of management and the board in investigating the matter and taking action (AU 316). Moreover, the Private Securities Litigation Reform Act of 1995, which applies to public companies, requires the auditor to report directly to the board these conclusions regarding lack of remedial action: that an illegal act materially affects the financial statements, that senior management has not taken appropriate remedial action, and that this failure will result in a modified report or the auditor's withdrawal. The company then has one business day to notify the SEC.

Answer (A) is incorrect because the auditor is usually under no obligation to report fraud to outside parties. The firm, however, is required to disclose the reason for a change in auditors on SEC Form 8-K. Answer (B) is incorrect because the auditor may wish to consult his/her legal counsel but not the client's counsel. Answer (C) is incorrect because the auditor is usually under no obligation to report fraud to outside parties. The firm, however, is required to disclose the reason for a change in auditors on SEC Form 8-K.

**87.** With respect to records in a CPA's possession, the *Code of Professional Conduct* provides that

A. An auditor may retain client records, after a demand is made for them, if fees due with respect to a completed engagement have not been paid.

B. Working papers that contain journal entries not reflected in the client's records need not be furnished to the client upon request.

C. Extensive schedules prepared by the client at the auditor's request are working papers that belong to the auditor and need not be furnished to the client upon request.

D. The auditor who returns client records must comply with any subsequent requests to again provide such information.

Answer (C) is correct. *(Publisher)*

**REQUIRED:** The true statement regarding records in the CPA's possession.

**DISCUSSION:** According to an Interpretation of Conduct Rule 501, "A member's workpapers – including, but not limited to, analyses and schedules prepared by the client at the request of the member – are the member's property, not client records, and need not be made available." However, the PCAOB's Auditing Standard No. 3, *Audit Documentation* relating to public clients is silent on property rights of working papers.

Answer (A) is incorrect because, after a demand is made for them, client records must be returned even if fees have not been paid. Answer (B) is incorrect because working papers containing client financial information not reflected in the client's books must be returned to the client upon request if the engagement is complete. Answer (D) is incorrect because, once the member has complied with the requirements for the return of client records, (s)he has no further obligation to provide such information.

**88.** A CPA's retention of client records after a demand has been made for them is an action that is

A. Not addressed by the AICPA *Code of Professional Conduct.*

B. Acceptable if sanctioned by state law.

C. Prohibited under the AICPA *Code of Professional Conduct.*

D. A violation of GAAS.

Answer (C) is correct. *(CPA, adapted)*

**REQUIRED:** The profession's policy concerning a CPA's retention of client records.

**DISCUSSION:** An Interpretation of Conduct Rule 501, *Acts Discreditable*, defines client records as "any accounting or other records belonging to the client that were provided to the member by or on behalf of the client." This interpretation prohibits the retention (after a demand is made for them) of client records to enforce payment or for any other purpose. Such an act is deemed to be discreditable to the profession.

Answer (A) is incorrect because Conduct Rule 501 prohibits retention of client records after a demand has been made for them. Answer (B) is incorrect because a state's grant of a lien on records in the CPA's possession does not change his/her duty under the Code. Answer (D) is incorrect because retention of client records after a demand has been made for them is prohibited by the *Code of Professional Conduct*, not by GAAS.

## 1.8 Code – Other Responsibilities and Practices

**89.** When a CPA is associated with financial statements that do not comply with promulgated GAAP because the statements would be misleading without the departure, the CPA is not required to disclose

A. The departure.

B. The approximate effects of the departure in comparison to the application of GAAP.

C. The reason the departure does not have a material effect on the statements.

D. The reasons compliance would be misleading.

Answer (C) is correct. *(Publisher)*

**REQUIRED:** The disclosure not required when application of promulgated GAAP would be misleading.

**DISCUSSION:** Under Conduct Rule 203, a CPA who performs services that require representations of conformity with promulgated GAAP is required to describe the departure, the approximate effects of the departure (if practicable), and the reasons compliance would result in misleading financial statements. But this requirement applies only if the effect on the statements or data is material.

Answer (A) is incorrect because the CPA is required to disclose the departure. Answer (B) is incorrect because the CPA is required to disclose the approximate effects of the departure in comparison with the application of GAAP. Answer (D) is incorrect because the CPA is required to disclose the reasons compliance would be misleading.

**90.** A CPA who is employed by a nonaccounting corporation performs services for the employer, including auditing the employer's financial statements. Reports issued with respect to such activities are distributed with the CPA's name and CPA designation appearing on the corporate letterhead. These reports should

A. Be restricted to internal use.

B. Make no reference to GAAS.

C. Be on plain paper (not on the corporate letterhead).

D. Refer to an audit.

Answer (B) is correct. *(Publisher)*

**REQUIRED:** The true statement about reports issued on the financial statements of a CPA's employer.

**DISCUSSION:** A CPA not in public practice who uses the CPA designation in a manner to imply that (s)he is independent of the employer has made a knowing misrepresentation of fact violating Conduct Rule 102. Thus, it is advisable that the employment title be clearly indicated. Moreover, an auditor who is not independent may not express an opinion. A reference to GAAS would imply independence.

Answer (A) is incorrect because, if a report is made available to third parties, it may indicate the CPA's professional designation if no implication of independence is conveyed. Answer (C) is incorrect because, if the report is to outsiders, it must be on the corporate letterhead. Answer (D) is incorrect because no reference should be made to GAAS, an audit, or a review. Such a reference might imply independence.

**91.** According to Conduct Rule 502, advertising or other forms of solicitation that are false, misleading, or deceptive are not in the public interest, and AICPA members in public practice must not seek to obtain clients in this manner. Such activities include all the following except those that

A. Indicate the CPA's educational and professional attainments.

B. Imply the ability to influence a court.

C. Claim to be able to save the taxpayer 20% of a determined tax liability.

D. Create unjustified expectations of favorable results.

Answer (A) is correct. *(Publisher)*

**REQUIRED:** The advertising activity not considered false, misleading, or deceptive.

**DISCUSSION:** Advertising and solicitation are acceptable as long as they do not involve falsehood or deception. Members may engage in self-laudatory, comparative, or endorsement advertising; in-person solicitation; and advertising that some may view as in bad taste. Thus, an accurate statement of educational and professional attainments is clearly permissible.

Answer (B) is incorrect because advertisement of influence over courts, tribunals, regulatory agencies, or a similar body or official is deceptive. Answer (C) is incorrect because a correct amount of tax liability exists and a claim to save a taxpayer part of that amount is deceptive. Answer (D) is incorrect because creating false and unjustified expectations of favorable results is misleading.

**92.** According to an Ethics Ruling based on the *Code of Professional Conduct*, a CPA

A. May not, upon leaving a firm, take any of the firm's client files without permission.

B. Is not associated with unaudited interim reports issued by clients even if the CPA's name is listed in the report.

C. Cannot undertake the responsibility of supervising and evaluating the work of specialists.

D. May disclose currently used Uniform CPA Examination questions.

Answer (A) is correct. *(Publisher)*

**REQUIRED:** The true statement concerning a CPA's responsibilities.

**DISCUSSION:** When the relationship of a member of the AICPA with a firm is terminated, and the member was not an owner of the firm, unless permitted by contract, the member may not take or retain originals or copies from the firm's client files or proprietary information without permission. Such behavior would be an act discreditable (Ethics Ruling under Conduct Rule 501).

Answer (B) is incorrect because a member is associated with financial statements of a public entity when (s)he has consented to the use of his/her name in a report, document, or written communication containing the statements (AU 504). Answer (C) is incorrect because CPAs must be able to define the tasks to be performed by specialists and evaluate the results. Answer (D) is incorrect because solicitation or knowing disclosure of currently used CPA examination questions is an act discreditable.

**93.** A member of the AICPA may render which service under a contingent fee arrangement?

A. An audit of the financial statements of a company that intends to issue securities for sale to the public, with the fee contingent upon the proceeds from the sale of the securities.

B. A compilation of the financial statements of a client seeking a loan, with the fee contingent upon the amount the client is able to borrow. The report does not disclose lack of independence.

C. An examination of the prospective financial statements of a client who intends to sell limited partnerships, with the CPA's fee contingent upon the proceeds.

D. A provision of investment advisory services, with the fee based on a percentage of the client's investment portfolio.

Answer (D) is correct. *(Publisher)*

**REQUIRED:** The service that may be rendered under a contingent fee arrangement.

**DISCUSSION:** According to an Ethics Ruling, the member is not in violation of Conduct Rule 302 regarding contingent fees if the fee is based on a specified percentage of the portfolio; the dollar amount of the portfolio on which the fee is based is determined at the beginning of each quarter (or longer periods, if agreed) and is adjusted only for client additions or withdrawals, and the fee arrangement is not renewed more often than quarterly.

Answer (A) is incorrect because a contingent fee is prohibited for an audit of financial statements. Answer (B) is incorrect because a contingent fee is prohibited for a compilation if the report does not disclose lack of independence and a third party is reasonably expected to use the financial statements. Answer (C) is incorrect because a contingent fee is prohibited for an examination of prospective financial statements.

**94.** The AICPA *Code of Professional Conduct* would be violated if a CPA accepted a fee for services and the fee was

A. Fixed by a public authority.

B. Based on a price quotation submitted in competitive bidding.

C. Based on the results of judicial proceedings in a tax matter.

D. Payable after a specified finding was attained in a review of financial statements.

Answer (D) is correct. *(CPA, adapted)*

**REQUIRED:** The fee arrangement that violates the *Code of Professional Conduct*.

**DISCUSSION:** A contingent fee is one that is dependent upon a specified finding. Conduct Rule 302, *Contingent Fees*, prohibits contingent fees (1) for the audit or review of a financial statement, (2) for a compilation if a third party is reasonably expected to use the financial statement and the report does not mention the member's lack of independence, (3) for an examination of prospective financial information, and (4) for the preparation of original or amended tax returns or claims for tax refunds. However, contingent fees may be accepted for other services.

Answer (A) is incorrect because Conduct Rule 302 states that fees fixed by courts or other public authorities are not contingent. Answer (B) is incorrect because competitive bidding is not prohibited. Answer (C) is incorrect because, in tax matters, fees determined based on the results of judicial proceedings or the findings of governmental agencies are not contingent.

**95.** The profession's ethical standards most likely are violated when a CPA represents that specific consulting services will be performed for a stated fee and it is apparent at the time of the representation that the

A. Actual fee will be substantially higher.

B. Actual fee will be substantially lower than the fees charged by other CPAs for comparable services.

C. CPA will not be independent.

D. Fee is a competitive bid.

Answer (A) is correct. *(CPA, adapted)*

**REQUIRED:** The action that violates ethical standards regarding fee representation.

**DISCUSSION:** Conduct Rule 502 prohibits forms of solicitation that are false, misleading, or deceptive. Under an Interpretation of Conduct Rule 502, a representation that specific services will be performed for a stated fee, when it is likely at the time that the actual fee will be substantially higher, is a prohibited form of solicitation.

Answer (B) is incorrect because a CPA is permitted to charge lower fees than other CPAs. Answer (C) is incorrect because independence is required in an audit, but not for consulting services. Answer (D) is incorrect because competitive bids for consulting services are allowed.

**96.** Inclusion of which of the following statements in a CPA's advertisement is not acceptable pursuant to the AICPA *Code of Professional Conduct*?

A. Paul Fall<br>Certified Public Accountant<br>Fluency in Spanish and French

B. Paul Fall<br>Certified Public Accountant<br>J.D., Evans Law School 1990

C. Paul Fall<br>Certified Public Accountant<br>Free Consultation

D. Paul Fall<br>Certified Public Accountant<br>Endorsed by AICPA

Answer (D) is correct. *(CPA, adapted)*

**REQUIRED:** The advertisement not in accordance with the AICPA *Code of Professional Conduct*.

**DISCUSSION:** A CPA may not claim to be endorsed by the Institute. A member may, however, state that (s)he is a member.

Answer (A) is incorrect because an accurate statement about fluency in languages is acceptable. Answer (B) is incorrect because an accurate statement about educational attainments is acceptable. Answer (C) is incorrect because advertising free consultation is acceptable.

**97.** A violation of the profession's ethical standards most likely occurs when a CPA

A. Purchases another CPA's accounting practice and bases the price on a percentage of the fees accruing from clients over a 3-year period.

B. Receives as a commission a percentage of the amounts invested by the CPA's audit clients in a tax shelter with the client's knowledge and approval.

C. Has a public accounting practice and also is the owner of a business that offers data processing services to the public.

D. Practices in a commercial corporation, a form of organization permitted by state law.

Answer (B) is correct. *(Publisher)*

**REQUIRED:** The most likely ethics violation.

**DISCUSSION:** Conduct Rule 503, *Commissions and Referral Fees*, states, "A member in public practice shall not for a commission recommend or refer to a client any product or service, or for a commission recommend or refer any product or service to be supplied by a client, or receive a commission, when the member or the member's firm also performs for that client" certain services. These include an audit or review of a financial statement, a compilation if a third party is reasonably expected to use the financial statement and the report does not indicate lack of independence, or an examination of prospective financial information.

Answer (A) is incorrect because a sales price based on expected future cash flows is appropriate. Answer (C) is incorrect because a CPA may own a business offering services of a type performed by public accountants. However, (s)he will be deemed to be in the practice of public accounting and must abide by the Rules of Conduct. Answer (D) is incorrect because the practice of public accounting may be any form permitted by law, provided the organization conforms to resolutions of the AICPA Council.

**98.** Which of the following is prohibited by the AICPA *Code of Professional Conduct*?

A. Practice of public accounting in the form of a professional corporation that uses a firm name indicating specialization.

B. Use of the partnership name for a limited period by one of the partners in a public accounting firm after the death or withdrawal of all other partners.

C. Failing to provide working papers to the client after a request has been made.

D. Prematurely expressing an opinion based on an audit because of time pressures from the client.

Answer (D) is correct. *(Publisher)*

**REQUIRED:** The action considered a code violation.

**DISCUSSION:** Conduct Rule 102 prohibits a member from subordinating his/her judgment to others. The auditor must complete the audit prior to signing the report.

Answer (A) is incorrect because the Code does not prohibit the use of a fictitious name or the indication of a specialization. However, the name or indication of specialization may not be misleading. In addition, the AICPA permits CPAs to use trade names (e.g., "Suburban Tax Services") that are not false or deceptive. Answer (B) is incorrect because names of one or more past owners may be included in the firm name of a successor organization as long as the name is not misleading. Answer (C) is incorrect because, according to the AICPA standards, the working papers are deemed to be the property of the CPA. However, working papers containing client financial information not reflected in the client's books must be returned to the client upon request if the engagement is complete.

**99.** Which of the following acts by a CPA who is not in public practice is most likely to be a violation of the ethical standards of the profession?

A. Using the CPA designation without disclosing employment status in connection with financial statements issued for external use by the CPA's employer.

B. Distributing business cards indicating the CPA designation and the CPA's title and employer.

C. Corresponding on the CPA's employer's letterhead, which contains the CPA designation and the CPA's employment status.

D. Compiling the CPA's employer's financial statements and making reference to the CPA's lack of independence.

Answer (A) is correct. *(CPA, adapted)*

**REQUIRED:** The action violating ethical standards.

**DISCUSSION:** According to an Ethics Ruling, a member not in public practice who uses the CPA designation in a manner implying that (s)he is independent of the employer has committed a knowing misrepresentation of fact in violation of Conduct Rule 102.

Answer (B) is incorrect because, as long as the CPA's title and the employer's name are on the business cards, their use is permissible. Answer (C) is incorrect because, as long as the CPA's title and the employer's name are on the letterhead, its use is permissible. Answer (D) is incorrect because an accountant may compile a nonpublic entity's financial statements if (s)he issues the appropriate report. The lack of independence, but not the reason therefore, should be disclosed (AR 100). If an accountant who is not independent is associated with the financial statements of a public entity (except a compilation report) but has not audited or reviewed them, (s)he must issue a disclaimer of opinion that states his/her lack of independence (AU 504).

**100.** Susan, CPA, performs compilation services for Dalstar, a nonpublic entity. The compilation reports issued by Susan disclose lack of independence and are not used by third parties. Susan has accepted a commission from a software company for recommending its products to Dalstar. The commission agreement was disclosed to Dalstar. Susan also refers Dalstar to Thomas, CPA, who is more competent with respect to engagements involving the industry in which Dalstar operates. Thomas performs an audit of Dalstar's financial statements and subsequently remits to Susan a portion of the fee collected. The referral fee agreement was likewise disclosed to Dalstar. Susan accepts the fee. Who, if anyone, has violated the *Code of Professional Conduct*?

A. Only Susan.

B. Both Susan and Thomas.

C. Only Thomas.

D. Neither Susan nor Thomas.

Answer (D) is correct. *(Publisher)*

**REQUIRED:** The violator(s) of the *Code of Professional Conduct* when a CPA pays a referral fee to another CPA.

**DISCUSSION:** A commission is "compensation, except a referral fee, for recommending or referring any product or service to be supplied by another person" (FTC Order dated August 3, 1990). Conduct Rule 503 prohibits receipt of a disclosed commission only if the CPA performs for the client an audit, a review, a compilation when the report will be used by third parties and the report does not disclose the CPA's lack of independence, or an examination of prospective financial information. A referral fee is "compensation for recommending or referring any service of a CPA to any person" (FTC Order cited above). Conduct Rule 503 permits referral fees if they are disclosed to the client. Consequently, Susan has not violated Conduct Rule 503 by accepting either the disclosed commission or the disclosed referral fee. Thomas has not violated the Code by paying the disclosed referral fee.

Answer (A) is incorrect because Susan has not violated the Code. Answer (B) is incorrect because Susan and Thomas have not violated the Code. Answer (C) is incorrect because Thomas has not violated the Code.

**101.** Ann Able, CPA, is considering forming a partnership with Jim Baker for the purpose of practicing public accounting. Which of the following is true?

A. The AICPA *Code of Professional Conduct* requires Baker to be a CPA.

B. Baker need not be a CPA if the partnership does not represent itself as a partnership of CPAs.

C. If Baker is not a CPA, he need not conform to the AICPA *Code of Professional Conduct*.

D. If Baker is not a CPA, he may not participate in the management of the partnership.

Answer (B) is correct. *(Publisher)*

**REQUIRED:** The true statement concerning a partnership with a non-CPA.

**DISCUSSION:** Conduct Rule 505 does not prohibit this arrangement, but the firm may designate itself as "Members of the AICPA" only if all CPA-owners are members. Moreover, this form of organization must be permitted by law or regulations, and it must conform to resolutions of the AICPA Council.

Answer (A) is incorrect because some state boards and CPA societies have rules prohibiting mixed partnerships, but the Code does not prohibit a member from forming a partnership with non-CPAs. Answer (C) is incorrect because all partners must conform to the Code. Answer (D) is incorrect because the non-CPA is not precluded from participating in management.

**102.** Under Conduct Rule 505, *Form of Organization and Name*, and the related resolution of the AICPA Council, which of the following is a characteristic of a form of organization in which a member may practice public accounting?

A. A CPA firm transfers all financial interests for attest services to another non-CPA firm through a leasing-of-employees arrangement.

B. The owners must be jointly and severally liable for the acts of the entity.

C. The entity must be a professional corporation.

D. A majority of the ownership of the firm must belong to CPAs.

Answer (D) is correct. *(Publisher)*

**REQUIRED:** The characteristic of an organization in which an AICPA member may practice public accounting.

**DISCUSSION:** A member may practice public accounting only in a form of organization permitted by law or regulation and only if such entity has specified characteristics. (1) CPAs must own a majority of the firm in terms of voting rights and financial interests. (2) A non-CPA owner, including an investor or commercial enterprise, must be actively engaged in providing services to clients as his/her principal occupation. (3) A CPA must have ultimate responsibility for all the services provided. (4) Any non-CPA owner must have a baccalaureate degree. (5) Non-CPA owners cannot hold themselves out to be CPAs, must abide by the Code, and must complete the work-related CPE requirements. (6) Owners must own their equity in their own right. (7) Ownership must be transferred to the firm or to other qualified owners if the non-CPA ceases to be actively engaged in the firm.

Answer (A) is incorrect because leasing arrangements may exist in alternative practice structures. However, the CPA-owners must remain financially responsible, under applicable laws or regulations, for the attest work performed. Answer (B) is incorrect because the relevant Council resolution does not address the question of liability. Answer (C) is incorrect because the entity may be in any form allowed under law or regulation.

**103.** A violation of the profession's ethical standards most likely occurs when a CPA who

A. Has been admitted to the Bar represents on letterhead to be an attorney and a CPA.

B. Has not prepared a newsletter permits the publisher to attribute it to the CPA.

C. Is controller of a bank permits the bank to use the controller's CPA title in the listing of officers in its publications.

D. Maintains a separate, distinct practice but forms an association with other CPAs for joint advertising. The group practices public accounting under the association's name.

Answer (D) is correct. *(Publisher)*

**REQUIRED:** The most likely ethics violation.

**DISCUSSION:** The practice of public accounting under the name of an association or group is not permitted. The public is likely to be confused about the actual relationship of the parties. Accordingly, each firm should practice in its own firm name, but it may indicate the name of the association elsewhere on its stationery.

Answer (A) is incorrect because, according to an Ethics Ruling, a single letterhead may be used. The Code does not prohibit the simultaneous practice of law and accounting. Answer (B) is incorrect because an Ethics Ruling permits attribution of a newsletter, tax booklet, or similar publication to a member if the member has a reasonable basis for concluding that information attributed to the member is not false, misleading, or deceptive. Answer (C) is incorrect because an Ethics Ruling permits the controller to be identified as a CPA in the listing of bank officers.

**104.** A violation of the profession's ethical standards most likely occurs when a CPA in public practice

A. Uses a records-retention agency to store the CPA's working papers and client records.

B. Serves as an expert witness in a damage suit and receives compensation based on the amount awarded to the plaintiff.

C. Refers life insurance prospects to the CPA's spouse, who is a life insurance agent.

D. Serves on a municipal board of income tax appeals, discloses that status to concerned parties and participates as a board member in a tax appeal involving a client but does not receive the client's consent for such action.

Answer (D) is correct. *(CPA, adapted)*

**REQUIRED:** The most likely ethics violation.

**DISCUSSION:** Under Interpretation 102-2, if the significant relationship creating a conflict of interest is disclosed to all appropriate parties who consent to the arrangement, Conduct Rule 102 does not prohibit performance of the professional service. Moreover, an Ethics Ruling has determined that service on a governmental body is within the Interpretation. However, disclosure and consent do not eliminate an impairment of independence. The failure to secure the client's consent means that the arrangement could be viewed as impairing the CPA's objectivity.

Answer (A) is incorrect because an Ethics Ruling permits the use of such a records center. Nevertheless, the responsibility for safeguarding the confidentiality of the client's records still rests with the CPA. Answer (B) is incorrect because contingent fees are allowed except in certain cases. Answer (C) is incorrect because the benefit (commission) received by the spouse as a result of the referral is ascribed to the CPA, but receipt of disclosed commissions is permissible in certain circumstances.

**105.** Which action is not considered a discreditable act under the Interpretations of Conduct Rule 501, *Acts Discreditable*?

A. A CPA-defendant has lost a final appeal of an adverse verdict in a sexual harassment suit in state court.

B. A CPA-defendant has lost a final appeal of an adverse verdict in a racial discrimination suit in federal court.

C. A CPA has a bank collect notes received from a client in payment of fees.

D. A CPA fails to follow standards and procedures established by governmental agencies in audits of grants by those agencies.

Answer (C) is correct. *(Publisher)*

**REQUIRED:** The action not a discreditable act.

**DISCUSSION:** An Ethics Ruling permits CPAs to assign client notes received in payment of fees to banks for collection.

Answer (A) is incorrect because a final adverse legal determination of culpability under antidiscrimination law creates a presumption that the member has committed an act discreditable. Answer (B) is incorrect because a final adverse legal determination of culpability under antidiscrimination law creates a presumption that the member has committed an act discreditable. Answer (D) is incorrect because a member must follow established governmental standards and procedures in addition to GAAS in auditing governmental agencies, grantees, etc. Thus, failing to follow standards and procedures established by governmental agencies in audits of grants by those agencies is a discreditable act.

**106.** Which of the following violates the *Code of Professional Conduct*?

A. A member not in public practice is a bank controller who is designated as a CPA on bank stationery and in bank advertisements listing officers of the bank.

B. A member contracts with a service provider to maintain a client's computer hardware and charges the client a higher servicing fee than that charged to the member by the service provider.

C. A partner in a CPA firm is elected to public office. After his/her withdrawal from the firm, the remaining partners continue to use a firm name that includes his/her name.

D. A member shares offices and a joint letterhead with another member although they are not partners.

Answer (D) is correct. *(Publisher)*

**REQUIRED:** The violation of the *Code of Professional Conduct.*

**DISCUSSION:** According to an Ethics Ruling, CPAs should not use a letterhead showing the names of two accountants when a partnership between them does not exist. Such a representation is misleading. Furthermore, some courts have held that such an arrangement may be a de facto partnership, and the individual CPAs may be liable for the obligations of the de facto partnership and of the de facto partners.

Answer (A) is incorrect because the bank controller's use of the CPA title is permitted by a specific Ethics Ruling. Answer (B) is incorrect because, according to an Ethics Ruling, the profit on the resale is not a commission. Answer (C) is incorrect because the name of a past owner may be included in the firm name of a successor organization.

**107.** Which is most likely a violation of the AICPA *Code of Professional Conduct*?

A. A member firm buys computer time at wholesale prices from another CPA firm and sells it at retail prices to clients.

B. A member does not timely file his/her own personal federal income tax return.

C. A tax booklet is attributed to a member firm even though it was prepared by an outside author.

D. A member forms a partnership for the practice of public accounting with non-CPAs.

Answer (B) is correct. *(Publisher)*

**REQUIRED:** The most likely ethics violation.

**DISCUSSION:** Under an Interpretation of Conduct Rule 501, acts discreditable to the profession include failing to comply with applicable law regarding timely filing of personal or firm tax returns or the timely remittance of payroll and other taxes collected on behalf of others.

Answer (A) is incorrect because a member may purchase a product from a third-party supplier and resell the product to a client. Answer (C) is incorrect because an Ethics Ruling permits a tax booklet to be attributed to the member in these circumstances given a reasonable basis for concluding that the information attributed to the member is not false, misleading, or deceptive. Answer (D) is incorrect because the partnership of a CPA with non-CPAs is not precluded by the Code.

## 1.9 Legal Liability

**108.** Contract law is the basis for the legal liability at common law of an auditor to his/her client. From which of the following may the auditor's liability arise?

A. Only fraudulent actions by the auditor.

B. Only gross negligence or fraudulent actions by the auditor.

C. Negligence, gross negligence, or fraudulent actions by the auditor.

D. Neither negligence nor fraudulent actions by the auditor.

Answer (C) is correct. *(Publisher)*

**REQUIRED:** The basis for an auditor's legal liability to a client at common law.

**DISCUSSION:** An auditor's liability to a client arises from their contract, which is usually documented in the audit engagement letter. The auditor is obligated to carry out the contract (perform the audit) by exercising reasonable care. (S)he will be liable to the client for any negligence or fraud.

Answer (A) is incorrect because the auditor will also be liable for negligence. Answer (B) is incorrect because the auditor will also be liable for failure to use reasonable care (ordinary negligence). Answer (D) is incorrect because both negligence and fraud will create a contractual liability. The contract implies a duty to exercise reasonable care.

**109.** Which of the following best describes litigation involving CPAs?

A. The Racketeer Influenced and Corrupt Organizations Act was specifically passed by Congress to address illegitimate actions by CPAs.

B. A CPA may successfully assert as a defense that the CPA had no motive to be part of a fraud.

C. A CPA may be exposed to criminal as well as civil liability.

D. A CPA is primarily responsible for a client's notes in an annual report filed with the SEC.

Answer (C) is correct. *(Publisher)*

**REQUIRED:** The best description of litigation involving CPAs.

**DISCUSSION:** A CPA may be exposed to criminal as well as civil liability under the Securities Act of 1933, the Securities Exchange Act of 1934, and the Racketeer Influenced and Corrupt Organizations Act (RICO).

Answer (A) is incorrect because RICO was enacted to curtail inroads of organized crime into legitimate business. Answer (B) is incorrect because, although absence of intent is a defense to fraud, motive is not relevant. Answer (D) is incorrect because management, not the CPA, is responsible for the financial statements, including the notes.

**110.** The prevailing legal view is that an auditor's liability to third parties at common law may be based on

A. Fraud only when such parties were in privity of contract with the auditor.

B. Gross negligence only if the auditor knew such parties were intended beneficiaries of the audit.

C. Ordinary negligence and that any third party who relied on the auditor's work may recover.

D. Ordinary negligence if such parties belonged to a specifically foreseen class but were not specifically known.

Answer (D) is correct. *(Publisher)*

**REQUIRED:** The basis for an auditor's legal liability to a third party at common law.

**DISCUSSION:** An auditor has not contracted with third parties, so the potential responsibility to them is not as great as to the client. Auditors may be liable to any third parties for gross negligence and intentional acts of deceit (fraud). However, auditors may be liable at common law for ordinary negligence to third parties in certain circumstances. The Restatement (Second) of Torts, an authoritative work published by the American Law Institute, provides for liability when a third party, although not specifically known at the time of the audit, belonged to a limited and foreseen class of financial statement users. For example, banks would be included in the class if the audit report were intended to be used by the client to obtain a bank loan. Other creditors, however, would be excluded from the class of potential plaintiffs.

Answer (A) is incorrect because the auditor may be liable for fraud to all third parties. Answer (B) is incorrect because the auditor may be liable for gross negligence to all third parties. Answer (C) is incorrect because the majority view precludes recovery on the basis of ordinary negligence unless the plaintiff belonged to a specifically foreseen class of users (intended beneficiaries).

**111.** Which is the true statement concerning an auditor's statutory legal liability?

A. The Securities Act of 1933 broadened the auditor's liability and the Securities Exchange Act of 1934 narrowed it.

B. The auditor has a greater burden of defense under the Securities Act of 1933 than the Securities Exchange Act of 1934.

C. Criminal liability only arises under state law.

D. The auditor may limit exposure to liability by destroying documents that might suggest an improper act.

Answer (B) is correct. *(Publisher)*

**REQUIRED:** The true statement concerning an auditor's statutory liability.

**DISCUSSION:** In general, the Securities Act of 1933 regulates initial sales of securities to the public. The Securities Exchange Act of 1934 regulates subsequent sales and exchanges of securities. Under the 1933 act, a purchaser need only prove damages resulting from the purchase of securities covered by a registration statement containing a false statement or omission in a section audited or prepared by the auditor. The auditor must then prove that (s)he was not negligent (or fraudulent), usually by showing that (s)he made a reasonable investigation (the "due diligence" defense). Under the 1934 act, the purchaser must prove that (s)he did not know the statement was false, that (s)he relied on it, and, under the antifraud provisions, that the auditor acted with intent or reckless disregard for the truth. Thus, gross negligence is the minimum basis for liability, and the auditor need not prove due diligence.

Answer (A) is incorrect because both securities statutes imposed greater liability on auditors than had existed under the common law. However, the 1934 act places a greater burden of proof on the plaintiff than the 1933 act. Answer (C) is incorrect because criminal liability can also arise under federal securities law. Answer (D) is incorrect because the Sarbanes-Oxley Act of 2002 makes it a felony to knowingly destroy or create documents to impede, obstruct, or influence any existing or contemplated federal investigation. The maximum prison term is 20 years. Moreover, a registered public accounting firm must retain audit working papers for at least 7 years. The documentation retained must be in sufficient detail to support the conclusions in the audit report.

**112.** How does the Securities Act of 1933, which imposes civil liability on auditors for misrepresentations or omissions of material facts in a registration statement, expand auditors' liability to purchasers of securities beyond that of common law?

A. Purchasers only have to prove loss caused by reliance on audited financial statements.

B. Privity with purchasers is not a necessary element of proof.

C. Purchasers have to prove either fraud or gross negligence as a basis for recovery.

D. Auditors are held to a standard of care described as professional skepticism.

Answer (B) is correct. *(CPA, adapted)*

**REQUIRED:** The expansion of auditor liability under the Securities Act of 1933.

**DISCUSSION:** Privity, i.e., being a party to the contract with the auditor, is not a required element of proof under Section 11, the most frequently invoked basis for recovery under the Securities Act of 1933. Privity is often the deciding factor in common law cases, however.

Answer (A) is incorrect because a plaintiff must simply prove that a loss occurred in a transaction involving the particular securities covered by the registration statement and that the registration statement contained a false statement or an omission of a material fact for which the auditors were responsible. If these elements are proven, the burden shifts to the auditors to prove that they exercised due diligence. Negligence, privity, and reliance are not elements of the plaintiff's case. Answer (C) is incorrect because the plaintiff need not prove fraud, gross negligence, negligence, privity, or reliance. Answer (D) is incorrect because auditors are held to the standard of due diligence, which may be satisfied by following GAAS in the conduct of the audit.

**113.** When engaged to compile unaudited financial statements for a nonpublic entity, the accountant's responsibility to detect errors, fraud, and illegal acts

A. Does not exist unless the parties have a written agreement.

B. Arises from the accountant's obligation to apply normal auditing procedures.

C. Is to design procedures to provide reasonable assurance of detecting material misstatements.

D. Is limited to informing the client that the engagement cannot be relied upon to disclose fraud.

Answer (D) is correct. *(Publisher)*

**REQUIRED:** The accountant's responsibility to detect errors, fraud, or illegal acts, when engaged to compile unaudited financial statements.

**DISCUSSION:** Under AR 100, the accountant's understanding with the entity should provide that (1) the engagement cannot be relied upon to detect errors, fraud, or illegal acts, and (2) (s)he will inform the entity of material errors or instances of fraud or illegal acts that come to his/her attention (unless clearly inconsequential).

Answer (A) is incorrect because a contract for services need not be in writing to be valid. Answer (B) is incorrect because the accountant need not apply auditing procedures to information gathered in the preparation of unaudited statements. Answer (C) is incorrect because AU 110 requires auditors "to plan and perform the audit to obtain reasonable assurance about whether the financial statements are free of material misstatement, whether caused by error or fraud."

**114.** The scope and nature of an auditor's contractual obligation to a client is ordinarily set forth in the

A. Management representation letter.

B. Scope paragraph of the auditor's report.

C. Engagement letter.

D. Introductory paragraph of the auditor's report.

Answer (C) is correct. *(CPA, adapted)*

**REQUIRED:** The form of the contractual agreement with a client.

**DISCUSSION:** An auditor should establish an understanding with the client regarding the services to be performed. The variety of matters that are included in the understanding may be communicated in an engagement letter (AU 310). Thus, the audit scope, responsibilities of management and the auditor, arrangements regarding the conduct of the audit, additional services to be provided, fees, and other matters should be set forth in a contract evidenced by an engagement letter. An engagement letter should be prepared for prospective clients on each engagement, audit or otherwise. Such a letter is highly recommended although not specifically required by GAAS. If the client agrees to the contractual relationship by signing a copy of the letter, it represents a written contract.

Answer (A) is incorrect because an auditor obtains a written management representation letter to complement other procedures, but it is not part of the engagement letter. Answer (B) is incorrect because the scope paragraph (1) states that the audit was conducted in accordance with GAAS, (2) sets forth the requirements of GAAS, (3) describes the nature of an audit, and (4) states that the audit provides a reasonable basis for the opinion. Answer (D) is incorrect because the introductory paragraph (1) states that the financial statements were audited and (2) describes the responsibilities of management and the auditor.

**115.** DMO Enterprises, Inc. engaged the accounting firm of Martin, Seals, & Anderson to perform its annual audit. The firm performed the audit in a competent, nonnegligent manner and billed DMO for $16,000, the agreed fee. Shortly after delivery of the audited financial statements, Hightower, the assistant controller, disappeared, taking with him $28,000 of DMO's funds. It was then discovered that Hightower had been engaged in a highly sophisticated, novel defalcation scheme during the past year. He had previously embezzled $35,000 of DMO funds. DMO has refused to pay the accounting firm's fee and is seeking to recover the $63,000 that was stolen by Hightower. Which of the following is most likely true?

A. The accountants cannot recover their fee and are liable for $63,000.

B. The accountants are entitled to collect their fee and are not liable for $63,000.

C. DMO is entitled to rescind the audit contract and thus is not liable for the $16,000 fee, but it cannot recover damages.

D. DMO is entitled to recover the $28,000 defalcation and is not liable for the $16,000 fee.

Answer (B) is correct. *(CPA, adapted)*

**REQUIRED:** The true statement concerning the disputed fee of auditors who failed to uncover a sophisticated embezzlement scheme.

**DISCUSSION:** An audit cannot guarantee that fraud will be detected. The auditor's opinion reflects that the audit is intended to give only reasonable assurance that the financial statements are free of material misstatement. Thus, AU 110 requires auditors "to plan and perform the audit to obtain reasonable assurance about whether the financial statements are free of material misstatement, whether caused by error or fraud." If the auditors planned and performed the audit in accordance with GAAS, including AU 110, the accounting firm fulfilled its contract with the client. The auditors should not be held liable for the loss and are entitled to their fee.

Answer (A) is incorrect because the accountants are entitled to the $16,000 in unpaid fees and are not liable for either the current embezzlement of $28,000 or the past embezzlement of $35,000. Answer (C) is incorrect because the client is liable for the $16,000 fee. Answer (D) is incorrect because the client is liable for the $16,000 fee and is not entitled to recover the $28,000 defalcation from the accountants.

**116.** Ocean and Associates, CPAs, audited the financial statements of Drain Corporation. As a result of Ocean's negligence in conducting the audit, the financial statements included material misstatements. Ocean was unaware of this fact. The financial statements and Ocean's unqualified opinion were included in a registration statement and prospectus for an original public offering of stock by Drain. Sharp purchased shares in the offering. Sharp received a copy of the prospectus prior to the purchase but did not read it. The shares declined in value as a result of the misstatements in Drain's financial statements becoming known. Under which of the following acts is Sharp most likely to prevail in a lawsuit against Ocean?

| | Securities Exchange Act of 1934, Section 10(b), Rule 10b-5 | Securities Act of 1933, Section 11 |
|---|---|---|
| A. | Yes | Yes |
| B. | Yes | No |
| C. | No | Yes |
| D. | No | No |

Answer (C) is correct. *(CPA, adapted)*

**REQUIRED:** The basis for recovery under securities law in a suit against negligent accountants.

**DISCUSSION:** Section 11 is the most frequently invoked basis for suit under the Securities Act of 1933. Under Section 11, the investor need prove only that (s)he suffered losses in a transaction involving the particular securities covered by the registration statement and that the registration statement contained a false statement or an omission of a material fact for which the CPAs were responsible, e.g., in the audited financial statements. Thus, under Section 11, Sharp need not prove reliance or negligence and will prevail if Ocean fails to prove due diligence. Sharp is unlikely to prevail under the antifraud provisions of the Securities Exchange Act of 1934 because of the absence of scienter.

**117.** Under Section 11 of the Securities Act of 1933, which of the following standards may a CPA use as a defense?

| | Generally Accepted Accounting Principles | Generally Accepted Fraud Detection Standards |
|---|---|---|
| A. | Yes | Yes |
| B. | Yes | No |
| C. | No | Yes |
| D. | No | No |

Answer (B) is correct. *(CPA, adapted)*

**REQUIRED:** The standards a CPA may use as a defense under Section 11.

**DISCUSSION:** A CPA is strictly liable to investors under Section 11 but will not be liable if (s)he can prove due diligence. This defense requires proof that a reasonable investigation was conducted and that the CPA reasonably believed that the financial statements were accurate on the effective date of the registration statement. Proof of adherence to GAAP and GAAS is the usual basis for such a due diligence defense.

**118.** Martin Corporation orally engages Dawson, CPA, to audit its year-end financial statements. The engagement is to be completed within 2 months after the close of Martin's fiscal year for a fixed fee of $2,500. Under these circumstances what obligation is assumed by Dawson?

A. None. The contract is unenforceable because it is not in writing.

B. An implied promise to exercise reasonable standards of competence and care.

C. An implied obligation to take extraordinary steps to discover all defalcations.

D. The obligation of an insurer of its work who is liable without fault.

Answer (B) is correct. *(CPA, adapted)*

**REQUIRED:** The obligation assumed by a CPA engaged to audit financial statements.

**DISCUSSION:** CPAs are required to adhere to reasonable standards of competence and care and perform an audit in accordance with GAAS. They are expected to complete the contract based upon the agreed terms.

Answer (A) is incorrect because an oral contract is enforceable (but subject to disagreement, which can be avoided with an engagement letter). Answer (C) is incorrect because an ordinary audit should be designed to provide reasonable assurance that material errors and fraud will be detected. Hence, it need not include extraordinary procedures to uncover all fraud, whether or not material. Answer (D) is incorrect because auditors are not insurers. They do not undertake to guarantee the results of their work regardless of fault. Rather, they are required to use due professional care.

**119.** You are a CPA retained by the manager of a cooperative retirement village to do write-up work. You are expected to prepare unaudited financial statements with each page marked "unaudited" and accompanied by a disclaimer of opinion stating no audit was made. In performing the work, you discover that there are no invoices to support $25,000 of the manager's claimed disbursements. The manager informs you that all the disbursements are proper. What should you do?

A. Submit the expected statements but omit the $25,000 of unsupported disbursements.

B. Include the unsupported disbursements in the statements because you are not expected to make an audit.

C. Obtain from the manager a written statement that you informed him/her of the missing invoices and that (s)he gave his/her assurance that the disbursements were proper.

D. Notify the owners that some of the claimed disbursements are unsupported and withdraw if the situation is not satisfactorily resolved.

Answer (D) is correct. *(CPA, adapted)*

**REQUIRED:** The appropriate action by a CPA who discovers a material irregularity while doing compilation work.

**DISCUSSION:** These facts are based on *1136 Tenants' Corp. v. Max Rothenburg & Co.* (1972), a case that imposed liability on a CPA doing compilation work for not pursuing an investigation of facts that appeared questionable on their face. Although the CPA need not audit the information, (s)he is responsible to take further action concerning information that is incorrect, incomplete, or otherwise unsatisfactory. Such action includes communication with the owners.

Answer (A) is incorrect because submitting the statements but omitting the unsupported disbursements is an inappropriate action on the part of the CPA. Answer (B) is incorrect because including the unsupported disbursements in the statements is an inappropriate action on the part of the CPA. Answer (C) is incorrect because obtaining the manager's statement is insufficient.

**120.** Under the antifraud provisions of Section 10(b) of the Securities Exchange Act of 1934, a CPA may be liable if the CPA acted

A. Negligently.

B. With independence.

C. Without due diligence.

D. Without good faith.

Answer (D) is correct. *(CPA, adapted)*
**REQUIRED:** The basis for a CPA's liability under Section 10(b).
**DISCUSSION:** The distinguishing element of fraud is scienter, which is the intent to deceive or defraud. Acting in good faith indicates lack of scienter. Hence, a CPA who acted without good faith cannot assert the good faith defense.
Answer (A) is incorrect because fraud entails an intent to deceive or defraud, not mere negligence. Answer (B) is incorrect because a CPA who performs attest services must be independent. Answer (C) is incorrect because lack of due diligence, per se, does not signify the existence of scienter.

## 1.10 Quality Control and Peer Review for CPA Firms

**121.** A CPA firm is reasonably assured of meeting its responsibility to provide services that conform with professional standards by

A. Adhering to generally accepted auditing standards.

B. Having an appropriate system of quality control.

C. Joining professional societies that enforce ethical conduct.

D. Maintaining an attitude of independence in its engagements.

Answer (B) is correct. *(CPA, adapted)*
**REQUIRED:** The means of reasonably assuring that a CPA firm's services meet professional standards.
**DISCUSSION:** A system of quality control should provide reasonable assurance that the firm's personnel comply with professional standards applicable to its audit and accounting practice. However, deficiencies in individual audit, attest, review, and compilation engagements do not, by themselves, signify that the firm's system of quality control is insufficient to provide it with reasonable assurance of compliance with the relevant standards (QC 20). GAAS apply to individual audit engagements. Quality control standards apply to the firm's practice as a whole (AU 161).
Answer (A) is incorrect because a firm must comply with all applicable standards, not merely GAAS. Answer (C) is incorrect because adhering to ethical standards is only one aspect of quality control. Answer (D) is incorrect because independence is included in the first of the five elements of quality control.

**122.** A firm of independent auditors must establish and follow quality control policies and procedures because these standards

A. Are necessary to meet increasing requirements of auditors' liability insurers.

B. Are required by the SEC for auditors of all firms.

C. Include formal filing of records of such policies and procedures.

D. Give reasonable assurance that the firm as a whole will conform with applicable auditing standards.

Answer (D) is correct. *(Publisher)*
**REQUIRED:** The reason a firm of independent auditors establishes a quality control system.
**DISCUSSION:** The system of quality control includes the organizational structure and the policies adopted and procedures established to provide reasonable assurance that the firm as a whole will comply with auditing standards and other applicable standards. Policies and procedures should be established with respect to the following elements: independence, integrity, and objectivity; personnel management; acceptance and continuance of clients and engagements; engagement performance; and monitoring (QC 20).
Answer (A) is incorrect because companies that insure CPAs against liability for malpractice establish their own requirements and insurance rates. Answer (B) is incorrect because all CPA firms are obligated to adhere to quality control standards issued by the ASB. The SEC has authority only over those firms that must report under the securities laws. Answer (C) is incorrect because quality control standards do not require formal records to be filed with the AICPA or any other body.

**123.** Quality control for a CPA firm, as referred to in Statements on Quality Control Standards (SQCS), applies to

A. Auditing services only.

B. Auditing and consulting services.

C. Auditing and tax services.

D. Auditing and accounting and review services.

Answer (D) is correct. *(CPA, adapted)*
**REQUIRED:** The applicability of the quality control standards.
**DISCUSSION:** According to QC 20, quality control for a CPA firm applies to all audit, attest, accounting and review, and other services for which professional standards have been established by the ASB and the Accounting and Review Services Committee. The SQCSs therefore do not apply to compliance with standards for consulting services and tax services, which are issued by different senior technical committees.

**124.** Which of the following are elements of a CPA firm's quality control that should be considered in establishing its quality control policies and procedures?

| | Personnel Management | Monitoring | Engagement Performance |
|---|---|---|---|
| A. | Yes | Yes | No |
| B. | Yes | Yes | Yes |
| C. | No | Yes | Yes |
| D. | Yes | No | Yes |

Answer (B) is correct. *(CPA, adapted)*

**REQUIRED:** The elements that should be considered in establishing quality control policies and procedures.

**DISCUSSION:** The quality control element of personnel management relates to assuring that employees have the skills needed for the responsibilities they are called upon to assume. The quality control element of monitoring is concerned with providing reasonable assurance that procedures related to the other elements are suitably designed and being effectively applied. The quality control element of engagement performance requires the firm to establish policies and procedures to ensure proper planning, performing, supervising, reviewing, documenting, and communicating the results of engagements. Such policies and procedures also should address the concurring partner review requirements applicable to SEC engagements established in the SECPS's membership requirements (QC 20).

**125.** The nature and extent of a CPA firm's quality control policies and procedures depend on

| | The CPA Firm's Size | The Nature of the CPA Firm's Practice | Cost-Benefit Considerations |
|---|---|---|---|
| A. | Yes | Yes | Yes |
| B. | Yes | Yes | No |
| C. | Yes | No | Yes |
| D. | No | Yes | Yes |

Answer (A) is correct. *(CPA, adapted)*

**REQUIRED:** The factors affecting a CPA firm's quality control policies and procedures.

**DISCUSSION:** The nature and extent of a firm's quality control policies and procedures depend on a number of factors, such as the firm's size, the degree of operating autonomy allowed, its personnel policies, the nature of its practice and organization, and appropriate cost-benefit considerations (QC 20).

**126.** Which of the following is an element of a CPA firm's quality control system that should be considered in establishing its quality control policies and procedures?

A. Complying with laws and regulations.

B. Using statistical sampling techniques.

C. Managing personnel.

D. Considering audit risk and materiality.

Answer (C) is correct. *(CPA, adapted)*

**REQUIRED:** The element of a CPA firm's quality control system.

**DISCUSSION:** The quality control element of personnel management requires establishment of policies and procedures to provide reasonable assurance that those hired have the appropriate characteristics to enable them to perform competently (e.g., maturity, integrity, leadership, and academic attainments), that work is assigned to persons with the degree of technical training and proficiency required, that personnel participate in required CPE and other professional development activities, and that personnel selected for advancement have the necessary qualifications (QC 20).

Answer (A) is incorrect because the auditor considers compliance with laws and regulations. However, this consideration is not an element of a CPA firm's quality control system. Answer (B) is incorrect because an auditing firm may use statistical or nonstatistical sampling techniques in performing audits. Answer (D) is incorrect because an auditor must consider audit risk and materiality in performing the audit, but this consideration is not an element of a quality control system.

**127.** The primary purpose of establishing quality control policies and procedures for deciding whether to accept a new client is to

A. Enable the CPA firm to attest to the reliability of the client.

B. Satisfy the CPA firm's duty to the public concerning the acceptance of new clients.

C. Minimize the likelihood of association with clients whose management lacks integrity.

D. Anticipate before performing any field work whether an unqualified opinion can be expressed.

Answer (C) is correct. *(CPA, adapted)*

**REQUIRED:** The primary purpose of establishing quality control policies and procedures for deciding whether to accept a new client.

**DISCUSSION:** CPA firms should have policies and procedures to determine whether to accept or continue a new client or to perform a specific engagement for a client. The objective is to minimize the likelihood of association with clients whose managers may lack integrity (QC 20).

Answer (A) is incorrect because the CPA firm attests to the fairness of the financial statements, not to the reliability of the client. Answer (B) is incorrect because the CPA firm has a duty to the public with regard to its reporting responsibilities but not client acceptance. Answer (D) is incorrect because the field work will indicate whether an unqualified opinion can be expressed.

**128.** In connection with the element of personnel management, a CPA firm's system of quality control should ordinarily provide that all personnel

A. Participate in professional development activities that enable them to fulfill responsibilities assigned.

B. Possess judgment, motivation, and adequate experience.

C. Seek assistance from persons having appropriate levels of knowledge, judgment, and authority.

D. Demonstrate compliance with peer review directives.

Answer (A) is correct. *(CPA, adapted)*

**REQUIRED:** The requirement for all personnel.

**DISCUSSION:** According to QC 20, the firm's policies and procedures should provide reasonable assurance that general and industry-specific CPE and other professional development activities should enable personnel to fulfill assigned responsibilities and satisfy CPE requirements of the AICPA and regulatory agencies, such as the GAO and state boards of accountancy.

Answer (B) is incorrect because motivation and judgment are often difficult to assess. Answer (C) is incorrect because seeking assistance from persons having appropriate levels of knowledge, judgment, and authority relates to the element of engagement performance. Answer (D) is incorrect because peer review directives may relate to any or all of the quality control elements.

**129.** Under the personnel management element of the AICPA's quality control standards, the practitioner-in-charge of an attest engagement ordinarily should have which of the following competencies?

I. Understanding of the organization's information technology systems

II. Adherence to the provisions of the Uniform Accountancy Act (UAA)

III. Experience in auditing the financial statements of a public company

A. I only.

B. I and II only.

C. II and III only.

D. I, II, and III.

Answer (A) is correct. *(Publisher)*

**REQUIRED:** The competency ordinarily required of a practitioner-in-charge of an attest engagement.

**DISCUSSION:** The practitioner-in-charge of an attest engagement ordinarily should understand "how the organization is dependent on or enabled by information technologies and the manner in which information systems are used to record and maintain financial information" (QC 40). Other competencies ordinarily required include understanding the role of the firm's system of quality control and the AICPA's *Code of Professional Conduct*, understanding the service to be rendered, technical proficiency, familiarity with the industry, and professional judgment. Other competencies may be required in particular circumstances.

Answer (B) is incorrect because CPAs must adhere to the accountancy laws of licensing jurisdictions, not the UAA. Answer (C) is incorrect because CPAs must adhere to the accountancy laws of licensing jurisdictions, not the UAA. Furthermore, a practitioner-in-charge may in some cases obtain the needed competencies other than through the practice of public accounting, for example, in relevant industry, governmental, and academic positions. Answer (D) is incorrect because CPAs must adhere to the accountancy laws of licensing jurisdictions, not the UAA. Furthermore, a practitioner-in-charge may in some cases obtain the needed competencies other than through the practice of public accounting, for example, in relevant industry, governmental, and academic positions.

**130.** In pursuing a CPA firm's quality control objectives, a CPA firm may maintain records indicating which partners or employees of the CPA firm were previously employed by the CPA firm's clients. Which quality control element is this procedure most likely to satisfy?

A. Professional relationship.

B. Experience requirements.

C. Independence, integrity, and objectivity.

D. Advancement.

Answer (C) is correct. *(CPA, adapted)*

**REQUIRED:** The quality control element associated with records of employment of personnel by the firm's clients.

**DISCUSSION:** CPA firms should avoid situations in which third parties might question the firm's independence. Thus, they should adhere to the independence standards established by the *Code of Professional Conduct*, state board of accountancy, state CPA society, the SEC, and any other law or regulation (QC 20).

Answer (A) is incorrect because a professional relationship is not a quality control element. Answer (B) is incorrect because experience requirements are not quality control elements. Answer (D) is incorrect because advancement is an aspect of the element of personnel management. It relates to assuring that employees selected for advancement have the skills needed for the responsibilities they will be called upon to assume.

**131.** Quality control policies and procedures should provide the firm with reasonable assurance that the policies and procedures relating to the other elements of quality control are being effectively applied. This statement defines the quality control element of

A. Planning.

B. Supervision.

C. Independence, integrity, and objectivity.

D. Monitoring.

Answer (D) is correct. *(Publisher)*

**REQUIRED:** The element concerned with effective application of all elements of quality control.

**DISCUSSION:** The quality control element of monitoring is concerned with providing reasonable assurance that policies and procedures related to the other elements are suitably designed and being effectively applied. Monitoring involves considering and evaluating the relevance and adequacy of policies and procedures, the appropriateness of guidance materials and practice aids, the effectiveness of professional development, and the compliance with policies and procedures (QC 20).

Answer (A) is incorrect because planning is an aspect of the element of engagement performance. This element encompasses all phases of the design and execution of an engagement. Answer (B) is incorrect because supervision is an aspect of the element of engagement performance. This element encompasses all phases of the design and execution of an engagement. Answer (C) is incorrect because the element of independence, integrity, and objectivity provides reasonable assurance that personnel at all levels remain independent in fact and appearance, perform all professional responsibilities with integrity, and maintain objectivity in discharging those responsibilities.

**132.** In connection with the element of monitoring, a CPA firm's system of quality control should ordinarily provide for the maintenance of

A. A file of minutes of staff meetings.

B. Updated personnel files.

C. Documentation to demonstrate compliance with its policies and procedures.

D. Documentation to demonstrate compliance with peer review directives.

Answer (C) is correct. *(CPA, adapted)*

**REQUIRED:** The item maintained in connection with the quality control element of monitoring.

**DISCUSSION:** The quality control element of monitoring is concerned with providing reasonable assurance that policies and procedures related to the other elements are suitably designed and being effectively applied. "Documentation should be retained for a period of time sufficient to enable those performing monitoring procedures and a peer review to evaluate the extent of the firm's compliance with its quality control standards" (QC 20).

Answer (A) is incorrect because a file of minutes of staff meetings is an example of the documentation of compliance. Answer (B) is incorrect because updated personnel files is an example of the documentation of compliance. Answer (D) is incorrect because documentation to demonstrate compliance with peer review directives is an example of the documentation of compliance.

**133.** Williams & Co. is a medium-sized CPA firm enrolled in Partnering for CPA Practice Success, the AICPA Alliance for CPA Firms (PCPS). The firm is to have a peer review under the AICPA Peer Review program. The review will most likely be performed by

A. Partners of Williams & Co. who are not associated with the particular audits being reviewed.

B. Audit review staff of the SEC.

C. Audit review staff of the AICPA.

D. Another CPA firm.

Answer (D) is correct. *(CPA, adapted)*

**REQUIRED:** The parties most likely to perform a peer review of a medium-sized CPA firm.

**DISCUSSION:** Peer review is a necessary part of the practice-monitoring requirement for AICPA membership. A peer review of a firm enrolled in the AICPA Peer Review program may be performed by a review team organized by (1) a firm engaged by the reviewed firm or (2) a state CPA society. Also, an association of firms may be authorized to aid its members by organizing review teams (PR 100). Furthermore, a PCPS firm need not perform the peer review of a PCPS firm, and the team captain need not be a PCPS member.

Answer (A) is incorrect because partners of the firm being reviewed are not considered independent for the purpose of peer review. Answer (B) is incorrect because the SEC does not perform peer reviews. Answer (C) is incorrect because the AICPA does not have professional staff to perform peer reviews.

**134.** AICPA members in the practice of public accounting with a firm that is registered and inspected by the Public Company Accounting Oversight Board (PCAOB) may be associated with that firm only if it is enrolled in the AICPA Center for Public Company Audit Firms' Peer Review Program (Center PRP). What is the purpose of the Center PRP?

A. It is a control check on the PCAOB inspection process.

B. It reviews and evaluates those portions of a firm's practice that are not inspected by the PCAOB.

C. It is a substitute for the inspection process of the PCAOB.

D. It is a part of the PCAOB inspection process.

Answer (B) is correct. *(Publisher)*

**REQUIRED:** The purpose of the Center PRP.

**DISCUSSION:** Inspections by the PCAOB entail evaluation over quality control related to the audits of public firms (issuers). The Center PRP provides an evaluation of quality control over other audit and attest engagements of the firm.

Answer (A) is incorrect because the PCAOB is responsible for controls over their inspections. Answer (C) is incorrect because the Center PRP complements the PCAOB inspection. Answer (D) is incorrect because the Center PRP is an AICPA program.

**135.** The AICPA peer review standards define three levels of peer review. The highest level, which includes an on-site review and provides the reviewer with a reasonable basis for expressing an opinion on the firm's quality control, is termed

A. A system review.

B. An engagement review.

C. A report review.

D. An inspection review.

Answer (A) is correct. *(Publisher)*

**REQUIRED:** The highest level of AICPA peer review.

**DISCUSSION:** A system review, defined by the AICPA peer review standards, is the highest level of peer review and allows the reviewer to express an opinion on quality control of the firm.

Answer (B) is incorrect because an engagement review is for a firm not required to have a system review but not qualifying for a report review. It provides the reviewer with a reasonable basis for expressing limited assurance on whether the financial statements and accountant's reports materially conform to professional standards. Answer (C) is incorrect because a report review is for a firm that performs only compilations omitting substantially all disclosures. It consists of comments and recommendations after review of a sample of engagements. Answer (D) is incorrect because the PCAOB does inspections of CPA firms that perform audits of public companies (issuers).

**136.** Inspections performed by the PCAOB focus on quality control of registered CPA firms that perform audits of public companies (issuers). As required by the Sarbanes-Oxley Act, inspections would determine all of the following except

A. The lead partner of a client is rotated every 5 years.

B. A second partner review is performed.

C. Independence is maintained by audit staff.

D. Only staff with prior experience work on audits.

Answer (D) is correct. *(Publisher)*

**REQUIRED:** The issue not considered in a PCAOB inspection.

**DISCUSSION:** Staff is required to be trained and supervised by auditing standards. However, there is no requirement that they have prior experience.

Answer (A) is incorrect because the lead partner must be rotated at least every 5 years. Answer (B) is incorrect because a second partner review is required for each audit engagement of an issuer. Answer (C) is incorrect because independence is a consideration of inspections by the PCAOB.

## 1.11 Responsibilities in Tax Practice

**137.** Statements on Standards for Tax Services (SSTSs) have been issued by the Tax Executive Committee of the AICPA. Which of the following is the true assertion about these statements?

A. They have also been approved by the Council of the AICPA.

B. They are applicable to all CPAs, not just members of the AICPA.

C. Compliance is required by the AICPA Code of Professional Conduct.

D. The statements apply only to federal income tax engagements.

Answer (C) is correct. *(Publisher)*

**REQUIRED:** The true statement concerning SSTSs.

**DISCUSSION:** AICPA Conduct Rule 201, *General Standards*, and Conduct Rule 202, *Compliance With Standards*, require members to comply with the SSTSs. Members who depart from the standards are required to justify those departures.

Answer (A) is incorrect because the standards have been approved by at least two-thirds of the members of the Tax Executive Committee by formal vote. However, they have not been considered and acted upon by the Council of the Institute. Answer (B) is incorrect because the SSTSs (codified as TS 100 through TS 800) are specifically enforceable only against members of the AICPA. Answer (D) is incorrect because the tax standards are applicable to all tax engagements, whether for preparing a federal income tax return or representing a client in a local sales tax appeal hearing.

**138.** When a member of the AICPA prepares a taxpayer's federal income tax return, the member has the responsibility to

A. Be an advocate for the entity's realistically sustainable position.

B. Verify the data to be used in preparing the return.

C. Take a position of independent neutrality.

D. Argue the position of the Internal Revenue Service.

Answer (A) is correct. *(CPA, adapted)*

**REQUIRED:** The responsibility of a member of the AICPA who prepares a federal income tax return.

**DISCUSSION:** A member of the AICPA engaged in tax practice has the right and responsibility to be an advocate for the client. But a member should not recommend a tax return position absent "a good faith belief that the position has a realistic possibility of being sustained administratively or judicially on its merits if challenged." However, a member may recommend a controversial position that is not frivolous if the member advises the taxpayer to make appropriate disclosures. The member may then prepare or sign the return if the position is appropriately disclosed (TS 100, *Tax Return Positions*). Such action by itself does not impair the objectivity and integrity requirements of Conduct Rule 102.

Answer (B) is incorrect because the data need not be verified unless the information seems incomplete, inconsistent, or incorrect. Answer (C) is incorrect because a member must be independent when performing attestation services, not for tax return preparation services. Answer (D) is incorrect because a member has the right and the responsibility to be an advocate of the client, not the IRS.

**139.** A member of the AICPA who is engaged to prepare an income tax return has a duty to prepare it in such a manner that the tax is

A. The legal minimum.

B. Computed in conformity with generally accepted accounting principles.

C. Supported by the client's audited financial statements.

D. Not subject to change upon audit.

Answer (A) is correct. *(CPA, adapted)*

**REQUIRED:** The duty of a member of the AICPA in preparing a client's income tax return.

**DISCUSSION:** A member of the AICPA should serve to the best of his/her ability and with professional concern for the taxpayer's best interests, consistent with responsibilities to the tax system. According to TS 100, "it is well established that the taxpayer has no obligation to pay more taxes than are legally owed, and a member has a duty to the taxpayer to assist in achieving that result." Within the limits of the law and ethical practice, the member should strive for the legal minimum tax, not for tax evasion.

Answer (B) is incorrect because the tax is computed based on statutes and pronouncements of the taxing authority, not GAAP. Answer (C) is incorrect because the tax expense, according to the statements, is based on GAAP. Moreover, the tax preparer need not audit the client's statements. Answer (D) is incorrect because discovery of errors may necessitate a change.

**140.** A CPA must sign the preparer's declaration on a federal income tax return

A. Only when the CPA prepares a tax return for compensation.

B. Only when the CPA can declare that a tax is based on information of which the CPA has personal knowledge.

C. Whenever the CPA prepares a tax return for others.

D. Only when the return is for an individual or corporation.

Answer (A) is correct. *(CPA, adapted)*

**REQUIRED:** The condition for signing the preparer's declaration on a federal income tax return.

**DISCUSSION:** Treasury Regulations require preparers to sign all the returns they prepare and to include their identification numbers. However, a preparer is defined as a person who prepares (or employs persons to prepare) for compensation any tax return or claim for refund of tax imposed by Subtitle A of the Internal Revenue Code (which covers income taxes on all entities).

Answer (B) is incorrect because the CPA may prepare a return based on information provided by the taxpayer. Personal knowledge of the information is not required. Answer (C) is incorrect because the CPA must sign only when (s)he receives compensation. Answer (D) is incorrect because the signature requirement applies to returns and claims for refund by all income tax-paying entities.

**141.** Which of the following is implied when a member of the AICPA signs the preparer's declaration on a federal income tax return?

A. The tax return is not misleading based on all information of which the member has knowledge.

B. The tax return and supporting schedules were prepared in accordance with GAAP.

C. The tax return was examined in accordance with standards established by the AICPA.

D. The tax return was prepared by a member who maintained an impartial attitude.

Answer (A) is correct. *(CPA, adapted)*

**REQUIRED:** The implication when a member signs the preparer's declaration on a federal income tax return.

**DISCUSSION:** Conduct Rule 102 states, "In the performance of any professional service, a member shall not knowingly misrepresent facts or subordinate his/her judgment to others."

Answer (B) is incorrect because the tax return and supporting schedules should be prepared in accordance with federal tax law. Answer (C) is incorrect because the member is not required to examine or review documents or other evidence supporting the taxpayer's information. Answer (D) is incorrect because a member in tax practice should take a position of client advocacy, barring any wrongdoing.

**142.** The preparer of a federal income tax return signs a preparer's declaration that states,

> Under penalties of perjury, I declare that I have examined this return, including accompanying schedules and statements, and to the best of my knowledge and belief, it is true, correct, and complete. Declaration of preparer (other than the taxpayer) is based on all information of which the preparer has any knowledge.

A member of the AICPA who signs this declaration as preparer of a client's tax return warrants that

A. Information furnished by the client was relied upon in preparing the tax return unless it appeared incorrect, inconsistent, or incomplete.

B. Information furnished by the client was audited in accordance with GAAS.

C. All available evidence in support of material assertions in the tax return was audited in accordance with GAAS.

D. All available evidence in support of material assertions in the tax return was documented.

Answer (A) is correct. *(CPA, adapted)*

**REQUIRED:** The warranty given by a member of the AICPA who signs the tax preparer's declaration on a federal income tax return.

**DISCUSSION:** The preparer's declaration should be understood to relate to information known by the member of the AICPA or made available to him/her in connection with the preparation of a return. The declaration should not imply an investigation in support of material furnished by the client. The member may ordinarily rely on the information furnished by the client unless, in light of his/her knowledge, the information presented appears to be "incorrect, incomplete, or inconsistent either on its face or on the basis of other facts known to the member" (TS 300, *Certain Procedural Aspects of Preparing Returns*).

Answer (B) is incorrect because the member does not perform an audit in accordance with GAAS of the information used to prepare the return. Answer (C) is incorrect because the member does not perform an audit in accordance with GAAS of the information used to prepare the return. Answer (D) is incorrect because the member need not examine or verify supporting data.

**143.** As part of an annual audit of a client, a member of the AICPA prepares the federal income tax return. What modifications should be made to the preparer's declaration when signing the return?

| | Modify to Conform to Audit Report | Modify to State That Information Was from Audited Financial Statements |
|---|---|---|
| A. | Yes | No |
| B. | No | No |
| C. | Yes | Yes |
| D. | No | Yes |

Answer (B) is correct. *(Publisher)*

**REQUIRED:** The modifications that the member should make to the preparer's declaration.

**DISCUSSION:** The member should make no modification of the preparer's declaration on a federal income tax return. Modification will not affect the signer's responsibilities as preparer. Unusual circumstances may be disclosed in a rider not constituting a modification. Furthermore, the member neither audits the information in the tax return nor warrants by signing as preparer that an investigation has been made.

**144.** In accordance with the AICPA's Statements on Standards for Tax Services, when a reasonable basis exists for omission of an answer to an applicable question on a tax return,

A. The member-preparer need not provide an explanation for the omission on the return.

B. A brief explanation of the reason for the omission must be provided on the return.

C. The question should be marked as nonapplicable.

D. A note on the return should state that the answer will be provided if the information is requested.

Answer (A) is correct. *(CPA, adapted)*

**REQUIRED:** The proper action when a reasonable basis exists for omission of an answer on a tax return.

**DISCUSSION:** According to TS 200, *Answers to Questions on Returns*, a member of the AICPA should sign the preparer's declaration when a question has not been answered only if the member has made "a reasonable effort to obtain from the taxpayer the information necessary to provide appropriate answers to all questions on a tax return." A possible disadvantage to the taxpayer does not justify omission of an answer. However, given reasonable grounds for the omission, the taxpayer is not required to provide an explanation on the return, although the member must consider whether the omission may cause the return to be incomplete.

Answer (B) is incorrect because, given reasonable grounds for the omission, the taxpayer is not required to provide an explanation on the return. Answer (C) is incorrect because an omission may be reasonable on grounds other than inapplicability. Answer (D) is incorrect because, given reasonable grounds for the omission, the taxpayer is not required to provide an explanation on the return.

**145.** According to the AICPA's standards, which of the following actions should be taken by a member tax preparer who discovers an error in a taxpayer's previously filed tax return?

A. Advise the IRS.

B. Correct the error.

C. Advise the taxpayer.

D. End the relationship with the taxpayer.

Answer (C) is correct. *(CPA, adapted)*

**REQUIRED:** The proper action by a member of the AICPA who discovers an error in a previously filed tax return.

**DISCUSSION:** According to TS 600, *Knowledge of Error: Return Preparation*, a member should inform the taxpayer promptly upon becoming aware of an error in a previously filed return and "recommend the corrective measures to be taken." In the case of a material understatement, an amended return should be filed by the taxpayer. A claim for refund is appropriate for a material overstatement. The advice may be given to the taxpayer orally.

Answer (A) is incorrect because a member should not inform the IRS without the taxpayer's permission, except if required by law. Answer (B) is incorrect because a member is not responsible for correcting a discovered error unless requested to do so by the taxpayer. Answer (D) is incorrect because a member need not end the relationship with the taxpayer over the discovery of a previous error.

**146.** Jones, a member of the AICPA, prepared Smith's federal income tax return and appropriately signed the preparer's declaration. Several months later, Jones learned that Smith improperly altered several figures before mailing the tax return to the IRS. Jones should communicate disapproval of this action to Smith and

A. Take no further action with respect to the current year's tax return but consider the implications of Smith's actions for any future relationship.

B. Inform the IRS of the unauthorized alteration.

C. File an amended tax return.

D. Refund any fee collected, return all relevant documents, and refuse any further association with Smith.

Answer (A) is correct. *(CPA, adapted)*

**REQUIRED:** The proper action of a tax preparer-member after the taxpayer improperly altered the return.

**DISCUSSION:** When the member discovers an error, (s)he must inform the taxpayer and recommend the corrective measures to be taken. It is then the taxpayer's responsibility to correct the error. If the IRS is likely to bring criminal charges, the taxpayer should be advised to seek legal counsel. If the error is not corrected, "the member should consider whether to withdraw from preparing the return and whether to continue a professional or employment relationship with the taxpayer" (TS 600).

Answer (B) is incorrect because the member may not inform the IRS, except if required by law. Answer (C) is incorrect because the member may not file an amended return without the taxpayer's permission. Answer (D) is incorrect because TS 600 does not mention refunding fees and returning documents.

**147.** Kopel was engaged to prepare Riff Raff's 20X1 federal income tax return. During the tax preparation interview, Raff told Kopel that he paid $3,000 in property taxes in 20X1. Actually, Raff's property taxes amounted to only $600. Based on Raff's word, Kopel deducted the $3,000 on Raff's return, resulting in an understatement of Raff's tax liability. Kopel had no reason to believe that the information was incorrect. Kopel did not request underlying documentation and was reasonably satisfied by Raff's representation that Raff had adequate records to support the deduction. Which of the following statements is true?

A. To avoid the preparer penalty for willful understatement of tax liability, Kopel was obligated to examine the underlying documentation for the deduction.

B. To avoid the preparer penalty for willful understatement of tax liability, Kopel should obtain Raff's representation in writing.

C. Kopel is not subject to the preparer penalty for willful understatement of tax liability because the deduction that was claimed was more than 25% of the actual amount that should have been deducted.

D. Kopel is not subject to the preparer penalty for willful understatement of tax liability because Kopel was justified in relying on Raff's representation.

Answer (D) is correct. *(CPA, adapted)*

**REQUIRED:** The true statement concerning tax return preparer liability.

**DISCUSSION:** A tax return preparer may rely, without verification, on information provided by the taxpayer when the preparer is reasonably justified in relying upon the taxpayer's representations. However, a preparer must make a reasonable inquiry if the information appears to be incorrect or incomplete.

Answer (A) is incorrect because the preparer is not subject to preparer penalties for willful understatement. (S)he is justified in relying on the data furnished by the taxpayer. The preparer is not a guarantor of the accuracy of the return. Answer (B) is incorrect because a preparer is not required to obtain a written representation from the taxpayer prior to preparing a taxpayer's return. Answer (C) is incorrect because preparer penalties are assessed only when the preparer has recommended a position that does not have a realistic possibility of success.

**148.** Elwyn, a member of the AICPA, is preparing a federal tax return for Emma, who stated that she had made about $150 of cash donations to charitable organizations for which she had no receipts. These donations had been given to solicitors at supermarkets, airports, and other similar settings. What should Elwyn do with this information when preparing the tax return?

A. Ignore it because the information cannot be verified.

B. Identify $150 as "Other miscellaneous contributions."

C. Request that Emma obtain receipts from the charitable organizations.

D. Increase one of the other specifically named contributions by $150.

Answer (B) is correct. *(Publisher)*

**REQUIRED:** The proper action by the CPA regarding the use of estimated tax data.

**DISCUSSION:** TS 400, *Use of Estimates*, permits a member of the AICPA to prepare tax returns involving the use of estimates if it is impracticable to obtain exact data and the amounts are reasonable. Estimates must not be presented so as to imply greater accuracy than exists. The member may therefore identify the approximate amount of the contribution as "Other miscellaneous contributions."

Answer (A) is incorrect because the use of estimates is not prohibited by the AICPA. Answer (C) is incorrect because the client is unable to obtain receipts. Answer (D) is incorrect because the information should not be presented in a manner implying greater accuracy than exists.

**149.** In accordance with *Statements on Standards for Tax Services*, which of the following is not considered a basis for a good faith belief that a tax return position is warranted under existing law?

A. A low probability that the return will be audited.

B. An administrative ruling of the taxing authority.

C. An attorney's opinion.

D. Well-reasoned articles by tax specialists.

Answer (A) is correct. *(Publisher)*

**REQUIRED:** The item not considered a basis for a good faith belief that a tax return position is warranted under existing law.

**DISCUSSION:** A member of the AICPA may not recommend a tax return position absent a good faith belief that the position "has a realistic possibility of being sustained administratively or judicially on its merits if challenged." But a member may recommend a position and prepare or sign the return if this standard is not met provided that the position is not frivolous and is appropriately disclosed. However, a member may never recommend a position that "exploits the audit selection process of a taxing authority" or serves solely as a bargaining position in negotiations with the taxing authority (TS 100).

A member may (1) conclude in good faith that a position is warranted in existing law or (2) conclude that a position can be supported by a good-faith argument for a change in the law. Such a conclusion may be based on (1) a well-reasoned statutory interpretation (e.g., by an attorney), (2) well-reasoned articles or treatises, or (3) pronouncements of the taxing authority.

**150.** According to the accounting profession's standards, which of the following statements is true regarding the standards a member of the AICPA should follow when recommending tax return positions and preparing tax returns?

A. A member may recommend a position that (s)he concludes is frivolous if the position is adequately disclosed on the return.

B. A member may recommend a position if (s)he has a good faith belief that the position has a realistic possibility of being sustained if challenged.

C. A member will usually not advise the taxpayer of the potential penalty consequences of the recommended tax return position.

D. A member may sign a tax return as preparer if the return takes a position that is frivolous, provided that the taxpayer wishes to take that position.

Answer (B) is correct. *(CPA, adapted)*

**REQUIRED:** The true statement about the standards followed in recommending tax return positions and preparing returns.

**DISCUSSION:** A member has the right and responsibility to be an advocate for the taxpayer. However, a member should not recommend a tax return position without "a good faith belief that the position has a realistic possibility of being sustained administratively or judicially on its merits if challenged." Nevertheless, a member may recommend a position that is not frivolous if (s)he advises the taxpayer to make appropriate disclosures (TS 100).

Answer (A) is incorrect because a member may not recommend a frivolous position, regardless of disclosure. Answer (C) is incorrect because a member should advise the taxpayer of the potential penalty consequences of an unrealistic position and the opportunity to avoid penalties through disclosure. Answer (D) is incorrect because a member should not prepare or sign a tax return if (s)he believes that a tax position taken is frivolous, that is, knowingly advanced in bad faith and patently improper.

**151.** Members of the AICPA often provide advice to taxpayers. When subsequent developments affect advice previously provided with respect to significant matters, a member

A. Must communicate this change whether or not (s)he is still employed by the taxpayer.

B. May not communicate this information to the taxpayer unless the taxpayer is a continuing taxpayer.

C. May communicate this information to the taxpayer whether or not (s)he is still engaged.

D. Should withdraw immediately.

Answer (C) is correct. *(Publisher)*

**REQUIRED:** The proper action when previous tax advice may no longer be appropriate.

**DISCUSSION:** The member is not obligated to communicate with a taxpayer when subsequent developments affect advice previously provided with respect to significant matters except (1) while assisting in implementing procedures or plans associated with advice provided or (2) in accordance with an obligation undertaken by specific agreement (TS 800, *Form and Content of Advice to Taxpayers*).

Answer (A) is incorrect because the member is under no obligation to initiate the communication unless (s)he is assisting the taxpayer in implementing the procedures or plans associated with the advice or has specifically agreed to undertake this obligation. Answer (B) is incorrect because a continuing taxpayer relationship is not a prerequisite of such communication. Answer (D) is incorrect because immediate withdrawal is a nonsense answer.

## 1.12 Consulting Services

**152.** Statements on Standards for Consulting Services are issued by the AICPA Management Consulting Services Executive Committee in connection with consulting services. Which statement concerning consulting services is false?

A. Consulting services differ fundamentally from the CPA's function of attesting to the assertions of other parties.

B. Consulting services ordinarily involve external reporting.

C. Most practitioners, including those who provide audit and tax services, also provide consulting services to their clients.

D. The performance of consulting services for attest clients does not, in and of itself, impair independence.

Answer (B) is correct. *(Publisher)*

**REQUIRED:** The false statement about consulting services.

**DISCUSSION:** The nature and scope of a consulting service is determined solely by the agreement between the practitioner and the client. The work is usually performed for the sole use and benefit of the client.

Answer (A) is incorrect because, in an attest service, the practitioner expresses a conclusion about the reliability of a written assertion that is the responsibility of another party. Answer (C) is incorrect because consulting services have evolved from accounting-related matters to a broad array of services involving many technical disciplines, industry knowledge, and consulting skills. Answer (D) is incorrect because the CPA can maintain independence in fact and appearance for attestation clients while performing many consulting services. In the case of a public client, consulting services must be approved by the audit committee.

**153.** According to the profession's standards, which of the following are considered consulting services?

| | Advisory Services | Implementation Services | Assurance Services |
|---|---|---|---|
| A. | Yes | Yes | Yes |
| B. | Yes | Yes | No |
| C. | Yes | No | Yes |
| D. | No | Yes | Yes |

Answer (B) is correct. *(CPA, adapted)*

**REQUIRED:** The services that are considered to be consulting services.

**DISCUSSION:** Consulting services include advisory services, which are performed to develop findings, conclusions, and recommendations for the client's consideration. They also include implementation services, which are performed to put a plan into effect. Other consulting services include consultations, transaction services, and staff and other support services (CS100). Assurance services differ from consulting services. They are "independent professional services that improve the quality of information, or its context, for decision makers."

**154.** A pervasive characteristic of a CPA's role in a consulting services engagement is that of being a(n)

A. Objective advisor.

B. Independent practitioner.

C. Computer specialist.

D. Confidential reviewer.

Answer (A) is correct. *(CPA, adapted)*

**REQUIRED:** The pervasive characteristic of a CPA's role in a consulting services engagement.

**DISCUSSION:** A consulting services practitioner should serve the client's interest by seeking to accomplish the objectives established by the understanding with the client while maintaining integrity and objectivity.

Answer (B) is incorrect because independence is not a requirement for consulting services. Answer (C) is incorrect because a consultant need not be a computer specialist to develop findings and provide recommendations. Answer (D) is incorrect because a review is an attestation service.

**155.** Ann Covington, CPA, has been asked to perform a consulting services engagement concerning the analysis of a potential merger. She has little experience with the industry involved. What is her most appropriate action?

A. Accept the engagement and perform it in accordance with auditing standards.

B. Accept the engagement and perform additional research or consult with others to obtain sufficient competence.

C. Accept the engagement and issue a report vouching for the achievability of the results of the merger.

D. Decline the engagement because she lacks sufficient knowledge.

Answer (B) is correct. *(Publisher)*
**REQUIRED:** The appropriate action by a CPA who has been asked to provide consulting services concerning unfamiliar matters.
**DISCUSSION:** The CPA may accept the engagement but should conduct research or consult with others to obtain a sufficient level of knowledge concerning the subject of the engagement. Conduct Rule 201 requires an AICPA member to "undertake only those professional services that the member or the member's firm can reasonably expect to be completed with professional competence."
Answer (A) is incorrect because audits, not consulting services engagements, are performed in accordance with auditing standards. Answer (C) is incorrect because an accountant's report on prospective financial information must always contain a caveat that the prospective results may not be achieved. Answer (D) is incorrect because the CPA need not decline the engagement if she does the research necessary to complete the engagement with professional competence.

**156.** The form of communication with a client in a consulting service should be

A. Either oral or written.

B. Oral with appropriate documentation.

C. Written, and copies should be sent to both management and the board of directors.

D. Written, and a copy should be sent to management alone.

Answer (A) is correct. *(CPA, adapted)*
**REQUIRED:** The form of communication with a client in a consulting service.
**DISCUSSION:** In a consulting service, reports may be written or oral depending on the understanding with the client, the need for a formal record, the intended use of results, the significance or sensitivity of material covered, and the degree results are communicated during the engagement.

**157.** Which of the following general standards apply to consulting services?

| | Due Professional Care | Independence in Mental Attitude | Planning and Supervision |
|---|---|---|---|
| A. | No | Yes | No |
| B. | No | Yes | Yes |
| C. | Yes | No | Yes |
| D. | Yes | No | No |

Answer (C) is correct. *(CPA, adapted)*
**REQUIRED:** The general standard(s) applicable to consulting services.
**DISCUSSION:** The general standards for consulting services include the general standards for the profession given in the AICPA's Conduct Rule 201: professional competence, due professional care, planning and supervision, and sufficient relevant data. In addition, CS 100 requires the following general standards for all consulting services:

1. Serve the client interest by seeking to accomplish the objectives established by the understanding with the client while maintaining integrity and objectivity.
2. Establish with the client a written or oral understanding about the responsibilities of the parties and the nature, scope, and limitations of the services to be performed.
3. Inform the client of conflicts of interest, significant reservations concerning the scope or benefits of the engagement, and significant engagement findings or events.

Independence standards apply to attestation services, not to consulting services.

**158.** According to the standards of the profession, which of the following events will require a CPA performing a consulting services engagement for a nonaudit client to withdraw from the engagement?

I. The CPA has a conflict of interest that is disclosed to the client, and the client consents to the CPA's continuing the engagement.

II. The CPA fails to obtain a written understanding from the client concerning the scope of the engagement.

A. I only.

B. II only.

C. Both I and II.

D. Neither I nor II.

Answer (D) is correct. *(CPA, adapted)*

**REQUIRED:** The event(s) that will require a CPA to withdraw from a consulting engagement for a nonaudit client.

**DISCUSSION:** The additional general standards for consulting services require serving the client interest with integrity and objectivity. If a conflict of interest is disclosed and consented to, objectivity is not deemed to be impaired, and the professional service may be performed. In addition, an accountant may establish either a written or an oral understanding with the client regarding the scope of the engagement. Thus, an accountant need not withdraw from an engagement when the understanding of the scope of the engagement is not in writing.

**159.** Which of the following statements applies to consultation services engagements?

A. A practitioner should obtain an understanding of the internal control to assess control risk.

B. A practitioner is not permitted to compile a financial forecast.

C. A practitioner should obtain sufficient relevant data to complete the engagement.

D. A practitioner is to maintain an appearance of independence.

Answer (C) is correct. *(CPA, adapted)*

**REQUIRED:** The statement applicable to consultation services engagements.

**DISCUSSION:** The general standards for consulting services include the general standards for the profession given in the AICPA's Conduct Rule 201: professional competence, due professional care, planning and supervision, and sufficient relevant data. Under Conduct Rule 201, a member should "obtain sufficient relevant data to afford a reasonable basis for conclusions or recommendations in relation to any professional services performed."

Answer (A) is incorrect because an assessment of control risk is irrelevant to many consulting services. Answer (B) is incorrect because a practitioner may perform a service regarding prospective financial information in conjunction with a consulting service. Answer (D) is incorrect because consulting services require integrity and objectivity but not independence.

## 1.13 Attestation Standards

**160.** In performing an attestation engagement, a CPA typically

A. Supplies litigation support services.

B. Assesses control risk at a low level.

C. Expresses a conclusion about an assertion.

D. Provides management consulting advice.

Answer (C) is correct. *(CPA, adapted)*

**REQUIRED:** The usual CPA's task in an attestation engagement.

**DISCUSSION:** When a CPA in the practice of public accounting performs an attest engagement, the engagement is subject to the Statements on Standards for Attestation Engagements (codified as AT 101 to AT 701). An attest engagement is one in which a practitioner is engaged to issue or does issue an examination, a review, or an agreed-upon procedures report on subject matter, or an assertion about the subject matter, that is the responsibility of another party.

Answer (A) is incorrect because litigation support services are consulting services. Answer (B) is incorrect because the CPA assesses control risk in an audit but not necessarily in all attest engagements. Furthermore, the assessment may not be at a low level. Answer (D) is incorrect because an attest engagement results in a conclusion about an assertion.

**161.** AT 101 states five general standards, two standards of field work, and four standards of reporting. These standards

A. Supersede the 10 standards adopted by the AICPA's membership.

B. Apply only to the expression of a positive opinion on historical financial statements.

C. Apply only to attest services rendered by a CPA in the practice of public accounting.

D. Must be followed by a practitioner engaged to provide compilation services on prospective financial information.

Answer (C) is correct. *(Publisher)*

**REQUIRED:** The proper application of the attestation standards.

**DISCUSSION:** A practitioner is a CPA in the practice of public accounting. The attestation standards apply only to attest engagements involving a practitioner. Thus, these standards apply only to attest services rendered by a CPA in the practice of public accounting.

Answer (A) is incorrect because the attestation standards do not supersede but are an extension of the 10 standards. Answer (B) is incorrect because the attestation standards were issued as a result of the growth in the types of attest services offered. CPAs now provide assurances regarding representations other than historical statements and in forms other than an opinion. Answer (D) is incorrect because AT 101 does not apply to compilations, which do not entail expression of a conclusion about the reliability of written assertions for which others are responsible. However, both AT 101 and other standards may apply to other services provided with respect to such information.

**162.** Which of the following professional services is considered an attest engagement?

A. A consulting service engagement to provide computer processing advice to a client.

B. An engagement to report on compliance with statutory requirements.

C. An income tax engagement to prepare federal and state tax returns.

D. The compilation of financial statements from a client's accounting records.

Answer (B) is correct. *(CPA, adapted)*

**REQUIRED:** The attest services offered by practitioners.

**DISCUSSION:** Attest services have traditionally been limited to expressing an opinion on historical financial statements on the basis of an audit in accordance with GAAS. But CPAs increasingly provide assurance on representations other than historical statements and in forms other than an opinion. AT 601, *Compliance Attestation*, provides guidance for engagements related to management's written assertion about compliance with specified laws, regulations, rules, contracts, or grants or about the effectiveness of internal control over such compliance.

Answer (A) is incorrect because consulting services in which the practitioner provides advice or recommendations to a client are not considered attest services. Answer (C) is incorrect because tax return preparation is not an attest service. Answer (D) is incorrect because a compilation of a financial statement is not an attest service according to AT 101.

**163.** Which of the following is not an attestation standard?

A. Sufficient evidence shall be obtained to provide a reasonable basis for the conclusion that is expressed in the report.

B. The report shall identify the assertion being reported on and state the character of the engagement.

C. The work shall be adequately planned and assistants, if any, shall be properly supervised.

D. A sufficient understanding of internal control shall be obtained to plan the engagement.

Answer (D) is correct. *(CPA, adapted)*

**REQUIRED:** The item not an attestation standard.

**DISCUSSION:** The attestation standards of field work do not mention internal control. However, the second standard of field work applicable to audits in accordance with GAAS states, "A sufficient understanding of internal control is to be obtained to plan the audit and to determine the nature, timing, and extent of tests to be performed."

Answer (A) is incorrect because the evidentiary requirement is contained in the second attestation standard of field work. Answer (B) is incorrect because the first attestation standard of reporting concerns the character of the engagement. Answer (C) is incorrect because the first attestation standard of field work concerns planning and supervision.

**164.** Which of the following field work or reporting standards included in GAAS explicitly corresponds to an attestation standard?

A. A sufficient understanding of internal control is to be obtained to plan the audit and to determine the nature, timing, and extent of tests to be performed.

B. The report shall identify those circumstances in which such principles (GAAP) have not been consistently observed in the current period in relation to the preceding period.

C. Informative disclosures in the financial statements are to be regarded as reasonably adequate unless otherwise stated in the report.

D. Sufficient competent evidential matter is to be obtained through inspection, observation, inquiries, and confirmations to afford a reasonable basis for an opinion regarding the financial statements under audit.

Answer (D) is correct. *(Publisher)*

**REQUIRED:** The auditing standard that corresponds to an attestation standard.

**DISCUSSION:** The third standard of field work included in GAAS parallels the second field work standard included in the attestation standards. AT 101 states, "Sufficient evidence shall be obtained to provide a reasonable basis for the conclusion that is expressed in the report."

Answer (A) is incorrect because the second auditing standard of field work has no explicit parallel in the attestation standards. One reason is that internal control may not be relevant to some assertions reported on by a practitioner. Answer (B) is incorrect because the second (consistency) and third (disclosure) auditing standards of reporting do not have analogues in the attestation standards. They are considered to be encompassed by the second attestation standard of reporting, which states, "The report shall state the practitioner's conclusion about the subject matter or the assertion in relation to the criteria against which the subject matter was evaluated." Thus, references to financial statements and GAAP are omitted. The reason for this omission is that the attestation standards are intended to provide a framework for the attest function beyond historical financial statements. Answer (C) is incorrect because the third standard of field work has no analogue in the attestation standards.

**165.** Which of the following is the authoritative body designated to promulgate attestation standards?

A. Auditing Standards Board.

B. Governmental Accounting Standards Board.

C. Financial Accounting Standards Board.

D. Government Accountability Office.

Answer (A) is correct. *(CPA, adapted)*

**REQUIRED:** The authoritative body designated to promulgate attestation standards.

**DISCUSSION:** Statements on Standards for Attestation Engagements are issued by the Auditing Standards Board, Accounting and Review Services Committee, and the Management Consulting Services Executive Committee. The Council of the AICPA granted these bodies, which also promulgate SASs, SSARSs, and SSCSs, respectively, the authority to interpret Conduct Rules 201 and 202. The attestation standards (AT 101 - AT 701) are issued pursuant to that authority.

Answer (B) is incorrect because the GASB issues accounting and reporting standards for local and state governments. Answer (C) is incorrect because the FASB establishes GAAP. Answer (D) is incorrect because the GAO issues *Government Auditing Standards.*

**166.** Which of the following is a conceptual difference between the attestation standards and generally accepted auditing standards?

A. The attestation standards provide a framework for the attest function beyond historical financial statements.

B. The requirement that the practitioner be independent in mental attitude is omitted from the attestation standards.

C. The attestation standards do not permit an attest engagement to be part of a business acquisition study or a feasibility study.

D. None of the standards of field work in generally accepted auditing standards are included in the attestation standards.

Answer (A) is correct. *(CPA, adapted)*

**REQUIRED:** The conceptual difference between the attestation standards and GAAS.

**DISCUSSION:** Two principal conceptual differences exist between the attestation standards and the 10 auditing standards adopted by the AICPA's membership. First, the attestation standards provide a framework for the attest function beyond historical financial statements. Second, the attestation standards accommodate the growing number of attest services in which the practitioner expresses assurances below the level that is expressed for the traditional audit (an opinion).

Answer (B) is incorrect because, in any attest engagement, the practitioner must be independent in mental attitude. Answer (C) is incorrect because attestation services may be provided in conjunction with other services provided to clients. Answer (D) is incorrect because the attestation standards and the 10 standards require that the work be adequately planned and that assistants be properly supervised. Both also require sufficient evidence.

**167.** The expansion of the attest function has resulted in attestation standards of reporting that are organized differently from the auditing standards of reporting. Consequently, the attestation standards of reporting

A. Cover one level and form of assurance.

B. Reflect the limitation of the use of certain reports to specified users.

C. Concern one basic presentation of assertions.

D. Are inapplicable when users have established the criteria against which assertions are measured.

Answer (B) is correct. *(Publisher)*

**REQUIRED:** The effect of the expansion of the attest function on the attestation standards of reporting.

**DISCUSSION:** Auditing standards contemplate issuance of a general-use audit report. The attestation standards reflect the expansion of the attest function to include engagements tailored to the needs of specified parties who have participated in establishing either the nature and scope of the engagement or the specified criteria against which the assertions were measured. Thus, the fourth attestation standard of reporting states, "The report shall state that the use of the report is restricted to specified parties under the following circumstances: 1) when the criteria used to evaluate the subject matter are determined by the practitioner to be appropriate only for a limited number of parties who either participated in their establishment or can be presumed to have an adequate understanding of the criteria, 2) when the criteria used to evaluate the subject matter are available only to specified users, 3) when reporting on subject matter and a written assertion has not been provided by the responsible party, 4) when the report is on an attest engagement to apply agreed-upon procedures to the subject matter."

Answer (A) is incorrect because the attest function covers more than one level and form of assurance on a variety of presentations of assertions and is no longer limited to expressing an opinion on historical financial statements presented in accordance with GAAP. Answer (C) is incorrect because the attestation standards cover a variety of assertions. Answer (D) is incorrect because user participation in establishing measurement criteria is a conceptual difference between auditing and attestation standards.

**168.** A CPA is required to comply with the provisions of Statements on Standards for Attestation Engagements (SSAE) when engaged to

A. Report on financial statements that the CPA generated through the use of computer software.

B. Review management's discussion and analysis (MD&A) prepared pursuant to rules and regulations adopted by the SEC.

C. Provide the client with a financial statement format that does not include dollar amounts.

D. Audit financial statements that the client prepared for use in another country.

Answer (B) is correct. *(CPA, adapted)*

**REQUIRED:** The services for which SSAEs establish standards or procedures.

**DISCUSSION:** An attest engagement is one in which the practitioner is engaged to issue or does issue an examination, review, or an agreed-upon procedures report on subject matter, or an assertion about the subject matter, that is the responsibility of another party. The SSAEs cover attest engagements, including the 11 attestation standards; agreed-upon procedures engagements; financial forecasts and projections; reporting on pro forma financial information; reporting on an entity's internal control over financial reporting; compliance attestation; and management's discussion and analysis.

Answer (A) is incorrect because Statements on Standards for Accounting and Review Services (SSARSs) apply when an accountant submits (e.g., by presenting financial statements that the accountant has prepared using software) unaudited statements of a nonpublic entity to a client or third party. Answer (C) is incorrect because compliance with the SSAEs is required if the financial statement format does include dollar amounts. Financial statements by definition contain financial data. Answer (D) is incorrect because AU 534 (SAS 51) applies to statements prepared for use in another country.

## 1.14 Assurance Services

**169.** Assurance services are best described as

A. Services designed for the improvement of operations, resulting in better outcomes.

B. Independent professional services that improve the quality of information, or its context, for decision makers.

C. The assembly of financial statements based on assumptions of a responsible party.

D. Services designed to express a positive opinion on historical financial statements based on the results of an audit.

Answer (B) is correct. *(Publisher)*
**REQUIRED:** The description of assurance services.
**DISCUSSION:** The AICPA defines assurance services as "independent professional services that improve the quality of information, or its context, for decision makers." Assurance services encompass audit and other attestation services as well as other, nonstandard, services, but they do not include consulting services. Assurance services should result in better information for decision making, with the form of output consisting of some form of communication. A formal written report need not be required. The level of assurance is flexible. For example, it may be at the compilation level, or it may be explicit assurance about the usefulness of information for the intended purpose. The assurance may also arise simply from the CPA's involvement.

Answer (A) is incorrect because the objective of consulting services is better outcomes, whereas the objective of assurance services is better decision making. Answer (C) is incorrect because compilation services involve the assembly of financial statements based on assumptions of a responsible party. Answer (D) is incorrect because the traditional audit is an attestation service. Assurance services include but are not limited to attest engagements.

**170.** The objective of assurance services is best described as

A. Providing more reliable information.

B. Enhancing decision making.

C. Comparing internal information and policies with those of other firms.

D. Improving the firm's outcomes.

Answer (B) is correct. *(Publisher)*
**REQUIRED:** The objective of assurance services.
**DISCUSSION:** The objective of assurance services, as stated by the AICPA, is to provide information that assists in better decision making. Assurance services encompass audit and other attestation services as well as other, nonstandard, services. Assurance services do not include consulting services.

Answer (A) is incorrect because providing more reliable information is the objective of attestation services. The objective of assurance services is broader. Answer (C) is incorrect because assurance services do not necessarily involve analysis of other organizations. Answer (D) is incorrect because providing information that results in better outcomes is an objective of consulting services.

**171.** Assurance services differ from consulting services in that they

| | Focus on Outcomes | Involve Monitoring of One Party by Another |
|---|---|---|
| A. | Yes | Yes |
| B. | Yes | No |
| C. | No | Yes |
| D. | No | No |

Answer (C) is correct. *(Publisher)*
**REQUIRED:** The way(s) in which assurance services differ from consulting services.
**DISCUSSION:** Assurance services encompass attestation services but not consulting services. Assurance services differ from consulting services because (1) they focus on improving information and decision making rather than outcomes, and (2) they usually involve situations in which one party has oversight responsibility for another rather than the two-party arrangements common in consulting engagements.

**172.** An AICPA special committee has developed business plans for assurance services covering which of the following?

A. Elder care, electronic commerce, and reporting on management's discussion and analysis.

B. Electronic commerce, development of financial forecasts, and risk assessment.

C. Information systems design, performance measurement, and health care delivery.

D. Assurances to underwriters, health care delivery, and elder care.

Answer (C) is correct. *(Publisher)*

**REQUIRED:** The areas in which business plans for assurance services have been developed by the AICPA.

**DISCUSSION:** An AICPA special committee has developed business plans for six assurance services: (1) providing assurance about whether care delivery goals for the elderly are met; (2) providing assurance about the integrity and security of electronic transactions, documents, and supporting systems; (3) assessing whether an organization's performance measures are relevant and reliable; (4) assessing health care providers' performance; (5) improving risk information through assessment of the probability and magnitude of significant adverse events; and (6) providing assurance about the design and operation of information systems.

Reporting on an MD&A, developing forecasts, and providing comfort letters to underwriters are not among the newly identified assurance services. It is subject to existing SSAEs or SASs.

**173.** Which of the following is a term for an attest engagement in which a CPA provides assurance concerning a client's commercial Internet site relating to the principles of security, processing integrity, availability, online privacy, and confidentiality?

A. ElectroNet.

B. EDIFACT.

C. TechSafe.

D. WebTrust.

Answer (D) is correct. *(CPA, adapted)*

**REQUIRED:** The attest engagement for an Internet site.

**DISCUSSION:** The WebTrust assurance service developed by the AICPA and the Canadian Institute of Chartered Accountants is an attestation engagement that assesses a client's Internet site against predefined criteria. WebTrust provides assurance regarding adherence to the principles of security, availability, processing integrity, online privacy, and confidentiality. It is a modular service that allows the practitioner to express an opinion and issue the corresponding seal regarding the site's adherence to individual principles or combinations of principles. (1) Security is protection against unauthorized access (both physical and logical). (2) Availability is assurance that the system is available for operation and use as committed or agreed. (3) Processing integrity is assurance that the processing is complete, accurate, timely, and authorized. (4) Online privacy is assurance that personal information obtained as a result of e-commerce being collected, used, and retained as committed or agreed. (5) Confidentiality is the protection of information. In a WebTrust examination engagement, the practitioner will perform tests of either management's assertion or the subject matter to which the assertion relates. The practitioner gathers evidence about the assertion's conformity with criteria (benchmarks) in the same way as is commonly done in other attest engagements.

Answer (A) is incorrect because ElectroNet is a nonsense term. Answer (B) is incorrect because EDIFACT (Electronic Data Interchange For Administration Commerce and Transport) is an ISO standard for electronic data interchange (EDI). Answer (C) is incorrect because TechSafe is a nonsense term.

**174.** An entity engaged a CPA to determine whether the client's web sites meet defined criteria for security and processing integrity. In performing this engagement, the CPA should comply with the provisions of

A. Statements on Assurance Standards.

B. Statements on Standards for Attestation Engagements.

C. Statements on Standards for Consulting Services.

D. Statements on Auditing Standards.

Answer (B) is correct. *(CPA, adapted)*

**REQUIRED:** The standards that apply to WebTrust.

**DISCUSSION:** WebTrust was developed from the attestation standards and requires a written assertion by management. Thus, SSAEs apply.

Answer (A) is incorrect because the AICPA has not issued specific Statements on Assurance Standards. Answer (C) is incorrect because WebTrust is not a consulting service. Assurance services differ from consulting services because (1) they focus on improving information and decision making rather than outcomes, and (2) they usually involve situations in which one party has oversight responsibility for another. Answer (D) is incorrect because SASs apply to audits of financial statements.

**175.** SysTrust is an assurance service developed by the AICPA and the Canadian Institute of Chartered Accountants. It is designed to

A. Increase the comfort of management and other stakeholders relative to an information system.

B. Provide an opinion on the fairness of an information system's output.

C. Provide the SEC with information used to administer the securities laws.

D. Allow a CPA to provide a consulting service to management relating to their information system.

Answer (A) is correct. *(Publisher)*

**REQUIRED:** The purpose of SysTrust.

**DISCUSSION:** The objective of SysTrust is an attestation report on management's assertion about the reliability of an information system that supports a business or a given activity. A CPA may also report directly on the reliability of the system. This assurance service is designed to increase the stakeholders' comfort relative to the system's satisfaction of the SysTrust principles. Although SysTrust and WebTrust share the same principles of security, availability, processing integrity, online privacy, and confidentiality, SysTrust can be applied to any system environment. WebTrust relates to websites. The service is modular, and the practitioner can be engaged to report on any one or more of the five principles.

Answer (B) is incorrect because SysTrust does not directly address the outputs of a system. Answer (C) is incorrect because the report is not specifically designed for any one user. Answer (D) is incorrect because assurance services are not consulting services.

**176.** The AICPA has identified a professional service it calls PrimePlus (formerly ElderCare). The fundamental purpose of this assurance service is to assist the elderly and their families by

A. Investing the funds of the elderly person.

B. Reporting whether specified objectives are being met by caregivers.

C. Choosing caregivers.

D. Performing operational audits of health care providers.

Answer (B) is correct. *(Publisher)*

**REQUIRED:** The fundamental purpose of PrimePlus.

**DISCUSSION:** The AICPA has developed business plans for six assurance services, one of which involves elder care. The fundamental purpose of elder care services is to gather evidence and report to concerned parties (e.g., adult children of an elderly parent) as to whether agreed-upon objectives have been met with regard to care delivery, such as medical, household, and financial services. PrimePlus services can involve three kinds of services: Direct services, assurance services, and consulting services. Direct services entail the more traditional aspects of accounting and financial services. Assurance services involve the measuring and reporting on achievement of prescribed goals in relation to stated criteria. Consulting services including planning and evaluation of client needs. Services provided directly to the elderly person or to the other concerned parties may include oversight of investments (but not investment of funds), assistance in the choice of caregivers, accounting for the elderly person's income and expenses, and arranging for care and services, such as transportation, meal delivery, or placement in a retirement facility.

Answer (A) is incorrect because the CPA might oversee, but not make, investments. Answer (C) is incorrect because the CPA might help in the choice of caregivers but would not make the decision. Answer (D) is incorrect because an operational audit is far beyond the limits of a PrimePlus service.

**177.** Which of the following is true regarding CPA training for PrimePlus services?

A. Financial oriented support staff may not require specific PrimePlus training.

B. Staff involved directly with the client do not need training similar to that of the engagement partner.

C. Additional training is not required for staff involved in preparing insurance claims.

D. PrimePlus courses are currently only offered through the AICPA.

Answer (A) is correct. *(Publisher)*

**REQUIRED:** The true statement about training of engagement personnel.

**DISCUSSION:** Because support staff are primarily involved in the financial aspects of the engagement, they may not need specific PrimePlus training.

Answer (B) is incorrect because any staff that are directly involved with the client will require the same type of training as the engagement partner. Answer (C) is incorrect because preparation of insurance claims requires specific training. Answer (D) is incorrect because state CPA societies also offer seminars on PrimePlus services.

**178.** The client of the practitioner providing PrimePlus services may be

| | The Elderly Person | An Attorney | A Family Member |
|---|---|---|---|
| A. | Yes | No | No |
| B. | Yes | Yes | No |
| C. | No | No | Yes |
| D. | Yes | Yes | Yes |

Answer (D) is correct. *(Publisher)*
**REQUIRED:** The client(s) of the practitioner providing PrimePlus.
**DISCUSSION:** The client varies with the engagement. The practitioner must understand who the client is and who has final authority to resolve issues in the engagement. If the client is a family member or some third party, that person must have power of attorney over the elderly person involved.

## 1.15 Personal Financial Planning

**179.** Which of the following services is a CPA generally required to perform when conducting a personal financial planning engagement?

A. Assisting the client to identify tasks that are essential in order to act on planning decisions.

B. Assisting the client to take action on planning decisions.

C. Monitoring progress in achieving goals.

D. Updating recommendations and revising planning decisions.

Answer (A) is correct. *(CPA, adapted)*
**REQUIRED:** The service a CPA generally is required to perform when conducting a personal financial planning engagement.
**DISCUSSION:** According to PFP 100, a PFP engagement includes defining the engagement objectives, planning specific procedures appropriate to the engagement, developing a basis for recommendations, communicating recommendations, and identifying the tasks for taking action on planning decisions. Thus, the CPA is responsible for assisting the client to identify tasks that are essential in order to act on planning decisions. The CPA also may help set target dates for completing such tasks and identifying responsible parties.
Answer (B) is incorrect because, unless undertaken by specific agreement, the CPA is not responsible for additional services, such as assisting the client to take action on planning decisions. Answer (C) is incorrect because, unless undertaken by specific agreement, the CPA is not responsible for additional services, such as monitoring progress in achieving goals. Answer (D) is incorrect because, unless undertaken by specific agreement, the CPA is not responsible for additional services, such as updating recommendations and revising planning decisions.

**180.** The guidance least likely to be applicable to personal financial planning (PFP) engagements is

A. Conduct Rule 301, *Confidential Client Information.*

B. Conduct Rule 101, *Independence.*

C. Statement on Standards for Consulting Services.

D. Statement on Standards for Attestation Engagements related to financial forecasts and projections.

Answer (B) is correct. *(Publisher)*
**REQUIRED:** The guidance least likely to be applicable to PFP engagements.
**DISCUSSION:** Personal financial planning is not a professional service that requires a CPA to be independent of the client. However, the CPA must follow the other pertinent Conduct Rules, including Rule 102, *Integrity and Objectivity*; Rule 201, *General Standards*; Rule 301, *Confidential Client Information*; and Rule 302, *Contingent Fees.*
Answer (A) is incorrect because PFP engagements require the CPA not to disclose confidential client information without the client's specific consent. Answer (C) is incorrect because the Statement on Standards for Consulting Services is relevant when a CPA values a business as part of a PFP engagement. Answer (D) is incorrect because a PFP engagement may entail preparation of financial forecasts or financial projections.

# STUDY UNIT TWO
# AUDIT PLANNING AND RISK ASSESSMENT



This study unit addresses various fundamental questions about the conduct of audits. **Acceptance of an engagement** depends on issues such as the timing of the auditor's appointment, the evaluation of the client's integrity, and predecessor-successor communication. **Audit planning** and **supervision** of assistants are required by the first standard of field work. Planning involves developing an overall strategy for the audit, particularly obtaining and evaluating evidence. Supervision includes directing assistants. **Audit risk** must be considered in every audit. The auditor must assess inherent and control risk and establish the level to which (s)he wishes to restrict overall audit risk. The auditor uses assessments to determine the acceptable level of detection risk. The auditor must also plan and perform the audit to obtain reasonable assurance that the financial statements are free of material misstatement, whether caused by error or fraud (irregularities). The auditor's responsibility is the same for **illegal acts** having a material direct effect on the financial statements. However, an audit in accordance with GAAS or PCAOB auditing standards provides no assurance that illegal acts having material but indirect effects will be detected. Furthermore, the auditor must specifically assess the identified risks of material misstatement due to **fraud**. Finally, every audit must be documented. **Audit documentation** provides the principal support for the audit. It shows that the engagement was adequately planned and supervised, that the auditor considered internal control, and that the evidence obtained was competent and sufficient.

## QUESTIONS

### 2.1 Engagement Acceptance

**1.** The scope and nature of an auditor's contractual obligation to a client is ordinarily set forth in the

A. Management representation letter.

B. Scope paragraph of the auditor's report.

C. Engagement letter.

D. Introductory paragraph of the auditor's report.

Answer (C) is correct. *(CPA, adapted)*

**REQUIRED:** The form of the contractual agreement with a client.

**DISCUSSION:** The audit scope, audit limitations and expectations, responsibilities of the parties, and fees for services should be set forth in a contract evidenced by an engagement letter. An engagement letter should be sent by the CPA to the prospective client on each engagement audit or otherwise. When signed, it represents a written contract. Although auditing standards do not require an engagement letter, the understanding with the client must be documented (AU 310, *Appointment of the Independent Auditor*).

Answer (A) is incorrect because a management representation letter is obtained to assure that management understands its responsibility for the financial statements. Answer (B) is incorrect because the scope paragraph describes the nature of the audit. Answer (D) is incorrect because the introductory paragraph states that the financial statements were audited and the responsibilities of management and the auditor.

**2.** An auditor's engagement letter most likely will include

A. Management's acknowledgment of its responsibility for maintaining effective internal control.

B. The auditor's preliminary assessment of the risk factors relating to misstatements arising from fraudulent financial reporting.

C. A reminder that management is responsible for illegal acts committed by employees.

D. A request for permission to contact the client's lawyer for assistance in identifying litigation, claims, and assessments.

Answer (A) is correct. *(CPA, adapted)*

**REQUIRED:** The item included in an auditor's engagement letter.

**DISCUSSION:** The primary purpose of an engagement letter is to provide a written record of the understanding with the client. Among the matters addressed are management's responsibility for (1) the financial statements, (2) establishing and maintaining effective internal control over financial reporting, (3) compliance with laws and regulations, (4) making financial records and related information available, (5) providing a representation letter, and (6) adjusting the statements to correct material misstatements (AU 310).

Answer (B) is incorrect because, prior to performing procedures, an auditor does not assess the risk factors relating to misstatements arising from fraudulent financial reporting. Answer (C) is incorrect because management is responsible for compliance with laws and regulations applicable to its activities. It is also responsible for acts of employees attributable to the entity. However, it is not responsible for other illegal acts of employees. Answer (D) is incorrect because management is responsible for adopting policies and procedures to identify, evaluate, and account for litigation, claims, and assessment (AU 337).

**3.** An auditor is required to establish an understanding with a client regarding the services to be performed for each engagement. This understanding generally includes

A. Management's responsibility for errors and the illegal activities of employees that may cause material misstatement.

B. The auditor's responsibility for ensuring that the audit committee is aware of any reportable conditions that come to the auditor's attention.

C. Management's responsibility for providing the auditor with an assessment of the risk of material misstatement due to fraud.

D. The auditor's responsibility for determining preliminary judgments about materiality and audit risk factors.

Answer (B) is correct. *(CPA, adapted)*

**REQUIRED:** The item required to be included in the understanding with the client.

**DISCUSSION:** The understanding with the client regarding services to be performed is typically documented in an engagement letter. An engagement letter should, among other things, include an understanding about reportable conditions. According to AU 310, "An audit is not designed to provide assurance on internal control or to identify reportable conditions. However, the auditor is responsible for ensuring that the audit committee or others with equivalent authority or responsibility are aware of any reportable conditions which come to his or her attention."

Answer (A) is incorrect because management is responsible for the financial statements and for maintaining effective internal control over financial reporting, not for the errors and illegal activities of employees. Answer (C) is incorrect because the auditor must assess the risk of material misstatement. Answer (D) is incorrect because the auditor must make judgments about risk and materiality in planning the audit, but responsibility for these matters is not required to be shared with the client.

**4.** Which of the following factors most likely would cause an auditor to decline a new audit engagement?

A. An inadequate understanding of the entity's internal control.

B. The close proximity to the end of the entity's fiscal year.

C. Concluding that the entity's management probably lacks integrity.

D. An inability to perform preliminary analytical procedures before assessing control risk.

Answer (C) is correct. *(CPA, adapted)*

**REQUIRED:** The factor most likely to cause an auditor to decline a new audit engagement.

**DISCUSSION:** During an audit, management makes many representations to the auditor. If management lacks integrity, the auditor's reliance on those representations would not be appropriate. Thus, the auditor should not accept an engagement if management lacks integrity.

Answer (A) is incorrect because the understanding of the entity's internal control is obtained subsequent to the acceptance of the engagement. Answer (B) is incorrect because, "although early appointment is preferable, an independent auditor may accept an engagement near or after the close of the fiscal year" (AU 310). Answer (D) is incorrect because analytical procedures are performed after the acceptance of the engagement.

**5.** Which of the following factors most likely would cause a CPA to reject a new audit engagement?

A. The prospective client has already completed its physical inventory count.

B. The CPA lacks an understanding of the prospective client's operations and industry.

C. The CPA is unable to review the predecessor auditor's working papers.

D. The prospective client is unwilling to make all financial records available to the CPA.

Answer (D) is correct. *(CPA, adapted)*

**REQUIRED:** The factor that would cause a CPA to reject an audit engagement.

**DISCUSSION:** According to AU 310, the understanding with the client should include such matters as management's responsibility "for making all financial records and related information available to the auditor." If the prospective client is unwilling to make all financial records available to the CPA, the result may be a scope limitation that would require qualification of the opinion or a disclaimer of an opinion should the engagement be accepted.

Answer (A) is incorrect because a physical inventory can be taken after year-end, and analytical procedures can be performed to reconcile the difference between the reported year-end balance and the actual count. Answer (B) is incorrect because the auditor must gain an understanding of the client's operations and industry prior to completing the audit but need not obtain it prior to acceptance of the engagement. Answer (C) is incorrect because, with the client's authorization, the predecessor ordinarily permits the successor to review working papers having continuing accounting significance, but valid business reasons may lead the predecessor to decide not to allow such a review. Moreover, no pronouncement requires the successor to review the predecessor's working papers.

**6.** In assessing whether to accept a client for an audit engagement, a CPA should consider the

| | Client's Business Risk | CPA's Business Risk |
|---|---|---|
| A. | Yes | Yes |
| B. | Yes | No |
| C. | No | Yes |
| D. | No | No |

Answer (A) is correct. *(CPA, adapted)*

**REQUIRED:** The issues related to client acceptance.

**DISCUSSION:** Before accepting an engagement, the CPA should consider the risks of being associated with the client. Auditor business risk relates to potential loss or injury to the auditor's professional practice from litigation and adverse publicity from the relationship with the client. The successful outcome of an audit and the ability to control auditor business risk often depends on the client's business risk. Thus, QC 20 states that policies and procedures should be established regarding acceptance and continuance of clients and engagements. They should provide reasonable assurance that the likelihood of association with a client whose management lacks integrity is minimized. Policies and procedures also should provide reasonable assurance that the firm considers the risks associated with providing services in specific situations.

**7.** Before accepting an engagement to audit a new client, an auditor is required to

A. Make inquiries of the predecessor auditor after obtaining the consent of the prospective client.

B. Obtain the prospective client's signature to the engagement letter.

C. Prepare a memorandum setting forth the staffing requirements and documenting the preliminary audit plan.

D. Discuss the management representation letter with the prospective client's audit committee.

Answer (A) is correct. *(CPA, adapted)*

**REQUIRED:** The step required of an auditor before accepting an engagement to audit a new client.

**DISCUSSION:** AU 315, *Communications between Predecessor and Successor Auditors*, requires the successor auditor to take the initiative in communicating with the predecessor auditor. A predecessor auditor includes an auditor engaged to audit the client, regardless of whether the audit was performed. Communication should be made only after obtaining the prospective client's permission, and the successor should request that the prospective client authorize the predecessor to respond fully to the successor's inquiries. The successor auditor should inquire about (1) reasons for the change in auditors; (2) disagreements with management about accounting principles and auditing procedures; (3) facts bearing on management's integrity; and (4) communications to audit committees or others regarding fraud, illegal acts by clients, and internal-control-related matters.

Answer (B) is incorrect because, although recommended, an engagement letter is not required for the auditor to accept an engagement. However, the auditor should establish and document an understanding with the prospective client (AU 310). Answer (C) is incorrect because planning the audit is not required to be performed prior to accepting an engagement. Answer (D) is incorrect because discussion of the management representation letter is not required prior to accepting an engagement.

**8.** A successor auditor ordinarily should request to review the predecessor's working papers relating to

| | Contingencies | Internal Control |
|---|---|---|
| A. | Yes | Yes |
| B. | Yes | No |
| C. | No | Yes |
| D. | No | No |

Answer (A) is correct. *(CPA, adapted)*

**REQUIRED:** The item(s), if any, a successor auditor ordinarily requests for review.

**DISCUSSION:** AU 315, *Communications between Predecessor and Successor Auditors*, requires the successor auditor to take the initiative in communicating with the predecessor. Communication should be made only after obtaining the prospective client's permission, and the successor should request that the prospective client authorize the predecessor to respond fully to the successor's inquiries. The predecessor usually allows the successor "to review working papers, including documentation of planning, internal control, audit results, and other matters of continuing accounting and auditing significance, such as the working paper analysis of balance sheet accounts, and those relating to contingencies."

**9.** Upon discovering material misstatements in a client's financial statements that the client would not revise, an auditor withdrew from the engagement. If asked by the successor auditor about the termination of the engagement, the predecessor auditor should

A. State that (s)he found material misstatements that the client would not revise.

B. Suggest that the successor ask the client.

C. Suggest that the successor obtain the client's permission to discuss the reasons.

D. Indicate that a misunderstanding occurred.

Answer (C) is correct. *(Publisher)*

**REQUIRED:** The appropriate response by a predecessor auditor when asked by a successor about his/her relationship with the client.

**DISCUSSION:** The successor auditor must obtain the client's permission before the predecessor auditor may discuss the reasons for termination of the previous relationship (AU 315). Furthermore, a member of the AICPA in public practice must not disclose confidential client information without the specific consent of the client (Conduct Rule 301).

Answer (A) is incorrect because the predecessor auditor should say nothing concerning the relationship until client permission is obtained. Answer (B) is incorrect because the predecessor is usually expected to cooperate with the successor, provided that the client consents. In unusual circumstances, such as pending litigation, the predecessor auditor may not respond fully to inquiries but should clearly state that his/her response is limited. The successor should then consider the implications for acceptance of the engagement. Answer (D) is incorrect because the predecessor auditor should say nothing concerning the relationship until client permission is obtained.

## 2.2 Audit Planning and Supervision

**10.** AU 311, *Planning and Supervision*, states that the auditor should consider the nature, extent, and timing of the work to be performed and should prepare a written audit program for every audit. Which audit standard is most closely related to this requirement?

A. The audit is to be performed by a person or persons having adequate technical training and proficiency as an auditor.

B. In all matters relating to the assignment, an independent mental attitude is to be maintained by the auditor(s).

C. Due professional care is to be exercised in the planning and performance of the audit and preparation of the report.

D. The work is to be adequately planned, and assistants, if any, are to be properly supervised.

Answer (D) is correct. *(Publisher)*

**REQUIRED:** The standard most closely related to the requirement for a written audit program.

**DISCUSSION:** The first standard of field work requires adequate planning and proper supervision. Audit planning involves developing an overall strategy for the expected conduct and scope of the audit. An audit program, which aids in instructing assistants in the work to be done, should set forth in reasonable detail the audit procedures the auditor believes necessary to accomplish audit objectives.

Answer (A) is incorrect because proper education and experience in the field of auditing are needed to provide services to the public (the first general standard). Answer (B) is incorrect because auditors must be unbiased and maintain an attitude of judicial impartiality (the second general standard). Answer (C) is incorrect because each professional within the independent auditor's organization must observe the standards of field work and reporting (the third general standard).

**11.** Which of the following is required documentation in an audit in accordance with auditing standards?

A. A flowchart or narrative of the information system describing the recording and classification of transactions for financial reporting.

B. An audit program setting forth in detail the procedures necessary to accomplish the engagement's objectives.

C. A planning memorandum establishing the timing of the audit procedures and coordinating the assistance of entity personnel.

D. An internal control questionnaire identifying policies and procedures that assure specific objectives will be achieved.

Answer (B) is correct. *(CPA, adapted)*

**REQUIRED:** The required documentation in an audit.

**DISCUSSION:** According to AU 311, in planning the audit, the auditor should consider the nature, extent, and timing of the work to be performed and should prepare a written audit program (or a set of written audit programs) for every audit. It sets forth in reasonable detail the specific audit procedures the auditor believes are necessary to accomplish the audit objectives.

Answer (A) is incorrect because the auditor should document the understanding of internal control, but a flowchart or narrative of the information system for financial reporting is just one method. For example, the auditor may use a questionnaire to document the understanding. Answer (C) is incorrect because the auditor may request and receive assistance from entity personnel, but a planning memorandum establishing the timing is not required by auditing standards. Answer (D) is incorrect because the auditor should document the understanding of internal control, but a questionnaire is only one method of accomplishing this objective. For example, flowcharts and narratives are other methods.

**12.** An auditor obtains knowledge about a new client's business and its industry to

A. Make constructive suggestions concerning improvements in the client's internal control.

B. Develop an attitude of professional skepticism concerning management's financial statement assertions.

C. Evaluate whether the aggregation of known misstatements causes the financial statements taken as a whole to be materially misstated.

D. Understand the events and transactions that may have an effect on the client's financial statements.

Answer (D) is correct. *(CPA, adapted)*

**REQUIRED:** The reason to obtain knowledge of a new client's business and industry.

**DISCUSSION:** The auditor should obtain a level of knowledge of the entity's business that will allow him/her to plan and perform the audit in accordance with auditing standards. That level of knowledge should enable him/her to obtain an understanding of the events, transactions, and practices that, in his/her judgment, may have a significant effect on the financial statements (AU 311).

Answer (A) is incorrect because communication of matters related to internal control occurs during and after the audit. Obtaining knowledge of the client's business occurs prior to audit planning. Answer (B) is incorrect because the auditor should adopt an attitude of professional skepticism in all phases of an engagement. Answer (C) is incorrect because evaluating whether the financial statements are materially misstated is done after the collection of evidence.

**13.** Prior to beginning the field work on a new audit engagement in which a CPA does not possess expertise in the industry in which the client operates, the CPA should

A. Reduce audit risk by lowering the preliminary levels of materiality.

B. Design special substantive tests to compensate for the lack of industry expertise.

C. Engage financial experts familiar with the nature of the industry.

D. Obtain a knowledge of matters that relate to the nature of the entity's business.

Answer (D) is correct. *(CPA, adapted)*

**REQUIRED:** The action taken by an auditor who lacks experience with the client's industry.

**DISCUSSION:** If the auditor lacks knowledge of the potential client's industry, (s)he should perform procedures to gain the knowledge. An Interpretation under Conduct Rule 201 states that if a CPA does not have or is unable to gain sufficient competence, (s)he should suggest the engagement of someone competent to perform the service either independently or as an associate.

Answer (A) is incorrect because the auditor cannot make judgments about materiality levels and design substantive tests until (s)he has sufficient knowledge of the entity's business. Answer (B) is incorrect because the auditor cannot make judgments about materiality levels and design substantive tests until (s)he has sufficient knowledge of the entity's business. Answer (C) is incorrect because engaging specialists is done only after the auditor has found that (s)he is not able to obtain sufficient knowledge through such normal procedures as inquiry of client personnel, review of previous audit documentation, and study of industry audit guides.

**14.** An auditor is planning an audit engagement for a new client in a business unfamiliar to the auditor. Which is the least useful source of information for the auditor during the preliminary planning stage, when the auditor is trying to obtain a general understanding of audit problems that might be encountered?

A. Textbooks and periodicals related to the industry.

B. AICPA Audit and Accounting Guides.

C. Financial statements of other entities in the industry.

D. Results of performing substantive tests.

Answer (D) is correct. *(CPA, adapted)*
**REQUIRED:** The least useful source of information for early planning of the audit.
**DISCUSSION:** The first standard of field work requires adequate planning of the audit. The auditor must acquire sufficient knowledge of the client's business to plan and perform the audit in accordance with auditing standards. However, substantive tests are performed to collect evidence to test management's assertions embodied in the financial statements. Most are performed after the planning stage of the audit.
Answer (A) is incorrect because textbooks and periodicals related to the industry are useful sources of information (AU 311). Answer (B) is incorrect because AICPA Audit and Accounting Guides are useful sources of information (AU 311). Answer (C) is incorrect because financial statements of other entities in the industry are useful sources of information (AU 311).

**15.** Which of the following is an auditor least likely to perform in planning a financial statement audit?

A. Coordinating the assistance of entity personnel in data preparation.

B. Discussing matters that may affect the audit with firm personnel responsible for non-audit services to the entity.

C. Selecting a sample of vendors' invoices for comparison with receiving reports.

D. Reading the current year's interim financial statements.

Answer (C) is correct. *(CPA, adapted)*
**REQUIRED:** The procedure an auditor is least likely to perform in planning a financial statement audit.
**DISCUSSION:** Selecting a sample of vendors' invoices for comparison with receiving reports is a substantive test. Substantive testing is performed in the field work stage of a financial statement audit, not in the planning stage.
Answer (A) is incorrect because coordinating the assistance of entity personnel is an example of planning procedures identified in AU 311. Answer (B) is incorrect because discussing matters that may affect the audit with firm personnel is an example of planning procedures identified in AU 311. Answer (D) is incorrect because reading the current year's interim financial statements is an example of planning procedures identified in AU 311.

**16.** Which of the following is an effective audit planning and control procedure that helps prevent misunderstandings and inefficient use of audit personnel?

A. Make copies, for inclusion in the audit documentation, of those client supporting documents examined by the auditor.

B. Provide the client with copies of the audit programs to be used during the audit.

C. Arrange a preliminary conference with the client to discuss audit objectives, fees, timing, and other information.

D. Arrange to have the auditor prepare and post any necessary adjusting or reclassification entries prior to final closing.

Answer (C) is correct. *(CPA, adapted)*
**REQUIRED:** The effective procedure to avoid misunderstandings and inefficient use of audit personnel.
**DISCUSSION:** A preliminary conference with the client to discuss various audit objectives, fees, timing, the reports to be prepared, the use of client personnel, etc., is an appropriate procedure to prevent misunderstandings during the audit. The arrangement should be documented in the engagement letter.
Answer (A) is incorrect because copies of client supporting documents are made during the audit itself, not during the planning stages. Also, not all documents need to be copied. Answer (B) is incorrect because the client should not be told which audit procedures are going to be used. Such information might be misused to circumvent the audit. Answer (D) is incorrect because the client (not the auditor) must prepare and post adjusting or reclassification entries.

**17.** Which of the following is most likely the first step an auditor will perform after accepting an initial audit engagement?

A. Prepare a rough draft of the financial statements and of the auditor's report.

B. Assess control risk for the assertions embodied in the financial statements.

C. Tour the client's facilities and review the general records.

D. Consult with and review the work of the predecessor auditor prior to discussing the engagement with the client management.

Answer (C) is correct. *(CPA, adapted)*
**REQUIRED:** The auditor's first step after accepting an initial audit engagement.
**DISCUSSION:** The first step after accepting an initial audit engagement should be to tour the client's facilities and review the general records to obtain an overview of the client's business. This overview provides information about the physical facilities, the location of accounting records, the extent of segregation of functions, the documentation of activities, the attitude of personnel, and a starting point for understanding the client's internal control.
Answer (A) is incorrect because preparing the report is one of the last steps performed in the engagement. Answer (B) is incorrect because the auditor must obtain an understanding of internal control before assessing control risk. Answer (D) is incorrect because consulting with the predecessor auditor is required by AU 315 before accepting the engagement.

**18.** In planning the audit engagement, the auditor should consider each of the following except

A. Matters relating to the entity's business and the industry in which it operates.

B. Risks of material misstatement due to fraud.

C. Anticipated levels of control risk and materiality.

D. The kind of opinion (unqualified, qualified, or adverse) that is likely to be expressed.

Answer (D) is correct. *(Publisher)*

**REQUIRED:** The factor not considered in planning the audit engagement.

**DISCUSSION:** Although AU 311 states that the nature of the report expected to be rendered (e.g., a report on consolidated or consolidating financial statements or special reports such as those on compliance with contractual provisions) should be considered in the planning phase, determining the kind of opinion to be expressed occurs after the completion of audit procedures.

Answer (A) is incorrect because AU 311 states that matters relating to the entity's business and the industry in which it operates should be considered in planning the audit. Other matters to be considered are the financial statement items likely to require adjustment, the conditions that may require extension or modification of audit tests, and the methods used to process significant accounting information, including the use of service organizations, such as outside service centers. Answer (B) is incorrect because, during planning, engagement personnel are required to discuss how and where the financial statements may be susceptible to material misstatements due to fraud. Answer (C) is incorrect because the anticipated levels of control risk and materiality should be considered during audit planning.

**19.** Which of the following factors does a CPA ordinarily consider in the planning stage of an audit engagement?

I. Financial statement accounts likely to contain a misstatement.

II. Conditions that require extension of audit tests.

A. I only.

B. II only.

C. Both I and II.

D. Neither I nor II.

Answer (C) is correct. *(CPA, adapted)*

**REQUIRED:** The factors a CPA ordinarily considers in the planning stage of an audit engagement.

**DISCUSSION:** According to AU 311, when planning an audit engagement, the auditor should consider, among other things, the financial statement accounts likely to require adjustment and the conditions that require extension or modification of audit tests (e.g., risk of material error or fraud).

**20.** In designing written audit programs, an auditor should establish specific audit objectives that relate primarily to the

A. Timing of audit procedures.

B. Cost-benefit of gathering evidence.

C. Selected audit techniques.

D. Financial statement assertions.

Answer (D) is correct. *(CPA, adapted)*

**REQUIRED:** The item to which specific audit objectives primarily relate.

**DISCUSSION:** Most audit work consists of obtaining and evaluating evidence about financial statement assertions, which are management representations embodied in financial statement components. AU 326 states, "In obtaining evidential matter in support of financial statement assertions, the auditor develops specific audit objectives in light of those assertions."

Answer (A) is incorrect because timing is important in meeting the objectives of the audit but does not relate to the audit objectives themselves. Answer (B) is incorrect because the cost-benefit of gathering evidence is important to the auditor but is not the primary consideration in determining the objectives of the audit. Answer (C) is incorrect because audit objectives determine the specific audit techniques.

**21.** Financial statement audit programs are modified to suit the circumstances of particular engagements. An audit program usually should be developed

A. Prior to beginning the actual audit work.

B. After the auditor has obtained an understanding of internal control and assessed risks.

C. After obtaining an understanding of the information and communication and control activities components of internal control.

D. When the engagement letter is prepared.

Answer (B) is correct. *(Publisher)*

**REQUIRED:** The time at which an audit program should be developed.

**DISCUSSION:** Only after the understanding of internal control is obtained and risks have been assessed can the auditor determine the nature, timing, and extent of substantive tests of financial statement assertions (AU 319). However, as the audit progresses, the auditor should consider necessary modifications in light of evidence collected.

Answer (A) is incorrect because the auditor cannot determine the necessary substantive tests until an understanding of internal control has been obtained and an assessment of risks has been made. This process is part of the audit work. Answer (C) is incorrect because the auditor must also obtain an understanding of the control environment, risk assessment, and monitoring components of internal control before planning the audit. Answer (D) is incorrect because the auditor must obtain an understanding of internal control and assess risks before preparing the audit program. This process follows the preparation of the engagement letter.

**22.** Which of the following ultimately determines the specific audit procedures necessary to provide an independent auditor with a reasonable basis for the expression of an opinion?

A. The audit program.

B. The auditor's judgment.

C. Auditing standards.

D. The audit documentation.

Answer (B) is correct. *(CPA, adapted)*

**REQUIRED:** The factor determining specific procedures.

**DISCUSSION:** The auditor's professional judgment must determine the necessary audit programs and the specific audit procedures that will gather sufficient competent evidence to afford a reasonable basis for an opinion.

Answer (A) is incorrect because audit programs are usually modified during the engagement to adapt to audit evidence as it is gathered. Answer (C) is incorrect because auditing standards, whether established by the AICPA's ASB or the PCAOB, are general objectives that are concerned with the quality of the auditor's performance. Answer (D) is incorrect because audit documentation demonstrates that the auditor has carried out the procedures (s)he has deemed necessary. The documentation does not determine the procedures undertaken.

**23.** One of the primary roles of an engagement work program is to

A. Serve as a tool for planning and conducting engagement work.

B. Document an internal auditor's evaluations of controls.

C. Provide for a standardized approach to the engagement.

D. Assess the risks associated with the activity under review.

Answer (A) is correct. *(CIA, adapted)*

**REQUIRED:** The item that states one of the primary roles of an engagement work program.

**DISCUSSION:** Work programs document procedures for collecting, analyzing, interpreting, and documenting information; state engagement objectives; set forth the scope and degree of testing needed to achieve objectives in each phase of the engagement; identify technical aspects, risks, processes, and transactions to be examined; state the nature and extent of testing required, and are prepared before work begins, with appropriate modification during the engagement (PA 2200-1).

Answer (B) is incorrect because engagement working papers include results of control evaluations. Answer (C) is incorrect because the work program should be logical, but it may not be consistent from year to year given the changing conditions to which the engagement client must adapt. The work program should be tailored to the current year's situation; thus, standardization may not be appropriate. Answer (D) is incorrect because the risk assessment in the planning phase helps to identify objectives, a step that must be taken before the work program can be developed.

**24.** Most of the independent auditor's work in formulating an opinion on financial statements consists of

A. Considering internal control.

B. Obtaining and examining evidential matter.

C. Examining cash transactions.

D. Comparing recorded accountability with assets.

Answer (B) is correct. *(CPA, adapted)*

**REQUIRED:** The principal activity of an auditor in formulating an opinion.

**DISCUSSION:** According to AU 326, *Evidential Matter*, most of the independent auditor's work in formulating an opinion on financial statements consists of obtaining and examining evidence. Evidence is the underlying accounting data and corroborating information available to the auditor.

Answer (A) is incorrect because considering internal control is an example of obtaining and examining evidence. Answer (C) is incorrect because examining cash transactions is an example of obtaining and examining evidence. Answer (D) is incorrect because comparing recorded accountability with assets is an example of obtaining and examining evidence.

**25.** Which of the following is the correct order of performing the steps A through C below?

A = Test of controls
B = Preparation of a flowchart documenting the understanding of the client's internal control
C = Substantive tests

A. ABC.

B. ACB.

C. BAC.

D. BCA.

Answer (C) is correct. *(CPA, adapted)*

**REQUIRED:** The correct order of audit steps.

**DISCUSSION:** The auditor first obtains an understanding of the client's internal control policies and procedures that are relevant to audit planning. This understanding may include flowcharting the system. Next, the auditor must assess control risk. This process will entail identifying specific control policies and procedures relevant to specific financial statement assertions and performing tests of controls to evaluate their effectiveness. The auditor uses the understanding obtained and the assessment of control risk to plan the nature, timing, and extent of substantive tests (AU 319).

**26.** Which of the following is an aspect of scheduling and controlling the audit engagement?

A. Including in the audit program a column for estimated and actual time.

B. Performing audit work only after the client's books of account have been closed for the period under examination.

C. Writing a conclusion in individual working papers indicating how the results of the audit will affect the auditor's report.

D. Including in the engagement letter an estimate of the minimum and maximum audit fee.

Answer (A) is correct. *(CPA, adapted)*

**REQUIRED:** The aspect of scheduling and controlling the audit engagement.

**DISCUSSION:** The audit program is a tool for scheduling and controlling the audit. It should contain a detailed set of procedures for accomplishing audit objectives, estimated times for each step, and the personnel required. Thus, it can be used to document the progress of the audit and the auditor's compliance with the first standard of field work (planning and supervision).

Answer (B) is incorrect because audit work may be done throughout the year before the books have been closed. Answer (C) is incorrect because writing a conclusion is an evaluation of the evidence rather than part of scheduling and controlling the audit. Answer (D) is incorrect because the engagement letter, describing the contractual agreement between the auditor and client, precedes the audit.

**27.** The element of the audit planning process most likely to be agreed upon with the client before implementation of the audit strategy is the determination of the

A. Timing of inventory observation procedures to be performed.

B. Evidence to be gathered to provide a sufficient basis for the auditor's opinion.

C. Procedures to be undertaken to discover litigation, claims, and assessments.

D. Pending legal matters to be included in the inquiry of the client's attorney.

Answer (A) is correct. *(CPA, adapted)*

**REQUIRED:** The element of audit planning most likely to be agreed upon with the client before implementation.

**DISCUSSION:** Auditing standards require auditors to observe or make at least some physical counts of inventory and to become satisfied about the effectiveness of the methods of inventory-taking and the client's representations concerning quantities and condition (AU 331). Observation of inventory necessitates coordination of the efforts of the auditors and the client prior to performance of the procedure.

Answer (B) is incorrect because the evidence to be gathered is not subject to the client's approval but to the auditor's professional judgment. Answer (C) is incorrect because the procedures to be undertaken to discover litigation, claims, and assessments are not subject to the client's approval but to the auditor's professional judgment. Answer (D) is incorrect because determination of the specific legal issues to be raised in the inquiry letter is not appropriate in the planning phase. It should await a more complete understanding of the client's affairs.

**28.** Which of the following is an engagement attribute for an audit of an entity that processes most of its financial data in electronic form without any paper documentation?

A. Discrete phases of planning, interim, and year-end field work.

B. Increased effort to search for evidence of management fraud.

C. Performance of audit tests on a continuous basis.

D. Increased emphasis on the completeness assertion.

Answer (C) is correct. *(CPA, adapted)*

**REQUIRED:** The engagement attribute for auditing in an electronic environment.

**DISCUSSION:** The audit trail for transactions processed in electronic form may be available only briefly. The auditor may conclude that audit procedures should be scheduled so that they correspond to the availability of the evidence. Thus, audit modules may be embedded in the client's software for this purpose.

Answer (A) is incorrect because this engagement attribute would be appropriate for any type of client. Answer (B) is incorrect because processing transactions in electronic form does not inherently increase the risk of management fraud. Answer (D) is incorrect because no inherent additional concern arises about the completeness assertion as a result of processing transactions in electronic form.

**29.** The audit work performed by each assistant should be reviewed to determine whether it was adequately performed and to evaluate whether the

A. Auditor's system of quality control has been maintained at a high level.

B. Results are consistent with the conclusions to be presented in the auditor's report.

C. Audit procedures performed are approved in the professional standards.

D. Audit has been performed by persons having adequate technical training and proficiency as auditors.

Answer (B) is correct. *(CPA, adapted)*

**REQUIRED:** The reason for reviewing the audit work of each assistant.

**DISCUSSION:** The first standard of field work requires assistants to be properly supervised. Thus, the "work performed by each assistant should be reviewed to determine whether it was adequately performed and to evaluate whether the results are consistent with the conclusions to be presented in the auditor's report" (AU 311).

Answer (A) is incorrect because the review of the audit work of each assistant is only a part of quality control. Answer (C) is incorrect because determination of whether the procedures are in accordance with professional standards is necessary in the planning stage. Answer (D) is incorrect because the selection of assistants having adequate technical training and proficiency concerns planning, not supervision.

**30.** The in-charge auditor most likely has a supervisory responsibility to explain to the staff assistants

A. That immaterial fraud is not to be reported to the client's audit committee.

B. How the results of various auditing procedures performed by the assistants should be evaluated.

C. What benefits may be attained by the assistants' adherence to established time budgets.

D. Why certain documents are being transferred from the current file to the permanent file.

Answer (B) is correct. *(CPA, adapted)*

**REQUIRED:** The responsibility of the audit supervisor.

**DISCUSSION:** AU 311 states "Assistants should be informed of their responsibilities and the objectives of the procedures that they are to perform." They should be informed about the matters that affect the nature, timing, and extent of procedures, including how the results of tests should be evaluated.

Answer (A) is incorrect because immaterial fraud may be reported to the client's audit committee. Answer (C) is incorrect because discussion of time budgets is not a responsibility under the auditing standards. Answer (D) is incorrect because, at the end of the audit, supervisors determine which documents are to be transferred to the permanent file. These decisions need not be justified to staff assistants.

**31.** The auditor with final responsibility for an engagement and one of the assistants have a difference of opinion about the results of an auditing procedure. If the assistant believes it is necessary to be disassociated from the matter's resolution, the CPA firm's procedures should enable the assistant to

A. Refer the disagreement to the AICPA's Peer Review Board.

B. Document the details of the disagreement with the conclusion reached.

C. Discuss the disagreement with the entity's management or its audit committee.

D. Report the disagreement to an impartial peer review monitoring team.

Answer (B) is correct. *(CPA, adapted)*

**REQUIRED:** The action permitted to an assistant who disagrees with the auditor in charge.

**DISCUSSION:** According to AU 311, audit personnel should be aware of the procedures to be followed when they have differences of opinion regarding accounting and auditing issues. An assistant should be able to document his/her disagreement with the conclusions reached if, after consultation, (s)he believes it is necessary to be disassociated from the resolution of the matter. Moreover, the basis for the final disposition of the disagreement should also be documented. The PCAOB's AS No. 3 requires working papers to document disagreements among members of the engagement team.

Answer (A) is incorrect because the Peer Review Board issues standards for performing and reporting on peer reviews. Answer (C) is incorrect because the client need not be informed of the disagreement about the results of an auditing procedure. Answer (D) is incorrect because there is no peer review monitoring team.

## 2.3 Risk Assessment

**32.** The audit risk against which the auditor and those who rely on his/her opinion require reasonable protection is a combination of three separate risks at the account-balance or class-of-transactions level. The first risk is inherent risk. The second risk is that material misstatements will not be prevented or detected by internal control. The third risk is that

A. The auditor will reject a correct account balance as incorrect.

B. Material misstatements that occur will not be detected by the audit.

C. The auditor will apply an inappropriate audit procedure.

D. The auditor will apply an inappropriate measure of audit materiality.

Answer (B) is correct. *(Publisher)*

**REQUIRED:** The component of audit risk in addition to inherent risk and control risk.

**DISCUSSION:** According to AU 312, one component of audit risk is detection risk, which is the risk that the auditor will not detect a material misstatement that exists in an assertion. Detection risk for a substantive test of details has two elements: (1) the risk that analytical procedures and other relevant substantive tests will fail to detect misstatements at least equal to tolerable misstatement and (2) the allowable risk of incorrect acceptance for the substantive test of details. The auditor assesses control risk (the second component) when considering the client s internal control. This assessment, the assessment of inherent risk, and the level to which the auditor wishes to restrict overall audit risk are the factors that the auditor uses to determine the acceptable level of detection risk.

**33.** Some account balances, such as those for pensions or leases, are the results of complex calculations. The susceptibility to material misstatements in these types of accounts is defined as

A. Audit risk.

B. Detection risk.

C. Sampling risk.

D. Inherent risk.

Answer (D) is correct. *(CMA, adapted)*

**REQUIRED:** The susceptibility to material misstatements in account balances resulting from complex calculations.

**DISCUSSION:** Inherent risk is the susceptibility of an assertion to a material misstatement in the absence of related controls. This risk is greater for some assertions and related balances or classes than others. For example, complex calculations are more likely to be misstated than simple ones, and cash is more likely to be stolen than an inventory of coal. Inherent risk exists independently of the audit (AU 312).

Answer (A) is incorrect because audit risk is the risk that the auditor may unknowingly fail to appropriately modify an opinion on financial statements that are materially misstated. Answer (B) is incorrect because detection risk is the risk that the auditor will not detect a material misstatement that exists in an assertion. Answer (C) is incorrect because sampling risk is the risk that a particular sample may contain proportionately more or fewer monetary misstatements or deviations from controls than exist in the population as a whole (AU 350).

**34.** As the acceptable level of detection risk decreases, an auditor may change the

A. Timing of substantive tests by performing them at an interim date rather than at year-end.

B. Nature of substantive tests from a less effective to a more effective procedure.

C. Timing of tests of controls by performing them at several dates rather than at one time.

D. Assessed level of inherent risk to a higher amount.

Answer (B) is correct. *(CPA, adapted)*

**REQUIRED:** The change resulting from a decrease in the acceptable level of detection risk.

**DISCUSSION:** The assurance provided by substantive tests must increase if the acceptable level of detection risk decreases. The auditor may (1) change from a less to a more effective procedure, for example, by directing tests toward independent parties outside the entity rather than toward client personnel; (2) change the timing of substantive tests, such as from an interim date to year-end; or (3) change the extent of testing, such as by using a larger sample (AU 319).

Answer (A) is incorrect because more assurance is provided by testing at year-end. Answer (C) is incorrect because the auditor tests controls when (s)he wishes to assess control risk below the maximum level. The resulting assessment is then used in the determination of the acceptable level of detection risk. Answer (D) is incorrect because the assessed level of inherent risk affects the acceptable level of detection risk but not vice versa.

**35.** The risk that an auditor's procedures will lead to the conclusion that a material misstatement does not exist in an account balance when, in fact, such misstatement does exist is

A. Audit risk.

B. Inherent risk.

C. Control risk.

D. Detection risk.

Answer (D) is correct. *(CPA, adapted)*
**REQUIRED:** The risk that audit procedures will fail to find a material misstatement.
**DISCUSSION:** Detection risk is "the risk that the auditor will not detect a material misstatement that exists in an assertion" (AU 312).
Answer (A) is incorrect because audit risk includes inherent risk and control risk, which are not affected by the auditor's procedures. Answer (B) is incorrect because inherent risk is the susceptibility of an assertion to material misstatement in the absence of related controls. Answer (C) is incorrect because control risk is the risk that a material misstatement in an assertion will not be prevented or detected on a timely basis by internal control.

**36.** Audit risk consists of inherent risk, control risk, and detection risk. Which of the following statements is true?

A. Cash is more susceptible to theft than an inventory of coal because it has a greater inherent risk.

B. The risk that material misstatement will not be prevented or detected on a timely basis by internal control can be reduced to zero by effective controls.

C. Detection risk is a function of the efficiency of an auditing procedure.

D. The existing levels of inherent risk, control risk, and detection risk can be changed at the discretion of the auditor.

Answer (A) is correct. *(Publisher)*
**REQUIRED:** The true statement about audit risk.
**DISCUSSION:** Inherent risk is the susceptibility of an assertion to material misstatement in the absence of related controls. Some assertions and related balances or classes of transactions have greater inherent risk. Thus, cash has a greater inherent risk than less liquid assets.
Answer (B) is incorrect because some control risk will always exist. Internal control has inherent limitations. Answer (C) is incorrect because detection risk is a function of auditing effectiveness (achieving results), not efficiency. Answer (D) is incorrect because the actual levels of inherent risk and control risk are independent of the audit process. Acceptable detection risk is a function of the desired level of overall audit risk and the assessed levels of inherent risk and control risk. Hence, detection risk can be changed at the discretion of the auditor, but inherent risk and control risk cannot. However, the auditor's preliminary judgments about inherent risk and control risk may change as the audit progresses.

**37.** The acceptable level of detection risk is inversely related to the

A. Assurance provided by substantive tests.

B. Risk of misapplying auditing procedures.

C. Preliminary judgment about materiality levels.

D. Risk of failing to discover material misstatements.

Answer (A) is correct. *(CPA, adapted)*
**REQUIRED:** The concept to which acceptable detection risk is inversely related.
**DISCUSSION:** An auditor considers internal control to assess control risk. The greater (lower) the assessed level of control risk, the lower (greater) the acceptable level of detection risk. In turn, the acceptable level of detection risk affects substantive testing. For example, as the acceptable level of detection risk decreases, the auditor changes the nature, timing, or extent of substantive tests to increase the assurance they provide. Hence, the relationship between substantive testing and acceptable detection risk is inverse.
Answer (B) is incorrect because the risk of misapplying auditing procedures is related to the auditor's training and experience. Answer (C) is incorrect because preliminary judgments about materiality levels are used by the auditor to determine the acceptable level of audit risk. Materiality and overall audit risk are inversely related. However, detection risk is just one component of audit risk (AU 312). Answer (D) is incorrect because the lower the level of detection risk acceptable to the auditor, the greater the assurance that should be provided by substantive testing. Given this additional assurance, the risk of failing to detect material misstatements (detection risk) should be decreased. Accordingly, the relationship of acceptable detection risk and the risk of failing to detect material misstatements is direct.

**38.** Which of the following audit risk components may be assessed in nonquantitative terms?

| | Control Risk | Detection Risk | Inherent Risk |
|---|---|---|---|
| A. | Yes | Yes | Yes |
| B. | No | Yes | Yes |
| C. | Yes | Yes | No |
| D. | Yes | No | Yes |

Answer (A) is correct. *(CPA, adapted)*

**REQUIRED:** The audit risk components that may be assessed in nonquantitative terms.

**DISCUSSION:** According to AU 312, the "components of audit risk may be assessed in quantitative terms such as percentages or in nonquantitative terms that range, for example, from a minimum to a maximum."

**39.** Which of the following would an auditor most likely use in determining the auditor's preliminary judgment about materiality?

A. The anticipated sample size of the planned substantive tests.

B. The entity's annualized interim financial statements.

C. The results of the internal control questionnaire.

D. The contents of the representation letter.

Answer (B) is correct. *(CPA, adapted)*

**REQUIRED:** The factor most likely used in determining the preliminary judgment about materiality.

**DISCUSSION:** AU 312 states that "the auditor's preliminary judgment about materiality might be based on the entity's annualized interim financial statements or financial statements of one or more prior periods, as long as recognition is given to the effect of major changes in the entity's circumstances (for example, a significant merger) and relevant changes in the economy as a whole or the industry in which the entity operates."

Answer (A) is incorrect because the auditor's preliminary judgment about materiality is used to determine the sample sizes for substantive tests. Sample sizes are calculated during evidence collection. Answer (C) is incorrect because results of the internal control questionnaire are considered during the assessment of control risk. Answer (D) is incorrect because the contents of the representation letter are determined near the end of the audit.

**40.** When expressing an unqualified opinion, the auditor who evaluates the audit findings should be satisfied that the

A. Amount of known misstatement is documented in the management representation letter.

B. Estimate of the total likely misstatement is less than a material amount.

C. Amount of known misstatement is acknowledged and recorded by the client.

D. Estimate of the total likely misstatement includes the adjusting entries already recorded by the client.

Answer (B) is correct. *(Publisher)*

**REQUIRED:** The audit findings that support an unqualified opinion.

**DISCUSSION:** The opinion paragraph of the standard auditor's report explicitly states that the financial statements present fairly, in all material respects, the financial position, results of operations, and cash flows of the entity in conformity with GAAP. It reflects the judgment that the effects (qualitative and quantitative) of uncorrected misstatements, individually or in the aggregate, do not cause the financial statements to be materially misstated. This evaluation requires the auditor to aggregate uncorrected misstatements to determine the best estimate of the total (likely misstatement), not just the amount specifically identified (known misstatement). The nature and effect of the aggregated misstatements and the conclusion as to whether they cause the financial statements to be materially misstated must be documented (AU 312). Furthermore, under the Sarbanes-Oxley Act of 2002, a financial report prepared under GAAP must reflect all correcting adjustments identified by a registered accounting firm.

Answer (A) is incorrect because the auditor's judgment regarding whether the financial statements are fairly presented, in all material respects, relates to his/her evaluation of likely misstatement, not known misstatement. Answer (C) is incorrect because the auditor's judgment regarding whether the financial statements are fairly presented, in all material respects, relates to his/her evaluation of likely misstatement, not known misstatement. Answer (D) is incorrect because total likely misstatement excludes material misstatements eliminated by, for example, adjusting entries.

**41.** According to AU 312, *Audit Risk and Materiality in Conducting an Audit*, the concepts of audit risk and materiality are interrelated and must be considered together by the auditor. Which of the following is true?

A. Audit risk is the risk that the auditor may unknowingly express a modified opinion when in fact the financial statements are fairly stated.

B. The phrase in the auditor's standard report "present fairly, in all material respects, in conformity with generally accepted accounting principles" indicates the auditor's belief that the financial statements taken as a whole are not materially misstated.

C. If misstatements are not important individually but are important in the aggregate, the concept of materiality does not apply.

D. Material fraud but not material errors cause financial statements to be materially misstated.

Answer (B) is correct. *(Publisher)*

**REQUIRED:** The true statement about the significance of audit risk and materiality.

**DISCUSSION:** The opinion paragraph of the standard report explicitly refers to materiality. Hence, financial statements that are presented fairly, in all material respects, in conformity with GAAP are not materially misstated. Material misstatement can result from errors or fraud.

Answer (A) is incorrect because audit risk is the risk the auditor may unknowingly fail to appropriately modify the opinion on financial statements that are materially misstated. Answer (C) is incorrect because the concept of materiality recognizes that some misstatements, either individually or in the aggregate, are important for the fair presentation of financial statements. Qualitative as well as quantitative factors affect materiality judgments. This concept is consistent with an SEC Staff Accounting Bulletin, which also states, "A matter is 'material' if there is substantial likelihood that a reasonable person would consider it important" (SAB 99). Answer (D) is incorrect because both material errors and material fraud cause financial statements to be materially misstated.

**42.** AU 350 gives a formula for risk relationships. Overall allowable audit risk (AR) is the risk that monetary misstatements equal to tolerable misstatement may remain undetected. Control risk (CR) is the auditor's assessment of the risk that internal control may not prevent or detect material misstatements. Inherent risk (IR) is the susceptibility of an assertion to material misstatement given no related controls. In the audit risk formula, AP is the auditor's assessment of the risk that analytical procedures and other relevant substantive tests will fail to detect material misstatements not detected by the relevant controls. TD is the allowable risk of incorrect acceptance for a substantive test of details given that material misstatements occur in an assertion and are not detected by internal control or by analytical procedures and other substantive tests. Which model represents the overall allowable audit risk?

A. $AR = IR \times CR \times AP \times TD$.

B. $AR = IR + CR + AP + TD$.

C. $AR = IR + CR - (AP + TD)$.

D. $AR = IR + CR - (AP \times TD)$.

Answer (A) is correct. *(Publisher)*

**REQUIRED:** The model associated with the overall allowable audit risk.

**DISCUSSION:** AU 350 states that the model for the overall allowable audit risk is not intended to be a mathematical formula including all factors that may influence the determination of individual risk components. However, the model is sometimes useful in considering and planning appropriate risk levels. AR is equal to the joint probability that material misstatements will occur in an assertion, that internal control will not prevent or detect material misstatements, and that subsequent procedures will also not detect them. Hence, AR is expressed as the product of IR, CR, AP, and TD.

**43.** The equation in AU 350 for the overall allowable audit risk (AR = IR × CR × AP × TD) is sometimes solved for TD (the allowable risk of incorrect acceptance associated with a test of details) because

A. The most important element is TD.

B. This version of the formula assists in planning a specific substantive test of details.

C. The overall allowable audit risk cannot be determined.

D. Auditors always consider tests of details first.

Answer (B) is correct. *(Publisher)*
**REQUIRED:** The reason the allowable audit risk formula is solved for TD.
**DISCUSSION:** The auditor first establishes the overall allowable audit risk (AR) with respect to a particular balance or class of transactions. After considering internal control, (s)he can assess control risk (CR) as well as inherent risk (IR). After applying analytical procedures and considering the results of other substantive tests, (s)he can then assess the risk (AP) that those procedures and tests did not detect misstatements in an assertion equal to tolerable misstatement. The auditor can then calculate the allowable risk of incorrect acceptance (TD) for a particular substantive test. Determination of this level of risk is necessary for planning the nature, timing, and extent of the substantive test.
Answer (A) is incorrect because the overall allowable audit risk is the most important element in planning appropriate audit tests. Answer (C) is incorrect because the auditor's professional judgment and experience is used to determine overall allowable audit risk. Answer (D) is incorrect because overall audit risk should be established and some analytical procedures should be performed at an early stage. Also, the assessment of control risk should ordinarily be made before the planning of most tests of details.

**44.** Which of the following models expresses the general relationship of the auditor's assessments of control risk (CR) and inherent risk (IR), the detection risk associated with analytical procedures and other relevant substantive tests (AP), and overall allowable audit risk (AR) that would lead the auditor to conclude that a substantive test of details of an account balance is not necessary?

| | AP | CR | AR | IR |
|---|---|---|---|---|
| A. | 20% | 40% | 10% | 100% |
| B. | 20% | 60% | 5% | 100% |
| C. | 10% | 70% | 4.5% | 100% |
| D. | 30% | 40% | 5.5% | 100% |

Answer (A) is correct. *(CPA, adapted)*
**REQUIRED:** The model expressing the relationship of risks not requiring an additional substantive test of details.
**DISCUSSION:** According to AU 350, the allowable risk of incorrect acceptance associated with a particular substantive test of details (TD) is equal to AR divided by the product of CR, AP, and IR. When the allowable level of AR exceeds the product of CR, AP, and IR, the planned substantive test of details may not be necessary because the relevant controls, analytical procedures, and other substantive tests may have reduced to an acceptable level the risk that monetary misstatements equal to tolerable misstatement will remain undetected. Thus, when AP is 20%, CR is 40%, and IR is 100%, risk is controlled at 8% (20% × 40% × 100%), which is less than a 10% AR.
Answer (B) is incorrect because, if AR is 5% and the product of AP, CR, and IR is 12% (20% × 60% × 100%), the additional substantive test will be necessary. Answer (C) is incorrect because, if AR is 4.5% and the product of AP, CR, and IR is 7% (10% × 70% × 100%), the additional substantive test will be necessary. Answer (D) is incorrect because, if AR is 5.5% and the product of AP, CR, and IR is 12% (30% × 40% × 100%), the additional substantive test will be necessary.

**45.** The concept of materiality with respect to the attest function

A. Applies only to publicly held firms.

B. Has greater application to the standards of reporting than the other generally accepted auditing standards.

C. Requires that relatively more effort be directed to those assertions that are more susceptible to misstatement.

D. Requires the auditor to make judgments as to whether misstatements affect the fairness of the financial statements.

Answer (D) is correct. *(Publisher)*
**REQUIRED:** The meaning of materiality with respect to the attest function.
**DISCUSSION:** The concept of materiality recognizes that some, but not all, matters are important to the fairness of the financial statements. "Audit risk is the risk that the auditor may unknowingly fail to appropriately modify the opinion on financial statements that are materially misstated" (AU 312). A decrease either in the amount of misstatements deemed to be material or in the acceptable level of audit risk requires the auditor to select more effective procedures, perform procedures closer to the balance sheet date, or increase the extent of procedures.
Answer (A) is incorrect because the concept of materiality applies to all auditees. Answer (B) is incorrect because materiality applies to all GAAS. Answer (C) is incorrect because the degree of inherent risk is the reason that more effort must be directed to assertions (e.g., cash) that are more susceptible to misstatement.

**46.** In considering materiality for planning purposes, an auditor believes that misstatements aggregating $10,000 would have a material effect on an entity's income statement but that misstatements would have to aggregate $20,000 to materially affect the balance sheet. Ordinarily, it would be appropriate to design auditing procedures that would be expected to detect misstatements that aggregate

A. $10,000

B. $15,000

C. $20,000

D. $30,000

Answer (A) is correct. *(CPA, adapted)*

**REQUIRED:** The materiality level used to design auditing procedures.

**DISCUSSION:** Because financial statements and the necessary audit tests are interrelated, as well as for reasons of efficiency, procedures should normally be designed to detect the smallest aggregate level of misstatements that could be material to any one statement. The smallest aggregate level of statements material to one statement is $10,000.

Answer (B) is incorrect because $15,000 is the average of the aggregate amounts material to the income statement and the balance sheet. Answer (C) is incorrect because $20,000 is the aggregate level of misstatements material to the balance sheet. Answer (D) is incorrect because $30,000 is the sum of the aggregate amounts material to the income statement and the balance sheet.

**47.** Madison Corporation has a few large accounts receivable that total $1,000,000. Nassau Corporation has a great number of small accounts receivable that also total $1,000,000. The importance of a misstatement in any one account is therefore greater for Madison than for Nassau. This is an example of the auditor's concept of

A. Materiality.

B. Comparative analysis.

C. Reasonable assurance.

D. Audit risk.

Answer (A) is correct. *(CPA, adapted)*

**REQUIRED:** The concept applicable to the relative size of individual accounts receivable.

**DISCUSSION:** The concept of materiality requires the auditor to evaluate the relative importance of items to users of financial statements. In an entity with few but large accounts receivable, the individual accounts are relatively more important and the possibility of material misstatement is greater than in an entity with many small accounts.

Answer (B) is incorrect because comparative analysis is a term that is associated with analytical procedures. Answer (C) is incorrect because reasonable assurance is implicit in the third field work standard: Sufficient evidence should be gathered to afford a reasonable basis for an opinion. Moreover, reasonable assurance is mentioned in the auditor's standard report. Answer (D) is incorrect because "audit risk is the risk that the auditor may unknowingly fail to appropriately modify the opinion on financial statements that are materially misstated" (AU 312).

## 2.4 Errors, Fraud, and Illegal Acts

**48.** Because of the risk of material misstatement due to fraud (fraud risk), an audit of financial statements in accordance with auditing standards should be planned and performed with an attitude of

A. Objective judgment.

B. Independent integrity.

C. Professional skepticism.

D. Impartial conservatism.

Answer (C) is correct. *(CPA, adapted)*

**REQUIRED:** The attitude with which an audit in accordance with auditing standards should be planned and performed.

**DISCUSSION:** "Due professional care requires the auditor to exercise professional skepticism" (AU 230). Professional skepticism is an attitude that includes a questioning mind and critical assessment of audit evidence. Regardless of past experience with the entity or belief in management's honesty, the audit must be conducted with (1) an awareness of the possible existence of fraud risk and (2) ongoing questioning of whether the evidence suggests that such fraud has occurred (AU 316, *Consideration of Fraud in a Financial Statement Audit*).

Answer (A) is incorrect because, although objective judgment is a quality appropriate for practitioners, it is not required to be applied specifically in an audit. Answer (B) is incorrect because, although independent integrity is a quality appropriate for practitioners, it is not required to be applied specifically in an audit. Answer (D) is incorrect because, although impartial conservatism is a quality appropriate for practitioners, it is not required to be applied specifically in an audit.

**49.** Which of the following statements reflects an auditor's responsibility for detecting fraud?

A. An auditor is responsible for detecting employee errors and simple fraud, but not for discovering fraudulent acts involving employee collusion or management override.

B. An auditor should plan the audit to detect fraud caused by departures from GAAP.

C. An auditor is not responsible for detecting fraud unless the application of auditing standards would result in such detection.

D. An auditor should design the audit to provide reasonable assurance of detecting errors and fraud that are material to the financial statements.

Answer (D) is correct. *(CPA, adapted)*

**REQUIRED:** The statement reflecting the auditor's responsibility for detecting fraud.

**DISCUSSION:** "The auditor has a responsibility to plan and perform the audit to obtain reasonable assurance about whether the financial statements are free of material misstatement, whether caused by error or fraud" (AU 110). Thus, the consideration of fraud should be logically integrated into the overall audit process in a manner consistent with other pronouncements, e.g., those on planning and supervision, audit risk and materiality, and internal control. This consideration entails (1) understanding fraud, (2) discussing fraud risks with members of the engagement team, (3) obtaining information needed to identify fraud risks, (4) identifying those risks, (5) assessing fraud risks, (6) responding to the assessments, (7) evaluating evidence at the end of the audit, (8) making appropriate communications about fraud, and (9) documenting the consideration (AU 316).

**50.** Certain individuals may have an attitude, character, or set of values that permit them to rationalize fraud. Moreover, individuals may have an incentive or be under pressure to commit fraud, or circumstances may provide an opportunity. The auditor's concern about the risk of material misstatements due to fraud is least likely to be heightened if management

A. Operating and financing decisions are made by numerous individuals.

B. Commits to unduly aggressive forecasts.

C. Has an excessive interest in increasing the entity's stock price through use of unduly aggressive accounting practices.

D. Is interested in inappropriate means of minimizing reported earnings for tax-motivated reasons.

Answer (A) is correct. *(Publisher)*

**REQUIRED:** The circumstances least likely to indicate increased fraud risk.

**DISCUSSION:** The auditor will identify a fraud risk factor if the decision process were dominated by one individual or a small group (an opportunity to commit fraud). In that case, compensating controls, e.g., effective oversight by the audit committee, reduce risk (AU 316, *Appendix*).

Answer (B) is incorrect because a commitment to third parties to achieve unduly aggressive or clearly unrealistic forecasts is a fraud risk factor that reflects an attitude or rationalization permitting fraudulent financial reporting. Answer (C) is incorrect because an excessive interest in improving the entity's stock price or earnings trend is a fraud risk factor that reflects an attitude or rationalization permitting fraudulent financial reporting. Answer (D) is incorrect because an interest in inappropriate means of minimizing earnings for tax purposes is a fraud risk factor that reflects an attitude or rationalization permitting fraudulent financial reporting.

**51.** Three conditions are generally present in the client's organization when fraud occurs. Those conditions include each of the following except a(n)

A. Incentive or pressure to commit fraud.

B. Professional skepticism about the likelihood of fraud.

C. Opportunity to commit fraud.

D. Attitude or rationalization about the act of fraud.

Answer (B) is correct. *(Publisher)*

**REQUIRED:** The condition not necessarily present when fraud occurs.

**DISCUSSION:** The auditor, not the client, should conduct the audit with professional skepticism, an attitude that requires an ongoing questioning of whether the information and evidence obtained suggest that fraud might exist.

Answer (A) is incorrect because incentives for, or pressures on, management or others to commit fraud ordinarily exists (whether or not observable) when fraud occurs. Answer (C) is incorrect because the opportunity to commit fraud ordinarily exists (whether or not observable) when fraud occurs. Answer (D) is incorrect because an attitude or rationalization that justifies the fraudulent action ordinarily exists (whether or not observable) when fraud occurs.

**52.** Which of the following circumstances most likely will cause an auditor to consider whether material misstatements due to fraud exist in an entity's financial statements?

A. Management places little emphasis on meeting earnings projections of external parties.

B. The board of directors oversees the financial reporting process and internal control.

C. Reportable conditions previously communicated to management are not corrected.

D. Transactions selected for testing are not supported by proper documentation.

Answer (D) is correct. *(CPA, adapted)*

**REQUIRED:** The circumstance most likely to cause an auditor to consider the existence of fraud risk.

**DISCUSSION:** Fraud risk factors relate to misstatements arising from (1) fraudulent financial reporting and (2) misappropriation of assets. Each of these categories may be further classified according to the three conditions that ordinarily exist when fraud occurs: (1) incentives/pressures, (2) opportunities, and (3) attitudes/rationalizations. For example, an opportunity for misappropriation of assets may arise because of inadequate control over assets reflected by a lack of timely and appropriate documentation of transactions, such as credit memos for returns of goods.

Answer (A) is incorrect because a risk factor exists when excessive pressure is placed on management to reach expectations of external parties. Answer (B) is incorrect because the board's involvement reduces the likelihood of material misstatements due to fraud. Answer (C) is incorrect because management may properly evaluate the costs and benefits in deciding whether to correct reportable conditions.

**53.** Which of the following characteristics most likely will heighten an auditor's concern about the risk of material misstatements due to fraud in an entity's financial statements?

A. The entity's industry is experiencing declining customer demand.

B. Employees who handle cash receipts are not bonded.

C. Internal auditors have direct access to the board of directors and the entity's management.

D. The audit committee is active in overseeing the entity's financial reporting policies.

Answer (A) is correct. *(CPA, adapted)*

**REQUIRED:** The characteristic most likely to increase the auditor's concern about fraud risk.

**DISCUSSION:** Certain risk factors are related to misstatements arising from fraudulent reporting. These factors may be grouped in three categories: (1) incentives/pressures, (2) opportunities, and (3) attitudes/rationalizations. One set of risk factors in the incentives/pressures category concerns threats to financial stability or profitability by economic, industry, or entity operating conditions, such as "significant declines in customer demand and increasing business failures in either industry or the overall economy" (AU 316).

Answer (B) is incorrect because failure to bond employees is a potential control weakness, but it may be compensated for. Answer (C) is incorrect because opportunities for fraudulent financial reporting are decreased when internal auditors have direct access to the board of directors. Answer (D) is incorrect because opportunities for fraudulent financial reporting are decreased when the audit committee is active in overseeing policies.

**54.** Which of the following circumstances most likely will cause an auditor to suspect that material misstatements exist in a client's financial statements?

A. The assumptions used in developing the prior year's accounting estimates have changed.

B. Differences between reconciliations of control accounts and subsidiary records are not investigated.

C. Negative confirmation requests yield fewer responses than in the prior year's audit.

D. Management consults with another CPA firm about complex accounting matters.

Answer (B) is correct. *(CPA, adapted)*

**REQUIRED:** The circumstances most likely causing an auditor to suspect that material misstatements exist in a client's financial statements.

**DISCUSSION:** Auditors must plan and perform audits to provide reasonable assurance about whether financial statements are free of material misstatements, whether caused by error or fraud. A deficiency in internal control is one of the risk factors that provides an opportunity for misstatements arising from fraudulent financial reporting or misappropriation of assets. For example, inadequate internal control may increase susceptibility to misappropriation of assets because of a lack of complete and timely reconciliation of assets.

Answer (A) is incorrect because the assumptions used in developing the prior year's accounting estimates are expected to change. Answer (C) is incorrect because a negative confirmation requests the recipient to respond only if (s)he disagrees with the information stated. A lower yield from such requests may simply indicate that control has improved and fewer balances are misstated. Answer (D) is incorrect because management's consultation with another CPA firm to obtain a second opinion about complex accounting matters is not necessarily an indicator of material misstatement. However, an auditor should communicate with the audit committee to discuss his/her views about those matters.

**55.** Which procedure must be performed during the planning stage of the audit concerning potential fraud?

A. Conduct discussions among the engagement personnel regarding the risks of material misstatement due to fraud.

B. Document the results of procedures used to address the risk of fraud.

C. Consider the characteristics of journal entries, particularly those made near year-end.

D. Consider whether estimates prepared and recorded by management could indicate a bias in reporting.

Answer (A) is correct. *(Publisher)*

**REQUIRED:** The procedure required during audit planning.

**DISCUSSION:** During planning, the key members of the audit team should discuss the potential for material misstatement due to fraud. The discussion should include (1) an exchange of ideas (brainstorming) concerning the susceptibility to fraud; (2) consideration of the entity's known fraud risk factors reflecting pressures/incentives to commit fraud, opportunities for fraud, and an environment that permits rationalization of fraud; and (3) an emphasis on the need to maintain professional skepticism.

Answer (B) is incorrect because the results of procedures are documented when evidence is collected. Answer (C) is incorrect because the auditor considers journal entries with characteristics indicative of fraud during evidence collection, not planning. Examples are entries (1) made to unrelated, unusual, or seldom-used accounts; (2) made by individuals who typically do not make journal entries; (3) recorded at the end of the period with no description; (4) made without account numbers during statement preparation; and (5) that include round numbers or a consistent ending number. Answer (D) is incorrect because estimates made by management are considered during evidence collection.

**56.** In every audit, the members of the audit team must discuss the potential for material misstatement due to fraud. This discussion

A. Must include all members of the audit team.

B. Includes brainstorming about how assets can be misappropriated.

C. Must be deferred until the auditor begins information-gathering procedures.

D. Normally excludes consideration of how fraud might be concealed.

Answer (B) is correct. *(Publisher)*

**REQUIRED:** The nature of the audit team's discussion of potential fraud.

**DISCUSSION:** Discussion among key engagement personnel about fraud risk is required. It should emphasize professional skepticism and continual alertness to potential fraud. The discussion may occur before or during information gathering, and communication should be ongoing. The discussion must include (1) brainstorming about factors that might create the conditions for fraud, (2) how and where the statements might be misstated, (3) how assets might be misappropriated or financial reports fraudulently misstated, (4) how fraud could be concealed, and (5) how the auditors might respond to fraud risk.

Answer (A) is incorrect because professional judgment should be exercised to determine the team members included. Answer (C) is incorrect because the discussion may be prior to or during information gathering to identify fraud risks. Answer (D) is incorrect because how fraud might be concealed is one topic covered when team members exchange ideas (brainstorm) about fraud.

**57.** Which of the following statements describes why a properly planned and performed audit may not detect a material misstatement due to fraud?

A. Audit procedures that are effective for detecting an error may be ineffective for detecting fraud that is concealed through collusion.

B. An audit is designed to provide reasonable assurance of detecting material errors, but there is no similar responsibility concerning material fraud.

C. The factors considered in assessing control risk indicated an increased risk of material misstatement due to fraud, but only a low risk of errors in the financial statements.

D. The auditor did not consider factors influencing audit risk for account balances that have effects pervasive to the financial statements taken as a whole.

Answer (A) is correct. *(CPA, adapted)*

**REQUIRED:** The reason a properly planned and performed audit may not detect a material fraud.

**DISCUSSION:** Absolute assurance is unattainable because of the characteristics of fraud and the limitations of audit evidence. Management may override controls in unpredictable ways or alter accounting records, and fraud may be concealed through collusion, falsifying documentation (including electronic approvals), or withholding evidence. Moreover, procedures that effectively detect an error (an unintentional misstatement) may not detect fraud (an intentional act that a perpetuation typically attempts to conceal).

Answer (B) is incorrect because the auditor's responsibility is the same for material misstatements due to fraud as for material errors. Answer (C) is incorrect because a properly planned and performed audit will result in a response to fraud risks that have been identified and assessed. Answer (D) is incorrect because an audit that is properly planned and performed should consider audit risk factors for accounts having pervasive effects on the statements.

**58.** During the consideration of fraud in a financial statement audit, the auditor should identify and assess risks that may result in material misstatements due to fraud. This assessment

A. Must state an overall judgment about whether an identified risk is high, medium, or low.

B. Requires an observation that the three fraud conditions are present.

C. Follows the auditor's determination that the entity's antifraud programs and controls are operating effectively.

D. Is based on evaluating whether the entity's antifraud programs and controls have been suitably designed and placed in operation.

Answer (D) is correct. *(Publisher)*

**REQUIRED:** The true statement about the assessment of identified fraud risks.

**DISCUSSION:** Identified fraud risks are assessed after the auditor's required evaluation of relevant antifraud programs and controls that relate to identified fraud risks. The entity may have broad programs or specific controls directed at specific risks. As part of the understanding of internal control, the auditor must evaluate whether programs and controls have been suitably designed and placed in operation. The auditor then determines whether the programs and controls reduce or increase the risks.

Answer (A) is incorrect because such an overall judgment is too broad to be useful. Answer (B) is incorrect because an auditor must not assume that failing to observe all three conditions signifies that no fraud risk is present. Answer (C) is incorrect because the assessment is made after evaluating whether antifraud programs and controls have been suitably designed and placed in operation.

**59.** In every audit, which of the following must be identified as a potential risk of material misstatement due to fraud?

A. Management override of controls.

B. Improper revenue recognition.

C. Collusion.

D. Falsification of documentation.

Answer (A) is correct. *(Publisher)*

**REQUIRED:** The potential fraud risk that must be identified in every audit.

**DISCUSSION:** The auditor must address the risk of management override of controls in all audits because of its unpredictability. Accordingly, even if specific fraud risks are not identified, the possibility of management override of controls is always deemed to exist. AU 316 states that the auditor's procedures "should address that risk apart from any conclusions regarding the existence of more specifically identifiable risks."

Answer (B) is incorrect because the auditor ordinarily assumes the existence of fraud risk relating to improper revenue recognition. If the assumption is rebuttable, the contrary conclusion must be documented. Answer (C) is incorrect because collusion is a means of concealing fraud, not a fraud risk required to be identified in every audit. Answer (D) is incorrect because falsification of documentation is a means of concealing fraud, not a fraud risk required to be identified in every audit.

**60.** If an independent audit leading to an opinion on financial statements causes the auditor to believe that a material misstatement due to fraud exists, (s)he should first

A. Consider the implications for other aspects of the audit and discuss the matter with appropriate levels of management.

B. Make the investigation necessary to determine whether fraud has actually occurred.

C. Request that management investigate to determine whether fraud has actually occurred.

D. Consider whether fraud was the result of a failure by employees to comply with existing controls.

Answer (A) is correct. *(CPA, adapted)*

**REQUIRED:** The appropriate action when the auditor believes that a material misstatement due to fraud exists.

**DISCUSSION:** The auditor should attempt to obtain additional evidence to determine whether material fraud has occurred or is likely to have occurred. (S)he then (1) considers the implications for other aspects of the audit; (2) discusses the matter with a level of management at least one level above those involved and with senior management; (3) attempts to obtain sufficient evidence to determine whether fraud exists; and (4), if appropriate, suggests that the client consult legal counsel (AU 316).

Answer (B) is incorrect because making the investigation necessary to determine whether fraud has actually occurred is not the first step to be taken when the auditor believes that material misstatement due to fraud exists. Answer (C) is incorrect because the auditor should not rely solely on management's investigation. Answer (D) is incorrect because considering whether fraud was the result of a failure by employees to comply with existing controls is not the first step to be taken.

**61.** Which of the following procedures will an auditor most likely perform when evaluating audit evidence at the completion of the audit?

A. Obtain assurance from the entity's attorney that all material litigation has been disclosed in the financial statements.

B. Verify the clerical accuracy of the entity's proof of cash and its bank cutoff statement.

C. Determine whether inadequate provisions for the safeguarding of assets have been corrected.

D. Consider whether the results of audit procedures affect the assessment of the identified risks of material misstatement due to fraud.

Answer (D) is correct. *(CPA, adapted)*

**REQUIRED:** The procedure most likely performed when evaluating audit evidence at the completion of the audit.

**DISCUSSION:** AU 316 states that the identified risks of material misstatement due to fraud must be specifically assessed. This assessment is ongoing. Thus, at the audit's conclusion, the results of the audit procedures and other observations should be evaluated to determine whether they alter the assessments. Furthermore, the auditor must evaluate whether analytical procedures performed as substantive tests or in the overall review indicate previously unidentified fraud risks.

Answer (A) is incorrect because obtaining assurances from the client's attorney is a procedure performed during the audit and therefore prior to its completion. Answer (B) is incorrect because conducting substantive tests of cash is a procedure performed during the audit and therefore prior to its completion. Answer (C) is incorrect because determining whether inadequate controls have been improved is a procedure performed during the audit and therefore prior to its completion.

**62.** Which of the following circumstances is most likely to cause an auditor to change an assessment of the risk of material misstatement of the financial statements due to fraud?

A. Property and equipment are usually sold at a loss before being fully depreciated.

B. Unusual discrepancies between the entity's records and confirmation replies.

C. Monthly bank reconciliations usually include several in-transit items.

D. Clerical errors are listed on a computer-generated exception report.

Answer (B) is correct. *(CPA, adapted)*

**REQUIRED:** The circumstance most likely to change an assessment of the risk of material misstatement due to fraud.

**DISCUSSION:** An auditor's assessment of fraud risks must be ongoing. Conditions may be encountered during the field work that support or change the auditor's judgments. An example of such a condition is "unusual discrepancies between the entity's records and confirmation replies" (AU 316).

Answer (A) is incorrect because sale at a loss before being fully depreciated suggests that the depreciation method is inadequate. Answer (C) is incorrect because in-transit items are normal. Answer (D) is incorrect because a listing of errors is an effective control.

**63.** Moor, CPA, discovers a likely fraud during an audit but concludes that its effects, if any, could not be so material as to affect the opinion. Moor should

A. Perform additional audit procedures to establish that fraud has occurred.

B. Report the finding to the appropriate representatives of the client with the recommendation that it be pursued to a conclusion.

C. Confer with the client about the additional audit procedures necessary to establish that fraud has occurred.

D. Notify the proper external authorities.

Answer (B) is correct. *(Publisher)*

**REQUIRED:** The auditor's proper action when suspected fraud is not so material as to affect the opinion.

**DISCUSSION:** The auditor should refer the matter of an immaterial fraud to an appropriate level of management. The appropriate level of management is at least one level above the highest level involved. However, any fraud involving senior management is reported to the audit committee. The auditor should also be satisfied that, in view of the organizational position of the likely perpetrator, the likely fraud has no implications for other aspects of the audit or that those implications have been adequately considered.

Answer (A) is incorrect because the auditor is not required to pursue immaterial errors. Answer (C) is incorrect because the auditor is not required to pursue fraud. Answer (D) is incorrect because the matter should be pursued with an appropriate level of management.

**64.** An auditor's consideration of the risk of material misstatement due to fraud and the results of audit tests indicate a significant risk of fraud. The auditor should

A. Express either a qualified or an adverse opinion.

B. Consider withdrawing from the engagement and communicating the reasons for withdrawal to the audit committee.

C. Express only an adverse opinion because of the strong possibility of fraud.

D. Inform proper authorities outside the entity.

Answer (B) is correct. *(Publisher)*

**REQUIRED:** The appropriate action by an auditor who has identified a significant risk of fraud.

**DISCUSSION:** If, after the application of appropriate procedures, the auditor is unable to conclude whether possible fraud may materially affect the financial statements, the auditor should consider withdrawing from the engagement and communicating his/her reasons to the audit committee or others with equivalent authority and responsibility. "Whether the auditor concludes that withdrawal from the engagement is appropriate may depend on (a) the implications about the integrity of management and (b) the diligence and cooperation of management or the board of directors in investigating the circumstances and taking appropriate action" (AU 316).

Answer (A) is incorrect because an adverse opinion is appropriate only when the financial statements are not fairly presented. Answer (C) is incorrect because an adverse opinion is appropriate only when the financial statements are not fairly presented. Answer (D) is incorrect because the auditor should communicate with an appropriate level of management and the audit committee.

**65.** Which of the following auditor concerns most likely could be so serious that the auditor concludes that a financial statement audit cannot be performed?

A. Management fails to modify prescribed internal controls for changes in information technology.

B. Internal control activities requiring segregation of duties are rarely monitored by management.

C. Management is dominated by one person who is also the majority shareholder.

D. There is a substantial risk of intentional misapplication of accounting principles.

Answer (D) is correct. *(CPA, adapted)*

**REQUIRED:** The auditor concern that is serious enough to lead the auditor to conclude that a financial statement audit cannot be performed.

**DISCUSSION:** According to AU 316, misstatements arising from fraudulent financial reporting are intentional misstatements or omissions to deceive financial statement users. The "intentional misapplication of accounting principles relating to amounts, classification, manner of presentation, or disclosure" is one such misstatement. The risk of material misstatement may be so significant that the auditor should consider withdrawing from the audit and notifying the audit committee.

Answer (A) is incorrect because a failure to modify prescribed internal controls does not necessarily indicate a lack of management integrity and require rejection of the engagement. However, the issue should be considered in assessing control risk. Answer (B) is incorrect because, depending on the nature of the duties, a lack of management monitoring does not necessarily indicate a lack of management integrity and require rejection of the engagement. However, the issue should be considered in assessing control risk. Answer (C) is incorrect because domination of management by a single individual without compensating controls, such as oversight by an active board of directors or audit committee, is a weakness in the control environment. However, it is not serious enough for the auditor to conclude that a financial statement audit cannot be performed.

**66.** Disclosure of possible fraud to parties other than the client's senior management and its audit committee ordinarily is not part of an auditor's responsibility. However, to which of the following outside parties may a duty to disclose possible fraud exist?

I. To the SEC when the client reports an auditor change

II. To a successor auditor when the successor makes appropriate inquiries

III. To a government funding agency from which the client receives financial assistance

A. I and II.

B. I and III.

C. II and III.

D. I, II, and III.

Answer (D) is correct. *(CPA, adapted)*

**REQUIRED:** The outside parties to whom a duty to disclose fraud exists.

**DISCUSSION:** A duty of disclosure to parties other than the client is imposed by a subpoena. It also may exist when the entity reports an auditor change to the SEC on Form 8-K; for example, the auditor may have withdrawn because the client failed to take appropriate remedial action, and the failure may be a "reportable event" or the source of a "disagreement." These requirements also apply to reports on material illegal acts that may be mandated by the Securities Exchange Act of 1934. Under AU 315, a predecessor auditor must respond promptly and fully, except in unusual circumstances, to inquiries by a successor if the prospective client gives its specific permission. Under *Government Auditing Standards*, an auditor may have a duty to report fraud directly if it involves assistance received from a governmental agency. For example, when management has not taken remedial action and the auditee does not report the fraud as soon as practicable to the entity that provided the assistance, the auditor must report the matter to that entity.

**67.** Which of the following must an auditor document with respect to the consideration of fraud in a financial statement audit?

A. Reasons for not identifying management override as a fraud risk.

B. Results of the retrospective review of accounting estimates for all years presented in the comparative statements.

C. Instances of the auditor's exercise of professional skepticism during the consideration of fraud.

D. Reasons for not identifying improper revenue recognition as a fraud risk.

Answer (D) is correct. *(Publisher)*

**REQUIRED:** The item that must be documented.

**DISCUSSION:** The auditor must document the following: (1) planning-stage discussions among the audit team about fraud risks, including how and when they occurred, the participants, and the subject matter; (2) procedures to obtain information to identify and assess fraud risks; (3) specifically identified fraud risks; (4) the response to those risks; (5) reasons in a given situation for not identifying improper revenue recognition as a fraud risk; (6) results of procedures for further addressing the risk of management override of controls; (7) other conditions and analytical relationships leading to further audit procedures and other responses; (8) those responses deemed to be appropriate with respect to the other conditions, etc.; and (9) fraud communications to management, the audit committee, and others.

Answer (A) is incorrect because management override is always identified as a fraud risk. Answer (B) is incorrect because the required retrospective review applies only to the prior year's significant accounting estimates. Answer (C) is incorrect because the auditor approaches every aspect of the audit with professional skepticism. Hence, specific, separate documentation of its exercise is not required.

**68.** Which of the following statements concerning illegal acts by clients is true?

A. An auditor's responsibility for material misstatements caused by illegal acts that have a direct and material effect on the financial statements is the same as that for errors and fraud.

B. An audit in accordance with auditing standards normally includes audit procedures specifically designed to detect illegal acts that have an indirect but material effect on the financial statements.

C. An auditor considers illegal acts from the perspective of the reliability of management's representations rather than their relation to audit objectives derived from financial statement assertions.

D. An auditor has no responsibility to detect illegal acts by clients that have an indirect effect on the financial statements.

Answer (A) is correct. *(CPA, adapted)*

**REQUIRED:** The true statement concerning illegal acts.

**DISCUSSION:** "The auditor has a responsibility to plan and perform the audit to provide reasonable assurance about whether the financial statements are free of material misstatement, whether caused by error or fraud" (AU 110). This standard also applies to illegal acts that have a direct and material effect on the financial statements.

Answer (B) is incorrect because certain illegal acts "relate more to an entity's operating aspects than to its financial and accounting aspects, and their financial statement effect is indirect." An audit in accordance with auditing standards is usually not specifically designed to detect illegal acts that have such indirect effects. Answer (C) is incorrect because the auditor considers illegal acts "from the perspective of their known relation to audit objectives derived from financial statement assertions rather than from the perspective of legality per se" (AU 317). Answer (D) is incorrect because, if illegal acts come to the auditor's attention, (s)he must undertake appropriate procedures. Absent such evidence, the auditor must make inquiries about compliance with laws and regulations and obtain written representations from management.

**69.** An auditor's document includes the following:

"Our audit is subject to the risk that errors, fraud, or illegal acts, including defalcations, if they exist, will not be detected. However, we will inform you of any such matters that come to our attention."

The above passage is most likely from

A. The explanatory paragraph of a "subject to" qualified auditor's report.

B. An engagement letter.

C. The explanatory paragraph of a compliance report on a government entity subject to GAO standards.

D. A comfort letter.

Answer (B) is correct. *(CPA, adapted)*

**REQUIRED:** The likely source of the quoted language.

**DISCUSSION:** The primary purpose of an engagement letter is to provide a written record of the agreement with the client as to the services to be provided by the auditor. It sets forth the rights and obligations under the contract between the client and the auditor. An engagement letter should also state the nature of the audit. Although not required by auditing standards, engagement letters are highly recommended.

Answer (A) is incorrect because "subject to" opinions may not be expressed (AU 508). Answer (C) is incorrect because an explanatory paragraph would contain specific information about compliance by the audited entity. Answer (D) is incorrect because a comfort letter, for example, one addressed to underwriters, is based on a review, not an audit.

**70.** The most likely reason an audit cannot reasonably be expected to bring all illegal acts by the client to the auditor's attention is that

A. Illegal acts are perpetrated by management override of the information and communication component of internal control.

B. Illegal acts by clients often relate to operating aspects rather than accounting aspects.

C. The information and communication component of the client's internal control procedures may be so effective that the auditor performs only minimal substantive testing.

D. Illegal acts may be perpetrated by the only person in the client's organization with access to both assets and the accounting records.

Answer (B) is correct. *(CPA, adapted)*

**REQUIRED:** The most likely reason an audit is not expected to detect all client illegal acts.

**DISCUSSION:** AU 317 states that some illegal acts, such as violations of tax law, have a direct and material effect on the financial statements. Other illegal acts, such as violations of environmental protection laws, "relate more to an entity's operating aspects than to its financial and accounting aspects, and their financial statement effect is indirect." An audit in accordance with auditing standards usually does not include audit procedures specifically designed to detect illegal acts that have such indirect effects.

Answer (A) is incorrect because many illegal acts are not subject to internal control; e.g., violations of insider trading rules may result from transactions that are recorded appropriately. Answer (C) is incorrect because illegal acts may involve matters outside the information and communication component so that even extensive substantive tests would not detect them. Answer (D) is incorrect because illegal acts may not involve manipulation of records.

**71.** Jones, CPA, is auditing the financial statements of XYZ Retailing, Inc. What assurance does Jones provide that direct-effect illegal acts that are material to XYZ's financial statements, and illegal acts that have a material but indirect effect on the financial statements, will be detected?

| | Direct-Effect Illegal Acts | Indirect-Effect Illegal Acts |
|---|---|---|
| A. | Reasonable | None |
| B. | Reasonable | Reasonable |
| C. | Limited | None |
| D. | Limited | Reasonable |

Answer (A) is correct. *(CPA, adapted)*

**REQUIRED:** The auditor assurance provided in connection with a client's potential illegal acts.

**DISCUSSION:** "The auditor has a responsibility to plan and perform the audit to provide reasonable assurance about whether the financial statements are free of material misstatement, whether caused by error or fraud" (AU 110). This standard also applies to illegal acts that have a direct and material effect on the financial statements. However, because of the nature of illegal acts that have an indirect effect on the financial statements, "an audit made in accordance with auditing standards provides no assurance that illegal acts will be detected or that any contingent liabilities that may result will be disclosed" (AU 317).

**72.** Some illegal acts (such as violations of the Occupational Safety and Health Act) relate to operating aspects of an entity more than to its financial or accounting aspects. In a financial statement audit,

A. Regular audit procedures can reasonably be expected to detect these acts.

B. The auditor should contact appropriate enforcement agencies.

C. The auditor should inquire of management about violations of laws and regulations.

D. Violations of laws having indirect effects on the financial statements are not of interest to the auditor.

Answer (C) is correct. *(Publisher)*

**REQUIRED:** The auditor's responsibility for illegal acts relating to operating aspects of an entity.

**DISCUSSION:** In the absence of evidence concerning illegal acts that have a material but indirect effect on financial statements, an audit in accordance with auditing standards will customarily not include procedures specifically designed to detect such acts. However, in an audit of financial statements presented in accordance with GAAP, the auditor should obtain specific written representations from management concerning "violations or possible violations of laws or regulations whose effects should be considered for disclosure in the financial statements or as a basis for recording a loss contingency" (AU 333).

Answer (A) is incorrect because the audit cannot be expected to detect all illegal acts. Answer (B) is incorrect because the auditor is customarily not responsible for contacting outside agencies either in search of or to disclose illegal acts. Answer (D) is incorrect because illegal acts relating to operating aspects of an entity are of interest to the auditor. They bear upon the integrity of management and may materially affect the financial statements.

**73.** When an auditor becomes aware of a possible client illegal act, the auditor should obtain an understanding of the nature of the act to

A. Consider whether other similar acts have occurred.

B. Recommend remedial actions to the audit committee.

C. Evaluate the effect on the financial statements.

D. Determine the reliability of management's representations.

Answer (C) is correct. *(CPA, adapted)*

**REQUIRED:** The reason the auditor obtains an understanding of the nature of a possible illegal act.

**DISCUSSION:** AU 317 states that when the auditor becomes aware of information concerning a possible illegal act, the auditor should obtain an understanding of the nature of the act, the circumstances in which it occurred, and sufficient other information to evaluate the effect on the financial statements. The auditor's ultimate purpose is to form an opinion on the fairness of the financial statements.

Answer (A) is incorrect because the auditor may consider whether other similar acts have occurred when applying any additional procedures necessary to obtain further understanding of the nature of the act. Answer (B) is incorrect because the auditor should communicate with the audit committee with respect to a discovered illegal act, but this purpose is a secondary objective of the audit. Answer (D) is incorrect because, if the auditor determines that an illegal act has occurred (s)he should assess the effects on the representations of management in other areas of the audit.

**74.** During the annual audit of Ajax Corp., a publicly held company, Jones, CPA, a continuing auditor, determined that illegal political contributions had been made during each of the past 7 years, including the year under audit. Jones notified the board of directors about the illegal contributions, but they refused to take any action because the amounts involved were immaterial to the financial statements. Jones should reconsider the intended degree of reliance to be placed on the

A. Letter of audit inquiry to the client's attorney.

B. Prior years' audit programs.

C. Management representation letter.

D. Preliminary judgment about materiality levels.

Answer (C) is correct. *(CPA, adapted)*

**REQUIRED:** The effect on the auditor of the client's failure to take corrective action for an illegal act.

**DISCUSSION:** Under AU 317, if the client does not take the remedial action considered necessary by the auditor, the auditor should consider withdrawal from the engagement even when the illegal act is not material. (S)he should weigh the effects on his/her ability to rely on management's representations and the possible results of continued association with the client. The auditor may also wish to seek legal advice.

Answer (A) is incorrect because the letter of audit inquiry to the client's attorney will be responded to by the client's attorney, not the client. Answer (B) is incorrect because the prior years' audit programs will not be relied upon in the current audit. Answer (D) is incorrect because the results of the acts have been judged immaterial to the financial statements, and no reconsideration is necessary.

**75.** An auditor concludes that a client has committed an illegal act that has not been properly accounted for or disclosed. The auditor should withdraw from the engagement if the

A. Auditor is precluded from obtaining sufficient competent evidence about the illegal act.

B. Illegal act has an effect on the financial statements that is both material and direct.

C. Auditor cannot reasonably estimate the effect of the illegal act on the financial statements.

D. Illegal act has a material effect on the financial statements, and the client refuses to accept the auditor's report as modified for the illegal act.

Answer (D) is correct. *(CPA, adapted)*

**REQUIRED:** The situation in which the auditor should withdraw from the engagement.

**DISCUSSION:** When an auditor concludes that a client has committed an illegal act that has not been properly accounted for or disclosed and the client refuses to accept the auditor's report as modified, "the auditor should withdraw from the engagement and indicate the reasons for withdrawal in writing to the audit committee or board of directors" (AU 317).

Answer (A) is incorrect because, if the auditor is precluded from obtaining sufficient competent evidence about an illegal act, a disclaimer should be issued. Answer (B) is incorrect because the auditor should express a qualified or adverse opinion if financial statements are not fairly presented. Answer (C) is incorrect because, if an auditor cannot reasonably estimate the effect of an illegal act on the financial statements, but no scope limitation or departure from GAAP exists, (s)he should consider either disclaiming an opinion or including an explanatory paragraph in a report expressing an unqualified opinion.

**76.** If the auditor considers an illegal act to be sufficiently serious to warrant withdrawing from the engagement, the auditor will likely

A. Notify all parties who may rely upon the company's financial statements of the company's illegal act.

B. Consult with legal counsel as to what other action, if any, should be taken.

C. Return all incriminating evidence and audit documentation to the client's audit committee for follow-up.

D. Contact the successor auditor to make the successor aware of the possible consequences of relying on management's representations.

Answer (B) is correct. *(CPA, adapted)*

**REQUIRED:** The action by an auditor who withdraws as a result of an illegal act.

**DISCUSSION:** According to AU 317, the auditor should consider consulting legal counsel in these circumstances. Such consultation may be necessary in assessing the effects of continued association with the client or determining whether the auditor may have a duty to notify parties outside the client that overrides his/her duty of confidentiality to the client.

Answer (A) is incorrect because notifying others is the responsibility of management. Answer (C) is incorrect because the auditor has no responsibility to return all incriminating evidence and audit documentation to the client's audit committee for follow-up. Answer (D) is incorrect because the successor auditor, with client approval, has the burden of initiating communication with the predecessor.

**77.** Under the Private Securities Litigation Reform Act of 1995, Baker, CPA, reported certain uncorrected illegal acts to Supermart's board of directors. Baker believed that failure to take remedial action would warrant a qualified audit opinion because the illegal acts had a material effect on Supermart's financial statements. Supermart failed to take appropriate remedial action, and the board of directors refused to inform the SEC that it had received such notification from Baker. Under these circumstances, Baker is required to

A. Resign from the audit engagement within ten business days.

B. Deliver a report concerning the illegal acts to the SEC within one business day.

C. Notify the shareholders that the financial statements are materially misstated.

D. Withhold an audit opinion until Supermart takes appropriate remedial action.

Answer (B) is correct. *(CPA, adapted)*

**REQUIRED:** The requirements under the Private Securities Litigation Reform Act of 1995.

**DISCUSSION:** Disclosure of illegal acts to outside parties is not normally the auditor's responsibility. However, under the Private Securities Litigation Reform Act of 1995, accountants must report illegal acts to the appropriate level of management and the audit committee unless they are clearly inconsequential. If senior management and the board fail to take action on reported material illegal acts, and this failure will result in a departure from a standard report or resignation from the audit, the accountants should report their conclusions to the board immediately. The board must then, within 1 business day, notify the SEC. If the accountants do not receive a copy of the notice within the 1-day period, they must furnish the SEC with a copy of their report within 1 business day.

Answer (A) is incorrect because the auditor is not required to resign from the engagement. Answer (C) is incorrect because a qualified audit opinion states that, except for the effects of the matter to which the qualification relates, the financial statements are presented fairly in all material respects. Any other notice to the shareholders is not required. Answer (D) is incorrect because the auditor should express a qualified opinion if it is justified by the lack of remedial action. Auditing standards do not provide for a delay in the report until remedial action is taken.

## 2.5 Working Papers and Documentation

**78.** The primary purpose of an internal auditor's working papers is to

A. Provide documentation of the planning and execution of engagement procedures performed.

B. Serve as a means with which to prepare the financial statements.

C. Document weaknesses in internal control with recommendations to management for improvement.

D. Comply with the International Standards for the Professional Practice of Internal Auditing.

Answer (A) is correct. *(CIA, adapted)*

**REQUIRED:** The primary purpose of an internal auditor's working papers.

**DISCUSSION:** Working papers provide the principal support for the engagement communications; aid in planning, performing, and reviewing the engagement; document whether engagement objectives were achieved; facilitate third-party review; provide a basis for evaluating the internal audit activity's quality program; aid in the professional development of the internal auditing staff; provide support in the event of fraud, litigation, insurance claims, etc.; and demonstrate compliance with the International IIA Standards (Practice Advisory 2330-1).

Answer (B) is incorrect because working papers do not provide the means for preparation of the financial statements. Answer (C) is incorrect because documentation of control weaknesses is only one example of working paper content, not the primary purpose for them. Answer (D) is incorrect because the preparation of adequate working papers is a requirement of the Standards but not the primary purpose for their existence.

**79.** Which of the following documentation is not required for an audit in accordance with auditing standards?

A. A written audit program setting forth the procedures necessary to accomplish the audit's objectives.

B. An indication that the accounting records agree or reconcile with the financial statements.

C. A client engagement letter that summarizes the timing and details of the auditor's planned field work.

D. The basis for the auditor's conclusions when the assessed level of control risk is below the maximum level.

Answer (C) is correct. *(CPA, adapted)*

**REQUIRED:** The documentation not required for an audit.

**DISCUSSION:** Although highly recommended, a client engagement letter is not required in an audit or any other engagement.

Answer (A) is incorrect because a written audit program is required by AU 311, *Planning and Supervision.* Answer (B) is incorrect because the audit documentation should demonstrate that the accounting records agree or reconcile with the financial statements. Answer (D) is incorrect because AU 319 requires the auditor to document the basis for the auditor's conclusions when the assessed level of control risk is below the maximum.

**80.** Audit documentation that records the procedures used by the auditor to gather evidence should be

A. Considered the primary support for the financial statements being audited.

B. Viewed as the connecting link between the books of account and the financial statements.

C. Designed to meet the circumstances of the particular engagement.

D. Destroyed when the audited entity ceases to be a client.

Answer (C) is correct. *(CPA, adapted)*

**REQUIRED:** The true statement concerning audit documentation.

**DISCUSSION:** AU 339 states that audit documentation should be designed to meet the circumstances of a particular engagement. Audit documentation serves mainly to provide the principal support for the auditor's report, including the representation regarding observance of the standards of field work, which is implied by the reference to auditing standards in the report.

Answer (A) is incorrect because the financial statements are primarily supported by the client's accounting records. Answer (B) is incorrect because working papers are not a part of, or a substitute for, the client's accounting records. Answer (D) is incorrect because the auditor should retain audit documentation for a period sufficient to meet the needs of his/her practice (AU 339). For public clients, audit documentation must be retained for at least 7 years (AS No. 3).

**81.** The PCAOB's AS No. 3, *Audit Documentation*, requires that a complete and final set of audit documentation be assembled for retention as of a date not more than 45 days after the audit report release date. After that date

A. Audit documentation may be deleted or discarded, but no information may be added.

B. Audit documentation may be added, but no audit documentation may be deleted or discarded.

C. No audit documentation may be deleted, discarded, or added.

D. Audit documentation may be deleted, discarded, or added as necessary.

Answer (B) is correct. *(Publisher)*

**REQUIRED:** Audit documentation responsibilities after the finalization date.

**DISCUSSION:** Circumstances may require additions to audit documentation after the report release date, for example, discovery of an audit issue after the financial statements have been issued. Any documentation added must indicate the date the information was added, the person who added it, and the reason for adding it. However, no audit documentation may be deleted or discarded after the document finalization date.

**82.** An auditor's working papers will ordinarily be least likely to include documentation showing how the

A. Client's schedules were prepared.

B. Engagement was planned.

C. Understanding of the client's internal control was obtained and control risk was assessed.

D. Unusual matters were resolved.

Answer (A) is correct. *(CPA, adapted)*

**REQUIRED:** The item least likely to be documented in the auditor's working papers.

**DISCUSSION:** AU 339 states that the audit documentation should demonstrate that (1) the engagement was adequately planned and supervised, (2) an understanding of internal control was obtained and control risk was assessed, and (3) sufficient competent evidence was obtained to afford a reasonable basis for an opinion. Documentation of the preparation of clients' schedules is not necessary because the schedules themselves represent how they were prepared.

Answer (B) is incorrect because the working papers show how the engagement was planned. Answer (C) is incorrect because the working papers show how the understanding of the client's internal control was obtained and control risk was assessed. Answer (D) is incorrect because the working papers show how unusual matters were resolved.

**83.** Which of the following is usually included or shown in the audit documentation?

A. The procedures used by the auditor to verify the personal financial status of members of the client's management team.

B. Analyses that are designed to be a part of, or a substitute for, the client's accounting records.

C. Excerpts from authoritative pronouncements that support the underlying generally accepted accounting principles used in preparing the financial statements.

D. The manner in which exceptions and unusual matters disclosed by the auditor's procedures were resolved or treated.

Answer (D) is correct. *(CPA, adapted)*

**REQUIRED:** The component of audit documentation.

**DISCUSSION:** The audit documentation should include information showing that the audit was properly planned and supervised, an understanding of internal control was obtained, control risk was assessed, and sufficient competent evidence was obtained to afford a reasonable basis for an opinion. All exceptions and unusual matters should be followed up, with the resolution or treatment included in the audit documentation. Management is responsible for making adjustments to correct material misstatements and for affirming to the auditor that the effects of uncorrected misstatements are immaterial, individually and in the aggregate (AU 310).

Answer (A) is incorrect because, although the auditor should consider incentives or pressures for the client's management to commit fraud, the personal financial status of managers is normally not verified. Answer (B) is incorrect because, as AU 339 notes, the audit documentation is not to be regarded as a part of, or a substitute for, the client's accounting records. Answer (C) is incorrect because management, not the auditor, must document and support the general acceptability of the accounting principles used by the client.

**84.** Although the quantity and content of audit documentation varies with each particular engagement, an auditor's permanent files most likely include

A. Schedules that support the current year's adjusting entries.

B. Prior years' accounts receivable confirmations that were classified as exceptions.

C. Documentation indicating that the audit work was adequately planned and supervised.

D. Analyses of capital stock and other equity accounts.

Answer (D) is correct. *(CPA, adapted)*

**REQUIRED:** The component of the permanent section of the audit documentation.

**DISCUSSION:** The permanent section of the audit documentation usually contains copies of important company documents. It may include the articles of incorporation, stock options, contracts, and bylaws; the engagement letter, which is the contract between the auditor and the client; analyses from previous audits of accounts of special importance to the auditor, such as long-term debt, PP&E, and equity; and information concerning internal control, e.g., flowcharts, organization charts, and questionnaires.

Answer (A) is incorrect because the schedules are included in the current files. Answer (B) is incorrect because confirmations are included in the current files. Answer (C) is incorrect because documentation indicating that the audit work was adequately planned and supervised is always included in the current files.

**85.** Audit working papers are indexed by means of reference numbers. The primary purpose of indexing is to

A. Permit cross-referencing and simplify supervisory review.

B. Support the audit report.

C. Eliminate the need for follow-up reviews.

D. Determine that working papers adequately support findings, conclusions, and reports.

Answer (A) is correct. *(CIA, adapted)*

**REQUIRED:** The primary purpose of indexing.

**DISCUSSION:** Indexing permits cross-referencing, which is important because it simplifies supervisory review either during the audit or subsequently by creating an audit trail of related items through the working papers. It thus facilitates preparation of the final report, later audits of the same auditee, and peer review.

Answer (B) is incorrect because the working papers as a whole should support the audit report. Answer (C) is incorrect because follow-up is necessitated by the auditee conditions, not the state of working papers. Answer (D) is incorrect because determining that working papers adequately support findings, conclusions, and reports is the purpose of supervisory review.

**86.** The audit working paper that reflects the major components of an amount reported in the financial statements is the

A. Interbank transfer schedule.

B. Carryforward schedule.

C. Supporting schedule.

D. Lead schedule.

Answer (D) is correct. *(CPA, adapted)*

**REQUIRED:** The working paper that reflects the major components of a financial statement amount.

**DISCUSSION:** Lead schedules help to eliminate detail from the auditor's working trial balance by classifying and summarizing similar or related items that are contained on the supporting schedules. A lead schedule contains the detailed accounts from the general ledger making up the line item total in the financial statements; e.g., the cash account might consist of petty cash, cash-general, cash-payroll, etc. Lead schedules and other elements of working papers should be cross-referenced.

Answer (A) is incorrect because an interbank transfer schedule is a working paper prepared for several days before and after the period under audit to determine that both parts of these transactions are recorded in the same period and in the appropriate period. Answer (B) is incorrect because a carryforward schedule is a continuing schedule of an account with a balance carried forward in the permanent file. Answer (C) is incorrect because supporting schedules provide details aggregated in the lead schedule.

**87.** An auditor ordinarily uses a working trial balance resembling the financial statements without footnotes, but containing columns for

A. Cash flow increases and decreases.

B. Audit objectives and assertions.

C. Reclassifications and adjustments.

D. Reconciliations and tickmarks.

Answer (C) is correct. *(CPA, adapted)*

**REQUIRED:** The columns contained on a working trial balance in the auditor's working papers.

**DISCUSSION:** A working trial balance is ordinarily used to record the year-end ledger balances prior to audit in the auditor's working papers. Reclassifications and adjustments are accumulated on the trial balance to reflect the final audited balances.

Answer (A) is incorrect because cash flow increases or decreases are reflected on the client's statement of cash flows. Answer (B) is incorrect because the audit objectives and tests of management's assertions are determined in the planning stage of the audit and reflected in the audit documentation. Answer (D) is incorrect because the working trial balance has no column for reconciliations and tickmarks.

**88.** In the course of the audit of financial statements for the purpose of expressing an opinion, the auditor will normally prepare a schedule of unadjusted differences for which (s)he did not propose adjustment when they were uncovered. The primary purpose served by this schedule is to

A. Point out to the responsible client officials the errors made by various company personnel.

B. Summarize the adjustments that must be made before the company can prepare and submit its federal tax return.

C. Identify the potential financial statement effects of errors or disputed items that were considered immaterial when discovered.

D. Summarize the errors made by the company so that corrections can be made after the audited financial statements are released.

Answer (C) is correct. *(CPA, adapted)*

**REQUIRED:** The purpose of the schedule of unadjusted differences for which the auditor did not propose adjustments.

**DISCUSSION:** The schedule of unadjusted differences identifies for management and the auditor the potential cumulative financial statement effect of errors or disputed items that were considered immaterial when discovered. The individual unadjusted differences may become material when viewed collectively. A summary of uncorrected misstatements is required to be included in or attached to the management representation letter with an acknowledgment by management that any uncorrected misstatements are immaterial. Moreover, the auditor must document (1) the nature and effect of the aggregated misstatements and (2) the conclusion about the aggregation material misstatement.

Answer (A) is incorrect because detection of errors by specific employees is not the primary purpose of the schedule. Answer (B) is incorrect because the unadjusted (immaterial) differences normally are not corrected for tax purposes. Answer (D) is incorrect because unadjusted items were judged immaterial and thus do not require correction. If corrections are necessary, i.e., if the collective unadjusted differences are material, the corrections should be made before the financial statements are released.

**89.** A difference of opinion concerning accounting and auditing matters relative to a particular phase of the audit arises between an assistant auditor and the auditor responsible for the engagement. After appropriate consultation, the assistant auditor asks to be dissociated from the resolution of the matter. The audit documentation would probably be

A. Silent on the matter because it is an internal matter of the auditing firm.

B. Expanded to note that the assistant auditor is completely dissociated from responsibility for the auditor's opinion.

C. Expanded to document the additional work required because all disagreements of this type will require expanded substantive testing.

D. Expanded to document the assistant auditor's position and the manner in which the difference of opinion was resolved.

Answer (D) is correct. *(CPA, adapted)*

**REQUIRED:** The proper action when the auditor and an assistant have a difference of opinion.

**DISCUSSION:** AU 311 states that differences of opinion concerning accounting and auditing issues should be included in the audit documentation, describing both the details of the disagreement and the basis for the resolution. The PCAOB's AS No. 3, *Audit Documentation*, requires working papers to document significant findings which include "Disagreements among members of the engagement team or with others consulted on the engagement about final conclusions reached on significant accounting or auditing matters."

Answer (A) is incorrect because auditing standards require documentation of the dispute and its resolution. Answer (B) is incorrect because the audit documentation should describe the assistant's position. Answer (C) is incorrect because not all disagreements require expanded testing.

**90.** An auditor who has accepted an engagement to audit financial statements wishes to review the predecessor's audit documentation. Such a review is

A. Permitted if the client and the predecessor auditor consent.

B. Permitted if the successor auditor refers in the audit report to the predecessor auditor's report and work.

C. Required if the successor auditor is to express an unqualified opinion.

D. Not permitted because the successor auditor should be independent.

Answer (A) is correct. *(Publisher)*

**REQUIRED:** The appropriate action concerning the review of a predecessor's audit documentation.

**DISCUSSION:** AU 315 states that the predecessor customarily makes him/herself available to the successor and makes available for review certain parts of the audit documentation. However, the successor should request that the client authorize such access to the predecessor's audit documentation, and the predecessor may want to request a consent and acknowledgment letter from the client to document this authorization. Moreover, the extent, if any, of the access allowed by the predecessor to the audit documentation is a matter of judgment.

Answer (B) is incorrect because referring to the work of the predecessor auditor as part of the basis for the successor auditor's opinion is an unacceptable practice. Answer (C) is incorrect because the successor is only required to inquire of the predecessor concerning information that will assist the successor in deciding whether to accept the engagement. Answer (D) is incorrect because reviewing the predecessor's audit documentation is not considered to affect the successor auditor's independence.

**91.** Which of the following analyses appearing in a predecessor's audit documentation is the successor auditor least likely to be interested in reviewing?

A. Analysis of noncurrent balance sheet accounts.

B. Analysis of current balance sheet accounts.

C. Analysis of contingencies.

D. Analysis of income statement accounts.

Answer (D) is correct. *(CPA, adapted)*

**REQUIRED:** The analysis from a predecessor's audit documentation in which a successor would be least interested.

**DISCUSSION:** The predecessor's analyses of balance sheet accounts, both current and noncurrent, and those relating to contingencies are of primary interest to the successor auditor because the successor must satisfy him/herself as to the reasonableness of the beginning balances. Analyses of income statement accounts are not needed because they have no beginning balances.

Answer (A) is incorrect because analyses of noncurrent balance sheet accounts reflect concern about beginning balances. Answer (B) is incorrect because analyses of current balance sheet accounts reflect concern about beginning balances. Answer (C) is incorrect because analyses of contingencies reflect concern about beginning balances.

**92.** Using personal computers in auditing may affect the methods used to review the work of staff assistants because

A. The audit field work standards for supervision may differ.

B. Documenting the supervisory review may require assistance of consulting services personnel.

C. Supervisory personnel may not have an understanding of the capabilities and limitations of personal computers.

D. Working paper documentation may not contain readily observable details of calculations.

Answer (D) is correct. *(CPA, adapted)*

**REQUIRED:** The reason using personal computers may affect the review of the work of staff assistants.

**DISCUSSION:** The first standard of field work requires assistants to be properly supervised. Thus, the "work performed by each assistant should be reviewed to determine whether it was adequately performed and to evaluate whether the results are consistent with the conclusions to be presented in the auditor's report" (AU 311). With the introduction of computers, accountants have been able to perform fewer manual calculations. Usually, the necessary numbers are entered into computer spreadsheets, and the answer is produced. Thus, the review of a staff assistant's work performed with a computer is different from that required when calculations are done manually.

Answer (A) is incorrect because the audit field work standards for supervision are the same whether or not a computer is used. Answer (B) is incorrect because audit staff typically have skills appropriate for the use of personal computers in documenting the work product of the audit. Answer (C) is incorrect because supervisors of the audit staff typically have the skills to evaluate the appropriate use of personal computers.

**93.** When reviewing engagement working papers, the primary responsibility of a supervisor of an auditing engagement is to determine that

A. Each worksheet is properly identified with a descriptive heading.

B. Working papers are properly referenced and kept in logical groupings.

C. Standard internal audit activity procedures are adhered to with regard to working paper preparation and technique.

D. Working papers adequately support the engagement observations, conclusions, and recommendations.

Answer (D) is correct. *(CIA, adapted)*

**REQUIRED:** The primary responsibility of an engagement supervisor when reviewing engagement working papers.

**DISCUSSION:** Engagement supervision includes reviewing all engagement working papers to ensure that they properly support engagement communications (Practice Advisory 2340-1). Engagement communications include observations, conclusions, and recommendations. This review is of primary importance because nothing reduces the credibility of an internal audit activity as much as ineptly developed engagement observations that collapse under attack.

Answer (A) is incorrect because descriptive headings are appropriate subjects for review, but they are not of primary importance. Answer (B) is incorrect because proper referencing and logical grouping are appropriate subjects for review, but they are not of primary importance. Answer (C) is incorrect because adherence to procedures is an appropriate subject for review, but it is not of primary importance.

**94.** Standardized working papers are often used, chiefly because they allow working papers to be prepared more

A. Efficiently.

B. Professionally.

C. Neatly.

D. Accurately.

Answer (A) is correct. *(CIA, adapted)*

**REQUIRED:** The reason for standardized working papers.

**DISCUSSION:** Use of standardized (pro forma) working papers improves audit efficiency by diminishing the time spent in their preparation. For example, standard forms may be developed for the audit program listing, records of the results of interviews, and worksheets.

Answer (B) is incorrect because standard forms do not necessarily result in greater professionalism. Answer (C) is incorrect because standard forms clearly reduce time spent in working paper preparation but do not necessarily result in greater neatness. Answer (D) is incorrect because standard forms do not necessarily result in greater accuracy.

**95.** After field work audit procedures are completed, a partner of the CPA firm who has not been involved in the audit performs a second or wrap-up working paper review. This second review usually focuses on

A. The fair presentation of the financial statements in conformity with GAAP.

B. Fraud involving the client's management and its employees.

C. The materiality of the adjusting entries proposed by the audit staff.

D. The communication of internal control weaknesses to the client's audit committee.

Answer (A) is correct. *(CPA, adapted)*

**REQUIRED:** The purpose of a second review by an audit partner.

**DISCUSSION:** Analytical procedures are required in an overall review and are typically performed by an audit partner. The purpose of these procedures is to assist the auditor in assessing the conclusions reached and in the evaluation of the overall financial statement presentation (AU 329). If the firm is a member of the SEC Practice Section of the Division for CPA Firms, a concurring review of the audit report and the financial statements is required. The reviewer must be a partner other than the audit partner-in-charge of an SEC engagement. In accordance with the Sarbanes-Oxley Act of 2002, these partners (and certain others) must be rotated every 5 years.

Answer (B) is incorrect because fraud involving the client's management and its employees is a matter to be resolved by the audit team. Answer (C) is incorrect because the materiality of the adjusting entries proposed by the audit staff is a matter to be resolved by the audit team. Answer (D) is incorrect because communication of reportable conditions is performed by the supervisor in charge of the audit.

# STUDY UNIT THREE
# INTERNAL CONTROL



The AICPA pronouncement on internal control is AU 319, *Consideration of Internal Control in a Financial Statement Audit*. This pronouncement defines concepts and terminology relevant to internal control and the assessment of control risk, including the second standard of field work:

> A sufficient understanding of internal control is to be obtained to plan the audit and to determine the nature, timing, and extent of tests to be performed.

AU 319 incorporates the management assertions model and the audit risk model developed in AU 326, *Evidential Matter*, and AU 312, *Audit Risk and Materiality*, respectively, into the standards on internal control.

The PCAOB's Auditing Standard No. 2, *An Audit of Internal Control over Financial Reporting Performed in Conjunction with an Audit of Financial Statements*, establishes requirements for firms ("issuers") subject to the reporting requirements of the Securities Exchange Act of 1934. The auditor's objective in an audit of internal control over financial reporting is to express an opinion on management's assessment of internal control.

Both AU 319 and AS No. 2 incorporate the concepts in the report on internal control issued by the Committee of Sponsoring Organizations (COSO) of the Commission on Fraudulent Financial Reporting. This document, *Internal Control -- Integrated Framework*, establishes definitions of internal control and of the components of internal control.

This chapter contains questions on the definitions of the components of internal control relevant to an audit of financial statements, the consideration of that internal control, and the controls relevant to the various accounting cycles. Additional questions relating to reporting on internal control are presented in Study Unit 8 (Subunit 8.5).

## QUESTIONS

### 3.1 Definition and Overview of Internal Control

**1.** Directors, management, external auditors, and internal auditors all play important roles in creating proper control processes. Senior management is primarily responsible for

A. Establishing and maintaining an organizational culture.

B. Reviewing the reliability and integrity of financial and operational information.

C. Ensuring that external and internal auditors oversee the administration of the system of risk management and control processes.

D. Implementing and monitoring controls designed by the board of directors.

Answer (A) is correct. *(CIA, adapted)*

**REQUIRED:** The best description of senior management's responsibility.

**DISCUSSION:** Management plans, organizes, and directs the performance of sufficient actions to provide reasonable assurance that goals and objectives will be achieved. Management periodically reviews its objectives and goals and modifies its processes to accommodate changes in internal and external conditions. Management also establishes and maintains an organizational culture, including an ethical climate that fosters control (PA 2100-1).

Answer (B) is incorrect because internal auditors are responsible for evaluating the adequacy and effectiveness of controls, including those relating to the reliability and integrity of financial and operational information (Standard 2120.A1). Answer (C) is incorrect because senior management's role is to oversee the establishment, administration, and assessment of the system of risk management and control processes (PA 2120.A1-1). Answer (D) is incorrect because the board has oversight responsibilities but ordinarily does not become involved in the details of operations.

**2.** Which of the following best describe the interrelated components of internal control?

A. Organizational structure, management philosophy, and planning.

B. Control environment, risk assessment, control activities, information and communication systems, and monitoring.

C. Risk assessment, backup facilities, responsibility accounting, and natural laws.

D. Legal environment of the firm, management philosophy, and organizational structure.

Answer (B) is correct. *(CMA, adapted)*

**REQUIRED:** The components of internal control.

**DISCUSSION:** Internal control has five components: the control environment, risk assessment, control activities, information and communication systems, and monitoring. The control environment sets the tone of an organization, influences control consciousness, and provides a foundation for the other components. Risk assessment is the identification and analysis of relevant risks to achievement of objectives. Control activities help ensure that management directives are executed. Information and communication systems facilitate the identification, capture, and exchange of information in a form and time frame that allow people to meet their responsibilities. Monitoring assesses the performance of internal control over time (AU 319 and AS No. 2).

Answer (A) is incorrect because planning is not a component of internal control. Organizational structure and management philosophy are factors in the control environment component. Answer (C) is incorrect because risk assessment is the only component listed. Answer (D) is incorrect because the legal environment of the firm, management philosophy, and organizational structure are factors in the control environment component.

**3.** As part of understanding internal control in planning an audit for a private company, an auditor is not required to

A. Consider factors that affect the risk of material misstatement.

B. Ascertain whether internal control policies and procedures have been placed in operation.

C. Identify the types of potential misstatements that can occur.

D. Obtain knowledge about the operating effectiveness of internal control.

Answer (D) is correct. *(CPA, adapted)*

**REQUIRED:** The step not required in obtaining the understanding of internal control.

**DISCUSSION:** Understanding internal control requires knowledge of the five components of internal control. It should include knowledge about not only the design of relevant controls but also whether they have been placed in operation by the entity and by service organizations whose services are part of the entity's information system. The auditor of a private company need not obtain knowledge about operating effectiveness as part of understanding internal control. However, if (s)he wishes to assess control risk below the maximum level, the auditor must identify controls relevant to specific assertions and perform tests of their effectiveness (AU 319).

Answer (A) is incorrect because the understanding of internal control is used to consider factors affecting the risk of material misstatements. Answer (B) is incorrect because the understanding of internal control is used to assure that controls have been placed in operation. Answer (C) is incorrect because the understanding of internal control is used to identify types of potential misstatements.

**4.** In an audit of financial statements, an auditor's primary consideration regarding a control is whether it

A. Reflects management's philosophy and operating style.

B. Affects management's financial statement assertions.

C. Provides adequate safeguards over access to assets.

D. Enhances management's decision-making processes.

Answer (B) is correct. *(CPA, adapted)*

**REQUIRED:** The primary audit consideration regarding a control.

**DISCUSSION:** An auditor's primary concern is to gather sufficient competent evidence to afford a reasonable basis for expressing an opinion on the financial statements. Audit evidence is obtained by performing audit procedures. These procedures are selected to achieve specific audit objectives. In turn, the objectives are determined in the light of management's financial statement assertions. Thus, the auditor is primarily concerned with whether a control affects financial statement assertions.

Answer (A) is incorrect because management's philosophy and operating style are important but not primary considerations in an audit of financial statements. Answer (C) is incorrect because adequate safeguards over access to assets are important but not primary considerations in an audit of financial statements. Answer (D) is incorrect because management's decision-making processes are important but not primary considerations in an audit of financial statements.

**5.** After obtaining a sufficient understanding of internal control in an audit of the financial statements, the auditor assesses

A. The need to apply auditing standards.

B. Detection risk to determine the acceptable level of inherent risk.

C. Detection risk and inherent risk to determine the acceptable level of control risk.

D. Control risk to determine the acceptable level of detection risk.

Answer (D) is correct. *(Publisher)*

**REQUIRED:** The step that follows obtaining the understanding.

**DISCUSSION:** The acceptable level of detection risk is a function of the assessed levels of inherent risk and control risk. Hence, as the latter increase, the acceptable level of detection risk decreases.

Answer (A) is incorrect because auditing standards must be applied in all financial statement audits. Answer (B) is incorrect because inherent risk and control risk, which depend on the entity's unique circumstances and not the auditor's procedures, must both be assessed to calculate the acceptable detection risk. Answer (C) is incorrect because the acceptable detection risk is a function of the assessments of inherent risk and control risk.

**6.** Which of the following are considered control environment factors?

| | Detection Risk | Personnel Policies and Practices |
|---|---|---|
| A. | Yes | Yes |
| B. | Yes | No |
| C. | No | Yes |
| D. | No | No |

Answer (C) is correct. *(CPA, adapted)*

**REQUIRED:** The factor(s), if any, considered to be part of the control environment.

**DISCUSSION:** Human resource policies and practices are part of the control environment. These policies and practices relate to hiring, orientation, training, evaluating, counseling, promoting, compensating, and remedial actions. The control environment is the component that sets the tone of an organization, influencing the control consciousness of its people. It is the foundation for the other components.

Answer (A) is incorrect because human resource policies and practices are part of the control environment, but detection risk is not. It is the risk that the audit procedures will fail to detect material misstatements. Thus, detection risk is a function of the effectiveness of the procedures used by the auditor. Answer (B) is incorrect because human resource policies and practices are part of the control environment, but detection risk is not. It is the risk that the audit procedures will fail to detect material misstatements. Thus, detection risk is a function of the effectiveness of the procedures used by the auditor. Answer (D) is incorrect because human resource policies and practices are part of the control environment, but detection risk is not. It is the risk that the audit procedures will fail to detect material misstatements. Thus, detection risk is a function of the effectiveness of the procedures used by the auditor.

**7.** Internal control cannot be designed to provide reasonable assurance regarding the achievement of objectives concerning

A. Reducing the cost of an external audit.

B. Elimination of all fraud.

C. Availability of reliable data for decision-making purposes and protection of important documents and records.

D. Compliance with the Foreign Corrupt Practices Act of 1977.

Answer (B) is correct. *(Publisher)*

**REQUIRED:** The objective that internal control cannot achieve.

**DISCUSSION:** Internal control is a process designed to provide reasonable assurance regarding the achievement of organizational objectives. It can provide reasonable assurance regarding reliability of financial reporting, compliance with applicable laws and regulations, and effectiveness and efficiency of operations. Because of inherent limitations, however, no system can be designed to eliminate all fraud.

Answer (A) is incorrect because a lower level of control risk permits the auditor to accept a higher level of detection risk and thus to reduce substantive tests. Answer (C) is incorrect because strong internal control will provide management with better data for decision-making purposes. The physical safety of important documents and records is also assured. Answer (D) is incorrect because strong internal control provides some assurance of compliance with the FCPA provisions regarding recordkeeping, internal control, and prohibition of corrupt payments.

**8.** Control activities constitute one of the five components of internal control. Control activities do not encompass

A. Performance reviews.

B. Information processing.

C. Physical controls.

D. An internal auditing function.

Answer (D) is correct. *(Publisher)*

**REQUIRED:** The item not belonging to the control activities component.

**DISCUSSION:** Control activities are policies and procedures that help ensure that management directives are carried out. They are intended to ensure that necessary actions are taken to address risks to achieve the entity's objectives. Control activities have various objectives and are applied at various organizational and functional levels. However, an internal auditing function is part of the monitoring component.

**9.** Monitoring is an important component of internal control. Which of the following items would not be an example of monitoring?

A. Management regularly compares divisional performance with budgets for the division.

B. Data processing management regularly generates exception reports for unusual transactions or volumes of transactions and follows up with investigation as to causes.

C. Data processing management regularly reconciles batch control totals for items processed with batch controls for items submitted.

D. Management has asked internal auditing to perform regular audits of the controls over cash processing.

Answer (C) is correct. *(CIA, adapted)*

**REQUIRED:** The item that is not an example of monitoring.

**DISCUSSION:** Monitoring assesses the quality of internal control over time. Management considers whether internal control is properly designed and operating as intended and modifies it to reflect changing conditions. Monitoring may be in the form of separate, periodic evaluations or of ongoing monitoring. Ongoing monitoring occurs as part of routine operations. It includes management and supervisory review, comparisons, reconciliations, and other actions by personnel as part of their regular activities. However, reconciling batch control totals is a processing control.

Answer (A) is incorrect because budgetary comparison is a typical example of a monitoring control. Answer (B) is incorrect because investigation of exceptions is a monitoring control used by lower-level management to determine when their operations may be out of control. Answer (D) is incorrect because internal auditing is a form of monitoring. It serves to evaluate management's other controls.

**10.** Effective internal control

A. Reduces the need for management to review exception reports on a day-to-day basis.

B. Eliminates risk and potential loss to the organization.

C. Cannot be circumvented by management.

D. Is unaffected by changing circumstances and conditions encountered by the organization.

Answer (A) is correct. *(CIA, adapted)*

**REQUIRED:** The service provided by effective control.

**DISCUSSION:** The need for management to spend time on a day-to-day basis reviewing exception reports is reduced when internal control is working effectively. Effective internal control should prevent as well as detect exceptions.

Answer (B) is incorrect because some risks are unavoidable and others can be eliminated only at excessive costs. Answer (C) is incorrect because the potential for management override is a basic limitation of internal control. Answer (D) is incorrect because controls should be modified as appropriate for changes in conditions.

**11.** A reason to establish internal control is to

A. Safeguard the resources of the organization.

B. Provide reasonable assurance that the objectives of the organization are achieved.

C. Encourage compliance with organizational objectives.

D. Ensure the accuracy, reliability, and timeliness of information.

Answer (B) is correct. *(Publisher)*

**REQUIRED:** The reason to establish internal control.

**DISCUSSION:** According to AU 319, "Internal control is a process, effected by an entity's board of directors, management, and other personnel, designed to provide reasonable assurance regarding the achievement of objectives in the following categories: reliability of financial reporting, effectiveness and efficiency of operations, and compliance with applicable laws and regulations."

Answer (A) is incorrect because safeguarding resources is subsumed under the overall purpose of providing reasonable assurance that the objectives of the organization are achieved. Answer (C) is incorrect because encouraging compliance with management's intentions is subsumed under the overall purpose of providing reasonable assurance that the objectives of the organization are achieved. Answer (D) is incorrect because ensuring the accuracy, reliability, and timeliness of information is subsumed under the overall purpose of providing reasonable assurance that the objectives of the organization are achieved.

**12.** Internal control is a function of management, and effective control is based upon the concept of charge and discharge of responsibility and duty. Which of the following is one of the overriding principles of internal control?

A. Responsibility for accounting and financial duties should be assigned to one responsible officer.

B. Responsibility for the performance of each duty must be fixed.

C. Responsibility for the accounting duties must be borne by the audit committee.

D. Responsibility for accounting must be assigned only to bonded employees.

Answer (B) is correct. *(CPA, adapted)*

**REQUIRED:** The principle of internal control.

**DISCUSSION:** Effective internal control may be obtained by decentralization of responsibilities and duties. Fixing the responsibility for each performance or duty makes it easier to trace problems to the person(s) responsible and hold them accountable for their actions.

Answer (A) is incorrect because accounting (record keeping) should be separated from finance (asset custody). Answer (C) is incorrect because the audit committee is responsible for overseeing the internal and external audits, not for accounting duties. Answer (D) is incorrect because bonding is not an overriding internal control principle. Employees having custodial, rather than accounting, responsibility are usually bonded.

**13.** The PCAOB's AS No. 2 indicates that internal controls may be preventive or detective. Which of the following controls is preventive?

A. Requiring two persons to open mail.

B. Reconciling the accounts receivable subsidiary file with the control account.

C. Using batch totals.

D. Preparing bank reconciliations.

Answer (A) is correct. *(Publisher)*

**REQUIRED:** The internal control that is preventive.

**DISCUSSION:** Preventive controls are designed to prevent errors or fraud. Detective controls attempt to identify errors or fraud that have already occurred. Assigning two individuals to open mail is an attempt to prevent misstatement of cash receipts.

Answer (B) is incorrect because reconciling the subsidiary file with the master file may detect and lead to the correction of errors, but the control does not prevent errors. Answer (C) is incorrect because the use of batch totals may detect a missing or lost document but will not necessarily prevent a document from becoming lost. Answer (D) is incorrect because bank reconciliations disclose errors in the accounts but have no preventive effect.

**14.** Which of the following statements about internal control is true?

A. Properly maintained internal control reasonably ensures that collusion among employees cannot occur.

B. The establishment and maintenance of internal control are important responsibilities of the internal auditor.

C. Exceptionally strong internal control is enough for the auditor to eliminate substantive tests on a significant account balance.

D. The cost-benefit relationship is a primary criterion that should be considered in designing internal control.

Answer (D) is correct. *(CPA, adapted)*

**REQUIRED:** The true statement about internal control.

**DISCUSSION:** The cost of a control should not exceed its benefits. Although the cost-benefit relationship is a primary criterion in designing internal control, precise measurement of costs and benefits is usually impossible, and management makes both quantitative and qualitative estimates and judgments in evaluating the relationship (AU 319).

Answer (A) is incorrect because collusion is an inherent limitation of internal control. Answer (B) is incorrect because establishment and maintenance of internal control are responsibilities of management. Answer (C) is incorrect because control risk ordinarily cannot be so low as to eliminate the need for substantive tests to restrict detection risk for all assertions related to significant account balances and classes of transactions.

**15.** Internal controls are designed to provide reasonable assurance that

A. Material errors or fraud will be prevented or detected and corrected within a timely period by employees in the course of performing their assigned duties.

B. Management's plans have not been circumvented by worker collusion.

C. The internal auditing department's guidance and oversight of management's performance is accomplished economically and efficiently.

D. Management's planning, organizing, and directing processes are properly evaluated.

Answer (A) is correct. *(CIA, adapted)*

**REQUIRED:** The purpose of internal controls.

**DISCUSSION:** Cost-effective controls should restrict deviations to a tolerable rate. Thus, material errors and improper or illegal acts should be prevented or detected and corrected within a timely period by employees in the normal course of performing their assigned duties. Accordingly, the cost-benefit relationship is considered by management during the design of systems, and the potential loss associated with any exposure or risk is weighed against the cost to control it.

Answer (B) is incorrect because collusion is an inherent limitation of internal control. Answer (C) is incorrect because the board of directors or a similar body is responsible for the guidance and oversight of management. Answer (D) is incorrect because the examination and evaluation of management processes is a function of the internal auditing department.

**16.** According to PCAOB AS No. 2, when "the design or operation of a control does not allow management or employees, in the normal course of performing their assigned functions, to prevent or detect misstatements on a timely basis," the result is a

A. Material weakness.

B. Significant deficiency.

C. Control deficiency.

D. Critical deficiency.

Answer (C) is correct. *(Publisher)*

**REQUIRED:** The control term matching the given definition.

**DISCUSSION:** A control deficiency may arise either in the design or operation of a control. It is the lowest level of deficiency identified in AS No. 2.

Answer (A) is incorrect because a material weakness is the highest level of deficiency. It is a significant deficiency, or combination of significant deficiencies, that results in more than a remote likelihood that a material misstatement of the annual or interim financial statement will not be prevented or detected. Answer (B) is incorrect because a significant deficiency is the midlevel deficiency defined in AS No. 2. It is a control deficiency, or combination of control deficiencies, that adversely affects the company's ability to initiate, authorize, record, process, or report financial data reliably in accordance with GAAP. Its effect is a more than remote likelihood that a misstatement of the company's annual or interim financial statements that is more than inconsequential will not be prevented or detected. Answer (D) is incorrect because AS No. 2 does not use the term critical deficiency.

## 3.2 Purpose of the Auditor's Consideration of Internal Control

**17.** The primary objective of procedures performed to obtain an understanding of internal control in a financial statement audit is to provide an auditor with

A. Evidence to use in reducing detection risk.

B. Knowledge necessary to plan the audit.

C. A basis for modifying tests of controls.

D. Information necessary to prepare flowcharts.

Answer (B) is correct. *(CPA, adapted)*

**REQUIRED:** The primary objective of procedures to obtain an understanding of internal control.

**DISCUSSION:** The second standard of field work states, "A sufficient understanding of internal control is to be obtained to plan the audit and to determine the nature, timing, and extent of tests to be performed."

Answer (A) is incorrect because the understanding is primarily directed toward audit planning. Substantive testing is concerned with gathering evidence to reduce detection risk to an acceptable level. Answer (C) is incorrect because the understanding is the basis for determining the nature, timing, and extent of both substantive tests and tests of controls. Answer (D) is incorrect because flowcharts are but one part of the documentation of the understanding.

**18.** An auditor should obtain sufficient knowledge of an entity's information system relevant to financial reporting to understand the

A. Safeguards used to limit access to computer facilities.

B. Process used to prepare significant accounting estimates.

C. Procedures used to assure proper authorization of transactions.

D. Programs and controls intended to address the risks of fraud.

Answer (B) is correct. *(CPA, adapted)*

**REQUIRED:** The purpose of obtaining sufficient knowledge of an entity's information system relevant to financial reporting.

**DISCUSSION:** The auditor should obtain sufficient knowledge of the information system relevant to financial reporting to understand (1) the classes of significant transactions; (2) the ways those transactions are initiated, recorded, processed, and reported; (3) the accounting records and supporting documents for those transactions; (4) the accounting processing involved; and (5) the financial reporting process used to prepare the entity's financial statements, including significant accounting estimates and disclosures (AU 319).

Answer (A) is incorrect because limiting access to computer facilities involves activity outside the information system relevant to financial reporting. Answer (C) is incorrect because assuring proper authorization of transactions involves activity outside the information system relevant to financial reporting. Answer (D) is incorrect because the auditor should make inquiries of management concerning the programs and controls the entity has established to mitigate specific fraud risks the entity has identified. However, these programs and controls may be included in any of the components of internal control, not just the information and communication component (which encompasses the information system relevant to financial reporting).

**19.** The ultimate purpose of assessing control risk is to contribute to the auditor's evaluation of the risk that

A. Tests of controls may fail to identify controls relevant to assertions.

B. Material misstatements may exist in the financial statements.

C. Specified controls requiring segregation of duties may be circumvented by collusion.

D. Entity policies may be overridden by senior management.

Answer (B) is correct. *(CPA, adapted)*

**REQUIRED:** The purpose of assessing control risk.

**DISCUSSION:** "The ultimate purpose of assessing control risk is to contribute to the auditor's evaluation of the risk that material misstatements exist in the financial statements" (AU 319).

Answer (A) is incorrect because tests of controls are performed when the auditor wishes to assess control risk below the maximum. An auditor must identify controls relevant to specific assertions before testing such controls. Answer (C) is incorrect because collusion is an inherent limitation of internal control. Answer (D) is incorrect because management override is an inherent limitation of internal control.

**20.** Firms subject to the reporting requirements of the Securities Exchange Act of 1934 are required by the Foreign Corrupt Practices Act of 1977 to maintain satisfactory internal control. Moreover, the Sarbanes-Oxley Act of 2002 requires that annual reports include (1) a statement of management's responsibility for establishing and maintaining adequate internal control and procedures for financial reporting, and (2) management's assessment of their effectiveness. The role of the registered auditor relative to the assessment made by management is to

A. Disclaim an opinion on the assessment and controls.

B. Report clients with unsatisfactory internal control to the SEC.

C. Express an opinion on whether the client is subject to the Securities Exchange Act of 1934.

D. Attest to, and report on, the assessment made by management.

Answer (D) is correct. *(Publisher)*

**REQUIRED:** The role of the auditor relative to reporting on the assessment by the management of a public client of internal control and procedures for financial reporting.

**DISCUSSION:** The registered auditor that issues the audit report for a public client must attest to, and report on, the assessment made by management in the internal control report. The attestation must be made in accordance with standards for attestation engagements issued or adopted by the Public Company Accounting Oversight Board (PCAOB). However, the auditor's evaluation must not be the subject of a separate engagement but in conjunction with an audit of the financial statements. The auditor must determine whether the entity's transactional records are (1) accurate and fair and (2) provide reasonable assurance that financial statements may be prepared in conformity with GAAP. The auditor also must describe material weaknesses in internal control.

Answer (A) is incorrect because the auditor is required to attest to internal control of a public client. Answer (B) is incorrect because the auditor's report on internal control is issued in conjunction with the audit report on the financial statements. Answer (C) is incorrect because public clients must report to the SEC, but the auditor need not express an opinion on whether the client is subject to the Securities Exchange Act of 1934.

**21.** An "issuer" subject to the Securities Exchange Act of 1934 would be required to include in its annual report an auditor's opinion whether internal control over financial reporting was

A. Sufficient to meet the needs of the shareholders.

B. Properly designed and operated effectively.

C. Adequate to eliminate fraud.

D. Complete and fair.

Answer (B) is correct. *(Publisher)*

**REQUIRED:** The purpose of an auditor's opinion on internal control.

**DISCUSSION:** The PCAOB's AS No. 2 requires an auditor's opinion on management's assertion that internal control over financial reporting was appropriately designed and operated effectively.

Answer (A) is incorrect because internal control should meet the needs of the company, not the shareholders. Answer (C) is incorrect because no system of internal control can be expected to eliminate all fraud. Answer (D) is incorrect because the terms "complete" and "fair" are more closely associated with the financial statements than internal control.

**22.** A CPA's consideration of internal control in a financial statement audit of a nonpublic company

A. Is usually more limited than that made in connection with an engagement to report on management's written assertion as to the effectiveness of internal control.

B. Is usually more extensive than that made in connection with an engagement to report on management's written assertion as to the effectiveness of internal control.

C. Will usually be identical to that made in connection with an engagement to report on management's written assertion as to the effectiveness of internal control.

D. Will usually result in a report on management's written assertion as to the effectiveness of internal control.

Answer (A) is correct. *(CPA, adapted)*

**REQUIRED:** The scope of the consideration of internal control in an audit.

**DISCUSSION:** The scope of the consideration of internal control in an audit of a nonpublic company is usually less than that in an engagement to report on management's written assertion as to the effectiveness of internal control. The auditor must test controls in such an engagement. In the consideration of internal control during an audit, the auditor may not test controls if (s)he assesses control risk for the related assertions at the maximum level.

Answer (B) is incorrect because the evaluation procedures are more extensive in an engagement to report on management's written assertion as to the effectiveness of internal control. However, in audits of public companies, the auditor must report on internal control. Answer (C) is incorrect because the evaluation procedures are more extensive in an engagement to report on management's written assertion as to the effectiveness of internal control. However, in audits of public companies, the auditor must report on internal control. Answer (D) is incorrect because an audit of a nonpublic company does not result in a report on management's written assertion as to the effectiveness of internal control unless the requirements of an engagement for that purpose are also met.

**23.** The Sarbanes-Oxley Act of 2002 requires management of publicly-traded corporations to do all of the following except

A. Establish and document internal control procedures and to include in their annual reports a report on the company's internal control over financial reporting.

B. Provide a report to include a statement of management's responsibility for internal control and of management's assessment of the effectiveness of internal control as of the end of the company's most recent fiscal year.

C. Provide an identification of the framework used to evaluate the effectiveness of internal control (such as the COSO report) and a statement that the external auditor has issued an attestation report on management's assessment.

D. Provide a statement that the board approves changes in internal control procedures.

Answer (D) is correct. *(Publisher)*

**REQUIRED:** The false statement with regard to management's responsibilities under the Sarbanes-Oxley Act of 2002.

**DISCUSSION:** The Sarbanes-Oxley Act of 2002 imposes many requirements on management, boards of directors, and auditors. Section 404 applies to internal controls and reports thereon. Section 404 requires management to establish and document internal control procedures and to include in their annual reports a report on the company s internal control over financial reporting. The report is to include a statement of management's responsibility for internal control, management's assessment of the effectiveness of internal control as of the end of the most recent fiscal year, identification of the framework used to evaluate the effectiveness of internal control (such as the COSO report), and a statement that the external auditor has issued an attestation report on management's assessment. Because of this requirement, there are two audit opinions: one on the internal controls and one on the financial statements. Section 301 does address activities of the board, but it does not require the board to approve.

**24.** A secondary result of the auditor's consideration of internal control in an audit of a private company's financial statements is that the consideration may

A. Provide a basis for determining the nature, timing, and extent of audit tests.

B. Assure that management's procedures to detect fraud are properly functioning.

C. Bring to the auditor's attention possible reportable conditions.

D. Develop evidence to support the assessed level of control risk.

Answer (C) is correct. *(CPA, adapted)*

**REQUIRED:** The secondary result of considering internal control.

**DISCUSSION:** The auditor is not required to search for reportable conditions, which are significant deficiencies in the design or operation of internal control that could adversely affect the organization's ability to initiate, record, process, and report financial data consistent with the financial statement assertions. However, the auditor may become aware of reportable conditions during the audit. Reportable conditions must be communicated to the audit committee or its equivalent (AU 325).

Answer (A) is incorrect because the auditor is required to consider internal control to plan the audit. Answer (B) is incorrect because obtaining evidence to provide assurance about the proper functioning of the client's internal control is necessary to document an assessment of control risk below the maximum level. Answer (D) is incorrect because gathering evidence to support the assessed level of control risk is required during the consideration of internal control.

## 3.3 Concepts and Characteristics of Internal Control

**25.** Which of the following most likely would not be considered an inherent limitation of the potential effectiveness of an entity's internal control?

A. Incompatible duties.

B. Management override.

C. Mistakes in judgment.

D. Collusion among employees.

Answer (A) is correct. *(CPA, adapted)*

**REQUIRED:** The item not considered an inherent limitation of internal control.

**DISCUSSION:** AU 319 lists the inherent limitations of internal control. The performance of incompatible functions, however, is a failure to separate duties properly, not an inevitable limitation on internal control. The segregation of functional responsibilities is an important category of control activities.

Answer (B) is incorrect because management establishes controls. Thus, it can override those policies and procedures. Answer (C) is incorrect because judgment in decision making can be faulty, and control may break down as a result of a simple error or mistake. Answer (D) is incorrect because controls based on segregation of duties may be circumvented by collusion among employees.

**26.** Internal control can provide only reasonable assurance of achieving entity control objectives. One factor limiting the likelihood of achieving those objectives is that

A. The auditor's primary responsibility is the detection of fraud.

B. The board of directors is active and independent.

C. The cost of internal control should not exceed its benefits.

D. Management monitors internal control.

Answer (C) is correct. *(Publisher)*

**REQUIRED:** The true statement about the limitation of internal control.

**DISCUSSION:** AU 319 states, "Internal control is influenced by the quantitative and qualitative estimates and judgments made by management in evaluating the cost-benefit relationship of an entity's internal control. Although the cost-benefit relationship is a primary criterion that should be considered in designing internal control, the precise measurement of costs and benefits usually is not possible."

Answer (A) is incorrect because the auditor's responsibility is "to plan and perform the audit to obtain reasonable assurance about whether the financial statements are free of material misstatement, whether caused by error or fraud" (AU 110). Answer (B) is incorrect because an active and independent board strengthens the control environment. Answer (D) is incorrect because monitoring strengthens internal control.

**27.** An entity should consider the cost of a control in relationship to the risk. Which of the following controls best reflects this philosophy for a large dollar investment in heavy machine tools?

A. Conducting a weekly physical inventory.

B. Placing security guards at every entrance 24 hours a day.

C. Imprinting a controlled identification number on each tool.

D. Having all dispositions approved by the vice president of sales.

Answer (C) is correct. *(Publisher)*

**REQUIRED:** The control appropriate for a large dollar investment in heavy machine tools.

**DISCUSSION:** A controlled identification number on each tool and periodic checking allow for an effective control at reasonable cost.

Answer (A) is incorrect because the cost of weekly inventories would likely outweigh the benefits derived. Answer (B) is incorrect because the cost of 24-hr. guards would likely outweigh the benefits derived. Answer (D) is incorrect because, although the disposition of assets should be approved, the vice president of sales, who is not familiar with the heavy equipment, would not be the appropriate officer to provide the authorization.

**28.** A financial statement auditor is considering internal control for a client with an information system that makes extensive use of information technology. Which of the following statements related to the assessment of control risk and the determination of detection risk for this client is false?

A. A lack of control at a single user entry point might compromise the security of a single database.

B. The auditor may find it necessary to assess control risk at less than the maximum for certain financial statement assertions.

C. The auditor must possess all the information technology skills necessary to complete the engagement.

D. Because of the inherent consistency of computer processing, the auditor may be able to reduce the extent of testing an automated control.

Answer (C) is correct. *(Publisher)*

**REQUIRED:** The false statement about the consideration of internal control if extensive use is made of information technology (IT).

**DISCUSSION:** The auditor should consider whether specialized skills are needed to determine the effect of IT on the audit, to understand the IT controls, and to design and perform tests of IT controls or substantive tests. A member of the auditor's staff or an outside service provider with IT skills can be employed to provide technical guidance.

Answer (A) is incorrect because the concentration of processing and data storage make information systems vulnerable to weaknesses in access controls. Answer (B) is incorrect because, once a programmed control is tested and found to be effective, the auditor may conclude that the control will continue to operative effectively absent change in the system. Answer (D) is incorrect because, once a programmed control is tested and found to be effective, the auditor may conclude that the control will continue to operative effectively absent change in the system.

**29.** Regardless of the assessed level of control risk, an auditor would perform some

A. Tests of controls to determine their effectiveness.

B. Analytical procedures to verify the design of controls.

C. Substantive tests to restrict detection risk for significant transaction classes.

D. Dual-purpose tests to evaluate both the risk of monetary misstatement and preliminary control risk.

Answer (C) is correct. *(CPA, adapted)*

**REQUIRED:** The procedures performed regardless of the assessed level of control risk.

**DISCUSSION:** AU 319 states, 'Although the inverse relationship between control risk and detection risk may permit the auditor to change the nature or the timing of substantive tests or limit their extent, ordinarily the assessed level of control risk cannot be sufficiently low to eliminate the need to perform any substantive tests to restrict detection risk for all of the assertions relevant to significant account balances or transaction classes."

Answer (A) is incorrect because, if control risk is assessed at the maximum, no tests of controls need be performed. Answer (B) is incorrect because, if control risk is assessed at the maximum, no tests of controls need be performed. Answer (D) is incorrect because, if control risk is assessed at the maximum, no tests of controls need be performed.

**30.** Control activities include procedures that pertain to physical controls over access to and use of assets and records. A departure from the purpose of such procedures is that

A. Access to the safe-deposit box requires two officers.

B. Only storeroom personnel and line supervisors have access to the raw materials storeroom.

C. The mail clerk compiles a list of the checks received in the incoming mail.

D. Only salespersons and sales supervisors use sales department vehicles.

Answer (B) is correct. *(Publisher)*

**REQUIRED:** The departure from the purpose of control activities that limit access to assets.

**DISCUSSION:** Storeroom personnel have custody of assets, while supervisors are in charge of execution functions. To give supervisors access to the raw materials storeroom is a violation of the essential internal control principle of segregation of functions.

Answer (A) is incorrect because it is appropriate for two officers to be required to open the safe-deposit box. One supervises the other. Answer (C) is incorrect because mail room clerks typically compile a prelisting of cash. The list is sent to the accountant as a control for actual cash sent to the cashier. Answer (D) is incorrect because use of sales department vehicles should be limited to sales personnel unless proper authorization is obtained.

**31.** Basic to a proper control environment are the quality and integrity of personnel who must perform the prescribed procedures. Which is not a factor in providing for competent personnel?

A. Segregation of duties.

B. Hiring practices.

C. Training programs.

D. Performance evaluations.

Answer (A) is correct. *(Publisher)*

**REQUIRED:** The factor not related to competence of personnel.

**DISCUSSION:** Human resource policies and practices are a factor in the control environment component of internal control. They affect the entity's ability to employ sufficient competent personnel to accomplish its objectives. Policies and practices include those for hiring, orientation, training, evaluating, promoting, compensating, and remedial actions. Although control activities based on the segregation of duties are important to internal control, they do not in themselves promote employee competence.

Answer (B) is incorrect because effective hiring practices result in selection of competent employees. Answer (C) is incorrect because effective training programs increase the competence of employees. Answer (D) is incorrect because performance evaluations improve competence by identifying substandard work and by serving as a basis for rewarding exceptional efforts.

**32.** Proper segregation of duties reduces the opportunities for persons to be in positions to both

A. Journalize entries and prepare financial statements.

B. Record cash receipts and cash disbursements.

C. Establish internal control and authorize transactions.

D. Perpetrate and conceal errors or fraud.

Answer (D) is correct. *(CPA, adapted)*

**REQUIRED:** The effects of the segregation of duties and responsibilities.

**DISCUSSION:** Proper segregation of duties and responsibilities reduces the opportunity for an individual to both perpetrate and conceal an error or fraud in the normal course of his/her duties. Hence, different people should be assigned the responsibilities for authorizing transactions, record keeping, and asset custody.

Answer (A) is incorrect because accountants typically journalize entries and prepare financial statements. Answer (B) is incorrect because accountants may record both cash receipts and cash disbursements as long as they do not have custody of the cash. Answer (C) is incorrect because management establishes internal control and ultimately has the responsibility to authorize transactions.

**33.** Management's aggressive attitude toward financial reporting and its emphasis on meeting projected profit goals most likely would significantly influence an entity's control environment when

A. The audit committee is active in overseeing the entity's financial reporting policies.

B. External policies established by parties outside the entity affect its accounting practices.

C. Management is dominated by one individual who is also a shareholder.

D. Internal auditors have direct access to the board of directors and entity management.

Answer (C) is correct. *(CPA, adapted)*

**REQUIRED:** The instance in which management's attitudes would most likely affect an entity's control environment.

**DISCUSSION:** Management philosophy and operating style is one factor affecting the control environment. Such characteristics as management's attitudes and actions toward financial reporting and its emphasis on meeting budget, profit, and other goals have a significant influence on the control environment, especially when management is dominated by one or a few individuals. When incentives or pressures are present to achieve certain performance goals, the auditor should heighten his/her concern about the possibility of fraud.

Answer (A) is incorrect because an active audit committee serves to mitigate the risks associated with certain management attitudes. Answer (B) is incorrect because external influences serve to mitigate the risks associated with certain management attitudes. Answer (D) is incorrect because an effective internal audit function serves to mitigate the risks associated with certain management attitudes.

**34.** Transaction authorization within an organization may be either specific or general. An example of specific transaction authorization is the

A. Setting of automatic reorder points for material or merchandise.

B. Approval of a detailed construction budget for a warehouse.

C. Establishment of requirements to be met in determining a customer's credit limits.

D. Establishment of sales prices for products to be sold to any customer.

Answer (B) is correct. *(CPA, adapted)*

**REQUIRED:** The example of a specific transaction authorization.

**DISCUSSION:** A specific transaction authorization is applicable to a unique decision. A general authorization establishes criteria and authorizes the routine making of decisions subject to the criteria. Approving a detailed construction budget for a warehouse is a one-time decision.

Answer (A) is incorrect because setting of automatic reorder points for material or merchandise is a general transaction authorization. Answer (C) is incorrect because establishment of requirements to be met in determining a customer's credit limits is a general transaction authorization. Answer (D) is incorrect because establishment of sales prices for products to be sold to any customer is a general transaction authorization.

**35.** It is important for the auditor to consider the competence of the audit client's employees, because their competence bears directly and importantly upon the

A. Cost-benefit relationship of internal control.

B. Achievement of the objectives of internal control.

C. Comparison of recorded accountability with assets.

D. Timing of the tests to be performed.

Answer (B) is correct. *(CPA, adapted)*

**REQUIRED:** The reason an auditor must consider the competence of employees.

**DISCUSSION:** Human resource policies and practices are a factor in the control environment component of internal control. For example, standards for hiring the most qualified individuals demonstrate a commitment to competent and trustworthy people. Human resource policies and practices concern hiring, orientation, training, evaluating, counseling, promoting, compensating, and remedial actions. Without sufficient competent employees, the auditee cannot achieve the objectives of internal control.

Answer (A) is incorrect because the cost-benefit relationship of the control system is a basic concept of internal control. Answer (C) is incorrect because comparison of recorded accountability with assets is an essential characteristic of internal control but is not directly related to the competence of employees. Answer (D) is incorrect because the timing of particular tests is dependent on such factors as the convenience of the auditor and client and the need for applying certain tests concurrently.

**36.** A proper segregation of duties requires

A. That an individual authorizing a transaction records it.

B. That an individual authorizing a transaction maintain custody of the asset that resulted from the transaction.

C. That an individual maintaining custody of an asset be entitled to access the accounting records for the asset.

D. That an individual recording a transaction not compare the accounting record of the asset with the asset itself.

Answer (D) is correct. *(CMA, adapted)*

**REQUIRED:** The item required by proper segregation of duties.

**DISCUSSION:** One person should not be responsible for all phases of a transaction, i.e., for authorization, recording, and custodianship of the related assets. These duties should be performed by separate individuals to reduce the opportunities for any person to be in a position of both perpetrating and concealing errors or fraud in the normal course of his/her duties. For instance, an employee who receives and lists cash receipts should not be responsible for comparing the recorded accountability for cash with existing amounts.

Answer (A) is incorrect because authorization and record keeping should be separate. Answer (B) is incorrect because authorization and asset custody should be separate. Answer (C) is incorrect because record keeping and asset custody should be separate.

**37.** If internal control is properly designed, the same employee may be permitted to

A. Receive and deposit checks and also approve write-offs of customer accounts.

B. Approve vouchers for payment and also sign checks.

C. Reconcile the bank statements and also receive and deposit cash.

D. Sign checks and also cancel supporting documents.

Answer (D) is correct. *(CPA, adapted)*

**REQUIRED:** The duties that are not incompatible with effective control.

**DISCUSSION:** Checks for disbursements should be signed by an officer, normally the treasurer, after necessary supporting evidence has been examined. The documentation typically consists of a voucher, a purchase order, a receiving report, and a vendor invoice. Canceling vouchers and supporting papers (with perforations, ink, etc.) upon payment of the voucher prevents the payment of a duplicate voucher. If the person signing the check cancels the documents, these documents cannot be recycled for duplicate payments.

Answer (A) is incorrect because authorization of transactions (write-offs of receivables) and custody of assets (checks) are incompatible duties. Answer (B) is incorrect because authorization (voucher approval) and custody of assets (checks) are incompatible functions. Answer (C) is incorrect because record keeping (reconciling the bank statements) and custody of cash are incompatible.

**38.** A small private entity may use less formal means to ensure that internal control objectives are achieved. For example, extensive accounting procedures, sophisticated accounting records, or formal controls are least likely to be needed if

A. Management is closely involved in operations.

B. The entity is involved in complex transactions.

C. The entity is subject to legal or regulatory requirements also found in larger entities.

D. Financial reporting objectives have been established.

Answer (A) is correct. *(Publisher)*

**REQUIRED:** The situation in which less formal means of achieving control objectives are appropriate.

**DISCUSSION:** Effective management involvement may obviate the need for more formal means of ensuring that internal control objectives are met. Thus, a smaller entity may not have formal policies regarding credit approval, information security, or competitive bidding. It also may not have a written code of conduct. Instead, a smaller entity may develop a culture emphasizing integrity and ethical behavior through management example. Moreover, an effective control environment may not require outside members on the board. In a small company, less detailed controls are possible when management retains authority for specific authorization of transactions and oversees employees performing incompatible tasks.

Answer (B) is incorrect because complex transactions may necessitate the more formal arrangements found in larger entities. Answer (C) is incorrect because legal or regulatory requirements may necessitate the more formal arrangements found in larger entities. Answer (D) is incorrect because all entities should establish financial reporting objectives. However, they may be recognized implicitly rather than explicitly in smaller entities. Management can assess the risks related to these objectives through direct personal involvement rather than a formal assessment process.

**39.** The frequency of the comparison of recorded accountability with assets (for the purpose of safeguarding assets) should be determined by

A. The amount of assets independent of the cost of the comparison.

B. The nature and amount of the asset and the cost of making the comparison.

C. The cost of the comparison and whether the susceptibility to loss results from errors or fraud.

D. The auditor in consultation with client management.

Answer (B) is correct. *(Publisher)*

**REQUIRED:** The factor(s) determining the frequency of comparing recorded accountability with assets.

**DISCUSSION:** Assets should be compared with the recorded accountability as frequently as the nature and amount of the assets require, within the limits of acceptable costs of comparison. The costs of safeguarding assets should not exceed the expected benefits.

Answer (A) is incorrect because the costs of controls should be considered when making the comparison. Answer (C) is incorrect because whether the susceptibility to loss arises from errors or fraud should have little bearing on the frequency of the comparison. Answer (D) is incorrect because management, not the auditor, has responsibility for internal control.

**40.** A company operates its own truck fleet. Rising operating costs have caused the company to reassess its internal control. Which one of the following controls may help to lower operating costs?

A. Preventive maintenance is performed independently of driver-requested maintenance.

B. Each driver has a control card for fuel use at the self-service diesel fuel dock.

C. Maintenance and repair part orders are determined and placed by using an EOQ system.

D. Parts and hand tools must be requisitioned from the parts department.

Answer (B) is correct. *(CIA, adapted)*

**REQUIRED:** The best control to help lower operating costs.

**DISCUSSION:** Requiring each driver to use a control card will permit the matching of fuel used by each driver with the miles driven. This practice should lower or control fuel (operating) costs as well as create an audit trail as evidence of the incurrence of fuel costs.

Answer (A) is incorrect because a combination of preventive and driver-requested maintenance is more effective. Answer (C) is incorrect because use of an EOQ system for parts orders is an effective control over maintenance rather than operating costs. Answer (D) is incorrect because requiring requisitions for parts is an effective control over maintenance rather than operating costs.

**41.** An audit of a depository institution discloses the existence of a personal loan to the president of that institution. The loan is both sizable and below market rate. Which of the following is a cost-effective policy that will help prevent a recurrence of this questionable practice?

A. Loans above a nominal dollar level will not be extended to directors or to executives above a specified organizational level.

B. Loans above a nominal dollar level will not be extended to any director or employee.

C. Below-market-rate loans will not be extended to directors or to executives above a specified organizational level.

D. Below-market-rate loans will not be extended under any circumstances.

Answer (A) is correct. *(CIA, adapted)*

**REQUIRED:** The policy that will help prevent a recurrence of an improper loan to an officer of a company.

**DISCUSSION:** High-ranking officials of an organization may be in a position to exercise undue influence over lower-level employees, for example, by bargaining for a reduced-rate loan in a negotiation that is clearly not at arm's length. A direct prohibition of any loans to high-ranking persons is a simple, cost-effective way of increasing the obstacles to self-serving behavior.

Answer (B) is incorrect because employees who are not in a position to bargain for below-market rates are appropriate institutional customers. Answer (C) is incorrect because not extending below-market-rate loans to directors or to executives above a specified organizational level leaves open the possibility of making loans at marginal rates that are favorable to the executive. Answer (D) is incorrect because not extending below-market-rate loans under any circumstances is neither cost effective nor prudent. Below-market-rate loans may be warranted, e.g., to prevent default.

## 3.4 Procedures for the Auditor's Consideration of Internal Control

**42.** The following are steps in the financial statement audit process:

I. Prepare flowchart
II. Gather exhibits of all documents
III. Interview personnel

The most logical sequence of steps is

A. I, II, III.
B. I, III, II.
C. III, II, I.
D. II, I, III.

Answer (C) is correct. *(CPA, adapted)*
**REQUIRED:** The order of the steps in the consideration of internal control.
**DISCUSSION:** AU 319 requires the auditor to gain an understanding of internal control and to document that understanding. For example, after making inquiries (interviewing client personnel), the auditor might gather client documents and then prepare a flowchart reflecting the information obtained about their flow.

**43.** Organizational charts are useful to an independent external auditor because they

A. Depict all lines of organizational communication.
B. Provide a starting point for assessing control risk.
C. Ensure the proper division of responsibilities.
D. Are essential to effective internal control.

Answer (B) is correct. *(Publisher)*
**REQUIRED:** The reason organizational charts are useful.
**DISCUSSION:** AU 319 identifies the organizational structure as a control environment factor to be considered in understanding internal control. An organizational chart depicts the assignment of authority and responsibility within an organization and is a consideration in evaluating the effectiveness of the organizational structure.
Answer (A) is incorrect because only formal lines of communication are shown on an organizational chart. Answer (C) is incorrect because the organizational chart does not ensure a proper allocation and performance of responsibilities. Answer (D) is incorrect because an organizational chart pictorially describes an entity's purported organization, but it does not in itself provide internal control.

**44.** In gaining an understanding of internal control, the auditor may trace several transactions through the control process, including how the transactions interface with any service organizations whose services are part of the information system. The primary purpose of this task is to

A. Replace substantive tests.
B. Determine whether the controls have been placed in operation.
C. Determine the effectiveness of the control procedures.
D. Detect fraud.

Answer (B) is correct. *(G. Fiebelkorn)*
**REQUIRED:** The reason an auditor traces several transactions through the control process.
**DISCUSSION:** The understanding should include knowledge about the design of relevant controls and determining whether they have been placed in operation by the entity and by service organizations whose services are part of the entity's information system. Tracing a few transactions through the control process should provide that evidence.
Answer (A) is incorrect because the auditor must perform at least some substantive testing for all material financial statement assertions. Answer (C) is incorrect because, in gaining the understanding, the auditor need not consider operating effectiveness. If the auditor wishes to assess control risk below the maximum, (s)he will test controls and evaluate their effectiveness. Answer (D) is incorrect because tracing a few transactions is not likely to detect fraud.

**45.** Audit evidence concerning segregation of duties ordinarily is best obtained by

A. Performing tests of transactions that corroborate management's financial statement assertions.
B. Observing the employees as they apply specific controls.
C. Obtaining a flowchart of activities performed by available personnel.
D. Developing audit objectives that reduce control risk.

Answer (B) is correct. *(CPA, adapted)*
**REQUIRED:** The best obtainable audit evidence concerning segregation of duties.
**DISCUSSION:** When documentary evidence does not exist, the auditor may rely on observation and inquiry about the effectiveness of the design or operation of a control, such as segregation of duties. Inquiry alone, however, will not ordinarily provide sufficient evidence to support the conclusion that the control significantly reduces the control risk for a specific assertion. Direct personal observation provides more assurance than inquiries.
Answer (A) is incorrect because tests of transactions to corroborate assertions are substantive tests, not tests of controls. Answer (C) is incorrect because a flowchart does not provide evidence that a control activity has been placed in operation or that it is effective. Answer (D) is incorrect because audit objectives are not audit evidence.

**46.** When considering an entity's internal control, an auditor should concentrate on the substance of controls rather than their form because

A. The controls may be operating effectively but may not be flowcharted.

B. Management may establish appropriate controls but not act on them.

C. The controls may be so inappropriate that no reliance is contemplated by the auditor.

D. Management may implement controls with costs in excess of benefits.

Answer (B) is correct. *(CPA, adapted)*

**REQUIRED:** The reason an auditor should concentrate on the substance of controls, not their form.

**DISCUSSION:** The auditor must concentrate on the substance rather than the form of controls because management may establish controls but not act on them. For example, management may develop a code of conduct but allow violations of the code (AU 319).

Answer (A) is incorrect because controls should be documented but need not be flowcharted. Answer (C) is incorrect because, if controls are so inappropriate that the auditor assesses control risk at the maximum, their substance is irrelevant. Answer (D) is incorrect because, when considering internal control in a financial statement audit, the auditor is primarily concerned with the effectiveness of controls, not their cost-benefit relationship.

**47.** Which of the following is a step in an auditor's decision to assess control risk below the maximum?

A. Apply analytical procedures to both financial data and nonfinancial information to detect conditions that may indicate weak controls.

B. Perform tests of details of transactions and account balances to identify potential errors and fraud.

C. Identify specific controls that are likely to detect or prevent material misstatements.

D. Document that the additional audit effort to perform tests of controls exceeds the potential reduction in substantive testing.

Answer (C) is correct. *(CPA, adapted)*

**REQUIRED:** The step necessary to assess control risk below the maximum.

**DISCUSSION:** Assessing control risk below the maximum requires identifying specific controls relevant to specific assertions that are likely to prevent or detect material misstatements. It also entails performing tests of controls to evaluate the effectiveness of such controls (AU 319).

Answer (A) is incorrect because analytical procedures are substantive tests. The auditor must perform tests of controls to assess control risk below the maximum. Answer (B) is incorrect because tests of details are substantive tests. The auditor must perform tests of controls to assess control risk below the maximum. Answer (D) is incorrect because, if the effort to perform tests of controls exceeds the potential reduction in substantive testing, assessing control risk at the maximum is justified.

**48.** Which of the following statements concerning control risk in a financial statement audit is true?

A. Assessing control risk and obtaining an understanding of an entity's internal control may be performed concurrently.

B. When control risk is at the maximum level, an auditor should reduce the amount of substantive testing.

C. Control risk may be assessed sufficiently low to eliminate substantive testing for significant transaction classes.

D. When assessing control risk, an auditor should not consider evidence obtained in prior audits about the operation of controls.

Answer (A) is correct. *(CPA, adapted)*

**REQUIRED:** The true statement concerning control risk.

**DISCUSSION:** According to AU 319, assessing control risk and understanding internal control may be performed concurrently. Procedures performed to achieve one objective may also pertain to the other. Moreover, for efficiency reasons, the auditor may plan to test some controls when obtaining the understanding.

Answer (B) is incorrect because the auditor should increase the amount of substantive testing if control risk is assessed at the maximum. Answer (C) is incorrect because some substantive tests must always be applied to significant assertions about material account balances or classes of transactions. Answer (D) is incorrect because evidence from previous audits may be considered subject to certain limitations, e.g., evidence obtained currently about changes in internal control.

**49.** In obtaining an understanding of an entity's internal control in a financial statement audit, an auditor is not obligated to

A. Determine whether the controls have been placed in operation.

B. Perform procedures to understand the design of controls.

C. Document the understanding of the entity's internal control components.

D. Search for significant deficiencies in the operation of internal control.

Answer (D) is correct. *(CPA, adapted)*

**REQUIRED:** The step an auditor need not take in obtaining an understanding of internal control.

**DISCUSSION:** The auditor should obtain a sufficient understanding of internal control to plan the audit. The understanding includes knowledge about the design of relevant controls and determining whether they have been placed in operation by the entity and by service organizations whose services are part of the entity's information system. In addition, the auditor should document the understanding of the entity's internal control. Though the auditor may become aware of deficiencies in the operation of internal control through gaining the understanding, (s)he is not obligated to search for such deficiencies.

**50.** According to AU 319, *Consideration of Internal Control in a Financial Statement Audit*, an entity's internal control addresses objectives related to reliability of financial reporting, compliance with applicable laws and regulations, and effectiveness and efficiency of operations. However, not all of these objectives and the related controls are relevant to a financial statement audit. Which one of the following would most likely be considered in an audit?

A. Timely reporting and review of quality control results.

B. Maintenance of control over unused checks.

C. Marketing analysis of sales generated by advertising projects.

D. Maintenance of statistical production analyses.

Answer (B) is correct. *(CMA, adapted)*

**REQUIRED:** The control most likely relevant to a financial statement audit.

**DISCUSSION:** Ordinarily, controls that are relevant to a financial statement audit pertain to the entity's objective of preparing financial statements for external purposes that are fairly presented in conformity with GAAP or another comprehensive basis of accounting. Maintenance of control over unused checks is an example of a relevant control because the objective is to provide assurance regarding the existence assertion for cash.

Answer (A) is incorrect because timely reporting and review of quality control results, marketing analysis, and maintenance of statistical production analyses concern the effectiveness, economy, and efficiency of management decision processes that ordinarily do not relate to an entity's ability to present fair financial statements. Answer (C) is incorrect because timely reporting and review of quality control results, marketing analysis, and maintenance of statistical production analyses concern the effectiveness, economy, and efficiency of management decision processes that ordinarily do not relate to an entity's ability to present fair financial statements. Answer (D) is incorrect because timely reporting and review of quality control results, marketing analysis, and maintenance of statistical production analyses concern the effectiveness, economy, and efficiency of management decision processes that ordinarily do not relate to an entity's ability to present fair financial statements.

**51.** The information and communication component of internal control includes the methods and records established to initiate, record, process, and report transactions and to maintain accountability. For which of the following transactions would the auditor ordinarily have the greatest difficulty in obtaining assurance that internal control objectives are met?

A. Collection of interest and dividends by a retailer.

B. Acquisition of production equipment by a manufacturer.

C. Collection of contributions from the public by a nonprofit organization.

D. Collection of credit sales by a retailer.

Answer (C) is correct. *(Publisher)*

**REQUIRED:** The transaction for which the auditor would have the greatest difficulty in gaining assurance that control objectives are met.

**DISCUSSION:** As part of the information and communication component, an accounting system should identify and record all valid transactions, permit their classification and recording at appropriately measured monetary values, determine the proper accounting period in which they should be recorded, and properly present them and related disclosures in the financial statements. Because corroborating documentation is often unavailable for contributions from the general public to a nonprofit organization, determining that these donations were properly accounted for is difficult.

Answer (A) is incorrect because collection of interest and dividends by a retailer is a transaction for which corroborating evidence (documentation) should be available. Answer (B) is incorrect because acquisition of production equipment by a manufacturer is a transaction for which corroborating evidence (documentation) should be available. Answer (D) is incorrect because collection of credit sales by a retailer is a transaction for which corroborating evidence (documentation) should be available.

**52.** Based on a consideration of internal control completed at an interim date, the auditor assessed control risk at a low level and performed interim substantive tests. The records and procedures would most likely be tested again at year-end if

A. Tests of controls were not performed by the internal auditor during the remaining period.

B. Internal control provides a basis for limiting the extent of substantive testing.

C. The auditor used nonstatistical sampling during the interim period testing of controls.

D. Inquiries and observations lead the auditor to believe that conditions have changed.

Answer (D) is correct. *(CPA, adapted)*

**REQUIRED:** The reason for retesting records and procedures at year-end.

**DISCUSSION:** Rapidly changing business conditions or other circumstances may predispose management to misstate financial statements in the remaining period. The auditor may then conclude that substantive tests covering the remaining period will be ineffective to control the incremental audit risk associated with testing at an interim date. In that case, the auditor should ordinarily decide to examine the relevant accounts as of the balance-sheet date (AU 313).

Answer (A) is incorrect because, by itself, the failure of the internal auditor to test controls during the remaining period does not require a change in audit strategy. Answer (B) is incorrect because a lower assessment of control risk increases the acceptable level of detection risk and decreases the necessary extent of tests. Answer (C) is incorrect because use of nonstatistical methods at the interim date does not necessitate retesting if sufficient competent evidence has been obtained.

**53.** An independent auditor of a client's financial statements might consider the procedures performed by the internal auditors because

A. They are employees whose work must be reviewed during substantive testing.

B. They are employees whose work may affect the nature, timing, and extent of audit procedures.

C. Their work affects the cost-benefit trade-off.

D. Their degree of independence may be inferred from the nature of their work.

Answer (B) is correct. *(CPA, adapted)*

**REQUIRED:** The reason an independent auditor might consider the procedures performed by internal auditors.

**DISCUSSION:** The work of the internal auditors cannot be substituted for the work of the independent auditor; however, the internal auditing function is part of the monitoring component of internal control. Consequently, the independent auditor should obtain an understanding of internal auditing sufficient to identify activities relevant to the audit (AU 322).

Answer (A) is incorrect because the independent auditor should obtain an understanding of internal auditing sufficient to identify activities relevant to the audit during the consideration of internal control. Answer (C) is incorrect because management is responsible for evaluating the cost-benefit relationship. Answer (D) is incorrect because internal auditors are not independent of the entity in the sense required by the *Code of Professional Conduct.*

**54.** Although substantive tests may support the accuracy of underlying records, these tests frequently provide no affirmative evidence of segregation of duties because

A. Substantive tests rarely guarantee the accuracy of the records if only a sample of the transactions has been tested.

B. The records may be accurate even though they are maintained by a person who performs incompatible functions.

C. Substantive tests relate to the entire period under audit, but tests of controls ordinarily are confined to the period during which the auditor is on the client's premises.

D. Many computerized procedures leave no audit trail of who performed them, so substantive tests may necessarily be limited to inquiries and observation of office personnel.

Answer (B) is correct. *(CPA, adapted)*

**REQUIRED:** The reason substantive tests may provide no affirmative evidence of segregation of duties.

**DISCUSSION:** Substantive tests, such as reconciliations or confirmations, may provide no affirmative evidence of segregation of duties because the records may be accurate even though maintained by a person who performs incompatible functions; that is, lack of segregation would not be revealed by substantive tests unless the detection of material inaccuracies resulted in performance of additional procedures.

Answer (A) is incorrect because properly applied sampling methods may provide reasonable assurance about the accuracy of records, including a quantification of the sampling risk. Answer (C) is incorrect because tests of the effectiveness of controls are concerned with the consistency of their application during the entire period under audit. Answer (D) is incorrect because, given computerized procedures, the auditor must perform substantive tests by auditing through the computer.

**55.** After obtaining an understanding of internal control and assessing control risk in the audit of a private company's financial statements, an auditor decided not to perform additional tests of controls. The auditor most likely concluded that the

A. Additional evidence to support a further reduction in control risk was not cost-beneficial to obtain.

B. Assessed level of inherent risk exceeded the assessed level of control risk.

C. Internal control was properly designed and justifiably may be relied on.

D. Evidence obtainable through test of controls would not support an increased assessment of control risk.

Answer (A) is correct. *(CPA, adapted)*

**REQUIRED:** The most likely reason the auditor decided not to perform additional tests of controls.

**DISCUSSION:** After obtaining the understanding of internal control and assessing control risk, the auditor may desire to seek a further reduction in the assessed level of control risk for certain assertions. In such cases, the auditor considers whether additional evidential matter sufficient to support a further reduction is likely to be available, and whether performing tests of controls to obtain that evidential matter is efficient (AU 319).

Answer (B) is incorrect because the assessment of inherent risk is independent of the assessment of control risk. Answer (C) is incorrect because gaining an understanding of internal control, i.e., obtaining knowledge about the design of controls and whether they have been placed in operation, is insufficient to assess control risk below the maximum. Answer (D) is incorrect because the issue is whether additional tests of controls will support a decreased assessment of control risk.

## 3.5 Tests of Controls

**56.** After gaining an understanding of internal control, the auditor may attempt to assess control risk at less than the maximum. For this purpose, the auditor should (1) identify specific controls that are likely to prevent or detect material misstatements in the relevant financial statement assertions, (2) perform procedures directed at the effectiveness of the design of the controls, and (3) perform tests of controls. The purpose of the tests of controls is to

A. Assure that the auditor has an adequate understanding of internal control.

B. Evaluate the effectiveness of such controls.

C. Provide recommendations to management to improve internal control.

D. Evaluate inherent risk.

Answer (B) is correct. *(Publisher)*

**REQUIRED:** The purpose of tests of controls.

**DISCUSSION:** The purpose of tests of controls is to evaluate the effectiveness of the operation of controls in preventing or detecting material misstatements. The auditor also tests how a control (whether manual or automated) was applied, by whom it was applied, and whether it was applied consistently during the audit period (AU 319).

Answer (A) is incorrect because the auditor gains an understanding of internal control primarily through previous experience with the entity, inquiries, inspection of documents and records, and observation of activities. Answer (C) is incorrect because the auditor is not obligated to search for reportable conditions but should communicate those of which (s)he becomes aware. Answer (D) is incorrect because inherent risk is the susceptibility of an assertion to a material misstatement in the absence of related controls.

**57.** Tests of controls are concerned primarily with each of the following questions except

A. How were the controls applied?

B. Were the controls approved by the board of directors?

C. Were the necessary controls consistently performed?

D. By whom were the controls applied?

Answer (B) is correct. *(CPA, adapted)*

**REQUIRED:** The question that is not directly relevant to tests of controls.

**DISCUSSION:** Tests of controls are undertaken to evaluate the effectiveness of the operation of controls. Management is responsible for designing and implementing the controls.

Answer (A) is incorrect because tests of controls directed toward operating effectiveness are concerned with how and by whom controls were applied and whether they were applied consistently during the audit period. Answer (C) is incorrect because tests of controls directed toward operating effectiveness are concerned with how and by whom controls were applied and whether they were applied consistently during the audit period. Answer (D) is incorrect because tests of controls directed toward operating effectiveness are concerned with how and by whom controls were applied and whether they were applied consistently during the audit period.

**58.** Tests of controls in a financial statement audit are least likely to be omitted with regard to

A. Accounts believed to be subject to ineffective controls.

B. Accounts representing few transactions.

C. Accounts representing many transactions.

D. Subsequent events.

Answer (C) is correct. *(Publisher)*

**REQUIRED:** The circumstances in which tests of controls are least likely to be omitted.

**DISCUSSION:** For high-volume accounts, the auditor usually must test controls because cost-benefit considerations preclude the review of all transactions. If the control risk for such accounts can be assessed at less than the maximum, the effect will be to reduce the assurance required by substantive tests.

Answer (A) is incorrect because if, as a result of obtaining the understanding of internal control, the auditor believes that controls are unlikely to be effective, (s)he may assess control risk at the maximum and omit tests of controls. Answer (B) is incorrect because, given few transactions, examining all transactions is more efficient than testing controls. Answer (D) is incorrect because each subsequent event that requires consideration by management and evaluation by the independent auditor should be examined. Hence, tests of relevant controls are likely to be omitted.

**59.** Which of the following procedures is not used in tests of controls over purchases?

A. Examine vouchers and supporting documents for authorization.

B. Trace vouchers to entries in the vouchers register.

C. Confirm inventory held in public warehouses.

D. Reperform calculations on some supporting documentation.

Answer (C) is correct. *(D. Wells)*

**REQUIRED:** The procedure that is not a test of controls over purchases.

**DISCUSSION:** The confirmation of inventory held in public warehouses is a substantive test of an account balance in the purchasing cycle.

**60.** The objective of tests of details of transactions performed as tests of controls is to

A. Monitor the design and use of entity documents such as prenumbered shipping forms.

B. Determine whether controls have been placed in operation.

C. Detect material misstatements in the account balances of the financial statements.

D. Evaluate whether controls operated effectively.

Answer (D) is correct. *(CPA, adapted)*

**REQUIRED:** The objective of the tests of the details of transactions performed as tests of controls.

**DISCUSSION:** Tests of controls are directed toward the operation of a control to assess its effectiveness in preventing or detecting material misstatements in a financial statement assertion.

Answer (A) is incorrect because the client's internal control should monitor the use of entity documents. Answer (B) is incorrect because determining whether controls have been placed in operation is part of obtaining the understanding of internal control. Answer (C) is incorrect because the purpose of substantive tests is to detect material misstatements in the account balances of the financial statements.

**61.** To obtain evidence about control risk, an auditor ordinarily selects tests from a variety of techniques, including

A. Analysis.

B. Confirmation.

C. Reperformance.

D. Comparison.

Answer (C) is correct. *(CPA, adapted)*

**REQUIRED:** The procedure most closely associated with tests of controls.

**DISCUSSION:** According to AU 319, the auditor selects tests of controls from a variety of techniques such as inquiry, observation, inspection, and reperformance of a control that pertains to an assertion. No one specific test of controls is always necessary, applicable, or equally effective in every circumstance.

Answer (A) is incorrect because analysis is more closely associated with substantive testing. Answer (B) is incorrect because confirmation is more closely associated with substantive testing. Answer (D) is incorrect because comparison is more closely associated with substantive testing.

**62.** An auditor wishes to evaluate the design and perform tests of controls over a client's cash disbursements procedures. If the controls leave no audit trail of documentary evidence, the auditor most likely will test the procedures by

A. Confirmation and observation.

B. Observation and inquiry.

C. Analytical procedures and confirmation.

D. Inquiry and analytical procedures.

Answer (B) is correct. *(CPA, adapted)*

**REQUIRED:** The tests of controls applied when controls leave no audit trail of documentary evidence.

**DISCUSSION:** Documentation of design or operation may not exist for some factors in the control environment, such as the assignment of authority and responsibility. In such circumstances, evidence about effectiveness of design or operation may be obtained through observation and inquiry.

Answer (A) is incorrect because analytical procedures and confirmation are substantive tests, not tests of controls. Answer (C) is incorrect because analytical procedures and confirmation are substantive tests, not tests of controls. Answer (D) is incorrect because analytical procedures and confirmation are substantive tests, not tests of controls.

**63.** Which of the following types of evidence will an auditor most likely examine to determine whether controls are operating as designed?

A. Confirmations of receivables verifying account balances.

B. Letters of representations corroborating inventory pricing.

C. Attorneys' responses to the auditor's inquiries.

D. Client records documenting the use of computer programs.

Answer (D) is correct. *(CPA, adapted)*

**REQUIRED:** The evidence most likely to provide assurance about the operating effectiveness of controls.

**DISCUSSION:** In testing controls over the computer processing function, the auditor should obtain evidence of proper authorization and recording of access to computer programs and files.

Answer (A) is incorrect because confirmations customarily request information regarding account balances. Thus, they are substantive tests, not tests of controls. Answer (B) is incorrect because representations about inventory pricing are obtained through substantive testing. Answer (C) is incorrect because inquiry of attorneys is a substantive test.

**64.** In a financial statement audit, the likelihood of assessing control risk too high is the risk that the sample selected to test controls

A. Does not support the auditor's planned assessed level of control risk when the true operating effectiveness of the control justifies such an assessment.

B. Contains misstatements that could be material to the financial statements when aggregated with misstatements in other account balances or transactions classes.

C. Contains proportionately fewer deviations from prescribed controls than exist in the balance or class as a whole.

D. Does not support the tolerable misstatement for some or all of management's assertions.

Answer (A) is correct. *(CPA, adapted)*

**REQUIRED:** The condition under which the auditor would assess control risk too high.

**DISCUSSION:** According to AU 350, one aspect of sampling risk in performing tests of controls is the risk of assessing control risk too high. It is the risk that the assessed level of control risk based on the sample is greater than the true operating effectiveness of the control. In other words, it is the risk that actual control risk is less than that indicated by the sample.

Answer (B) is incorrect because substantive tests are directed towards misstatements in management's assertions. Answer (C) is incorrect because, if the sample deviation rate is lower than the population rate, the auditor may assess control risk too low. Answer (D) is incorrect because substantive tests are directed towards misstatements in management's assertions.

**65.** Which of the following procedures concerning accounts receivable is an auditor most likely to perform to obtain evidential matter in support of an assessed level of control risk below the maximum level?

A. Observing an entity's employee prepare the schedule of past due accounts receivable.

B. Sending confirmation requests to an entity's principal customers to verify the existence of accounts receivable.

C. Inspecting an entity's analysis of accounts receivable for unusual balances.

D. Comparing an entity's uncollectible accounts expense to actual uncollectible accounts receivable.

Answer (A) is correct. *(CPA, adapted)*

**REQUIRED:** The procedure used to obtain evidential matter in support of an assessed level of control risk below the maximum level.

**DISCUSSION:** To assess control risk below the maximum, an auditor must perform tests of controls. Tests of controls include inquiry, observation, inspection, and reperformance of a control by the auditor. Thus, observing an entity's employee prepare the schedule of past due accounts receivable provides evidence of the effectiveness of certain controls over accounts receivable.

Answer (B) is incorrect because sending confirmation requests to verify the existence of accounts receivable is a test of the details of balances, which is a substantive test. Answer (C) is incorrect because inspecting an entity's analysis of accounts receivable for unusual balances is a test of the details of balances, which is a substantive test. Answer (D) is incorrect because comparing uncollectible accounts expense to actual uncollectible accounts receivable is a form of analytical procedure, which is used to determine if the auditor's expectation is supported by client data.

**66.** An auditor is least likely to test controls that provide for

A. Approval of the purchase and sale of trading securities.

B. Classification of revenue and expense transactions by product line.

C. Segregation of the functions of recording disbursements and reconciling the bank account.

D. Comparison of receiving reports and vendors' invoices with purchase orders.

Answer (B) is correct. *(CPA, adapted)*

**REQUIRED:** The controls least likely to be tested.

**DISCUSSION:** The independent auditor is primarily concerned with the fairness of external financial reporting. (S)he would be less likely to test controls over records used solely for internal management purposes. If items in financial statements are not classified by product line, the independent auditor would thus be unlikely to expend significant audit effort in testing such classifications.

Answer (A) is incorrect because a basic management objective of internal control is proper authorization of transactions. Answer (C) is incorrect because a basic management objective of establishing internal control is to provide for comparing recorded accountability with existing assets at reasonable intervals, such as by reconciling bank statements with the accounting records. Such reconciliations should be performed by an independent employee. Answer (D) is incorrect because comparison of receiving reports and vendors' invoices with purchase orders is a basic control over the purchasing function.

**67.** In performing tests of controls, the auditor will normally find that

A. The level of inherent risk is directly proportional to the rate of error.

B. The rate of deviations in the sample exceeds the rate of error in the accounting records.

C. The rate of error in the sample exceeds the rate of deviations.

D. All unexamined items result in errors in the accounting records.

Answer (B) is correct. *(CPA, adapted)*

**REQUIRED:** The normal finding by an auditor during tests of controls.

**DISCUSSION:** When testing controls, the auditor is directly concerned with deviations from specific controls. Failure to comply with a control does not necessarily result in an error in the records; e.g., the absence of an authorization signature does not necessarily mean that the transaction was improperly recorded. Accordingly, the rate of deviations from a control normally exceeds the error rate in the records.

Answer (A) is incorrect because inherent risk and the rate of error are not necessarily correlated. Effective controls may minimize the error rate even though inherent risk is high. Answer (C) is incorrect because the sample error rate should approximate the rate of total deviations from the control tested. Answer (D) is incorrect because unaudited items are not necessarily in error.

## 3.6 Internal Control of the Sales-Receivables-Cash Receipts Cycle

**68.** The internal control objectives of the revenue cycle include all of the following except

A. Revenue cycle transactions are properly executed.

B. Appropriate goods are ordered so that sales can be made.

C. Transactions relating to revenue are properly recorded.

D. Custody over assets resulting from the revenue cycle is properly maintained.

Answer (B) is correct. *(Publisher)*

**REQUIRED:** The internal control objective not directly related to the revenue cycle.

**DISCUSSION:** The revenue cycle contains the activities pertaining to exchanges with customers and the collection in cash of the amounts paid for the goods or services provided. Ordering appropriate goods, which is an objective of the purchases-payables cycle, is only indirectly related to the revenue cycle.

Answer (A) is incorrect because an internal control objective of the revenue cycle is that revenue-cycle transactions be properly executed. Answer (C) is incorrect because an internal control objective of the revenue cycle is that transactions relating to revenue be properly recorded. Answer (D) is incorrect because an internal control objective of the revenue cycle is that custody over assets resulting from the revenue cycle be properly maintained.

**69.** When evaluating internal control of an entity that processes sales transactions on the Internet, an auditor should be most concerned about the

A. Lack of sales invoice documents as an audit trail.

B. Potential for computer disruptions in recording sales.

C. Inability to establish an integrated test facility.

D. Frequency of archiving and data retention.

Answer (B) is correct. *(CPA, adapted)*

**REQUIRED:** The greatest concern about Internet controls.

**DISCUSSION:** Processing sales on the Internet (often called e-commerce) creates new and additional risks for clients. The client should use effective controls to ensure proper acceptance, processing, and storage of sales transactions. Threats include not only attacks from hackers but also system overload and equipment failure.

Answer (A) is incorrect because e-commerce sales transactions do not typically result in sales invoice documents. Answer (C) is incorrect because an integrated test facility is just one of many techniques for testing sales processing controls and transactions. Answer (D) is incorrect because, although archival and data retention are disaster recovery concerns, the question relates to controls over sales processing.

**70.** Which of the following are not directly involved in the revenue cycle?

A. Sales manager and the credit manager.

B. Treasurer and controller.

C. Billing clerk.

D. Receiving department clerk.

Answer (D) is correct. *(Publisher)*

**REQUIRED:** The person(s) not directly involved in the revenue cycle.

**DISCUSSION:** The receiving department clerk is involved in the purchases-payables cycle. The clerk counts the goods and prepares receiving reports that provide partial authorization for invoice payment.

Answer (A) is incorrect because the sales manager is responsible for executing sales transactions, and the credit manager authorizes sales. Answer (B) is incorrect because the treasurer has custody of cash receipts from sales, and the controller maintains records for the sales and billing cycle. Answer (C) is incorrect because the billing clerk is responsible for the preparation of invoices and the billing process.

**71.** Which of the following employees should report to the treasurer?

A. Internal auditor.

B. Sales clerk.

C. Bookkeeper.

D. Credit manager.

Answer (D) is correct. *(Publisher)*

**REQUIRED:** The person who should report to the treasurer.

**DISCUSSION:** The treasurer's primary responsibility is to safeguard assets. Although credit approval is an authorization process, assets are lost if credit is improperly granted. Thus, the credit manager should be responsible to one who has no vested interest in the granting of credit.

Answer (A) is incorrect because the internal auditor is part of internal control and should report to the audit committee. Answer (B) is incorrect because the sales clerk is involved with the execution of sales transactions and would more appropriately report to the sales manager. Answer (C) is incorrect because record keeping should be separated from authorization and asset custody.

**72.** An auditor tests an entity's policy of obtaining credit approval before shipping goods to customers in support of management's financial statement assertion of

A. Valuation or allocation.

B. Completeness.

C. Existence or occurrence.

D. Rights and obligations.

Answer (A) is correct. *(CPA, adapted)*

**REQUIRED:** The assertion related to the credit policy.

**DISCUSSION:** The proper approval of credit provides assurance that the account receivable will be collectible; thus, it is related to the valuation assertion that accounts receivable are recorded at net realizable value.

Answer (B) is incorrect because completeness concerns whether all transactions and accounts have been presented. Answer (C) is incorrect because existence or occurrence concerns whether assets or liabilities exist and whether recorded transactions have occurred. Answer (D) is incorrect because rights and obligations assertions deal with whether assets are the rights of the entity and obligations are liabilities of the entity at a given date.

**73.** At which point in an ordinary sales transaction of a wholesaling business is a lack of specific authorization of least concern to the auditor in the conduct of an audit?

A. Granting of credit.

B. Shipment of goods.

C. Determination of discounts.

D. Selling of goods for cash.

Answer (D) is correct. *(CPA, adapted)*

**REQUIRED:** The point in an ordinary sales transaction at which specific authorization is of least concern to an auditor.

**DISCUSSION:** Selling goods for cash is the consummation of a transaction that would likely be covered by a general authorization. Thus, the risk of loss arising from lack of specific authorization of cash sales is minimal.

Answer (A) is incorrect because granting of credit in a sales transaction may require specific authorization, i.e., special consideration before approval by the appropriate person. Answers (B) and (C) are incorrect because shipment of goods and determination of discounts in sales transactions may require specific authorization.

**74.** Which of the following most likely would be the result of ineffective controls in the revenue cycle?

A. Final authorization of credit memos by personnel in the sales department could permit an employee defalcation scheme.

B. Fictitious transactions could be recorded, causing an understatement of revenues and an overstatement of receivables.

C. Irregularities in recording transactions in the subsidiary accounts could result in a delay in goods shipped.

D. Omission of shipping documents could go undetected, causing an understatement of inventory.

Answer (A) is correct. *(CPA, adapted)*

**REQUIRED:** The most likely result of ineffective controls in the revenue cycle.

**DISCUSSION:** Ineffective controls in the revenue cycle, such as inappropriate division of duties and responsibilities, inadequate supervision, or deficient authorization, may result in the ability of employees to perpetrate irregularities. Thus, sales personnel should approve sales returns and allowances but not the related credit memos. Moreover, no authorization for the return of goods, defective or otherwise, should be considered complete until the goods are returned as evidenced by a receiving report.

Answer (B) is incorrect because recording fictitious sales overstates revenues. Answer (C) is incorrect because the customers' accounts are not posted until after goods are shipped. Answer (D) is incorrect because, if shipping documents are omitted, shipments of goods may not be credited to inventory, which overstates the account.

**75.** Which of the following credit approval procedures would be the basis for developing a deficiency finding for a wholesaler?

A. Trade-credit standards are reviewed and approved by the finance committee of the board of directors.

B. Customers not meeting trade-credit standards are shipped merchandise on a cash-on-delivery (C.O.D.) basis only.

C. Salespeople are responsible for evaluating and monitoring the financial condition of prospective and continuing customers.

D. An authorized signature from the credit department denoting approval of the customer's credit is to appear on all credit-sales orders.

Answer (C) is correct. *(CIA, adapted)*

**REQUIRED:** The credit approval procedure justifying a deficiency finding.

**DISCUSSION:** Salespeople should be responsible for generating sales and providing service to customers. For effective control purposes, the credit department should be responsible for monitoring the financial condition of prospective and continuing customers in the credit approval process.

Answer (A) is incorrect because trade-credit standards may be evaluated and approved by a committee of the board or delegated to management. Answer (B) is incorrect because shipping merchandise on a cash-on-delivery (C.O.D.) basis only is customary if trade-credit standards are not met. Answer (D) is incorrect because, the credit department should approve transactions based upon credit information before sales are processed.

**76.** Alpha Company uses its sales invoices for posting perpetual inventory records. Inadequate internal control over the invoicing function allows goods to be shipped that are not invoiced. The inadequate controls could cause an

A. Understatement of revenues, receivables, and inventory.

B. Overstatement of revenues and receivables, and an understatement of inventory.

C. Understatement of revenues and receivables, and an overstatement of inventory.

D. Overstatement of revenues, receivables, and inventory.

Answer (C) is correct. *(CPA, adapted)*

**REQUIRED:** The result of shipping goods that are not invoiced.

**DISCUSSION:** If goods are shipped before the sales are invoiced, inventory will not be credited for the shipments, thus overstating inventory. Moreover, if the accounting function does not receive copies of the invoices, sales and receivables will not be recorded, with the consequent understatement of those accounts.

Answer (A) is incorrect because shipping goods that are not invoiced could cause an overstatement of inventory. Answer (B) is incorrect because shipping goods that are not invoiced could cause an overstatement of inventory and an understatement of revenues and receivables. Answer (D) is incorrect because shipping goods that are not invoiced could cause an understatement of revenues and receivables.

**77.** Which of the following controls most likely would help ensure that all credit sales transactions of an entity are recorded?

A. The billing department supervisor sends copies of approved sales orders to the credit department for comparison to authorized credit limits and current customer account balances.

B. The accounting department supervisor independently reconciles the accounts receivable subsidiary ledger to the accounts receivable control account monthly.

C. The accounting department supervisor controls the mailing of monthly statements to customers and investigates any differences reported by customers.

D. The billing department supervisor matches prenumbered shipping documents with entries in the sales journal.

Answer (D) is correct. *(CPA, adapted)*

**REQUIRED:** The control to detect unrecorded sales.

**DISCUSSION:** The sequential numbering of documents provides a standard control over transactions. The numerical sequence should be accounted for by an independent party. A major objective is to detect unrecorded and unauthorized transactions. Moreover, comparing shipments with the sales journal also will detect unrecorded transactions.

Answer (A) is incorrect because credit approval does not ensure that sales have been recorded. Answer (B) is incorrect because the reconciliation will not detect sales that were never recorded. Answer (C) is incorrect because customers are unlikely to report understatement of their accounts.

Questions 78 and 79 are based on the following information. A flowchart of a client's revenue cycle appears below.

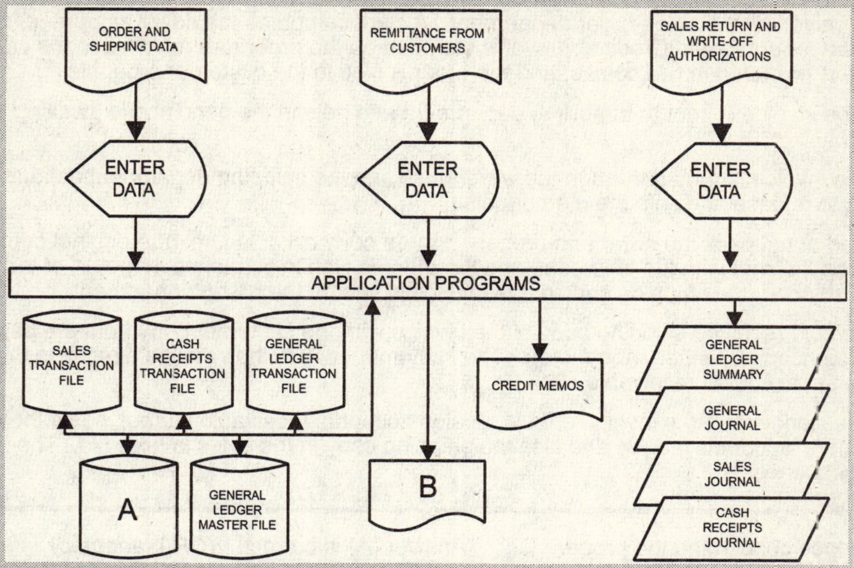


**78.** Symbol A most likely represents

A. Remittance advice file.
B. Receiving report file.
C. Accounts receivable master file.
D. Cash disbursements transaction file.

Answer (C) is correct. *(CPA, adapted)*
**REQUIRED:** The file accessed during processing a client's revenue transactions.
**DISCUSSION:** During the processing of sales orders and remittances from customers, as well as sales returns and write-off authorizations, the accounts receivable master file is accessed and updated. Thus, symbol A represents the accounts receivable master file.

Answer (A) is incorrect because the remittance advice file is represented by the cash receipts transaction file. Answer (B) is incorrect because the receiving report file relates to the purchasing cycle. Answer (D) is incorrect because the cash disbursements transaction file relates to the purchasing cycle.

**79.** Symbol B most likely represents

A. Customer orders.
B. Receiving reports.
C. Customer checks.
D. Sales invoices.

Answer (D) is correct. *(CPA, adapted)*
**REQUIRED:** The document represented by symbol B.
**DISCUSSION:** One output of the revenue cycle is the generation of sales invoices to be sent to customers.

Answer (A) is incorrect because customer orders are entered online and not outputted from the system. Answer (B) is incorrect because receiving reports are generated from the purchasing cycle, not the revenue cycle. Answer (C) is incorrect because customer checks are represented by remittances from customers and entered online. However, the customer checks are safeguarded and deposited daily into the bank account.

Questions 80 through 83 are based on the following information. Sales procedures that were encountered during the regular annual audit of Marvel Wholesale Distributing Company are as follows:

Customer orders are received by the sales-order department. A clerk computes the dollar amount of the order and sends it to the credit department for approval. Credit approval is stamped on the order and returned to the sales-order department. An invoice is prepared in two copies, and the order is filed in the customer order file.

The customer copy of the invoice is sent to the billing department and held in the pending file awaiting notification that the order has been shipped.

The shipping copy of the invoice is routed through the warehouse and the shipping department as authority for the respective departments to release and ship the merchandise.

Shipping department personnel pack the order and prepare a three-copy bill of lading: the original copy is mailed to the customer, the second copy is sent with the shipment, and the other is filed in sequence in the bill of lading file. After the merchandise has been shipped, the shipping copy of the invoice is sent to the billing department.

The billing clerk matches the received shipping copy of the invoice with the customer copy from the pending file. Both copies of the invoice are priced, extended, and footed. The customer copy is then mailed directly to the customer, and the shipping copy is sent to the accounts receivable clerk.

The accounts receivable clerk enters the invoice data in a sales-accounts receivable journal, posts the customer's account in the subsidiary customers' accounts ledger, and files the shipping copy in the sales invoice file. The invoices are numbered and filed in sequence.

**80.** To gather audit evidence concerning the proper credit approval of sales, the auditor would select a sample of transaction documents from the population represented by the

A. Customer order file.

B. Bill of lading file.

C. Subsidiary customers' accounts ledger.

D. Sales invoice file.

Answer (A) is correct. *(CPA, adapted)*

**REQUIRED:** The file or ledger containing evidence of proper issuance of credit sale approvals.

**DISCUSSION:** The customer order is first sent to the credit department, and credit approval is stamped on it. It is then returned to the sales department and filed. The customer order file thus contains the only documentation for credit approvals.

Answer (B) is incorrect because the bill of lading file contains no evidence of credit approvals. Answer (C) is incorrect because the subsidiary customers' accounts ledger contains no evidence of credit approvals. Answer (D) is incorrect because the sales invoice file contains no evidence of credit approvals.

**81.** To determine whether internal control operated effectively to minimize errors of failure to post invoices to the customers' accounts ledger, the auditor should select a sample of transactions from the population represented by the

A. Customer order file.

B. Bill of lading file.

C. Subsidiary customers' accounts ledger.

D. Sales invoice file.

Answer (D) is correct. *(CPA, adapted)*

**REQUIRED:** The source of data to ascertain whether internal control minimized accounts receivable posting errors.

**DISCUSSION:** The auditor should trace sales according to the sales invoices to the accounts receivable subsidiary ledger. Sales invoices in the sales invoice file without corresponding entries in the subsidiary ledger represent transactions not posted.

Answer (A) is incorrect because the customer order file does not necessarily contain sales information. Customer orders may not be accepted or shipped. Answer (B) is incorrect because the bill of lading file does not necessarily contain sales information. All shipments do not necessarily pertain to customer orders. Answer (C) is incorrect because the items in the subsidiary ledger represent those transactions that have been posted. The direction of the testing should be from sales invoice to subsidiary ledger, not subsidiary ledger to sales invoice.

**82.** To gather audit evidence that uncollected items in customers' accounts represented valid trade receivables, the auditor should select a sample of items from the population represented by the

A. Customer order file.

B. Bill of lading file.

C. Subsidiary customers' accounts ledger.

D. Sales invoice file.

Answer (C) is correct. *(CPA, adapted)*

**REQUIRED:** The test appropriate for determining the validity of accounts receivable.

**DISCUSSION:** The auditor should sample from records of open accounts receivable to determine if they represent valid assets. The open accounts receivable are maintained in the subsidiary customers' accounts ledger. Items would be confirmed directly with the debtors.

Answer (A) is incorrect because the customer order file is not updated for shipment or payment. Answer (B) is incorrect because the bill of lading file is not updated for shipment or payment. Answer (D) is incorrect because the sales invoice file is not updated for shipment or payment.

**83.** To determine whether internal control operated effectively to minimize errors of failure to invoice a shipment, the auditor should select a sample of transactions from the population represented by the

A. Customer order file.

B. Bill of lading file.

C. Subsidiary customers' accounts ledger.

D. Sales invoice file.

Answer (B) is correct. *(CPA, adapted)*

**REQUIRED:** The appropriate test to ascertain whether internal control minimized failures to invoice shipments.

**DISCUSSION:** The auditor should match bill of lading file copies relating to customer shipments to sales invoices (or possibly to the accounts receivable subsidiary ledger) to determine if shipments were not billed.

Answer (A) is incorrect because the customer order file may contain orders that were not approved and shipped. Answer (C) is incorrect because an inconsistency between a customer balance and an invoice may result from payment, not necessarily from failure to invoice a shipment. Answer (D) is incorrect because the direction of the testing is wrong. To test for failure to invoice, the auditor should not be sampling from a file containing only invoiced orders. Comparing sales invoices with corresponding bills of lading provides evidence that they represent actual shipments. Shipment provides evidence that the transactions were valid.

**84.** Proper authorization of write-offs of uncollectible accounts should be approved in which of the following departments?

A. Accounts receivable.

B. Credit.

C. Accounts payable.

D. Treasurer.

Answer (D) is correct. *(CPA, adapted)*

**REQUIRED:** The department authorizing write-offs of uncollectible accounts.

**DISCUSSION:** The write-off of uncollectible accounts requires strong controls. The initiation of the write-off is performed by the credit manager. However, approval should be made by an independent party, typically the treasurer. The credit manager will be evaluated, in part, on the amount of bad debt written off and should require significant evidence before initiating a write-off.

Answer (A) is incorrect because accounts receivable is an accounting function and should not be involved with the authorization of transactions. Answer (B) is incorrect because write-offs of uncollectible accounts should be approved by someone outside the credit department who does not have a record-keeping function. Answer (C) is incorrect because accounts payable is an accounting function and should not be involved with the authorization of transactions.

**85.** An auditor observes the mailing of monthly statements to a client's customers and reviews evidence of follow-up on errors reported by the customers. This test of controls most likely is performed to support management's financial statement assertion(s) of

| | Presentation and Disclosure | Existence or Occurrence |
|---|---|---|
| A. | Yes | Yes |
| B. | Yes | No |
| C. | No | Yes |
| D. | No | No |

Answer (C) is correct. *(CPA, adapted)*

**REQUIRED:** The financial statement assertion(s), if any, related to observing the client's follow-up on errors reported.

**DISCUSSION:** The existence assertion concerns whether assets or liabilities exist at the balance sheet date. Observation of the mailing of monthly statements, as well as observing the correction of reported errors, provides evidence that controls may be effective in ensuring that the client's customers are bona fide.

Answer (A) is incorrect because the observation of client activities related to customer statements provides little evidence concerning presentation or disclosure in the financial statements. Answer (B) is incorrect because the observation of client activities related to customer statements provides little evidence concerning presentation or disclosure in the financial statements. Answer (D) is incorrect because the mailing and follow-up procedures provide evidence that controls may be effective in ensuring that the client's customers are bona fide.

**86.** In a retail cash sales environment, which of the following controls is often absent?

A. Competent personnel.

B. Segregation of functions.

C. Supervision.

D. Asset access limited to authorized personnel.

Answer (B) is correct. *(Publisher)*

**REQUIRED:** The control often absent in a cash sales environment.

**DISCUSSION:** In the usual retail cash sales situation, the sales clerk authorizes and records the transactions and takes custody of assets. However, management ordinarily employs other compensating controls to minimize the effects of the failure to segregate functions. The cash receipts function is closely supervised, cash registers provide limited access to assets, and an internal recording function maintains control over cash receipts.

**87.** An auditor noted that the accounts receivable department is separate from other accounting activities. Credit is approved by a separate credit department. Control accounts and subsidiary ledgers are balanced monthly. Similarly, accounts are aged monthly. The accounts receivable manager writes off delinquent accounts after 1 year, or sooner if a bankruptcy or other unusual circumstances are involved. Credit memoranda are prenumbered and must correlate with receiving reports. Which of the following areas could be viewed as an internal control weakness of the above organization?

A. Write-offs of delinquent accounts.

B. Credit approvals.

C. Monthly aging of receivables.

D. Handling of credit memos.

Answer (A) is correct. *(CIA, adapted)*

**REQUIRED:** The area viewed as an internal control weakness of the organization.

**DISCUSSION:** The accounts receivable manager has the ability to perpetrate fraud because (s)he performs incompatible functions. Authorization and recording of transactions should be separate. Thus, an employee outside the accounts receivable department should authorize write-offs.

Answer (B) is incorrect because credit approval is an authorization function that is properly segregated from the record-keeping function. Answer (C) is incorrect because monthly aging is appropriate. Answer (D) is incorrect because the procedures regarding credit memoranda are standard controls.

**88.** One of two office clerks in a small company prepares a sales invoice for $4,300; however, the invoice is incorrectly entered by the bookkeeper in the general ledger and the accounts receivable subsidiary ledger as $3,400. The customer subsequently remits $3,400, the amount on the monthly statement. Assuming there are only three employees in the department, the most effective control to prevent this type of error is

A. Assigning the second office clerk to independently check the sales invoice prices, discounts, extensions, and footings, and to account for the invoice serial number.

B. Requiring that monthly statements be prepared by the bookkeeper and verified by one of the other office clerks prior to mailing.

C. Using predetermined totals to control posting routines.

D. Requiring the bookkeeper to perform periodic reconciliations of the accounts receivable subsidiary ledger and the general ledger.

Answer (C) is correct. *(CIA, adapted)*

**REQUIRED:** The most effective control to prevent posting errors.

**DISCUSSION:** A control total should be generated for the transactions to be posted. It should then be compared with the total of items posted to the individual accounts.

Answer (A) is incorrect because the misposting was an error that occurred subsequent to assigning the second office clerk to independently check the sales invoice prices, discounts, extensions, and footings, and to account for the invoice serial number. Answer (B) is incorrect because requiring that monthly statements be prepared by the bookkeeper and verified by one of the other office clerks prior to mailing would not detect an initial misposting. The statements are based on the misposted records. Answer (D) is incorrect because requiring the bookkeeper to perform periodic reconciliations of the accounts receivable subsidiary ledger and the general ledger would not detect an initial misposting. The reconciliations are based on the misposted records.

**89.** Which of the following is the best protection for a company that wishes to prevent the lapping of trade accounts receivable?

A. Segregate duties so that the bookkeeper in charge of the general ledger has no access to incoming mail.

B. Segregate duties so that no employee has access to both checks from customers and currency from daily cash receipts.

C. Have customers send payments directly to the company's depository bank.

D. Request that customers' payment checks be made payable to the company and addressed to the treasurer.

Answer (C) is correct. *(CPA, adapted)*

**REQUIRED:** The best protection from lapping of accounts receivable.

**DISCUSSION:** Lapping is the delayed recording of cash receipts to cover a cash shortage. Current receipts are posted to the accounts of customers who paid one or two days previously to avoid complaints (and discovery) when monthly statements are mailed. The best protection is for the customers to send payments directly to the company's depository bank. This procedure precludes client personnel from having access to the money.

Answer (A) is incorrect because having payments sent directly to the depository bank is the best protection. Cash receipts are not physically received by firm personnel. Answer (B) is incorrect because all monies should be entrusted to the treasurer for safekeeping. Answer (D) is incorrect because having payments sent directly to the depository bank is the best protection. Cash receipts are not physically received by firm personnel.

**90.** To conceal defalcations involving receivables, an experienced bookkeeper would be expected to charge which of the following accounts?

A. Miscellaneous income.

B. Petty cash.

C. Miscellaneous expense.

D. Sales returns.

Answer (D) is correct. *(CPA, adapted)*

**REQUIRED:** The account charged to conceal defalcations.

**DISCUSSION:** If monies have been abstracted from customers paying on account, a bookkeeper would debit sales returns and credit accounts receivable. If accounts receivable are not credited, the customer will continue to be billed and will complain.

Answer (A) is incorrect because debiting miscellaneous income and crediting accounts receivable results in an unusual entry that is likely to be reviewed and discovered. Answer (B) is incorrect because debiting petty cash and crediting accounts receivable results in an unusual entry that is likely to be reviewed and discovered. Answer (C) is incorrect because debiting miscellaneous expense and crediting accounts receivable results in an unusual entry that is likely to be reviewed and discovered.

**91.** Upon receipt of customers' checks in the mail room, a responsible employee should prepare a remittance listing that is forwarded to the cashier. A copy of the listing should be sent to the

A. Internal auditor to investigate the listing for unusual transactions.

B. Treasurer to compare the listing with the monthly bank statement.

C. Accounts receivable bookkeeper to update the subsidiary accounts receivable records.

D. Entity's bank to compare the listing with the cashier's deposit slip.

Answer (C) is correct. *(CPA, adapted)*

**REQUIRED:** The use of the client's remittance listing.

**DISCUSSION:** Individuals with record-keeping responsibility should not have custody of cash. They should use either the remittance advices or a listing of remittances to make entries to the cash and accounts receivable control accounts and to the subsidiary accounts receivable records. Having different people make entries in the control accounts and subsidiary records is an effective control.

Answer (A) is incorrect because the internal auditors should have no ongoing control responsibilities. The investigation of unusual transactions is first conducted in the treasurer's department. Answer (B) is incorrect because the monthly bank statement should be reconciled by someone outside of the treasury function. Answer (D) is incorrect because the entity's bank will supply a validated deposit slip based on the deposit for the day.

**92.** Cash receipts from sales on account have been misappropriated. Which of the following acts would conceal this defalcation and be least likely to be detected by an auditor?

A. Understating the sales journal.

B. Overstating the accounts receivable control account.

C. Overstating the accounts receivable subsidiary ledger.

D. Understating the cash receipts journal.

Answer (A) is correct. *(CPA, adapted)*

**REQUIRED:** The act that would conceal theft of cash receipts from credit sales and be least likely to be detected.

**DISCUSSION:** Not recording sales on account in the books of original entry is the most effective way to conceal a subsequent theft of cash receipts. The accounts will be incomplete but balanced, and procedures applied to the accounting records will not detect the defalcation. Moreover, customers are not likely to alert the auditor to the fraud because an unrecorded sale will not be billed and an unrecorded receivable will not be confirmed.

Answer (B) is incorrect because the discrepancy between the accounts receivable control account and the accounts receivable subsidiary ledger would alert the auditor to the misstatement. Answer (C) is incorrect because the discrepancy between the accounts receivable control account and the accounts receivable subsidiary ledger would alert the auditor to the misstatement. Answer (D) is incorrect because understating the cash receipts journal will not conceal the defalcation. Cash receipts will not reconcile with the credits to accounts receivable. If accounts receivable are not credited, confirmation will detect the fraud.

**93.** For the purpose of proper accounting control, postdated checks remitted by customers should be

A. Restrictively endorsed.

B. Returned to customer.

C. Recorded as a cash sale.

D. Placed in the joint custody of two officers.

Answer (A) is correct. *(CPA, adapted)*

**REQUIRED:** The appropriate procedure for handling postdated checks remitted by customers.

**DISCUSSION:** All checks remitted by customers should be restrictively endorsed with the phrase "For Deposit Only" in the company account regardless of their date. They should be physically safeguarded until deposit.

Answer (B) is incorrect because acceptance of a postdated check may be the firm's best (only) chance to collect cash from the customer. Answer (C) is incorrect because a postdated check does not represent cash. Answer (D) is incorrect because the postdated check should be kept by the treasurer and accounted for by the controller.

**94.** Which of the following controls is most likely to deter lapping of collections from customers?

A. Independent internal verification of dates of entry in the cash receipts journal with dates of daily cash summaries.

B. Authorization of write-offs of uncollectible accounts by a supervisor independent of credit approval.

C. Segregation of duties between receiving cash and posting the accounts receivable ledger.

D. Supervisory comparison of the daily cash summary with the sum of the cash receipts journal entries.

Answer (C) is correct. *(CPA, adapted)*

**REQUIRED:** The best protection from lapping of collections from customers.

**DISCUSSION:** Lapping is the delayed recording of cash receipts to cover a cash shortage. Lapping is possible when an employee who maintains the accounts receivable ledger also has physical custody of the cash receipts. The best protection is to require customers to send payments directly to the company's depository bank. The next best procedure is to assure that the accounts receivable clerk has no access to cash received by the mail room. Thus, the duties of receiving cash and posting the accounts receivable ledger are segregated.

Answer (A) is incorrect because lapping delays recording cash receipts so that posting the cash receipts journal and recording in the cash summary occur on the same date and in the same amounts. Answer (B) is incorrect because lapping involves delayed posting of cash payments, not bad debt write-offs. Moreover, the credit manager should approve write-offs. Answer (D) is incorrect because lapping delays recording cash receipts so that posting the cash receipts journal and recording in the cash summary occur on the same date and in the same amounts.

---

Questions 95 and 96 are based on the following information. Management discovers that a supervisor at one of its restaurant locations removes excess cash and resets sales totals throughout the day on the point of sale (POS) system. At closing, the supervisor deposits cash equal to the recorded sales on the POS system and keeps the rest.

The supervisor forwards the close-of-day POS reports from the POS system along with a copy of the bank deposit slip to the company's revenue accounting department. The revenue accounting department records the sales and the cash for the location in the general ledger and verifies the deposit slip to the bank statement. Any differences between sales and deposits are recorded in an over/short account and, if necessary, followed up with the location supervisor. The customer food order checks are serially numbered, and it is the supervisor's responsibility to see that they are accounted for at the end of each day. Customer checks and the transaction journal tapes from the POS system are kept by the supervisor for one week at the location and then destroyed.

---

**95.** Which of the following controls allowed the fraud to occur?

A. The accounting for customer food checks by the supervisor.

B. The deposit of cash receipts by the supervisor.

C. The matching of the bank deposit slips to the bank statement by revenue accounting.

D. The forwarding of the close-of-day POS reports to revenue accounting.

Answer (A) is correct. *(CIA, adapted)*

**REQUIRED:** The control that allowed the fraud to occur.

**DISCUSSION:** An inappropriate segregation of duties existed because the supervisor was responsible for accounting for customer food checks and depositing receipts and had the ability to reset POS totals throughout the day.

Answer (B) is incorrect because the depositing of receipts by the supervisor is not the problem. The supervisor's access to cash and ability to reset POS totals throughout the day allowed the fraud. Answer (C) is incorrect because an independent verification of the deposits made by the supervisor is appropriate. Answer (D) is incorrect because the forwarding of the close-of-day POS reports to revenue accounting is a step in the process of independently verifying sales.

**96.** Which of the following audit procedures would have detected the fraud?

A. Flowcharting the controls over the verification of bank deposits.

B. Comparing a sample of the close-of-day POS reports to copies of the bank deposit slips.

C. On a test basis, verifying that the serial-numbered customer food checks are accounted for.

D. For selected days, reconciling the total of customer food checks to daily bank deposits.

Answer (D) is correct. *(CIA, adapted)*

**REQUIRED:** The audit procedure that would have detected the fraud.

**DISCUSSION:** Using the total of the customer food checks as a confirmation of sales would have detected the shortage in the bank deposit.

Answer (A) is incorrect because the fraud involved receipts, not deposits. Answer (B) is incorrect because the fraud involved altering the amounts on the close-of-day POS reports by resetting the POS system totals to zero. Answer (C) is incorrect because the accounting for individual customer food checks would not have detected the fraud. It did not involve manipulation of these documents.

**97.** For effective internal control, employees maintaining the accounts receivable subsidiary ledger should not also approve

A. Employee overtime wages.

B. Credit granted to customers.

C. Write-offs of customer accounts.

D. Cash disbursements.

Answer (C) is correct. *(CPA, adapted)*

**REQUIRED:** The activity incompatible with maintaining the accounts receivable subsidiary ledger.

**DISCUSSION:** An employee who authorizes a transaction, such as the write-off of a receivable, ordinarily should not be responsible for recording the same transaction. Segregating the functions of authorization, record keeping, and custody of assets reduces the possibility that an employee may be able to both perpetrate and conceal a fraud in the normal course of his/her duties.

Answer (A) is incorrect because authorization of cash disbursements, e.g., for overtime, is not related to receivables. Answer (B) is incorrect because, although credit approval effectively authorizes a debit to receivables, combining that function with keeping the receivables records is less likely to result in fraud than approving write-offs. Answer (D) is incorrect because authorization of cash disbursements, e.g., for overtime, is not related to receivables.

**98.** To safeguard the assets through proper internal control, accounts receivable that are written off should be transferred to

A. A separate ledger.

B. An attorney for evidence in collection proceedings.

C. A tax deductions file.

D. A credit manager, since customers may seek to reestablish credit by paying.

Answer (A) is correct. *(CPA, adapted)*

**REQUIRED:** The proper disposition of accounts receivable that are written off.

**DISCUSSION:** Accounts receivable that are written off should be transferred to a separate ledger, which should be maintained by the accounting department and periodically reviewed to determine if accounts have become collectible.

Answer (B) is incorrect because, if collection proceedings are initiated, the expectation is that the accounts will be collected and therefore should not be written off. Answer (C) is incorrect because the tax effects of accounts receivable are reflected in bad debt expense. Answer (D) is incorrect because the credit manager should not control the accounts receivable. The credit manager's function is to authorize credit, not maintain custody of assets.

**99.** Sound internal control procedures dictate that defective merchandise returned by customers should be presented initially to the

A. Accounts receivable supervisor.

B. Receiving clerk.

C. Shipping department supervisor.

D. Sales clerk.

Answer (B) is correct. *(CPA, adapted)*

**REQUIRED:** The individual to whom customers should return defective merchandise.

**DISCUSSION:** For control purposes, all receipts of goods or materials should be handled by the receiving clerk. Receiving reports should be prepared for all items received.

**100.** When an office supply company is unable to fill an order completely, it marks the out-of-stock items as back ordered on the customer's order and enters these items in a back order file that management can view or print. Customers are becoming disgruntled with the company because it seems unable to keep track of and ship out-of-stock items as soon as they are available. The best approach for ensuring prompt delivery of out-of-stock items is to

A. Match the back order file to goods received daily.

B. Increase inventory levels to minimize the number of times that stockouts occur.

C. Implement electronic data interchange with supply vendors to decrease the time to replenish inventory.

D. Reconcile the sum of filled and back orders with the total of all orders placed daily.

Answer (A) is correct. *(CIA, adapted)*

**REQUIRED:** The best approach for ensuring prompt delivery of out-of-stock items.

**DISCUSSION:** Reconciling the back order file to shipments received daily would identify unfilled orders for appropriate action.

Answer (B) is incorrect because increasing inventory levels might minimize the number of times that out-of-stock conditions occur but will not affect delivery of the items that are out of stock. Answer (C) is incorrect because implementing electronic data interchange with supply vendors may decrease the time to replenish inventory but will not affect delivery of the items that are out of stock. Answer (D) is incorrect because reconciling the sum of filled and back orders with the total of all orders placed daily ensures that orders are either filled or back ordered but will not affect delivery of the items that are out of stock.

**101.** Cash receipts should be deposited on the day of receipt or the following business day. Select the most appropriate audit procedure to determine that cash is promptly deposited.

A. Review cash register tapes prepared for each sale.

B. Review the functions of cash handling and maintaining accounting records for proper separation of duties.

C. Compare the daily cash receipts totals with the bank deposits.

D. Review the functions of cash receiving and disbursing for proper separation of duties.

Answer (C) is correct. *(CIA, adapted)*

**REQUIRED:** The most appropriate audit procedure to determine that cash is promptly deposited.

**DISCUSSION:** A standard control over the cash receipts function is to require that daily cash receipts be deposited promptly and intact. Hence, the total of cash receipts for a day should equal the bank deposit because no cash disbursements are made from the daily receipts. To determine whether cash receipts are promptly deposited, the auditor should compare the daily cash receipts totals with bank deposits.

Answer (A) is incorrect because reviewing the cash register tapes will not ensure that cash is deposited. Answer (B) is incorrect because separating functions will not ensure that cash is deposited. Answer (D) is incorrect because separating functions will not ensure that cash is deposited.

**102.** To establish illegal slush funds, corporations may divert cash received in normal business operations. An auditor would encounter the greatest difficulty in detecting the diversion of proceeds from

A. Scrap sales.

B. Dividends.

C. Purchase returns.

D. C.O.D. sales.

Answer (A) is correct. *(CPA, adapted)*

**REQUIRED:** The transaction from which the diversion of proceeds is most difficult to detect.

**DISCUSSION:** Because scrap sales often provide little documentary evidence to corroborate cash receipts, it is difficult to detect abstraction of proceeds from unrecorded sales.

Answer (B) is incorrect because the auditor can ordinarily reconcile the expected dividends from securities held with the actual amounts received. Answer (C) is incorrect because purchase returns are usually well documented and controlled. Answer (D) is incorrect because C.O.D. sales are usually well documented and controlled.

## 3.7 Internal Control of the Purchases-Payables-Cash Disbursements Cycle

**103.** The primary audit objective regarding the purchasing of materials by the client is to

A. Ascertain that materials paid for are on hand.

B. Observe the annual physical count.

C. Investigate the recording of unusual transactions regarding materials.

D. Determine the reliability of financial reporting by the purchasing function.

Answer (D) is correct. *(Publisher)*

**REQUIRED:** The auditor's primary objective in reviewing a client's materials purchasing cycle.

**DISCUSSION:** The auditor must obtain an understanding of the client's controls over the purchasing cycle and assess control risk to determine the nature, timing, and extent of substantive testing of details of purchasing cycle account balances and transactions.

Answer (A) is incorrect because materials not on hand may have been sold or used in production. Answer (B) is incorrect because this question relates to purchasing, not the inventory function. Answer (C) is incorrect because investigating the recording of unusual transactions is an audit procedure rather than an objective.

**104.** Which of the following questions is inappropriate on an internal control questionnaire concerning purchase transactions?

A. Are an approved purchase requisition and a signed purchase order required for each purchase?

B. Are prenumbered purchase orders and receiving reports used and accounted for?

C. Are all goods received in a centralized receiving department and counted, inspected, and compared with purchase orders on receipt?

D. Are intact cash receipts deposited daily in the bank?

Answer (D) is correct. *(Publisher)*

**REQUIRED:** The question not associated with purchase transactions.

**DISCUSSION:** The question concerning the daily deposit of intact cash receipts is related to the cash receipts cycle, not the purchases-payables-cash disbursements cycle.

Answer (A) is incorrect because a question concerning the requirement of an approved purchase requisition and a signed purchase order is appropriate relative to internal control over purchase transactions. Answer (B) is incorrect because a question concerning the use of prenumbered purchase orders and receiving reports is appropriate relative to internal control over purchase transactions. Answer (C) is incorrect because a question concerning activities of a centralized receiving department is appropriate relative to internal control over purchase transactions.

**105.** If internal control is well-designed, employees in the same department most likely will approve purchase orders and also

A. Reconcile the open invoice file.

B. Inspect goods upon receipt.

C. Authorize requisitions of goods.

D. Negotiate terms with vendors.

Answer (D) is correct. *(CPA, adapted)*

**REQUIRED:** The task appropriately performed by employees who approve purchase orders.

**DISCUSSION:** To prevent or detect errors or fraud in the performance of assigned responsibilities, duties are often segregated. Approving purchase orders and negotiating terms with vendors are part of the authorization process performed by the purchasing department.

Answer (A) is incorrect because reconciling the open invoice file is the accounting department's function. Answer (B) is incorrect because inspection of goods upon receipt is the receiving department's function. Answer (C) is incorrect because authorization of the requisition is inventory control's function.

**106.** To minimize the risk that agents in the purchasing department will use their positions for personal gain, the organization should

A. Require competitive bidding.

B. Request internal auditors to confirm selected purchases and accounts payable.

C. Specify that all items purchased must pass value-per-unit-of-cost reviews.

D. Direct the purchasing department to maintain records on purchase prices paid, with review of such records required every 6 months.

Answer (A) is correct. *(CIA, adapted)*

**REQUIRED:** The control that will minimize the risk that purchasing agents will use their positions for personal gain.

**DISCUSSION:** The primary function of a purchasing department is to ensure the authorized acquisition of goods of a specified quality on a timely basis at an economical price. Competitive bidding procedures should reduce both costs and the likelihood that a purchasing agent will show favoritism to a vendor.

Answer (B) is incorrect because confirmation establishes the existence of the liabilities but does not test the choice of vendor. Answer (C) is incorrect because specifying that all items purchased must pass value-per-unit-of-cost reviews is essentially a detective, not a preventive, control. Answer (D) is incorrect because directing the purchasing department to maintain records on purchase prices paid, with review of such records required every 6 months, is essentially a detective, not a preventive, control.

**107.** A university does not have a centralized receiving function for departmental purchases of books, supplies, and equipment. Which of the following controls will most effectively prevent payment for goods not received, if performed prior to invoice payment?

A. Vendor invoices should be matched with department purchase orders.

B. Names and addresses on vendor invoices should be compared to a list of department-authorized vendors.

C. Vendor invoices should be approved by a departmental supervisor other than the employee ordering the goods.

D. Invoices over a specified amount should be approved by the vice president of finance.

Answer (C) is correct. *(CIA, adapted)*

**REQUIRED:** The control that would most effectively prevent payment for goods not received, if performed prior to invoice payment.

**DISCUSSION:** The departmental supervisors are the most likely to be aware of the goods received by their departments. Moreover, segregating ordering authority from payment authority will prevent unauthorized purchases.

Answer (A) is incorrect because purchase orders do not provide evidence that the goods were received. Answer (B) is incorrect because comparison with lists of authorized vendors does not provide evidence that goods were received. Answer (D) is incorrect because the vice president of finance is unlikely to have knowledge of goods received by the departments.

**108.** The principal function of a cash budget is to

A. Ensure that the accounting principles relevant to cash transactions are applied consistently from period to period.

B. Ensure that the accounting records are accurate.

C. Physically safeguard cash.

D. Implement asset and liability maturity matching.

Answer (D) is correct. *(Publisher)*

**REQUIRED:** The principal function of a cash budget.

**DISCUSSION:** Financial management customarily matches asset and liability maturities. Hence, long-term assets are usually financed with long-term debt and equity, and short-term financing is matched with temporary current assets. The purpose of maturity matching is to reduce the risk that the entity will be unable to pay its obligations as they become due.

Answer (A) is incorrect because the budget is ordinarily considered a financial tool, not an accounting check. Answer (B) is incorrect because the budget is ordinarily considered a financial tool, not an accounting check. Answer (C) is incorrect because the cash budget plans for the sources and uses of cash, whereas safes and bank accounts physically safeguard cash.

**109.** Your objective is to determine that nonrecurring purchases, initiated by various user organizations, have been properly authorized. If all purchases are made through the purchasing department, to which of the following documents should you vouch purchases?

A. Purchase requisitions.

B. Purchase orders.

C. Invoices.

D. Receiving reports.

Answer (A) is correct. *(CIA, adapted)*

**REQUIRED:** The document to which purchases should be vouched.

**DISCUSSION:** When the auditor tests for unauthorized nonrecurring purchases, (s)he should vouch purchases to the purchase requisitions. The initiating authorization by the user department is embodied in a properly authorized purchase requisition.

Answer (B) is incorrect because the purchase order does not contain the crucial initiating authorization. Answer (C) is incorrect because the authorization for a purchase is not contained in the vendor's invoice. Answer (D) is incorrect because the authorization for a purchase is not contained in the receiving report.

**110.** Effective controls relevant to purchasing of raw materials should usually include all of the following except

A. Systematic reporting of product changes that will affect raw materials.

B. Determining the need for the raw materials prior to preparing the purchase order.

C. Obtaining third-party written quality and quantity reports prior to payment for the raw materials.

D. Obtaining financial approval prior to making a commitment.

Answer (C) is correct. *(CPA, adapted)*

**REQUIRED:** The procedure that is not an effective control over usual purchases.

**DISCUSSION:** Obtaining third-party written quality and quantity reports prior to payment for raw materials is unnecessary. Only in exceptional cases when client personnel are not sufficiently knowledgeable about the purchased goods would outside advice be necessary.

Answer (A) is incorrect because the latest product changes should be incorporated in the bill of materials records so that obsolete materials are not ordered. Answer (B) is incorrect because only needed items should be ordered. Answer (D) is incorrect because financial approval before making a commitment is important so that funds will be available when payment is required.

**111.** In assessing control risk for purchases, an auditor vouches a sample of entries in the voucher register to the supporting documents. Which assertion would this test of controls most likely support?

A. Completeness.

B. Existence or occurrence.

C. Valuation or allocation.

D. Rights and obligations.

Answer (B) is correct. *(CPA, adapted)*

**REQUIRED:** The assertion tested by vouching.

**DISCUSSION:** A voucher signifies a liability. Its issuance is recorded in the voucher register after comparison of the vendor's invoice with the purchase requisition, purchase order, and receiving report. The direction of testing is an important consideration in meeting specific audit objectives. Selecting a sample of recorded entries in the voucher register and vouching them to the supporting documentation provides evidence that the transactions occurred.

Answer (A) is incorrect because this procedure does not test for unrecorded transactions. Answer (C) is incorrect because this procedure provides evidence regarding the amount owed and whether the entry reflects an obligation of the company, but it most strongly supports the assertion about existence. Answer (D) is incorrect because this procedure provides evidence regarding the amount owed and whether the entry reflects an obligation of the company, but it most strongly supports the assertion about existence.

**112.** Based on observations made during a financial statement audit, the independent auditor should discuss with management the effectiveness of the company's controls that protect against the purchase of

A. Required supplies provided by a vendor who offers no trade or cash discounts.

B. Inventory items acquired based on an economic order quantity (EOQ) inventory management concept.

C. New equipment that is needed but does not qualify for an accelerated write-off under the class life rules.

D. Supplies individually ordered, without considering possible volume discounts.

Answer (D) is correct. *(CPA, adapted)*

**REQUIRED:** The potential weakness in the controls relevant to purchasing.

**DISCUSSION:** Because an auditor must communicate to the audit committee or its equivalent any reportable conditions observed during an audit (AU 325), (s)he should discuss procedures with management that permit the avoidable loss of assets. (S)he should therefore be concerned with whether the failure to consider possible volume discounts is attributable to an error or fraud.

Answer (A) is incorrect because the firm may consider other factors such as quality and service, not just whether a discount is offered on the required supplies. Answer (B) is incorrect because inventory management is appropriately based on EOQ concepts. It minimizes the sum of inventory ordering costs and inventory carrying costs. Answer (C) is incorrect because equipment acquisition should be based on need for the equipment, not on whether the purchase qualifies for preferential tax treatment.

**113.** In assessing control risk for the purchasing cycle, the auditor will be least influenced by

A. The effectiveness of controls in other cycles, e.g., the sales-receivables-cash receipts cycle.

B. The existence within the purchasing cycle of internal control strengths that offset weaknesses.

C. The audit work performed in the purchasing cycle by the company's internal auditor.

D. The availability of a company manual describing policies and procedures for the purchasing cycle.

Answer (A) is correct. *(Publisher)*

**REQUIRED:** The least influential factor in the assessment of control risk for the purchasing cycle.

**DISCUSSION:** The auditor must (1) obtain sufficient evidence to support the assessed level of control risk and (2) document the conclusion and the basis for it (AU 319). The effectiveness of internal control in other areas of an organization should not affect the assessment of control risk for the purchasing cycle. Each area should be judged upon its own merits.

Answer (B) is incorrect because the availability of a company manual describing policies and procedures for the purchasing cycle, the scope and results of audit work by the company's internal auditor, and the existence of internal control strengths that offset weaknesses are important in the assessment of control risk. Answer (C) is incorrect because the availability of a company manual describing policies and procedures for the purchasing cycle, the scope and results of audit work by the company's internal auditor, and the existence of internal control strengths that offset weaknesses are important in the assessment of control risk. Answer (D) is incorrect because the availability of a company manual describing policies and procedures for the purchasing cycle, the scope and results of audit work by the company's internal auditor, and the existence of internal control strengths that offset weaknesses are important in the assessment of control risk.

**114.** Effective controls relevant to the economy and efficiency of purchases will result in proper evaluation of the time for ordering merchandise. When making this evaluation, the purchasing company should give primary consideration to

A. The price differences that exist among various vendors who can supply the merchandise at the required time.

B. The borrowing cost of money (interest) that the company must incur as a consequence of acquiring the merchandise.

C. The trade-off between the cost of owning and storing excess merchandise and the risk of loss by not having merchandise on hand.

D. The flow of funds within the company that indicates when money is available to pay for merchandise.

Answer (C) is correct. *(CPA, adapted)*

**REQUIRED:** The primary consideration regarding the timing of purchase orders.

**DISCUSSION:** Effective purchasing departments should use the basic economic order quantity (EOQ) calculation that minimizes both the cost of owning and storing excess merchandise and the cost of ordering merchandise (and thus the timing of ordering). This model assumes the demand is constant and does not consider the cost of stockouts. Probabilistic models have been developed to incorporate the risk of loss (cost) by not having merchandise on hand.

Answer (A) is incorrect because the price differences that exist among various vendors does not address the question of when to order. Answer (B) is incorrect because the borrowing cost of money (interest) that the company must incur as a consequence of acquiring the merchandise does not address the question of when to order. Answer (D) is incorrect because, if the merchandise is needed, the treasurer is responsible for assuring that financing, which may be external, is arranged.

**115.** Which of the following constitutes the best evidence of the transfer of accountability for incoming material from the receiving department to other departments or activities?

A. The physical evidence of that type of material in other departments.

B. Oral evidence from personnel in both receiving and other departments.

C. An authorized signature on the prescribed transfer form.

D. Documentary evidence in the form of entries in journals and ledgers.

Answer (C) is correct. *(CIA, adapted)*

**REQUIRED:** The best evidence of the transfer of accountability for incoming material.

**DISCUSSION:** Internal control must maintain effective accountability for assets. The signature on a prescribed form documents the transfer of accountability for assets and thus permits the recorded accountability to be compared with the existing assets when necessary.

Answer (A) is incorrect because the physical evidence of that type of material in other departments provides evidence of the physical transfer of material, not of accountability. Answer (B) is incorrect because a paper trail is preferable to oral evidence. Answer (D) is incorrect because the entries must be supported by documentation.

**116.** An internal control questionnaire indicates that an approved receiving report is required to accompany every check request for payment of merchandise. Which of the following procedures provides the greatest assurance that this control is operating effectively?

A. Select and examine receiving reports and ascertain that the related canceled checks are dated no earlier than the receiving reports.

B. Select and examine receiving reports and ascertain that the related canceled checks are dated no later than the receiving reports.

C. Select and examine canceled checks and ascertain that the related receiving reports are dated no earlier than the checks.

D. Select and examine canceled checks and ascertain that the related receiving reports are dated no later than the checks.

Answer (D) is correct. *(CPA, adapted)*

**REQUIRED:** The procedure providing assurance that an approved receiving report is required to accompany every check request for payment of merchandise.

**DISCUSSION:** The best procedure is to test whether any checks have been issued without receiving reports. An appropriate sample of canceled checks and the related supporting documentation should be examined. The checks should not have been written before the dates on the receiving reports.

Answer (A) is incorrect because selecting and examining receiving reports and ascertaining that the related canceled checks are dated no earlier than the receiving reports tests in the wrong direction. This procedure determines whether receiving reports resulted in issuance of checks. Answer (B) is incorrect because selecting and examining receiving reports and ascertaining that the related canceled checks are dated no later than the receiving reports tests in the wrong direction. This procedure determines whether receiving reports resulted in issuance of checks. Answer (C) is incorrect because the dates on the checks should be later than the dates on the receiving reports.

**117.** A receiving department receives copies of purchase orders for use in identifying and recording inventory receipts. The purchase orders list the name of the vendor and the quantities of the materials ordered. A possible error that this system could allow is

A. Payment to unauthorized vendors.

B. Payment for unauthorized purchases.

C. Overpayment for partial deliveries.

D. Delay in recording purchases.

Answer (C) is correct. *(CIA, adapted)*

**REQUIRED:** The error that may occur in a purchasing system.

**DISCUSSION:** To ensure a fair count, the copy of the purchase order sent to the receiving clerk should not include quantities. The receiving clerk should count the items in the shipment and prepare a receiving report. Copies are sent to inventory control and accounts payable.

Answer (A) is incorrect because comparing receipts with purchase orders will help detect unauthorized vendors. Answer (B) is incorrect because comparing receipts with purchase orders will help detect unauthorized purchases. Answer (D) is incorrect because using purchase orders to identify receipts will not delay recording purchases.

**118.** Which of the following observations made during the preliminary survey of a local department store's disbursement cycle reflects a control strength?

A. Individual department managers use prenumbered forms to order merchandise from vendors.

B. The receiving department is given a copy of the purchase order complete with a description of goods, quantity ordered, and extended price for all merchandise ordered.

C. The treasurer's office prepares checks for suppliers based on vouchers prepared by the accounts payable department.

D. Individual department managers are responsible for the movement of merchandise from the receiving dock to storage or sales areas as appropriate.

Answer (C) is correct. *(CIA, adapted)*

**REQUIRED:** The observation about the disbursement cycle indicative of a control strength.

**DISCUSSION:** Accounting for payables is a recording function. The matching of the supplier's invoice, the purchase order, and the receiving report (and usually the purchase requisition) should be the responsibility of the accounting department. These are the primary supporting documents for the payment voucher prepared by the accounts payable section that will be relied upon by the treasurer in making payment.

Answer (A) is incorrect because the managers should submit purchase requisitions to the purchasing department. The purchasing function should be separate from operations. Answer (B) is incorrect because, to encourage a fair count, the receiving department should receive a copy of the purchase order from which the quantity has been omitted. Answer (D) is incorrect because the receiving department should transfer goods directly to the storeroom to maintain security. A copy of the receiving report should accompany the goods to the storeroom so that the amount stored can be compared with the amount in the report.

**119.** During the audit of a construction contract, it was discovered that the contractor was being paid for each ton of dirt removed. The contract called for payment based on cubic yards removed. Which internal control might have prevented this error?

A. Comparison of invoices with purchase orders or contracts.

B. Comparison of invoices with receiving reports.

C. Comparison of actual costs with budgeted costs.

D. Extension checks of invoice amounts.

Answer (A) is correct. *(CIA, adapted)*

**REQUIRED:** The internal control that might have prevented use of an incorrect measure of work done.

**DISCUSSION:** The contractor's invoice would have stated a unit of measure different from that in the contract. Thus, a comparison of the invoice with the original contract would have disclosed the error.

Answer (B) is incorrect because the dirt removed would not have been received by the company; hence, no receiving reports would have existed. Answer (C) is incorrect because this comparison would not have directly detected the specific reason for a variance. However, the cost comparison would have detected the variance and prompted an investigation of its cause. Answer (D) is incorrect because the problem was not a mathematical error but an erroneous basis for payment.

**120.** The procedure that best discourages the resubmission of vendor invoices after they have been paid is

A. A requirement for double endorsement of checks.

B. The cancelation of vouchers by accounting personnel.

C. The cancelation of vouchers by treasurer personnel.

D. The mailing of payments directly to payees by accounting personnel.

Answer (C) is correct. *(CMA, adapted)*

**REQUIRED:** The procedure best discouraging resubmission of vendor invoices after payment.

**DISCUSSION:** Canceling vouchers and supporting papers (with perforations, ink, etc.) upon payment prevents the payment of a duplicate voucher. If the person signing the check does the canceling, the documents cannot be recycled for duplicate payments. Securing the paid-voucher file from access by the accounts payable clerk is another effective control.

Answer (A) is incorrect because a single endorsement is not a control weakness if the person who signs does not have incompatible functions and if proper documentation is required before signing. Answer (B) is incorrect because the vouchers should not be canceled before payment. Answer (D) is incorrect because mailing payments directly to payees does not prevent a second use of invoices by unethical personnel. Also, record keepers should not have access to signed checks.

**121.** Which of the following controls is not usually performed with regard to vouchers payable in the accounting department?

A. Determining the mathematical accuracy of the vendor's invoice.

B. Having an authorized person approve the voucher.

C. Controlling the mailing of the check and remittance advice.

D. Matching the receiving report with the purchase order.

Answer (C) is correct. *(CPA, adapted)*

**REQUIRED:** The control not usually applied to vouchers payable by the accounting department.

**DISCUSSION:** The treasurer has an asset custody function that should be segregated from the recording function of the accounting department. Consequently, checks for disbursements should be signed by an officer, normally the treasurer, after necessary supporting evidence has been examined. The treasurer should also be responsible for canceling the supporting documentation and mailing the signed checks and remittance advices. The documentation typically consists of a payment voucher, a purchase order, a receiving report, and a vendor invoice.

Answer (A) is incorrect because the accounting department determines the mathematical accuracy of the vendor's invoice. Answer (B) is incorrect because the accounting department has an authorized person approve the voucher. Answer (D) is incorrect because the accounting department matches the receiving report with the purchase order.

**122.** Propex Corporation uses a voucher register and does not record invoices in a subsidiary ledger. Propex will probably benefit most from the additional cost of maintaining a subsidiary ledger if

A. There are usually invoices in an unmatched invoice file.

B. Vendors' requests for confirmation of receivables often go unanswered for several months until paid invoices can be reviewed.

C. Partial payments to vendors are continuously made in the ordinary course of business.

D. It is difficult to reconcile vendors' monthly statements.

Answer (C) is correct. *(CPA, adapted)*

**REQUIRED:** The situation in which an accounts payable subsidiary ledger is useful.

**DISCUSSION:** If a firm makes partial payments to vendors, it may be difficult to keep track of the amounts still due on vouchers. An accounts payable subsidiary ledger provides a continuous record of amounts due to vendors.

Answer (A) is incorrect because some unmatched invoices will usually be awaiting appropriate receiving reports in any organization. Answer (B) is incorrect because Propex will benefit only to the extent of good vendor relations if it promptly answers confirmation requests. Answer (D) is incorrect because, under a voucher system, there is no need to reconcile vendors' monthly statements unless problems arise.

**123.** Which of the following controls is not usually performed in the vouchers payable department?

A. Matching the vendor's invoice with the related receiving report.

B. Approving vouchers for payment by having an authorized employee sign the vouchers.

C. Indicating the asset and expense accounts to be debited.

D. Accounting for unused prenumbered purchase orders and receiving reports.

Answer (D) is correct. *(CPA, adapted)*

**REQUIRED:** The control not usually performed in the vouchers payable department.

**DISCUSSION:** Employees in the vouchers payable department should have no responsibilities related to purchasing or receiving goods. The purchasing department accounts for unused prenumbered purchase orders. The receiving department accounts for unused prenumbered receiving reports.

**124.** Fraudulent use of corporate credit cards will be minimized by which of the following controls?

A. Establishing a corporate policy on the issuance of credit cards to authorized employees.

B. Periodically reviewing the validity of the need for credit cards at executive and operating levels.

C. Reconciling the monthly statement from the credit card company with the submitted copies of the cardholders' charge slips.

D. Subjecting credit card charges to the same expense controls as those used on regular company expense forms.

Answer (D) is correct. *(CIA, adapted)*

**REQUIRED:** The control minimizing fraudulent use of corporate credit cards.

**DISCUSSION:** Credit card charges should be controlled in much the same manner as expense accounts and other expense reports, including use of limitations on specific kinds of expenditures. These charges should be compared with supporting documentation, such as receiving reports and invoices.

Answer (A) is incorrect because establishing a corporate policy on the issuance of credit cards to authorized employees concerns the question of credit card availability, not credit card use. Answer (B) is incorrect because periodically reviewing the validity of the need for credit cards at executive and operating levels concerns the question of credit card availability, not credit card use. Answer (C) is incorrect because reconciling the monthly statement from the credit card company with the submitted copies of the cardholders' charge slips is a check on the billing of charges.

**125.** Which of the following questions should not appear in an internal control questionnaire relating to cash disbursements?

A. Are all disbursements except for petty cash made by check?

B. Are imprinted and prenumbered checks used and is a check protection device used in printing the check amount?

C. Is each check supported by an approved voucher?

D. Are prelistings made of all cash receipts?

Answer (D) is correct. *(Publisher)*

**REQUIRED:** The question not appearing in a questionnaire about cash disbursements.

**DISCUSSION:** Prelisting of cash receipts is performed in the mail room as part of the sales-receivables-cash receipts cycle. This question is inappropriate in a questionnaire relating to cash disbursements. The questionnaire should list inquiries as to whether supporting documentation is mutilated upon signing; issuing a check to cash or bearer is prohibited; signing blank checks is prohibited; unused checks are controlled; voided checks are retained and accounted for; and the check signer is responsible for mailing signed checks.

**126.** If internal control is well-designed, the same employee may be permitted to

A. Mail signed checks and also cancel supporting documents.

B. Prepare receiving reports and also approve purchase orders.

C. Approve vouchers for payment and also have access to unused purchase orders.

D. Mail signed checks and also prepare bank reconciliations.

Answer (A) is correct. *(CPA, adapted)*

**REQUIRED:** The functions the same employee may be permitted to perform.

**DISCUSSION:** The cash disbursements department has an asset custody function. Consequently, this department is responsible for signing checks after verification by reference to the supporting documents. The supporting documents should then be canceled and the checks mailed. Cancelation prevents the documentation from being used to support duplicate payments. Moreover, having the party who signs the checks place them in the mail reduces the risk that they will be altered or diverted.

Answer (B) is incorrect because receiving should not know how many units have been ordered. Answer (C) is incorrect because accounts payable is responsible for approving vouchers, and purchasing should be the only department with access to purchase orders. Answer (D) is incorrect because the bank reconciliation is performed by someone with no asset custody function, e.g., an accounting department employee.

**127.** Which of the following is a standard control over cash disbursements?

A. Checks should be signed by the controller and at least one other employee of the company.

B. Checks should be sequentially numbered and the numerical sequence should be accounted for by the person preparing bank reconciliations.

C. Checks and supporting documents should be marked "Paid" immediately after the check is returned with the bank statement.

D. Checks should be sent directly to the payee by the employee who prepares documents that authorize check preparation.

Answer (B) is correct. *(CPA, adapted)*

**REQUIRED:** The standard control over cash disbursements.

**DISCUSSION:** The sequential numbering of checks provides a standard control over cash disbursements. The numerical sequence of canceled checks should be accounted for by the person preparing bank reconciliations. Physical control over blank checks should be maintained by the treasurer.

Answer (A) is incorrect because, to separate custody of and accounting for cash, the controller should not have the authority to sign checks. Answer (C) is incorrect because supporting documents (but not the check) should be marked "Paid" immediately upon signing the check to preclude resubmission with a duplicate invoice. Answer (D) is incorrect because the check signer (not the check preparer) should oversee the mailing of the checks.

**128.** Operating control of the check-signing machine normally should be the responsibility of the

A. General accounting function.

B. Treasury function.

C. Legal counsel.

D. Internal audit function.

Answer (B) is correct. *(CPA, adapted)*

**REQUIRED:** The department that should have operating control of the check-signing machine.

**DISCUSSION:** The operating control of a check-signing machine normally should be the responsibility of the treasurer, who maintains custody of assets.

Answer (A) is incorrect because cash custody should not be assigned to a department that maintains accounting records. Answer (C) is incorrect because legal counsel should not have access to the check-signing machine. Legal counsel performs a staff function without operational authority. Answer (D) is incorrect because, to maintain its objectivity, the internal audit department should not have any responsibility for operations.

**129.** Which of the following items in a communication about reportable conditions in internal control over cash receipts and disbursements is least significant?

A. Cash receipts are not deposited intact daily.

B. Treasurer fails to verify the names and addresses of check payees.

C. Signed checks are distributed by the controller to approved payees.

D. Checks are signed by one person.

Answer (D) is correct. *(Publisher)*

**REQUIRED:** The reportable condition concerning cash transactions that is of least significance

**DISCUSSION:** The auditor should be least concerned that the checks are signed by only one person as long as that person is not assigned other incompatible functions and proper documentation is required before signing.

Answer (A) is incorrect because cash receipts should be deposited intact daily. Answer (B) is incorrect because the treasurer should sign checks based on proper documentation. The accounting function, which prepares the voucher (authorization for payment), should verify the payees' names and addresses. Answer (C) is incorrect because the controller, who is responsible for accounting for cash, should not have access to signed checks.

**130.** Which of the following questions will an auditor most likely include on an internal control questionnaire for notes payable?

A. Are assets that collateralize notes payable critically needed for the entity's continued existence?

B. Are two or more authorized signatures required on checks that repay notes payable?

C. Are the proceeds from notes payable used for the purchase of noncurrent assets?

D. Are direct borrowings on notes payable authorized by the board of directors?

Answer (D) is correct. *(CPA, adapted)*

**REQUIRED:** The question most likely included on an internal control questionnaire for notes payable.

**DISCUSSION:** Control is enhanced when different persons or departments authorize, record, and maintain custody of assets for a class of transactions. Authorization of notes payable is best done by the board of directors.

Answer (A) is incorrect because the importance of specific assets to the entity is an operational matter and not a primary concern of an auditor in the consideration of internal control. Answer (B) is incorrect because questions about the payment function are likely to be included on the questionnaire relating to cash disbursements. Answer (C) is incorrect because the use of funds is an operating decision made by management and is not a primary concern of the auditor in the consideration of internal control.

**131.** Under which of the following circumstances is an auditor most likely to intensify an audit of a $500 impress petty cash fund?

A. Reimbursement vouchers are not prenumbered.

B. Reimbursement occurs twice each week.

C. The custodian occasionally uses the cash fund to cash employee checks.

D. The custodian endorses reimbursement checks.

Answer (B) is correct. *(CPA, adapted)*

**REQUIRED:** The circumstance in which the auditor would intensify an audit of a petty cash fund.

**DISCUSSION:** If the auditor determines that reimbursement occurs twice each week, (s)he would intensify the audit of the imprest cash fund. The frequent need for reimbursement suggests that the fund is not functioning as planned.

Answer (A) is incorrect because, although failure to prenumber vouchers is not a preferable practice, it does not suggest errors or fraud. Answer (C) is incorrect because use of the cash fund to cash employee checks is not a preferable practice, but it does not suggest errors or fraud. Answer (D) is incorrect because the custodian's endorsement of reimbursement checks is an appropriate procedure to obtain cash for the fund.

## 3.8 Internal Control of Personnel and Payroll

**132.** Which of the following is an operating control over the staffing function?

A. Making background checks on all new hires.

B. Maintaining records of the department's accomplishments.

C. Encouraging new hires to participate in professional organizations.

D. Requiring personnel to participate in firm-sponsored external activities.

Answer (A) is correct. *(CIA, adapted)*

**REQUIRED:** The operating control over staffing.

**DISCUSSION:** Staffing concerns providing the necessary personnel to achieve organizational objectives economically. Because honest and capable personnel also help create an environment conducive to effective internal control, hiring policies and procedures are crucial. Background checks, for example, may screen out potential hirees of questionable character.

Answer (B) is incorrect because maintaining records is an accounting control. Answer (C) is incorrect because professional development activities concern the directing function, that is, motivating people in an organization to contribute effectively to achieve goals. Answer (D) is incorrect because professional development activities concern the directing function, that is, motivating people in an organization to contribute effectively to achieve goals.

**133.** Effective controls over the payroll function may include

A. Reconciliation of totals on job time tickets with job reports by employees responsible for those specific jobs.

B. Verification of agreement of job time tickets with employee clock card hours by a payroll department employee.

C. Preparation of payroll transaction journal entries by an employee who reports to the supervisor of the personnel department.

D. Custody of rate authorization records by the supervisor of the payroll department.

Answer (B) is correct. *(CPA, adapted)*

**REQUIRED:** The effective control over payroll.

**DISCUSSION:** The total time spent on jobs should closely approximate the total time indicated on time cards. Comparing these records should therefore provide an independent check of the accuracy of time reported on the time cards.

Answer (A) is incorrect because an independent party should perform the review function; employees should not review themselves. Answer (C) is incorrect because the functions of authorization, custody of assets, and record keeping should not be performed (or controlled) by the same parties. The payroll department should prepare the payroll transaction journal entries. If the personnel department performed this task, authorization and record keeping would be combined. Answer (D) is incorrect because personnel authorizes the pay rates used in the payroll calculation.

**134.** In manufacturing environments, employees are often required to use time cards and job time tickets. Which is the false statement related to the use of these documents?

A. Job time tickets are completed by employees for each job worked on, and an employee may have one or many job time tickets in a day.

B. Only one time card should exist for each employee.

C. Time reported on job time tickets should be reconciled to time cards.

D. Payroll should be prepared from job time tickets.

Answer (D) is correct. *(Publisher)*

**REQUIRED:** The false statement about job time tickets and time cards.

**DISCUSSION:** The payroll should be prepared from the time cards, which are the official records of time worked. The allocation of direct labor to the various jobs and the identification of indirect labor that should be charged to overhead is determined from the job time tickets.

Answer (A) is incorrect because a different job time ticket should be prepared for each employee task, and an employee may work on one or many jobs in a day. Answer (B) is incorrect because each employee should have only one time card, which is the official record of hours worked. Answer (C) is incorrect because the time reported on the time tickets should be reconciled to the time cards.

**135.** Organizational independence in the processing of payroll is achieved by functional separations that are built into the system. Which one of the following functional separations is not required for internal control purposes?

A. Separation of timekeeping from payroll preparation.
B. Separation of personnel function from payroll preparation.
C. Separation of payroll preparation and paycheck distribution.
D. Separation of payroll preparation and maintenance of year-to-date records.

Answer (D) is correct. *(CMA, adapted)*

**REQUIRED:** The functional separation that is not required for internal control purposes.

**DISCUSSION:** Most companies have their payrolls prepared by the same individuals who maintain the year-to-date records. There is no need for this functional separation because both duties involve record-keeping.

Answer (A) is incorrect because separating timekeeping and payroll preparation is an effective control. It prevents one person from claiming that an employee worked certain hours and then writing a check to that employee. Payment to an absent or fictitious employee would therefore require collusion between two employees. Answer (B) is incorrect because personnel should be separate from payroll. The former authorizes the calculation of the payroll by the latter. Answer (C) is incorrect because separating paycheck preparation from distribution makes it more difficult for fictitious employees to receive checks.

**136.** Which of the following controls is most effective in providing reasonable assurance that salary, wage, and benefit expenses are incurred only for work performed?

A. All time cards and reports are reviewed and approved in writing by immediate line supervisors having no responsibilities for paycheck distribution.
B. The accuracy of extensions of hours worked and pay rates is rechecked by an independent party, and pay rate and other key payroll information is changed only upon the receipt of a written authorization from the personnel department.
C. Actual payroll amounts are regularly compared against budgeted amounts by management, with all material budget variances being investigated.
D. The payroll register is used as the source document for posting employment-related expenses to the general ledger.

Answer (A) is correct. *(CIA, adapted)*

**REQUIRED:** The most effective control providing reasonable assurance that salary, wage, and benefit expenses are incurred only for work performed.

**DISCUSSION:** Review and approval of time cards by line supervisors is appropriate because these supervisors should know whether work has been performed. Also, they do not distribute paychecks, so they are not in a position to divert falsely authorized checks.

Answer (B) is incorrect because an arithmetic check of payroll calculations provides no control over the actual hours reported, which is the basis for compensating work performed. Also, proper authority for pay rate changes controls the level of pay, not the reporting of hours of work performed. Answer (C) is incorrect because comparisons between actual and budgeted labor expense may reveal overall inefficient labor use, but probably not particular improprieties. Answer (D) is incorrect because posting to the general ledger from the payroll register controls recording of the expense, not the propriety of the labor hours reported.

**137.** In the audit of which of the following types of profit-oriented enterprises is the auditor most likely to place special emphasis on testing the controls over proper classification of payroll transactions?

A. A manufacturing organization.
B. A retailing organization.
C. A wholesaling organization.
D. A service organization.

Answer (A) is correct. *(CPA, adapted)*

**REQUIRED:** The organization in which payroll transaction classifications are most important to the auditor.

**DISCUSSION:** A manufacturing organization is characteristically labor intensive with a high frequency and volume of payroll transactions requiring classification into direct labor and overhead. Payroll information is important in the costing of work-in-process, finished goods inventory, and cost of goods sold.

Answer (B) is incorrect because retailing organizations are normally not as labor intensive and do not require as many payroll transactions as a manufacturer. Furthermore, their labor costs are typically expensed rather than capitalized as part of inventory. Answer (C) is incorrect because wholesaling organizations are normally not as labor intensive and do not require as many payroll transactions as a manufacturer. Furthermore, their labor costs are typically expensed rather than capitalized as part of inventory. Answer (D) is incorrect because service organizations are normally not as labor intensive and do not require as many payroll transactions as a manufacturer. Furthermore, their labor costs are typically expensed rather than capitalized as part of inventory.

**138.** Which of the following departments most likely approves changes in pay rates and deductions from employee salaries?

A. Personnel.

B. Treasurer.

C. Controller.

D. Payroll.

Answer (A) is correct. *(CPA, adapted)*

**REQUIRED:** The department that most likely approves changes in pay rates and deductions.

**DISCUSSION:** The personnel department provides the authorization for payroll-related transactions, e.g., hiring, termination, and changes in pay rates and deductions.

Answer (B) is incorrect because the treasurer performs a custody function for payroll-related transactions. Answer (C) is incorrect because the payroll department, which is overseen by the controller, has a record keeping function for payroll-related transactions. Answer (D) is incorrect because the payroll department has a record-keeping function for payroll-related transactions.

**139.** Which of the following controls is most likely to prevent direct labor hours from being charged to manufacturing overhead?

A. Periodic independent counts of work-in-process for comparison with recorded amounts.

B. Comparison of daily journal entries with approved production orders.

C. Use of time tickets to record actual labor worked on production orders.

D. Reconciliation of work-in-process inventory with periodic cost budgets.

Answer (C) is correct. *(CPA, adapted)*

**REQUIRED:** The control to prevent direct labor hours from being charged to manufacturing overhead.

**DISCUSSION:** Time tickets should specifically identify labor hours as direct or indirect.

Answer (A) is incorrect because independent counts of work-in-process for comparison with recorded amounts provide assurance that all inventories are accounted for but do not assure proper classification of the costs within the account. Answer (B) is incorrect because comparison of daily journal entries with approved production orders only provides assurance that costs are being assigned to production orders. Answer (D) is incorrect because reconciliation of work-in-process inventory with periodic cost budgets is an analytical procedure that might detect the problem but would not prevent it.

**140.** The purpose of segregating the duties of hiring personnel and distributing payroll checks is to separate the

A. Human resources function from the controllership function.

B. Cash receipts function from the cash disbursements function.

C. Authorization of transactions from the custody of related assets.

D. Operational responsibility from the record keeping responsibility.

Answer (C) is correct. *(CPA, adapted)*

**REQUIRED:** The purpose of segregating the duties of hiring personnel and distributing payroll checks.

**DISCUSSION:** In principle, the payroll function should be divided into its authorization, recording, and custody functions. Authorization of hiring, wage rates, and deductions is provided by personnel. Authorization of hours worked is provided by production. Based upon these authorizations, accounting calculates and records the payroll. Based on the calculated amounts, the treasurer prepares and distributes payroll checks.

Answer (A) is incorrect because neither the controller (accounting function) nor the personnel department (human resources function) should distribute checks. Answer (B) is incorrect because the payroll function does not include the cash receipts function. Answer (D) is incorrect because neither hiring personnel (authorization) nor distributing checks (asset custody) is a record-keeping activity.

**141.** Which of the following situations represents an internal control weakness in the payroll department?

A. Payroll department personnel are rotated in their duties.

B. Paychecks are distributed by the employees' immediate supervisors.

C. Payroll records are reconciled with quarterly tax reports.

D. The timekeeping function is independent of the payroll department.

Answer (B) is correct. *(CMA, adapted)*

**REQUIRED:** The internal control weakness in the payroll department.

**DISCUSSION:** A supervisor who distributes payroll checks is in a position to divert paychecks of fictitious employees if (s)he also has access to personnel records. This opportunity results from being assigned the incompatible functions of authorization, record keeping, and custodianship. A person unrelated to either payroll record keeping or the operating department should distribute checks. Many organizations use "direct deposit" programs to transfer pay directly to employees' bank accounts, eliminating the distribution process.

Answer (A) is incorrect because periodic rotation of payroll personnel inhibits the perpetration and concealment of fraud. Answer (C) is incorrect because reconciling payroll records with quarterly tax reports is an analytical procedure that may detect a discrepancy. Answer (D) is incorrect because timekeeping should be independent of employee records.

**142.** Which of the following personnel department procedures reduces the risk of payroll fraud and represents an appropriate responsibility for the department?

A. Distributing paychecks.

B. Authorizing overtime hours.

C. Authorizing the addition or deletion of employees from the payroll.

D. Collection and retention of unclaimed paychecks.

Answer (C) is correct. *(CIA, adapted)*

**REQUIRED:** The procedure reducing the risk of fraud that is the responsibility of the personnel department.

**DISCUSSION:** The payroll department is responsible for assembling payroll information (record keeping). The personnel department is responsible for authorizing employee transactions such as hiring, firing, and changes in pay rates and deductions. Segregating the recording and authorization functions helps prevent fraud.

Answer (A) is incorrect because the treasurer should perform the asset custody function regarding payroll. Answer (B) is incorrect because authorizing overtime is a responsibility of operating management. Answer (D) is incorrect because unclaimed checks should be in the custody of the treasurer until they can be deposited in a special bank account.

**143.** Which of the following procedures most likely would be considered a weakness in an entity's internal control over payroll?

A. A voucher for the amount of the payroll is prepared in the general accounting department based on the payroll department's payroll summary.

B. Payroll checks are prepared by the payroll department and signed by the treasurer.

C. The employee who distributes payroll checks returns unclaimed payroll checks to the payroll department.

D. The personnel department sends employees' termination notices to the payroll department.

Answer (C) is correct. *(CPA, adapted)*

**REQUIRED:** The ineffective control over payroll.

**DISCUSSION:** The payroll department assembles payroll information, which is a recording function. Custody of assets such as unclaimed payroll checks is incompatible with record keeping.

Answer (A) is incorrect because preparation of a voucher is appropriately performed by the accounting department, which has a record keeping function. Answer (B) is incorrect because the treasurer's signing of checks is consistent with the asset custody function. Answer (D) is incorrect because the personnel department properly performs the authorization function regarding employment transactions.

**144.** Each Friday afternoon, payroll checks are distributed by the shift superintendent. The plant is so large and the turnover is so great that the superintendent does not know many of the workers. Undelivered checks are returned to the payroll clerk, from whom the workers can obtain them at some later time. The payroll clerk routinely continues the payroll record for workers one week after their departure from the firm, ultimately cashes the unclaimed checks, and keeps the money. Which of the following is a control designed to prevent this misappropriation?

A. Require the shift superintendent to know all the workers by name.

B. Require the timekeeper to compute the weekly pay of each worker and to make distribution of the checks received from the treasurer's office.

C. Require the treasurer's office to prepare checks only on the basis of supporting documentation from both the timekeeper and payroll office.

D. Periodically rotate the shift superintendent.

Answer (C) is correct. *(CIA, adapted)*

**REQUIRED:** The control designed to prevent a misappropriation by a payroll clerk.

**DISCUSSION:** The payroll should be prepared from the time cards, which are the official records of time worked, and the authorized pay rates and deductions. After the payroll is prepared, it should be independently verified. Also, the payroll department has a recording function and should not be charged with custody of related assets (undelivered paychecks) even temporarily. Undelivered checks should be sent to the treasurer for deposit in a bank account after a reasonable period of time.

Answer (A) is incorrect because requiring the shift superintendent to know all workers by name is a control that would be difficult to execute. Answer (B) is incorrect because the timekeeper should not perform these incompatible functions. (S)he should neither compute weekly pay nor have custody of assets. Answer (D) is incorrect because the payroll clerk's fraud does not depend on the identity of the shift superintendent.

**145.** Proper internal control over the cash payroll function mandates which of the following?

A. The payroll clerk should fill the envelopes with cash and a computation of the net wages.

B. Unclaimed pay envelopes should be retained by the paymaster.

C. Each employee should be asked to sign a receipt.

D. A separate checking account for payroll should be maintained.

Answer (C) is correct. *(CPA, adapted)*
**REQUIRED:** The most appropriate control over cash payroll.
**DISCUSSION:** Under a cash payroll system, the receipt signed by the employee, which is the only document in support of payment, is essential to verify proper payment.
Answer (A) is incorrect because a person (e.g., a cashier) other than the one computing net wages should put the cash in the envelope. Answer (B) is incorrect because unclaimed cash payroll should be deposited in a special bank account for safekeeping. Answer (D) is incorrect because effective internal control does not require that a separate account be maintained. A cash payroll requires only a limited number of checks.

**146.** A large retail enterprise has established a policy that requires the paymaster to deliver all unclaimed payroll checks to the internal auditing department at the end of each payroll distribution day. This policy was most likely adopted to

A. Assure that employees who were absent on a payroll distribution day are not paid for that day.

B. Prevent the paymaster from cashing checks that are unclaimed for several weeks.

C. Prevent a bona fide employee's check from being claimed by another employee.

D. Detect any fictitious employee who may have been placed on the payroll.

Answer (D) is correct. *(CPA, adapted)*
**REQUIRED:** The reason for delivering unclaimed payroll checks to the internal auditing department.
**DISCUSSION:** A follow-up of unclaimed checks may result in identification of fictitious or terminated employees, thus eliminating an employee's opportunity to claim a paycheck belonging to a terminated employee. The unclaimed checks should then be turned over to a custodian so the internal auditing function does not assume operating responsibilities.
Answer (A) is incorrect because assuring that employees are not paid for absences is an operating responsibility, which should not be undertaken by the internal auditing department. Answer (B) is incorrect because preventing the paymaster from cashing checks can be achieved by immediately turning the unclaimed checks over to a custodian. Answer (C) is incorrect because preventing a bona fide employee's check from being claimed by another employee is a control that applies only to unclaimed checks and thus would not identify checks claimed by the wrong employees.

**147.** Employers bond employees who handle cash receipts because fidelity bonds reduce the possibility of employing dishonest individuals and

A. Protect employees who make unintentional errors from possible monetary damages resulting from their errors.

B. Deter dishonesty by making employees aware that insurance companies may investigate and prosecute dishonest acts.

C. Facilitate an independent monitoring of the receiving and depositing of cash receipts.

D. Force employees in positions of trust to take periodic vacations and rotate their assigned duties.

Answer (B) is correct. *(CPA, adapted)*
**REQUIRED:** The purpose of bonding employees.
**DISCUSSION:** Effective internal control, including personnel practices that stress the hiring of trustworthy people, does not guarantee against losses from embezzlement and other fraudulent acts committed by employees. Accordingly, an employer may obtain a fidelity bond to insure against losses arising from illegal acts by the covered employees. Blanket policies that cover groups of employees are often obtained by larger employers. Prior to issuing this form of insurance, the underwriters investigate the individuals to be covered, a practice that prevents the hiring of employees whose past misdeeds can be uncovered in this way. Also, employees should be informed that bonding companies are diligent in prosecuting bonded individuals who commit fraud.
Answer (A) is incorrect because bonding insures employers against intentional wrongdoing. Answer (C) is incorrect because bonding is irrelevant to an independent monitoring of the receiving and depositing of cash receipts. Answer (D) is incorrect because bonding is irrelevant to forcing trusted employees to take periodic vacations and rotate their assigned duties.

**148.** An auditor will ordinarily ascertain whether payroll checks are properly endorsed during the audit of

A. Time cards.

B. The voucher system.

C. Cash in bank.

D. Accrued payroll.

Answer (A) is correct. *(CPA, adapted)*
**REQUIRED:** The phase in the audit when payroll check endorsements are audited.
**DISCUSSION:** Ordinarily, the auditor examines the endorsements on payroll checks while obtaining an understanding of and testing the payroll cycle, which includes consideration of time cards.
Answer (B) is incorrect because the voucher system is usually not integral to the payroll cycle. Answer (C) is incorrect because cash in bank is usually not integral to the payroll cycle. Answer (D) is incorrect because accrued payroll implies that payroll checks were not issued, e.g., for a partial payroll period just prior to year-end.

### 3.9 Internal Control of Securities

**149.** Each of the following is a proper control over securities and investments except

A. Proper authorization of transactions.

B. Custodian bonded and separate from investment records.

C. Storage in a safe-deposit box.

D. Custodian separate from treasury function.

Answer (D) is correct. *(Publisher)*
**REQUIRED:** The improper control over securities and investments.
**DISCUSSION:** The custody of cash and securities should be placed with the treasury function. The treasurer should therefore not be separated from custody of securities and investments.
Answer (A) is incorrect because proper authorization of transactions is a proper control over securities and investments. Answer (B) is incorrect because the custodian should be bonded and should not have access to records. Answer (C) is incorrect because storage in a safe-deposit box is a proper control over securities and investments.

**150.** Which of the following controls is an entity most likely use to assist in satisfying the completeness assertion related to long-term investments?

A. Senior management verifies that securities in the bank safe-deposit box are registered in the entity's name.

B. The internal auditor compares the securities in the bank safe-deposit box with recorded investments.

C. The treasurer vouches the acquisition of securities by comparing brokers' advices with canceled checks.

D. The controller compares the current market prices of recorded investments with the brokers' advices on file.

Answer (B) is correct. *(CPA, adapted)*
**REQUIRED:** The control to test the completeness assertion for long-term investments.
**DISCUSSION:** An interpretation of AU 326 states, "Substantive tests designed primarily to obtain evidence about the completeness assertion include analytical procedures and tests of details of related populations." The related population consists of the assets in the safe-deposit box. This population should be compared with the records of the investments to provide assurance that the balance is complete, that is, contains all long-term investments.
Answer (A) is incorrect because verification that securities are registered in the entity's name relates to the rights assertion. Answer (C) is incorrect because comparing canceled checks with brokers' advices pertains to the rights assertion. Answer (D) is incorrect because comparing market prices with brokers' advices relates most directly to the valuation assertion.

**151.** Which of the following questions is not appropriate for an internal control questionnaire concerning securities?

A. Is there a periodic reconciliation of the detail of securities with the security control account?

B. Is there a record of all identification numbers of securities, and are securities held in the name of the company?

C. Do the internal auditors periodically test controls over securities?

D. All of the questions are appropriate.

Answer (D) is correct. *(Publisher)*
**REQUIRED:** The question not appropriate for a control questionnaire on securities.
**DISCUSSION:** Each item listed is an important control regarding securities.
Answer (A) is incorrect because there should be a periodic reconciliation of the individual securities with the control account in the general ledger. Answer (B) is incorrect because all aspects of the securities, including the identification numbers, should be recorded, and the securities should be in the name of the firm rather than held in bearer form or in the name of an individual. Answer (C) is incorrect because the internal auditors should periodically test the controls over securities.

**152.** An internal auditor is reviewing the company's policy regarding investing in financial derivatives. The auditor would normally expect to find all of the following in the policy except

A. A statement indicating whether derivatives are to be used for hedging or speculative purposes.

B. A specific authorization limit for the amount and types of derivatives that can be used by the organization.

C. A specific limit on the amount authorized for any single trader.

D. A statement requiring board review of each transaction because of the risk involved in such transactions.

Answer (D) is correct. *(CIA, adapted)*
**REQUIRED:** The item not normally expected to be found in a policy regarding investing in financial derivatives.
**DISCUSSION:** Policies are general statements that guide managers' decision making. They are developed by the board of directors to provide guidelines for achieving objectives. Management is responsible for daily operations and should abide by the policies. Consequently, the board would not review each transaction.

**153.** The client has equity securities classified as available for sale. The auditor is most concerned about controls related to

A. The determination of the fair value measurements of the securities.

B. The accrued interest receivable for the securities.

C. Why specific securities were purchased.

D. When the securities will be sold.

Answer (A) is correct. *(Publisher)*

**REQUIRED:** The auditor's control concern about available-for-sale securities.

**DISCUSSION:** The auditor should obtain an understanding of (1) the client's process for the determination of fair value measurements and disclosures and (2) the relevant controls. This understanding should be sufficient to plan the audit. Available-for-sale and trading securities are required to be reported at fair value by GAAP (AU 328, *Auditing Fair Value Measurements and Disclosures*).

Answer (B) is incorrect because equity securities do not accrue interest. Answer (C) is incorrect because the reasons for the acquisition of specific securities and their uses are management's operating decisions. The auditor is only marginally interested in these decisions. Answer (D) is incorrect because the reasons for the acquisition of specific securities and their uses are management's operating decisions. The auditor is only marginally interested in these decisions.

**154.** When an entity uses a trust company as custodian of its trading securities, the possibility of concealing fraud most likely will be reduced if the

A. Trust company has no direct contact with the entity employees responsible for maintaining investment accounting records.

B. Securities are registered in the name of the trust company rather than the entity itself.

C. Interest and dividend checks are mailed directly to an entity employee who is authorized to sell securities.

D. Trust company places the securities in a bank safe-deposit vault under the custodian's exclusive control.

Answer (A) is correct. *(CPA, adapted)*

**REQUIRED:** The condition that most likely will reduce the possibility of the concealment of fraud.

**DISCUSSION:** To conceal fraud related to trading securities, collusion between those responsible for record keeping and custody is required. The possibility of collusion is reduced if no direct contact between responsible parties exists.

Answer (B) is incorrect because the securities should be registered in the name of the owner. Answer (C) is incorrect because interest and dividends should be sent to the trust company custodian. Answer (D) is incorrect because use of a bank safe-deposit vault under the custodian's exclusive control is an appropriate control but does not minimize the possibility of collusion.

**155.** An employee should not be able to visit the corporate safe-deposit box containing investment securities without being accompanied by another corporate employee. What is a possible consequence of an employee's being able to visit the safe-deposit box unaccompanied?

A. The employee could pledge corporate investments as security for a short-term personal bank loan.

B. The employee could steal securities, and the theft would never be discovered.

C. It would be impossible to obtain a fidelity bond on the employee.

D. There would be no record of when company personnel visited the safe-deposit box.

Answer (A) is correct. *(CIA, adapted)*

**REQUIRED:** The possible result of an unaccompanied visit to the safe-deposit box.

**DISCUSSION:** The bank should maintain a record, which can be inspected by company personnel, of all safe-deposit box visits. Access should be limited to authorized officers. Firms typically require the presence of two authorized persons for access to the box. This precaution provides supervisory control over, for example, the temporary removal of the securities to serve as a pledge for a loan (hypothecation of securities).

Answer (B) is incorrect because an audit would eventually uncover an outright theft assuming no alteration of the asset records. Answer (C) is incorrect because obtaining a fidelity bond is contingent upon the character of the employee, not the presence of a specific control. Answer (D) is incorrect because the bank maintains a record of visits.

**156.** Which of the following procedures is most likely to give the greatest assurance that securities held as investments are safeguarded?

A. There is no access to securities between year-end and the date of the auditor's security count.

B. Proceeds from the sale of investments are received by an employee who does not have access to securities.

C. Investment acquisitions are authorized by a member of the board of directors before execution.

D. Access to securities requires the signatures and presence of two designated officials.

Answer (D) is correct. *(CPA, adapted)*

**REQUIRED:** The control procedure that best safeguards securities held as investments.

**DISCUSSION:** The presence of two authorized individuals is usually required for access to securities, especially those held in safe-deposit boxes. This precaution provides supervisory control.

Answer (A) is incorrect because denying access to authorized officials is not conducive to successful financial management. Moreover, the procedure is effective for a short period only. Answer (B) is incorrect because other employees may have improper access. Answer (C) is incorrect because the issue is the physical safety of assets already held, not authorization of acquisitions.

## 3.10 Internal Control of Inventory

**157.** Internal control over inventories is important for all of the following reasons except

A. Inventories are often the largest current asset.

B. Inventories directly affect the results of operations.

C. Inventories are the most liquid asset.

D. Inventories are a material component of total assets.

Answer (C) is correct. *(Publisher)*

**REQUIRED:** The statement not a reason internal control over inventories is important.

**DISCUSSION:** Cash is considered the most liquid asset and most subject to inherent risk.

Answer (A) is incorrect because inventories typically represent an extremely large component of current assets. Answer (B) is incorrect because inventories, once sold, become cost of goods sold, and therefore are an important component of the results of operations. Answer (D) is incorrect because inventories typically represent a large portion of the total assets of a firm.

**158.** Which of the following questions would not be appropriate for an internal control questionnaire concerning inventory?

A. Are goods stored in locked storage areas?

B. Are disbursement vouchers approved before payment?

C. Is access to the storeroom limited to authorized personnel?

D. Are there independent, periodic comparisons of inventory records with goods on hand?

Answer (B) is correct. *(Publisher)*

**REQUIRED:** The question inappropriate for an internal control questionnaire on inventory.

**DISCUSSION:** Disbursement vouchers should be prepared for all types of expenditures, not just inventory. Thus, a question about vouchers would be more appropriately asked in the cash disbursements questionnaire.

Answer (A) is incorrect because goods in locked storage areas relates directly to the internal controls over the inventory function. Answer (C) is incorrect because limitation of access to the storeroom to authorized personnel relates directly to the internal controls over the inventory function. Answer (D) is incorrect because independent, periodic comparisons of inventory records with goods on hand relates directly to the controls over the inventory function.

**159.** An essential procedural control to ensure the accuracy of the recorded inventory quantities is

A. Performing a gross profit test.

B. Testing inventory extensions.

C. Calculating unit costs and valuing obsolete or damaged inventory items in accordance with inventory policy.

D. Establishing a cutoff for goods received and shipped.

Answer (D) is correct. *(CIA, adapted)*

**REQUIRED:** The control over recorded inventory quantities.

**DISCUSSION:** A proper cutoff point for goods received and shipped assures that only goods owned by the client are included in inventory.

Answer (A) is incorrect because performing a gross profit test is primarily concerned with the dollar valuation of inventory rather than with the quantity of items in inventory. Answer (B) is incorrect because testing inventory extensions is primarily concerned with the dollar valuation of inventory rather than with the quantity of items in inventory. Answer (C) is incorrect because calculating unit costs and valuing obsolete or damaged inventory items in accordance with inventory policy is primarily concerned with the dollar valuation of inventory rather than with the quantity of items in inventory.

**160.** Apex Manufacturing Corporation mass produces eight different products. The controller who is interested in strengthening internal control over the accounting for materials used in production is most likely to implement

A. An economic order quantity (EOQ) system.

B. A job-order cost accounting system.

C. A perpetual inventory system.

D. A separation of duties among production personnel.

Answer (C) is correct. *(CPA, adapted)*
**REQUIRED:** The best system to strengthen internal control over accounting for materials.
**DISCUSSION:** A perpetual inventory system provides for continuous updating of inventory records and thus accounts for materials used. Close and continuous attention must be paid to materials usage to keep a perpetual system up to date.
Answer (A) is incorrect because EOQ makes reordering more cost effective but does not strengthen the control over accounting for materials used. Answer (B) is incorrect because a job-order cost system determines the cost of special order products. Also, a process-cost system, not a job-order system, is applicable to mass production. Answer (D) is incorrect because separation of duties among production workers does not improve control over accounting for materials unless the functions of authorization, asset custody, and recording are also separated.

**161.** An internal auditor is examining inventory control in a merchandising division with annual sales of $3,000,000 and a 40% gross profit rate. Tests show that 2% of the dollar amount of purchases do not get into inventory because of breakage and employee theft. Adding certain controls costing $35,000 annually could reduce these losses to .5% of purchases. Should the controls be recommended?

A. Yes, because the projected saving exceeds the cost of the added controls.

B. No, because the cost of the added controls exceeds the projected savings.

C. Yes, because the ideal system of internal control is the most extensive one.

D. Yes, regardless of cost-benefit considerations, because the situation involves employee theft.

Answer (B) is correct. *(CIA, adapted)*
**REQUIRED:** The correct decision as to whether to add inventory controls and the reason.
**DISCUSSION:** Controls must be subject to the cost-benefit criterion. The annual cost of these inventory controls is $35,000, but the cost saving is only $27,000 {(2% – .5%) × [$3,000,000 sales × (100% – 40% gross profit rate)]}. Hence, the cost exceeds the benefit, and the controls should not be recommended.
Answer (A) is incorrect because cost exceeds the benefit. Answer (C) is incorrect because the ideal system is not likely to be feasible on account of its cost. Answer (D) is incorrect because cost-benefit considerations apply even to employee theft.

**162.** The objectives of internal control for a production cycle are to provide assurance that transactions are properly executed and recorded, and that

A. Independent internal verification of activity reports is established.

B. Transfers to finished goods are documented by a completed production report and a quality control report.

C. Production orders are prenumbered and signed by a supervisor.

D. Custody of work-in-process and of finished goods is properly maintained.

Answer (D) is correct. *(CPA, adapted)*
**REQUIRED:** The objectives of internal control for a production cycle.
**DISCUSSION:** A principal objective of internal control is to safeguard assets. In the production cycle, control procedures must be in place to ensure that inventory is protected from misuse and theft. Accordingly, inventories should be in the custody of a storekeeper, and transfers should be properly documented and recorded to establish accountability.
Answer (A) is incorrect because independent internal verification of activity reports is a control procedure, not an objective. Answer (B) is incorrect because documenting transfers to finished goods is a control procedure, not an objective. Answer (C) is incorrect because the use of prenumbered production orders signed by a supervisor is a control procedure, not an objective.

**163.** To determine if an organization is purchasing excess raw materials, an internal auditor should

A. Be sure that standards are established for quality, quantity, and sourcing for raw materials.

B. Ascertain that production budgets and economic order quantities are integrated and have been used in determining quantities purchased.

C. Obtain assurance that purchasing agent assignments are rotated periodically.

D. Determine that the purchasing department has a written charter with a set of procedures and guidelines covering purchasing operations.

Answer (B) is correct. *(CIA, adapted)*

**REQUIRED:** The procedure to determine if an organization is purchasing excess raw materials.

**DISCUSSION:** An economic order quantity (EOQ) model can be used to determine the order quantity (or production run) that minimizes the sum or order costs (or setup costs for production) and carrying costs, given annual demand. Production needs and the EOQ model should be coordinated to ascertain the optimal levels of raw materials purchases.

Answer (A) is incorrect because these standards are beneficial, but excess inventory will still result if production, EOQs, and purchasing are not coordinated. Answer (C) is incorrect because rotation of purchasing agents is a control intended to prevent conflicts of interest, not excessive purchasing. Answer (D) is incorrect because the existence of procedures and guidelines is not proof that they are being followed.

**164.** A purchasing agent places an order for inventory whenever a requisition is received from the warehouse. The warehouse clerk issues requisitions based on periodic physical counts because no perpetual records are maintained. Numerous duplicate orders have been placed for goods previously ordered but not received. To prevent this excess ordering, the firm should

A. Keep an adequate record of open purchase orders and review it before ordering.

B. Count goods in the warehouse less often.

C. Use prenumbered purchase orders.

D. Not use purchase requisitions.

Answer (A) is correct. *(Publisher)*

**REQUIRED:** The procedure by which a company using a monthly physical inventory as a basis for purchase orders can prevent excess ordering.

**DISCUSSION:** A well-kept open purchase order file will provide information on outstanding orders and, if reviewed prior to ordering, will prevent duplicate orders.

Answer (B) is incorrect because, to requisition needed goods on a timely basis, goods must be counted often. Answer (C) is incorrect because prenumbered purchase orders fail to provide information on purchase orders placed but not received. Answer (D) is incorrect because purchase requisitions are authorizations for purchases and should be the basis for a purchase order.

**165.** A company uses an MRP (materials requirement planning) system to control inventory. One objective is to minimize raw material inventories while avoiding production shutdowns. One way to achieve this objective using MRP is to

A. Regularly update the authorized master production schedule.

B. Use an EOQ (economic order quantity) model.

C. Take a physical inventory monthly instead of annually.

D. Use a second-order exponential smoothing model with seasonality factors.

Answer (A) is correct. *(CIA, adapted)*

**REQUIRED:** The means of minimizing raw material inventories.

**DISCUSSION:** MRP is a computer-based information system designed to plan and control materials used in production. It determines the quantity of finished goods that will be required and the point when they will be needed. The system requires prompt notice of changes in production schedules.

Answer (B) is incorrect because an EOQ system is a general inventory management model that attempts to balance ordering and carrying costs. Answer (C) is incorrect because taking inventory does not reduce the amount on hand. Answer (D) is incorrect because an MRP system must be concerned with very short-term rather than seasonal variations in production requirements.

**166.** For several years, a client's physical inventory count has been lower than the books have shown at the time of the count, and downward adjustments of the inventory account have been required. Contributing to the inventory problem could be weaknesses in internal control that led to the failure to record some

A. Purchases returned to vendors.

B. Sales returns received.

C. Sales discounts allowed.

D. Cash purchases.

Answer (A) is correct. *(CPA, adapted)*

**REQUIRED:** The transaction that results in an overstatement of inventory.

**DISCUSSION:** Purchases returned to the vendor but not recorded overstate inventory records. The goods are reflected in inventory but are not on hand.

Answer (B) is incorrect because unrecorded sales returns are included in the physical count but do not appear on the books, resulting in an understatement (not overstatement) of inventory. Answer (C) is incorrect because failure to record sales discounts overstates sales figures but has no effect on inventory. Answer (D) is incorrect because unrecorded cash purchases are included in the physical count but do not appear on the books, resulting in an understatement (not overstatement) of inventory.

**167.** A firm's inventory consisted of 1,000 different items, 20 of which accounted for 70% of the dollar value. The most recent regular quarterly manual count revealed an unnecessary 2 years' supply of several of the more expensive items. The control that would best help to correct this oversupply problem is

A. Use of a control total over the number of unique inventory items.

B. Limit check on the total dollar value of the inventory.

C. Use of authorizing signatures on requisitions for inventory requested by production.

D. Perpetual inventory of the larger dollar value items in the inventory.

Answer (D) is correct. *(CIA, adapted)*

**REQUIRED:** The control to prevent oversupply.

**DISCUSSION:** In a perpetual system, purchases (or transfers from work-in-process) are recorded directly in the inventory account when they are made. Inventory is correspondingly reduced as sales occur. Thus, a running total of inventory can be monitored throughout the period.

Answer (A) is incorrect because a control total would verify that no inventory records were lost or that no new ones were added. It would not aid in the solution of the inventory acquisition problem. Answer (B) is incorrect because a limit test on the total inventory value would provide information as to when the inventory dollar level reached a certain point but not on the makeup of the inventory. Answer (C) is incorrect because use of authorizing signatures would provide control over requisitions but not over the rest of the inventory acquisition process.

**168.** Which of the following controls most likely would be used to maintain accurate inventory records?

A. Perpetual inventory records are periodically compared with the current cost of individual inventory items.

B. A just-in-time inventory ordering system keeps inventory levels to a desired minimum.

C. Requisitions, receiving reports, and purchase orders are independently matched before payment is approved.

D. Periodic inventory counts are used to adjust the perpetual inventory records.

Answer (D) is correct. *(CPA, adapted)*

**REQUIRED:** The control most useful in maintaining accurate inventory records.

**DISCUSSION:** The recorded accountability for assets should be compared with existing assets at reasonable intervals. If assets are susceptible to loss through errors and fraud, the comparison should be made independently. Thus, periodic inventory counts should be reconciled to the perpetual inventory records to provide assurance that the inventory records properly reflect the inventory on hand.

Answer (A) is incorrect because periodic comparison of inventory records with current cost information may provide assurance that inventories are maintained at lower of cost or market but does not assure the accuracy of the records. Answer (B) is incorrect because a JIT system may provide assurance that inventory levels are maintained at the desired minimum but does not assure the accuracy of records. Answer (C) is incorrect because matching documents provides assurance that only goods that are authorized and received are paid for but does not assure the accuracy of records.

**169.** EOQ formulas, ABC analysis, and two-bin systems are commonly used elements of the control cycle for the stores process. These controls primarily relate to what part of the cycle?

A. Determination of need.

B. Acceptance of materials.

C. Storage of materials.

D. Release of materials.

Answer (A) is correct. *(CIA, adapted)*

**REQUIRED:** The part of the control cycle for stores in which the listed techniques are used.

**DISCUSSION:** ABC analysis divides inventory into high-, medium-, and low-value items for purposes of frequency of review and reordering. EOQ models determine the economic order quantity that minimizes order and carrying costs. Once the reorder point is established, a two-bin system may be used to signal the time to reorder when perpetual records are not kept: an inventory item is divided into two groups; when the first is depleted, the order is placed and the second protects against stockout until replenishment. Thus, each technique is concerned with determination of need.

**170.** Appropriate control over obsolete materials requires that they be

A. Carried at cost in the accounting records until the actual disposition takes place.

B. Sorted, treated, and packaged before disposition in order to obtain the best selling price.

C. Determined by an approved authority to be unusable for their normal purposes.

D. Retained within the regular storage area.

Answer (C) is correct. *(CIA, adapted)*

**REQUIRED:** The appropriate control over obsolete materials.

**DISCUSSION:** Because auditors, storekeepers, etc., may not have the requisite expertise to determine whether materials are usable, that decision must often be made by a designated independent authority. To provide effective control of materials, this determination, asset custody, and authorization for disposal are functions that should be segregated.

Answer (A) is incorrect because obsolete materials should be carried at net realizable value. Answer (B) is incorrect because costs of sorting, etc., may be greater than disposal value. Answer (D) is incorrect because obsolete materials frequently should be segregated.

**171.** Which of the following organizational controls related to the processing of scrap would you recommend?

A. Separate the responsibility for processing scrap materials from the operational activities that produce the scrap materials.

B. Define each manager's responsibility for processing scrap and authorize one person in each production department to perform this function.

C. Specify detailed procedures for each manager to follow in determining the quantity, grade, and packaging of scrap.

D. Give the managers the authority to obtain competitive bids for the disposal of scrap.

Answer (A) is correct. *(CIA, adapted)*

**REQUIRED:** The most appropriate organizational control relating to processing scrap.

**DISCUSSION:** Organizational controls concern the separation of functional responsibilities: custodianship, record keeping, authorization, and execution. Thus, those who generate the scrap should not subsequently process it.

Answer (B) is incorrect because managers with operational responsibility over scrap should not also have the authority to process it. Answer (C) is incorrect because managers with operational responsibility over scrap should not also have the authority to process it. Answer (D) is incorrect because managers with operational responsibility over scrap should not also have the authority to dispose of it.

## 3.11 Internal Control of Property, Plant, and Equipment

**172.** Which of the following questions is an auditor least likely to include on an internal control questionnaire concerning the initiation and execution of equipment transactions?

A. Are requests for major repairs approved at a higher level than the department initiating the request?

B. Are prenumbered purchase orders used for equipment and periodically accounted for?

C. Are requests for purchases of equipment reviewed for consideration of soliciting competitive bids?

D. Are procedures in place to monitor and properly restrict access to equipment?

Answer (D) is correct. *(CPA, adapted)*

**REQUIRED:** The question least likely to be included on an internal control questionnaire concerning initiation and execution of equipment transactions.

**DISCUSSION:** Although access to equipment should be restricted to authorized personnel only, the issue is the initiation and execution of equipment transactions, not custody of the assets.

Answer (A) is incorrect because approval of major repairs is related to the issue of transaction initiation and execution. Answer (B) is incorrect because use of prenumbered purchase orders is related to the issue of transaction initiation and execution. Answer (C) is incorrect because competitive bidding is related to the issue of transaction initiation and execution.

**173.** Which control is not appropriate for property, plant, and equipment?

A. Disposal of fully depreciated assets.

B. Proper authority for acquisition and retirement of assets.

C. Detailed property records and physical controls over assets.

D. Written policies for capitalization and expenditure and review of application of depreciation methods.

Answer (A) is correct. *(Publisher)*

**REQUIRED:** The improper control over property, plant, and equipment.

**DISCUSSION:** No control should require disposal of fully depreciated assets. Such assets may still be productive and used in the business and should remain on the books until disposal.

Answer (B) is incorrect because proper authority for acquisition and retirement of assets is a proper control over property, plant, and equipment. Answer (C) is incorrect because detailed property records and physical controls over assets are proper controls over property, plant, and equipment. Answer (D) is incorrect because written policies for capitalization and expenditure and review of application of depreciation methods are proper controls over property, plant, and equipment.

**174.** Equipment acquisitions that are misclassified as maintenance expense most likely will be detected by a control that provides for

A. Segregation of duties of employees in the accounts payable department.

B. Independent verification of invoices for disbursements recorded as equipment acquisitions.

C. Investigation of variances within a formal budgeting system.

D. Authorization by the board of directors of significant equipment acquisitions.

Answer (C) is correct. *(CPA, adapted)*

**REQUIRED:** The control to detect misclassification of equipment acquisitions as maintenance expense.

**DISCUSSION:** A formal planning and budgeting system that estimates maintenance expense at a certain level will report a significant variance if capital expenditures are charged to the account. Investigation of the variance is likely to disclose the misclassification.

Answer (A) is incorrect because accounts payable assembles the required payment documentation but is unlikely to question the classification of the expenditure. Answer (B) is incorrect because testing the population of recorded equipment acquisitions will not detect items misclassified as maintenance expense. Answer (D) is incorrect because the misclassification would occur subsequent to authorization.

**175.** One objective of internal control is to record property, plant, and equipment (PPE) additions correctly as to account, amount, and period. Which of the following environmental considerations indicates that the risk of material misstatement of these additions is high?

A. Most construction is performed in-house.

B. All material additions are required to be approved by the board of directors.

C. Recently acquired loans preclude further plant acquisition for 3 years.

D. Gross property, plant, and equipment increased 36% during the current period.

Answer (A) is correct. *(K.M. Macur)*

**REQUIRED:** The environmental consideration indicating a high risk of material misstatement.

**DISCUSSION:** The inherent risk of misstatement for in-house construction is high. For example, the company must allocate overhead, allocate labor costs between regular and construction labor, and estimate the interest cost to be capitalized. An outside construction company would send an invoice, and determining the amount to record would therefore be relatively easy.

Answer (B) is incorrect because approval of all material additions by the board of directors is a control consideration relating to authorization, not recording. Answer (C) is incorrect because reducing the amount of construction is most likely to decrease risk. Answer (D) is incorrect because the increase in PPE does not necessarily significantly increase the risk of misstatement, especially if valuation is based on vendors' prices rather than the entity's own estimates of the costs of in-house construction.

**176.** Which of the following is an internal control weakness related to factory equipment?

A. Checks issued in payment of purchases of equipment are not signed by the controller.

B. All purchases of factory equipment are required to be made by the department in need of the equipment.

C. Factory equipment replacements are usually made when estimated useful lives, as indicated in depreciation schedules, have expired.

D. Proceeds from sales of fully depreciated equipment are credited to other income.

Answer (B) is correct. *(CPA, adapted)*

**REQUIRED:** The internal control weakness related to factory equipment.

**DISCUSSION:** Making purchases of factory equipment is a function incompatible with the production activities of user departments. Satisfactory internal control requires separation of incompatible functions, so purchases of factory equipment should be made by a separate purchasing department.

Answer (A) is incorrect because controllers who perform a record-keeping function should not sign checks. Answer (C) is incorrect because, if estimated useful lives are accurate, replacing equipment at the end of those lives is a reasonable policy, not a control weakness. Answer (D) is incorrect because gains (all proceeds of fully depreciated equipment) from sales other than of inventory should be credited to other income or gain on sale of equipment.

**177.** Which of the following controls most likely would justify a reduced assessed level of control risk concerning plant and equipment acquisitions?

A. Periodic physical inspection of plant and equipment by the internal audit staff.

B. Comparison of current-year plant and equipment account balances with prior-year actual balances.

C. The review of prenumbered purchase orders to detect unrecorded trade-ins.

D. Approval of periodic depreciation entries by a supervisor independent of the accounting department.

Answer (A) is correct. *(CPA, adapted)*

**REQUIRED:** The control that would justify reducing an assessed level of control risk.

**DISCUSSION:** A periodic physical inspection by the internal audit staff is the best procedure for verifying the existence of plant and equipment. Direct observation by an independent, competent, and objective internal audit staff helps to reduce the potential for fictitious acquisitions or other fraudulent activities. The result is a lower assessed level of control risk.

Answer (B) is incorrect because comparing records of assets may not detect nonexistent assets. Answer (C) is incorrect because reviewing purchase orders is less effective than direct verification. Answer (D) is incorrect because depreciation is based on recorded amounts. If they are misstated, depreciation will also be misstated.

**178.** Which of the following procedures is most likely to prevent the improper disposition of equipment?

A. A separation of duties between those authorized to dispose of equipment and those authorized to approve removal work orders.

B. The use of serial numbers to identify equipment that could be sold.

C. Periodic comparison of removal work orders with authorizing documentation.

D. A periodic analysis of the scrap sales and the repairs and maintenance accounts.

Answer (A) is correct. *(CPA, adapted)*

**REQUIRED:** The procedure most likely to prevent the improper disposition of equipment.

**DISCUSSION:** Segregation of duties reduces the opportunity for an individual to both perpetrate and conceal errors or fraud. Accordingly, the authorization, recording, and asset custody functions should be separated. Thus, the same individual should not approve removal work orders (authorization) and dispose of equipment (asset custody).

Answer (B) is incorrect because the use of serial numbers to identify equipment that could be sold may detect but will not prevent improper dispositions. Answer (C) is incorrect because periodic comparison of removal work orders with authorizing documentation may detect but will not prevent improper dispositions. Answer (D) is incorrect because a periodic analysis of the scrap sales and the repairs and maintenance accounts may detect but will not prevent improper dispositions.

**179.** An auditor notes year-to-year increases of over $200,000 for small tool expense at a manufacturing facility that has produced the same amount of identical product for the last 3 years. Production inventory is kept in a controlled staging area adjacent to the receiving dock, but the supply of small tools is kept in an unsupervised area near the exit to the plant employees' parking lot. After determining that all of the following alternatives are equal in cost and are also feasible for local management, the auditor can best address the security issue by recommending that plant management

A. Move the small tools inventory to the custody of the production inventory staging superintendent and implement the use of a special requisition to issue small tools.

B. Initiate a full physical inventory of small tools on a monthly basis.

C. Place supply of small tools in a secured area, install a key-access card system for all employees, and record each key-access transaction on a report for the production superintendent.

D. Close the exit to the employee parking lot and require all plant employees to use a doorway by the receiving dock that also provides access to the plant employees' parking area.

Answer (A) is correct. *(CIA, adapted)*

**REQUIRED:** The best preventive control to reduce the risk of loss of small tools.

**DISCUSSION:** Physical control of assets is a preventive control that reduces the likelihood of theft or other loss. Giving responsibility for custody of small tools to one individual establishes accountability. Requiring that requisitions be submitted ensures that tool use is properly authorized.

Answer (B) is incorrect because a full physical inventory is a periodic, detective control that would only be effective in determining the amount of losses. Answer (C) is incorrect because recording each key-access transaction is a preventive and detective control that does not record the number or type of tools removed from the inventory. Answer (D) is incorrect because requiring all plant employees to use a doorway by the receiving dock is a preventive control that does not limit access to the small tools inventory.

**180.** Which of the following controls will most likely allow for a reduction in the scope of the auditor's tests of depreciation expense?

A. Review and approval of the periodic equipment depreciation entry by a supervisor who does not actively participate in its preparation.

B. Comparison of equipment account balances for the current year with the current-year budget and prior-year actual balances.

C. Review of the miscellaneous income account for salvage credits and scrap sales of partially depreciated equipment.

D. Authorization of payment of vendors' invoices by a designated employee who is independent of the equipment receiving function.

Answer (A) is correct. *(CPA, adapted)*

**REQUIRED:** The control permitting reduction in tests of depreciation.

**DISCUSSION:** A reduction in control risk and the consequent increase in the acceptable level of detection risk may permit the auditor to alter the nature, timing, or extent of substantive tests. An independent check on the validity and accuracy of depreciation expense clearly enhances the effectiveness of internal control and is thus likely to reduce the external auditor's assessment of control risk.

Answer (B) is incorrect because comparison of equipment account balances for the current year with the current-year budget and prior-year actual balances is an auditor's analytical procedure to test the completeness of the current-year equipment balance. Answer (C) is incorrect because review of the miscellaneous income account for salvage credits and scrap sales of partially depreciated equipment is an audit procedure to detect unrecorded fixed asset disposals. Answer (D) is incorrect because authorization of payment of invoices by a designated employee independent of the receiving function relates to authorization of cash disbursements.

## 3.12 Communication with Audit Committees

**181.** Reportable conditions are matters that come to an auditor's attention that should be communicated to an entity's audit committee because these conditions represent

A. Disclosures of information that significantly contradict the auditor's going concern assumption.

B. Material fraud or illegal acts perpetrated by high-level management.

C. Significant deficiencies in the design or operation of internal control.

D. Manipulation or falsification of accounting records or documents from which financial statements are prepared.

Answer (C) is correct. *(CPA, adapted)*

**REQUIRED:** The definition of a reportable condition.

**DISCUSSION:** Reportable conditions are matters coming to the auditor's attention that represent significant deficiencies in the design or operation of internal control that, in the auditor's judgment, could adversely affect the organization's ability to initiate, record, process, and report financial data consistent with the assertions of management in the financial statements (AU 325).

Answer (A) is incorrect because disclosures indicating a substantial doubt about the going concern assumption pertain not to internal control but to conditions and events such as operating losses, loan defaults, and labor difficulties. Answer (B) is incorrect because reportable conditions include more than fraud or illegal acts. Answer (D) is incorrect because reportable conditions include more than fraud or illegal acts.

**182.** Which of the following factors should an auditor consider in making a judgment about whether an internal control deficiency is so significant that it is a reportable condition?

I. Diversity of the entity's business.
II. Size of the entity's operations.

A. I only.

B. II only.

C. Both I and II.

D. Neither I nor II.

Answer (C) is correct. *(CPA, adapted)*

**REQUIRED:** The factor(s), if any, an auditor should consider before identifying an internal control deficiency as a reportable condition.

**DISCUSSION:** In judging which matters are reportable, the auditor should consider various factors. Examples of these factors include the size, complexity, and diversity of the entity; organizational structure; and ownership characteristics (AU 325).

**183.** Which of the following best describes the auditor's responsibility with respect to reportable conditions under AU 325?

A. The auditor must report the conditions whether or not the audit committee knows of them.

B. The auditor must exercise due diligence in searching for reportable conditions.

C. The auditor may report the conditions orally, but reporting in writing is preferable.

D. The auditor's report is a general-use report and may be distributed to the shareholders.

Answer (C) is correct. *(D. Finkbiner)*

**REQUIRED:** The best description of the auditor's responsibility for reportable conditions.

**DISCUSSION:** The report should preferably be in writing. If it is oral, the auditor should detail the communication in the audit documentation.

Answer (A) is incorrect because, if the audit committee has acknowledged its understanding and consideration of such deficiencies and the associated risks, the auditor may decide the matters do not need to be reported. Answer (B) is incorrect because the auditor is not obligated to search for reportable conditions; however, (s)he may become aware of conditions through the application of audit procedures or otherwise. Answer (D) is incorrect because the report is intended solely for the information and use of the audit committee, management, and others within the organization (or specified regulatory agency) and is not intended to be and should not be used by anyone other than the specified parties.

**184.** Which of the following statements concerning an auditor's communication of internal control related matters (reportable conditions) noted in an audit is true?

A. The auditor may issue a written report to the audit committee representing that no reportable conditions were noted.

B. Reportable conditions should be recommunicated each year even if the audit committee has acknowledged its understanding of such deficiencies.

C. Reportable conditions may not be communicated in a document that contains suggestions regarding activities that concern other topics such as business strategies or administrative efficiencies.

D. The auditor may choose to communicate significant internal-control-related matters either during the course of the audit or after the audit is concluded.

Answer (D) is correct. *(CPA, adapted)*
**REQUIRED:** The true statement concerning communication of reportable conditions noted in an a
**DISCUSSION:** Timely communication of reportable conditions may be desirable. Hence, the auditor has the optic of making an interim communication before conclusion of the engagement. The timing of the communication is determined by the significance of the matters noted and the urgency of corrective action.
Answer (A) is incorrect because AU 325 prohibits issuance of a report declaring that no reportable conditions were noted. The limited assurance that would be provided could easily be misinterpreted. However, this restriction does not apply in an audit under *Government Auditing Standards.* Answer (B) is incorrect because reportable conditions may be known to management, and their existence may reflect a decision to accept the risk because of cost or other considerations. If the audit committee has acknowledged the deficiencies and their risks, the auditor may choose not to report such matters. Answer (C) is incorrect because items beneficial to the client may be communicated even though they are not control related.

**185.** When communicating internal-control-related matters noted in a financial statement audit, an auditor's report issued on reportable conditions should indicate that

A. Errors or fraud may occur and not be detected because of the inherent limitations of internal control.

B. The expression of an unqualified opinion on the financial statements may be dependent on corrective follow-up action.

C. The deficiencies noted were not detected within a timely period by employees in the normal course of performing their assigned functions.

D. The purpose of the audit was to report on the financial statements and not to provide assurance on internal control.

Answer (D) is correct. *(CPA, adapted)*
**REQUIRED:** The content of an auditor's report issued on reportable conditions.
**DISCUSSION:** AU 325 states, "Any report issued on reportable conditions should indicate that the purpose of the audit was to report on the financial statements and not to provide assurance on internal control."
Answer (A) is incorrect because the report on reportable conditions identifies significant deficiencies in the design or operation of internal control, not errors or fraud. Answer (B) is incorrect because the opinion on the financial statements should be supported by evidence collected by the auditor, not subsequent corrective actions by management. Answer (C) is incorrect because the report on reportable conditions identifies significant deficiencies in the design or operation of internal control, not errors or fraud.

**186.** Based on AU 325, which of the following statements concerning material weaknesses and reportable conditions is true?

A. An auditor should identify and communicate material weaknesses separately from reportable conditions.

B. All material weaknesses are reportable conditions.

C. An auditor should report immediately material weaknesses and reportable conditions discovered during an audit.

D. All reportable conditions are material weaknesses.

Answer (B) is correct. *(CPA, adapted)*
**REQUIRED:** The true statement concerning reportable conditions.
**DISCUSSION:** A material weakness is a reportable condition "in which the design or operation of one or more of the internal control components does not reduce to a relatively low level the risk that errors or fraud in amounts that would be material in relation to the financial statements being audited may occur and not be detected within a timely period by employees in the normal course of performing their assigned functions" (AU 325). Reportable conditions include but are not limited to material weaknesses.
Answer (A) is incorrect because an auditor may, but is not required to, identify material weaknesses separately. Answer (C) is incorrect because whether an interim communication is made depends on the relative significance of the matters noted and the urgency of corrective action. Answer (D) is incorrect because not all reportable conditions are material weaknesses.

**187.** Which of the following representations should not be included in a report on internal-control-related matters noted in an audit under the auditing standards?

A. Reportable conditions related to the design of internal control exist, but none is deemed to be a material weakness.

B. There are no significant deficiencies in the design or operation of internal control.

C. Corrective follow-up action is recommended due to the relative significance of material weaknesses discovered during the audit.

D. The auditor's consideration of internal control would not necessarily disclose all reportable conditions that exist.

Answer (B) is correct. *(CPA, adapted)*

**REQUIRED:** The item not included in a report on internal control related matters.

**DISCUSSION:** No report should be issued if no reportable conditions were noted. The potential for misinterpretation would exist if the auditor issued a report representing that no reportable conditions were found (AU 325). However, this restriction does not apply in an audit under *Government Auditing Standards*.

Answer (A) is incorrect because the report may state that the reportable conditions noted are not material weaknesses. Answer (C) is incorrect because an interim communication may be the appropriate means for recommending corrective follow-up action on significant matters noted. Answer (D) is incorrect because the language in the report may state that the consideration of internal control might not disclose all reportable conditions.

**188.** Which of the following statements concerning an auditor's required communication of reportable conditions is true?

A. A reportable condition previously communicated during the prior year's audit that remains uncorrected causes a scope limitation.

B. An auditor should perform tests of controls on reportable conditions before communicating them to the client.

C. An auditor's report on reportable conditions should include a restriction on the distribution of the report.

D. An auditor should communicate reportable conditions after tests of controls but before commencing substantive tests.

Answer (C) is correct. *(CPA, adapted)*

**REQUIRED:** The true statement concerning the auditor's required communication of reportable conditions.

**DISCUSSION:** A report on reportable conditions should (1) state that the purpose of the audit was to report on the financial statements, not to provide assurance on internal control; (2) give the definition of reportable conditions; and (3) state that the report is intended solely for the information and use of the audit committee, management, and others within the organization (or specified regulatory agency) and is not intended to be and should not be used by anyone other than the specified parties.

Answer (A) is incorrect because, although a reportable condition previously communicated may require continued communication in the following year, it does not necessarily cause a limitation on the scope of the audit. Answer (B) is incorrect because tests of controls are performed on internal control, not on reportable conditions. Answer (D) is incorrect because reportable conditions are typically reported at the conclusion of the audit. However, they may be communicated during the audit if this information is considered useful to the client.

**189.** A CPA had previously communicated a reportable condition in connection with an audit of prior financial statements. As of the current audit date, the condition has not been corrected, and the audit committee has not acknowledged its understanding and consideration of the risks involved. What communication should be made by the CPA?

A. None, because management has been previously put on notice and now has sole responsibility.

B. A new communication is required only if it involves an area in which the auditor has assessed control risk below the maximum level.

C. A new communication is required only if the auditor has assessed control risk at the maximum level.

D. The condition should be reported.

Answer (D) is correct. *(Publisher)*

**REQUIRED:** The effect on the auditor of a previously communicated reportable condition.

**DISCUSSION:** AU 325 requires communication about reportable conditions and makes no exception solely for previous reporting of a condition. However, "provided the audit committee has acknowledged its understanding and consideration of such deficiencies and the associated risks, the auditor may decide the matter does not need to be reported."

Answer (A) is incorrect because, even though internal control is the responsibility of management, the auditor has the responsibility to report the condition to the audit committee. Answer (B) is incorrect because the auditor should report the condition regardless of the assessment of control risk. Answer (C) is incorrect because the auditor should report the condition regardless of the assessment of control risk.

**190.** Which of the following matters is an auditor required to communicate to an entity's audit committee?

I. Disagreements with management about matters significant to the entity's financial statements that have been satisfactorily resolved

II. The nature of the assurance provided by an audit

A. I only.

B. II only.

C. Both I and II.

D. Neither I nor II.

Answer (C) is correct. *(CPA, adapted)*

**REQUIRED:** The matter(s), if any, to be communicated to the audit committee.

**DISCUSSION:** AU 380, *Communication with Audit Committees*, states that the matters to be discussed with the audit committee include (1) the auditors' responsibilities under the auditing standards; (2) significant accounting policies; (3) sensitive accounting estimates; (4) audit adjustments; (5) the quality of the entity's accounting principles (in SEC engagements); (6) other information in documents containing audited statements; (7) auditor disagreements with management, whether or not satisfactorily resolved; (8) management's consultations with other accountants; (9) issues discussed with management prior to the retention of the auditors; and (10) any serious difficulties the auditors may have had with management during the audit. Under the Sarbanes-Oxley Act of 2002, a registered audit firm must communicate (1) critical accounting policies, (2) all alternative treatments of GAAP information discussed with management, (3) the ramifications of using such treatments, and (4) the treatment preferred by the firm.

**191.** Which of the following matters will an auditor most likely communicate to an entity's audit committee?

A. A list of negative trends that may lead to working capital deficiencies and adverse financial ratios.

B. The level of responsibility assumed by management for the preparation of the financial statements.

C. Difficulties encountered in achieving a satisfactory response rate from the entity's customers in confirming accounts receivables.

D. The effects of significant accounting policies adopted by management in emerging areas for which there is no authoritative guidance.

Answer (D) is correct. *(CPA, adapted)*

**REQUIRED:** The matter an auditor will most likely communicate to an entity's audit committee.

**DISCUSSION:** AU 380, *Communication with Audit Committees*, requires the auditor to inform the audit committee "about the initial selection of and changes in significant accounting policies or their application." The communication also extends to "methods used to account for significant unusual transactions and the effect of significant accounting policies in controversial or emerging areas for which there is a lack of authoritative guidance or consensus." An example of such an area is revenue recognition.

Answer (A) is incorrect because a list of negative trends that may lead to working capital deficiencies and adverse financial ratios is more likely to be communicated to management. Answer (B) is incorrect because the engagement letter should state that management is responsible for the financial statements. Moreover, the audit committee presumably understands management's responsibilities. Answer (C) is incorrect because the difficulties encountered in performing the audit that are communicated to the audit committee are more likely to involve dealings with management and other client personnel.

**192.** In identifying matters for communication with an entity's audit committee, an auditor is most likely to ask management whether

A. The turnover in the accounting department was unusually high.

B. It consulted with another CPA firm about accounting matters.

C. There were any subsequent events of which the auditor was unaware.

D. It agreed with the auditor's assessed level of control risk.

Answer (B) is correct. *(CPA, adapted)*

**REQUIRED:** The matter communicated to the audit committee.

**DISCUSSION:** The auditor may, but is not required to, inquire of management concerning any consultations with other accountants. However, if the auditor becomes aware that management has consulted with other accountants, the auditor should discuss with the audit committee his/her views about significant matters involved in that consultation (AU 380).

Answer (A) is incorrect because a high turnover of employees may increase the assessed control risk but does not require communication with the audit committee. Answer (C) is incorrect because the subsequent events discovered by the auditor need not be communicated to the audit committee. Answer (D) is incorrect because the assessed level of control risk is a matter of auditor judgment and is not negotiated with the client.

**193.** Which of the following matters is an auditor required to communicate to an entity's audit committee?

A. The basis for assessing control risk below the maximum.

B. The process used by management in formulating sensitive accounting estimates.

C. The auditor's preliminary judgments about materiality levels.

D. The justification for performing substantive procedures at interim dates.

Answer (B) is correct. *(CPA, adapted)*

**REQUIRED:** The required communication to an entity's audit committee.

**DISCUSSION:** Certain management estimates are particularly sensitive because they are significant to the financial statements, and future events affecting them may differ from current judgments. The audit committee should be informed about the process used in formulating sensitive estimates and the basis for the auditor's conclusions concerning their reasonableness (AU 380).

**194.** An auditor is obligated to communicate a proposed audit adjustment to an entity's audit committee if the adjustment

A. Has not been recorded before the end of the auditor's field work.

B. Has a significant effect on the entity's financial reporting process.

C. Is a recurring matter that was proposed to management the prior year.

D. Related to an uncorrected misstatement, was determined to be immaterial by management, and pertained to the earliest period presented.

Answer (B) is correct. *(CPA, adapted)*

**REQUIRED:** The circumstances in which a proposed audit adjustment must be communicated.

**DISCUSSION:** The auditor should inform the audit committee about adjustments arising from the audit that could, in his/her judgment, have a significant effect on the entity's financial reporting process, either individually or in the aggregate. Furthermore, the auditor should communicate to the audit committee any uncorrected misstatements aggregated during the current engagement and pertaining to the latest period presented that management determined to be immaterial, either individually or in the aggregate (AU 380).

Answer (A) is incorrect because the entries affecting the year-end financial statement balances may be made subsequent to year-end. Answer (C) is incorrect because the oral or written communication of recurring matters ordinarily need not be repeated. Answer (D) is incorrect because the auditor should communicate such an adjustment if it pertained to the latest period presented.

**195.** In an SEC engagement, should an auditor communicate the following matters to the audit committee of a public entity?

| | Auditor's Judgments About the Quality of the Client's Accounting Principles | Issues Discussed with Management Prior to the Auditor's Retention |
|---|---|---|
| A. | Yes | Yes |
| B. | Yes | No |
| C. | No | Yes |
| D. | No | No |

Answer (A) is correct. *(CPA, adapted)*

**REQUIRED:** The matter(s), if any, to be communicated to the audit committee.

**DISCUSSION:** The matters to be discussed with the audit committee include the quality of the accounting principles used by management in SEC engagements. Management is normally a participant in the discussion. Matters covered may include (1) the consistency of principles and their application; (2) the clarity and completeness of the statements; and (3) items significantly affecting representational faithfulness, verifiability, and neutrality. Given the lack of objective criteria for consistent evaluation of the application of principles, the discussion should address the unique circumstances of the auditee. Under the Sarbanes-Oxley Act of 2002, a registered audit firm must communicate (1) critical accounting policies, (2) all alternative treatments of GAAP information discussed with management, (3) the ramifications of using such treatments, and (4) the treatment preferred by the firm. Furthermore, in any audit engagement, the auditor and the audit committee should discuss any major issues discussed with management in connection with the initial or recurring retention of the auditors, for example, issues concerning the application of accounting principles and auditing standards.

## 3.13 External Auditors' Relations with Internal Auditors

**196.** The independent auditor should understand the internal audit function as it relates to internal control because

A. The audit programs, working papers, and reports of internal auditors may often be used as a substitute for the work of the independent auditor's staff.

B. The procedures performed by the internal audit staff may eliminate the independent auditor's need for considering internal control.

C. The work performed by internal auditors may be a factor in determining the nature, timing, and extent of the independent auditor's procedures.

D. The understanding of the internal audit function is an important substantive test to be performed by the independent auditor.

Answer (C) is correct. *(CPA, adapted)*

**REQUIRED:** The reason the independent auditor must understand the internal audit function.

**DISCUSSION:** AU 322, *The Auditor's Consideration of the Internal Audit Function in an Audit of Financial Statements*, states that the independent auditor should obtain an understanding of the internal audit function when obtaining an understanding of a client's internal control. The understanding should be sufficient to identify internal audit activities relevant to audit planning. Thus, an internal audit function is one of many factors to be considered in determining the nature, timing, and extent of audit procedures.

Answer (A) is incorrect because programs, working papers, and reports of internal auditors may never be used to substitute for the work of the independent auditor's staff. Answer (B) is incorrect because AU 319 requires the independent auditor to obtain an understanding of internal control and to assess control risk. Answer (D) is incorrect because the understanding of the internal audit function is part of the independent auditor's consideration of internal control, not a substantive test.

**197.** If the independent auditors decide that it is efficient to consider how the work performed by the internal auditors may affect the nature, timing, and extent of audit procedures, they should assess the internal auditors'

A. Competence and objectivity.

B. Efficiency and experience.

C. Independence and review skills.

D. Training and supervisory skills.

Answer (A) is correct. *(CPA, adapted)*

**REQUIRED:** The internal auditors' traits that the independent auditors should consider.

**DISCUSSION:** If the external auditors decide that it is efficient to consider how the internal auditors' work may affect the nature, timing, and extent of audit procedures, the competence and objectivity of the internal auditors should be assessed. Assessing competence entails obtaining information about education and experience; professional certification and CPE; audit policies, programs, and procedures; assignment of internal auditors; supervision and review of their activities; quality of working papers, reports, and recommendations; and evaluation of internal auditors' performance. Assessing objectivity includes obtaining information about organizational status (the level to which the internal auditors report; access to the board, audit committee, or the owner-manager; and whether these individuals oversee employment decisions related to the internal auditors) and about policies to maintain internal auditors' objectivity concerning the areas audited (AU 322).

Answer (B) is incorrect because competence encompasses the traits of efficiency, experience, training, and supervisory skills. Moreover, objectivity must also be assessed. Answer (C) is incorrect because internal auditors are not independent in the sense intended by the *Code of Professional Conduct* and GAAS. Answer (D) is incorrect because competence encompasses the traits of efficiency, experience, training, and supervisory skills. Moreover, objectivity must also be assessed.

**198.** In assessing the competence and objectivity of an entity's internal auditor, an independent auditor is least likely to consider information obtained from

A. Discussions with management personnel.

B. External peer reviews of the internal auditor's activities.

C. Previous experience with the internal auditor.

D. The results of analytical procedures.

Answer (D) is correct. *(CPA, adapted)*

**REQUIRED:** The least likely procedure in assessing the competence and objectivity of an entity's internal auditor.

**DISCUSSION:** Analytical procedures are evaluations of financial information made by a study of plausible relationships among both financial and nonfinancial data, using models that range from simple to complex. They are substantive tests used by the auditor to gather evidence about the fairness of the financial statements.

Answer (A) is incorrect because, in "assessing competence and objectivity, the auditor usually considers information obtained from previous experience with the internal audit function, from discussions with management personnel, and from a recent external quality review, if performed" (AU 322). Answer (B) is incorrect because, in "assessing competence and objectivity, the auditor usually considers information obtained from previous experience with the internal audit function, from discussions with management personnel, and from a recent external quality review, if performed" (AU 322). Answer (C) is incorrect because, in "assessing competence and objectivity, the auditor usually considers information obtained from previous experience with the internal audit function, from discussions with management personnel, and from a recent external quality review, if performed" (AU 322).

**199.** For which of the following judgments may an independent auditor share responsibility with an entity's internal auditor who is assessed to be both competent and objective?

| | Materiality of Misstatements | Evaluation of Accounting Estimates |
|---|---|---|
| A. | Yes | No |
| B. | No | Yes |
| C. | No | No |
| D. | Yes | Yes |

Answer (C) is correct. *(CPA, adapted)*

**REQUIRED:** The judgment(s), if any, for which an independent auditor may share responsibility with an internal auditor.

**DISCUSSION:** The responsibility to report on the financial statements rests solely with the independent auditor and cannot be shared with the internal auditors. Because the auditor has the ultimate responsibility to express an opinion on the financial statements, judgments about assessments of inherent and control risk, the materiality of misstatements, the sufficiency of tests performed, the evaluation of significant accounting estimates, and other matters affecting the auditor's report should always be those of the external auditor.

**200.** Internal auditing can affect the scope of the external auditor's audit of financial statements by

A. Decreasing the external auditor's need to perform detailed tests.

B. Allowing the external auditor to limit his/her audit to substantive testing.

C. Limiting direct testing by the external auditor to assertions not directly tested by internal auditing.

D. Eliminating the need to be on hand during the physical count of inventory.

Answer (A) is correct. *(CIA, adapted)*

**REQUIRED:** The effect of internal auditing on the scope of the external audit.

**DISCUSSION:** The work of the internal auditors may affect the nature, timing, and extent of the audit procedures, which include those for understanding internal control, assessing control risk, and conducting substantive tests.

Answer (B) is incorrect because the external auditor must always obtain an understanding of internal control and assess control risk. Answer (C) is incorrect because the auditor must perform direct tests of assertions related to material financial statement amounts if the risk of material misstatement or the subjectivity involved in the evaluation of audit evidence is high. Answer (D) is incorrect because the external auditor must observe the client's physical inventory.

**201.** In assessing the competence of an internal auditor, an independent CPA most likely would obtain information about the

A. Quality of the internal auditor's documentation.

B. Organization's commitment to integrity and ethical values.

C. Influence of management on the scope of the internal auditor's duties.

D. Organizational levels to which the internal auditor reports.

Answer (A) is correct. *(CPA, adapted)*

**REQUIRED:** The information needed to assess the competence of an internal auditor.

**DISCUSSION:** In assessing the competence of an internal auditor, the auditor should consider such factors as educational level and professional experience; professional certification and continuing education; audit policies, programs and procedures; supervision and review of the internal auditor's activities; departmental practices regarding assignments; quality of documentation, reports, and recommendations; and evaluation of the internal auditor's performance.

Answer (B) is incorrect because the organization's commitment to integrity and ethical values relates to objectivity rather than competence. Answer (C) is incorrect because the influence of management on the scope of the internal auditor's duties relates to objectivity rather than competence. Answer (D) is incorrect because the organizational levels to which the internal auditor reports relates to objectivity rather than competence.

**202.** In assessing the objectivity of internal auditors, the independent CPA who is auditing the entity's financial statements most likely considers the

A. Internal auditing standards developed by The Institute of Internal Auditors.

B. Tests of internal control activities that could detect errors and fraud.

C. Materiality of the accounts recently inspected by the internal auditors.

D. Results of the tests of transactions recently performed by the internal auditors.

Answer (A) is correct. *(Publisher)*

**REQUIRED:** The factor an independent CPA most likely considers when assessing the objectivity of an entity's internal auditors.

**DISCUSSION:** According to AU 322, the external auditor should obtain an understanding of the internal audit function as part of the understanding of internal control. The purpose is to identify internal audit activities relevant to a financial statement audit. One inquiry customarily made is about the application of professional standards by the internal auditors. If the internal audit function is deemed relevant to the audit, and if it is efficient to consider how the internal auditors' work may affect the audit, the external auditor must assess the competence and objectivity of the internal auditors. This assessment is also made if direct assistance from the internal auditors is sought. Compliance with the internal auditing standards developed by The Institute of Internal Auditors or by the Government Accountability Office is one measure of the competence and objectivity of internal auditors. These standards require internal auditors to be objective in performing their work.

Answer (B) is incorrect because tests of internal control activities that could detect errors and fraud concern the effects of the internal auditor's work on the audit. Answer (C) is incorrect because materiality of the accounts recently inspected by the internal auditors concerns the effects of the internal auditor's work on the audit. Answer (D) is incorrect because results of the tests of transactions recently performed by the internal auditors concern the effects of the internal auditor's work on the audit.

**203.** Which of the following is a false statement about the relationship of the internal auditor and the scope of the external audit of a company's financial statements?

A. The nature, timing, and extent of the external auditor's substantive tests may be affected by the work of the internal auditors.

B. The internal auditors may assist the external auditor in performing substantive tests and tests of controls under certain circumstances.

C. The external auditor is not required to give consideration to the internal audit function beyond obtaining an understanding sufficient to identify activities relevant to planning the audit.

D. The internal auditors may determine the extent to which audit procedures should be employed by the external auditor.

Answer (D) is correct. *(CMA, adapted)*

**REQUIRED:** The false statement about the relationship between the internal auditor and external auditor.

**DISCUSSION:** According to AU 322, the independent external auditor is required to obtain an understanding of the internal audit function to identify activities relevant to the audit. If internal audit activities are relevant, (s)he should then determine whether it is efficient to consider the internal auditors' work further. If it is efficient, the auditor should assess the competence and objectivity of the internal auditors. If they are sufficiently competent and objective, the auditor may then consider how (not whether) their work will affect the audit.

Answer (A) is incorrect because the work of the internal auditors may affect the substantive procedures performed by the external auditor. Answer (B) is incorrect because internal auditors may directly assist in substantive tests and tests of controls if their competence and objectivity are assessed and their work is properly supervised, reviewed, evaluated, and tested. Answer (C) is incorrect because the auditor must obtain an understanding of the internal audit function but may conclude that the activities of the internal auditors are not relevant to the audit. The auditor may also conclude that further consideration of their activities is not efficient or that they lack sufficient competence and objectivity.

**204.** During an audit of a client's financial statements, an internal auditor may provide direct assistance to an independent CPA in

| | Obtaining an Understanding of Internal Control | Performing Tests of Controls | Performing Substantive Tests |
|---|---|---|---|
| A. | No | No | No |
| B. | Yes | No | No |
| C. | Yes | Yes | No |
| D. | Yes | Yes | Yes |

Answer (D) is correct. *(CPA, adapted)*

**REQUIRED:** The types of direct assistance an internal auditor may provide to an independent CPA.

**DISCUSSION:** The auditor may request direct assistance from the internal auditor when performing the audit. Thus, the auditor may appropriately request the internal auditor's assistance in obtaining the understanding of internal control, performing tests of controls, or performing substantive tests (AU 322).

**205.** The coordination of activities between internal and external auditors

A. Results in no duplication of audit efforts.

B. Includes the exchange of audit reports and management letters.

C. Prohibits internal auditors from using the same audit techniques as external auditors, and vice versa.

D. Prevents external auditors from having access to the programs used by internal auditors.

Answer (B) is correct. *(CIA, adapted)*

**REQUIRED:** The true statement about coordination of internal and external audit activities.

**DISCUSSION:** The chief audit executive should coordinate internal and external audit efforts to ensure adequate audit coverage and to minimize duplicate efforts. Coordination involves periodic meetings to discuss matters of mutual interest, access to each other's audit programs and working papers, exchange of audit reports and management letters, and common understanding of audit techniques, methods, and terminology (PA 2050-1).

Answer (A) is incorrect because some duplication is unavoidable. Answer (C) is incorrect because common techniques should often be used. Answer (D) is incorrect because internal auditors often make their programs and working papers available to the external auditor.

### 3.14 Internal Control Documentation

**206.** The auditor's consideration of the client's internal control is documented to substantiate

A. Conformity of the accounting records with generally accepted accounting principles.

B. Compliance with auditing standards.

C. Adherence to procedures for economic, effective, and efficient management decision making.

D. The fairness of the financial statement presentation.

Answer (B) is correct. *(CPA, adapted)*

**REQUIRED:** The reason for the auditor's documentation of the consideration of the client's internal control.

**DISCUSSION:** Audit documentation should show that the field work standards have been followed, e.g., obtaining a sufficient understanding of internal control to plan the audit and gathering sufficient competent evidence to provide a basis for the opinion. Thus, the auditor should document the understanding of internal control, the conclusions about the assessed levels of control risk for specific assertions, and the bases for those assessments.

Answer (A) is incorrect because the entire audit process, not just the consideration of internal control, establishes the fairness of the financial statement presentation, including conformity with GAAP. Answer (C) is incorrect because adherence to procedures for certain decision-making processes, such as those relating to product pricing, may not be relevant to a financial statement audit. Answer (D) is incorrect because the entire audit process, not just the consideration of internal control, establishes the fairness of the financial statement presentation, including conformity with GAAP.

**207.** Which of the following statements regarding auditor documentation of the client's internal control is true?

A. Documentation must include flowcharts.

B. Documentation must include procedural write-ups.

C. No documentation is necessary, although it is desirable.

D. No one particular form of documentation is necessary, and the extent of documentation may vary.

Answer (D) is correct. *(CPA, adapted)*

**REQUIRED:** The true statement about the auditor's documentation of the client's internal control.

**DISCUSSION:** The auditor may document his/her understanding of internal control in the form of answers to a questionnaire, narrative memoranda, flowcharts, decision tables, or any other form that the auditor considers appropriate in the circumstances.

Answer (A) is incorrect because flowcharts are not required. Answer (B) is incorrect because procedural write-ups are not required. Answer (C) is incorrect because documentation is required but not in any specific form.

**208.** When assessing control risk, an auditor is required to document the auditor's understanding of the

I. Entity's control activities that help ensure management directives are carried out.

II. Entity's control environment factors that help the auditor plan the engagement.

A. I only.

B. II only.

C. Both I and II.

D. Neither I nor II.

Answer (C) is correct. *(CPA, adapted)*

**REQUIRED:** The items that should be documented when assessing control risk.

**DISCUSSION:** The understanding of the components of internal control (control environment, risk assessment, control activities, information and communication systems, and monitoring) and the conclusions about the assessed levels of control risk for specific assertions should be documented. The auditor should also document the bases for conclusions that the effectiveness of the design and operation of controls supports the assessed levels. The auditor's documentation depends on the assessed levels of control risk, the nature of internal control, and the nature of the entity's documentation.

**209.** Which of the following is not a medium that can normally be used by an auditor to record information concerning a client's internal control?

A. Narrative memorandum.

B. Procedures manual.

C. Flowchart.

D. Decision table.

Answer (B) is correct. *(CPA, adapted)*

**REQUIRED:** The medium not used by an auditor to record information concerning a client's internal control.

**DISCUSSION:** A procedures manual is one source of information about the client's internal control. However, the auditor normally does not prepare this manual and record information in it. The accounting procedures manual is a client document that explains the client's accounting system and how to implement it.

Answer (A) is incorrect because memoranda are means of documenting the understanding of internal control (AU 319). Answer (C) is incorrect because flowcharts are means of documenting the understanding of internal control (AU 319). Answer (D) is incorrect because decision tables are means of documenting the understanding of internal control (AU 319).

**210.** When documenting the understanding of a client's internal control, the independent auditor sometimes uses a systems flowchart, which can best be described as a

A. Pictorial presentation of the flow of instructions in a client's internal computer system.

B. Diagram that clearly indicates an organization's internal reporting structure.

C. Graphic illustration of the flow of operations that is used to replace the auditor's internal control questionnaire.

D. Symbolic representation of a system or series of sequential processes.

Answer (D) is correct. *(CPA, adapted)*

**REQUIRED:** The best description of a systems flowchart.

**DISCUSSION:** A systems flowchart is a symbolic representation of the flow of documents and procedures through a series of steps in the accounting process of the client's organization.

Answer (A) is incorrect because a pictorial presentation of the flow of instructions in a client's internal computer system is a computer program flowchart. Answer (B) is incorrect because the organizational chart depicts the client's internal reporting structure. Answer (C) is incorrect because a flowchart does not necessarily replace the auditor's internal control questionnaire. Controls beyond those depicted on the systems flowchart must also be considered by the auditor, and information obtained from the questionnaire may be used to develop the flowchart.

**211.** The normal sequence of documents and operations on a well-prepared systems flowchart is

A. Top to bottom and left to right.

B. Bottom to top and left to right.

C. Top to bottom and right to left.

D. Bottom to top and right to left.

Answer (A) is correct. *(CPA, adapted)*

**REQUIRED:** The normal sequence of documents and operations on a well-prepared systems flowchart.

**DISCUSSION:** The direction of flow in the normal sequence of documents and operations on a well-prepared systems flowchart is from top to bottom and from left to right.

Answer (B) is incorrect because the normal vertical movement is top to bottom. Answer (C) is incorrect because the normal horizontal movement is left to right. Answer (D) is incorrect because the normal sequence is top to bottom and left to right.

**212.** An advantage of using systems flowcharts to document information about internal control instead of using internal control questionnaires is that systems flowcharts

A. Identify internal control weaknesses more prominently.

B. Provide a visual depiction of clients' activities.

C. Indicate whether control procedures are operating effectively.

D. Reduce the need to observe clients' employees performing routine tasks.

Answer (B) is correct. *(CPA, adapted)*

**REQUIRED:** The advantage of systems flowcharts over internal control questionnaires.

**DISCUSSION:** Systems flowcharts provide a visual representation of a series of sequential processes, that is, of a flow of documents, data, and operations. In many instances, a flowchart is preferable to a questionnaire because a picture is usually more easily comprehended.

Answer (A) is incorrect because a systems flowchart can present the flow of information and documents in a system, but does not specifically identify the weaknesses. Answer (C) is incorrect because the flowchart does not provide evidence of how effectively the procedures are actually operating. Answer (D) is incorrect because the flowchart is useful in documenting the understanding of control, but it does not reduce the need for observation of employees performing tasks if those tests of controls are deemed necessary.

**213.** The diamond-shaped symbol is commonly used in flowcharting to show or represent a

A. Process or a single step in a procedure or program.

B. Terminal output display.

C. Decision point, conditional testing, or branching.

D. Predefined process.

Answer (C) is correct. *(CIA, adapted)*

**REQUIRED:** The meaning of the diamond-shaped symbol used in flowcharting.

**DISCUSSION:** Flowcharts illustrate in pictorial fashion the flow of data, documents, and/or operations in a system. Flowcharts may summarize a system or present great detail, e.g., as found in program flowcharts. According to the American National Standards Institute, the diamond-shaped symbol represents a decision point or test of a condition in a program flowchart, that is, the point at which a determination must be made as to which logic path (branch) to follow. The diamond is also sometimes used in systems flowcharts.

Answer (A) is incorrect because the rectangle is the appropriate symbol for a process or a single step in a procedure or program. Answer (B) is incorrect because a terminal display is signified by a symbol similar to the shape of a cathode ray tube. Answer (D) is incorrect because a predefined processing step is represented by a rectangle with double lines on either side.

**214.** In connection with the consideration of internal control, an auditor encounters the following flowcharting symbols:

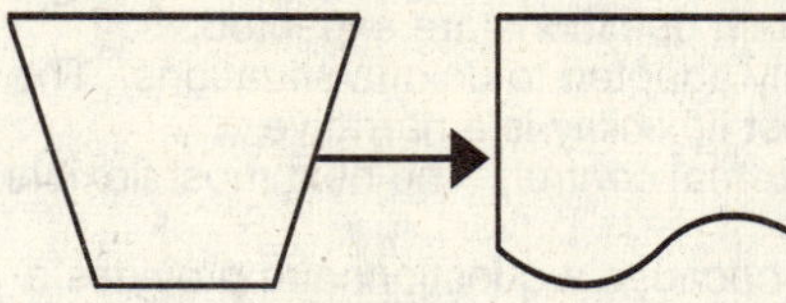

The auditor should conclude that a

A. Master file has been created by a manual operation.

B. Master file has been created by a computer operation.

C. Document has been generated by a computer operation.

D. Document has been generated by a manual operation.

Answer (D) is correct. *(CPA, adapted)*

**REQUIRED:** The meaning of the flowcharting symbols shown.

**DISCUSSION:** The symbol on the left represents a manual operation and the symbol on the right a document. The arrow's direction suggests that a document is prepared through a manual operation.

Answer (A) is incorrect because a master file is depicted by a parallelogram (input/output), or a symbol for the type of storage device used (e.g., magnetic tape or disk). Answer (B) is incorrect because a computer operation is depicted by a rectangle. Answer (C) is incorrect because a computer operation is depicted by a rectangle.

**215.** The following is a section of a system flowchart for a payroll application.

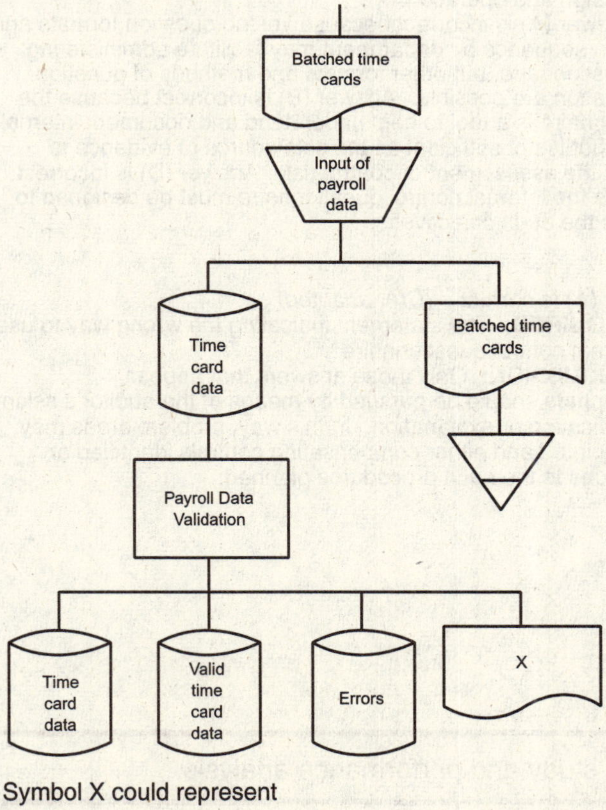


Symbol X could represent

A. Erroneous time cards.

B. An error report.

C. Batched time cards.

D. Unclaimed payroll checks.

Answer (B) is correct. *(CPA, adapted)*

**REQUIRED:** The item represented by Symbol X.

**DISCUSSION:** Symbol X is a document, that is, hard copy output of the validation routine shown. The time card data, the validated data, and the errors are recorded on magnetic disk after the validation process. Thus, either an error report or the valid time card information is represented by Symbol X.

Answer (A) is incorrect because time cards were stored offline before the validation process. Answer (C) is incorrect because time cards were stored offline before the validation process. Answer (D) is incorrect because no payroll checks are shown.

**216.** A questionnaire consists of a series of questions relating to controls normally required to prevent or detect errors and fraud that may occur for each type of transaction. Which of the following is not an advantage of a questionnaire?

A. A questionnaire provides a framework that minimizes the possibility of overlooking aspects of internal control.

B. A questionnaire can be easily completed.

C. A questionnaire is flexible in design and application.

D. The completed questionnaire provides documentation that the auditor understands internal control for planning purposes.

Answer (C) is correct. *(Publisher)*

**REQUIRED:** The item that is not considered an advantage of a questionnaire.

**DISCUSSION:** Questionnaires are designed to be inflexible in that the responses to certain questions are expected. Questionnaires are not easily adapted to unique situations. The approach that offers the most flexibility is a narrative memorandum describing internal control. The next most flexible approach is a flowchart.

Answer (A) is incorrect because a questionnaire provides a framework to assure that control concerns are not overlooked. Answer (B) is incorrect because a questionnaire is relatively easy to complete. For the most part, only yes/no responses are elicited from management and employees. Answer (D) is incorrect because the completed questionnaire can become part of the documentation of the auditor's understanding of internal control.

**217.** A well-designed internal control questionnaire should

A. Elicit "yes" or "no" responses rather than narrative responses and be organized by department.

B. Be a sufficient source of data for assessment of control risk.

C. Help evaluate the effectiveness of internal control.

D. Be independent of the objectives of the audit.

Answer (C) is correct. *(CIA, adapted)*

**REQUIRED:** The function of a well-designed internal control questionnaire.

**DISCUSSION:** An internal control questionnaire consists of a series of questions about the firm's controls designed to prevent or detect errors or fraud. Answers to the questions help the auditor identify specific controls relevant to specific assertions and to design tests of controls to evaluate the effectiveness of their design and operation.

Answer (A) is incorrect because yes/no question formats and question sequence by department may facilitate administering the questionnaire, but other formats and methods of question organization are possible. Answer (B) is incorrect because the questionnaire is a tool to help understand and document internal control but is not sufficient as the sole source of evidence to support the assessment of control risk. Answer (D) is incorrect because the internal control questionnaire must be designed to achieve the audit objectives.

**218.** Which of the following statements indicates the wrong way to use an internal control questionnaire?

A. Clarifying all answers with written remarks and explanations.

B. Filling out the questionnaire during an interview with the person who has responsibility for the area that is being audited.

C. Constructing the questionnaire so that a no response requires attention.

D. Supplementing the completed questionnaire with a narrative description or flowchart.

Answer (A) is correct. *(CIA, adapted)*

**REQUIRED:** The statement indicating the wrong way to use an internal control questionnaire.

**DISCUSSION:** Only those answers that appear inappropriate should be pursued by means of the auditor's asking for clarification or explanation. In this way, problem areas may be pinpointed and either compensating controls identified or extensions to the audit procedures planned.

# STUDY UNIT FOUR
# AUDIT EVIDENCE AND PROCEDURES



This study unit concerns auditing procedures, the resulting audit evidence, and related matters. The emphasis is on financial audits as performed by both internal and external auditors. Questions on audit procedures and audit evidence unique to internal auditing, especially efficiency, compliance, operational, and other audits, are found in Study Unit 9, Internal Auditing.

## QUESTIONS

### 4.1 Nature, Competence, and Sufficiency

**1.** Which of the following is a false statement about financial statement audit objectives?

A. There should be a one-to-one relationship between audit objectives and procedures.

B. Audit objectives should be developed in light of management assertions about the financial statement components.

C. Selection of tests to meet audit objectives should depend upon the understanding of internal control.

D. The auditor should resolve any substantial doubt about any of management's material financial statement assertions.

Answer (A) is correct. *(Publisher)*

**REQUIRED:** The false statement concerning audit objectives.

**DISCUSSION:** AU 326, *Evidential Matter*, states, "There is not necessarily a one-to-one relationship between audit objectives and procedures. Some auditing procedures may relate to more than one objective. On the other hand, a combination of auditing procedures may be needed to achieve a single objective."

Answer (B) is incorrect because the assertions made by management should be considered when the auditor develops audit objectives. Answer (C) is incorrect because the understanding of internal control and the assessed control risk affect the nature, timing, and extent of the auditor's substantive tests (AU 319, *Consideration of Internal Control in a Financial Statement Audit*). Answer (D) is incorrect because the auditor must consider whether specific audit objectives have been achieved; all substantial doubts about material assertions by management should be resolved before an opinion is formed.

**2.** The third standard of field work requires the auditor to collect sufficient competent evidence in support of the opinion. Which procedure is not listed in this standard?

A. Inspection.

B. Inquiries.

C. Observation.

D. Reconciliation.

Answer (D) is correct. *(Publisher)*

**REQUIRED:** The procedure not listed in the third standard of field work.

**DISCUSSION:** The third standard of field work lists the following procedures: inspection, observation, inquiries, and confirmations. Although reconciliations are often made by the auditor in collecting evidence, the procedure is not explicitly mentioned in the third standard of field work.

**3.** AU 326 states that management makes certain assertions that are embodied in financial statement components. For example, two such categories of assertions are completeness and valuation or allocation. Which of the following is not a broad category of management assertions according to AU 326?

A. Rights and obligations.

B. Presentation and disclosure.

C. Existence or occurrence.

D. Errors or fraud.

Answer (D) is correct. *(Publisher)*

**REQUIRED:** The category of assertions not explicitly listed in AU 326.

**DISCUSSION:** Management implicitly represents that the financial statements are free from material misstatements. But this representation is not explicitly noted in AU 326 as a category of assertions. AU 326 describes five categories of assertions. Assertions about completeness address whether all transactions and accounts that should be represented in the financial statements are included. Assertions about valuation or allocation address whether asset, liability, revenue, and expense components have been included in the financial statements at appropriate amounts. Assertions about rights and obligations address whether assets are the rights of the entity and liabilities are the obligations of the entity at the balance sheet date. Assertions about presentation and disclosure address whether particular components of the financial statements are properly classified, described, and disclosed. Assertions about existence or occurrence address whether assets or liabilities of the entity exist at a given date and whether recorded transactions have occurred during a given period.

**4.** Which of the following statements concerning audit evidence is true?

A. To be competent, audit evidence should be either persuasive or relevant, but need not be both.

B. The measure of the validity of audit evidence lies in the auditor's judgment.

C. The difficulty and expense of obtaining audit evidence concerning an account balance is a valid basis for omitting the test.

D. A client's accounting data can be sufficient audit evidence to support the financial statements.

Answer (B) is correct. *(CPA, adapted)*

**REQUIRED:** The true statement about audit evidence.

**DISCUSSION:** AU 326 states, "The measure of the validity of such evidence for audit purposes lies in the judgment of the auditor." Unlike legal evidence, audit evidence is not circumscribed by rigid rules. In determining whether evidence is competent and sufficient, the auditor must make many judgments about issues such as relevance, objectivity, timeliness, and the existence of corroboration.

Answer (A) is incorrect because, to be competent, audit evidence must be both valid and relevant. Moreover, an auditor usually must rely on evidence that is persuasive rather than convincing. Answer (C) is incorrect because, although the cost of obtaining evidence and its usefulness should be rationally related, the matter of difficulty and expense is not itself a valid basis for omitting a test. Answer (D) is incorrect because accounting data must be supported by corroborating information.

**5.** Which of the following is the best explanation of the difference, if any, between engagement objectives and procedures?

A. Procedures establish broad general goals; objectives specify the detailed work to be performed.

B. Objectives are tailor-made for each engagement; procedures are generic in application.

C. Objectives define specific desired accomplishments; procedures provide the means of achieving objectives.

D. Procedures and objectives are essentially the same.

Answer (C) is correct. *(CIA, adapted)*

**REQUIRED:** The difference between objectives and procedures.

**DISCUSSION:** According to PA 2210-1, "Planning should be documented. Engagement objectives and scope of work should be established. Engagement objectives are broad statements developed by internal auditors and define what the engagement is intended to accomplish. Engagement procedures are the means to attain engagement objectives. Engagement objectives and procedures, taken together, define the scope of the internal auditor's work."

Answer (A) is incorrect because objectives are specific goals, and procedures specify the detailed work. Answer (B) is incorrect because both objectives and procedures must be defined specifically for each engagement. Answer (D) is incorrect because procedures are the means of collecting, analyzing, interpreting, and documenting information during the engagement to achieve the objectives.

**6.** In gathering evidence in the performance of substantive tests, the auditor

A. Should use the test month approach.

B. Relies on persuasive rather than convincing evidence in the majority of cases.

C. Would consider the client's documentary evidence more competent than evidence gathered from observation and physical inspection.

D. Would express an adverse opinion if (s)he has substantial doubt as to any assertion of material significance.

Answer (B) is correct. *(Publisher)*

**REQUIRED:** The correct assumption about the performance of substantive tests.

**DISCUSSION:** Given the limits of time and cost to which evidence gathering is subject, even an experienced auditor is rarely convinced beyond all doubt regarding all aspects of the financial statements. Hence, the auditor must usually rely on persuasive rather than convincing evidence.

Answer (A) is incorrect because there is no requirement to select specific months for detail testing. "Test month approach" is a nonexistent term. Answer (C) is incorrect because evidence from physical inspection or observation is usually judged more competent than documentary evidence for the existence assertion. Answer (D) is incorrect because the auditor must be convinced that the financial statements, taken as a whole, are not presented fairly before (s)he expresses an adverse opinion.

**7.** JP Industries has significant information that is transmitted, processed, maintained, and accessed electronically. The auditor has concluded that it is not possible to reduce detection risk to an acceptable level by performing only substantive tests for a number of financial statement assertions. The auditor's alternative strategy is to

A. Increase the acceptable audit risk.

B. Focus audit tests on other assertions for which substantive tests prove to be effective.

C. Require management to change its information system to provide appropriate evidence.

D. Perform tests of controls to gather evidential matter to use in assessing control risk related to those assertions.

Answer (D) is correct. *(Publisher)*

**REQUIRED:** The appropriate audit strategy when the client processes significant information electronically.

**DISCUSSION:** When significant information is transmitted, processed, maintained, or accessed electronically, reducing detection risk to an acceptable level by performing substantive tests alone may not be feasible. For example, the risk of improper initiation or alteration of information is increased when information is produced, maintained, or accessed only in electronic form. Thus, in such cases, the auditor should perform tests of controls or consider the consequences for the report (AU 326).

Answer (A) is incorrect because the auditor has already established an acceptable level of audit risk. Answer (B) is incorrect because the auditor cannot express an unqualified opinion if (s)he remains in substantial doubt about any material assertion. Answer (C) is incorrect because the auditor should not expect management to change its information system solely to accommodate the audit.

**8.** The primary difference between an audit of the balance sheet and an audit of the income statement is that the audit of the income statement addresses the verification of

A. Transactions.

B. Authorizations.

C. Costs.

D. Cutoffs.

Answer (A) is correct. *(CPA, adapted)*

**REQUIRED:** The difference between the audit of the income statement and the balance sheet.

**DISCUSSION:** The audit of the income statement focuses on the propriety of handling transactions because most income statement accounts represent large volumes of transactions. The audit of the balance sheet is focused on verification of account balances.

Answer (B) is incorrect because all transactions must be authorized. Answer (C) is incorrect because the auditor is equally concerned with the costs reflected in the income statement and the balance sheet. Answer (D) is incorrect because cutoffs to verify that only current period transactions are reflected apply to both statements.

**9.** The competence of evidence available to an auditor is least likely to be affected by

A. The relevance of such evidence to the financial statement assertion being investigated.

B. The relationship of the preparer of such evidence to the entity being audited.

C. The timeliness of such audit evidence.

D. The sampling method employed by the auditor to obtain a sample of such evidence.

Answer (D) is correct. *(Publisher)*

**REQUIRED:** The factor that does not affect the competence of audit evidence.

**DISCUSSION:** Competent evidence is both valid and relevant. Ordinarily, evidence obtained from independent sources, developed under effective control, or generated through the auditor's personal experience is presumed to be the most competent (AU 326). The sample selection method does not affect the competence of evidence as long as the sample is representative of the population.

Answer (A) is incorrect because competent evidence must be valid and relevant. Answer (B) is incorrect because the independence of the source (or preparer) of the evidence from the auditee provides greater assurance of its reliability. Answer (C) is incorrect because timeliness is an aspect of relevance. Competent evidence must be relevant.

**10.** Which of the following statements concerning evidence is true?

A. Competent evidence supporting management's assertions should be convincing rather than merely persuasive.

B. Effective internal control contributes little to the reliability of the evidence created within the entity.

C. The cost of obtaining evidence is not an important consideration to an auditor in deciding what evidence should be obtained.

D. A client's accounting data cannot be considered sufficient audit evidence to support the financial statements.

Answer (D) is correct. *(CPA, adapted)*

**REQUIRED:** The true statement concerning evidence.

**DISCUSSION:** Evidence supporting the financial statements consists of underlying accounting data (books of original entry, ledgers, accounting manuals, spreadsheets, etc.) and corroborating information (written and electronic checks, EFT records, confirmations, information obtained by inquiry, etc.). AU 326 states, "Accounting data alone cannot be considered sufficient support for financial statements; on the other hand, without adequate attention to the propriety and accuracy of the underlying accounting data, an opinion on financial statements would not be warranted."

Answer (A) is incorrect because the auditor must usually rely on evidence that is merely persuasive. Answer (B) is incorrect because the more effective internal control, the more assurance it provides about the reliability of the accounting data and financial statements. Answer (C) is incorrect because the auditor will consider the cost of evidence relative to its usefulness. If the auditor deems necessary evidence too costly, a scope limitation results.

**11.** Which of the following procedures would provide the most reliable audit evidence?

A. Inquiries of the client's internal audit staff held in private.

B. Inspection of prenumbered client purchase orders filed in the vouchers payable department.

C. Analytical procedures performed by the auditor on the entity's trial balance.

D. Inspection of bank statements obtained directly from the client's financial institution.

Answer (D) is correct. *(CPA, adapted)*

**REQUIRED:** The procedure that provides the most reliable audit evidence.

**DISCUSSION:** When documentation is prepared solely by client personnel, its persuasiveness will be less than that prepared by the auditor or an independent party. Ordinarily, the most reliable documentation is created outside the entity and has never been within the client's control, e.g., statements obtained from the bank, letters from attorneys, and letters from insurance brokers.

Answer (A) is incorrect because the internal audit staff is not independent. Answer (B) is incorrect because the purchase orders are internally generated. Answer (C) is incorrect because analytical procedures are based on the entity's internal records.

**12.** The most reliable forms of documentary evidence are those documents that are

A. Prenumbered.

B. Internally generated.

C. Easily duplicated.

D. Authorized by a responsible official.

Answer (D) is correct. *(CMA, adapted)*

**REQUIRED:** The most reliable forms of documentary evidence.

**DISCUSSION:** Externally generated documents are deemed to be more reliable than those produced by the auditee. However, the evidentiary value of the latter is enhanced if they are subject to effective control. Accordingly, authorization by an appropriate party lends credibility to a document because it increases the probability that the underlying transaction is valid.

Answer (A) is incorrect because the use of prenumbered and sequentially issued documents is an effective control, but such documents may be accessible to an employee who is perpetrating fraud. Answer (B) is incorrect because internally generated documents are readily available to those attempting to commit fraud. Answer (C) is incorrect because easily duplicated documents are readily available to those attempting to commit fraud.

**13.** Which of the following presumptions does not relate to the competence of audit evidence?

A. The more effective internal control, the more assurance it provides about the accounting data and financial statements.

B. An auditor's opinion, to be economically useful, is formed within a reasonable time and based on evidence obtained at a reasonable cost.

C. Evidence obtained from independent sources outside the entity is more reliable than evidence secured solely within the entity.

D. The independent auditor's direct personal knowledge obtained through observation and inspection is more persuasive than information obtained indirectly.

Answer (B) is correct. *(CPA, adapted)*

**REQUIRED:** The presumption not relating to the competence of audit evidence.

**DISCUSSION:** Competent evidence is both valid and relevant. Ordinarily, evidence obtained from independent sources, developed under effective internal control, or generated through the auditor's personal experience is presumed to be the most competent (AU 326). However, cost-benefit considerations relate to the sufficiency, not the competence, of evidence.

Answer (A) is incorrect because the more effective internal control, the more assurance it provides about the reliability of the accounting data and financial statements. Answer (C) is incorrect because evidence obtained from independent sources outside an entity provides greater assurance of reliability than evidence secured solely within the entity. Answer (D) is incorrect because the independent auditor's direct personal knowledge obtained through physical examination, observation, computation, and inspection is more persuasive than information obtained indirectly.

**14.** AU 326 describes three presumptions concerning the validity of evidence. The situations given below indicate the relative degrees of assurance provided by two types of evidence obtained in different situations. Which describes an exception to one of the general presumptions?

A. The auditor has obtained greater assurance about the balance of sales at Plant A where (s)he has made limited tests of transactions because of effective internal control than at Plant B where (s)he has made extensive tests of transactions because of ineffective internal control.

B. The auditor's computation of interest payable on outstanding bonds provides greater assurance than reliance on the client's calculation.

C. The report of an expert regarding the valuation of a collection of paintings held as an investment provides greater assurance than the auditor's physical observation of the paintings.

D. The schedule of insurance coverage obtained from the company's insurance agent provides greater assurance than one prepared by the internal audit staff.

Answer (C) is correct. *(Publisher)*

**REQUIRED:** The exception to the presumptions concerning validity of audit evidence.

**DISCUSSION:** AU 326 describes three presumptions concerning the validity of evidence. Evidence is usually more valid when (1) it is obtained from independent sources, (2) accounting data and financial statements are developed under effective internal control, and (3) it consists of the auditor's direct knowledge obtained by examination, observation, computation, or inspection. Preference for the report of a specialist over the auditor's physical observation of works of art is acceptable because the auditor is not expected to have such expertise. Physical observation provides evidence of the existence of assets but often does not verify their value, ownership, cost, or condition. Consequently, the presumption in favor of the auditor's direct knowledge is overcome in this case.

Answer (A) is incorrect because control risk should be lower when control is effective, and judging that greater assurance has been provided about sales at Plant A is consistent with the second presumption stated above. Answer (B) is incorrect because the auditor's direct knowledge should be preferred to indirect knowledge. Answer (D) is incorrect because information obtained from independent sources is more valid than that prepared by the client's staff.

**15.** Observation is considered a reliable audit procedure, but one that is limited in usefulness. However, it is used in a number of different audit situations. Which of the following statements is true regarding observation as an audit technique?

A. It is the most effective audit methodology to use in filling out internal control questionnaires.

B. It is the most persuasive methodology to learn how transactions are really processed during the period under audit.

C. It is rarely sufficient to satisfy any audit assertion other than existence.

D. It is the most persuasive audit technique for determining if fraud has occurred.

Answer (C) is correct. *(CIA, adapted)*

**REQUIRED:** The true statement about the audit technique of observation.

**DISCUSSION:** Observation is effective for verifying whether particular assets such as inventory or equipment exist at a given date. However, it is of limited use in addressing other assertions. Thus, it provides less persuasive evidence about the assertions of completeness, rights, valuation, and presentation and disclosure. For example, merely observing inventory does not determine whether the auditee has rights in it.

Answer (A) is incorrect because interviews are the most effective method to fill out questionnaires. The interview results should be supplemented with observations. Answer (B) is incorrect because observation provides information on how transactions are processed at one moment in time, not how they are processed throughout the period under audit investigation. Answer (D) is incorrect because the auditor will very seldom be able to observe a fraud.

**16.** Which of the following elements ultimately determines the specific auditing procedures that are necessary in the circumstances to afford a reasonable basis for an opinion?

A. Auditor judgment.

B. Materiality.

C. Audit risk.

D. Reasonable assurance.

Answer (A) is correct. *(CPA, adapted)*

**REQUIRED:** The ultimate determinant of specific auditing procedures.

**DISCUSSION:** The third standard of field work states, "Sufficient competent evidential matter is to be obtained through inspection, observation, inquiries, and confirmations to afford a reasonable basis for an opinion regarding the financial statements." The nature, timing, and extent of the specific procedures to be applied to obtain sufficient competent evidential matter are matters of professional judgment (AU 326).

Answer (B) is incorrect because materiality is among the considerations in exercising professional judgment. Answer (C) is incorrect because audit risk is among the considerations in exercising professional judgment. Answer (D) is incorrect because, although the audit should be planned and performed to obtain reasonable assurance about whether the financial statements are free of material misstatement, whether such assurance has been obtained is itself ultimately a matter of auditor judgment.

**17.** Assuming a low assessed level of control risk, which of the following audit procedures is least likely to be performed?

A. Physical inspection of a sample of inventory.

B. Search for unrecorded cash receipts.

C. Obtainment of a client representation letter.

D. Confirmation of accounts receivable.

Answer (B) is correct. *(CPA, adapted)*

**REQUIRED:** The procedure least necessary when control risk is low.

**DISCUSSION:** Auditing standards do not specifically require a search for unrecorded cash receipts. Given a low assessed level of control risk, the auditor might decide to reduce the audit effort devoted to substantive tests of assertions about cash and omit the procedure.

Answer (A) is incorrect because AU 331, *Inventories*, states that observation of inventories is a generally accepted auditing procedure. An auditor who expresses an opinion when inventories have not been observed must justify the opinion expressed. Answer (C) is incorrect because AU 333, *Management Representations*, requires written representations from management. Answer (D) is incorrect because, according to AU 330, *The Confirmation Process*, confirmation of accounts receivable is a generally accepted auditing procedure. There is a presumption in favor of confirmation.

**18.** You have been assigned to audit the maintenance department of an organization. Which of the following is likely to produce the least reliable audit evidence?

A. Notes on discussions with mechanics in the maintenance operation.

B. A schedule comparing actual maintenance expenses with budgeted expenses and those of the prior period and disclosing important differences.

C. A narrative covering review of user reports on maintenance service.

D. An analysis of changes in certain maintenance department ratios.

Answer (A) is correct. *(CIA, adapted)*

**REQUIRED:** The procedure that is likely to produce the least reliable evidence in an audit of a maintenance department.

**DISCUSSION:** Although representations by personnel of the auditee are evidence, auditor observation and analysis of documents provide more reliable evidence.

Answer (B) is incorrect because the comparison provides more reliable evidence relative to the maintenance department's operations. Such documentary evidence is presumably prepared independently of the audited department. Answer (C) is incorrect because reports by users of maintenance services are likewise independent evidence. They are of interest to internal auditors because they bear on the quality of performance. Answer (D) is incorrect because analytical procedures are typically considered more reliable than representations by client personnel.

**19.** If an auditor conducts an audit of financial statements in accordance with applicable auditing standards, which of the following will the auditor most likely detect?

A. Misposting of recorded transactions.

B. Unrecorded transactions.

C. Forgery.

D. Collusive fraud.

Answer (A) is correct. *(Publisher)*

**REQUIRED:** The error or fraud most likely to be detected.

**DISCUSSION:** Until a transaction is recorded leaving an audit trail, standard audit procedures are often ineffective. A misposting of previously recorded transactions is therefore the most likely item to be detected.

Answer (B) is incorrect because unrecorded transactions leave no audit trail. Answer (C) is incorrect because auditors usually are not qualified to detect forgery. Answer (D) is incorrect because the possibility of collusion is an inherent limitation of internal control. The purpose of segregation of duties can be circumvented if two or more persons agree to commit an irregularity.

**20.** Each of the following might, by itself, form a valid basis for an auditor to decide to omit a test except for the

A. Difficulty and expense involved in testing a particular item.

B. Assessment of control risk at a low level.

C. Inherent risk involved.

D. Relationship between the cost of obtaining evidence and its usefulness.

Answer (A) is correct. *(CPA, adapted)*

**REQUIRED:** The consideration that is not a valid reason for omission of an audit test.

**DISCUSSION:** The costs and benefits of obtaining evidence should have a rational relationship. However, the difficulty and expense of performing a test are not in themselves considered valid reasons for omitting it if the test is necessary to obtain sufficient competent evidence to afford a reasonable basis for an opinion (AU 326).

Answer (B) is incorrect because the lower the control risk, the higher the acceptable detection risk, and the greater the justification for omitting a substantive test. Answer (C) is incorrect because a test might be omitted if the susceptibility to errors and fraud is slight. Answer (D) is incorrect because the cost of obtaining evidence and its usefulness should have a rational relationship.

**21.** Which of the following auditing procedures is ordinarily performed last?

A. Reading of the minutes of the directors' meetings.

B. Confirming accounts payable.

C. Obtaining a management representation letter.

D. Testing of the purchasing function.

Answer (C) is correct. *(CPA, adapted)*

**REQUIRED:** The auditing procedure ordinarily performed last.

**DISCUSSION:** Written representations by management should be dated no earlier than the date of the report because the auditor is concerned with events occurring through that date that may require adjustment to or disclosure in the financial statements (AU 333).

Answer (A) is incorrect because reading the minutes is customarily done in the preliminary or planning phase of the audit. Answer (B) is incorrect because confirming accounts payable is done at interim dates or year-end. Answer (D) is incorrect because testing of the purchasing function is done at interim dates or year-end.

**22.** Before applying substantive tests to the details of asset accounts at an interim date, an auditor should assess

A. Control risk below the maximum level.

B. Inherent risk at the maximum level.

C. The difficulty in controlling the incremental audit risk.

D. Materiality for the accounts tested as insignificant.

Answer (C) is correct. *(CPA, adapted)*

**REQUIRED:** The assessment made prior to applying substantive tests at an interim date.

**DISCUSSION:** Before substantive tests of details are performed at interim dates, the auditor should assess the difficulty of controlling the incremental audit risk. Factors to be considered include the cost of substantive tests to cover the remaining period; the possible impairment of the effectiveness of those tests, if the auditor assesses control risk at the maximum; the existence of rapidly changing business conditions or circumstances that might lead management to misstate the financial statements; the predictability of year-end balances; the propriety of the auditee's procedures for adjusting accounts and establishing cutoffs; and the question of whether the financial reporting information system permits investigation of unusual transactions or entries, other causes of significant fluctuations, and changes in the composition of balances (AU 313, *Substantive Tests prior to the Balance Sheet Date*).

Answer (A) is incorrect because assessing control risk below the maximum is not required. Answer (B) is incorrect because inherent risk at the maximum is not required. Answer (D) is incorrect because the accounts need not be tested if they are not material.

**23.** In evaluating an entity's accounting estimates, one of an auditor's objectives is to determine whether the estimates are

A. Not subject to bias.

B. Consistent with industry guidelines.

C. Based on objective assumptions.

D. Reasonable in the circumstances.

Answer (D) is correct. *(CPA, adapted)*

**REQUIRED:** The objective of evaluating an entity's accounting estimates.

**DISCUSSION:** "The auditor is responsible for evaluating the reasonableness of accounting estimates made by management in the context of the financial statements taken as a whole" (AU 342, *Auditing Accounting Estimates*).

Answer (A) is incorrect because accounting estimates are based on subjective as well as objective factors and may be subject to bias. Answer (B) is incorrect because there are few industry guidelines relative to accounting estimates. Answer (C) is incorrect because estimates may be based on subjective factors.

**24.** Before applying principal substantive tests to the details of accounts at an interim date prior to the balance sheet date, an auditor should

A. Assess control risk as below the maximum for the assertions embodied in the accounts selected for interim testing.

B. Determine that the accounts selected for interim testing are not material to the financial statements taken as a whole.

C. Consider whether the amounts of the year-end balances selected for interim testing are reasonably predictable.

D. Obtain written representations from management that all financial records and related data will be made available.

Answer (C) is correct. *(CPA, adapted)*

**REQUIRED:** The auditor action prior to applying principal substantive tests at an interim date.

**DISCUSSION:** Among the auditor's considerations is whether the year-end balances of accounts selected for interim examination are reasonably predictable as to amount, relative significance, and composition.

Answer (A) is incorrect because assessing control risk below the maximum is not required. However, if the auditor assesses control risk at the maximum for the remaining period, (s)he should consider whether the effectiveness of certain substantive tests to cover that period will be impaired. Answer (B) is incorrect because the accounts selected for interim testing are likely to be material. Answer (D) is incorrect because written representations will be obtained from the client regardless of when testing is done.

**25.** A client uses a suspense account for unresolved questions whose final accounting has not been determined. If a balance remains in the suspense account at year-end, the auditor would be most concerned about

A. Suspense debits that management believes will benefit future operations.

B. Suspense debits that the auditor verifies will have realizable value to the client.

C. Suspense credits that management believes should be classified as "current liability."

D. Suspense credits that the auditor determines to be customer deposits.

Answer (A) is correct. *(CPA, adapted)*

**REQUIRED:** The accounting disposition of year-end suspense items most troublesome for an auditor.

**DISCUSSION:** Although the auditor is concerned about management's assertions about all accounts, the greatest risks are overstated assets or understated liabilities. The unverified suspense debits represent assets that may not exist.

Answer (B) is incorrect because the auditor has verified that the debits (assets) have future value; thus, they are properly classified as assets. Answer (C) is incorrect because, for each suspense credit, a liability is reflected. Consequently, liabilities are not understated. Answer (D) is incorrect because, for each suspense credit, a liability is reflected. Consequently, liabilities are not understated.

**26.** In evaluating the reasonableness of an accounting estimate, an auditor is most likely to concentrate on key factors and assumptions that are

A. Consistent with prior periods.

B. Similar to industry guidelines.

C. Objective and not susceptible to bias.

D. Deviations from historical patterns.

Answer (D) is correct. *(CPA, adapted)*

**REQUIRED:** The focus of an auditor when evaluating the reasonableness of an accounting estimate.

**DISCUSSION:** "In evaluating the reasonableness of an accounting estimate, an auditor normally concentrates on key factors and assumptions that are (1) significant to the accounting estimate, (2) sensitive to variations, (3) deviations from historical patterns, and (4) subjective and susceptible to misstatement and bias" (AU 342).

Answer (A) is incorrect because the auditor would concentrate on estimates that are deviations from historical patterns. Answer (B) is incorrect because key factors and assumptions similar to industry guidelines would not help evaluate the reasonableness of an accounting estimate. Answer (C) is incorrect because the auditor would concentrate on key factors and assumptions that are subjective and susceptible to misstatement and bias.

**27.** Which of the following procedures will most likely assist an auditor in determining whether management has identified all accounting estimates that could be material to the financial statements?

A. Inquire about the existence of related-party transactions.

B. Determine whether accounting estimates deviate from historical patterns.

C. Confirm inventories at locations outside the entity.

D. Review the lawyer's letter for information about litigation.

Answer (D) is correct. *(CPA, adapted)*

**REQUIRED:** The procedures to determine whether management has identified all material accounting estimates.

**DISCUSSION:** The auditor should consider the financial statement assertions and make inquiries of management to determine the need for estimates. (S)he should also evaluate (1) changes in the entity's business and the industry in which it operates; (2) changes in the methods of accumulating information; (3) litigation, claims, and assessments; (4) available minutes; and (5) regulatory or examination reports, supervisory correspondence, and similar materials. Thus, the response to the letter of audit inquiry sent to the client's lawyer may help the auditor to determine whether material estimates have been identified concerning litigation, claims, and assessments (AU 342).

Answer (A) is incorrect because a related-party transaction may not involve an accounting estimate. Information about the outcome of pending litigation helps to estimate the amount of the recovery or liability. Answer (B) is incorrect because determination of whether accounting estimates deviate from historical patterns helps evaluate the reasonableness of accounting estimates, not their existence. Answer (C) is incorrect because confirming inventories at locations outside the entity (e.g., public warehouses) tests the count of those inventories, not an estimate, such as the net realizable value.

**28.** During the audit of fair value measurements and disclosures (FVMD), the auditor must

A. Understand the components of internal control, but need not specifically obtain an understanding of the entity's process for determining FVMD.

B. Use the understanding of the audited entity's process for determining FVMD to assess the risk of material misstatement.

C. Determine that the entity has measured fair values using discounted cash flows whenever feasible.

D. Address only the initial recording of transactions.

Answer (B) is correct. *(Publisher)*

**REQUIRED:** The necessary procedure in an audit of FVMD.

**DISCUSSION:** To meet its responsibility to make the FVMD included in the financial statements, management may need to adopt an accounting and financial reporting process that consists of (1) choosing valuation methods, (2) identifying significant assumptions, (3) preparing the valuations, and (4) ensuring conformity with GAAP. The auditor must obtain an understanding of this process and the relevant controls that is sufficient for an effective audit of FVMD. The understanding is used to assess the risk of material misstatement and to determine the nature, timing, and extent of audit procedures (AU 328, *Auditing Fair Value Measurements and Disclosures*).

Answer (A) is incorrect because the auditor must obtain such an understanding. Answer (C) is incorrect because GAAP do not require a specific method for measuring fair value. Answer (D) is incorrect because fair value measurements also are necessary for changes in value subsequent to initial recording.

**29.** As part of the audit of fair value measurements and disclosures (FVMD), an auditor may need to test the entity's significant assumptions. In these circumstances, the auditor must

A. Verify that the entity has used its own assumptions, not those of marketplace participants.

B. Obtain sufficient evidence to express an opinion on the assumptions.

C. Evaluate whether the assumptions individually and as a whole form a reasonable basis for the FVMD.

D. Identify especially sensitive assumptions.

Answer (C) is correct. *(Publisher)*

**REQUIRED:** The necessary step in an audit of FVMD when the auditor tests significant assumptions.

**DISCUSSION:** When observable market prices are not available, the entity uses valuation methods based on the assumptions that the market would employ to estimate fair values, if obtainable without excessive cost. Accordingly, the auditor must evaluate whether the significant assumptions are consistent with (1) economic conditions, (2) existing market data, (3) the entity's plans, (4) past experience, (5) prior-period assumptions, (6) cash flow risks, and (7) other factors (AU 328).

Answer (A) is incorrect because valuation methods preferably should be based on the assumptions that the market would use. Answer (B) is incorrect because the auditor is required merely to evaluate whether, in the context of the audit as a whole, the assumptions form a reasonable basis for the FVMD. Answer (D) is incorrect because the auditor considers the sensitivity of valuations to changes in assumptions, but is not always required to identify especially sensitive assumptions.

## 4.2 Analytical Procedures

**30.** Analytical procedures can best be categorized as

A. Substantive tests.

B. Tests of controls.

C. Qualitative tests.

D. Budget comparisons.

Answer (A) is correct. *(CIA, adapted)*

**REQUIRED:** The best classification of analytical procedures.

**DISCUSSION:** According to AU 329, *Analytical Procedures*, analytical procedures "consist of evaluations of financial information made by a study of plausible relationships among both financial and nonfinancial data." They "involve comparisons of recorded amounts, or ratios developed from recorded amounts, to expectations developed by the auditor."

Answer (B) is incorrect because tests of controls are used to evaluate the effectiveness of control activities. Answer (C) is incorrect because analytical procedures tend to be quantitative even when nonfinancial information is considered. Answer (D) is incorrect because budget comparisons are only one of many types of analytical procedures.

**31.** Analytical procedures enable the auditor to predict the balance or quantity of an item under audit. Information to develop this estimate can be obtained from all of the following except

A. Tracing transactions through the system to determine whether procedures are being applied as prescribed.

B. Comparison of financial data with data for comparable prior periods, anticipated results (e.g., budgets and forecasts), and similar data for the industry in which the entity operates.

C. Study of the relationships of elements of financial data that would be expected to conform to a predictable pattern based upon the entity's experience.

D. Study of the relationships of financial data with relevant nonfinancial data.

Answer (A) is correct. *(Publisher)*

**REQUIRED:** The procedure that is not a source of information for analytical procedures.

**DISCUSSION:** Tracing transactions through the system is a test of controls directed toward the operating effectiveness of internal control, not an analytical procedure.

Answer (B) is incorrect because the basic premise of analytical procedures is that plausible relationships among data may be reasonably expected to exist and continue in the absence of known conditions to the contrary. Well-drafted budgets and forecasts prepared at the beginning of the year should therefore be compared with actual results, and client information should be compared with data for the industry in which the client operates. Answer (C) is incorrect because the auditor should expect financial ratios and relationships to exist and to remain relatively stable in the absence of reasons for variation. Answer (D) is incorrect because financial information is related to nonfinancial information; e.g., salary expense should be related to the number of hours worked.

**32.** The objective of performing analytical procedures in planning an audit is to identify the existence of

A. Unusual transactions and events.

B. Illegal acts that went undetected because of internal control weaknesses.

C. Related party transactions.

D. Recorded transactions that were not properly authorized.

Answer (A) is correct. *(CPA, adapted)*

**REQUIRED:** The objective of analytical procedures.

**DISCUSSION:** The objective of analytical procedures "is to identify such things as the existence of unusual transactions and events, and amounts, ratios, and trends that might indicate matters that have financial statement and audit planning ramifications" (AU 329).

Answer (B) is incorrect because the objective of performing analytical procedures to plan the audit is to identify areas of specific risk, not specific illegal acts. Answer (C) is incorrect because, although the auditor should evaluate disclosures about related party transactions, analytical procedures performed to plan the audit would not necessarily detect such transactions. Answer (D) is incorrect because tests of controls would be necessary to determine whether transactions were properly authorized.

**33.** Analytical procedures used in planning an audit should focus on

A. Evaluating the adequacy of evidence gathered concerning unusual balances.

B. Testing individual account balances that depend on accounting estimates.

C. Enhancing the auditor's understanding of the client's business.

D. Identifying material weaknesses in internal control.

Answer (C) is correct. *(CPA, adapted)*

**REQUIRED:** The focus of analytical procedures used in planning.

**DISCUSSION:** Analytical procedures used in planning an audit should focus on enhancing the auditor's understanding of the client's business and identifying unusual relationships and unexpected fluctuations in data that may indicate areas of greater risk of misstatement (AU 329).

Answer (A) is incorrect because evaluation of evidence is done in the final stage of the audit. Answer (B) is incorrect because analytical procedures are predictions or expectations of account balances or ratios but are not specifically designed to test estimates. Answer (D) is incorrect because the auditor's understanding of internal control and tests of controls may identify material weaknesses.

**34.** Which of the following statements concerning analytical procedures is true?

A. Analytical procedures may be omitted entirely for some financial statement audits.

B. Analytical procedures used in planning the audit should not use nonfinancial information.

C. Analytical procedures usually are effective and efficient for tests of controls.

D. Analytical procedures alone may provide the appropriate level of assurance for some assertions.

Answer (D) is correct. *(CPA, adapted)*

**REQUIRED:** The true statement concerning analytical procedures.

**DISCUSSION:** AU 329 states, "For some assertions, analytical procedures are effective in providing the appropriate level of assurance." The decision is based on the auditor's judgment about the expected effectiveness and efficiency of the available procedures. The auditor must then decide which procedure(s) can provide the desired level of assurance for particular assertions.

Answer (A) is incorrect because analytical procedures are required in the planning and review stages of the audit. Answer (B) is incorrect because analytical procedures used in planning the audit often use financial data only, but relevant nonfinancial information may also be considered. Answer (C) is incorrect because analytical procedures may be used as substantive tests but not as tests of controls.

**35.** For all audits of financial statements made in accordance with auditing standards, the use of analytical procedures is required to some extent

| | In the Planning Stage | As a Substantive Test | In the Review Stage |
|---|---|---|---|
| A. | Yes | No | Yes |
| B. | No | Yes | No |
| C. | No | Yes | Yes |
| D. | Yes | No | No |

Answer (A) is correct. *(CPA, adapted)*

**REQUIRED:** The required use(s) of analytical procedures.

**DISCUSSION:** The auditor is required to apply analytical procedures in planning the nature, timing, and extent of other auditing procedures. However, analytical procedures may be, but are not required to be, used as substantive tests to provide competent evidence about specific financial statement assertions. Analytical procedures give supervisors and reviewers an overall perspective on the financial information being audited and are required in the final review.

**36.** Which of the following statements is true concerning analytical procedures?

A. Analytical procedures usually involve comparisons of ratios developed from recorded amounts with assertions developed by management.

B. Analytical procedures used in planning an audit ordinarily use data aggregated at a high level.

C. Analytical procedures can replace tests of controls in gathering evidence to support the assessed level of control risk.

D. Analytical procedures are more efficient, but not more effective, than tests of details and transactions.

Answer (B) is correct. *(CPA, adapted)*

**REQUIRED:** The true statement concerning analytical procedures.

**DISCUSSION:** Analytical procedures applied in planning the audit focus on enhancing the understanding of the business and the transactions and events since the last audit, identify areas that may represent specific audit risks, and ordinarily use data aggregated at a high level.

Answer (A) is incorrect because analytical procedures involve comparisons of recorded amounts, or ratios developed therefrom, with expectations developed by the auditor. Answer (C) is incorrect because tests of controls are required if control risk is to be assessed at below the maximum. Analytical procedures are used as substantive tests but not as tests of controls. Answer (D) is incorrect because, for many assertions, analytical procedures may not be as effective or efficient as tests of details in providing the desired level of assurance.

**37.** Which of the following statements about analytical procedures is true?

A. Analytical procedures performed in the final review stage of the audit should focus on identifying specific risks.

B. Analytical procedures performed in the final review stage of the audit should achieve audit objectives related to specific assertions in the financial statements.

C. Analytical procedures performed in the planning stage of the audit should address the risk of material misstatement of revenue due to fraudulent financial reporting.

D. Analytical procedures performed in the planning stage of the audit should assist in assessing the validity of the conclusions reached.

Answer (C) is correct. *(Publisher)*

**REQUIRED:** The usage of analytical procedures.

**DISCUSSION:** Analytical procedures applied in planning the audit (1) focus on enhancing the understanding of the business and the transactions and events since the last audit, (2) identify areas that may represent specific audit risks, and (3) ordinarily use data aggregated at a high level (AU 319). Analytical procedures performed in the planning stage may yield unusual or unexpected results that the auditor should consider when identifying fraud risks. In the planning stage, analytical procedures must be performed on revenue accounts to identify unusual or unexpected relationships that are indicative of material misstatement due to fraudulent financial reporting. Furthermore, the results of these procedures pertaining to revenue must be updated in the overall review stage. For example, a comparison of sales volume based on recorded revenue with production capacity may suggest that fictitious sales have been reported (AU 316).

Answer (A) is incorrect because analytical procedures in the final stage assist in assessing the conclusions reached and in evaluating the overall financial presentation. Answer (B) is incorrect because analytical procedures used as substantive tests achieve audit objectives related to specific assertions. Answer (D) is incorrect because analytical procedures in the final review stage assist in assessing the validity of the conclusions reached.

**38.** Which of the following items tend to be the most predictable for purposes of analytical procedures applied as substantive tests?

A. Relationships involving balance sheet accounts.

B. Transactions subject to management discretion.

C. Relationships involving income statement accounts.

D. Data subject to audit testing in the prior year.

Answer (C) is correct. *(CPA, adapted)*

**REQUIRED:** The most predictable item for purposes of analytical procedures applied as substantive tests.

**DISCUSSION:** According to AU 329, "Relationships involving income statement accounts tend to be more predictable than relationships involving only balance sheet accounts because income statement accounts represent transactions over a period of time, whereas balance sheet accounts represent amounts at a moment in time."

Answer (A) is incorrect because relationships involving balance sheet accounts tend to be less predictable. Balance sheet accounts represent amounts at a moment in time. Answer (B) is incorrect because transactions subject to management discretion are often unpredictable. Answer (D) is incorrect because data subject to audit testing in the prior year may not reflect changed conditions.

**39.** According to professional standards, analytical procedures are least likely to be applied to

A. Test disclosures about reportable operating segments.

B. Review financial statements or interim financial information.

C. Compile financial statements.

D. Plan an audit and assist in the final review.

Answer (C) is correct. *(Publisher)*

**REQUIRED:** The inappropriate use of analytical procedures.

**DISCUSSION:** AR 100, *Compilation and Review of Financial Statements*, states that no audit procedures need be applied in a compilation of financial statements. The accountant is only required to read the financial statements to identify obvious errors.

Answer (A) is incorrect because an Interpretation of AU 326 states that an auditor should consider applying analytical procedures consisting of comparisons of information about segments with comparable information for the prior year and with budgeted information. Answer (B) is incorrect because analytical procedures ordinarily should be applied in a review of interim financial information (AU 722, *Interim Financial Information*) and in a review of financial statements of a private entity (AR 100). Answer (D) is incorrect because AU 329 requires analytical procedures to be applied in the planning and final review stages of an audit.

**40.** Analytical procedures performed in the overall review stage of an audit suggest that several accounts have unexpected relationships. The results of these procedures most likely indicate that

A. Misstatements exist in the relevant account balances.

B. Internal control activities are not operating effectively.

C. Additional tests of details are required.

D. The communication with the audit committee should be revised.

Answer (C) is correct. *(CPA, adapted)*

**REQUIRED:** The implication when analytical procedures applied in the overall review stage of the audit have unexpected results.

**DISCUSSION:** Analytical procedures are required to be performed in the final review stage of the audit. They assist in assessing the conclusions reached and in evaluating the overall financial presentation. When analytical procedures have unexpected results, the auditor should investigate the causes. Thus, additional tests of details should be performed to gather additional evidence (AU 329).

Answer (A) is incorrect because analytical procedures can identify unexpected relationships but not their causes. Answer (B) is incorrect because tests of controls are conducted to determine the effectiveness of their design and operation. Answer (D) is incorrect because, until the auditor determines the cause of the unexpected relationships, the auditor does not know whether the communication with the audit committee should be revised.

**41.** A basic premise underlying analytical procedures is that

A. These procedures cannot replace tests of balances and transactions.

B. Statistical tests of financial information may lead to the discovery of material misstatements in the financial statements.

C. The study of financial ratios is an acceptable alternative to the investigation of unusual fluctuations.

D. Plausible relationships among data may reasonably be expected to exist and continue in the absence of known conditions to the contrary.

Answer (D) is correct. *(CPA, adapted)*

**REQUIRED:** The premise underlying analytical procedures.

**DISCUSSION:** AU 329 states, "A basic premise underlying the application of analytical procedures is that plausible relationships among data may reasonably be expected to exist and continue in the absence of known conditions to the contrary." Variability in these relationships can be explained by, for example, unusual events or transactions, business or accounting changes, misstatements, or random fluctuations.

Answer (A) is incorrect because, for some assertions, analytical procedures alone may provide the auditor with the level of assurance (s)he desires. Answer (B) is incorrect because analytical procedures, such as simple comparisons, do not necessarily require statistical testing. Answer (C) is incorrect because the objective of analytical procedures, such as ratio analysis, is to identify significant differences for evaluation and possible investigation.

**42.** Which of the following factors will influence an auditor's consideration of the reliability of data for purposes of analytical procedures least?

A. Whether the data were processed in a computer system or in a manual accounting system.

B. Whether sources within the entity were independent of those who are responsible for the amount being audited.

C. Whether the data were subjected to audit testing in the current or prior year.

D. Whether the data were obtained from independent sources outside the entity or from sources within the entity.

Answer (A) is correct. *(CPA, adapted)*

**REQUIRED:** The factor least likely to influence an auditor's consideration of the reliability of data for purposes of analytical procedures.

**DISCUSSION:** The consideration of the reliability of data should include sources of the data and the conditions under which the data were gathered. The factors influencing this consideration include the other answer choices. Other factors include whether the auditor's expectations were developed using data from a variety of sources and whether the data were developed under a reliable system with adequate controls. The mode of processing is less influential than the other factors. Whether sources within the entity were independent of those who are responsible for the amount being audited, whether the data were subjected to audit testing in the current or prior year, and whether the data were obtained from independent sources outside the entity or from sources within the entity are more influential than the other factor.

**43.** As a result of analytical procedures, the independent auditor determines that the gross profit percentage has declined from 30% in the preceding year to 20% in the current year. The auditor should

A. Document management's intentions with respect to plans for reversing this trend.

B. Evaluate management's performance in causing this decline.

C. Require footnote disclosure.

D. Consider the possibility of a misstatement in the financial statements.

Answer (D) is correct. *(CPA, adapted)*

**REQUIRED:** The appropriate action when the auditor has identified a decline in the gross profit rate.

**DISCUSSION:** AU 329 indicates that the auditor should consider the possibility of a misstatement when (s)he has identified unexpected differences between recorded amounts and expectations. Because a change of 10% is likely to be judged significant, the auditor should reconsider the expectations used and make inquiries of management. If the difference still cannot be explained, additional procedures should be performed.

Answer (A) is incorrect because an auditor appropriately considers management's plans for dealing with adverse conditions that create a substantial doubt about the ability of the entity to continue as a going concern (AU 341, *The Auditor's Consideration of an Entity's Ability to Continue as a Going Concern*). In the absence of this doubt, however, the auditor's scope of work does not include consideration of management's plans to reverse the trend. Answer (B) is incorrect because the auditor typically does not evaluate management's performance. Answer (C) is incorrect because requiring disclosure is premature. The auditor must first determine the cause of the decline.

**44.** Which of the following is the most reliable analytical approach to verification of the year-end financial statement balances of a wholesale business?

A. Verify depreciation expense by multiplying the depreciable asset balances by one divided by the depreciation rate.

B. Verify commission expense by multiplying sales revenue by the company's standard commission rate.

C. Verify interest expense, which includes imputed interest, by multiplying long-term debt balances by the year-end prevailing interest rate.

D. Verify FICA tax liability by multiplying total payroll costs by the FICA contribution rate in effect during the year.

Answer (B) is correct. *(CPA, adapted)*

**REQUIRED:** The reliable analytical procedure to verify balances of a wholesale business.

**DISCUSSION:** If the wholesaler uses a standard commission rate, commission expense should be related to sales revenue. The auditor should also compare actual with budgeted and prior year amounts.

Answer (A) is incorrect because one divided by the life of the asset is the formula for the straight-line depreciation rate. The client may also use other depreciation methods. Answer (C) is incorrect because interest expense is not related to the prevailing rate but to contracted and imputed rates. Answer (D) is incorrect because FICA tax is withheld from individual wages up to a ceiling amount. No tax liability exists for amounts above the ceiling, so the test will probably overstate the liability.

**45.** An auditor's decision either to apply analytical procedures as substantive tests or to perform tests of transactions and account balances usually is determined by the

A. Availability of data aggregated at a high level.

B. Relative effectiveness and efficiency of the tests.

C. Timing of tests performed after the balance sheet date.

D. Auditor's familiarity with industry trends.

Answer (B) is correct. *(CPA, adapted)*

**REQUIRED:** The basis for choosing between analytical procedures and tests of details.

**DISCUSSION:** The decision is based on the auditor's judgment about the expected effectiveness and efficiency of the available procedures. The auditor considers the level of assurance required to be provided by substantive testing for a particular audit objective related to a particular assertion. (S)he must then decide which procedure or combination of procedures can provide that level of assurance. "For some assertions, analytical procedures are effective in providing the appropriate level of assurance" (AU 329).

Answer (A) is incorrect because availability of data is among the factors in evaluating effectiveness and efficiency. Answer (C) is incorrect because timing of tests is among the factors in evaluating effectiveness and efficiency. Answer (D) is incorrect because familiarity with industry trends is among the factors in evaluating effectiveness and efficiency.

**46.** Which result of an analytical procedure suggests the existence of obsolete merchandise?

A. Decrease in the inventory turnover rate.

B. Decrease in the ratio of gross profit to sales.

C. Decrease in the ratio of inventory to accounts payable.

D. Decrease in the ratio of inventory to accounts receivable.

Answer (A) is correct. *(CIA, adapted)*

**REQUIRED:** The analytical procedure that might uncover obsolete merchandise.

**DISCUSSION:** Inventory turnover is equal to cost of sales divided by average inventory. If inventory is increasing at a faster rate than sales, the turnover rate decreases and suggests a buildup of unsalable inventory.

Answer (B) is incorrect because the ratio of gross profit to sales does not necessarily change when obsolete merchandise is on hand. Answer (C) is incorrect because the ratio of inventory to accounts payable does not necessarily change when obsolete merchandise is on hand. Answer (D) is incorrect because the ratio of inventory to accounts receivable does not necessarily change when obsolete merchandise is on hand.

**47.** An auditor's preliminary analysis of accounts receivable turnover revealed the following rates over these accounting periods:

| 20X2 | 20X1 | 20X0 |
|---|---|---|
| 4.3 | 6.2 | 7.3 |

Which of the following is the most likely cause of the decrease in accounts receivable turnover?

A. Increase in the cash discount offered.

B. Liberalization of credit policy.

C. Shortening of due date terms.

D. Increased cash sales.

Answer (B) is correct. *(CIA, adapted)*

**REQUIRED:** The most likely cause of a decrease in accounts receivable turnover.

**DISCUSSION:** The accounts receivable turnover ratio equals net credit sales over average accounts receivable. Accounts receivable turnover will decrease if net credit sales decrease or average accounts receivable increase. Liberalization of credit policy will increase receivables.

Answer (A) is incorrect because an increase in cash sales that reduces credit sales as a result of an increased cash discount has an indeterminate effect on the turnover ratio. Both the numerator and denominator are decreased but not necessarily by the same amount. An increase in cash sales not affecting credit sales has no effect on the ratio. Answer (C) is incorrect because shortening due dates decreases the average accounts receivable outstanding and increases the ratio if other factors are held constant. Answer (D) is incorrect because increased cash sales have an indeterminate effect on the turnover ratio.

**48.** Which of the following is least likely to be comparable between similar companies in the same industry line of business?

A. Earnings per share.

B. Return on total assets before interest and taxes.

C. Accounts receivable turnover.

D. Operating cycle.

Answer (A) is correct. *(CPA, adapted)*

**REQUIRED:** The measure least likely to be comparable between similar companies.

**DISCUSSION:** Similar companies in the same industry that are equally profitable may have quite different earnings per share because of differences in shares outstanding and in other aspects of their capital structures.

Answer (B) is incorrect because similar companies should have a comparable return on total assets. Answer (C) is incorrect because similar companies should have a comparable accounts receivable turnover. Answer (D) is incorrect because similar companies should have a comparable operating cycle.

**49.** Auditors sometimes use comparison of ratios as audit evidence. For example, an unexplained decrease in the ratio of gross profit to sales suggests which of the following possibilities?

A. Unrecorded purchases.

B. Unrecorded sales.

C. Merchandise purchases being charged to selling and general expense.

D. Fictitious sales.

Answer (B) is correct. *(CPA, adapted)*

**REQUIRED:** The reason for a decrease in the gross profit ratio.

**DISCUSSION:** Error or fraud that decreases gross profit relative to sales (or increases sales relative to gross profit) causes the ratio to decline. Unrecorded sales cause inventory to decrease and cost of sales to increase with no increase in sales, thereby decreasing gross profit relative to sales and lowering the ratio.

Answer (A) is incorrect because unrecorded or misrecorded purchases result in a lower recorded cost of sales, a greater gross profit, and an increase in the ratio. Answer (C) is incorrect because unrecorded or misrecorded purchases result in a lower recorded cost of sales, a greater gross profit, and an increase in the ratio. Answer (D) is incorrect because fictitious sales increase sales with no associated cost; hence, gross profit is inflated and the ratio increases.

**50.** An auditor discovers that a client's accounts receivable turnover is substantially lower for the current year than for the prior year. This trend may indicate that

A. Fictitious credit sales have been recorded during the year.

B. Employees have stolen inventory just before year-end.

C. The client recently tightened its credit-granting policies.

D. An employee has been lapping receivables in both years.

Answer (A) is correct. *(CPA, adapted)*

**REQUIRED:** The most likely cause of a decrease in accounts receivable turnover.

**DISCUSSION:** The accounts receivable turnover ratio equals net credit sales divided by average accounts receivable. Accounts receivable turnover will decrease if net credit sales decrease or average accounts receivable increases. Fictitious sales increase both the numerator and denominator. Adding an equal amount to both the numerator and denominator decreases a fraction greater than 1.0. For example, adding 1 to both parts of the fraction $3 \div 2$ decreases it to $4 \div 3$. The turnover ratio will decrease still more in the next period because fictitious items will continue to increase receivables (a real account) but not sales (a nominal account).

Answer (B) is incorrect because stolen inventory has no effect on accounts receivable turnover. It affects inventory turnover. Answer (C) is incorrect because tightening of credit-granting policies will decrease net credit sales and receivables. Subtracting an equal amount from the numerator and denominator increases a fraction greater than 1.0. Answer (D) is incorrect because lapping is the delayed recording of cash receipts to cover a cash shortage. Current receipts are posted to accounts of customers who paid one or two days previously. If lapping occurs in both years, the turnover ratio is not affected.

**51.** The auditor is evaluating the effectiveness of a sales commission plan adopted 12 months earlier. An audit procedure likely to provide strong evidence of the plan's effectiveness is to

A. Calculate the percentage change in monthly sales by product line for the last 3 years.

B. Compare monthly selling costs of this year with those of the 2 preceding years.

C. Regress monthly indices of external economic conditions against sales for the 2 preceding years and compare predictions with reported sales.

D. Compare the ratio of selling costs per dollar of sales each month for the past year with that of other companies in the industry.

Answer (C) is correct. *(CIA, adapted)*

**REQUIRED:** The technique to determine the effectiveness of a newly installed sales commission plan.

**DISCUSSION:** The auditor requires evidence as to whether sales have increased more than could be expected from changes in external economic conditions. Regression analysis is a statistical tool to generate predictions based on projections of current economic conditions. It provides benchmarks whereby current sales may be compared with expected sales to evaluate the effect of the sales commission variable.

Answer (A) is incorrect because simple comparison of month-to-month sales figures does not take into account changes in external economic factors. Answer (B) is incorrect because the effectiveness of the sales commission plan should be measured by the sales generated, not by costs. Answer (D) is incorrect because the effectiveness of the sales commission plan should be measured by the sales generated, not by costs.

**52.** Analytical procedures used in the overall review stage of an audit generally include

A. Considering unusual or unexpected account balances that were not previously identified.

B. Performing tests of transactions to corroborate management's financial statement assertions.

C. Gathering evidence concerning account balances that have not changed from the prior year.

D. Retesting controls that appeared to be ineffective during the assessment of control risk.

Answer (A) is correct. *(CPA, adapted)*

**REQUIRED:** The analytical procedure used in the final review stage.

**DISCUSSION:** Analytical procedures are required to be used as an overall review in the final review stage of the audit. They are useful in assessing the conclusions reached by the auditor and in evaluating financial statement presentation. Procedures ordinarily should include reading the statements and notes and considering (1) the adequacy of evidence regarding previously identified unusual or unexpected balances and (2) unusual or unexpected balances or relationships not previously noted (AU 329).

Answer (B) is incorrect because analytical procedures are not tests of transactions. Answer (C) is incorrect because the lack of change from the prior year may not be unusual or unexpected. Answer (D) is incorrect because analytical procedures are substantive tests, not tests of controls.

## 4.3 Sales-Receivables Cycle

**53.** Which of the following is not a principal objective of the auditor in the audit of revenues?

A. To verify cash deposited during the year.

B. To obtain an understanding of internal control and assess control risk, with particular emphasis on the use of accrual accounting to record revenue.

C. To verify that earned revenue has been recorded and recorded revenue has been earned.

D. To identify and interpret significant trends and variations in the amounts of various categories of revenue.

Answer (A) is correct. *(CPA, adapted)*

**REQUIRED:** The statement not a principal objective of an auditor when auditing revenues.

**DISCUSSION:** The verification of cash deposits during the year is not part of the audit of revenues. Verification of cash and marketable securities is undertaken as a separate part of the audit program.

Answer (B) is incorrect because the auditor must obtain an understanding of internal control sufficient to plan the audit. (S)he must also assess control risk to determine the acceptable detection risk. Answer (C) is incorrect because proper verification that accrual accounting has been properly applied is an important objective of the audit of revenues. Answer (D) is incorrect because the heavy volume of transactions in revenue accounts may result in substantial audit risk, which may be reduced by use of analytical procedures.

**54.** In the audit of which of the following general ledger accounts will tests of controls be particularly appropriate?

A. Equipment.

B. Bonds payable.

C. Bank charges.

D. Sales.

Answer (D) is correct. *(CPA, adapted)*

**REQUIRED:** The account for which tests of controls are most appropriate.

**DISCUSSION:** In auditing the sales or revenue account, tests of controls are particularly appropriate, provided the auditor believes that control risk can be assessed at less than the maximum. Because of the large number of transactions, examining all items will seldom be cost-effective.

Answer (A) is incorrect because the ease of verifying the physical existence of equipment and computing depreciation may make it inefficient to evaluate the effectiveness of controls. Answer (B) is incorrect because the ready availability of evidence in the contractual agreements and the infrequency of transactions make tests of controls less necessary for bonds payable. Answer (C) is incorrect because evidence of bank charges is easily obtainable from an independent source. Bank charges are usually reported as a single amount on each monthly bank statement.

**55.** Auditors are often concerned with the possibility of overstatement of sales and receivables. However, management may also have reasons for understating these balances. Which of the following would explain understatement of sales and receivables?

A. To window-dress the financial statements.

B. To avoid paying taxes.

C. To meet budgets and forecasts.

D. All of the answers are correct.

Answer (B) is correct. *(Publisher)*

**REQUIRED:** The reason(s) for understating sales and receivables.

**DISCUSSION:** State sales taxes and federal and state income taxes are based upon sales or profits, respectively. Management may attempt to reduce or avoid tax liability by not recording and reporting all sales and receivables.

Answer (A) is incorrect because sales and receivables would be overstated to window-dress the statements. Answer (C) is incorrect because management may attempt to overstate sales to achieve forecasts or to meet budgets. Answer (D) is incorrect because only one of the choices is correct.

**56.** An auditor observed that a client mails monthly statements to customers. Subsequently, the auditor reviewed evidence of follow-up on the errors reported by the customers. This test of controls was most likely performed to support management's financial statement assertion(s) of

| | Presentation and Disclosure | Rights and Obligations |
|---|---|---|
| A. | Yes | Yes |
| B. | Yes | No |
| C. | No | Yes |
| D. | No | No |

Answer (C) is correct. *(CPA, adapted)*

**REQUIRED:** The financial statement assertion(s) related to observing the client's follow-up on errors reported in monthly statements.

**DISCUSSION:** The rights and obligations assertion relates to whether the related assets are the rights of the entity and the related liabilities are the obligations of the entity at the balance sheet date. Observation of the mailing of monthly statements and the correction of reported errors provides evidence that controls may be effective in ensuring that receivables are genuine. However, these procedures provide little or no evidence about whether particular financial statement components are properly classified, described, and disclosed.

**57.** Material misstatements due to fraudulent financial reporting often result from an overstatement of revenues (for example, through premature revenue recognition or recording of fictitious revenues) or an understatement of revenues (for example, through improperly shifting revenues to a later period). To address the risk of improper revenue recognition, the auditor most likely should

A. Increase the assessment of control risk.

B. Assume the existence of a risk of material misstatement due to fraud relating to revenue recognition.

C. Focus testing of journal entries on those made during the reporting period rather than at the end of the reporting period.

D. Focus testing on the actions of the client's staff-level employees.

Answer (B) is correct. *(Publisher)*

**REQUIRED:** The auditor response to the risk of misstated revenues.

**DISCUSSION:** Management may be subject to incentives or pressures to misstate revenues. Given management's opportunity to override controls, the auditor ordinarily should assume the existence of a fraud risk relating to revenue recognition (AU 316).

Answer (A) is incorrect because the auditor assesses control risk based on the audit evidence regarding the effectiveness of the client's controls, not on the need to adjust for an unspecified risk of improper revenue recognition. Answer (C) is incorrect because focus of testing should be on the end of the reporting period, when it is most likely that fraudulent adjustments to revenue will be made. Answer (D) is incorrect because the focus should be on management-level employees or those with both the incentive pressure and opportunity to commit frauds related to revenue.

**58.** Tracing bills of lading to sales invoices provides evidence that

A. Shipments to customers were invoiced.

B. Shipments to customers were recorded as sales.

C. Recorded sales were shipped.

D. Invoiced sales were shipped.

Answer (A) is correct. *(CPA, adapted)*

**REQUIRED:** The evidence provided by tracing bills of lading to sales invoices.

**DISCUSSION:** Comparing the seller's copies of shipping documents (such as bills of lading) with billing documents (sales invoices) provides evidence that the amounts shipped were billed to customers. The absence of invoices for goods shipped suggests that the related sales were unrecorded at the balance sheet date.

Answer (B) is incorrect because the shipping documents would have to be traced to the sales records, not the sales invoices, to obtain direct proof that shipments were recorded as sales. Answer (C) is incorrect because the proper direction of testing to determine whether recorded sales were shipped is from the sales records to the bills of lading. A sales record without a related shipping document might indicate a fictitious sale or an improper sales cutoff. Answer (D) is incorrect because the proper direction of testing to determine whether invoiced sales were shipped is from the sales records to the bills of lading. A sales record without a related shipping document might indicate a fictitious sale or an improper sales cutoff.

**59.** An auditor most likely will review an entity's periodic accounting for the numerical sequence of shipping documents and invoices to support management's financial statement assertion of

A. Existence or occurrence.

B. Rights and obligations.

C. Valuation or allocation.

D. Completeness.

Answer (D) is correct. *(CPA, adapted)*

**REQUIRED:** The assertion supported by reviewing the numerical sequence of shipping documents and invoices.

**DISCUSSION:** The completeness assertion concerns whether all transactions and accounts that should be presented in the financial statements are included. Testing the numerical sequence of shipping documents and invoices may detect omitted items.

Answer (A) is incorrect because the existence or occurrence assertion addresses whether assets or liabilities exist at a given date and whether recorded transactions have occurred. Answer (B) is incorrect because the rights and obligations assertion concerns whether assets are rights of the entity and liabilities are obligations at a given date. Answer (C) is incorrect because the valuation or allocation assertion concerns whether assets, liabilities, revenues, and expenses have been included at appropriate amounts.

**60.** Which of the following might be detected by an auditor's review of the client's sales cutoff?

A. Excessive goods returned for credit.

B. Unrecorded sales discounts.

C. Lapping of year-end accounts receivable.

D. Inflated sales for the year.

Answer (D) is correct. *(CPA, adapted)*

**REQUIRED:** The condition that might be detected by review of the client's sales cutoff.

**DISCUSSION:** A cutoff review of sales is designed to detect the client's manipulation of sales for the period under audit. By examining recorded sales for several days before and after the balance sheet date and comparing them with sales invoices and shipping documents, the auditor may detect the recording of a sale in a period other than that in which title passed. The completeness assertion is the primary focus of the cutoff tests.

Answer (A) is incorrect because sales returns are not recorded in the sales journal and thus are not examined in the sales cutoff test. Answer (B) is incorrect because examination of cash receipts would reveal unrecorded discounts. Answer (C) is incorrect because lapping may be detected by the confirmation of customer balances and tracing amounts received according to duplicate deposit slips to the accounts receivable subsidiary ledger. Lapping is the concealment of a cash shortage by a delayed recording of cash receipts.

**61.** Cutoff tests designed to detect credit sales made before the end of the year that have been recorded in the subsequent year provide assurance about management's assertion of

A. Presentation.

B. Completeness.

C. Rights.

D. Existence.

Answer (B) is correct. *(CPA, adapted)*

**REQUIRED:** The management assertion about which assurance is provided by cutoff tests.

**DISCUSSION:** The completeness assertion is tested by examining recorded sales for several days before and after the balance sheet date and comparing them with sales invoices and shipping documents. The auditor may detect the recording of a sale in a period other than that in which title passed.

Answer (A) is incorrect because the assertion about presentation and disclosure concerns whether financial statement components are properly classified, described, and disclosed. Answer (C) is incorrect because the rights and obligations assertion concerns whether assets are the rights of the entity and liabilities are obligations at a given date. Answer (D) is incorrect because the existence or occurrence assertion concerns whether assets or liabilities exist at a given date and whether recorded transactions have occurred.

**62.** A company's sales cutoff is December 31. All goods sold are shipped FOB destination, and the company records sales 3 days after shipment. The following sales were recorded as indicated:

| | | (Amounts in Thousands) | |
|---|---|---|---|
| Date Shipped | Month Recorded | Selling Price | Cost |
| December 28 | December | $182 | $190 |
| December 29 | December | 60 | 50 |
| December 30 | January | 144 | 145 |
| January 2 | December | 230 | 215 |
| January 5 | January | 182 | 174 |

Ignoring tax effects, the net effect on income for the month ended December 31 of any failures to observe a proper cutoff was

A. $(1,000)

B. $15,000

C. $24,000

D. $25,000

Answer (D) is correct. *(Publisher)*

**REQUIRED:** The net effect on income of the failure to observe a proper cutoff.

**DISCUSSION:** FOB destination means that title and risk of loss do not pass to the buyer until the goods are tendered at the specified place. The December 29 shipment (which resulted in a $10,000 gain) should have been recorded in January because the company records sales 3 days after shipment. Because the selling price of this shipment was greater than its cost, the effect of the error was to overstate income for December by the $10,000 difference. The January 2 shipment (which resulted in a $15,000 gain) was also erroneously recorded in December. Because its selling price was more than cost, the effect of the error was to overstate income for December by the $15,000 gain. The net effect of these errors is that income for the month ended December 31 was overstated by $25,000.

**63.** An auditor observed the auditee's annual physical inventory on December 15. The auditee adjusted the inventory balance and detailed perpetual inventory records to agree with the count. Goods are shipped FOB shipping point. Listed below are four material items discovered when the auditor tested the sales cutoff as of the client's fiscal year-end at December 31. Which item does not require an adjusting entry on the auditee's books?

| | Shipped | Recorded as Sale | Credited to Inventory |
|---|---|---|---|
| A. | 1/1 | 12/31 | 12/31 |
| B. | 12/31 | 1/3 | 12/31 |
| C. | 12/14 | 12/16 | 12/16 |
| D. | 12/9 | 12/20 | 12/12 |

Answer (D) is correct. *(Publisher)*

**REQUIRED:** The item not requiring an adjusting entry.

**DISCUSSION:** Goods shipped on 12/9 would have been properly recorded as a sale on 12/20, a date within the same accounting period. Moreover, the credit to inventory on 12/12 preceded the physical count on 12/15. No adjustment is necessary.

Answer (A) is incorrect because the 1/1 shipment should have been recorded as a sale in the same period or year. Answer (B) is incorrect because the 12/31 shipment should have been recorded as a sale in the same period or year. Answer (C) is incorrect because items shipped on 12/14 should have been excluded from the 12/15 inventory, and no credit would have been necessary on 12/16.

**64.** The auditor finds a situation in which one person has the ability to collect receivables, make deposits, issue credit memos, and record receipt of payments. The auditor suspects the individual may be stealing from cash receipts. Which of the following audit procedures will be most effective in discovering fraud in this scenario?

A. Send positive confirmations to a random selection of customers.

B. Send negative confirmations to all outstanding accounts receivable customers.

C. Perform a detailed review of debits to customer discounts, sales returns, or other debit accounts, excluding cash posted to the cash receipts journal.

D. Take a sample of bank deposits and trace the detail in each bank deposit back to the entry in the cash receipts journal.

Answer (C) is correct. *(CIA, adapted)*

**REQUIRED:** The audit procedure most effective in detecting theft from cash receipts.

**DISCUSSION:** The most effective procedure is to perform a detailed review of debits to customer discounts, sales returns, and other debit accounts. These accounts could be used to conceal a theft of cash payments without alerting customers.

Answer (A) is incorrect because an employee who performs asset custody, authorization, and recording functions can conceal the theft by debiting customer discounts or sales returns. Customers would be unaware of the activity because their balances would reflect their expectations. Answer (B) is incorrect because an employee who performs asset custody, authorization, and recording functions can conceal the theft by debiting customer discounts or sales returns. Customers would be unaware of the activity because their balances would reflect their expectations. Answer (D) is incorrect because bank deposits will agree with journal entries. The stolen amounts are never recorded.

**65.** A large university has relatively ineffective internal control. The university's auditor seeks assurance that all tuition revenue has been recorded. The auditor could best obtain the desired assurance by

A. Confirming a sample of tuition payments with the students.

B. Observing tuition payment procedures on a surprise basis.

C. Comparing business office revenue records with registrar's office records of students enrolled.

D. Preparing a year-end bank reconciliation.

Answer (C) is correct. *(CIA, adapted)*

**REQUIRED:** The best procedure for testing whether all tuition revenue has been recorded.

**DISCUSSION:** To be assured that all tuition revenue is being recorded, the auditor must perform substantive tests, which are tests of details and analytical procedures to detect misstatements in an account balance, transaction class, or disclosure component. Comparing business office revenue records with registrar's office records of students enrolled provides analytical evidence based on independently generated records.

Answer (A) is incorrect because confirmations of payments do not detect unrecorded receipts. Answer (B) is incorrect because observation is a test of controls, not a substantive test of the completeness assertion for the revenue balance. Answer (D) is incorrect because preparing a year-end bank reconciliation would only detect an unrecorded deposit or other cash accounting error.

**66.** If the objective of a test of details of transactions is to detect overstatements of sales, the auditor's direction of testing should be from the

A. Cash receipts journal to the sales journal.

B. Sales journal to the cash receipts journal.

C. Source documents to the accounting records.

D. Accounting records to the source documents.

Answer (D) is correct. *(CPA, adapted)*

**REQUIRED:** The appropriate test to detect an overstatement of sales.

**DISCUSSION:** Overstatements of sales likely result from entries in sales with no supporting documentation. The proper direction of sampling is to select entries in the sales account and vouch them to the shipping documents. The source documents represent the valid sales.

Answer (A) is incorrect because the cash receipts journal is a book of original entry, not a source document. Answer (B) is incorrect because the sales journal is a book of original entry, not a source document. Answer (C) is incorrect because the proper direction of testing is from the accounting records to the source documents.

**67.** One objective of an audit of a water utility for a small city is to determine whether all customers are being billed. The best direction of testing is from the

A. Meter department records to the sales register.

B. Sales register to the meter department records.

C. Accounts receivable ledger to the sales register.

D. Sales register to the accounts receivable ledger.

Answer (A) is correct. *(Publisher)*

**REQUIRED:** The best direction of testing to determine whether all customers are being billed.

**DISCUSSION:** The best direction of testing is to proceed from the meter department records, which indicate those customers who have received service, to the sales register. Comparing services rendered with billings is the best way to detect omitted billings.

Answer (B) is incorrect because comparing the sales register with the meter records is useful for verifying the amounts billed for which service was not provided. Answer (C) is incorrect because comparisons between the accounts receivable ledger and the sales register are useful for verifying the accuracy of the posting of accounts receivable. Answer (D) is incorrect because comparisons between the accounts receivable ledger and the sales register are useful for verifying the accuracy of the posting of accounts receivable.

**68.** An inappropriate audit objective relative to accounts receivable is to determine that

A. The accounts exist and are properly valued.

B. The accounts represent the complete transaction process.

C. The accounts are collected by the balance sheet date.

D. The client has rights in the accounts receivable.

Answer (C) is correct. *(Publisher)*

**REQUIRED:** The determination that is not an audit objective relative to accounts receivable.

**DISCUSSION:** Accounts receivable represent the amounts due the client at the balance sheet date. The auditor should not expect the accounts to be collected at the balance sheet date.

Answer (A) is incorrect because the determination that accounts exist and are properly valued is an appropriate audit objective relating to management assertions or representations (existence and valuation) made in financial statement components (AU 326). The auditor's responsibility is to obtain and evaluate evidence concerning the assertions made by management. Answer (B) is incorrect because an audit objective may appropriately relate to the completeness assertion. Answer (D) is incorrect because an audit objective may be developed in the light of an assertion about rights.

**69.** Which of the following will most likely give the most assurance concerning the valuation assertion of accounts receivable?

A. Vouching amounts in the subsidiary ledger to details on shipping documents.

B. Comparing receivable turnover ratios with industry statistics for reasonableness.

C. Inquiring about receivables pledged under loan agreements.

D. Assessing the allowance for uncollectible accounts for reasonableness.

Answer (D) is correct. *(CPA, adapted)*

**REQUIRED:** The procedure providing the most assurance about the valuation of accounts receivable.

**DISCUSSION:** Assertions about valuation or allocation concern whether financial statement components have been included at appropriate amounts. For example, management asserts that trade accounts receivable are stated at net realizable value (gross accounts receivable minus allowance for uncollectible accounts). Hence, assessing the allowance provides assurance about the valuation of the account.

Answer (A) is incorrect because vouching amounts in the subsidiary ledger to details on shipping documents provides evidence about the occurrence assertion for transactions. Answer (B) is incorrect because comparing receivable turnover ratios with industry statistics for reasonableness provides evidence as to completeness. Answer (C) is incorrect because inquiring about receivables pledged under loan agreements pertains to presentation and disclosure assertions.

**70.** In confirming accounts receivable, an auditor decided to confirm customers' account balances rather than individual invoices. Which of the following most likely will be included with the client's confirmation letter?

A. An auditor-prepared letter explaining that a nonresponse may cause an inference that the account balance is correct.

B. A client-prepared letter reminding the customer that a nonresponse will cause a second request to be sent.

C. An auditor-prepared letter requesting the customer to supply missing and incorrect information directly to the auditor.

D. A client-prepared statement of account showing the details of the customer's account balance.

Answer (D) is correct. *(CPA, adapted)*

**REQUIRED:** The nature of a confirmation of an accounts receivable balance.

**DISCUSSION:** A confirmation must be requested by the client because the receiving party has no relationship with the client's auditor. In confirming the customer's receivables account balance, display of the details of the balance will likely help the customer in reconciling the amount and may increase response rates.

Answer (A) is incorrect because the request should come from the client. Answer (B) is incorrect because no threats should be included in a confirmation. Answer (C) is incorrect because the request should come from the client.

**71.** Which of the following statements will an auditor most likely add to the negative form of confirmations of accounts receivable to encourage timely consideration by the recipient?

A. "This is not a request for payment; remittances should not be sent to our auditors in the enclosed envelope."

B. "Report any differences on the enclosed statement directly to our auditors; no reply is necessary if this amount agrees with your records."

C. "If you do not report any differences within 15 days, it will be assumed that this statement is correct."

D. "The following invoices have been selected for confirmation and represent amounts that are overdue."

Answer (C) is correct. *(CPA, adapted)*

**REQUIRED:** The statement to encourage timely consideration of a negative form of receivables confirmation.

**DISCUSSION:** An issue with respect to negative confirmation requests is whether recipients are likely to give them consideration (AU 330). Providing a time limit tends to encourage recipients to respond in a timely manner.

Answer (A) is incorrect because, although the statement is appropriate for a confirmation, it does not encourage a timely response. Answer (B) is incorrect because, although the statement is appropriate for a confirmation, it does not encourage a timely response. Answer (D) is incorrect because noting that an amount is overdue could discourage a customer from replying in a timely manner.

**72.** Auditing standards define a confirmation as "the process of obtaining and evaluating a direct communication from a third party in response to a request for information about a particular item affecting financial statement assertions." Two assertions for which confirmation of accounts receivable balances provides primary evidence are

A. Completeness and valuation.

B. Valuation and rights and obligations.

C. Rights and obligations and existence.

D. Existence and completeness.

Answer (C) is correct. *(CPA, adapted)*

**REQUIRED:** The assertions tested by confirming receivables.

**DISCUSSION:** Confirmation by means of direct (independent) communication with debtors is the generally accepted auditing procedure for accounts receivable. Confirmations are most likely to be effective for the existence and rights-and-obligations assertions. Assertions about existence or occurrence address whether assets or liabilities of the entity exist at a given date and whether recorded transactions have occurred during a given period. Assertions about rights and obligations address whether assets are the rights of the entity and liabilities are the obligations of the entity at the balance sheet date. Thus, confirmation provides evidence that receivables exist and that the client has the right of collection. The valuation assertion concerns whether items have been included in the financial statements at appropriate amounts. For receivables, net realizable values are appropriate. The completeness assertion concerns whether all items that should be presented are so included, for example, whether all receivables have been recorded. Unrecorded receivables are usually not discovered by confirmation. Thus, confirmation provides insufficient evidence about both the valuation assertion and the completeness assertion.

**73.** Auditors may use positive or negative forms of confirmation requests for accounts receivable. An auditor most likely will use

A. The positive form to confirm all balances regardless of size.

B. A combination of the two forms, with the positive form used for large balances and the negative form for the small balances.

C. A combination of the two forms, with the positive form used for trade receivables and the negative form for other receivables.

D. The positive form when the combined assessed level of inherent and control risk for assertions related to receivables is acceptably low, and the negative form when it is unacceptably high.

Answer (B) is correct. *(CPA, adapted)*

**REQUIRED:** The true statement about the use of positive and negative confirmations.

**DISCUSSION:** A positive confirmation asks the debtor for a reply. It may ask the respondent to state whether (s)he agrees with the information given or request that the recipient fill in the account balance or provide other information. The latter type of positive confirmation is called a blank form. The negative confirmation asks for a response only when the debtor disagrees. A combination of the two forms is often used.

Answer (A) is incorrect because the negative form is often used, especially when many small balances are involved. Answer (C) is incorrect because the choice of confirmation does not depend on the nature of the receivable. Answer (D) is incorrect because the positive form is used when control risk is high.

**74.** In the confirmation of accounts receivable, the auditor will most likely

A. Request confirmation of a sample of the inactive accounts.

B. Seek to obtain positive confirmations for at least 50% of the total dollar amount of the receivables.

C. Require confirmation of all receivables from agencies of the federal government.

D. Require that confirmation requests be sent within 1 month of the fiscal year-end.

Answer (A) is correct. *(CPA, adapted)*

**REQUIRED:** The most likely auditor action regarding confirmation of receivables.

**DISCUSSION:** When the combined assessed level of inherent and control risk is at an acceptably low level, the auditor will confirm only a sample of receivables. The sample should include inactive or past due accounts. If such accounts are to be regarded as assets, acknowledgment of the debts must be obtained. Confirming inactive accounts may also detect lapping or establish what amounts are in dispute.

Answer (B) is incorrect because auditing standards do not establish a percentage dollar amount to be confirmed. Confirming all large balances, however, may account for a substantial dollar value of the receivables. Answer (C) is incorrect because the record systems and operating procedures of governmental agencies may not permit confirmation. Answer (D) is incorrect because, when internal control is effective, confirmations may be sent more than 1 month before year-end.

**75.** The negative request form of accounts receivable confirmation may be used when the

| | Combined Assessed Level of Inherent and Control Risk Is | Number of Small Balances Is | Consideration by the Recipient Is |
|---|---|---|---|
| A. | Low | Many | Likely |
| B. | Low | Few | Unlikely |
| C. | High | Few | Likely |
| D. | High | Many | Likely |

Answer (A) is correct. *(CPA, adapted)*

**REQUIRED:** The conditions appropriate for use of negative accounts receivable confirmation.

**DISCUSSION:** AU 330 states, "Negative confirmation requests may be used to reduce audit risk to an acceptable level when (1) the combined assessed level of inherent and control risk is low, (2) a large number of small balances is involved, and (3) the auditor has no reason to believe that the recipients of the requests are unlikely to give them consideration." Returned negative confirmations provide evidence about assertions in the financial statements, but unreturned negative confirmation requests rarely provide significant evidence about assertions other than some aspects of existence. Negative confirmations should not be used when the combined assessed level of control and inherent risk is high, small balances are few, or consideration by recipients is unlikely.

**76.** Negative confirmation of accounts receivable is less effective than positive confirmation of accounts receivable because

A. A majority of recipients usually lack the willingness to respond objectively.

B. Some recipients may report incorrect balances that require extensive follow-up.

C. The auditor cannot infer that all nonrespondents have verified their account information.

D. Negative confirmations do not produce evidence that is statistically quantifiable.

Answer (C) is correct. *(CPA, adapted)*

**REQUIRED:** The reason negative confirmations are less effective than positive confirmations.

**DISCUSSION:** Because a failure to reply is assumed to indicate the debtor's agreement when negative confirmations are used, no auditor follow-up occurs, and no explicit evidence is provided that the intended parties received their requests and verified the information. Thus, unreturned negative confirmation requests rarely provide significant evidence about assertions other than existence. Positive confirmations require a reply, whether or not the debtor agrees with the balance. Alternative procedures are applied to the nonresponses to obtain the evidence necessary to reduce audit risk to an acceptable level (AU 330).

Answer (A) is incorrect because the assumed lack of objectivity to which this answer refers would affect both forms of confirmation. Answer (B) is incorrect because inaccurate reporting would affect positive and negative confirmations. Answer (D) is incorrect because both forms of confirmation produce evidence that is quantifiable.

**77.** To reduce the risks associated with accepting fax responses to requests for confirmations of accounts receivable, an auditor most likely would

A. Examine the shipping documents that provide evidence for the existence assertion.

B. Verify the sources and contents of the faxes in telephone calls to the senders.

C. Consider the faxes to be nonresponses and evaluate them as unadjusted differences.

D. Inspect the faxes for forgeries or alterations and consider them to be acceptable if none are noted.

Answer (B) is correct. *(CPA, adapted)*

**REQUIRED:** The procedure to reduce the risk of accepting false confirmations by fax.

**DISCUSSION:** Because establishing the source of a fax is often difficult, the auditor should ensure that the confirmations returned by fax are genuine. One way is to verify the sources by following up with telephone calls to the senders.

Answer (A) is incorrect because the purpose of the confirmation is to test the existence of the receivable by direct communication with the debtor. Answer (C) is incorrect because a fax is considered a valid response if the source can be verified. Answer (D) is incorrect because faxes may not be signed. Furthermore, the auditor is unlikely to be qualified to recognize forgeries.

**78.** An auditor confirms a representative number of open accounts receivable as of December 31 and investigates respondents' exceptions and comments. By this procedure, the auditor is most likely to learn of which of the following?

A. One of the cashiers has been covering a personal embezzlement by lapping.

B. One of the sales clerks has not been preparing charge slips for credit sales to family and friends.

C. One of the computer processing control clerks has been removing all sales invoices applicable to his account from the data file.

D. The credit manager has misappropriated remittances from customers whose accounts have been written off.

Answer (A) is correct. *(CPA, adapted)*

**REQUIRED:** The fraud most likely to be detected by confirming receivables.

**DISCUSSION:** Lapping is the theft of a cash payment from one customer concealed by crediting that customer's account when a second customer makes a payment. When lapping exists at the balance sheet date, the confirmation of customer balances will probably detect the fraud because the customers' and company's records of lapped accounts will differ.

Answer (B) is incorrect because, if a charge slip has not been prepared, no accounts receivable balance will exist to be confirmed. Answer (C) is incorrect because, if a sales invoice is not processed, no account balance will appear in the records. Answer (D) is incorrect because, once the account has been written off, the account is no longer open.

**79.** An auditor who has confirmed accounts receivable may discover that the sales journal was held open past year-end if

A. Positive confirmations sent to debtors are not returned.

B. Negative confirmations sent to debtors are not returned.

C. Most of the returned negative confirmations indicate that the debtor owes a larger balance than the amount being confirmed.

D. Most of the returned positive confirmations indicate that the debtor owes a smaller balance than the amount being confirmed.

Answer (D) is correct. *(Publisher)*

**REQUIRED:** The result of confirmation indicating that the sales journal was held open past year-end.

**DISCUSSION:** When the majority of the returned positive confirmations indicate smaller balances at year-end than those in the client's records, the client may have held open the sales journal after year-end and debited customers' accounts for the period under audit rather than for the subsequent period. The effect would be to overstate sales and receivables.

Answer (A) is incorrect because the failure to receive replies to positive confirmations may cause the auditor concern about the existence assertion. Answer (B) is incorrect because the failure to return negative confirmations provides some evidence about the existence assertion. Answer (C) is incorrect because replies indicating balances larger than those confirmed suggest that the sales journal was closed prior to year-end.

**80.** During the process of confirming receivables as of December 31, 20X1, a positive confirmation was returned indicating the "balance owed as of December 31 was paid on January 9, 20X2." The auditor would most likely

A. Determine whether there were any changes in the account between January 1 and January 9, 20X2.

B. Determine whether a customary trade discount was taken by the customer.

C. Reconfirm the zero balance as of January 10, 20X2.

D. Verify that the amount was received.

Answer (D) is correct. *(CPA, adapted)*

**REQUIRED:** The auditor action when a confirmation response states that the year-end balance was paid.

**DISCUSSION:** Responses to confirmations that involve significant differences are investigated by the auditor. Others are delegated to client employees with a request that explanations be given to the auditor. Such differences often arise because of recent cash payments. In that event, the auditor should trace remittances to verify that stated amounts were received.

Answer (A) is incorrect because the auditor wishes to confirm a year-end balance, not transactions in the subsequent period. Also, the reply does not suggest a discrepancy in the account. Answer (B) is incorrect because the auditor is more concerned with confirming the balance due at year-end than with whether a customer took a discount. Answer (C) is incorrect because reconfirmation is not required.

**81.** Confirmation of accounts receivable is a generally accepted auditing procedure. The presumption that an auditor will confirm accounts receivable is not overcome if

A. Based on prior years' audit experience, response rates will be inadequate.

B. Based on experience with similar engagements, responses are expected to be unreliable.

C. The combined assessed level of inherent and control risk is high.

D. The accounts receivable are immaterial.

Answer (C) is correct. *(Publisher)*

**REQUIRED:** The condition not sufficient to overcome the presumption that an auditor will confirm accounts receivable.

**DISCUSSION:** The presumption may be overcome if the combined assessed level of inherent and control risk is low, and the assessed level, together with the evidence expected to be obtained from performance of other procedures, is sufficient to reduce audit risk to an acceptably low level for the applicable assertions. An auditor who has decided not to request confirmations must document how the presumption was overcome.

Answer (A) is incorrect because the presumption may be overcome if confirmations would be ineffective. Answer (B) is incorrect because the presumption may be overcome if confirmations would be ineffective. Answer (D) is incorrect because confirmations are not required if accounts receivable are not material to the financial statements.

**82.** A company has computerized sales and cash receipts journals. The computer programs for these journals have been properly debugged. The auditor discovered that the total of the accounts receivable subsidiary accounts differs materially from the accounts receivable control account. This discrepancy could indicate

A. Credit memoranda being improperly recorded.

B. Lapping of receivables.

C. Receivables not being properly aged.

D. Statements being intercepted prior to mailing.

Answer (A) is correct. *(CIA, adapted)*

**REQUIRED:** The reason the accounts receivable subsidiary ledger may differ from the control account.

**DISCUSSION:** Sales returns and allowances require the crediting of accounts receivable. The recording of unauthorized credit memoranda is one explanation for the discrepancy if sales and cash receipts are properly recorded.

Answer (B) is incorrect because lapping entails the theft of cash receipts and the use of subsequent receipts to conceal the theft. The effect is to overstate receivables, but no difference between the control total and the total of subsidiary accounts would arise. Answer (C) is incorrect because aging does not involve accounting entries. Answer (D) is incorrect because interception of customer statements might indicate fraudulent receivables but would not cause the subsidiary ledger discrepancy.

**83.** Which of the following is the greatest drawback of using subsequent collections evidenced only by a deposit slip as an alternative procedure when responses to positive accounts receivable confirmations are not received?

A. Checking of subsequent collections can never be used as an alternative auditing procedure.

B. By examining a deposit slip only, the auditor does not know whether the payment is for the receivable at the balance sheet date or a subsequent transaction.

C. A deposit slip is not received directly by the auditor.

D. A customer may not have made a payment on a timely basis.

Answer (B) is correct. *(Publisher)*

**REQUIRED:** The greatest drawback of using subsequent collections as an alternative to confirmation.

**DISCUSSION:** The deposit slip does not indicate which receivables are being paid. The deposits may not be from the collection of accounts receivable, or the receipts may be for sales made after year-end.

Answer (A) is incorrect because the auditor may use alternative procedures. Indeed, the alternative procedures may be omitted when no unusual qualitative factors or systematic characteristics are related to the nonresponses and when treating the nonresponses as 100% misstatements does not affect the auditor's decision about whether the financial statements are materially misstated (AU 330). If an account receivable is paid, an account receivable presumably existed. Answer (C) is incorrect because copies of the deposit slips can be provided to the auditor by the bank. Also, the bank proofs the original of the deposit slip when received. Answer (D) is incorrect because, although late payment may cause a problem, the auditor typically performs field work 45 to 60 days after year-end.

**84.** Which of the following procedures will an auditor most likely perform for year-end accounts receivable confirmations when the auditor did not receive replies to second requests?

A. Review the cash receipts journal for the month prior to year-end.

B. Intensify the study of internal control concerning the revenue cycle.

C. Increase the assessed level of detection risk for the existence assertion.

D. Inspect the shipping records documenting the merchandise sold to the debtors.

Answer (D) is correct. *(CPA, adapted)*

**REQUIRED:** The most appropriate audit procedure when customers fail to reply to second requests.

**DISCUSSION:** When customers fail to answer a second request for a positive confirmation, the accounts may be disputed, uncollectible, or fictitious. The auditor should then use alternative procedures (examination of subsequent cash receipts, shipping documents, or other client documentation of existence) to obtain evidence about the validity of nonresponding accounts.

Answer (A) is incorrect because previous collections cannot substantiate year-end balances. Answer (B) is incorrect because nonresponse to a confirmation request is not proof of ineffective control. Nonresponses do occur and are expected. Answer (C) is incorrect because control risk and inherent risk are assessed, but detection risk is not. However, the acceptable level of detection risk may be decreased if the assessment of inherent risk or control risk is increased as a result of reassessment of risks.

**85.** An auditor learns that collections of accounts receivable during the last 10 days of December were not recorded. The effect will be to

A. Leave both working capital and the current ratio unchanged at December 31.

B. Overstate both working capital and the current ratio at December 31.

C. Overstate working capital with no effect on the current ratio at December 31.

D. Overstate the current ratio with no effect on working capital at December 31.

Answer (A) is correct. *(Publisher)*

**REQUIRED:** The effect of failing to record year-end collections.

**DISCUSSION:** Working capital is equal to current assets minus current liabilities, and the current ratio is equal to current assets divided by current liabilities. Because cash and accounts receivable are both current assets, the error has no effect on working capital and the current ratio at December 31 because it did not change total current assets.

Answer (B) is incorrect because neither working capital nor the current ratio is affected by failing to record cash collections. The only effects are that cash is understated and accounts receivable overstated. Answer (C) is incorrect because working capital is not affected. Answer (D) is incorrect because the current ratio is not affected.

**86.** The most effective audit procedure for determining the collectibility of an account receivable is the

A. Confirmation of the account.

B. Examination of the related sales invoice(s).

C. Review of the subsequent cash collections.

D. Review of authorization of credit sales to the customer and the previous history of collections.

Answer (C) is correct. *(CMA, adapted)*

**REQUIRED:** The most effective audit procedure for determining collectibility.

**DISCUSSION:** Collectibility pertains to the assertion of valuation. It is the principal issue with regard to the adequacy of the allowance for doubtful accounts. The best way to determine collectibility is to learn whether the receivable was subsequently collected. A confirmation provides evidence that a contract exists and that the debtor acknowledges the debt, but the subsequent collection of the receivable is the only means of gaining complete assurance that the amount will be paid.

Answer (A) is incorrect because confirmation tends to be more effective in providing evidence about the existence than the valuation (collectibility) assertion. Answer (B) is incorrect because examination of the related sales invoice(s) is a test of the validity, not the collectibility, of a receivable. Answer (D) is incorrect because experience is a good indicator of collectibility but is not as good as collection.

**87.** All of the following are examples of substantive tests to verify the valuation of net accounts receivable except the

A. Recomputation of the allowance for bad debts.

B. Inspection of accounts for current versus noncurrent status in the statement of financial position.

C. Inspection of the aging schedule and credit records of past due accounts.

D. Comparison of the allowance for bad debts with past records.

Answer (B) is correct. *(CMA, adapted)*

**REQUIRED:** The item that is not an example of a test of valuation.

**DISCUSSION:** The inspection of accounts for current versus noncurrent status is a test of management's assertion relating to statement presentation and disclosure. It is not a test of valuation.

Answer (A) is incorrect because recomputation of the allowance for bad debts tests the valuation of the account balance. Answer (C) is incorrect because inspection of the aging schedule and credit records of past due accounts tests the valuation of the account balance. Answer (D) is incorrect because comparison of the allowance for bad debts with past records tests the valuation of the account balance.

**88.** Once an auditor has determined that accounts receivable have increased because of slow collections in a tight money environment, the auditor is likely to

A. Increase the balance in the allowance for bad debts account.

B. Review the going concern ramifications.

C. Review the credit and collection policy.

D. Expand tests of collectibility.

Answer (D) is correct. *(CPA, adapted)*

**REQUIRED:** The appropriate audit response when receivables have increased because of slow collections.

**DISCUSSION:** Whenever collections of receivables have slowed, the auditor should determine the effects on the allowance for doubtful accounts. (S)he should therefore expand tests of collectibility, e.g., with a review of collections subsequent to the balance sheet date and investigation of credit ratings.

Answer (A) is incorrect because an increase in the allowance account may not be required if the accounts are collectible as in the past. Answer (B) is incorrect because questioning whether the client is a going concern is necessary only if the client is on the verge of bankruptcy or some other form of cessation. Answer (C) is incorrect because a review of credit and collection policy is only one part of the expansion of tests of collectibility.

**89.** An auditor reconciles the total of the accounts receivable subsidiary ledger to the general ledger control account as of October 31. By this procedure, the auditor is most likely to learn of which of the following?

A. An October invoice was improperly computed.

B. An October check from a customer was posted in error to the account of another customer with a similar name.

C. An opening balance in a subsidiary ledger account was improperly carried forward from the previous accounting period.

D. An account balance is past due and should be written off.

Answer (C) is correct. *(CPA, adapted)*

**REQUIRED:** The error detected by reconciling the subsidiary ledger to the general ledger.

**DISCUSSION:** By reconciling the accounts receivable ledger to the general ledger control account, transfer errors will be identified.

Answer (A) is incorrect because reconciliation of the subsidiary ledger and control account will not detect an error if entries to both are based on the same erroneous document. Only recalculation of invoices will detect this error. Answer (B) is incorrect because posting to the wrong account will most likely be detected by confirmation. The trial balance total and the control account are not affected by such an error. Answer (D) is incorrect because uncollectibility will most probably be detected through aging receivables.

**90.** An auditor suspects that a client's customer, whose accounts receivable balance represents a material proportion of the client's total receivables, is fictitious. The evidence that provides the strongest proof that the auditor's suspicion is unfounded, given the existence of weaknesses in the client's internal control over accounts receivable, is

A. Receipt of a positive confirmation response.

B. Subsequent posting of the collection of the account balance.

C. Nonresponse to a negative confirmation request.

D. Location of the customer's name and address in a published industry directory.

Answer (D) is correct. *(Publisher)*

**REQUIRED:** The best evidence that a client's customer is not fictitious.

**DISCUSSION:** Verifying that the debtor exists and has the same address as appears in the client's records provides evidence that the customer is not fictitious. A published industry directory is an independent source of evidence of the customer's existence. Taken together with the return of a positive confirmation, the industry directory provides strong proof of the validity of the account.

Answer (A) is incorrect because confirmation responses can be falsified to conceal fraud. A false address may be given at which the confirmation request will be intercepted by a participant in the fraud. Answer (B) is incorrect because the payment may be either entirely fictitious or the posting of another customer's payment (lapping). Answer (C) is incorrect because a negative confirmation request may be intercepted by a party to fraud.

## 4.4 Purchases-Payables Cycle

**91.** In auditing accounts payable, an auditor's procedures most likely will focus primarily on management's assertion of

A. Existence or occurrence.

B. Presentation and disclosure.

C. Completeness.

D. Valuation or allocation.

Answer (C) is correct. *(CPA, adapted)*

**REQUIRED:** The assertion that is the focus of an audit of accounts payable.

**DISCUSSION:** The primary audit risk for accounts payable is the potential for understatement of the liability. Thus, the auditor will most likely focus on the completeness assertion.

Answer (A) is incorrect because the existence or occurrence assertion concerns whether liabilities exist at a given date and whether transactions occurred during the period. The audit risk for accounts payable is not great for that assertion. Answer (B) is incorrect because the risk of inappropriate presentation and disclosure on the financial statements is not as great as the risk that some items are not included. Answer (D) is incorrect because the risk that accounts payable are not valued in accordance with GAAP is less than the risk that the balance may not be complete.

**92.** An auditor performs a test to determine whether all merchandise for which the client was billed was received. The population for this test consists of all

A. Merchandise received.

B. Vendors' invoices.

C. Canceled checks.

D. Receiving reports.

Answer (B) is correct. *(CPA, adapted)*

**REQUIRED:** The population for a test to determine whether all merchandise for which the client was billed was received.

**DISCUSSION:** Vendors' invoices are the billing documents received by the client. They describe the items purchased, the amounts due, and the payment terms. The auditor should trace these invoices to the related receiving reports.

Answer (A) is incorrect because testing merchandise received will not detect merchandise billed but not received. Answer (C) is incorrect because tracing canceled checks to the related receiving reports tests whether goods paid for, not goods billed, were received. Answer (D) is incorrect because tracing receiving reports to vendors' invoices tests whether all goods received were billed.

**93.** The primary audit test to determine if accounts payable are valued properly is

A. A confirmation of accounts payable.

B. Vouching accounts payable to supporting documentation.

C. An analytical procedure.

D. Verification that accounts payable are reported as a current liability in the balance sheet.

Answer (B) is correct. *(Publisher)*

**REQUIRED:** The audit test to determine if accounts payable are properly valued.

**DISCUSSION:** Relatively few problems are encountered by the auditor in meeting the objective of determining the proper valuation of accounts payable. The auditor vouches the recorded accounts payable to the supporting documentation, the invoice and purchase order, to determine if the accounts are accurately valued.

Answer (A) is incorrect because the confirmation of accounts payable cannot be relied on to reveal unrecorded liabilities. Answer (C) is incorrect because analytical procedures provide an overall review of the payables, but they are not specifically directed at valuation of individual accounts. Answer (D) is incorrect because whether accounts payable are reported as a current liability is related to the audit objective concerning statement presentation and disclosure rather than proper valuation.

**94.** Which of the following procedures is least likely to be performed before the balance sheet date?

A. Observation of inventory.

B. Testing internal control over cash.

C. Search for unrecorded liabilities.

D. Confirmation of receivables.

Answer (C) is correct. *(CPA, adapted)*

**REQUIRED:** The procedure least likely to be performed before the balance sheet date.

**DISCUSSION:** The search for unrecorded liabilities will probably be performed after the balance sheet date. The auditor will review cash disbursements made subsequent to year-end to determine if payments are for previously unrecorded liabilities.

Answer (A) is incorrect because, if control is effective and the client maintains well-kept perpetual records, the auditor's observation procedures usually can be performed during or at the end of the period under audit (AU 331). Answer (B) is incorrect because the understanding of internal control is customarily obtained prior to the balance sheet date to permit the auditor to plan the audit and determine the nature, extent, and timing of tests. Answer (D) is incorrect because receivables confirmation may be made either during (if control is effective), at the end of, or after the period.

**95.** An audit assistant found a purchase order for a regular supplier in the amount of $5,500. The purchase order was dated after receipt of the goods. The purchasing agent had forgotten to issue the purchase order. Also, a disbursement of $450 for materials did not have a receiving report. The assistant wanted to select additional purchase orders for investigation but was unconcerned about the lack of a receiving report. The audit director should

A. Agree with the assistant because the amount of the purchase order exception was considerably larger than the receiving report exception.

B. Agree with the assistant because the cash disbursement clerk had been assured by the receiving clerk that the failure to fill out a report didn't happen very often.

C. Disagree with the assistant because the two problems have an equal risk of loss associated with them.

D. Disagree with the assistant because the lack of a receiving report has a greater risk of loss associated with it.

Answer (D) is correct. *(CIA, adapted)*

**REQUIRED:** The implications of a missing purchase order and a missing receiving report.

**DISCUSSION:** The risk of a material fraud is greater for the missing receiving report than for the postdated purchase order. In the latter case, the goods were received, and the company has obtained what it paid for. Because the goods come from a regular supplier, the likelihood is that the purchase was actually authorized. However, the lack of a receiving report in support of a disbursement is a much more serious matter. It suggests potential fraud because an approved payment voucher should be accompanied by a purchase order, supplier's invoice, and a receiving report. One possibility is that duplicate payments are being made.

Answer (A) is incorrect because the potential for fraud and heightened control risk made the absence of a receiving report a material matter despite its dollar amount. Answer (B) is incorrect because the hearsay testimony of the cash disbursement clerk has very little evidentiary value. Answer (C) is incorrect because the missing receiving report indicates a much greater risk than the postdated purchase order.

**96.** When using confirmations to provide evidence about the completeness assertion for accounts payable, the appropriate population most likely is

A. Vendors with whom the entity has previously done business.

B. Amounts recorded in the accounts payable subsidiary ledger.

C. Payees of checks drawn in the month after the year end.

D. Invoices filed in the entity's open invoice file.

Answer (A) is correct. *(CPA, adapted)*

**REQUIRED:** The appropriate population when confirmations of accounts payable are used to test the completeness assertion.

**DISCUSSION:** When sending confirmations for accounts payable, the population of accounts should include small and zero balances as well as large tested balances. The auditor should use the activity in the account as a gauge for selection. That is, if orders are placed with a vendor on a consistent basis, the confirmation should be sent to that vendor regardless of the recorded balance due.

Answer (B) is incorrect because the auditor, in testing the completeness assertion, is concerned with balances that have not been recorded or invoices that have not been filed. Answer (C) is incorrect because, although this is an auditing concern, this would not be the population for the confirmation process. Answer (D) is incorrect because the auditor, in testing the completeness assertion, is concerned with balances that have not been recorded or invoices that have not been filed.

**97.** Which of the following is a substantive test that an auditor is most likely to perform to verify the existence and valuation of recorded accounts payable?

A. Investigating the open purchase order file to ascertain that prenumbered purchase orders are used and accounted for.

B. Receiving the client's mail, unopened, for a reasonable period of time after year-end to search for unrecorded vendor's invoices.

C. Vouching selected entries in the accounts payable subsidiary ledger to purchase orders and receiving reports.

D. Confirming accounts payable balances with known suppliers who have zero balances.

Answer (C) is correct. *(CPA, adapted)*

**REQUIRED:** The substantive test for the existence and valuation of recorded accounts payable.

**DISCUSSION:** Vouching a sample of recorded accounts payable to purchase orders and receiving reports provides evidence that the obligations exist at a given date. The purchase orders evidence the initiation of the transactions, and the receiving reports indicate that goods were received and that liabilities were thereby incurred. Thus, these documents provide evidence that amounts are owed to others, that the transactions occurred, and that the liabilities have been included at appropriate amounts.

Answer (A) is incorrect because ascertaining that prenumbered documents are used and accounted for relates most directly to the completeness assertion. Answer (B) is incorrect because searching for unrecorded liabilities relates most directly to completeness. Answer (D) is incorrect because confirming payables with known suppliers having zero balances is a procedure for detecting unrecorded liabilities. Thus, it relates most directly to completeness.

**98.** Which of the following four statements, which compare confirmation of accounts payable with suppliers and confirmation of accounts receivable with debtors, is false?

A. Confirmation of accounts receivable with debtors is a more widely accepted auditing procedure than is confirmation of accounts payable with suppliers.

B. Statistical sampling techniques are more widely accepted in the confirmation of accounts payable than in the confirmation of accounts receivable.

C. As compared with the confirmation of accounts receivable, the confirmation of accounts payable will tend to emphasize accounts with zero balances at the balance sheet date.

D. It is less likely that the confirmation request sent to the supplier will show the amount owed than that the request sent to the debtor will show the amount due.

Answer (B) is correct. *(Publisher)*

**REQUIRED:** The false statement concerning confirmation of accounts payable and receivable.

**DISCUSSION:** In both cases, the use of statistical sampling is appropriate for relatively large populations with common characteristics.

Answer (A) is incorrect because externally generated evidence usually obviates the need for the confirmation of accounts payable. The self-interest of creditors protects against understatement of client liabilities. Also, confirming payables does not detect unrecorded liabilities, whereas confirming receivables may detect fictitious or overstated accounts. Answer (C) is incorrect because the audit of accounts payable, not accounts receivable, may focus attention on accounts with zero balances to discover understatements of payables. Answer (D) is incorrect because the creditor may be in the process of billing a client for current shipments, the amounts in the client's records may not reflect all liabilities. Hence, the auditor may refrain from stating an amount in the confirmation request so that all purchases may be confirmed. For receivables, only payments in transit will need to be reconciled by the auditor.

**99.** Confirmation of accounts payable with creditors is most appropriate when

A. The majority of accounts payable balances are owed to related parties.

B. Creditor statements are not available, and internal control over accounts payable is unsatisfactory.

C. Accounts payable balances are immaterial.

D. Internal control over accounts payable is effective, and sufficient evidence exists to minimize the risk of a material misstatement.

Answer (B) is correct. *(Publisher)*

**REQUIRED:** The reason for confirming accounts payable.

**DISCUSSION:** When internal control relevant to assertions about accounts payable is ineffective, control risk is increased. The auditor may need to change the nature, timing, or extent of substantive tests and consider the use of confirmations. The auditor should also confirm accounts payable when documentary evidence is lacking, individual creditors have relatively large balances, the client has made a major purchase from the creditor regardless of the size of the balance, unusual transactions are involved, or the account is secured.

Answer (A) is incorrect because the auditor only needs to give particular consideration to confirming the accounts with related parties in the presence of other indications that the payables should be confirmed. Answer (C) is incorrect because confirmation of accounts payable is usually unnecessary when the payables are immaterial. Answer (D) is incorrect because the confirmation of accounts payable is usually not considered when internal control is effective.

**100.** Purchase cutoff procedures test the completeness assertion. A company should include goods in its inventory if it

A. Has sold the goods.

B. Holds legal title to the goods.

C. Has physical possession of the goods.

D. Has paid for the goods.

Answer (B) is correct. *(Publisher)*

**REQUIRED:** The purpose of a purchase cutoff.

**DISCUSSION:** In general, a cutoff ensures that transactions are recorded in the appropriate period. A proper purchase cutoff is intended to assure inclusion of the goods in inventory and the recognition of a liability in the period in which the client acquired title to the goods.

Answer (A) is incorrect because sold goods should be removed from inventory. Answer (C) is incorrect because title can pass without actual possession (e.g., shipments to the client FOB shipping point). Answer (D) is incorrect because the goods may be purchased on credit and need not be paid for by the cutoff date.

**101.** When title to merchandise in transit has passed to the audit client, the auditor engaged in the performance of a purchase cutoff will encounter the greatest difficulty in gaining assurance with respect to the

A. Quantity.

B. Quality.

C. Price.

D. Terms.

Answer (B) is correct. *(CPA, adapted)*

**REQUIRED:** The greatest audit difficulty when title to merchandise in transit passes to the client.

**DISCUSSION:** The purpose of the cutoff is to ensure that the asset and related liability are recognized in the correct period. Accordingly, merchandise that is included in ending inventory but has not yet arrived may not be available for inspection. The quality of such merchandise cannot be assured until the inspection has been conducted after the goods are received. The auditor should be able to determine the quantity, the price, and the terms of the agreement from supporting documentation.

**102.** Which of the following audit procedures is least likely to detect an unrecorded liability?

A. Analysis and recomputation of interest expense.

B. Analysis and recomputation of depreciation expense.

C. Mailing of standard bank confirmation forms.

D. Reading of the minutes of meetings of the board of directors.

Answer (B) is correct. *(CPA, adapted)*

**REQUIRED:** The procedure least likely to detect an unrecorded liability.

**DISCUSSION:** The analysis and recomputation of depreciation expense is useful in determining whether the expense and asset accounts have been properly stated. Liabilities are not part of the depreciation recording process, so analysis and recomputation of depreciation would not detect unrecorded liabilities.

Answer (A) is incorrect because the recomputation of interest expense may reveal greater interest expense than expected based upon the recorded debt of the organization. Answer (C) is incorrect because the standard bank confirmation form requests information about other accounts not listed on the form that may come to the attention of the bank. Answer (D) is incorrect because a significant liability often requires approval by the board of directors.

**103.** A firm has recently converted its purchasing cycle from a manual system to an online computer system. The internal auditor in charge of the first post-implementation audit of the new system has access to a generalized audit software package. One audit objective is to determine whether all material liabilities for trade accounts payable have been recorded. Which of the following is most useful in achieving this objective?

A. A listing of all purchase transactions processed after the cutoff date.

B. A listing of all accounts payable ledger accounts with a post office box given as the vendor mailing address.

C. A listing of all duplicate purchase orders, receiving reports, and vendor invoices.

D. A listing of all vendors with a debit balance in the accounts payable ledgers.

Answer (A) is correct. *(CIA, adapted)*

**REQUIRED:** The procedure for determining whether all liabilities for trade accounts payable have been recorded.

**DISCUSSION:** Examining a listing of all purchase transactions processed after the cutoff date tests the completeness of accounts payable. It investigates the possibility that accounts payable have been recorded in the wrong period.

Answer (B) is incorrect because listing payables with post office boxes is useful in the detection of fraud, but has little efficacy in the determination of the completeness of accounts payable. Answer (C) is incorrect because listing duplicate documents is not helpful in the search for all legitimate accounts payable. Answer (D) is incorrect because liability accounts typically have a credit balance. An account payable with a debit balance is often the result of the misclassification of a receivable. The result of such an error is the overstatement of accounts payable. The internal auditor is testing for an understatement of accounts payable.

**104.** Unrecorded liabilities are most likely to be found during the review of which of the following documents?

A. Unpaid bills.

B. Shipping records.

C. Bills of lading.

D. Unmatched sales invoices.

Answer (A) is correct. *(CPA, adapted)*

**REQUIRED:** The documents that should be reviewed to detect unrecorded liabilities.

**DISCUSSION:** The auditor examines unvouchered invoices (unpaid bills) because they could represent payables that should have been recorded prior to year-end. This procedure should be carried out through the last day of field work.

Answer (B) is incorrect because shipping records relate to the client's sales. Answer (C) is incorrect because bills of lading relate to the client's sales. Answer (D) is incorrect because unmatched sales invoices relate to the client's sales.

**105.** In a payables application, checks are authorized and paid based on matching purchase orders, receiving reports, and vendor invoices. Partial payments are common. An appropriate audit procedure for verifying that a purchase order has not been paid twice is to sort the

A. Receiving report file by purchase order, compute total amounts received by purchase order, compare total amounts received with purchase order amounts, and investigate any discrepancies between the total amounts received and purchase order amounts.

B. Vendor invoice file by purchase order, compute total amounts invoiced by purchase order, compare total amounts invoiced with purchase order amounts, and investigate any discrepancies between the total amounts invoiced and purchase order amounts.

C. Receiving report file by vendor invoice amounts and investigate any discrepancies between the total amounts received and vendor invoice amounts.

D. Check register file by purchase order, compute total amounts paid by purchase order, compare total amounts paid with purchase order amounts, and investigate any discrepancies between the total amounts paid and purchase order amounts.

Answer (D) is correct. *(CIA, adapted)*

**REQUIRED:** The appropriate audit procedure for verifying that a purchase order has not been paid twice.

**DISCUSSION:** The audit objectives for payables include the discovery of unrecorded liabilities and overpayments. Effective internal control over payments avoids these problems by matching supporting documents, using proper check preparation methods, and providing for stringent authorization procedures. The audit process described tests the effectiveness of internal control over payments in a way that merely tracing a sample of checks to purchase orders could not.

Answer (A) is incorrect because the procedure described compares goods received with goods ordered. Answer (B) is incorrect because the procedure described compares goods invoiced by the vendor and goods ordered. Answer (C) is incorrect because the procedure described compares goods received and goods invoiced.

**106.** Which of the following audit procedures is best for identifying unrecorded trade accounts payable?

A. Reviewing cash disbursements recorded subsequent to the balance sheet date to determine whether the related payables apply to the prior period.

B. Investigating payables recorded just prior to and just subsequent to the balance sheet date to determine whether they are supported by receiving reports.

C. Examining unusual relationships between monthly accounts payable balances and recorded cash payments.

D. Reconciling vendors' statements to the file of receiving reports to identify items received just prior to the balance sheet date.

Answer (A) is correct. *(CPA, adapted)*
**REQUIRED:** The procedure most likely to reveal unrecorded liabilities.
**DISCUSSION:** The greatest risk in the audit of payables is that unrecorded liabilities exist. Omission of an entry to record a payable is more difficult to detect than an inaccurate or false entry. The search for unrecorded payables should include examining cash disbursements made after the balance sheet date and comparing them with the accounts payable trial balance, sending confirmations to vendors with zero balances, and reconciling payable balances with vendors' documentation.
Answer (B) is incorrect because investigating recorded payables to determine whether they are supported by receiving reports tests only the amounts that have been recorded. Answer (C) is incorrect because examining unusual relationships between monthly accounts payable balances and recorded cash payments tests only the amounts that have been recorded. Answer (D) is incorrect because reconciling vendors' statements to the file of receiving reports to identify items received just prior to the balance sheet date does not determine whether these items are recorded.

**107.** In an audit of a public warehouse, which of the following is the most important audit procedure with respect to disclosing unrecorded liabilities?

A. Confirmation of negotiable receipts with holders.

B. Review of outstanding receipts.

C. Inspection of receiving and issuing procedures.

D. Observation of inventory.

Answer (C) is correct. *(CPA, adapted)*
**REQUIRED:** The most important audit procedure to disclose unrecorded liabilities of a public warehouse.
**DISCUSSION:** When auditing a public warehouse, the inspection of receiving and issuing procedures is the most important procedure for disclosing unrecorded liabilities. Shipping orders and receiving reports that are not reflected in the records suggest that transactions are not being properly recorded.
Answer (A) is incorrect because the auditor is not likely to know the names of the holders when receipts are negotiable. Answer (B) is incorrect because a review of outstanding receipts only furnishes audit evidence concerning recorded receipts, not whether the liabilities have been recorded. Answer (D) is incorrect because observation of inventory provides evidence that the inventory exists but not that the related liabilities are unrecorded.

**108.** One objective of an audit of the purchasing function is to determine the cost of late payment of invoices containing trade discounts. The appropriate population from which a sample would be drawn is the file of

A. Receiving reports.

B. Purchase orders.

C. Canceled checks.

D. Paid vendor invoices.

Answer (D) is correct. *(CIA, adapted)*
**REQUIRED:** The sample to determine the cost of late payment of invoices containing trade discounts.
**DISCUSSION:** A vendor invoice shows both the amount and terms of payment for purchase. Failure to pay within the discount period is normally not advantageous. Hence, lost discounts may signify inefficiency in the purchases-payables-cash disbursements function or a shortage of cash.
Answer (A) is incorrect because receiving reports indicate the date and quantity received but not whether discounts were offered or taken. Answer (B) is incorrect because purchase orders show only the quantity and expected price of a purchase. Answer (C) is incorrect because canceled checks show only the total paid, not whether a discount was offered or taken.

**109.** In an audit of a purchasing department, which of the following usually is considered a risk factor?

A. Purchase specifications are developed by the department requesting the material.

B. Purchases are made against blanket or open purchase orders for certain types of items.

C. Purchases are made from parties related to buyers or other company officials.

D. Purchases are not rotated among suppliers included on an approved vendor list.

Answer (C) is correct. *(CIA, adapted)*
**REQUIRED:** The item considered to be a risk factor.
**DISCUSSION:** Purchasing from parties related to buyers or other company officials is a risk factor because it suggests the possibility of fraud. Such conflicts of interest may result in transactions unfavorable to the company.
Answer (A) is incorrect because the requesting department normally develops specifications. Answer (B) is incorrect because open purchase orders are customary for high-use items. Answer (D) is incorrect because an approved vendor list is often maintained as a control to help ensure that purchases are made only from reliable vendors. However, rotation is not usually appropriate.

**110.** In verifying debits to perpetual inventory records of a nonmanufacturing firm, the auditor is most interested in examining the purchase

A. Journal.

B. Requisitions.

C. Orders.

D. Invoices.

Answer (D) is correct. *(CPA, adapted)*

**REQUIRED:** The document(s) most useful to the auditor when verifying debits to perpetual inventory records.

**DISCUSSION:** Vendor invoices, which state the items purchased, the amount due, and the payment terms, document inventory cost when compared with purchase orders and receiving reports.

Answer (A) is incorrect because the purchase journal is created from the information on the vendor invoices. Answer (B) is incorrect because purchase requisitions, which are requests by authorized personnel to order goods, other assets, or services, do not authoritatively state vendor prices. Answer (C) is incorrect because, although the purchase order is a formal written offer to buy specified goods and serves as a purchase authorization, it may not state the price the vendor ultimately charges.

**111.** Which of the following procedures relating to the examination of accounts payable may the auditor delegate entirely to the client's employees?

A. Test footings in the accounts payable ledger.

B. Reconcile unpaid invoices to vendors' statements.

C. Prepare a schedule of accounts payable.

D. Mail confirmations for selected account balances.

Answer (C) is correct. *(CPA, adapted)*

**REQUIRED:** The procedure that may be delegated entirely to the client's employees.

**DISCUSSION:** Preparation of schedules is usually delegated to the client's employees. The auditor should review and test the schedules prepared by the client, however.

Answer (A) is incorrect because the auditor should perform test footings in the accounts payable ledger to assure proper addition. Answer (B) is incorrect because reconciliation of unpaid invoices to vendors' statements might disclose unrecorded liabilities and should be performed by the auditor. Answer (D) is incorrect because the auditor should mail all confirmations to the creditors.

**112.** An auditor's purpose in reviewing the renewal of a note payable shortly after the balance sheet date most likely is to obtain evidence concerning management's assertions about

A. Existence or occurrence.

B. Presentation and disclosure.

C. Completeness.

D. Valuation or allocation.

Answer (B) is correct. *(CPA, adapted)*

**REQUIRED:** The auditor's purpose in reviewing the renewal of a note payable shortly after year-end.

**DISCUSSION:** Events such as the renewal of a note payable do not require adjustment of the financial statements but may require disclosure (AU 560). Accordingly, the auditor should determine that the renewal had essentially the same terms and conditions as the recorded debt at year-end. A significant change may affect the presentation of notes payable (e.g., as current or noncurrent), the interpretation of the statements, and the required disclosures.

Answer (A) is incorrect because the renewal does not raise an issue as to whether the note existed. Answer (C) is incorrect because the renewal does not raise an issue as to whether all notes were reported. Answer (D) is incorrect because the renewal does not affect the valuation of notes payable.

## 4.5 Cash

**113.** Which of the following is not an audit objective related to cash?

A. Reported cash exists.

B. The client has ownership rights in the reported cash.

C. Compensating cash balances are reported as other current assets.

D. The reported cash balance includes all cash transactions that should have been recorded.

Answer (C) is correct. *(Publisher)*

**REQUIRED:** The item not considered an objective of the audit of cash.

**DISCUSSION:** Normally, cash should be identified as a current asset. When compensating balances exist, however, any cash balances legally restricted under loan or line of credit agreements should be segregated on the balance sheet and classified according to the appropriate classification of the related debt, either current or noncurrent.

Answer (A) is incorrect because one objective is to verify management's assertion that cash exists. Answer (B) is incorrect because the auditor should establish that the client has ownership rights in the cash balances. Answer (D) is incorrect because the completeness objective requires the auditor to gather evidence that the reported cash balance includes all cash transactions that should have been recorded.

**114.** Normally, the audit objective of valuation is of minimum concern during the audit of cash. However, the auditor's concern about the valuation objective will most likely increase when

A. Both currency and negotiable securities are on hand.

B. The client uses a demand deposit account.

C. The proof of cash cannot be reconciled.

D. The client has foreign currency accounts.

Answer (D) is correct. *(Publisher)*

**REQUIRED:** The most likely reason for the auditor to be concerned about the valuation of cash.

**DISCUSSION:** Foreign currency accounts must be converted to U.S. dollars based upon the current exchange rate. Changes in the conversion rate and restrictions on the movement of foreign currency create problems of valuation for the auditor.

Answer (A) is incorrect because the auditor is more concerned about the existence than the valuation of cash. The latter is ordinarily easily determined once the former is established. Thus, currency can usually be valued at its face amount, and negotiable securities normally have readily ascertainable market values. Answer (B) is incorrect because a demand deposit account, which is simply a checking account, is used by most organizations for cash disbursements. Answer (C) is incorrect because the inability to reconcile a proof of cash affects the auditor's concern about the existence, not the valuation, of cash.

**115.** When counting cash on hand, the auditor must exercise control over all cash and other negotiable assets to prevent

A. Theft.

B. Irregular endorsement.

C. Substitution.

D. Deposits in transit.

Answer (C) is correct. *(CPA, adapted)*

**REQUIRED:** The reason for controlling cash and negotiable assets.

**DISCUSSION:** Simultaneous verification of cash and cash equivalents, such as trading securities, avoids the possibility of conversion of negotiable assets to cash to conceal a cash shortage. The auditor should control and verify all liquid assets at one time (AU 313).

Answer (A) is incorrect because simultaneous verification does not directly prevent theft except during the time the auditor controls the assets. Rather, it helps to uncover a fraud that has already occurred by making its concealment more difficult. Answer (B) is incorrect because simultaneous verification does not directly prevent irregular endorsement except during the time the auditor controls the assets. Rather, it helps to uncover a fraud that has already occurred by making its concealment more difficult. Answer (D) is incorrect because deposits in transit (those recorded on the client's but not the bank's books) are a normal result of business activity.

**116.** The AICPA Standard Form to Confirm Account Balance Information with Financial Institutions requests all of the following except

A. Due date of a direct liability.

B. The principal amount paid on a direct liability.

C. Description of collateral for a direct liability.

D. The interest rate of a direct liability.

Answer (B) is correct. *(Publisher)*

**REQUIRED:** The item not requested on a standard bank account balance confirmation form.

**DISCUSSION:** The principal amount paid on a direct liability is not listed on the AICPA standard form. The auditor is not concerned with the amount of a liability already paid. The form confirms account number/description, balance, due date, interest rate, date through which interest is paid, and description of collateral. The due date, a description of the collateral, and the interest rate are requested on a standard bank cash confirmation form to obtain third-party evidence concerning the client's liability.

**117.** An auditor ordinarily sends a standard confirmation request to all banks with which the client has done business during the year under audit, regardless of the year-end balance. A purpose of this procedure is to

A. Provide the data necessary to prepare a proof of cash.

B. Request that a cutoff bank statement and related checks be sent to the auditor.

C. Detect kiting activities that may otherwise not be discovered.

D. Seek information about other deposit and loan amounts that come to the attention of the institution in the process of completing the confirmation.

Answer (D) is correct. *(CPA, adapted)*

**REQUIRED:** The reason confirmations are sent.

**DISCUSSION:** The AICPA Standard Form to Confirm Account Balance Information with Financial Institutions is used to confirm certain basic information about deposits and direct liabilities on loans. To confirm other matters, such as contingent liabilities and security agreements, auditors send a separate letter, signed by the client, to a responsible official. The standard form is designed to substantiate only the information that is stated on the confirmation request. It is not designed to provide assurance about accounts not listed on the form and does not provide significant evidence about the completeness assertion. Nevertheless, the standard form contains this language: "Although we do not request or expect you to conduct a comprehensive, detailed search of your records, if during the process of completing this confirmation, additional information about other deposit and loan accounts we may have with you comes to your attention, please include such information below."

Answer (A) is incorrect because the data for a proof of cash are in the month-end bank statement. Answer (B) is incorrect because the client must sign a letter requesting the bank to send a cutoff bank statement directly to the auditor shortly after year-end. Answer (C) is incorrect because the auditor should prepare a bank transfer schedule for a few days before and after the balance sheet date to determine whether transfers among the client's accounts have been recorded in the proper periods.

**118.** Bank teller supervisors might manipulate accounts using their privileged computer access codes. They could withdraw money for their own use and move money among accounts when depositors complain to the bank about errors. The audit procedure most likely to detect this is

A. Reviewing transactions on privileged access codes.

B. Reviewing transactions for employees' accounts.

C. Verifying proof records for teller access codes.

D. Testing the accuracy of account posting programs.

Answer (A) is correct. *(CIA, adapted)*

**REQUIRED:** The audit procedure most likely to detect the fraud.

**DISCUSSION:** A basic control problem in a computer system is the absence of the separation of functions found in manual systems. Thus, the supervisors' possession of privileged codes allows access to both deposits and related records. Controls must be implemented to compensate for this lack of segregation. Reviewing the system access log for transactions involving the supervisors' codes is one such control.

Answer (B) is incorrect because reviewing transactions for employees' accounts will not detect transfers to accounts not in the employees' names. Answer (C) is incorrect because verifying proof records for teller access codes determines whether daily transactions balance. Answer (D) is incorrect because the issue is whether transactions are authorized, not whether the postings are accurate.

**119.** During the examination of a cutoff bank statement, an auditor noticed that the majority of checks listed as outstanding at the preceding December 31 had not cleared the bank. Which of the following is not a likely explanation of this finding?

A. Checks were written prior to year-end but were not mailed on a timely basis.

B. Kiting was used to cover a shortage of cash.

C. The cash disbursements journal had been held open past year-end.

D. The cutoff bank statement was requested too soon after year-end.

Answer (B) is correct. *(Publisher)*

**REQUIRED:** The unwarranted conclusion when the majority of checks outstanding at year-end have not cleared.

**DISCUSSION:** Kiting is an attempt to conceal a cash shortage by recording a deposit in the current period from an interbank transfer but failing to record the disbursement until the following period. The check is returned in the cutoff bank statement with no record in the cash disbursements journal or on the bank reconciliation.

Answer (A) is incorrect because, if the checks were held after year-end, they would not likely have cleared the bank prior to receipt of the cutoff bank statement. Answer (C) is incorrect because the cash disbursements journal could have been held open, thus permitting disbursements actually made in the subsequent period to be predated and recorded in the period under audit. Answer (D) is incorrect because, if the cutoff bank statement is requested too soon after year-end, the checks mailed at year-end may not have had time to clear the bank and be returned.

**120.** On receiving a client's bank cutoff statement, an auditor most likely will trace

A. Prior-year checks listed in the cutoff statement to the year-end outstanding checklist.

B. Deposits in transit listed in the cutoff statement to the year-end bank reconciliation.

C. Checks dated after year-end listed in the cutoff statement to the year-end outstanding checklist.

D. Deposits recorded in the cash receipts journal after year-end to the cutoff statement.

Answer (A) is correct. *(CPA, adapted)*

**REQUIRED:** The search an auditor most likely performs after receiving a client's bank cutoff statement.

**DISCUSSION:** A cutoff bank statement should be used to test reconciling items on the year-end bank reconciliation, e.g., deposits in transit and outstanding checks. Analysis of a cutoff bank statement is a procedure that entails consideration of a bank statement for part of a month that includes canceled checks and other debit/credit memos. The cutoff bank statement covers at least 7 business days following the client's year-end, thus permitting the auditor to verify that deposits in transit and checks outstanding listed on the client's year-end bank reconciliation have been recorded by the bank. Tracing prior-year checks listed in the cutoff statement to the year-end outstanding checklist in the bank reconciliation helps the auditor to detect outstanding but unrecorded checks at year-end (an overstatement of cash).

Answer (B) is incorrect because the auditor is more likely to vouch the deposits in transit on the reconciliation of the cutoff statement to determine that the recorded amount was actually deposited. Overstatement is a greater risk than the understatement of cash resulting from an unrecorded deposit in transit. Answer (C) is incorrect because checks dated after year-end are not listed in the year-end checklist. Answer (D) is incorrect because the auditor's primary concern with regard to the deposits is that amounts recorded as in transit at year-end were not actually received by the bank.

**121.** A proof of cash used by an auditor

A. Proves that the client's year-end balance of cash is fairly stated.

B. Confirms that the client has properly separated the custody function from the recording function with respect to cash.

C. Validates that the client's bank did not make an error during the period being examined.

D. Determines whether any unauthorized disbursements or unrecorded deposits were made for the given time period.

Answer (D) is correct. *(CMA, adapted)*

**REQUIRED:** The purpose of a proof of cash.

**DISCUSSION:** A proof of cash consists of a four-column worksheet, with bank reconciliations in the first and fourth columns for the beginning and end of the period and reconciliations of cash receipts and disbursements in the middle columns. The amounts per books and per bank should reconcile both horizontally and vertically. The proof of cash thus detects unauthorized disbursements or unrecorded deposits for the period. It is useful when internal control over cash transactions is ineffective.

Answer (A) is incorrect because a proof of cash only reconciles one bank account. Other procedures are necessary to provide evidence concerning the fairness of the cash balance, e.g., examination of cash on hand and cash in foreign countries. Answer (B) is incorrect because the auditor must obtain an understanding of internal control relevant to cash to determine whether the custody function is properly separated from the recording function. Answer (C) is incorrect because a proof of cash may detect an error made by the client's bank, but that is not the reason the auditor performs the proof.

**122.** A bank cutoff statement is least likely to detect

A. Including a nonexistent deposit in transit on the bank reconciliation.

B. Omitting checks, which were written prior to year-end, from the outstanding check list on the bank reconciliation.

C. Writing and dating of checks prior to year-end but not releasing the checks until after year-end.

D. Applying cash receipts from one customer to another customer's account (lapping).

Answer (D) is correct. *(D. Wells)*

**REQUIRED:** The purpose not served by a bank cutoff statement.

**DISCUSSION:** Lapping is detected through confirmation of accounts receivable and comparing information on remittance advices and deposit slips with the cash receipts journal.

Answer (A) is incorrect because the cutoff bank statement would not show the nonexistent deposit. Answer (B) is incorrect because some checks returned with the cutoff bank statement dated prior to year-end would not appear on the year-end bank reconciliation. Answer (C) is incorrect because few, if any, of the checks that appear as outstanding on the bank reconciliation at year-end would have cleared the bank and be included in the cutoff bank statement.

**123.** Which of the following cash transfers results in a misstatement of cash at December 31, 20X0?

Bank Transfer Schedule

| | Disbursement | | Receipt | |
|---|---|---|---|---|
| | Recorded in Books | Paid by Bank | Recorded in Books | Received by Bank |
| A. | 12/31/X0 | 1/4/X1 | 12/31/X0 | 12/31/X0 |
| B. | 1/4/X1 | 1/5/X1 | 12/31/X0 | 1/4/X1 |
| C. | 12/31/X0 | 1/5/X1 | 12/31/X0 | 1/4/X1 |
| D. | 1/4/X1 | 1/11/X1 | 1/4/X1 | 1/41/X1 |

Answer (B) is correct. *(CPA, adapted)*
**REQUIRED:** The interbank cash transfer that indicates an error in cash cutoff.
**DISCUSSION:** An error in cash cutoff occurs if one-half of the transaction is recorded in the current period and one-half in the subsequent period. Transfer B was recorded as a receipt on 12/31/X0 but not as a disbursement until 1/4/X1. This discrepancy is an error in cutoff called kiting. It overstates the cash balance because the amount of the transfer is included in both bank accounts at year-end. The disbursement and the receipt are recorded in the books in the same month.

Questions 124 and 125 are based on the following information. This data was taken from the bank transfer schedule prepared during the audit of Fox Co.'s financial statements for the year ended December 31. Assume all checks are dated and issued on December 30.

| | Bank Accounts | | Disbursement Date | | Receipt Date | |
|---|---|---|---|---|---|---|
| Check No. | From | To | Per Books | Per Bank | Per Books | Per Bank |
| 101 | National | Federal | Dec. 30 | Jan. 4 | Dec. 30 | Jan. 3 |
| 202 | County | State | Jan. 3 | Jan. 2 | Dec. 30 | Dec. 31 |
| 303 | Federal | American | Dec. 31 | Jan. 3 | Jan. 2 | Jan. 2 |
| 404 | State | Republic | Jan. 2 | Jan. 2 | Jan. 2 | Dec. 31 |

**124.** Which of the following checks might indicate kiting?

A. #101 and #303.

B. #202 and #404.

C. #101 and #404.

D. #202 and #303.

Answer (B) is correct. *(CPA, adapted)*
**REQUIRED:** The checks that might indicate kiting.
**DISCUSSION:** Kiting is the recording of a deposit from an interbank transfer in the current period, while failing to record the related disbursement until the next period. It is a fraud that exploits the lag (float period) between the deposit of a check in one account and the time it clears the bank on which it is drawn. Checks #202 and #404 may indicate kiting because they were recorded by the receiving banks before year-end, although the disbursing banks did not record the payments until the next year. Checks #101 and #303 were recorded as received after year-end.

**125.** Which of the following checks illustrate deposits/transfers in transit at December 31?

A. #101 and #202.

B. #101 and #303.

C. #202 and #404.

D. #303 and #404.

Answer (B) is correct. *(CPA, adapted)*
**REQUIRED:** The checks indicating deposits/transfers in transit.
**DISCUSSION:** A deposit/transfer in transit is one recorded in the entity's books as a receipt by the balance sheet date but not recorded as a deposit by the bank until the next period. Check #101 is a deposit/transfer in transit because the check was recorded in the books before the end of the year but not recorded by either bank until January. Check #303 is also a deposit/transfer in transit, because the check was deducted from Federal's balance in December, but was not added to American's balance until January. Checks #202 and #404 were recorded in the books after the balance sheet date.

Questions 126 and 127 are based on the following information.

Miles Company
Bank Transfer Schedule
December 31

| Check Number | Bank Accounts From | Bank Accounts To | Amount | Date Disbursed per Books | Date Disbursed per Bank | Date Deposited per Books | Date Deposited per Bank |
|---|---|---|---|---|---|---|---|
| 2020 | 1st Natl. | Suburban | $32,000 | 12/31 | 1/5# | 12/31 | 1/3† |
| 2021 | 1st Natl. | Capital | 21,000 | 12/31 | 1/4# | 12/31 | 1/3† |
| 3217 | 2nd State | Suburban | 6,700 | 1/3 | 1/5 | 1/3 | 1/6 |
| 0659 | Midtown | Suburban | 5,500 | 12/30 | 1/5# | 12/30 | 1/3† |

**126.** The tick mark # most likely indicates that the amount was traced to the

A. December cash disbursements journal.

B. Outstanding check list of the applicable bank reconciliation.

C. January cash disbursements journal.

D. Year-end bank confirmations.

Answer (B) is correct. *(CPA, adapted)*

**REQUIRED:** The meaning of the tick mark # in the bank transfer schedule.

**DISCUSSION:** The tick marks indicate the dates that amounts were disbursed according to the bank. In each case, the amount was recorded in the books at the end of the preceding period. Because the checks traced had not cleared at December 31, they were not included in the December bank statement. Thus, these outstanding checks are reconciling items (differences between the books and the December bank statements for the respective drawee banks).

Answer (A) is incorrect because the transfer schedule already indicates that the marked transactions were recorded in the December cash disbursements journal. Tracing to the bank reconciliation serves the more useful purpose of determining whether these checks were included as reconciling items. Answer (C) is incorrect because the marked disbursements were recorded in December. Answer (D) is incorrect because the bank confirmation requests information about the year-end balance, which would not include the outstanding checks.

**127.** The tick mark † most likely indicates that the amount was traced to the

A. Deposits in transit of the applicable bank reconciliation.

B. December cash receipts journal.

C. January cash receipts journal.

D. Year-end bank confirmations.

Answer (A) is correct. *(CPA, adapted)*

**REQUIRED:** The meaning of the tick mark † in the bank transfer schedule.

**DISCUSSION:** The tick marks indicate transfers recorded by the depository banks in January that were recorded in the books in December. Accordingly, these transactions were deposits in transit at December 31 and should have been included in the appropriate bank reconciliations.

Answer (B) is incorrect because the marked amounts were known to be recorded in the books. Answer (C) is incorrect because the December cash receipts journal includes the marked transactions. Answer (D) is incorrect because the bank confirmation at year-end would not include items recorded by the bank in January.

**128.** Which of the following characteristics is most likely indicative of check kiting?

A. High turnover of employees who have access to cash.

B. Many large checks that are recorded on Mondays.

C. Low average balance compared with high level of deposits.

D. Frequent ATM checking account withdrawals.

Answer (C) is correct. *(CPA, adapted)*

**REQUIRED:** The item most likely to indicate check kiting.

**DISCUSSION:** Kiting is the recording of a deposit from an interbank transfer in the current period, while failing to record the related disbursement until the next period. It overstates the cash balance because the amount of the transfer is included in both bank accounts at year-end. A low average balance compared with a high level of deposits is an indication of check kiting.

Answer (A) is incorrect because high turnover of employees who have access to cash indicates susceptibility to theft. Answer (B) is incorrect because recording of large checks on Mondays has no necessary connection with check kiting. Answer (D) is incorrect because the frequency of ATM checking account withdrawals has no necessary connection with check kiting.

**129.** On the last day of the fiscal year, the cash disbursements clerk drew a company check on Bank A and deposited the check in the company account at Bank B to cover a previous theft of cash. The disbursement has not been recorded. The auditor will best detect this form of kiting by

A. Comparing the detail of cash receipts as shown by the cash receipts records with the detail on the confirmed duplicate deposit tickets for 3 days prior to and subsequent to year-end.

B. Preparing from the cash disbursements book a summary of bank transfers for one week prior to and subsequent to year-end.

C. Examining the composition of deposits in both Bank A and B subsequent to year-end.

D. Examining paid checks returned with the bank statement of the next accounting period after year-end.

Answer (D) is correct. *(CPA, adapted)*

**REQUIRED:** The best audit procedure to detect kiting.

**DISCUSSION:** Because the check used to make the bank transfer is not recorded in the current period, the check is not listed as outstanding on the reconciliation of the bank account on which it was drawn. The auditor detects kiting by comparing paid checks, returned in the next period and dated prior to year-end, with the checks listed as outstanding on the related bank reconciliation. In other words, the auditor searches for checks that should have been listed as outstanding but were not.

Answer (A) is incorrect because the deposits and receipts records are accounted for correctly in kiting. Answer (B) is incorrect because the cash disbursements book would not contain this disbursement at year-end. Answer (C) is incorrect because the deposit records are accounted for correctly in kiting.

**130.** An internal auditor is concerned about the possibility of fraud if

A. Cash receipts, net of the amounts used to pay petty cash-type expenditures, are deposited in the bank daily.

B. The monthly bank statement reconciliation is performed by the same employee who maintains the perpetual inventory records.

C. The accounts receivable subsidiary ledger and accounts payable subsidiary ledger are maintained by the same person.

D. One person, acting alone, has sole access to the petty cash fund (except for a provision for occasional surprise counts by a supervisor or auditor).

Answer (A) is correct. *(CIA, adapted)*

**REQUIRED:** The reason an internal auditor is concerned about the possibility of fraud.

**DISCUSSION:** Paying petty cash expenditures from cash receipts facilitates the unauthorized removal of cash before deposit. All cash receipts should be deposited intact daily. Petty cash expenditures should be handled through an imprest fund.

Answer (B) is incorrect because the monthly bank reconciliation should not be performed by a person who makes deposits or writes checks, but the inventory clerk does not have these responsibilities. Answer (C) is incorrect because there is no direct relationship between the transactions posted to the accounts receivable and accounts payable subsidiary ledgers. Having the same person maintain both ledgers does not create a control weakness. Answer (D) is incorrect because, to establish accountability for petty cash, only one person should have access to the fund.

**131.** Using a wide variety of solicitation techniques, a large public charity raises funds for medical research from the general public. In an audit of donations, the internal auditor is least likely to use which of the following audit procedures?

A. Written confirmation of a sample of direct mail pledges.

B. Reconciliation of depository bank accounts.

C. Surprise observation of door-to-door solicitation teams.

D. Reconciliation of raffle tickets sold to amounts deposited in the bank.

Answer (C) is correct. *(CIA, adapted)*

**REQUIRED:** The least likely audit procedure in an audit of donations.

**DISCUSSION:** An analysis of the instructions given to door-to-door solicitation teams is more appropriate than a surprise observation. The lack of materiality of individual donations, the presence of other controls, and the inability to sample enough teams all make direct observation an inefficient audit procedure.

Answer (A) is incorrect because written confirmation of mail pledges provides evidence of existence. Answer (B) is incorrect because reconciliation of depository bank accounts provides evidence of the completeness of cash. Answer (D) is incorrect because reconciliation of raffle tickets sold to amounts deposited in the bank tests completeness of the raffle revenues.

## 4.6 Inventories

**132.** Observation of inventories is a generally accepted auditing procedure. Which of the following statements about this accepted auditing procedure is false?

A. Regardless of the inventory system maintained by the client, an annual physical count must be made of each item in the inventory, and test counts must be made by the auditor.

B. The independent auditor, when asked to audit financial statements covering the current period and one or more periods for which (s)he had not observed or made some physical counts, may be able to become satisfied as to such prior inventories through appropriate alternative procedures.

C. When the well-kept perpetual inventory records are checked by the client periodically by comparisons with physical counts, the auditor's observation procedures usually can be performed either during or after the end of the period under audit.

D. Inventories, which in the ordinary course of business are physically located in public warehouses, may be verified by direct confirmation in writing from the custodians, provided that, when the amount involved is a significant portion of the current assets or the total assets, additional procedures are applied as deemed necessary.

Answer (A) is correct. *(Publisher)*

**REQUIRED:** The false statement about observation of inventory.

**DISCUSSION:** Firms may use methods of determining inventories, such as statistical sampling, that are highly effective and sufficiently reliable to make an annual physical count of each item in inventory unnecessary. The auditor should, however, be present to observe such counts as (s)he deems necessary to become satisfied as to the effectiveness of the procedures (AU 331).

Answer (B) is incorrect because, if the auditor is able to become satisfied as to the fairness of the current year's inventory, (s)he may be able to apply tests of prior transactions, review records of prior counts, and employ other procedures to become satisfied as to the prior year's inventory. Answer (C) is incorrect because, if the client's controls are effective, the physical count and auditor observation may take place before, at, or after year-end. Answer (D) is incorrect because AU 331 and AU 901, *Public Warehouses -- Controls and Auditing Procedures for Goods Held*, indicate that direct confirmation of goods held in public warehouses is appropriate. However, other procedures should be applied when such inventories represent a significant proportion of the client's current or total assets. These may include (1) obtaining an understanding of the client's internal control and testing the controls relevant to investigating the warehouseman and evaluating its performance, (2) obtaining an independent accountant's report on the warehouseman's relevant controls or applying alternative procedures to gain reasonable assurance that information received from the warehouseman is reliable, (3) observing physical counts whenever practicable, and (4) securing confirmations from lenders when warehouse receipts have been pledged as collateral.

**133.** In an audit of inventories, an auditor is least likely to verify that

A. The financial statement presentation of inventories is appropriate.

B. Damaged goods and obsolete items have been properly accounted for.

C. All inventory owned by the client is on hand at the time of the count.

D. The client has used proper inventory pricing.

Answer (C) is correct. *(CPA, adapted)*

**REQUIRED:** The item that is not an objective of an audit of inventories.

**DISCUSSION:** An auditor does not expect all inventory to which the auditee has title to be on hand at the date of the count. Some purchased goods may still be in transit at that time. Also, some inventory may be away from the premises on consignment but still properly included in the count.

Answer (A) is incorrect because the auditor should test management's assertions about presentation. Answer (B) is incorrect because the auditor should test assertions about valuation. Answer (D) is incorrect because the auditor should test assertions about valuation.

**134.** Which of the following audit procedures probably provides the most reliable evidence concerning the entity's assertion of rights and obligations related to inventories?

A. Trace test counts noted during the entity's physical count to the entity's summarization of quantities.

B. Inspect contracts and agreements to determine whether any inventory is pledged as collateral or subject to any liens.

C. Select the last few shipping advices used before the physical count and determine whether the shipments were recorded as sales.

D. Inspect the open purchase order file for significant commitments that should be considered for disclosure.

Answer (B) is correct. *(CPA, adapted)*

**REQUIRED:** The procedure providing the most reliable evidence concerning rights and obligations related to inventories.

**DISCUSSION:** The major audit objective of testing the assertion of rights and obligations for inventories is to determine that the entity has legal title or similar rights of ownership to the inventories. Typically, the auditor will examine paid vendors' invoices, consignment agreements, and contracts.

Answer (A) is incorrect because tracing test counts to the summarization of quantities tests the assertion of completeness. Answer (C) is incorrect because examining cutoff procedures tests the assertion of completeness. Answer (D) is incorrect because determining whether commitments should be disclosed in the footnotes deals with the assertion of statement presentation and disclosure.

**135.** An auditor is most likely to inspect loan agreements under which an entity's inventories are pledged to support management's financial statement assertion of

A. Existence or occurrence.

B. Completeness.

C. Presentation and disclosure.

D. Valuation or allocation.

Answer (C) is correct. *(CPA, adapted)*

**REQUIRED:** The assertion tested by inspection of loan agreements under which inventories are pledged.

**DISCUSSION:** According to AU 326, "Assertions about presentation and disclosure address whether particular components of the financial statements are properly classified, described, and disclosed." Determining that the pledge or assignment of inventories is appropriately disclosed is an audit objective related to the presentation and disclosure assertion.

Answer (A) is incorrect because inspection of loan agreements does not determine whether inventories physically exist. Answer (B) is incorrect because inspection of loan agreements does not determine whether the inventory includes all items owned by the company. Answer (D) is incorrect because inspection of loan agreements does not determine whether inventory is included at proper amounts, e.g., at LCM.

**136.** An auditor selected items for test counts while observing a client's physical inventory. The auditor then traced the test counts to the client's inventory listing. This procedure most likely obtained evidence concerning management's assertion of

A. Rights and obligations.

B. Completeness.

C. Existence or occurrence.

D. Valuation.

Answer (B) is correct. *(CPA, adapted)*

**REQUIRED:** The assertion relevant to tracing test counts to the client's inventory listing.

**DISCUSSION:** Tracing the details of test counts to the final inventory schedule assures the auditor that items in the observed physical inventory are included in the inventory records. The auditor should compare the inventory tag sequence numbers in the final inventory schedule with those in the records of his/her test counts made during the client's physical inventory.

Answer (A) is incorrect because the reconciliation of the test counts with the inventory listing does not provide assurance that the inventory is owned by the client. Answer (C) is incorrect because, although the observation of inventory provides evidence as to existence, specifically tracing test counts to the inventory listing provides assurance of completeness. Answer (D) is incorrect because the valuation assertion is tested by determining whether items are included in inventory at LCM.

**137.** Periodic or cycle counts of selected inventory items are made at various times during the year rather than a single inventory count at year-end. Which of the following is necessary if the auditor plans to observe inventories at interim dates?

A. Complete recounts by independent teams are performed.

B. Perpetual inventory records are maintained.

C. Unit cost records are integrated with production accounting records.

D. Inventory balances are rarely at low levels.

Answer (B) is correct. *(CPA, adapted)*

**REQUIRED:** The precondition for observing inventories at interim dates.

**DISCUSSION:** "When the well-kept perpetual inventory records are checked by the client periodically by comparisons with physical counts, the auditor's observation procedures usually can be performed either during or after the end of the period under audit" (AU 331). If substantive tests are applied at an interim date, the audit risk that misstatements existing at the balance sheet date will not be detected is increased. The incremental risk may be reduced if substantive tests can be designed both to cover the remaining period and to permit the extension to year-end of audit conclusions made at the interim date (AU 313).

Answer (A) is incorrect because complete recounts of inventory by independent teams is rarely necessary. Answer (C) is incorrect because, although integrating cost records into the production records may provide for increased coordination, the process is not necessary to rely on cycle counts of inventory. Answer (D) is incorrect because inventory counts are typically easier when inventory balances are at low levels.

**138.** A client maintains perpetual inventory records in both quantities and dollars. If the assessed level of control risk is high, an auditor will probably

A. Apply gross profit tests to ascertain the reasonableness of the physical counts.

B. Increase the extent of tests of controls relevant to the inventory cycle.

C. Request the client to schedule the physical inventory count at the end of the year.

D. Insist that the client perform physical counts of inventory items several times during the year.

Answer (C) is correct. *(CPA, adapted)*

**REQUIRED:** The auditor's action if control risk for inventory is high.

**DISCUSSION:** If control risk is high, extending work done on an interim basis to year-end might be inappropriate. Thus, observation of inventory at year-end provides the best evidence as to existence.

Answer (A) is incorrect because comparing the gross profit test results with the prior year's results provides evidence about sales and cost of goods sold but not inventory. Answer (B) is incorrect because, if the auditor believes controls are unlikely to be effective, tests of controls would not be performed. Answer (D) is incorrect because the risk is that year-end inventory would be misstated.

**139.** When outside firms of nonaccountants specializing in the taking of physical inventories are used to count, list, price, and subsequently compute the total dollar amount of inventory on hand at the date of the physical count, the auditor will ordinarily

A. Consider the report of the outside inventory-taking firm to be an acceptable alternative procedure to the observation of physical inventories.

B. Make or observe some physical counts of the inventory, recompute certain inventory calculations, and test certain inventory transactions.

C. Not reduce the extent of work on the physical count of inventory.

D. Consider the reduced audit effort with respect to the physical count of inventory as a scope limitation.

Answer (B) is correct. *(CPA, adapted)*

**REQUIRED:** The auditor's responsibility when an outside firm has taken the inventory.

**DISCUSSION:** The taking of inventory by an outside firm of nonaccountants does not substitute for the auditor's own observation or performing some test counts. The extent of his/her procedures may be reduced, but only after a proper evaluation of the outside firm's work, including examining its program, observing its procedures and controls, recomputing calculations, and applying tests to subsequent transactions.

Answer (A) is incorrect because the use of experts to count the inventory may reduce the extent of the auditor's other work on the inventory, but it cannot be a complete substitute. Answer (C) is incorrect because the independent auditor may be able to reduce the extent of his/her procedures but only after a proper evaluation of the outside firm's work. Answer (D) is incorrect because a scope limitation should not be reported unless the auditor's judgment concerning the extent of contact with the inventory is restricted; i.e., the client limits the CPA's involvement in the observation and review of the inventory count.

**140.** After accounting for a sequence of inventory tags, an auditor traces a sample of tags to the physical inventory listing to obtain evidence that all items

A. Included in the listing have been counted.

B. Represented by inventory tags are included in the listing.

C. Included in the listing are represented by inventory tags.

D. Represented by inventory tags are bona fide.

Answer (B) is correct. *(CPA, adapted)*

**REQUIRED:** The reason for tracing a sample to the physical inventory listing.

**DISCUSSION:** The auditor should observe the counting process, determine that proper procedures are followed, and make selected test counts. Because the auditor does not make a complete count, not every misstatement will be detected, but (s)he should be able to determine that no large block of inventory has been omitted. Having accounted for a sequence of inventory tags, the auditor should trace a sample of the tags to the physical inventory sheets. The purpose is to test the completeness assertion: all inventory listed on a tag should be reflected in the sheets.

Answer (A) is incorrect because the direction of testing must be from the listing to the tags to obtain evidence that all items included in the listing have been counted. Answer (C) is incorrect because the direction of testing must be from the listing to the tags to obtain evidence that all items included in the listing are represented by inventory tags. Answer (D) is incorrect because the validity of the tags is determined by examining the inventory itself.

**141.** If the perpetual inventory records show lower quantities of inventory than the physical count, an explanation of the difference might be unrecorded

A. Sales.

B. Sales discounts.

C. Purchases.

D. Purchase discounts.

Answer (C) is correct. *(CPA, adapted)*

**REQUIRED:** The reason the physical count might exceed the perpetual inventory amount.

**DISCUSSION:** In a perpetual system, purchases are debited directly to inventory at the time of the transaction rather than to a purchases account. A sale requires an immediate credit to inventory. Hence, failure to record a purchase would understate inventory.

Answer (A) is incorrect because an unrecorded sale would overstate inventory. Answer (B) is incorrect because sales discounts affect neither the quantity nor the valuation of inventory. Answer (D) is incorrect because unrecorded purchase discounts affect the valuation but not the quantity of inventory.

**142.** An independent auditor may accept a client's sampling method for the performance of physical inventory only if

A. The client is willing to accept a qualification of the auditor's opinion because of a scope limitation.

B. Control risk is assessed at the maximum.

C. The sampling plan has statistical validity.

D. Over half of the dollar value of the inventory is counted.

Answer (C) is correct. *(Publisher)*

**REQUIRED:** The basis for an auditor's acceptance of a sampling method for inventory.

**DISCUSSION:** According to AU 331, "If statistical sampling methods are used by the client in the taking of the physical inventory, the auditor must be satisfied that the sampling plan is reasonable and statistically valid, that it has been properly applied, and that the results are reasonable in the circumstances." But the auditor still should be present to observe such counts as (s)he deems necessary to assure that the inventory exists.

Answer (A) is incorrect because a scope limitation does not exist unless the auditor is precluded from evaluating the client's sampling plan or observing the counts. Answer (B) is incorrect because the auditor is more likely to accept the method when controls are effective and control risk is assessed at less than the maximum. Answer (D) is incorrect because the extent of the counts depends on the circumstances and the auditor's judgment. No fixed percentage of the inventory must be counted.

**143.** The physical count of inventory of a retailer was higher than shown by the perpetual records. Which of the following could explain the difference?

A. Inventory items had been counted but the tags placed on the items had not been taken off the items and added to the inventory accumulation sheets.

B. Credit memos for several items returned by customers had not been recorded.

C. No journal entry had been made on the retailer's books for several items returned to its suppliers.

D. An item purchased "FOB shipping point" had not arrived at the date of the inventory count and had not been reflected in the perpetual records.

Answer (B) is correct. *(CPA, adapted)*

**REQUIRED:** The reason that the physical count exceeded the amount in the perpetual records.

**DISCUSSION:** If credit memos for items returned by customers have not been prepared and recorded, the returned items will be reflected in the physical inventory but not in the perpetual records.

Answer (A) is incorrect because items counted but not added to the inventory accumulation sheets will understate the physical count. Answer (C) is incorrect because, if no journal entry has been made for items returned to vendors, the perpetual records will be overstated. Answer (D) is incorrect because, if an entry has not been made in the perpetual records and the item has not been received, both the records and physical inventory will be understated by the same amount. FOB shipping point means that title passes when the items are shipped, and they should be included in both inventory and accounts payable at that time.

**144.** An auditor is most likely to learn of slow-moving inventory through

A. Inquiry of sales personnel.

B. Inquiry of warehouse personnel.

C. Physical observation of inventory.

D. Review of perpetual inventory records.

Answer (D) is correct. *(CPA, adapted)*

**REQUIRED:** The procedure most likely to detect slow-moving inventory.

**DISCUSSION:** In a perpetual inventory system, receipts and issuances of goods are recorded as the transactions occur, both as to quantities and prices. By comparing the dates of receipt and issuance, the auditor is readily able to identify slow-moving and possibly obsolete inventory.

Answer (A) is incorrect because inquiries are less reliable and comprehensive than a review of perpetual inventory records. Answer (B) is incorrect because inquiries are less reliable and comprehensive than a review of perpetual inventory records. Answer (C) is incorrect because observation will prove useful only if the appearance of the items suggested the length of time they were held.

**145.** Which of the following procedures will best detect the theft of valuable items from an inventory that consists of hundreds of different items selling for $1 to $10 and a few items selling for hundreds of dollars?

A. Maintain a perpetual inventory of only the more valuable items with frequent periodic verification of the validity of the perpetual inventory record.

B. Have an independent auditing firm examine and report on management's assertion about the design and operating effectiveness of the control activities relevant to inventory.

C. Have separate warehouse space for the more valuable items with sequentially numbered tags.

D. Require an authorized officer's signature on all requisitions for the more valuable items.

Answer (A) is correct. *(CPA, adapted)*

**REQUIRED:** The best procedure to detect the theft of valuable items from an inventory.

**DISCUSSION:** The costs of maintaining perpetual records for a large volume of inexpensive items are likely to exceed the benefits of more accurate and timely information and better safeguards against theft. For high value items, maintaining such records, with frequent reconciliations to physical counts, may prove cost beneficial.

Answer (B) is incorrect because the engagement would not necessarily result in detection of theft, although it might identify material weaknesses or other reportable conditions that encourage theft. Answer (C) is incorrect because separate warehouse space for the more valuable items with sequentially numbered tags is helpful but not as effective in detecting (as opposed to preventing) theft as a system whereby the quantity that should be on hand is known with reasonable accuracy at all times. Answer (D) is incorrect because requiring an authorized officer's signature on all requisitions for the more valuable items is useful but less effective than maintaining perpetual inventory records.

**146.** Which of the following is the best audit test to evaluate the accuracy of the inventory records for materials inventory in a production operation?

A. Trace selected inventory receipts to perpetual inventory records.

B. Vouch selected postings in the perpetual inventory records to source documents.

C. Perform turnover tests for materials inventory.

D. Reconcile quantities on hand per physical counts of selected items with perpetual inventory records and verify pricing.

Answer (D) is correct. *(CIA, adapted)*

**REQUIRED:** The best audit test for evaluating the accuracy of the inventory records for materials inventory.

**DISCUSSION:** The objectives in designing an audit test should be to verify both the quantity on hand and the dollar value of inventory. By reconciling the quantities on hand determined by the physical count with the perpetual inventory records and verifying pricing, both objectives are met. The auditor's observation of the physical count is an indispensable audit procedure.

Answer (A) is incorrect because tracing selected inventory receipts to perpetual inventory records provides less reliable evidence than observation of the physical count. Answer (B) is incorrect because vouching selected postings in the perpetual inventory records to source documents provides less reliable evidence than observation of the physical count. Answer (C) is incorrect because analytical procedures do not provide direct evidence of inventory amounts.

**147.** For the week before Moore Company's physical count, all receiving reports include a notation that they have been prepared prior to the count. For the week after the physical count, all receiving reports indicate that they have been prepared after the count. The receiving department continues to receive goods after the cutoff time while the physical count is in process. To determine the accuracy of the cutoff, the auditor should

A. Trace a sample of receiving reports issued after the last receiving report to the physical items to see that they have been included in the physical count.

B. Trace a sample of receiving reports issued before the last receiving report to the physical items to see that they have not been included in the physical count.

C. Observe that the receiving clerk is stamping the receiving reports properly.

D. List the number of the last receiving report for items included in the physical count.

Answer (D) is correct. *(Publisher)*

**REQUIRED:** The procedure for testing the inventory cutoff.

**DISCUSSION:** The numbers of the last receiving and shipping reports should be recorded so that the auditor may determine whether an accurate cutoff was made. For example, merchandise represented by receiving reports numbered after the cutoff should not be included in inventory.

Answer (A) is incorrect because receiving reports prepared after the cutoff should be traced on a test basis to the inventory records to determine that the items have not been included. Answer (B) is incorrect because receiving reports prepared before the cutoff should be traced on a test basis to the inventory records to determine that the items have been included. Answer (C) is incorrect because the least effective method of checking the accuracy of the cutoff of inventory is to observe that the receiving clerk is stamping the receiving reports properly. The auditor is primarily concerned with the dates on the receiving reports in order to verify that goods received or shipped near year-end are accounted for in the proper reporting period.

**148.** Purchase cutoff procedures should be designed to test whether all inventory

A. Purchased and received before year-end was paid for.

B. Ordered before year-end was received.

C. Purchased and received before year-end was recorded.

D. Owned by the company is in the possession of the company at year-end.

Answer (C) is correct. *(CPA, adapted)*

**REQUIRED:** The purpose of a purchase cutoff.

**DISCUSSION:** A purchase cutoff is an audit procedure related to the audit objective of testing the completeness assertion about inventories. It is performed to obtain evidence that all goods owned by the client at the balance sheet date are included in inventory and that the related liability is recorded. Legal title to goods in transit is determined by whether the shipping terms are FOB shipping point or destination.

Answer (A) is incorrect because items may be included in inventory although not yet paid for. Answer (B) is incorrect because the company may not have title to goods on order. Answer (D) is incorrect because the company may have title to goods in transit or held on consignment.

**149.** The audit of year-end physical inventories should include steps to verify that the client's purchases and sales cutoffs were adequate. The audit steps should be designed to detect whether merchandise included in the physical count at year-end was not recorded as a

A. Sale in the subsequent period.

B. Purchase in the current period.

C. Sale in the current period.

D. Purchase return in the subsequent period.

Answer (C) is correct. *(CPA, adapted)*

**REQUIRED:** The error detected by the audit of purchases and sales cutoffs.

**DISCUSSION:** Goods on hand and counted in the year-end inventory should not also have been recorded as sold during the current audit period. If they were sold, they could not have been owned by the client at year-end. Cutoff tests include comparison of the records of sales and purchases for several days before and after the balance sheet date with duplicate sales invoices and shipping records.

Answer (A) is incorrect because year-end inventory most likely will be sold in the subsequent period. Answer (B) is incorrect because year-end inventory most likely was purchased in the current period. Answer (D) is incorrect because unreturned items are owned by the client and should be in ending inventory.

**150.** An auditor's observation of physical inventories at the main plant at year-end provides direct evidence to support which of the following objectives?

A. Accuracy of the priced-out inventory.

B. Evaluation of lower of cost or market test.

C. Identification of obsolete or damaged merchandise to evaluate allowance (reserve) for obsolescence.

D. Determination of goods on consignment at another location.

Answer (C) is correct. *(CIA, adapted)*

**REQUIRED:** The objective supported by observation of inventory.

**DISCUSSION:** One way to discover damaged or obsolete merchandise is to observe the client's physical inventory count and inspect the merchandise during the inventory process. The auditor should check for dusty packages, rusted metal, physical damage to the merchandise, etc. The auditor may also need to consult a specialist regarding the quality or condition of merchandise.

Answer (A) is incorrect because observation verifies physical existence and condition, not price accuracy. Answer (B) is incorrect because observation verifies physical existence and condition, not cost accuracy. Answer (D) is incorrect because observation at the main plant is not evidence of the existence of goods at another site.

**151.** Some firms that dispose of only a small part of their total output by consignment shipments fail to make any distinction between consignment shipments and regular sales. Which of the following suggests that the client's goods have been shipped on consignment?

A. Numerous shipments of small quantities.

B. Numerous shipments of large quantities and few returns.

C. Large debits to accounts receivable and small periodic credits.

D. Large debits to accounts receivable and large periodic credits.

Answer (C) is correct. *(CPA, adapted)*

**REQUIRED:** The condition indicative of goods shipped on consignment.

**DISCUSSION:** A consignment is a shipment of inventory by the owner to a sales agent (the consignee), who sells the goods and then pays the consignor. Goods on consignment are owned by the consignor. Large debits to accounts receivable and small periodic credits suggest that large quantities have been "sold," but smaller quantities are being "paid for." Typically, consignment payments are remitted periodically as the consignee makes sales. Failing to distinguish sales and consignments overstates net income and understates inventory.

Answer (A) is incorrect because fewer but larger shipments with many returns indicate consignments. Answer (B) is incorrect because fewer but larger shipments with many returns indicate consignments. Answer (D) is incorrect because consigned goods are normally paid for in small amounts as they are sold.

**152.** An auditor concluded that no excessive costs for an idle plant were charged to inventory. This conclusion most likely related to the auditor's objective to obtain evidence about the financial statement assertions regarding inventory, including presentation and disclosure and

A. Valuation and allocation.

B. Completeness.

C. Existence or occurrence.

D. Rights and obligations.

Answer (A) is correct. *(CPA, adapted)*

**REQUIRED:** The assertion related to the conclusion that no excessive costs for an idle plant were inventoried.

**DISCUSSION:** Inventory should properly include the costs of direct labor, direct materials, and manufacturing overhead. Thus, to be properly valued, an appropriate amount of manufacturing overhead should be charged to inventory. Costs of an idle plant should not be included in manufacturing overhead.

Answer (B) is incorrect because excessive costs for an idle plant do not affect the completeness assertion. Answer (C) is incorrect because excessive costs for an idle plant do not affect the existence or occurrence assertions. Answer (D) is incorrect because excessive costs for an idle plant do not affect the rights and obligations assertions.

**153.** During an investigation of unexplained inventory shrinkage, an internal auditor is testing inventory additions as recorded in the perpetual inventory records. Because of internal control weaknesses, the information recorded on receiving reports may not be reliable. Under these circumstances, which of the following documents provides the best evidence of additions to inventory?

A. Purchase orders.

B. Purchase requisitions.

C. Vendors' invoices.

D. Vendors' statements.

Answer (C) is correct. *(CIA, adapted)*

**REQUIRED:** The best evidence of additions to inventory when receiving reports are unreliable.

**DISCUSSION:** Vendors' invoices state the quantities and costs of goods shipped. Thus, they provide an external source of evidence of additions to inventory. However, an adjustment must be made for purchase returns.

Answer (A) is incorrect because the quantity ordered may not equal the quantity shipped by the vendor. Answer (B) is incorrect because the quantity requested in a purchase requisition may not equal the quantity actually ordered or the quantity shipped by the vendor. Answer (D) is incorrect because vendors' statements normally list only the invoice number, date, and total. They do not list invoice detail such as quantities shipped.

**154.** To obtain evidence as to the reasonableness and completeness of inventory balances, auditors often perform analytical procedures. Which of the following quantitative relationships is not applicable to inventory balances?

A. The gross profit percentage.

B. Debt-to-equity ratio.

C. Inventory turnover ratios.

D. Number of days' sales in inventory.

Answer (B) is correct. *(Publisher)*

**REQUIRED:** The quantitative relationship not applicable to inventory balances.

**DISCUSSION:** The debt-to-equity ratio, a measure of leverage, relates to corporate financing, not inventory. It equals total debt divided by total equity.

Answer (A) is incorrect because the gross profit percentage (gross profit ÷ net sales) provides information about inventories. Gross profit is equal to net sales minus cost of goods sold, and inventories affect cost of goods sold. Any significant unexplained variance in the percentage may be the result of an inventory misstatement. Answer (C) is incorrect because inventory ratios, such as cost of goods sold divided by average inventory, should remain relatively constant in the absence of known conditions to the contrary. Answer (D) is incorrect because the number of days' sales in inventory (360 ÷ inventory turnover) is a measure that can be monitored by the auditor. The number of days' sales in inventories should be relatively constant.

**155.** During the preliminary survey phase of an audit of the organization's production cycle, management stated that the sale of scrap was well controlled. Evidence to verify that assertion can best be gained by

A. Comparing current revenue from scrap sales with that of prior periods.

B. Interviewing persons responsible for collecting and storing the scrap.

C. Comparing the quantities of scrap expected from the production process with the quantities sold.

D. Comparing the results of a physical inventory of scrap on hand with perpetual inventory records.

Answer (C) is correct. *(CIA, adapted)*

**REQUIRED:** The best procedure to verify the assertion that the sale of scrap is well controlled.

**DISCUSSION:** If the sale of scrap is well controlled, a large amount will not be on hand. Most scrap will be sold when produced. Hence, if the quantities sold are approximately the same as those expected, an auditor can assume that the controls over the sale of scrap are effective.

Answer (A) is incorrect because comparing current revenue from scrap sales with that of prior periods presumes that prior periods' amounts were correct and that no change has occurred in quantity produced. Answer (B) is incorrect because the persons responsible for collecting and storing the scrap can only describe the safeguards in place to handle scrap before its sale. Answer (D) is incorrect because comparing the physical count with perpetual inventory records verifies only the accuracy of perpetual inventory records.

## 4.7 Property, Plant, and Equipment

**156.** Property, plant, and equipment (PPE) is typically judged to be one of the accounts least susceptible to fraud because

A. The amounts recorded on the balance sheet for most companies are immaterial.

B. The inherent risk is usually low.

C. The depreciated values are always smaller than cost.

D. Internal control is inherently effective regarding this account.

Answer (B) is correct. *(Publisher)*

**REQUIRED:** The reason PPE is not susceptible to fraud.

**DISCUSSION:** Property, plant, and equipment is one of the accounts least susceptible to material misstatement in the absence of related controls. Inherent risk is low because of the infrequency of transactions in the account, the relative ease with which the existence of these assets can be verified, the slow turnover, and the simplicity of cutoff procedures.

Answer (A) is incorrect because PPE amounts are often quite large. Answer (C) is incorrect because some PPE items (e.g., land) are not depreciated. Answer (D) is incorrect because the susceptibility to misstatement is a matter of inherent risk, not control risk.

**157.** Which is the best audit procedure to obtain evidence to support the legal ownership of real property?

A. Examination of corporate minutes and board resolutions with regard to approvals to acquire real property.

B. Examination of closing documents, deeds, and ownership documents registered and on file at the county courthouse.

C. Discussion with corporate legal counsel concerning the acquisition of a specific piece of property.

D. Confirmation with the title company that handled the escrow account and disbursement of proceeds for the closing of the property.

Answer (B) is correct. *(CIA, adapted)*

**REQUIRED:** The best audit procedure for obtaining evidence to support the legal ownership of real property.

**DISCUSSION:** Examination of title documents, the deed, and any other supporting documents, such as closing documents, will be helpful in verifying ownership. But these are not conclusive. An inspection of public records will determine if there are any interests in the property (e.g., mortgages, judgment liens, or claims to the title) that do not appear in the auditee's records.

Answer (A) is incorrect because an examination of corporate minutes and board resolutions will not provide evidence of actual ownership, only approval to acquire the property. Answer (C) is incorrect because the testimony of corporate legal counsel provides only corroborating evidence. Answer (D) is incorrect because confirmation with an escrow agent is evidence only of the closing. It does not provide evidence regarding subsequent transactions, such as a mortgage liability not recorded in the company books.

**158.** In the audit of property, plant, and equipment, the auditor tries to do all of the following except to

A. Obtain an understanding of internal control.

B. Determine the extent of property abandoned during the year.

C. Assess the adequacy of replacement funds.

D. Judge the reasonableness of the depreciation.

Answer (C) is correct. *(CPA, adapted)*

**REQUIRED:** The determination not made during an audit of PPE.

**DISCUSSION:** In performing the attest function, the external auditor is not directly concerned with evaluating the soundness of the client's business practices or financial prospects. Whether replacement funds are adequate does not bear on the question of whether the financial statements are fairly presented in conformity with GAAP.

Answer (A) is incorrect because, in all audits, auditing standards require the auditor to obtain an understanding sufficient to plan the audit and to determine the nature, timing, and extent of tests. Answer (B) is incorrect because the auditor should determine whether abandonments of property were properly recorded so as to avoid overstatement of assets. Answer (D) is incorrect because depreciation affects both asset valuation and income.

**159.** Which of the following combinations of procedures is an auditor most likely to perform to obtain evidence about fixed asset additions?

A. Inspecting documents and physically examining assets.

B. Recomputing calculations and obtaining written management representations.

C. Observing operating activities and comparing balances to prior period balances.

D. Confirming ownership and corroborating transactions through inquiries of client personnel.

Answer (A) is correct. *(CPA, adapted)*

**REQUIRED:** The combination of procedures most likely to obtain evidence about fixed asset additions.

**DISCUSSION:** The auditor's direct observation of fixed assets is one means of determining whether additions have been made. Tracing to the detailed records determines whether additions have been recorded. Inspection of such documents as deeds, lease agreements, insurance policies, invoices, canceled checks, and tax notices may also reveal additions.

Answer (B) is incorrect because recomputations are based on book amounts and will not reveal unrecorded additions. Management representations may also be incomplete. Answer (C) is incorrect because analytical procedures may not detect additions offset by disposals. Answer (D) is incorrect because the auditor must become aware of additions before confirming ownership or corroborating transactions.

**160.** When few property and equipment transactions occur during the year, the continuing auditor usually obtains an understanding of internal control and performs

A. Tests of controls to assess control risk at less than the maximum.

B. Analytical procedures to verify current year additions to property and equipment.

C. A thorough examination of the balances at the beginning of the year.

D. Extensive tests of current year property and equipment transactions.

Answer (D) is correct. *(CPA, adapted)*

**REQUIRED:** The PPE procedures performed by a continuing auditor.

**DISCUSSION:** Testing the details of transactions is the preferable procedure for property and equipment because the beginning balance would have been subjected to audit procedures and the number of subsequent transactions in the account is normally minimal. The auditor may choose to assess control risk at the maximum level after obtaining the understanding of internal control because (s)he believes that evaluating the effectiveness of the relevant controls would be inefficient.

Answer (A) is incorrect because assessment of control risk below the maximum is unnecessary if the auditor does extensive testing of details. Answer (B) is incorrect because analytical procedures are unnecessary as substantive tests if the auditor does extensive testing of details. Answer (C) is incorrect because a continuing auditor would already have examined the beginning balances.

**161.** If an auditor tours a production facility, which of the misstatements or questionable practices is most likely to be detected?

A. Depreciation expense on fully depreciated machinery has been recognized.

B. Overhead has been overapplied.

C. Necessary facility maintenance has not been performed.

D. Insurance coverage on the facility has lapsed.

Answer (C) is correct. *(CIA, adapted)*

**REQUIRED:** The misstatement or questionable practice uncovered by touring the client's plant.

**DISCUSSION:** The auditor is likely to discover that necessary plant maintenance was not performed during the year through direct observation of asset condition.

Answer (A) is incorrect because only inspection of depreciation records will reveal depreciation recorded for fully depreciated machines. Answer (B) is incorrect because the auditor compares actual overhead incurred with overhead applied to determine whether overhead was underapplied. Answer (D) is incorrect because the auditor inspects the insurance contracts to detect lapsed insurance coverage.

**162.** Treetop Corporation acquired a building and arranged mortgage financing during the year. Verification of the related mortgage acquisition costs is least likely to include an examination of the related

A. Deed.

B. Canceled checks.

C. Closing statement.

D. Interest expense.

Answer (A) is correct. *(CPA, adapted)*

**REQUIRED:** The item that the auditor is least likely to inspect to verify mortgage acquisition costs.

**DISCUSSION:** A deed provides evidence concerning ownership rights and obligations relative to mortgaged property. However, it typically does not contain information about costs of mortgages.

Answer (B) is incorrect because canceled checks provide evidence concerning the cost of a mortgage. Answer (C) is incorrect because a closing statement provides evidence concerning the cost of a mortgage. Answer (D) is incorrect because interest expense provides evidence concerning the cost of a mortgage.

**163.** In testing for unrecorded retirements of equipment, an auditor is most likely to

A. Select items of equipment from the accounting records and then locate them during the plant tour.

B. Compare depreciation journal entries with similar prior-year entries in search of fully depreciated equipment.

C. Inspect items of equipment observed during the plant tour and then trace them to the equipment subsidiary ledger.

D. Scan the general journal for unusual equipment additions and excessive debits to repairs and maintenance expense.

Answer (A) is correct. *(CPA, adapted)*

**REQUIRED:** The procedure most useful in detecting unrecorded retirements of equipment.

**DISCUSSION:** The completeness assertion is that all transactions and accounts that should be presented are so included. Thus, the equipment account should reflect all retirement transactions as well as all additions. To test for unrecorded retirements, the auditor inspects selected items chosen from the records. However, unlike confirmation of receivables or observation of inventories, inspection of equipment, especially a complete physical inventory, is not a generally accepted auditing procedure. But a high assessment of control risk may induce the auditor to inspect a sample of items.

Answer (B) is incorrect because fully depreciated equipment may not be physically retired. Answer (C) is incorrect because, to detect unrecorded retirements, the direction of testing should be from the records to the physical assets. Answer (D) is incorrect because the concern is with retirements of equipment, not additions.

**164.** One audit procedure for an audit of facilities and equipment is to test the accuracy of recorded depreciation. Which of the following is the best source of evidence that the equipment in question is in service?

A. A review of depreciation policies and procedures.

B. A comparison of depreciation schedules with a listing of insurance appraisals for the same equipment.

C. A comparison of depreciation schedules with the maintenance and repair logs for the same equipment.

D. A review of inventory documentation for the equipment.

Answer (C) is correct. *(CIA, adapted)*

**REQUIRED:** The best source of evidence that the equipment in question is in service.

**DISCUSSION:** The maintenance and repair records provide evidence that equipment exists and is in use. Equipment in service is more likely to require maintenance than retired equipment. However, the best evidence is the auditor's direct observation.

Answer (A) is incorrect because a review of policies and procedures provides no evidence about the existence assertion for specific assets. Answer (B) is incorrect because a comparison with current insurance records would be inconclusive. Retired equipment could still be insured. Answer (D) is incorrect because retired equipment could still be in the inventory.

**165.** The auditor is least likely to learn of retirements of equipment through which of the following?

A. Review of the purchase return and allowance account.

B. Review of depreciation.

C. Analysis of the debits to the accumulated depreciation account.

D. Review of insurance policy riders.

Answer (A) is correct. *(CPA, adapted)*

**REQUIRED:** The procedure least likely to provide evidence about retirements of equipment.

**DISCUSSION:** Review of the purchase return and allowance account offers no information about the retirement of equipment. This account is used to record the return of purchased inventory and is unaffected by the entries to record the acquisition, depreciation, and disposition of fixed assets.

Answer (B) is incorrect because review of depreciation may reveal equipment retirements. Answer (C) is incorrect because analysis of the debits may reveal equipment retirements. Answer (D) is incorrect because reduction in insurance coverage may indicate a retirement of equipment.

**166.** Determining that proper amounts of depreciation are expensed provides assurance about management's assertions of valuation or allocation and

A. Presentation and disclosure.

B. Completeness.

C. Rights and obligations.

D. Existence or occurrence.

Answer (A) is correct. *(CPA, adapted)*

**REQUIRED:** The assertion tested by consideration of the amounts of depreciation that are expensed.

**DISCUSSION:** The presentation and disclosure assertion concerns whether particular components of the financial statements are properly classified, described, and disclosed. For example, if cost of sales includes depreciation, the auditor should determine that this classification is appropriate and that it is properly disclosed.

Answer (B) is incorrect because the completeness assertion addresses whether all transactions and accounts that should be presented are included. Answer (C) is incorrect because the rights and obligations assertion addresses whether assets are rights, and obligations are liabilities, of the entity at a specified time. Answer (D) is incorrect because the existence or occurrence assertion addresses whether assets or liabilities exist at a given time and whether recorded transactions occurred during the period.

**167.** The auditor may conclude that depreciation charges are insufficient by noting

A. Insured values greatly in excess of carrying amounts.

B. Large numbers of fully depreciated assets.

C. Continuous trade-ins of relatively new assets.

D. Excessive recurring losses on assets retired.

Answer (D) is correct. *(CPA, adapted)*

**REQUIRED:** The condition indicating insufficient depreciation charges.

**DISCUSSION:** Excessive recurring losses on assets retired indicate excess carrying amounts at the dates of disposition. The implication is that the method of cost allocation has not been sufficient. The effect of such understating of depreciation in prior periods would have been to overstate income in those periods and understate income in the period of retirement.

Answer (A) is incorrect because the insured values of assets should reflect fair values. Carrying amounts reflect historical cost. Answer (B) is incorrect because large numbers of fully depreciated assets indicate excessive, not insufficient, depreciation charges. Answer (C) is incorrect because trade-ins of relatively new assets suggest rapid technological change in the client's industry.

**168.** The most appropriate reason for a decrease in accumulated depreciation is that

A. Depreciation for prior periods was understated.

B. Major repairs have lengthened the life of an asset.

C. A depreciable asset has been recorded at current cost.

D. Retained earnings have been appropriated for a possible loss on retirement.

Answer (B) is correct. *(Publisher)*

**REQUIRED:** The reason for a decrease in accumulated depreciation.

**DISCUSSION:** If major repairs have lengthened the life of an asset, the company should reduce the amount of accumulated depreciation to increase the carrying amount of the asset. This practice is acceptable for representing the increased life of an asset.

Answer (A) is incorrect because an adjustment for understated depreciation requires a credit, not a debit, to accumulated depreciation. Answer (C) is incorrect because depreciable assets ordinarily should be recorded at historical cost. Answer (D) is incorrect because an appropriation affects retained earnings accounts only.

**169.** An auditor analyzes repairs and maintenance accounts primarily to obtain evidence in support of the audit assertion that all

A. Noncapitalizable expenditures for repairs and maintenance have been recorded in the proper period.

B. Expenditures for property and equipment have been recorded in the proper period.

C. Noncapitalizable expenditures for repairs and maintenance have been properly charged to expense.

D. Expenditures for property and equipment have not been charged to expense.

Answer (D) is correct. *(CPA, adapted)*

**REQUIRED:** The reason an auditor analyzes repairs and maintenance expense.

**DISCUSSION:** The auditor should vouch significant debits from the repairs and maintenance expense account to determine whether any should have been capitalized.

Answer (A) is incorrect because an improper cutoff of repairs and maintenance expenses is not a major risk. Answer (B) is incorrect because the repairs and maintenance expense accounts are not the appropriate sources of evidence regarding the cutoff of expenditures for property and equipment. Answer (C) is incorrect because vouching additions to plant, property, and equipment provides evidence of whether any expense has been inappropriately charged as a capital item.

**170.** In violation of a company policy, Lowell Company erroneously capitalized the cost of painting its warehouse. The auditor examining Lowell's financial statements will most likely detect this misstatement when

A. Discussing capitalization policies with Lowell's controller.

B. Examining maintenance expense accounts.

C. Observing, during the physical inventory observation, that the warehouse had been painted.

D. Examining the construction work orders supporting items capitalized during the year.

Answer (D) is correct. *(CPA, adapted)*

**REQUIRED:** The procedure to detect the capitalization of a maintenance expense.

**DISCUSSION:** The audit program for PPE includes verification of additions by vouching them to the original documents. The entries in the journals are supported by authorizations, vendors' invoices, contracts, deeds, and construction work orders. Inspection of the work order for painting the warehouse will alert the auditor that an expense had been incorrectly capitalized.

Answer (A) is incorrect because, given that the policy of the firm is to expense painting costs, discussion with the controller will not uncover the misstatement. Answer (B) is incorrect because items capitalized will not be reflected in maintenance accounts. Answer (C) is incorrect because the auditor will not detect improper accounting for the cost by observing the painted warehouse.

**171.** Which of the following costs should not be capitalized?

A. Major reconditioning of a delivery truck.

B. Machine operator's wages during a period of testing and adjusting new machinery.

C. Fencing the plant parking lot.

D. Maintenance of an unused stand-by plant.

Answer (D) is correct. *(Publisher)*

**REQUIRED:** The cost that should not be capitalized.

**DISCUSSION:** Keeping an unused plant on stand-by for current operations suggests that maintenance on the plant should be reflected in current costs. The plant, even though unused, is not the same as a nonproductive asset. If the idle plant is not expected to be used, however, it should be written down to net realizable value and excluded from the fixed assets accounts. Maintenance costs might then be considered as costs of disposal.

Answer (A) is incorrect because the costs of a major reconditioning of a delivery truck should be capitalized. Improvements, additions, and replacements benefit several periods by extending the useful life of an asset or by increasing future service potential. Answer (B) is incorrect because costs of putting a capital asset into service are capitalized according to GAAP. Answer (C) is incorrect because the costs of fencing the plant parking lot should be capitalized and depreciated as land improvements.

**172.** An audit client has leased an asset and appropriately recorded a capital lease. Because of the existence of a bargain purchase option, the auditor should determine

A. Whether the sum of the minimum lease payments equals the fair value of the property.

B. That the leased property is being depreciated over the life of the lease.

C. Whether the interest rate used in discounting the minimum lease payments is the client's incremental borrowing rate or the lessor's implicit rate.

D. That the cost of the property to the lessor is the cost recorded by the client.

Answer (C) is correct. *(Publisher)*

**REQUIRED:** The appropriate audit procedure relative to a capital lease.

**DISCUSSION:** A leased asset should be capitalized at the sum of the discounted minimum lease payments. Thus, the interest rate used in the discounting process is an important consideration in determining whether the asset is fairly presented in the balance sheet. The interest rate is the client's incremental borrowing rate, unless the lessor's implicit rate is known and is less than the client's incremental rate.

Answer (A) is incorrect because the total amount of lease payments represents both the cost of the asset and interest expense. Answer (B) is incorrect because the asset should be depreciated over its estimated life, which is not necessarily the life of the lease (given that the lease is capitalized or a result of a bargain purchase option). Answer (D) is incorrect because the lessee does not capitalize the asset at the cost to the lessor.

## 4.8 Other Assets

**173.** The primary audit objectives for other assets include all of the following except to

A. Determine that the asset is written off on a periodic basis.

B. Confirm that the asset exists.

C. Determine the basis of the carrying amount of the asset.

D. Determine whether the asset is fairly presented in the financial statements.

Answer (A) is correct. *(Publisher)*

**REQUIRED:** The item not considered an audit objective for other assets.

**DISCUSSION:** The auditor should be concerned that each asset is presented fairly in accordance with GAAP. If GAAP require periodic allocation of costs, then determining that the asset is written off on a periodic basis is an appropriate audit objective. However, for nondepreciable assets, e.g., land, verification of the write-off is not an audit objective.

Answer (B) is incorrect because confirming the asset's existence is an appropriate audit objective for other assets. Answer (C) is incorrect because determining the basis of the carrying amount of the asset is an appropriate audit objective for other assets. Answer (D) is incorrect because determining whether the asset is fairly presented in the financial statements is an appropriate audit objective for other assets.

**174.** A client has a large and active investment portfolio that is kept in a bank safe-deposit box. If the auditor is unable to count the securities at the balance sheet date, the auditor most likely will

A. Request the bank to confirm to the auditor the contents of the safe-deposit box at the balance sheet date.

B. Examine supporting evidence for transactions occurring during the year.

C. Count the securities at a subsequent date and confirm with the bank whether securities were added or removed since the balance sheet date.

D. Request the client to have the bank seal the safe-deposit box until the auditor can count the securities at a subsequent date.

Answer (D) is correct. *(CPA, adapted)*

**REQUIRED:** The procedure most likely performed if the auditor cannot count securities at the balance sheet date.

**DISCUSSION:** Securities should be inspected simultaneously with the verification of cash and the count of other liquid assets to prevent transfers among asset categories for the purpose of concealing a shortage. If this procedure is not possible but the securities are kept by a custodian in a bank safe-deposit box, the client may instruct the custodian that no one is to have access to the securities unless in the presence of the auditor. Thus, when the auditor finally inspects the securities, (s)he may conclude that they represent what was on hand at the balance sheet date. However, some securities may be uncertificated, and physical inspection may be impossible.

Answer (A) is incorrect because the bank does not have access to the contents of the client's safe-deposit box. Answer (B) is incorrect because supporting evidence for transactions occurring during the year is not a substitute for inspection of the securities. Answer (C) is incorrect because the bank does not have access to the contents of the client's safe-deposit box.

**175.** Which of the following is not one of the auditor's primary objectives in an audit of trading securities?

A. To determine whether securities are authentic.

B. To determine whether securities are the property of the client.

C. To determine whether securities actually exist.

D. To determine whether securities are properly classified on the balance sheet.

Answer (A) is correct. *(CPA, adapted)*

**REQUIRED:** The item that is not one of the auditor's primary objectives in auditing trading securities.

**DISCUSSION:** The objectives of the audit of trading securities are to determine whether (1) the controls relevant to the securities and the revenue therefrom are effective, (2) the securities actually exist and are owned by the client, (3) all transactions and accounts that should be presented are included in the financial statements, (4) the securities are properly accounted for in conformity with GAAP, and (5) the securities' balance sheet classification is accurate. The auditor is not expected, however, to have the expertise to evaluate the authenticity of securities. If forgery is suspected, (s)he should engage a specialist.

Answer (B) is incorrect because determining whether securities are the property of the client is one of the auditor's primary objectives in auditing trading securities. Answer (C) is incorrect because determining whether securities actually exist is one of the auditor's primary objectives in auditing trading securities. Answer (D) is incorrect because determining whether securities are properly classified on the balance sheet is one of the auditor's primary objectives in auditing trading securities.

**176.** Ann Melton, CPA, observes the count of securities on December 31. She records the serial numbers of the securities and reconciles them and the number of shares with company records. Which fraud should be detected by this procedure?

A. An investee company declared and paid a stock dividend on December 15. The stock certificate for the additional shares was received directly by the treasurer who made no record of the receipt and embezzled the shares.

B. The treasurer embezzled and sold securities on April 4. She speculated successfully with the proceeds and replaced the securities on December 29.

C. The treasurer borrowed securities on July 15 to use as collateral for a personal loan. He repaid the loan and returned the securities on December 2.

D. The treasurer embezzled interest receipts from bonds by having the payments mailed directly to him.

Answer (B) is correct. *(Publisher)*

**REQUIRED:** The fraud likely to be detected by reconciling the serial numbers of securities and the number of shares with company records.

**DISCUSSION:** The auditor is most likely to discover that the company's securities had been misappropriated and then later replaced by using this procedure. The company records will indicate securities with serial numbers different from those counted by the auditor.

Answer (A) is incorrect because information concerning stock splits, stock dividends, and cash dividends from publications such as the *Wall Street Journal* or other similar sources would have to be consulted to determine the client's holdings. Answer (C) is incorrect because a surprise interim count or joint control of securities would be necessary to detect or prevent the temporary misappropriation of the securities. Answer (D) is incorrect because tests of interest income accounts, not serial numbers of securities, would show whether interest had been misappropriated.

**177.** Which of the following statements regarding the audit of negotiable notes receivable is false?

A. Confirmation from the debtor is an acceptable alternative to inspection.

B. Materiality of the amount involved is a factor considered when selecting the accounts to be confirmed.

C. Physical inspection of a note by the auditor does not provide conclusive evidence.

D. Notes receivable discounted with recourse need to be confirmed.

Answer (A) is correct. *(CPA, adapted)*

**REQUIRED:** The false statement about the audit of negotiable notes receivable.

**DISCUSSION:** Although notes receivable should be confirmed, negotiable notes are akin to stocks and bonds in that they must also be inspected to determine whether the client has custody. Confirmation also does not establish collectibility. For this purpose, the auditor should examine cash receipts records to determine promptness of interest and principal payments.

Answer (B) is incorrect because the auditor should usually attempt to confirm a substantial amount of the dollar value of receivables. Answer (C) is incorrect because inspection by auditors may not detect forgery or establish ownership. Answer (D) is incorrect because receivables discounted with recourse should be confirmed. Those discounted without recourse need not be because the client then has no contingent liability.

**178.** Which of the following is the least effective audit procedure regarding the existence assertion for the securities held by the auditee?

A. Examination of paid checks issued in payment of securities purchased.

B. Vouching all changes during the year to supporting documents.

C. Simultaneous count of liquid assets.

D. Confirmation from the custodian.

Answer (A) is correct. *(Publisher)*
**REQUIRED:** The audit procedure giving the least assurance of the existence of securities.
**DISCUSSION:** Paid checks issued in payment for securities do not assure that the investments are in existence and still owned by the client at the balance sheet date.
Answer (B) is incorrect because vouching changes in the account to supporting documents provides evidence of both purchases and sales. Answer (C) is incorrect because a simultaneous count of securities, cash, and other liquid assets is the ideal way to verify the investment balance. Answer (D) is incorrect because a confirmation request sent by the auditor directly to a bank, broker, or other holder is a means of independently identifying which securities are in existence and owned by the client.

**179.** A company makes a practice of investing excess short-term cash in trading securities that are traded regularly on national exchanges. A reliable test of the valuation of these securities is

A. Consideration of current market quotations.

B. Confirmation of securities held by the broker.

C. Recalculation of investment value using a valuation model.

D. Calculation of premium or discount amortization.

Answer (A) is correct. *(CIA, adapted)*
**REQUIRED:** The reliable test of the valuation of trading securities.
**DISCUSSION:** Trading and available-for-sale securities should be measured on the statement of financial position at fair value. If market quotations are based on sufficient market activity, they usually provide sufficient competent evidence regarding valuation (AU 332, *Auditing Derivative Investments, Hedging Activities, and Investments in Securities*).
Answer (B) is incorrect because, although confirmation of securities held by the broker addresses the existence and rights and obligations assertions, it does not determine the valuation of the securities. Answer (C) is incorrect because valuation models may be used for certain securities when no quoted market prices exist. In that case, the auditor should assess the reasonableness and appropriateness of the model. Answer (D) is incorrect because any discount or premium on trading securities is not amortized.

**180.** An auditee is holding equity securities as collateral for a debt. The auditor should

A. Determine from data published in the financial press that the auditee has recorded dividend income from the collateral.

B. Ascertain the value of the securities.

C. Ascertain that the amount recorded for the collateral in the investment account is equal to its fair value at the balance sheet date.

D. Verify that the client has taken title to the securities.

Answer (B) is correct. *(Publisher)*
**REQUIRED:** The proper audit procedure for securities held as collateral.
**DISCUSSION:** A client may hold an asset of another company as security for an outstanding debt. If the asset is important for evaluating the fair value and collectibility of the investment (the debt), the auditor should obtain evidence about the client's rights and the existence, fair value, and transferability of the collateral. Current market quotations from financial publications or from national exchanges and NASDAQ usually provide sufficient evidence of the value of regularly traded securities.
Answer (A) is incorrect because the client (creditor) has no dividend income from the collateral. The debtor still owns the securities and earns the income, although the client may apply cash dividends to reduce the debt. Answer (C) is incorrect because the collateral is not recorded as a client investment until the debtor defaults and the client obtains title. Answer (D) is incorrect because the client will take title from the debtor only if the debt is not paid.

**181.** Which of the following is the most effective audit procedure for verification of dividends earned on investments in equity securities?

A. Tracing deposited dividend checks to the cash receipts book.

B. Reconciling amounts received with published dividend records.

C. Comparing the amounts received with preceding year dividends received.

D. Recomputing selected extensions and footings of dividend schedules and comparing totals to the general ledger.

Answer (B) is correct. *(CPA, adapted)*

**REQUIRED:** The most effective audit procedure for verification of dividends earned.

**DISCUSSION:** Standard investment advisory services publish dividend records for all listed stocks. They show amounts and payment dates for dividend declarations and permit the auditor to independently recompute the client's reported dividend income.

Answer (A) is incorrect because tracing deposited checks does not test whether all checks were deposited. Answer (C) is incorrect because dividends may vary from period to period. Answer (D) is incorrect because recomputation tests the arithmetic accuracy of the records, not their validity.

**182.** Auditors may need to plan and perform auditing procedures for financial statement assertions about derivatives and hedging activities. Which of the following substantive procedures most clearly tests the completeness assertion about derivatives?

A. Assessing the reasonableness of the use of an option-pricing model.

B. Determining whether changes in the fair value of derivatives designated and qualifying as hedging instruments have been reported in earnings or in other comprehensive income.

C. Requesting counterparties to provide information about them, such as whether side agreements have been made.

D. Physically inspecting the derivative contract.

Answer (C) is correct. *(Publisher)*

**REQUIRED:** The substantive procedure that most clearly tests the completeness assertion about derivatives.

**DISCUSSION:** An audit of completeness assertions addresses whether derivatives are recognized or disclosed in the financial statements, that is, in earnings, other comprehensive income, or cash flows or through disclosure. An example of a substantive procedure for the completeness assertion about derivatives and securities is a request to the counterparty to a derivative or the holder of a security for information about it, for example, whether an agreement exists to repurchase securities sold or whether side agreements have been made. A request might also be made to counterparties or holders who are frequently used, but who the accounting records indicate do not currently stand in that relationship to the reporting entity (AU 332).

Answer (A) is incorrect because assessing the reasonableness of the use of an option-pricing model tests the valuation assertion. Answer (B) is incorrect because determining whether changes in the fair value of derivatives designated and qualifying as hedging instruments have been reported in earnings or in other comprehensive income tests the presentation assertion. Answer (D) is incorrect because physically inspecting the derivative contract tests the existence assertion.

**183.** In establishing the existence and ownership of an investment held by a corporation in the form of publicly traded stock, an auditor should inspect the securities or

A. Obtain written representations from management confirming that the securities are properly classified as trading securities.

B. Inspect the audited financial statements of the investee company.

C. Confirm the number of shares owned that are held by an independent custodian.

D. Determine that the investment is carried at the lower of cost or market.

Answer (C) is correct. *(CPA, adapted)*

**REQUIRED:** The procedure to establish the existence and ownership of an investment in stock.

**DISCUSSION:** To test the existence assertion and the rights and obligations (ownership) assertion, the auditor should perform one or more of the following procedures depending on the nature of the investments and the assessment of audit risk: inspection; confirmation with the issuer, custodian, or counterparty; confirmation of unsettled transactions with the broker-dealer; or reading partnership or similar agreements (AU 332). Thus, brokers, banks, agents, or others holding securities for the client should be requested by the client to respond directly to the auditor's confirmation requests.

Answer (A) is incorrect because the classification of securities relates to the presentation and disclosure assertion. Furthermore, equity securities held for long-term investment purposes are classified as available-for-sale, not trading. Answer (B) is incorrect because an investment accounted for using the equity method might require the auditor to inspect audited financial statements of the investee to test the assertion about valuation. Answer (D) is incorrect because determining the carrying amount does not test the existence and rights and obligations assertions. Furthermore, equity securities with readily determinable fair values accounted for under SFAS 115, *Accounting for Certain Investments in Debt and Equity Securities*, are recorded at fair value.

**184.** In connection with an audit of the prepaid insurance account, which of the following procedures is usually not performed by the auditor?

A. Recompute the portion of the premium that expired during the year.

B. Prepare excerpts of insurance policies for audit documentation.

C. Confirm premium rates with an independent insurance broker.

D. Examine support for premium payments.

Answer (C) is correct. *(CPA, adapted)*

**REQUIRED:** The procedure not usually performed when auditing prepaid insurance.

**DISCUSSION:** The objectives of the audit of prepayments include determining that amounts shown reflect all prepayments, are properly valued according to GAAP, apply to future periods, are expected to be realized (to provide future benefits), and are accurately classified. Ascertaining that a prepayment is properly valued involves verifying the amount of the expenditure by examining invoices from insurers, canceled checks, and the insurance policy. The auditor does not usually confirm premium rates with an independent insurance broker. Paid checks and other documents are sufficient evidence of the amounts paid.

Answer (A) is incorrect because recomputing the portion of the premium that expired during the year is an appropriate procedure. Answer (B) is incorrect because preparing excerpts of insurance policies for audit documentation is an appropriate procedure. Answer (D) is incorrect because examining support for premium payments is an appropriate procedure.

**185.** When auditing prepaid insurance, an auditor discovers that the original insurance policy on plant equipment is not available for inspection. The policy's absence most likely indicates the possibility of a(n)

A. Insurance premium due but not recorded.

B. Deficiency in the coinsurance provision.

C. Lien on the plant equipment.

D. Understatement of insurance expense.

Answer (C) is correct. *(CPA, adapted)*

**REQUIRED:** The likely reason an insurance policy is not available for inspection.

**DISCUSSION:** When liens are placed on equipment or property, the lienholder often requires that the assets be insured and that the lienholder be named as the beneficiary of the insurance. Hence, the policy would likely be held by the lienholder even though the client is required to pay the premiums.

Answer (A) is incorrect because the premium has been paid and recorded as prepaid insurance. Answer (B) is incorrect because coinsurance provisions require that the policy holder maintain coverage of a certain percentage of the value of the property (often 80-90%). Answer (D) is incorrect because the issue is not the recording of insurance, but the physical existence of the policy.

**186.** An auditor is most likely to verify the interest earned on bond investments by

A. Verifying the receipt and deposit of interest checks.

B. Confirming the bond interest rate with the issuer of the bonds.

C. Recomputing the interest earned on the basis of face amount, interest rate, and period held.

D. Testing controls relevant to cash receipts.

Answer (C) is correct. *(CPA, adapted)*

**REQUIRED:** The method most likely used to verify bond interest earned.

**DISCUSSION:** The audit program for investments includes making an independent computation of revenue (such as dividends and interest). For example, bond certificates contain information about interest rates, payment dates, issue date, and face amount that the auditor can use to recalculate bond interest earned, including amounts accrued but not collected, during the period the auditee has held the investment.

Answer (A) is incorrect because verifying the receipt and deposit of interest checks does not consider accrued interest. Answer (B) is incorrect because confirming the bond interest rate does not, by itself, verify interest earned; the interest earned must be recomputed. Answer (D) is incorrect because verification of interest earned requires substantive testing, not tests of controls.

**187.** Deferred charges, such as issue cost of debt or cost of factory rearrangement, should usually be

A. Disallowed by the auditor.

B. Reported on the balance sheet as a noncurrent asset.

C. Written off immediately as a current operating expense.

D. Converted to deferred credits by periodic transactions.

Answer (B) is correct. *(Publisher)*

**REQUIRED:** The proper disposition of deferred charges.

**DISCUSSION:** Deferred charges that are allocable to the operations of several years should be classified separately as noncurrent assets. The auditor's objective in examining deferred charges is to determine that they are proper charges to future operations and that their amounts and allocation are reported fairly in accordance with GAAP.

Answer (A) is incorrect because deferred charges established in accordance with GAAP are proper assets and may be presented in the balance sheet. Answer (C) is incorrect because deferred charges are assets. They provide probable future economic benefits controllable by the entity that arise from past transactions or events. Answer (D) is incorrect because deferred charges cannot be converted into deferred credits.

**188.** The auditor, in determining whether the client has adopted the appropriate accounting method for an investment in the voting stock of an investee that is not consolidated, should obtain evidence primarily by

A. Inquiries to the client as to whether the client can exercise significant influence over the investee.

B. Direct confirmation with the investee concerning the control or influence that can be exercised by the client.

C. Comparison of the number of shares held by the investor with the investee's number of shares outstanding according to the written confirmation.

D. An independent, third party's opinion concerning the potential influence or control that can be exercised by the client over the investee.

Answer (A) is correct. *(Publisher)*

**REQUIRED:** The procedure to be used in assessing whether the client has properly accounted for investments.

**DISCUSSION:** An entity that is not required to consolidate an investee may nevertheless exercise significant influence over it. Significant influence, which is rebuttably presumed if the investor holds 20% to 50% of the voting stock, requires the entity to account for the investee using the equity method (APB 18, *Equity Method for Investments in Common Stock*). Thus, the auditor should inquire of the investor's management concerning the client's ability to exercise significant influence over the investee. The auditor should also inquire as to the circumstances serving as a basis for management's conclusions.

Answer (B) is incorrect because inquiry should be made of the client. The investee might not want to disclose that the client has such influence. Answer (C) is incorrect because significant influence may depend more upon the diversity of ownership of the investee than the number of shares held by the client. Answer (D) is incorrect because the auditor normally considers management's responses to inquiries in conjunction with the attendant circumstances as a basis for the conclusion.

**189.** Which of the following provides the best form of evidence pertaining to the annual valuation of an investment in which the independent auditor's client owns a 30% voting interest?

A. Market quotations of the investee company's stock.

B. Current fair value of the investee company's assets.

C. Historical cost of the investee company's assets.

D. Audited financial statements of the investee company.

Answer (D) is correct. *(CPA, adapted)*

**REQUIRED:** The best evidence for valuation of a 30% voting interest.

**DISCUSSION:** Because a 30% voting interest creates a presumption that the investor is able to exercise significant influence over the investee, the equity method of accounting for the investment must be used. This method requires the investor to recognize the appropriate percentage of the investee's earnings as a debit to the investment and a credit to income. Dividends reduce the investment. Audited financial statements of the investee are usually sufficient evidence regarding the investor's equity.

Answer (A) is incorrect because market quotations may provide sufficient evidence regarding the fair value of the securities but not the equity in net assets and results of operations of the investee. Answer (B) is incorrect because the relevant valuation is of the equity in net assets and results of operations. Answer (C) is incorrect because an equity method investment is not carried at historical cost.

**190.** A corporate balance sheet indicates that one of the corporate assets is a patent. An auditor will most likely obtain evidence regarding the continuing validity and existence of this patent by obtaining a written representation from

A. A patent attorney.

B. A regional state patent office.

C. The patent inventor.

D. The patent owner.

Answer (A) is correct. *(CPA, adapted)*

**REQUIRED:** The appropriate source of evidence of the validity and existence of a patent.

**DISCUSSION:** A patent is an intangible asset representing a governmental grant of rights to an invention for a specified time. Its lack of physical substance makes it hard to verify its existence and ownership. To obtain evidence regarding the continuing validity and existence of a patent, the auditor should obtain a written representation from a patent attorney, an independent specialist who has expertise not normally possessed by auditors. The attorney can perform the necessary research and express an opinion on which the auditor may reasonably rely.

Answer (B) is incorrect because patents are obtained from the U.S. Patent and Trademark Office of the Department of Commerce. There are no state or regional patent offices in the United States. Answer (C) is incorrect because the inventor may have no current knowledge of the status of the patent. Answer (D) is incorrect because the owner is usually the client. The auditor needs independent evidence to corroborate client representations.

**191.** In verifying the amount of goodwill recorded by a client in the current period, the most convincing evidence an auditor can obtain is by comparing the recorded amounts of assets acquired and liabilities assumed with the

A. Assessed values as evidenced by tax bills.

B. Seller's carrying amounts as evidenced by financial statements.

C. Insured values as evidenced by insurance policies.

D. Fair values as evidenced by independent appraisals.

Answer (D) is correct. *(CPA, adapted)*

**REQUIRED:** The most convincing evidence concerning goodwill recorded by a client.

**DISCUSSION:** Goodwill is recorded in a business combination when the price paid for the net assets acquired exceeds the sum of their fair values. If the carrying amount of an investment reflects (1) factors, such as goodwill, not recognized by the investee, or (2) fair values materially different from the investee's carrying amounts, the auditor should consider obtaining current appraisals of these amounts. Evaluations by persons independent of the investor and investee usually provide greater assurance of reliability than those by persons associated with those companies, although evaluations by associated parties may be acceptable. The acquiring entity should subsequently test goodwill for impairment at least annually.

Answer (A) is incorrect because a tax bill is an assessment on physical asset value only, not on the entity's going concern value. Answer (B) is incorrect because the seller's financial statements reflect the historical cost to the acquired company, not current fair value. Answer (C) is incorrect because the client may not even have insured the full fair value of the physical assets, much less the presumably greater going concern value of the business.

**192.** The auditor can best verify a client's bond sinking-fund transactions and year-end balance by

A. Confirmation with individual holders of retired bonds.

B. Confirmation with the bond trustee.

C. Recomputation of interest expense, interest payable, and amortization of bond discount or premium.

D. Examination and count of the bonds retired during the year.

Answer (B) is correct. *(CPA, adapted)*

**REQUIRED:** The best way to verify a client's bond sinking-fund transactions.

**DISCUSSION:** The bond trustee is an outside, independent agent responsible for maintaining subsidiary ledgers and paying dividends. (S)he also often keeps the sinking-fund accounts. Consequently, the auditor should verify bond sinking-fund transactions with this trustee.

Answer (A) is incorrect because confirmation with individual holders of retired bonds provides some evidence relative to the retirement process, but not of the balance in the sinking fund or of the transactions during the year. Answer (C) is incorrect because it is only part of the overall procedure of which trustee confirmation is the most important step. Answer (D) is incorrect because examination and count of the bonds retired during the year provides some evidence relative to the retirement process, but not of the balance in the sinking fund or of the transactions during the year.

**193.** The best audit procedure for determining the existence of open commodity futures contracts at year-end is the review of

A. Canceled checks in the subsequent period.

B. Available broker trade advices.

C. The replies to the standard confirmation requests sent to financial institutions.

D. Direct confirmations with the client's commodity traders.

Answer (D) is correct. *(CPA, adapted)*

**REQUIRED:** The best audit procedure for determining the existence of open commodity futures contracts.

**DISCUSSION:** Direct confirmation with the client's commodity traders provides independent verification of open commodity futures contracts and may reveal undisclosed liabilities.

Answer (A) is incorrect because payment for futures would have been made when the contract was made. Answer (B) is incorrect because the auditor is concerned that obligations be fairly represented. It is possible to lose or destroy trade advices. Answer (C) is incorrect because the standard form inquires specifically about deposit balances and direct liabilities to the financial institution. The client's bank or other financial institution would not likely have information relative to open commodity futures contracts. The client's broker is the independent party with first-hand knowledge.

## 4.9 Long-Term Debt and Other Liabilities

**194.** An auditor's program to audit long-term debt should include steps that require

A. Examining bond trust indentures.

B. Inspecting the accounts payable subsidiary ledger.

C. Investigating credits to the bond interest income account.

D. Verifying the existence of the bondholders.

Answer (A) is correct. *(CPA, adapted)*

**REQUIRED:** The procedure to be included in the audit program for long-term debt.

**DISCUSSION:** The bond trust indenture contains information concerning contractual arrangements made with bondholders, such as the face amount of the bonds, interest rates, payment dates, descriptions of collateral, provisions for conversion or retirement, trustee duties, and sinking-fund requirements. The auditor should examine any bond trust indenture to determine that the client is complying with its terms and with the law.

Answer (B) is incorrect because accounts payable are current liabilities, not long-term debt. Answer (C) is incorrect because credits to bond interest income do not pertain to long-term debt (income relates to investments, not debt). Answer (D) is incorrect because the existence of bondholders is implied by the reporting of bonded debt.

**195.** In an audit of bonds payable, an auditor expects the trust indenture to include the

A. Auditee's debt-to-equity ratio at the time of issuance.

B. Effective yield of the bonds issued.

C. Subscription list.

D. Description of the collateral.

Answer (D) is correct. *(Publisher)*

**REQUIRED:** The information in a bond trust indenture.

**DISCUSSION:** A bond trust indenture is the contractual agreement between the bondholders and the bond issuer. It contains the date of issue and the date of maturity of the bond issue as well as the amount of the bonds, interest rates, payment dates, descriptions of collateral, provisions for conversion or retirement, trustee duties, sinking-fund requirements, and restrictions on the borrower.

Answer (A) is incorrect because current financial ratios are usually not included, but restrictive ratios may be; e.g., the debt-to-equity ratio might not be permitted to exceed 2 to 1. Answer (B) is incorrect because the effective yield to maturity of the bonds issued may be calculated from the premium or discount and the stated interest rate, but is not included in the trust indenture. Answer (C) is incorrect because the subscriptions list contains the names of the original subscribers, but these names are not normally included in the trust indenture.

**196.** During an audit of a publicly held company, the auditor should obtain written confirmation regarding debenture transactions from the

A. Debenture holders.

B. Client's attorney.

C. Internal auditors.

D. Trustee.

Answer (D) is correct. *(CPA, adapted)*

**REQUIRED:** The source of confirmation of debenture transactions.

**DISCUSSION:** Debentures are bonds backed by the general credit of the issuer and not secured by specific assets. A bond issuer normally employs the services of an independent financial institution as trustee. The bond trustee is responsible for executing bond transactions, e.g., distributing or paying interest, and protecting the interests of bondholders. Accordingly, the auditor should confirm transactions with the trustee.

Answer (A) is incorrect because direct communication with bondholders is unnecessary when a trustee is used. Answer (B) is incorrect because the client's attorney does not have the information necessary to furnish independent evidence regarding bond transactions. Answer (C) is incorrect because internal auditors are not knowledgeable about bond transaction details or independent.

**197.** With respect to bonds issued during the period under audit, the independent external auditor should

A. Inspect the records maintained by the bond trustee.

B. Determine that the net cash received equaled the face amount of the bonds payable.

C. Determine that the amount sold does not exceed the amount authorized.

D. Confirm the existence of the bondholders.

Answer (C) is correct. *(Publisher)*

**REQUIRED:** The proper audit procedure for a new issue of bonds.

**DISCUSSION:** Bonds issued during the year under audit should be traced to the minutes of the shareholders' or board of directors' meetings to check for proper authorization. The amount sold should be no greater than the amount authorized in the minutes.

Answer (A) is incorrect because an auditor usually can rely on the confirmation of information with the bond trustee (who is usually an independent third party). Answer (B) is incorrect because the credit to the bonds payable account should be for the face value of the bonds. The debit to cash will not ordinarily equal face value because bonds are usually issued at a premium or a discount. Answer (D) is incorrect because bondholder rights exist on the basis of the sale of bonds; a liability for interest and principal exists irrespective of who and where the bondholders are.

**198.** With respect to bonds issued during the period under audit, the auditor should

A. Review proper presentation and disclosure in the financial statements.

B. Consider whether the bond issue complied with applicable laws and regulations.

C. Calculate the effective interest rate to see if it is substantially the same as the rates for similar issues.

D. Determine that bonds are not owned by directors or officers of the company.

Answer (A) is correct. *(Publisher)*

**REQUIRED:** The audit procedure relevant to the audit of bonds payable currently being issued.

**DISCUSSION:** The objectives of the audit of long-term debt are to obtain an understanding of the relevant controls and to assess control risk; ascertain that all long-term debt has been recorded and constitutes bona fide liabilities; verify that federal and state laws relative to financial reporting have been complied with; determine that premium, discount, interest payable, and interest expense are accurately recorded; monitor compliance with debt contracts; and review proper presentation and disclosure in the financial statements.

Answer (B) is incorrect because the opinion of counsel on the legality of the issue should address these matters. Answer (C) is incorrect because the effective interest rate for similar issues changes with the overall interest rate. Answer (D) is incorrect because directors or officers of a company may invest in company bonds.

**199.** An auditor's purpose in reviewing the renewal of a note payable shortly after the balance-sheet date most likely is to obtain evidence concerning management's assertions about

A. Existence or occurrence.

B. Presentation and disclosure.

C. Completeness.

D. Valuation or allocation.

Answer (B) is correct. *(CPA, adapted)*

**REQUIRED:** The purpose in reviewing the renewal of a note payable shortly after the balance-sheet date.

**DISCUSSION:** The auditor should be aware of transactions occurring shortly after year-end to determine the impact on the year-end balances and disclosures. Subsequent events occur after the balance-sheet date but prior to the issuance of the financial statements. They provide information about conditions that did or did not exist at the balance-sheet date. Events that did not exist at the balance sheet date, such as the renewal of the note payable, do not require adjustment of the financial statements but may require disclosure (AU 560, *Subsequent Events*). Accordingly, the auditor should determine that the note payable renewal had essentially the same terms and conditions as the recorded debt at year-end. A significant change may affect the presentation of notes payable, the interpretation of the year-end financial statements, and the required disclosures in the notes.

Answer (A) is incorrect because the renewal does not significantly affect the other noted assertions about existence or occurrence. Answer (C) is incorrect because the renewal does not significantly affect the other noted assertions about completeness. Answer (D) is incorrect because the renewal does not significantly affect the other noted assertions about valuation or allocation.

**200.** During the year under audit, a company has completed a private placement of a substantial amount of bonds. Which of the following is the most important step in the auditor's program for the audit of bonds payable?

A. Confirming the amount issued with the bond trustee.

B. Tracing the cash received from the issue to the accounting records.

C. Examining the bond records maintained by the transfer agent.

D. Recomputing the annual interest cost and the effective yield.

Answer (B) is correct. *(CPA, adapted)*

**REQUIRED:** The most important step in auditing a private placement of bonds.

**DISCUSSION:** In a private placement of bonds, one not involving the use of an independent trustee, the auditor is most concerned that the cash received from the issue is accurately recorded. The auditor is also concerned that the cash is adequately safeguarded by the treasurer's department. Failure to employ a trustee substantially increases control risk for all aspects of bond issues.

Answer (A) is incorrect because a bond trustee is not apt to be used by the issuer if bonds are privately placed. Answer (C) is incorrect because a transfer agent is not apt to be used by the issuer if bonds are privately placed. Answer (D) is incorrect because the mathematical check of the accuracy of the annual interest cost and the effective yield is not as important as the auditor's verification that cash received is properly accounted for.

**201.** During an audit, Wicks learns that the audit client was granted a 3-month waiver of the repayment of principal on the installment loan with Blank Bank without an extension of the maturity date. With respect to this loan, the audit program used by Wicks is least likely to include a verification of the

A. Interest expense for the year.

B. Balloon payment.

C. Total liability at year-end.

D. Installment loan payments.

Answer (B) is correct. *(CPA, adapted)*

**REQUIRED:** The item least likely to be verified in the audit of an installment loan.

**DISCUSSION:** The auditor's primary concern is that the liability is reported correctly in the financial statements. The amount of the balloon payment falling due in a future period as a result of the waiver is of less importance.

Answer (A) is incorrect because the auditor should verify interest expense to determine that it is recorded properly and determine the applicability of SFAS 15, *Accounting by Debtors and Creditors for Troubled Debt Restructurings*. Answer (C) is incorrect because becoming satisfied as to the total liability at year-end is a primary objective of the auditor. Answer (D) is incorrect because the amount of installment loan payments determines the amount of the current liability at year-end.

**202.** Several years ago, Conway, Inc. secured a conventional real estate mortgage loan. Which of the following audit procedures is least likely to be performed by an auditor auditing the mortgage balance?

A. Examine the current year's canceled checks.

B. Review the mortgage amortization schedule.

C. Inspect public records of lien balances.

D. Recompute mortgage interest expense.

Answer (C) is correct. *(CPA, adapted)*

**REQUIRED:** The audit procedure least likely to be performed regarding a mortgage loan.

**DISCUSSION:** Public real estate records will not disclose the current balance. They only disclose the original amount of the mortgage. Other evidence is normally available, such as receipts for payments to the mortgagee and confirmations with payees.

Answer (A) is incorrect because canceled checks represent the decrease in the mortgage balance and should be inspected by the auditor. Answer (B) is incorrect because the mortgage amortization schedule is evidence of the amount that should have been paid during the period as well as the principal balance at year-end. Answer (D) is incorrect because the recomputation of interest expense and interest payable is an important means of verifying the amount of outstanding liabilities.

**203.** In auditing long-term bonds payable, an auditor most likely will

A. Perform analytical procedures on the bond premium and discount accounts.

B. Examine documentation of assets purchased with bond proceeds for liens.

C. Compare interest expense with the bond payable amount for reasonableness.

D. Confirm the existence of individual bondholders at year-end.

Answer (C) is correct. *(CPA, adapted)*

**REQUIRED:** The appropriate procedure for testing long-term bonds payable.

**DISCUSSION:** The recorded interest expense should reconcile with the outstanding bonds payable. If interest expense appears excessive relative to the recorded bonds payable, unrecorded liabilities may exist.

Answer (A) is incorrect because analytical procedures on the bond premium and discount accounts are not likely to be effective in uncovering potential unrecorded payables. Answer (B) is incorrect because the examination of documentation related to assets is considered in the audit of assets, not bonds payable. Answer (D) is incorrect because a confirmation tests existence, but the greatest audit risk is that the bonds payable balance is not complete.

**204.** The audit procedures used to verify accrued liabilities differ from those employed for the verification of accounts payable because

A. Accrued liabilities usually pertain to services of a continuing nature while accounts payable are the result of completed transactions.

B. Accrued liability balances are less material than accounts payable balances.

C. Evidence supporting accrued liabilities is nonexistent while evidence supporting accounts payable is readily available.

D. Accrued liabilities at year-end will become accounts payable during the following year.

Answer (A) is correct. *(CPA, adapted)*

**REQUIRED:** The difference between audit procedures used to verify accrued liabilities and those used to verify accounts payable.

**DISCUSSION:** The procedures differ because the balances result from different transactional processes. Liabilities are accrued for such continuing transactions as rent, salaries, and interest. Accounts payable are short-term obligations arising from the purchase of goods and services in the ordinary course of business.

Answer (B) is incorrect because one balance is not inherently more or less material than the other. Answer (C) is incorrect because supporting documentary evidence exists for both. Answer (D) is incorrect because, once accrued liabilities become accounts payable (not necessarily at year-end), the audit procedures do not differ.

**205.** The auditor is most likely to verify accrued commissions payable in conjunction with the

A. Sales cutoff test.

B. Verification of contingent liabilities.

C. Review of post balance sheet date disbursements.

D. Examination of trade accounts payable.

Answer (A) is correct. *(CPA, adapted)*

**REQUIRED:** The audit step performed concurrently with verifying accrued commissions payable.

**DISCUSSION:** Sales commissions and accrued sales commissions payable are based upon sales of the period. The auditor verifies accrued commissions payable in conjunction with procedures applied to the sales cutoff test. The purpose is to obtain reasonable assurance that revenues and related liabilities are recorded in the same period in accordance with the matching principle.

Answer (B) is incorrect because the auditor would review the minutes of board meetings, send an inquiry letter to the client's legal counsel, send bank confirmations, obtain a representation letter from the client, and review correspondence with financial institutions to verify or detect contingent liabilities. Answer (C) is incorrect because the review of disbursements in the subsequent period is performed to detect unrecorded liabilities. Answer (D) is incorrect because the examination of trade accounts payable is performed in conjunction with the audit of inventories, purchases, and cash disbursements.

**206.** SFAS 5, *Accounting for Contingencies*, defines a loss contingency and states the requirements for recognition as a charge to income and a credit to an accrued liability. An accrual could not be made as a result of

A. Guarantees of indebtedness incurred by others.

B. Repurchase commitments.

C. Pending litigation or threats of expropriation.

D. General business risks.

Answer (D) is correct. *(Publisher)*

**REQUIRED:** The impermissible basis for accruing a contingent liability and recognizing a loss.

**DISCUSSION:** General business risks do not provide a possible basis for accrual of a contingent liability because "not all uncertainties inherent in the accounting process give rise to contingencies" (SFAS 5). General or unspecified business risks cannot meet the conditions for accrual: the loss is probable at the balance-sheet date, and it can be reasonably estimated.

Answer (A) is incorrect because guarantees of indebtedness incurred by others are listed in SFAS 5 as loss contingencies. Furthermore, if the conditions for accrual of a loss contingency are not met, the guarantor still must record a liability (a noncontingent obligation) for the fair value of the guarantee. If the conditions are met, the greater of the amount of the contingent liability or the fair value of the guarantee is recorded (FASB Interpretation No. 45). Answer (B) is incorrect because repurchase commitments are listed in SFAS 5 as loss contingencies. Answer (C) is incorrect because pending litigation or threats of expropriation are listed in SFAS 5 as loss contingencies.

**207.** In an audit for the fiscal year ended on December 31, 20X0, the auditor discovered that a debit had been made on January 15, 20X1, to a notes receivable account from the cash disbursements journal. This entry may indicate that a

A. Receivable has been established from a party for whom the client has guaranteed a debt.

B. Provision for contingencies is required.

C. Contingent liability was created in 20X1.

D. Contingent asset has been recognized.

Answer (A) is correct. *(Publisher)*

**REQUIRED:** The implication of a debit made to notes receivable and a credit made to cash.

**DISCUSSION:** The entry suggests that a contingent liability has become a real liability and has been settled. The payment of the debt upon default of the party would be recognized in the accounts by a debit to notes receivable and a credit to cash.

Answer (B) is incorrect because no provision for contingencies is needed if the liability has been paid. Answer (C) is incorrect because the entry suggests that a contingent liability became an actual liability and has been paid. Answer (D) is incorrect because contingent assets are never recognized in the accounts until realized. Contingent liabilities are recognized when they are probable and they are subject to reasonable estimation.

## 4.10 Equity

**208.** In an audit of equity, an auditor is most concerned that

A. Capital stock transactions are properly authorized.

B. Stock splits are capitalized at par or stated value on the dividend declaration date.

C. Dividends during the year under audit were approved by the shareholders.

D. Changes in the accounts are verified by a bank serving as a registrar and stock transfer agent.

Answer (A) is correct. *(Publisher)*

**REQUIRED:** The most important consideration when auditing the equity section.

**DISCUSSION:** A primary concern of the auditor is that all capital stock transactions are properly authorized. Accordingly, all entries in the capital stock account should be vouched to the minutes of the board of directors' meetings. The articles of incorporation, by-laws, and minutes of shareholders' meetings should also be reviewed. The auditor requires information about the number and rights of shares authorized and issued, the par or stated value, conversion and call features, stock dividends, and stock splits. The auditor also determines whether transactions are properly accounted for and equity items are presented in accordance with GAAP.

Answer (B) is incorrect because stock splits require no transfer from retained earnings. Answer (C) is incorrect because the board of directors usually approves dividends. Answer (D) is incorrect because the registrar and transfer agent, who is responsible for increases and exchanges of stock, is not responsible for monitoring all changes in the accounts.

**209.** In the audit of a medium-sized manufacturing concern, which one of the following areas can be expected to require the least amount of audit time?

A. Equity.

B. Revenue.

C. Assets.

D. Liabilities.

Answer (A) is correct. *(CPA, adapted)*

**REQUIRED:** The area requiring the least audit time for a medium-sized company.

**DISCUSSION:** Transactions affecting equity are usually few even though they may be significant in amount. Consequently, the audit time required will probably be small compared to that needed for active accounts. Equity will ordinarily be affected only by stock issuances, treasury stock transactions, dividends, and closing entries.

Answer (B) is incorrect because the auditor will usually spend more time on revenues than on equity. Answer (C) is incorrect because the auditor will usually spend more time on assets than on equity. Answer (D) is incorrect because the auditor will usually spend more time on liabilities than on equity.

**210.** Mayer, CPA, is auditing equity. Tests typically include all the following except

A. Reviewing the bank reconciliation for the imprest dividend account.

B. Tracing individual dividend payments to the capital stock records.

C. Verifying the authorization of dividends by inspecting the directors' minutes.

D. Determining that dividend declarations comply with debt agreements.

Answer (B) is correct. *(Publisher)*

**REQUIRED:** The procedure not normally performed in an audit of equity.

**DISCUSSION:** An auditor does not normally trace individual dividend payments to the capital stock records. (S)he may test certain large dividend payments but, because the amount of each dividend is usually small, detail checking is minimal. The need for extensive checking is reduced when the client uses an independent financial institution as its agent for dividend payments. The stock transfer agent often performs this function because it maintains detailed records of shareholders.

Answer (A) is incorrect because reviewing the bank reconciliation for the imprest dividend account is an appropriate auditing procedure. Answer (C) is incorrect because verifying the authorization of dividends is an appropriate auditing procedure. Answer (D) is incorrect because determining that dividend declarations comply with debt agreements is an appropriate auditing procedure.

**211.** When a corporate client maintains its own stock records, the auditor primarily will rely upon

A. Confirmation with the company secretary of shares outstanding at year-end.

B. Review of the corporate minutes for data as to shares outstanding.

C. Confirmation of the number of shares outstanding at year-end with the appropriate state official.

D. Inspection of the stock book at year-end and accounting for all certificate numbers.

Answer (D) is correct. *(Publisher)*

**REQUIRED:** The appropriate procedure when a company is its own registrar and transfer agent.

**DISCUSSION:** When an independent registrar and a stock transfer agent are employed by the client, the auditor may simply confirm the shares issued and outstanding at year-end. But when the client acts as its own registrar and transfer agent, the auditor should perform procedures equivalent to independent confirmations. (S)he should account for stock certificate numbers, examine all canceled certificates, and reconcile the subsidiary shareholder ledger with the general ledger.

Answer (A) is incorrect because confirmations are usually sent to independent parties. Answer (B) is incorrect because the minutes indicate the number of shares authorized, not the number outstanding. Answer (C) is incorrect because state officials and officers do not maintain records as to the number of a corporation's outstanding shares.

**212.** When a client company does not maintain its own stock records, the auditor should obtain written confirmation from the transfer agent and registrar concerning

A. Restrictions on the payment of dividends.

B. The number of shares issued and outstanding.

C. Guarantees of preferred stock liquidation value.

D. The number of shares subject to agreements to repurchase.

Answer (B) is correct. *(CPA, adapted)*

**REQUIRED:** The information confirmed by the transfer agent and registrar.

**DISCUSSION:** The independent stock registrar is a financial institution employed to prevent improper issuances of stock, especially over-issuances. It verifies that each issue is properly authorized by the articles of incorporation and properly issued by the stock transfer agent. New stock certificates are examined and registered by the registrar before being issued. The stock transfer agent maintains detailed shareholder records and facilitates transfer of shares. Both are independent and reliable sources of evidence concerning total shares issued and outstanding at year-end. The trend has been to combine their functions.

Answer (A) is incorrect because the articles of incorporation, bylaws, and minutes of directors' and shareholders' meetings are potential sources of this information. Answer (C) is incorrect because guarantees of preferred stock liquidation value are beyond the purview of the transfer agent and registrar. Answer (D) is incorrect because the number of shares subject to agreements to repurchase is approved by the board of directors.

**213.** A company declared and paid a stock dividend. Its independent external auditor should determine that

A. The officers authorized the issuance of the stock dividend.

B. The stock dividend was properly recorded by means of a memorandum entry only.

C. Shareholders received their additional shares by confirming year-end holdings with them.

D. Appropriate amounts were transferred from retained earnings to capital stock and additional paid-in capital.

Answer (D) is correct. *(Publisher)*

**REQUIRED:** The appropriate audit procedure when a company has declared a stock dividend.

**DISCUSSION:** The auditor should gather evidence that the stock dividend was properly authorized by the board of directors and does not result in the issuance of shares in excess of the number permitted by the articles of incorporation. The auditor must also verify the amounts transferred from retained earnings to capital stock and additional paid-in capital.

Answer (A) is incorrect because, usually, only the board of directors authorizes stock and cash dividends. Answer (B) is incorrect because large stock dividends (issuances in excess of 20-25% of the shares outstanding) are capitalized at an amount specified by the applicable state statute, which is usually the par value. Small stock dividends are recorded at fair value. Answer (C) is incorrect because the auditor does not usually confirm holdings with shareholders. Instead, the auditor confirms the total shares issued and outstanding with the independent registrar and stock transfer agent.

**214.** The auditor is concerned with establishing that dividends are paid to client corporation shareholders owning stock as of the

A. Issue date.

B. Declaration date.

C. Record date.

D. Payment date.

Answer (C) is correct. *(CPA, adapted)*

**REQUIRED:** The date that establishes the right to receive a declared dividend.

**DISCUSSION:** Persons who hold stock in the corporation as of the record date are entitled to payment of the dividend. The auditor should test the dividend payment list to gather evidence that dividends were paid to the appropriate shareholders. The integrity of the dividend payment process is enhanced when an independent agent (usually a financial institution) is used to disburse dividends.

Answer (A) is incorrect because the issue date is the date the stock was issued. Answer (B) is incorrect because the declaration date is the date the company declares the amount of a dividend and specifies the date of record. Answer (D) is incorrect because, on the payment date, the dividends are paid to those shareholders who owned stock as of the record date.

**215.** The auditor does not expect the client to debit retained earnings for which of the following transactions?

A. A 10% stock dividend.

B. A 60% stock dividend.

C. A 4-for-1 stock split.

D. An appropriation of retained earnings for treasury stock.

Answer (C) is correct. *(Publisher)*

**REQUIRED:** The transaction not requiring a debit to retained earnings.

**DISCUSSION:** A 4-for-1 stock split results in an increase in the number of shares and a proportionate decrease in the par or stated value per share. No entry is recorded for a stock split. A memo entry, however, is made indicating that the par value has been changed.

Answer (A) is incorrect because a small stock dividend should be capitalized at fair value. Answer (B) is incorrect because a large stock dividend is normally capitalized at par value. Answer (D) is incorrect because crediting appropriations for treasury stock and debiting retained earnings is a necessary entry.

**216.** An audit program for the retained earnings account should include a step that requires verification of the

A. Fair value used to charge retained earnings to account for a two-for-one stock split.

B. Approval of the adjustment to the beginning balance as a result of a write-down of an account receivable.

C. Authorization for both cash and stock dividends.

D. Gain or loss resulting from disposition of treasury shares.

Answer (C) is correct. *(CPA, adapted)*

**REQUIRED:** The step that should be performed in the audit of retained earnings.

**DISCUSSION:** The auditor should determine from the minutes of the board of directors' meetings that proper authorization has been made for both cash and stock dividends. All dividends require transfers from (debits to) retained earnings. Thus, dividends should be audited in conjunction with retained earnings.

Answer (A) is incorrect because no change is made in retained earnings for stock splits. Answer (B) is incorrect because a write-down of accounts receivable is taken through the income statement, not directly to retained earnings. Answer (D) is incorrect because only losses on treasury stock transactions can be charged to retained earnings. Gains and some losses are taken to additional paid-in-capital accounts.

**217.** During an audit of an entity's equity accounts, the auditor determines whether there are restrictions on retained earnings resulting from loans, agreements, or state law. This audit procedure most likely is intended to verify management's assertion of

A. Existence or occurrence.

B. Completeness.

C. Valuation or allocation.

D. Presentation and disclosure.

Answer (D) is correct. *(CPA, adapted)*

**REQUIRED:** The assertion that the auditor tests relative to restrictions on retained earnings.

**DISCUSSION:** The presentation and disclosure assertion concerns the classification, description, and disclosure of financial statement components (AU 326). Hence, when restrictions have been placed on retained earnings, the auditor should determine that they are properly disclosed in the notes to the financial statements.

Answer (A) is incorrect because restrictions on retained earnings have little relevance to existence or occurrence. Answer (B) is incorrect because restrictions on retained earnings have little relevance to completeness. Answer (C) is incorrect because restrictions on retained earnings have little relevance to presentation and disclosure.

**218.** With respect to treasury stock, the auditor should not object to which of the following?

A. Restrictions on retained earnings have not been met.

B. Dividends have been paid on treasury stock.

C. The treasury stock certificates have been destroyed.

D. Treasury stock is recorded at cost rather than par value.

Answer (D) is correct. *(Publisher)*

**REQUIRED:** The appropriate treatment of treasury stock.

**DISCUSSION:** Treasury stock may be valued at cost or at par value according to GAAP.

Answer (A) is incorrect because certain states restrict retained earnings relative to treasury stock. The auditor should take exception to the failure to comply with the restriction. Answer (B) is incorrect because dividends are only paid on shares issued and outstanding. Answer (C) is incorrect because the auditor should inspect the treasury stock or confirm the stock with the custodian or registrar. Even after retirement, the certificates should be kept to provide evidence that they have not been reissued.

**219.** If the auditee has a material amount of treasury stock on hand at year-end, the auditor should

A. Count the certificates at the same time other securities are counted.

B. Count the certificates only if the company had treasury stock transactions during the year.

C. Not count the certificates if treasury stock is a deduction from equity.

D. Count the certificates only if the company classifies treasury stock with other assets.

Answer (A) is correct. *(Publisher)*

**REQUIRED:** The true statement about the audit of treasury stock.

**DISCUSSION:** All capital transactions should be verified. Thus, the auditor must count the certificates of treasury stock on hand at year-end at the same time the other securities are counted. This procedure provides direct evidence that the treasury stock exists and is in the possession of the client. Any treasury stock certificates not on hand are confirmed with the holders.

Answer (B) is incorrect because the auditor should inspect treasury stock certificates at year-end. Answer (C) is incorrect because the auditor should inspect treasury stock certificates at year-end. Answer (D) is incorrect because treasury stock is never classified as an asset.

**220.** In performing tests concerning the granting of stock options, an auditor should

A. Confirm the transaction with the Secretary of State in the state of incorporation.

B. Verify the existence of option holders in the entity's payroll records or stock ledgers.

C. Determine that sufficient treasury stock is available to cover any new stock issued.

D. Trace the authorization for the transaction to a vote of the board of directors.

Answer (D) is correct. *(CPA, adapted)*

**REQUIRED:** The tests performed by the auditor concerning the granting of stock options.

**DISCUSSION:** Equity transactions, for example, issuances of stock, purchases of treasury stock, declarations of dividends, and the issuance of stock options to employees or others, require authorization by the board of directors. Hence, the auditor should inspect minutes of board meetings to verify that stock options were granted.

Answer (A) is incorrect because the Secretary of State is not likely to have knowledge of the granting of stock options within a particular entity. Answer (B) is incorrect because the existence of option holders is not a major risk concerning the audit of stock options. Answer (C) is incorrect because the firm need not hold treasury stock at the time of granting stock options if the shares are publicly traded and can be acquired as needed or if the firm has the ability to issue new shares.

**221.** In an examination of equity, the auditor should determine that the entity reports accumulated other comprehensive income in the balance sheet in the

A. Liabilities section.

B. Equity section as a component separate from retained earnings and additional paid-in capital.

C. Retained earnings section.

D. Other assets section.

Answer (B) is correct. *(Publisher)*

**REQUIRED:** The treatment of accumulated other comprehensive income.

**DISCUSSION:** According to SFAS 130, *Reporting Comprehensive Income*, if an enterprise that reports a full set of financial statements has items of other comprehensive income, it must display comprehensive income and its components in a financial statement having the same prominence as the other statements included in the full set. No particular format is required, but net income must be shown as a component of comprehensive income in that statement. However, absent items of other comprehensive income, e.g., foreign currency items, minimum pension liability adjustments, or unrealized gains and losses on certain securities, an enterprise need not report comprehensive income. Furthermore, the total of other comprehensive income for a period is reported as a component of equity in the balance sheet separate from retained earnings and additional paid-in capital.

## 4.11 Personnel and Payroll

**222.** In an audit of payroll, an auditor is primarily concerned about

A. Excess FICA and income tax withholding.

B. Errors in employee time records.

C. Misposted payroll amounts.

D. Errors or fraud in the amount of payments.

Answer (D) is correct. *(Publisher)*

**REQUIRED:** The auditor's primary concern in an audit of payroll.

**DISCUSSION:** The auditor is primarily concerned about the possibility of errors or fraud in the amount of payment when auditing payroll transactions. Employee compensation is a major item of expense and is especially susceptible to fraud unless internal control is effective. The inherent risk for payroll transactions is increased by the need for rapid processing of a large amount of information.

Answer (A) is incorrect because excess FICA and income tax withholding is an important, but secondary, consideration. Answer (B) is incorrect because errors in employee time records is an important, but secondary, consideration. Answer (C) is incorrect because misposted payroll amounts is an important, but secondary, consideration.

**223.** In auditing payroll, an auditor most likely will

A. Verify that checks representing unclaimed wages are mailed.

B. Trace individual employee deductions to entity journal entries.

C. Observe entity employees during a payroll distribution.

D. Compare payroll costs with entity standards or budgets.

Answer (D) is correct. *(CPA, adapted)*

**REQUIRED:** The procedure used in the audit of payroll.

**DISCUSSION:** Comparing payroll costs with budgeted amounts is a standard analytical procedure that should be performed in any audit of the payroll function.

Answer (A) is incorrect because checks representing unclaimed wages should be maintained by the treasurer until claimed by the appropriate employees. Answer (B) is incorrect because the individual employee deductions will not result in entity journal entries, but the sum of the payroll will result in cumulative journal entries. Answer (C) is incorrect because observation of payroll distribution is a standard procedure but one that might not be necessary when assessed control risk is low.

**224.** Which of the following audit procedures provides the least relevant evidence in determining that payroll payments were made to bona fide employees?

A. Reconcile time cards in use to employees on the job.

B. Examine canceled checks for proper endorsement and compare with personnel records.

C. Test for segregation of the authorization for payment from the hire/fire authorization.

D. Test the payroll account bank reconciliation by tracing outstanding checks to the payroll register.

Answer (D) is correct. *(CIA, adapted)*

**REQUIRED:** The procedure that provides the least relevant evidence that payroll payments were made to bona fide employees.

**DISCUSSION:** A payroll account proof tests for completeness of the recorded transactions, not for their validity.

Answer (A) is incorrect because verification that an employee is actually working is a common procedure to test for nonexistent employees. Answer (B) is incorrect because examining for proper endorsements and comparing with records may detect improper payments. Answer (C) is incorrect because segregation of payroll authorization from employment decisions helps to eliminate the conditions in which one person can arrange payment to fictitious employees.

**225.** An auditor is most likely to perform substantive tests of details on payroll transactions and balances when

A. Cutoff tests indicate a substantial amount of accrued payroll expense.

B. The assessed level of control risk relative to payroll transactions is low.

C. Analytical procedures indicate unusual fluctuations in recurring payroll entries.

D. Accrued payroll expense consists primarily of unpaid commissions.

Answer (C) is correct. *(CPA, adapted)*

**REQUIRED:** The best reason for substantive tests of details on payroll.

**DISCUSSION:** The auditor should evaluate significant unexpected differences revealed by analytical procedures. The first step is to reconsider the methods and factors used in developing the expectations and to make inquiries of management. If a suitable explanation is not received, additional procedures to investigate the differences are necessary.

Answer (A) is incorrect because a substantial amount of accrued payroll expense is not an abnormal condition. Answer (B) is incorrect because a low assessed level of control risk may permit the auditor to devote less effort to substantive tests. Answer (D) is incorrect because the existence of unpaid earned commissions provides no indication of a misstatement.

**226.** To check the accuracy of hours worked, an auditor would ordinarily compare clock cards with

A. Personnel records.

B. Shop job time tickets.

C. Labor variance reports.

D. Time recorded in the payroll register.

Answer (B) is correct. *(CPA, adapted)*

**REQUIRED:** The item with which the auditor compares clock cards to verify hours worked.

**DISCUSSION:** The auditor should compare shop job time tickets with the clock cards to determine the accuracy of the hours worked. The job tickets, which contain the total hours worked on each job, should not vary significantly from the employee time cards used to compute payroll.

Answer (A) is incorrect because the personnel department is responsible for authorizing employment, pay rates, and employee reclassifications. The timekeeping function should be performed separately. Answer (C) is incorrect because labor variance reports only show the difference between the time budgeted and the time charged to certain jobs. Answer (D) is incorrect because the time recorded in the payroll register is taken from clock time cards.

**227.** Analytical procedures may be applied to payroll to detect unusual items. Which of the following is an appropriate analytical procedure for payroll?

A. Compare the relationship of hours worked to payroll with that of the preceding year.

B. Inspect authorizations on time cards.

C. Compare rates authorized under a union contract with payroll records.

D. Review payroll bank account reconciliation.

Answer (A) is correct. *(Publisher)*

**REQUIRED:** The analytical procedure for payroll.

**DISCUSSION:** Analytical procedures involve comparisons of recorded amounts with expectations developed by the auditor. Sources of information for developing these expectations include financial information for comparable prior periods; anticipated results, e.g., budgets and forecasts; relationships of elements of financial information within the period; industry information; and relationships of financial information with relevant nonfinancial information (AU 329). Evaluating the relationship of hours worked and payroll for the current and preceding years involves comparing financial information with relevant nonfinancial information in the light of an expectation developed based on data from a comparable prior period.

Answer (B) is incorrect because inspecting authorizations on time cards is a test of controls. Answer (C) is incorrect because comparing rates authorized under a union contract with payroll records directly tests the validity of payroll. Answer (D) is incorrect because reviewing the payroll bank account reconciliation directly tests the validity of payroll.

**228.** An auditor found that employee time cards in one department are not properly approved by the supervisor. Which of the following could result?

A. Duplicate paychecks might be issued.

B. The wrong hourly rate could be used to calculate gross pay.

C. Employees might be paid for hours they did not work.

D. Payroll checks might not be distributed to the appropriate payees.

Answer (C) is correct. *(CIA, adapted)*

**REQUIRED:** The misstatement that could occur if time cards are not approved by a supervisor.

**DISCUSSION:** The time cards report the number of hours worked. Failure to approve the time worked could result in an amount of pay inconsistent with actual hours worked.

Answer (A) is incorrect because each employee would have one time card and be issued one check based on the time card. Answer (B) is incorrect because the authorized pay rates should be provided by the personnel department. Answer (D) is incorrect because the paymaster should assure that only authorized employees receive a paycheck.

**229.** One payroll audit objective is to determine whether the employees received pay in amounts recorded in the payroll journal. To satisfy this objective, the auditor should

A. Reconcile the payroll bank account.

B. Request that a company official distribute all paychecks.

C. Determine whether a proper segregation of duties exists between recording payroll and reconciling the payroll bank account.

D. Compare canceled payroll checks with the payroll journal.

Answer (D) is correct. *(CIA, adapted)*

**REQUIRED:** The procedure to verify that employees received pay in amounts recorded in the payroll journal.

**DISCUSSION:** To test the accuracy of the payroll journal, the auditor should vouch a sample of the entries to supporting documents, i.e., the canceled checks, timekeeping information, and records of wage rates and authorized deductions.

Answer (A) is incorrect because reconciling the payroll bank account should be part of the audit program for payroll, but does not test the agreement of amounts received by employees with the payroll journal entries. Answer (B) is incorrect because a company official should distribute all paychecks, but this procedure does not assure the agreement of amounts received by employees with the payroll journal entries. Answer (C) is incorrect because determining whether a proper segregation of duties exists between recording payroll and reconciling the payroll bank account should be part of the audit program for payroll, but does not test the agreement of amounts received by employees with the payroll journal entries.

**230.** An internal auditor wishes to determine whether salaried employees in the division being audited are taking more paid vacation time than they have earned. Which of the following audit procedures will be most effective?

A. Observing which employees were absent because of vacations and tracing those absences through the payroll records to subtractions from accumulated vacation time.

B. Comparing total vacation time taken by selected employees in the most recent 12 months per payroll records to the time taken by the same employees in the preceding 12 months.

C. Sending confirmations to selected employees, asking them to verify the accuracy of the number of days of vacation used during the year and the number of remaining unused days as obtained from the payroll records.

D. Comparing the accrued vacation pay liability as computed for the firm's most recent balance sheet with the corresponding amount for 1 year earlier and investigating any significant change.

Answer (A) is correct. *(CIA, adapted)*

**REQUIRED:** The audit procedure to test for excessive vacation time.

**DISCUSSION:** Salaried employees do not punch a clock to create a record of their presence, so observation by the auditor may be necessary to determine whether they are present. The time such an employee is absent may be compared with vacation pay and the payroll charged to vacation time to determine whether an excessive amount is being taken.

Answer (B) is incorrect because many reasons may justify the year-to-year change; for example, increased employee seniority or use of time accumulated from the previous year. Also, comparison of payroll records tests recorded amounts only. Answer (C) is incorrect because a confirmation sent to a wrongdoer is not likely to elicit an incriminating reply. Answer (D) is incorrect because comparing the accrued vacation pay liability with the corresponding amount for 1 year earlier tests recorded amounts only.

**231.** The client's bookkeeper perpetrated a theft by preparing erroneous W-2 forms. The bookkeeper's FICA withholding was overstated by $500 and the FICA withholding from all other employees was understated. Which of the following is an audit procedure to detect such a fraud?

A. Multiplication of the applicable rate by the individual gross taxable earnings.

B. Using Form W-4 and withholding charts to determine whether deductions authorized per pay period agree with amounts deducted per pay period.

C. Footing and crossfooting of the payroll register followed by tracing postings to the general ledger.

D. Vouching canceled checks to federal tax Form 941.

Answer (A) is correct. *(CPA, adapted)*

**REQUIRED:** The audit procedure to detect a manipulation of withholding taxes.

**DISCUSSION:** One objective of the audit of payroll is to verify the client's compliance with various legal requirements, e.g., income tax withholding, Social Security taxes, workers' compensation, unemployment insurance, and wage and hour laws. The auditor should perform tests of controls by sampling payroll transactions. The deductions authorized by employees or required by law should be compared with those actually made. By comparing the recorded amounts withheld on individual employees' W-2 forms with those independently calculated by the auditor, (s)he should detect any misstatement of FICA withholding.

Answer (B) is incorrect because the misstatement was not in the records for each pay period but in the year-end summaries of withholding (W-2). Answer (C) is incorrect because the total amount of FICA taxes is correct, so the records will foot and crossfoot correctly. Answer (D) is incorrect because the total amount of FICA taxes remitted with the Form 941 was correct.

**232.** An auditor reviews the reconciliation of payroll tax forms that a client is responsible for filing to

A. Verify that payroll taxes are deducted from employees' gross pay.

B. Determine whether internal control activities are operating effectively.

C. Uncover fictitious employees who are receiving payroll checks.

D. Identify potential liabilities for unpaid payroll taxes.

Answer (D) is correct. *(CPA, adapted)*

**REQUIRED:** The reason an auditor reviews the reconciliation of payroll tax forms that a client is responsible for filing.

**DISCUSSION:** To satisfy the completeness assertion, payroll tax expense should be reconciled with payroll tax returns (income tax, FICA, and unemployment taxes). Moreover, to satisfy the rights and obligations assertion, the auditor must determine whether the assets, expenses, and payables (liabilities) are the client's. Thus, the review of the reconciliation of payroll tax forms identifies the client's potential liabilities for unpaid payroll taxes. Detection of unrecorded amounts is a primary objective of an audit of liabilities.

Answer (A) is incorrect because payroll records indicate whether deductions have been made. Answer (B) is incorrect because the reconciliation is just one control. Answer (C) is incorrect because examination of payroll records and a surprise observation of payroll distribution are typical procedures for detecting fictitious employees.

## 4.12 Management Representations

**233.** A purpose of a management representation letter is to reduce

A. Audit risk to an aggregate level of misstatement that could be considered material.

B. An auditor's responsibility to detect material misstatements only to the extent that the letter is relied on.

C. The possibility of a misunderstanding concerning management's responsibility for the financial statements.

D. The scope of an auditor's procedures concerning related party transactions and subsequent events.

Answer (C) is correct. *(CPA, adapted)*

**REQUIRED:** The purpose of a management representation letter.

**DISCUSSION:** Management's written representations confirm oral representations given to the auditor, indicate and document their continuing appropriateness, and reduce the possibility of misunderstanding about the subject matter of the representations. That subject matter includes management's acknowledgment of responsibility for the financial statements. A letter of representations is not a substitute for the procedures necessary to afford a reasonable basis for an opinion.

**234.** When an audit is made in accordance with auditing standards, the auditor should always

A. Document the understanding of the client's internal control but not the bases for the conclusions about the assessed levels of control risk for financial statement assertions.

B. Employ analytical procedures as substantive tests to obtain evidence about specific assertions related to account balances.

C. Obtain certain written representations from management.

D. Observe the taking of physical inventory on the balance sheet date.

Answer (C) is correct. *(CPA, adapted)*

**REQUIRED:** The requirement of an audit made in accordance with auditing standards.

**DISCUSSION:** AU 333 requires that the auditor obtain certain written representations from management. These representations corroborate information received orally from management, but they do not substitute for the procedures necessary to afford a reasonable basis for the opinion.

Answer (A) is incorrect because the auditor should document the support for the risk assessments. Answer (B) is incorrect because analytical procedures are required to be applied in the planning and final review stages of an audit, but not as a substitute for tests of details. Answer (D) is incorrect because, when well-kept perpetual inventory records are checked by the client periodically through comparisons with physical counts, the auditor's observation procedures usually can be performed either during or after the end of the period under audit.

**240.** A written management representation letter is most likely to be an auditor's best source of corroborative information of a client's intention to

A. Terminate an employee pension plan.

B. Make a public offering of its common stock.

C. Settle an outstanding lawsuit for an amount less than the accrued loss contingency.

D. Discontinue a line of business.

Answer (D) is correct. *(CPA, adapted)*

**REQUIRED:** The client's intention that is best corroborated by a management representation letter.

**DISCUSSION:** Written management representations are audit evidence but do not ordinarily substitute for other auditing procedures. However, the client's plan for discontinuing a line of business is an example of a matter about which other procedures may provide little evidence. Accordingly, the written representation will be necessary as confirmation of management's intent.

Answer (A) is incorrect because minutes of directors' meetings document a client's intention to terminate an employee pension plan. Answer (B) is incorrect because minutes of directors' meetings document a client's intention to make a public offering of its common stock. Answer (C) is incorrect because an inquiry of the client's lawyer provides more reliable evidence about litigation.

**241.** A written representation from a client's management that, among other matters, acknowledges responsibility for the fair presentation of financial statements, should normally be signed by the

A. Chief executive officer and the chief financial officer.

B. Chief financial officer and the chair of the board of directors.

C. Chair of the audit committee of the board of directors.

D. Chief executive officer, the chair of the board of directors, and the client's lawyer.

Answer (A) is correct. *(CPA, adapted)*

**REQUIRED:** The persons who normally should sign the management representation letter.

**DISCUSSION:** The management representation letter should be signed by members of management with overall responsibility for financial and operating matters who, the auditor believes, are responsible for and knowledgeable about the areas covered in the representations. AU 333 states that these members are normally the chief executive officer and the chief financial officer. Although others may hold high positions in the firm, they are not ultimately responsible or do not have as broad a knowledge as the chief executive officer and chief financial officer. The auditor is not precluded from obtaining representations from others in the firm, however.

**242.** Key Co. plans to present comparative financial statements for the years ended December 31, 20X1 and 20X2, respectively. Smith, CPA, audited Key's financial statements for both years and plans to report on the comparative financial statements on May 1, 20X3. Key's current management team was not present until January 1, 20X2. What period of time should be covered by Key's management representation letter?

A. January 1, 20X1 through December 31, 20X2.

B. January 1, 20X1 through May 1, 20X3.

C. January 1, 20X2 through December 31, 20X2.

D. January 1, 20X2 through May 1, 20X3.

Answer (B) is correct. *(CPA, adapted)*

**REQUIRED:** The dates to be covered by a management representation letter.

**DISCUSSION:** "Because the auditor is concerned with events occurring through the date of his or her report that may require adjustment to or disclosure in the financial statements, the representations should be made as of a date no earlier than the date of the auditor's report." Moreover, "If current management was not present during all periods covered by the auditor's report, the auditor should nevertheless obtain written representations from current management on all such periods" (AU 333).

**243.** An auditor frequently asks the client's personnel questions about the accounts under audit. Although this evidence may be useful, it is weak and should be corroborated by the auditor. Which of the following replies is most useful to the auditor?

A. "Yes, that's how we record that item."

B. "No, I always perform that procedure."

C. "No, we don't always require authorization."

D. "Yes, all inventory is counted."

Answer (C) is correct. *(Publisher)*

**REQUIRED:** The response most likely to be useful.

**DISCUSSION:** Although oral evidence furnished by client personnel should not be relied upon exclusively, the results of inquiries may help the auditor to identify areas that require additional audit attention. For example, the reply to the question about authorization indicates that the client may not be complying with authorization requirements. Assurances by client personnel that procedures have been performed provide audit evidence of limited value.

**244.** If management refuses to furnish certain written representations that the auditor believes are essential, which of the following is appropriate?

A. The auditor can rely on oral evidence relating to the matter as a basis for an unqualified opinion.

B. The client's refusal does not constitute a scope limitation that may lead to a modification of the opinion.

C. The client's refusal may have an effect on the auditor's ability to rely on other representations of management.

D. The auditor should express an adverse opinion because of management's refusal.

Answer (C) is correct. *(CPA, adapted)*

**REQUIRED:** The effect of management's refusal to furnish essential written representations.

**DISCUSSION:** The refusal constitutes a scope limitation sufficient to preclude an unqualified opinion and is ordinarily sufficient to support a disclaimer of an opinion or a withdrawal from the engagement. The auditor must also consider the effects of the refusal on his/her ability to rely on management's other representations (AU 333).

Answer (A) is incorrect because oral representations must be confirmed in writing. Answer (B) is incorrect because the auditor must modify the opinion, disclaim an opinion, or withdraw from the engagement. Answer (D) is incorrect because a qualified opinion or a disclaimer is more appropriate than an adverse opinion unless the auditor knows that the financial statements are not fairly presented.

**245.** An auditor should obtain written representations from management concerning unasserted claims and assessments that the client's lawyer has advised are probable of assertion. These representations may be limited to matters that are considered either individually or collectively material, provided an understanding on the limits of materiality for this purpose has been reached by

A. The auditor and the client's lawyer.

B. Management and the auditor.

C. Management, the client's lawyer, and the auditor.

D. The auditor independently of management.

Answer (B) is correct. *(CPA, adapted)*

**REQUIRED:** The materiality limitation on the scope of management's representations.

**DISCUSSION:** Management's representations may be limited to matters that are considered individually or collectively material on the condition that management and the auditor have reached an understanding concerning the limits of materiality. Such limitations do not apply to certain representations not directly related to amounts in the financial statements, e.g., acknowledgment of responsibility for fair presentation, availability of records, and fraud involving management and persons with significant roles in financial reporting (AU 333).

Answer (A) is incorrect because the lawyer and the auditor (not the client) jointly determine the limits of materiality for purposes of the lawyer's response, not management's. This question, however, relates to representations by management. Answer (C) is incorrect because the lawyer and the auditor (not the client) jointly determine the limits of materiality for purposes of the lawyer's response, not management's. This question, however, relates to representations by management. Answer (D) is incorrect because the auditor and management must reach an understanding.

**246.** A client requests that a predecessor auditor reissue the report on financial statements of a prior period to be presented comparatively with the financial statements of a subsequent period. If no filings with the SEC are contemplated, the auditor

A. May reissue the report without performing additional procedures.

B. Should obtain an updating management representation letter before reissuing the report.

C. Should refuse to reissue the report because (s)he is not a continuing auditor.

D. May reissue the report only if it refers to the successor auditor's work.

Answer (B) is correct. *(Publisher)*

**REQUIRED:** The true statement about reissuance of an audit report.

**DISCUSSION:** When a predecessor auditor is requested to reissue the report on prior-period financial statements to be presented comparatively with the audited statements of a subsequent period, (s)he must obtain an updating representation letter from the former client's management. This requirement applies even if no SEC filings are necessary. The letter should state whether any information has come to management's attention requiring modification of prior representations and whether subsequent events have occurred that necessitate adjustment to or disclosure in the current financial statements (AU 333). The predecessor auditor should also obtain a representation letter from the successor auditor.

Answer (A) is incorrect because various procedures must be performed (AU 508). For example, updating representations must be obtained (AU 333). Answer (C) is incorrect because a predecessor auditor may reissue a report. Answer (D) is incorrect because no reference should be made to the successor auditor's report or work (AU 508).

## 4.13 Litigation Involving the Client

**247.** The primary source of information to be reported about litigation, claims, and assessments is the

A. Client's lawyer.

B. Court records.

C. Client's management.

D. Independent auditor.

Answer (C) is correct. *(CPA, adapted)*

**REQUIRED:** The primary source of information to be reported about litigation, claims, and assessments.

**DISCUSSION:** "Management is responsible for adopting policies and procedures to identify, evaluate, and account for litigation, claims, and assessments as a basis for the preparation of financial statements in conformity with generally accepted accounting principles" (AU 337, *Inquiry of a Client's Lawyer Concerning Litigation, Claims, and Assessments*).

Answer (A) is incorrect because the client's lawyer is the auditor's primary source of evidence to corroborate the information furnished by management. Answer (B) is incorrect because the auditor does not ordinarily examine court records. Answer (D) is incorrect because the auditor collects evidence to support management's assertions concerning litigation, claims, and assessments.

**248.** The primary reason an auditor requests that letters of inquiry be sent to a client's attorneys is to provide the auditor with

A. The probable outcome of asserted claims and pending or threatened litigation.

B. Corroboration of the information furnished by management about litigation, claims, and assessments.

C. The attorneys' opinions of the client's historical experiences in recent similar litigation.

D. A description and evaluation of litigation, claims, and assessments that existed at the balance-sheet date.

Answer (B) is correct. *(CPA, adapted)*

**REQUIRED:** The primary reason that letters of audit inquiry are sent to a client's attorneys.

**DISCUSSION:** A letter of audit inquiry to a client's lawyer is the auditor's primary means of corroborating information furnished by management concerning litigation, claims, and assessments. Evidence obtained from the client's legal department may provide the needed corroboration, but it does not substitute for information that outside counsel refuses to furnish (AU 337).

Answer (A) is incorrect because management provides a description and evaluation of litigation, claims, and assessments that existed at the balance-sheet date. The letter of audit inquiry corroborates that information. Answer (C) is incorrect because the auditor is concerned with current litigation, not recent similar litigation. Answer (D) is incorrect because management provides a description and evaluation of litigation, claims, and assessments that existed at the balance-sheet date. The letter of audit inquiry corroborates that information.

**249.** The letter of audit inquiry addressed to the client's lawyer will not ordinarily be

A. Sent to a lawyer who was engaged by the audit client during the year and soon thereafter resigned the engagement.

B. Used to corroborate the information originally obtained from management concerning litigation, claims, and assessments.

C. Limited to references concerning only pending or threatened litigation in connection with which the lawyer has been engaged.

D. Needed during the audit of clients whose securities are not registered with the SEC.

Answer (C) is correct. *(CPA, adapted)*

**REQUIRED:** The false statement about the letter of audit inquiry to the client's lawyer.

**DISCUSSION:** A letter of audit inquiry to a client's lawyer includes, but is not limited to, management-prepared lists of unasserted claims and assessments as well as pending or threatened litigation, claims, and assessments in connection with which the lawyer has been engaged. The lawyer is expected to respond appropriately (within the limits of materiality) if (s)he has given substantive attention to any of these matters on behalf of the company in the form of legal consultation or representation.

Answer (A) is incorrect because the auditor should communicate with all lawyers engaged by the client during the year. Answer (B) is incorrect because management is the auditor's primary source of information concerning litigation, claims, and assessments. The inquiry letter is the primary means of corroboration. Answer (D) is incorrect because the lawyer's letter is customary in all audits.

**250.** Which of the following is not an audit procedure that the independent auditor performs with respect to litigation, claims, and assessments?

A. Inquire of and discuss with management the policies and procedures adopted for litigation, claims, and assessments.

B. Obtain from management a description and evaluation of litigation, claims, and assessments that existed at the balance-sheet date.

C. Obtain assurance from management that it has disclosed all unasserted claims that its lawyer has advised are probable of assertion and must be disclosed.

D. Confirm directly with the client's lawyer that all claims have been recorded in the financial statements.

Answer (D) is correct. *(CPA, adapted)*

**REQUIRED:** The procedure that is not performed regarding litigation.

**DISCUSSION:** Under SFAS 5, a loss contingency is recorded in the financial statements only if it is probable and its amount can be reasonably estimated. Hence, many contingent claims will not be recorded.

Answer (A) is incorrect because inquiring of and discussing with management the policies and procedures adopted for litigation, claims, and assessments is a procedure required by AU 337. Answer (B) is incorrect because obtaining from management a description and evaluation of litigation, claims, and assessments that existed at the balance-sheet date is a procedure required by AU 337. Answer (C) is incorrect because obtaining assurance from management that it has disclosed all unasserted claims that the lawyer has advised are probable of assertion is a procedure required by AU 337.

**251.** A CPA has received a lawyer's letter in which no significant disagreements with the client's assessments of contingent liabilities were noted. The resignation of the client's lawyer shortly after receipt of the letter should alert the auditor that

A. Undisclosed unasserted claims may have arisen.

B. The lawyer was unable to form a conclusion with respect to the significance of litigation, claims, and assessments.

C. The auditor must begin a completely new examination of contingent liabilities.

D. An adverse opinion will be necessary.

Answer (A) is correct. *(CPA, adapted)*

**REQUIRED:** The implication of the resignation of the client's lawyer soon after responding to the inquiry letter.

**DISCUSSION:** A lawyer may be required to resign an engagement under his/her code of professional responsibility if the client disregards advice concerning financial accounting and reporting for litigation, claims, and assessments. Given that the response to the letter of audit inquiry stated that the client's assessment of contingent liabilities was satisfactory, the source of disagreement may be undisclosed, unasserted claims.

Answer (B) is incorrect because inability to form a legal conclusion does not ordinarily cause an ethical conflict with the client sufficient to cause the lawyer's resignation. Answer (C) is incorrect because much of the auditor's work, particularly that performed on client records, may still be valid. Answer (D) is incorrect because an adverse opinion is expressed only when the financial statements or related disclosures are not presented fairly.

**252.** Which of the following statements concerning litigation, claims, and assessments extracted from a letter from a client's lawyer is most likely to cause the auditor to request clarification?

A. "I believe that the possible liability to the company is nominal in amount."

B. "I believe that the action can be settled for less than the damages claimed."

C. "I believe that the plaintiff's case against the company is without merit."

D. "I believe that the company will be able to defend this action successfully."

Answer (B) is correct. *(CPA, adapted)*

**REQUIRED:** The lawyer's statement most likely causing an auditor's request for clarification.

**DISCUSSION:** The letter of audit inquiry requests, among other things, that the lawyer evaluate the likelihood of unfavorable outcomes of pending or threatened litigation, claims, and assessments. It also requests that the lawyer estimate, if possible, the amount or range of potential loss (AU 337). Thus, the auditor is concerned about the amount of the expected settlement as well as the likelihood of the outcome.

Answer (A) is incorrect because the lawyer's statement that the amount of possible liability will not be material states an amount or range of loss. Answer (C) is incorrect because the lawyer has stated that no liability is expected. Answer (D) is incorrect because the lawyer has stated that no liability is expected.

**253.** A lawyer's response to an auditor's inquiry concerning litigation, claims, and assessments may be limited to matters that are considered individually or collectively material to the client's financial statements. Which parties should reach an understanding on the limits of materiality for this purpose?

A. The auditor and the client's management.

B. The client's audit committee and the lawyer.

C. The client's management and the lawyer.

D. The lawyer and the auditor.

Answer (D) is correct. *(CPA, adapted)*

**REQUIRED:** The parties responsible for setting materiality limits for a lawyer's response to an auditor's inquiry concerning litigation, claims, and assessments.

**DISCUSSION:** The letter of audit inquiry requests a statement about the nature of, and reasons for, any limitation on the lawyer's response. The lawyer may limit the response to matters to which (s)he has given substantive attention in the form of legal consultation or representation. Furthermore, the lawyer's response may be limited to those matters that are considered individually or collectively material to the financial statements, provided the lawyer and auditor have reached an understanding on the limits of materiality for this purpose (AU 337).

Answer (A) is incorrect because the auditor and the client should have an understanding about the limits of materiality for the purpose of the inquiry. The lawyer and the auditor should agree about materiality for the purpose of the response.
Answer (B) is incorrect because the auditor must judge whether items are material relative to the financial statements.
Answer (C) is incorrect because the auditor must judge whether items are material relative to the financial statements.

**254.** An auditor should obtain evidence relevant to all the following factors concerning third-party litigation against a client except the

A. Period in which the underlying cause for legal action occurred.

B. Probability of an unfavorable outcome.

C. Jurisdiction in which the matter will be resolved.

D. Existence of a situation indicating an uncertainty as to the possible loss.

Answer (C) is correct. *(CPA, adapted)*

**REQUIRED:** The least important audit consideration when obtaining evidence regarding litigation.

**DISCUSSION:** When performing audit procedures after year-end, the auditor is least interested in determining where the particular matter in litigation will be resolved. The major concern is the impact of the event on the fair presentation of the year-end financial statements. Accordingly, the auditor should obtain evidence of the existence, amount, degree of probability, and timing of the cause of the litigation.

**255.** The appropriate date for the client to specify as the effective date in the audit inquiry to a lawyer is

A. The balance-sheet date.

B. Seven working days after the request is received by the lawyer.

C. The date of the audit inquiry itself.

D. The expected date of the completion of audit field work.

Answer (D) is correct. *(Publisher)*

**REQUIRED:** The appropriate effective date of the letter of inquiry to a lawyer.

**DISCUSSION:** According to an interpretation of AU 337, the date of the lawyer's response "should be as close to the completion of the field work as practicable." The auditor is concerned with events occurring through the date of the report that may require adjustment to, or disclosure in, the financial statements.

Answer (A) is incorrect because the balance-sheet date is not ordinarily as close as practicable to the completion of field work. Answer (B) is incorrect because 7 working days after the request is received by the lawyer is not ordinarily as close as practicable to the completion of field work. Answer (C) is incorrect because the date of the audit inquiry itself is not ordinarily as close as practicable to the completion of field work.

**256.** The refusal of a client's lawyer to provide a representation on the legality of a particular act committed by the client is ordinarily

A. Sufficient reason to issue a "subject to" opinion.

B. Considered to be a scope limitation.

C. Insufficient reason to modify the auditor's report because of the lawyer's obligation of confidentiality.

D. Proper grounds to withdraw from the engagement.

Answer (B) is correct. *(CPA, adapted)*

**REQUIRED:** The auditor's conclusion when the client's lawyer refuses to corroborate information.

**DISCUSSION:** The lawyer's refusal either orally or in writing to provide the requested information is a scope limitation sufficient to preclude an unqualified opinion, because the letter of audit inquiry to the client's lawyer is the primary means of corroborating management's representations about litigation, claims, and assessments. However, a statement in the letter such as, "It would be inappropriate for this firm to respond to a general inquiry relating to the existence of unasserted possible claims and assessments," is not considered a scope limitation.

Answer (A) is incorrect because "subject to" is an unacceptable phrase in an audit opinion. Answer (C) is incorrect because an unqualified opinion cannot be expressed when a material scope limitation has been imposed. Answer (D) is incorrect because the failure could preclude an unqualified opinion but would not likely be grounds for withdrawal.

## 4.14 Use of Specialists

**257.** Which of the following statements is true about the auditor's use of the work of a specialist?

A. The specialist should not have an understanding of the auditor's corroborative use of the specialist's findings.

B. The auditor is required to perform substantive procedures to verify the specialist's assumptions and findings.

C. The client should not have an understanding of the nature of the work to be performed by the specialist.

D. The auditor should obtain an understanding of the methods and assumptions used by the specialist.

Answer (D) is correct. *(CPA, adapted)*

**REQUIRED:** The true statement about the auditor's use of the work of a specialist.

**DISCUSSION:** AU 336, *Using the Work of a Specialist*, states that the auditor should obtain an understanding of the methods and assumptions used to determine whether the findings are suitable for corroborative purposes. The auditor should consider whether the specialist's findings support the assertions and should test the accounting data provided by the client to the specialist.

Answer (A) is incorrect because the auditor, the client, and the specialist should have an understanding about the nature of the work to be performed. Answer (B) is incorrect because, if the specialist's findings support the assertions, the auditor may reasonably conclude that sufficient, competent evidence has been obtained. Answer (C) is incorrect because the auditor, the client, and the specialist should have an understanding about the nature of the work to be performed.

**258.** Which of the following statements concerning the auditor's use of the work of a specialist is true?

A. If the auditor believes that the determinations made by the specialist are unreasonable, only a qualified opinion may be expressed.

B. If the specialist is related to the client, the auditor is still permitted to use the specialist's findings as corroborative evidence.

C. The specialist may not be related to the client.

D. The specialist is identified in the auditor's report when the auditor expresses an unqualified opinion.

Answer (B) is correct. *(CPA, adapted)*

**REQUIRED:** The true statement about use of a specialist.

**DISCUSSION:** A related specialist may be acceptable under certain circumstances. The auditor should assess the risk that the specialist's objectivity may be impaired. If the auditor believes that objectivity might be impaired, the auditor should perform additional audit procedures or hire another specialist (AU 336).

Answer (A) is incorrect because, if the findings are unreasonable, additional procedures should be applied. If they do not resolve the matter, the opinion of another specialist should be sought. If the issue is still not resolved, a qualified opinion or a disclaimer should ordinarily be expressed. An adverse opinion should be expressed only when the auditor concludes the financial statements are materially misstated. Answer (C) is incorrect because a related specialist may be acceptable under certain circumstances. Answer (D) is incorrect because the specialist may be identified whenever the auditor modifies the standard report as a result of the work of a specialist.

**259.** Which of the following is not a specialist upon whose work an auditor may rely?

A. Actuary.

B. Appraiser.

C. Internal auditor.

D. Engineer.

Answer (C) is correct. *(CPA, adapted)*

**REQUIRED:** The individual not considered a specialist.

**DISCUSSION:** For the purposes of AU 336, a specialist is a person or firm possessing special skill or knowledge in a particular field other than accounting or auditing. The external auditor should consider the work of internal auditors but should not deem them to be specialists in the sense contemplated by AU 336. Specialists include, but are not limited to, actuaries, appraisers, engineers, environmental consultants, geologists, and attorneys (if not engaged to provide services to the client regarding litigation, claims, or assessments).

**260.** In using the work of a specialist, an auditor referred to the specialist's findings in the auditor's report. This is an appropriate reporting practice if the

A. Auditor is not familiar with the professional certification, personal reputation, or particular competence of the specialist.

B. Auditor, as a result of the specialist's findings, adds an explanatory paragraph emphasizing a matter regarding the financial statements.

C. Specialist is aware that his/her work will be used to evaluate the assertions in the financial statements.

D. Auditor, as a result of the specialist's findings, decides to indicate a division of responsibility with the specialist.

Answer (B) is correct. *(CPA, adapted)*

**REQUIRED:** The instance in which an auditor may refer to a specialist's findings.

**DISCUSSION:** An auditor ordinarily should not refer to the work or findings of a specialist. However, "The auditor may, as a result of the report or findings of the specialist, decide to add explanatory language to his/her standard report or depart from an unqualified opinion." The specialist may be identified "if the auditor believes the reference will facilitate an understanding of the reason for the explanatory paragraph or the departure from the unqualified opinion" (AU 336). Emphasizing a matter is a basis for adding an explanatory paragraph that may justify referring to a specialist.

Answer (A) is incorrect because the auditor is required to evaluate the professional qualifications of the specialist. Answer (C) is incorrect because the specialist's awareness of the use of his/her work is independent of the decision to refer to the specialist. Answer (D) is incorrect because a division of responsibility with the specialist is inappropriate.

**261.** In using the work of a specialist, an understanding should exist among the auditor, the client, and the specialist as to the nature of the specialist's work. The documentation of this understanding should cover

A. A statement that the specialist assumes no responsibility to update the specialist's report for future events or circumstances.

B. The conditions under which a division of responsibility may be necessary.

C. The specialist's understanding of the auditor's corroborative use of the specialist's findings.

D. The auditor's disclaimer as to whether the specialist's findings corroborate the representations in the financial statements.

Answer (C) is correct. *(CPA, adapted)*

**REQUIRED:** The matter covered in the understanding about the work of the specialist.

**DISCUSSION:** The understanding should be documented and should cover the objectives and scope of the work, the specialist's representations as to his/her relationship to the client, the methods or assumptions to be used, and a comparison with those used in the preceding period. Documentation should also include the specialist's understanding of the auditor's corroborative use of the findings in relation to the assertions in the financial statements, and the form and content of the specialist's report that would enable the auditor to evaluate the specialist's work (AU 336).

Answer (A) is incorrect because the understanding need not contain a disclaimer about the specialist's responsibility to update the report. Answer (B) is incorrect because the auditor may, in some cases, refer to a specialist but may not divide responsibility with him/her. Answer (D) is incorrect because the understanding need not contain a disclaimer about whether the findings corroborate the representations.

**262.** When an outside specialist has assumed full responsibility for taking the client's physical inventory, reliance on the specialist's report is acceptable if

A. The auditor is satisfied through application of appropriate procedures as to the reputation and competence of the specialist.

B. Circumstances made it impracticable or impossible for the auditor to either do the work personally or observe the work done by the inventory firm.

C. The auditor conducted the same audit tests and procedures as would have been applicable if the client employees took the physical inventory.

D. The auditor's report contains a reference to the assumption of full responsibility.

Answer (C) is correct. *(CPA, adapted)*

**REQUIRED:** The basis for relying on the work of an outside inventory specialist.

**DISCUSSION:** AU 331 charges the auditor with responsibility for the observation of inventories. The auditor must perform this procedure whether the client or an outside specialist takes the physical inventory. The auditor must still examine the outside firm's program, observe its procedures and controls, make or observe some physical counts, recompute calculations, and test intervening transactions.

Answer (A) is incorrect because, although the auditor is concerned with the reputation and competence of the specialist, (s)he still must become satisfied as to the existence of the inventory. Answer (B) is incorrect because the auditor usually cannot express an unqualified opinion unless (s)he has made or observed some physical counts. Answer (D) is incorrect because the auditor cannot assign responsibility to a specialist.

## 4.15 Subsequent Events

**263.** Which of the following procedures can be performed only in the subsequent period?

A. Examination of data to determine that a proper cutoff has been made.

B. Tests of the details of balances.

C. Tests of the details of transactions.

D. Reading of the minutes of the board of directors' meetings.

Answer (A) is correct. *(Publisher)*

**REQUIRED:** The procedure that can be performed only in the subsequent period.

**DISCUSSION:** The objective of a cutoff test is to determine that transactions are reported in the correct period. A cutoff test can be performed only after year-end when all transactions for the year can be identified.

Answer (B) is incorrect because the tests of the details of balances and most other audit procedures can be performed during the year. Answer (C) is incorrect because the tests of the details of transactions and most other audit procedures can be performed during the year. Answer (D) is incorrect because minutes of meetings during the subsequent period through the date of the audit report should be considered.

**264.** Which of the following procedures will an auditor most likely perform to obtain evidence about the occurrence of subsequent events?

A. Confirming a sample of material accounts receivable established after year-end.

B. Comparing the financial statements being reported on with those of the prior period.

C. Investigating personnel changes in the accounting department occurring after year-end.

D. Inquiring as to whether any unusual adjustments were made after year-end.

Answer (D) is correct. *(CPA, adapted)*

**REQUIRED:** The subsequent events procedure.

**DISCUSSION:** Procedures performed at or near the completion of field work normally include inquiring of management as to (1) whether the interim statements were prepared on the same basis as the statements being reported on, (2) whether any substantial contingent liabilities or commitments existed at the date of the balance sheet, (3) whether any significant change had occurred in equity, (4) whether any unusual adjustments had been made during the subsequent period, and (5) the current status of items that were accounted for on a basis of tentative, preliminary, or inconclusive data.

Answer (A) is incorrect because the auditor confirms receivables before year-end. Answer (B) is incorrect because this analytical procedure is performed at the beginning of the audit. Answer (C) is incorrect because personnel changes after year-end do not typically relate to the recording of subsequent events.

**265.** An auditor is concerned with completing various phases of the audit after the balance-sheet date. This work relating to subsequent events should be extended to the date of the

A. Auditor's report.

B. Final review of the audit documentation.

C. Public issuance of the financial statements.

D. Delivery of the auditor's report to the client.

Answer (A) is correct. *(CPA, adapted)*

**REQUIRED:** The date to which subsequent events work should be extended.

**DISCUSSION:** Subsequent events occur after the balance-sheet date and prior to the issuance of the financial statements. Audit work relating to subsequent events should be performed at or near the completion of the field work (AU 560). Because the audit report is normally dated as of the last day of the field work (AU 530, *Dating of the Independent Auditor's Report*), the "subsequent period" for audit report purposes normally extends from the balance-sheet date to the date of the audit report.

Answer (B) is incorrect because subsequent events work should be extended to the date of the report. Answer (C) is incorrect because the date of the public issuance of the financial statements is later than the date of the report. Answer (D) is incorrect because the delivery of the auditor's report to the client occurs after the date of the report.

**266.** Which of the following statements best expresses the auditor's responsibility with respect to events occurring after the balance-sheet date?

A. The auditor has no responsibility for events occurring in the subsequent period unless these events affect transactions recorded on or before the balance-sheet date.

B. The auditor's responsibility is to determine that transactions recorded on or before the balance-sheet date actually occurred.

C. The auditor is fully responsible for events occurring in the subsequent period and should extend all detailed procedures through the last day of field work.

D. The auditor is responsible for determining that a proper cutoff has been made and for performing a general review of events occurring in the subsequent period.

Answer (D) is correct. *(Publisher)*

**REQUIRED:** The best description of the auditor's subsequent events responsibility.

**DISCUSSION:** AU 560 states that events and transactions sometimes occur subsequent to the balance-sheet date but prior to the issuance of the financial statements that have a material effect on the financial statements, and therefore require adjustment or disclosure in the statements. Certain specific procedures, such as the determination that proper cutoffs have been made and the examination of data to aid in evaluating assets and liabilities as of the balance-sheet date, are normally applied in the subsequent events period. Other phases of the audit, however, will have been substantially completed by year-end. The auditor is responsible for performing a general subsequent events review but not for continuously reviewing matters about which (s)he has already become satisfied.

Answer (A) is incorrect because the auditor is responsible for conditions not existing at year-end that must be disclosed to prevent the statements from being misleading. Answer (B) is incorrect because transactions occurring prior to year-end are not subsequent events. Answer (C) is incorrect because the auditor is only expected to apply the subsequent events procedures described in AU 560.

**267.** Which of the following procedures should an auditor ordinarily perform regarding subsequent events?

A. Compare the latest available interim financial statements with the financial statements being audited.

B. Send second requests to the client's customers who failed to respond to initial accounts receivable confirmation requests.

C. Communicate material weaknesses in internal control to the client's audit committee.

D. Review the cutoff bank statements for several months after the year-end.

Answer (A) is correct. *(CPA, adapted)*

**REQUIRED:** The subsequent events procedure.

**DISCUSSION:** Subsequent events procedures include (1) reading the latest interim statements and comparing them with the statements being reported on; (2) inquiring about and discussing with management various financial and accounting matters; (3) reading the minutes of directors', shareholders', and committee meetings; (4) obtaining a letter of representations from management; (5) inquiring of client's legal counsel; and (6) performing any further procedures deemed necessary.

Answer (B) is incorrect because second confirmation requests do not disclose subsequent events. Answer (C) is incorrect because communication of material weaknesses is not a subsequent events procedure. Answer (D) is incorrect because cutoff bank statements are requested from banks 7 to 10 days after year-end. They are used to verify the client's bank reconciliations and detect kiting.

**268.** After the date of the report, an auditor has no obligation to make continuing inquiries or perform other procedures concerning the audited financial statements, unless

A. Information, which existed at the report date and may affect the report, comes to the auditor's attention.

B. The control environment changes after the date of the report.

C. Information about an event that occurred after the end of field work comes to the auditor's attention.

D. Final determinations or resolutions are made of contingencies that had been disclosed in the financial statements.

Answer (A) is correct. *(CPA, adapted)*

**REQUIRED:** The basis for the obligation to perform procedures after the report date.

**DISCUSSION:** Although the auditor may need to extend subsequent events procedures when public companies make filings under the Securities Act of 1933 (AU 711, *Filings under Federal Securities Statutes*), (s)he ordinarily need not apply any procedures after the date of the report. But, if the auditor becomes aware of information that relates to the financial statements previously reported on, that (s)he did not know at the date of the report, and that is of such a nature and from such a source that (s)he would have investigated it had it come to light during the course of the audit, (s)he should, as soon as practicable, determine whether the information is reliable and whether the facts existed at the date of the report (AU 561, *Subsequent Discovery of Facts Existing at the Date of the Auditor's Report*).

Answer (B) is incorrect because the auditor has no responsibility to consider changes in controls after the report date. Answer (C) is incorrect because the subsequent event must have occurred prior to the date of the auditor's report for the auditor to have reporting responsibility. Answer (D) is incorrect because the auditor has no responsibility to monitor disclosed contingencies after the report date.

**269.** Which of the following events occurring after the date of the report most likely will cause the auditor to make further inquiries about the previously issued financial statements?

A. A technological development that could affect the entity's future ability to continue as a going concern.

B. The discovery of information regarding a contingency that existed before the financial statements were issued.

C. The entity's sale of a subsidiary that accounts for 30% of the entity's consolidated sales.

D. The final resolution of a lawsuit explained in a separate paragraph of the auditor's report.

Answer (B) is correct. *(CPA, adapted)*

**REQUIRED:** The event occurring after the date of the report most likely resulting in further inquiries.

**DISCUSSION:** When the auditor becomes aware of information that relates to prior financial statements but that was not known to him/her at the date of the report and that (s)he would have investigated if it had been discovered during the audit, the auditor should undertake to determine whether the information is reliable and whether the facts existed at the report date (AU 561).

Answer (A) is incorrect because an event occurring after the date of the report need not be considered by the auditor if it would not affect the report. Answer (C) is incorrect because an event occurring after the date of the report need not be considered by the auditor if it would not affect the report. Answer (D) is incorrect because the auditor need not consider final determinations or resolutions of contingencies that were disclosed in the financial statements or that resulted in a departure from the auditor's standard report.

**270.** Subsequent to the date of the auditor's report, the auditor became aware of facts existing at the report date that would have affected the report had the auditor then been aware of such facts. After determining that the information is reliable, the auditor should next

A. Notify the board of directors that the auditor's report must no longer be associated with the financial statements.

B. Determine whether there are persons relying or likely to rely on the financial statements who would attach importance to the information.

C. Request that management disclose the effects of the newly discovered information by adding a footnote to subsequently issued financial statements.

D. Issue revised pro forma financial statements taking into consideration the newly discovered information.

Answer (B) is correct. *(CPA, adapted)*

**REQUIRED:** The next step after determining the reliability of a subsequently discovered fact.

**DISCUSSION:** When new information that existed at the report date has been found to be reliable, appropriate action must be taken if the matter would have affected the report and was not reflected in the financial statements, provided the auditor "believes there are persons currently relying or likely to rely on the financial statements who would attach importance to the information" (AU 561). The time elapsed since the date of the report is a factor to be weighed.

Answer (A) is incorrect because notifying the board of directors that the auditor's report must no longer be associated with the financial statements is only necessary when the client refuses to make necessary disclosures. Answer (C) is incorrect because the appropriate action will depend on such factors as whether the effects of the new information can be promptly determined and whether issuance of statements for a subsequent period is imminent. Answer (D) is incorrect because the appropriate action will depend on such factors as whether the effects of the new information can be promptly determined and whether issuance of statements for a subsequent period is imminent.

**271.** After an audit report containing an unqualified opinion on a nonpublic client's financial statements was dated and the financial statements issued, the client decided to sell the shares of a subsidiary that accounts for 30% of its revenue and 25% of its net income. The auditor should

A. Determine whether the information is reliable and, if determined to be reliable, request that revised financial statements be issued.

B. Notify the entity that the auditor's report may no longer be associated with the financial statements.

C. Describe the effects of this subsequently discovered information in a communication with persons known to be relying on the financial statements.

D. Take no action because the auditor has no obligation to make any further inquiries.

Answer (D) is correct. *(CPA, adapted)*

**REQUIRED:** The auditor's responsibility after the report date when the client sells shares of its subsidiary.

**DISCUSSION:** AU 561 states, "After the date of the report, the auditor has no obligation to make any further or continuing inquiry or perform any other auditing procedures with respect to the audited financial statements covered by that report, unless new information that may affect the report comes to his/her attention."

Answer (A) is incorrect because it is an action that might be appropriate if (s)he had subsequently discovered facts that existed at the date of the report. Answer (B) is incorrect because it is an action that might be appropriate if (s)he had subsequently discovered facts that existed at the date of the report. Answer (C) is incorrect because it is an action that might be appropriate if (s)he had subsequently discovered facts that existed at the date of the report.

**272.** An auditor concludes that the omission of a substantive procedure considered necessary at the time of the audit may impair the auditor's current ability to support the previously expressed opinion. The auditor need not apply the omitted procedure if

A. The risk of adverse publicity or litigation is low.

B. The results of other procedures that were applied tend to compensate for the procedure omitted.

C. The auditor's opinion was qualified because of a departure from generally accepted accounting principles.

D. The results of the subsequent period's tests of controls make the omitted procedure less important.

Answer (B) is correct. *(CPA, adapted)*

**REQUIRED:** The circumstances in which an auditor need not apply an omitted procedure.

**DISCUSSION:** According to AU 390, *Consideration of Omitted Procedures after the Report Date*, the results of other procedures applied or audit evidence obtained in a later audit (possibly at an interim date) may compensate for an omitted procedure. Furthermore, the auditor should assess the importance of the omitted procedure to the support of the audit opinion in relation to the overall engagement and the circumstances of the audit.

Answer (A) is incorrect because a low risk of adverse consequences to the auditor does not justify failing to apply the omitted procedure. Answer (C) is incorrect because the omission may have resulted in an inappropriate report or affected a matter not the basis for the qualification. Thus, the nature of the opinion does not justify failure to correct the omission. Answer (D) is incorrect because the results of the tests of controls in a subsequent period do not necessarily apply to the earlier period.

**273.** On March 15, 20X1, Kent, CPA, expressed an unqualified opinion on a client's audited financial statements for the year ended December 31, 20X0. On May 4, 20X1, Kent's internal inspection program disclosed that engagement personnel failed to observe the client's physical inventory. Omission of this procedure impairs Kent's current ability to support the unqualified opinion. If the shareholders are currently relying on the opinion, Kent should first

A. Advise management to disclose to the shareholders that Kent's unqualified opinion should not be relied on.

B. Undertake to apply alternative procedures that would provide a satisfactory basis for the unqualified opinion.

C. Reissue the auditor's report and add an explanatory paragraph describing the departure from auditing standards.

D. Compensate for the omitted procedure by performing tests of controls to reduce audit risk to a sufficiently low level.

Answer (B) is correct. *(CPA, adapted)*

**REQUIRED:** The appropriate action when an auditor discovers that a necessary audit procedure was not performed during the previous audit.

**DISCUSSION:** If the auditor determines that the omission impairs his/her current ability to support the opinion and (s)he believes persons are currently relying or are likely to rely on the report, the auditor should promptly undertake to apply the omitted procedure or alternative procedures that would provide a satisfactory basis for the opinion (AU 390).

Answer (A) is incorrect because notification of users would only be necessary if the auditor could not become satisfied upon applying the procedure. Answer (C) is incorrect because the auditor has followed auditing standards in becoming satisfied with the application of the procedure. Answer (D) is incorrect because tests of controls do not substitute for required substantive tests.

## 4.16 Related-Party Transactions

**274.** When auditing related-party transactions, an auditor places primary emphasis on

A. Confirming the existence of the related parties.

B. Verifying the valuation of the related-party transactions.

C. Evaluating the disclosure of the related-party transactions.

D. Ascertaining the rights and obligations of the related parties.

Answer (C) is correct. *(CPA, adapted)*

**REQUIRED:** The primary concern of the auditor about related-party transactions.

**DISCUSSION:** The auditor's primary emphasis with regard to related-party transactions should be on the presentation and disclosure assertions with respect to their nature and their effect on the financial statements. However, the FASB requires that transactions with related parties be accounted for on the same basis as would be appropriate if the parties were not related.

Answer (A) is incorrect because, in an audit of related-party transactions, the auditor places no special emphasis on the existence assertions. Answer (B) is incorrect because, in an audit of related-party transactions, the auditor places no special emphasis on the valuation assertions. Answer (D) is incorrect because, in an audit of related-party transactions, the auditor places no special emphasis on the rights and obligations assertions.

**275.** After determining that a related-party transaction has actually occurred, an auditor should

A. Add a separate paragraph to the auditor's standard report to explain the transaction.

B. Perform analytical procedures to verify whether similar transactions occurred, but were not recorded.

C. Obtain an understanding of the business purpose of the transaction.

D. Substantiate that the transaction was consummated on terms equivalent to an arm's-length transaction.

Answer (C) is correct. *(CPA, adapted)*

**REQUIRED:** The procedure performed after determining that a related-party transaction has occurred.

**DISCUSSION:** After identifying related-party transactions, the auditor should become satisfied about their purpose, nature, extent, and effect. Among other things, the auditor should obtain an understanding of the business purpose of the transaction (AU 334, *Related Parties*).

Answer (A) is incorrect because, if the related-party transaction has been accounted for properly, no modification of the standard report is necessary. However, in some cases, the auditor may wish to add a separate paragraph emphasizing that the entity has had significant related-party transactions (AU 508). Answer (B) is incorrect because the auditor is not responsible for undisclosed, unrecorded related-party transactions. Answer (D) is incorrect because the auditor normally cannot determine whether a transaction was consummated on terms equivalent to an arm's-length transaction. The auditor's primary concern is with disclosure of related-party transactions.

**276.** Which of the following events most likely indicates the existence of related parties?

A. Borrowing a large sum of money at a variable rate of interest.

B. Selling real estate at a price that differs significantly from its carrying amount.

C. Making a loan without scheduled terms for repayment of the funds.

D. Discussing merger terms with a company that is a major competitor.

Answer (C) is correct. *(CPA, adapted)*

**REQUIRED:** The item that most likely indicates the existence of related parties.

**DISCUSSION:** AU 334 gives examples of transactions that suggest a related-party relationship. Exchanging property for similar property in a nonmonetary transaction, borrowing or lending at rates significantly above or below market rates, selling realty at a price materially different from its appraised value, and making loans with no scheduled repayment terms suggest related-party transactions.

Answer (A) is incorrect because large sums of money are often borrowed at fluctuating interest rates, especially when the debt is long term. Answer (B) is incorrect because real estate's fair value is normally significantly higher than its carrying amount. Answer (D) is incorrect because discussing merger terms indicates only that the parties may be related in the future.

**277.** An auditor searching for related-party transactions should obtain an understanding of each subsidiary's relationship to the total entity because

A. This may permit the audit of intercompany account balances to be performed as of concurrent dates.

B. Intercompany transactions may have been consummated on terms equivalent to arm's-length transactions.

C. This may reveal whether particular transactions would have taken place if the parties had not been related.

D. The business structure may be deliberately designed to obscure related-party transactions.

Answer (D) is correct. *(CPA, adapted)*

**REQUIRED:** The reason for understanding parent-subsidiary relationships.

**DISCUSSION:** AU 334 states that "the auditor should obtain an understanding of management responsibilities and the relationship of each component to the total entity." The auditor should also consider internal control and the business purpose of each component of the entity. The auditor should be aware that sometimes "business structure and operating style are occasionally deliberately designed to obscure related-party transactions."

Answer (A) is incorrect because a concurrent audit is not required. Answer (B) is incorrect because the auditor's concern is that related-party transactions were not at arm's-length. Answer (C) is incorrect because, except for routine transactions, determining whether a transaction would have occurred and what the terms would have been if the parties were unrelated is ordinarily not possible.

**278.** Which of the following would not necessarily be a related-party transaction?

A. A sale to another corporation with a similar name.

B. A purchase from another corporation that is controlled by the corporation's chief shareholder.

C. A loan from the corporation to a major shareholder.

D. Sale of land to the corporation by the spouse of a director.

Answer (A) is correct. *(CPA, adapted)*

**REQUIRED:** The transaction not necessarily with a related party.

**DISCUSSION:** Principal owners, management, and members of their immediate families are parties related to the enterprise. Other parties with which the enterprise may deal are related if one party can control or significantly influence the management or operating policies of the other to the extent that one of the parties might be prevented from fully pursuing its own interests. A corporation that merely has a similar name is not necessarily related.

Answer (B) is incorrect because a purchase from another corporation that is controlled by the corporation's chief shareholder is a related-party transaction. Answer (C) is incorrect because a loan from the corporation to a major shareholder is a related-party transaction. Answer (D) is incorrect because the sale of land to the corporation by the spouse of a director is a related-party transaction.

**279.** Which of the following statements is true about related-party transactions?

A. In the absence of evidence to the contrary, related-party transactions should be assumed to be outside the ordinary course of business.

B. An auditor should determine whether a particular transaction would have occurred if the parties had not been related.

C. An auditor should substantiate that related-party transactions were consummated on terms equivalent to those that prevail in arm's-length transactions.

D. The audit procedures directed toward identifying related-party transactions should include considering whether transactions are occurring but are not being given proper accounting recognition.

Answer (D) is correct. *(CPA, adapted)*

**REQUIRED:** The true statement about related-party transactions.

**DISCUSSION:** According to AU 334, the audit procedures directed toward identifying related-party transactions should include considering whether transactions are occurring but are not being given proper accounting recognition, for example, receiving or providing accounting, management, or other services at no charge or a major stockholder's payment of corporate expenses.

Answer (A) is incorrect because, in the absence of contrary evidence, related-party transactions are assumed to be in the ordinary course of business. Answer (B) is incorrect because determining whether a particular transaction would have occurred if the parties had not been related is ordinarily not possible unless the transaction is routine. Answer (C) is incorrect because related-party transactions need not be consummated on terms equivalent to those that prevail in arm's-length transactions.

**280.** In the absence of evidence to the contrary, transactions with related parties should not be assumed to be outside the ordinary course of business. The auditor should, however, be aware of the possibility that transactions with related parties may have been motivated solely or in large part by extraordinary conditions. Which of the following is not normally a condition motivating a transaction outside of the ordinary course of business?

A. Lack of sufficient working capital or credit to continue business.

B. An urgent desire for a continued favorable earnings record in the hope of supporting the price of the company's stock.

C. Dependence on a single or relatively few products, customers, or transactions for the ongoing success of the venture.

D. Mutual benefit to both parties.

Answer (D) is correct. *(Publisher)*

**REQUIRED:** The condition not considered a motive for a transaction outside the ordinary course of business.

**DISCUSSION:** Parties customarily execute transactions that are mutually beneficial. These are considered within the ordinary course of business. The absence of mutual benefit is an indication that the transaction is not at arm's-length and that special disclosure is required to prevent the statements from being misleading.

Answer (A) is incorrect because lack of sufficient working capital or credit to continue business is a condition suggesting that transactions resulting from related-party activities are in substance different from their form. Other such conditions include an overly optimistic earnings forecast; a declining industry characterized by a large number of business failures; excess capacity; significant litigation, especially litigation between shareholders and management; and significant danger of obsolescence because the company is in a high-technology industry. Answer (B) is incorrect because it is a condition motivating a transaction outside of the ordinary course. Answer (C) is incorrect because it is a condition motivating a transaction outside of the ordinary course.

**281.** Which of the following auditing procedures is most likely to assist an auditor in identifying related-party transactions?

A. Retesting ineffective controls previously reported to the audit committee.

B. Sending second requests for unanswered positive confirmations of accounts receivable.

C. Reviewing accounting records for nonrecurring transactions recognized near the balance sheet date.

D. Inspecting communications with law firms for evidence of unreported contingent liabilities.

Answer (C) is correct. *(CPA, adapted)*

**REQUIRED:** The procedure that is most likely to assist the auditor in identifying related-party transactions.

**DISCUSSION:** AU 334 identifies a number of procedures intended to provide guidance for identifying material transactions with parties known to be related and for identifying material transactions that may be indicative of the existence of previously undetermined relationships. One of those procedures is reviewing accounting records for large, unusual, or nonrecurring transactions or balances, paying particular attention to transactions recognized at or near the end of the reporting period.

Answer (A) is incorrect because retesting ineffective controls is not an effective use of audit resources. Answer (B) is incorrect because confirmations typically do not provide effective evidence as to related-party transactions. Answer (D) is incorrect because inspecting communications with law firms for evidence of unreported contingent liabilities is for the purpose of identifying potential litigations, claims, and assessments requiring disclosure in the financial statements.

**282.** Which of the following is an unusual procedure that may be deemed necessary to discover the effect of a related-party transaction?

A. Examine invoices and other pertinent documents such as receiving or shipping reports.

B. Confirm or discuss significant information with intermediaries, such as banks, guarantors, or agents.

C. Determine whether the transaction has been approved by the board of directors or other appropriate officials.

D. Inspect or confirm the transferability and value of collateral.

Answer (B) is correct. *(Publisher)*

**REQUIRED:** The unusual procedure to discover the effect of a related-party transaction.

**DISCUSSION:** AU 334 suggests that, to understand fully a related-party transaction, certain procedures not otherwise required to comply with auditing standards should be considered. The confirmation or discussion of significant information with intermediaries, such as banks, guarantors, attorneys, or agents, is an unusual procedure that might be applied when necessary to understand a related-party transaction.

Answer (A) is incorrect because it is a normal procedure that may be performed by an auditor to obtain satisfaction as to the purpose, nature, and extent of related-party transactions and their effects. Answer (C) is incorrect because it is a normal procedure that may be performed by an auditor to obtain satisfaction as to the purpose, nature, and extent of related-party transactions and their effects. Answer (D) is incorrect because it is a normal procedure that may be performed by an auditor to obtain satisfaction as to the purpose, nature, and extent of related-party transactions and their effects.

**283.** Disclosure in financial statements of a reporting entity that has participated in related-party transactions that are material, individually or in the aggregate, should include all of the following except

A. The nature of the relationship.

B. A description of the transactions for the period reported upon including amounts, if any, and such other information necessary to an understanding of the effects on the financial statements.

C. A statement that the transactions would have taken place regardless of whether the parties were related.

D. The dollar volume of the transactions, amounts due from or to related parties and, if not otherwise apparent, the terms and manner of settlement.

Answer (C) is correct. *(Publisher)*

**REQUIRED:** The item concerning related-party transactions not required to be disclosed.

**DISCUSSION:** It is ordinarily not possible to determine whether a particular transaction would have taken place if the parties had not been related or, assuming it would have taken place, what the terms and the manner of settlement would have been. Accordingly, representations to the effect that "a transaction was consummated on terms equivalent to those that prevail in arm's-length transactions" are difficult to substantiate and should not be included in the disclosures.

Answer (A) is incorrect because the nature of the relationship is information that is of interest to readers of the financial statements in determining the effects of related-party transactions on those statements (SFAS 57, *Related-Party Disclosures*). Answer (B) is incorrect because a description of the transactions for the period reported upon including amounts, if any, and such other information necessary to an understanding of the effects on the financial statements require disclosure. Answer (D) is incorrect because the dollar volume of the transactions, amounts due from or to related parties and, if not otherwise apparent, the terms and manner of settlement require disclosure.

**284.** Ajax, Inc. is an affiliate of the audit client and is audited by another firm of auditors. Which of the following is most likely to be used by the auditor of the client to obtain assurance that all guarantees of the affiliate's indebtedness have been detected?

A. Send the standard bank confirmation request to all of the client's lender banks.

B. Review client minutes and obtain a representation letter.

C. Examine supporting documents for all entries in intercompany accounts.

D. Obtain written confirmation of indebtedness from the auditor of the affiliate.

Answer (B) is correct. *(CPA, adapted)*

**REQUIRED:** The procedure used to determine that all guarantees of indebtedness have been detected.

**DISCUSSION:** The client's independent auditor should review minutes of board of directors and relevant committee meetings and obtain a representation letter to gain assurance that all guarantees of the affiliate's indebtedness have been detected.

Answer (A) is incorrect because bank confirmations sent to the client's lender banks would not detect guarantees of indebtedness to nonbank creditors. Answer (C) is incorrect because guarantees are not reflected in the accounts. Answer (D) is incorrect because confirmations, per se, are not typically obtained from other auditors.

## 4.17 Statement of Cash Flows

**285.** When auditing a client's statement of cash flows, an auditor will rely primarily upon

A. Determination of the amount of cash at year-end.

B. Cross-referencing to balances and transactions considered in connection with the audit of the other financial statements.

C. Analysis of significant ratios of prior years as compared to the current year.

D. The audit guidance provided by SFAS 95, *Statement of Cash Flows*.

Answer (B) is correct. *(CPA, adapted)*

**REQUIRED:** The evidence on which the auditor will primarily rely when auditing a statement of cash flows.

**DISCUSSION:** The statement of cash flows represents balances taken from the other statements as well as analysis of changes in those balances. Consequently, this statement is audited in conjunction with the balance sheet and income statement accounts.

Answer (A) is incorrect because the statement reflects the changes in the cash balance rather than the balance in the account at year-end. Answer (C) is incorrect because analysis of ratios (an analytical procedure) used as a substantive test may be effective and efficient for testing some assertions but not all of those encompassed by a statement of cash flows. Answer (D) is incorrect because SFAS 95 prescribes GAAP for the statement of cash flows, not audit guidance.

**286.** Which of the following procedures would an auditor most likely perform in auditing the statement of cash flows?

A. Compare the amounts included in the statement of cash flows to similar amounts in the prior year's statement of cash flows.

B. Reconcile the cutoff bank statements to verify the accuracy of the year-end bank balances.

C. Vouch all bank transfers for the last week of the year and first week of the subsequent year.

D. Reconcile the amounts included in the statement of cash flows to the other financial statements' balances and amounts.

Answer (D) is correct. *(CPA, adapted)*

**REQUIRED:** The procedure useful in auditing the statement of cash flows.

**DISCUSSION:** The information presented on a statement of cash flows is taken from the income statement and balance sheet. Indeed, a reconciliation of net income and net operating cash flow is required to be presented. Thus, reconciliation of amounts in the statement of cash flows with other financial statements' balances and amounts is an important procedure in the audit of the statement of cash flows.

Answer (A) is incorrect because analytical procedures for cash are not usually effective. Cash is a managed account. Answer (B) is incorrect because reconciling the cutoff bank statements to verify the accuracy of year-end bank balances is an appropriate procedure to audit the cash account but not necessarily the statement of cash flows. Answer (C) is incorrect because vouching all bank transfers for the last week of the year and the first week of the subsequent year is effective for detecting cutoff misstatements, such as those arising from kiting, but not for auditing the statement of cash flows.

**287.** An auditor is reviewing a corporate client's statement of cash flows. The auditor should expect the cash flows to be classified according to

A. Fund inflows and fund outflows.

B. Cash inflows and cash outflows.

C. Operating activities, sources, and uses.

D. Investing, financing, and operating activities.

Answer (D) is correct. *(Publisher)*

**REQUIRED:** The activities into which cash receipts and cash payments should be classified.

**DISCUSSION:** To provide the most useful information about cash receipts and cash payments to investors, creditors, and others, a statement of cash flows should report the cash effects of an entity's operations, its investing transactions, and its financing transactions during the period. In addition, the related disclosures should report the effects of investing and financing transactions that do not directly affect cash.

Answer (A) is incorrect because a statement of cash flows is based on cash. Answer (B) is incorrect because the cash flows must be classified according to investing, financing, and operating activities. Answer (C) is incorrect because sources and uses were used in the now-superseded statement of changes in financial position.

**288.** Many of the Granada Corporation's convertible bondholders have converted their bonds into stock during the year under audit. The independent auditor should review the Granada Corporation's statement of cash flows and related disclosures to ascertain that they show

A. Only the cash used to reduce the convertible debt.

B. Only the cash provided by the issuance of stock.

C. The issuance of the stock and reduction in convertible debt.

D. Nothing relating to the conversion because it does not affect cash.

Answer (C) is correct. *(CPA, adapted)*

**REQUIRED:** The proper reporting of the conversion of bonds to stock.

**DISCUSSION:** Information about noncash financing and investing activities must be reported in related disclosures but not on the face of the statement of cash flows. Exclusion of such transactions from the statement avoids complicating it and emphasizes the entity's cash receipts and payments (SFAS 95). The issuance of stock and the reduction of convertible debt should therefore be disclosed in a related but separate schedule. All financing (and investing) activities during the period should be reported, including those that do not directly affect cash.

Answer (A) is incorrect because, although both parts of the financing activity should be reported, neither involves a cash flow. Answer (B) is incorrect because, although both parts of the financing activity should be reported, neither involves a cash flow. Answer (D) is incorrect because all financing and investing activities should be reported.

# STUDY UNIT FIVE
# INFORMATION SYSTEMS



This study unit covers computers, computer operations, computer systems, and the auditing of computer operations and systems. The first seven subunits are definitional. Subunit 5.1 is an introduction, and Subunits 5.2 through 5.7 relate to computer system attributes, development, and design. Subunits 5.8 through 5.12 address computer processing controls and their evaluation. Subunit 5.13 describes the auditor's understanding and testing of a client's computer processing internal control. Subunit 5.14 involves the use of the computer to assist the auditor in gathering evidence. Subunit 5.15 introduces concepts of artificial intelligence. Subunit 5.16 presents some limited Certified Information Systems Auditor (CISA) concepts. The following discussion provides an overview of computer processing controls.

## COMPUTER PROCESSING CONTROLS

A variety of controls may be performed to assure the accuracy, completeness, and authorization of transactions. The two broad groupings of information systems control activities are general and application controls.

**General controls** include controls over data center operations, system software acquisition and maintenance, applications system development and maintenance, and access security. These controls apply to mainframe, server, and end-user environments (AU 319).

1. **Data center operation controls** include the plan of the organization and the operation of the computer processing activity. They are concerned with the proper segregation of duties and responsibilities within the computer processing environment. The responsibilities of systems analysts, programmers, operators, file librarians, and the control group should be performed by different individuals, and proper supervision should be provided. Operating controls ensure efficient and effective operation within the computer processing department. These controls also assure proper procedures in the event of data loss caused by error or disaster. Typical operating controls include the proper labeling of all files both internally and externally, halt and error procedures, duplicate files, and reconstruction procedures for files. We term these **operating and organizational controls**, and they are covered in Subunit 5.9.
2. **System software acquisition and maintenance controls** and **application system development and maintenance controls** are concerned with the proper planning, procurement, testing, and documentation of systems. These controls also provide for security and virus protection of software including operating systems, utility programs, and application software. Maintenance controls include authorizations, program change controls, and documentation, including proper use of flowcharts. We term these **program development and documentation controls**, and they are covered in Subunit 5.10.
3. **Access security controls** provide assurance that only authorized individuals have access to computer equipment and data files. These controls include physical safeguards of equipment, proper library security, and passwords. They are covered in Subunit 5.11.

**Application controls** apply to the processing of individual applications. These controls help ensure that transactions are valid, properly authorized, and completely and accurately processed. They can be classified into input, processing, and output controls. They are covered in Subunit 5.12.

1. **Input controls** are designed to provide reasonable assurance that data received for computer processing have been properly authorized and are in a form suitable for processing. Input controls also include those that relate to rejection, correction, and resubmission of data that were initially incorrect.
2. **Processing controls** are designed to provide reasonable assurance that data submitted for processing have been processed appropriately, i.e., that all transactions are processed as authorized, no authorized transactions are omitted, and no unauthorized transactions are added.
3. **Output controls** are designed to assure that the processing results are accurate and that only authorized personnel receive the output.

## QUESTIONS

### 5.1 Introduction to the Information Systems Environment

**1.** A management information system

A. Can exist only with computers.

B. Primarily processes data and produces reports.

C. Supports the operations, management, and decision-making functions in an organization.

D. Is a single large system in an organization.

Answer (C) is correct. *(CIA, adapted)*

**REQUIRED:** The description of a management information system.

**DISCUSSION:** A management information system (MIS) is a system of resources within the organization that processes data to generate information useful in operations and management. It provides the most comprehensive support for decision making involving structured tasks.

Answer (A) is incorrect because an MIS rarely exists without computers except in small businesses. Answer (B) is incorrect because the data processing cycle (processing of data and production of reports) generates information for use in the MIS. Answer (D) is incorrect because the MIS consists of many subsystems, including the accounting information system.

**2.** Early decision models used with structured decisions, such as inventory reordering and production scheduling, emphasized finding the structure of the decision and programming as much of it as possible. More recent models have been developed to support unstructured decision processes. Models of the latter type are called

A. Decision support systems.

B. Management information systems.

C. Systems analysis techniques.

D. Rational decision models.

Answer (A) is correct. *(CIA, adapted)*

**REQUIRED:** The term for models developed to support unstructured decision processes.

**DISCUSSION:** A decision support system (DSS) assists middle- and upper-level managers in long-term, nonroutine, and often unstructured decision making. The system combines data, decision models, and user-friendly software to provide end users with capabilities for analysis rather than specified information flows. It is an aid to decision making, not the automation of a decision process.

Answer (B) is incorrect because an MIS does not normally include subsystems that provide support for unstructured decisions. Answer (C) is incorrect because systems analysis techniques are used to design the DSS. Answer (D) is incorrect because all decision models are rational.

**3.** The first phase in the evolutionary development of information systems occurs when

A. Management discovers it is losing money.

B. Resources permit the hiring of a system staff.

C. The decision is made to acquire a computer system.

D. The growth of an enterprise brings about the need for improved administrative planning and control.

Answer (D) is correct. *(CDP, adapted)*

**REQUIRED:** The first phase in the evolutionary development of an information system.

**DISCUSSION:** As its information needs change, an organization requires improved methods of processing data to provide information for managerial decisions and to control the implementation of those decisions. When this need is recognized, firms begin systems development activities.

Answer (A) is incorrect because management may lose money for many reasons other than the lack of systems development. Answer (B) is incorrect because the need for improved processing should be the deciding criterion, not whether resources permit the hiring of additional staff. Answer (C) is incorrect because the need should precede the decision to acquire a computer system.

**4.** Management activities can be classified in three levels: strategic planning, management control, and operational control. Information requirements vary with the level of management activity. Which of the following best describes the information requirements for strategic planning?

A. Frequent use, external, aggregate information.

B. Future-oriented, outdated, detailed information.

C. Highly current, accurate, largely internal information.

D. Wide scope, aggregate, future-oriented information.

Answer (D) is correct. *(CIA, adapted)*

**REQUIRED:** The best description of the information requirements for strategic planning.

**DISCUSSION:** Strategic planning concerns development of the entity's long-range mission and objectives and the means for accomplishing them. Such plans are often stated in general terms and exclude operational detail because of uncertainty about future conditions. Strategic planning is commonly defined as having a planning horizon of 1 to 10 years. The information needed for strategic planning tends to come from external sources, to be very wide in scope, and to be highly aggregated (not detailed). Moreover, this information is future oriented, much less current than that needed for operational or management control, relatively less accurate, and infrequently used.

Answer (A) is incorrect because information needed for strategic planning is not frequently used. Answer (B) is incorrect because information needed for strategic planning is not detailed or necessarily outdated. Answer (C) is incorrect because information needed for operational control needs to be highly current and accurate and is largely internal.

**5.** Who is ultimately responsible for the implementation of cost-effective controls in an automated system?

A. The director of internal auditing.

B. Operating management.

C. The computer processing audit manager.

D. The control group in the computer processing department.

Answer (B) is correct. *(CIA, adapted)*

**REQUIRED:** The party or parties primarily responsible for the implementation of cost-effective controls.

**DISCUSSION:** Operating management should assure that effective controls are implemented in all parts of an organization. Management is ultimately responsible for establishing systems to provide reasonable assurance of achieving organizational objectives and goals.

Answer (A) is incorrect because internal auditing is responsible for evaluating, but not establishing, internal controls. Answer (C) is incorrect because the computer processing audit manager is only one member of operating management. Answer (D) is incorrect because the control group acts as a liaison between system users and the computer department and implements many controls on an operational basis, but it is not responsible for the development of controls.

**6.** Regardless of the nature of the client's information processing system, the auditor must consider internal control. In a computer environment, the auditor must, at a minimum, have

A. A basic familiarity with the computer's operating system.

B. A sufficient understanding of the entire computer system.

C. An expertise in computer systems analysis.

D. A background in programming procedures.

Answer (B) is correct. *(Publisher)*

**REQUIRED:** The degree of understanding an auditor must have of a client's computer processing system.

**DISCUSSION:** The first general standard (GAAS) requires the audit to be performed by a person having adequate technical training and proficiency as an auditor. The second standard of field work requires that a sufficient understanding of internal control be obtained to plan the audit and determine the nature, timing, and extent of substantive tests. Hence, the auditor should have the training and proficiency that are necessary to understand control activities relevant to the computer processing system. This understanding must be sufficient for audit planning and testing.

Answer (A) is incorrect because familiarity with the computer's operating system is less important than understanding the entire processing system. Answer (C) is incorrect because auditors usually do not need to be experts in computer systems analysis, although certain audit procedures may require special expertise. Answer (D) is incorrect because auditors usually do not need to have a background in programming procedures, although certain audit procedures may require special expertise.

**7.** Which of the following statements most likely represents a disadvantage for an entity that keeps data files on a server rather than on a manual system?

A. Attention is focused on the accuracy of the programming process rather than errors in individual transactions.

B. It is usually easier for unauthorized persons to access and alter the files.

C. Random error associated with processing similar transactions in different ways is usually greater.

D. It is usually more difficult to compare recorded accountability with the physical count of assets.

Answer (B) is correct. *(CPA, adapted)*

**REQUIRED:** The disadvantage of server-based data files.

**DISCUSSION:** In a manual system, one individual is usually assigned responsibility for maintaining and safeguarding the records. However, in a server environment, the data files may be subject to change by others without documentation or an indication of who made the changes.

Answer (A) is incorrect because the focus on programming is an advantage of using a server. A software program allows transactions to be processed uniformly. Answer (C) is incorrect because it describes a disadvantage of a manual system. Answer (D) is incorrect because the method of maintaining the files is independent of the ability to compare this information in the file with the physical count of assets.

**8.** The most common computer-related problem confronting organizations is

A. Hardware malfunction.

B. Input errors and omissions.

C. Disruption to computer processing caused by natural disasters.

D. Fraud.

Answer (B) is correct. *(CIA, adapted)*

**REQUIRED:** The most common problem confronting an organization using computers.

**DISCUSSION:** The most common problem confronting an organization in its use of computers is erroneous or incomplete input. Input is especially susceptible to errors and omissions because of the substantial human intervention required. Comprehensive and effective input controls are necessary to ensure that data stored in files or used in processing are not contaminated.

Answer (A) is incorrect because hardware malfunction is not considered a major problem once the development and testing phase is complete. Answer (C) is incorrect because the second most common problem is the disruption to processing caused by natural disasters such as fire or power failures. Answer (D) is incorrect because the third most common problem is computer abuse, e.g., fraud.

**9.** Which one of the following statements about an accounting information system (AIS) is false?

A. An AIS supports day-to-day operations by collecting and sorting data about an organization's transactions.

B. The information produced by an AIS is made available to all levels of management for use in planning and controlling an organization's activities.

C. An AIS is best suited to solve problems where there is great uncertainty and ill-defined reporting requirements.

D. An AIS is often referred to as a transaction processing system.

Answer (C) is correct. *(CMA, adapted)*

**REQUIRED:** The false statement about an AIS.

**DISCUSSION:** An AIS is a subsystem of a management information system that processes financial and transactional data relevant to managerial and financial accounting. The AIS supports operations by collecting and sorting data about an organization's transactions. An AIS is concerned not only with external parties, but also with the internal activities needed for management decision making at all levels. An AIS is best suited to solve problems when reporting requirements are well defined. A decision support system is a better choice for problems in which decision making is less structured.

Answer (A) is incorrect because it is an attribute of an AIS. Answer (B) is incorrect because it is an attribute of an AIS. Answer (D) is incorrect because it is an attribute of an AIS.

**10.** The two broad groupings of information systems control activities are general controls and application controls. General controls include controls

A. Designed to assure that only authorized users receive output from processing.

B. For developing, modifying, and maintaining computer programs.

C. Relating to the correction and resubmission of faulty data.

D. Designed to ensure that all data submitted for processing have been properly authorized.

Answer (B) is correct. *(Publisher)*

**REQUIRED:** The general controls.

**DISCUSSION:** General controls are policies and procedures that relate to many information systems applications and support the effective functioning of application controls by helping to ensure the continued proper operation of information systems. General controls include controls over (1) data center and network operations, (2) systems software acquisition and maintenance, (3) access security, and (4) application systems acquisition, development, and maintenance (AU 319).

Answer (A) is incorrect because control over report distribution (output) is an application control. Answer (C) is incorrect because correction of input errors is an application control. Answer (D) is incorrect because authorization of input is an application control.

**11.** Which of the following risks are greater in computerized systems than in manual systems?

I. Erroneous data conversion
II. Erroneous source document preparation
III. Repetition of errors
IV. Concentration of data

A. I and II.
B. II and III.
C. I, III, and IV.
D. I, II, III, and IV.

Answer (C) is correct. *(CISA, adapted)*

**REQUIRED:** The risks that are greater in a computer system than a manual system.

**DISCUSSION:** Unlike a manual system, a computer system converts data to machine-readable form so that transactions can be processed. This additional step increases the risk of input error. Moreover, if an error exists in the program, systematic, repetitive errors will occur in processing transactions. Finally, data are typically stored magnetically on tapes or disks. This concentration of data increases the risk of loss from natural and other disasters.

Answer (A) is incorrect because source document preparation either precedes processing or is eliminated altogether in a computerized system. Thus, the risk of erroneous source document preparation in computerized systems is the same as or less than the equivalent risk in manual systems. Answer (B) is incorrect because source document preparation either precedes processing or is eliminated altogether in a computerized system. Thus, the risk of erroneous source document preparation in computerized systems is the same as or less than the equivalent risk in manual systems. Answer (D) is incorrect because source document preparation either precedes processing or is eliminated altogether in a computerized system. Thus, the risk of erroneous source document preparation in computerized systems is the same as or less than the equivalent risk in manual systems.

**12.** Compared with closed systems, open systems are characterized by

A. Less expensive components.
B. Decreased interoperability.
C. More dependence on particular vendors.
D. More restricted portability.

Answer (A) is correct. *(CIA, adapted)*

**REQUIRED:** The item that characterizes open systems.

**DISCUSSION:** Open systems consist of components produced in conformity with nonproprietary public standards. Since the 1980s, government agencies have demanded that suppliers provide components with interfaces defined by public standards. These standards apply especially to operating systems and telecommunications protocols. Thus, they permit systems from different suppliers to work together (interoperability). Moreover, open systems can be sized to an entity's needs (scalability), relocated to new platforms (portability), and used for years to come (compatibility). Another result of product interchangeability is the formation of a commodity market and a decline in prices. Less product differentiation means that competition is increasingly based solely on price.

Answer (B) is incorrect because open systems have increased interoperability. Answer (C) is incorrect because users of open systems have a wider range of vendors available. Answer (D) is incorrect because open systems are more portable.

**13.** Expert systems consist of

A. Software packages with the ability to make judgment decisions.
B. A panel of outside consultants.
C. Hardware designed to make judgment decisions.
D. Hardware and software used to automate routine tasks.

Answer (A) is correct. *(CIA, adapted)*

**REQUIRED:** The definition of expert systems.

**DISCUSSION:** Artificial intelligence and its subfield, expert systems, have been identified as one of the major issues facing the accounting profession. Expert systems enable a computer to make decisions in a human way. An expert system is an interactive system that asks a series of questions and uses knowledge gained from a human expert to analyze answers and come to a decision, that is, to exercise judgment. Expert systems were originally developed to make decisions in areas that did not have enough human experts to satisfy the need to make decisions. Some of the earliest expert systems were used by doctors to diagnose diseases. Work is being done with expert systems in taxation, financial accounting, managerial accounting, and auditing.

Answer (B) is incorrect because expert systems do not require outside consultants. Answer (C) is incorrect because hardware does not make judgment decisions. Answer (D) is incorrect because automation of routine tasks is not the purpose of expert systems.

## 5.2 Basic Hardware Concepts

**14.** Which of the following is not an element of hardware?

A. Monitors.

B. Application programs.

C. CD-ROM drive.

D. Scanners.

Answer (B) is correct. *(Publisher)*

**REQUIRED:** The item that is not considered hardware.

**DISCUSSION:** Computer hardware consists of the configuration of physical equipment. Application software consists of programs written for or by users to perform certain ultimate tasks specified by the users.

Answer (A) is incorrect because monitors are output devices for display of data or graphics. Answer (C) is incorrect because a CD-ROM (compact disk-read only memory) is a laser optical disk. It provides high capacity storage, is movable, has a rapid data transfer rate, and is very durable. Furthermore, the newest versions are rewritable. Answer (D) is incorrect because scanners are input devices that digitize documents and graphics.

**15.** Which of the following is a hardware device not usually associated with input?

A. Printer.

B. Optical scanner.

C. Touch screen.

D. Mouse.

Answer (A) is correct. *(Publisher)*

**REQUIRED:** The hardware device not usually associated with input.

**DISCUSSION:** A printer is used to produce a hard copy of information output. Printers may print one character, one line, or one page at a time. They also vary with respect to speed and quality.

Answer (B) is incorrect because an optical scanner reads characters directly from source documents based upon the shapes of the characters. Answer (C) is incorrect because touch screen technology provides another limited alternative to keyboard input. Commands or data can be entered by touching the sensitized surface of a monitor. Answer (D) is incorrect because a mouse is a pointing device used for input.

**16.** Which of the following computer hardware devices allows for an immediate update of merchandise inventory in a retail environment?

A. Inventory control terminal.

B. CD-RW.

C. Video display terminal.

D. Point-of-sale terminal.

Answer (D) is correct. *(CIA, adapted)*

**REQUIRED:** The computer hardware device that allows for an immediate update of merchandise inventory.

**DISCUSSION:** Point-of-sale terminals have replaced cash registers in retail stores. They capture data by optical scanning or by keying. The data are then transmitted to a CPU. The system facilitates collection of sales data, updating and ordering of inventory, pricing at the point of sale, and checking of customer credit cards.

Answer (A) is incorrect because the term inventory control terminal is not meaningful in this context. Answer (B) is incorrect because CD-RW is the acronym for a compact disk that is rewritable. Answer (C) is incorrect because video display terminal is a generic term for any device with a keyboard and a visual display that interacts with a computer.

**17.** Banks are required to process many transactions from paper documents (e.g., checks, deposit slips) during the course of an average business day. This requires a reliable, yet economical form of input. The most common source automation device used by banks is

A. A disk pack.

B. Magnetic tape.

C. Bar coding.

D. Magnetic ink character recognition.

Answer (D) is correct. *(CMA, adapted)*

**REQUIRED:** The most common source automation device used by banks.

**DISCUSSION:** Magnetic ink character recognition (MICR) is used by banks to read the magnetic ink on checks and deposit slips. MICR is a form of data entry device.

Answer (A) is incorrect because a disk pack is a storage device. Answer (B) is incorrect because magnetic tape is used as a secondary storage medium. It is low cost and reusable, but data retrieval is relatively slow because it uses sequential access. Answer (C) is incorrect because bar coding is a data entry technique often used by manufacturers, wholesalers, and retailers, but it is rarely used by banks.

**18.** Which of the following statements about personal computers, midrange computers, and mainframe computers is true?

A. Personal computers usually cost more than midrange computers but less than mainframes.

B. Because of the increased use of personal computers, there will be little need for mainframes in the near future.

C. Midrange computers must be programmed directly in machine language while mainframes use higher-level language.

D. The cost per transaction to process on each type of computer has decreased in recent years.

Answer (D) is correct. *(Publisher)*

**REQUIRED:** The true statement concerning personal, midrange, and mainframe computers.

**DISCUSSION:** Advances in technology have resulted in less expensive computers and increased computing power. The cost to process transactions on all kinds of computers has therefore decreased.

Answer (A) is incorrect because personal computers may cost less than $1,000. Relative to personal computers, midrange computers are more costly, more powerful, have more memory, and are able to interface with more peripheral equipment. Mainframes are large computers with many peripheral devices and large memories. There is virtually no upper limit on the cost of a mainframe. Answer (B) is incorrect because, although personal computers have become extremely popular, e.g., for word processing, databases, other business-related activities, and Internet use, large mainframes are still necessary for simulations and processing not possible on smaller computers. Midrange computers fill the gap between personal and mainframe computers, and a relatively strong demand also exists for these types of processors, particularly for servers used in networks. Answer (C) is incorrect because all three computers ordinarily may be programmed in higher-level languages.

**19.** Internal auditors may encounter different personal computer platforms in separate operating divisions or geographic locations. Which of the following statements is true?

I. Most data and programs from one personal computer platform are transferable to another platform only through translation and emulation programs.

II. Neither data nor programs are transferable when the hardware is not identical.

III. Neither data nor programs are transferable when the operating systems are not identical.

IV. Most data and many programs are transferable among environments through shareware programs.

A. I.

B. I, IV.

C. III.

D. II, III.

Answer (A) is correct. *(CIA, adapted)*

**REQUIRED:** The true statement(s) about personal computer platforms.

**DISCUSSION:** An emulator is a hardware device that permits one system to imitate another, that is, to use the same data and programs and obtain the same results as the other system. A translator is a program that translates from one programming language into another.

Answer (B) is incorrect because shareware is not available to meet most conversion needs. Shareware is a program that can be freely copied and tested before purchase. If the party obtaining the shareware continues to use it, there is an obligation to send payment to the author. Shareware typically is found on bulletin boards and online information systems. Answer (C) is incorrect because there are facilities to transfer data and programs between some environments. Answer (D) is incorrect because there are facilities to transfer data and programs between some environments.

**20.** A piece of hardware that takes the computer's digital information and transforms it into signals that can be sent over ordinary telephone lines is called a(n)

A. Terminal emulator.

B. Communications control unit.

C. Intelligent terminal.

D. Modem.

Answer (D) is correct. *(CIA, adapted)*

**REQUIRED:** The hardware that transforms digital information into analog signals.

**DISCUSSION:** Modems are used to communicate between terminals and a CPU, usually across telephone lines. The modem (modulator-demodulator) converts the digital form of data storage in a computer into analog or sound waves that can be communicated across telephone lines. The modem at the receiving end converts the analog signal back to the digital form used by the terminal or CPU.

Answer (A) is incorrect because a terminal emulator permits a personal computer to interface with a mainframe. Answer (B) is incorrect because communications control units include communications processors (front-end processors), multiplexors, and concentrators. Communications processors are small computers that perform communications tasks (storing and moving data, editing, message switching, etc.). Multiplexors combine signals from different terminals into one signal to be sent to the CPU or other point. A concentrator is essentially a more advanced multiplexor. Answer (C) is incorrect because an intelligent terminal is hardware that has processing ability.

**21.** Many personal computers (PCs) have both a floppy disk drive and a hard disk drive. The major difference between the two types of storage is that a hard disk

A. Has a much larger storage capacity than a floppy disk and can also access information much more quickly.

B. Is a direct-access storage medium, and a floppy disk is a sequential-access storage medium.

C. Provides an automatic audit trail, and a floppy disk does not.

D. Is suitable for an online system, but a floppy disk is not.

Answer (A) is correct. *(CIA, adapted)*

**REQUIRED:** The difference between floppy disk and hard disk storage.

**DISCUSSION:** Floppy disks were developed by IBM out of plastic film that rotates the desired stored data to an opening in its cover where it is accessed by the computer's read-write device. Hard disks are used in larger systems as well as in personal computers. They require much less power and maintenance than floppies and can store far more data. Also, the read-write operations and disk rotation are much faster with hard disks.

Answer (B) is incorrect because both floppy disk and hard disk are direct-access storage media. Answer (C) is incorrect because neither hard disk nor floppy disk provides an automatic audit trail. Answer (D) is incorrect because both floppy disk and hard disk are suited for an online system.

**22.** A manufacturer of complex electronic equipment such as oscilloscopes and microscopes has been shipping its products with thick paper manuals but wants to reduce the cost of producing and shipping this documentation. Of the following, the best medium for the manufacturer to use to accomplish this result is

A. VCR tape.

B. Digital audiotape (DAT).

C. Compact disk (CD).

D. Computer output to microfilm (COM).

Answer (C) is correct. *(CIA, adapted)*

**REQUIRED:** The best way to reduce the cost of producing and shipping documentation.

**DISCUSSION:** CDs are cheaper to produce and ship than the existing paper, yet it permits large volumes of text and images to be reproduced. Users of the electronic equipment are likely to have access to CD readers on PCs for using such documentation.

Answer (A) is incorrect because a VCR tape is mainly useful for watching video. Answer (B) is incorrect because DAT is primarily used as a backup medium in imaging systems and as a master for CDs. Answer (D) is incorrect because COM is used for frequent access to archived documents, such as canceled checks in banking applications.

**23.** Uninterruptible power supplies are used in computer centers to reduce the likelihood of

A. Failing to control concurrent access to data.

B. Losing data stored in main memory.

C. Dropping bits in data transmission.

D. Crashing disk drive read-write heads.

Answer (B) is correct. *(CIA, adapted)*

**REQUIRED:** The reason for uninterruptible power supplies in computer centers.

**DISCUSSION:** Fully protected systems have generator or battery backup to prevent data destruction and downtime from electrical power disturbances. Loss of electrical power or voltage fluctuations need not disturb the vulnerable contents of main memory if an uninterruptible system is in place.

Answer (A) is incorrect because concurrency controls serve this purpose. Answer (C) is incorrect because hardware controls built into the system avoid errors in transmission. Answer (D) is incorrect because disk drives are currently designed to protect against crashing read-write heads.

**24.** When evaluating the downsizing of the plant materials inventory system, data center personnel considered redundant array of inexpensive (or independent) disks (RAID) for the inventory database. One reason to use RAID is to ensure that

A. If one drive fails, all data can still be reconstructed.

B. All data are split evenly across pairs of drives.

C. Before-and-after images are stored for all transactions.

D. Write time is minimized to avoid concurrency conflicts.

Answer (A) is correct. *(CIA, adapted)*

**REQUIRED:** The reason to use RAID.

**DISCUSSION:** A disk array expedites data transfer and provides fault tolerance. It combines two or more drives with special controller circuitry and software to execute reads and writes as if only one disk drive existed. When files are stored on RAID, data can be reconstructed even if one drive fails.

Answer (B) is incorrect because splitting data evenly across pairs of drives (data striping) results in faster reads and writes but reduced reliability. The failure of one drive causes loss of all data. Answer (C) is incorrect because writing before-and-after images is a means of creating a transaction log for database transactions, which can be implemented with or without RAID. Answer (D) is incorrect because minimizing write time is not an advantage of RAID.

**25.** The location in the central processing unit (CPU) where data and programs are temporarily stored during processing is the

A. Floppy disk drive.

B. Magnetic tape drive.

C. Random-access memory (RAM).

D. Magnetic disk drive.

Answer (C) is correct. *(CMA, adapted)*

**REQUIRED:** The location in the CPU where data and programs are temporarily stored during processing.

**DISCUSSION:** The CPU is the part of the computer system that manipulates numbers, symbols, and letters. Primary storage is the area in the CPU where programs and data are temporarily stored during processing. Internal primary storage is also known as random-access memory because each memory location therein can be randomly accessed in the same amount of time.

Answer (A) is incorrect because a floppy disk drive is a random access storage medium for personal computers that permits permanent storage of data. Answer (B) is incorrect because a magnetic tape drive is not for temporary storage. Answer (D) is incorrect because a magnetic disk drive is a secondary storage medium for permanent storage of data.

**26.** In a computer system, the place where parts of the operating system program and language translator program are permanently stored is

A. Read only memory (ROM).

B. Magnetic disk drive.

C. Random access memory (RAM).

D. Magnetic tape drive.

Answer (A) is correct. *(CMA, adapted)*

**REQUIRED:** The place where parts of the operating system and language translator are stored.

**DISCUSSION:** ROM consists of semiconductor chips that come from the manufacturer with programs already stored in them. These chips can be read from but not written to and therefore constitute permanent storage. Start up instructions are permanently stored in ROM in a personal computer to initiate processing and prevent users from accidentally erasing or changing the system. Some personal computers, however, have erasable, programmable ROM (EPROM). EPROM may be erased by an ultraviolet technique (but not by the computer) after which new instructions may be entered.

Answer (B) is incorrect because a magnetic disk is a temporary storage device. Answer (C) is incorrect because RAM is a temporary storage device. Answer (D) is incorrect because magnetic tape is a temporary storage device.

**27.** Access time in relation to computer processing is the amount of time it takes to

A. Transmit data from a remote terminal to a central computer.

B. Complete a transaction from initial input to output.

C. Perform a computer instruction.

D. Retrieve data from memory.

Answer (D) is correct. *(CMA, adapted)*

**REQUIRED:** The definition of access time.

**DISCUSSION:** Access time is the interval between the moment at which an instruction control unit initiates a call for data and the moment at which delivery of the data is completed. For example, direct access memory is typically faster than sequential access memory.

Answer (A) is incorrect because access time refers to the speed of data retrieval not data transmittal. Answer (B) is incorrect because throughput time is the time to complete a transaction from initial input to output. Answer (C) is incorrect because access time is much slower than the time required to execute an instruction.

**28.** Which of the following measures indicates the computational power of a microprocessor?

A. Capacity of the hard disk.

B. Main memory storage capacity.

C. Number of bits processed per second.

D. Read only memory.

Answer (C) is correct. *(CIA, adapted)*

**REQUIRED:** The measure indicating the computational power of a microprocessor.

**DISCUSSION:** Processing speed is commonly calculated in terms of arithmetic-logic operations performed per second. This measure is a function of the main processing chip's cycle speed stated in gigahertz.

Answer (A) is incorrect because capacity of the hard disk is a measure of memory. Answer (B) is incorrect because main memory storage capacity is a measure of memory. Answer (D) is incorrect because read only memory is main memory that ordinarily cannot be modified by the user. It is not a performance measure.

**29.** The significance of hardware controls is that they

A. Ensure correct programming of operating system functions.

B. Assure the correct execution of machine instructions.

C. Reduce the incidence of user input errors in online systems.

D. Ensure that run-to-run totals in application systems are consistent.

Answer (B) is correct. *(CIA, adapted)*
**REQUIRED:** The significance of hardware controls.
**DISCUSSION:** Hardware controls are built into the equipment by the manufacturer to detect and control errors arising from the use of the equipment. Examples include parity checks, read-after-write checks, and echo checks.
Answer (A) is incorrect because programmers and/or analysts must correct errors in computer programs. Answer (C) is incorrect because use of input screens, limit tests, self-checking digits, and other input controls can reduce the incidence of input errors in online systems. Answer (D) is incorrect because run-to-run totals ensure the completeness of update in an online system by accumulating separate totals for all transactions processed throughout a period. This total is compared with the total of items accepted for processing.

**30.** In a data center, many hardware controls assure the accuracy of data processed. One hardware control used to evaluate stored data by counting the number of on bits in each character and then determining whether the total obtained is odd or even is a

A. Programmed check.

B. Header label check.

C. Check digit routine.

D. Parity check.

Answer (D) is correct. *(CIA, adapted)*
**REQUIRED:** The hardware control that counts on bits.
**DISCUSSION:** Hardware controls are built into the computer by the manufacturer. A parity check adds the on bits in a byte and determines whether the sum is odd or even, depending on whether the computer has odd or even parity, respectively. This check verifies that all data have been transferred without loss. For example, if the computer has even parity, the parity bit added to a byte will be turned on if the byte contains an odd number of on bits. The parity bit is turned off if the byte has an even number of on bits. Accordingly, if the number of on bits, including the parity bit, is not even, an error has occurred.
Answer (A) is incorrect because a programmed check is an edit test performed by a program (software). Answer (B) is incorrect because a header label identifies a file on a tape or disk. Software makes this check. Answer (C) is incorrect because a self-checking digit is a suffix digit related algorithmically to the preceding digit(s) of an identification number. It is an application control to verify that the number has been transferred correctly from one medium or device to another.

**31.** A manufacturer is considering using bar-code identification for recording information on parts used by the manufacturer. A reason to use bar codes rather than other means of identification is to ensure that

A. The movement of all parts is recorded.

B. The movement of parts is easily and quickly recorded.

C. Vendors use the same part numbers.

D. Vendors use the same identification methods.

Answer (B) is correct. *(CIA, adapted)*
**REQUIRED:** The reason to use bar codes.
**DISCUSSION:** Bar-code scanning is a form of optical character recognition. Bar codes are a series of bars of different widths that represent critical information about the item. They can be read and the information can be instantly recorded using a scanner. Thus, bar coding records the movement of parts with minimal labor costs.
Answer (A) is incorrect because any identification method may fail to record the movement of some parts. Answer (C) is incorrect because each vendor has its own part-numbering scheme. Answer (D) is incorrect because each vendor has its own identification method, although vendors in the same industry often cooperate to minimize the number of bar-code systems they use.

## 5.3 Basic Software and Data Organization Concepts

**32.** A highly confidential file needs to be properly deleted from a computer. The best way to accomplish this task is to use a(n)

A. Security card.

B. Encryption routine.

C. Disk utility.

D. Multiplexor.

Answer (C) is correct. *(CIA, adapted)*
**REQUIRED:** The best way to delete a confidential file.
**DISCUSSION:** Unknown copies of sensitive data may exist in the hard drive or in memory. Most delete utilities erase file pointers but not underlying data. However, some utilities are available for this purpose.
Answer (A) is incorrect because security cards are used during logons. Answer (B) is incorrect because encryption routines are mathematical algorithms and keys used to encode sensitive information so that it is unintelligible until decrypted. Answer (D) is incorrect because a multiplexor is used to control multiple transmissions from linked terminals and modems.

**33.** Several language interfaces exist in a database management system. These typically include a data-definition language (DDL), a data control language (DCL), a data-manipulation language (DML), and a database query language (DQL). What language interface would a database administrator use to establish the structure of database tables?

A. DDL.

B. DCL.

C. DML.

D. DQL.

Answer (A) is correct. *(CIA, adapted)*

**REQUIRED:** The language interface used by a database administrator to establish the structure of database tables.

**DISCUSSION:** The data-definition language defines the database structure and content, especially the schema (the description of the entire database) and subschema (logical views of the database). The schema specifies characteristics such as the names of the data elements contained in the database and their relationship to each other. The subschema defines the logical data views required for applications. Thus, it limits the data elements and functions available to each application.

Answer (B) is incorrect because DCL is used to specify privileges and security rules. Answer (C) is incorrect because DML provides programmers with a facility to update the database. Answer (D) is incorrect because DQL is used for ad hoc queries.

**34.** Computer manufacturers install software programs permanently inside the computer as part of its main memory to provide protection from erasure or loss if electrical power is interrupted. This concept is known as

A. File integrity.

B. Software control.

C. Firmware.

D. Random access memory (RAM).

Answer (C) is correct. *(CMA, adapted)*

**REQUIRED:** The term for software installed permanently in the computer.

**DISCUSSION:** Firmware consists of software programs permanently installed in the computer hardware. Firmware can be used to monitor internal conditions, e.g., by making signal counts (such as accesses to the computer) or taking snapshots of indicators. Thus, ROM (read only memory) is firmware.

Answer (A) is incorrect because file integrity is achieved by implementing controls that protect the completeness, accuracy, and physical security of files. Answer (B) is incorrect because software control refers to library control of programs. Answer (D) is incorrect because RAM is a computer's main memory.

**35.** Software offered to users on a "try before you buy" basis is called

A. Shareware.

B. Firmware.

C. Middleware.

D. Freeware.

Answer (A) is correct. *(Publisher)*

**REQUIRED:** The software offered on a "try before you buy" basis.

**DISCUSSION:** Shareware is commercial software offered to users without initial charge. It is traditionally offered by less established software developers. Shareware often comes with some features disabled. Ordinarily, it can only be used without charge for a limited time. Users pay a fee to "register" the software, in return for which they receive a license to use it with all features enabled.

Answer (B) is incorrect because firmware is permanently wired into the hardware. Answer (C) is incorrect because middleware oversees the interaction between disparate systems. Answer (D) is incorrect because freeware is software that, although usually copyrighted, may be used without any licensing fee on a much less limited basis than shareware.

**36.** A program that edits a group of source language statements for syntax errors and translates the statements into an object program is a(n)

A. Interpreter.

B. Compiler.

C. Debugger.

D. Encrypter.

Answer (B) is correct. *(CIA, adapted)*

**REQUIRED:** The program that edits and translates source language statements into an object program.

**DISCUSSION:** A compiler is a form of software that performs language translation. It translates higher-level language (source code) programs into machine language object programs. The instructions in object code are grouped into modules. Prior to execution, the modules are joined by the linkage editor to form the load module. The load module is what the computer actually executes.

Answer (A) is incorrect because an interpreter translates and executes source language statements one at a time. Answer (C) is incorrect because a debugger is a program that traces program execution or captures variable values for the purpose of helping the developer find program errors. Answer (D) is incorrect because an encrypter is a program that converts ordinary text to encoded text that cannot be deciphered without access to the encryption key and procedure.

**37.** Specialized programs that perform generalized functions such as sorting and data comparison are called

A. Utility programs.

B. Communication programs.

C. Object programs.

D. Source programs.

Answer (A) is correct. *(CISA, adapted)*

**REQUIRED:** The term describing programs that perform generalized functions such as sorting.

**DISCUSSION:** Utility programs are standardized subroutines that can be incorporated into other programs, e.g., to alphabetize or to find square roots. These routines are ordinarily supplied by the manufacturer and are part of the operating system.

Answer (B) is incorrect because communication programs provide interface between remote computer sites. Answer (C) is incorrect because object programs are not limited to utility functions. Programmers write programs in source languages to be converted into object programs that can be processed by the computer. Source languages include assembly languages that use symbols and codes dependent on the specific computer and compiler languages (e.g., COBOL and FORTRAN) consisting of English-like statements that are machine independent. Answer (D) is incorrect because source programs are not limited to utility functions. Programmers write programs in source languages to be converted into object programs that can be processed by the computer. Source languages include assembly languages that use symbols and codes dependent on the specific computer and compiler languages (e.g., COBOL and FORTRAN) consisting of English-like statements that are machine independent.

**38.** A computer program produces periodic payrolls and reports. The program is a(n)

A. Operating system.

B. Application program.

C. Report generator.

D. Utility program.

Answer (B) is correct. *(CIA, adapted)*

**REQUIRED:** The term associated with a program used to produce user reports.

**DISCUSSION:** Application programs are written to solve specific user problems; that is, they perform the ultimate computer functions required by system users. Thus, a program designed to process payroll is an application program.

Answer (A) is incorrect because an operating system is a set of programs used by the CPU to control operations. Answer (C) is incorrect because a report generator is a component of a database management system that produces customized reports using data stored in the database. Answer (D) is incorrect because utility programs are standardized subroutines that can be incorporated into other programs.

**39.** BASIC, FORTRAN, and COBOL are all examples of

A. Application programs.

B. Machine languages.

C. High-level languages.

D. Operating systems.

Answer (C) is correct. *(CIA, adapted)*

**REQUIRED:** The proper classification of BASIC, FORTRAN, and COBOL.

**DISCUSSION:** A procedure-oriented or higher-level language allows specification of processing steps in terms of highly aggregated operations. They are ordinarily user-friendly. Translation to an object program is performed by a compiler program. COBOL (COmmon Business Oriented Language) consists of a series of English-like statements. FORTRAN (FORmula TRANslation) is very effective for solving mathematics and engineering problems but is less so for business applications. BASIC (Beginner's All-purpose Symbolic Instruction Code) is a widely used language for personal computers but not for large business application processing.

Answer (A) is incorrect because BASIC, FORTRAN, and COBOL are languages, not application programs. Answer (B) is incorrect because machine language is a programming language made up of instructions that a computer can directly recognize and execute. Answer (D) is incorrect because an operating system is a set of programs and routines used by the CPU to control the operations of the computer and its peripheral equipment.

**40.** Structured Query Language (SQL) is best defined as a

A. Programming language in which UNIX is written.

B. Report generator used to produce customized business reports.

C. Programming language in which many business applications are written.

D. Data manipulation language used in conjunction with a database management system (DBMS).

Answer (D) is correct. *(Publisher)*

**REQUIRED:** The definition of SQL.

**DISCUSSION:** SQL is the most common standard data manipulation language for relational DBMSs. A data manipulation language is used for accessing and processing data from a database to satisfy requests for data and to create applications.

Answer (A) is incorrect because C is the language used in much of the UNIX operating system. Answer (B) is incorrect because a report generator has a greater emphasis on data formats, organization, and display than a query language. Answer (C) is incorrect because COBOL is the programming language in which many business applications are written.

**41.** Regardless of the language in which an application program is written, its execution by a computer requires that primary memory contain

A. A utility program.

B. An operating system.

C. Compiler.

D. Assembly.

Answer (B) is correct. *(D. Payne)*

**REQUIRED:** The item necessary to execute an application program.

**DISCUSSION:** An operating system (e.g., UNIX or Windows) is required in all computerized systems to oversee the elements of the CPU and the interaction of the hardware components.

Answer (A) is incorrect because utility programs are application programs that are usually attached to larger programs. They perform various activities, such as sorting data, merging files, converting data from one medium to another, and printing. Answer (C) is incorrect because a compiler converts (compiles) a program written in a source language, such as FORTRAN, into machine language. Answer (D) is incorrect because an assembler translates an assembly language program into machine language. Assembly language uses mnemonic codes for each machine language instruction.

**42.** Object oriented programming is characterized by an emphasis on objects and the procedures performed upon them. Which of the following programming languages is most closely associated with object oriented programming?

A. Pascal.

B. Fortran.

C. C.

D. C++.

Answer (D) is correct. *(Publisher)*

**REQUIRED:** The programming language most closely associated with object oriented programming.

**DISCUSSION:** C++ is sometimes referred to as "C with classes." As the name implies, C is its foundation. Classes provide a means of encapsulating the objects used by the program (which ordinarily represent the program's data) into a well-organized, modular format that is easy to reuse and maintain. Through a process called inheritance, new objects can be derived from existing objects by adding new elements to the existing object design. C++ was specifically designed with these features in mind. Because code segments can be reused in other programs, the time and cost of writing software is reduced.

Answer (A) is incorrect because Pascal traditionally emphasizes procedures rather than objects. Answer (B) is incorrect because Fortran traditionally emphasizes procedures rather than objects. Answer (C) is incorrect because C traditionally emphasizes procedures rather than objects.

**43.** Computers containing more than one central processing unit (CPU) are increasingly common. This feature enables a computer to execute multiple instructions from multiple programs simultaneously. This process is

A. Time sharing.

B. Multitasking.

C. Multiprocessing.

D. Batch processing.

Answer (C) is correct. *(Publisher)*

**REQUIRED:** The term for executing multiple programs with multiple CPUs.

**DISCUSSION:** Multiprocessing greatly increases system efficiency by executing multiple programs on the same computer at the same time. In systems with only one CPU, although multiple programs may be active simultaneously, program instructions are only executed for one program at a time.

Answer (A) is incorrect because, in time sharing, the CPU spends a fixed amount of time on each program. Answer (B) is incorrect because multitasking is multiprogramming on a single-user operating system. It is the process of having multiple programs active at a given time, although the CPU is executing instructions from only one program at a time. Answer (D) is incorrect because batch processing entails execution of a list of instructions from beginning to end without interruption.

**44.** Structured programming is best described as a technique that

A. Makes the order of the coding reflect as closely as possible the dynamic execution of the program.

B. Reduces the maintenance time of programs by the use of small-scale program modules.

C. Provides knowledge of program functions to other programmers via peer reviews.

D. Controls the coding and testing of the high-level functions of the program in the development process.

Answer (B) is correct. *(CISA, adapted)*

**REQUIRED:** The best description of structured programming.

**DISCUSSION:** Structured programming is an approach for creating a series of standardized, interrelated subroutines or modules. Guidelines are followed by programmers to create programs that are easy to read, maintain, and modify because changes in one module do not affect others.

Answer (A) is incorrect because the instructions coded by programmers do not necessarily reflect the actual order of the processing steps performed during execution by the computer. Answer (C) is incorrect because structured programming does allow other programmers to understand the coding but not via peer reviews. Answer (D) is incorrect because structured programming does not provide for testing during the development process.

**45.** The primary purpose of a macro program in a spreadsheet application is to allow the end user to

A. Reduce keystrokes.

B. Merge files with two different formats.

C. Delete redundant files from the root directory.

D. Rearrange data elements.

Answer (A) is correct. *(CIA, adapted)*

**REQUIRED:** The purpose of a macro program.

**DISCUSSION:** A macro program records keystrokes and commands used in repetitious jobs, which reduces the necessary keystrokes.

Answer (B) is incorrect because a merge file is a system software utility. Answer (C) is incorrect because deleting files is a system software utility. Answer (D) is incorrect because rearranging data elements is a possible macro application but is not the primary purpose of macros.

**46.** Computers understand codes that represent letters of the alphabet, numbers, or special characters. These codes require that data be converted into predefined groups of binary digits. Such chains of digits are referred to as

A. Registers.

B. ASCII code.

C. Input.

D. Bytes.

Answer (D) is correct. *(CIA, adapted)*

**REQUIRED:** The term for the chains of digits that a computer is capable of understanding.

**DISCUSSION:** A byte is a grouping of bits required to define one unit of data, such as a letter or an integer.

Answer (A) is incorrect because a register is a location within the CPU where data and instructions are temporarily stored. Answer (B) is incorrect because ASCII (American Standard Code for Information Interchange) refers to the coding convention itself. Answer (C) is incorrect because input is the data placed into processing (noun) or the act of placing the data in processing (verb).

**47.** In an inventory system on a database management system (DBMS), one stored record contains part number, part name, part color, and part weight. These individual items are called

A. Fields.

B. Stored files.

C. Bytes.

D. Occurrences.

Answer (A) is correct. *(CIA, adapted)*

**REQUIRED:** The term for the data elements in a record.

**DISCUSSION:** A record is a collection of related data items (fields). A field (data item) is a group of characters representing one unit of information.

Answer (B) is incorrect because a file is a group or set of related records ordered to facilitate processing. Answer (C) is incorrect because a byte is a group of bits (binary digits). It represents one character. Answer (D) is incorrect because occurrences is not a meaningful term in this context.

**48.** An inventory clerk, using a computer terminal, views the following on screen: part number, part description, quantity on-hand, quantity on-order, order quantity and reorder point for a particular inventory item. Collectively, these data make up a

A. Field.

B. File.

C. Database.

D. Record.

Answer (D) is correct. *(CIA, adapted)*

**REQUIRED:** The term for the collection of data described.

**DISCUSSION:** A record is a collection of related data items (fields). A field (data item) is a group of characters representing one unit of information. The part number, part description, and other items are represented by fields.

Answer (A) is incorrect because field refers to a single data item. Answer (B) is incorrect because file refers to multiple records. Answer (C) is incorrect because database refers to multiple files.

**49.** Block codes

A. Are generally used to identify missing items from a set of documents or records.

B. Allow a user to number items sequentially.

C. Allow a user to assign meaning to particular segments of a coding scheme.

D. Are randomly calculated groups of numbers used as a control check.

Answer (C) is correct. *(CMA, adapted)*

**REQUIRED:** The true statement about block codes.

**DISCUSSION:** Coding of data is the assignment of alphanumeric symbols consistent with a classification scheme. Block coding assigns blocks of numbers in a sequence to classes of items. For example, in a chart of accounts, assets may be assigned numbers 100-199, liabilities the numbers 200-299, etc.

Answer (A) is incorrect because some items in a block code may be unassigned to allow for flexibility. Answer (B) is incorrect because some items in a block code may be unassigned to allow for flexibility. Answer (D) is incorrect because block codes are assigned judgmentally, not at random.

**50.** A file containing relatively permanent information used as a source of reference and periodically updated with detail is termed a

A. Transaction file.

B. Record layout.

C. Master file.

D. Dump.

Answer (C) is correct. *(Publisher)*

**REQUIRED:** The file containing relatively permanent information.

**DISCUSSION:** A master file containing relatively permanent information, such as an inventory file listing the part number, description, quantities on hand, quantities on order, etc., is used in a file processing run. Transactions are processed against the master file, thus periodically updating it.

Answer (A) is incorrect because a transaction file (detail file) contains current transaction information used to update the master file, such as the number of items shipped to be removed from inventory. Answer (B) is incorrect because a record layout is a representation of the format of the records on the file. It would show the position and length of the fields in the file. The layout of every record in the file is the same. Answer (D) is incorrect because a dump is a listing of the contents of memory.

**51.** With two letters (upper case only) or digits followed by three digits, how many codes can be created if the letters O, Q, and I are not to be used to avoid confusion errors with 0 and 1?

A. 66,000

B. 100,000

C. 1,089,000

D. 1,296,000

Answer (C) is correct. *(CDP, adapted)*

**REQUIRED:** The number of unique codes possible in the situation given.

**DISCUSSION:** The first two items in the code may consist of any combination of 23 letters (26 characters in the alphabet minus O, Q, and I) and 10 numbers. Each of the next three positions can contain only one of 10 digits (0 to 9). The maximum number of unique codes is therefore 1,089,000 (33 × 33 × 10 × 10 × 10).

## 5.4 File Structures and Modes of Processing

**52.** What type of computer processing system is characterized by data that are assembled from more than one location and records that are updated immediately?

A. Personal computer systems.

B. Data compression systems.

C. Batch processing systems.

D. Online, real-time systems.

Answer (D) is correct. *(CPA, adapted)*

**REQUIRED:** The system allowing data entry from multiple locations and immediate updating.

**DISCUSSION:** Real-time processing involves processing an input record and receiving the output soon enough to affect a current decision-making process. In a real-time system, the user interacts with the system to control an ongoing activity. Online indicates that the decision maker is in direct communication with the computer. Online, real-time systems usually permit access to the main computer (for example, a mid-range computer used as a server) from multiple remote terminals.

Answer (A) is incorrect because access from multiple locations is more typical of mid-range or larger computer systems than of personal computer systems. Answer (B) is incorrect because data compression systems encode data to take up less storage space. Answer (C) is incorrect because batching of transactions requires assembly of data at one place and a delay in updating.

**53.** Misstatements in a batch computer system caused by incorrect programs or data may not be detected immediately because

A. Errors in some transactions may cause rejection of other transactions in the batch.

B. The identification of errors in input data typically is not part of the program.

C. There are time delays in processing transactions in a batch system.

D. The processing of transactions in a batch system is not uniform.

Answer (C) is correct. *(CPA, adapted)*

**REQUIRED:** The reason errors may not be detected immediately in a batch computer system.

**DISCUSSION:** Transactions in a batch computer system are grouped together, or batched, prior to processing. Batches may be processed either daily, weekly, or even monthly. Thus, considerable time may elapse between the initiation of the transaction and the discovery of an error.

Answer (A) is incorrect because the transactions within the batch are typically not contingent upon one another. Answer (B) is incorrect because edit checks can be incorporated into batch processing environments. However, the edit checks are used to test the transactions in batches. Answer (D) is incorrect because a batch of transactions is typically processed uniformly.

**54.** The relationship between online, real-time database systems and batch processing systems is that

A. A firm will have only one processing mode because a single computer cannot do both.

B. A firm will not use batch processing if it has a large computer.

C. A firm may use both processing modes concurrently.

D. A firm will always prefer an online, real-time processing system because batch processing is slow.

Answer (C) is correct. *(Publisher)*

**REQUIRED:** The relationship between online, real-time systems and batch processing systems.

**DISCUSSION:** Firms may find it beneficial to incorporate both processing modes into one system. A database may be established for information that must be obtained quickly, for instance, a sales processing system in which credit information must be available to sales personnel on an ongoing basis. However, other processing requirements may take advantage of the speed and control provided in a batch processing system. For example, payroll transactions may be processed quickly and efficiently in a batch mode.

Answer (A) is incorrect because one computer can operate in both modes. Answer (B) is incorrect because firms with large computers find it both cost effective and efficient to group transactions and process them periodically. Answer (D) is incorrect because a firm will not automatically prefer an online, real-time system. When transactions, e.g., payroll, can be conveniently grouped, processing is extremely fast and efficient in a batch mode.

**55.** Sequential access means that

A. Data must be stored on magnetic tape.

B. The address of the location of data is found through the use of either an algorithm or an index.

C. Each record can be accessed in the same amount of time.

D. To read record 500, records 1 through 499 must be read first.

Answer (D) is correct. *(CIA, adapted)*

**REQUIRED:** The characteristic of sequential access.

**DISCUSSION:** Sequential access means that records are stored in logical or physical order, and the only way to retrieve a record is to read the preceding records. Records may be sequentially ordered despite being physically separate. Thus, they may be linked via pointers.

Answer (A) is incorrect because magnetic tape is not the only medium on which data are stored sequentially. For instance, data storage on disk drives may also be sequential. Answer (B) is incorrect because locating data through a hashing function or index is a characteristic of direct or random file access. Answer (C) is incorrect because, given sequential access storage, less time is needed to retrieve the first record than subsequent records.

**56.** Which of the following features is least likely to be found in a real-time application?

A. User manuals.

B. Preformatted screens.

C. Automatic error correction.

D. Turnaround documents.

Answer (D) is correct. *(CISA, adapted)*

**REQUIRED:** The feature not likely to be used in a real-time application.

**DISCUSSION:** Turnaround documents are source documents typically printed by the computer system as output and then later returned for use as machine-readable input. Real-time systems normally do not use source documents.

Answer (A) is incorrect because user manuals are an important component of a real-time system. They explain how to use the system properly. Answer (B) is incorrect because preformatted screens are usually the means by which users interact with real-time systems. Answer (C) is incorrect because automatic error correction is a prime advantage of real-time systems. It allows immediate error detection and correction.

**57.** Which of the following is usually not a consideration specifically relevant to real-time computer systems implementation?

A. Queues.

B. Interrupts.

C. Priority allocation.

D. Hardware diagnostics.

Answer (D) is correct. *(CDP, adapted)*

**REQUIRED:** The item irrelevant to real-time computer systems implementation.

**DISCUSSION:** Hardware diagnostic routines are used to identify hardware problems. They are applicable to all computer systems and not relevant solely to real-time systems. An example of a hardware diagnostic is a parity check to test data for validity each time data are transmitted internally in the system.

Answer (A) is incorrect because deciding which jobs have priority in processing (queuing) is an important factor in real-time systems when the CPU must decide which transaction updates are most important. Answer (B) is incorrect because interrupts permit high-priority jobs entering the system to obtain immediate action. In multiprogramming, work on one program is interrupted so the processor may attend to another. Answer (C) is incorrect because deciding which jobs have priority in processing (queuing) is an important factor in real-time systems when the CPU must decide which transaction updates are most important.

**58.** A business has decided to use magnetic disks to store accounts receivable information. What data file concepts should be used to provide the ability to answer customer inquiries as they are received?

A. Sequential storage and chains.

B. Sequential storage and indexes.

C. Record keys, indexes, and pointers.

D. Inverted file structure, indexes, and internal labels.

Answer (C) is correct. *(CIA, adapted)*

**REQUIRED:** The data file concepts needed to answer customer inquiries as they are received.

**DISCUSSION:** A record key is an attribute that uniquely identifies or distinguishes each record from the others. An index is a table listing storage locations for attributes, often including those other than the unique record key attribute. A pointer is a data item that indicates the physical address of the next logically related record.

Answer (A) is incorrect because the ability to respond immediately to customers requires direct access. Answer (B) is incorrect because the ability to respond immediately to customers requires direct access. Answer (D) is incorrect because internal labels are used to indicate various things to the computer, such as the contents of various types of data storage media, the beginning of each file (with identification information), and the end of each file. However, they do not provide information for locating specific records in a file. An inverted file structure (inverted list) is an index based on a secondary key, for example, years of experience rather than an employee number (the primary key).

**59.** Data processing assigns a unique identification code or key to each data record. Which one of the following statements about coding is false?

A. A primary key is the main code used to store and locate records within a file.

B. Records can be sorted, and temporary files created, using codes other than their primary keys.

C. Secondary keys are used when the primary keys cannot be found.

D. Secondary keys are used for alternative purposes, including inverted files, and a given data record may have more than one secondary key.

Answer (C) is correct. *(CMA, adapted)*

**REQUIRED:** The statement about coding that is false.

**DISCUSSION:** A primary key is the main code used to store and locate records within a file. However, records can be sorted, and temporary files created, using codes other than the primary keys. Secondary keys are used for other purposes, including inverted files. An inverted file allows access to records by means of a key other than the primary key. A given data record can have more than one secondary key. Secondary keys are not substituted by the computer when primary keys cannot be found.

Answer (A) is incorrect because a primary key is the main code used to store and locate records within a file. Answer (B) is incorrect because records can be sorted, and temporary files created, using codes other than their primary keys. Answer (D) is incorrect because secondary keys are used for alternative purposes, including inverted files, and a given data record may have more than one secondary key.

**60.** A system in which the master files are updated in batch mode overnight and duplicated copies of the files are updated and queried during the day best describes which of the following online systems?

A. Memo updating.

B. Online updating.

C. Remote job entry.

D. Inquiry.

Answer (A) is correct. *(CISA, adapted)*

**REQUIRED:** The correct term.

**DISCUSSION:** Memo updating minimizes the risk of damage to the database during processing transactions. A copy of the database is updated upon data entry, but a log of each transaction is also stored. Periodically, the transaction log is used to update the actual database and a new "memo" copy is established.

Answer (B) is incorrect because online updating requires master files to be updated a short time after the transaction is entered. Answer (C) is incorrect because remote job entry is the initiation of an application program from a remote terminal. Answer (D) is incorrect because inquiry provides users with a response to a request in a timely manner with no file update.

**61.** Which of the following is most likely characteristic of a direct access file that uses indexes or dictionaries as its addressing technique when processing randomly?

A. A randomizing formula is used.

B. Two accesses are required to retrieve each record.

C. Synonyms will be generated that will result in extra accesses.

D. There will be a high incidence of gaps or unassigned physical records within the file.

Answer (B) is correct. *(CDP, adapted)*

**REQUIRED:** The most likely characteristic of a direct access file using indexes.

**DISCUSSION:** Typically, indexed files will use tables or indexes for locating the address of a record. For example, in accessing an alphabetic record, first the index must be accessed and searched (in much the same way as finding a telephone number in a directory) to locate the pointer or address of the record. Next, the record must be accessed at the address location.

Answer (A) is incorrect because a randomizing formula or hashing scheme is used to obtain direct access without consulting an index (direct access method). The procedure determines the address of a record by transforming the primary key of the record into a random number (the desired address). Answer (C) is incorrect because synonyms may be generated when access is obtained without indexation. If the randomizing formula generates the same address for two different keys (a synonym), the record is placed in the next higher available address. Answer (D) is incorrect because indexing permits elimination of most gaps. The direct access method leaves gaps because the randomizing procedure may not generate the numbers corresponding to many storage addresses.

## 5.5 Databases

**62.** Of the following, the greatest advantage of a database (server) architecture is

A. Data redundancy can be reduced.

B. Conversion to a database system is inexpensive and can be accomplished quickly.

C. Multiple occurrences of data items are useful for consistency checking.

D. Backup and recovery procedures are minimized.

Answer (A) is correct. *(CIA, adapted)*

**REQUIRED:** The greatest advantage of a database architecture.

**DISCUSSION:** Data organized in files and used by the organization's various applications programs are collectively known as a database. In a database system, storage structures are created that render the applications programs independent of the physical or logical arrangement of the data. Each data item has a standard definition, name, and format, and related items are linked by a system of pointers. The programs therefore need only to specify data items by name, not by location. A database management system handles retrieval and storage. Because separate files for different applications programs are unnecessary, data redundancy can be substantially reduced.

Answer (B) is incorrect because conversion to a database is often costly and time consuming. Answer (C) is incorrect because a traditional flat-file system, not a database, has multiple occurrences of data items. Answer (D) is incorrect because, given the absence of data redundancy and the quick propagation of data errors throughout applications, backup and recovery procedures are just as critical in a database as in a flat-file system.

**63.** One advantage of a database management system (DBMS) is

A. Each organizational unit takes responsibility and control for its own data.

B. The cost of the data processing department decreases as users are now responsible for establishing their own data handling techniques.

C. A decreased vulnerability as the database management system has numerous security controls to prevent disasters.

D. The independence of the data from the application programs, which allows the programs to be developed for the user's specific needs without concern for data capture problems.

Answer (D) is correct. *(CMA, adapted)*

**REQUIRED:** The advantage of a DBMS.

**DISCUSSION:** A fundamental characteristic of databases is that applications are independent of the database structure; when writing programs or designing applications to use the database, only the name of the desired item is necessary. Programs can be developed for the user's specific needs without concern for data capture problems. Reference can be made to the items using the data manipulation language, after which the DBMS takes care of locating and retrieving the desired items. The physical or logical structure of the database can be completely altered without having to change any of the programs using the data items; only the schema requires alteration.

Answer (A) is incorrect because each organizational unit develops programs to make use of elements of a broad database. Answer (B) is incorrect because data handling techniques are still the responsibility of the data processing department; it is the use of the data that is departmentalized. Answer (C) is incorrect because the DBMS is no safer than any other database system.

**64.** Which of the following is a false statement about a database management system application environment?

A. Data are used concurrently by multiple users.

B. Data are shared by passing files between programs or systems.

C. The physical structure of the data is independent of user needs.

D. Data definition is independent of any one program.

Answer (B) is correct. *(CISA, adapted)*

**REQUIRED:** The false statement about data in a DBMS environment.

**DISCUSSION:** In this kind of system, applications use the same database. There is no need to pass files between applications.

Answer (A) is incorrect because the advantage of a DBMS is that data can be used concurrently by multiple users. Answer (C) is incorrect because, when a DBMS is used, the physical structure of the data is independent of user needs. Answer (D) is incorrect because, when a DBMS is used, the data are defined independently of the needs of any one program.

**65.** An organization uses a database management system (DBMS) as a repository of data. The DBMS in turn supports a number of end-user-developed applications. Some of the applications update the database. In evaluating the control procedures over access and use of the database, the auditor will be most concerned that

A. End users have their read-only applications approved by data processing before accessing the database.

B. Concurrency update controls are in place.

C. End-user applications are developed and tested on personal computers before being ported to the mainframe.

D. A relational database model is adopted so that multiple users can be served at the same time.

Answer (B) is correct. *(CIA, adapted)*

**REQUIRED:** The greatest concern in evaluating controls over access to and use of a database.

**DISCUSSION:** Concurrency controls manage situations in which two or more users attempt to access a file or database simultaneously. As such, the purpose of concurrency controls is to protect data integrity.

Answer (A) is incorrect because end-user computing frees the end user from the need to have requests approved by data processing, including end-user applications that use large mainframe databases. Answer (C) is incorrect because the distinction between testing on mainframe versus personal computers is not important here. Answer (D) is incorrect because relational data models are popular but are not needed to support multiple users or end-user computing.

**66.** In a database system, locking of data helps preserve data integrity by permitting transactions to have control of all the data needed to complete the transactions. However, implementing a locking procedure could lead to

A. Inconsistent processing.

B. Rollback failures.

C. Unrecoverable transactions.

D. Deadly embraces (retrieval contention).

Answer (D) is correct. *(CIA, adapted)*

**REQUIRED:** The potential disadvantage of a locking procedure.

**DISCUSSION:** In a distributed processing system, the data and resources a transaction may update or use should be held in their current status until the transaction is complete. A deadly embrace occurs when two transactions need the same resource at the same time. If the system does not have a method to cope with the problem efficiently, response time worsens or the system eventually fails. The system should have an algorithm for undoing the effects of one transaction and releasing the resources it controls so that the other transaction can run to completion.

Answer (A) is incorrect because inconsistent processing occurs when a transaction has different effects depending on when it is processed. Data locking ensures consistent processing. Answer (B) is incorrect because rollback failure is the inability of the software to undo the effects of a transaction that could not be run to completion. A rollback failure is not caused by data locking. However, data locking may lead to situations in which rollback is required. Answer (C) is incorrect because unrecoverable transactions are not a typical symptom of locking procedures.

**67.** An internal auditor encounters a batch-processed payroll in which each record contains the same type of data elements, in the same order, with each data element needing the same number of storage spaces. Which file structure most appropriately supports this set of records?

A. Single flat file structure.

B. Hierarchical structure.

C. Network structure.

D. Relational structure.

Answer (A) is correct. *(CIA, adapted)*

**REQUIRED:** The file structure in which each record has the same type and order of data elements and the same storage requirements.

**DISCUSSION:** In a single flat file structure, all attributes and field lengths in a record are identical to those in the other records. The structure is typically a table or spreadsheet with records for rows and attributes for columns.

Answer (B) is incorrect because a hierarchical or tree structure is used to express relationships in which one attribute or item is related to many others in layers of subordinate records. Answer (C) is incorrect because a network structure expresses complex relationships in which many attributes are related to many others. Answer (D) is incorrect because a relational structure is not unlike the flat structure but is far more sophisticated. It gives the system the ability to handle many data relationships that were not anticipated by the designers. It uses a series of tables in which each table defines a relationship.

**68.** A flat file structure is used in database management systems (DBMS) when

A. A complex network structure is employed.

B. A network based structure is used and a complex database schema is developed.

C. A simple network structure is employed.

D. A relational database model is selected for use.

Answer (D) is correct. *(CMA, adapted)*

**REQUIRED:** The situation in which a flat file structure is used with a DBMS.

**DISCUSSION:** A flat file structure is used with a relational database model. A relational structure organizes data in conceptual tables. One relation (table or file) can be joined together or related to another without pointers or linked lists if each contains one or more of the same fields (also known as columns or attributes). The relational structure has become popular because it is relatively easy to construct and yet very powerful.

Answer (A) is incorrect because a complex network structure requires something more intricate than a flat file structure. Answer (B) is incorrect because a network structure reduces redundancy by arranging data through development of many-to-many relationships; that is, each item may have multiple antecedent as well as successive relationships, which would preclude a simple flat file structure. Answer (C) is incorrect because a network structure reduces redundancy by arranging data through development of many-to-many relationships; that is, each item may have multiple antecedent as well as successive relationships, which would preclude a simple flat file structure.

Questions 69 through 74 are based on the following information. Five brand managers in a consumer food products company met regularly to figure out what price points were being lowered by their competitors and how well coupon promotions did. The data they needed to analyze consisted of about 50 gigabytes of daily point-of-sale (POS) data from major grocery chains for each month. The brand managers are competent users of spreadsheet and database software on personal computers. They considered several alternative software options to access and manipulate data to answer their questions.

**69.** The selected option is unlikely to use a hierarchical database system because

A. A hierarchical database system requires multiple joins.

B. Programming queries for it are too costly and time consuming.

C. Point-of-sale data are too sensitive for routine access.

D. Summarization of point-of-sale data will not answer the questions.

Answer (B) is correct. *(CIA, adapted)*

**REQUIRED:** The reason the selected option is unlikely to use a hierarchical database system.

**DISCUSSION:** A hierarchical structure is tree-like. A record is divided into segments that are connected in one-to-many relationships. Because all of the paths through the data must be prespecified, a hierarchical structure is inflexible and does not support ad hoc queries. Thus, programming queries for a hierarchical database are often costly and time consuming.

Answer (A) is incorrect because hierarchical database systems do not have commands for joins, which are standard features in relational systems. Answer (C) is incorrect because the point-of-sale information is clearly proprietary, but brand managers must use it to manage the business. Answer (D) is incorrect because point-of-sale data contain precisely the information that, if summarized appropriately, will answer questions about product sales and product use.

**70.** The limiting factor in the brand managers' use of a relational database system to answer their ad hoc questions will most likely be

A. Understanding what individual data records represent.

B. Obtaining computer resources for complicated queries.

C. Distinguishing primary and foreign keys in the data.

D. Lack of management interest in using the results.

Answer (B) is correct. *(CIA, adapted)*

**REQUIRED:** The limiting factor in the use of a relational database to answer ad hoc queries.

**DISCUSSION:** The limiting factor will likely be the availability of computer resources for complicated queries about the large volume (50 gigabytes) of data. The disadvantage of relational databases is low processing efficiency. Many accesses may be needed to execute the select, join, and project commands.

Answer (A) is incorrect because the brand managers understand the data that point-of-sale terminals capture in grocery stores. Answer (C) is incorrect because distinguishing primary and foreign keys in the data will be relatively straightforward. The brand managers are already familiar with the data. Answer (D) is incorrect because management is highly interested in the results.

**71.** The organization's senior management was pleased that its brand managers were taking the initiative to use sales data creatively. The information systems director, however, was concerned that the brand managers might be creating standard queries that would provide erroneous results for decision making. The best approach for ensuring the correctness of the brand managers' queries is

A. A source code review of the queries.

B. A code comparison audit.

C. A transaction retrieval and analysis.

D. An input-output analysis.

Answer (A) is correct. *(CIA, adapted)*

**REQUIRED:** The best approach for ensuring correctness of queries.

**DISCUSSION:** A source code review, that is, a review of the programs written in a high-level language, will detect erroneous queries written by the managers, which may then be corrected.

Answer (B) is incorrect because a code comparison audit is used to compare two versions of the same program to verify that only authorized code is executed. Answer (C) is incorrect because a transaction retrieval and analysis is a sampling approach to collecting data about transactions to verify correct processing. Answer (D) is incorrect because an input-output analysis traces transactions from input to output.

**72.** The brand managers tried to import the POS data into personal computer spreadsheets for analysis. Their efforts were unsuccessful, most likely because of

A. The complexity of the mainframe data structure and the large volume of data.

B. The difficulty of establishing access privileges for each subset of the mainframe data.

C. Inconsistencies in the mainframe data due to lack of integrity constraints on the data files.

D. Error-prone transmission links for downloading the data from the mainframe data files.

Answer (A) is correct. *(CIA, adapted)*

**REQUIRED:** The reason efforts to include POS data in spreadsheets were not successful.

**DISCUSSION:** The managers' efforts were unsuccessful because of the high complexity of the mainframe data structure and the large volume of data. Because spreadsheets lack SQL (structured query language) query capabilities, there is no way to manipulate the huge volume of data into two-dimensional views that can be readily imported into spreadsheets. SQL is the standard data manipulation language for relational databases. A data manipulation language is used in conjunction with a conventional third- or fourth-generation programming language to extract data from databases and develop applications.

Answer (B) is incorrect because access privileges for the POS data would have to be established, but this operation is routine. Answer (C) is incorrect because lack of integrity constraints on data files might result in inaccurate data but would not affect downloading and subsequent analysis. Answer (D) is incorrect because transmission links for downloading the data from the mainframe data files can be made sufficiently error free to accomplish the downloading.

**73.** Eventually, the brand managers chose a data analysis tool and report writer that permitted multidimensional views of the data. The tool could support different views, such as actual versus projected sales by region, actual versus projected sales by product, and projected sales by product and by region. In order to see the data in such views, the brand managers would need to specify

A. A protocol for data transmission.

B. Access privileges by user number.

C. Integrity constraints for the data.

D. Criteria for retrieving the data.

Answer (D) is correct. *(CIA, adapted)*

**REQUIRED:** The item that must be specified to see the data.

**DISCUSSION:** In the mainframe database, the data exist in files or tables, not in the formats interesting to brand managers. Thus, before users can see views of the data, the data must be retrieved and reconfigured in appropriate ways.

Answer (A) is incorrect because protocols for data transmission will be determined by IS and telecommunications personnel, not by users. Answer (B) is incorrect because different access privileges may be granted to different users, but specifying access privileges by user number does not cause data to be retrieved in a specified format. Answer (C) is incorrect because integrity constraints will be established for data entering the original database on the mainframe, but they are independent of how data views will be presented to users.

**74.** After abandoning spreadsheets as their analysis tool, the brand managers were successful in downloading limited subsets of the POS and using the data to populate relational database files on their personal computers. They could then access the data using a relational query language. One of the downloaded files contained actual sales by product by store, and another contained projected sales by product by store. In order to compare actual and projected sales by product by store, a query would have to include

A. Projecting the two tables on product and store identification codes.

B. Projecting the two tables on product identification codes.

C. Joining the two tables on product and store identification codes.

D. Joining the two tables on product identification codes.

Answer (C) is correct. *(CIA, adapted)*

**REQUIRED:** The operation required to compare data in relational database files.

**DISCUSSION:** The join operation combines relational tables. Thus, joining the two tables on product and store identification codes combines the two files containing those codes. The next step is to project a subset of the joined table that includes the desired data.

Answer (A) is incorrect because projecting is the relational operation that creates column subsets from a file. Projecting the tables on identification codes would still leave actual and projected sales in different files. Answer (B) is incorrect because projecting is the relational operation that creates column subsets from a file. Projecting the tables on identification codes would still leave actual and projected sales in different files. Answer (D) is incorrect because joining the two tables on product identification codes does not achieve the necessary combination with store identification codes.

**75.** To trace data through several application programs, an auditor needs to know what programs use the data, which files contain the data, and which printed reports display the data. If data exist only in a database system, the auditor could probably find all of this information in a

A. Data dictionary.

B. Database schema.

C. Data encryptor.

D. Decision table.

Answer (A) is correct. *(CIA, adapted)*

**REQUIRED:** The information source in a database needed to trace data through several application programs.

**DISCUSSION:** The data dictionary is a file (possibly manual but usually computerized) in which the records relate to specified data items. It contains definitions of data items, the list of programs used to process them, and the reports in which data are found. Only certain persons or entities are permitted to retrieve data or to modify data items. Accordingly, these access limitations are also found in the data dictionary.

Answer (B) is incorrect because the schema describes the structure of the database. Answer (C) is incorrect because an encryptor encodes data. Answer (D) is incorrect because a decision table is a type of logic diagram that presents in matrix form the decision points and related actions reflected in a computer program.

**76.** All of the following are methods for distributing a relational database across multiple servers except

A. Snapshot (making a copy of the database for distribution).

B. Replication (creating and maintaining replica copies at multiple locations).

C. Normalization (separating the database into logical tables for easier user processing).

D. Fragmentation (separating the database into parts and distributing where they are needed).

Answer (C) is correct. *(CIA, adapted)*

**REQUIRED:** The item not a method for distributing a relational database across multiple servers.

**DISCUSSION:** Normalization is the term for determining how groups of data items in a relational structure are arranged in records in a database. This process relies on "normal forms," that is, conceptual definitions of data records and specified design rules. Normalization is intended to prevent inconsistent updating of data items. It is a process of breaking down a complex data structure by creating smaller, more efficient relations, which minimizes or eliminates the repeating groups in each relation.

Answer (A) is incorrect because the replication technique makes duplicates to be stored at multiple locations. Changes are periodically copied and sent to each location. If a database is small, storing multiple copies may be cheaper than retrieving records from a central site. Answer (B) is incorrect because the snapshot technique makes duplicates to be stored at multiple locations. Changes are periodically copied and sent to each location. If a database is small, storing multiple copies may be cheaper than retrieving records from a central site. Answer (D) is incorrect because fragmentation or partitioning stores specific records where they are most needed. For example, a financial institution may store a particular customer's data at the branch where (s)he usually transacts his/her business. If the customer executes a transaction at another branch, the pertinent data are retrieved via communications lines.

**77.** Which of the following database models is considered to be the most versatile?

A. The hierarchical model.

B. The tree model.

C. The network model.

D. The relational model.

Answer (D) is correct. *(CIA, adapted)*

**REQUIRED:** The most versatile database model.

**DISCUSSION:** Because data are organized in two-dimensional tables, the relational database models are easier to construct than the complex architectures that result when using the hierarchical and network models. The tables (relations) provide flexibility because they can be combined (joined) in many ways to permit a wide variety of inquiries. They also permit data to be more readily added to or omitted from the data structures.

Answer (A) is incorrect because the tree model organizes data through the development of relationships that are strictly one to many. Construction of this model is difficult because the data are hard coded. When data are added to the database, the index must be completely redefined. In the relational model, however, new relations can be created by joining tables. Answer (B) is incorrect because the hierarchical model organizes data through the development of relationships that are strictly one to many. Construction of this model is difficult because the data are hard coded. When data are added to the database, the index must be completely redefined. In the relational model, however, new relations can be created by joining tables. Answer (C) is incorrect because the network model organizes data through the development of relationships that are many to many. Construction is therefore difficult.

**78.** Users making queries in a relational database often need to combine several tables to get the information they want. One approach to combining tables is known as

A. Joining.
B. Merging.
C. Projecting.
D. Pointing.

Answer (A) is correct. *(CIA, adapted)*
**REQUIRED:** The approach to combining tables when making database queries.
**DISCUSSION:** Joining is the combining of two or more relational tables based on a common data element. For example, if a supplier table contains information about suppliers and a parts table contains information about parts, the two tables can be joined using the supplier number (assuming both tables contain this attribute) to give information about the supplier of particular parts.
Answer (B) is incorrect because the three basic operations in a relational database are selecting, joining, and projecting. Answer (C) is incorrect because projecting is the basic operation in a relational database that results in a subset consisting of columns (fields) in a table. This operation creates a new table containing only the required information. Answer (D) is incorrect because a pointer is a data element attached to a record that gives the address of another record.

## 5.6 Networks and Data Communication

**79.** An electronic meeting conducted among several parties at remote sites is referred to as

A. Teleprocessing.
B. Interactive processing.
C. Telecommuting.
D. Teleconferencing.

Answer (D) is correct. *(CMA, adapted)*
**REQUIRED:** The process of holding an electronic meeting among several parties at remote sites.
**DISCUSSION:** Conducting an electronic meeting among several parties at remote sites is called teleconferencing. It can be accomplished by telephone or electronic mail group communication software. Videoconferencing permits the conferees to see each other on video screens. These practices have grown in recent years as companies have attempted to cut their travel costs.
Answer (A) is incorrect because teleprocessing refers to connections in an online system. Answer (B) is incorrect because interactive processing allows users to converse directly with the system. It requires online processing and direct access to stored information. Answer (C) is incorrect because telecommuting refers to the practice of individuals working out of their homes by communicating with their offices via the computer.

**80.** Which of the following is considered a component of a local area network (LAN)?

A. Program flowchart.
B. Loop verification.
C. Transmission media.
D. Input routine.

Answer (C) is correct. *(CPA, adapted)*
**REQUIRED:** The component of a LAN.
**DISCUSSION:** A LAN connects a variety of computing resources for data sharing and communications purposes within a localized area such as an office complex. LANs contain computers for processing and data storage, transmission media (communications channels) to transmit information, communications electronics for message switching and routing, and various software to accomplish the network tasks.
Answer (A) is incorrect because a program flowchart is a medium to document the understanding of internal control. Answer (B) is incorrect because a closed loop verification is an application control. Answer (D) is incorrect because an input routine captures the data as the initial phase of a transaction cycle.

**81.** Which of the following is considered to be a server in a local area network (LAN)?

A. The cabling that physically interconnects the nodes of the LAN.
B. A device that stores program and data files for users of the LAN.
C. A device that connects the LAN to other networks.
D. A workstation that is dedicated to a single user on the LAN.

Answer (B) is correct. *(CIA, adapted)*
**REQUIRED:** The server in a local area network.
**DISCUSSION:** A server is a computer in a network that operates as a librarian. It stores programs and data files for users of the LAN and manages access to them.
Answer (A) is incorrect because the cabling that interconnects the nodes of the LAN is the telecommunications link. Answer (C) is incorrect because a device that connects the LAN to other networks is a network gateway. Answer (D) is incorrect because a workstation dedicated to a single user of the LAN is a client.

**82.** Audit team members can use the same database and programs when their personal computers share a hard disk and printer on a local area network (LAN). Which communication device enables a personal computer to connect to a LAN?

A. A network interface card that plugs into the motherboard.

B. An internal modem that plugs into the motherboard.

C. An external modem with a cable connection to a serial port.

D. A fax modem that sends signals through telephone lines.

Answer (A) is correct. *(CIA, adapted)*

**REQUIRED:** The communication device that enables a personal computer to connect to a LAN.

**DISCUSSION:** A local area network is a local, distributed computer system. A network interface card links personal computers and printers in a local area network that is connected by coaxial cable, twisted pair, or optical fiber. The card creates an address for the personal computer, transmits data, and monitors incoming messages.

Answer (B) is incorrect because modems are used to connect personal computers to regular telephone lines. Answer (C) is incorrect because modems are used to connect personal computers to regular telephone lines. Answer (D) is incorrect because modems are used to connect personal computers to regular telephone lines.

**83.** In distributed data processing, a ring network

A. Has all computers linked to a host computer, and each linked computer routes all data through the host computer.

B. Links all communication channels to form a loop, and each link passes communications through its neighbor to the appropriate location.

C. Attaches all channel messages along one common line with communication to the appropriate location via direct access.

D. Organizes itself along hierarchical lines of communication usually to a central host computer.

Answer (B) is correct. *(CMA, adapted)*

**REQUIRED:** The true statement about a ring network in a distributed data processing system.

**DISCUSSION:** In a distributed system, an organization's processing needs are examined in their totality. The decision is not whether an application should be done centrally or locally, but rather which parts are better performed by small local computers as intelligent terminals, and which parts are better performed at some other, possibly centralized, site. The key distinction between decentralized and distributed systems is the interconnection among the nodes in the network. A ring network links all communication channels to form a loop and each link passes communications through its neighbor to the appropriate location.

Answer (A) is incorrect because a star network routes all data through the host computer. Answer (C) is incorrect because a bus network attaches all channel messages along one common line with communication to the appropriate location via direct access. Answer (D) is incorrect because a tree configuration is organized along hierarchical lines to a host computer.

**84.** When two devices in a data communications system are communicating, there must be agreement as to how both data and control information are to be packaged and interpreted. Which of the following terms is commonly used to describe this type of agreement?

A. Asynchronous communication.

B. Synchronous communication.

C. Communication channel.

D. Communication protocol.

Answer (D) is correct. *(CIA, adapted)*

**REQUIRED:** The agreement as to how both data and control information are to be packaged and interpreted.

**DISCUSSION:** A protocol is the set of formal rules or conventions governing communication between a sending and a receiving device. It prescribes the manner by which data are transmitted between these communications devices. In essence, a protocol is the envelope within which each message is transmitted throughout a data communications network.

Answer (A) is incorrect because asynchronous communication is a mode of transmission. Communication is in disjointed segments, typically character by character, preceded by a start code and ended by a stop code. Answer (B) is incorrect because synchronous communication is a mode of transmission in which a continuous stream of blocks of characters result in faster communications. Answer (C) is incorrect because a communication channel is a transmission link between devices in a network. The term is also used for a small processor that controls input-output devices.

**85.** Large organizations often have their own telecommunications networks for transmitting and receiving voice, data, and images. Very small organizations, however, are unlikely to be able to make the investment required for their own networks and are more likely to use

A. Public switched lines.

B. Fast-packet switches.

C. Standard electronic mail systems.

D. A WAN.

Answer (A) is correct. *(CIA, adapted)*

**REQUIRED:** The telecommunications networks likely to be used by small organizations.

**DISCUSSION:** Companies can use public switched lines (phone lines) on a per-transmission basis. This option is the most cost-effective way for low-volume users to conduct telecommunications.

Answer (B) is incorrect because fast-packet switches receive transmissions from various devices, break the data into packets, and route them over a network to their destination. They are typically installed by telecommunication utility companies and other large companies that have their own networks. Answer (C) is incorrect because electronic mail systems do not allow for voice transmissions. Answer (D) is incorrect because large organizations use wide area networks.

**86.** An insurance firm uses a wide area network (WAN) to allow agents away from the home office to obtain current rates and client information and to submit approved claims using notebook computers and dial-in modems. In this situation, which of the following methods will provide the best data security?

A. Dedicated phone lines.

B. Call-back features.

C. Frequent changes of user IDs and passwords.

D. End-to-end data encryption.

Answer (D) is correct. *(CIA, adapted)*

**REQUIRED:** The best data security method for a wide area network.

**DISCUSSION:** Encryption of data is a security procedure in which a program encodes data prior to transmission and another program decodes the data after transmission. Encoding is important when confidential data that can be electronically monitored are transmitted between geographically separated locations. The question defines what is termed "tunneling" or a "virtual private network."

Answer (A) is incorrect because dedicated phone lines are not available to agents in the field. Answer (B) is incorrect because call-back features are used to authenticate the user but do not otherwise protect the transmitted data. Answer (C) is incorrect because frequent changes of user IDs and passwords are used to authenticate the user but do not otherwise protect the transmitted data.

**87.** Advantages of using fiber optic cable are that

I. The signal is attenuated.

II. Data are transmitted rapidly.

III. It is small and flexible.

IV. It is unaffected by electrical interference.

A. I and III.

B. I and IV.

C. I, II, and III.

D. II, III, and IV.

Answer (D) is correct. *(CISA, adapted)*

**REQUIRED:** The advantages of fiber optics.

**DISCUSSION:** A fiber optic cable uses light impulses that travel through clear flexible tubing half the size of a human hair. Fiber optic cables are not subject to electrical interference and are highly reliable. They provide for extremely flexible and fast data transmission. The signal remains strong across long distances; i.e., it does not tend to weaken (attenuate).

**88.** A real estate brokerage firm is moving into a building that is already equipped with extensive telephone wiring. The firm is considering the installation of a digital private branch exchange (PBX) to connect computers and other office devices such as copying machines, printers, and facsimile machines. A limitation of using a PBX-based system for this network is that

A. The firm becomes dependent on others for system maintenance.

B. The system cannot easily handle large volumes of data.

C. Coaxial cabling must be installed throughout the building.

D. Relocating devices in the office would be difficult and expensive.

Answer (B) is correct. *(CIA, adapted)*

**REQUIRED:** The limitation of a PBX system.

**DISCUSSION:** A PBX has the advantage of using existing telephone lines and therefore does not need special wiring. Moreover, equipment can be moved without necessitating rewiring. However, because PBX-based systems use telephone wiring (most often copper wire), they cannot easily handle large volumes of data.

Answer (A) is incorrect because the firm is responsible for all maintenance of the equipment in a PBX-based system, although it could contract for service. Answer (C) is incorrect because PBXs use telephone wiring. LANs typically require their own coaxial cabling. Answer (D) is incorrect because PBX-based systems do not require rewiring when devices are moved.

**89.** The Internet consists of a series of networks that include

A. Gateways to allow personal computers to connect to mainframe computers.

B. Bridges to direct messages through the optimum data path.

C. Repeaters to physically connect separate local area networks (LANs).

D. Routers to strengthen data signals between distant computers.

Answer (A) is correct. *(CIA, adapted)*

**REQUIRED:** The composition of the Internet.

**DISCUSSION:** The Internet facilitates information transfer between computers. Gateways are hardware or software products that allow translation between two different protocol families. For example, a gateway can be used to exchange messages between different e-mail systems.

Answer (B) is incorrect because routers are used to determine the best path for data. Answer (C) is incorrect because bridges connect LANs. Answer (D) is incorrect because repeaters strengthen signals.

**90.** Which of the following is true concerning HTML?

A. The acronym stands for HyperText Material Listing.

B. The language is among the most difficult to learn.

C. The language is independent of hardware and software.

D. HTML is the only language that can be used for Internet documents.

Answer (C) is correct. *(Publisher)*

**REQUIRED:** The true statement concerning HTML.

**DISCUSSION:** HTML is the most popular language for authoring Web pages. It is hardware and software independent, which means that it can be read by several different applications and on many different kinds of computer operating systems. HTML uses tags to mark information for proper display on browsers.

Answer (A) is incorrect because HTML is the acronym for HyperText Markup Language. Answer (B) is incorrect because the language is relatively easy to learn. Almost anyone can learn and use HTML, not just computer programmers. Answer (D) is incorrect because a number of other languages can be used for Internet transmissions, including JAVA and XML.

**91.** XML

A. Is focused on the content of the data.

B. Has become less important as new languages on the Internet are developed.

C. Uses standardized tags.

D. Is useful to display highly unstructured data.

Answer (A) is correct. *(Publisher)*

**REQUIRED:** The true statement about XML.

**DISCUSSION:** XML, which stands for eXtensible Markup Language, is useful for putting structured data into a text file. It can be used to extract and tag information from a database for transmission and subsequent use in other applications, e.g., display on the Internet or imported into a spreadsheet.

Answer (B) is incorrect because XML has become very popular for use on the Internet. Information tagged in XML can be integrated into HTML and other presentations. Answer (C) is incorrect because XML is very flexible and allows the user to design customized tags. Answer (D) is incorrect because the data must conform to a structure to be properly tagged.

**92.** Which of the following is a false statement about XBRL?

A. XBRL is freely licensed.

B. XBRL facilitates the automatic exchange of information.

C. XBRL is used primarily in the U.S.

D. XBRL is designed to work with a variety of software applications.

Answer (C) is correct. *(Publisher)*

**REQUIRED:** The false statement concerning XBRL.

**DISCUSSION:** XBRL stands for eXtensible Business Reporting Language. It is being developed for business and accounting applications. It is an XML-based application used to create, exchange, and analyze financial reporting information and is being developed for worldwide use.

Answer (A) is incorrect because the AICPA-led consortium that developed XBRL has promoted the application as a freely licensed product. Answer (B) is incorrect because XBRL will facilitate the exchange of information, for example, for reporting to the SEC. Answer (D) is incorrect because XBRL will allow exchange of data across many platforms and will soon be integrated into accounting software applications and products.

**93.** The firewall system that limits access to a computer network by routing users to replicated Web pages is

A. A packet filtering system.
B. Kerberos.
C. A proxy server.
D. An authentication system.

Answer (C) is correct. *(Publisher)*
**REQUIRED:** The firewall system that routes users to replicated web pages.
**DISCUSSION:** A proxy server maintains copies of web pages to be accessed by specified users. Outsiders are directed there, and more important information is not available from this access point.
Answer (A) is incorrect because a packet filtering system examines each incoming IP packet. Answer (B) is incorrect because Kerberos is encryption and authentication software that uses DES encryption techniques. Answer (D) is incorrect because an authentication system verifies a user's identity and is often an application provided by a firewall system, but it is not a firewall system itself.

**94.** An Internet firewall is designed to provide adequate protection against which of the following?

A. A computer virus.
B. Unauthenticated logins from outside users.
C. Insider leaking of confidential information.
D. A Trojan horse application.

Answer (B) is correct. *(Publisher)*
**REQUIRED:** The protection provided by an Internet firewall.
**DISCUSSION:** A firewall is a device that separates two networks and prevents passage of specific types of network traffic while maintaining a connection between the networks. Generally, an Internet firewall is designed to protect a system from unauthenticated logins from outside users, although it may provide several other features as well.
Answer (A) is incorrect because a firewall cannot adequately protect a system against computer viruses. Answer (C) is incorrect because industrial spies need not leak information through the firewall. A telephone or floppy disk are much more common means of sharing confidential information. Answer (D) is incorrect because a firewall cannot adequately protect against a Trojan horse (a program, such as a game, that appears friendly but that actually contains applications destructive to the computer system) or any other program that can be executed in the system by an internal user.

**95.** The most difficult aspect of using Internet resources is

A. Making a physical connection.
B. Locating the best information source.
C. Obtaining the equipment required.
D. Getting authorization for access.

Answer (B) is correct. *(CIA, adapted)*
**REQUIRED:** The most difficult aspect of using Internet resources.
**DISCUSSION:** The Internet is a series of networks throughout the world that facilitates information transfer between computers. Gateways allow mainframe computers to interface with personal computers. The graphics-rich environment of the World Wide Web (WWW) has been largely responsible for bringing the Internet out of the static realm of e-mail and text-only documents. The WWW continues to grow faster than any other segment of the Internet. Businesses, schools, government, and nonprofit organizations (in addition to millions of individuals) are gravitating to the Internet to promote themselves and their products to an audience spanning the entire planet. Accordingly, given the vast scope of the Internet, the most difficult aspect of its use is locating the best information sources. One solution has been the development of programs, including browsers and search engines, for accessing the WWW.
Answer (A) is incorrect because there is no limitation on the number of access ports. Answer (C) is incorrect because the only requirements for accessing Internet resources are a computer, a modem, a telephone line, a service provider, and basic communications software. Answer (D) is incorrect because organizations routinely provide Internet access to their employees, and individuals can obtain access through individual subscriptions to commercial information service providers.

**96.** Which of the following statements is (are) true regarding electronic mail security?

I. Electronic mail can be no more secure than the computer system on which it operates.

II. Confidential electronic mail messages should be stored on the mail server as electronic mail for the same length of time as similar paper-based documents.

III. In larger organizations, there may be several electronic mail administrators and locations with varying levels of security.

A. I only.

B. I and II.

C. I and III.

D. III only.

Answer (C) is correct. *(CIA, adapted)*

**REQUIRED:** The true statement(s) about electronic mail security.

**DISCUSSION:** The database that maintains all electronic messages or that permits linkages to all such messages ordinarily resides on a network file server. Consequently, network security is responsible for preventing unauthorized access to stored messages. Another problem arises in large, decentralized organizations with several electronic mail administrators. In these circumstances, electronic mail security and administrative procedures may not be as well understood and applied as in a centralized environment with fewer administrators.

Answer (A) is incorrect because statements I and III are true. Answer (B) is incorrect because a confidential mail message should not be retained on the server once the user has downloaded it to a personal computer. Furthermore, even if messages have been removed from the server, they may pose a security risk if they remain in personal databases or in data file backups. Answer (D) is incorrect because statements I and III are true.

## 5.7 Electronic Data Interchange (EDI)

**97.** Which of the following is usually a benefit of using electronic funds transfer (EFT) for international cash transactions?

A. Improvement of the audit trail for cash receipts and disbursements.

B. Creation of self-monitoring access controls.

C. Reduction of the frequency of data entry errors.

D. Off-site storage of source documents for cash transactions.

Answer (C) is correct. *(CPA, adapted)*

**REQUIRED:** The benefit of using EFT for international cash transactions.

**DISCUSSION:** The processing and transmission of electronic transactions, such as EFTs, virtually eliminates human interaction. This process not only helps eliminate errors but also allows for the rapid detection and recovery from errors when they do occur.

Answer (A) is incorrect because the audit trail is typically less apparent in an electronic environment than in a manual environment. Answer (B) is incorrect because a key control is management's establishment and monitoring of access controls. Answer (D) is incorrect because source documents are often eliminated in EFT transactions.

**98.** Which of the following statements is true concerning the security of messages in an electronic data interchange (EDI) system?

A. When confidentiality of data is the primary risk, message authentication is the preferred control rather than encryption.

B. Encryption performed by physically secure hardware devices is more secure than encryption performed by software.

C. Message authentication in EDI systems performs the same function as segregation of duties in other information systems.

D. Security in the transaction phase in EDI systems is not necessary because problems at that level will usually be identified by the service provider.

Answer (B) is correct. *(CPA, adapted)*

**REQUIRED:** The true statement about the security of messages in an EDI system.

**DISCUSSION:** Physically secure hardware devices for performing encryption are under the direct control of the client. Software is not easily controlled because it is portable. More control is achieved with the hardware approach.

Answer (A) is incorrect because, when confidentiality is of concern, encryption and access controls should be used. Answer (C) is incorrect because authentication relates to authorization, not message security. Answer (D) is incorrect because security in the EDI transaction phase is also an issue. The transmission of information to the service provider, such as a VAN, is subject to a variety of problems, for example, interception or alteration, that may not be detected by the service provider.

**99.** Which of the following is usually a benefit of transmitting transactions in an electronic data interchange (EDI) environment?

A. A compressed business cycle with lower year-end receivables balances.

B. A reduced need to test computer controls related to sales and collections transactions.

C. An increased opportunity to apply statistical sampling techniques to account balances.

D. No need to rely on third-party service providers to ensure security.

Answer (A) is correct. *(CPA, adapted)*

**REQUIRED:** The benefit of EDI.

**DISCUSSION:** EDI transactions are typically transmitted and processed in real time. Thus, EDI compresses the business cycle by eliminating delays. The time required to receive and process an order, ship goods, and receive payment is greatly reduced compared with that of a typical manual system. Accordingly, more rapid receipt of payment minimizes receivables and improves cash flow.

Answer (B) is incorrect because use of a sophisticated processing system would increase the need to test computer controls. Answer (C) is incorrect because computer technology allows all transactions to be tested rather than just a sample. Answer (D) is incorrect because EDI often uses a VAN (value-added network) as a third-party service provider, and reliance on controls provided by the VAN may be critical.

**100.** Which of the following are essential elements of the audit trail in an electronic data interchange (EDI) system?

A. Network and sender/recipient acknowledgments.

B. Message directories and header segments.

C. Contingency and disaster recovery plans.

D. Trading partner security and mailbox codes.

Answer (A) is correct. *(CPA, adapted)*

**REQUIRED:** The essential element in an EDI audit trail.

**DISCUSSION:** An audit trail allows for the tracing of a transaction from initiation to conclusion. Network and sender/recipient acknowledgments relate to the transaction flow and provide for the tracking of transactions.

Answer (B) is incorrect because message directories and header segments provide information controlling the message, such as originating and destination stations, message type and priority level, which are part of the message and not the audit trail. Answer (C) is incorrect because, although contingency and disaster recovery plans are important controls, they do not relate to the audit trail. Answer (D) is incorrect because, although maintaining control over security and mailbox codes is an important control, it does not relate to the audit trail.

**101.** A control that a company can use to detect forged EDI messages is to

A. Acknowledge all messages initiated externally with confirming messages.

B. Permit only authorized employees to have access to transmission facilities.

C. Delay action on orders until a second order is received for the same goods.

D. Write all incoming messages to a write-once/read-many device for archiving.

Answer (A) is correct. *(CIA, adapted)*

**REQUIRED:** The control to detect forged EDI messages.

**DISCUSSION:** If the company acknowledges messages initiated externally, the alleged sender will have the opportunity to recognize that it had not sent the message and will then be able to notify the company of the potential forgery. Then corrective action can be taken by the company.

Answer (B) is incorrect because permitting only authorized employees to have access to transmission facilities controls for unauthorized access to the facilities but would not detect forged EDI messages. Answer (C) is incorrect because delaying action on orders until a second order is received for the same goods defeats the purpose of using EDI, namely, rapid communication followed by rapid response. Answer (D) is incorrect because writing all incoming messages to a write-once/read-many device is a good practice, but it will not detect forgeries.

**102.** In a review of an EDI application using a third-party service provider, the auditor should

I. Ensure encryption keys meet ISO standards

II. Determine whether an independent review of the service provider's operation has been conducted

III. Verify that only public-switched data networks are used by the service provider

IV. Verify that the service provider's contracts include necessary clauses, such as the right to audit

A. I and II.

B. I and IV.

C. II and III.

D. II and IV.

Answer (D) is correct. *(CIA, adapted)*

**REQUIRED:** The auditor's procedures in a review of an EDI application.

**DISCUSSION:** An auditor should review trading partner agreements and contracts with third-party service providers. These documents should contain necessary clauses and appropriately limit liabilities. Moreover, legal counsel should have reviewed the agreements or contracts. An auditor should also determine whether the third-party service provider's operations and controls have been independently reviewed (e.g., by public accountants).

Answer (A) is incorrect because using a third-party service provider does not require encryption. Answer (B) is incorrect because using a third-party service provider does not require encryption. Answer (C) is incorrect because use of public-switched data networks is not a requirement of EDI.

**103.** Electronic data interchange (EDI) offers significant benefits to organizations, but it is not without certain major obstacles. Successful EDI implementation begins with which of the following?

A. Mapping the work processes and flows that support the organization's goals.

B. Purchasing new hardware for the EDI system.

C. Selecting reliable vendors for translation and communication software.

D. Standardizing transaction formats and data.

Answer (A) is correct. *(CIA, adapted)*

**REQUIRED:** The initial phase of EDI implementation.

**DISCUSSION:** Marked benefits arise when EDI is tied to strategic efforts that alter, not mirror, previous practices. Applying EDI to an inefficient process results in continuing to do things the wrong way, only faster. Hence, the initial phase of EDI implementation includes understanding the organization's mission and an analysis of its activities as part of an integrated solution to the organization's needs.

Answer (B) is incorrect because the prerequisite for EDI success is an understanding of the mission of the business and the processes and flows that support its goals, followed by cooperation with external partners. Purchasing new hardware is a subsequent step. Answer (C) is incorrect because, before applying EDI technology to the business, EDI must be viewed as part of an overall integrated solution to organizational requirements. Answer (D) is incorrect because EDI is not a solution by itself. Instead of considering how to transmit and receive transactions, a company must first analyze the entire process.

**104.** A company using EDI made it a practice to track the functional acknowledgments from trading partners and to issue warning messages if acknowledgments did not occur within a reasonable length of time. What risk was the company attempting to address by this practice?

A. Transactions that have not originated from a legitimate trading partner may be inserted into the EDI network.

B. Transmission of EDI transactions to trading partners may sometimes fail.

C. There may be disagreement between the parties as to whether the EDI transactions form a legal contract.

D. EDI data may not be accurately and completely processed by the EDI software.

Answer (B) is correct. *(CIA, adapted)*

**REQUIRED:** The EDI risk addressed by tracking functional acknowledgments from trading partners.

**DISCUSSION:** Tracking of customers' functional acknowledgments, when required, will help to ensure successful transmission of EDI transactions. Some possible controls include the provision of end-to-end acknowledgments, particularly when multiple, interconnected networks are involved, and maintenance of a tickler file of outstanding functional acknowledgments, with issuance of warnings for those that are overdue.

Answer (A) is incorrect because unauthorized access to the EDI system should be prevented by procedures that ensure the effective use of passwords, and data integrity and privacy should be maintained through the use of encryption and authentication measures. Answer (C) is incorrect because contractual issues should be resolved by the company and its trading partners before EDI is implemented. Answer (D) is incorrect because the risk that EDI data may not be completely and accurately processed is minimized by system-based controls, not by acknowledgments from trading partners.

**105.** Before sending or receiving EDI messages, a company should

A. Execute a trading partner agreement with each of its customers and suppliers.

B. Reduce inventory levels in anticipation of receiving shipments.

C. Demand that all its suppliers implement EDI capabilities.

D. Evaluate the effectiveness of its use of EDI transmissions.

Answer (A) is correct. *(CIA, adapted)*

**REQUIRED:** The process to be performed before sending or receiving EDI messages.

**DISCUSSION:** Before sending or receiving EDI messages, a company should execute a trading partner agreement with its customers and suppliers. All parties should understand their responsibilities, the messages each will initiate, how they will interpret messages, the means of authenticating and verifying the completeness and accuracy of messages, the moment when the contract between the parties is effective, the required level of security, etc.

Answer (B) is incorrect because the company may intend to reduce inventory levels, but that intention is unrelated to the timing of its first EDI messages. Answer (C) is incorrect because the company may want to demand or encourage all its customers and suppliers to implement EDI capabilities, but that request is independent of sending and receiving messages. Answer (D) is incorrect because it is not possible to evaluate the effectiveness of EDI transmissions until after they occur.

**106.** The best approach for minimizing the likelihood of software incompatibilities leading to unintelligible messages is for a company and its customers to

A. Acquire their software from the same software vendor.

B. Agree to synchronize their updating of EDI-related software.

C. Agree to use the same software in the same ways indefinitely.

D. Each write their own version of the EDI-related software.

Answer (B) is correct. *(CIA, adapted)*

**REQUIRED:** The best approach for minimizing the likelihood of software incompatibilities leading to unintelligible messages.

**DISCUSSION:** EDI entails the exchange of common business data converted into standard message formats. Thus, two crucial requirements are that the participants agree on transaction formats and that translation software be developed to convert messages into a form understandable by other companies. Thus, if one company changes its software, its trading partners must also do so.

Answer (A) is incorrect because the company and its customers may obtain their EDI-related software from the same vendor but still have software incompatibility problems if they do not synchronize their installation of updated versions. Answer (C) is incorrect because, as business requirements change, it may not be possible to use the same software in the same ways indefinitely. Answer (D) is incorrect because, even if the company and its customers each write their own versions, synchronization problems will arise from updates.

**107.** Organizations that move to implement EDI often use value-added networks (VANs). Which of the following would not normally be performed by a VAN?

A. Store electronic purchase orders of one organization to be accessed by another organization.

B. Provide common interfaces across organizations thereby eliminating the need for one organization to establish direct computer communication with a trading partner.

C. Maintain a log of all transactions of an organization with its trading partner.

D. Provide translations from clients' computer applications to a standard protocol used for EDI communication.

Answer (D) is correct. *(CIA, adapted)*

**REQUIRED:** The function not performed by a VAN.

**DISCUSSION:** Companies must purchase their own software to translate their data to a national standard protocol for EDI purposes, either ANSI X.12 in the U.S. or EDIFACT in Europe and most of the rest of the world. Once the data are in the standard format, the VAN handles all aspects of the communication. VANs are privately owned telecommunications carriers that sell capacity to outside users. Among other things, a VAN provides a mailbox service permitting EDI messages to be sent, sorted, and held until needed in the recipient's computer system.

Answer (A) is incorrect because VANs normally provide mailbox services. Answer (B) is incorrect because VANs normally provide common communication interfaces. Answer (C) is incorrect because VANs normally provide logs of transactions.

## 5.8 System Planning and Design

**108.** The proper sequence of activities in the systems development life cycle is

A. Design, analysis, implementation, and operation.

B. Design, implementation, analysis, and operation.

C. Analysis, design, implementation, and operation.

D. Programming, analysis, implementation, and operation.

Answer (C) is correct. *(CMA, adapted)*

**REQUIRED:** The sequential steps in a systems development life cycle.

**DISCUSSION:** The first step in systems development is identification and definition of a need relative to organizational objectives. The next step is to determine the scope of the required study and to proceed with a thorough analysis of the existing system. These steps lead to the general design of a new system. If the new system proves to be justified, the decision is then made to proceed with its implementation. Detailed systems design, including development and design of data files, is part of the implementation phase. Following implementation and operation, systems maintenance must be undertaken by analysts and programmers throughout the life of a system. Maintenance is the redesign of the system and programs to meet new needs or to correct design flaws.

Answer (A) is incorrect because analysis precedes design. Answer (B) is incorrect because analysis precedes design. Answer (D) is incorrect because it does not include the design step.

**109.** An MIS manager has only enough resources to install either a new payroll system or a new data security system, but not both. Which of the following actions is most appropriate?

A. Giving priority to the security system.

B. Leaving the decision to the MIS manager.

C. Increasing MIS staff output in order for both systems to be installed.

D. Having the information systems steering committee set the priority.

Answer (D) is correct. *(CISA, adapted)*

**REQUIRED:** The appropriate action given inadequate resources.

**DISCUSSION:** The needs assessment and cost-benefit analysis should be conducted by those responsible for making the decision. In this case, the information systems steering committee is the appropriate decision maker.

Answer (A) is incorrect because not enough information is given to conclude that priority should be given to the security system. Answer (B) is incorrect because the MIS manager should not be the only decision maker. Answer (C) is incorrect because the question indicates that development of both systems is not possible.

**110.** Which one of the following is not considered a typical risk associated with outsourcing (the practice of hiring an outside company to handle all or part of the data processing)?

A. Inflexibility.

B. Loss of control.

C. Loss of confidentiality.

D. Less availability of expertise.

Answer (D) is correct. *(CMA, adapted)*

**REQUIRED:** The item that is not considered a typical risk associated with outsourcing.

**DISCUSSION:** Some companies have outsourced their data processing function because of the economies provided, superior service quality, avoidance of changes in the organization's IS infrastructure, cost predictability, the freeing of human and financial capital, avoidance of fixed costs, and the greater expertise offered by outside vendors. The risks of outsourcing include the inflexibility of the relationship, the loss of control, the vulnerability of important information, and often dependency on a single vendor.

**111.** The strengths of the bottom-up approach to systems development are that it

I. Supports evolutionary growth of organizational functions

II. Minimizes the cost of systems development and maintenance

III. Incorporates the existing organizational systems

IV. Identifies the factors crucial to organizational success

A. I and III.

B. I and IV.

C. II and III.

D. II and IV.

Answer (A) is correct. *(CIA, adapted)*

**REQUIRED:** The strengths of the bottom-up approach to systems development.

**DISCUSSION:** The bottom-up approach begins at the operational level, designs each functional unit, and then ties these units together at each management level of the organization. This approach builds on existing capabilities and allows for evolutionary growth of organizational functions.

Answer (B) is incorrect because identifying crucial factors at the organizational level is a strength of the top-down approach. It begins with organizational objectives and goals, then breaks them into functional requirements to be implemented at lower levels of the organization. Answer (C) is incorrect because the bottom-up approach may not be the least costly in all circumstances. Answer (D) is incorrect because the bottom-up approach may not be the least costly in all circumstances.

**112.** Enterprise resource planning (ERP) software packages, such as SAP and Oracle, are all-inclusive systems that attempt to provide entity-wide information. ERP systems provide advantages to the auditor because they

A. Have proven difficult for some firms to install.

B. Typically require firms to reduce the division of duties and responsibilities found in traditional systems.

C. Typically have built-in transaction logs and ability to produce a variety of diagnostic reports.

D. Have been installed by smaller firms so, to date, few auditors have encountered them.

Answer (C) is correct. *(Publisher)*

**REQUIRED:** The advantage of an ERP system for the auditor.

**DISCUSSION:** ERP systems have a variety of controls and report generation functions that allow the auditor to abstract and monitor data collected and processed. Some ERP systems have built-in audit functions.

Answer (A) is incorrect because the difficulty of installing ERP systems is a disadvantage to the auditor. Answer (B) is incorrect because ERP systems often require the client to depart from the traditional functional division of duties such as accounting, finance, and marketing. The result is increased audit risk. Answer (D) is incorrect because ERP systems are very costly and therefore have been implemented only by large organizations. However, the trend is for more and more organizations to install these systems.

**113.** Which of the following should be emphasized before designing any system elements in a top-down approach to new systems development?

A. Types of processing systems being used by competitors.

B. Computer equipment to be used by the system.

C. Information needs of managers for planning and control.

D. Controls in place over the current system.

Answer (C) is correct. *(CIA, adapted)*

**REQUIRED:** The matter to be emphasized before designing a new system.

**DISCUSSION:** The top-down method begins with analysis of broad organizational goals, objectives, and policies as a basis for the design process. This step requires an understanding of the entity's environment and significant activities. The next step is to determine the decisions made by managers and the information required to make them. The necessary reports, databases, inputs, processing methods, and equipment specifications can then be defined. The weakness of the top-down approach is that it tends to concentrate on managers' information needs at the expense of the design of efficient transaction processing at the operational level.

Answer (A) is incorrect because the needs of the organization should be the overriding factor in systems development. Answer (B) is incorrect because the equipment selection should be a function of the processing needs, not vice versa. Answer (D) is incorrect because functional controls should be designed for the new system.

**114.** Using a telecommunications provider affects in-house networks. To prepare for changes resulting from enhanced external network services, management should

A. Optimize in-house networks to avoid bottlenecks that would limit the benefits offered by the telecommunications provider.

B. Plan for rapid implementation of new capabilities in anticipation of ready acceptance of the new technology.

C. Downsize the company's disaster recovery plan to recognize the increasing role of the telecommunications provider.

D. Enhance the in-house network management to minimize dependence on the telecommunications provider for network management.

Answer (A) is correct. *(CIA, adapted)*

**REQUIRED:** The appropriate action to prepare for changes resulting from enhanced external network services.

**DISCUSSION:** To prepare the company for changes resulting from the enhanced external network services, management should take appropriate action. A number of bottlenecks may limit the benefits that can be derived from the external network. For example, conversion from analog to digital technology is necessary to achieve rapid improvements in bandwidth and speed and to improve access to telecommunications services. Furthermore, applications, systems software, and communications protocols must be able to process information in a format and in a manner acceptable to end users. Communications security also has heightened importance as greater amounts of data are transmitted from remote sites.

Answer (B) is incorrect because resistance to change, inflexible organizational structures, and skepticism about the technology should be expected and must be successfully managed if the company is to reap the benefits. Answer (C) is incorrect because a company's disaster recovery plan should be enhanced to ensure the reliability of the network. Answer (D) is incorrect because network management may now be primarily a function, yet it will become more of a partnership arrangement with the communications carrier.

**115.** Many companies and government organizations would like to convert to open systems in order to

A. Get volume discounts from equipment vendors.

B. Achieve more economies of scale for equipment.

C. Use less expensive computing equipment.

D. Facilitate the integration of proprietary components.

Answer (C) is correct. *(CIA, adapted)*

**REQUIRED:** The reason for converting to open systems.

**DISCUSSION:** Open systems are those for which suppliers provide components whose interfaces are defined by public standards. For example, the U.S. government specifies that its suppliers adhere to the Unix operating system and the telecommunications protocols developed for the Internet. In contrast, a closed system's components are built to proprietary standards so that the equipment made by other suppliers cannot interface with the existing system. Accordingly, converting to open systems increases the number of vendors from which substitutable components can be acquired, which increases price competition for equipment.

Answer (A) is incorrect because running open systems tends to increase the number of vendors and decrease the amount of the average purchase from any one vendor. The result is a decrease in the opportunities for volume discounts from vendors. Answer (B) is incorrect because, in general, running open systems allows organizations to scale their computing facilities to a precise size, which may be inconsistent with attempting to achieve economies of scale due to larger volumes concentrated in fewer sites. Answer (D) is incorrect because running open systems tends to reduce an organization's reliance on proprietary components and reduce the need for their integration into existing systems.

**116.** The implementation of a client-server architecture offers significant potential benefits but also introduces certain management and control issues. For this architecture, which of the following is true?

A. The client part of the application should be designed to peripheral devices.

B. Organizations with decentralized information technology staff are best suited to meet the challenges of managing this architecture.

C. The training needs of end users are reduced because the client workstations will support graphical user interfaces, which are self-explanatory.

D. The diagnosis and resolution of system problems may be difficult because client-server systems can rarely be constructed without products from a number of vendors.

Answer (D) is correct. *(CIA, adapted)*

**REQUIRED:** The true statement about implementation of a client-server architecture.

**DISCUSSION:** A client-server system divides processing of an application between a client machine on a network and a file server. This division depends on which tasks each is best suited to perform. However, user interaction is ordinarily restricted to the client part of the application. This portion normally consists of the user interface, data entry, queries, and receipt of reports. The file server customarily manages peripheral hardware and controls access to shared databases. Thus, a client-server application must be designed as separate software components that run on different machines but appear to be one application. Multiple vendors are ordinarily involved in the many facets of client-server systems, and problems with the systems often cannot be traced easily to a single vendor's product or service.

Answer (A) is incorrect because the file server customarily manages peripheral hardware. Answer (B) is incorrect because, due to the need to obtain consensus regarding the management of client-server systems and to coordinate information technology expertise and end-user initiatives, organizations with strong, centralized IT departments are less likely to experience severe management problems. Answer (C) is incorrect because training needs of end-user staff may be substantial. The client-server platform extends certain development capabilities to the users and increases the ability of users to access and manipulate data.

**117.** Which of the following is the most appropriate activity for an internal auditor to perform during a review of systems development activity?

A. Serve on the MIS steering committee that determines what new systems are to be developed.

B. Review the methodology used to monitor and control the system development function.

C. Recommend specific automated procedures to be incorporated into new systems that will provide reasonable assurance that all data submitted to an application are converted to machine-readable form.

D. Recommend specific operational procedures that will ensure that all data submitted for processing are converted to machine-readable form.

Answer (B) is correct. *(CIA, adapted)*

**REQUIRED:** The procedure to perform during a review of systems development activity.

**DISCUSSION:** Auditor objectivity is not impaired when (s)he recommends standards of control for systems or reviews procedures before implementation. However, drafting procedures for systems and designing, installing, and operating systems are not audit functions. Thus, reviewing the methodology used by an organization is an appropriate activity that enables the internal auditor to determine whether (s)he can rely on the systems development activity to design and implement appropriate automated controls within applications.

Answer (A) is incorrect because service on a management decision-making committee is an operating responsibility and would impair audit objectivity. Answer (C) is incorrect because making recommendations for specific procedures is an operating responsibility. Answer (D) is incorrect because making recommendations for specific procedures is an operating responsibility.

**118.** Even though an organization is committed to using its mainframe for its manufacturing plant operations, it has been looking for ways to downsize other applications. The purpose of downsizing is to

A. Improve reliability.

B. Improve security.

C. Reduce complexity.

D. Decrease costs.

Answer (D) is correct. *(CIA, adapted)*

**REQUIRED:** The purpose of downsizing.

**DISCUSSION:** The purpose of downsizing is to reduce costs of applications by abandoning larger, more expensive systems in favor of smaller, less expensive systems that are more versatile. However, downsized applications are less reliable than their mainframe predecessors because they are new and have not been used extensively. Typically, downsized client-server implementations lack the monitoring and control features that permit recovery from minor processing interruptions.

Answer (A) is incorrect because client-server technology used in downsizing is less reliable. Answer (B) is incorrect because security is usually better on a mainframe. Answer (C) is incorrect because downsizing applications often increases their complexity. The data files become fragmented across multiple systems.

**119.** Object technology provides a new and better way of enabling developers and users to build and tailor applications. In light of this technology, what action should management take with respect to its older (legacy) systems?

A. Plan for rapid migration of legacy systems to object-based applications.

B. Consider the more stable legacy systems as initial candidates for conversion.

C. Investigate the integration of object-based capabilities with legacy systems.

D. Defer the use of object technology until the legacy systems need replacement.

Answer (C) is correct. *(CIA, adapted)*

**REQUIRED:** The approach to introducing object technology.

**DISCUSSION:** Object technology is an approach to writing computer programs that expedites development. Objects are self-contained, reusable parts that are especially helpful for developing interactive and graphical programs. A legacy system is an older system that has been operating for years. Legacy systems represent a significant investment and may still provide adequate service. To balance the need for meeting changes in the corporate and technical environments with the economic imperative represented by the investment in legacy systems, information systems departments should seek opportunities to add object-oriented capabilities to existing systems.

Answer (A) is incorrect because the costs of migrating legacy systems and retraining the personnel who are to develop and maintain them preclude rapid transition. Answer (B) is incorrect because legacy systems that are difficult to modify and maintain are better candidates for conversion to object technology. Answer (D) is incorrect because object technology should be explored as a better approach for implementing business applications.

**120.** Object technology has become more important in companies' strategic use of information systems because of its potential to

A. Permit quicker and more reliable development of systems.

B. Maintain programs written in procedural languages.

C. Minimize data integrity violations in hierarchical databases.

D. Streamline the traditional "waterfall" systems development methodology.

Answer (A) is correct. *(CIA, adapted)*

**REQUIRED:** The reason object technology has become more important.

**DISCUSSION:** An object-oriented approach is intended to produce reusable code. Because code segments can be reused in other programs, the time and cost of writing software should be reduced.

Answer (B) is incorrect because object technology has the potential to support faster maintenance of programs written in object-oriented, but not procedural, languages. Answer (C) is incorrect because object technology is being applied to relational, but not hierarchical, databases. Answer (D) is incorrect because object technology is typically implemented in a prototyping environment.

**121.** User acceptance testing is more important in an object-oriented development process than in a traditional environment because of the implications of the

A. Absence of traditional design documents.

B. Lack of a tracking system for changes.

C. Potential for continuous monitoring.

D. Inheritance of properties in hierarchies.

Answer (D) is correct. *(CIA, adapted)*

**REQUIRED:** The reason user acceptance testing is more important in an object-oriented development process.

**DISCUSSION:** In object-oriented development, all objects in a class inherit the properties of higher classes in the hierarchy. Thus, changes in one object may affect many other objects, and the extent and effects of errors significantly increase. Testing one object provides no assurance that the objects are properly coordinated. Accordingly, user acceptance testing to verify correct functioning of the whole system becomes more important.

Answer (A) is incorrect because, instead of traditional design documents, items such as the business model, narratives of process functions, iterative development screens, computer processes and reports, and product descriptions guides are produced in object-oriented development. Answer (B) is incorrect because, in general, object-oriented development systems include tracking systems for changes made in objects and hierarchies. Answer (C) is incorrect because object-oriented systems are usually developed in client-server environments, so the potential exists for continuous monitoring of system use. However, continuous monitoring typically occurs during system operation, not during development.

**122.** An electronics firm has decided to implement a new system through the use of rapid application development techniques. Which of the following should be included in the development of the new system?

A. Deferring the need for system documentation until the final modules are completed.

B. Removing project management responsibilities from the development teams.

C. Creating the system module by module until completed.

D. Using object development techniques to minimize the use of previous code.

Answer (C) is correct. *(CIA, adapted)*

**REQUIRED:** The step in the development of a new system using rapid application development techniques.

**DISCUSSION:** Rapid application development includes automated design and development methods (computer-aided software engineering) and joint application development. It emphasizes human management, user involvement, and development of systems incrementally. A related concept is rapid prototyping. Thus, the new system is developed module by module.

Answer (A) is incorrect because system documentation is not eliminated or deferred by using rapid application development. Answer (B) is incorrect because project management involves development teams. Answer (D) is incorrect because, if object development is useful, it will increase usage of previous code.

**123.** Which of the following risks is more likely to be encountered in an end-user computing (EUC) environment as compared with a mainframe computer system?

A. Inability to afford adequate uninterruptible power supply systems.

B. User input screens without a graphical user interface (GUI).

C. Applications that are difficult to integrate with other information systems.

D. Lack of adequate utility programs.

Answer (C) is correct. *(CIA, adapted)*

**REQUIRED:** The risk more likely to be encountered in an EUC environment.

**DISCUSSION:** The risk of allowing end users to develop their own applications is decentralization of control. End-user developed applications may not be subject to an independent outside review by systems analysts and are not created in the context of a formal development methodology. These applications may lack appropriate standards, controls, and quality assurance procedures. Moreover, when end users create their own applications and files, private information systems may proliferate in which data are largely uncontrolled. These systems may contain the same information, but end-user applications may update and define the data in different ways. Thus, determining the location of data and ensuring data consistency become more difficult because the applications are difficult to integrate.

Answer (A) is incorrect because inability to afford adequate uninterruptible power supply systems is a risk in all computing environments. Answer (B) is incorrect because lack of a GUI is a risk in all computing environments. Answer (D) is incorrect because lack of adequate utility programs is a risk in all computing environments.

**124.** As the internal auditor reviewing personal computer operations, your first step should be to determine the existence of

A. Procedures for training accounting department personnel in the uses of personal computers, including the use of modems.

B. Backup procedures for computer processing when equipment is down or software is not operational.

C. Physical security for hardware and software.

D. Standards, policies, and procedures for acquiring, operating, and replacing hardware and software.

Answer (D) is correct. *(CIA, adapted)*

**REQUIRED:** The primary first step in reviewing personal computer operations.

**DISCUSSION:** A primary purpose of an operational audit is to determine whether standards are being met and policies and procedures are being followed. A fundamental first step is to ascertain whether management has met its responsibility of establishing these policies (general guides to decision making), procedures (specific ways to accomplish work), and operating standards (defined performance measures).

Answer (A) is incorrect because training procedures are encompassed by standards, policies, and procedures for acquiring, operating, and replacing hardware and software to achieve the primary objective. Answer (B) is incorrect because backup procedures are encompassed by standards, policies, and procedures for acquiring, operating, and replacing hardware and software to achieve the primary objective. Answer (C) is incorrect because physical security is encompassed by standards, policies, and procedures for acquiring, operating, and replacing hardware and software to achieve the primary objective.

**125.** Two major retail companies, both publicly traded and operating in the same geographic area, have recently merged. The companies are approximately the same size and have audit departments. Company A has little EDI experience. Company B has invested heavily in information technology and has EDI connections with its major vendors. Which of the following is the least important risk factor when considering the ability to integrate the two companies' computer systems?

A. The number of programmers and systems analysts employed by each company.

B. The extent of EDI connections with vendors.

C. The compatibility of existing operating systems and database structures.

D. The size of company databases and the number of database servers used.

Answer (A) is correct. *(CIA, adapted)*

**REQUIRED:** The least important risk factor when integrating two companies' computer systems.

**DISCUSSION:** The number of systems personnel employed may reflect differences in operating philosophy (outsourcing vs. in-house development of applications). However, the number of personnel in each company is a less serious concern than the compatibility of hardware and software.

Answer (B) is incorrect because Company A has little EDI experience. Hence, the greater the number of vendors that must be connected with Company A, the greater the risk exposure. Answer (C) is incorrect because the difficulty and expense of conversion will be increased if the computer systems have significant compatibility problems. Answer (D) is incorrect because the greater the complexity of the systems to be integrated, the greater the risk exposure.

**126.** A systems development approach used to quickly produce a model of user interfaces, user interactions with the system, and process logic is called

A. Neural networking.

B. Prototyping.

C. Reengineering.

D. Application generation.

Answer (B) is correct. *(CIA, adapted)*

**REQUIRED:** The approach used to produce a model of user interfaces, user interactions with the system, and process logic.

**DISCUSSION:** Prototyping produces the first model(s) of a new system. This technique usually employs a software tool for quick development of a model of the user interface (such as by report or screen), interaction of users with the system (for example, a menu-screen approach or data entry), and processing logic (the executable module). Prototyping stimulates user participation because the model allows quick exploration of concepts and development of solutions with quick results.

Answer (A) is incorrect because neural networking involves hardware or software that imitates the processing activities of the human brain. Answer (C) is incorrect because reengineering salvages reusable components of existing systems and restructures them to develop new systems or to improve the old systems. Answer (D) is incorrect because an application generator is software that can be used to develop an application simply by describing its requirements to the computer rather than by writing a procedural program.

**127.** Which of the following is not an audit objective in the review of hardware acquisition?

A. Ensuring that adequate information for sound management decision making is available prior to contracting for the purchase, rent, or lease of new equipment.

B. Ensuring that vendors are provided with appropriate and uniform data for submission of bids according to management approved specifications and guidelines.

C. Ensuring that appropriate hardware is selected, installed, and tested in accordance with management approved specifications.

D. Ensuring that provisions are made to minimize damage or abuse to hardware and to maintain the hardware in good operating condition.

Answer (D) is correct. *(CISA, adapted)*

**REQUIRED:** The audit objective not related to the review of hardware acquisition.

**DISCUSSION:** Determining whether controls are in place to minimize damage or abuse to equipment is considered in the evaluation of the firm's operating environment. This step occurs subsequent to the acquisition of the equipment.

Answer (A) is incorrect because ensuring that adequate information for sound management decision making is available is an objective of a hardware acquisition review. Answer (B) is incorrect because ensuring that vendors are provided with appropriate and uniform data is an objective of a hardware acquisition review. Answer (C) is incorrect because ensuring that appropriate hardware is selected, installed, and tested is an objective of a hardware acquisition review.

**128.** Management's enthusiasm for computer security tends to vary with changes in the environment, particularly the occurrence of other computer disasters. Which of the following concepts should be addressed when making a comprehensive recommendation regarding the costs and benefits of computer security?

I. Potential loss if security is not implemented

II. Probability of occurrences

III. Cost and effectiveness of the implementation and operation of computer security

A. I only.

B. I and II only.

C. III only.

D. I, II, and III.

Answer (D) is correct. *(CIA, adapted)*

**REQUIRED:** The concept(s) that should be addressed in an analysis of cost-benefit considerations.

**DISCUSSION:** Potential loss is the amount of dollar damages associated with a security problem or loss of assets. Potential loss times the probability of occurrence is an estimate (expected value) of the exposure associated with lack of security. It represents a potential benefit associated with the implementation of security measures. To perform a cost-benefit analysis, the costs should be considered. Thus, all three items need to be addressed.

Answer (A) is incorrect because potential loss of security measures is an important element of the analysis. Answer (B) is incorrect because the probability of loss is an important element of the analysis. Answer (C) is incorrect because the cost and effectiveness of security measures is an important element of the analysis.

Questions 129 through 131 are based on the following information. The state administration has just appointed a new director of the Department of Information Systems (DIS). DIS is responsible for information systems for state functions and maintains large computers located in the state capital and distributed facilities in each county. In cooperation with staff in other state departments and agencies, DIS oversees the contracting process for outside contractors who develop major systems. After major systems have been installed and accepted, DIS is responsible for their maintenance.

One major system installed just as the new director of DIS was being appointed was the Integrated Public Assistance System (IPAS), which integrated record keeping, collections, and disbursements for food stamps, welfare, and child support for over one million recipients. At the time this system was developed, most of the costs for information systems for public assistance were paid by the federal government if a state's system met federal requirements. IPAS was designed for online entry of case information in county offices and overnight batch generation of checks to recipients.

Initially, when only a few counties had been converted to the system, response time on terminals in county offices was about 3 seconds. Now, with about half the counties converted, response time is at least 30 seconds and sometimes as long as 10 minutes. All data records appear to be correct despite the response time, and transmission errors have been negligible. The same computer also supports other online application systems that have been operating normally.

The long response times have delayed conversion of existing cases to the new system. During the conversion period, any new cases for public assistance were to be entered into the new system, but the lengthening response time has caused many new applicants to wait several months before their cases were entered, thus delaying the start of their authorized benefits.

The governor of the state is aware of the status of IPAS and has asked the new director of DIS to propose remedies for the situation. Realizing the need for assessing the system, the director of DIS has asked the state's internal auditing department to investigate the system configuration and recommend ways to improve online response.

**129.** If the response time were caused by application software, the most likely cause would be application programs that

A. Make erroneous updates of transactions to the master files.

B. Require more printing than the installed printers can accommodate.

C. Invoke more input-output operations than are necessary for the specified functions.

D. Contain infinite loops that degrade response time.

Answer (C) is correct. *(CIA, adapted)*

**REQUIRED:** The most likely cause of slow response time if application software is to blame.

**DISCUSSION:** Processing is relatively more rapid than input and output. Thus, invoking more input-output operations than are necessary for the specified functions is the most likely application software cause of lengthening response time.

Answer (A) is incorrect because, despite the response time, all data records appear to be correct, so the programs are not likely to make erroneous updates of transactions to the master files. Answer (B) is incorrect because requiring more printing than the installed printers can accommodate does not appear to be the problem. Online terminal response is independent of printer use. Answer (D) is incorrect because the presence of infinite loops in application programs would cause the program to stop rather than just run more slowly.

**130.** If the response time is caused by central site hardware, the most likely cause is

A. A malfunctioning CPU.

B. Inadequate disk access.

C. Defective disk volumes.

D. Failing disk channels.

Answer (B) is correct. *(CIA, adapted)*

**REQUIRED:** The most likely cause of slow response time if central site hardware is to blame.

**DISCUSSION:** As more records are added to the system, the disk space becomes saturated and degrades the system. Overhead time related to management of disk space takes more and more computer cycles and can degrade response time.

Answer (A) is incorrect because the symptom of a malfunctioning CPU is complete failure or unusual results, neither of which is present here. Answer (C) is incorrect because a symptom of defective disk volumes is unrecoverable or erroneous data on disk files, neither of which occurred here. Answer (D) is incorrect because a symptom of failing disk channels is unrecoverable or erroneous data on disk files, neither of which occurred here.

**131.** If the response time is a function of the communications network, the most likely cause is

A. Defective terminals in county offices.

B. Insufficient transmission capacity.

C. A malfunctioning front-end controller.

D. Transient errors in transmission lines.

Answer (B) is correct. *(CIA, adapted)*

**REQUIRED:** The most likely cause if the response time is a function of the communications network.

**DISCUSSION:** As more and more sites (counties) are added to the network, the transmission capacity may be overloaded. Transmission capacity is based on the technology used, e.g., telephone lines, microwave, and satellite. Directly tied to the technology is the communication equipment, e.g., the use of concentrators and front-end processors (controllers).

Answer (A) is incorrect because a symptom of defective terminals in county offices would be transmission errors, which are not present. Answer (C) is incorrect because a symptom of a malfunctioning front-end controller would be transmission or data errors, which are not present. Answer (D) is incorrect because a symptom of transient errors in transmission lines would be transmission errors, which are not present.

**132.** All of the following are included in the systems implementation process except

A. Training.

B. Documentation.

C. Systems design.

D. Testing and conversion.

Answer (C) is correct. *(CMA, adapted)*

**REQUIRED:** The item not included in the systems implementation process.

**DISCUSSION:** Systems implementation includes training and educating users, documenting the systems, testing the systems' programs and procedures, systems conversion (including final testing and switchover), and systems follow-up. General systems design is not a part of the implementation stage of the life cycle, but the detailed systems design, such as the line-by-line coding of computer programs, is accomplished at this stage.

Answer (A) is incorrect because training is a part of the implementation stage. Answer (B) is incorrect because documentation is a part of the implementation stage. Answer (D) is incorrect because testing and conversion is a part of the implementation stage.

**133.** Which of the following is not an important element in deciding whether to lease or purchase computer equipment?

A. Cost of money.

B. Tax considerations.

C. Maintenance expense.

D. Parallel operations cost.

Answer (D) is correct. *(CDP, adapted)*

**REQUIRED:** The unimportant element in deciding whether to lease or purchase computer equipment.

**DISCUSSION:** Any cost that is not affected by the decision need not be considered. Parallel operations costs (costs of operating both the old and new systems during the checkout period of the new system) are incurred whether the firm leases or purchases the equipment.

Answer (A) is incorrect because high interest rates may favor the lease option. Answer (B) is incorrect because the amount and availability of the investment tax credit, deductions for interest and depreciation, and other tax-planning factors will vary depending on the option chosen. Answer (C) is incorrect because maintenance expense will vary depending on the terms of the lease or purchase.

**134.** The cost-effectiveness of information technology is affected by how efficiently it is used. One procedure designed to help ensure efficiency is to

A. Control access to sensitive output.

B. Provide for backup and disaster recovery.

C. Monitor the change environment for software in use.

D. Delete copies of data files when the information is no longer needed.

Answer (D) is correct. *(CIA, adapted)*

**REQUIRED:** The procedure designed to ensure the cost-effectiveness of information technology.

**DISCUSSION:** Efficiency is not achieved when facilities are underused, work is nonproductive, or procedures are uneconomical. Efficiency will be improved by freeing media and disk space for other uses, thus reducing data storage costs.

Answer (A) is incorrect because access to sensitive output is a security concern. Answer (B) is incorrect because backup and disaster recovery is an operational integrity issue. Answer (C) is incorrect because the change environment is a security and independence concern.

**135.** Which of the following steps should be included in an action plan covering privacy concerns?

I. Preparation of a plan to ensure that necessary privacy controls are integrated into the design of computer systems

II. Training of employees in the awareness of privacy and company policies

III. Preparation of a plan to inform customers of the organization's privacy policies

IV. Preparation of an analysis of the potential impact that privacy would have on the computer system

A. IV.

B. I and III.

C. II and IV.

D. I, II, III, and IV.

Answer (D) is correct. *(CISA, adapted)*

**REQUIRED:** The step(s) that should be included in a privacy-related action plan.

**DISCUSSION:** Privacy considerations are among the many reasons for developing effective computer security. Failure to safeguard the privacy of confidential client information may result in both loss of business and litigation. Other information, such as trade secrets, must be shielded from disclosure to competitors. Moreover, some firms, e.g., defense contractors, may have access to information affecting national security. Accordingly, each of the listed steps is appropriate. Establishing a company code of ethics and a strong internal audit function are among the other aspects of a control environment that stresses concern for privacy issues.

Answer (A) is incorrect because steps I, II, and III should also be included. Answer (B) is incorrect because steps II and IV should also be included. Answer (C) is incorrect because steps I and III should also be included.

## 5.9 Operating and Organizational Controls

**136.** An auditor anticipates assessing control risk at a low level in a computerized environment. Under these circumstances, on which of the following procedures should the auditor initially focus?

A. Programmed control procedures.

B. Application control procedures.

C. Output control procedures.

D. General control procedures.

Answer (D) is correct. *(CPA, adapted)*

**REQUIRED:** The initial concern when the auditor anticipates assessing control risk at less than the maximum in a computer environment.

**DISCUSSION:** Some computer controls relate to all computer activities (general controls), and some relate to specific tasks (application controls). Because general controls are pervasive in their effect, they should be tested before application controls. If the general controls are ineffective, tests of the application controls over input, processing, and output will be unlikely to permit the auditor to assess control risk at less than the maximum.

Answer (A) is incorrect because programmed procedures relate to application controls, which should be tested for effectiveness once the general controls prove to be effective. Answer (B) is incorrect because general controls are tested before application controls. Answer (C) is incorrect because output controls are application controls, which are tested after general controls.

**137.** Which of the following statements is true concerning internal control in an electronic data interchange (EDI) system?

A. Preventive controls generally are more important than detective controls in EDI systems.

B. Control objectives for EDI systems generally are different from the objectives for other information systems.

C. Internal controls in EDI systems rarely permit control risk to be assessed at below the maximum.

D. Internal controls related to the segregation of duties generally are the most important controls in EDI systems.

Answer (A) is correct. *(CPA, adapted)*

**REQUIRED:** The true statement about EDI controls.

**DISCUSSION:** In general, preventive controls are more important than detective controls because the benefits typically outweigh the costs. In electronic processing, once a transaction is accepted, there is often little opportunity to apply detective controls. Thus, it is important to prevent errors or frauds before they happen.

Answer (B) is incorrect because the basic control objectives are the same regardless of the nature of the processing: to ensure the integrity of the information and to safeguard the assets. Answer (C) is incorrect because, to gather sufficient evidence in a sophisticated computer system, it is often necessary to rely on the controls. Control risk may be assessed at below the maximum if relevant controls are identified and tested and if the resulting evidential matter provides the degree of assurance necessary to support the assessed level of control risk. Answer (D) is incorrect because the level of segregation of duties achieved in a manual system is usually not feasible in a computer system.

**138.** In the organization of the information systems function, the most important separation of duties is

A. Not allowing the data librarian to assist in data processing operations.

B. Assuring that those responsible for programming the system do not have access to data processing operations.

C. Having a separate information officer at the top level of the organization outside of the accounting function.

D. Using different programming personnel to maintain utility programs from those who maintain the application programs.

Answer (B) is correct. *(CMA, adapted)*

**REQUIRED:** The most important separation of duties in the information systems function.

**DISCUSSION:** Separation of duties is a general control that is vital in a computerized environment. Some separation of duties common in noncomputerized environments may not be feasible in a computer environment. However, certain tasks should not be combined. Systems analysts and programmers should be separate from computer operators. Both programmers and analysts may be able to modify programs, files, and controls, and should therefore have no access to those programs nor to computer equipment. Operators should not be assigned programming duties or responsibility for systems design, and should have no opportunity to make changes in programs and systems.

Answer (A) is incorrect because librarians maintain control over documentation, programs, and data files; they should have no access to equipment, but they can assist in data processing operations. Answer (C) is incorrect because a separate information officer outside of the accounting function would not be as critical a separation of duties as that between programmers and processors. Answer (D) is incorrect because programmers usually handle all types of programs.

**139.** Your firm has recently converted its purchasing cycle from a manual process to an online computer system. Which of the following is a probable result associated with conversion to the new automatic system?

A. Processing errors are increased.

B. The firm's risk exposures are reduced.

C. Processing time is increased.

D. Traditional duties are less segregated.

Answer (D) is correct. *(CIA, adapted)*

**REQUIRED:** The probable result associated with conversion to the new automatic system.

**DISCUSSION:** In a manual system with appropriate internal control, separate individuals are responsible for authorizing transactions, recording transactions, and custody of assets. These checks and balances prevent fraud and detect inaccurate or incomplete transactions. In a computer environment, however, this segregation of duties is not always feasible. For example, a computer may print checks, record disbursements, and generate information for reconciling the account balance.

Answer (A) is incorrect because a computer system decreases processing errors. Answer (B) is incorrect because the conversion to a new system does not reduce the number of risk exposures. Answer (C) is incorrect because processing time is decreased.

**140.** The organization chart is a graphic representation of the

A. Power structure.

B. Communications channels.

C. Locus of decision making.

D. Formal authority structure.

Answer (D) is correct. *(CDP, adapted)*

**REQUIRED:** The relationship graphically represented by an organization chart.

**DISCUSSION:** An organization chart represents pictorially the formal lines of authority within an organization. It depicts the organizational structure and the hierarchical relationships of the functional units in the organization.

Answer (A) is incorrect because the power structure concerns personalities more than assigned responsibilities. Answer (B) is incorrect because, although the organization chart customarily shows communication lines, it does not represent the informal channels that operate within an organization. Answer (C) is incorrect because the organization chart depicts responsibility and authority, which includes more than the loci of decision making.

**141.** It is important to maintain proper segregation of duties in a computer environment. Which of the following access setups is appropriate?

| | Update Access for Production Data | | Update Access for Production Programs | |
|---|---|---|---|---|
| | Users Have? | Application Programmers Have? | Users Have? | Application Programmers Have? |
| A. | Yes | No | No | No |
| B. | Yes | No | No | Yes |
| C. | No | Yes | Yes | No |
| D. | No | Yes | Yes | Yes |

Answer (A) is correct. *(CIA, adapted)*

**REQUIRED:** The appropriate access setup.

**DISCUSSION:** Incompatible duties should be separated for effective control. End users need access to applications data and functions but not to systems software, applications programs, and most computer equipment. Application programmers should be segregated from computer operations, technical support staff, computer equipment, systems software, production versions of programs, and production data.

**142.** A systems analyst should have access to each of the following except

A. Source code.

B. Password identification tables.

C. User procedures.

D. Edit criteria.

Answer (B) is correct. *(CISA, adapted)*

**REQUIRED:** The item to which a systems analyst should not have access.

**DISCUSSION:** If the systems analyst has access to password identification tables, (s)he is in a position to access and change application programs and files without proper authorization.

Answer (A) is incorrect because the analyst needs access to source code for approved projects in progress. Answer (C) is incorrect because the analyst needs access to user procedures to determine how input is entered and output is used. Answer (D) is incorrect because the analyst needs access to edit criteria to obtain assurance that the system design criteria and objectives are incorporated in applications.

**143.** For a specific computer application jobstream, an explanation of the purpose, identification of computer components used, identification of input-output forms and media, and identification of programmed terminations and prescribed restart instructions are found in the

A. Systems flowchart.

B. Program documentation.

C. Console log.

D. Computer run book.

Answer (D) is correct. *(CIA, adapted)*

**REQUIRED:** The document meeting the given definition.

**DISCUSSION:** Documentation is a general control. All programs, procedures, and operating instructions should be documented before final approval. The computer (or console) run book provides operations documentation regarding the matters described in the question.

Answer (A) is incorrect because a systems flowchart shows the flow of information through the system, not the detailed operating instructions found in the computer run book. Answer (B) is incorrect because program documentation includes a statement of the purpose of the program, flowcharts and listings for the program, decision tables, controls, formats for records, inputs and outputs, program operating instructions, and program changes. It should be part of the computer run book. Answer (C) is incorrect because computer console logs typically contain information about jobs processed, job start and stop times, and problems encountered.

**144.** One of the major problems in a computer system is that incompatible functions may be performed by the same individual. One compensating control is the use of

A. Echo checks.

B. A self-checking digit system.

C. Computer-generated hash totals.

D. A computer log.

Answer (D) is correct. *(CPA, adapted)*

**REQUIRED:** The control compensating for inadequate segregation of duties in a computer system.

**DISCUSSION:** A computer (console) log is a record of computer and software usage usually produced by the operating system. Proper monitoring of the log is a compensating control for the lack of segregation of duties. For instance, the log should contain a list of interventions by the operators.

Answer (A) is incorrect because echo checks are hardware controls used to determine if the correct message was received by an output device. Answer (B) is incorrect because a self-checking digit system is an input control that tests identification numbers. Answer (C) is incorrect because hash totals are control totals used to check for losses or inaccuracies arising during data movement.

**145.** Which of the following represents an internal control weakness in a computer-based system?

A. Computer programmers write and revise programs designed by analysts.

B. The data control group is solely responsible for distributing reports and other output.

C. The computer librarian maintains custody and record keeping for computer application programs.

D. Computer operators have access to operator instructions and the authority to change programs.

Answer (D) is correct. *(CIA, adapted)*

**REQUIRED:** The control weakness in a computer-based system.

**DISCUSSION:** Computer operators need access to operator instructions. Otherwise, they could not perform their duties. Operators, however, should not have the authority to change computer programs.

Answer (A) is incorrect because writing and revising computer programs are appropriate functions for programmers. Answer (B) is incorrect because distributing computer reports is an appropriate function of the control group. Answer (C) is incorrect because maintaining custody and related record keeping for computer programs is appropriate for a computer librarian.

**146.** In a large organization, the biggest risk in not having an adequately staffed information center help desk is

A. Increased difficulty in performing application audits.

B. Inadequate documentation for application systems.

C. Increased likelihood of use of unauthorized program code.

D. Persistent errors in user interaction with systems.

Answer (D) is correct. *(CIA, adapted)*

**REQUIRED:** The biggest risk in not having an adequately staffed information center help desk.

**DISCUSSION:** Help desk personnel should be properly trained to log problems, resolve minor problems, and forward more difficult problems to appropriate individuals. An effective help desk minimizes user frustration and delays in processing, continuation of errors in user interaction with the information systems, processing mistakes necessitating later correction or reruns, and failures to log errors and analysis of their causes.

Answer (A) is incorrect because application audits are largely unaffected by help desk staffing. Answer (B) is incorrect because preparation of documentation is a development function. Answer (C) is incorrect because prevention of use of unauthorized program code is a function of change control.

**147.** In planning the physical location of a computer facility, the primary consideration for selecting a site is that it should

A. Maximize the visibility of the computer.

B. Minimize the distance that data control personnel must travel to deliver data and reports and be easily accessible by a majority of company personnel.

C. Be in the basement or on the ground floor.

D. Provide security.

Answer (D) is correct. *(J. Brooks)*

**REQUIRED:** The primary consideration in selecting a site for a computer.

**DISCUSSION:** The primary criterion for selecting a site should be the security of the environment of the computer. The computer must be protected from disasters such as fire, windstorm, sabotage, and improper access.

Answer (A) is incorrect because a highly visible site is usually not physically secure. Answer (B) is incorrect because, although minimizing travel distance is important, it is not the primary consideration. Additionally, only authorized personnel should be allowed in the computer site; thus, easy access by a majority of company personnel is not necessary. Answer (C) is incorrect because the basement or the ground floor is not always the best location. In certain geographic areas, these locations are subject to flooding.

**148.** Which of the following statements regarding security concerns for notebook computers is true?

A. The primary methods of control usually involve general controls.

B. Centralized control over the selection and acquisition of hardware and software is not a major concern.

C. Some traditional controls such as segregation of duties become more important.

D. As their use becomes more sophisticated, the degree of concern regarding physical security decreases.

Answer (A) is correct. *(CIA, adapted)*

**REQUIRED:** The true statement about security concerns for notebook computers.

**DISCUSSION:** General controls apply to all computer activities. General controls to prevent theft of equipment and data and to restrict access to the use of equipment and data are the primary consideration, given the nature of notebook computers.

Answer (B) is incorrect because, to assure compatibility with other computers, files, and databases, and to control expenditures, it is necessary to have centralized control over the selection and acquisition of hardware and software. Answer (C) is incorrect because, given the nature and uses of notebook computers, segregation of duties may not be feasible. Answer (D) is incorrect because, as the use of notebook computers becomes more sophisticated, the degree of concern regarding physical security increases.

**149.** Which of the following should not be the responsibility of a database administrator?

A. Design the content and organization of the database.

B. Develop applications to access the database.

C. Protect the database and its software.

D. Monitor and improve the efficiency of the database.

Answer (B) is correct. *(CIA, adapted)*

**REQUIRED:** The item not the responsibility of a database administrator.

**DISCUSSION:** The database administrator (DBA) is the person who has overall responsibility for developing and maintaining the database. One primary responsibility is for designing the content of the database. Another responsibility of the DBA is to protect and control the database. A third responsibility is to monitor and improve the efficiency of the database. The responsibility of developing applications to access the database belongs to systems analysts and programmers.

Answer (A) is incorrect because designing the content and organization of the database is a responsibility of the database administrator. Answer (C) is incorrect because protecting the database and its software is a responsibility of the database administrator. Answer (D) is incorrect because monitoring and improving the efficiency of the database is a responsibility of the database administrator.

**150.** The responsibilities of a data administrator (DA) include monitoring

A. The database industry.

B. The performance of the database.

C. Database security.

D. Backup of the system.

Answer (A) is correct. *(Publisher)*

**REQUIRED:** The responsibilities of a data administrator.

**DISCUSSION:** The DA handles administrative issues that arise regarding the database. The DA acts as an advocate by suggesting new applications and standards. One of the DA's responsibilities is to monitor the database industry for new developments. In contrast, the database administrator (DBA) deals with the technical aspects of the database.

**151.** The operational responsibility for the accuracy and completeness of computer-based information should be placed on which of the following groups?

A. Top management.

B. External auditors.

C. Internal auditors.

D. Users.

Answer (D) is correct. *(CIA, adapted)*

**REQUIRED:** The group operationally responsible for the accuracy and completeness of computer-based information.

**DISCUSSION:** The operational responsibility for the accuracy and completeness of computer-based information should be placed on users. Users are in the best position to review output in relation to the input provided and determine whether the results of processing are reasonable.

Answer (A) is incorrect because top management is charged with the overall control of computer-based information systems. Operational control resides in the users. Answer (B) is incorrect because external auditing is an independent appraisal function. Its principal purpose is the expression of an opinion about financial statements. Answer (C) is incorrect because internal auditing is an independent appraisal function. Internal auditors should not have operational responsibility.

**152.** Operating controls include all of the following except

A. Halt and error controls.

B. Batch controls.

C. Library security and use of proper file labels.

D. Duplicate files and backup procedures.

Answer (B) is correct. *(Publisher)*

**REQUIRED:** The control not an operating control.

**DISCUSSION:** A batch total is the sum of information that results from adding a field from each record in a batch or group. It provides for control over the movement or processing of the batch and is considered an application control.

Answer (A) is incorrect because halt and error condition controls include explicit instructions that should appear in run manuals for handling halts and error messages for programs. Answer (C) is incorrect because library security controls include the organization and operation of a library to preclude misplacement or theft of tapes, programs, and other file media. In addition, internal and external labels should be used so that the proper files are processed. Answer (D) is incorrect because operating controls also include provisions for backup and reconstruction of files if data are lost as a result of processing errors or catastrophes.

**153.** Which of the following is most important when there is a lack of adequate fire detection and control equipment in the computer areas?

A. Adequate fire insurance.

B. Regular hardware maintenance.

C. Offsite storage of transaction and master files.

D. Fully tested backup processing facilities.

Answer (C) is correct. *(CISA, adapted)*

**REQUIRED:** The most important control given a lack of fire detection and control equipment.

**DISCUSSION:** One of the primary risks against which a computer operation must be protected is the loss of programs and files. Backup procedures, including offsite storage of backup copies, are necessary to protect against loss.

Answer (A) is incorrect because, although adequate fire insurance is an important element for recovery, offsite storage of transaction and master files is essential to recovery. Answer (B) is incorrect because regular hardware maintenance does not relate to recovery. Answer (D) is incorrect because, although a fully tested backup processing facility is an important element for recovery, without offsite storage, recovery is ordinarily not feasible.

**154.** Because of a power surge, a read-write head damaged the surface of the disk volume containing the savings account master file used by an online savings account update and inquiry program. At the time of the failure, there were 20 active teller terminals connected to the program. The disk damage was the only physical damage resulting from the power fluctuation. Possible recovery steps are

1. Restart the online update and inquiry program.
2. Restore the savings account master file from the good records on the original disk.
3. Restore the savings account master file from the most recent file backup.
4. Display each teller's last transaction and prompt each teller to reenter any subsequent transactions.
5. Apply transactions occurring since the last complete file backup to the master file.
6. Prompt tellers to reenter their last transaction.

The best recovery procedure consists of which sequence of steps?

A. 2, 5, 1, 6

B. 2, 5, 1, 4

C. 3, 5, 1, 4

D. 3, 5, 1, 6

Answer (C) is correct. *(CIA, adapted)*

**REQUIRED:** The sequence of steps in the best recovery procedure.

**DISCUSSION:** The use of restart and recovery procedures eliminates the need to reprocess all data in the event of a processing failure. If checkpoints are established during a processing run (e.g., by periodically copying necessary data and program indicators onto a storage medium), the run may be restarted from the checkpoint. Restart and recovery procedures can also be used in an online system. Accordingly, the recovery procedure should begin with updating the most recent copy of the damaged master file from the transactions log. The online update and inquiry program can then be activated and each teller told to reenter transactions after the last recorded transaction.

Answer (A) is incorrect because the original disk was damaged, thus preventing a full update from that source. Also, each teller should begin with the transaction following the last one logged before the power surge. Answer (B) is incorrect because the original disk was damaged, thus preventing a full update from that source. Answer (D) is incorrect because each teller should begin with the transaction following the last one logged before the power surge.

**155.** Contingency plans for information systems should include appropriate backup agreements. Which of the following arrangements is considered too vendor-dependent when vital operations require almost immediate availability of computer resources?

A. A "hot site" arrangement.

B. A "cold site" arrangement.

C. A "cold and hot site" combination arrangement.

D. Using excess capacity at another data center within the organization.

Answer (B) is correct. *(CIA, adapted)*

**REQUIRED:** The contingency plan that is too vendor-dependent.

**DISCUSSION:** Organizations should maintain contingency plans for operations in the case of a disaster. These plans usually include off-site storage of important backup data and an arrangement for the continuation of operations at another location. A "cold site" has all needed assets in place except the needed computer equipment and is vendor-dependent for timely delivery of equipment.

Answer (A) is incorrect because a "hot site" has all needed assets in place and is not vendor-dependent. Answer (C) is incorrect because a "cold and hot site" combination allows the "hot site" to be used until the "cold site" is prepared and is thus not too vendor-dependent. Answer (D) is incorrect because excess capacity would ensure that needed assets are available and would not be vendor-dependent.

**156.** Which two of the following are part of a review to ensure that machine malfunctions, error recovery, and stop/restart procedures are clearly documented and periodically reviewed as a security precaution?

I. Reviewing for completeness the list of abnormal operations that require documented records

II. Reviewing the adequacy of procedures for processing on backup hardware

III. Interviewing management responsible for reviewing the records of abnormal operations and determining the adequacy of steps taken to assure the credibility and continuity of processing

IV. Interviewing the operations supervisor to determine the extent of rotation of personnel between shifts

A. I and III.

B. I and IV.

C. II and III.

D. II and IV.

Answer (A) is correct. *(CISA, adapted)*

**REQUIRED:** The two procedures that would be part of a review to ensure that machine malfunctions, error recovery, and stop/restart procedures are clearly documented and reviewed.

**DISCUSSION:** The auditor should review the completeness of the list of typical abnormal operations for which documented records are required. But the mere existence of documentation does not assure that the described procedures would be carried out. Hence, the auditor should interview management to determine the adequacy of the procedures employed in case of malfunctions.

Answer (B) is incorrect because rotation of personnel is not a procedure to aid recovery from either a malfunction or an outright catastrophe. Answer (C) is incorrect because auxiliary processing is part of a disaster (e.g., a flood, fire, or other interrupting regular operations) plan rather than a restart procedure (needed because of human errors or machine breakdowns). Answer (D) is incorrect because rotation of personnel is not a procedure to aid recovery from either a malfunction or an outright catastrophe. Moreover, auxiliary processing is part of a disaster plan rather than a restart procedure.

**157.** At a remote computer center, management installed an automated scheduling system to load data files and execute programs at specific times during the day. The best approach for verifying that the scheduling system performs as intended is to

A. Analyze job activity with a queuing model to determine workload characteristics.

B. Simulate the resource usage and compare the results with actual results of operations.

C. Use library management software to track changes to successive versions of applications programs.

D. Audit job accounting data for file accesses and job initiation/termination messages.

Answer (D) is correct. *(CIA, adapted)*

**REQUIRED:** The best approach for verifying that the scheduling system performs as intended.

**DISCUSSION:** Job accounting data analysis permits programmatic examination of job initiation and termination, record counts, and processing times. Auditing job accounting data for file accesses and job initiation/termination messages will reveal whether the correct data files were loaded/dismounted at the correct times and the correct programs were initiated/terminated at the correct times.

Answer (A) is incorrect because analyzing job activity with a queuing model to determine workload characteristics gives information about resource usage. Answer (B) is incorrect because a simulation helps management characterize the workload. Answer (C) is incorrect because using library management software to track changes to successive versions of application programs permits control of production and test versions.

**158.** All of the following are examples of corrective controls except

A. Transaction trails.

B. Passwords.

C. Upstream resubmission.

D. Automatic error correction.

Answer (B) is correct. *(CISA, adapted)*

**REQUIRED:** The item not a corrective control.

**DISCUSSION:** Passwords are controls over unauthorized access to the computer or to data files. They are a preventive, not a corrective, control.

Answer (A) is incorrect because a transaction trail is primarily a corrective rather than a detective control in computer systems given the difficulty of manual review of a large volume of transactions. The transaction trail (an audit trail) is principally used to follow up and correct exceptions. Answer (C) is incorrect because upstream resubmission is the input of error corrections under more stringent controls than those over the original transactions. Error corrections are especially error prone. Answer (D) is incorrect because automatic error correction is a nonsense term.

**159.** A company updates its accounts receivable master file weekly and retains the master files and corresponding update transactions for the most recent 2-week period. The purpose of this practice is to

A. Verify run-to-run control totals for receivables.

B. Match internal labels to avoid writing on the wrong volume.

C. Permit reconstruction of the master file if needed.

D. Validate groups of update transactions for each version.

Answer (C) is correct. *(CIA, adapted)*

**REQUIRED:** The purpose of periodic retention of master files and transaction data.

**DISCUSSION:** The grandfather-father-son approach normally employs magnetic tapes to furnish backup in a batch processing system. The procedure involves creation and retention of three generations of master files so that lost or destroyed data may be regenerated from the remaining master files and transaction data. In this case, a master file (the grandfather) and the first week's transactions are used to generate a second master file (the father). This file and the second week's transactions are the basis for the current master file (the son). Online systems employ rollback and recovery procedures; i.e., the master file is periodically dumped onto a storage medium. Reconstruction is then possible using the backup copy and the transactions log.

Answer (A) is incorrect because comparison of batch totals is a control over the completeness of processing, not a recovery procedure. Answer (B) is incorrect because internal labels may avoid destruction of data but do not aid in recovery. Answer (D) is incorrect because validation may avoid destruction of data but does not aid in recovery.

**160.** A company's management has expressed concern over the varied system architectures that the organization uses. Potential security and control concerns include all of the following except

A. Users may have different user ID codes and passwords to remember for the several systems that they use.

B. There are difficulties in developing uniform security standards for the various platforms.

C. Backup file storage administration is often decentralized.

D. Having data distributed across many computers throughout the organization increases the risk that a single disaster would destroy large portions of the organization's data.

Answer (D) is correct. *(CIA, adapted)*

**REQUIRED:** The item not a security and control risk resulting from use of varied system architectures.

**DISCUSSION:** The use of distributed systems with different architectures throughout the organization decreases the risk that a single disaster will destroy large portions of data. Centralization of data in a single mainframe environment would pose greater risk of data loss.

Answer (A) is incorrect because password proliferation is a considerable security concern. Users may be tempted to record their passwords or make them overly simple. Answer (B) is incorrect because consistent security across varied platforms is challenging as a result of the different features of various systems and the decentralization of security administration. Answer (C) is incorrect because decentralization of backup file storage administration may lead to lack of consistency and difficulty in monitoring compliance.

**161.** Good planning will help an organization restore computer operations after a processing outage. Good recovery planning should ensure that

A. Backup/restart procedures have been built into job streams and programs.

B. Change control procedures cannot be bypassed by operating personnel.

C. Planned changes in equipment capacities are compatible with projected workloads.

D. Service level agreements with owners of applications are documented.

Answer (A) is correct. *(CIA, adapted)*

**REQUIRED:** The condition ensured by good recovery planning.

**DISCUSSION:** The disaster plan should embrace data center recovery, critical application recovery, and network recovery. It should be updated and current with regard to recent test results and new applications, equipment, and network configurations. The plan should also ensure that backup facilities are still able to process critical applications and that end-user responsibility is established. Another essential component of a disaster recovery plan is that backup/restart procedures have been anticipated and provided for in the application systems.

Answer (B) is incorrect because whether change control procedures can be bypassed is not usually a consideration in disaster recovery planning. Answer (C) is incorrect because planned rather than actual changes in equipment capacities are not relevant in disaster recovery planning. Answer (D) is incorrect because ensuring that service level agreements with owners of critical applications are adequate is not a function of disaster recovery planning.

**162.** Each day, after all processing is finished, a bank performs a backup of its online deposit files and retains it for 7 days. Copies of each day's transaction files are not retained. This approach is

A. Valid, in that having a week's worth of backups permits recovery even if one backup is unreadable.

B. Risky, in that restoring from the most recent backup file would omit subsequent transactions.

C. Valid, in that it minimizes the complexity of backup/recovery procedures if the online file has to be restored.

D. Risky, in that no checkpoint/restart information is kept with the backup files.

Answer (B) is correct. *(CIA, adapted)*

**REQUIRED:** The true statement about retention of backup files but not each day's transaction files.

**DISCUSSION:** At appropriate intervals, the disk files should be copied on magnetic tape so that restart procedures can begin at those points if data are lost or destroyed. However, not retaining each day's transaction files is risky because information processed since the last backup file was created will be lost.

Answer (A) is incorrect because the practice of not retaining daily transaction data is unsound in that the bank loses a day's transactions for each backup that is unreadable. Answer (C) is incorrect because the practice of not retaining daily transaction data certainly minimizes complexity but at the expense of losing transaction data if the online file must be restored from the backup. Answer (D) is incorrect because checkpoint/restart information is not needed. The backups are created after all processing is finished for the day.

**163.** An inexperienced computer operator loaded an incorrect version of the accounts receivable master file in a tape drive during processing. Because of this error, the entire processing run had to be repeated at a significant cost. Which of the following software controls is most effective in preventing this type of operator error from affecting the processing of files?

A. Data transmission check.

B. File header label check.

C. Memory isolation protection.

D. Unauthorized access protection.

Answer (B) is correct. *(CIA, adapted)*

**REQUIRED:** The software control for preventing use of an incorrect version of a master file.

**DISCUSSION:** The use of external, header, and trailer labels should be enforced to ensure the proper access and protection of files. A header label is a machine-readable record at the beginning of a file that identifies the file. Software makes this check. A trailer label is a machine-readable label at the end of a file containing record counts and control totals. An external label is a human-readable identifying label affixed to the outside of a file holder, such as a magnetic tape file.

Answer (A) is incorrect because a data transmission check verifies only the accuracy of the communication. Answer (C) is incorrect because memory isolation protection (boundary protection) protects programs or data from interference (unauthorized reading and/or writing) caused by activity related to other programs or data stored on the same medium. Answer (D) is incorrect because access controls (passwords, etc.) prevent unauthorized access from remote locations, not authorized use by an operator.

**164.** The use of external labels with floppy disks is least likely to prevent which of the following?

A. Formatting a disk that was used for a backup of hard disk files.

B. Using a version of a file that has been subsequently revised.

C. Erasing an important file on a disk.

D. Spilling liquid on a disk and losing the files.

Answer (D) is correct. *(Publisher)*

**REQUIRED:** The error or problem not likely prevented by external labels on floppy disks.

**DISCUSSION:** Proper handling of magnetic media requires safeguards from excessive heat, accidental magnetic contact, and physical abuse such as liquid spills. External labels do not prevent such occurrences.

Answer (A) is incorrect because all external file media, e.g., magnetic tapes and disks, should be properly labeled so that the user can determine the proper use of the files. Formatting the wrong disk and thereby erasing its contents could therefore be prevented by use of external labels. Answer (B) is incorrect because use of the wrong version of a file can be prevented by use of external labels. Answer (C) is incorrect because erasing an important file on a disk can be prevented by use of external labels.

## 5.10 System and Application Software Acquisition and Maintenance

**165.** In the computer program development process, a problem will most likely result when

A. Programmers take a longer amount of time to perform programming tasks than expected.

B. Written specifications from the user are used to develop detail program code.

C. Programmers use specialized application tools to simulate the system being programmed.

D. User specifications are inadvertently misunderstood.

Answer (D) is correct. *(CMA, adapted)*

**REQUIRED:** The most likely cause of a problem during computer program development.

**DISCUSSION:** Program development entails coding programs in accordance with the specifications established in the physical design phase of the systems development life cycle. The physical system design includes creating specifications for, among other things, work flow and programs (but not coding) that are consistent with the general or conceptual design. The general design incorporates user descriptions of the applications. Accordingly, a misunderstanding about user specifications can have fundamental and far-reaching consequences.

Answer (A) is incorrect because, although a programming delay is undesirable, it does not necessarily impair the achievement of objectives. Answer (B) is incorrect because user specifications are the foundation of the program development process. Answer (C) is incorrect because using specialized application tools should avert problems.

**166.** Each of the following will help ensure development of an effective application system except

A. Active participation by user departments in the development stage.

B. Management involvement in the development stage.

C. Prioritization of applications to be developed.

D. Post-implementation reviews.

Answer (C) is correct. *(CISA, adapted)*

**REQUIRED:** The step that would not help ensure the development of an effective system.

**DISCUSSION:** Effectiveness relates to the ability to meet the objectives set forth by the organization. The nature of the applications themselves, not necessarily the order in which they are implemented, would influence their effectiveness.

Answer (A) is incorrect because active participation by user departments in the development stage helps assure that the objectives of the system are identified. Answer (B) is incorrect because management involvement helps assure that proper resources are directed to development. Answer (D) is incorrect because post-implementation reviews are important for ensuring that a newly developed application includes the appropriate controls and effectively meets management's needs. If the system is not controlled or effective, the post-implementation review should identify the weaknesses for further correction.

**167.** Program documentation is a control designed primarily to ensure that

A. Programmers have access to the tape library or information on disk files.

B. Programs do not make mathematical errors.

C. Programs are kept up-to-date and perform as intended.

D. No one has made use of the computer hardware for personal reasons.

Answer (C) is correct. *(CMA, adapted)*

**REQUIRED:** The purpose of program documentation.

**DISCUSSION:** Complete, up-to-date documentation of all programs and associated operating procedures is necessary for efficient operation of a computer installation. Maintenance of programs is important to provide for continuity and consistency of data processing services to users. Program documentation (the program run manual) consists of problem statements, systems flowcharts, operating instructions, record layouts, program flowcharts, program listings, test data, and approval and change sheets.

Answer (A) is incorrect because programmers should not have access to operational materials. Answer (B) is incorrect because editing routines check for arithmetic errors prior to processing, and debugging should uncover errors in programs. Answer (D) is incorrect because documentation cannot ensure computer security.

**168.** The process of monitoring, evaluating, and modifying a system as needed is referred to as systems

A. Analysis.

B. Feasibility study.

C. Maintenance.

D. Implementation.

Answer (C) is correct. *(CMA, adapted)*

**REQUIRED:** The term for the process of monitoring, evaluating, and modifying a system.

**DISCUSSION:** Systems maintenance must be undertaken by systems analysts and applications programmers continually throughout the life of a system. Maintenance is the redesign of the system and programs to meet new needs or to correct design flaws. These changes should be part of a regular program of preventive maintenance.

Answer (A) is incorrect because systems analysis is the process of determining user problems and needs, surveying the organization's present system, and analyzing the facts. Answer (B) is incorrect because a feasibility study determines whether a proposed system is technically, operationally, and economically feasible. Answer (D) is incorrect because implementation involves training and educating users, testing, conversion, and follow-up.

**169.** Effective internal control for application development should provide for which of the following?

I. A project steering committee to initiate and oversee the system

II. A technical systems programmer to evaluate systems software

III. Feasibility studies to evaluate existing systems

IV. The establishment of standards for systems design and programming

A. I and III.

B. I, II, and IV.

C. I, III, and IV.

D. II, III, and IV.

Answer (C) is correct. *(CISA, adapted)*

**REQUIRED:** The components of effective internal control for application development.

**DISCUSSION:** Effective systems development requires participation by top management. This can be achieved through a steering committee composed of higher-level representatives of system users. The committee approves or recommends projects and reviews their progress. Studies of the economic, operational, and technical feasibility of new applications necessarily entail evaluations of existing systems. Another necessary control is the establishment of standards for system design and programming. Standards represent user and system requirements determined during systems analysis.

Answer (A) is incorrect because standards must be established. Answer (B) is incorrect because a technical systems programmer has a role in the development and modification of the operating system but not necessarily in applications development. The technical support in this area would be provided by systems analysts rather than programmers. Answer (D) is incorrect because a technical systems programmer has a role in the development and modification of the operating system but not necessarily in applications development.

**170.** Use of unlicensed software in an organization

I. Increases the risk of introducing viruses into the organization

II. Is not a serious exposure if only low-cost software is involved

III. Can be detected by software checking routines that run from a network server

A. I only.

B. I and II only.

C. I, II, and III.

D. I and III only.

Answer (D) is correct. *(CIA, adapted)*

**REQUIRED:** The true statement(s) about use of unlicensed software.

**DISCUSSION:** Antivirus measures should include strict adherence to software acquisition policies. Unlicensed software is less likely to have come from reputable vendors and to have been carefully tested. Special software is available to test software in use to determine whether it has been authorized.

Answer (A) is incorrect because use of unlicensed software increases the risk of viral infection, and its use can be detected by software checking routines. Moreover, the cost of the software is not relevant. Any software may contain a virus. Answer (B) is incorrect because use of unlicensed software increases the risk of viral infection, and its use can be detected by software checking routines. Moreover, the cost of the software is not relevant. Any software may contain a virus. Answer (C) is incorrect because use of unlicensed software increases the risk of viral infection, and its use can be detected by software checking routines. Moreover, the cost of the software is not relevant. Any software may contain a virus.

**171.** An insurance company is planning to implement new standard software in all of its local offices. The new software has a fast response time, is very user friendly, and was developed with extensive user involvement. The new software captures, consolidates, edits, validates, and finally transfers standardized transaction data to the headquarters mainframe. Local managers, who were satisfied with existing locally written personal computer applications, opposed the new approach because they anticipated

A. Increased workloads.

B. Lengthy retraining.

C. More accountability.

D. Less computer equipment.

Answer (C) is correct. *(CIA, adapted)*

**REQUIRED:** The reason for opposing introduction of new software.

**DISCUSSION:** Cooperative processing implies a tighter coupling than previously existed between the personal computers and the mainframe. The result may threaten the managers' perceived autonomy by increasing the control exercised by headquarters and therefore the accountability of local managers.

Answer (A) is incorrect because, given that only existing systems would be converted, the transaction volume would likely remain relatively constant. Answer (B) is incorrect because retraining would probably be needed, but PC-based transaction capture applications with graphical interfaces are often easy to learn with minimal training. Answer (D) is incorrect because, compared with mainframe-only processing, cooperative processing typically requires more computer equipment at distributed locations.

**172.** A benefit of using computer-aided software engineering (CASE) technology is that it can ensure that

A. No obsolete data fields occur in files.

B. Users become committed to new systems.

C. All programs are optimized for efficiency.

D. Data integrity rules are applied consistently.

Answer (D) is correct. *(CIA, adapted)*

**REQUIRED:** The benefit of CASE.

**DISCUSSION:** CASE is an automated technology (at least in part) for developing and maintaining software and managing projects. A benefit of using CASE technology is that it can ensure that data integrity rules, including those for validation and access, are applied consistently across all files.

Answer (A) is incorrect because obsolete data fields must be recognized by developers or users. Once recognized, obsolete data fields can be treated consistently in CASE procedures. Answer (B) is incorrect because using CASE will not ensure user commitment to new systems if they are poorly designed or otherwise do not meet users' needs. Answer (C) is incorrect because, although it has the potential to accelerate system development, CASE cannot ensure that all programs are optimized for efficiency. In fact, some CASE-developed modules may need to be optimized by hand to achieve acceptable performance.

**173.** CASE (computer-aided software engineering) is the use of the computer to aid in the development of computer-based information systems. Which of the following could not be automatically generated with CASE tools and techniques?

A. Information requirements determination.

B. Program logic design.

C. Computer program code.

D. Program documentation.

Answer (A) is correct. *(CIA, adapted)*

**REQUIRED:** The item not automatically generated by CASE.

**DISCUSSION:** CASE applies the computer to software design and development. It maintains on the computer a library of standard program modules and all of the system documentation, e.g., data flow diagrams, data dictionaries, and pseudocode (structured English); permits development of executable input and output screens; and generates program code in at least skeletal form. Thus, CASE facilitates the creation, organization, and maintenance of documentation and permits some automation of the coding process. However, information requirements must be determined prior to using CASE.

Answer (B) is incorrect because CASE may generate program logic design. Answer (C) is incorrect because CASE may generate computer program code. Answer (D) is incorrect because CASE may generate program documentation.

---

Questions 174 through 176 are based on the following information. Baker Manufacturing Co. has the following nine master files:

- Accounts payable
- Accounts receivable
- Bill of materials (material requirements for producing a product)
- Finished goods inventory
- Open production orders
- Open purchase orders
- Raw materials inventory
- Work-in-process inventory
- Production operations list (labor operations and machine requirements)

---

**174.** Master files maintained as part of the sales order processing system are

A. Accounts receivable, bill of materials.

B. Accounts payable, accounts receivable, finished goods inventory.

C. Accounts receivable, sales summary, production operations list.

D. Accounts receivable, finished goods inventory.

Answer (D) is correct. *(Publisher)*

**REQUIRED:** The master files maintained as part of the sales order processing system.

**DISCUSSION:** A sales order processing cycle involves taking customers' orders and updating amounts owed by customers (accounts receivable) and the amount of inventory left after shipment (finished goods inventory).

Answer (A) is incorrect because the bill of materials file is used in production planning. Answer (B) is incorrect because the accounts payable files are used to process purchases. Answer (C) is incorrect because the production operations list file is used in production planning.

**175.** Master files maintained as part of the processing of purchase transactions are

A. Accounts payable, bill of materials, finished goods inventory, and open purchase orders.

B. Accounts payable, open purchase orders, raw materials inventory, and work-in-process inventory.

C. Accounts payable, bill of materials, and open purchase orders.

D. Accounts payable, open purchase orders, and raw materials inventory.

Answer (D) is correct. *(Publisher)*

**REQUIRED:** The master files maintained as part of the processing of purchases.

**DISCUSSION:** The processing of purchase transactions involves preparing purchase orders and updating raw materials inventory on order (raw materials inventory) and purchase orders not yet received (open purchase orders). Upon receipt of the purchased item, updating is required for the amount on hand (raw material inventory), open purchase orders since the item was received (open purchase orders), and the amount owed to the vendor (accounts payable).

Answer (A) is incorrect because the bill of materials file is used in production planning, and finished goods inventory is part of the sales order processing cycle. Answer (B) is incorrect because the work-in-process inventory file is used in production planning. Answer (C) is incorrect because the bill of materials file is used in production planning.

**176.** Master files used to plan and report on the resources required for the coming period include

A. Bill of materials, open production orders, work-in-process inventory, and production operations list.

B. Finished goods inventory, open production orders, open purchase orders, and work-in-process inventory.

C. Finished goods inventory, open purchase orders, raw materials inventory, and work-in-process.

D. Bill of materials, open production orders, accounts payable, and production operations list.

Answer (A) is correct. *(Publisher)*

**REQUIRED:** The master files used to plan and report on resources required for the coming period.

**DISCUSSION:** Production planning involves determining what needs to be produced (open production orders and finished goods inventory), what materials are required (bill of materials), what labor and machine operations are needed (production operations list), what resources are tied up in production (work-in-process), and what raw materials are available (raw materials inventory). Based on this evaluation, new production orders (open production orders) are issued.

Answer (B) is incorrect because the open purchase orders file is used in the processing of purchases. Answer (C) is incorrect because the open purchase orders file is used in the processing of purchases. Answer (D) is incorrect because the accounts payable file is used in the processing of purchases.

**177.** The accountant who prepared a spreadsheet model for workload forecasting left the company, and the accountant's successor was unable to understand how to use the spreadsheet. The best control for preventing such situations from occurring is to ensure that

A. Use of end-user computing resources is monitored.

B. End-user computing efforts are consistent with strategic plans.

C. Documentation standards exist and are followed.

D. Adequate backups are made for spreadsheet models.

Answer (C) is correct. *(CIA, adapted)*

**REQUIRED:** The best control to permit new employees to understand internally developed programs.

**DISCUSSION:** The accountant's successor could not use the forecasting model because of inadequate documentation. By requiring that documentation standards exist and are followed, the company will enable new employees to understand internally developed programs when the developer leaves the organization.

Answer (A) is incorrect because monitoring concerns controlling the use of resources. Answer (B) is incorrect because consistency with strategic plans concern evaluation of the system. Answer (D) is incorrect because maintaining adequate backups for spreadsheet models is necessary, but lack of adequate backup is not the reason the accountant's successor could not use the forecasting model.

**178.** Which of the following controls will best protect production programs from unauthorized modification?

A. Requiring two operators to be present during equipment operation.

B. Implementing management review of daily run logs.

C. Limiting program access solely to operators.

D. Restricting programmer access to the computer room.

Answer (C) is correct. *(CISA, adapted)*

**REQUIRED:** The best control to provide protection against unauthorized changes in production programs.

**DISCUSSION:** Operators require access to production programs in order to run the programs. However, systems programmers and others should be denied access to the resident production programs to limit the risk of unauthorized changes.

Answer (A) is incorrect because unauthorized modifications can be made by programmers at terminals regardless of whether two operators are present during operation. Answer (B) is incorrect because an effective control would be a management review of console logs, not run logs. Answer (D) is incorrect because unauthorized modifications can be made by programmers at terminals regardless of whether programmers are denied access to the computer room.

**179.** An entrepreneur purchases a copy of spreadsheet software for use on a single office personal computer. Which of the following actions would most likely not violate the software license agreement?

A. Making a backup copy.

B. Installing the spreadsheet software on a multi-user network.

C. Using the spreadsheet software at home for personal business.

D. Reselling the spreadsheet software.

Answer (A) is correct. *(CIA, adapted)*

**REQUIRED:** The action that would not violate a software license agreement.

**DISCUSSION:** A software agreement usually allows one backup copy to be made. Installing the software on multiple computers and making additional copies are likely copyright violations.

Answer (B) is incorrect because installing the spreadsheet software on a multi-user network makes it available to multiple users. Answer (C) is incorrect because not all software vendors allow use on different machines. Answer (D) is incorrect because agreements typically prohibit resale.

**180.** Managers at a consumer products company purchased personal computer software only from recognized vendors and prohibited employees from installing nonauthorized software on their personal computers. To minimize the likelihood of computer viruses infecting any of its systems, the company should also

A. Restore infected systems with authorized versions.

B. Recompile infected programs from source code backups.

C. Institute program change control procedures.

D. Test all new software on a stand-alone personal computer.

Answer (D) is correct. *(CIA, adapted)*
**REQUIRED:** The best protection against viruses.
**DISCUSSION:** Software from recognized sources should be tested in quarantine (for example, in a test/development machine or a stand-alone personal computer) because even vendor-supplied software may be infected with viruses. The software should be run with a vaccine program and tested for the existence of logic bombs, and other viral agents.
Answer (A) is incorrect because, if viruses infect a system, the company should restore the system with authorized software, but this procedure does not minimize the likelihood of initial infection. Answer (B) is incorrect because, if viruses infect programs that the company wrote, it should recompile the programs from source code backups, but this procedure does not minimize the likelihood of initial infection. Answer (C) is incorrect because instituting program change control procedures is good practice but does not minimize the likelihood of the system's being infected initially.

**181.** Which of the following is an indication that a computer virus is present?

A. Frequent power surges that harm computer equipment.

B. Unexplainable losses of or changes to data.

C. Inadequate backup, recovery, and contingency plans.

D. Numerous copyright violations due to unauthorized use of purchased software.

Answer (B) is correct. *(CIA, adapted)*
**REQUIRED:** The indicator of a computer virus.
**DISCUSSION:** The effects of computer viruses range from harmless messages to complete destruction of all data within the system. A symptom of a virus is the unexplained loss of or change to data.
Answer (A) is incorrect because power surges are caused by hardware or power supply problems. Answer (C) is incorrect because inadequate backup, recovery, and contingency plans are operating policy weaknesses. Answer (D) is incorrect because copyright violations represent policy or compliance problems.

**182.** Which of the following operating procedures increases an organization's exposure to computer viruses?

A. Encryption of data files.

B. Frequent backup of files.

C. Downloading public-domain software from websites.

D. Installing original copies of purchased software on hard disk drives.

Answer (C) is correct. *(CIA, adapted)*
**REQUIRED:** The procedure that increases exposure to viruses.
**DISCUSSION:** Viruses are spread through shared data. Downloading public-domain software carries a risk that contaminated data may enter the computer.
Answer (A) is incorrect because viruses are spread through the distribution of contaminated programs. Answer (B) is incorrect because backing up files does not increase the chances of a virus entering the computer system. Answer (D) is incorrect because original copies of purchased software on hard disk drives should be free of viruses.

**183.** An organization installed antivirus software on all its personal computers. The software was designed to prevent initial infections, stop replication attempts, detect infections after their occurrence, mark affected system components, and remove viruses from infected components. The major risk in relying on antivirus software is that antivirus software may

A. Not detect certain viruses.

B. Make software installation overly complex.

C. Interfere with system operations.

D. Consume too many system resources.

Answer (A) is correct. *(CIA, adapted)*
**REQUIRED:** The major risk in relying on antivirus software.
**DISCUSSION:** Antivirus software designed to identify and remove known viruses is sometimes known as a vaccine. A vaccine works only for known viruses and may not be completely effective for variants of those viruses.
Answer (B) is incorrect because having antivirus software is unlikely to make software installation overly complex.
Answer (C) is incorrect because antivirus software need not interfere with system operations. Its execution can be scheduled in advance so as not to interfere with running programs.
Answer (D) is incorrect because antivirus software can be set to execute at times when it would not consume too many system resources, e.g., at startup.

**184.** The graphic portrayal of the flow of data and the information processing of a system, including computer hardware, is best displayed in a

A. Data-flow diagram.

B. System flowchart.

C. Gantt chart.

D. Program flowchart.

Answer (B) is correct. *(CMA, adapted)*

**REQUIRED:** The best method of displaying the flow of data and the information processing of a system.

**DISCUSSION:** A system flowchart is a graphic analysis of a data processing application, usually prepared by a systems analyst. The system flowchart is general and stresses flows of data, not computer program logic. A program flowchart is a graphic representation of the detailed steps and logic of an individual computer program.

Answer (A) is incorrect because a data-flow diagram shows only the flow of data, not the total system. Answer (C) is incorrect because a Gantt chart is a bar chart used to monitor the progress of large projects. Answer (D) is incorrect because a program flowchart shows only the details of a single program, not the entire computer system.

**185.** Decision tables differ from program flowcharts in that decision tables emphasize

A. Ease of manageability for complex programs.

B. Logical relationships among conditions and actions.

C. Cost-benefit factors justifying the program.

D. The sequence in which operations are performed.

Answer (B) is correct. *(CPA, adapted)*

**REQUIRED:** The distinction between decision tables and flowcharts.

**DISCUSSION:** A decision table identifies the contingencies considered in the description of a problem and the appropriate actions to be taken relative to those contingencies. Decision tables are logic diagrams presented in matrix form. Unlike flowcharts, they do not present the sequence of the actions described.

Answer (A) is incorrect because neither flowcharts nor decision tables emphasize ease of manageability. Answer (C) is incorrect because neither flowcharts nor decision tables emphasize cost-benefit factors. Answer (D) is incorrect because, unlike flowcharts, decision tables do not present the sequence of the actions described.

**186.** Which one of the following best reflects the basic elements of a data flow diagram?

A. Data sources, data flows, computer configurations, flowchart, and data storage.

B. Data source, data destination, data flows, transformation processes, and data storage.

C. Data flows, data storage, and program flowchart.

D. Data flows, program flowchart, and data destination.

Answer (B) is correct. *(CMA, adapted)*

**REQUIRED:** The best description of the basic elements of a data flow diagram.

**DISCUSSION:** Structured analysis is a graphical method of defining the inputs, processes, and outputs of a system and dividing it into subsystems. It is a top down approach that specifies the interfaces between modules and the transformations occurring within each. Data flow diagrams are used in structured analysis. The basic elements of a data flow diagram include data source, data destination, data flows, transformation processes, and data storage.

Answer (A) is incorrect because computer configuration is not an element of a data flow diagram. Answer (C) is incorrect because a program flowchart is not an element of a data flow diagram. Answer (D) is incorrect because a program flowchart is not an element of a data flow diagram.

**187.** A document flowchart represents

A. The sequence of logical operations performed during the execution of a computer program.

B. The possible combinations of alternative logic conditions and corresponding courses of action for each condition in a computer program.

C. The flow of data through a series of operations in an automated data processing system.

D. The flow of forms that relate to a particular transaction through an organization.

Answer (D) is correct. *(CMA, adapted)*

**REQUIRED:** The definition of a document flowchart.

**DISCUSSION:** A document flowchart graphically presents the flow of forms (documents) through a system that relate to a given transaction, e.g., the processing of a customer's order. It shows the source, flow, processing, and final disposition of the various copies of all related documents.

Answer (A) is incorrect because a program flowchart represents the sequence of logical operations performed during the execution of a computer program. Answer (B) is incorrect because a decision table consists of the possible combinations of alternative logic conditions and corresponding courses of action for each condition in a computer program. Answer (C) is incorrect because a system flowchart is used to represent the flow of data through an automated data processing system.

**188.** An internal auditor is reviewing the following computer logic diagram:

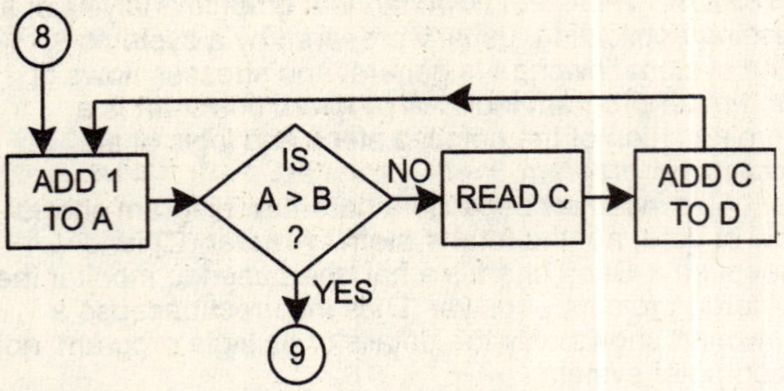


This diagram represents which of the following?

A. Program loop step.

B. Data validity check.

C. Balance test.

D. Limit test.

Answer (A) is correct. *(CIA, adapted)*

**REQUIRED:** The operation described by the computer logic diagram.

**DISCUSSION:** Variable A will be increased by 1 and C will be added to D repetitively until A exceeds B. The diagram illustrates a program loop, a technique for performing repeated iterations of an instruction a specified number of times.

Answer (B) is incorrect because a data validity check compares the bits of each transmitted character with the valid combinations of bits. Answer (C) is incorrect because a balance test compares a gross amount with its components. Answer (D) is incorrect because a limit test ascertains whether a number falls within a predetermined range of reasonable values.

**189.** The correct labeling, in order, for the following flowchart symbols is

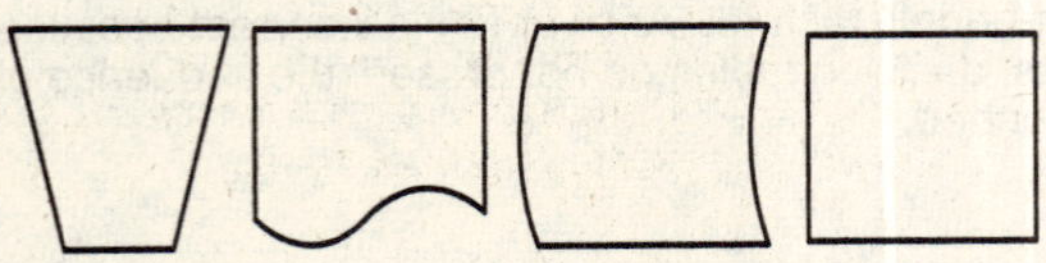

A. Document, display, online storage, and entry operation.

B. Manual operation, processing, offline storage, and input-output activity.

C. Display, document, online storage, and entry operation.

D. Manual operation, document, online storage, and entry operation.

Answer (D) is correct. *(CMA, adapted)*

**REQUIRED:** The correct sequence of labels of four flowchart symbols.

**DISCUSSION:** The first symbol indicates a manual operation, which is an offline process. The second symbol represents a document, and the third symbol indicates online storage (e.g., a disk drive). The final symbol represents an operation. An operation is defined as a process resulting in a change in the information or the flow direction. In other words, it can be an entry operation.

Answer (A) is incorrect because the first symbol, a trapezoid, is for a manual operation. Answer (B) is incorrect because the third symbol is for online storage. Answer (C) is incorrect because the first symbol does not represent display.

**190.** The symbol employed to determine if an employee's wages are above or below the maximum limit for FICA taxes is

A. 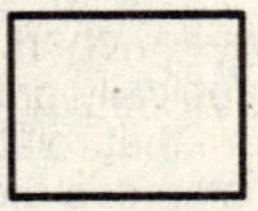

B. 

C. 

D. 

Answer (B) is correct. *(CMA, adapted)*

**REQUIRED:** The symbol to determine if an employee's wages are within a limit.

**DISCUSSION:** The question implies a decision, for which a diamond is the flowcharting symbol.

Answer (A) is incorrect because a rectangle is the general symbol for a process or operation. Answer (C) is incorrect because a trapezoid symbolizes a manual operation. Answer (D) is incorrect because a square represents an auxiliary operation performed by a machine other than a computer.

**191.** The symbol employed to represent the printing of the employees' paychecks by the computer is

A. 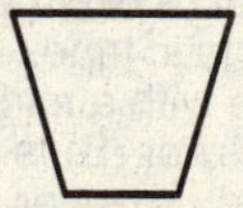

B. 

C. 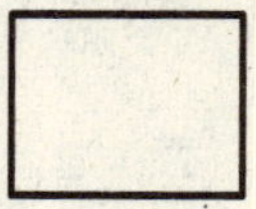

D. 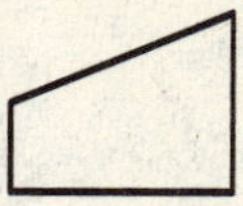

Answer (C) is correct. *(CMA, adapted)*

**REQUIRED:** The flowchart symbol for the printing of paychecks by a computer.

**DISCUSSION:** The printing of paychecks by the computer is an operation depicted by the general processing symbol, which is a rectangle.

Answer (A) is incorrect because a trapezoid depicts a manual operation. Answer (B) is incorrect because a square is an auxiliary operation performed by a machine other than a computer. Answer (D) is incorrect because this symbol indicates manual input, e.g., entry of a proper code through a computer console.

**192.** The symbol employed to represent the employees' checks printed by the computer is

A. 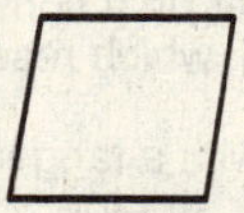

B. 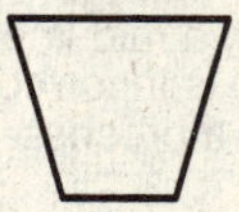

C. 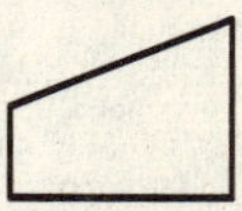

D. 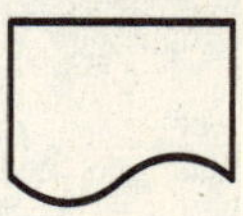

Answer (D) is correct. *(CMA, adapted)*

**REQUIRED:** The symbol used to represent employee checks printed by a computer.

**DISCUSSION:** Employee checks printed by the computer are depicted by the document symbol, which resembles the top of a grand piano.

Answer (A) is incorrect because a parallelogram is the general symbol for input or output. Answer (B) is incorrect because a trapezoid indicates a manual operation. Answer (C) is incorrect because this symbol indicates manual input.

**193.** The symbol used to represent the physical act of collecting employees' time cards for processing is

A. 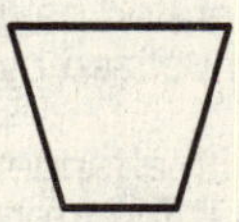

B. 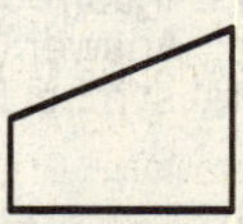

C. 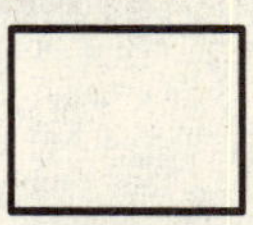

D. 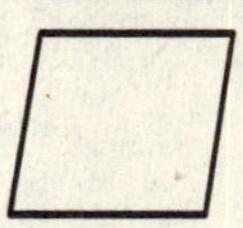

Answer (A) is correct. *(CMA, adapted)*

**REQUIRED:** The symbol used to represent the physical act of collecting employees' time cards for processing.

**DISCUSSION:** Collecting employees' time cards is a manual operation represented by a trapezoid with equal nonparallel sides.

Answer (B) is incorrect because this symbol represents manual input. Answer (C) is incorrect because a rectangle is the general symbol for processing. Answer (D) is incorrect because a parallelogram is the general symbol for input or output.

**194.** The symbol used to represent the employees' payroll records stored on magnetic tape is

A. 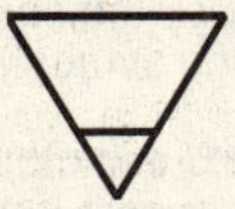

B. 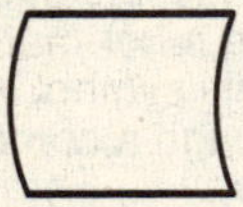

C. 

D. 

Answer (D) is correct. *(CMA, adapted)*

**REQUIRED:** The symbol representing employees' payroll records stored on magnetic tape.

**DISCUSSION:** The magnetic tape symbol (a circle with a tangent at its base) indicates storage on magnetic tape.

Answer (A) is incorrect because a triangle with a mid-line parallel to its base depicts offline storage. Answer (B) is incorrect because this symbol represents online storage. Answer (C) is incorrect because this symbol represents punched paper tape.

**195.** The symbol used to represent the weekly payroll register generated by the computer is

A. 

B. 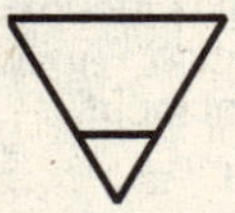

C. 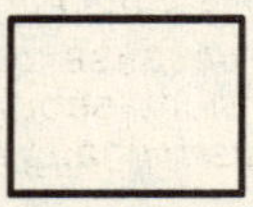

D. 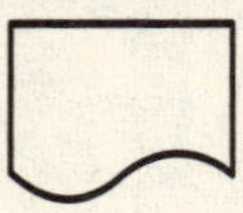

Answer (D) is correct. *(CMA, adapted)*

**REQUIRED:** The symbol used to represent a weekly payroll register printed by a computer.

**DISCUSSION:** The weekly payroll register on a computer printout is represented by a document symbol, which resembles the top of a grand piano.

Answer (A) is incorrect because a circle with a tangent at its base represents magnetic tape input-output or storage. Answer (B) is incorrect because a triangle with a mid-line parallel to its base depicts offline storage. Answer (C) is incorrect because a rectangle is the general symbol for a process.

**196.** The symbol used to represent the file of hard-copy, computer-generated payroll reports kept for future reference is

A. 

B. 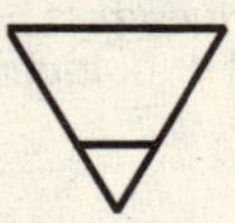

C. 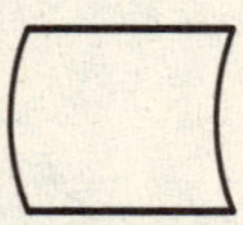

D. 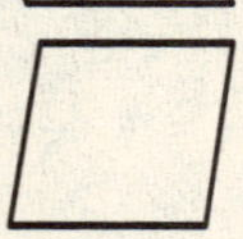

Answer (B) is correct. *(CMA, adapted)*

**REQUIRED:** The symbol used to represent the kept file of hard-copy, computer-generated payroll reports.

**DISCUSSION:** Hard-copy, computer-generated payroll reports are kept in offline storage, which is symbolized by a triangle with a mid-line parallel to its base.

Answer (A) is incorrect because a circle with a tangent at its base represents a magnetic tape. Answer (C) is incorrect because this symbol represents online storage. Answer (D) is incorrect because a parallelogram is the general symbol for input or output.

**197.** Which of the following symbolic representations indicates that a sales invoice has been filed?

A. 

B. 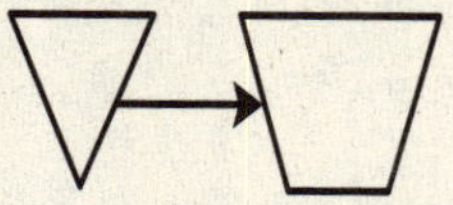

C. 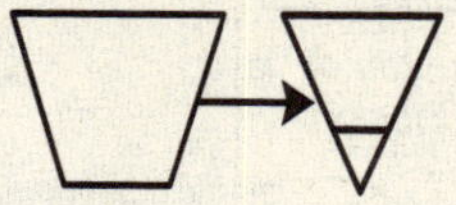

D. 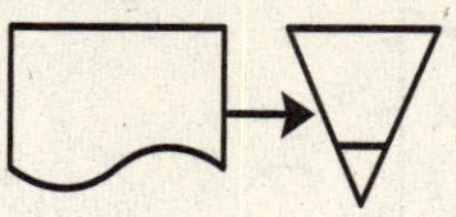

Answer (D) is correct. *(CPA, adapted)*

**REQUIRED:** The symbols indicating filing of a document.

**DISCUSSION:** The arrow from the document symbol to the triangle with the mid-line parallel to its base indicates that a document has been stored in an offline file.

Answer (A) is incorrect because the arrow from the document symbol to the trapezoid indicates manual (offline) processing of the document. Answer (B) is incorrect because the arrow from offline storage to the manual operation symbol signifies manual (offline) processing of an offline file. Answer (C) is incorrect because the arrow from the trapezoid to the triangle with a mid-line indicates that manual (offline) processing is followed by offline file storage of the result.

**198.** An auditor should review the procedures within a program change control group to determine whether it does which of the following?

A. Makes programs available to programmers for change only on receiving written authorization.

B. Reviews user documentation for any necessary changes resulting from a program change.

C. Codes the necessary program changes.

D. Estimates the time and cost involved in a program change.

Answer (A) is correct. *(CISA, adapted)*

**REQUIRED:** The function of a program change control group.

**DISCUSSION:** A program change control group is responsible for determining that proper procedures are carried out relative to controlling programming changes. This includes assuring that written authorizations are received for changes. To avoid fraud and to ensure compatibility with other programs, programmers should not be able to make unauthorized changes.

Answer (B) is incorrect because the systems analyst has the operational responsibility to assure that documentation is changed to reflect the modification. Answer (C) is incorrect because programmers, not the control group, should code the necessary changes. Answer (D) is incorrect because the systems analyst, in conjunction with management, should estimate the time and cost involved in a program change.

Questions 199 through 203 are based on the following information. This flowchart depicts the processing of daily cash receipts for Rockmart Manufacturing.

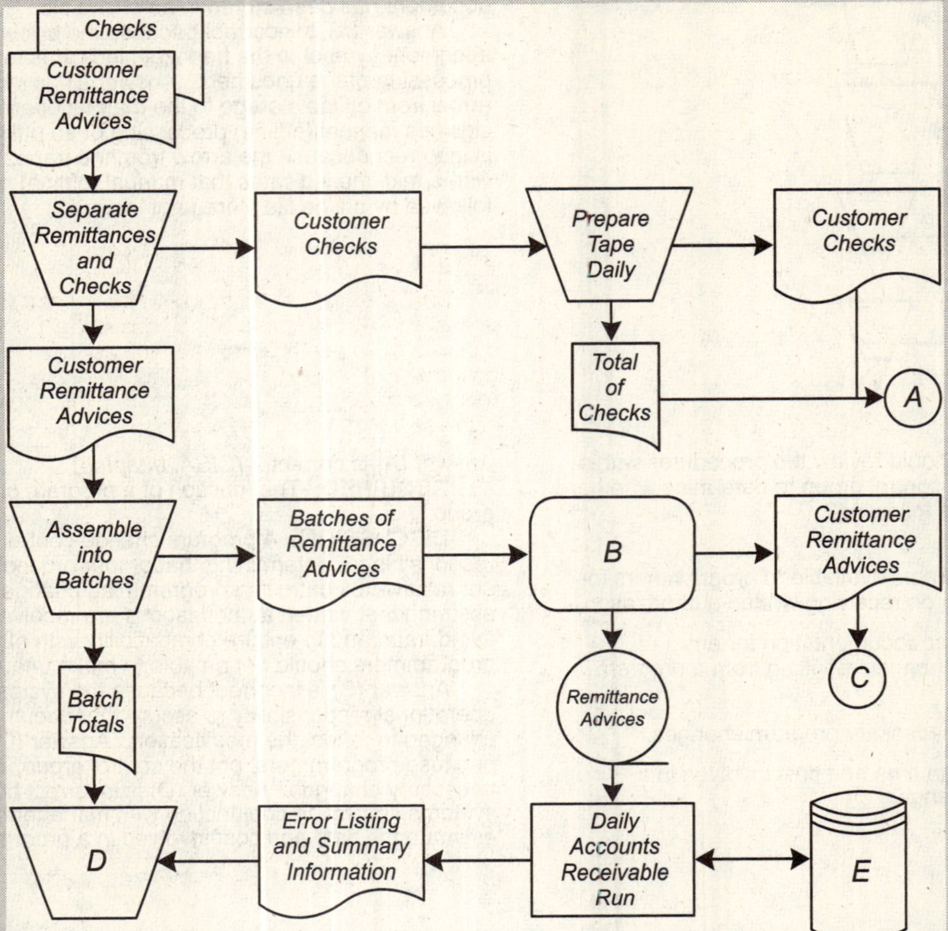


**199.** The customer checks accompanied by the control tape (refer to symbol A) should be

A. Forwarded daily to the billing department for deposit.

B. Taken by the mail clerk to the bank for deposit daily.

C. Forwarded to the treasurer for deposit daily.

D. Accumulated for a week and then forwarded to the treasurer for deposit weekly.

Answer (C) is correct. *(CMA, adapted)*

**REQUIRED:** The proper procedure for handling customer checks and the related control tape.

**DISCUSSION:** Symbol A is a connector between a point on this flowchart and another part of the flowchart not shown. The checks and the adding machine control tape should flow through symbol A to the treasurer's office. The treasurer is the custodian of funds and is responsible for deposit of daily receipts.

Answer (A) is incorrect because record keepers perform functions that should be separate from custody of assets. Answer (B) is incorrect because the mail clerk should prepare a list of checks received before they are forwarded to the treasurer for deposit. Answer (D) is incorrect because daily receipts should be deposited intact daily and then reconciled with the bank deposit records.

**200.** The appropriate description that should be placed in symbol B is

A. Keying and verifying.

B. Error correction.

C. Collation of remittance advices.

D. Batch processing.

Answer (A) is correct. *(CMA, adapted)*

**REQUIRED:** The appropriate description for symbol B.

**DISCUSSION:** The figure below symbol B signifies magnetic tape, so the operation represented by symbol B must be keying the information onto the tape. Verifying the keyed data should also occur at this step.

Answer (B) is incorrect because error correction other than for keying errors should occur subsequently. Answer (C) is incorrect because collation has already occurred. Answer (D) is incorrect because batch processing describes the entire system.

**201.** The next action to take with the customer remittance advices (refer to symbol C) would be to

A. Discard them immediately.

B. File them daily by batch number.

C. Forward them to the internal audit department for internal review.

D. Forward them to the treasurer to compare with the monthly bank statement.

Answer (B) is correct. *(CMA, adapted)*

**REQUIRED:** The action taken at symbol C.

**DISCUSSION:** All activity with respect to the paper documents most likely ceases at symbol C. Thus, the batched documents must be filed.

Answer (A) is incorrect because the documents should be kept for reference and audit. Answer (C) is incorrect because internal auditors cannot feasibly review all documents regarding transactions even in an audit. Answer (D) is incorrect because comparison by the treasurer would be inappropriate. (S)he has custody of cash.

**202.** The appropriate description that should be placed in symbol D is

A. Attach batch total to report and file.

B. Reconcile cash balances.

C. Compare batch total and correct as necessary.

D. Proof report.

Answer (C) is correct. *(CMA, adapted)*

**REQUIRED:** The appropriate description for symbol D.

**DISCUSSION:** This flowcharting symbol indicates a manual operation or offline process. Because the input to this operation consists of an adding machine tape containing batch totals and a document containing summary information about the accounts receivable update and an error listing, the operation apparently involves comparing these items.

Answer (A) is incorrect because no filing symbol is given. Answer (B) is incorrect because the flowchart concerns daily receipts, not the reconciliation of cash balances. Answer (D) is incorrect because symbol D indicates a comparison, not output in the form of a report.

**203.** The appropriate description that should be placed in symbol E is

A. Accounts receivable master file.

B. Bad debts master file.

C. Remittance advice master file.

D. Cash projection file.

Answer (A) is correct. *(CMA, adapted)*

**REQUIRED:** The appropriate description of symbol E.

**DISCUSSION:** The flowcharting figure at symbol E indicates magnetic disk storage. Given that it is an input and output for the daily computer processing of accounts receivable, it must be the accounts receivable master file.

Answer (B) is incorrect because bad debts are not a part of processing daily receipts. Answer (C) is incorrect because the remittance advice master file was not used for the daily accounts receivable run. Answer (D) is incorrect because the cash projection file was not used for the daily accounts receivable run.

## 5.11 Access and Security Controls

**204.** The primary objective of security software is to

A. Control access to information system resources.

B. Restrict access to prevent installation of unauthorized utility software.

C. Detect the presence of viruses.

D. Monitor the separation of duties within applications.

Answer (A) is correct. *(CIA, adapted)*

**REQUIRED:** The primary objective of security software.

**DISCUSSION:** The objective of security software is to control access to information system resources, such as program libraries, data files, and proprietary software. Security software identifies and authenticates users, controls access to information, and records and investigates security related events and data.

Answer (B) is incorrect because security software will control the use of utilities, not their installation. Answer (C) is incorrect because antivirus software detects the presence of viruses. Answer (D) is incorrect because security software may be a tool to establish, but does not monitor, separation of duties.

**205.** Assigning passwords to computer users is a control to prevent unauthorized access. Because a password does not conclusively identify a specific individual, it must be safeguarded from theft. A method used to protect passwords is to

A. Require that they be displayed on computer screens but not printed on hard copy output.

B. Set maximum character lengths.

C. Require a minimum retention period.

D. Eliminate all records of old passwords.

Answer (C) is correct. *(Publisher)*

**REQUIRED:** The password security technique.

**DISCUSSION:** Security measures include changing passwords frequently, that is, establishing a relatively short maximum retention period; not displaying or printing passwords; setting minimum lengths; prohibiting the use of certain words, character strings, or names; mandating a minimum retention period, so users cannot promptly change passwords back to their old and convenient values; and retaining old passwords to prevent their use.

Answer (A) is incorrect because a password should not be displayed. Answer (B) is incorrect because a minimum length requirement is more likely. Answer (D) is incorrect because retention of old passwords prevents their reuse.

**206.** An equipment manufacturer maintains a secure website for access to its order-entry system for the convenience of its pre-approved customers worldwide so they may order parts. Because of the cost and sensitive nature of certain electronic parts, the manufacturer maintains secure access to its order-entry system. The best technique for monitoring the security of access is

A. Integrated test facility for the order-entry system.

B. Tracing of transactions through the order-entry system.

C. Transaction selection of order-entry transactions.

D. Logging of unsuccessful access attempts.

Answer (D) is correct. *(CIA, adapted)*

**REQUIRED:** The best technique for monitoring the security of access.

**DISCUSSION:** Pre-approved customers should be assigned passwords. An access log should be used to record all attempts to use the system. The date and time, codes used, and data involved are recorded. The system should monitor unsuccessful attempts because repeated attempts suggest that someone is trying random or patterned character sequences in order to identify a password.

Answer (A) is incorrect because an integrated test facility (ITF) is a technique by which an auditor selects transactions and processing functions and applies the transactions to a fictitious entity during a normal processing cycle along with regular transactions. Answer (B) is incorrect because tracing follows the path of a transaction during processing. Answer (C) is incorrect because transaction selection uses an independent computer program to monitor and select transactions for internal audit review. Like tracing, it fails to determine whether a transaction is legitimate. It would be an appropriate technique to apply to transactions suspected to be illegitimate.

**207.** Data access security related to applications may be enforced through all the following except

A. User identification and authentication functions incorporated in the application.

B. Utility software functions.

C. User identification and authentication functions in access control software.

D. Security functions provided by a database management system.

Answer (B) is correct. *(CIA, adapted)*

**REQUIRED:** The functions through which data access security cannot be enforced.

**DISCUSSION:** Utility programs perform routine functions (e.g., sorting and copying), are available to all users, and are promptly available for many different applications. Utility programs can actually be a serious weakness in data access security because some can bypass normal access controls.

Answer (A) is incorrect because, although the trend is for this type of control function to be performed by other software, most such controls still reside in application software. Answer (C) is incorrect because access control software has as one of its primary objectives improving data access security for all data on the system. Answer (D) is incorrect because most database management systems provide for improved data access security while they are running.

**208.** The duties properly assigned to an information security officer could include all of the following except

A. Developing an information security policy for the organization.

B. Maintaining and updating the list of user passwords.

C. Commenting on security controls in new applications.

D. Monitoring and investigating unsuccessful access attempts.

Answer (B) is correct. *(CIA, adapted)*

**REQUIRED:** The duty not properly assigned to an information security office.

**DISCUSSION:** The information security officer should not know user passwords. Passwords are normally stored on a computer in encrypted format, and users change them directly.

Answer (A) is incorrect because developing an information security policy for the organization is an appropriate duty of the information security officer. Answer (C) is incorrect because commenting on security controls in new applications is an appropriate duty of the information security officer. Answer (D) is incorrect because monitoring and investigating unsuccessful access attempts is an appropriate duty of the information security officer.

**209.** All administrative and professional staff in a corporate legal department prepare documents on terminals connected to a host LAN file server. The best control over unauthorized access to sensitive documents in the system is

A. Required entry of passwords for access to the system.

B. Physical security for all disks containing document files.

C. Periodic server backup and storage in a secure area.

D. Required entry of passwords for access to individual documents.

Answer (D) is correct. *(CIA, adapted)*

**REQUIRED:** The best control over unauthorized access to sensitive documents in a local area network.

**DISCUSSION:** Different passwords may be required to access the system, to read certain files, and to perform certain other functions. Required entry of passwords for access to individual documents is the best single control over unauthorized access to sensitive documents.

Answer (A) is incorrect because password security for access to the system permits all departmental employees access to all documents in the system. Answer (B) is incorrect because this system uses no floppy disks. Answer (C) is incorrect because periodic server backup and storage in a secure area is a good security/backup procedure, but it would not prevent access to sensitive documents online.

**210.** An auditor has just completed a physical security audit of a data center. Because the center engages in top-secret defense contract work, the auditor has chosen to recommend biometric authentication for workers entering the building. The recommendation might include devices that verify all of the following except

A. Fingerprints.

B. Retina patterns.

C. Speech patterns.

D. Password patterns.

Answer (D) is correct. *(CIA, adapted)*

**REQUIRED:** The method that does not provide biometric authentication.

**DISCUSSION:** Biometric technologies are automated methods of establishing an individual's identity using physiological or behavioral traits. These characteristics include fingerprints, retina patterns, hand geometry, signature dynamics, speech, and keystroke dynamics.

Answer (A) is incorrect because verifying fingerprints is a biometric measure. Answer (B) is incorrect because verifying retina patterns is a biometric measure. Answer (C) is incorrect because verifying speech patterns is a biometric measure.

**211.** Authentication is the process by which the

A. System verifies that the user is entitled to enter the transaction requested.

B. System verifies the identity of the user.

C. User identifies him/herself to the system.

D. User indicates to the system that the transaction was processed correctly.

Answer (B) is correct. *(CISA, adapted)*

**REQUIRED:** The definition of authentication.

**DISCUSSION:** Identification is the process of uniquely distinguishing one user from all others. Authentication is the process of determining that individuals are who they say they are. For example, a password may identify but not authenticate its user if it is known by more than one individual.

Answer (A) is incorrect because authentication involves verifying the identity of the user. This process does not necessarily confirm the functions the user is authorized to perform. Answer (C) is incorrect because user identification to the system does not imply that the system has verified the identity of the user. Answer (D) is incorrect because this procedure is an application control for accuracy of the transaction.

**212.** As organizations become more computer integrated, management is becoming increasingly concerned with the quality of access controls to the computer system. Which of the following provides the most accountability?

| | Option I | Option II | Option III | Option IV |
|---|---|---|---|---|
| Restrict access by: | Individuals | Groups | Individuals | Departments |
| Identify computer data at: | Field level | Workstation | Workstation | Individual record level |
| Restrict access: | Need to know | Right to know | Normal processing by employee type | Items identified as processed by department |
| Identify users by: | Password | Password | Key access to workstation, or password on workstation | Departmental password |
| Limit ability to: | Delete, add, or modify data | Add or delete files | Add, delete, or modify data stored at workstation | Add, delete, or modify data normally processed by department |

A. Option I.

B. Option II.

C. Option III.

D. Option IV.

Answer (A) is correct. *(CIA, adapted)*

**REQUIRED:** The access control option providing the most accountability.

**DISCUSSION:** Access should be limited to those whose activities necessitate access to the computer system. Moreover, the degree of access allowed should be consistent with an individual's responsibilities. Restricting access to particular individuals rather than groups or departments clearly establishes specific accountability. Not everyone in a group will need access or the same degree of access. Thus, passwords assigned to individuals should be required for identification of users by the system. Furthermore, data should be restricted at the field level, not the workstation level. It may be possible to limit access to a workstation, but most workstations are connected to larger mainframe or network databases. Thus, the security at the workstation level only is insufficient.

**213.** Which of the following is a control that will prevent accessing the accounts receivable files from a hardwired terminal located in a manufacturing department?

A. An echo check.

B. A device authorization table.

C. Providing only dial-up terminals.

D. Using data encryption.

Answer (B) is correct. *(J. Brooks)*

**REQUIRED:** The control that will prevent access via a hardwired terminal.

**DISCUSSION:** A device authorization table restricts file access to those physical devices that logically need access. Because it is illogical for anyone to access the accounts receivable file from a manufacturing terminal, the device authorization table will deny access even when a valid password is used.

Answer (A) is incorrect because an echo check relates to the accuracy of signals sent from or to a terminal. Answer (C) is incorrect because dial-up terminals provide less security than hardwired terminals. Any terminal may dial into the communications port using public telephones. Answer (D) is incorrect because, although data encryption (transmitting data in code form) might make the data unusable, it would not prevent access.

**214.** The use of message encryption software

A. Guarantees the secrecy of data.

B. Requires manual distribution of keys.

C. Increases system overhead.

D. Reduces the need for periodic password changes.

Answer (C) is correct. *(CIA, adapted)*

**REQUIRED:** The effect of message encryption software.

**DISCUSSION:** Encryption software uses a fixed algorithm to manipulate plain text and an encryption key (a set of random data bits used as a starting point for application of the algorithm) to introduce variation. The machine instructions necessary to encrypt and decrypt data constitute system overhead. As a result, processing speed may be slowed.

Answer (A) is incorrect because no encryption approach absolutely guarantees the secrecy of data. Answer (B) is incorrect because keys may also be distributed electronically via secure key transporters. Answer (D) is incorrect because periodic password changes are needed. Passwords are the typical means of validating users' access to unencrypted data.

**215.** The encryption technique that requires two keys, a public key that is available to anyone for encrypting messages and a private key that is known only to the recipient for decrypting messages, is

A. Rivest, Shamir, and Adelman (RSA).

B. Advanced encryption standard (AES).

C. Modulator-demodulator.

D. A cypher lock.

Answer (A) is correct. *(CIA, adapted)*

**REQUIRED:** The encryption technique requiring two keys.

**DISCUSSION:** RSA is an encryption standard licensed to hardware and software vendors. Public-key encryption requires management of fewer keys for a given client-server environment than does private-key encryption. However, compared with AES, RSA entails more complex computations and therefore has a higher processing overhead. RSA requires two keys: The public key for encrypting messages is widely known, but the private key for decrypting messages is kept secret by the recipient.

Answer (B) is incorrect because AES is a shared private-key method developed for the U.S. government. It encrypts data using a choice of three key sizes: 128, 192, and 256 bits. AES requires only a single key for each pair of parties that want to send each other encrypted messages. Answer (C) is incorrect because a modem is used for telecommunications. Answer (D) is incorrect because a cypher lock is a physical device.

**216.** The telecommunication control of dial-up/disconnect/dial-back can be circumvented by using

A. Dedicated line technology.

B. Automatic call forwarding.

C. Encryption algorithms.

D. High baud rate lines.

Answer (B) is correct. *(CISA, adapted)*

**REQUIRED:** The technique that would circumvent callback control procedures.

**DISCUSSION:** Automatic call forwarding can circumvent the control if the authorized user has this telephone service and the computer callback is forwarded to an unauthorized user.

Answer (A) is incorrect because dedicated line technology strengthens controls, not circumvents them. Answer (C) is incorrect because encryption algorithms strengthen controls, not circumvent them. Answer (D) is incorrect because the speed of the lines does not directly contribute to the strength or weakness of telecommunication controls.

## 5.12 Application Controls

**217.** Application control objectives do not normally include assurance that

A. Authorized transactions are completely processed once and only once.

B. Transaction data are complete and accurate.

C. Review and approval procedures for new systems are set by policy and adhered to.

D. Processing results are received by the intended user.

Answer (C) is correct. *(CISA, adapted)*
**REQUIRED:** The assurance not provided by an application control.
**DISCUSSION:** Application controls provide reasonable assurance that the recording, processing, and reporting of data are properly performed. Review and approval procedures for new systems are among the general controls known as system software acquisition and maintenance controls.
Answer (A) is incorrect because an objective of application controls is that authorized transactions are completely processed once and only once. Answer (B) is incorrect because an objective of application controls is that transaction data is complete and accurate. Answer (D) is incorrect because an objective of application controls is that processing results are received by the intended user.

**218.** Data processing activities may be classified in terms of three stages or processes – input, processing, and output. An activity that is not normally associated with the input stage is

A. Batching.

B. Recording.

C. Verifying.

D. Reporting.

Answer (D) is correct. *(CMA, adapted)*
**REQUIRED:** The process not associated with input.
**DISCUSSION:** Reporting is normally associated with output, not input. Output is the processing result, e.g., account listings or displays, reports, magnetic files, invoices, or checks.
Answer (A) is incorrect because batching is closely associated with input. Answer (B) is incorrect because recording is closely associated with input. Answer (C) is incorrect because verifying is closely associated with input.

**219.** Many customers, managers, employees, and suppliers have blamed computers for making errors. In reality, computers make very few mechanical errors. The most likely source of errors in a fully operational computer-based system is

A. Operator error.

B. Systems analysis and programming.

C. Processing.

D. Input.

Answer (D) is correct. *(CMA, adapted)*
**REQUIRED:** The most common cause of error.
**DISCUSSION:** GIGO is the acronym for garbage-in, garbage-out. Inappropriate input results in inappropriate output.
Answer (A) is incorrect because, although there is a chance of operator error, operators are typically guided by run manuals. Answer (B) is incorrect because, if programs are properly designed and tested before implementation, most bugs (errors) can be removed. Answer (C) is incorrect because, once programs are operationally tested, the processing usually does not result in errors.

**220.** A mail-order retailer of low-cost novelty items is receiving an increasing number of complaints from customers about the wrong merchandise being shipped. The order code for items has the format *wwxxyyzz*. The major category is *ww*, *xx* is the minor category, *yy* identifies the item, and *zz* identifies the catalog. In many cases, the wrong merchandise was sent because adjacent characters in the order code had been transposed. The best control for decreasing the number of orders with the wrong merchandise is to

A. Require customers to specify the name for each item they order.

B. Add check-digits to the order codes and verify them for each order.

C. Separate the parts of the order code with hyphens to make the characters easier to read.

D. Use a master file reference for all order codes to verify the existence of items.

Answer (B) is correct. *(CIA, adapted)*
**REQUIRED:** The control that prevents erroneous input.
**DISCUSSION:** Self-checking digits may be used to detect incorrect codes. The digit is generated by applying an algorithm to the code. During the input process, the check digit is recomputed by applying the same algorithm to the code actually entered.
Answer (A) is incorrect because having customers specify the name for each item they order would let the company correct erroneous order codes once they had been detected, but would not, in general, detect erroneous codes. Answer (C) is incorrect because separating the parts of the order code with hyphens would make the characters easier to read, but would not cure the problem of transposed characters. Answer (D) is incorrect because using a master file reference for all order codes would verify the existence of items, but would not detect erroneous order codes in which transposed characters in an order code match other items.

**221.** The purpose of input controls is to ensure the

A. Authorization of access to data files.

B. Authorization of access to program files.

C. Completeness, accuracy, and validity of updating.

D. Completeness, accuracy, and validity of input.

Answer (D) is correct. *(CIA, adapted)*

**REQUIRED:** The purpose of input controls.

**DISCUSSION:** Input controls provide reasonable assurance that data received for computer processing have been properly authorized and are in a form suitable for processing, i.e., complete, accurate, and valid. Input controls also relate to rejection, correction, and resubmission of data that were initially incorrect.

Answer (A) is incorrect because access controls authorize access to data files. Answer (B) is incorrect because access controls authorize access to program files. Answer (C) is incorrect because processing controls ensure the completeness, accuracy, and validity of updating.

**222.** Data conversion is the translation of data into a form the computer can accept. What method of data conversion is most difficult to audit?

A. Keying data to disk for online processing.

B. Keying data to disk for batch processing.

C. Keying data to source documents for magnetic-ink character recognition.

D. Reading source data using optical-character recognition.

Answer (A) is correct. *(CIA, adapted)*

**REQUIRED:** The type of data conversion that is most difficult to audit.

**DISCUSSION:** Data conversion in an online environment is difficult to audit because the audit trail is often invisible. Hard-copy source documents are often lacking.

Answer (B) is incorrect because keying to disk creates records readily available for testing. Answer (C) is incorrect because magnetic-ink character recognition provides batch control capability and hard-copy source documents. Answer (D) is incorrect because optical-character recognition retains hard-copy source documents and reduces the risks associated with the manual data conversion process.

**223.** The most valuable information for detecting unauthorized input from a terminal is provided by the

A. Console log printout.

B. Transaction journal.

C. Automated suspense file listing.

D. User error report.

Answer (B) is correct. *(CISA, adapted)*

**REQUIRED:** The control to detect unauthorized input from a terminal.

**DISCUSSION:** A transaction log records all transactions received by the computer processing facility. The log can be subsequently compared with authorized transactions (e.g., authorized source documents) to assure validity of the transactions.

Answer (A) is incorrect because a console log does not record the individual transactions transmitted from a terminal. Answer (C) is incorrect because the suspense file only lists transaction activity if an edit error occurs. Answer (D) is incorrect because a user error report lists only input that results in an edit error.

**224.** Which of the following computerized control procedures is most effective in ensuring that data uploaded from personal computers to a mainframe are complete and that no additional data are added?

A. Self-checking digits to ensure that only authorized part numbers are added to the database.

B. Batch control totals, including control totals and hash totals.

C. Passwords that effectively limit access to only those authorized to upload the data to the mainframe computer.

D. Field-level edit controls that test each field for alphanumerical integrity.

Answer (B) is correct. *(CIA, adapted)*

**REQUIRED:** The control over completeness of data uploaded from personal computers.

**DISCUSSION:** Batch control totals for the data transferred can be reconciled with the batch control totals in the existing file. This comparison provides information on the completion of the data transfer. Batch totals may include record counts, totals of certain critical amounts, or hash totals. A hash total is a control total without a defined meaning, such as the total of employee numbers or invoice numbers, that is used to verify the completeness of data. Thus, the hash total for the employee listing by the personnel department could be compared with the total generated during the payroll run.

Answer (A) is incorrect because self-checking digits detect inaccurate identification numbers. They are an effective control to ensure that the appropriate part has been identified but not that data transfer is complete. Answer (C) is incorrect because passwords help ensure that only authorized personnel make the transfer, not that data transfer is complete. Answer (D) is incorrect because field checks are effective input controls, but they do not ensure completeness of data transfer.

**225.** A wholesaling firm has a computerized billing system. Because of a clerical error while entering information from the sales order, one of its customers was billed for only three of the four items ordered and received. Which of the following controls could have prevented or resulted in prompt detection of this situation?

A. Matching line control counts produced by the computer with predetermined line control counts.

B. Periodic comparison of total accounts receivable per accounts receivable master file with total accounts receivable per accounts receivable control account.

C. A completeness check that does not allow a sales invoice to be processed if key fields are blank.

D. Prenumbered shipping documents together with a procedure for follow-up any time there is not a one-to-one relationship between shipping documents and sales invoices.

Answer (A) is correct. *(CIA, adapted)*

**REQUIRED:** The control to prevent or promptly detect the clerical error.

**DISCUSSION:** Detective controls, such as a line control count, identify undesirable events as they occur. A line control count counts individual line items on documents. These counts are compared to predetermined line control counts for each document to detect missing lines.

Answer (B) is incorrect because a comparison of the accounts receivable master file and the control account will show no discrepancy. Both would be based on the three-item invoice. Answer (C) is incorrect because a completeness check could not be used to catch the billing error. Many invoices would properly include three or fewer items. Answer (D) is incorrect because all four items were included in the same shipment, so a sales invoice corresponding to the shipping document would exist.

**226.** If a control total were to be computed on each of the following data items, which would best be identified as a hash total for a payroll computer application?

A. Hours worked.

B. Total debits and total credits.

C. Net pay.

D. Department numbers.

Answer (D) is correct. *(CPA, adapted)*

**REQUIRED:** The example of a hash total.

**DISCUSSION:** The three types of control totals are record counts, financial (amount) totals, and hash totals. Record counts establish the number of source documents and reconcile it to the number of output records. Financial (amount) totals compute dollar or amount totals from source documents (e.g., the total dollar amount of invoices processed) and reconcile them with the output records. Hash totals add numbers on input documents that are not normally added (e.g., department numbers for payroll processing) and reconcile them with output records.

Answer (A) is incorrect because hours worked would be identified as a financial total. Answer (B) is incorrect because total debits and total credits would be identified as a financial total. Answer (C) is incorrect because net pay would be identified as a financial total.

**227.** If, in reviewing an applications system, it is noted that batch controls are not used, which of the following statements by the user of the system is acceptable as a compensating control?

A. "The supervisor must approve all inputs."

B. "We do a 100% key verification of all data input."

C. "We do a 100% physical review of the input document to the output document."

D. "The volume of transactions prohibits batching."

Answer (C) is correct. *(CISA, adapted)*

**REQUIRED:** The control that compensates for the lack of batch controls.

**DISCUSSION:** If the application provides for matching each input document with an output document, the need for batch totals is minimized. The physical review provides evidence that all records were processed.

Answer (A) is incorrect because approval of input does not assure that all input records are processed. Answer (B) is incorrect because key verification does not assure that the initial keypunching was done for all records. Answer (D) is incorrect because the greater the volume, the more appropriate batch totals become.

**228.** A company's labor distribution report requires extensive corrections each month because of labor hours charged to inactive jobs. Which of the following data processing input controls appears to be missing?

A. Completeness test.

B. Validity test.

C. Limit test.

D. Control total.

Answer (B) is correct. *(CIA, adapted)*

**REQUIRED:** The data processing input control not met when labor hours are charged to inactive jobs.

**DISCUSSION:** Validity tests are used to ensure that transactions contain valid transaction codes, valid characters, and valid field size. If the jobs are checked first for validity, hours are not mistakenly assigned to them.

Answer (A) is incorrect because completeness tests are used to ensure that the input has the prescribed amount of data in all data fields. Answer (C) is incorrect because limit tests are used to determine whether the data exceed certain predetermined limits. Answer (D) is incorrect because control totals are used to reconcile computer input to the source document totals.

**229.** An online bank teller system permitted withdrawals from inactive accounts. The best control for denying such withdrawals is a

A. Proof calculation.

B. Check-digit verification.

C. Master file lookup.

D. Duplicate record check.

Answer (C) is correct. *(CIA, adapted)*

**REQUIRED:** The best control for denying withdrawals from inactive accounts.

**DISCUSSION:** The master file will contain information about the status of bank accounts (i.e., active or inactive). By looking up the account numbers in the master file, the teller can verify that the account is active.

Answer (A) is incorrect because a proof calculation is the use of a predefined algorithm to be performed on the information in a telecommunications transmission to verify that no transmission errors occurred. Answer (B) is incorrect because a check-digit verification is used to control the accuracy of input of reference numbers but does not deny access to an inactive but valid account. Answer (D) is incorrect because a duplicate record check ensures that duplicate records are not processed.

**230.** Omen Company is a manufacturer of men's shirts. It distributes weekly sales reports to each sales manager. The quantity 2R5 appeared in the quantity sold column for one of the items on the weekly sales report for one of the sales managers. The most likely explanation for what has occurred is that

A. The output quantity has been stated in hexadecimal numbers.

B. The computer has malfunctioned during execution.

C. The printer has malfunctioned and the "R" should have been a decimal point.

D. The program did not contain a data-checking routine for input data.

Answer (D) is correct. *(CMA, adapted)*

**REQUIRED:** The probable reason for reporting a quantity item using an alphabetic character.

**DISCUSSION:** The probable explanation for reporting a quantity using a character other than a digit is that the data were incorrectly encoded and the computer program did not perform a field check, which would have detected the error. A field check tests whether a field consists of the proper characters, such as alphabetic, numeric, special, or combinations.

Answer (A) is incorrect because R is not a hexadecimal character. Hexadecimal characters are 0-9 and A-F representing 0 to 15 in decimal. Answer (B) is incorrect because the probability of a computer malfunction's resulting in the printing of an R is slight. Answer (C) is incorrect because 2.5 would not be appropriate for a quantity of shirts sold.

**231.** An employee in the receiving department keyed in a shipment from a remote terminal and inadvertently omitted the purchase order number. The best systems control to detect this error is

A. Completeness test.

B. Sequence check.

C. Reasonableness test.

D. Compatibility test.

Answer (A) is correct. *(CMA, adapted)*

**REQUIRED:** The control to detect the omission of a purchase order number keyed in from a remote terminal.

**DISCUSSION:** A completeness test checks that all data elements are entered before processing. An interactive system can be programmed to notify the user to enter the number before accepting the receiving report.

Answer (B) is incorrect because a sequence check tests for the ordering, not omission, of records. Answer (C) is incorrect because a limit or reasonableness test checks the values of data items against established limits. Answer (D) is incorrect because a compatibility test (field check) determines whether characters are appropriate to a field.

**232.** Which one of the following input validation routines is not likely to be appropriate in a real-time operation?

A. Sign check.

B. Reasonableness check.

C. Sequence check.

D. Redundant data check.

Answer (C) is correct. *(CMA, adapted)*

**REQUIRED:** The input validation routine not appropriate in a real-time operation.

**DISCUSSION:** The program controls listed prescreen or edit data prior to processing, but the sequence check is most likely to be used only in batch processing. A sequence check tests to determine that records are in proper order. For example, a payroll input file can be sorted into Social Security number order. A sequence check can then be performed to verify record order. This control would not apply in a real-time operation because records are not processed sequentially.

Answer (A) is incorrect because sign checks test data for the appropriate arithmetic sign. For instance, hours worked in a payroll should always be a positive number. Answer (B) is incorrect because reasonableness tests verify that amounts fall within predetermined limits. Answer (D) is incorrect because a redundancy check requires sending additional data items to serve as a check on the other transmitted data; for example, part of a customer name can be matched against the name associated with the transmitted customer number.

**233.** As part of an audit, the auditor was studying a computer flowchart containing the logic diagram shown below. Which of the following controls is represented by this diagram?

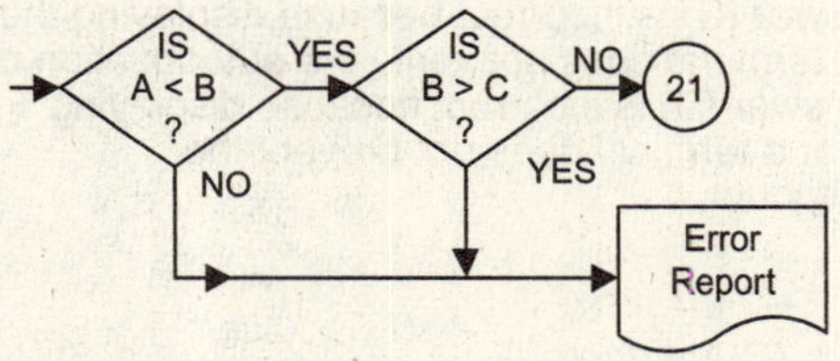


A. Field check.

B. Limit check.

C. Control total.

D. Password check.

Answer (B) is correct. *(CIA, adapted)*

**REQUIRED:** The control represented by the flowchart.

**DISCUSSION:** A limit check (often termed a reasonableness or range test) determines whether an amount is within a predetermined limit for given information. The first decision block asks if A, the lower limit, is less than B, the value of interest. The second decision block asks if B is greater than the upper limit. The purpose of this test is to determine if B is within an acceptable or reasonable range. If it is not, an error report is generated.

Answer (A) is incorrect because a field check (valid character check) examines a field to test whether it contains an improper kind of character. Answer (C) is incorrect because a control total is used to control the completeness and accuracy of processing, not to evaluate the reasonableness of results. Answer (D) is incorrect because passwords restrict unauthorized access to the computer.

**234.** The online data entry control called preformatting is

A. A program initiated prior to regular input to discover errors in data before entry so that the errors can be corrected.

B. A check to determine if all data items for a transaction have been entered by the terminal operator.

C. A series of requests for required input data that requires an acceptable response to each request before a subsequent request is made.

D. The display of a document with blanks for data items to be entered by the terminal operator.

Answer (D) is correct. *(CMA, adapted)*

**REQUIRED:** The definition of preformatting.

**DISCUSSION:** To avoid data entry errors in online systems, a preformatted screen approach may be used. It is a screen prompting approach that involves the display on a monitor of a set of boxes for entry of specified data items. The format may even be in the form of a copy of a transaction document. This technique is best suited to conversion of data from a source document.

Answer (A) is incorrect because an edit routine is a program initiated prior to regular input to discover errors in data before entry so that the errors can be corrected. Answer (B) is incorrect because a completeness check tests whether all data items for a transaction have been entered by the terminal operator. Answer (C) is incorrect because the dialogue approach is another screen prompting method for data entry. It is most appropriate when information is received orally, e.g., by phone.

**235.** When erroneous data are detected by computer program controls, such data may be excluded from processing and printed on an error report. This error report should be reviewed and followed up by the

A. Computer operator.

B. Systems analyst.

C. Data control group.

D. Computer programmer.

Answer (C) is correct. *(CPA, adapted)*

**REQUIRED:** The individual or group responsible.

**DISCUSSION:** Some entities use a data control group that acts as liaison between the users and the processing center. This group records input data in a control log, follows the progress of processing, distributes output, and establishes control totals. It is also responsible for following up error reports and assuring that erroneous records are reprocessed. The data control group must be organizationally independent of computer operations within the data processing function to allow for proper control.

Answer (A) is incorrect because computer operators are not independent of the computer processing operation. Answer (B) is incorrect because systems analysts are not independent of the computer processing operation. Answer (D) is incorrect because computer programmers are not independent of the computer processing operation.

**236.** In the accounting system of Acme Company, the amounts of cash disbursements entered at a computer terminal are transmitted to the computer, which immediately transmits the amounts back to the terminal for display on the terminal screen. This display enables the operator to

A. Establish the validity of the account number.

B. Verify the amount was entered accurately.

C. Verify the authorization of the disbursement.

D. Prevent the overpayment of the account.

Answer (B) is correct. *(CPA, adapted)*

**REQUIRED:** The effect of displaying the amounts entered at a terminal.

**DISCUSSION:** The display of the amounts entered is an input control that permits visual verification of the accuracy of the input by the operator. This procedure is closed-loop verification.

Answer (A) is incorrect because displaying the amounts entered at a terminal does not establish the validity of the account number. Answer (C) is incorrect because displaying the amounts entered at a terminal does not verify the authorization of the disbursement. Answer (D) is incorrect because displaying the amounts entered at a terminal does not prevent the overpayment of the account.

**237.** The key verification process associated with keying computer records for input to a computer system is

A. Effectively used to detect the erroneous recording of data on source documents.

B. Inexpensive and therefore widely used.

C. Used to detect errors introduced by the keying process.

D. Ordinarily used with a computer program written to check the data.

Answer (C) is correct. *(CIA, adapted)*

**REQUIRED:** The purpose of key verification.

**DISCUSSION:** Key verification is a procedure to determine if the keying process was performed properly. Information from source documents is rekeyed on a special keyboard by another operator and compared with that previously recorded.

Answer (A) is incorrect because key verification does not detect errors in the source documents. Answer (B) is incorrect because, although widely used, key verification effectively doubles the work and therefore is expensive. Answer (D) is incorrect because key verification is a manual process.

**238.** If a payroll system continues to pay employees who have been terminated, control weaknesses most likely exist because

A. Procedures were not implemented to verify and control the receipt by the computer processing department of all transactions prior to processing.

B. There were inadequate manual controls maintained outside the computer system.

C. Programmed controls such as limit checks should have been built into the system.

D. Input file label checking routines built into the programs were ignored by the operator.

Answer (B) is correct. *(CISA, adapted)*

**REQUIRED:** The control weakness allowing terminated employees to continue being paid.

**DISCUSSION:** The authorization to pay employees comes from outside the computer department. Thus, inadequate controls external to the computer processing department are most likely the cause of allowing the payments to terminated employees to continue without detection.

Answer (A) is incorrect because batch totals constitute adequate controls over properly authorized transactions but provide no control over unauthorized transactions. Answer (C) is incorrect because a limit check tests the reasonableness of a particular transaction but not whether it was authorized. Answer (D) is incorrect because paying proper attention to input file labels (header labels) will not detect unauthorized transactions.

## 5.13 The Auditor's Understanding and Testing of Controls

**239.** The major purpose of the auditor's study and evaluation of the company's computer processing operations is to

A. Evaluate the competence of computer processing operating personnel.

B. Ensure the exercise of due professional care.

C. Evaluate the reliability and integrity of financial information.

D. Become familiar with the company's means of identifying, measuring, classifying, and reporting information.

Answer (C) is correct. *(CIA, adapted)*

**REQUIRED:** The major purpose of the auditor's study and evaluation of the company's computer operations.

**DISCUSSION:** Information systems provide data for decision making, control, and compliance with external requirements. Thus, auditors should examine information systems and, as appropriate, ascertain whether financial records and reports contain accurate, reliable, timely, complete, and useful information, and controls over record keeping and reporting are adequate and effective.

Answer (A) is incorrect because determining the competence of computer processing operating personnel is not the major purpose of the evaluation. Answer (B) is incorrect because due professional care should be exercised in all audits. Answer (D) is incorrect because becoming familiar with the company's information system is a means to an end.

**240.** Which of the following statements concerning the assessment of control risk in a client's computer environment is true?

A. The auditor's objectives with respect to the assessment of control risk are the same as in a manual system.

B. The auditor must obtain an understanding of the internal control and test controls in computer environments.

C. If the general controls are ineffective the auditor ordinarily can assess control risk at a low level if the application controls are effective.

D. The auditor usually can ignore the computer system if (s)he can obtain an understanding of the controls outside the computer system.

Answer (A) is correct. *(Publisher)*

**REQUIRED:** The true statement about the auditor's assessment of control risk in a computer environment.

**DISCUSSION:** The auditor is required to obtain an understanding of internal control and assess control risk to plan the audit. Whether the control system is manual or computerized does not affect this objective.

Answer (B) is incorrect because the auditor need not test the effectiveness of the controls if control risk is assessed at the maximum. Answer (C) is incorrect because, if general controls are weak, the auditor is unlikely to assess control risk at a low level, no matter how effective the application controls appear to be. Answer (D) is incorrect because, when computer applications are significant, the auditor must consider the relevant control activities as an integral part of the assessment of control risk.

**241.** After reviewing terminal security controls, the auditor has concluded that the controls are insufficient. Which of the following audit techniques could the auditor have used to reach this conclusion?

I. Observation
II. Generalized audit software
III. Internal control questionnaires
IV. Control flowcharting

A. I.

B. II and III.

C. I, III, and IV.

D. I, II, III, and IV.

Answer (C) is correct. *(CISA, adapted)*

**REQUIRED:** The audit techniques that could be the basis for concluding that security controls are insufficient.

**DISCUSSION:** An auditor reads documentation, observes the actions of employees, makes inquiries, prepares questionnaires, and develops flowcharts to gain an understanding of the controls. (S)he may then conclude that controls are inappropriate or insufficient, even without testing their effectiveness.

Answer (A) is incorrect because observation alone will not provide sufficient evidence for an audit conclusion about terminal security. Answer (B) is incorrect because generalized audit software is typically used to perform substantive tests but is not appropriate for testing terminal security. Answer (D) is incorrect because generalized audit software is typically used to perform substantive tests but is not appropriate for testing terminal security.

**242.** For audit reliance to be placed on the results of processing in an application system, the auditor should be reasonably satisfied that

A. The system was tested before implementation.

B. An audit trail exists.

C. The system is well documented.

D. The system is functioning properly.

Answer (D) is correct. *(CISA, adapted)*

**REQUIRED:** The assurance the auditor should obtain.

**DISCUSSION:** The most important element of assurance that the auditor should obtain is that the system is functioning properly. If this is the case, reliance can be placed upon the results of processing.

Answer (A) is incorrect because, although testing before implementation is an important consideration, even well-tested systems may not be functioning properly. Answer (B) is incorrect because audit trails are desirable but not absolutely necessary to place reliance on a system. Answer (C) is incorrect because full documentation is desirable but not absolutely necessary.

**243.** The auditor's primary concern with an auditee programmer's writing a program to age inventory is

A. The auditor's programming expertise.

B. Loss of independence.

C. Saving valuable audit time.

D. The programmer's access to confidential information.

Answer (B) is correct. *(CIA, adapted)*

**REQUIRED:** The auditor's primary concern with an auditee programmer's writing a program to age inventory.

**DISCUSSION:** If the auditor uses a program written by the auditee's programmer to perform an audit function (aging receivables), the independence of the auditor may be questioned. The auditor must therefore take appropriate steps to evaluate the program and control its use.

Answer (A) is incorrect because the auditor is concerned with the programmer's expertise and integrity. The auditor does not necessarily need programming ability. Answer (C) is incorrect because saving audit time is secondary to the need for objectivity in conducting the audit. Answer (D) is incorrect because the development of an inventory aging program typically does not involve access to confidential input information.

**244.** The auditor plans to select a sample of transactions to assess the extent that purchase discounts may have been lost by the company. After assessing the risks associated with lost purchase discounts, the auditor was most likely to select a sample from which one of the following populations?

A. Open purchase orders.

B. Paid EDI invoices.

C. Paid non-EDI invoices.

D. Paid EDI and non-EDI invoices.

Answer (C) is correct. *(CIA, adapted)*

**REQUIRED:** The population sampled to assess the extent of lost purchase discounts.

**DISCUSSION:** Manual input and processing increase the risk of delayed payments and loss of purchase discounts. Furthermore, an EDI system is unlikely to offer cash discounts. Thus, the proper population from which to sample consists of paid invoices not processed through the EDI system.

Answer (A) is incorrect because open purchase orders have not yet been invoiced or paid. Answer (B) is incorrect because an EDI system is unlikely to offer cash discounts. In addition, the auditor was involved in the design and testing of the EDI system and presumably has knowledge of the EDI system's procedures. Answer (D) is incorrect because an EDI system is unlikely to offer cash discounts. In addition, the auditor was involved in the design and testing of the EDI system and presumably has knowledge of the EDI system's procedures.

**245.** When an accounting application is processed by computer, an auditor cannot verify the reliable operation of programmed controls by

A. Manually comparing detail transaction files used by an edit program with the program's generated error listings to determine that errors were properly identified by the edit program.

B. Constructing a processing system for accounting applications and processing actual data from throughout the period through both the client's program and the auditor's program.

C. Manually reperforming, as of a moment in time, the processing of input data and comparing the simulated results with the actual results.

D. Periodically submitting auditor-prepared test data to the same computer process and evaluating the results.

Answer (C) is correct. *(CPA, adapted)*

**REQUIRED:** The procedure by which an auditor cannot verify the reliable operation of programmed controls.

**DISCUSSION:** This procedure describes auditing around the computer. The computer is treated as a black box, and only the inputs and outputs are evaluated. Because the actual controls may not be understood or tested, the technique is ordinarily inappropriate if the effectiveness of programmed controls is an important component of internal control and the assessment of control risk.

Answer (A) is incorrect because a manual comparison of the computer-generated output of an auditor-controlled edit program with the error listings generated by the client's program would provide evidence that the client's programmed controls were operating as planned. Answer (B) is incorrect because parallel simulation can be an effective method of testing the reliability of controls. Answer (D) is incorrect because submitting auditor-prepared test data to the client's computer process is an effective method of evaluating the reliability of control procedures.

**246.** Which of the following could the auditor examine only in online systems?

A. Results of test decks.

B. Resolution of errors.

C. Levels of terminal access.

D. Tests of transactions.

Answer (C) is correct. *(CIA, adapted)*

**REQUIRED:** The item an auditor could examine only in online systems.

**DISCUSSION:** Online operation implies direct communication with the CPU, and this typically requires computer terminals. Thus, only in online systems could the auditor examine levels of terminal access.

Answer (A) is incorrect because the auditor could examine results of test decks in offline systems. Answer (B) is incorrect because the auditor could examine resolution of errors in offline systems. Answer (D) is incorrect because the auditor could examine tests of transactions in offline systems.

**247.** Which of the following is necessary to audit balances in an online computer system in an environment of destructive updating?

A. Periodic dumping of transaction files.

B. Year-end use of audit hooks.

C. An integrated test facility (ITF).

D. A well-documented audit trail.

Answer (D) is correct. *(CPA, adapted)*

**REQUIRED:** The condition necessary to audit balances in an online computer system.

**DISCUSSION:** The processing of input records in an online, real-time computer system typically destroys the previous master file entry in an environment of destructive updating. Thus, a well-documented audit trail is especially important for the auditor.

Answer (A) is incorrect because periodic dumping of transaction files may be a way of monitoring transactions, but the auditor would not find it beneficial in the audit. Answer (B) is incorrect because an audit hook is a part of a program that allows for attachment of an audit module to allow continuous monitoring. However, given destructive updating, capturing values only at year-end is much less useful than a well-documented audit trail. Answer (C) is incorrect because an ITF is a possible but unnecessary approach to auditing computer systems.

**248.** Which of the following is likely to be least important to an auditor who is considering internal control for the automated data processing function?

A. Ancillary program functions.

B. Disposition of source documents.

C. Operator competence.

D. Disk capacity.

Answer (D) is correct. *(CPA, adapted)*

**REQUIRED:** The least important item in the consideration of internal control.

**DISCUSSION:** Disk capacity relates to the number of characters the system can store. This is of little or no concern to an auditor considering internal control.

Answer (A) is incorrect because ancillary or auxiliary program functions affect internal control. Answer (B) is incorrect because the auditor should inspect source documents. Answer (C) is incorrect because an entity must employ sufficient competent personnel to accomplish its goals and objectives. Thus, human resource policies and practices are a factor in the control environment that should be considered.

**249.** In a distributed database (DDB) environment, which of the following is a test of control for access control administration?

A. Reconciliation of batch control totals.

B. Examination of logged activity.

C. Prohibition of random access.

D. Analysis of system-generated core dumps.

Answer (B) is correct. *(CIA, adapted)*

**REQUIRED:** The access control in a distributed database (DDB) environment.

**DISCUSSION:** A computer log could provide information concerning users who have accessed the system, the files accessed, the processing accomplished, the time of access, and the amount of time the processing took. The log thus provides data allowing an auditor to evaluate the effectiveness of the system's access controls.

Answer (A) is incorrect because batch totals are unlikely to be calculated in a DDB environment, which is characterized by online processing. Answer (C) is incorrect because DDB systems must provide for random access so that users can obtain information from the files as needed. Answer (D) is incorrect because core dumps, which represent information stored in the memory of the computer, provide little information for access control analysis.

**250.** Tests of controls in an advanced computer system

A. Can be performed using only actual transactions because testing of simulated transactions is of no consequence.

B. Can be performed using actual transactions or simulated transactions.

C. Is impracticable because many procedures within the computer processing activity leave no visible evidence of having been performed.

D. Is inadvisable because it may distort the evidence in live online files.

Answer (B) is correct. *(CPA, adapted)*

**REQUIRED:** The true statement about tests of controls in an advanced computer system.

**DISCUSSION:** Tests of controls determine the effectiveness of the design and operation of internal controls. They can be performed using either actual or simulated transactions. For example, the integrated test facility (ITF) method uses both actual and simulated transactions.

Answer (A) is incorrect because the auditor is concerned with the effectiveness of a control, not the processing of a particular transaction. Answer (C) is incorrect because many procedures that leave no visible evidence may leave machine-readable evidence. Answer (D) is incorrect because master files can be protected during tests of controls. An ITF, for example, uses dummy records so that test transactions will not contaminate live online files.

**251.** After gaining an understanding of a client's computer processing internal control, a financial statement auditor may decide not to test the effectiveness of the computer processing control procedures. Which of the following is not a valid reason for choosing to omit tests of controls?

A. The controls duplicate operative controls existing elsewhere in the system.

B. There appear to be major weaknesses that would preclude assessing control risk at less than the maximum level.

C. The time and dollar costs of testing exceed the time and dollar savings in substantive testing if the tests of controls show the controls to be operative.

D. The controls appear effective enough to support a reduced level of control risk.

Answer (D) is correct. *(CPA, adapted)*

**REQUIRED:** The invalid reason for omitting tests of controls.

**DISCUSSION:** Although controls appear to be effective based on the understanding of internal control, the auditor must perform tests of controls for those control activities for which control risk is to be assessed at less than the maximum level. Control risk affects the acceptable level of detection risk used in determining the nature, timing, and extent of substantive tests.

Answer (A) is incorrect because compensating controls may appropriately limit control risk. Answer (B) is incorrect because, if the auditor intends to assess control risk at the maximum level, tests of controls are unnecessary. Answer (C) is incorrect because, if tests of controls are not cost effective, the auditor should expand substantive testing.

**252.** Auditing through the computer is required when

A. Input transactions are batched and system logic is straightforward.

B. Processing primarily consists of sorting the input data and updating the master file sequentially.

C. Processing is primarily online and updating is real-time.

D. Generalized audit software is not available.

Answer (C) is correct. *(CIA, adapted)*

**REQUIRED:** The condition requiring auditing through the computer.

**DISCUSSION:** When the computer plays a significant role in processing, storing, and reporting the information being audited, the auditor should audit through the computer. In highly sophisticated systems, the auditor may find it necessary to be able to assess control risk less than the maximum. AU 319 states "When evidence of an entity's initiation, recording, and processing of financial data exists only in electronic form, the auditor's ability to obtain the desired assurance only from substantive tests would significantly diminish."

Answer (A) is incorrect because, in a straightforward batch system, printouts and other documentation may be sufficient for adequate testing outside the computer. Answer (B) is incorrect because, when files are stored sequentially and processed in that manner, printouts and other documentation may be sufficient for adequate testing outside the computer. Answer (D) is incorrect because, whether or not generalized audit software is available, the auditor should consider the consequences of auditing around, rather than through, the computer.

**253.** When an auditor tests a computerized accounting system, which of the following is true of the test data approach?

A. Test data must consist of all possible valid and invalid conditions.

B. The program tested is different from the program used throughout the year by the client.

C. Several transactions of each type must be tested.

D. Test data are processed by the client's computer programs under the auditor's control.

Answer (D) is correct. *(CPA, adapted)*

**REQUIRED:** The true statement concerning the test data approach.

**DISCUSSION:** Using the test data approach, the auditor develops and processes a set of valid and invalid transactions using the client's application programs. Based on the understanding of the programmed controls, the auditor has an expectation of the results of the processing. The auditor can determine if the client's controls are working effectively to reject and report invalid and questionable transactions.

Answer (A) is incorrect because the auditor should test those controls that must be evaluated to assess control risk below the maximum level. Answer (B) is incorrect because the program tested should be the same one used by management throughout the year; otherwise the auditor has no assurance concerning the effectiveness of the controls that were actually in place. Answer (C) is incorrect because only one of each type of transaction needs to be tested. The computer can be expected to test all similar transactions in the same manner.

**254.** The following flowchart depicts

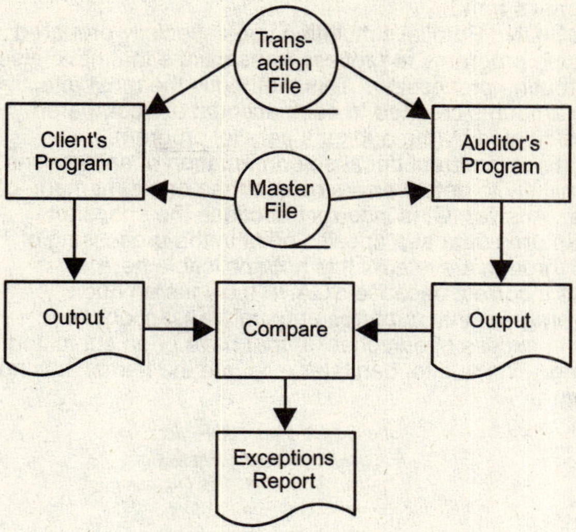


A. Program code checking.

B. Parallel simulation.

C. Integrated test facility.

D. Controlled reprocessing.

Answer (B) is correct. *(CPA, adapted)*

**REQUIRED:** The audit technique depicted by the flowchart.

**DISCUSSION:** Parallel simulation is a test of the controls in a client's application program. An auditor-developed program is used to process actual client data and compare the output and the exceptions report with those of the client's application program. If the client's programmed controls are operating effectively, the two sets of results should be reconcilable.

Answer (A) is incorrect because program code checking refers to desk checking the client's application program code to determine if it contains the appropriate controls. Answer (C) is incorrect because an ITF introduces dummy records into the client's files and then processes dummy transactions to update the records. The auditor can test the controls by including various types of transactions to be processed. Answer (D) is incorrect because controlled reprocessing is a variant of parallel simulation that uses an authenticated copy of the auditee's program. The flowchart indicates that the auditor's program is being used.

**255.** Parallel simulation (the audit model technique) is an appropriate audit approach for

A. Testing for the presence of authorized signatures on documents.

B. Summarizing the results of accounts receivable confirmation work.

C. Calculating amounts for declining-balance depreciation charges.

D. Scanning the general ledger file for unusual transactions.

Answer (C) is correct. *(CIA, adapted)*

**REQUIRED:** The proper use of parallel simulation.

**DISCUSSION:** Parallel simulation involves duplicate processing of the client's data using a program developed by the auditor. The auditor's program simulates the logic of the client's application program. The auditor may thus enter data and compare simulated test results with those from the auditee's program. Parallel simulation is appropriate for auditing depreciation because controls such as limit or reasonableness tests can be tested by the auditor.

Answer (A) is incorrect because testing for the presence of authorized signatures on documents is a test of controls that cannot be done by a program. Answer (B) is incorrect because confirmations provide auditor-developed data from sources external to the auditee. Parallel simulation seeks to duplicate auditee processing. Answer (D) is incorrect because scanning the general ledger file for unusual transactions does not replicate auditee processing.

**256.** To determine whether any unauthorized program changes have been made since the last authorized program update, the best computer audit technique is for the auditor to conduct a(n)

A. Code comparison.

B. Code review.

C. Test data run.

D. Analytical review.

Answer (A) is correct. *(CIA, adapted)*

**REQUIRED:** The best technique to determine whether unauthorized program changes have been made.

**DISCUSSION:** Code comparison is the process of comparing two versions of the same program to determine whether the two correspond. It is an efficient technique because it is performed by software.

Answer (B) is incorrect because code review is the process of reading program source code listings to determine whether the code contains potential errors or inefficient statements. Code review can be used as a means of code comparison but is inefficient. Answer (C) is incorrect because test data runs permit the auditor to verify the processing of preselected transactions. They provide no evidence about unexecuted portions of the program. Answer (D) is incorrect because analytical review is the process of creating and evaluating ratios between numbers, often in the context of financial statements.

**257.** Auditors have learned that increased computerization has created more opportunities for computer fraud but has also led to the development of computer audit techniques to detect frauds. A type of fraud that has occurred in the banking industry is a programming fraud in which the programmer designs a program to calculate daily interest on savings accounts to four decimal points. The programmer then truncates the last two digits and adds it to his or her account balance. Which of the following computer audit techniques would be most effective in detecting this type of fraud?

A. Parallel simulation.

B. Generalized audit software that selects account balances for confirmation with the depositor.

C. Snapshot.

D. SCARF (Systems Control and Audit Review File).

Answer (A) is correct. *(CIA, adapted)*

**REQUIRED:** The audit technique most effective in detecting the programmer's fraud.

**DISCUSSION:** Parallel simulation uses specially prepared application-type programs to process transactions that have also been run in routine processing. This method is the most effective because the amounts credited to each account are compared with those calculated by the auditor's parallel program.

Answer (B) is incorrect because confirmation of an account balance is unlikely to detect errors of less than one cent made on a daily basis. Answer (C) is incorrect because the snapshot technique captures data at a specific point in the processing of transactions through a system. It is not applicable here. Answer (D) is incorrect because SCARF includes an audit module in a program that captures unusual transactions (or transactions in excess of edit checks) that have been submitted for processing. The auditor can later evaluate the items. It is not applicable here.

**258.** A mail-order retailer has just modified its processing programs to charge each customer the appropriate sales tax. The best approach for detecting whether sales taxes are applied correctly is to

A. Move the program code that computes sales taxes to a single program and make this program part of the processing sequence.

B. Change the operator input screens to show the computation of sales taxes so the operator can verify the computation.

C. Modify the program code to prompt the operator to ask customers whether their areas have sales taxes and enter the appropriate rates.

D. Add the program code that will sort orders by area, compute taxes in the aggregate, and compare the amount with the sum of individual taxes charged for each area.

Answer (D) is correct. *(CIA, adapted)*

**REQUIRED:** The best approach for detecting whether sales taxes are applied correctly.

**DISCUSSION:** Sales taxes vary from one jurisdiction to another. Hence, the program should sort orders by area. Verification of the accuracy of the tax charges can then be obtained by calculating the total taxes for each area in two ways: applying the tax rate to the aggregate sales and summing the taxes charged on individual sales.

Answer (A) is incorrect because moving the program code that computes sales taxes to a single program is a good system design approach, but it does not guarantee that sales tax processing is complete. Answer (B) is incorrect because changing the operator input screens does not ensure correct application of sales taxes. The operator may not know what the appropriate computation is. Answer (C) is incorrect because customers may not know the proper rates or may deny that their areas impose the taxes.

**259.** To obtain evidence that online access controls are properly functioning, an auditor is most likely to

A. Create checkpoints at periodic intervals after live data processing to test for unauthorized use of the system.

B. Examine the transaction log to discover whether any transactions were lost or entered twice because of a system malfunction.

C. Enter invalid identification numbers or passwords to ascertain whether the system rejects them.

D. Vouch a random sample of processed transactions to assure proper authorization.

Answer (C) is correct. *(CPA, adapted)*

**REQUIRED:** The procedure to obtain evidence that user online access controls are functioning.

**DISCUSSION:** Employees with access authority to process transactions that change records should not also have asset custody or program modification responsibilities. The auditor should determine that password authority is consistent with other assigned responsibilities. The auditor can directly test whether password controls are working by attempting entry into the system by using invalid identifications and passwords.

Answer (A) is incorrect because checkpoints are used as a recovery procedure in batch processing applications. Answer (B) is incorrect because testing for missing or duplicate transactions would not determine whether online access controls were functioning effectively. Answer (D) is incorrect because unauthorized transactions may be entered by anyone who knows valid passwords, etc.

**260.** Which of the following computer-assisted auditing techniques allows fictitious and real transactions to be processed together without the knowledge of client operating personnel?

A. Integrated test facility (ITF).

B. Input controls matrix.

C. Parallel simulation.

D. Data entry monitor.

Answer (A) is correct. *(CPA, adapted)*

**REQUIRED:** The technique that processes fictitious and real transactions without the knowledge of client personnel.

**DISCUSSION:** Using an ITF, the auditor creates a test record within the client's actual system. Fictitious transactions affecting the test record along with actual transactions are processed. Client operating personnel need not be aware of the testing process.

Answer (B) is incorrect because input controls matrix is not a method typically used by auditors to test a client's computer systems. Answer (C) is incorrect because parallel simulation reprocesses only real, not fictitious, transactions. Answer (D) is incorrect because data entry monitor is not a method typically used by auditors to test a client's computer systems.

**261.** A primary reason auditors are reluctant to use an ITF (minicompany technique) is that it requires them to

A. Reserve specific master file records and process them at regular intervals.

B. Collect transaction and master file records in a separate file.

C. Notify user personnel so they can make manual adjustments to output.

D. Identify and reverse the fictitious entries to avoid contamination of control totals.

Answer (D) is correct. *(CIA, adapted)*

**REQUIRED:** The reason for not using an ITF.

**DISCUSSION:** An ITF permits dummy transactions to be processed with live transactions but requires additional programming to ensure that programs will recognize the specially coded test data. Also, dummy files must be established (the test facility or dummy entity). Nevertheless, output (for example, control totals) is affected by the existence of the ITF transactions. One way to avoid the problem is to use immaterial transactions. However, the resulting differences between control totals may be troublesome, and the inability to use large numbers may preclude auditing limit tests. An alternative is to submit reversing entries. However, reversals (1) threaten data integrity if they are inaccurate, (2) must be submitted in the same run, and (3) may allow users to obtain contaminated data before the entries are made.

Answer (A) is incorrect because reserving specific master file records and processing them at regular intervals is typical of the base case system of evaluation. Answer (B) is incorrect because the embedded audit module technique involves selection of items of audit interest by the audit module included in an application program. These items are recorded in a separate audit log. Answer (C) is incorrect because making manual adjustments to output does not reverse the fictitious entries in the master file.

**262.** The audit effort most likely to yield relevant evidence in determining the adequacy of an organization's disaster-recovery plan should focus on

A. The completeness of the plan as to facilities, operations, communications, security, and data processing.

B. The sufficiency of the list of replacement equipment needed in event of a disaster.

C. The question of whether the plan is in the planning or developmental stage.

D. The role of the internal auditing department in developing and testing the plan.

Answer (A) is correct. *(CIA, adapted)*

**REQUIRED:** The focus of the audit effort regarding a disaster recovery plan.

**DISCUSSION:** A computer center should have a comprehensive (complete) reconstruction and recovery plan that will allow it to regenerate important programs and data files and continue operations in the event of disasters, equipment failures, or errors. The center should create backup (duplicate) copies of data files, databases, programs, and documentation, store backup copies off-site, and plan for auxiliary processing at another site.

Answer (B) is incorrect because consideration of the adequacy of the plan must extend to numerous factors other than the sufficiency of the list of replacement equipment. Answer (C) is incorrect because consideration of the adequacy of the plan must extend to numerous factors other than the question of whether the plan is in the planning or development stage. Answer (D) is incorrect because the involvement of internal auditing does not assure adequacy.

**263.** In auditing an online perpetual inventory system, an auditor selected certain file-updating transactions for detailed testing. The audit technique that will provide a computer trail of all relevant processing steps applied to a specific transaction is described as

A. Simulation.

B. Snapshot.

C. Code comparison.

D. Tagging and tracing.

Answer (D) is correct. *(CIA, adapted)*

**REQUIRED:** The audit technique that provides a computer trail for processing a specific transaction.

**DISCUSSION:** Tagging and tracing describes the selection of specific transactions to which an indicator is attached at input. A computer trail of all relevant processing steps of these tagged transactions in the application system can be printed or stored in a computer file for auditor evaluation.

Answer (A) is incorrect because simulation permits comparisons of live data but does not produce a trail of all relevant processing steps. Answer (B) is incorrect because a snapshot is a technique for recording the content of computer memory to aid in verifying a decision process. Answer (C) is incorrect because a code comparison is used to verify that program changes and computer maintenance procedures are correctly followed.

**264.** To decrease overall inventory costs, a manufacturer has implemented a distributed database system for maintaining all inventory records at each plant. Each plant can requisition inventory from other plants. Management believes, however, that materials requisitions that require inventory from multiple plants are not being entered in the database correctly; i.e., the inventory is shipped, but the counts remain the same. The best approach for investigating the situation is

A. An embedded audit module.

B. An audit hook.

C. A snapshot.

D. SCARF (Systems Control Audit Review File).

Answer (C) is correct. *(CIA, adapted)*

**REQUIRED:** The best approach for investigating a database system in which data are not entered correctly.

**DISCUSSION:** To determine why the inventory count has not changed, the processing must be tested. The best approach is to use the snapshot technique. It involves capturing the data used in processing at a specific point in the stream of processing. The snapshot technique will permit analysis of all data pertinent to a complex database update so that the correctness or deficiencies of updating can be determined.

Answer (A) is incorrect because an embedded audit module selects transactions meeting specific criteria. It permits continuous monitoring of the system but is not helpful in debugging this potential updating error. Answer (B) is incorrect because an audit hook is useful in calling audit routines to perform processing for audit activity but is not helpful in debugging this potential updating error. Answer (D) is incorrect because the SCARF method is used to identify outliers (transactions with unusual characteristics or transactions that are processed when they do not pass normal edit controls). It simply writes these transactions to a file for further audit investigation.

**265.** A service organization processes payroll data having a material effect on the financial statements of an audit client. The client has established certain internal control activities over input and output data. If the financial statement auditor wishes to assess control risk at less than the maximum, which of the following statements is false?

A. The auditor may decide that obtaining evidence of the operating effectiveness of the service organization's activities is not necessary or efficient and still be able to assess control risk at less than the maximum.

B. The auditor may need to perform tests of the service organization's processing controls that would provide a basis for assessing control risk below the maximum.

C. If certain relevant controls exist only at the service organization, the client's auditor must evaluate the operating effectiveness of those controls to assess control risk at less than the maximum.

D. If certain relevant controls exist only at the service organization and a service auditor issues a report on activities placed in operation, the client's auditor may use the report to assess control risk below the maximum.

Answer (D) is correct. *(Publisher)*

**REQUIRED:** The false statement about assessing control risk at less than the maximum when a service organization processes transactions for an audit client.

**DISCUSSION:** The use of a computer service organization reduces control risk through increased segregation of functions. If the client's controls over the data are effective, the auditor may be able to audit around the service organization's computer. The arrangement usually provides an adequate audit trail for this purpose. If controls necessary to achieve specific entity objectives are located at the service organization, the user auditor must either apply appropriate procedures at the service organization or obtain a report by a service auditor for the purpose of assessing control risk below the maximum. The service auditor's report must report on activities placed in operation and on tests of operating effectiveness (AU 324).

Answer (A) is incorrect because the client's auditor may be able to assess control risk at less than the maximum after testing the relevant client controls over the service organization's activities. Answer (B) is incorrect because, if the relevant controls are at the service organization and an appropriate service auditor's report is not available or is not used, the auditor must test controls at the service organization if control risk is to be assessed below the maximum. Answer (C) is incorrect because the evaluation of operating effectiveness must be based on the auditor's tests of controls at the service organization or on an appropriate service auditor's report if control risk is to be assessed below the maximum level.

**266.** What information would the auditor expect to find in the data dictionary that would assist in a payroll application audit?

A. Programs that access the data.

B. Type of operating system.

C. Online user identification.

D. System network architecture and flowcharts.

Answer (A) is correct. *(CIA, adapted)*

**REQUIRED:** The information found in the data dictionary that would assist in the payroll audit.

**DISCUSSION:** The data dictionary is a file (possibly manual but usually computerized) in which the records relate to specified data items. It contains definitions of data records and files and the list of programs used to process them. Only certain persons or entities are permitted to retrieve data or to modify data items. Accordingly, these access limitations are also found in the data dictionary.

Answer (B) is incorrect because the type of operating system is not customarily part of the data dictionary. Answer (C) is incorrect because online user identification is not customarily part of the data dictionary. Answer (D) is incorrect because system network architecture and flowcharts are not customarily part of the data dictionary.

**267.** Matthews Corp. has changed from a system of recording time worked on clock cards to a computerized payroll system in which employees record time in and out with magnetic cards. The computer system automatically updates all payroll records. Because of this change

A. A generalized computer audit program must be used.

B. Part of the audit trail is altered.

C. The potential for payroll-related fraud is diminished.

D. Transactions must be processed in batches.

Answer (B) is correct. *(CPA, adapted)*

**REQUIRED:** The effect of computerization of a payroll system.

**DISCUSSION:** In a manual payroll system, a paper trail of documents is created to provide audit evidence that controls over each step in processing are in place and functioning. One element of a computer system that differentiates it from a manual system is that a transaction trail useful for auditing purposes might exist only for a brief time or only in computer-readable form.

Answer (A) is incorrect because use of generalized audit software is only one of many ways of auditing through a computer. Answer (C) is incorrect because conversion to a computer system may actually increase the chance of fraud by eliminating segregation of incompatible functions and other controls. Answer (D) is incorrect because automatic updating indicates that processing is not in batch mode.

**268.** An audit of the electronic data interchange (EDI) area of a banking group revealed the facts listed below. Which one indicates the need for improved internal control?

A. Employees may only access the computer system via an ID and an encrypted password.

B. The system employs message sequencing as a way to monitor data transmissions.

C. Certain types of transactions may only be made at specific terminals.

D. Branch office employees may access the mainframe with a single call via modem.

Answer (D) is correct. *(CIA, adapted)*

**REQUIRED:** The condition that indicates the need for improved internal control.

**DISCUSSION:** The system should employ automatic dial-back to prevent intrusion by unauthorized parties. This procedure accepts an incoming modem call, disconnects, and automatically dials back a prearranged number to establish a permanent connection for data transfer or inquiry.

Answer (A) is incorrect because employee access to the computer system via an ID and an encrypted password is considered acceptable. Encrypted passwords further decrease the likelihood of unauthorized access. Answer (B) is incorrect because message sequencing detects unauthorized access by numbering each message and incrementing each message by one more than the last one sent. This procedure will detect a gap or duplicate. Answer (C) is incorrect because allowing certain types of transactions (such as payroll transactions) to be made only at specific terminals minimizes the likelihood of unauthorized access.

## 5.14 Computer-Assisted Auditing

**269.** An auditor is least likely to use computer software to

A. Construct parallel simulations.

B. Access client data files.

C. Prepare spreadsheets.

D. Assess computer control risk.

Answer (D) is correct. *(CPA, adapted)*

**REQUIRED:** The task least likely to be done with computer software.

**DISCUSSION:** The auditor is required to obtain an understanding of internal control and assess control risk to plan the audit. This assessment is a matter of professional judgment that cannot be accomplished by a computer.

Answer (A) is incorrect because parallel simulation involves using an auditor's program to reproduce the logic of the client's program. Answer (B) is incorrect because computer software makes accessing client files much faster and easier. Answer (C) is incorrect because many audit spreadsheet programs are available.

**270.** Computer technology makes it possible to perform paperless audits. For example, in an audit of computer-processed customer accounts receivable balances, an auditor might use a personal computer to access the accounts receivable files directly and copy selected customer records into the computer for audit analysis. Which of the following is an advantage of this type of paperless audit of accounts receivable balances?

A. It reduces the amount of substantive testing required.

B. It allows immediate processing of audit data on a spreadsheet working paper.

C. It increases the amount of technical skill required of the auditor.

D. It allows direct confirmation of customer account balances.

Answer (B) is correct. *(CIA, adapted)*

**REQUIRED:** The advantage of a paperless audit of accounts receivable balances.

**DISCUSSION:** Electronic spreadsheets are software packages that display multicolumn worksheets, which may be used as automated audit working papers. A major advantage of this type of auditing is the ability to process data immediately using personal computer software without first having to enter the data manually into the computer.

Answer (A) is incorrect because audit technology has no direct effect on the amount of substantive testing required. Answer (C) is incorrect because the need for increased expertise is not an advantage. Answer (D) is incorrect because processing computer files does not in itself provide confirmation of customer account balances, although software may assist in preparing confirmation requests.

**271.** A primary advantage of using generalized audit software (GAS) packages in auditing the financial statements of a client that uses a computer system is that the auditor may

A. Substantiate the accuracy of data through self-checking digits and hash totals.

B. Reduce the level of required tests of controls to a relatively small amount.

C. Access information stored on computer files without a complete understanding of the client's hardware and software features.

D. Consider increasing the use of substantive tests of transactions in place of analytical procedures.

Answer (C) is correct. *(CPA, adapted)*

**REQUIRED:** The advantage of using GAS.

**DISCUSSION:** The primary use of GAS is to select and summarize a client's records for additional testing. These packages permit the auditor to audit through the computer; to extract, compare, analyze, and summarize data; and to generate output for use in the audit. They allow the auditor to exploit the computer to examine many more records than otherwise possible with far greater speed and accuracy. Although GAS requires the auditor to provide certain specifications about the particular client's records, computer equipment, and file formats, a detailed knowledge of the client's system may be unnecessary because the audit package is designed to be used in many environments. The leading audit software packages are currently ACL (Audit Command Language) and IDEA (Interactive Data Extraction and Analysis).

Answer (A) is incorrect because self-checking digits and hash totals are application controls used by clients. Answer (B) is incorrect because GAS may permit far more comprehensive tests of controls than in a manual audit. Answer (D) is incorrect because the auditor is required to apply analytical procedures in the planning and overall review phases of the audit.

**272.** Specialized audit software

A. Is written to interface with many different client systems.

B. May be written while its purposes and users are being defined.

C. Requires the auditor to have less computer expertise than generalized audit software.

D. May be written in a procedure-oriented language.

Answer (D) is correct. *(Publisher)*

**REQUIRED:** The true statement regarding specialized audit software.

**DISCUSSION:** Specialized audit software is written in a procedure- or problem-oriented language to fulfill a specific set of audit tasks. The purposes and users of the software are well defined before the software is written. Auditors develop specialized audit software for the following reasons:

1. Unavailability of alternative software
2. Functional limitations of alternative software
3. Efficiency considerations
4. Increased understanding of systems
5. Opportunity for easy implementation
6. Increased auditor independence and prestige

Answer (A) is incorrect because generalized audit software is written to interface with many different client systems. Answer (B) is incorrect because the purposes and users of this software must be defined before it is written. Answer (C) is incorrect because generalized audit software purchased "off the shelf" requires less computer expertise than specialized software created by the auditor.

**273.** The two requirements crucial to achieving audit efficiency and effectiveness with a personal computer are selecting

A. The appropriate audit tasks for personal computer applications and the appropriate software to perform the selected audit tasks.

B. The appropriate software to perform the selected audit tasks and client data that can be accessed by the auditor's personal computer.

C. Client data that can be accessed by the auditor's personal computer and audit procedures that are generally applicable to several clients in a specific industry.

D. Audit procedures that are generally applicable to several clients in a specific industry and the appropriate audit tasks for personal computer applications.

Answer (A) is correct. *(CPA, adapted)*

**REQUIRED:** The two requirements for audit efficiency and effectiveness using a personal computer.

**DISCUSSION:** The question relates to using the computer as an audit tool. To use a personal computer for this purpose effectively and efficiently, the auditor must have the appropriate hardware and software.

Answer (B) is incorrect because access to client data does not relate directly to the efficient and effective use of a personal computer. Answer (C) is incorrect because access to the client's records and selection of standardized audit procedures pertain more to using generalized audit software to perform substantive tests than to using the personal computer as an audit tool. Answer (D) is incorrect because selection of standardized procedures for the industry does not relate directly to the efficient and effective use of a personal computer.

**274.** Smith Corporation has numerous customers. A customer file is kept on disk storage. Each customer record contains the name, address, credit limit, and account balance. The auditor wishes to test this file to determine whether credit limits are being exceeded. The best procedure for the auditor to follow is to

A. Develop test data that would cause some account balances to exceed the credit limit and determine if the system properly detects such situations.

B. Develop a program to compare credit limits with account balances and print out the details of any account with a balance exceeding its credit limit.

C. Request a printout of all account balances so they can be manually checked against the credit limits.

D. Request a printout of a sample of account balances so they can be individually checked against the credit limits.

Answer (B) is correct. *(CPA, adapted)*

**REQUIRED:** The best technique to test a customer computer file to determine whether credit limits are being exceeded.

**DISCUSSION:** The auditor should consider developing a program to compare the balances with the credit limits and to print out the exceptions. The auditor can then focus on those customers whose credit limits may have been exceeded.

Answer (A) is incorrect because the auditor only needs to abstract information already available in the client's files. Answer (C) is incorrect because requesting a printout of all account balances so they can be manually checked against the credit limits would entail extensive manual work that could be done far more quickly and accurately by the computer. Answer (D) is incorrect because, although a sample may be useful, the information is available and the speed and power of the computer allows the auditor to identify all customers exceeding the credit limit.

**275.** An auditor using audit software probably would be least interested in which of the following fields in a computerized perpetual inventory file?

A. Economic order quantity.

B. Warehouse location.

C. Date of last purchase.

D. Quantity sold.

Answer (A) is correct. *(CPA, adapted)*

**REQUIRED:** The field from an inventory record that would be least interesting to an auditor.

**DISCUSSION:** The economic order quantity, which is based on the most cost-effective combination of ordering and carrying costs, is a management decision with little impact on the fairness of the inventory balance on the financial statements.

Answer (B) is incorrect because the auditor would be interested in the storage location of the inventory item for test-count purposes. Answer (C) is incorrect because the auditor would be interested in the date of last purchase for various reasons. For example, if the date is not relatively recent, the item may be slow-moving or obsolete, with consequent implications for its lower-of-cost-or-market valuation. On the other hand, a date of purchase near year-end suggests the need for cutoff tests. Answer (D) is incorrect because the quantity sold is obviously significant for determining the accuracy of the inventory balance, sales, cost of sales, and related accounts.

**276.** Which of the following represents a limitation on the use of generalized audit software (GAS)?

A. It requires lengthy detailed instructions in order to accomplish specific tasks.

B. It has limited application without significant modification.

C. It requires significant programming knowledge to be used effectively.

D. It can only be used on hardware with compatible operating systems.

Answer (D) is correct. *(CIA, adapted)*

**REQUIRED:** The disadvantage of using GAS.

**DISCUSSION:** Diversity of programming languages, computers, systems designs, and differing data structures makes generalized audit software impossible to apply in some situations.

Answer (A) is incorrect because the use of GAS is normally more efficient. Less time is required to write instructions to accomplish a function than to manually select and examine items. Answer (B) is incorrect because the program is generalized, i.e., designed to be used on a variety of systems without significant modifications. Answer (C) is incorrect because an advantage is that GAS requires minimal knowledge of computer technology.

**277.** When an auditor performs tests on a computerized inventory file containing over 20,000 line items, that auditor can maintain independence and perform most efficiently by

A. Asking the console operator to print every item that cost more than $100.

B. Using a generalized audit software package.

C. Obtaining a printout of the entire file and then selecting each nth item.

D. Using the systems department's programmer to write an extraction program.

Answer (B) is correct. *(CIA, adapted)*

**REQUIRED:** The method to maintain independence and perform efficiently in testing an inventory file.

**DISCUSSION:** Independence can be preserved when the auditor acquires general audit software (GAS) from an external source rather than relying on auditee-developed audit software. Also, efficiency is enhanced to the extent GAS can be used (as compared to manual auditing or writing special audit programs).

Answer (A) is incorrect because independence is jeopardized when an operator is involved in the process. Answer (C) is incorrect because printing out the entire file is both unnecessary and inefficient. Answer (D) is incorrect because overreliance on an auditee's programmer impairs independence.

**278.** Which of the following strategies will a CPA most likely consider in auditing an entity that processes most of its financial data only in electronic form, such as a paperless system?

A. Continuous monitoring and analysis of transaction processing with an embedded audit module.

B. Increased reliance on internal control activities that emphasize the segregation of duties.

C. Verification of encrypted digital certificates used to monitor the authorization of transactions.

D. Extensive testing of firewall boundaries that restrict the recording of outside network traffic.

Answer (A) is correct. *(CPA, adapted)*

**REQUIRED:** The audit strategy for an electronic environment.

**DISCUSSION:** An audit module embedded in the client's software routinely selects and abstracts certain transactions. They may be tagged and traced through the information system. An alternative is recording in an audit log, that is, in a file accessible only by the auditor.

Answer (B) is incorrect because the same level of segregation of duties as in a manual system is not feasible in highly sophisticated computer systems. Answer (C) is incorrect because encrypted digital signatures help ensure the authenticity of the sender of information, but verifying them is a less pervasive and significant procedure than continuous monitoring of transactions. Answer (D) is incorrect because firewalls exclude unauthorized activity from entering a system; however, such activity would be independent of the internal processing of financial information.

**279.** Which of the following is the primary reason that many auditors hesitate to use embedded audit modules?

A. Embedded audit modules cannot be protected from computer viruses.

B. Auditors are required to monitor embedded audit modules continuously to obtain valid results.

C. Embedded audit modules can easily be modified through management tampering.

D. Auditors are required to be involved in the system design of the application to be monitored.

Answer (D) is correct. *(CPA, adapted)*

**REQUIRED:** The primary reason many auditors hesitate to use embedded audit modules.

**DISCUSSION:** Continuous monitoring and analysis of transaction processing can be achieved with an embedded audit module. For example, an auditor may establish an audit module that counts the number of times the credit manager overrides established credit limits. A disadvantage of an embedded audit module is that audit hooks must be programmed into the operating system and applications. An alternative is embedding code in the auditee's programs to routinely extract/select certain transactions or details to be recorded in a file accessible only by the auditors. These methods require that an auditor have a working understanding of the computer system and be involved in its design. Designing the system may impair independence unless the client makes all management decisions.

Answer (A) is incorrect because embedded audit modules are protected from computer viruses. Answer (B) is incorrect because auditors are not required to monitor audit modules continuously to obtain valid results. Answer (C) is incorrect because embedded audit modules cannot be easily modified through management tampering.

**280.** Auditors often make use of computer programs that perform routine processing functions, such as sorting and merging. These programs are made available by computer companies and others and are specifically referred to as

A. Compiler programs.

B. Supervisory programs.

C. Utility programs.

D. User programs.

Answer (C) is correct. *(CPA, adapted)*

**REQUIRED:** The term for programs used to perform routine functions.

**DISCUSSION:** Utility programs are provided by manufacturers of equipment to perform routine processing tasks required by both clients and auditors, such as extracting data, sorting, merging, and copying. Utility programs are pretested, are independent of the client's own programming efforts, and furnish useful information without the trouble of writing special programs for the engagement.

Answer (A) is incorrect because compiler programs convert source programs written in a higher-level language into computer-readable object programs, i.e., into machine language. Answer (B) is incorrect because supervisory programs, also termed operating systems, are master programs responsible for controlling operations within a computer system. Answer (D) is incorrect because user programs are those prepared for a particular application.

**281.** Which of the following concepts distinguishes the retention of computerized audit documentation from the traditional hard copy form?

A. Analyses, conclusions, and recommendations are filed on electronic media and are therefore subject to computer system controls and security procedures.

B. Evidential support for all findings is copied and provided to local management during the closing conference and to each person receiving the final report.

C. Computerized data files can be used in computer audit procedures.

D. Audit programs can be standardized to eliminate the need for a preliminary survey at each location.

Answer (A) is correct. *(CIA, adapted)*

**REQUIRED:** The distinction between computerized audit documentation and the traditional hard copy.

**DISCUSSION:** The only difference between the computerized audit documentation and hard copy form is how the working papers are stored. Electronic audit documentation is saved either on disks or hard drive, whereas hard copy is stored in a file cabinet. Unlike computerized audit documentation, hard copies are not subject to computer controls and security procedures.

Answer (B) is incorrect because evidential support would be retained and provided on the basis of the nature of the finding and not the media used for storing audit documentation. Answer (C) is incorrect because this capability is not an exclusive function of computerized audit documentation. Answer (D) is incorrect because, though the nature of the preliminary survey may change in some cases, the requirement for this phase of the audit is not eliminated by computerized audit documentation.

## 5.15 Artificial Intelligence

**282.** Prudent managers will recognize the limits within which expert systems can be effectively applied. An expert system is most appropriately used to

A. Compensate for the lack of certain technical knowledge within the organization.

B. Help make customer-service jobs easier to perform.

C. Automate daily managerial problem-solving.

D. Emulate human expertise for strategic planning.

Answer (B) is correct. *(CIA, adapted)*

**REQUIRED:** The most appropriate use for an expert system.

**DISCUSSION:** Expert systems are systems that allow a computer to make decisions in a human way. Expert systems allow even small companies to perform activities and provide services previously only available from larger firms. The use of expert systems has helped to improve the quality of customer service in applications such as maintenance and scheduling by automating them and making them easy to perform.

Answer (A) is incorrect because expert systems codify and apply existing knowledge, but they do not create knowledge. Answer (C) is incorrect because expert systems do best in automating lower-level clerical functions. Answer (D) is incorrect because expert systems concern problems with relatively few possible outcomes that are all known in advance.

**283.** The processing in knowledge-based systems is characterized by

A. Algorithms.

B. Deterministic procedures.

C. Heuristics.

D. Simulations.

Answer (C) is correct. *(CIA, adapted)*

**REQUIRED:** The characteristic of processing in knowledge-based systems.

**DISCUSSION:** Knowledge-based (expert) systems contain a knowledge base for a limited domain of human expertise and inference procedures for the solution of problems. They use symbolic processing based on heuristics rather than algorithms. A heuristic procedure is an exploratory problem-solving technique that uses self-education methods, e.g., the evaluation of feedback, to improve performance. These systems are often very interactive and provide explanations of their problem-solving behavior.

Answer (A) is incorrect because algorithms are defined procedures used in typical computer programs. Answer (B) is incorrect because deterministic procedures are procedures used in computer programs that permit no uncertainty in outcomes. Answer (D) is incorrect because simulations are computer programs that permit experimentation with logical and mathematical models.

**284.** A bank implemented an expert system to help account representatives consolidate the bank's relationships with each customer. The expert system has

A. A sequential control structure.

B. Distinct input-output variables.

C. A knowledge base.

D. Passive data elements.

Answer (C) is correct. *(CIA, adapted)*

**REQUIRED:** The component of an expert system.

**DISCUSSION:** An expert system relies on a computer's ability to make decisions in a human way. There are six components to the expert system: knowledge base, domain database, database management system, inference engine, user interface, and knowledge acquisition facility. The knowledge base contains the rules used when making decisions.

Answer (A) is incorrect because traditional programs, e.g., in COBOL, have sequential control structures; expert systems do not. Answer (B) is incorrect because traditional programs, not expert systems, have distinct input-output variables. Answer (D) is incorrect because traditional programs, not expert systems, have passive data elements.

**285.** For which of the following applications would the use of a fuzzy logic system be the most appropriate artificial intelligence (AI) choice?

A. Assigning airport gates to arriving airline flights.

B. Forecasting demand for spare auto parts.

C. Ventilating expressway tunnels.

D. Diagnosing computer hardware problems.

Answer (C) is correct. *(CIA, adapted)*

**REQUIRED:** The most appropriate use for fuzzy logic.

**DISCUSSION:** Fuzzy logic is a superset of conventional (Boolean) logic that has been extended to handle the concept of partial truth. Because they use nonspecific terms (membership functions) characterized by well-defined imprecision, fuzzy logic systems can create rules to address problems with many solutions. Fuzzy logic can be used when values are approximate or subject and data are incomplete or ambiguous. These systems have been applied successfully to applications such as ventilating expressway tunnels, selecting companies for business combinations, or detecting fraud in medical insurance claims.

Answer (A) is incorrect because assigning airport gates to arriving airline flights requires an expert system that uses precise data for quick and consistent decisions. Answer (B) is incorrect because neural networks provide the technology to undertake sophisticated forecasting and analysis. They emulate the processing patterns of the brain and therefore can learn from experience. Answer (D) is incorrect because diagnosing problems with computer hardware could be accomplished by an expert system.

## 5.16 CISA Concepts

NOTE: The Information Systems Audit and Control Association offers the Certified Information Systems Auditor (CISA) exam. It has one process area (The IS Audit Process - 10%) and six content areas (Management, Planning, and Organization of IS - 11%; Technical Infrastructure and Operational Practices - 13%; Protection of Information Assets - 25%; Disaster Recovery and Business Continuity - 10%; Business Application System Development, Acquisition, Implementation, and Maintenance - 10%; and Business Process Evaluation and Risk Management - 15%). Additional information about the CISA program is available at www.gleim.com.

**286.** Which of the following are typical responsibilities of a Certified Information Systems Auditor?

I. Evaluation of the IS strategy and the processes for its development
II. Evaluation of the IS policies, standards, and procedures
III. Evaluation of management practices

A. I and III.

B. I and II.

C. II and III.

D. I, II, and III.

Answer (D) is correct. *(CISA, adapted)*

**REQUIRED:** The responsibilities of an IS auditor.

**DISCUSSION:** According to the Information Systems Audit and Control Association (ISACA), the responsibilities of a CISA identified in the content area of *Management, Planning, and Organization of IS* include all items listed as well as evaluation of the IS organization and structure and evaluation of the selection and management of third-party services.

**287.** Which of the following statements best describes the data processing technical requirements for IS auditors? IS auditors should

A. Be as technically proficient as the people they audit.

B. Conduct audits in accordance with generally accepted IS audit standards.

C. Only possess a limited amount of technical knowledge, mainly in the area of current buzzwords.

D. Only possess a knowledge of auditing and controls.

Answer (B) is correct. *(CISA, adapted)*

**REQUIRED:** The statement that best describes the technical requirements of IS auditors.

**DISCUSSION:** According to ISACA, the IS auditor should conduct audits in accordance with generally accepted IS audit standards and guidelines to ensure that the organization's information technology and business systems are adequately controlled, monitored, and assessed.

Answer (A) is incorrect because IS auditors can rely on the work of technical specialists in those areas for which they are not as proficient as the people they are auditing. Answer (C) is incorrect because IS auditors need more than a limited amount of data processing knowledge. Answer (D) is incorrect because IS auditors need more than knowledge of auditing and controls.

**288.** The first step the IS audit manager should take when preparing the annual IS audit plan is to

A. Meet with the audit committee members to discuss the IS audit plan for the upcoming year.

B. Ensure that the IS audit staff is competent in areas that are likely to appear on the plan and provide training as necessary.

C. Assess the overall risks and develop objectives.

D. Begin with the prior year's IS audit plan and carry over any IS audit steps that have not been completed.

Answer (C) is correct. *(CISA, adapted)*

**REQUIRED:** The first step in the annual audit plan.

**DISCUSSION:** The first step in an IS audit is to assess the overall risks and develop an audit program which consists of control objectives and audit procedures which should satisfy those objectives.

Answer (A) is incorrect because the IS audit manager would not meet with the audit committee until a risk analysis of areas of exposure has been completed. Answer (B) is incorrect because the IS audit manager does not know what areas are to appear on the IS audit plan until a risk analysis is completed and discussions are held with the audit committee members. Answer (D) is incorrect because a risk analysis would be the first step before any IS audit effort is expended.

**289.** In which of the following areas is an internal IS auditor expected to draw upon the work of an external auditor?

A. Safeguarding of company assets.

B. Accuracy and reliability of accounting records.

C. Promotion of operational efficiency.

D. Adherence to company policies and legal obligations.

Answer (B) is correct. *(CISA, adapted)*

**REQUIRED:** The area in which the IS auditor would draw on the work of the external auditor.

**DISCUSSION:** External auditors express opinions on the fairness of the financial statements. Thus, the internal IS auditor would most likely draw on the work of the external auditor for assurances about the reliability of the accounting records.

Answer (A) is incorrect because an external auditor would not be relied upon to safeguard company assets. Answer (C) is incorrect because external auditors typically do not evaluate operational efficiencies unless specifically engaged to do so. External auditors' procedures are limited to those considered necessary to form an opinion on the fairness of the financial statements. Answer (D) is incorrect because, whereas external auditors may review adherence to company policies and legal obligations in specific situations, their review is limited to those procedures considered necessary to express an audit opinion.

**290.** Monitoring environmental controls includes which of the following?

I. Evaluating digital signature techniques
II. Evaluating fire suppression systems
III. Evaluating the uninterruptible power supply (UPS)

A. I and III.

B. I and II.

C. I, II, and III.

D. II and III.

Answer (D) is correct. *(CISA, adapted)*

**REQUIRED:** The activities related to environmental controls.

**DISCUSSION:** Environmental controls relate to the physical aspects of the IT infrastructure and include fire suppression and the uninterruptible power supply.

**291.** The audit objective of an IS resource management evaluation is to provide assurance that

A. The IS manager practices effective, efficient, and economic support to the organization's business objectives.

B. Organizational resources of time and money are used in the most economical manner during the acquisition of hardware and software.

C. Appropriate control features are included in systems hardware and software.

D. All tasks have been computerized.

Answer (A) is correct. *(CISA, adapted)*

**REQUIRED:** The audit objective of an IS resource management evaluation.

**DISCUSSION:** The audit objective of an IS resource management evaluation is to analyze and evaluate the information systems (IS) strategy, policies and procedures, management practices, and organization structures. The process includes evaluation of management's actions relating to the use of resources.

Answer (B) is incorrect because the audit objective of an IS resource management review is not limited to acquisition of hardware and software. Answer (C) is incorrect because whether appropriate control features are included in systems hardware and software does not relate to resource management but to control issues. Answer (D) is incorrect because proper processing methods should be evaluated using cost and benefit criteria.

**292.** A primary purpose of an input-output control module in an operating system is to assure that

A. Read and write requests are properly executed.

B. A record is maintained of all file accesses.

C. Control modules are held to near size.

D. Hardware errors are recorded promptly.

Answer (A) is correct. *(CISA, adapted)*

**REQUIRED:** The purpose of an input-output control module in an operating system.

**DISCUSSION:** Input-output controls are concerned with the reading and writing of data. They should be used to determine if read and write requests are properly executed.

Answer (B) is incorrect because a console log is used to record file accesses and processing. Answer (C) is incorrect because holding control modules to near size is nonsensical in this context. Answer (D) is incorrect because hardware errors are detected by hardware controls, not by input-output controls.

**293.** To ensure privacy in a public key encryption system, knowledge of which of the following keys is required to decode the received message?

I. Private
II. Public

A. I.
B. II.
C. Both I and II.
D. Neither I nor II.

Answer (A) is correct. *(CISA, adapted)*

**REQUIRED:** The key(s) required to decode messages in a public key system to ensure privacy.

**DISCUSSION:** In a public key system, the public key is used to encrypt the message prior to transmission, and the private key is needed to decrypt (decode) the message.

Answer (B) is incorrect because the private key, not the public key, is needed to decrypt (decode) the message. Answer (C) is incorrect because the public key is not needed. Answer (D) is incorrect because the private key is needed to decrypt (decode) the message.

**294.** Which of the following types of transmission media are most secure against unauthorized access or tapping?

A. Copper wire.
B. Twisted pair.
C. Fiber-optic cables.
D. Coaxial cables.

Answer (C) is correct. *(CISA, adapted)*

**REQUIRED:** The most secure transmission medium.

**DISCUSSION:** Fiber-optic cables have been proven to be more tamper resistant than the other media listed. Optical transmissions cannot be wiretapped.

Answer (A) is incorrect because copper wire can be tapped easily with inexpensive equipment. Answer (B) is incorrect because twisted pair can be tapped easily with inexpensive equipment. Answer (D) is incorrect because coaxial cables can be tapped easily with inexpensive equipment.

**295.** Each of the following statements about distributed data processing (DDP) systems is true except

A. From the IS auditor's perspective, it is a desirable trend in DDP systems design to off-load operating system and communication functions from software into hardware or microcode.
B. DDP systems are essentially unauditable because of the complexity of network software.
C. DDP systems increase the need for effective risk analysis.
D. An important design goal of DDP systems is to provide more power and flexibility to the end users even though inadequate controls may exist in some of the end-user software.

Answer (B) is correct. *(CISA, adapted)*

**REQUIRED:** The false statement concerning DDP systems.

**DISCUSSION:** Technical complexity is not a valid reason for failing to audit a processing system. The IS auditor should have sufficient technical knowledge and training to audit complex networks.

Answer (A) is incorrect because hardware or microcode functions have the advantage of being less prone to unauthorized modification than software. Answer (C) is incorrect because processing may be distributed to numerous user areas, each with varied risk levels and degrees of control, requiring an effective risk analysis methodology to ensure adequate audit coverage for critical functions. Answer (D) is incorrect because end-user software is usually designed for rapid development and ease of modification. It could be susceptible to errors in the hands of an inexperienced user.

**296.** An IS auditor is called as an expert witness by the plaintiff in litigation involving the misuses of a service bureau's computer by an unauthorized individual who used another's password to manipulate data. The IS auditor's testimony regarding security issues should include descriptions of each of the following except the

A. Access control.
B. Method of assignment of passwords.
C. Methods that could prevent similar misuse.
D. Controls that were overridden to gain access.

Answer (C) is correct. *(CISA, adapted)*

**REQUIRED:** The inappropriate testimony by an IS auditor in a case involving unauthorized access to a plaintiff's files.

**DISCUSSION:** The IS auditor is not likely to be able to provide testimony that another method of control would have prevented the unauthorized action. Such testimony is mere speculation by the auditor.

Answer (A) is incorrect because access control concerns procedures germane to the litigation. The auditor's assessments will be important to the plaintiff's case. Answer (B) is incorrect because the method of assignment of passwords is germane to the litigation. Answer (D) is incorrect because controls that were overridden to gain access are germane to the litigation.

**297.** A data center that has installed online communications, a database management system, access control software, and a sophisticated network is planning its first test at the hot site. The first test should include recovery of

A. All systems and application software.

B. Only the operating system.

C. All system software and the network.

D. Only the access control software.

Answer (B) is correct. *(CISA, adapted)*

**REQUIRED:** The purpose of an initial test at a data center's hot site.

**DISCUSSION:** A hot site is typically a service bureau where a data center can obtain processing services in case of a disaster. The more common commercial hot sites limit the amount of time a subscriber can be present to perform testing. Thus, an organization's best approach is to attempt to recover the operating system first because it is the nucleus of all processing.

Answer (A) is incorrect because the operating system should be recovered before other software. Answer (C) is incorrect because the operating system should be recovered before the network. Answer (D) is incorrect because the operating system should be recovered before the access control software.

**298.** Which of the following is of most concern when contracting for a hot site as the alternative processing facility?

A. The number of other subscribers to the hot site.

B. Possession by the hot site of the most current version of the operating software.

C. Location of the hot site's offsite storage facility.

D. Number of years the hot site has been in operation.

Answer (A) is correct. *(CISA, adapted)*

**REQUIRED:** The item of most concern when contracting for a hot site.

**DISCUSSION:** The number of other subscribers would affect the availability of facilities at the hot site. The computer resources provided should be adequate to perform necessary processing.

Answer (B) is incorrect because, if the last update to the operating system is very recent, the hot site may not have upgraded to it. Hence, the company will not want to deal with upgrading the operating system during recovery. Answer (C) is incorrect because assurance as to adequate protection of files, rather than the location of the hot site's offsite storage facility, are of concern. Answer (D) is incorrect because capabilities of a hot site are of greater concern.

**299.** Which of the following are features of security software packages?

I. Provision of an audit trail
II. Backup of critical files
III. Establishment of various levels of protection
IV. Monitoring of accesses to protected resources

A. I and IV.

B. II and III.

C. I, III, and IV.

D. I, II, III, and IV.

Answer (C) is correct. *(CISA, adapted)*

**REQUIRED:** The control features included in security software packages.

**DISCUSSION:** Security software packages typically provide safeguards over unauthorized access and use of hardware and software. Passwords, console logs, dial-up/callback are techniques used to protect an installation.

Answer (A) is incorrect because establishment of various levels of protection is also a feature of security software packages. Answer (B) is incorrect because security software packages do not provide for backing up critical files. However, there may be a feature for backing up the security software files. Answer (D) is incorrect because security software packages do not provide for backing up critical files.

**300.** The critical recovery time period is the length of time

A. The company will process at the alternative site before returning to the data center.

B. The company can do without IS services before business is significantly affected.

C. Covered by the offsite rotation cycle for backup files.

D. The recovery team will need to work together in a disaster condition.

Answer (B) is correct. *(CISA, adapted)*

**REQUIRED:** The definition of critical recovery time.

**DISCUSSION:** The critical recovery time period is the time in which the company must recover IS services before the disaster has a significant negative effect on its ability to continue in existence.

Answer (A) is incorrect because the time the company will process at the alternative site before returning to the data center is less critical than the time the company can do without IS services before business is significantly affected. Answer (C) is incorrect because the time covered by the offsite rotation cycle for backup files is less critical than the time the company can do without IS services before business is significantly affected. Answer (D) is incorrect because the time the recovery team will need to work together in a disaster condition is less critical than the time the company can do without IS services before business is significantly affected.

**301.** The IS auditor finds that data communications are subject to message encryption and that effective controls have been designed for the encryption and decryption processes. Based on this finding, tests of controls should be carried out to ensure that

A. The network has an effective mechanism for determining whether all parts of a message sent are received.

B. The X.25 interface standard is being correctly applied during encryption and decryption.

C. Authorized encryption and decryption procedures are being adhered to in practice.

D. Messages sent by way of satellite transmissions are not dispersed over too wide a receiving area.

Answer (C) is correct. *(CISA, adapted)*

**REQUIRED:** The purpose of compliance tests (tests of controls).

**DISCUSSION:** Tests of controls evaluate the effectiveness of the operation of controls. The auditor has concluded that the encryption controls have been adequately designed, but tests must be conducted to see if they are being applied as intended.

Answer (A) is incorrect because testing to ensure that the network has an effective mechanism for determining whether all parts of a message sent are received can be performed during the evaluation of the design of the controls. Answer (B) is incorrect because the X.25 interface standard is only one of many controls that should be tested for effectiveness. Answer (D) is incorrect because determining that messages sent by way of satellite transmissions are not dispersed over too wide a receiving area is only one of many tests of effectiveness that should be performed.

**302.** An appropriate control technique for a data communications security review is to ensure that

A. Messages transmitted over secure media are always encrypted.

B. User authentication mechanisms are used with stand-alone personal computer installations.

C. Telecommunication system commands can be entered only from the master console.

D. Sensitive messages are always transmitted bit by bit, enclosed between a start bit and a stop bit.

Answer (C) is correct. *(CISA, adapted)*

**REQUIRED:** The appropriate technique for a data communications security review.

**DISCUSSION:** To assure security, systems commands should be made only from the master control console. In addition, a computer-generated log should be maintained of all systems modifications.

Answer (A) is incorrect because encryption may not be cost beneficial for nonsensitive data. Answer (B) is incorrect because user authentication mechanisms should be used on all systems, not just personal computer installations. Answer (D) is incorrect because transmissions are usually in packets of data rather than bit by bit.

**303.** As transactions to update an online sales order system are processed, the transactions are copied to a transaction log. At the end of the day, the sales order entry disk files are copied to a backup tape. During the backup procedure, the disk file containing the sales order system failed, and the file was lost. Which, if any, of the following are required to restore the online sales order system?

I. The previous day's backup file.
II. The previous day's transaction log.
III. The current day's transaction log.
IV. None. The system cannot be restored.

A. IV only.

B. I and III.

C. I and II.

D. I, II, and III.

Answer (B) is correct. *(CISA, adapted)*

**REQUIRED:** The file(s) required to restore the online sales order system.

**DISCUSSION:** The previous day's backup file will be the most current backup of the result of processing up until that time. The current day's transaction log will contain all of the activity since that time. The combination of these two files will allow restoration of the system.

Answer (A) is incorrect because restoration is possible. Answer (C) is incorrect because the previous day's transaction file includes the activity that has been included on the previous day's system backup file. Answer (D) is incorrect because the previous day's transaction file includes the activity that has been included on the previous day's system backup file.

**304.** Why would the IS auditor of a company that is considering contracting its data processing needs to a service bureau request a copy of each candidate bureau's financial statements?

A. To evaluate the fairness of each service bureau's charges on the basis of relative profit margins.

B. To determine whether each service bureau is affiliated with a company that might represent a conflict of interests.

C. To evaluate each service bureau's financial stability and ability to fulfill the contract.

D. To obtain an understanding of the processing performed by each service bureau and the controls within the system.

Answer (C) is correct. *(CISA, adapted)*

**REQUIRED:** The purpose of requesting financial statements from a service bureau.

**DISCUSSION:** A primary concern of a company contracting for its data processing needs is whether the service bureau has the financial stability to perform its contract. One means of assessing financial stability is to analyze the bureau's financial statements.

Answer (A) is incorrect because the financial statements do not disclose the relative profit margins by types of service provided. Answer (B) is incorrect because the financial statements are not the best source of such information. Answer (D) is incorrect because marketing literature of the service bureau provides a description of the services offered.

**305.** The results of a generalized audit software simulation of the aging of accounts receivable revealed substantial differences in the aging distribution, even though grand totals reconciled. Which of the following should the IS auditor do first to resolve the discrepancy?

A. Recreate the test, using different software.

B. List a sample of actual data to verify the accuracy of the test program.

C. Ignore the discrepancy because the grand totals reconcile and instruct the controller to correct the program.

D. Create test transactions and run test data on both the production and simulation programs.

Answer (B) is correct. *(CISA, adapted)*

**REQUIRED:** The first step an IS auditor should take when illogical results are obtained from a GAS package.

**DISCUSSION:** Actual data are easily obtained and can be compared with the aging schedule to assess the integrity of the simulation program's logic.

Answer (A) is incorrect because only if it were determined that the program was corrupted would substitute software be required. Answer (C) is incorrect because the auditor has reason to believe that errors may exist and should determine the reasons for the discrepancy. Answer (D) is incorrect because this expensive procedure will not be justified until the data from the simulation have been checked.

# STUDY UNIT SIX
# STATISTICAL SAMPLING



This study unit covers statistical sampling applications for auditing. Statistical sampling permits auditors to measure and control the risk associated with examining only a part (a sample) of the items (the population) under audit.

Consider the following when performing a **test of controls** involving sampling:

1. Planning the sample requires consideration of
   a. The relation of the sample to the objective of the test
   b. The tolerable rate of deviations that would support the assessed level of control risk
   c. Allowable risk of assessing control risk too low
   d. Characteristics of the population
2. Sample selection should be representative. All items should have a chance to be selected.
3. Performance and evaluation
   a. The effects of limitations on tests of controls should be considered.
   b. The sample deviation rate is the best estimate of the population deviation rate.
   c. If the sample does not support the planned assessed level of control risk for an assertion, the nature, timing, and extent of substantive tests may need to be reevaluated.

Consider the following when performing a **substantive test** involving sampling:

1. Planning the sample requires consideration of
   a. The relevant audit objectives and characteristics of the population
   b. Preliminary materiality judgments as to tolerable misstatement
   c. Allowable risk of incorrect acceptance for the substantive test of details
2. Sample selection should be conducted so that the sample represents the population. Consequently, all items should have an opportunity to be chosen.
3. Performance and evaluation
   a. Appropriate audit procedures are applied to each sample item.
   b. The auditor must project the quantitative misstatement results of the sample to the population and compare it with tolerable misstatement.
   c. Projected misstatements, known misstatements detected by nonsampling tests, and other audit evidence should be considered in the aggregate in determining whether the financial statements are materially misstated.

Textbooks, firm literature, professional exams, and auditing standards often use different vocabulary for the same concept. However, if you study the questions and answer explanations in this study unit, you should be able to cope effectively with differences among the terms you encounter. The two terms defined on the next page cause considerable misunderstanding.

**Confidence level or reliability** is the estimated percentage of repeated simple random samples of size n that will adequately represent a normally distributed population. Thus, a confidence level of 90% indicates that samples should adequately represent the population about 90% of the time. Confidence level is related to audit risk. When an auditor accepts a confidence level of 90%, it indicates that the auditor is accepting a risk of 10% (100% – 90%) that the sample will not represent the population.

In sampling for variables (substantive testing), the primary concern is the "risk of incorrect acceptance," or "the risk that the sample supports the conclusion that the recorded account balance is not materially misstated when it is materially misstated" (AU 350, *Audit Sampling*). In sampling for attributes (tests of controls), the primary concern is "the risk of assessing control risk too low," or "the risk that the assessed level of control risk based on the sample is less than the true operating effectiveness of the control." In other words, the risk of assessing control risk too low is that internal control is actually less effective than indicated by the sample. These wrong conclusions relate to effectiveness issues. They are termed Type II or beta errors.

**Precision or confidence interval (allowance for sampling risk)** is an interval around the sample statistic (for example, the mean) that is expected to contain the true value of the population. In principle, given repeated sampling and a normally distributed population, the confidence level is the percentage of all the precision intervals that may be constructed from simple random samples of size n that will include the population value. In practice, the confidence level is regarded as the probability that a precision interval will contain the population value.

The estimated size of the precision interval is based upon the tolerable deviation rate for a test of controls. In sampling for attributes (tests of controls), precision may be estimated by subtracting the expected deviation rate from the tolerable rate in the population.

In sampling for variables (substantive testing), planned precision is determined by considering tolerable misstatement in conjunction with the risks of incorrect acceptance and incorrect rejection. Tolerable misstatement should not exceed the auditor's preliminary judgments about materiality. The risk of incorrect acceptance is defined above. The risk of incorrect rejection is defined as "the risk that the sample supports the conclusion that the recorded account balance is materially misstated when it is not materially misstated" (a Type I or alpha error). The risk of incorrect rejection relates to efficiency issues because the auditor will likely continue auditing until the balance is finally supported. A table is typically consulted to determine the appropriate precision as a percentage of tolerable misstatement.

The following symbols and abbreviations are used in this study unit:

P -- required precision interval
C -- confidence coefficient
σ -- (sigma) population standard deviation
s -- sample standard deviation
p -- deviation rate
q -- 100% minus p
n -- sample size
N -- population size
μ -- population mean or average
x -- an observed value

$\bar{x}$ -- mean of a sample
FPC -- finite population correction factor
Σ -- summation symbol
AR -- allowable audit risk
CR -- control risk
TD -- allowable risk of incorrect acceptance for a test of details
AP -- detection risk for analytical procedures and other relevant substantive tests of details
IR -- inherent risk

## QUESTIONS

### 6.1 Purpose and Rationale of Statistical Sampling

**1.** AU 350, *Audit Sampling,* identifies two general approaches to audit sampling. They are

A. Random and nonrandom.

B. Statistical and nonstatistical.

C. Precision and reliability.

D. Risk and nonrisk.

Answer (B) is correct. *(Publisher)*

**REQUIRED:** The two approaches to audit sampling.

**DISCUSSION:** Statistical sampling allows the auditor to control and measure risk associated with observing only a portion of a population. However, the choice of nonstatistical or statistical sampling does not directly affect the auditor's decisions about the auditing procedures to be applied, the competence of the evidence obtained with respect to sample items, or the actions that might be taken given the nature and causes of particular misstatements. Either approach, properly applied, can provide sufficient competent evidence.

Answer (A) is incorrect because random selection is necessary in statistical sampling so that the sample will represent the population. Answer (C) is incorrect because precision is the allowance for sampling risk, and reliability is the degree to which the sample is expected to be representative. Answer (D) is incorrect because all sampling involves risk.

**2.** In a sampling application, the group of items about which the auditor wants to estimate some characteristic is called the

A. Population.

B. Attribute of interest.

C. Sample.

D. Sampling unit.

Answer (A) is correct. *(CIA, adapted)*

**REQUIRED:** The group of items about which an auditor wants to draw conclusions.

**DISCUSSION:** The population is the group of items about which an auditor wishes to draw conclusions. However, the difference between the targeted population (the population about which information is desired) and the sampled population (the population from which the sample is actually drawn) should be understood.

Answer (B) is incorrect because the attribute is the characteristic of the population the auditor wants to estimate. Answer (C) is incorrect because the sample is a subset of the population used to estimate the characteristic. Answer (D) is incorrect because a sampling unit is the item that is actually selected for examination. It is a subset of the population.

**3.** An advantage of statistical sampling over nonstatistical sampling is that statistical sampling helps an auditor to

A. Minimize the failure to detect errors and fraud.

B. Eliminate nonsampling risk.

C. Reduce the level of audit risk and materiality to a relatively low amount.

D. Measure the sufficiency of the evidential matter obtained.

Answer (D) is correct. *(CPA, adapted)*

**REQUIRED:** The advantage of statistical sampling.

**DISCUSSION:** Statistical sampling helps the auditor to design an efficient sample, to measure the sufficiency of the evidence obtained, and to evaluate the sample results. The third standard of field work requires auditors to obtain sufficient competent evidence. Sufficiency relates to the design and size of the sample. Statistical sampling permits the auditors to measure sampling risk and therefore to design more efficient samples, that is, samples of a size necessary to provide sufficient evidence.

Answer (A) is incorrect because, in some circumstances, professional judgment may indicate that nonstatistical methods are preferable to minimize the failure to detect errors and fraud. Answer (B) is incorrect because statistical sampling is irrelevant to nonsampling risk. Answer (C) is incorrect because statistical sampling does not reduce materiality.

**4.** When using sampling for substantive tests of details, the auditor must do all but which of the following?

A. Determine the tolerable misstatement.

B. Project sample misstatement results to the population.

C. Compute the sample standard deviation.

D. Select a representative sample.

Answer (C) is correct. *(J. Swearingen)*

**REQUIRED:** The procedure not required in sampling.

**DISCUSSION:** AU 350 does not require that the sample standard deviation be calculated. The computation would be necessary if parametric statistical sampling were used, but statistical sampling is not required by AU 350.

Answer (A) is incorrect because evaluation in monetary terms of the sample results is related to the auditor's judgments. The maximum monetary misstatement that does not cause the financial statements to be materially misstated is the tolerable misstatement. An estimate of tolerable misstatement is vital to planning the audit. Answer (B) is incorrect because AU 350 requires that misstatement projected from the sample be compared with tolerable misstatement, with appropriate consideration given to sampling risk. Answer (D) is incorrect because AU 350 also requires that samples be representative. Thus, all population items should have an opportunity to be chosen.

**5.** The application of statistical sampling techniques is least related to which of the following generally accepted auditing standards?

A. The work is to be adequately planned and assistants, if any, are to be properly supervised.

B. In all matters relating to the assignment, an independence in mental attitude is to be maintained by the auditor.

C. A sufficient understanding of internal control is to be obtained to plan the audit and to determine the nature, timing, and extent of tests to be performed.

D. Sufficient competent evidential matter is to be obtained through inspection, observation, inquiries, and confirmations to afford a reasonable basis for an opinion regarding the financial statements under audit.

Answer (B) is correct. *(CPA, adapted)*

**REQUIRED:** The standard to which statistical sampling is least related.

**DISCUSSION:** The second general standard (independence) concerns the mental attitude to be maintained by an auditor in all matters pertaining to the assignment. The application of statistical sampling techniques is more closely related to the standards of field work.

Answer (A) is incorrect because auditors should plan to use statistical sampling and supervise its implementation. Answer (C) is incorrect because statistical methods may be used for tests of controls as well as substantive tests. Answer (D) is incorrect because auditing standards contemplate the use of statistical techniques in gathering evidential matter.

**6.** An auditor suspects that the invoices from a small number of vendors contain serious misstatements and therefore limits the sample to those vendors only. A major disadvantage of selecting such a directed sample of items to examine is the

A. Difficulty in obtaining sample items.

B. Inability to quantify the sampling error related to the total population of vendor invoices.

C. Absence of a normal distribution.

D. Tendency to sample a greater number of units.

Answer (B) is correct. *(CIA, adapted)*

**REQUIRED:** The disadvantage of a directed sample.

**DISCUSSION:** Judgment sampling uses the auditor's subjective judgment to determine the sample size (number of items examined) and sample selection (which items to examine). This subjectivity is not always a weakness. The auditor, based on other audit work, may be able to test the most material and risky transactions and to emphasize the types of transactions subject to high control risk. Probability (random) sampling provides an objective method of determining sample size and selecting the items to be examined. Unlike judgment sampling, it also provides a means of quantitatively assessing precision and reliability.

Answer (A) is incorrect because obtaining invoices for a small number of vendors should be simple. Answer (C) is incorrect because the sampling distribution is expected to be normal even if the population distribution is not. Answer (D) is incorrect because judgment sampling provides no objective means for determining the appropriate sample size. Thus, it has no tendency to sample a greater number of units.

## 6.2 Sampling Concepts

**7.** If the size of the sample to be used in a particular test of attributes has not been determined by using statistical concepts, but the sample has been chosen in accordance with random selection procedures,

A. No inferences can be drawn from the sample.

B. The auditor has caused nonsampling risk to increase.

C. The auditor may or may not achieve desired precision at the desired level of confidence.

D. The auditor will have to evaluate the results by reference to the principles of discovery sampling.

Answer (C) is correct. *(CPA, adapted)*

**REQUIRED:** The significance of choosing sample size without regard to statistical concepts.

**DISCUSSION:** According to the sample size formula for attribute sampling, the size of an attribute sample is a function of the auditor's desired precision, his/her desired level of confidence, the expected deviation rate, and the size of the population. When the auditor does not use these criteria to determine sample size, (s)he runs a risk of not meeting the audit objectives.

Answer (A) is incorrect because inferences can be drawn from both statistical and nonstatistical samples. Answer (B) is incorrect because nonsampling risk includes all aspects of audit risk not arising from sampling, e.g., misapplying a procedure or choosing an inappropriate procedure. Answer (D) is incorrect because discovery sampling is a special form of attribute sampling used to discover critical deviations.

**8.** An auditee uses statistical sampling in the taking of its physical inventory. The independent external auditor should

A. Either observe a statistical inventory count each year or qualify or disclaim an opinion.

B. Either observe a complete inventory count sometime during the year and become satisfied that the statistical procedures are valid or qualify or disclaim an opinion.

C. Observe such test counts as (s)he deems necessary and become satisfied with the statistical validity of the sample, the precision, and the confidence level.

D. Insist that the company take a complete physical inventory annually and observe the count.

Answer (C) is correct. *(Publisher)*

**REQUIRED:** The responsibility of an auditor regarding statistical sampling in the taking of physical inventory.

**DISCUSSION:** Statistical methods for determining inventory quantities are sufficiently reliable to make a complete annual physical count unnecessary. However, "the auditor must be satisfied that the sampling plan is reasonable and statistically valid, that it has been properly applied, and that the results are reasonable in the circumstances." The auditor should still make or observe test counts as (s)he deems necessary (AU 331, *Inventories*).

Answer (A) is incorrect because the auditor must be present only to observe such test counts as (s)he deems necessary and must be satisfied as to the effectiveness of the counting procedures used. Answer (B) is incorrect because observation of a complete count may not be necessary. Answer (D) is incorrect because, if the auditor determines the statistical plan to be valid, etc., (s)he will not insist that the client take a complete annual physical inventory.

**9.** To quantify the risk that sample evidence leads to erroneous conclusions about the sampled population,

A. Each item in the sampled population must have an equal chance of being selected.

B. Each item in the sampled population must have a chance of being selected that is proportional to its book value.

C. Each item in the sampled population must have an equal or known probability of being selected.

D. The precise number of items in the population must be known.

Answer (C) is correct. *(CIA, adapted)*

**REQUIRED:** The requirement for quantifying sampling risk.

**DISCUSSION:** Probability (random) sampling is used in any sampling plan in which every item in the population has an equal (or known) and nonzero probability of being chosen. A probability sample permits the use of statistical methods based on the laws of probability to quantify an estimate of sampling risk.

Answer (A) is incorrect because sampling risk can be quantified when purely random sampling is not used if the probability of selection is known and nonzero. Stratified random sampling is an example. Answer (B) is incorrect because each item in the sampled population must have a chance of being selected that is proportional to its book value in dollar-unit sampling, but this characteristic does not apply to other methods. Answer (D) is incorrect because sampling risk for an infinite population is quantifiable.

**10.** Each time an auditor draws a conclusion based on evidence from a sample, an additional risk, sampling risk, is introduced. An example of sampling risk is

A. Projecting the results of sampling beyond the population tested.

B. Properly applying an improper audit procedure to sample data.

C. Improperly applying a proper audit procedure to sample data.

D. Drawing an erroneous conclusion from sample data.

Answer (D) is correct. *(CIA, adapted)*

**REQUIRED:** The example of sampling risk.

**DISCUSSION:** Sampling risk arises from the possibility that the conclusion drawn may differ from that reached if the test had been applied to all items in the population. It is the risk that a particular sample may contain proportionately more or fewer monetary misstatements or deviations from prescribed controls than exist in the balance or class as a whole (AU 350).

Answer (A) is incorrect because sample results are relevant only to the population tested. Improper projection of results is a nonsampling risk. Answer (B) is incorrect because sampling risk arises even though the proper procedure is correctly applied and the results are evaluated appropriately. Thus, choice of the wrong procedure is a nonsampling risk. Answer (C) is incorrect because sampling risk arises even though the proper procedure is correctly applied and the results are evaluated appropriately. Thus, improper application of the right procedure is a nonsampling risk.

**11.** Several risks are inherent in the evaluation of audit evidence that has been obtained through the use of statistical sampling. An example of a beta or Type II error related to sampling risk is the failure to

A. Properly define the population to be sampled.

B. Draw a random sample from the population.

C. Reject the statistical hypothesis that a carrying amount is not materially misstated when the true carrying amount is materially misstated.

D. Accept the statistical hypothesis that a carrying amount is not materially misstated when the true carrying amount is not materially misstated.

Answer (C) is correct. *(CIA, adapted)*

**REQUIRED:** The example of beta or Type II error.

**DISCUSSION:** In hypothesis testing, the rejection of a true hypothesis is an alpha or Type I error. Failure to reject a false hypothesis is a beta or Type II error. Both kinds of errors are aspects of sampling risk. Incorrect acceptance, for example, is a beta or Type II error. If an account balance is erroneously accepted as fairly stated based upon a sample, additional audit work and the chances of exposing the mistake will probably be minimal. Hence, a beta error is more serious than an alpha (Type I) error (incorrect rejection leading to further audit work).

Answer (A) is incorrect because sampling risk is defined narrowly as the risk that audit conclusions based on a sample may differ from those based on testing all items in a population. Nonsampling risk consists of all other aspects of audit risk. Thus, the risk of mistakes in taking a sample is an aspect of nonsampling risk. Answer (B) is incorrect because failure to draw a random sample is related to nonsampling risk. Answer (D) is incorrect because incorrect rejection of a value is an alpha error.

**12.** A confidence level of 90% means that

A. The expected deviation rate is equal to 10%.

B. The point estimate obtained is within 10% of the true population value.

C. The probability is 90% that the sample results will not vary from the true characteristics of the population by more than a specified amount.

D. A larger sample size is required than if the desired confidence level were equal to 95%.

Answer (C) is correct. *(CIA, adapted)*

**REQUIRED:** The meaning of a 90% confidence level.

**DISCUSSION:** A 90% confidence level signifies that, in repeated sampling from a normally distributed population, the precision intervals constructed around the results of simple random samples of size n will contain the true population value approximately 90% of the time.

Answer (A) is incorrect because the confidence level is a probability, not a deviation rate or a range of values. For attribute sampling (used in tests of controls), the complement of a 90% confidence level is a 10% risk of assessing control risk too low. For variables sampling (used in substantive testing), the complement of a 90% confidence level is a 10% risk of incorrect rejection. Answer (B) is incorrect because the confidence level is a probability, not a deviation rate or a range of values. For attribute sampling (used in tests of controls), the complement of a 90% confidence level is a 10% risk of assessing control risk too low. For variables sampling (used in substantive testing), the complement of a 90% confidence level is a 10% risk of incorrect rejection. Answer (D) is incorrect because a smaller sample is required if the desired confidence level is 90% rather than 95%.

**13.** When planning a sample for a substantive test of details, an auditor should consider tolerable misstatement for the sample. This consideration should

A. Be related to the auditor's business risk.

B. Not be adjusted for qualitative factors.

C. Be related to preliminary judgments about materiality levels.

D. Not be changed during the audit process.

Answer (C) is correct. *(CPA, adapted)*

**REQUIRED:** The true statement about tolerable misstatement.

**DISCUSSION:** When planning a sample for substantive tests, the auditor should consider how much monetary misstatement in the related account balance or class of transactions may exist without causing the financial statements to be materially misstated. This maximum monetary misstatement is the tolerable misstatement for the sample. It is used in audit planning to determine the necessary precision and sample size. Tolerable misstatement, combined for the entire audit plan, should not exceed the auditor's preliminary judgments about materiality (AU 350).

Answer (A) is incorrect because the auditor's business risk is irrelevant. Answer (B) is incorrect because qualitative factors should be considered; for example, the nature and cause of misstatements and their relationship to other phases of the audit. Answer (D) is incorrect because, if sample results suggest that planning assumptions were unsound, the auditor should take appropriate action.

**14.** As lower acceptable levels of both audit risk and materiality are established, the auditor should plan more work on individual accounts to

A. Find smaller misstatements.

B. Find larger misstatements.

C. Increase the tolerable misstatement in the accounts.

D. Decrease the risk of assessing control risk too low.

Answer (A) is correct. *(CPA, adapted)*

**REQUIRED:** The result of lowering acceptable audit risk and materiality.

**DISCUSSION:** A lower acceptable level of materiality means that the tolerable misstatement in an account is smaller. As a result, the auditor must plan for a larger sample size and therefore more audit work on the accounts to discover smaller misstatements. Moreover, the lower the allowable audit risk that tolerable misstatement will be undetected after the auditor has completed all procedures deemed necessary, the lower the allowable risk of incorrect acceptance, and the greater the required sample size.

Answer (B) is incorrect because the auditor should plan to find smaller misstatements. Answer (C) is incorrect because, as the size of a material misstatement decreases, the level of tolerable misstatement decreases. Answer (D) is incorrect because, during substantive testing of an account balance, the auditor is ultimately concerned with decreasing the risk of incorrectly accepting the balance. Tests of controls, not substantive tests, are designed to decrease the risk of assessing control risk too low.

**15.** An auditor's statistical sample drawn from a population of invoices indicates a mean value of $150 and sampling precision of ± $30 at a 95% confidence level. Which of the following statements correctly interprets these sample data?

A. In repeated sampling, the point estimate of the true population mean will be $150 about 95% of the time.

B. The probability is 95% that the true population mean is $150.

C. In repeated sampling, intervals with precision ± $30 around the sample mean will always contain the true population mean.

D. The probability is 95% that the range $120 to $180 contains the true population mean.

Answer (D) is correct. *(CIA, adapted)*

**REQUIRED:** The interpretation of the sample data.

**DISCUSSION:** The relationship between the estimated mean, the precision interval, and the confidence level is that the auditor can state, at the desired confidence level given a simple random sample of size n taken from a normally distributed population, that the precision interval (the sample mean ± the precision amount) contains the true population mean. Here, the auditor is 95% confident that the interval $120 to $180 ($150 ± $30) contains the true population mean.

Answer (A) is incorrect because repeated samples will result in many different point estimates. Answer (B) is incorrect because the probability is 95% that the range $120 to $180 contains the true population value, not that this value is equal to the point estimate of $150. Answer (C) is incorrect because the probability is 95%, not 100%.

**16.** In statistical sampling for variables, setting the appropriate confidence level and desired sample precision are decisions made by the auditor that will affect sample size for a substantive test. Which of the following should not be a factor in the choice of desired precision?

A. The sampling risk.

B. The size of an account balance misstatement considered material.

C. The audit resources available for execution of the sampling plan.

D. The objective of the audit test being conducted.

Answer (C) is correct. *(CIA, adapted)*

**REQUIRED:** The factor not considered when selecting desired precision.

**DISCUSSION:** The basic sample size equation for variables sampling is

$$n = \frac{C^2 \sigma^2}{P^2}$$

P is the average precision (per item in the population), C is the confidence coefficient, $\sigma$ is the population standard deviation, and n is the sample size. C is the number of standard deviations in the standard normal distribution that corresponds to the specified confidence level. Thus, it controls sampling risk. The tolerable misstatement is related to materiality judgments. It determines the estimated precision. A table is ordinarily consulted to determine precision as a percentage of tolerable misstatement. The objective of the audit sample affects both sampling risk and precision. The audit resources available determine whether the test will be undertaken but should not affect the process once the audit procedure is undertaken.

Answer (A) is incorrect because sampling risk is a factor in calculating desired precision. Answer (B) is incorrect because materiality is a factor in calculating desired precision. Answer (D) is incorrect because the objective of the audit test is a factor in calculating desired precision.

**17.** Which one of the following statements is true regarding two random samples drawn in the same way from the same population, one of size 30 and one of size 300?

A. The two samples would have the same expected value.

B. The larger sample is more likely to produce a large sample mean.

C. The smaller sample will have a smaller 95% confidence interval for the mean.

D. The smaller sample will, on the average, produce a lower estimate of the variance of the population.

Answer (A) is correct. *(CIA, adapted)*

**REQUIRED:** The true statement about random samples of different size.

**DISCUSSION:** The expected value of a random sample of any size is equal to the population mean.

Answer (B) is incorrect because the larger sample is more reliable but both samples will produce an unbiased estimate of the population mean. Answer (C) is incorrect because the smaller sample is less reliable and therefore will have a wider 95% confidence interval. Answer (D) is incorrect because the variance is also a population parameter, and the expected value of the sample variance does not change with sample size.

**18.** The accounting department reports the accounts payable balance as $175,000. You are willing to accept that balance if it is within $15,000 of the actual balance. Using a variables sampling plan, you compute a 95% confidence interval of $173,000 to $190,000. You would therefore

A. Find it impossible to determine the acceptability of the balance.

B. Accept the balance but with a lower level of confidence.

C. Take a larger sample before totally rejecting the balance and requiring adjustments.

D. Accept the $175,000 balance because the confidence interval is within the materiality limits.

Answer (D) is correct. *(CIA, adapted)*

**REQUIRED:** The conclusion regarding a balance that is within the computed confidence interval.

**DISCUSSION:** The auditor is willing to accept the carrying amount if it is within $15,000 (the tolerable misstatement) of the population value. The sample mean used to estimate the population value must be $181,500 [($173,000 + $190,000) ÷ 2] because it is at the midpoint of the computed (achieved) confidence interval (precision). This interval is based on a precision (± $8,500) that is well within the tolerable misstatement (materiality limits) of ± $15,000. Thus, the auditor should accept the $175,000 value. The interval based on tolerable misstatement and the narrower achieved precision limits contain this value.

Answer (A) is incorrect because the achieved confidence interval ($173,000 to $190,000) contains the accounts payable balance at the 95% confidence level. Answer (B) is incorrect because the achieved confidence interval ($173,000 to $190,000) contains the accounts payable balance at the 95% confidence level. Answer (C) is incorrect because the auditor does not need to take a larger sample. The carrying amount is acceptable based on the initial sample.

**19.** The measure of variability of a statistical sample that serves as an estimate of the population variability is the

A. Basic precision.

B. Range.

C. Standard deviation.

D. Confidence interval.

Answer (C) is correct. *(CIA, adapted)*

**REQUIRED:** The measure of population variability.

**DISCUSSION:** Variability (dispersion) is measured by the variance, standard deviation, quartile deviations, range, etc., of a sample or population. The population standard deviation (σ) is a measure of the degree of compactness of values. It is used to determine appropriate sample sizes. Given that N equals population size, μ is the population mean, and $x_i$ is an observed value of a population item, the formula is

$$\sigma = \sqrt{\frac{\Sigma (x_i - \mu)^2}{N}}$$

Answer (A) is incorrect because basic precision is the range around the sample value that is expected to contain the true population value. Answer (B) is incorrect because the range is the difference between the largest and smallest values in a sample. It is a crude measure of variability but is not used to estimate population variability. Answer (D) is incorrect because confidence interval is a synonym for precision.

**20.** The variability of a population, as measured by the standard deviation, is the

A. Extent to which the individual values of the items in the population are spread about the mean.

B. Degree of asymmetry of a distribution.

C. Tendency of the means of large samples (at least 30 items) to be normally distributed.

D. Measure of the closeness of a sample estimate to a corresponding population characteristic.

Answer (A) is correct. *(CIA, adapted)*

**REQUIRED:** The definition of standard deviation.

**DISCUSSION:** Standard deviation is a mathematical measure (denoted by σ) of the dispersion of items in a population about its mean.

Answer (B) is incorrect because skewness or asymmetry means that extreme values at one end of the distribution are not balanced by large values at the other end. Answer (C) is incorrect because the central limit theorem states that the distribution of sample means for large samples should be normally distributed even if the underlying population is not. Answer (D) is incorrect because precision is the interval about the sample value that is expected to contain the true value of the population.

**21.** In a sampling application, the standard deviation represents a measure of the

A. Expected deviation rate.

B. Level of confidence desired.

C. Degree of data variability.

D. Extent of precision achieved.

Answer (C) is correct. *(CIA, adapted)*

**REQUIRED:** The definition of standard deviation.

**DISCUSSION:** The standard deviation is a measure of data variability. The population standard deviation is a parameter that equals the square root of the population variance, which equals (for a finite population) the sum of the squared deviations from the mean, divided by the number of items in the population.

Answer (A) is incorrect because the expected deviation rate is associated with attribute sampling. The standard deviation is calculated for variables sampling. Answer (B) is incorrect because the confidence level is determined by auditor judgment. Answer (D) is incorrect because achieved precision in variables sampling is computed using the standard deviation.

**22.** The concept of standard deviation is significant in statistical sampling because

A. The central limit theorem states that repeated samples from a population will produce sample standard deviations that cluster around the actual standard deviation of the population.

B. The sample size for variables estimation is directly related to the magnitude of the population standard deviation.

C. The magnitude of the finite population correction factor is directly related to the magnitude of the standard deviation of the population.

D. Statistical sampling is inappropriate if the standard deviation is very small relative to the mean of the population.

Answer (B) is correct. *(CIA, adapted)*

**REQUIRED:** The significance of the standard deviation.

**DISCUSSION:** The standard deviation is used to calculate sample size in variables sampling applications. The formula is

$$n = \frac{C^2 \sigma^2}{P^2}$$

n is the sample size, C is the confidence coefficient, σ is the standard deviation of the population, and P is the average precision (per item in the population) specified by the auditor. As the population dispersion increases, so does the required sample size.

Answer (A) is incorrect because the central limit theorem relates to means, not standard deviations, of samples. Answer (C) is incorrect because the finite population correction factor is used to adjust the sample size for small populations. Answer (D) is incorrect because, if the standard deviation of the population is small, the result is very accurate estimation.

**23.** The standard deviation of the population is required in the sample size determination formula. However, the true value for the standard deviation of the population is not likely to be known. The auditor usually employs an estimate of this value based upon all the following except

A. A pre-sample.

B. The prior year's audit.

C. The available carrying amounts.

D. Inquiries of management.

Answer (D) is correct. *(Publisher)*

**REQUIRED:** The item not involved in estimating the standard deviation of the population.

**DISCUSSION:** Although inquiries of management are important, management is unlikely to be able to estimate the standard deviation of the population under audit.

Answer (A) is incorrect because one acceptable approach is to determine an estimated population standard deviation from testing a pre-sample of 30-50 items. Once the total sample required is calculated, the pre-sample items can be included as part of the sample. Answer (B) is incorrect because the prior year's audit may provide evidence that might be used as an estimate for the current period. Answer (C) is incorrect because the available carrying amounts (e.g., the accounts receivable balances) may be used to determine the standard deviation of the carrying amounts, which in turn may be employed as a surrogate for the actual but unknown population standard deviation.

**24.** An auditor has taken a large sample from an audit population that is skewed in the sense that it contains a large number of small dollar balances and a small number of large dollar balances. The auditor can conclude

A. The sampling distribution is not normal; thus, PPS sampling based on the Poisson distribution more accurately defines the nature of the population.

B. The sampling distribution is normal; thus, the Z value can be used in evaluating the sample results.

C. The sampling distribution is not normal; thus, attribute sampling is the only alternative statistical tool that can appropriately be used.

D. None of the answers are correct.

Answer (B) is correct. *(CIA, adapted)*

**REQUIRED:** The auditor's conclusion about a skewed population.

**DISCUSSION:** The central limit theorem states that, regardless of the distribution of the population from which random samples are taken, the shape of the sampling distribution of the means approaches the normal distribution as the sample size increases. Hence, Z values (the number of standard deviations in the standard normal distribution needed to provide specified levels of confidence) can be used. Z (sometimes designated as C in the sample-size formula) values represent areas under the curve for the standard normal distribution.

Answer (A) is incorrect because the sampling distribution is deemed to be normal (a continuous distribution). The Poisson distribution approaches the binomial distribution (a discrete distribution) for large samples and thus is related to attribute sampling. Answer (C) is incorrect because the sampling distribution can be normally distributed if a large enough sample size is taken. Moreover, attribute sampling is not appropriate for estimating population values. Answer (D) is incorrect because the sampling distribution is normal.

**25.** Using the following results from a variables sample, compute the standard error of the mean.

Population size = 10,000
Sample size = 144
Sample standard deviation = $24.00
Confidence level = 90% (C = 1.65)
Mean = $84.00

A. $60.00

B. $7.00

C. $3.30

D. $2.00

Answer (D) is correct. *(CIA, adapted)*

**REQUIRED:** The standard error of the mean given results from a variables sample.

**DISCUSSION:** The standard error of the mean equals the population standard deviation divided by the square root of the sample size. To determine achieved precision, the standard error of the mean is multiplied by the confidence coefficient. If the sample standard deviation is used as an estimate of the population standard deviation, the standard error of the mean is

$$\frac{\$24.00}{\sqrt{144}} = \$2.00$$

Answer (A) is incorrect because $60 is a nonsensical number in this context. Answer (B) is incorrect because $7.00 equals the mean ($84) divided by the square root of the sample size (square root of 144). Answer (C) is incorrect because $3.30 is the estimated precision $[(1.65 \times \$24) \div \sqrt{144}]$.

**26.** In performing substantive tests, the auditor is concerned with two risks or errors of sampling:

1. The risk of incorrect rejection (an alpha or Type I error)
2. The risk of incorrect acceptance (a beta or Type II error)

Which of the following is true about alpha and beta errors?

A. The alpha error is of greater concern to the auditor than the beta error.

B. The beta error is of greater concern to the auditor than the alpha error.

C. The beta error and the alpha error are of equal importance to the auditor.

D. Neither the alpha error nor the beta error need be considered by the auditor.

Answer (B) is correct. *(Publisher)*
**REQUIRED:** The relative importance of alpha and beta errors.
**DISCUSSION:** The risk of beta error, that is the risk of incorrect acceptance, relates directly to the ability to detect material misstatements and is therefore of primary concern to the auditor. The risk of incorrect rejection (an alpha error) is that an account balance will be rejected as not fairly presented even though it is not materially misstated. Because the auditor will require additional audit evidence regarding a misstatement, an alpha error is not as serious as a beta error. Conversely, if an account balance is incorrectly accepted as fairly presented based upon a sample (a beta error), additional audit work will probably be minimal, and the chances of detecting the misstatement will be correspondingly reduced.

**27.** While performing a substantive test of details during an audit, the auditor determined that the sample results supported the conclusion that the recorded account balance was materially misstated. It was, in fact, not materially misstated. This situation illustrates the risk of

A. Assessing control risk too low.

B. Assessing control risk too high.

C. Incorrect rejection.

D. Incorrect acceptance.

Answer (C) is correct. *(CPA, adapted)*
**REQUIRED:** The risk of erroneously concluding that a balance is materially misstated.
**DISCUSSION:** The two aspects of sampling risk for a substantive test of details are the risk of incorrect acceptance and the risk of incorrect rejection. The latter "is the risk that the sample supports the conclusion that the recorded account balance is materially misstated when it is not materially misstated" (AU 350).
Answer (A) is incorrect because the risk of assessing control risk too low is an aspect of sampling risk for tests of controls. Answer (B) is incorrect because the risk of assessing control risk too high is an aspect of sampling risk for tests of controls. Answer (D) is incorrect because the risk of incorrect acceptance is the risk that an auditor will erroneously conclude that a balance is not materially misstated.

**28.** In conducting a substantive test of an account balance, an auditor hypothesizes that no material misstatement exists. The risk that sample results will support the hypothesis when a material misstatement actually does exist is the risk of

A. Incorrect rejection.

B. Alpha error.

C. Incorrect acceptance.

D. Type I error.

Answer (C) is correct. *(CIA, adapted)*
**REQUIRED:** The type of risk.
**DISCUSSION:** For a substantive test, the two aspects of sampling risk are the risk of incorrect rejection (alpha or Type I error) and the risk of incorrect acceptance (beta or Type II error). The latter "is the risk that the sample supports the conclusion that the recorded account balance is not materially misstated when it is materially misstated" (AU 350).

**29.** The auditor failed to recognize a deviation included in a sample intended to test controls related to a transaction process. This failure best reflects

A. Statistical risk.

B. Sampling risk.

C. Audit risk.

D. Nonsampling risk.

Answer (D) is correct. *(Publisher)*
**REQUIRED:** The term for the failure to recognize a control deviation.
**DISCUSSION:** Nonsampling risk includes the possibility of the auditor's failure to recognize a misstatement or deviation. Sampling risk results from the application of statistical sampling techniques. Sampling risk arises because fewer than 100% of the items are evaluated. Nonsampling risk includes all the aspects of audit risk that are not caused by sampling (AU 350).
Answer (A) is incorrect because, without examining every item, the exact population parameter cannot be determined, and a statistical risk will result. Answer (B) is incorrect because, without examining every item, the exact population parameter cannot be determined, and a sampling risk will result. Answer (C) is incorrect because audit risk is the risk of concluding that the financial statements are fairly stated when they are not.

**30.** An auditor of a manufacturing company analyzes cost variances incurred in the manufacturing process to determine their statistical significance. Which of the following techniques is most likely to be used for this purpose?

A. Markov chains.

B. Monte Carlo method.

C. Application of probability theory.

D. Sensitivity analysis.

Answer (C) is correct. *(CIA, adapted)*

**REQUIRED:** The technique used to determine the statistical significance of cost variances.

**DISCUSSION:** An auditor may use statistical control charts to determine the significance of variances in a cost accounting system. Control limits are established using probability theory to determine the likelihood that an observed variance indicates the system is out of control. If an observation falls outside the limits, an investigation should be made to determine the cause of the deviation.

Answer (A) is incorrect because Markov chains relate to a decision process. Answer (B) is incorrect because the Monte Carlo method is used in simulation models. Answer (D) is incorrect because sensitivity analysis studies the effect of changing a variable or parameter in a decision process.

**31.** In appraising the results of a statistical sample, the finite population correction (FPC) factor

A. Can be greater than one.

B. Has less effect as the sample becomes a larger proportion of the population.

C. Is needed when sampling is performed with replacement.

D. Is applied to reduce the size of the sample.

Answer (D) is correct. *(CIA, adapted)*

**REQUIRED:** The use of the FPC factor.

**DISCUSSION:** The FPC factor reduces the sample size when it is large relative to the population size (N). The larger the sample size, the greater the probability that extreme values (which greatly affect the sample result) will be included in the sample. Hence, a somewhat smaller sample size is needed than if the population were infinite. An approximation of the FPC formula is

$$\sqrt{\frac{N-n}{N}}$$

Answer (A) is incorrect because the FPC factor cannot be greater than one. Answer (B) is incorrect because the FPC factor has a greater effect as the sample becomes larger. Answer (C) is incorrect because using the FPC factor is independent of whether sampling is performed with replacement.

## 6.3 Sampling Methods

**32.** Which of the following sampling methods is used to estimate a numerical measurement of a population, such as a dollar value?

A. Attribute sampling.

B. Stop-or-go sampling.

C. Variables sampling.

D. Random-number sampling.

Answer (C) is correct. *(CPA, adapted)*

**REQUIRED:** The sampling method used to estimate a numerical measurement of a population.

**DISCUSSION:** Variables sampling samples dollar values or other quantities. The purpose of variables sampling is to estimate the value of a population.

Answer (A) is incorrect because attribute sampling is a method to test the control structure. Answer (B) is incorrect because stop-or-go sampling is a method to test the control structure. Answer (D) is incorrect because random-number sampling is a generic term relating to the selection of the sampling units.

**33.** The auditor uses variables and attribute sampling to make accounting estimates. These methods estimate, respectively,

A. Deviation rate and quantities.

B. Quantities and deviation rate.

C. Constants and dollars.

D. Dollars and constants.

Answer (B) is correct. *(Publisher)*

**REQUIRED:** The use of variables and attribute sampling.

**DISCUSSION:** Variables sampling is used by auditors to estimate quantities or dollar amounts in substantive testing. Attribute sampling applies to tests of controls and is used to estimate a deviation rate (occurrence rate) for a population.

Answer (A) is incorrect because the proper order is reversed. Answer (C) is incorrect because the terms are nonsense in this context. Answer (D) is incorrect because the terms are nonsense in this context.

**34.** The appropriate sampling plan to use to identify at least one deviation, assuming some number of such deviations exist in a population, and then to discontinue sampling when one irregularity is observed is

A. Stop-or-go sampling.

B. Discovery sampling.

C. Variables sampling.

D. Attribute sampling.

Answer (B) is correct. *(CIA, adapted)*

**REQUIRED:** The sampling plan that should be used.

**DISCUSSION:** Discovery sampling is a form of attribute sampling applied when a control is critical and a single deviation is important, for example, commission of a material fraud. The expected deviation rate should be at or near zero, and the sample size is calculated so that the sample will include at least one example of a deviation if it occurs in the population at a given rate.

Answer (A) is incorrect because stop-or-go sampling is a variant of attribute sampling intended to reduce sample sizes when the population is relatively deviation free. It allows for discontinuing sampling when few or no deviations are found or for expanding the sample if the initial sample does not provide sufficient assurance. Answer (C) is incorrect because variables sampling estimates the value of a population. Answer (D) is incorrect because most attribute sampling applications are not discontinued when a single deviation is found.

**35.** In performing tests of controls over authorization of cash disbursements, which of the following statistical sampling methods is most appropriate?

A. Variables.

B. Stratified.

C. Ratio.

D. Attribute.

Answer (D) is correct. *(CPA, adapted)*

**REQUIRED:** The sampling method most appropriate for tests of controls.

**DISCUSSION:** The auditor uses attribute sampling to test the effectiveness of controls. The auditor is concerned with the occurrence rate of procedural deviations in the population. Attribute sampling enables the auditor to estimate the occurrence rates and to determine whether the estimated rates are within an acceptable range.

Answer (A) is incorrect because variables sampling is concerned with quantities and dollar values (population totals). Answer (B) is incorrect because stratified sampling relates to variables estimation. Answer (C) is incorrect because ratio estimation is a method of variables sampling.

**36.** An auditor for the state highway and safety department needs to estimate the average highway weight of tractor-trailer trucks using the state's highway system. Which estimation method must be used?

A. Mean-per-unit (MPU).

B. Difference.

C. Ratio.

D. Probability-proportional-to-size.

Answer (A) is correct. *(CIA, adapted)*

**REQUIRED:** The best sampling estimation method to estimate an average weight.

**DISCUSSION:** MPU estimation estimates the average value of population items. MPU averages the audit values of the sample items and multiplies the result by the number of items in the population.

Answer (B) is incorrect because difference is a technique that compares book with audit values. Answer (C) is incorrect because ratio estimation is a technique that compares book with audit values. Answer (D) is incorrect because PPS sampling selects items denominated in dollars using individual dollars as sampling units.

**37.** When would difference estimation or ratio estimation sampling methods be inappropriate?

A. If differences between the carrying amounts and audit values of a population are rare.

B. If the average difference between the audit value and carrying amount of a population is small.

C. If differences between the carrying amount and audit value of a population are numerous.

D. If the average difference between the audit value and carrying amount of a population is large.

Answer (A) is correct. *(CIA, adapted)*

**REQUIRED:** The circumstances in which difference or ratio estimation is inappropriate.

**DISCUSSION:** Difference estimation approximates total misstatement in the population by calculating the mean difference between the audited and carrying amounts in the sample and then multiplying by the number of population items. Ratio estimation approximates the total population misstatement by multiplying the proportion of the sample misstatement times the population carrying amount. These methods are not reliable when misstatements are few or tend to be in one direction.

Answer (B) is incorrect because the frequency and direction of misstatements rather than their size determine whether difference and ratio estimation are reliable. However, difference estimation is preferable when the size of misstatements is independent of the recorded values. Answer (C) is incorrect because difference and ratio estimation are more reliable when misstatement rates are high. Answer (D) is incorrect because the frequency and direction of misstatements rather than their size determine whether difference and ratio estimation are reliable. However, difference estimation is preferable when the size of misstatements is independent of the recorded values.

**38.** Which sampling method is most appropriate for the audit of the parts inventory of a wholesale electronic supply house when many small over- and understatements are expected?

A. Dollar-unit sampling.

B. Ratio or difference estimation.

C. Mean-per-unit sampling.

D. Stratified mean-per-unit sampling.

Answer (B) is correct. *(J. Heian)*

**REQUIRED:** The appropriate sampling method when many small over- and understatements are expected.

**DISCUSSION:** Difference estimation of population misstatement entails determining the differences between the audit and carrying amounts for items in the sample, adding the differences, calculating the mean difference, and multiplying the mean by the number of items in the population. An allowance for sampling risk is also calculated. Ratio estimation is similar except that it estimates the population misstatement by multiplying the carrying amount of the population by the ratio of the total audit value of the sample items to their total carrying amount. Both methods are reliable and efficient when misstatements are relatively frequent, small misstatements predominate, and they do not tend to be in one direction (they are not skewed).

Answer (A) is incorrect because dollar-unit sampling is not appropriate when many misstatements are expected or the population contains understatements. Answer (C) is incorrect because MPU is considered less efficient than either ratio or difference estimation when many misstatements are present. Answer (D) is incorrect because MPU is considered less efficient than either ratio or difference estimation when many misstatements are present.

**39.** The major reason that the difference and ratio estimation methods are expected to produce audit efficiency is that the

A. Number of members of the populations of differences or ratios is smaller than the number of members of the population of carrying amounts.

B. Beta risk may be completely ignored.

C. Calculations required in using difference or ratio estimation are less arduous and fewer than those required when using direct estimation.

D. Variability of the populations of differences or ratios is less than that of the populations of carrying amounts or audited values.

Answer (D) is correct. *(CPA, adapted)*

**REQUIRED:** The reason for increased audit efficiency.

**DISCUSSION:** Difference estimation approximates total misstatement in the population by calculating the mean difference between the audited and carrying amounts in the sample and then multiplying by the number of population items. Ratio estimation approximates the total population misstatement by multiplying the proportion of the sample misstatement times the population carrying amount. The variability in both of these estimates will likely be smaller than the variability within the population. Because the sample size varies directly with the variability of the population, the use of differences or ratios will usually allow for smaller sample sizes and greater efficiency in sampling.

Answer (A) is incorrect because the number of members in the population does not change if the sampling method changes. Answer (B) is incorrect because beta risk, the risk of accepting the carrying amount when it is materially misstated, is present in any sampling method. Answer (C) is incorrect because the sample size must be calculated using basically the same formula for any sampling method employed.

**40.** Which of the following best describes an inherent limitation of the probability-proportional-to-size (PPS) sampling method?

A. It can only be used for substantive testing of asset accounts.

B. It is complicated and always requires the use of a computer system to perform the calculations.

C. Misstatement rates must be large and the misstatements must be overstatements.

D. Misstatement rates must be small and the misstatements must be overstatements.

Answer (D) is correct. *(CIA, adapted)*

**REQUIRED:** The inherent limitation of PPS sampling.

**DISCUSSION:** PPS sampling combines attribute sampling and variables sampling concepts to estimate dollar amounts instead of deviation rates. Efficient use of PPS sampling requires misstatement rates to be small. The PPS sample size increases with the expected misstatement. Hence, the PPS sample size may be greater than that for classical variables sampling. Moreover, PPS sampling is not designed to address understatements or negative values without special modifications. Another disadvantage of PPS sampling is that misstatement estimates may be overly conservative, thereby increasing the risk of incorrect rejection.

Answer (A) is incorrect because PPS sampling is appropriate for substantive testing of most accounts when overstatement is of concern. Answer (B) is incorrect because PPS sampling is relatively simple and can be used with a table of the Poisson distribution. Answer (C) is incorrect because misstatement rates should be small.

**41.** An auditor is preparing to sample accounts receivable for overstatement. A statistical sampling method that automatically provides stratification when using systematic selection is

A. Attribute sampling.

B. Ratio-estimation sampling.

C. Dollar-unit sampling.

D. Mean-per-unit (MPU) sampling.

Answer (C) is correct. *(CIA, adapted)*

**REQUIRED:** The sampling method that automatically stratifies accounts receivable.

**DISCUSSION:** Dollar-unit or probability-proportional-to-size (PPS) sampling combines attribute sampling and variables sampling concepts to estimate dollar amounts instead of deviation rates. It is a procedure for selecting items from a population using each dollar as a sampling unit. The procedure is applied by selecting every nth dollar in the population (the population consists of dollars in ascending value from $1 to the total value of the population). The item that contains the dollar selected is included in the sample. It effectively stratifies the population because the larger the account balance, the greater the chance of selection. Moreover, PPS sampling is not designed to address understatements or negative values without special modifications.

Answer (A) is incorrect because attribute sampling estimates deviation rates, not dollar amounts. Answer (B) is incorrect because ratio-estimation sampling uses the ratio of audited amounts to recorded amounts and does not automatically stratify. Answer (D) is incorrect because MPU averages the audit values of sample items and multiplies by the number in the population to estimate the population value. It does not automatically stratify.

**42.** Using statistical sampling to assist in verifying the year-end accounts payable balance, an auditor has accumulated the following data:

| | Number of Accounts | Book Balance | Balance Determined by the Auditor |
|---|---|---|---|
| Population | 4,100 | $5,000,000 | ? |
| Sample | 200 | 250,000 | $300,000 |

Using the ratio estimation technique, the auditor's estimate of year-end accounts payable balance is

A. $6,150,000

B. $6,000,000

C. $5,125,000

D. $5,050,000

Answer (B) is correct. *(CPA, adapted)*

**REQUIRED:** The estimated balance using ratio estimation.

**DISCUSSION:** Ratio estimation estimates the total population misstatement by multiplying the proportion of the sample misstatement times the population carrying amount. Here, the proportion of the sample misstatement is 20% [($300,000 – $250,000) ÷ $250,000]. The estimated population misstatement is $1,000,000 (.2 × $5,000,000). The estimated year-end balance is therefore $6,000,000 ($5,000,000 book balance + $1,000,000 estimated misstatement).

Answer (A) is incorrect because $6,150,000 assumes that the ratio is 23% [($6,150,000 – $5,000,000) ÷ $5,000,000]. Answer (C) is incorrect because $5,125,000 assumes that the ratio is 2.5% [($5,125,000 – $5,000,000) ÷ $5,000,000]. Answer (D) is incorrect because $5,050,000 equals the carrying amount of the population ($5,000,000) plus the understatement error of the sample ($50,000).

**43.** In which sampling method is the probability of selection of an item proportional to the size or the value of the item (e.g., a $1,000 item is 10 times more likely to be selected than a $100 item)?

A. Discovery sampling.

B. Ratio estimation.

C. Dollar-unit sampling.

D. Stratified sampling.

Answer (C) is correct. *(Publisher)*

**REQUIRED:** The sampling method in which the probability of selection of an item is proportional to its size.

**DISCUSSION:** Dollar-unit or probability-proportional-to-size (PPS) sampling defines individual dollars within an item or balance as the sampling units. Thus, an item containing 1,000 sampling units ($1,000) has a 10 times greater chance of being selected for audit than a balance with 100 sampling units ($100).

Answer (A) is incorrect because discovery sampling is a sampling plan to search for critical deviations. Answer (B) is incorrect because ratio estimation estimates the population misstatement by multiplying the proportion of sample misstatement times the population carrying amount. Answer (D) is incorrect because stratification divides a population into subpopulations so that variability can be minimized and a more efficient sample can be drawn.

**44.** An internal auditor plans to test the accuracy of recorded quantities-on-hand in an inventory file against the actual quantities-on-hand. Under which of the following conditions is the auditor least likely to use a stop-or-go sampling plan?

A. The population to be sampled is very large.

B. The auditor expects the population to contain a high rate of deviations.

C. The auditor plans to draw a relatively small sample size.

D. The auditor plans to determine an upper precision limit for the estimated percentage of deviations contained in the population.

Answer (B) is correct. *(CIA, adapted)*

**REQUIRED:** The condition in which stop-or-go sampling is least likely to be used.

**DISCUSSION:** Stop-or-go sampling is an attribute sampling model that helps prevent oversampling by allowing the auditor to halt an audit test at the earliest possible moment. It is used when the auditor believes that the population contains relatively few deviations.

Answer (A) is incorrect because stop-or-go sampling is appropriate for populations of any size. Answer (C) is incorrect because stop-or-go sampling is designed to reduce sample size. Answer (D) is incorrect because the purpose of stop-or-go sampling is to state that a deviation rate is below a prespecified rate (upper precision limit) with a prespecified level of confidence.

**45.** A statistical sampling technique that will minimize sample size whenever a low deviation rate is expected is

A. Ratio-estimation sampling.

B. Difference-estimation sampling.

C. Stratified mean-per-unit sampling.

D. Stop-or-go sampling.

Answer (D) is correct. *(CIA, adapted)*

**REQUIRED:** The technique that minimizes sample size.

**DISCUSSION:** Stop-or-go sampling is typically used when a low deviation rate is expected. It is a version of acceptance sampling, which, like other attribute sampling methods, is used to test the effectiveness of controls. Stop-or-go sampling is unlike acceptance sampling in that it does not rely on a fixed sample size. Thus, it may reduce the sample size because sample items are examined only until enough evidence has been gathered to reach the desired conclusion.

Answer (A) is incorrect because deviation rate is irrelevant to variables sampling methods such as ratio-estimation sampling. Answer (B) is incorrect because deviation rate is irrelevant to variables sampling methods such as difference estimation. Answer (C) is incorrect because deviation rate is irrelevant to variables sampling methods such as MPU.

## 6.4 Sample Selection

**46.** A distinguishing characteristic of random number sample selection is that

A. Each item is selected from a stratum having minimum variability.

B. Each item's chance for selection is proportional to its dollar value.

C. Each item in the population has a known and nonzero chance of being selected.

D. Each stratum in the population has an equal number of items selected.

Answer (C) is correct. *(CIA, adapted)*

**REQUIRED:** The distinguishing characteristic of random number sample selection.

**DISCUSSION:** Probability sampling is possible if every item in the population has a known and nonzero chance of being drawn. Simple random sampling is a special case of probability sampling in which every possible sample of a given size has the same probability of being chosen, and every item in the population has an equal probability of being chosen. Random selection can be used for stratified and other samples in which items do not have an equal chance of being selected.

Answer (A) is incorrect because stratifying the population is not required for random selection. Answer (B) is incorrect because dollar values are not used in random selection. Answer (D) is incorrect because stratifying the population is not required for random selection.

**47.** Which of the following sample planning factors would influence the sample size for a substantive test of details for a specific account?

| | Expected Amount of Misstatements | Measure of Tolerable Misstatement |
|---|---|---|
| A. | No | No |
| B. | Yes | Yes |
| C. | No | Yes |
| D. | Yes | No |

Answer (B) is correct. *(CPA, adapted)*

**REQUIRED:** The factors that would influence the sample size for a substantive test of details.

**DISCUSSION:** Certain variables sampling plans, for example, probability-proportional-to-size sampling, specifically consider the expected amount of misstatement and the measure of tolerable misstatement or materiality in the determination of sample size.

**48.** An auditor wishes to sample 200 sales receipts from a population of 5,000 receipts issued during the last year. The receipts have preprinted serial numbers and are arranged in chronological (and thus serial number) order. The auditor randomly chooses a receipt from the first 25 receipts and then selects every 25th receipt thereafter. The sampling procedure described here is called

A. Systematic random sampling.

B. Dollar-unit sampling.

C. Judgment interval sampling.

D. Variables sampling.

Answer (A) is correct. *(CIA, adapted)*

**REQUIRED:** The sampling plan that selects a random start and then chooses each nth item.

**DISCUSSION:** Systematic (interval) sampling is accomplished by selecting a random start and taking every nth item in the population. The value of n is computed by dividing the population by the size of the sample. The random start should be in the first interval. An advantage of systematic sampling is its relative ease. It requires merely counting items in the population, not assigning a random number to each item. However, a systematic sampling plan assumes the items are arranged randomly in the population. If the auditor discovers that this condition does not exist, a random selection method should be used.

Answer (B) is incorrect because dollar-unit sampling selects individual dollars within an item or balance as the sampling units. Answer (C) is incorrect because judgment sampling uses the auditor's subjective judgment to determine the sample size (number of items examined) and sample selection (which items to examine). Answer (D) is incorrect because the sampling procedure described can be used for attribute as well as variables sampling.

**49.** To test compliance with a policy regarding sales returns recorded during the most recent year, an auditor systematically selected 5% of the actual returns recorded in March and April. Returns during these two busiest months of the year represented about 25% of total annual returns. Projections of deviation rates from this sample have limited usefulness because

A. The small size of the sample relative to the population makes sampling risk unacceptable.

B. The failure to stratify the population according to sales volume results in bias.

C. The systematic selection of returns during the 2 months is not sufficiently random.

D. The deviation rates during the 2 busiest months may not be representative of the whole year.

Answer (D) is correct. *(CIA, adapted)*

**REQUIRED:** The reason for the limited usefulness of projections of deviation rates.

**DISCUSSION:** By selecting a sample from only 2 months, the auditor may be able to draw conclusions about the overall deviation rate during those months, but the sample does not provide sufficient information to draw conclusions about the overall rate for the year.

Answer (A) is incorrect because, although sampling risk is related to sample size, it is not related to the ratio of sample size to the population size. In addition, this problem does not contain sufficient information to evaluate the acceptability of sampling risk. Answer (B) is incorrect because the objective of stratifying a population is to decrease the sampling risk, not bias. This problem does not give enough information to decide whether stratification might have enabled the auditor to use a smaller sample. Answer (C) is incorrect because systematic selection with a random start is unbiased if the population is randomly organized.

**50.** Internal auditing is conducting an operational audit of the organization's mailroom activities to determine whether the use of express mail service is limited to cases of necessity. To test cost-effectiveness, the auditor selects the 100 most recent express-mail transactions for review. A major limitation of such a sampling technique is that it

A. Does not allow a statistical generalization about all express-mail transactions.

B. Results in a sample size that is too small to project to the population.

C. Does not evaluate existing controls in this area.

D. Does not describe the population from which it was drawn.

Answer (A) is correct. *(CIA, adapted)*

**REQUIRED:** The major limitation of selecting a sample of the most recent transactions for review.

**DISCUSSION:** The last 100 express-mail transactions may not be representative of all express-mail transactions. The sample is a judgment rather than a statistical (probability or random) sample. Every item in the population (all express-mail transactions of the organization) does not have an equal (or known) and nonzero probability of being chosen. Thus, sampling risk cannot be quantified.

Answer (B) is incorrect because a sample of 100 may be sufficient. Answer (C) is incorrect because the auditor is testing for cost effectiveness. Answer (D) is incorrect because the last 100 transactions may describe the population from which they were drawn.

**51.** An auditor is conducting a survey of perceptions and beliefs of employees concerning an organization health care plan. The best approach to selecting a sample is to

A. Focus on people who are likely to respond so that a larger sample can be obtained.

B. Focus on managers and supervisors because they can also reflect the opinions of the people in their departments.

C. Use stratified sampling when the strata are defined by marital and family status, age, and salaried/hourly status.

D. Use monetary-unit sampling according to employee salaries.

Answer (C) is correct. *(CIA, adapted)*

**REQUIRED:** The best way to sample employee beliefs.

**DISCUSSION:** Stratified sampling divides a population into subpopulations, thereby permitting the application of different techniques to each stratum. This approach reduces the effect of high variability if the strata are selected so that variability among the strata is greater than variability within each stratum. For example, one expects to find greater similarities among married people than between married people and unmarried people.

Answer (A) is incorrect because this convenience sample is likely to emphasize people with the time to respond. It tends to omit employees who are too busy to respond. Answer (B) is incorrect because managers and supervisors often do not have the same needs and perceptions as their subordinates and also often misperceive the views of employees. Answer (D) is incorrect because the survey tests perceptions and beliefs, not monetary amounts.

**52.** An entity wishes to determine inventory value by counting a sample of inventory items. If a stratified random sample is to be drawn, the strata should be identified in such a way that

A. The overall population is divided into subpopulations of equal size so that each subpopulation can be given equal weight when estimates are made.

B. Each stratum differs as much as possible with respect to unit costs, but the unit costs for items within each stratum are as similar as possible.

C. The sample means and standard deviation of each individual stratum will be equal to the means and standard deviations of all other strata.

D. The items in each stratum will follow a normal distribution so that probability theory can be used in making inferences from the sample data.

Answer (B) is correct. *(Publisher)*

**REQUIRED:** The proper way to stratify a population of inventory items.

**DISCUSSION:** When the items in a population are heterogeneous, stratifying the population into homogeneous subpopulations may be advantageous. Each stratum should differ from the others, but the items within each stratum should be similar.

Answer (A) is incorrect because the purpose of stratification is to divide the population so that homogeneous items are grouped together, not to create subpopulations of equal size. Answer (C) is incorrect because the individual strata should be as different from each other as possible. Thus, the means and standard deviations of the strata should differ. Answer (D) is incorrect because whether an item should be included in a stratum is based upon the characteristic used for stratifying, not upon the distribution of the items within the stratum.

**53.** To use stratified sampling to evaluate a large, heterogeneous inventory, which of the following is least likely to be used as a criterion to classify inventory items into strata?

A. Dollar value.

B. Number of items.

C. Turnover volume.

D. Storage locations.

Answer (B) is correct. *(CIA, adapted)*

**REQUIRED:** The least likely criterion to classify inventory items into strata.

**DISCUSSION:** Stratifying a population means dividing it into subpopulations, which permits application of different sampling techniques to each subpopulation or stratum. Stratifying allows for greater emphasis on larger or more important items. When the items in a population are heterogeneous, stratifying the population into homogeneous subpopulations may be advantageous. Each stratum should differ from the others, but the items within each stratum should be similar. Number of items is not usually associated with the risk of misstatement.

Answer (A) is incorrect because the risk of misstatement is correlated with dollar value. Answer (C) is incorrect because the risk of misstatement is correlated with turnover. Answer (D) is incorrect because the risk of misstatement is correlated with location.

**54.** Stratified mean-per-unit (MPU) sampling is a statistical technique that may be more efficient than unstratified MPU because it usually

A. May be applied to populations in which many monetary misstatements are expected to occur.

B. Produces an estimate having a desired level of precision with a smaller sample size.

C. Increases the variability among items in a stratum by grouping sampling units with similar characteristics.

D. Yields a weighted sum of the strata standard deviations that is greater than the standard deviation of the population.

Answer (B) is correct. *(CPA, adapted)*

**REQUIRED:** The reason for using stratification.

**DISCUSSION:** The primary objective of stratification is to reduce the effect of high variability by dividing the population into subpopulations. Reducing the variance within each subpopulation allows the auditor to sample a smaller number of items while holding precision and confidence level constant.

Answer (A) is incorrect because the number of misstatements in the population is independent of the advantages of stratification. Answer (C) is incorrect because stratification is used to decrease the effects of variation within the strata. Answer (D) is incorrect because the standard deviation, which measures variation, should be less within the strata than for the population as a whole.

**55.** Which of the following is not a criterion for a good stratified random sampling plan?

A. Every item must belong to one and only one stratum.

B. The original population of items must be normally distributed.

C. An identifiable means of subdividing a heterogeneous population into groups with more homogeneous characteristics must be available.

D. The number of items in each group must be known or determinable.

Answer (B) is correct. *(CIA, adapted)*

**REQUIRED:** The condition not a criterion for stratified sampling.

**DISCUSSION:** The population need not be normally distributed. Indeed, the purpose of stratification is to overcome skewness of distribution in the original population by defining subpopulations that are as nearly homogeneous as possible.

Answer (A) is incorrect because a necessary condition for stratification is that every item belong to one and only one stratum. Answer (C) is incorrect because a necessary condition for stratification is that an identifiable means of subdividing a heterogeneous population into groups with more homogeneous characteristics be available. Answer (D) is incorrect because a necessary condition for stratification is that the number of items in each group be known or determinable.

**56.** An accounts receivable aging schedule was prepared on 300 pages with each page containing the aging data for 50 accounts. The pages were numbered from 1 to 300, and the accounts listed on each were numbered from 1 to 50. An auditor selected accounts receivable for confirmation using a table of numbers as illustrated:

| Select Column from Table of Numbers | Separate Five Digits: First Three Digits Last Two Digits | |
|---|---|---|
| 02011 | 020-11 | x |
| 85393 | 853-93 | * |
| 97265 | 972-65 | * |
| 61680 | 616-80 | * |
| 16656 | 166-56 | * |
| 42751 | 427-51 | * |
| 69994 | 699-94 | * |
| 07942 | 079-42 | y |
| 10231 | 102-31 | z |
| 53988 | 539-88 | * |

x Mailed confirmation to account 11 listed on p. 20.
y Mailed confirmation to account 42 listed on p. 79.
z Mailed confirmation to account 31 listed on p. 102.
* Rejected.

This procedure is an example of

A. Acceptance sampling.

B. Systematic sampling.

C. Sequential sampling.

D. Random sampling.

Answer (D) is correct. *(CPA, adapted)*

**REQUIRED:** The appropriate term associated with the sampling method illustrated.

**DISCUSSION:** This sampling method is random. When random sampling is used, each item in the population has an equal or known and nonzero chance of being selected for inclusion in the sample. The auditor in this instance selected a random sample using a random number table. Before this approach can be used, a correspondence between the random numbers and the items in the population must be established. In this example, the relationship was established by designating the first three digits from the random number table as corresponding to the page number and the last two digits as corresponding to the item number. The number 85393 is rejected because (1) the page number (853) does not lie between 1 and 300, and (2) the item number (93) does not lie between 1 and 50. If either of these conditions occurs, the random number is rejected. If the random number falls within both ranges (e.g., 02011), the item corresponding to the random number is included in the sample. The eleventh item on page 20 is therefore chosen for confirmation.

Answer (A) is incorrect because acceptance sampling is a form of attribute sampling. The described plan is concerned with the value of the account and is therefore an example of variables sampling. Answer (B) is incorrect because systematic sampling is a special type of random sampling that needs no correspondence between random numbers and items in the population. Answer (C) is incorrect because sequential (stop-or-go) sampling needs no correspondence between random numbers and items in the population.

**57.** In a regional survey of suburban households to obtain data on television viewing habits, a statistical sample of suburban areas is first selected. Within the chosen areas, statistical samples of whole blocks are selected, and within the selected blocks, random samples of households are selected. This type of sample selection can best be described as

A. Attribute sampling.

B. Stratified sampling.

C. Cluster sampling.

D. Interval sampling.

Answer (C) is correct. *(CIA, adapted)*

**REQUIRED:** The sampling method used to select random samples from statistically selected groups.

**DISCUSSION:** Block (cluster) sampling selects groups of items rather than individual items. For this plan to be effective, dispersion within clusters should be greater than dispersion among clusters. If blocks of homogeneous items are selected, the sample will be biased. Cluster sampling is most appropriate when each group is representative of the entire population.

Answer (A) is incorrect because attribute sampling is not a selection technique. Answer (B) is incorrect because stratified sampling separates the population into several strata, with the elements in each stratum possessing some common attribute. The sample is then chosen using a statistical sampling approach. Answer (D) is incorrect because interval sampling selects every nth item for sampling with a randomized starting point.

**58.** An auditor is designing a sampling plan to test the accuracy of daily production reports over the past 3 years. All of the reports contain the same information except that Friday reports also contain weekly totals and are prepared by managers rather than by supervisors. Production normally peaks near the end of a month. If the auditor wants to select two reports per month using an interval sampling plan, which of the following techniques reduces the likelihood of bias in the sample?

A. Estimating the rate of misstatements in the population.

B. Using multiple random starts.

C. Increasing the confidence level.

D. Increasing the precision.

Answer (B) is correct. *(CIA, adapted)*

**REQUIRED:** The technique that reduces the chance of bias in the sample.

**DISCUSSION:** Systematic (interval) sample entails choosing a random start and then selecting subsequent items at fixed intervals. However, if the population is not random, for example, because it exhibits cyclical variation, the results will be biased. This bias may be overcome by taking repeated systematic samples, each with a random start. In effect, each possible systematic sample in the population is a cluster. Thus, the repeated systematic samples, each with a random start, constitute a random sample of clusters.

Answer (A) is incorrect because estimating the rate of misstatements in the population has no effect on bias. Bias is related to the selection method. Answer (C) is incorrect because increasing the confidence level has no effect on bias. Answer (D) is incorrect because increasing the precision has no effect on bias.

**59.** Which of the following is a false statement about cluster sample selection?

A. Every item in the sample must correspond to a random number.

B. Sample groups of items rather than individual items are selected.

C. Cluster sampling is normally used when the sampling units (documents) are filed sequentially.

D. Dispersion within clusters should be greater than between clusters.

Answer (A) is correct. *(Publisher)*

**REQUIRED:** The false statement.

**DISCUSSION:** Because cluster sampling entails selection of groups rather than individual items from a population, random numbers are not assigned to individual items within the population. Rather, clusters or blocks are randomly selected for audit.

Answer (B) is incorrect because cluster sampling selects blocks or clusters of items rather than individual items for audit. Answer (C) is incorrect because, when documents are sequentially filed, time can be saved by selecting blocks rather than individual items from the population. Answer (D) is incorrect because dispersion within the clusters should be large and dispersion among the clusters should be small.

**60.** The advantage of selecting a sample by cluster is that this method

A. Increases the precision and confidence level of the sample.

B. Reduces the time required to locate the individual items chosen for examination.

C. Decreases the standard deviation of the sample.

D. Decreases sample size.

Answer (B) is correct. *(Publisher)*

**REQUIRED:** The advantage of cluster sampling.

**DISCUSSION:** The use of cluster or block sampling may allow the auditor to select on a random basis a large set of data (a block) to be examined. Because the auditor need not establish a correspondence between random numbers and items in the population, time may be saved.

Answer (A) is incorrect because the precision and confidence level of the sample are independent of the sample selection method. Answer (C) is incorrect because the standard deviation of the sample is independent of the sample selection method. Answer (D) is incorrect because sample size is independent of the sample selection method.

**61.** An auditor desires to use a table of random digits to select a sample from a population of documents that have the following broken number sequences: 0001-1000, 2000-5000, and 8000-11000. Which of the following is the most efficient approach to overcome the problem of the broken number sequences?

A. Deduct four-digit constant values from the second and third sequences, choose the appropriate random numbers, and add the constants back to the individual numbers.

B. Skip through the entire random number tables until large blocks of digits appear that will fit within the three different number sequences.

C. Choose appropriate random numbers from the tables without modifying the approach and recognize that a large selection of unusable numbers will occur.

D. Select three different starting points in the random tables and vary the selection pattern to obtain needed numbers in the three different sequences.

Answer (A) is correct. *(CIA, adapted)*

**REQUIRED:** The most efficient approach to overcoming the problem of broken number sequences when using a random digits table.

**DISCUSSION:** Efficient use of random digits tables often requires that constants be subtracted from the items in the population so that it more closely matches the numbers in the table. After an acceptable number is found in the table, the constant is added back to determine which item is selected. Randomness of selection is not impaired by this technique.

Answer (B) is incorrect because random digits tables do not contain large blocks of usable numbers. Answer (C) is incorrect because selecting many unusable numbers is inefficient. Answer (D) is incorrect because use of random digits tables requires a single starting point and a consistent selection pattern.

## 6.5 Attribute Sampling

**62.** Statistical sampling may be used to test the effectiveness of controls. The auditor's procedures should result in a statistical conclusion concerning

A. Population characteristics occurring at least once in the population.

B. The population value not being misstated by more than a fixed amount.

C. Monetary precision exceeding a certain predetermined amount.

D. The relation of the population deviation rate to the tolerable rate.

Answer (D) is correct. *(Publisher)*

**REQUIRED:** The conclusion that can be drawn from statistical tests of controls.

**DISCUSSION:** The auditor uses attribute sampling to test the effectiveness of controls. The auditor is concerned with the occurrence rate of procedural deviations in the population. Attribute sampling enables the auditor to estimate the occurrence rate of deviations and to determine the relation of the estimated rate to the tolerable rate.

Answer (A) is incorrect because the only way to be certain that a characteristic occurs at least once is to examine items until one is located. Answer (B) is incorrect because variables sampling is concerned with quantities (e.g., population totals). Answer (C) is incorrect because variables sampling is concerned with dollar values (e.g., monetary precision), whereas attribute sampling is concerned with deviation rates.

**63.** An auditor plans to examine a sample of 20 purchase orders for proper approvals as prescribed by the client's internal control. One of the purchase orders in the chosen sample of 20 cannot be found, and the auditor is unable to use alternative procedures to test whether that purchase order was properly approved. The auditor should

A. Choose another purchase order to replace the missing purchase order in the sample.

B. Consider this test of controls invalid and proceed with substantive tests because internal control is ineffective.

C. Treat the missing purchase order as a deviation for the purpose of evaluating the sample.

D. Select a completely new set of 20 purchase orders.

Answer (C) is correct. *(CPA, adapted)*

**REQUIRED:** The effect of failure to locate a sample item.

**DISCUSSION:** According to AU 350, "If the auditor is not able to apply the planned audit procedures or appropriate alternative procedures to selected items, (s)he should consider the reasons for this limitation, and (s)he should ordinarily consider those selected items to be deviations from the procedures for the purpose of evaluating the sample."

Answer (A) is incorrect because the auditor would choose another purchase order only if an item in the sample were not used, e.g., if it were properly voided. Answer (B) is incorrect because the sampling plan could be completed by counting the missing purchase order as a deviation. Answer (D) is incorrect because selecting a new sample is unnecessary.

**64.** An auditor planning an attribute sample from a large number of invoices intends to estimate the actual rate of deviations. Which factor below is the most important for the auditor to consider?

A. Audit objective.

B. Population size.

C. Desired confidence level.

D. Population variance.

Answer (A) is correct. *(CIA, adapted)*

**REQUIRED:** The most important factor in planning an attribute sample.

**DISCUSSION:** Attribute sampling enables the auditor to estimate the occurrence rate in a population and to determine the relation of the estimated rate to the tolerable rate. However, the audit objective must be known before audit procedures can be designed and their results evaluated.

Answer (B) is incorrect because knowing the population is large is sufficient. Answer (C) is incorrect because the desired confidence level is a function of the purposes to be served by the audit. Answer (D) is incorrect because the variance is calculated in variables, not attribute, sampling applications.

**65.** Statistical sampling usually may be applied in tests of controls when the client's controls

A. Permit detection of material misstatements in the accounting records.

B. Leave an audit trail.

C. Are described in accounting manuals.

D. Depend primarily on segregation of duties.

Answer (B) is correct. *(Publisher)*

**REQUIRED:** The condition permitting use of statistical sampling in tests of controls.

**DISCUSSION:** Sampling techniques are useful when a population from which to sample can be identified. When attribute sampling is applied in tests of controls, an audit trail of documents and notations (such as signatures) must exist to provide evidence of the effectiveness of the control.

Answer (A) is incorrect because the client's controls, if appropriate, are always expected to detect material misstatements. Answer (C) is incorrect because the auditor is more concerned with the existence and effectiveness of controls rather than with their documentation. Answer (D) is incorrect because segregation of duties is tested through inquiry and observation rather than through sampling.

**66.** For which of the following audit tests will an auditor most likely use attribute sampling?

A. Making an independent estimate of the amount of a LIFO inventory.

B. Examining invoices in support of the valuation of fixed asset additions.

C. Selecting accounts receivable for confirmation of account balances.

D. Inspecting employee time cards for proper approval by supervisors.

Answer (D) is correct. *(CPA, adapted)*

**REQUIRED:** The appropriate use of attribute sampling.

**DISCUSSION:** The approvals represent the application of a control. Attribute sampling enables the auditor to estimate the occurrence rate of control deviations and to determine its relation to the tolerable rate. Thus, a control such as proper approval of time cards by supervisors can be tested for effectiveness using attribute sampling.

Answer (A) is incorrect because variables sampling is useful in estimating the amount of inventory. Answer (B) is incorrect because examining invoices in support of the valuation of fixed asset additions is a substantive test for which variables sampling is appropriate. Answer (C) is incorrect because the selection of accounts receivable for confirmation is a substantive test.

**67.** In testing payroll transactions, an auditor discovers that four out of a statistical sample of 100 selected time cards were not signed by the appropriate supervisor. To evaluate the materiality or significance of this control deficiency, the auditor should

A. Compare the tolerable deviation rate with the expected deviation rate.

B. Compute an upper precision limit and compare with the tolerable deviation rate.

C. Evaluate the dollar amount of the four time cards in relation to the financial statements.

D. Report the deviations and let management assess the significance because they are in the best position to know.

Answer (B) is correct. *(CIA, adapted)*

**REQUIRED:** The procedure applied to evaluate the materiality of the control deficiency.

**DISCUSSION:** After specifying the confidence level and tolerable rate of deviations, the auditor determines the sample size and precision. The tolerable rate is the rate the auditor is willing to accept without altering the assessed level of control risk. The achieved precision is the range of values constructed based on a statistic derived from a random sample. At the stated confidence level, the auditor expects this range to contain the true population value. In this attribute sampling application, the upper, but not the lower, precision limit is of interest. This limit should be compared with the maximum tolerable rate.

Answer (A) is incorrect because both the expected deviation rate and the tolerable rate are known before sampling. Answer (C) is incorrect because any monetary misstatement in the sample must first be extrapolated to the population before the significance can be assessed. Answer (D) is incorrect because the auditor should determine the significance of detected deviations.

**68.** The tolerable rate for a test of controls depends primarily on which of the following?

A. The cause of the deviations.

B. The effect on substantive tests of assessing control risk at a certain level.

C. The amount of any substantive misstatement.

D. The limit used in audits of similar clients.

Answer (B) is correct. *(L.M. Bailey)*

**REQUIRED:** The determinant of the tolerable rate.

**DISCUSSION:** The tolerable rate is the maximum rate of deviations from a prescribed control that the auditor is willing to accept without altering the assessment of control risk for the assertions related to the activity. The tolerable rate is determined based on two considerations: the planned assessed level of control risk and the assurance desired to be provided by the evidence in the sample (AU 350). The lower the assessed control risk, the higher the acceptable level of detection risk. Because substantive tests are performed to reduce detection risk to the acceptable level, the nature, timing, and extent of such tests will be affected if audit evidence indicates that a higher assessed level of control risk and thus a lower acceptable level of detection risk are necessary.

Answer (A) is incorrect because the cause of the deviations is unknown prior to testing. The auditor sets the tolerable rate prior to such tests. Answer (C) is incorrect because the misstatement is unknown prior to testing. Answer (D) is incorrect because audit clients are unlikely to be so similar that the same tolerable rate can be used.

**69.** In addition to evaluating the frequency of deviations in tests of controls, an auditor also considers certain qualitative aspects of the deviations. The auditor most likely will give broader consideration to the implications of a deviation if it is

A. The only deviation discovered in the sample.

B. Identical to a deviation discovered during the prior year's audit.

C. Caused by an employee's misunderstanding of instructions.

D. Initially concealed by a forged document.

Answer (D) is correct. *(CPA, adapted)*

**REQUIRED:** The aspect of a deviation requiring broader consideration.

**DISCUSSION:** The discovery of fraud ordinarily requires broader consideration than the discovery of an unintentional deviation. The discovery of an initially concealed forged document raises concerns because it indicates that the integrity of employees may be in doubt.

Answer (A) is incorrect because a single deviation discovered in a sample may not cause major concern. Answer (B) is incorrect because deviations are often repetitive. Discovery of an identical deviation in a subsequent year is not unusual. Answer (C) is incorrect because a misunderstanding is not fraud and does not necessarily arouse concern.

**70.** The diagram below depicts the auditor's estimated maximum deviation rate compared with the tolerable rate, and also depicts the true population deviation rate compared with the tolerable rate.

| Auditor's Estimate Based on Sample Results | True State of Population: Deviation Rate Exceeds Tolerable Rate | True State of Population: Deviation Rate Is Less Than Tolerable Rate |
|---|---|---|
| Maximum Deviation Rate Exceeds Tolerable Rate | I. | III. |
| Maximum Deviation Rate Is Less Than Tolerable Rate | II. | IV. |

As a result of testing controls, the auditor assesses control risk too high and increases substantive testing as a result. This is illustrated by situation

A. I.

B. II.

C. III.

D. IV.

Answer (C) is correct. *(CPA, adapted)*

**REQUIRED:** The situation that involves assessing control risk too high.

**DISCUSSION:** The risk of assessing control risk too high is one aspect of sampling risk in testing controls. According to AU 350, it "is the risk that the assessed level of control risk based on the sample is greater than the true operating effectiveness of the control." Thus, the risk is that the control is actually more effective than indicated by the sample. Like the risk of incorrect rejection in substantive testing, the risk of assessing control risk too high is a form of alpha (Type I) error. Alpha error concerns the efficiency, not the effectiveness, of the audit because it ordinarily leads to application of further audit procedures and ultimate arrival at the correct conclusion.

Answer (A) is incorrect because, in situation I, the auditor would properly assess control risk at a high level. Answer (B) is incorrect because, in situation II, the sample might lead to assessing control risk too low. Answer (D) is incorrect because, in situation IV, the auditor would properly assess control risk at less than the maximum level.

**71.** Which of the following statements is true concerning statistical sampling in tests of controls?

A. As the population size increases, the sample size should increase proportionately.

B. Deviations from specific controls at a given rate ordinarily result in misstatements at a lower rate.

C. The relationship between the expected population deviation rate and the sample size is inverse.

D. In determining the tolerable rate, an auditor considers detection risk and the sample size.

Answer (B) is correct. *(CPA, adapted)*

**REQUIRED:** The true statement concerning statistical sampling and tests of controls.

**DISCUSSION:** Deviations from a specific control increase the risk of misstatements in the accounting records. However, deviations do not always result in misstatements. Thus, deviations from a specific control at a given rate ordinarily result in misstatements at the financial statement level at a lower rate (AU 350).

Answer (A) is incorrect because, as population size increases, the required sample size increases at a decreasing rate. Answer (C) is incorrect because the relationship between the expected population deviation rate and the required sample size is direct. Answer (D) is incorrect because the tolerable rate depends on the planned assessed level of control risk and the assurance to be provided by the evidence in the sample.

**72.** As a result of sampling procedures applied as tests of controls, an auditor incorrectly assesses control risk too low. The most likely explanation for this situation is that

A. The deviation rates of both the auditor's sample and the population exceed the tolerable rate.

B. The deviation rates of both the auditor's sample and the population are less than the tolerable rate.

C. The deviation rate in the auditor's sample is less than the tolerable rate, but the deviation rate in the population exceeds the tolerable rate.

D. The deviation rate in the auditor's sample exceeds the tolerable rate, but the deviation rate in the population is less than the tolerable rate.

Answer (C) is correct. *(CPA, adapted)*

**REQUIRED:** The most likely explanation for assessing control risk too low.

**DISCUSSION:** When the deviation rate in the sample is less than the tolerable rate, the auditor concludes that the controls tested are effective. If, in fact, the true deviation rate in the population is greater than the tolerable rate, the auditor will assess control risk too low because control is less effective than indicated by the sample.

Answer (A) is incorrect because, if the sample rate and the population rate are both greater than the tolerable rate, the auditor's conclusion should be accurate. Answer (B) is incorrect because, if the sample rate and the population rate are both less than the tolerable rate, the auditor's conclusion should be accurate. Answer (D) is incorrect because, if the sample rate exceeds the population rate, the auditor is likely to assess control risk too high.

**73.** A test of 200 invoices randomly selected by the auditor revealed that 35 had not been approved for payment. At the 95% confidence level, what precision can be assigned?

A. 6.9%

B. 5.3%

C. 9.1%

D. 3.5%

Answer (B) is correct. *(CIA, adapted)*

**REQUIRED:** The achieved precision.

**DISCUSSION:** The following sample size formula for an attribute sampling application can be solved for precision:

$$n = \frac{C^2 pq}{P^2}$$

C is the confidence coefficient, p is the expected deviation rate, q is 1 – p, P is the specified precision rate, and n is the sample size.

$$P^2 = \frac{(1.96)^2 \times (35 \div 200) \times [1 - (35 \div 200)]}{200}$$

$$P^2 = .0028$$

$$P = .053 \text{ or } 5.3\%$$

Questions 74 through 77 are based on the following information.

| Confidence Level | Deviation Rate | Field Size | +1% | +2% | +3% | +4% | +5% | +6% | +8% | +10% |
|---|---|---|---|---|---|---|---|---|---|---|
| | | | Sample Sizes for Precision of | | | | | | | |
| 95% | 10% | 200 | | | | | 82 | 65 | | |
| | | 400 | | | 196 | 140 | 103 | 77 | | |
| | | 500 | | | 217 | 151 | 108 | 81 | | |
| | | 1,000 | | 464 | 278 | 178 | 121 | 88 | 51 | 50 |
| | | 2,000 | | 604 | 322 | 195 | 129 | 92 | 53 | 51 |
| 99% | 10% | 200 | | | | | | 91 | 64 | |
| | | 400 | | | | 193 | 149 | 117 | 76 | 52 |
| | | 500 | | | | 214 | 162 | 124 | 79 | 53 |
| | | 1,000 | | | 399 | 272 | 193 | 142 | 85 | 56 |
| | | 2,000 | | 854 | 498 | 314 | 213 | 153 | 89 | 58 |

**74.** You are using attribute sampling to test the effectiveness of a control over a file of 1,000 purchase orders. You expect a 10% deviation rate in the population and would like to select a sample sufficiently large to provide a precision of 10% with a 99% level of confidence. What sample size is needed?

A. 50
B. 56
C. 121
D. 193

Answer (B) is correct. *(CIA, adapted)*
**REQUIRED:** The determined sample size.
**DISCUSSION:** For a population of 1,000, an expected deviation rate of 10%, a confidence level of 99%, and a precision of 10%, the attribute sampling table specifies a minimum sample size of 56.
Answer (A) is incorrect because 50 is the minimum sample size for a confidence level of 95%. Answer (C) is incorrect because 121 is the minimum sample size for a confidence level of 95% and a precision of 5%. Answer (D) is incorrect because 193 is the minimum sample size for a population of 400 and a precision of 4%.

**75.** You are using attribute sampling to test the effectiveness of a control over a file of 1,000 purchase orders. You expect a 10% deviation rate in the population and would like your sample results to vary by no more than 40 purchase orders. If you selected a sample size of 178, how reliable will you conclude your sample results to be?

A. 90%
B. 95%
C. 96%
D. 99%

Answer (B) is correct. *(CIA, adapted)*
**REQUIRED:** The determined reliability.
**DISCUSSION:** For a population of 1,000, an expected deviation rate of 10%, a precision of 4% (40 ÷ 1,000), and a sample size of 178, the attribute sampling table specifies a 95% confidence level or reliability.
Answer (A) is incorrect because the table gives no values for a confidence level of 90%. Answer (C) is incorrect because the table gives no values for a confidence level of 96%. Answer (D) is incorrect because 272 is the sample size for a population of 1,000, precision of 4%, and a 10% deviation rate.

**76.** You used attribute sampling to test a population of 1,000 purchase orders, and the results showed a deviation rate of 9%. If your sample size was 85 and your confidence level was 99%, what was the upper occurrence limit?

A. 17%
B. 9%
C. 8%
D. 1%

Answer (A) is correct. *(CIA, adapted)*
**REQUIRED:** The determined upper occurrence limit.
**DISCUSSION:** For a population size of 1,000, a confidence level of 99%, and a sample size of 85, the precision is +8%. Given the deviation rate of 9%, the upper occurrence limit is 17% (8% + 9%).
Answer (B) is incorrect because 9% is the deviation rate. Answer (C) is incorrect because 8% is the precision. Answer (D) is incorrect because 1% is the difference between the precision and the deviation rate, which has no relevance.

**77.** Refer to the information preceding question 74. You used attribute sampling to test a population of 2,000 purchase orders. Using a reliability level of 99%, an expected deviation rate of 10%, and a sample size of 195, the precision is

A. More than 5%.

B. More than 3% but less than 5%.

C. More than 6% but less than 8%.

D. Indeterminable from the data given.

Answer (A) is correct. *(CIA, adapted)*

**REQUIRED:** The determined precision.

**DISCUSSION:** At the 99% confidence level and population size of 2,000, the attribute sampling table shows that a sample size of 195 has a precision of between 5% and 6%.

Answer (B) is incorrect because, at the 95% confidence level and a population size of 2,000, a sample size of 195 has a precision of 4%. Answer (C) is incorrect because a sample of 195 has a precision of less than 6% for all values in the table. Answer (D) is incorrect because the precision is determinable from the data given.

**78.** In evaluating an attribute sample, the estimated range that is expected to contain the population characteristic is the

A. Confidence level.

B. Precision.

C. Upper deviation limit.

D. Expected deviation rate.

Answer (B) is correct. *(CIA, adapted)*

**REQUIRED:** The range within which the estimate of the population characteristic is expected to fall.

**DISCUSSION:** Precision, or the confidence interval, is an interval around the sample statistic that is expected to contain the true population value. Precision for an attribute sample is based upon the tolerable rate of deviation. The upper limit of the interval is of greatest interest in attribute sampling applications.

Answer (A) is incorrect because the confidence level is the specified measure of how reliable the auditor wants the sample results to be. Answer (C) is incorrect because precision is the range between the lower and upper deviation limits. Answer (D) is incorrect because the expected deviation rate is a measure of how frequently the auditor expects the characteristic of interest to exist in the population prior to selecting and evaluating the sample.

**79.** What is an auditor's evaluation of a statistical sample for attributes when a test of 50 documents results in three deviations if the tolerable rate is 7%, the expected population deviation rate is 5%, and the allowance for sampling risk is 2%?

A. Modify the planned assessed level of control risk because the tolerable rate plus the allowance for sampling risk exceeds the expected population deviation rate.

B. Accept the sample results as support for the planned assessed level of control risk because the sample deviation rate plus the allowance for sampling risk exceeds the tolerable rate.

C. Accept the sample results as support for the planned assessed level of control risk because the tolerable rate minus the allowance for sampling risk equals the expected population deviation rate.

D. Modify the planned assessed level of control risk because the sample deviation rate plus the allowance for sampling risk exceeds the tolerable rate.

Answer (D) is correct. *(CPA, adapted)*

**REQUIRED:** The evaluation of an attribute sample given the sample deviation, sampling risk, tolerable rate, and expected rate.

**DISCUSSION:** The sample has a 6% (3 ÷ 50) deviation rate. The auditor's upper precision limit is 8% (6% + the 2% allowance for sampling risk, which is the difference between the tolerable rate of 7% and the expected rate of 5%). Thus, the true deviation rate could be as large as 8% and exceed the tolerable rate. Accordingly, the auditor should revise his/her consideration of the planned assessed level of control risk for the relevant assertions and possibly alter the nature, timing, and extent of substantive tests (AU 350).

Answer (A) is incorrect because precision (allowance for sampling risk) is the difference between the tolerable rate and the expected rate, and the precision interval is constructed around the sample rate, not the tolerable rate. Answer (B) is incorrect because a deviation rate that may be as large as 8% is a reason for revising the consideration of the planned assessed level of control risk. Answer (C) is incorrect because the sample deviation rate, which is the best estimate of the true rate, must not be ignored.

## 6.6 Variables Sampling

**80.** Very small random samples (fewer than 30) should normally be avoided when using a variables sampling plan because

A. The estimated standard deviation of the population will increase disproportionately.

B. The skew of the distribution of sample means cannot be determined.

C. The estimated population mean value will increase disproportionately.

D. The size of the sampling risk will increase disproportionately.

Answer (D) is correct. *(CIA, adapted)*

**REQUIRED:** The reason to avoid small sample sizes.

**DISCUSSION:** When small samples are selected from a population, the chance is greater that the sample will not adequately represent the population. Small samples (fewer than 30) should therefore be avoided because of the increase in sampling risk.

Answer (A) is incorrect because, if the sample is too small and is therefore not representative, the misstatement may lie in either direction depending on the sample. Answer (B) is incorrect because the results of a small sample can be statistically evaluated, but they are usually not as precise or reliable as those achieved when the sample is larger. Thus, the mean, standard error, skewness, etc., are less useful for very small samples. Answer (C) is incorrect because, if the sample is too small and is therefore not representative, the misstatement may lie in either direction depending on the sample.

**81.** In applying variables sampling, an auditor attempts to

A. Estimate a qualitative characteristic of interest.

B. Determine various rates of occurrence for specified attributes.

C. Discover at least one instance of a critical deviation.

D. Predict a monetary population value within a range of precision.

Answer (D) is correct. *(CIA, adapted)*

**REQUIRED:** The purpose of variables sampling.

**DISCUSSION:** Variables sampling is used to estimate the value of a population. In auditing, this process entails estimating the monetary value of an account balance or other accounting total. The result is often stated in terms of a point estimate plus or minus a stated dollar value (the range of precision at the desired level of confidence).

Answer (A) is incorrect because the estimate is quantitative. Answer (B) is incorrect because determining various rates of occurrence for specified attributes applies to attribute sampling. Answer (C) is incorrect because discovering at least one instance of a critical deviation is the purpose of discovery sampling.

**82.** In estimation sampling for variables, which of the following must be known in order to estimate the appropriate sample size required to meet the auditor's needs in a given situation?

A. The qualitative aspects of misstatements.

B. The total dollar amount of the population.

C. The acceptable level of risk.

D. The estimated deviation rate in the population.

Answer (C) is correct. *(CPA, adapted)*

**REQUIRED:** The factor that must be known to estimate sample size.

**DISCUSSION:** Variables sampling is employed in substantive testing because it may be used to estimate the amount of a variable, such as an account balance, and to quantify the risk that the estimate may not approximate the true value. AU 350 states, "When planning a particular sample for a substantive test of details, the auditor should consider the relationship of the sample to the audit objective, preliminary estimates of materiality levels, the auditor's allowable risk of incorrect acceptance, and characteristics of the population."

Answer (A) is incorrect because qualitative aspects of misstatements are a matter for sample evaluation, not sample size selection. Answer (B) is incorrect because estimating the population value is the objective of the sample. Also, some sampling methods, e.g., mean-per-unit sampling, ignore the carrying amounts of individual sample items. Answer (D) is incorrect because attribute sampling is concerned with deviation rates.

**83.** An auditor selected a random sample of 100 items from a population of 2,000 items. The total dollars in the sample were $10,000, and the standard deviation was $10. If the achieved precision based on this sample was plus or minus $4,000, the minimum acceptable value of the population would be

A. $204,000

B. $196,000

C. $199,000

D. $199,800

Answer (B) is correct. *(CIA, adapted)*

**REQUIRED:** The minimum acceptable value of the population.

**DISCUSSION:** The mean value of a sample item is $100 ($10,000 ÷ 100), so the estimated population value is $200,000. Given achieved precision of $4,000, the minimum acceptable value of the population is $196,000 ($200,000 – $4,000).

Answer (A) is incorrect because $204,000 results from adding $4,000. Answer (C) is incorrect because $199,000 subtracts the total standard deviation of the sample, assuming $10 is the standard deviation per sample item. Answer (D) is incorrect because $199,800 subtracts the standard deviation of the population, assuming $10 is the total standard deviation of the 100-item sample.

**84.** An auditor used a mean-per-unit sampling plan to estimate the average cost of repairing photocopy machines. The sample size was 50, and population size was 2,000. The mean of the sample was \$75. The standard deviation was \$14, and the standard error of the mean was \$2. What is the achieved confidence interval at a 95% confidence level (Z = 2)?

A. \$47 to \$103.

B. \$71 to \$79.

C. \$61 to \$89.

D. \$73 to \$75.

Answer (B) is correct. *(CIA, adapted)*

**REQUIRED:** The achieved confidence interval for a given confidence level.

**DISCUSSION:** If C is the confidence coefficient, n is the sample size, and σ is the standard deviation, the following is the basic variables sampling formula solved for precision (P):

$$P = \frac{C\sigma}{\sqrt{n}}$$

If C is given as 2 (Z = 2), the confidence interval equals the mean plus or minus two times the standard error of the mean $\left(\sigma \div \sqrt{n} = \$2\right)$. Thus, the achieved confidence interval equals \$75 ± \$4, or \$71 to \$79.

Answer (A) is incorrect because \$47 to \$103 equals two standard deviations above and below the mean. Answer (C) is incorrect because \$61 to \$89 equals one standard deviation above and below the mean. Answer (D) is incorrect because \$73 to \$75 equals one standard error below the mean.

**85.** In an application of mean-per-unit sampling, the following information has been obtained:

| | |
|---|---|
| Reported carrying amount | \$600,000 |
| Point estimate (estimated total value) | 591,000 |
| Allowance for sampling risk (precision) | ± 22,000 |
| Tolerable misstatement | ± 45,000 |

The appropriate conclusion is that the reported carrying amount is

A. Acceptable only if the risk of incorrect rejection is at least twice the risk of incorrect acceptance.

B. Acceptable.

C. Not acceptable.

D. Acceptable only if the risk of incorrect acceptance is at least twice the risk of incorrect rejection.

Answer (B) is correct. *(CIA, adapted)*

**REQUIRED:** The correct conclusion given an application of mean-per-unit sampling.

**DISCUSSION:** In mean-per-unit sampling, the audit estimate of the population value is obtained by multiplying the number of items in the population by the average value of the audited sample items. The precision interval is constructed around the audited value of the sample items. When the point estimate of the audited population value is \$591,000 with a precision interval of plus or minus \$22,000, a carrying amount of \$600,000 is acceptable because it falls within the allowance for sampling risk (precision). The precision is determined by considering the tolerable misstatement in conjunction with the allowable risk of incorrect acceptance (an issue related to audit effectiveness) and allowable risk of incorrect rejection (an efficiency issue). A table is typically consulted that gives the ratio of the precision to tolerable misstatement for the specified risks of incorrect rejection and incorrect acceptance. For example, the table sets precision at 50% of tolerable misstatement, or approximately \$22,000, when the specified risk of incorrect acceptance is 50% of the risk of incorrect rejection.

Answer (A) is incorrect because the allowable risk of incorrect rejection is separately determined by the auditor based on professional judgment. Answer (C) is incorrect because the reported value is acceptable. Answer (D) is incorrect because the allowable risk of incorrect acceptance is separately determined by the auditor based on professional judgment.

**86.** In a variables sampling application, an auditor draws random samples from two equal-sized groups of inventory items. The mean value of the inventory in the first group was calculated to be \$3,000, with a standard deviation of \$500. The mean value of inventory in the second group was estimated to be \$1,000, with a standard deviation of \$90. If the auditor had drawn an unstratified sample from the entire population, the expected mean value of inventory would be \$2,000, and the expected standard deviation would be

A. Between \$90 and \$500, but not \$295.

B. Less than \$90.

C. Greater than \$500.

D. \$295.

Answer (C) is correct. *(Publisher)*

**REQUIRED:** The standard deviation given an unstratified sample.

**DISCUSSION:** The standard deviation is a measure of variability within a population. That the population was stratified indicates that each stratum has a smaller standard deviation than the population as a whole. If the two diverse populations are combined, the resulting standard deviation is likely to be larger than that of either of the separate strata. Because the standard deviations of the two strata were \$500 and \$90, the expected standard deviation is likely to be greater than \$500.

Answer (A) is incorrect because the resulting standard deviation is likely to be larger than that of either of the separate strata. Answer (B) is incorrect because the resulting standard deviation is likely to be larger than that of either of the separate strata. Answer (D) is incorrect because \$295 is the simple average of the standard deviations of the two strata. The resulting standard deviation is likely to be larger than that of either of the separate strata.

**87.** An auditor's finding was stated as follows: "Twenty of one hundred randomly selected items tested revealed that $200 of cash discounts on purchases were lost." This variables sampling finding is deficient because the

A. Recommendation specifies no action.

B. Sampling methodology is not defined.

C. Amount is not material.

D. Probable effect on the entire population is not provided.

Answer (D) is correct. *(CIA, adapted)*

**REQUIRED:** The reason the variables sampling finding is deficient.

**DISCUSSION:** The finding states the number of population items selected and the total amount of purchase discounts lost but does not extend the sample results to the population.

Answer (A) is incorrect because no action may be necessary if there is a reason for the loss of purchase discounts or if the amount is immaterial. Answer (B) is incorrect because the methodology was stated to be random sampling. Answer (C) is incorrect because the amount may or may not be material.

## 6.7 Dollar-Unit (PPS) Sampling

**88.** An auditor is planning to use monetary-unit sampling for testing the dollar value of a large accounts receivable population. The advantages of using monetary-unit sampling (MUS) include all of the following except

A. It is an efficient model for establishing that a low error rate population is not materially misstated.

B. It does not require the normal distribution approximation required by variables sampling.

C. It can be applied to a group of accounts because the sampling units are homogenous.

D. It results in a smaller sample size than classical variables sampling for larger numbers of misstatements.

Answer (D) is correct. *(CIA, adapted)*

**REQUIRED:** The item not an advantage of MUS.

**DISCUSSION:** MUS is also known as probability-proportional-to-size (PPS) sampling or dollar-unit sampling. It is a combination of attribute sampling and variables sampling that arrives at a result stated as a dollar amount instead of a deviation rate. It uses the dollar as the sampling unit. MUS is appropriate for testing account balances, such as those for inventory and receivables, in which some items may be far larger than others in the population. In effect, it stratifies the population because the larger account balances have a greater chance of being selected. MUS is most useful if few misstatements are expected. Moreover, it is designed to detect overstatements. It is not effective for estimating understatements because, the greater the understatement, the less likely the item will be selected. Furthermore, as the number of expected misstatements increases, MUS requires a larger sample size than classical variables sampling.

Answer (A) is incorrect because MUS is efficient when few misstatements are expected. Answer (B) is incorrect because MUS does not assume normally distributed populations. Answer (C) is incorrect because MUS uses dollars as sampling units.

**89.** When an auditor uses dollar-unit statistical sampling to examine the total value of invoices, each invoice

A. Has an equal probability of being selected.

B. Can be represented by no more than one dollar unit.

C. Has an unknown probability of being selected.

D. Has a probability proportional to its dollar value of being selected.

Answer (D) is correct. *(CIA, adapted)*

**REQUIRED:** The effect of using dollar-unit sampling to examine invoices.

**DISCUSSION:** Dollar-unit sampling results in the selection of every nth dollar; thus, a $1,000 item is 1,000 times more likely to be selected than a $1 item. The probability of selection of a sampled item is directly proportional to the size of the item.

Answer (A) is incorrect because each dollar, but not each invoice, has an equal probability of being selected unless all invoices are for the same amount. Answer (B) is incorrect because it is possible for two or more dollars to be selected from the same item; e.g., a $4,500 item will be represented by four dollars if every 1,000th dollar is selected. Answer (C) is incorrect because the probability of selection can be calculated using the dollar value of the item and the dollar value of the population.

**90.** Which of the following most likely would be an advantage in using classical variables sampling rather than probability-proportional-to-size (PPS) sampling?

A. An estimate of the standard deviation of the population's recorded amounts is not required.

B. The auditor rarely needs the assistance of a computer program to design an efficient sample.

C. Inclusion of zero and negative balances usually does not require special design considerations.

D. Any amount that is individually significant is automatically identified and selected.

Answer (C) is correct. *(CPA, adapted)*

**REQUIRED:** The advantage of using classical variables sampling rather than PPS sampling.

**DISCUSSION:** PPS is most useful if few misstatements are expected and if overstatement is the most likely kind of misstatement. One disadvantage of PPS sampling is that it is designed to detect overstatements. It is not effective for estimating understatements. The smaller the item, the less likely it will be selected in the sample, but the more likely the item is understated.

Answer (A) is incorrect because the sample size formula for estimation of variables includes the standard deviation of the population. Answer (B) is incorrect because a computer program is helpful in many sampling applications. Answer (D) is incorrect because, in classical variables sampling, every item has an equal and nonzero probability of selection.

**91.** Monetary-unit sampling (MUS) is most useful when the auditor

A. Is testing the accounts payable balance.

B. Cannot cumulatively arrange the population items.

C. Expects to find several material misstatements in the sample.

D. Is concerned with overstatements.

Answer (D) is correct. *(CIA, adapted)*

**REQUIRED:** The best use of MUS.

**DISCUSSION:** MUS is also known as probability-proportional-to-size (PPS) sampling or dollar-unit sampling. It combines attribute sampling and variables sampling to arrive at a dollar amount instead of a deviation rate. It uses the dollar as the sampling unit. MUS sampling is appropriate for testing account balances, such as those for inventory and receivables, in which some items may be far larger than others in the population. In effect, it stratifies the population because the larger account balances have a greater chance of being selected. MUS is most useful if few misstatements are expected. Moreover, it is designed to detect overstatements. It is not effective for estimating understatements because, the greater the understatement, the less likely the item will be selected. Special design considerations are required if the auditor anticipates understatements or zero or negative balances.

Answer (A) is incorrect because an audit of accounts payable is primarily concerned with understatements. Answer (B) is incorrect because the items in the population must be arranged by cumulative dollar total. The first dollar is chosen randomly, the second equals the random start plus the sample interval in dollars, etc. Answer (C) is incorrect because, as the expected amount of misstatement increases, the MUS sample size increases. MUS may also overstate the upper misstatement limit when misstatements are found. The result might be rejection of an acceptable balance.

**92.** Which of the following is an improper technique when using dollar-unit statistical sampling in an audit of accounts receivable?

A. Combining negative and positive dollar misstatements in the appraisal of a sample.

B. Using a sampling technique in which the same account balance could be selected more than once.

C. Selecting a random starting point and then sampling every nth dollar unit (systematic sampling).

D. Defining the sampling unit in the population as an individual dollar and not as an individual account balance.

Answer (A) is correct. *(CIA, adapted)*

**REQUIRED:** The improper technique when using dollar-unit sampling in an audit of receivables.

**DISCUSSION:** When using dollar-unit sampling, the auditor may calculate the gross projected likely misstatement (GPLM) and the gross upper misstatement limit (GUML) for overstatements, ignoring understatements. (S)he then calculates these values for understatements, ignoring overstatements. The net upper misstatement limits are then determined by subtracting the GPLM for one kind of misstatement from the GUML for the other. The resulting net upper misstatement limits for overstatements and understatements define the precision interval. However, more complicated computations may be appropriate in certain extreme cases. The GUMLs may not be netted, and individual positive and negative misstatements also cannot be netted.

Answer (B) is incorrect because two or more dollars may be selected from the same item; e.g., a $10,000 item will be represented twice if every 5,000th dollar is selected. Answer (C) is incorrect because dollar-unit sampling consists of selecting a random start and then sampling every nth dollar unit. Answer (D) is incorrect because dollar-unit sampling defines the sampling unit in the population as an individual dollar and not as an individual account balance.

**93.** The use of probability-proportional-to-size sampling is inefficient if

A. Bank accounts are being audited.

B. Statistical inferences are to be made.

C. Each account is of equal importance.

D. The number of sampling units is large.

Answer (C) is correct. *(CIA, adapted)*

**REQUIRED:** The inefficient use of probability-proportional-to-size (PPS) sampling.

**DISCUSSION:** Probability-proportional-to-size sampling gives greater weight to larger, more significant items. If all items are of the same importance, PPS is inappropriate.

Answer (A) is incorrect because PPS sampling could be appropriate in an audit of bank accounts if larger items are more important than smaller items (which is usually true in variables sampling). Answer (B) is incorrect because PPS sampling permits statistical inferences to be made. Answer (D) is incorrect because PPS sampling could be appropriate with a large number of sampling units if larger items are more important than smaller items.

**94.** In selecting a sample using dollar-unit sampling, the dollar is the sampling unit. Thus, if the 300th dollar of invoices is selected,

A. Only that dollar is audited.

B. Only an invoice with exactly $300 is audited.

C. An invoice of less than $300 cannot be selected.

D. The invoice containing the 300th dollar is audited.

Answer (D) is correct. *(Publisher)*

**REQUIRED:** The item sampled.

**DISCUSSION:** The dollar selected is a basis for choosing the sales invoice to be audited. Thus, the 300th dollar identifies an invoice on which all dollars will be audited.

Answer (A) is incorrect because, not only is the 300th dollar audited, but also all other dollars on the invoice selected. Answer (B) is incorrect because an invoice with any amount may be selected by the technique, not just those for exactly $300. Answer (C) is incorrect because an invoice with any amount may be selected by the technique, not just those for $300 or more.

**95.** In a probability-proportional-to-size sample with a sampling interval of $5,000, an auditor discovered that a selected account receivable with a recorded amount of $10,000 had an audit amount of $8,000. If this were the only error discovered by the auditor, the projected misstatement of this sample would be

A. $1,000

B. $2,000

C. $4,000

D. $5,000

Answer (B) is correct. *(CPA, adapted)*

**REQUIRED:** The total projected misstatement of the PPS sample.

**DISCUSSION:** PPS (or dollar-unit) sampling is a commonly used method of statistical sampling for tests of details of balances because it provides a simple statistical result expressed in dollars. The projected misstatement in this sampling method equals the actual misstatement of the sampled item when the carrying amount of the item ($10,000) equals or exceeds the sampling interval ($5,000). Thus, the projected misstatement is $2,000 ($10,000 recorded amount – $8,000 audit amount).

Answer (A) is incorrect because $1,000 equals the amount of the misstatement divided by the carrying amount, times the sampling interval. Answer (C) is incorrect because $4,000 is twice the projected misstatement. Answer (D) is incorrect because $5,000 is the sampling interval.

Questions 96 through 99 are based on the following information. Edwards has decided to use probability-proportional-to-size (PPS) sampling in the audit of a client's accounts receivable balance. Few, if any, account balance overstatements are expected. Edwards plans to use the following PPS sampling table:

Reliability Factors for Overstatements

| Number of Overstatements | Risk of Incorrect Acceptance | | | | |
|---|---|---|---|---|---|
| | 1% | 5% | 10% | 15% | 20% |
| 0 | 4.61 | 3.00 | 2.31 | 1.90 | 1.61 |
| 1 | 6.64 | 4.75 | 3.89 | 3.38 | 3.00 |
| 2 | 8.41 | 6.30 | 5.33 | 4.72 | 4.28 |

The following information was also available:

| | |
|---|---|
| Tolerable misstatement | $15,000 |
| Risk of incorrect acceptance | 5% |
| Recorded amount of accounts receivable | $300,000 |

Three overstatements were discovered in a PPS sample:

| | Recorded Amount | Audit Amount |
|---|---|---|
| 1st | $ 400 | $ 320 |
| 2nd | 500 | 0 |
| 3rd | 3,000 | 2,500 |

**96.** Edwards should use a sampling interval of

A. $20,000

B. $15,000

C. $10,000

D. $5,000

Answer (D) is correct. *(Publisher)*

**REQUIRED:** The sampling interval for a PPS sample.

**DISCUSSION:** Because the dollar amount of anticipated misstatement is not given, it must be assumed to be zero. In that case, the PPS sample size formula is

$$n = \frac{RM \times RF}{TM}$$

n is the sample size, RM the recorded or carrying amount of the population, RF the reliability factor (always from the zero line of the table), and TM the tolerable misstatement. The sampling interval equals RM divided by n. Solving the formula for this value establishes that the interval also equals TM divided by RF, or $5,000 ($15,000 ÷ 3.00 at 5% risk of incorrect acceptance and zero overstatements).

Answer (A) is incorrect because $20,000 equals the $15,000 TM divided into the $300,000 BV. Answer (B) is incorrect because $15,000 is the tolerable misstatement. Answer (C) is incorrect because the derivation of $10,000 cannot be readily determined.

**97.** Given a sampling interval of $5,000, Edwards should use a sample size of

A. 60

B. 50

C. 40

D. 30

Answer (A) is correct. *(Publisher)*

**REQUIRED:** The sample size for a PPS sample.

**DISCUSSION:** The sample size equals the recorded amount of the population divided by the sampling interval, or 60 ($300,000 ÷ $5,000).

Answer (B) is incorrect because a sample size of 50 assumes an interval of $6,000, not $5,000. Answer (C) is incorrect because a sample size of 40 assumes an interval of $7,500. Answer (D) is incorrect because a sample size of 30 assumes an interval of $10,000.

**98.** Assume that the sampling interval is $1,000. What is the total projected misstatement given the three misstatements discovered?

A. $1,750

B. $1,700

C. $1,200

D. $1,000

Answer (B) is correct. *(Publisher)*

**REQUIRED:** The total projected misstatement.

**DISCUSSION:** The total projected misstatement is the sum of the misstatements projected based on the respective logical sampling units (accounts receivable) containing misstatements. If a logical unit has a recorded amount less than the sampling interval, a tainting percentage [(recorded amount – audit amount) ÷ recorded amount] is calculated for that misstatement and then multiplied by the sampling interval. The percentage taint in the logical unit is extended to all dollars in the sampling interval it represents. If the recorded amount is equal to or greater than the sampling interval, the misstatement in the logical unit is the projected misstatement.

| Recorded Amount | Audit Amount | Tainting % | Sampling Interval | Projected Misstatement |
|---|---|---|---|---|
| $ 400 | $ 320 | 20% | $1,000 | $ 200 |
| 500 | 0 | 100% | 1,000 | 1,000 |
| 3,000 | 2,500 | -- | -- | 500 |
| | | | | $1,700 |

Answer (A) is incorrect because the derivation of $1,750 cannot be readily determined. Answer (C) is incorrect because $1,200 is the total projected misstatement for the first two items. Answer (D) is incorrect because $1,000 is the projected misstatement for item two.

**99.** Assuming a sampling interval of $1,000, what is the upper misstatement limit (UML) based on this sample?

A. $1,700

B. $3,000

C. $5,560

D. $5,790

Answer (C) is correct. *(Publisher)*

**REQUIRED:** The upper misstatement limit (UML).

**DISCUSSION:** The first component of the UML is basic precision: the product of the sampling interval ($1,000) and the reliability factor (3.00) for zero misstatements at the specified risk of incorrect acceptance (5%). The second is the total projected misstatement ($1,700). The third is an allowance for widening the precision gap as a result of finding more than zero misstatements. This allowance is determined only with respect to logical sampling units with recorded amounts less than the sampling interval. If a sample item is equal to or greater than the sampling interval, the taint for that interval is certain, and no further allowance is necessary. Calculating this allowance requires determining the adjusted incremental changes in the reliability factors (these factors increase, and precision widens, as the number of misstatements increases). The factors are from the 5% column in the table. To prevent double counting of amounts included in basic precision, in projected misstatement, and in the adjustments for higher-ranked misstatements, the preceding reliability factor plus 1.0 is subtracted from each factor. The projected misstatements are then ranked from highest to lowest, each adjusted incremental reliability factor is multiplied by the related projected misstatement, and the products are summed.

| | | |
|---|---|---|
| Basic precision ($1,000 × 3.00) | | $3,000 |
| Total projected misstatement | | 1,700 |
| Allowance for precision gap widening: | | |
| (4.75 – 3.00 – 1.00) × $1,000 = | $750 | |
| (6.30 – 4.75 – 1.00) × $ 200 = | 110 | 860 |
| UML | | $5,560 |

Answer (A) is incorrect because $1,700 is the total projected misstatement given the misstatements found. Answer (B) is incorrect because $3,000 is basic precision. Answer (D) is incorrect because $5,790 {$5,560 + [(7.76 – 6.30 – 1.00) × $500]} includes an allowance for precision gap widening for a third misstatement.

Questions 100 and 101 are based on the following information.

The work of an auditor has been assigned to take a dollar-unit sample of a population of vouchers in the purchasing department. The population has a total recorded amount of $300,000. The auditor believes that a maximum misstatement of $900 is acceptable and wants to have 95% confidence in the results. (The reliability factor at 95% and zero misstatements = 3.00).

Table of First 10 Vouchers in Population

| Voucher # | Balance | Cumulative Balance |
|---|---|---|
| 1 | $100 | $ 100 |
| 2 | 150 | 250 |
| 3 | 40 | 290 |
| 4 | 200 | 490 |
| 5 | 10 | 500 |
| 6 | 290 | 790 |
| 7 | 50 | 840 |
| 8 | 190 | 1,030 |
| 9 | 20 | 1,050 |
| 10 | 180 | 1,230 |

**100.** Given a random start of $50 as the first dollar amount, what is the number of the fourth voucher to be selected, assuming that the sample size will be 1,000?

A. 4

B. 6

C. 7

D. 8

Answer (D) is correct. *(CIA, adapted)*

**REQUIRED:** The number of the fourth voucher selected using dollar-unit sampling.

**DISCUSSION:** The vouchers have a recorded amount of $300,000 and 1,000 items are to be sampled, so every 300th dollar will be chosen. Given a random start of $50, the vouchers containing the 50th, 350th, 650th, and 950th dollars will be selected. The cumulative amount of the first eight vouchers is $1,030. Accordingly, voucher 8 is the fourth voucher audited. It contains the 950th dollar.

Answer (A) is incorrect because voucher 4 contains the 350th dollar and is the second voucher selected. Answer (B) is incorrect because voucher 6 contains the 650th dollar and is the third voucher selected. Answer (C) is incorrect because voucher 7 is not selected.

**101.** In examining the sample, one overstatement was detected, causing an extension of $270 to the tolerable misstatement. Assuming that the sample size was 1,000 and that the maximum dollar amount of overstatement if no misstatements were found was established to be $900 before the sampling analysis, what conclusion can the auditor now make from the sampling evidence?

A. (S)he is 95% confident that the dollar amount of overstatement in the population of vouchers is between $900 and $1,170.

B. (S)he is 95% confident that the dollar amount of overstatement in the population of vouchers exceeds $1,170.

C. (S)he is 95% confident that the dollar amount of overstatement in the population of vouchers is less than $1,170.

D. An insufficient number of misstatements was detected to warrant a conclusion.

Answer (C) is correct. *(CIA, adapted)*

**REQUIRED:** The conclusion from the audit evidence given an extension of tolerable misstatement.

**DISCUSSION:** Had the internal auditor detected no misstatements in the sample, (s)he could have been 95% confident that the dollar amount of overstatement in the balance was less than $900. Given discovery of an overstatement causing an extension to the tolerable misstatement of $270, the auditor could conclude with 95% confidence that the overstatement is less than $1,170 ($900 + $270).

Answer (A) is incorrect because the auditor is 95% confident that the overstatement is less than $1,170. Answer (B) is incorrect because the auditor is 95% confident that the overstatement is less than $1,170. Answer (D) is incorrect because a conclusion would have been warranted even if no misstatements had been found.

**102.** Which of the following statements is true concerning probability-proportional-to-size (PPS) sampling, also known as dollar-unit sampling?

A. The sampling distribution should approximate the normal distribution.

B. Overstated units have a lower probability of sample selection than units that are understated.

C. The auditor controls the risk of incorrect acceptance by specifying that risk level for the sampling plan.

D. The sampling interval is calculated by dividing the number of physical units in the population by the sample size.

Answer (C) is correct. *(CPA, adapted)*

**REQUIRED:** The true statement about PPS sampling.

**DISCUSSION:** AU 350 considers PPS sampling to be an appropriate random-based method. Thus, it is a technique the auditor may use to measure and control the risks associated with observing fewer than 100% of the population. The auditor can quantify and measure beta risk, i.e., the risk of accepting a recorded (carrying) amount as fair when it is materially misstated.

Answer (A) is incorrect because PPS requires no assumptions about the population or sampling distribution. Answer (B) is incorrect because, as the size of the units in the population increases, so does the probability of selection. Answer (D) is incorrect because the sampling interval is calculated by dividing the total dollars, not units, in the population by the sample size. Every nth dollar is then selected after a random start.

## 6.8 Relationships -- Sample Size Determinants

**103.** A number of factors influence the sample size for a substantive test of details of an account balance. All other factors being equal, which of the following would lead to a larger sample size?

A. A lower assessed level of control risk.

B. Increased use of analytical procedures to obtain evidence about particular assertions.

C. Smaller expected frequency of deviations.

D. Smaller measure of tolerable misstatement.

Answer (D) is correct. *(CPA, adapted)*

**REQUIRED:** The factor increasing sample size.

**DISCUSSION:** Holding the risk of incorrect acceptance constant, a reduction in acceptable tolerable misstatement requires the auditor to select a larger sample. The larger sample reduces the allowance for sampling risk.

Answer (A) is incorrect because, as control risk decreases, the acceptable level of detection risk increases. Substantive tests are applied to reduce detection risk to the acceptable level. As that level rises, the assurance that must be provided by substantive tests declines. Smaller samples may therefore be appropriate when acceptable detection risk increases. Answer (B) is incorrect because "the auditor's reliance on substantive tests to achieve an audit objective related to a particular assertion may be derived from tests of details, from analytical procedures, or from a combination of both" (AU 329, *Analytical Procedures*). Thus, use of analytical procedures might reduce or eliminate the need for tests of details. Answer (C) is incorrect because frequency of deviations concerns sampling for attributes, not for variables. Moreover, a smaller expected deviation rate permits a smaller sample.

**104.** The size of a sample designed for dual-purpose testing should be

A. The larger of the samples that would otherwise have been designed for the two separate purposes.

B. The smaller of the samples that would otherwise have been designed for the two separate purposes.

C. The combined total of the samples that would otherwise have been designed for the two separate purposes.

D. More than the larger of the samples that would otherwise have been designated for the two separate purposes, but less than the combined total of the samples that would otherwise have been designed for the two separate purposes.

Answer (A) is correct. *(CPA, adapted)*

**REQUIRED:** The true statement about sample size for dual-purpose testing.

**DISCUSSION:** According to AU 350, dual-purpose testing is the use of a sample for both tests of controls and substantive testing. It is customarily employed when the auditor believes that "there is an acceptably low risk that the rate of deviations from the prescribed control in the population exceeds the tolerable rate." Hence, a related substantive test might be planned at a level of risk that anticipates an assessed level of control risk below the maximum. The sample size "should be the larger of the samples that would otherwise have been designed for the two separate purposes."

**105.** Which of the following combinations results in a decrease in sample size in an attribute sample?

| | Allowable Risk of Assessing Control Risk Too Low | Tolerable Rate | Expected Population Deviation Rate |
|---|---|---|---|
| A. | Increase | Decrease | Increase |
| B. | Decrease | Increase | Decrease |
| C. | Increase | Increase | Decrease |
| D. | Increase | Increase | Increase |

Answer (C) is correct. *(CPA, adapted)*

**REQUIRED:** The combination that results in a decrease in the size of an attribute sample.

**DISCUSSION:** To determine the sample size for a test of controls, the auditor considers (1) the tolerable rate of deviations, (2) the expected actual rate of deviations, and (3) the allowable risk of assessing control risk too low. An increase in the allowable risk of assessing control risk too low, an increase in the tolerable rate, and a decrease in the expected rate have the effect of diminishing the degree of assurance to be provided by the sample. Thus, each factor is a basis for reducing sample size.

**106.** An auditor should consider the tolerable rate of deviation when determining the number of check requests to select for a test to obtain assurance that all check requests have been properly authorized. The auditor should also consider

| | The Average Dollar Value of the Check Requests | The Allowable Risk of Assessing Control Risk Too Low |
|---|---|---|
| A. | Yes | Yes |
| B. | Yes | No |
| C. | No | Yes |
| D. | No | No |

Answer (C) is correct. *(CPA, adapted)*

**REQUIRED:** The issue(s), if any, to consider in determining the size of a sample in a test of controls.

**DISCUSSION:** Tests of controls, such as tests of proper authorization of check requests, are binary; that is, the auditor determines whether the control has been applied. Dollar values are irrelevant in this form of testing. However, the determination of the sample size for a test of controls (an attribute sample) is based on the following formula:

$$n = C^2 pq \div P^2$$

C is the coefficient for the specified confidence level (1 – the allowable risk of assessing control risk too low), p is the expected population deviation rate, q is 100% minus p, and P is the specified precision (tolerable deviation rate – the expected population deviation). Moreover, if the population is not large (less than 5,000 items), a correction factor would be included in the calculation.

**107.** An auditor seeks to determine the misstatements made in recording sales invoices. Which of the following factors will usually be most significant in determining the number of sales invoices to select for testing?

A. The total number of invoices for the period.

B. The estimated loss being incurred by the division.

C. The dollars of sales considered to be material.

D. The precision desired.

Answer (D) is correct. *(CIA, adapted)*

**REQUIRED:** The factor most significant in determining the required sample size.

**DISCUSSION:** The auditor's precision is usually the most important factor in determining the number of sales invoices to be selected. The precision is squared before it is used in the sample size formula. Accordingly, relatively small changes in the desired precision have a great effect on the required sample size.

Answer (A) is incorrect because the population size has a relatively small effect on the required sample size. The finite population correction factor reduces the required sample size for samples that are large relative to the population. Answer (B) is incorrect because the estimated loss being incurred by the division is not a factor used in calculating sample size. Answer (C) is incorrect because the amount of sales considered to be material is not a factor used in calculating sample size.

**108.** In an audit of a governmental agency, you are searching for expenditures that are improperly classified. Assuming a statistical sampling plan is adopted, which of the factors listed below most directly affects the number of items that you seek to review?

A. Magnitude of the dollar budget for the agency.

B. Number of items you found misclassified in last year's audit.

C. Quality of internal control.

D. Estimated deviation rate.

Answer (D) is correct. *(CIA, adapted)*

**REQUIRED:** The most significant factor used in determining the size of the sample.

**DISCUSSION:** In the attribute sample size formula, the estimated deviation rate, its complement, and the square of the confidence coefficient are factors appearing in the numerator. The square of the precision is in the denominator.

Answer (A) is incorrect because attribute sampling is concerned with deviation rates, not quantities or dollar values. Answer (B) is incorrect because, although the number of items misclassified in the previous period may be helpful, the auditor still must calculate the estimated deviation rate for the current period. Answer (C) is incorrect because the quality of internal control is not explicitly recognized in the sample size formula. However, the estimation of the deviation rate may be influenced by the auditor's understanding of internal control.

**109.** An auditor is determining the sample size for an inventory observation using mean-per-unit estimation, which is a variables sampling plan. To calculate the required sample size, the auditor usually determines the

| | Variability in the Dollar Amounts of Inventory Items | Risk of Incorrect Acceptance |
|---|---|---|
| A. | Yes | Yes |
| B. | Yes | No |
| C. | No | Yes |
| D. | No | No |

Answer (A) is correct. *(CPA, adapted)*

**REQUIRED:** The factor(s), if any, used to determine a mean-per-unit sample size.

**DISCUSSION:** Four factors are considered in determining sample size for mean-per-unit estimation. Those factors include the population size, an estimate of population variation (the standard deviation), the risk of incorrect rejection (its complement is the confidence level), and the tolerable misstatement (precision is a percentage thereof, and the percentage is a function of the risk of incorrect rejection and the allowable risk of incorrect acceptance).

**110.** An auditor is considering a sample size of 50 to estimate the average amount per invoice in a large trucking company. How will the precision of the sample results be affected if the sample size is increased to 200?

A. The larger sample will be about two times as precise as the smaller sample.

B. The larger sample will be about four times as precise as the smaller sample.

C. Although precision will not be increased that much, a possible downward bias in the estimate of the average per invoice would be corrected.

D. Both sample sizes are larger than 30, so the increase will not have that much of an effect on precision.

Answer (A) is correct. *(CIA, adapted)*

**REQUIRED:** The effect on precision of increasing the sample size.

**DISCUSSION:** In variables sampling, the precision of the sample results is inversely proportional to the square root of the sample size. Thus, increasing the sample by a factor of four decreases (tightens) the precision by a factor of two.

Answer (B) is incorrect because the precision of sample results does not increase at the same rate as sample size. Answer (C) is incorrect because the expected value of the sample mean is the same regardless of sample size. Answer (D) is incorrect because precision will tighten by a factor of two.

Questions 111 through 115 are based on the following information. The following table shows comparative population characteristics and audit specifications of two populations:

| | Characteristics of Population 1 Relative to Population 2 | | Audit Specifications as to a Sample from Population 1 Relative to a Sample from Population 2 | |
|---|---|---|---|---|
| | Size | Variability | Specified Precision | Specified Confidence Level |
| Case 1 | Equal | Equal | Equal | Higher |
| Case 2 | Equal | Larger | Wider | Equal |
| Case 3 | Larger | Equal | Tighter | Lower |
| Case 4 | Smaller | Smaller | Equal | Lower |
| Case 5 | Larger | Equal | Equal | Higher |

For this question (this case), you are to indicate the required sample size to be selected from population 1 relative to the sample from population 2.

**REQUIRED:** The effects on sample size of changing the characteristics and specifications of two populations.

**DISCUSSION:** In general, four factors affect sample size for a variables sampling application: population size, variability of the population, specified precision (allowance for sampling risk), and specified confidence level (reliability). Increases in population size, variability, and specified confidence level cause sample sizes to become larger. Increases in specified precision cause sample sizes to become smaller.

**111.** In Case 1, the required sample size from Population 1 is

A. Larger than the required sample size from Population 2.

B. Equal to the required sample size from Population 2.

C. Smaller than the required sample size from Population 2.

D. Indeterminate relative to the required sample size from Population 2.

Answer (A) is correct. *(CPA, adapted)*

**REQUIRED:** The effects on sample size of changing the characteristics and specifications of two populations.

**DISCUSSION:** In Case 1, all other characteristics are the same except that Population 1 will have a higher specified confidence level. A higher confidence level has a higher confidence coefficient, which varies directly with sample size. Thus, the auditor must take a larger sample size from Population 1 than from Population 2.

**112.** In Case 2, the required sample size from Population 1 is

A. Larger than the required sample size from Population 2.

B. Equal to the required sample size from Population 2.

C. Smaller than the required sample size from Population 2.

D. Indeterminate relative to the required sample size from Population 2.

Answer (D) is correct. *(CPA, adapted)*

**REQUIRED:** The effects on sample size of changing the characteristics and specifications of two populations.

**DISCUSSION:** In Case 2, variability in Population 1 is larger and the specified precision is wider. Larger variability (a larger $\sigma$) requires a larger sample size, but the wider precision decreases the sample size. The magnitudes are unknown, so the relative required sample size is not determinable.

**113.** In Case 3, the required sample size from Population 1 is

A. Larger than the required sample size from Population 2.

B. Equal to the required sample size from Population 2.

C. Smaller than the required sample size from Population 2.

D. Indeterminate relative to the required sample size from Population 2.

Answer (D) is correct. *(CPA, adapted)*

**REQUIRED:** The effects on sample size of changing the characteristics and specifications of two populations.

**DISCUSSION:** Case 3 specifies a larger population size, a tighter specified precision, and a lower confidence level. The larger size of Population 1 and the tighter precision require a larger sample size; however, the lower specified confidence level requires a smaller sample size. Because the magnitudes are unknown, the effect on sample size is not determinable.

**114.** In Case 4, the required sample size from Population 1 is

A. Larger than the required sample size from Population 2.

B. Equal to the required sample size from Population 2.

C. Smaller than the required sample size from Population 2.

D. Indeterminate relative to the required sample size from Population 2.

Answer (C) is correct. *(CPA, adapted)*

**REQUIRED:** The effects on sample size of changing the characteristics and specifications of two populations.

**DISCUSSION:** In Case 4, Population 1 is smaller than Population 2, the variability is smaller, and the required specified confidence level is lower. Smaller population size indicates a smaller sample size. The smaller variability and lower confidence level also decrease the sample size. Thus, the sample required from Population 1 is smaller than that from Population 2.

**115.** In Case 5, the required sample size from Population 1 is

A. Larger than the required sample size from Population 2.

B. Equal to the required sample size from Population 2.

C. Smaller than the required sample size from Population 2.

D. Indeterminate relative to the required sample size from Population 2.

Answer (A) is correct. *(CPA, adapted)*

**REQUIRED:** The effects on sample size of changing the characteristics and specifications of two populations.

**DISCUSSION:** In Case 5, Population 1 is larger and has a higher specified confidence level. Both attributes are directly related to sample size. Thus, the sample from Population 1 will be larger than that from Population 2.

**116.** In attribute sampling, a 10% change in which of the following factors normally will have the least effect on the size of a statistical sample?

A. Population size.

B. Precision (confidence interval).

C. Reliability (confidence level).

D. Standard deviation.

Answer (A) is correct. *(CPA, adapted)*

**REQUIRED:** The factor having the least effect on sample sizes in attribute sampling.

**DISCUSSION:** A change in the size of the population has a very small effect on the required sample size when the population is large. This conclusion can be shown by analyzing the finite population correction factor sometimes applied to the standard sample size formula. An approximation of the FPC formula is

$$n = n'\sqrt{\frac{N - n'}{N}}$$

where n' equals the preliminary sample size, n equals the determined sample size, and N is the population size. Changes in N cause very little change in the expression; e.g., a reduction in the population such that the former sample size now constitutes about 20% of the reduced population only decreases the required sample size by about 10%.

Answer (B) is incorrect because precision (confidence interval) has a major effect on sample size. Answer (C) is incorrect because reliability (confidence level) has a major effect on sample size. Answer (D) is incorrect because standard deviation has a major effect on sample size.

**117.** In testing a control, an auditor established an upper precision limit of 6% and a confidence level of 95%. The expected deviation rate was 4%. If the auditor expects a deviation rate of only 2% but wishes to retain the same upper precision limit and confidence level, the sample size should approximate

A. 518

B. 412

C. 369

D. 47

Answer (D) is correct. *(Publisher)*

**REQUIRED:** The effect of a change in occurrence rate on sample size.

**DISCUSSION:** In attribute sampling, the expected deviation rate varies directly with sample size. Thus, a reduction in the deviation rate should cause a reduction in the required sample size. Based on the attribute sampling formula below, the sample size should be the number calculated with the formula for sample size.

$$n = \frac{C^2 pq}{P^2} = \frac{1.96^2 \times .02 \times .98}{.04^2} = 47$$

C is the confidence coefficient, p is the deviation rate, q is 100% – p, P is the specified precision interval (tolerable rate minus the expected occurrence rate), and n is the sample size. The specified precision is equal to the desired upper precision limit minus the occurrence rate. In this example, P increases from 2% to 4%.

**118.** If all other sample size planning factors were exactly the same in attribute sampling, changing the confidence level from 95% to 90% and changing the desired precision from 2% to 5% would result in a revised sample size that is

A. Larger.

B. Smaller.

C. Unchanged.

D. Indeterminate.

Answer (B) is correct. *(CIA, adapted)*

**REQUIRED:** The sample size effect of decreasing the confidence level and widening the desired precision interval.

**DISCUSSION:** If C is the confidence coefficient, p is the expected deviation rate, q is 100% minus p, and P is the desired precision, the basic sample-size formula for attribute sampling is

$$n = \frac{C^2 pq}{P^2}$$

Thus, if the confidence level is reduced (the numerator item C is lower) and precision is widened (the denominator item P is greater), sample size will be smaller.

Answer (A) is incorrect because increasing C and narrowing P would result in a larger sample size. Answer (C) is incorrect because decreasing C and widening P decreases the sample size. Answer (D) is incorrect because decreasing C and widening P decreases the sample size.

**119.** What effect does an increase in the standard deviation have on the required sample size of mean-per-unit estimation and dollar-unit sampling? Assume no change in any of the other characteristics of the population and no change in desired precision and confidence.

| | Mean-per-Unit Estimation | Dollar-Unit Sampling |
|---|---|---|
| A. | Decrease in sample size | No change in sample size |
| B. | No change in sample size | Decrease in sample size |
| C. | Increase in sample size | No change in sample size |
| D. | No change in sample size | Increase in sample size |

Answer (C) is correct. *(CIA, adapted)*

**REQUIRED:** The effect of an increase in the standard deviation on the required sample size.

**DISCUSSION:** An increase in the standard deviation represents an increase in the variability of the population. It therefore requires increasing the sample size when MPU is used. A sample for an MPU application is determined from the standard variables sampling sample size formula. The DUS sample size formula does not include the population standard deviation or other measure of variability. The sampling units consist of individual dollars. Hence, they are homogeneous, and no measure of their variability is necessary.

**120.** Hill has decided to use probability-proportional-to-size (PPS) sampling, sometimes called dollar-unit sampling, in the audit of a client's accounts receivable balances. Hill plans to use the following PPS sampling table:

TABLE 1
Reliability Factors for Overstatements

| Number of Overstatements | Risk of Incorrect Acceptance 1% | 5% | 10% | 15% | 20% |
|---|---|---|---|---|---|
| 0 | 4.61 | 3.00 | 2.31 | 1.90 | 1.61 |
| 1 | 6.64 | 4.75 | 3.89 | 3.38 | 3.00 |
| 2 | 8.41 | 6.30 | 5.33 | 4.72 | 4.28 |

TABLE 2
Expansion Factors for Expected Errors

| | Risk of Incorrect Acceptance 1% | 5% | 10% | 15% | 20% |
|---|---|---|---|---|---|
| Factor | 1.9 | 1.6 | 15 | 1.4 | 1.3 |

| Additional Information | |
|---|---|
| Tolerable misstatement | $ 24,000 |
| Anticipated misstatement | $ 5,000 |
| Risk on incorrect acceptance | 5% |
| Recorded amount of accounts receivable | $240,000 |
| Number of accounts | 360 |

What sample size should Hill use?

A. 120
B. 108
C. 45
D. 30

Answer (C) is correct. *(Publisher)*
**REQUIRED:** The size of the PPS sample.
**DISCUSSION:** PPS sampling is appropriate for account balances that may include a few overstated items, such as inventory and receivables. PPS sampling relies on an attribute sampling approach (Poisson distribution) to reach a conclusion regarding the probability of overstating an account balance by a specified amount of dollars. The PPS sample size formula is

$$n = \frac{RM \times RF}{TM - (AM \times EF)}$$

n equals sample size, RM is the recorded or carrying amount of the account, RF is the appropriate reliability factor (always from the zero line of Table 1), TM is tolerable misstatement, AM is the anticipated misstatement, and EF is the expansion factor (from Table 2).

$$n = \frac{\$240,000 \times 3.00}{\$24,000 - (\$5,000 \times 1.6)}$$

**121.** An auditor initially planned to use unrestricted random sampling with replacement in the audit of accounts receivable. Later, the auditor decided to use unrestricted random sampling without replacement. As a result of this decision, the sample size should

A. Increase.
B. Remain the same.
C. Decrease.
D. Be indeterminate.

Answer (C) is correct. *(CPA, adapted)*
**REQUIRED:** The effect of sampling without replacement on the sample size.
**DISCUSSION:** Unrestricted random sampling means each item in the population has an equal and nonzero chance of being selected. Sampling with replacement means an item may be included more than once in the sample. Sampling without replacement removes an item from the population after selection. Sampling without replacement uses information about the population more efficiently. It results in a smaller sample, if other things are held constant, because the sample size formula for sampling without replacement is multiplied by the finite population correction factor (always less than 1.0).

Questions 122 through 126 are based on the following information. Robert Lambert is a CPA of Rainbow Manufacturing Corporation. Rainbow manufactures two products: Product A and Product B. Product A requires raw materials that have a very low per-item cost, and Product B requires raw materials that have a very high per-item cost. Raw materials for both products are stored in a single warehouse. In year 1, Rainbow established the total value of raw materials stored in the warehouse by physically inventorying an unrestricted random sample of items selected without replacement. Mr. Lambert is evaluating the statistical validity of alternative sampling plans Rainbow is considering for year 2. Lambert knows the size of the year 1 sample and that Rainbow did not use stratified sampling in year 1. Assumptions about the population, variability, specified precision (confidence interval), and specified reliability (confidence level) for a possible year 2 sample are given in individual cases. You are to indicate in each case the effect upon the size of the year 2 sample as compared to the year 1 sample. Each case is independent of cases presented in other questions relating to this fact pattern.

**122.** Rainbow wants to use stratified sampling in year 2 (the total population will be divided into two strata, one each for the raw materials for Product A and Product B). Compared with year 1, the population size of the raw materials inventory is approximately the same, and the variability of the items in the inventory is approximately the same. The specified precision and specified reliability are to remain the same. Under these assumptions, the required sample size for year 2 should be

A. Larger than the year 1 sample size.

B. Equal to the year 1 sample size.

C. Smaller than the year 1 sample size.

D. Of a size that is indeterminate based upon the information given.

Answer (C) is correct. *(CPA, adapted)*

**REQUIRED:** The effects of changing population size, variability of population, specified precision, specified reliability, and sample selection methods on sample size.

**DISCUSSION:** In this case, all factors are held constant except that the population is to be stratified. One subpopulation will contain materials with a very low per-item cost, while the other subpopulation will include raw materials that have a high per-item cost. By dividing the population into two strata, the variability within each subpopulation will probably be greatly reduced compared to that of the single population sampled in year 1. Because the variability is less, the sample sizes will be smaller. The sum of the two samples will likely be less than the prior year's sample size.

**123.** Rainbow wants to use stratified sampling in year 2. Compared with year 1, the population size of the raw materials inventory is approximately the same, and the variability of the items in the inventory is approximately the same. Rainbow specified the same precision but desires to change the specified reliability from 90% to 95%. Under these assumptions, the required sample size for year 2 should be

A. Larger than the year 1 sample size.

B. Equal to the year 1 sample size.

C. Smaller than the year 1 sample size.

D. Of a size that is indeterminate based upon the information given.

Answer (D) is correct. *(CPA, adapted)*

**REQUIRED:** The effects of changing population size, variability of population, specified precision, specified reliability, and sample selection methods on sample size.

**DISCUSSION:** Stratification allows smaller sample sizes when the total population contains a high amount of variability. The purpose of stratification is to create strata, each of which has less variability than the total population. However, the effect of increasing the specified reliability from 90% to 95% is to increase sample size. Because the magnitude of the variability change is unknown, the effect on the sample size is not determinable.

**124.** Rainbow wants to use unrestricted random sampling without replacement in year 2. Compared with year 1, the population size of the raw materials inventory is approximately the same, and the variability of the items in the inventory is approximately the same. Rainbow specifies the same precision but desires to change the specified reliability from 90% to 95%. Under these assumptions, the required sample size for year 2 should be

A. Larger than the year 1 sample size.

B. Equal to the year 1 sample size.

C. Smaller than the year 1 sample size.

D. Of a size that is indeterminate based upon the information given.

Answer (A) is correct. *(CPA, adapted)*

**REQUIRED:** The effects of changing population size, variability of population, specified precision, specified reliability, and sample selection methods on sample size.

**DISCUSSION:** The only change from year 1 to year 2 is that the specified reliability (confidence level) will increase from 90% to 95%. Because reliability varies directly with sample size, a larger sample will be required for year 2.

**125.** Rainbow wants to use unrestricted random sampling without replacement in year 2. Compared with year 1, the population size of the raw materials inventory has increased, and the variability of the items in the inventory has increased. The specified precision and specified reliability are to remain the same. Under these assumptions, the required sample size for year 2 should be

A. Larger than the year 1 sample size.

B. Equal to the year 1 sample size.

C. Smaller than the year 1 sample size.

D. Of a size that is indeterminate based upon the information given.

Answer (A) is correct. *(CPA, adapted)*

**REQUIRED:** The effects of changing population size, variability of population, specified precision, specified reliability, and sample selection methods on sample size.

**DISCUSSION:** The increase in population size and in variability are directly related to sample size. Because both changes increase the necessary sample size, the sample for year 2 will be larger than that for year 1.

**126.** Rainbow wants to use unrestricted random sampling without replacement in year 2. Compared with year 1, the population size of the raw materials inventory has increased, but the variability of the items in the inventory has decreased. The specified precision and specified reliability are to remain the same. Under these assumptions, the required sample size for year 2 should be

A. Larger than the year 1 sample size.

B. Equal to the year 1 sample size.

C. Smaller than the year 1 sample size.

D. Of a size that is indeterminate based upon the information given.

Answer (D) is correct. *(CPA, adapted)*

**REQUIRED:** The effects of changing population size, variability of population, specified precision, specified reliability, and sample selection methods on sample size.

**DISCUSSION:** Population size and variability are directly related to sample size. The increase in population dictates an increase in sample size, while the decrease in variability requires a decrease in sample size. Because the magnitudes of the changes are not given, the change in the size of the sample is indeterminate.

Questions 127 and 128 are based on the following information.

Determination of Sample Size
RISK LEVEL -- 10% (90% RELIABILITY)

| Sample Size | Occurrence Rate (%) | | | | |
|---|---|---|---|---|---|
| | 1.0 | 2.0 | 3.0 | 4.0 | 5.0 |
| | Upper Precision Limit (%) | | | | |
| 100 | 3.3 | 5.2 | 6.6 | 7.8 | 9.1 |
| 200 | 2.6 | 4.0 | 5.2 | 6.4 | 7.6 |
| 300 | 2.2 | 3.5 | 4.7 | 5.9 | 7.0 |
| 350 | | 3.3 | | 5.7 | |
| 400 | 2.0 | 3.2 | 4.4 | 5.6 | 6.7 |
| 450 | | 3.1 | | 5.5 | |
| 500 | 1.8 | 3.1 | 4.2 | 5.4 | 6.5 |
| 550 | | 3.0 | | 5.3 | |
| 600 | 1.7 | 2.9 | 4.1 | 5.2 | 6.3 |
| 700 | 1.7 | 2.9 | 4.0 | 5.1 | 6.2 |

**127.** If 10% risk (90% reliability) is acceptable with an expected occurrence rate of 3% and an upper precision limit (tolerable ràte) of 5%, the minimum sample size should be

A. 117

B. 240

C. 300

D. 550

Answer (B) is correct. *(CIA, adapted)*

**REQUIRED:** The minimum sample size given risk, expected occurrence rate, and an upper precision limit.

**DISCUSSION:** At an occurrence rate of 3%, the sample size for an upper precision limit of 5.2% is 200. For a limit of 4.7%, the sample size is 300. For a limit of 5%, interpolation yields a sample size of 240.

$$\left[\frac{(5.2-5.0)}{(5.2-4.7)} \times (300-200)\right] + 200 = 240$$

Answer (A) is incorrect because a sample size of 117 signifies an upper precision limit between 6.6% and 5.2%. Answer (C) is incorrect because a sample size of 300 corresponds to an upper precision limit of 4.7%. Answer (D) is incorrect because a sample size of 550 relates to an upper precision limit between 4.2% and 4.1%.

**128.** At 10% risk (90% reliability), a sample of 200 items has been drawn and tested. The upper precision limit (tolerable rate) is 3%. Which of the following statements is true?

A. If four deviations were found, the population would be acceptable.

B. If two deviations were found, the population would be acceptable.

C. A tolerable rate of 3% indicates a high planned assessed level of control risk for the control tested.

D. The auditor should assume that each deviation results in a misstatement in the accounting records.

Answer (B) is correct. *(CIA, adapted)*

**REQUIRED:** The true statement given risk, sample size, and the tolerable rate.

**DISCUSSION:** If the sample consists of 200 items and two deviations are found, the occurrence rate is 1%. At 90% reliability, the upper precision limit for an occurrence rate of 1% is 2.6%. The population is acceptable because one can state with 90% reliability that the true occurrence rate is 2.6% or less, which is less than the tolerable rate of 3%.

Answer (A) is incorrect because, at an occurrence rate of 2% (four deviations in a sample of 200), the upper precision limit (4%) exceeds the tolerable rate (3%). Answer (C) is incorrect because a low tolerable rate suggests that the planned assessed level of control risk is low. Answer (D) is incorrect because a deviation does not signify a misstatement in the records.

# STUDY UNIT SEVEN
# AUDIT REPORTS



This study unit includes questions on audit reports covering most of AU Sections 400 and 500. Study Unit 8, Special Reports and Other Reporting Issues, addresses the remaining matters relevant to external auditing, and internal audit reports are covered in Study Unit 9.

Thus, Study Unit 7 concerns reports issued on the results of financial statement audits performed in accordance with auditing standards by independent, external auditors. The language of audit reports for "nonissuers" (private companies) is determined by the four standards of reporting (given below) and Statements on Auditing Standards (SASs) issued by the Auditing Standards Board. SASs are codified within the framework of the 10 general, field work, and reporting standards adopted by the AICPA membership. An auditor who is an AICPA member must comply with SASs. In general, the PCAOB has adopted the existing SASs. However, for reports on "issuers" (public companies), the report language is determined by the PCAOB.

<u>GAAS Standards of Reporting</u>

1. The report shall state whether the financial statements are presented in accordance with generally accepted accounting principles.
2. The report shall identify those circumstances in which such principles have not been consistently observed in the current period in relation to the preceding period.
3. Informative disclosures in the financial statements are to be regarded as reasonably adequate unless otherwise stated in the report.
4. The report shall contain either an expression of opinion regarding the financial statements, taken as a whole, or an assertion to the effect that an opinion cannot be expressed. When an overall opinion cannot be expressed, the reasons therefore should be stated. In all cases in which an auditor's name is associated with financial statements, the report should contain a clear-cut indication of the character of the auditor's work, if any, and the degree of responsibility the auditor is taking.

## QUESTIONS

### 7.1 Purposes

**1.** The AICPA's GAAS encompass four reporting standards. They include all but which of the following?

A. The report shall state whether the financial statements are presented in accordance with GAAP.

B. The report shall state that GAAS have been followed in the conduct of the audit.

C. The report should identify those circumstances in which GAAP have not been consistently applied.

D. Informative disclosures in the financial statements are to be regarded as reasonably adequate unless otherwise stated in the report.

Answer (B) is correct. *(Publisher)*

**REQUIRED:** The item not a reporting standard.

**DISCUSSION:** Although the auditor's standard report for nonissuers must state in the scope paragraph that GAAS have been followed, the four generally accepted reporting standards do not explicitly require such a statement. All the other answers state reporting standards.

Answer (A) is incorrect because the first standard of reporting requires a statement as to whether the financial statements are in accordance with GAAP. Answer (C) is incorrect because the requirement to identify lack of consistency is contained in the second reporting standard. Answer (D) is incorrect because the requirement to report on lack of adequate disclosure is stated in the third reporting standard.

**2.** The objective of the traditional audit of financial statements is

A. To make suggestions as to the form or content of the financial statements or to draft them in whole or in part.

B. To express an opinion on the fairness with which the statements present financial position, results of operations, and cash flows in accordance with generally accepted accounting principles.

C. To assure adoption of sound accounting policies and the establishment and maintenance of internal control.

D. To express an opinion on the accuracy with which the statements present financial position, results of operations, and cash flows in accordance with generally accepted accounting principles.

Answer (B) is correct. *(Publisher)*

**REQUIRED:** The objective of an audit.

**DISCUSSION:** Based on a traditional audit, the independent auditor expresses an opinion (or a disclaimer of opinion) on the fairness, in all material respects, of the presentation of financial statements, i.e., on whether they will be misleading to users. The report should state whether the audit was in accordance with auditing standards and whether, in the auditor's opinion, the statements are presented in conformity with GAAP (AU 110, *Responsibilities and Functions of the Independent Auditor*).

Answer (A) is incorrect because the auditor may make suggestions concerning the statements or help prepare them, but (s)he is responsible only for expressing an opinion as to their fairness. The statements remain the representations of management. Answer (C) is incorrect because management is responsible for adopting sound accounting policies and establishing and maintaining internal control. Answer (D) is incorrect because the auditor expresses an opinion on the fairness of financial statements, not their accuracy.

**3.** Which of the following best describes why an independent auditor is asked to express an opinion on the fair presentation of financial statements?

A. It is difficult to prepare financial statements that fairly present a company's financial position, results of operations, and cash flows without the expertise of an independent auditor.

B. It is management's responsibility to seek available independent aid in the appraisal of the financial information shown in its financial statements.

C. The opinion of an independent party is needed because a company may not be objective with respect to its own financial statements.

D. It is a customary courtesy that all shareholders receive an independent report on management's stewardship in managing the affairs of the business.

Answer (C) is correct. *(CPA, adapted)*

**REQUIRED:** The best reason for an independent auditor's opinion.

**DISCUSSION:** The opinion of a suitably qualified, independent, outside party lends credibility to the financial statements. The opinion contained in the audit report, which accompanies the audited financial statements, is the result of the auditor's performance of the attest function: the gathering of evidence during the audit and the expression of an opinion on the fairness of the statements.

Answer (A) is incorrect because the auditor's independence is vital to the performance of the attest function, not his/her preparation of financial statements. Under the Sarbanes-Oxley Act of 2002, a registered public accounting firm may not provide to a public client certain nonaudit services such as bookkeeping or other services related to its accounting records or financial statements. Also, the assertions in the statements are the sole responsibility of management. Answer (B) is incorrect because management does not seek an appraisal of the financial statements, only an opinion as to whether they are presented fairly. Answer (D) is incorrect because, although the distribution of information to shareholders is customary, it is not the primary reason for an auditor's report.

**11.** The auditor's judgment concerning the overall fairness of the presentation of financial position, results of operations, and cash flows is applied within the framework of

A. Quality control.

B. Auditing standards, which include the concept of materiality.

C. The auditor's assessment of control risk.

D. Generally accepted accounting principles.

Answer (D) is correct. *(CPA, adapted)*

**REQUIRED:** The framework within which the auditor judges the financial statements.

**DISCUSSION:** The first standard of reporting requires the auditor to state whether the audited entity's financial statements are presented in conformity with GAAP (AU 150). Without this framework, the auditor would have no uniform standard for judging fairness of presentation (AU 411).

Answer (A) is incorrect because quality control standards relate to the conduct of a CPA firm's audit practice as a whole. A firm of independent auditors must adopt a system of quality control to provide reasonable assurance that its personnel comply with auditing standards. Answer (B) is incorrect because, although the auditor must comply with auditing standards, (s)he must specifically judge whether the statements are presented fairly in accordance with GAAP. Answer (C) is incorrect because the assessment of control risk is but one step in an audit. The ultimate purpose is to express an opinion on the fair presentation of the statements in conformity with GAAP.

**12.** The auditor's opinion refers to generally accepted accounting principles (GAAP). Which of the following best describes GAAP?

A. The interpretations of accounting rules and procedures by certified public accountants on audit engagements.

B. The pronouncements of the Financial Accounting Standards Board and its predecessor, the Accounting Principles Board.

C. The guidelines set forth by various governmental agencies that derive their authority from Congress.

D. The conventions, rules, and procedures that are necessary to define accepted accounting practice at a particular time.

Answer (D) is correct. *(CPA, adapted)*

**REQUIRED:** The statement that best describes GAAP.

**DISCUSSION:** GAAP are the "conventions, rules, and procedures necessary to define accepted accounting practice at a particular time." They include both the broad guidelines and the detailed practices and procedures promulgated by the profession that provide uniform standards to measure financial presentations (AU 411).

Answer (A) is incorrect because interpretations of GAAP made by CPAs on audit engagements are judgments about the application of GAAP to particular circumstances. Answer (B) is incorrect because GAAP include but are not limited to pronouncements of the APB and FASB. Answer (C) is incorrect because, although the federal government can require disclosures by public companies, for example, through regulations of the SEC, GAAP are much broader. They apply to all entities, whether public or private and regardless of size.

**13.** Which of the following is a source of officially established accounting principles for nongovernmental entities?

A. International Accounting Standards.

B. FASB Concepts Statements.

C. FASB Interpretations. → Tech Bulletins

D. AICPA Issues Papers.

Answer (C) is correct. *(Publisher)*

**REQUIRED:** The source of GAAP as designated by the AICPA for nongovernmental entities.

**DISCUSSION:** For nongovernmental entities, the Financial Accounting Standards Board is responsible for identifying the sources of accounting principles and the framework for selecting the principles used in the preparation of financial statements. The nongovernmental hierarchy has five tiers. The first tier [category (a)] consists of sources of officially established accounting principles (FASB Statements and Interpretations, APB Opinions, FASB Staff Positions, and AICPA Accounting Research Bulletins). The next three tiers [categories (b), (c), and (d)] contain other sources of established accounting principles. The fifth tier includes other accounting literature.

Answer (A) is incorrect because International Accounting Standards (the new International Accounting Standards Board will designate its standards as International Financial Reporting Standards) are considered other accounting literature rather than established accounting principles. Answer (B) is incorrect because FASB Concepts Statements are considered other accounting literature rather than established accounting principles. Answer (D) is incorrect because AICPA Issues Papers are considered other accounting literature rather than established accounting principles.

**14.** The standards provide separate GAAP hierarchies for nongovernmental entities, state and local governments, and federal governmental entities. Which of the following is true concerning the GAAP hierarchy for state and local governments?

A. Not all FASB Statements and Interpretations are at the top of the hierarchy.

B. GASB Concepts Statements are considered established accounting principles.

C. Not all GASB Statements and Interpretations are at the top of the hierarchy.

D. All AICPA Audit and Accounting Guides are considered established accounting principles.

Answer (A) is correct. *(Publisher)*

**REQUIRED:** The true statement about the GAAP hierarchy for state and local governments.

**DISCUSSION:** The GAAP hierarchy for state and local governments has five tiers. The first tier [category (a)] consists of sources of officially established accounting principles (GASB Statements and Interpretations, and, if specifically made applicable to state and local governments by GASB Statements or Interpretations, AICPA and FASB pronouncements). The next three tiers [categories (b), (c), and (d)] contain other sources of established accounting principles. The fifth tier includes other accounting literature. If a FASB or AICPA pronouncement is not specifically made applicable to state and local governments by the GASB, it is treated as other accounting literature. Thus, widely recognized and prevalent industry practice [category (d)] prevails over such a pronouncement (AU 411).

Answer (B) is incorrect because GASB Concepts Statements not specifically made applicable to state and local governments are considered other accounting literature. Answer (C) is incorrect because all GASB Statements and Interpretations are in the top tier. Answer (D) is incorrect because AICPA Audit and Accounting Guides not specifically made applicable to state and local governments are considered other accounting literature.

**15.** Which of the following is a source of officially established accounting principles for federal governmental entities?

A. FASAB Technical Bulletins.

B. AICPA pronouncements specifically made applicable to federal governmental entities by the FASAB.

C. FASB pronouncements specifically made applicable to federal governmental entities by the FASB.

D. Technical releases of the Accounting and Auditing Policy Committee of the FASAB.

Answer (B) is correct. *(Publisher)*

**REQUIRED:** The source of officially established accounting principles for federal governmental entities.

**DISCUSSION:** The GAAP hierarchy for federal governmental entities has five tiers. The first tier [category (a)] consists of officially established accounting principles [Federal Accounting Standards Advisory Board (FASAB) Statements and Interpretations, and, if specifically made applicable to federal entities by the FASAB, AICPA and FASB pronouncements]. The next three tiers [categories (b), (c), and (d)] contain other sources of established accounting principles. The fifth tier includes other accounting literature (AU 411).

Answer (A) is incorrect because Category (b) includes FASAB Technical Bulletins, and, if specifically made applicable to federal entities by the AICPA and cleared by the FASAB Statements or Interpretations, AICPA Audit and Accounting Guides and AICPA SOPs. Answer (C) is incorrect because, to be treated as a source of category (a) principles, FASB pronouncements must be specifically made applicable to federal entities by FASAB Statements or Interpretations. Answer (D) is incorrect because technical releases of the Accounting and Auditing Policy Committee of the FASAB belong in category (c) along with AICPA AcSEC Practice Bulletins specifically made applicable to federal entities and cleared by the FASAB. Category (d) pronouncements include FASAB staff implementation guides and practices widely recognized and prevalent in the federal government.

**16.** When criteria to select among alternative accounting principles have not been established to relate accounting methods to circumstances, the auditor

A. Must treat all alternative principles as acceptable.

B. May concur with management's selection of an accounting principle that appears appropriate when applied in a manner similar to the application of an established principle to a similar event.

C. Is required by current authoritative literature to obtain a ruling from the AICPA.

D. Is required by the SEC to seek advice from the FASB about the proper accounting method.

Answer (B) is correct. *(Publisher)*

**REQUIRED:** The auditor's responsibility absent criteria for selection from alternative accounting principles.

**DISCUSSION:** Specifying the circumstances in which one principle should be selected from alternatives is the function of authoritative bodies. But criteria may not yet exist to provide guidance in certain situations. In these cases, management may be able to select an accounting principle that appears appropriate when applied in a manner similar to the application of an established principle to an analogous transaction or event (AU 411).

Answer (A) is incorrect because alternative accounting principles may be applicable, but a principle is unacceptable if it does not result in fair reporting. Answer (C) is incorrect because a ruling from the AICPA is not required. Answer (D) is incorrect because advice from the FASB is not required.

**17.** When the financial statements contain a departure from generally accepted accounting principles, the effect of which is material, the auditor should

A. Qualify the opinion and explain the effect of the departure from GAAP in a separate paragraph.

B. Qualify the opinion and describe the departure from GAAP within the opinion paragraph.

C. Disclaim an opinion and explain the effect of the departure from GAAP in a separate paragraph.

D. Disclaim an opinion and describe the departure from GAAP within the opinion paragraph.

Answer (A) is correct. *(CPA, adapted)*

**REQUIRED:** The auditor's report when the statements contain a material departure from GAAP.

**DISCUSSION:** When the financial statements are materially affected by a departure from GAAP, the auditor should express a qualified or adverse opinion. The opinion will contain a separate explanatory paragraph(s) preceding the opinion paragraph. The explanation should state the auditor's substantive reasons for the conclusions about the departure and disclose the principal effects of the subject matter of the qualification or adverse opinion, if practicable. If the effects are not reasonably determinable, the report should so state. The opinion paragraph should refer to the separate explanation (AU 508).

Answer (B) is incorrect because a separate explanatory paragraph(s) is required. Answer (C) is incorrect because a material departure from GAAP justifies expression of a qualified or adverse opinion. A disclaimer of opinion is appropriate when the audit scope is insufficient to permit the auditor to form an opinion. Answer (D) is incorrect because a material departure from GAAP justifies expression of a qualified or adverse opinion. A disclaimer of opinion is appropriate when the audit scope is insufficient to permit the auditor to form an opinion.

**18.** A CPA engaged to audit financial statements observes that the accounting for a certain material item is not in conformity with GAAP, although the departure is prominently disclosed in a note to the financial statements. The CPA should

A. Express an unqualified opinion but insert a separate paragraph emphasizing the matter by reference to the note.

B. Disclaim an opinion.

C. Not allow the accounting treatment for this item to affect the type of opinion because the departure from GAAP was disclosed.

D. Qualify the opinion because of the departure from GAAP.

Answer (D) is correct. *(CPA, adapted)*

**REQUIRED:** The effect on the audit opinion of a material departure from GAAP.

**DISCUSSION:** When financial statements are materially affected by a departure from GAAP and the audit has been in accordance with auditing standards, the auditor should express a qualified or an adverse opinion, stating the basis for the opinion in the report, even though full and prominent note disclosure has been made.

Answer (A) is incorrect because an unqualified opinion cannot be expressed when the statements are materially affected by a departure from GAAP. Answer (B) is incorrect because a disclaimer is appropriate when the audit scope was insufficient to form an opinion. Answer (C) is incorrect because note disclosure of the departure from GAAP does not overcome the need for a modified opinion.

**19.** Eagle Company's financial statements contain a departure from generally accepted accounting principles because, due to unusual circumstances, the statements would otherwise be misleading. The auditor should express an opinion that is

A. Qualified and describe the departure in a separate paragraph.

B. Unqualified but not mention the departure in the auditor's report.

C. Qualified or adverse, depending on materiality, and describe the departure in a separate paragraph.

D. Unqualified and describe the departure in a separate paragraph.

Answer (D) is correct. *(CPA, adapted)*

**REQUIRED:** The opinion expressed when a departure from GAAP results in fairly presented financial statements.

**DISCUSSION:** Conduct Rule 203, *Accounting Principles*, prohibits expression of an opinion that financial statements are in conformity with GAAP if they contain a material departure from GAAP. However, an exception is permitted when the auditor can demonstrate that because of unusual circumstances the statements would otherwise be misleading. Given these circumstances, and if no other basis for modifying the opinion exists, the CPA may express an unqualified opinion, with a separate paragraph that describes the departure, its effects, and the reasons compliance with GAAP would be misleading.

Answer (A) is incorrect because a qualified opinion is not expressed when the statements are fairly presented. Answer (B) is incorrect because an explanatory paragraph must be added even though the opinion is unqualified. Answer (C) is incorrect because an adverse or qualified opinion is not expressed when the statements are fairly presented.

**20.** According to the profession's ethical standards, which of the following events may justify a departure from a Statement of Financial Accounting Standards?

| | New Legislation | Evolution of a New Form of Business Transaction |
|---|---|---|
| A. | No | Yes |
| B. | Yes | No |
| C. | Yes | Yes |
| D. | No | No |

Answer (C) is correct. *(CPA, adapted)*

**REQUIRED:** The event(s), if any, that may justify departure from an SFAS.

**DISCUSSION:** In general, strict compliance with accounting principles is required. However, Conduct Rule 203 recognizes that, due to unusual circumstances, adhering to GAAP may cause financial statements to be misleading. An Interpretation under Conduct Rule 203 lists new legislation and the evolution of a new form of business transaction as events that may justify departure from an SFAS and other officially established accounting principles.

**21.** Patentex developed a new secret formula that is of great value because it has resulted in a virtual monopoly. Patentex has capitalized all research and development costs associated with this formula. Greene, CPA, who is auditing this account, will probably

A. Confer with management regarding transfer of the amount from the balance sheet to the income statement.

B. Confirm that the secret formula is registered and on file with the county clerk's office.

C. Confer with management regarding a change in the title of the account to goodwill.

D. Confer with management regarding ownership of the secret formula.

Answer (A) is correct. *(CPA, adapted)*

**REQUIRED:** The auditor's proper response upon discovering the capitalization of R&D costs.

**DISCUSSION:** SFAS 2, *Accounting for Research and Development Costs*, requires that R&D costs be expensed "when incurred." The auditor should confer with management about this departure from GAAP. If management refuses to adopt the accepted principle, the auditor will express a qualified or an adverse opinion if the departure has a material effect on the statements taken as a whole. The correction is to expense the amounts capitalized.

Answer (B) is incorrect because confirming that the formula is registered is relevant to the existence, rights, and valuation assertions but not to the choice of accounting principle. Answer (C) is incorrect because reclassifying R&D costs as goodwill would be misleading. The costs must be expensed. Answer (D) is incorrect because conferring with management about ownership of the formula is relevant to the rights assertion, not to the choice of accounting principle.

**22.** When an auditor expresses an opinion stating that financial statements intended for the use of the general public are in accordance with prescribed accounting regulations of a regulatory authority, the auditor

A. Is expressing a piecemeal opinion.

B. Should issue a standard report except for substitution of "prescribed accounting regulations of . . . regulatory body" in place of generally accepted accounting principles.

C. Should also express a qualified or adverse opinion as to material variances from generally accepted accounting principles as appropriate.

D. Need only observe the general and field work standards in expressing an opinion.

Answer (C) is correct. *(Publisher)*

**REQUIRED:** The reporting when statements are based on regulations prescribed by a regulatory body.

**DISCUSSION:** GAAP also apply to companies whose accounting practices are prescribed by governmental regulations, e.g., utilities, insurance companies, and financial institutions. The first standard of reporting is thus applicable to opinions on the statements of such companies presented for purposes other than filings with their respective supervisory agencies. Consequently, the auditor should express a qualified or an adverse opinion if the statements contain a material departure from GAAP (AU 544, *Lack of Conformity with GAAP*). But if the statements are intended solely for the information and use of those within the entity and the regulatory agency, AU 623, *Special Reports*, applies, and an unqualified opinion based on the prescribed methods is a possibility.

Answer (A) is incorrect because piecemeal opinions are prohibited (AU 508). Answer (B) is incorrect because, if financial statements are prepared in accordance with a basis of accounting prescribed by a regulatory body and are not intended solely for filing with that body, the auditor must use the standard form of report modified for departures from GAAP (AU 544). Answer (D) is incorrect because the reporting standards also apply.

**23.** To which of the following material asset balances should an auditor object as not in accordance with GAAP?

A. Franchise fees paid.

B. Increase in goodwill resulting from annual testing.

C. Excess of the cost over the fair value of the net assets of an acquired entity.

D. Research and development costs that will be billed to a customer at a subsequent date.

Answer (B) is correct. *(CPA, adapted)*

**REQUIRED:** The material asset balance that is not in accordance with GAAP.

**DISCUSSION:** Goodwill should be tested for impairment at the reporting-unit level at least annually. If goodwill is impaired, the asset should be written down to fair value. However, goodwill should not be increased. Goodwill is recognized only in a business combination.

Answer (A) is incorrect because the cost of a franchise should be capitalized and accounted for subsequently depending whether the asset has a finite or indefinite life. Answer (C) is incorrect because the excess of cost over the fair value of the net assets acquired in a business combination is recorded as goodwill. Answer (D) is incorrect because costs incurred in conducting R&D activities under contractual arrangements are not covered by SFAS 2 and may be capitalized.

**24.** On January 2, 20X1, the Retail Auto Parts Co. received a notice from its primary suppliers that effective immediately all wholesale prices would be increased 10%. On the basis of the notice, Retail Auto Parts Co. revalued its December 31, 20X0 inventory to reflect the higher costs. The inventory constituted a material proportion of total assets; however, the effect of the revaluation was material to current assets but not to total assets or net income. In reporting on the company's financial statements for the year ended December 31, 20X0, in which inventory is valued at the adjusted amounts, the auditor would most likely

A. Express an unqualified opinion provided the nature of the adjustment and the amounts involved are disclosed in notes.

B. Express a qualified opinion

C. Disclaim an opinion.

D. Express an adverse opinion.

Answer (B) is correct. *(CPA, adapted)*

**REQUIRED:** The effect on the opinion of the client's revaluation of inventory.

**DISCUSSION:** The auditor should express a qualified opinion and disclose that the financial statements have not been presented in conformity with GAAP. Inventory should be recorded at lower of cost or market. Holding gains should not be recognized until realized, i.e., when inventory is sold.

Answer (A) is incorrect because Conduct Rule 203 prohibits expression of an unqualified opinion in these circumstances even though full disclosure is made. Answer (C) is incorrect because a disclaimer is proper only when evidence is insufficient to form an opinion. Answer (D) is incorrect because an adverse opinion is probably not appropriate. The effect of revaluation was not material to total assets or net income.

**25.** The client includes in the determination of net income certain material items properly classifiable as other comprehensive income. In this situation, the auditor must express a(n)

A. Unqualified opinion.

B. Qualified opinion.

C. Adverse opinion.

D. Qualified or adverse opinion.

Answer (D) is correct. *(Publisher)*

**REQUIRED:** The opinion when a client includes other comprehensive income items in the determination of net income.

**DISCUSSION:** Other comprehensive income items (for example, foreign currency translation adjustments, minimum pension liability adjustments, unrealized gains and losses on available-for-sale securities, and net gain or loss on derivatives designated and qualifying as cash flow hedges) are excluded from the determination of net income. The total of other comprehensive income for a period is transferred to a component of equity that is displayed separately from retained earnings and additional paid-in capital in the balance sheet (SFAS 130, *Reporting Comprehensive Income*). Given that the departure from GAAP is material, the auditor should express either a qualified or an adverse opinion (AU 508).

Answer (A) is incorrect because the report must be modified for the failure to apply GAAP. Answer (B) is incorrect because, if the auditor concludes that the financial statements taken as a whole are not presented fairly, an adverse opinion is justified. Answer (C) is incorrect because the auditor may conclude that, except for the effects of the departure from GAAP, the financial statements are presented fairly. In that case, a qualified opinion is justified.

**26.** The following appeared in an audit report: "As described in Note 4, these financial statements were prepared on the basis of accounting that the partnership used for income tax purposes, which is a comprehensive basis of accounting other than generally accepted accounting principles." This sentence is

A. Unacceptable in any audit report.

B. Acceptable in a special report.

C. An indication that the partnership is in liquidation.

D. In a report that must be approved by the IRS.

Answer (B) is correct. *(Publisher)*

**REQUIRED:** The true statement about the quoted language.

**DISCUSSION:** When financial statements are prepared on a comprehensive basis other than GAAP, a paragraph should be included in the auditor's report referring to a note describing the basis and indicating that it departs from GAAP. The auditor's opinion should indicate whether the statements are presented fairly in the context of the comprehensive basis described (AU 623).

Answer (A) is incorrect because the quoted wording is standard in a special report. Answer (C) is incorrect because an entity in liquidation would likely record assets at net realizable value. Answer (D) is incorrect because the IRS need not be consulted about audit reports.

**27.** Garden Apartments, Inc. completed construction and began to rent a 250-unit apartment complex on November 25, 20X1. During December, 75 units were leased, and an additional 125 units were leased in January 20X2. During the month of November 20X1, the company charged to expense $23,000 for the cost of advertising, a grand opening party, and the advertising agency fee for planning the promotional campaign. As a part of the campaign, all tenants signing leases received gifts. At June 30, 20X2, the balance sheet reflected $15,200 of deferred costs associated with these gifts, and a note stated that the costs were being amortized over the life of the related lease. During the audit of the financial statements of Garden Apartments, Inc. for the year ended June 30, 20X2, no facts other than those above came to the auditor's attention that might preclude expression of an unqualified opinion. The report on the financial statements should contain

A. An adverse opinion.

B. An unqualified opinion.

C. A "subject to" opinion.

D. A disclaimer of opinion.

Answer (B) is correct. *(Publisher)*

**REQUIRED:** The effect of the accounting treatment of certain costs on the auditor's opinion.

**DISCUSSION:** Advertising and promotion costs ordinarily should be expensed, and the direct costs of leasing the apartments may be capitalized and expensed over the lives of the leases. These transactions were accounted for in conformity with GAAP, and an unqualified opinion is appropriate.

Answer (A) is incorrect because an adverse opinion states that the financial statements are not presented fairly in accordance with GAAP. Answer (C) is incorrect because AU 508 states, "Phrases such as 'subject to' are not clear or forceful enough and should not be used." Answer (D) is incorrect because a disclaimer is appropriate only when the auditor has collected insufficient evidence to express an opinion.

**28.** A client owning 18% of the voting stock of an investee has accounted for the investment under the equity method. The effect of using the equity method rather than the fair value method is material. In this instance,

A. The client is definitely in violation of GAAP.

B. A decision as to whether an 18% interest provides an ability to exercise significant influence rests with management, and the auditor should consider the equity method to be the appropriate valuation method.

C. Because an interest of less than 20% implies that the investor cannot exercise significant influence over the investee, the auditor will need to obtain evidence to support a claim to the contrary.

D. If the equity method is used in the published financial statements, and the auditor agrees that this method is appropriate, no disclosure that the 20% presumption was set aside is required.

Answer (C) is correct. *(Publisher)*

**REQUIRED:** The true statement about accounting for an 18% ownership interest under the equity method.

**DISCUSSION:** Accounting for a less than 20% investment under the equity method is a violation of GAAP unless the client can exercise significant influence over the investee. APB 18, *The Equity Method of Accounting for Investments in Common Stock*, establishes a rebuttable presumption of no significant influence when less than 20% of the investee's voting stock is held. If the client cannot demonstrate significant influence, given the material effect of using the equity rather than the fair value method, the auditor should express a qualified or an adverse opinion.

Answer (A) is incorrect because the equity method is appropriate if the client exercises significant influence over the investee. Answer (B) is incorrect because the auditor is responsible for determining whether the client has demonstrated that it exercises significant influence. Answer (D) is incorrect because GAAP require disclosure of the accounting method used and, in this case, the reason the equity method was chosen.

**29.** The client's general use financial statements do not reflect a provision for a deferred income tax liability because this accounting procedure is not required by the regulatory commission that prescribes uniform accounting procedures for the industry in which this company operates. A note accompanying the financial statements correctly discloses the amount of the deferred tax liability at the statement date as $2,200,000, an amount material to the financial statements taken as a whole. What is the effect of these circumstances on the auditor's opinion?

A. They will not affect the auditor's opinion because the client's accounting procedures conform to the uniform accounting procedures applicable to the industry of which the client is a part.

B. The auditor should express either an adverse opinion or a qualified opinion depending on his/her judgment as to the effects of the departure from GAAP on the overall fairness of the financial statements.

C. They will not affect the auditor's opinion because the note disclosure provides the reader with the information necessary for a proper interpretation of the client's financial position and results of operations.

D. They will affect the auditor's opinion only if (s)he believes the content of the note is insufficient to meet the requirements of adequate disclosure.

Answer (B) is correct. *(Publisher)*

**REQUIRED:** The effect of a material departure from GAAP resulting from the client's adherence to uniform procedures prescribed by a regulatory agency.

**DISCUSSION:** AU 623 defines the elements of the auditor's report when (s)he is reporting on financial statements prepared in accordance with a comprehensive basis of accounting other than GAAP. This form of reporting does not include an opinion concerning adherence to GAAP. But when reporting on statements prepared in accordance with the requirements of a regulatory body, the auditor must use the standard form of report, unless the statements are intended solely for the information and use of a regulatory agency (AU 544). Thus, given that the statements are for general use, the standard form of report should be used. The auditor should express either an adverse or a qualified opinion, depending on the effects of the departure from GAAP and the fairness with which the financial statements are presented. The opinion must be modified because recognition of a deferred tax liability is required by SFAS 109, *Accounting for Income Taxes*.

Answer (A) is incorrect because, given that a general-use report based on the requirements of a regulatory body is to be issued, the auditor may not express an opinion solely on conformity with the other comprehensive basis of accounting. (S)he must state whether the statements are in accordance with GAAP. An opinion on conformity with the prescribed basis of accounting should be expressed in an additional paragraph. Answer (C) is incorrect because failure to adhere to GAAP is not remedied by note disclosure. Answer (D) is incorrect because failure to adhere to GAAP is not remedied by note disclosure.

**30.** An auditor's client is a nonprofit organization. GAAP for this type of nonprofit organization have been clearly defined, and the client has followed such practices. The preferred method of reporting on the client's adherence to such practices is to

A. Use the phrase "In conformity with generally accepted accounting principles" in the opinion paragraph.

B. Use the phrase "In conformity with generally accepted accounting practices for a nonprofit organization in the . . . field" in the opinion paragraph.

C. Describe the accounting practices in a separate paragraph, with appropriate reference thereto in the opinion paragraph.

D. Make no reference because accounting practices differ for each nonprofit organization.

Answer (A) is correct. *(Publisher)*

**REQUIRED:** The preferred method of stating that a nonprofit organization uses GAAP.

**DISCUSSION:** Because the auditee uses GAAP, the language in the standard audit report is appropriate.

Answer (B) is incorrect because the standard opinion paragraph does not require modification for the type of organization being reported on. Answer (C) is incorrect because the client should describe the accounting principles employed in a summary of significant accounting policies preceding the notes or as the first note to the statements. Answer (D) is incorrect because GAAS, including the first standard of reporting, must be adhered to when an auditor reports on any statement. The auditor must therefore indicate whether the statements are presented in conformity with GAAP.

**31.** AU 625, *Reports on the Application of Accounting Principles*, provides guidance to a reporting accountant who

A. Has been engaged to report on financial statements.

B. Is preparing a written report on the application of accounting principles to specific transactions.

C. Intends to give oral advice in the form of a position paper not related to specific transactions or financial statements.

D. Is requested to provide expert testimony in litigation involving accounting matters.

Answer (B) is correct. *(Publisher)*

**REQUIRED:** The applicability of AU 625.

**DISCUSSION:** Management and others may consult accountants about the applicability of accounting principles. AU 625 guides the reporting accountant when (s)he prepares a written report on (1) the application of accounting principles to specified transactions (completed or proposed) involving facts and circumstances of a particular entity or (2) the type of opinion that may be expressed on a specific entity's financial statements. The accountant may not provide a written report on the application of accounting principles to a hypothetical transaction.

Answer (A) is incorrect because AU 625 does not apply to engagements to report on financial statements or to advise other public accountants. Answer (C) is incorrect because AU 625 is not applicable to position papers, e.g., articles or speeches, unless they are intended to provide guidance on specific transactions or on the opinion to be expressed on a specific entity's statements. Answer (D) is incorrect because AU 625 does not apply to assist in litigation or provide expert testimony.

**32.** Blue, CPA, has been asked to report on the application of accounting principles to a specific transaction by an entity that is audited by another CPA. Blue may accept this engagement but should

A. Consult with the continuing CPA to obtain information relevant to the transaction.

B. Report the engagement's findings to the entity's audit committee, the continuing CPA, and management.

C. Disclaim any opinion that the hypothetical application of accounting principles conforms with generally accepted accounting principles.

D. Notify the entity that the report is for general use.

Answer (A) is correct. *(CPA, adapted)*

**REQUIRED:** The proper action of a CPA who accepts an engagement to report on the application of accounting principles.

**DISCUSSION:** The reporting accountant should consult with the continuing accountant to determine the available facts relevant to a professional judgment. The continuing accountant may provide information not otherwise available to the reporting accountant. The latter should (1) explain the need to consult with the continuing accountant to the entity's management, (2) request permission, and (3) request authorization for the continuing accountant to respond fully (AU 625).

Answer (B) is incorrect because the accountant's written report should be addressed to the requesting entity (e.g., management or the board). Answer (C) is incorrect because the report should contain a statement describing the appropriate accounting principles to be applied. If appropriate, the report should state reasons for the conclusions, not an opinion or a disclaimer. Also, the engagement may not involve reporting on the application of accounting principles to a hypothetical transaction. Answer (D) is incorrect because the use of the report is restricted to specified parties.

**33.** In connection with a proposal to obtain a new client, an accountant in public practice is asked to prepare a written report on the application of accounting principles to a specific transaction. The accountant's report should include a statement that

A. Any difference in the facts, circumstances, or assumptions presented may change the report.

B. The engagement was performed in accordance with Statements on Standards for Consulting Services.

C. The guidance provided is for general use.

D. Nothing came to the accountant's attention that caused the accountant to believe that the accounting principles violated GAAP.

Answer (A) is correct. *(CPA, adapted)*

**REQUIRED:** The statement included in a report on the application of accounting principles to a specific transaction.

**DISCUSSION:** The accountant's report is addressed to the requesting entity. The report should contain (1) a description of the engagement and whether it was in accordance with AICPA standards; (2) a description of the transaction; (3) a description of the accounting principles applied (including their country of origin); (4) a statement that the responsibility for proper accounting is with the preparers of the financial statements; and (5) a statement that any difference in facts, circumstances, or assumptions may change the report (AU 625).

Answer (B) is incorrect because the accountant's report should state that the engagement is conducted in accordance with applicable AICPA standards. Answer (C) is incorrect because the use of the report is restricted to specified parties. Answer (D) is incorrect because the report does not provide for negative assurance.

**34.** Before reporting on the financial statements of a U.S. entity that have been prepared in conformity with another country's accounting principles, an auditor practicing in the U.S. should

A. Understand the accounting principles generally accepted in the other country.

B. Be certified by the appropriate auditing or accountancy board of the other country.

C. Notify management that the auditor is required to disclaim an opinion on the financial statements.

D. Receive a waiver from the auditor's state board of accountancy to perform the engagement.

Answer (A) is correct. *(CPA, adapted)*

**REQUIRED:** The requirement for reporting on financial statements of a U.S. entity prepared in conformity with another country's accounting principles.

**DISCUSSION:** AU 534, *Reporting on Financial Statements Prepared for Use in Other Countries*, states that an independent auditor practicing in the U.S. may report on the financial statements of a U.S. entity prepared in conformity with accounting principles generally accepted in another country. However, the auditor must clearly understand, and obtain written representations from management about, the purpose and uses of the statements. (S)he must also comply with the AICPA's general and field work standards. According to AU 508, the standard audit report should identify the country of origin of the accounting standards used to prepare the statements. It should also identify the country of origin of the auditing standards followed in performing the audit.

Answer (B) is incorrect because the accountant needs to be a CPA in the U.S. Answer (C) is incorrect because the accountant can express an opinion on the fairness of the financial statements. Answer (D) is incorrect because no waiver is required to perform this service.

## 7.3 Consistency Issues

**35.** The objective of the consistency standard is to provide assurance that

A. There are no variations in the format and presentation of financial statements.

B. Substantially different transactions and events are not accounted for on an identical basis.

C. The auditor is consulted before material changes are made in the application of accounting principles.

D. The comparability of financial statements between periods is not materially affected by changes in accounting principles without disclosure.

Answer (D) is correct. *(CPA, adapted)*

**REQUIRED:** The objective of the standard of reporting relating to consistency.

**DISCUSSION:** The second standard of reporting concerns the consistency of application of GAAP: "The report shall identify those circumstances in which such principles have not been consistently observed in the current period in relation to the preceding period" (AU 508). The objective is to assure that the comparability of financial statements has not been materially affected by changes in accounting principles or, if comparability has been affected, to require proper reporting. Implicit in the objective is that principles are consistently observed within each period (AU 420, *Consistency of Application of GAAP*).

Answer (A) is incorrect because variations in the format and presentation of financial statements (e.g., changes in classification) are not considered to be changes affecting consistency within the meaning of AU 420. Answer (B) is incorrect because the auditor reports on whether accounting practices were consistent, not identical. Answer (C) is incorrect because consultation is not required.

**36.** Seripak Corporation made a material change in accounting principle with which the auditor concurs. The auditor should express

A. An unqualified opinion with a separate explanatory paragraph.

B. A "subject to" opinion with a separate explanatory paragraph.

C. A "subject to" opinion without a separate explanatory paragraph.

D. An "except for" opinion without a separate explanatory paragraph.

Answer (A) is correct. *(K.J. Plucinski)*

**REQUIRED:** The appropriate report when the auditor concurs with a change in accounting principle.

**DISCUSSION:** A material change in accounting principle raises a consistency issue. Thus, a report with a separate explanatory paragraph is required. Unless the change is unjustified, it does not require a modification of the opinion.

Answer (B) is incorrect because the phrase "subject to" is not acceptable in any report. Such language is not clear or forceful enough. Answer (C) is incorrect because the phrase "subject to" is not acceptable in any report. Such language is not clear or forceful enough. Answer (D) is incorrect because the report should contain a separate explanatory paragraph but no qualification. If the auditor does not concur with the change, the opinion should be modified because of the departure from GAAP.

**37.** If management fails to provide adequate justification for a change from one generally accepted accounting principle to another, the auditor should

A. Add an explanatory paragraph and express a qualified or an adverse opinion for lack of conformity with generally accepted accounting principles.

B. Disclaim an opinion because of uncertainty.

C. Disclose the matter in a separate explanatory paragraph(s) but not modify the opinion paragraph.

D. Neither modify the opinion nor disclose the matter because both principles are generally accepted.

Answer (A) is correct. *(Publisher)*

**REQUIRED:** The effect of management's failure to justify a change in accounting principle.

**DISCUSSION:** If management has not provided reasonable justification for a change, the new principle is not generally accepted, or the method of accounting for the effect of the change does not conform with GAAP, the auditor should express a qualified or an adverse opinion in the report for the year of change and add (an) explanatory paragraph(s) preceding the opinion paragraph (AU 508). The presumption that an entity should not change an accounting principle is overcome only when it justifies use of an acceptable alternative as preferable (APB 20, *Accounting Changes*).

Answer (B) is incorrect because a disclaimer may be issued for a scope limitation but not for failure to justify a change in GAAP. Answer (C) is incorrect because a modified opinion must be expressed. Answer (D) is incorrect because a modified opinion must be expressed.

**38.** The following explanatory paragraph was included in an auditor's report to indicate a lack of consistency:

> As discussed in note T to the financial statements, the company changed its method of computing depreciation in 20X1.

How should the auditor report on this matter if the auditor concurred with the change?

| | Type of Opinion | Location of Explanatory Paragraph |
|---|---|---|
| A. | Unqualified | Before opinion paragraph |
| B. | Unqualified | After opinion paragraph |
| C. | Qualified | Before opinion paragraph |
| D. | Qualified | After opinion paragraph |

Answer (B) is correct. *(CPA, adapted)*

**REQUIRED:** The reporting of a lack of consistency.

**DISCUSSION:** AU 508 states that a change in accounting principles or in the method of their application having a material effect on comparability requires the auditor to refer to the change in an explanatory paragraph of the report. This paragraph should follow the opinion paragraph and identify the nature of the change and refer to a note that discusses the change.

**39.** Below are lists of accounting changes affecting consistency and comparability. All items are material. Which list does not contain a change requiring recognition in the audit report?

A. Correction of an error in an accounting principle; change in accounting estimate; a reclassification.

B. Reclassification; a substantially different transaction; an accounting change having no material effect on the financial statements in the current year but having a substantial effect in subsequent years.

C. Substantially different transactions; changes in the items treated as cash equivalents in the presentation of cash flows; a change in reporting entity not resulting from a transaction or event.

D. Correction of an error not involving an accounting principle; change in accounting estimate; a change in reporting entity not resulting from a transaction or event.

Answer (B) is correct. *(Publisher)*

**REQUIRED:** The set of items requiring no reference in the auditor's report as to consistency.

**DISCUSSION:** Five accounting changes affect consistency and require an additional paragraph in the auditor's report (AU 420): (1) changes in accounting principle, (2) changes in the reporting entity not resulting from a transaction or event, (3) correction of an error in principle, (4) changes in principle inseparable from a change in estimate, and (5) changes in the presentation of cash flows that involve determination of the items treated as cash equivalents. Five other changes affect comparability but not consistency and require no modification of the report: (1) changes in accounting estimate, (2) error corrections not involving a principle, (3) changes in classification and reclassification, (4) substantially different transactions or events, and (5) changes having no material effect in the current year but expected to have a material future effect.

**40.** APB 20 indicates that a number of accounting changes should be handled on a retroactive or restatement basis. These exceptions are typically comprehensive and substantially affect reported net income. Which of the following is not an exception requiring restatement of prior financial statements for comparative purposes in the year of an accounting change?

A. A change in the useful lives of depreciable assets.

B. A change from the LIFO inventory valuation method to another method.

C. A change in the method of accounting for long-term construction-type contracts.

D. Issuance of financial statements by a company for the first time to obtain additional equity capital to effect a business combination or to register securities.

Answer (A) is correct. *(Publisher)*

**REQUIRED:** The accounting change not applied retroactively to the statements of prior years.

**DISCUSSION:** A change in the useful lives of depreciable assets is a change in estimate that does not affect consistency and should be accounted for prospectively.

Answer (B) is incorrect because the change from LIFO by a firm that has used the method for a number of years would have a significant effect on the current year's income. LIFO cost of goods sold would likely reflect low inventory values. A change to LIFO from any other method, however, would not require restatement. Answer (C) is incorrect because a change from the completed-contract method to the percentage-of-completion method, or vice versa, has a significant effect on the comparability of the financial statements. Answer (D) is incorrect because private companies selling equity securities for the first time should make their prior financial statements as meaningful as possible.

**41.** Under APB 20, which of the following is not a requirement for ordinary accounting changes?

A. The cumulative effect of the adjustment should be reported in income between extraordinary items and net income.

B. The items should be reported on a net of tax basis.

C. The adjustment to retained earnings should be clearly marked in the balance sheet as "adjustment for the cumulative effect on prior years of retroactively applying the new method of accounting."

D. Income before extraordinary items and net income computed on a pro forma basis should be shown on the face of the income statement for all periods presented as if the newly adopted principle had been applied during all periods affected.

Answer (C) is correct. *(Publisher)*

**REQUIRED:** The requirement not established for ordinary accounting changes by APB 20.

**DISCUSSION:** No adjustments are necessary to the retained earnings account because the cumulative effect of the change on net income is reported in the income statement of the current year, and no prior period financial statements are restated. Restatement and direct adjustment of retained earnings would be appropriate if one of the exceptions to APB 20 requiring retroactive treatment of accounting changes is applicable, e.g., a change in the method of accounting for long-term construction contracts or a change from LIFO to another inventory method.

Answer (A) is incorrect because the cumulative effect of the adjustment should be reported in the income statement between extraordinary items and net income. Answer (B) is incorrect because items should be reported on a net of tax basis in a manner similar to that used for an extraordinary item. Answer (D) is incorrect because income before extraordinary items and net income computed on a pro forma basis should be shown on the face of the income statement. Related earnings per share data should also be reported.

**42.** Tread Corp. accounts for the effect of a material accounting change prospectively when the inclusion of the cumulative effect of the change is required in the current year. The auditor should choose between expressing a(n)

A. Qualified opinion or a disclaimer of opinion.

B. Disclaimer of opinion or an unqualified opinion with an explanatory paragraph.

C. Unqualified opinion with an explanatory paragraph and an adverse opinion.

D. Adverse opinion and a qualified opinion.

Answer (D) is correct. *(CPA, adapted)*

**REQUIRED:** The auditor's reporting options when a client fails to comply with GAAP.

**DISCUSSION:** APB 20 defines accounting changes and GAAP for reporting an accounting change. When an audit client's financial statements contain a material departure from GAAP, the auditor should express a qualified or an adverse opinion.

Answer (A) is incorrect because a disclaimer is expressed only when the audit scope is insufficient to form an opinion. Answer (B) is incorrect because a disclaimer or an unqualified opinion is inappropriate for a GAAP violation. Answer (C) is incorrect because an unqualified opinion can be expressed only if the financial statements contain no material departure from GAAP.

**43.** When there has been a change in accounting principles, but the effect of the change on the comparability of the financial statements is not material, the auditor should

A. Refer to the change in an explanatory paragraph.

B. Explicitly concur that the change is preferred.

C. Not refer to consistency in the auditor's report.

D. Refer to the change in the opinion paragraph.

Answer (C) is correct. *(CPA, adapted)*

**REQUIRED:** The reference, if any, in the auditor's report to a change in accounting principle not considered material.

**DISCUSSION:** The standard report implies that comparability between or among periods has not been materially affected by changes in accounting principles because either no change has occurred or there has been a change in principles or in the method of their application, but its effect on comparability is not material (AU 508).

Answer (A) is incorrect because an additional paragraph is added following the opinion paragraph only if the change is material. Answer (B) is incorrect because the auditor should not refer to consistency when the effect on comparability is immaterial. Answer (D) is incorrect because the auditor should refer to the change in the opinion paragraph only if (s)he takes exception to it in expressing the opinion.

**44.** If the auditor is reporting on several periods and a change in accounting principle from straight-line to declining-balance depreciation occurred in the earliest period reported upon, the auditor should

A. Refer to the change in the report even though there is no inconsistency subsequent to the change.

B. Qualify the opinion for the first year reported on but express an unqualified opinion for the subsequent years.

C. Not refer to the change.

D. Require restatement of the financial statements for the period immediately preceding the period of change in addition to referring to the change in the report.

Answer (A) is correct. *(Publisher)*

**REQUIRED:** The effect on the report when a change in principle occurs in the earliest period reported upon.

**DISCUSSION:** The auditor must add a separate explanatory paragraph following the opinion paragraph to reflect the inconsistency. This paragraph is required in reports on financial statements of subsequent years as long as the year of change is presented and reported on. The paragraph is necessary, although the year of the change is the earliest year reported on and there is no inconsistency in the application of principles in years subsequent to the change. However, the paragraph may be omitted when a change not requiring a cumulative-effect type adjustment is made at the beginning of the earliest year presented and reported on (AU 508).

Answer (B) is incorrect because the auditor must add an explanatory paragraph, but, if (s)he concurs with the change, it will not be a basis for departing from an unqualified opinion. Answer (C) is incorrect because the auditor must add an explanatory paragraph. Answer (D) is incorrect because cumulative-effect type changes do not require restatement of prior periods' financial statements.

**45.** The ABC Manufacturing Co. in 20X0 and 20X1 included certain factory administrative expenses in the general and administrative expense category. For the year ended December 31, 20X2, ABC has decided that these expenses should be allocated to units produced as part of factory overhead. The amount involved is material. The auditor should regard this change as

A. A classification change that does not require special treatment or comment.

B. A change in an accounting principle that requires management justification.

C. A change in an accounting estimate that requires note explanation.

D. A change from the absorption costing inventory method to the direct costing inventory method.

Answer (B) is correct. *(Publisher)*

**REQUIRED:** The auditor's treatment of a change in accounting for certain expenses.

**DISCUSSION:** The change in the treatment of these expenses is a change in accounting principle, that is, a change in a convention, rule, or procedure applied in accounting practice. A change in accounting principle requires reasonable justification by the client and a separate explanatory paragraph in the auditor's report. The auditor must also become satisfied that the new principle is generally accepted and that the method of accounting for the effect of the change conforms with GAAP (AU 508).

Answer (A) is incorrect because classification changes result from changes in account titles or items included within account classifications. Answer (C) is incorrect because changes in estimates require no modification of the auditor's report unless they are inseparable from a change in principle. However, a material change in estimate may require note disclosure. Answer (D) is incorrect because a change to direct costing would entail treating fixed manufacturing costs as period costs (immediate expenses), not as product (inventoriable) costs.

**46.** If an accounting change has no material effect on the financial statements in the current year but the change is reasonably certain to have a material effect in later years, the change should be

A. Treated as a consistency modification of the opinion in the auditor's report for the current year.

B. Disclosed in the notes to the financial statements of the current year.

C. Disclosed in the notes to the financial statements and referred to in the auditor's report for the current year.

D. Treated as a subsequent event.

Answer (B) is correct. *(CPA, adapted)*

**REQUIRED:** The treatment of a change with no material current effect.

**DISCUSSION:** AU 420 states, "If an accounting change has no material effect on the financial statements in the current year, but the change is reasonably certain to have substantial effects in later years, the change should be disclosed in the notes to the financial statements whenever the statements of the period of change are presented, but the independent auditor need not recognize the change in the report as to consistency."

Answer (A) is incorrect because the auditor should modify the opinion for lack of adequate disclosure if the change is not included in the notes by the client. By itself, however, lack of consistency does not necessitate modification of the opinion paragraph. Answer (C) is incorrect because the auditor need not recognize the change in the audit report. Answer (D) is incorrect because changes in accounting methods are not subsequent events.

**47.** A company has changed its method of inventory valuation from an unacceptable one to one in conformity with generally accepted accounting principles. The auditor's report on the financial statements of the year of the change should include

A. No reference to consistency.

B. A reference to a prior-period adjustment.

C. A note explaining the change.

D. Justification for the change and the impact of the change on reported net income.

Answer (B) is correct. *(CPA, adapted)*

**REQUIRED:** The effect on the report when a change is made from an unacceptable to an acceptable principle.

**DISCUSSION:** Such a change is a correction of an error in accounting principle, but it also requires recognition in the auditor's report as to consistency (AU 420). An error correction requires a prior-period adjustment, and the change is identified in a separate paragraph of the auditor's report following the opinion paragraph.

Answer (A) is incorrect because a reference should be made in a separate explanatory paragraph. Answer (C) is incorrect because an auditor's report should not contain notes. Answer (D) is incorrect because justification for the change in principle is the responsibility of management, and the impact of those changes should be reflected in management's financial statements.

**48.** An entity changed from the straight-line method to the declining-balance method of depreciation for all newly acquired assets. This change has no material effect on the current year's financial statements but is reasonably certain to have a substantial effect in later years. If the change is disclosed in the notes to the financial statements, the auditor should issue a report with a(n)

A. Qualified opinion.

B. Explanatory paragraph.

C. Unqualified opinion.

D. Consistency modification.

Answer (C) is correct. *(CPA, adapted)*

**REQUIRED:** The report issued when a change in accounting principle has no material current effect.

**DISCUSSION:** If a change in accounting principle has no material effect on the current financial statements, but is reasonably certain to have a substantial effect in future years, the change should be disclosed but need not be recognized in the report (AU 420).

Answer (A) is incorrect because a justified change in accounting principle does not result in a qualified opinion. Answer (B) is incorrect because, if an accounting change has no material effect on the current financial statements but is likely to affect future financial statements, the auditor need not modify the report. Answer (D) is incorrect because, if an accounting change has no material effect on the current financial statements but is likely to affect future financial statements, the auditor need not modify the report.

**49.** Green Company uses the first-in, first-out method of costing for its international subsidiary's inventory and the last-in, first-out method of costing for its domestic inventory. The different costing methods will cause Green's auditor to issue a report with a(n)

A. Explanatory paragraph as to consistency.

B. Qualified opinion.

C. Opinion modified as to consistency.

D. Unqualified opinion.

Answer (D) is correct. *(CPA, adapted)*

**REQUIRED:** The audit report when two business segments use different inventory methods.

**DISCUSSION:** A difference between the accounting principles used by two segments of an entity does not raise a consistency issue. The second standard of reporting concerns the consistent observation of principles in the current period in relation to the preceding period, that is, between periods. Thus, the use of two different cost flow assumptions does not, by itself, affect the comparability of the entity's financial statements between periods if no accounting changes have occurred.

Answer (A) is incorrect because no explanatory paragraph as to consistency is necessary. Answer (B) is incorrect because an unqualified opinion is possible even in the event of a lack of consistency. Answer (C) is incorrect because the use of different principles does not require modification of the opinion.

**50.** A change in the method of determining the items to be treated as cash equivalents in the statement of cash flows

A. Is treated as a reclassification for both disclosure and reporting purposes and ordinarily requires no reference in the auditor's report.

B. Requires disclosure in the financial statements and reference in the auditor's report.

C. Must be disclosed in the notes to the financial statements and usually is not referred to in the auditor's report.

D. Is considered an accounting change not affecting consistency.

Answer (B) is correct. *(Publisher)*

**REQUIRED:** The correct treatment of a change in the policy regarding determination of cash equivalents.

**DISCUSSION:** SFAS 95, *Statement of Cash Flows*, requires disclosure of the enterprise's policy regarding determination of the items to be treated as cash equivalents. A change in that policy is a change in principle requiring retroactive restatement. AU 420 states that this type of change in presentation of cash flows requires an explanatory paragraph in the audit report.

Answer (A) is incorrect because a change in policy determining cash equivalents is a change in principle, not a reclassification. Answer (C) is incorrect because the change affects consistency and requires an explanatory paragraph. Answer (D) is incorrect because the change affects consistency and requires an explanatory paragraph.

**51.** In which of the following situations concerning consistency should the auditor appropriately issue the standard report?

A. A change in the specific subsidiaries included in the group of companies for which consolidated statements are presented.

B. A change from an accounting principle that is not generally accepted to one that is generally accepted.

C. A change in the percentage used to calculate the provision for warranty expense.

D. The correction of a mistake in the application of a generally accepted accounting principle.

Answer (C) is correct. *(CPA, adapted)*

**REQUIRED:** The situation in which the standard report is appropriate.

**DISCUSSION:** A change in the calculation of warranty expense is a change in accounting estimate. Changes that affect comparability but not the consistent application of accounting principles do not require recognition in the auditor's report (AU 508).

Answer (A) is incorrect because this change in the reporting entity affects consistency. It does not result from a transaction or event and therefore requires an explanatory paragraph. Answer (B) is incorrect because a change from an accounting principle that is not generally accepted to one that is generally accepted is a correction of an error in principle and requires recognition in the report. Answer (D) is incorrect because correction of a mistake in the application of GAAP is an error correction requiring recognition in the report.

**52.** An accounting change may result in financial statements that are actually those of a different reporting entity. The change should be reported by restating the financial statements of all prior periods presented. Which of the following is a change in the reporting entity that does not require an explanatory paragraph about consistency to be added to the audit report?

A. Presenting consolidated or combined statements in place of statements of individual companies.

B. Changing specific subsidiaries included in the group of companies for which consolidated financial statements are presented.

C. Creation, cessation, purchase, or disposition of a subsidiary or other business unit.

D. Changing the companies included in combined financial statements.

Answer (C) is correct. *(Publisher)*

**REQUIRED:** The change in reporting entity not requiring a consistency reference.

**DISCUSSION:** The users of financial statements have a right to expect that changes in account balances are the results of transactions or events. If changes in account balances arise from changes in accounting principles, including certain changes in the reporting entity, rather than transactions or events, the auditor has a responsibility to report accordingly. However, a change in the reporting entity caused by the creation, cessation, purchase, or disposition of a subsidiary or other business unit is considered to be a change in the reporting entity resulting from a transaction or event. This kind of change in the reporting entity does not require an explanatory paragraph about consistency in the audit report (AU 420).

Answer (A) is incorrect because presenting consolidated or combined statements in place of statements of individual companies does not result from a transaction or event. Hence, they require recognition in the auditor's report as to consistency. Answer (B) is incorrect because changing specific subsidiaries included in the group of companies for which consolidated financial statements are presented does not result from a transaction or event. Hence, they require recognition in the auditor's report as to consistency. Answer (D) is incorrect because changing the companies included in combined financial statements does not result from a transaction or event. Hence, they require recognition in the auditor's report as to consistency.

**53.** If a change in accounting principle is inseparable from the effect of a change in estimate, this material event should be accounted for as a change in

A. Estimate, and the auditor should report on consistency.

B. Principle, and the auditor should report on consistency.

C. Estimate, and the auditor should not recognize the change in the report.

D. Principle, and the auditor should not recognize the change in the report.

Answer (A) is correct. *(CPA, adapted)*

**REQUIRED:** The true statement about a change in principle inseparable from a change in estimate.

**DISCUSSION:** When the effect of a change in accounting principle is inseparable from the effect of a change in estimate, APB 20 requires that it be accounted for in the same manner as a change in estimate only. However, because a change in principle is involved, this type of change requires recognition in the independent auditor's report as to consistency (AU 420). An example is the change from deferring and amortizing a cost to recording it as an expense when incurred because its future benefits are doubtful. Because the new method recognizes a change in estimated future benefits, the effect of the change in principle is inseparable from the change in estimate.

## 7.4 Disclosure Considerations

**54.** Notes that are included with financial statements are the responsibility of the

A. Securities and Exchange Commission.

B. Company's management.

C. Independent auditor.

D. Internal auditor.

Answer (B) is correct. *(Publisher)*

**REQUIRED:** The person(s) primarily responsible for the accuracy of notes.

**DISCUSSION:** The notes are considered part of the basic financial statements (AU 551, *Reporting on Information Accompanying the Basic Financial Statements in Auditor-Submitted Documents*). Because management has the primary responsibility for the financial statements, it also has the primary responsibility for the fairness of information included in notes.

Answer (A) is incorrect because the SEC is responsible for assuring that firms comply with federal securities laws. Answer (C) is incorrect because the independent external auditor is responsible for expressing an opinion on the fairness of the financial statements. Answer (D) is incorrect because the internal auditor advises management.

**55.** When an auditor qualifies an opinion because of inadequate disclosure, the auditor should describe the nature of the omission in a separate explanatory paragraph and modify the

| | Introductory Paragraph | Scope Paragraph | Opinion Paragraph |
|---|---|---|---|
| A. | Yes | No | No |
| B. | Yes | Yes | No |
| C. | No | Yes | Yes |
| D. | No | No | Yes |

Answer (D) is correct. *(CPA, adapted)*

**REQUIRED:** The effect(s) on the auditor's report of inadequate disclosure.

**DISCUSSION:** If management fails to disclose information required by GAAP, the auditor should express a qualified opinion or an adverse opinion because of the departure from GAAP. (S)he should also provide the information in the report, if practicable, unless omission is appropriate under a specific SAS. If the opinion is qualified, only the opinion paragraph should include the appropriate qualifying language and refer to the explanatory paragraph(s) preceding the opinion paragraph.

**56.** The standard independent auditor's report names the basic financial statements in the introductory paragraph. They include the statements of financial position,

A. Income, and cash flows.

B. Income, changes in retained earnings, and cash flows.

C. Income, retained earnings, and cash flows.

D. Income, and retained earnings.

Answer (C) is correct. *(Publisher)*

**REQUIRED:** The basic financial statements.

**DISCUSSION:** The statements of financial position, income, retained earnings, and cash flows are the basic financial statements upon which the auditor reports (AU 508). When both financial position and results of operations are presented, disclosure of changes in equity accounts (other than retained earnings) and in the number of shares of equity securities is required to be made in the basic financial statements, the notes, or in a separate statement of changes in equity (APB 12, *Omnibus Opinion-1967*). Furthermore, SFAS 130 requires an enterprise that has items of other comprehensive income and that reports financial position, results of operations, and cash flows to display comprehensive income and its components. These items should be presented in a financial statement that is given the same prominence as the other statements constituting the full set. However, no specific format is required for this statement as long as net income is displayed as a component of comprehensive income.

**57.** If financial statements are to meet the requirements of adequate disclosure,

A. All information pertaining to the company must be disclosed in the statements or related notes, even though some of the disclosures are potentially detrimental to the company or its shareholders.

B. All information believed by the auditor to be essential to the fair presentation of the financial statements must be disclosed, no matter how confidential management believes the data to be.

C. Statement notes should be written in very technical language to avoid misinterpretation by the reader.

D. A statement note must clearly detail any deficiencies contained in the financial statements themselves.

Answer (B) is correct. *(Publisher)*

**REQUIRED:** The true statement about the requirements of adequate disclosure.

**DISCUSSION:** In considering the adequacy of disclosure, the auditor necessarily uses confidential client information. Otherwise, forming an opinion on the statements would be difficult. To the extent required by GAAP, such information must be disclosed (AU 431, *Adequacy of Disclosure in Financial Statements*). But beyond these requirements, the auditor who discloses confidential information without specific consent violates Conduct Rule 301, *Confidential Client Information.*

Answer (A) is incorrect because only the information required by GAAP must be disclosed. Answer (C) is incorrect because notes need only be written so that the informative disclosures are reasonably adequate. Answer (D) is incorrect because notes do not list deficiencies contained in the financial statements. The financial statements must conform with GAAP.

**58.** If the basic financial statements are accompanied by a separate statement of changes in equity, this statement should

A. Not be identified in the introductory paragraph but should be reported on separately in the opinion paragraph.

B. Be excluded from both the introductory and opinion paragraphs.

C. Be identified in the introductory paragraph of the report but need not be reported on separately in the opinion paragraph.

D. Be identified in the introductory paragraph of the report and must be reported on separately in the opinion paragraph.

Answer (C) is correct. *(CPA, adapted)*

**REQUIRED:** The effect on the report of presenting a separate statement of changes in equity.

**DISCUSSION:** If the basic statements are accompanied by a separate statement of changes in equity, it should be identified in the introductory paragraph. It need not be reported on separately in the opinion paragraph, however, because such changes are included in the presentation of financial position, results of operations, and cash flows (AU 508).

**59.** Adequate disclosure means that sufficient information is presented so that financial statements are not misleading. The decisions concerning adequate disclosure should reflect the needs of

A. Reasonably prudent investors.

B. Any and all readers of the financial statements.

C. Experts in accounting and finance.

D. Governmental regulatory agencies.

Answer (A) is correct. *(Publisher)*

**REQUIRED:** The parties toward whom the adequate disclosure requirement is directed.

**DISCUSSION:** The definition of a reasonably prudent investor is a difficult matter. Nevertheless, adequate disclosure is usually deemed to encompass the amount and quality of information necessary for a reasonably well-informed individual to make investment decisions.

Answer (B) is incorrect because, even if financial statements are general-purpose, they are not expected to meet the needs of any and all readers. Answer (C) is incorrect because the disclosure should be such that expertise in accounting or finance is not required to interpret the statements. Answer (D) is incorrect because regulatory bodies exist to protect the public, who are the ultimate beneficiaries of the disclosure requirements.

**60.** Which of the following statements is false regarding disclosure in a client's financial statements?

A. Information essential for a fair presentation should be set forth in the financial statements.

B. Omission of a statement of cash flows is considered inadequate disclosure.

C. Inadequate disclosure normally results in the auditor including the required information in the report.

D. The auditor should never disclose information in the report that the client has not shown in the financial statements.

Answer (D) is correct. *(Publisher)*

**REQUIRED:** The false statement regarding disclosure in the financial statements.

**DISCUSSION:** AU 431 states, "If management omits from the financial statements, including the accompanying notes, information that is required by generally accepted accounting principles, the auditor should express a qualified or an adverse opinion and should provide the information in the report, if practicable."

Answer (A) is incorrect because information essential for a fair presentation should be set forth in the financial statements. Answer (B) is incorrect because omission of a statement of cash flows is considered inadequate disclosure. Answer (C) is incorrect because inadequate disclosure normally results in the auditor's including the required information in the report.

**61.** If a publicly held company issues financial statements that purport to present its financial position and results of operations but omits the statement of cash flows, the auditor ordinarily will express a(n)

A. Disclaimer of opinion.

B. Qualified opinion.

C. Review report.

D. Unqualified opinion with a separate explanatory paragraph.

Answer (B) is correct. *(CPA, adapted)*

**REQUIRED:** The opinion expressed when a client fails to present a statement of cash flows.

**DISCUSSION:** Under SFAS 95, an entity that reports financial position and results of operations must provide a statement of cash flows. Thus, the omission of the cash flow statement is normally a basis for qualifying the opinion. If the statements fail to disclose information required by GAAP, the auditor should provide the information in the report, if practicable. However, the auditor is not required to prepare a basic financial statement. Accordingly, (s)he should qualify the opinion and explain the reason in a separate paragraph (AU 508).

Answer (A) is incorrect because the question concerns disclosure rather than a scope limitation. Answer (C) is incorrect because the engagement is an audit. Answer (D) is incorrect because the lack of disclosure normally requires qualification of the opinion.

**62.** Notes to financial statements may be used to

A. Describe the nature and type of auditing procedures applied to the financial statements.

B. Make an unsubstantiated claim that related party transactions were consummated on terms equivalent to those that prevail in arm's-length transactions.

C. Correct an improper financial statement presentation.

D. Indicate bases for valuing assets.

Answer (D) is correct. *(Publisher)*

**REQUIRED:** The purpose of notes.

**DISCUSSION:** Notes should be used to describe the valuation bases for the assets on the balance sheet. For example, it should be stated that property is recorded at historical cost and that such cost is systematically allocated to appropriate accounting periods.

Answer (A) is incorrect because the financial statements should not refer to the audit or the work of the auditor. Answer (B) is incorrect because SFAS 57, *Related Party Disclosures*, states that the representations "shall not imply that related party transactions were consummated on terms equivalent to those that prevail in arm's-length transactions unless such representations can be substantiated." Answer (C) is incorrect because notes are not a substitute for recognition in financial statements of items that meet recognition criteria.

**63.** Which of the following concepts is not encompassed by the phrase "present fairly in all material respects, in conformity with generally accepted accounting principles"?

A. The appropriateness of the principles.

B. The adequacy of informative disclosures.

C. The reflection of changes in the purchasing power of the monetary unit.

D. The form and content of the financial statements.

Answer (C) is correct. *(Publisher)*

**REQUIRED:** The concept not encompassed by the phrase "present fairly in conformity with GAAP."

**DISCUSSION:** Enterprises are encouraged but not required to disclose supplemental information on the effects of changing prices (SFAS 89, *Financial Reporting and Changing Prices*).

Answer (A) is incorrect because the auditor's opinion concerning the fairness of presentation in conformity with GAAP is based on certain judgments, e.g., about whether the accounting principles selected and applied are appropriate in the circumstances (AU 411). Answer (B) is incorrect because GAAP require adequate disclosure of material matters related to the form, content, and arrangement of the financial statements and their notes (AU 431). Answer (D) is incorrect because the form and content of the financial statements are encompassed by the phrase "present fairly in conformity with GAAP."

**64.** A closely held manufacturing company must disclose all of the following information in audited financial statements except

A. Replacement cost of inventory.

B. Pledged inventory.

C. LIFO reserves.

D. Changes in methods of accounting for inventory.

Answer (A) is correct. *(CPA, adapted)*

**REQUIRED:** The disclosure not required of a closely held manufacturing company.

**DISCUSSION:** A manufacturing company should report inventory at full absorption cost unless the fair value is less than cost. Whether they are closely or publicly held, companies need not report replacement cost of inventory.

Answer (B) is incorrect because pledged inventory is a disclosure required of all companies. Answer (C) is incorrect because LIFO reserves are disclosures required of all companies using LIFO. Answer (D) is incorrect because changes in methods of accounting for inventory are disclosures required of all companies.

**65.** In which of the following situations will an auditor ordinarily choose between expressing a qualified opinion or an adverse opinion?

A. The auditor did not observe the entity's physical inventory and is unable to become satisfied as to its balance by other auditing procedures.

B. The financial statements fail to disclose information that is required by generally accepted accounting principles.

C. The auditor is asked to report only on the entity's balance sheet and not on the other basic financial statements.

D. Events disclosed in the statements cause the auditor to have substantial doubt about the entity's ability to continue as a going concern.

Answer (B) is correct. *(CPA, adapted)*

**REQUIRED:** The situation in which a qualified or an adverse opinion is expressed.

**DISCUSSION:** Departures from GAAP, including inadequate disclosures, may result in either a qualified or an adverse opinion. The auditor must exercise judgment as to the materiality of the departure, weighing factors such as dollar magnitude, significance to the entity, pervasiveness of misstatements, and impact on the statements taken as a whole (AU 508). If the departure from GAAP is not sufficiently material to require an adverse opinion, the auditor should express a qualified opinion.

Answer (A) is incorrect because a scope limitation is not a basis for an adverse opinion. Answer (C) is incorrect because a limited reporting engagement may result in the expression of an unqualified opinion. Answer (D) is incorrect because substantial doubt about the entity's ability to continue as a going concern normally results in the addition of a paragraph to the end of the report.

**66.** On January 15, 20X1, before the Mapleview Co. released its financial statements for the year ended December 31, 20X0, it settled a long-standing lawsuit. A material loss resulted and no prior liability had been recorded. How should this loss be disclosed or recognized?

A. The loss should be disclosed in notes to the financial statements, but the financial statements themselves need not be adjusted.

B. The loss should be disclosed in an explanatory paragraph in the auditor's report.

C. No disclosure or recognition is required.

D. The financial statements should be adjusted to recognize the loss.

Answer (D) is correct. *(Publisher)*

**REQUIRED:** The proper disclosure of a material loss on an existing lawsuit after year-end.

**DISCUSSION:** Subsequent events that provide additional evidence with respect to conditions that existed at the balance sheet date and that affect the estimates inherent in the process of preparing the financial statements should be reflected in the current financial statements. Settlement of a lawsuit is indicative of conditions existing at year-end and calls for adjustment of the statements (AU 560, *Subsequent Events*).

Answer (A) is incorrect because the financial statements should be adjusted to reflect the loss. Answer (B) is incorrect because the audit report need not be modified. Answer (C) is incorrect because failure to adjust the statements for a material loss on an asset that existed at year-end would be misleading.

**67.** A major customer of an audit client suffers a fire just prior to completion of year-end field work. The audit client believes that this event could have a significant direct effect on the financial statements. The auditor should

A. Advise management to disclose the event in notes to the financial statements.

B. Disclose the event in the auditor's report.

C. Withhold submission of the auditor's report until the extent of the direct effect on the financial statements is known.

D. Advise management to adjust the financial statements.

Answer (A) is correct. *(CPA, adapted)*

**REQUIRED:** The appropriate action by the auditor concerning a subsequent event.

**DISCUSSION:** Subsequent events, such as a fire or other casualty, that provide evidence with respect to conditions that did not exist at the balance sheet date should not result in adjustment of the financial statements, but such events should be disclosed in the notes if necessary to keep the statements from being misleading (AU 560).

Answer (B) is incorrect because subsequent events, such as a fire or other casualty, that provide evidence with respect to conditions that did not exist at the balance sheet date are rarely disclosed in the audit report. Answer (C) is incorrect because an unreasonable amount of time may elapse before all the effects are known. Answer (D) is incorrect because adjustment of the financial statements is inappropriate. The fire damage did not exist at the balance sheet date.

**68.** Green, CPA, concludes that there is substantial doubt about JKL Co.'s ability to continue as a going concern. If JKL's financial statements adequately disclose its financial difficulties, Green's auditor's report should

| | Include an Explanatory Paragraph Following the Opinion Paragraph | Specifically Use the Words "Going Concern" | Specifically Use the Words "Substantial Doubt" |
|---|---|---|---|
| A. | Yes | Yes | Yes |
| B. | Yes | Yes | No |
| C. | Yes | No | Yes |
| D. | No | Yes | Yes |

Answer (A) is correct. *(CPA, adapted)*
**REQUIRED:** The effect of a substantial doubt about the going concern assumption.
**DISCUSSION:** According to AU 341, *The Auditor's Consideration of an Entity's Ability to Continue as a Going Concern*, an evaluation must be made as to whether substantial doubt exists "about the entity's ability to continue as a going concern for a reasonable period of time, not to exceed 1 year beyond the date of the financial statements." If the auditor reaches this conclusion after identifying conditions and events that create such doubt and after evaluating management's plans to mitigate their effects, (s)he should consider the adequacy of disclosure and include an explanatory paragraph (after the opinion paragraph) in the report. The auditor must use language in the explanatory paragraph that includes the phrases "substantial doubt" and "going concern." Also, the explanatory paragraph should not use conditional language in expressing its conclusion about the existence of a substantial doubt. The substantial doubt is not a basis for a qualified or an adverse opinion, but a disclaimer is not precluded in the case of such a material uncertainty.

**69.** Which of the following conditions or events is most likely to cause an auditor to have substantial doubt about an entity's ability to continue as a going concern?

A. Cash flows from operating activities are negative.
B. Research and development projects are postponed.
C. Significant related party transactions are pervasive.
D. Stock dividends replace annual cash dividends.

Answer (A) is correct. *(CPA, adapted)*
**REQUIRED:** The basis for substantial doubt about the going concern assumption.
**DISCUSSION:** The significance of conditions or events depends on circumstances, and some conditions or events may be significant only in conjunction with others. Such conditions and events include negative trends, financial difficulties, internal matters, and external matters. Negative cash flows from operating activities provide evidence of negative trends and financial difficulties.
Answer (B) is incorrect because an entity may postpone R&D and not raise doubts about its ability to continue as a going concern. Answer (C) is incorrect because the auditor's concern is with the adequacy of disclosure for related party transactions. Answer (D) is incorrect because stock dividends preserve cash and are not indicative of going concern problems.

**70.** Grant Company's financial statements adequately disclose uncertainties that concern future events, the outcome of which are not susceptible to reasonable estimation. The auditor's report should include

A. An unqualified opinion.
B. A "subject to" qualified opinion.
C. An "except for" qualified opinion.
D. An adverse opinion.

Answer (A) is correct. *(CPA, adapted)*
**REQUIRED:** The opinion when financial statements adequately disclose uncertainties.
**DISCUSSION:** In the absence of a scope limitation or a departure from GAAP, an uncertainty does not require modification of the report.
Answer (B) is incorrect because a "subject to" qualified opinion is never permissible. Answer (C) is incorrect because a qualified opinion related to an uncertainty is appropriate given a scope limitation or a departure from GAAP. Answer (D) is incorrect because, absent a departure from GAAP, an uncertainty does not result in an adverse opinion.

**71.** Which of the following phrases will an auditor most likely include in the auditor's report when expressing a qualified opinion because of inadequate disclosure?

A. Subject to the departure from generally accepted accounting principles, as described above.
B. With the foregoing explanation of these omitted disclosures.
C. Except for the omission of the information discussed in the preceding paragraph.
D. Does not present fairly in all material respects.

Answer (C) is correct. *(CPA, adapted)*
**REQUIRED:** The phrase included when the opinion is qualified because of inadequate disclosure.
**DISCUSSION:** A report qualified for inadequate disclosure includes a separate paragraph preceding the opinion paragraph. The opinion paragraph states, "In our opinion, except for the omission of information discussed in the preceding paragraph, the financial statements referred to above present fairly . . ."
Answer (A) is incorrect because a "subject to" opinion should not be expressed in any circumstance. Answer (B) is incorrect because the phrase "with the foregoing explanation" is not forceful enough, lacks clarity, and should not be used.
Answer (D) is incorrect because the phrase "does not present fairly" indicates an adverse opinion.

**72.** Zero Corp. suffered a loss having a material effect on its financial statements as a result of a customer's bankruptcy that rendered a trade receivable uncollectible. This bankruptcy occurred suddenly because of a natural disaster 10 days after Zero's balance sheet date, but one month before the issuance of the financial statements and the auditor's report. Under these circumstances, the

| | Financial Statements Should Be Adjusted | Event Requires Financial Statement Disclosure, but No Adjustment | Auditor's Report Should Be Modified for a Lack of Consistency |
|---|---|---|---|
| A. | Yes | No | No |
| B. | Yes | No | Yes |
| C. | No | Yes | Yes |
| D. | No | Yes | No |

Answer (D) is correct. *(CPA, adapted)*

**REQUIRED:** The effect on the financial statements and the auditor's report of a subsequent event.

**DISCUSSION:** Certain subsequent events may provide additional evidence about conditions at the date of the balance sheet and affect estimates inherent in the preparation of the statements. These events require adjustment by the client in the financial statements at year-end. Other subsequent events provide evidence about conditions not existing at the date of the balance sheet but arising subsequent to that date and affecting the interpretation of the year-end financial statements. These events may require disclosure in notes to the financial statements but do not require adjustment of financial statement balances. In this case, the financial statements should not be adjusted, but disclosure should be made in the notes. The report is unaffected if disclosure is made.

**73.** If the auditor discovers that the fair value of a client's investments in trading securities has increased, the auditor should insist that the

A. Investments be reported at lower of cost or market.

B. Investments be classified as long-term for balance sheet purposes with full disclosure in the notes.

C. Holding gain be recognized in the financial statements of the client.

D. Equity section of the balance sheet separately show a credit equal to the amount of the gain.

Answer (C) is correct. *(Publisher)*

**REQUIRED:** The auditor's action when (s)he discovers that the fair value of trading securities has increased.

**DISCUSSION:** According to SFAS 115, *Accounting for Certain Investments in Debt and Equity Securities*, unrealized holding gains and losses on trading securities are included in earnings. Failure to adhere to SFAS 115 is a departure from GAAP and requires a qualified or adverse opinion if material.

Answer (A) is incorrect because the gain must be recognized in the income statement and the investment reported at fair value. Answer (B) is incorrect because no reclassification is necessary for a change in fair value of an investment. Answer (D) is incorrect because an unrealized gain or loss on available-for-sale securities is reported as a separate component of equity until realized.

**74.** An auditor most likely will modify an unqualified opinion if the entity's financial statements include a note on related party transactions

A. Disclosing loans to related parties at interest rates significantly below prevailing market rates.

B. Describing an exchange of real estate for similar property in a nonmonetary related party transaction.

C. Stating that a particular related party transaction occurred on terms equivalent to those that would have prevailed in an arm's-length transaction.

D. Presenting the dollar volume of related party transactions and the effects of any change from prior periods in the method of establishing the terms.

Answer (C) is correct. *(CPA, adapted)*

**REQUIRED:** The note on related party transactions that would most likely result in a modified opinion.

**DISCUSSION:** The auditor's primary concern regarding related party transactions is for adequate disclosure because the accounting treatment of these transactions is ordinarily the same as for other transactions. It is difficult to substantiate representations that the related party transactions were consummated on terms equivalent to those that prevail in arm's-length transactions. An auditor who believes the representations to be unsubstantiated should express a qualified or an adverse opinion (AU 334, *Related Parties*).

Answer (A) is incorrect because loans are common related party transactions that do not require an opinion modification. However, the auditor may wish to include an explanatory paragraph to emphasize such matters. Answer (B) is incorrect because exchanges of real estate are common related party transactions that do not require an opinion modification. However, the auditor may wish to include an explanatory paragraph to emphasize such matters. Answer (D) is incorrect because the dollar amount of related party transactions and the effects of changes in the method of establishing the terms should be disclosed.

**75.** When an independent auditor wishes to include in the report additional explanatory matter (not required for adequate disclosure) to highlight certain circumstances or to aid in the interpretation of the financial statements, this additional disclosure should be referred to in

A. The scope paragraph only.

B. Neither the scope paragraph nor the opinion paragraph.

C. The introductory paragraph and the opinion paragraph.

D. The opinion paragraph only.

Answer (B) is correct. *(Publisher)*

**REQUIRED:** The proper treatment in the audit report of additional information not required for adequate disclosure.

**DISCUSSION:** An auditor may wish to emphasize a matter affecting the statements even though (s)he intends to express an unqualified opinion. This information should be contained in a separate explanatory paragraph (AU 508).

Answer (A) is incorrect because the scope paragraph should remain unchanged. Answer (C) is incorrect because the introductory and opinion paragraphs should remain unchanged. Answer (D) is incorrect because the opinion paragraph should remain unchanged.

**76.** An auditor's standard report expresses an unqualified opinion and includes an explanatory paragraph that emphasizes a matter included in the notes to the financial statements. The auditor's report is deficient if the explanatory paragraph states that the entity

A. Is a component of a larger business enterprise.

B. Has omitted a statement of cash flows.

C. Has had a significant subsequent event.

D. Has accounting reclassifications that enhance the comparability between years.

Answer (B) is correct. *(CPA, adapted)*

**REQUIRED:** The statement in an explanatory paragraph indicating a deficiency in the report.

**DISCUSSION:** The statement of cash flows is a basic financial statement. Its omission when financial position and results of operations are presented is a departure from GAAP that requires the auditor to modify the opinion paragraph.

Answer (A) is incorrect because the entity's position as a component of a larger business enterprise may be emphasized in an explanatory paragraph expressing an unqualified opinion. Answer (C) is incorrect because an entity having had a significant subsequent event may be emphasized in an explanatory paragraph expressing an unqualified opinion. Answer (D) is incorrect because accounting reclassifications that enhance the comparability between years may be emphasized in an explanatory paragraph expressing an unqualified opinion.

**77.** When a publicly held company refuses to include in its audited financial statements any of the segment disclosures that the auditor believes are required, the auditor should express

A. An unqualified opinion with a separate explanatory paragraph emphasizing the matter.

B. A qualified opinion because of inadequate disclosure.

C. An adverse opinion because of a significant uncertainty.

D. A disclaimer of opinion because of the significant scope limitation.

Answer (B) is correct. *(CPA, adapted)*

**REQUIRED:** The effect on the report.

**DISCUSSION:** SFAS 131, *Disclosures about Segments of an Enterprise and Related Information,* requires an operating-segment approach to disclosure. The change to an operating-segment approach is similar to a reclassification of prior-period information made for comparative purposes. According to an Interpretation of AU 326 that addresses segment disclosures, the auditor's standard report implicitly applies to segment information included in those statements. The auditor should not refer to segment information unless the audit reveals a related material misstatement or omission, or unless the audit was subject to a scope limitation. If material information is not included that the auditor believes should be disclosed, the auditor should modify the opinion for inadequate disclosure and describe the information omitted (AU 508). The auditor should include this information in the report, if practicable, unless a specific SAS allows its omission. The auditor need not assume the position of a preparer of financial information.

Answer (A) is incorrect because inadequate disclosure requires an opinion modification if it is material. Answer (C) is incorrect because the issue is disclosure, not an uncertainty. Moreover, by itself, an uncertainty does not result in a required report modification. Answer (D) is incorrect because inadequate disclosure is not a scope limitation.

## 7.5 Unqualified, Qualified, and Adverse Opinions

**78.** Which paragraphs of an auditor's standard report on financial statements of a private company (nonissuer) should refer to generally accepted auditing standards (GAAS) and generally accepted accounting principles (GAAP)?

| | GAAS | GAAP |
|---|---|---|
| A. | Opening | Scope |
| B. | Scope | Scope |
| C. | Scope | Opinion |
| D. | Opening | Opinion |

Answer (C) is correct. *(CPA, adapted)*

**REQUIRED:** The paragraphs of the standard report that refer to GAAS and GAAP.

**DISCUSSION:** The auditor's report should contain a clear-cut indication of the character of the auditor's work, if any, and state the degree of responsibility assumed (AU 150). GAAS are referred to only in the scope paragraph because they relate to the nature of the audit. The opinion paragraph contains an opinion as to whether the statements as a whole are fairly presented, in all material respects, in conformity with GAAP. Neither GAAS nor GAAP are mentioned in the introductory paragraph, which identifies the financial statements audited and describes the responsibilities of management and of the auditor (AU 508). For an audit report of a company subject to reporting to the SEC, the scope paragraph should refer to the standards of the PCAOB rather than GAAS.

**79.** A United States auditor is aware that the report on the financial statements will be available on the Internet to parties outside the United States. In the standard audit report, how should the auditor make reference to the country of origin of the accounting principles used to prepare the financial statements?

A. Modify the scope and opinion paragraphs.

B. Modify the scope and introductory paragraphs.

C. Modify the opinion paragraph only.

D. Modify the introductory paragraph only.

Answer (C) is correct. *(Publisher)*

**REQUIRED:** The standard report modification(s) to refer to the country of origin of the accounting principles.

**DISCUSSION:** According to AU 508, the country of origin of the accounting principles used to prepare the financial statements should be identified in the opinion paragraph. For example, if that country is the United States, the end of the last sentence should be worded as follows: ". . . the year then ended in conformity with accounting principles generally accepted in the United States of America." The auditor should also identify the country of origin of the auditing standards followed in performing the audit. In that case, for a private company, the first sentence of the scope paragraph is worded as follows: "We conducted our audit in accordance with auditing standards generally accepted in the United States of America." For an issuer, the first sentence of the scope paragraph is worded as follows: "We conducted our audit in accordance with the standards of the Public Company Accounting Oversight Board (United States)."

**80.** Which of the following circumstances is not considered a departure from the auditor's standard report?

A. The auditor wishes to emphasize a particular matter regarding the financial statements.

B. The auditor's opinion is based in part on the report of another auditor.

C. The financial statements are affected by a departure from a generally accepted accounting principle.

D. The auditor is asked to report only on the balance sheet but has unlimited access to information underlying all the basic financial statements.

Answer (D) is correct. *(CPA, adapted)*

**REQUIRED:** The circumstance not resulting in a departure from the auditor's standard report.

**DISCUSSION:** When the auditor is asked to report only on the balance sheet, has unlimited access to information underlying all the basic financial statements, and applies all the procedures (s)he considers necessary, only the reporting objectives are limited, and the report is not considered a departure from the standard report.

Answer (A) is incorrect because emphasis of a matter requires an additional paragraph but not a modified opinion. Answer (B) is incorrect because, if the principal auditor does not assume responsibility for the other auditor's work, (s)he should make the appropriate disclosure in the introductory and scope paragraphs and refer to it in the opinion paragraph. If the CPA accepts responsibility for the work of the other CPA, no report modification is necessary. Answer (C) is incorrect because a material departure from GAAP requires a modified opinion.

**81.** An auditor includes a separate paragraph in an otherwise unmodified report to emphasize that the entity being reported on had significant transactions with related parties. The inclusion of this separate paragraph

A. Is considered a qualification of the opinion.

B. Violates auditing standards if this information is already disclosed in notes to the financial statements.

C. Necessitates a revision of the opinion paragraph to include the phrase "with the foregoing explanation."

D. Is appropriate and would not negate the unqualified opinion.

Answer (D) is correct. *(CPA, adapted)*

**REQUIRED:** The effect of a separate paragraph in an otherwise unmodified report.

**DISCUSSION:** An auditor may emphasize a matter in an explanatory paragraph and express an unqualified opinion. Matters to be emphasized might include that the entity is a component of a larger enterprise or that it has had significant related party transactions. Subsequent events and accounting matters affecting comparability (e.g., a divestiture) are other matters suitable for this treatment.

Answer (A) is incorrect because emphasis of a matter in a separate paragraph is not inconsistent with an unqualified opinion. Answer (B) is incorrect because the auditor can emphasize a matter without violating GAAS or the PCAOB standards. Answer (C) is incorrect because "with the foregoing explanation" creates doubt as to whether the report was intended to be qualified.

**82.** Without affecting the CPA's willingness to express an unqualified opinion on the client's financial statements, corporate management may refuse a request to

A. Authorize its attorney to confirm that a list of pending or threatened litigation prepared by management includes all items known to the attorney.

B. Change its basis of accounting for inventories from FIFO to LIFO because, in the opinion of the CPA, the FIFO method fails to give adequate recognition to the extraordinary increases in prices of merchandise acquired and held by the company.

C. Write down to salvage value certain equipment that is no longer useful.

D. Allow the CPA to examine tax returns for years prior to that of the financial statements being audited.

Answer (B) is correct. *(CMA, adapted)*

**REQUIRED:** The request from an auditor that the client could refuse without jeopardizing an unqualified opinion.

**DISCUSSION:** FIFO (first-in, first-out) and LIFO (last-in, first-out) are both generally accepted methods of accounting for inventories. LIFO has the advantage during periods of inflation of matching current costs with current revenues. An independent auditor who has requested a change from FIFO to LIFO is likely to express an unqualified opinion even if management refuses to do so because the financial statements would still conform with GAAP.

Answer (A) is incorrect because a lawyer's refusal to furnish the information requested in the inquiry letter is a scope limitation sufficient to preclude an unqualified opinion (AU 337, *Inquiry of a Client's Lawyer Concerning Litigation, Claims, and Assessments*). Answer (C) is incorrect because refusal to write down obsolete equipment is a departure from GAAP that will result in modification of the opinion if the resulting misstatement is material. Answer (D) is incorrect because a scope limitation concerning tax liabilities may require qualifying or disclaiming an opinion depending on the importance of the omitted procedures to the auditor's ability to form an opinion.

**83.** Which of the following phrases should be included in the opinion paragraph when an auditor expresses a qualified opinion?

| | When Read in Conjunction with Note X | With the Foregoing Explanation |
|---|---|---|
| A. | Yes | No |
| B. | No | Yes |
| C. | Yes | Yes |
| D. | No | No |

Answer (D) is correct. *(CPA, adapted)*

**REQUIRED:** The phrase(s) used in a qualified opinion.

**DISCUSSION:** The auditor should use a phrase such as "with the exception of" or "except for" to qualify an opinion, followed by the basis for the qualification and a reference to the explanatory paragraph(s) preceding the opinion paragraph. The explanatory paragraph(s) should state the substantive reasons for the qualification and disclose the principal effects of the subject matter of the qualification, if practicable, or refer to a note including such disclosures. However, the notes are part of the financial statements, and a phrase such as "when read in conjunction with the notes" in the opinion paragraph is likely to be misunderstood. Moreover, wording such as "with the foregoing explanation" is neither clear nor forceful enough.

**84.** An auditor's report includes an additional paragraph disclosing a difference of opinion between the auditor and the client for which the auditor believes an adjustment to the financial statements should be made. The opinion paragraph of the auditor's report most likely expresses

A. An unqualified opinion.

B. A qualified opinion.

C. A "subject to" opinion.

D. A disclaimer of opinion.

Answer (B) is correct. *(CPA, adapted)*

**REQUIRED:** The opinion most likely expressed given a dispute between the auditor and the client.

**DISCUSSION:** The most likely reason for a separate paragraph disclosing a difference of opinion with the client is a departure from GAAP. Such a disagreement is usually the basis for a qualified opinion. If the departure from GAAP causes the statements, taken as a whole, not to be fairly presented, an adverse opinion expressed.

Answer (A) is incorrect because the auditor cannot express an unqualified opinion if (s)he believes the statements contain a material departure from GAAP. Answer (C) is incorrect because the wording "subject to" is unacceptable in any report. Answer (D) is incorrect because an opinion must be expressed if one is formed by the auditor.

**85.** An auditor may not express a qualified opinion when

A. A scope limitation prevents the auditor from completing an important audit procedure.

B. The auditor's report refers to the work of a specialist.

C. An accounting principle at variance with generally accepted accounting principles is used.

D. The auditor lacks independence with respect to the audited entity.

Answer (D) is correct. *(CPA, adapted)*

**REQUIRED:** The situation in which an auditor may not express a qualified opinion.

**DISCUSSION:** A CPA may not express an opinion when not independent. (S)he should disclaim an opinion and state that (s)he is not independent (AU 504, *Association with Financial Statements*).

Answer (A) is incorrect because a scope limitation is the basis for a qualified opinion or a disclaimer depending upon the auditor's assessment of the importance of the omitted procedure(s) (AU 508). Answer (B) is incorrect because the report may refer to and identify a specialist if the auditor departs from an unqualified opinion or adds an explanatory paragraph as a result of the specialist's report or findings (AU 336, *Using the Work of a Specialist*). Answer (C) is incorrect because a material departure from GAAP requires a modified opinion.

**86.** An auditor's report includes the following statement: "The financial statements do not present fairly the financial position, results of operations, or cash flows in conformity with generally accepted accounting principles." This auditor's report was most likely issued in connection with financial statements that are

A. Inconsistent.

B. Based on prospective financial information.

C. Misleading.

D. Affected by a material uncertainty.

Answer (C) is correct. *(CPA, adapted)*

**REQUIRED:** The nature of the financial statements on which the quoted report was issued.

**DISCUSSION:** The language quoted states an adverse opinion. The essence of an adverse opinion is that the statements reported on, taken as a whole, are not fairly presented in accordance with GAAP (AU 508). The financial statements should be based on principles having general acceptance that are appropriate in the circumstances. They should also be (1) informative about matters affecting their use, understanding, and interpretation; (2) neither too detailed nor too condensed; and (3) presented to reflect the underlying transactions and events within a range of acceptable limits (AU 411). If financial statements fail to meet these standards, they are misleading.

Answer (A) is incorrect because an inconsistency, by itself, results in no modification of the opinion but in an explanatory paragraph. Answer (B) is incorrect because the standard examination report on a financial forecast or projection refers to guidelines established by the AICPA, not to GAAP (AT 301). Answer (D) is incorrect because a material uncertainty does not, by itself, result in a required report modification.

**87.** When financial statements are presented that are not in conformity with generally accepted accounting principles, an auditor may express a

| | Qualified Opinion | Disclaimer of an Opinion |
|---|---|---|
| A. | Yes | No |
| B. | Yes | Yes |
| C. | No | Yes |
| D. | No | No |

Answer (A) is correct. *(CPA, adapted)*

**REQUIRED:** The proper report when statements do not conform with GAAP.

**DISCUSSION:** Departures from GAAP may result in either a qualified or an adverse opinion. The auditor must exercise judgment as to the materiality of the departure, weighing factors such as dollar magnitude, significance to the entity, pervasiveness of misstatements, and impact on the statements taken as a whole (AU 508). If the departure from GAAP is not sufficiently material to require an adverse opinion, the auditor should express a qualified opinion.

**88.** An auditor will express an adverse opinion if

A. A severe scope limitation has been imposed by the client.

B. A violation of GAAP is sufficiently material that a qualified opinion is not justified.

C. A qualified opinion cannot be expressed because the auditor lacks independence.

D. The company's ability to continue as a going concern is subject to substantial doubt.

Answer (B) is correct. *(K.J. Plucinski)*

**REQUIRED:** The circumstances in which the auditor will express an adverse opinion.

**DISCUSSION:** The auditor will express a qualified opinion when the statements are fairly presented in accordance with GAAP except for the effects of the matter to which the qualification relates. When the statements as a whole are not fairly presented in conformity with GAAP, a qualified opinion will be inappropriate, and an adverse opinion must be expressed (AU 508).

Answer (A) is incorrect because a severe client-imposed scope limitation will result in a disclaimer of opinion. Answer (C) is incorrect because a lack of independence will result in a disclaimer of opinion. Answer (D) is incorrect because such a doubt will result in a separate explanatory paragraph or a disclaimer of opinion.

**89.** When an auditor expresses an adverse opinion, the opinion paragraph should include

A. The principal effects of the departure from generally accepted accounting principles.

B. A direct reference to a separate paragraph disclosing the basis for the opinion.

C. The substantive reasons for the financial statements being misleading.

D. A description of the uncertainty or scope limitation that prevents an unqualified opinion.

Answer (B) is correct. *(CPA, adapted)*

**REQUIRED:** The matter included in the opinion paragraph when an adverse opinion is expressed.

**DISCUSSION:** An adverse opinion states that the financial statements are not fairly presented in accordance with GAAP. When an adverse opinion is expressed, the opinion paragraph should include a direct reference to a separate paragraph that discloses the basis for the adverse opinion. This paragraph should precede the opinion paragraph and state (1) all the substantive reasons for the adverse opinion and (2) the principal effects of the subject matter of the adverse opinion, if practicable (AU 508).

Answer (A) is incorrect because the principal effects of the subject matter of the adverse opinion, if practicable, should be stated in the explanatory paragraph. Answer (C) is incorrect because all the substantive reasons for the adverse opinion should be stated in the explanatory paragraph. Answer (D) is incorrect because an adverse opinion is not expressed as a result of an uncertainty or scope limitation.

**90.** An auditor may reasonably express a "subject to" qualified opinion for

| | Lack of Consistency | Departure from Generally Accepted Accounting Principles |
|---|---|---|
| A. | Yes | Yes |
| B. | Yes | No |
| C. | No | Yes |
| D. | No | No |

Answer (D) is correct. *(CPA, adapted)*

**REQUIRED:** The type of opinion that uses the phrase "subject to."

**DISCUSSION:** The phrase "subject to" should not be used in any report. It is not clear or forceful enough (AU 508).

**91.** The opinion paragraph of an independent auditor's report begins, "In our opinion, based upon our audit and the report of other auditors, the financial statements referred to above present fairly, in all material respects, the financial position . . ." This language states

A. A disclaimer of opinion.

B. An unqualified opinion.

C. An "except for" opinion.

D. A qualified opinion.

Answer (B) is correct. *(Publisher)*

**REQUIRED:** The opinion expressed when the report refers to the report of another auditor.

**DISCUSSION:** When the auditor refers to the report of another auditor as a basis, in part, for his/her opinion, (s)he must clearly indicate the division of responsibility by disclosure in the introductory paragraph and by reference to the report of the other auditor in the scope and opinion paragraphs (AU 508 and AU 543, *Part of Audit Performed by Other Independent Auditors*). These references do not in themselves constitute a disclaimer or a modification of the opinion expressed. This is an unqualified opinion even though it varies from the standard report.

Answer (A) is incorrect because an opinion is being expressed. Answer (C) is incorrect because the quotation contains no qualifying language. Answer (D) is incorrect because the quotation contains no qualifying language.

**92.** An auditor is in compliance with the fourth standard of reporting when (s)he issues a report containing

A. A piecemeal opinion and a disclaimer on the statements as a whole.

B. An unqualified opinion in which (s)he explains that, to a limited extent, (s)he is not fully independent of the client.

C. A qualified opinion with respect to the income statement and the statement of cash flows and an unqualified opinion with respect to the statement of financial position.

D. An opinion qualified with respect to the degree of responsibility accepted for the accompanying financial statements.

Answer (C) is correct. *(Publisher)*

**REQUIRED:** The report in compliance with the fourth standard of reporting.

**DISCUSSION:** The fourth standard of reporting requires an expression of opinion regarding the statements taken as a whole or an assertion to the effect that an opinion cannot be expressed. The phrase "taken as a whole" applies equally to a complete set of statements and to an individual statement. The auditor may thus express different opinions on different statements (AU 508).

Answer (A) is incorrect because opinions on identified items in the statements (piecemeal opinions) are inappropriate when the auditor has expressed a disclaimer of opinion or an adverse opinion on the statements taken as a whole. Piecemeal opinions tend to overshadow or contradict a disclaimer or an adverse opinion. Answer (B) is incorrect because the auditor must be independent to express any opinion. Answer (D) is incorrect because an auditor may not qualify an opinion with respect to responsibility. Opinions are qualified as to the fairness of financial presentation.

**93.** An auditor may express a qualified opinion under which of the following circumstances?

| | Lack of Sufficient Competent Evidential Matter | Restrictions on the Scope of the Audit |
|---|---|---|
| A. | Yes | Yes |
| B. | Yes | No |
| C. | No | Yes |
| D. | No | No |

Answer (A) is correct. *(CPA, adapted)*

**REQUIRED:** The circumstances in which the auditor may express a qualified opinion.

**DISCUSSION:** A qualified opinion is expressed because of a departure from GAAP, a lack of sufficient competent evidence, or a restriction on the scope of the audit. The auditor may be required to qualify the opinion or disclaim an opinion because of scope restrictions, "whether imposed by the client or by circumstances, such as the timing of the work, the inability to obtain sufficient competent evidential matter, or an inadequacy in the records" (AU 508).

**94.** When qualifying an opinion because of an insufficiency of audit evidence, an auditor should refer to the situation in the

| | Scope Paragraph | Notes to the Financial Statements |
|---|---|---|
| A. | Yes | Yes |
| B. | Yes | No |
| C. | No | Yes |
| D. | No | No |

Answer (B) is correct. *(CPA, adapted)*

**REQUIRED:** The effect on the auditor's report when the opinion is qualified because of an insufficiency of evidence.

**DISCUSSION:** When an opinion is qualified for a scope limitation or insufficient evidence, the notes to the financial statements are unchanged because they were not drafted by the auditor. The scope paragraph is unchanged except that it begins with the clause, "Except as discussed in the following paragraph." An explanatory paragraph is added, followed by the opinion paragraph with appropriate qualifying language (AU 508).

**95.** If the independent auditor has not become satisfied by means of other auditing procedures with respect to opening inventories, (s)he should

A. Disclaim an opinion or qualify the opinion on the statements taken as a whole.

B. Either disclaim an opinion on the statement of income or qualify the opinion thereon, depending on the degree of materiality of the amounts involved.

C. Either disclaim an opinion on the statement of income or qualify the opinion thereon, regardless of the degree of materiality of the amounts involved.

D. Express an adverse opinion on the statements taken as a whole when the amount in question is material.

Answer (B) is correct. *(Publisher)*

**REQUIRED:** The opinion expressed when the auditor is not satisfied as to opening inventories.

**DISCUSSION:** An unqualified opinion is possible only if the audit has been conducted in accordance with GAAS or the PCAOB standards and if the auditor has applied all procedures (s)he deems necessary. A scope restriction, e.g., on the observation of inventories, may prevent the auditor from obtaining the evidence required to support an unqualified opinion. If (s)he has become satisfied as to current inventory, the auditor may use alternate procedures to become satisfied as to opening inventories (AU 331, *Inventories*). But if (s)he cannot become satisfied regarding inventories, a qualified opinion or a disclaimer of opinion must be expressed, depending on the importance of the omitted procedure. Because cost of goods sold is dependent on opening inventories, an unqualified opinion on the income statement is not possible.

Answer (A) is incorrect because the restriction may apply only to the income statement. Answer (C) is incorrect because the materiality of the amounts involved determines the opinion expressed. Answer (D) is incorrect because an adverse opinion is inappropriate for a scope limitation.

**96.** A separate paragraph of an auditor's report describes an uncertainty as follows:

As discussed in Note X to the financial statements, the Company is a defendant in a lawsuit alleging infringement of certain patent rights and claiming damages. Discovery proceedings are in progress.

What type of opinion should the auditor express under these circumstances?

A. Unqualified.

B. "Subject to" qualified.

C. "Except for" qualified.

D. Disclaimer.

Answer (A) is correct. *(CPA, adapted)*

**REQUIRED:** The opinion that should be expressed because of an uncertainty.

**DISCUSSION:** AU 508 does not require the addition of an uncertainties paragraph. However, standards provide the auditor with the option of emphasizing a matter regarding the financial statements by adding a separate paragraph to the report. This separate paragraph does not affect the opinion expressed on the financial statements.

Answer (B) is incorrect because the phrase "subject to" is not permitted in any report. Answer (C) is incorrect because, by itself, an uncertainty does not result in an opinion modification. Answer (D) is incorrect because a disclaimer is less likely than an unqualified opinion on these facts. Moreover, an auditor's report containing a disclaimer would give all the substantive reasons for the disclaimer.

**97.** In which of the following circumstances would an auditor most likely add an explanatory paragraph to the standard report while expressing an unqualified opinion?

A. The auditor is asked to report on the balance sheet but not on the other basic financial statements.

B. There is substantial doubt about the entity's ability to continue as a going concern.

C. Management's estimates of the effects of future events are unreasonable.

D. Certain transactions cannot be tested because of management's records retention policy.

Answer (B) is correct. *(CPA, adapted)*

**REQUIRED:** The situation most likely resulting in an explanatory paragraph and an unqualified opinion.

**DISCUSSION:** If the auditor reaches this conclusion after identifying conditions and events that create such doubt and after evaluating management's plans to mitigate their effects, (s)he should consider the adequacy of disclosure and include an explanatory paragraph (after the opinion paragraph) in the report. The auditor must use language in the explanatory paragraph that includes the words "substantial doubt" and "going concern."

Answer (A) is incorrect because an auditor may be asked to report on one financial statement. In that event, (s)he may appropriately express an unqualified opinion without adding an explanatory paragraph. Answer (C) is incorrect because the statements are not fairly presented if the estimates included in them are unreasonable. An unqualified opinion could not be expressed. Answer (D) is incorrect because a qualification or disclaimer of opinion is appropriate when the scope of the audit is limited.

**98.** If an auditor is satisfied that sufficient evidence supports management's assertions about an uncertainty and its presentation or disclosure, the auditor should

A. Express an unqualified opinion.

B. Express an unqualified opinion with a separate explanatory paragraph.

C. Disclaim an opinion.

D. Express a qualified opinion or disclaim an opinion, depending upon the materiality of the loss.

Answer (A) is correct. *(CPA, adapted)*

**REQUIRED:** The opinion expressed when the likelihood is remote that an uncertainty will have a material effect.

**DISCUSSION:** In the absence of a departure from GAAP, for example, because of inadequate disclosure, or a scope limitation, an uncertainty does not require modification of the report.

Answer (B) is incorrect because a separate paragraph is not required. Answer (C) is incorrect because a disclaimer is appropriate only when the scope of the audit was too limited to warrant expression of an opinion. Answer (D) is incorrect because a disclaimer is appropriate only when the scope of the audit was too limited to warrant expression of an opinion. Moreover, an uncertainty does not, by itself, require any report modification.

**99.** An external auditor discovers that a payroll supervisor of the firm being audited has misappropriated $10,000. The firm's total assets and before-tax net income are $14 million and $3 million, respectively. Assuming no other issues affect the report, the external auditor's report will most likely contain a(n)

A. Disclaimer of opinion.

B. Adverse opinion.

C. Scope qualification.

D. Unqualified opinion.

Answer (D) is correct. *(CMA, adapted)*

**REQUIRED:** The audit report issued after detection of a misappropriation.

**DISCUSSION:** The auditor is likely to express an unqualified opinion for two reasons. First, the misappropriated amount is immaterial relative to assets and income. Second, as long as the misappropriation is accounted for properly, the financial statements will be fairly presented in accordance with GAAP.

Answer (A) is incorrect because a disclaimer is appropriate when the audit is insufficient to permit formation of an opinion. Answer (B) is incorrect because an adverse opinion states that the statements are not fairly presented. An immaterial item, properly accounted for, does not impair the fairness of presentation. Answer (C) is incorrect because the audit scope has not been limited.

**100.** During the year ended December 31, Price Corporation reported its fixed assets at lower of cost or market (LCM) because their fair value had declined. The loss has been included as an extraordinary item in the income statement and the adjustment has been fully disclosed in the notes. If a CPA believes that the values reported in the financial statements are reasonable, what opinion should be expressed?

A. An unqualified opinion.

B. A "subject to" qualified opinion.

C. An adverse opinion.

D. A disclaimer of opinion.

Answer (C) is correct. *(Publisher)*

**REQUIRED:** The opinion expressed when fixed assets are reported at LCM.

**DISCUSSION:** The fixed assets of a company should be recorded at historical cost minus accumulated depreciation. Recording them at LCM is therefore a departure from GAAP. The CPA should express either a qualified opinion or an adverse opinion, assuming that the effects of the departure are material (AU 508).

Answer (A) is incorrect because a material departure from GAAP precludes an unqualified opinion. Answer (B) is incorrect because a "subject to" qualified opinion is an unacceptable form of reporting. Answer (D) is incorrect because a disclaimer is proper when the audit is not sufficient in scope to permit formation of an opinion.

**101.** If a company is experiencing financial difficulty that raises substantial doubt about its ability to continue as a going concern, auditing standards require the auditor to

A. Withdraw from the engagement.

B. Value the assets on a liquidation basis.

C. Plan to conduct a complete audit rather than perform procedures on a test basis.

D. Include in the report a paragraph describing the nature of the difficulties.

Answer (D) is correct. *(N. Schmukler)*

**REQUIRED:** The auditor's responsibility when the entity may not be able to continue as a going concern.

**DISCUSSION:** Auditing standards require the auditor to alert financial statement users to the existence of doubt about the ability of an auditee to continue in existence. AU 341 is intended to reduce the instances when, shortly after the expression of an unqualified opinion, the auditee becomes bankrupt. Hence, the auditor's substantial doubt requires inclusion of an explanatory paragraph in the report. This paragraph should include the words "substantial doubt" and "going concern."

Answer (A) is incorrect because the auditor need not withdraw. Answer (B) is incorrect because the existence of a substantial doubt does not require that assets be presented on a liquidation basis; they may continue to be presented on a going concern basis unless liquidation is imminent. Answer (C) is incorrect because, even when the entity may not be able to continue as a going concern, the audit will normally be performed on a test basis.

**102.** During the year, the research staff of Dermoplex, Inc. devoted its entire efforts toward developing a skin cancer ointment. All costs that could be attributed directly to the project were accounted for as deferred charges and classified on the balance sheet as an asset. If the amounts involved are material, the auditor should

A. Express an unqualified opinion with a separate paragraph explaining the uncertainty of cost recovery.

B. Disclaim an opinion.

C. Express an adverse opinion.

D. Express an unqualified opinion provided that the uncertainty about ultimate realization of the deferred charges is disclosed in the notes.

Answer (C) is correct. *(Publisher)*

**REQUIRED:** The appropriate opinion when the client has capitalized R&D costs.

**DISCUSSION:** Capitalizing R&D costs is not permitted according to GAAP. Ordinarily, they must be expensed in the period in which they were incurred (SFAS 2). Because capitalizing R&D costs is a departure from GAAP and the amounts involved are material, the auditor should express an adverse opinion if the statements as a whole are not fairly presented in conformity with GAAP. A qualified opinion might be appropriate, however, depending on the materiality of the exception.

Answer (A) is incorrect because the issue is not uncertainty but the departure from GAAP. Answer (B) is incorrect because the auditor has sufficient evidence to express an opinion that the financial statements are materially misstated. Answer (D) is incorrect because the issue is not uncertainty but the departure from GAAP.

**103.** In which circumstance will the auditor not consider the need to modify the report?

A. The client's legal counsel is requested to advise whether a material act is legal or illegal but refuses to do so.

B. The auditor concludes that the effect of an illegal act creates substantial doubt about the entity's ability to continue as a going concern.

C. The auditor concludes that the effect of an illegal act, taken alone or with similar acts, is material in amount and has not been properly accounted for or disclosed in the financial statements.

D. All of the circumstances require modification of the auditor's report.

Answer (D) is correct. *(Publisher)*

**REQUIRED:** The circumstance in which the auditor would not consider modifying the report.

**DISCUSSION:** All of the answer choices given describe circumstances in which the report should be modified.

Answer (A) is incorrect because the auditor may be unable to determine the legality of certain acts or the amounts associated with them as a result of an inability to gather sufficient competent evidence; e.g., the client's legal counsel may have refused to give advice. In these circumstances, the scope limitation may require a qualified opinion or a disclaimer. Answer (B) is incorrect because, if the effects of an illegal act create substantial doubt about the entity's ability to continue as a going concern, a separate explanatory paragraph is required. Answer (C) is incorrect because, if the effects of an illegal act are material but have not been properly accounted for or disclosed, the departure from GAAP may result in a qualified or an adverse opinion (AU 317, *Illegal Acts by Clients*).

**104.** The federal government alleges that your client has overcharged on certain contracts and is demanding a material refund. If the client is compelled to return this sum, the current ratio of 2:1 in the present financial statements would be reduced to 1.2:1, and a substantial reduction in retained earnings would occur. No decision has been reached at the end of field work, and a note adequately describing the event and negotiations has been written by the client. The auditor should most likely

A. Express an adverse opinion because of the material uncertainty.

B. Issue an unmodified report because adequate disclosure of the uncertainty has been made in the notes.

C. Express a qualified opinion because of the material uncertainty.

D. Express a piecemeal opinion.

Answer (B) is correct. *(Publisher)*

**REQUIRED:** The appropriate report when a properly disclosed loss contingency exists.

**DISCUSSION:** When a material uncertainty exists, the auditor need only modify the report when a scope limitation exists or the financial statements depart from GAAP. Given that disclosure is in conformity with GAAP and that no indication is given of a scope limitation, the auditor need not modify the report.

Answer (A) is incorrect because an adverse opinion is not appropriate if the financial statements are presented fairly. Answer (C) is incorrect because a qualified opinion is not expressed solely on the basis of an uncertainty. Answer (D) is incorrect because a piecemeal opinion is never appropriate.

Questions 105 through 110 are based on the following information.

An audit was performed by Leo Scott, CPA, of the financial statements of Lectronic Leasing Company for the year ended December 31.

A cash advance to Computer Credit Corporation is material to the presentation of Lectronic's financial position. Computer Credit's unaudited financial statements show negative working capital, negative equity, and losses in each of the 5 preceding years. Mr. Scott has suggested an allowance for the uncollectibility of the advance to Computer Credit.

All of the capital stock of both Lectronic and Computer Credit is owned by Paul McRae and his family. Mr. McRae adamantly refuses to consider an allowance for uncollectibility. He insists that Computer Credit eventually will be profitable and be able to repay the advance.

Mr. McRae proposes the following note to Lectronic's statements:

Note 1 to Financial Statements

At December 31, the Company had advanced $500,000 to Computer Credit Corporation. We obtained written confirmation of this debt from Computer Credit Corporation and reviewed unaudited financial statements of Computer Credit Corporation. Computer Credit Corporation is not in a position to repay this advance at this time, but the Company has informed us that it is optimistic as to the future of Computer Credit Corporation. Computer Credit Corporation's capital stock is wholly owned by Lectronic Leasing Company's common shareholders.

**105.** Assume that Mr. Scott concludes, based upon appropriate audit procedures, that Mr. McRae's optimism concerning Computer Credit can be neither substantiated nor disproved and that evidence to form an opinion is not available because of the auditee's record retention policies. His report will include a(n)

A. Disclaimer of opinion.

B. Qualified opinion for the failure to follow GAAP.

C. Separate explanatory paragraph based on the uncertainty or an adverse opinion.

D. Adverse opinion only.

Answer (A) is correct. *(CPA, adapted)*

**REQUIRED:** The report issued given an uncertainty.

**DISCUSSION:** If the auditor has not obtained sufficient evidential matter to support management's assertions concerning an uncertainty, an unqualified opinion is not appropriate. A qualification or disclaimer of opinion because of a scope limitation is appropriate when sufficient evidential matter related to an uncertainty does or did exist but was not available for reasons such as management's record retention policies or a restriction imposed by management.

Answer (B) is incorrect because no departure from GAAP is described. Answer (C) is incorrect because an adverse opinion is expressed only when the auditor believes the statements are not fairly presented in conformity with GAAP. Answer (D) is incorrect because an adverse opinion is expressed only when the auditor believes the statements are not fairly presented in conformity with GAAP.

**106.** Assume that Mr. Scott introduces the opinion paragraph of his report as follows: "With the explanation given in Note 1, in our opinion the aforementioned financial statements present fairly . . ." This is a(n)

A. Unqualified opinion.

B. Adverse opinion.

C. Qualified opinion.

D. Improper type of reporting.

Answer (D) is correct. *(CPA, adapted)*

**REQUIRED:** The proper characterization of the phrase "With the explanation given in Note 1."

**DISCUSSION:** Because the notes are part of the financial statements, reporting that those statements are fairly presented when read in conjunction with a cited note is likely to be misunderstood and accordingly should not be done. But a separate explanatory paragraph may be shortened by a reference to a note (AU 508).

**107.** Assume that, subsequent to the completion of field work (but prior to issuance of Mr. Scott's report), Mr. McRae and his family sell all of their stock in Computer Credit and the new owners repay the advance from Lectronic. Mr. Scott's opinion as to Lectronic's financial statements will be

A. Unaffected because the sale of Computer Credit stock occurred subsequent to the audit date.

B. Unaffected because the sale of Computer Credit stock occurred subsequent to the completion of field work.

C. Qualified unless the repayment of the advance is recorded by Lectronic as a December 31 transaction.

D. Unqualified because the issue of collectibility is now settled.

Answer (D) is correct. *(CPA, adapted)*

**REQUIRED:** The effect on the report of a subsequent event that resolves a material uncertainty.

**DISCUSSION:** The subsequent event provides additional evidence with respect to conditions existing at the balance sheet date. Such an event may require adjustment of the financial statements and consequently may affect the audit report (AU 560). Here, the auditor can now express an unqualified opinion, assuming no other basis exists for modifying the opinion. The subsequent event has eliminated the uncertainty as to collectibility of the receivable.

Answer (A) is incorrect because the auditor is responsible for subsequent events occurring prior to the issuance of the report. Answer (B) is incorrect because the auditor is responsible for subsequent events occurring prior to the issuance of the report. Answer (C) is incorrect because no qualification as to collectibility of the receivable is necessary. The best evidence of collectibility is payment.

**108.** With respect to Lectronic's advance to Computer Credit, Mr. Scott

A. Needs no disclosure in his auditor's report because the common ownership of the two companies has been adequately disclosed.

B. Needs no disclosure in his auditor's report because the auditor is not expected to be an expert appraiser of property values.

C. Should be concerned in formulating his auditor's opinion primarily with the issue of collectibility from Lectronic's viewpoint.

D. Should be concerned in formulating his auditor's opinion primarily with the consolidated financial position of the two companies.

Answer (C) is correct. *(CPA, adapted)*

**REQUIRED:** The treatment in the report of a material advance to a related party, collectibility of which is doubtful.

**DISCUSSION:** The auditor has apparently concluded that a material receivable is uncollectible. Management refuses to create an allowance for the bad debt; thus, the auditor may conclude that Lectronic's statements are misleading, requiring a modification of the opinion. The debt also represents a material transaction with a related party. The auditor will expect the client to disclose (1) the nature of the relationship, (2) a description of the transaction, (3) the amounts due, and (4) the terms and manner of settlement of the debt (AU 334).

Answer (A) is incorrect because both the related party transaction and uncollectibility of the receivable must be mentioned in the audit report. The basis for the modification of the opinion must be explained. Answer (B) is incorrect because, although not expected to be an appraiser of property values, the auditor must modify the opinion unless convinced that the financial statements are fairly presented. Answer (D) is incorrect because the scope of the engagement extends only to Lectronic's statements.

**109.** A deficiency in the given note is that it

A. Does not identify the auditor.

B. Is worded as a representation of the auditor.

C. Does not state the auditor's conclusion or opinion.

D. Includes the client's representation as to collectibility.

Answer (B) is correct. *(CPA, adapted)*

**REQUIRED:** The deficiency in the given note.

**DISCUSSION:** The financial statements and notes are the representations of management. The assertions of the auditor are made in the audit report, although the report may refer to the notes in certain cases.

Answer (A) is incorrect because notes should not identify the auditor. Answer (C) is incorrect because notes should not restate his/her conclusions. Answer (D) is incorrect because the client may properly include a representation as to the collectibility of a debt in the notes.

**110.** Assume that Mr. Scott concludes, based upon appropriate audit procedures, that the advance to Computer Credit will not be repaid. His report will include a

A. Disclaimer of opinion.

B. Qualified opinion or disclaimer of opinion.

C. "Subject to" opinion or adverse opinion.

D. Qualified opinion or adverse opinion.

Answer (D) is correct. *(CPA, adapted)*

**REQUIRED:** The type of report if the auditor concludes that the advance will not be repaid.

**DISCUSSION:** If the advance is treated as uncollectible, the financial statements are not in accordance with GAAP because management has refused to establish an allowance account. The auditor should express a qualified opinion or an adverse opinion depending on the materiality of the debt (AU 508).

Answer (A) is incorrect because a disclaimer of opinion is appropriate only when the auditor is unable to form an opinion. Answer (B) is incorrect because a disclaimer of opinion is appropriate only when the auditor is unable to form an opinion. Answer (C) is incorrect because a "subject to" opinion is not an acceptable form of reporting.

**111.** The introductory paragraph of an auditor's report is not modified when the

A. Entity declines to include in the financial statements segment information that the auditor believes is required to be disclosed.

B. Financial statements of a prior period that are presented for comparative purposes have been audited by a predecessor auditor whose report is not given.

C. Principal auditor indicates the division of responsibility by making reference to the audit of a consolidated subsidiary by another auditor.

D. Auditor was engaged to express an opinion on the balance sheet only.

Answer (A) is correct. *(C.J. Skender)*

**REQUIRED:** The situation in which the introductory paragraph is not modified.

**DISCUSSION:** Failure to include segment information is a departure from GAAP because of inadequate disclosure. The auditor should modify the opinion and provide the information in the report, if practicable, unless a specific SAS allows its omission from the report (AU 508). However, no currently effective pronouncement addresses the issue of whether omitted segment disclosures must be included in the audit report. Accordingly, at a minimum, the auditor will include an explanatory paragraph describing the omitted matter and will also modify the opinion paragraph but not the introductory paragraph.

Answer (B) is incorrect because, if the predecessor auditor's report is not presented, the successor auditor should indicate in the introductory paragraph that the financial statements were audited by another auditor, the date of his/her report, the type of report issued, and the substantive reasons for the opinion if it was not unqualified (AU 508). Answer (C) is incorrect because an opinion based in part on the report of another auditor requires modification of the introductory, scope, and opinion paragraphs of the report to indicate the division of responsibility. Answer (D) is incorrect because only the statements audited are identified in the introductory paragraph.

**112.** During the course of an audit of the financial statements of Excellent Corporation, Smart, CPA, discovered that the company vice-president had misrepresented one of the company's products before the Food and Drug Administration by falsifying test results. Unasserted claims, material in amount, loom in the near future. Management refuses to permit the inclusion of a liability for such claims even though it is probable that they will be asserted and the amount of loss can be reasonably estimated. Smart should issue a report with a(n)

A. Explanatory paragraph and either an adverse opinion or a qualified opinion.

B. Qualified opinion and an explanatory paragraph but should not consider expressing an adverse opinion.

C. Qualified opinion and no explanatory paragraph.

D. Unqualified opinion and an explanatory paragraph.

Answer (A) is correct. *(Publisher)*

**REQUIRED:** The opinion that should be expressed when the client improperly refuses to provide for a material loss contingency.

**DISCUSSION:** According to SFAS 5, *Accounting for Contingencies*, a loss contingency should be recognized in the accounts if its occurrence is probable and its amount can be reasonably estimated. The client's refusal to do so is a departure from GAAP. Given that the amount involved is material, the auditor should express a qualified opinion or an adverse opinion. The report should also include a separate paragraph disclosing the substantive reasons for the modified opinion and the principal effects of the subject matter of the opinion, if determinable (AU 508).

Answer (B) is incorrect because the matter may be sufficiently material to require an adverse rather than a qualified opinion. Answer (C) is incorrect because a separate explanatory paragraph will be necessary. Answer (D) is incorrect because a material departure from GAAP requires a qualified or an adverse opinion.

**113.** A client makes test counts on the basis of a statistical plan. The auditor observes such counts as are deemed necessary and is able to become satisfied as to the reliability of the client's procedures. In reporting on the results of the audit, the auditor

A. Can express an unqualified opinion.

B. Must comment in the scope paragraph as to the inability to observe year-end inventories.

C. Is required to disclaim an opinion if the inventories were material.

D. Must qualify the opinion if the inventories were material.

Answer (A) is correct. *(Publisher)*

**REQUIRED:** The report when a client uses statistical sampling to count inventory.

**DISCUSSION:** When the client uses statistical sampling to determine inventory quantities, the auditor must become satisfied that the procedures are reliable. The auditor must observe at least some counts and must be satisfied that the sampling plan is reasonable and statistically valid, that it has been properly applied, and that its results are reasonable (AU 331). Given no significant scope limitation, the report need not refer to failure to observe a year-end physical count or to the alternative procedures employed. The auditor may express an unqualified opinion (AU 508).

Answer (B) is incorrect because comment in the scope paragraph on the omission of a procedure is unnecessary if the auditor has become satisfied by applying alternative procedures. Answer (C) is incorrect because no significant scope limitation existed. Answer (D) is incorrect because the auditor need not qualify the opinion if the financial statements are fairly stated.

**114.** When a scope limitation has precluded the auditor from obtaining sufficient competent evidential matter to determine whether certain client acts are illegal, (s)he would most likely express

A. An unqualified opinion with a separate explanatory paragraph.

B. Either a qualified opinion or an adverse opinion.

C. Either a disclaimer of opinion or a qualified opinion.

D. Either an adverse opinion or a disclaimer of opinion.

Answer (C) is correct. *(CPA, adapted)*

**REQUIRED:** The report issued when evidence about illegal client acts is insufficient.

**DISCUSSION:** The auditor may be unable to determine the legality of certain acts or the amounts associated with them because of an inability to gather sufficient competent evidence; e.g., internal control may have been circumvented, resulting in failure to record or properly document the acts, or client's legal counsel may have refused to give advice. In these circumstances, the scope limitation requires a qualified opinion or a disclaimer, although a client-imposed scope limitation ordinarily results in a disclaimer.

Answer (A) is incorrect because a material scope limitation results in a qualified opinion or a disclaimer. Answer (B) is incorrect because an adverse opinion is only appropriate when the statements as a whole are not fairly presented. Answer (D) is incorrect because an adverse opinion is only appropriate when the statements as a whole are not fairly presented.

**115.** Late in December, Tech Products Company sold available-for-sale securities that had appreciated in value and then repurchased them the same day. The sale and purchase transactions resulted in a large gain. Without the gain, the company would have reported a loss for the year. Which statement with respect to the auditor is true?

A. If the sale and repurchase are disclosed, an unqualified opinion should be expressed.

B. The repurchase transaction is a sham and the auditor should insist upon a reversal or express an adverse opinion.

C. The auditor should withdraw from the engagement and refuse to be associated with the company.

D. A disclaimer of opinion should be expressed.

Answer (A) is correct. *(CPA, adapted)*

**REQUIRED:** The auditor's proper reaction to a sale and repurchase of appreciated securities.

**DISCUSSION:** Unrealized holding gains and losses on available-for-sale securities are recorded in other comprehensive income. Thus, to include the appreciation in the determination of net income, the company had to sell the securities. Because a transaction occurred, the proper accounting is to record the gain realized on the sale. Although management has indulged in obvious window-dressing, an unqualified opinion may still be expressed if disclosure is adequate to prevent the financial statements from being misleading.

Answer (B) is incorrect because the transactions should be recorded. Answer (C) is incorrect because no legal or ethical principle requires the auditor to withdraw. Answer (D) is incorrect because the transactions do not preclude forming an opinion on the statements and accompanying notes.

**116.** A note to the financial statements of the First Security Bank indicates that all of the records relating to the bank's business operations are stored on magnetic disks, and that no emergency backup systems or duplicate disks are stored because the bank and its auditors consider the occurrence of a catastrophe to be remote. Based upon this note, the auditor's report should express

A. A "subject to" opinion.

B. A qualified opinion.

C. An unqualified opinion.

D. An adverse opinion.

Answer (C) is correct. *(CPA, adapted)*

**REQUIRED:** The opinion the auditor should render when a client fails to provide for backup records.

**DISCUSSION:** Failure to provide for backup records does not affect the fairness of the financial statements, regardless of the negative implications for the client's internal control. The auditor should therefore express an unqualified opinion in the absence of other indications to the contrary.

Answer (A) is incorrect because the wording "subject to" is not acceptable in any report. Answer (B) is incorrect because the absence of backup records is not a basis for expressing a qualified opinion if the financial statements are fairly presented in conformity with GAAP. Answer (D) is incorrect because the absence of backup records is not a basis for expressing an adverse opinion if the financial statements are fairly presented in conformity with GAAP.

**117.** An auditor who uses the work of a specialist may refer to and identify the specialist in the auditor's report if the

A. Specialist is also considered to be a related party.

B. Auditor indicates a division of responsibility related to the work of the specialist.

C. Specialist's work provides the auditor greater assurance of reliability.

D. Auditor expresses a qualified opinion or an adverse opinion related to the work of the specialist.

Answer (D) is correct. *(CPA, adapted)*

**REQUIRED:** The circumstance in which an auditor may refer to a specialist.

**DISCUSSION:** The report or findings of the specialist may cause the auditor to add an explanatory paragraph to the standard report or to depart from an unqualified opinion. In these cases, the report may refer to and identify the specialist to facilitate understanding of the reason for the paragraph or departure (AU 336).

Answer (A) is incorrect because the work of an unrelated specialist ordinarily provides greater assurance of reliability, but a related specialist may be acceptable in some circumstances. However, whether the specialist is a related party is irrelevant to the decision to refer to him/her in the report. Answer (B) is incorrect because an auditor can divide responsibility with another auditor who performed part of the audit but not with a specialist. Answer (C) is incorrect because the auditor's use of a specialist is intended to provide greater assurance regarding the conclusions in the audit report, but reference to his/her work is justified only in certain circumstances.

**118.** When would the auditor refer to the work of an appraiser in the auditor's report?

A. An unqualified opinion is expressed and no explanatory paragraph is added, but the auditor wishes to disclose the use of a specialist.

B. A qualified opinion is expressed because of a matter unrelated to the work of the appraiser.

C. An adverse opinion is expressed based on a difference of opinion between the client and the outside appraiser as to the value of certain assets.

D. A disclaimer of opinion is expressed because of a scope limitation imposed on the auditor by the appraiser.

Answer (C) is correct. *(CPA, adapted)*

**REQUIRED:** The basis for reference to an appraiser.

**DISCUSSION:** Given a material difference between the specialist's findings and the assertions in the statements, the auditor should apply additional procedures, possibly including obtaining the opinion of another specialist. If the auditor concludes that the client's assertions are not in conformity with GAAP, a qualified or an adverse opinion should be expressed. The report may refer to and identify the specialist to facilitate understanding of the reason for the modification (AU 336).

Answer (A) is incorrect because the auditor should not refer to a specialist when an unqualified opinion is expressed unless an explanatory paragraph is added. Answer (B) is incorrect because the qualification must be related to the work of the specialist. Answer (D) is incorrect because an appraiser cannot impose a scope limitation on the auditor. The auditor can consult another appraiser.

## 7.6 Disclaimers of Opinion

**119.** Statements on Auditing Standards (SASs) describe the CPA's reporting responsibility for unaudited financial statements of public companies, while Statements on Standards for Accounting and Review Services (SSARSs) describe the CPA's reporting responsibilities for unaudited financial statements of nonpublic entities. Which of the following is a false statement about the responsibilities of a CPA when associated with unaudited financial statements?

A. Unaudited financial statements of nonpublic entities should include either a compilation report or review report.

B. Unaudited financial statements of public entities should include a disclaimer.

C. The CPA must be independent to issue disclaimers, compilation reports, or review reports.

D. Whatever the report form, the primary concern should be to indicate the degree of responsibility the CPA is assuming.

Answer (C) is correct. *(Publisher)*

**REQUIRED:** The false statement about the CPA's association with unaudited financial statements.

**DISCUSSION:** When a CPA is associated with the financial statements of a public entity and either lacks independence or fails to collect sufficient competent evidential matter, (s)he should disclaim an opinion on the financial statements (AU 504 and AU 508). When associated with the unaudited statements of a private entity, a CPA who lacks independence may be asked to compile financial statements. A compilation report may be issued despite the lack of independence because no assurance is being offered and, in effect, a disclaimer is being presented in the report. The CPA must be independent, however, when (s)he issues a review report because it provides limited assurances to users (AR 100, *Compilation and Review of Financial Statements*).

Answer (A) is incorrect because, when a CPA is associated with the financial statements of a private entity, (s)he should issue either a compilation report or, if a review is performed, a review report. Answer (B) is incorrect because the CPA should issue a disclaimer when (s)he is associated with the financial statements of a public entity for which (s)he has not performed an audit or a review. Answer (D) is incorrect because part of the CPA's obligation to the users of the report is to indicate the degree of responsibility assumed.

**120.** A disclaimer of opinion on the financial statements that was issued because of a scope limitation on an audit differs from a compilation report on the unaudited statements of a nonpublic entity in that

A. A compilation report offers some assurances. A disclaimer offers none.

B. A compilation relates only to income statements and balance sheets. A disclaimer pertains to all financial statements presented.

C. Any procedures applied in a compilation should be described in the report, but procedures applied when a disclaimer is issued should not be described.

D. A compilation report states what service was performed. A disclaimer states what service was to be performed.

Answer (D) is correct. *(Publisher)*

**REQUIRED:** The difference between a disclaimer and a compilation report.

**DISCUSSION:** The standard disclaimer of opinion issued because of a scope limitation on an audit begins, "We were engaged to audit the accompanying" financial statements (AU 508). A standard compilation report begins, "I(we) have compiled the accompanying" financial statements (AR 100).

Answer (A) is incorrect because neither report offers any form of assurance. Answer (B) is incorrect because both reports refer to all financial statements presented. Answer (C) is incorrect because the procedures performed should not be described in either report.

**121.** In which of the following circumstances will an auditor usually choose between expressing a qualified opinion and disclaiming an opinion?

A. Departure from generally accepted accounting principles.

B. Inadequate disclosure of accounting policies.

C. Inability to obtain sufficient competent evidential matter.

D. Unreasonable justification for a change in accounting principle.

Answer (C) is correct. *(CPA, adapted)*

**REQUIRED:** The circumstance in which the auditor chooses between a disclaimer and a qualified opinion.

**DISCUSSION:** Scope restrictions, whether client-imposed or the result of circumstances such as the timing of the work, the inability to obtain sufficient competent evidence, or inadequate accounting records, may require a qualification of the opinion or a disclaimer. The choice depends on the assessment of the importance of the omitted procedure(s).

Answer (A) is incorrect because a departure from GAAP usually requires a choice between a qualified and an adverse opinion. Answer (B) is incorrect because inadequate disclosure usually requires a choice between a qualified and an adverse opinion. Answer (D) is incorrect because an unreasonable justification for a change in accounting principle usually requires a choice between a qualified and an adverse opinion.

**122.** Under which of the following circumstances might an auditor disclaim an opinion?

A. The financial statements contain a departure from generally accepted accounting principles, which has a material effect.

B. The principal auditor decides to refer to the report of another auditor who audited a subsidiary.

C. There has been a material change between periods in the method of application of accounting principles.

D. The auditor is unable to obtain sufficient evidence to support management's assertions concerning an uncertainty.

Answer (D) is correct. *(CPA, adapted)*

**REQUIRED:** The reason for a disclaimer.

**DISCUSSION:** AU 508 states that a qualification or disclaimer of opinion is appropriate for a scope limitation relating to an uncertainty if sufficient evidence does or did exist but was not available to the auditor for reasons such as management's record retention policies or a restriction imposed by management.

Answer (A) is incorrect because the auditor should express a qualified or an adverse opinion when the statements contain a material departure from GAAP. Answer (B) is incorrect because reference to the report of another auditor as a partial basis for the opinion is not even a qualification of the opinion, much less a disclaimer. It is a sharing of responsibility. Answer (C) is incorrect because, if the auditor concurs in the change, lack of consistency requires only an explanatory paragraph.

**123.** A CPA is associated with client-prepared financial statements but is not independent. With respect to the CPA's lack of independence, which of the following actions by the CPA might confuse a reader of such financial statements?

A. Stamping the word unaudited on each page of the financial statements.

B. Disclaiming an opinion and stating that independence is lacking.

C. Issuing a modified auditor's report explaining the reason for the auditor's lack of independence.

D. Preparing an accountant's report that includes essential data that are not disclosed in the financial statements.

Answer (C) is correct. *(CPA, adapted)*

**REQUIRED:** The confusing action by a CPA who is not independent and is associated with financial statements.

**DISCUSSION:** When a CPA lacks independence, (s)he should disclaim an opinion and state specifically that (s)he is not independent. The reasons for lack of independence and any procedures performed should not be described. Issuing a modified report improperly implies that an audit was performed (AU 504).

Answer (A) is incorrect because marking each page of unaudited financial statements clearly and conspicuously as unaudited would not confuse a reader. Answer (B) is incorrect because, when an auditor is not independent, a disclaimer is appropriate. Answer (D) is incorrect because, if management omits data required by GAAP, the accountant must urge the client to revise the presentation. If the client refuses, a CPA who is not independent should modify the disclaimer to disclose the departure and, if practicable, its effect on the financial statements.

**124.** A CPA is concerned about association with unaudited financial statements because

A. Users may be misled regarding the degree of responsibility the CPA is accepting.

B. A fee cannot be charged unless the CPA is associated with financial statements.

C. Association is necessary for compliance with the requirement of due professional care.

D. An audit must be performed if the CPA is associated with financial statements.

Answer (A) is correct. *(Publisher)*

**REQUIRED:** The reason for concern about association with unaudited financial statements.

**DISCUSSION:** The association of a CPA with financial statements may lead users to attribute undeserved credibility to them. When the statements are unaudited or unreviewed, the CPA should make clear the degree of responsibility assumed by including a disclaimer of opinion in the report (AU 504).

Answer (B) is incorrect because fees should be based on the extent and degree of difficulty of the services performed, not on whether the CPA is associated with statements. Answer (C) is incorrect because a member of the AICPA must perform all services with due care. Answer (D) is incorrect because a CPA may be associated with financial statements without auditing or reviewing them if (s)he disclaims an opinion.

**125.** Under which of the following circumstances is a disclaimer of opinion inappropriate?

A. The auditor is engaged after fiscal year-end and is unable to observe physical inventories or apply alternative procedures to verify their balances.

B. The auditor is unable to determine the amounts associated with fraud committed by the client's management.

C. The financial statements fail to contain adequate disclosure concerning related party transactions.

D. The client refuses to permit its attorney to furnish information requested in a letter of audit inquiry.

Answer (C) is correct. *(CPA, adapted)*

**REQUIRED:** The circumstances in which a disclaimer is inappropriate.

**DISCUSSION:** A disclaimer is inappropriate when the auditor believes that the financial statements contain material departures from GAAP. Inadequacy of the disclosures required by GAAP is such a departure. Because SFAS 57 requires certain disclosures about related party transactions, the inadequacy of such disclosures is a basis for expressing a qualified or an adverse opinion and providing the information in the report, if practicable, unless omission from the report is recognized as appropriate by a specific SAS (AU 431 and AU 508).

Answer (A) is incorrect because a significant scope limitation, such as a failure to perform a generally accepted auditing procedure (observing inventory) and not becoming satisfied by alternative procedures, may result in a qualified opinion or in a disclaimer. Answer (B) is incorrect because a disclaimer or qualified opinion (and communication with the audit committee or the board) should be expressed in these circumstances (AU 316, *Consideration of Fraud in a Financial Statement Audit*). Answer (D) is incorrect because a client-imposed scope limitation ordinarily results in a disclaimer.

**126.** When Auditee Company was formed, Bill Larson, CPA, performed professional services for which he accepted common stock as a portion of his compensation. Currently, he owns 2% of Auditee's outstanding common stock, an amount that is immaterial to both his firm's and his own personal net worth. What is Larson's reporting responsibility in these circumstances?

A. If Larson is satisfied as to the fairness of the financial statements, he may express an unqualified opinion because his financial interest in the client is immaterial.

B. It is not possible for Larson's audit to meet the requirements of the auditing standards. He must disclaim an opinion and state that he is not independent.

C. Larson must disclaim an opinion and state his lack of independence and the reason for his lack of independence so that the reader will be able to evaluate all of the relevant facts of the case.

D. If Larson is satisfied as to the fairness of the financial statements, he may express an unqualified opinion, but he should note in a separate paragraph that he holds a nominal interest in the client's common stock.

Answer (B) is correct. *(Publisher)*

**REQUIRED:** The reporting responsibility of a CPA who has an immaterial financial interest in a client.

**DISCUSSION:** According to Interpretation 101-1 of Conduct Rule 101, *Independence*, independence is considered to be impaired if, "during the period of the professional engagement, a covered member had or was committed to acquire any direct or material indirect financial interest in the client" (see also the second general auditing standard). Larson's interest in the client is immaterial but direct; hence, he is not independent. When a CPA lacks independence, (s)he must disclaim an opinion and explicitly state his/her lack of independence but not the reasons for it (AU 504).

Answer (A) is incorrect because any direct financial interest in the client, regardless of its materiality, prevents an auditor from being independent. Lack of independence precludes the expression of any opinion. Answer (C) is incorrect because the CPA should not state the reasons for lack of independence. They might mislead the reader concerning the importance of the impairment of independence. Answer (D) is incorrect because any direct financial interest in the client, regardless of its materiality, prevents an auditor from being independent.

**127.** Which of the following is an example of a CPA's being associated with unaudited financial statements?

A. A client of a CPA consults with the CPA on a data processing matter prior to preparing and submitting input data to an independent computer service company for preparation of unaudited financial statements.

B. Computer input data are prepared by the CPA's client and are submitted to an independent computer service company that was recommended by the CPA. The resulting unaudited financial statements are returned to the client.

C. The CPA analyzes the client's input data before sending the data to an independent computer service company, and the processed financial statements are returned directly to the client.

D. A CPA recommends that a client use the client's computer to process data that generate unaudited financial statements.

Answer (C) is correct. *(CPA, adapted)*

**REQUIRED:** The example of an association of a CPA with unaudited financial statements.

**DISCUSSION:** According to AU 504, if a CPA helps prepare or consents to the use of his/her name with unaudited financial statements, (s)he is associated with them. A CPA who reviews the client's input data has assisted in the preparation of the statements and is deemed to be associated with them.

Answer (A) is incorrect because consulting with the client does not constitute preparation of the financial statements by the CPA. Answer (B) is incorrect because recommending a computer service company does not constitute preparation of the financial statements by the CPA. Answer (D) is incorrect because recommending that a client use its own computer does not constitute preparation of the financial statements by the CPA.

**128.** When an independent CPA assists in preparing the financial statements of a publicly held entity but has not audited or reviewed them, the CPA should disclaim an opinion. In such situations, the CPA has no responsibility to apply any procedures beyond

A. Documenting that internal control is not being relied on.

B. Reading the financial statements for obvious material misstatements.

C. Ascertaining whether the financial statements are in conformity with GAAP.

D. Determining whether management has elected to omit substantially all required disclosures.

Answer (B) is correct. *(CPA, adapted)*

**REQUIRED:** The CPA's responsibility for unaudited financial statements.

**DISCUSSION:** According to AU 504, if a CPA helps prepare or consents to the use of his/her name with unaudited financial statements, (s)he is associated with them. In this situation, the CPA's responsibility is to issue a report stating that (s)he has not audited the statements and expresses no opinion on them. The CPA has no responsibility to apply any procedures beyond reading the financial statements for obvious material misstatements.

Answer (A) is incorrect because the CPA need not document procedures either applied or not applied. Answer (C) is incorrect because the CPA does not ascertain whether the financial statements are in conformity with GAAP. Answer (D) is incorrect because the CPA must read the financial statements for obvious material misstatements, which include, but are not limited to, inadequate disclosure.

**129.** Because of a scope limitation, an auditor disclaimed an opinion on the financial statements taken as a whole, but the auditor's report included a statement that the current asset portion of the entity's balance sheet was fairly stated. The inclusion of this statement is

A. Not appropriate because it may tend to overshadow the auditor's disclaimer of opinion.

B. Not appropriate because the auditor is prohibited from reporting on only one basic financial statement.

C. Appropriate provided the auditor's scope paragraph adequately describes the scope limitation.

D. Appropriate provided the statement is in a separate paragraph preceding the disclaimer of opinion paragraph.

Answer (A) is correct. *(CPA, adapted)*

**REQUIRED:** The suitability of a statement in an auditor's disclaimer concerning whether an element of the balance sheet was stated fairly.

**DISCUSSION:** "Piecemeal opinions (expressions of opinion as to certain identified items in financial statements) should not be expressed when the auditor has disclaimed an opinion or has expressed an adverse opinion on the financial statements taken as a whole because piecemeal opinions tend to overshadow or contradict a disclaimer of opinion or an adverse opinion" (AU 508).

Answer (B) is incorrect because the auditor can report on one basic financial statement and not on others. Such a limited reporting engagement is acceptable. Answer (C) is incorrect because a piecemeal opinion is inappropriate in this circumstance. Answer (D) is incorrect because a piecemeal opinion is inappropriate in this circumstance.

**130.** If an accountant concludes that unaudited financial statements of a public entity on which the accountant is disclaiming an opinion also lack adequate disclosure, the accountant should suggest appropriate revision. If the client does not accept the accountant's suggestion, the accountant should

A. Express an adverse opinion and describe the appropriate revision in the report.

B. Refer to the appropriate revision and issue a modified report expressing limited assurance.

C. Describe the appropriate revision to the financial statements in the accountant's disclaimer of opinion.

D. Accept the client's inaction because the statements are unaudited and the accountant has disclaimed an opinion.

Answer (C) is correct. *(CPA, adapted)*

**REQUIRED:** The action when the client refuses to revise unaudited statements to provide adequate disclosure.

**DISCUSSION:** Inadequate disclosure is a departure from GAAP. When an accountant who is associated with the unaudited statements of a public entity suggests revision because of such a departure and the client refuses, the disclaimer should be modified to describe the departure. The "description should refer specifically to the nature of the departure and, if practicable, state the effects on the financial statements or include the necessary information for adequate disclosure" (AU 504).

Answer (A) is incorrect because an opinion may be expressed only if an audit has been performed. Answer (B) is incorrect because a disclaimer expresses no assurance. Answer (D) is incorrect because the accountant must modify the disclaimer if the client does not act. If the client will not accept the modified disclaimer, the accountant should refuse to be associated with the statements and, if necessary, withdraw from the engagement (AU 504).

**131.** Harris, CPA, performed the audit of the 20X1 financial statements of Lanco, Inc. The unaudited 20X0 financial statements were to be presented with the 20X1 financial statements for comparative purposes. Harris prepared a report to accompany both sets of financial statements. The statements are not to be presented in documents filed with the SEC. The presentation should not include

A. Marking the 20X0 columns as unaudited.

B. A separate paragraph.

C. The language "except for" in the scope paragraph.

D. A statement in the report that the 20X0 financial statements were not audited by Harris.

Answer (C) is correct. *(L.M. Bailey)*

**REQUIRED:** The improper aspect of a report on audited and unaudited statements presented in comparative form.

**DISCUSSION:** The phrase "except for" is used to qualify an opinion on audited financial statements. It appears in the opinion, not the scope, paragraph.

Answer (A) is incorrect because the unaudited statements should be clearly marked to identify their status. Answer (B) is incorrect because the prior period's report should be reissued, or the current period's report should include a separate paragraph describing the responsibility assumed for the prior period's statements. However, when unaudited statements are presented in comparative form with audited statements in an SEC filing, the unaudited statements need not be referred to in the auditor's report (AU 504). Answer (D) is incorrect because, if the 20X0 report is reissued, it should contain a statement that the 20X0 financial statements were not audited by Harris.

## 7.7 Scope Limitations

**132.** Limitation on the scope of the audit may require the auditor to express a qualified opinion or to disclaim an opinion. Which of the following is usually a limitation on the scope of the audit?

A. The unavailability of sufficient competent evidential matter.

B. The engagement of the auditor to report on only one basic financial statement.

C. The audit of a subsidiary's financial statements by an auditor other than the one who audits and reports on the consolidated financial statements.

D. The engagement of the auditor after year-end.

Answer (A) is correct. *(CPA, adapted)*

**REQUIRED:** The limitation on the scope of the audit.

**DISCUSSION:** Restrictions on the audit may be imposed by the client or by circumstances, such as the timing of the work, inadequacy of the accounting records, or an inability to obtain sufficient competent evidence. Scope limitations prevent the auditor from applying all procedures deemed necessary and result in either a qualified opinion or a disclaimer. The auditor's decision depends on the importance of the omitted procedure(s).

Answer (B) is incorrect because reports on one financial statement do not involve scope limitations if the auditor's access to information is not limited and if (s)he applies all the procedures deemed necessary. Answer (C) is incorrect because reference to another auditor's report as a partial basis for an opinion is not a qualification or a scope limitation. Answer (D) is incorrect because the auditor engaged after year-end may be able to become satisfied as to the fairness of the financial statements through the use of alternative procedures.

**133.** An auditor decides to express a qualified opinion on an entity's financial statements because a major inadequacy in its computerized accounting records prevents the auditor from applying necessary procedures. The opinion paragraph of the auditor's report should state that the qualification pertains to

A. A client-imposed scope limitation.

B. A departure from auditing standards.

C. The possible effects on the financial statements.

D. Inadequate disclosure of necessary information.

Answer (C) is correct. *(CPA, adapted)*

**REQUIRED:** The wording in the opinion paragraph when the opinion is qualified because of a scope limitation.

**DISCUSSION:** AU 508 states that, when an auditor qualifies the opinion because of a scope limitation, the wording in the opinion paragraph should indicate that the qualification pertains to the possible effects on the financial statements and not to the scope limitation itself.

Answer (A) is incorrect because the qualification should not pertain to the scope limitation. Answer (B) is incorrect because the auditor apparently has followed auditing standards in the conduct of the audit. Answer (D) is incorrect because the lack of sufficient competent evidence does not constitute inadequate disclosure.

**134.** An auditor's opinion reads as follows: "In our opinion, except for the above-mentioned limitation on the scope of our audit..." This is an example of an

A. Acceptable review opinion.

B. Acceptable emphasis of a matter.

C. Acceptable qualified opinion.

D. Unacceptable reporting practice.

Answer (D) is correct. *(CPA, adapted)*

**REQUIRED:** The true statement about combining the phrases "except for" and "limitation on the scope."

**DISCUSSION:** When an opinion is qualified because of a scope limitation, the opinion paragraph should indicate that the qualification pertains to the possible effects on the statements (AU 508). The language given in the question bases the qualification on the restriction itself and is unacceptable.

Answer (A) is incorrect because the standard review report states that no opinion is expressed. Answer (B) is incorrect because a matter is emphasized in a separate explanatory paragraph. Emphasis of a matter is consistent with an unqualified opinion. Answer (C) is incorrect because a qualified opinion should include language such as: "In our opinion, except for the effects of such adjustments, if any, as might have been determined to be necessary had we been able to examine evidence..."

**135.** Which action should be taken by a CPA who has been asked to audit the financial statements of a company whose fiscal year has ended?

A. Discuss with the client the possibility of an adverse opinion because of the late engagement date.

B. Ascertain whether circumstances are likely to permit an adequate audit and expression of an unqualified opinion.

C. Inform the client of the need to issue a qualified opinion if the physical inventory has already been taken.

D. Ascertain whether an understanding of internal control can be obtained and control risk can be assessed after completion of the field work.

Answer (B) is correct. *(CPA, adapted)*

**REQUIRED:** The proper action when the CPA is engaged after the end of the fiscal year.

**DISCUSSION:** According to AU 310, *Appointment of the Independent Auditor*, the auditor should ascertain whether circumstances are likely to permit an adequate audit. If they do not, the auditor should discuss with the client the possible necessity for a qualified opinion or disclaimer of opinion.

Answer (A) is incorrect because a scope limitation, by itself, cannot result in an adverse opinion. Answer (C) is incorrect because a qualified opinion is not inevitable. The auditor may consider the application of alternative procedures if observing the physical inventory is impracticable. Answer (D) is incorrect because the consideration of internal control should precede other aspects of the field work.

**136.** Park, CPA, was engaged to audit the financial statements of Tech Co., a new client, for the year ended December 31, 20X0. Park obtained sufficient audit evidence for all of Tech's financial statement items except Tech's opening inventory. Due to inadequate financial records, Park could not verify Tech's January 1, 20X0 inventory balances. Park's opinion on Tech's 20X0 financial statements most likely will be

| | Balance Sheet | Income Statement |
|---|---|---|
| A. | Disclaimer | Disclaimer |
| B. | Unqualified | Disclaimer |
| C. | Disclaimer | Adverse |
| D. | Unqualified | Adverse |

Answer (B) is correct. *(CPA, adapted)*

**REQUIRED:** The appropriate opinion on each financial statement when the auditor cannot verify opening inventory.

**DISCUSSION:** Because the balance sheet presents information as of a specific moment in time, the auditor should be satisfied with the balances presented at year-end. However, beginning inventory enters materially into the determination of the statements of income, retained earnings, and cash flows. Thus, the auditor will probably not be able to form an opinion as to the fairness of these statements and should issue a disclaimer on them.

**137.** Green, CPA, was engaged to audit the financial statements of Essex Co. after its fiscal year had ended. The timing of Green's appointment as auditor and the start of field work made confirmation of accounts receivable by direct communication with the debtors ineffective. However, Green applied other procedures and was satisfied as to the reasonableness of the account balances. Green's auditor's report most likely contained a(n)

A. Unqualified opinion.

B. Unqualified opinion with an explanatory paragraph.

C. Qualified opinion because of a scope limitation.

D. Qualified opinion because of a departure from auditing standards.

Answer (A) is correct. *(CPA, adapted)*

**REQUIRED:** The opinion expressed when an auditor becomes satisfied as to receivables by using alternate procedures.

**DISCUSSION:** Because the CPA is satisfied as to the amounts of receivables, no scope limitation exists. Accordingly, the report need not refer to the omission of the procedures or the use of alternative procedures, and the CPA may express an unqualified opinion (AU 508).

Answer (B) is incorrect because no basis is given for including an explanatory paragraph. Answer (C) is incorrect because no scope limitation exists. Answer (D) is incorrect because the auditor has not departed from auditing standards. The presumption that confirmation requests will be made is overcome if the use of confirmations would be ineffective (AU 330, *The Confirmation Process*).

**138.** When disclaiming an opinion because of a client-imposed scope limitation, an auditor should indicate in a separate paragraph why the audit did not comply with generally accepted auditing standards. The auditor should also omit the

| | Scope Paragraph | Opinion Paragraph |
|---|---|---|
| A. | No | Yes |
| B. | Yes | Yes |
| C. | No | No |
| D. | Yes | No |

Answer (D) is correct. *(CPA, adapted)*

**REQUIRED:** The paragraph(s), if any, omitted from a disclaimer.

**DISCUSSION:** When a scope limitation exists, the auditor may express a qualified opinion or disclaimer of opinion, depending on the materiality of the scope limitation. If an opinion is disclaimed, the introductory and opinion paragraphs are modified, and the scope paragraph is omitted.

**139.** If the auditor obtains satisfaction with respect to the accounts receivable balance by alternative procedures because it is impracticable to confirm accounts receivable, the auditor's report should be unqualified and could be expected to

A. Disclose that alternative procedures were used because of a client-imposed scope limitation.

B. Disclose in the opinion paragraph that confirmation of accounts receivable was impracticable.

C. Not mention the alternative procedures.

D. Refer to a note that discloses the alternative procedures.

Answer (C) is correct. *(CPA, adapted)*

**REQUIRED:** The proper reference in the report to alternative means of obtaining satisfaction about receivables.

**DISCUSSION:** If the auditor cannot confirm receivables but is able to become satisfied by applying alternative procedures, there is no significant scope limitation, and the report need not refer to the omission of the procedures or the use of alternative procedures.

Answer (A) is incorrect because the report need not refer to the alternative procedures. Answer (B) is incorrect because reference to the omitted procedure is not necessary. Answer (D) is incorrect because reference to a note that discloses the alternative procedures is not appropriate.

**140.** A limitation on the scope of an audit sufficient to preclude an unqualified opinion will always result when management

A. Engages the auditor after the year-end physical inventory count is completed.

B. Fails to correct a material internal control weakness that had been identified during the prior year's audit.

C. Refuses to furnish a management representation letter to the auditor.

D. Prevents the auditor from reviewing the audit documentation of the predecessor auditor.

Answer (C) is correct. *(CPA, adapted)*

**REQUIRED:** The scope limitation that is always sufficient to preclude an unqualified opinion.

**DISCUSSION:** According to AU 333, *Management Representations*, "Management's refusal to furnish written representations constitutes a limitation on the scope of the audit sufficient to preclude an unqualified opinion and is ordinarily sufficient to cause an auditor to disclaim an opinion or withdraw from the engagement." However, the circumstances may permit a qualified opinion. Furthermore, the auditor should consider the effects of management's refusal on his/her ability to rely on other management representations.

Answer (A) is incorrect because a limitation sufficient to preclude an unqualified opinion will not arise if the auditor becomes satisfied as to inventory by other procedures. Answer (B) is incorrect because failure to correct a previously identified material internal control weakness is not a limitation on the auditor's ability to apply necessary procedures. Answer (D) is incorrect because review of the predecessor's audit documentation may not be necessary to the audit.

**141.** Morris, CPA, suspects that a pervasive scheme of illegal bribes exists throughout the operations of Worldwide Import-Export, Inc., a new audit client. Morris notified the audit committee and Worldwide's legal counsel, but neither could assist Morris in determining whether the amounts involved were material to the financial statements or whether senior management was involved in the scheme. Under these circumstances, Morris should

A. Express an unqualified opinion with a separate explanatory paragraph.

B. Disclaim an opinion on the financial statements.

C. Express an adverse opinion on the financial statements.

D. Issue a special report regarding the illegal bribes.

Answer (B) is correct. *(CPA, adapted)*

**REQUIRED:** The auditor action when (s)he cannot determine the amounts involved in illegal acts or the extent of management's involvement.

**DISCUSSION:** Bribery is an illegal act within the meaning of AU 317, that is, a violation of laws or governmental regulations. Under AU 317, if the auditor is precluded by the client from obtaining sufficient evidence to evaluate whether an illegal act has occurred, the auditor ordinarily should disclaim an opinion.

Answer (A) is incorrect because an unqualified opinion is not justified. Answer (C) is incorrect because an adverse opinion is expressed only when the financial statements are not presented fairly. Answer (D) is incorrect because special reports as defined in AU 623 are not issued on such topics.

**142.** The auditor will most likely disclaim an opinion because of

A. The client's failure to present supplementary information required by the FASB.

B. Inadequate disclosure of material information.

C. A client-imposed scope limitation.

D. The qualification of an opinion by the other auditor of a subsidiary when responsibility has been divided.

Answer (C) is correct. *(CPA, adapted)*

**REQUIRED:** The most likely basis for a disclaimer.

**DISCUSSION:** Restrictions on the audit may be imposed by the client or by circumstances, such as the timing of the work, inadequacy of the accounting records, or an inability to obtain sufficient competent evidence. They result in either a qualified opinion or a disclaimer. When restrictions that significantly limit the scope of the audit are imposed by the client, the auditor normally should disclaim an opinion (AU 508).

Answer (A) is incorrect because the omission does not affect the opinion. The required information does not change accounting and reporting standards for preparing basic financial statements (AU 558, *Required Supplementary Information*). But the auditor should include an explanatory paragraph. Answer (B) is incorrect because inadequate disclosure of material matters is a departure from GAAP requiring a qualified or an adverse opinion. Answer (D) is incorrect because the nature and significance of the subject of the qualification may vary substantially. Thus, the principal auditor may have no need to modify the report because of such a qualification.

**143.** A limitation on the scope of an audit sufficient to preclude an unqualified opinion will usually result when management

A. Presents financial statements that are prepared in accordance with the cash receipts and disbursements basis of accounting.

B. States that the financial statements are not intended to be presented in conformity with generally accepted accounting principles.

C. Does not make the minutes of the board of directors' meetings available to the auditor.

D. Asks the auditor to report on the balance sheet and not on the other basic financial statements.

Answer (C) is correct. *(CPA, adapted)*

**REQUIRED:** The basis for a scope limitation sufficient to preclude an unqualified opinion.

**DISCUSSION:** According to AU 508, an auditor should ordinarily disclaim an opinion because of a client-imposed scope limitation.

Answer (A) is incorrect because, if the auditor is issuing a special report on financial statements prepared on a comprehensive basis of accounting other than GAAP, for example, the cash basis, an unqualified opinion may be expressed (AU 623). Answer (B) is incorrect because stating that the financial statements are not intended to be presented in conformity with GAAP does not constitute a scope limitation. Answer (D) is incorrect because a limitation on the reporting engagement is not a scope limitation if the auditor is able to apply necessary procedures and his/her access to information is not limited.

**144.** A limitation on the scope of the audit sufficient to preclude an unqualified opinion will always result when management

A. Asks the auditor to report on the balance sheet and not on the other basic financial statements.

B. Refuses to permit its lawyer to respond to the letter of audit inquiry.

C. Discloses material related party transactions in the notes to the financial statements.

D. Knows that confirmation of accounts receivable is not feasible.

Answer (B) is correct. *(CPA, adapted)*

**REQUIRED:** The limitation on the scope of the audit sufficient to preclude an unqualified opinion.

**DISCUSSION:** Inquiry of a client's lawyer is a necessary audit procedure. The refusal to permit the lawyer to furnish the information requested in an inquiry letter, either in writing or orally, would be a limitation on the scope of the audit sufficient to preclude an unqualified opinion (AU 337).

Answer (A) is incorrect because a limited reporting engagement is not considered a scope limitation if the auditor's access to information is not limited and (s)he applies the procedures (s)he considers necessary. Answer (C) is incorrect because disclosure of material related party transactions is required by SFAS 57. Answer (D) is incorrect because, when circumstances other than a client-imposed limitation preclude confirmation of receivables, the auditor need not qualify the opinion or disclaim an opinion if (s)he can become satisfied about receivables by applying alternative procedures.

**145.** A limitation on the scope of an audit sufficient to preclude an unqualified opinion will usually result when management

A. Is unable to obtain audited financial statements supporting the entity's investment in a foreign subsidiary.

B. Refuses to disclose in the notes to the financial statements related party transactions authorized by the board of directors.

C. Does not sign an engagement letter specifying the responsibilities of both the entity and the auditor.

D. Fails to correct a reportable condition communicated to the audit committee after the prior year's audit.

Answer (A) is correct. *(CPA, adapted)*

**REQUIRED:** The scope limitation sufficient to preclude an unqualified opinion.

**DISCUSSION:** A common scope restriction is the inability to obtain audited financial statements of an investee. A restriction on the application of procedures to important financial statement elements requires the auditor to determine whether (s)he has examined sufficient competent evidence to permit expression of an unqualified or a qualified opinion or whether (s)he should disclaim an opinion.

Answer (B) is incorrect because refusal to make related party disclosures is a departure from GAAP, not a scope limitation. Answer (C) is incorrect because failure to sign an engagement letter is not sufficient to preclude an unqualified opinion. Answer (D) is incorrect because failure to correct a reportable condition is not a limitation of scope.

## 7.8 Addressing and Dating the Report

**146.** The auditor's report may be addressed to the company whose financial statements are being audited or to that company's

A. Chief operating officer.

B. President.

C. Board of directors.

D. Chief financial officer.

Answer (C) is correct. *(CPA, adapted)*

**REQUIRED:** The addressee of the auditor's report.

**DISCUSSION:** The auditor's report should be addressed to the company whose statements are being audited or to its board of directors or shareholders. If the client is an unincorporated entity, the report should be addressed as circumstances dictate, e.g., to the partners or the proprietor. If the statements audited are not those of the client, the client is the proper addressee (AU 508).

**147.** An auditor has been engaged by the State Bank to audit the XYZ Corporation in conjunction with a loan commitment. The report would most likely be addressed to

A. The shareholders, XYZ Corporation.

B. The State Bank.

C. The board of directors, XYZ Corporation.

D. To whom it may concern.

Answer (B) is correct. *(Publisher)*

**REQUIRED:** The proper addressee of the report when the auditee is not the client.

**DISCUSSION:** AU 508 states that occasionally an auditor is retained to audit the financial statements of a company that is not his/her client. In such a case, the report customarily is addressed to the client and not to the board of directors or shareholders of the company whose financial statements are being audited.

Answer (A) is incorrect because the State Bank is the CPA's client and the report should be addressed to it. Answer (C) is incorrect because the State Bank is the CPA's client and the report should be addressed to it. Answer (D) is incorrect because an audit report should not be addressed to whom it may concern.

**148.** On February 13, 20X1, Fox, CPA, met with the audit committee of the Gem Corporation to review the draft of Fox's report on the company's financial statements as of and for the year ended December 31, 20X0. On February 16, 20X1, Fox completed all remaining field work at the Gem Corporation's headquarters. On February 17, 20X1, Fox typed and signed the final version of the auditor's report. On February 18, 20X1, the final report was mailed to Gem's audit committee. What date should have been used on Fox's report?

A. February 13, 20X1

B. February 16, 20X1

C. February 17, 20X1

D. February 18, 20X1

Answer (B) is correct. *(CPA, adapted)*

**REQUIRED:** The date that should be used on the auditor's report.

**DISCUSSION:** February 16, 20X1 is the date that all field work was completed. This date is usually the date of the report according to AU 530, *Dating of the Independent Auditor's Report.* The auditor is not responsible for making any inquiries or carrying out any audit procedures for the period after the date of the report (but see AU 711, *Filings under Federal Securities Statutes*, regarding filings under the Securities Act of 1933).

**149.** The date of the audit report is important because

A. The user has a right to expect that the auditor has performed certain procedures to detect subsequent events that would materially affect the financial statements through the date of the report.

B. The auditor bills time to the client up to and including the audit report date, and the statement to the client should reflect this date.

C. Auditing standards require all audits to be performed on a timely basis.

D. It should coincide with the date of the financial statements.

Answer (A) is correct. *(Publisher)*

**REQUIRED:** The importance of the audit report date.

**DISCUSSION:** AU 560 states that the auditor should perform certain procedures at or near the date of the completion of field work, which usually is the date of the auditor's report. These procedures include (1) reading the latest available interim financial statements and comparing them with the year-end statements; (2) inquiring of and discussing with officers and other executives (a) whether any substantial contingent liabilities or commitments existed at the balance sheet date, (b) whether there was any significant change in capital stock, long-term debt, or working capital, (c) the current status of items in the financial statements being reported upon that were accounted for on a basis of tentative, preliminary, or inconclusive data, and (d) whether any unusual adjustments had been made during the period from the balance sheet date to the date of inquiry; (3) reading the available minutes of meetings of shareholders, directors, and appropriate committees; (4) inquiring of the client's legal counsel concerning litigation, claims, and assessments; and (5) obtaining a letter of representations from the officers.

Answer (B) is incorrect because the auditor may bill the client for services after the report date. Answer (C) is incorrect because the auditor must use due care, but no standard requires the audit to be performed on a timely basis. Answer (D) is incorrect because the report should usually be dated as of the end of field work.

**150.** An auditor's report on comparative financial statements should be dated as of the date of the

A. Issuance of the financial statements with the attached audit report.

B. Completion of the auditor's recent field work.

C. Latest financial statements being reported on.

D. Last subsequent event disclosed in the statements.

Answer (B) is correct. *(CPA, adapted)*

**REQUIRED:** The date of the report on comparative financial statements.

**DISCUSSION:** According to AU 508, "Ordinarily, the auditor's report on comparative financial statements should be dated as of the date of completion of field work for the most recent audit."

Answer (A) is incorrect because using the date of issuance of the financial statements implies that the auditor performed audit procedures up to that date. Answer (C) is incorrect because the report should be dated as of the last day of the latest field work so as to encompass the subsequent events period, not the end of the period under audit. Answer (D) is incorrect because, if an event requiring disclosure occurs after the completion of field work, the auditor may dual date the report, i.e., date the report as of the completion of field work except for the note disclosing the subsequent event, which would be dated as of its occurrence.

**151.** An audit report was dual dated for a subsequent event disclosed in the financial statements that occurred after the completion of field work but before issuance of the financial statements. The auditor's responsibility for events occurring subsequent to the completion of field work was

A. Limited to include only events occurring before the date of the last subsequent event referred to.

B. Limited to the specific event referred to.

C. Extended to subsequent events occurring through the date of issuance of the financial statements.

D. Extended to include all events occurring since the completion of field work.

Answer (B) is correct. *(CPA, adapted)*

**REQUIRED:** The auditor's responsibility for events occurring subsequent to the completion of field work when the report is dual dated.

**DISCUSSION:** Subsequent to the completion of field work, the auditor is responsible only for the specific subsequent event. (S)he is responsible for other subsequent events only up to the date of the completion of field work (AU 530). However, if the report is not dual dated, it is dated as of the post-field-work subsequent event. If procedures are extended, the auditor's responsibility is extended to the later report date.

**152.** An auditor's decision about whether to dual date the audit report is based upon the auditor's willingness to

A. Extend auditing procedures.

B. Accept responsibility for subsequent events.

C. Permit inclusion of a note captioned: Event (Unaudited) Subsequent to the Date of the Auditor's Report.

D. Assume responsibility for events subsequent to the date of the auditor's report.

Answer (A) is correct. *(CPA, adapted)*

**REQUIRED:** The factor upon which the decision to dual date the audit report is based.

**DISCUSSION:** When a subsequent event disclosed in the financial statements occurs after the completion of field work but before the issuance of the related financial statements, the auditor may use dual dating. (S)he may date the report as of the completion of field work except for the matters affected by the subsequent event, which are assigned the appropriate later date. In that case, the auditor's responsibility for events after the completion of field work would be limited to the specific event. If the auditor is willing to accept responsibility to the later date and accordingly extends subsequent events procedures to that date, the auditor may choose the later date as the date for the entire report (AU 530 and AU 560).

Answer (B) is incorrect because the auditor must assume responsibility for subsequent events occurring between the balance sheet date and the date of the report. Answer (C) is incorrect because a caption regarding an unaudited event subsequent to the date of the auditor's report is appropriate for a reissuance of an auditor's report, not for the original report (AU 530). Answer (D) is incorrect because the auditor does not assume responsibility for events subsequent to the date of the report.

**153.** Normally, an independent accountant's responsibility for subsequent events work ends at the date of the report. However, when registration filings with the SEC contain audited financial statements, the accountant must extend subsequent events work to

A. The prospectus date.

B. The filing date.

C. The effective date.

D. The date the final security is sold.

Answer (C) is correct. *(Publisher)*

**REQUIRED:** The date to which the auditor should extend subsequent events work for a registration statement.

**DISCUSSION:** The auditor should extend procedures to the effective date or as close to it as reasonable and practicable. In addition to the subsequent-events procedures outlined in AU 560, the accountant should also (1) read the entire prospectus and other pertinent portions of the registration statement and (2) inquire of and obtain written representations from officers and other executives responsible for financial and accounting matters about whether any significant events have occurred other than those reflected or disclosed in the registration statement (AU 711). The registration statement speaks as of the effective date, which differs from the prospectus date (the date the document is prepared for first submission to the SEC), the filing date (the date the prospectus and other documents are submitted to the SEC), and the date the last security is sold.

**154.** In May 20X2, an auditor reissues the auditor's report on the 20X0 financial statements at a continuing client's request. The 20X0 financial statements are not restated and the auditor does not revise the wording of the report. The auditor should

A. Dual date the reissued report.

B. Use the release date of the reissued report.

C. Use the original report date on the reissued report.

D. Use the current-period auditor's report date on the reissued report.

Answer (C) is correct. *(CPA, adapted)*

**REQUIRED:** The date of a reissued report.

**DISCUSSION:** Under AU 530, use of the original date in a reissued report removes any implication that records, transactions, or events after such date have been audited or reviewed. The auditor will thus have no responsibility to carry out procedures relating to the period between original issuance and reissuance.

Answer (A) is incorrect because the report is dual dated only if it has been revised since the original reissue date. Answer (B) is incorrect because the release date of the reissued report implies that additional audit procedures have been applied. Answer (D) is incorrect because use of the current report date implies that the report has been updated for additional audit procedures applied between the original issue date and the current auditor's report date.

**155.** On September 30, 20X1, Miller was asked to reissue an auditor's report, dated March 31, 20X1, on a client's financial statements for the year ended December 31, 20X0. Miller will submit the reissued report to the client in a document that contains information in addition to the client's basic financial statements. However, Miller discovered that the client suffered substantial losses on receivables resulting from conditions that occurred since March 31, 20X1. Miller should

A. Request the client to disclose the event in a separate, appropriately labeled note to the financial statements and reissue the original report with its original date.

B. Request the client to restate the financial statements and reissue the original report with a dual date.

C. Reissue the original report with its original date without regard to whether the event is disclosed in a separate note.

D. Not reissue the original report but express a "subject to" qualified opinion that discloses the event in a separate paragraph.

Answer (A) is correct. *(CPA, adapted)*

**REQUIRED:** The auditor action regarding reissuance of a report and a disclosable subsequent event.

**DISCUSSION:** The subsequent event concerned conditions that arose after the balance sheet date and thus required disclosure only (AU 560). If an event of this kind occurs between the date of the report and the date of its reissuance, and it comes to the auditor's attention, it may be disclosed in a note. The caption may be as follows: Event (Unaudited) Subsequent to the Date of the Independent Auditor's Report. In this case, the auditor's report would have the same date as the original report (AU 530).

Answer (B) is incorrect because restatement is not necessary. The conditions arose after the balance sheet date. Also, the auditor is not assuming responsibility for the subsequent event and thus should not dual date the report. Answer (C) is incorrect because, when financial statements are reissued, a note is required if disclosure of the subsequent event is necessary to prevent the statements from being misleading (AU 560). Answer (D) is incorrect because a "subject to" opinion is never permissible.

## 7.9 Comparative Financial Statements

**156.** When comparative financial statements are presented, the fourth standard of reporting, which refers to financial statements "taken as a whole," should be considered to apply to the financial statements of the

A. Periods presented plus one preceding period.

B. Current period only.

C. Current period and those of the other periods presented.

D. Current and immediately preceding period only.

Answer (C) is correct. *(CPA, adapted)*

**REQUIRED:** The periods to which the fourth standard of reporting applies.

**DISCUSSION:** The fourth standard of reporting requires expression of an opinion on the statements taken as a whole or an assertion that an opinion cannot be expressed. The phrase "taken as a whole" applies not only to the current period's statements but also to those of prior periods presented on a comparative basis (AU 508).

**157.** When financial statements of a prior period are presented on a comparative basis with financial statements of the current period, the continuing auditor is responsible for

A. Expressing dual dated opinions.

B. Updating the report on the previous financial statements only if there has not been a change in the opinion.

C. Updating the report on the previous financial statements only if the previous opinion was qualified and the reasons for the qualification no longer exist.

D. Updating the report on the previous financial statements regardless of the opinion previously expressed.

Answer (D) is correct. *(CPA, adapted)*

**REQUIRED:** The responsibility of a continuing auditor relative to comparative statements.

**DISCUSSION:** The reference in the fourth reporting standard to expression of an opinion on the financial statements taken as a whole should be considered to apply not only to the statements of the current period but also to those of one or more prior periods being presented comparatively with those of the current period. Thus, a continuing auditor should update the report on the individual statements of one or more prior periods presented on a comparative basis. Hence, the auditor's report on comparative statements should usually be dated as of the completion of the field work for the most recent audit (AU 508).

Answer (A) is incorrect because dual-dated reports relate to events that occur between the last day of field work (the normal date of the auditor's report) and the report's release date. Answer (B) is incorrect because the report must be updated regardless of whether the opinion has changed. Answer (C) is incorrect because the report must be updated regardless of whether the opinion has changed.

**158.** Which of the following is a true statement concerning the auditor's report on comparative financial statements?

A. A continuing auditor may under certain circumstances express an opinion different from the previous opinion.

B. The report should not express an opinion different from that previously expressed on the statements of a prior period because the differences would lessen the public's confidence in the integrity of the auditor's report.

C. A predecessor auditor may reissue the report on the financial statements of a prior period provided (s)he performs certain procedures, including obtaining representation letters from the successor auditor and from management, and provided (s)he refers in the reissued report to the work of the successor auditor.

D. If the financial statements of the prior period have been audited, but those of the current period have not, the auditor should update the report on the prior period and include as a separate paragraph in the report a disclaimer of opinion on the unaudited financial statements.

Answer (A) is correct. *(Publisher)*

**REQUIRED:** The true statement about reports on comparative financial statements.

**DISCUSSION:** A continuing auditor should update the report on the statements of one or more prior periods presented comparatively with the statements of the current period. A continuing auditor is one who has audited the current period's statements and those of one or more consecutive periods immediately preceding the current period. An updated report is distinguishable from the reissuance of a prior report because the continuing auditor considers information acquired during the audit of the current period's statements and issues the updated report in conjunction with the report on the current period statements. An updated report may contain an opinion different from that expressed in the previous report because the auditor may have become aware during the current audit of circumstances or events affecting a prior period's statements, e.g., restatement in the current period to correct a prior departure from GAAP (AU 508).

Answer (B) is incorrect because the auditor is required to be alert during the current audit for circumstances and events that affect the prior period statements presented or the adequacy of disclosures therein. Answer (C) is incorrect because the predecessor auditor should perform certain procedures, including obtaining representation letters from the successor auditor and from management, but should not refer to the report or work of the successor auditor. Answer (D) is incorrect because updating implies that the auditor has considered information obtained during the current year's audit.

**159.** When reporting on comparative financial statements, which of the following circumstances ordinarily should cause the auditor to change the previously expressed opinion on the prior year's financial statements?

A. The prior year's financial statements are restated to reflect a change in an account title from "Trade Receivables" to "Accounts Receivable."

B. A departure from generally accepted accounting principles caused an adverse opinion on the prior year's financial statements and those statements have been properly restated.

C. A change in accounting principle caused the auditor to make a consistency modification in the current year's auditor's report.

D. A scope limitation caused a qualified opinion on the prior year's financial statements but the current year's opinion was properly unqualified.

Answer (B) is correct. *(CPA, adapted)*

**REQUIRED:** The event that causes an auditor to change a previously expressed opinion.

**DISCUSSION:** AU 508 states that, if an opinion in an updated report is different from the one previously expressed, the auditor should disclose all the substantive reasons for the different opinion in a separate paragraph preceding the opinion paragraph of the report. The explanatory paragraph should include (1) the date of the auditor's previous report, (2) the type of opinion previously expressed, (3) the circumstances or events that caused the auditor to express a different opinion, and (4) a statement that the auditor's updated opinion on the statements of the prior period is different from the previous opinion.

Answer (A) is incorrect because a change in classification has no effect on the auditor's report. Answer (C) is incorrect because a change in accounting principle in the current period has no effect on the opinion on the prior year's statements. The auditor should add a paragraph at the end of the current year's report identifying the change. Answer (D) is incorrect because the scope limitation from the prior year requires the auditor to express a qualified opinion on the prior year's financial statements.

**160.** An auditor expressed a qualified opinion on the prior year's financial statements because of a lack of adequate disclosure. These financial statements are properly restated in the current year and presented in comparative form with the current year's financial statements. The auditor's updated report on the prior year's financial statements should

A. Be accompanied by the auditor's original report on the prior year's financial statements.

B. Continue to express a qualified opinion on the prior year's financial statements.

C. Make no reference to the type of opinion expressed on the prior year's financial statements.

D. Express an unqualified opinion on the restated financial statements of the prior year.

Answer (D) is correct. *(CPA, adapted)*

**REQUIRED:** The effect on the auditor's updated report when the opinion has changed from the previous year.

**DISCUSSION:** During the audit, an auditor may become aware of circumstances or events affecting the statements of a prior period and should consider them when updating the report. For example, if the opinion was modified because of a departure from GAAP and the statements are restated in the current period to conform with GAAP, the updated report should indicate the restatement and express an unqualified opinion. The opinion should contain an explanatory paragraph preceding the opinion paragraph to describe the previous report and the reasons for the change in opinion.

Answer (A) is incorrect because the original report should not be reissued. Answer (B) is incorrect because the opinion has changed and the auditor should not continue to express the previous opinion. Answer (C) is incorrect because an explanatory paragraph should be added to the current audit report explaining the reason for the change and the type of opinion previously expressed.

**161.** Which of the following portions of a continuing auditor's standard report on comparative financial statements is improper?

A. "In our opinion, the financial statements referred to above present fairly, in all material respects, the financial position."

B. "Of XYZ Company as of December 31, 20X1 and 20X0 and the results of its operations and its cash flows."

C. "For the years then ended in conformity with generally accepted accounting principles."

D. "Applied on a basis consistent with that of the preceding year."

Answer (D) is correct. *(CPA, adapted)*

**REQUIRED:** The improper portion of a continuing auditor's standard report on comparative statements.

**DISCUSSION:** The auditor's standard three-paragraph report is silent as to consistency. If the comparability of the financial statements has been materially affected by a change in accounting principles or in the method of their application, the change should be referred to in an explanatory paragraph following the opinion paragraph. Agreement with the change is implied unless the auditor takes exception to it (AU 508).

Answer (A) is incorrect because the opinion paragraph in a standard report on comparative statements states an opinion. Answer (B) is incorrect because the opinion paragraph in a standard report on comparative statements identifies the auditee. Answer (C) is incorrect because the opinion paragraph in a standard report on comparative statements mentions GAAP.

**162.** When single-year financial statements are presented, an auditor ordinarily expresses an unqualified opinion in an unmodified report if the

A. Auditor is unable to obtain audited financial statements supporting the entity's investment in a foreign affiliate.

B. Entity declines to present a statement of cash flows with its balance sheet and related statements of income and retained earnings.

C. Auditor wishes to emphasize an accounting matter affecting the comparability of the financial statements with those of the prior year.

D. Prior year's financial statements were audited by another CPA whose report expressing an unqualified opinion is not presented.

Answer (D) is correct. *(CPA, adapted)*

**REQUIRED:** The conditions under which an unqualified opinion is expressed in an unmodified report.

**DISCUSSION:** When single-year financial statements are presented, the auditor's reporting responsibility is limited to those statements. If the prior year's financial statements are not presented for comparative purposes, the current-year auditor should not refer to the prior year's statements and the report thereon. Furthermore, the failure to present comparative statements is not a basis for modifying the opinion or the report.

Answer (A) is incorrect because an inability to obtain audited financial statements supporting an entity's investment in a foreign affiliate is a scope limitation requiring either a qualified opinion or a disclaimer of opinion. Answer (B) is incorrect because, if the entity declines to present a statement of cash flows, the auditor should express a qualified opinion. Answer (C) is incorrect because adding an additional paragraph to emphasize a matter results in a modified report.

**163.** Unaudited financial statements for the prior year presented in comparative form with audited financial statements for the current year should be clearly marked to indicate their status and

I. The report on the prior period should be reissued to accompany the current period report.

II. The report on the current period should include as a separate paragraph a description of the responsibility assumed for the prior period's financial statements.

A. I only.

B. II only.

C. Both I and II.

D. Either I or II.

Answer (D) is correct. *(CPA, adapted)*

**REQUIRED:** The true statement(s) about comparative presentation of unaudited prior year's statements with audited current year's statements.

**DISCUSSION:** In these circumstances, the audit report on comparative statements presented in documents filed with the SEC would not refer to the unaudited statements, and these statements should be clearly marked as unaudited. In all other cases, the unaudited statements (that may have been reviewed or compiled) should also be clearly marked to indicate their status, and either the report on the prior period should be reissued (AU 530) or the report on the current period should include as a separate paragraph a description of the responsibility assumed for the prior period's statements (AU 504).

**164.** Gole, CPA, is engaged to review the 20X1 financial statements of North Co., a nonpublic entity. Previously, Gole audited North's 20X0 financial statements and expressed an unqualified opinion. Gole decides to include a separate paragraph in the 20X1 review report because North plans to present comparative financial statements for 20X1 and 20X0. This separate paragraph should indicate that

A. The 20X1 review report is intended solely for the information of management and the board of directors.

B. The 20X0 auditor's report may no longer be relied on.

C. No auditing procedures were performed after the date of the 20X0 auditor's report.

D. There are justifiable reasons for changing the level of service from an audit to a review.

Answer (C) is correct. *(CPA, adapted)*

**REQUIRED:** The reference in a separate paragraph in a review report when comparative statements are presented and an audit was performed in the previous year.

**DISCUSSION:** A continuing accountant who performs a lower level of service should include a separate paragraph describing the responsibility assumed for the financial statements of the prior period or reissue the previous report. The paragraph included in the review report should indicate that no auditing procedures were performed after the date of the auditor's report.

Answer (A) is incorrect because a review report may be distributed to any user. Answer (B) is incorrect because the previous auditor's report may still be relied upon. Answer (D) is incorrect because no mention of the reasons for the change of service should be made in the review report.

**165.** Audited financial statements of the prior period are presented comparatively with unaudited statements of the current period in a document not filed with the SEC, and the report on the current period is to contain a separate paragraph describing the responsibility assumed for the financial statements of the prior period. The report on the current period should not indicate

A. That the financial statements of the prior period were audited previously and no auditing procedures were performed after the previous report date.

B. The date of the previous report and the type of opinion expressed previously.

C. The substantive reasons for any modification of the opinion on the prior-period statements.

D. That nothing has come to the auditors' attention to lead them to believe that material changes have taken place since that date.

Answer (D) is correct. *(Publisher)*

**REQUIRED:** The disclosure not required in the report.

**DISCUSSION:** When unaudited financial statements are presented in comparative form with audited financial statements, the financial statements that have not been audited should be clearly marked to indicate their status. In an SEC filing, the unaudited statements should not be referred to in the auditor's report. But in any other document, either (1) the report on the prior period should be reissued or (2) the report on the current period should include a separate paragraph describing the responsibility assumed for the financial statements of the prior period. When the statements of the prior period have been audited and the report on the current period is to contain a separate paragraph, it should include all of the information specified in answers (A) through (C) (AU 504). Negative assurances are not permissible in general-use attest reports except in certain contexts, e.g., in letters for underwriters (AU 634) or in other attest engagements in which attestation risk is reduced only to a moderate level, e.g., a review of a private company's financial statements (AT 101, *Attest Engagements*).

Answer (A) is incorrect because the report should state that the financial statements of the prior period were audited previously. Answer (B) is incorrect because the report should state the date of the previous report and the type of opinion expressed. Answer (C) is incorrect because the report should state the substantive reasons for any modification of the opinion.

**166.** When management does not provide reasonable justification that a change in accounting principle is preferable and it presents comparative financial statements, the auditor should express a qualified opinion

A. Only in the year of the accounting principle change.

B. Each year that the financial statements initially reflecting the change are presented.

C. Each year until management changes back to the accounting principle formerly used.

D. Only if the change is to an accounting principle that is not generally accepted.

Answer (B) is correct. *(CPA, adapted)*

**REQUIRED:** The year(s) or circumstance in which an unjustified accounting change requires a qualified opinion.

**DISCUSSION:** If management has not provided reasonable justification for a change, the new principle is not generally accepted, or the method of accounting for the effect of the change does not conform with GAAP, the auditor should express a qualified or an adverse opinion in the report for the year of change and add (an) explanatory paragraph(s) preceding the opinion paragraph. Also, "the auditor should continue to express the exception with respect to the financial statements for the year of change as long as they are presented and reported on" (AU 508).

Answer (A) is incorrect because the qualified opinion should be expressed each year the statements for the year of change are presented. Answer (C) is incorrect because the qualified opinion should be expressed regardless of any future change in principle. Answer (D) is incorrect because a qualified opinion may be appropriate if the auditor determines that the change to an acceptable principle is unjustified.

**167.** Comparative financial statements include the prior year's statements that were audited by a predecessor auditor whose report is not presented. If the predecessor's report was unqualified, the successor should

A. Express an opinion on the current year's statements alone and make no reference to the prior year's statements.

B. Indicate in the auditor's report that the predecessor auditor expressed an unqualified opinion.

C. Obtain a letter of representations from the predecessor concerning any matters that might affect the successor's opinion.

D. Request the predecessor auditor to reissue the prior year's report.

Answer (B) is correct. *(CPA, adapted)*

**REQUIRED:** The successor auditor's disclosure about the report of a predecessor.

**DISCUSSION:** The successor auditor should state in the introductory paragraph that the prior year's financial statements were audited by another auditor. (S)he should give the date and the type of report and, if the report was modified, the reasons for modification. If the predecessor auditor expressed an unqualified opinion but included an explanatory paragraph, the nature of and reasons for such paragraph should be described (AU 508).

Answer (A) is incorrect because the prior year's financial statements presented comparatively must be considered in an auditor's report. Answer (C) is incorrect because the successor should communicate with the predecessor prior to accepting the engagement. Answer (D) is incorrect because the predecessor's report may be reissued and the successor's report would then be silent as to the predecessor. However, the question indicates that the predecessor's report is not presented.

**168.** Comparative financial statements include the financial statements of the prior year that were audited by a predecessor auditor whose report is not presented. If the predecessor's report was qualified, the successor should

A. Indicate the substantive reasons for the qualification in the predecessor auditor's opinion.

B. Request the client to reissue the predecessor's report on the prior year's statements.

C. Issue an updated comparative audit report indicating the division of responsibility.

D. Express an opinion only on the current year's statements and make no reference to the prior year's statements.

Answer (A) is correct. *(CPA, adapted)*

**REQUIRED:** The successor auditor's action if the predecessor's qualified report is not presented.

**DISCUSSION:** When the predecessor's report is not presented, the successor's report should include in the introductory paragraph (1) a statement that the financial statements of the prior period were audited by another auditor, (2) the date of the report, (3) the type of report issued, and (4) the substantive reasons if the report was other than a standard report.

Answer (B) is incorrect because, although the report may be reissued, the question states that the report is not presented. Answer (C) is incorrect because division of responsibility is only appropriate when other auditors have audited a portion of the current statements being reported on. Answer (D) is incorrect because the statements presented in comparative form must be reported on or a disclaimer must be presented.

**169.** After properly communicating with the predecessor auditor, Seal & Co., CPAs, accepted the engagement to audit Mass Company's annual financial statements. Mass desires that comparative statements from years audited by the predecessor auditor be presented in the annual report. The predecessor auditor's report will not be presented. In its report, Seal should

A. Not refer to the report of the predecessor auditor in the introductory paragraph.

B. Refer to the report of the predecessor auditor in both the introductory and opinion paragraphs.

C. Refer to the report of the predecessor auditor in the opinion paragraph only.

D. Not refer to the report of the predecessor auditor in the opinion paragraph.

Answer (D) is correct. *(CPA, adapted)*

**REQUIRED:** The auditor action when the previous year's financial statements were audited by another auditor.

**DISCUSSION:** According to AU 508, when the prior period's statements have been audited by a predecessor auditor whose report is not presented, the introductory paragraph of the successor's report should include (1) a statement that other auditors audited the prior period's statements, (2) the date of their report, (3) the type of report issued, and (4) the substantive reasons if the report was other than a standard report. Also, "The successor auditor should not name the predecessor auditor in the report; however, the successor auditor may name the predecessor auditor if the predecessor auditor's practice was acquired by, or merged with, that of the successor auditor."

**170.** When unaudited financial statements are presented in comparative form with audited financial statements in a document filed with the Securities and Exchange Commission, such statements should be

| | Marked as "Unaudited" | Withheld until Audited | Referred to in the Auditor's Report |
|---|---|---|---|
| A. | Yes | No | No |
| B. | Yes | No | Yes |
| C. | No | Yes | Yes |
| D. | No | Yes | No |

Answer (A) is correct. *(CPA, adapted)*

**REQUIRED:** The treatment of unaudited statements presented comparatively with audited statements in a document filed with the SEC.

**DISCUSSION:** AU 504 states, "When unaudited financial statements are presented in comparative form with audited statements in documents filed with the Securities and Exchange Commission, such statements should be clearly marked as 'unaudited' but should not be referred to in the auditor's report." Moreover, such statements should not be withheld until audited.

**171.** The predecessor auditor, who is satisfied after properly communicating with the successor auditor, has reissued a report because the audit client desires comparative financial statements. The predecessor auditor's report should

A. Refer to the report of the successor auditor only in the scope paragraph.

B. Refer to the work of the successor auditor in the scope and opinion paragraphs.

C. Refer to both the work and the report of the successor auditor only in the opinion paragraph.

D. Not refer to the report or the work of the successor auditor.

Answer (D) is correct. *(CPA, adapted)*

**REQUIRED:** The true statement about reference to the successor auditor in a reissued report.

**DISCUSSION:** A predecessor auditor who has been asked to reissue his/her report should (1) read the current-period statements, (2) compare the statements (s)he reported on with other statements to be presented comparatively, (3) obtain a representation letter from the successor auditor, and (4) obtain an updating representation letter from the management of the former client. The predecessor auditor may also wish to consider the professional reputation and standing of the successor auditor and other matters discussed in AU 543, but the reissued report should not refer to the report or work of the successor auditor.

Answer (A) is incorrect because the reissued report should not refer to the report of the successor auditor. Answer (B) is incorrect because the reissued report should not refer to the work of the successor auditor. Answer (C) is incorrect because the reissued report should not refer to the report or the work of the successor auditor.

**172.** When a predecessor auditor reissues the report on the prior period's financial statements at the request of the former client, the predecessor auditor should

A. Indicate in the introductory paragraph of the reissued report that the financial statements of the subsequent period were audited by another CPA.

B. Read the current period's statements and compare them with those for the prior period.

C. Obtain a representation letter from the client's lawyer.

D. Add an explanatory paragraph to the reissued report stating that the predecessor has not performed additional auditing procedures concerning the prior period's financial statements.

Answer (B) is correct. *(CPA, adapted)*

**REQUIRED:** The procedure performed by the predecessor auditor before reissuing a report.

**DISCUSSION:** AU 508 requires performance of certain procedures by the predecessor auditor before reissuing a report on prior-period financial statements. (S)he should (1) read the current period's financial statements, (2) compare the prior and current financial statements, (3) obtain a representation letter from the successor auditor, and (4) obtain an updating representation letter from the management of the former client.

Answer (A) is incorrect because the reissued report should not refer to the successor auditor. Answer (C) is incorrect because the predecessor auditor should obtain representation letters from the successor auditor and management but not from the client's lawyer. However, the successor auditor must inquire of the client's outside counsel to corroborate management's representations about litigation, claims, and assessments (AU 337). Answer (D) is incorrect because the report should not be modified unless the auditor's previous conclusions have changed since the prior report was issued.

## 7.10 Related Party Transactions

**173.** An audit in accordance with auditing standards cannot be expected to provide assurance that all related party transactions will be discovered. Nevertheless, during the course of the audit, the auditor should be aware of the possible existence of material related party transactions that could affect the financial statements. The primary concern of the auditor regarding related party transactions is that

A. They are accounted for using the standards set forth by the FASB for related party transactions.

B. Their existence and significance be adequately disclosed.

C. They are reported to the SEC because they are illegal.

D. Their form be emphasized rather than their economic substance.

Answer (B) is correct. *(Publisher)*

**REQUIRED:** The auditor's responsibility with regard to related party transactions.

**DISCUSSION:** Established accounting principles ordinarily do not require transactions with related parties to be accounted for on a basis different from what would be appropriate if the parties were not related. Until applicable accounting standards are established by authoritative bodies, the auditor should view related party transactions within the framework of existing pronouncements, with emphasis on the adequacy of disclosure (AU 334).

Answer (A) is incorrect because GAAP ordinarily do not establish specific requirements for the recording of related party transactions. Answer (C) is incorrect because related party transactions, per se, are not illegal. Answer (D) is incorrect because the substance of the transactions should be emphasized, not their form.

**174.** When one party has the ability to significantly influence the management or operating policies of the other to the extent that one of the transacting parties might be prevented from fully pursuing its separate interests, the parties are related for purposes of AU 334. Which of the following is not usually regarded as a party related to a firm?

A. Affiliates, principal owners, and entities for which investments are accounted for by the equity method.

B. Third parties that can significantly influence the operating policies of the transacting parties.

C. Management and members of their immediate families.

D. The U.S. government.

Answer (D) is correct. *(Publisher)*

**REQUIRED:** The party not considered a related party.

**DISCUSSION:** Although the U.S. government regulates many aspects of business activity, it is not considered a related party when dealing with a firm.

Answer (A) is incorrect because affiliates, owners, and those related through investment interests may exercise influence to the extent that one (or more) of the transacting parties might be prevented from pursuing its separate interests (AU 334). Answer (B) is incorrect because parties that can significantly influence the operating policies of the transacting parties by definition are related parties. Answer (C) is incorrect because management and members of their immediate families may exercise influence to the extent that one (or more) of the transacting parties might be prevented from pursuing its separate interests.

**175.** The auditor should be aware of the possibility of related party transactions. Examples of transactions that raise questions as to their substance and may be indicative of the existence of related party transactions include all of the following except

A. Borrowing or lending on an interest-free basis or at a rate of interest significantly above or below current market rates.

B. Selling real estate at a price that differs significantly from its appraised value or exchanging property for similar property in a nonmonetary transaction.

C. The purchase of particularly small quantities of an item based upon current market price.

D. Making loans with no scheduled terms as to when or how the funds will be repaid.

Answer (C) is correct. *(Publisher)*

**REQUIRED:** The item not indicative of the existence of related party transactions.

**DISCUSSION:** The purchase of very large quantities at market prices might be indicative of related party transactions because the related party may influence the purchaser to buy large quantities of its excess production. However, the purchase of small quantities at regular prices does not indicate the existence of a related party transaction.

Answer (A) is incorrect because borrowing or lending on an interest-free basis or at a rate of interest significantly above or below current market rates may be indicative of related parties (AU 334). Answer (B) is incorrect because selling real estate at a price that differs significantly from its appraised value or exchanging property for similar property in a nonmonetary transaction may be indicative of related parties. Answer (D) is incorrect because making loans with no scheduled terms may be indicative of related parties.

**176.** For a reporting entity that has participated in related party transactions that are material, disclosure in the financial statements should include

A. The nature of the relationship and the terms and manner of settlement.

B. Details of the transactions within major classifications.

C. A statement to the effect that a transaction was consummated on terms equivalent to those that prevail in arm's-length transactions.

D. A reference to deficiencies in the entity's internal control.

Answer (A) is correct. *(CPA, adapted)*

**REQUIRED:** The financial statement disclosures required for related party transactions.

**DISCUSSION:** Disclosure in financial statements of a reporting entity that has participated in material related party transactions should include (1) the nature of the relationship, (2) a description of the transactions, (3) the dollar value of the transactions, (4) the amounts due from or to related parties, and (5), if not otherwise apparent, the terms and manner of settlement (SFAS 57).

Answer (B) is incorrect because the client need not separate the transactions into major classifications. Answer (C) is incorrect because a statement that transactions approximated those at arm's-length is not required. If such a representation is made, the auditor must reach a conclusion as to its propriety. Answer (D) is incorrect because the client is not obligated to provide disclosures about its internal control.

**177.** Current authoritative literature ordinarily requires material related party transactions to be

A. Accounted for differently from transactions between unrelated parties but not separately disclosed.

B. Accounted for on the same basis as transactions between unrelated parties and not separately disclosed.

C. Separately disclosed but not accounted for differently from transactions between unrelated parties.

D. Separately disclosed and accounted for differently from transactions between unrelated parties.

Answer (C) is correct. *(Publisher)*

**REQUIRED:** The accounting treatment of material related party transactions.

**DISCUSSION:** AU 334 states, "Certain accounting pronouncements prescribe accounting treatment when related parties are involved. However, established accounting principles ordinarily do not require transactions with related parties to be accounted for on a basis different from what would be appropriate if the parties were not related."

**178.** In the absence of evidence to the contrary, transactions with related parties should not be assumed to be outside the ordinary course of business. The auditor should, however, be aware of the possibility that transactions with related parties may have been motivated solely, or in a large measure, by certain conditions. The auditor should evaluate these conditions to identify related parties and related party transactions. Which of the following is not one of those conditions?

A. A lack of sufficient working capital or credit to continue business.

B. An urgent desire for a continued favorable earnings record to support the price of the company stock.

C. Dependence upon a single or relatively few products, customers, or transactions.

D. Reduction in number and dollar value of accounts receivable.

Answer (D) is correct. *(Publisher)*

**REQUIRED:** The item not a likely motivation for related party transactions.

**DISCUSSION:** A reduction in accounts receivable does not necessarily have negative implications for a business. It may simply reflect improved collection procedures or tighter credit policies. Hence, the reduction is not, per se, a condition likely to motivate related party transactions. In addition to those cited in the question, conditions indicative of related party transactions include an overly optimistic earnings forecast; a declining industry characterized by a large number of business failures; excess capacity; significant litigation, especially between shareholders and management; and significant risk of obsolescence, e.g., in a high-technology industry.

Answer (A) is incorrect because a lack of sufficient working capital or credit may motivate a related party transaction. Answer (B) is incorrect because a desire for a continued favorable earnings record may motivate a related party transaction. Answer (C) is incorrect because a dependence upon a single or relatively few products, customers, or transactions may motivate a related party transaction.

**179.** While expressing an unqualified opinion, an auditor includes a separate paragraph in the report to emphasize that the entity being reported upon had significant transactions with related parties. This inclusion

A. Violates auditing standards if this information is already disclosed in notes to the financial statements.

B. Necessitates a revision of the opinion paragraph to include the phrase "with the foregoing explanation."

C. Is appropriate and would not negate the unqualified opinion.

D. Is considered a qualification of the opinion.

Answer (C) is correct. *(CPA, adapted)*

**REQUIRED:** The effect of emphasizing related party transactions in a separate paragraph of the report.

**DISCUSSION:** An auditor may emphasize a matter in a separate paragraph while expressing an unqualified opinion. Significant related party transactions, the status of the entity as a component of a larger enterprise, an accounting matter affecting comparability, and an unusually important subsequent event are examples of matters that might be emphasized (AU 508).

Answer (A) is incorrect because auditing standards permit emphasis of a matter without qualifying the opinion. Answer (B) is incorrect because the opinion paragraph should not refer to the separate paragraph. Answer (D) is incorrect because auditing standards permit emphasis of a matter without qualifying the opinion.

**180.** An auditor refers to significant related party transactions in a separate paragraph of the report. If the ensuing opinion paragraph contains the words "with the foregoing explanation," the auditor is considered to have

A. Expressed an unqualified opinion with appropriate reference to the separate paragraph.

B. Expressed an adverse opinion.

C. Expressed a negative assurance opinion.

D. Reported inappropriately.

Answer (D) is correct. *(CPA, adapted)*

**REQUIRED:** The true statement about use of the phrase "with the foregoing explanation."

**DISCUSSION:** A separate explanatory paragraph is used when the auditor wishes to emphasize a matter, to describe uncertainties, to identify lack of consistency in applying GAAP, to express a qualified opinion, etc. The phrase "with the foregoing explanation" should never be used because it may be misunderstood as an attempt to qualify the opinion or, when a qualified opinion is expressed, because it is not clear or forceful enough (AU 508).

**181.** An auditor would be most likely to consider modifying an otherwise unqualified opinion if the client's financial statements include a note on related party transactions

A. Representing that certain related party transactions were consummated on terms equivalent to those obtainable in transactions with unrelated parties.

B. Presenting the dollar volume of related party transactions and the effects of any change in the method of establishing terms from that used in the prior period.

C. Explaining the business purpose of the sale of real property to a related party.

D. Disclosing compensating balance arrangements maintained for the benefit of related parties.

Answer (A) is correct. *(CPA, adapted)*

**REQUIRED:** The most likely basis for expressing a qualified opinion.

**DISCUSSION:** According to AU 334, "Except for routine transactions, it will ordinarily not be possible to determine whether a particular transaction would have taken place if the parties had not been related, or, assuming it would have taken place, what the terms and manner of settlement would have been." Accordingly, representations concerning such matters are difficult to substantiate. If the auditor is unable to reach a conclusion as to their propriety, (s)he should consider including in the report a comment to that effect and expressing a qualified opinion or a disclaimer.

Answer (B) is incorrect because the dollar volume of related party transactions and the effects of any change in the method of establishing terms are required disclosures. Answer (C) is incorrect because the business purpose of the sale of real property to a related party is a required disclosure. Answer (D) is incorrect because compensating balance arrangements maintained for the benefit of related parties is a required disclosure.

## 7.11 Subsequent Events and Subsequently Discovered Facts

**182.** Subsequent events for reporting purposes are defined as events that occur subsequent to the

A. Balance sheet date.

B. Date of the auditor's report.

C. Balance sheet date but prior to the issuance of the financial statements.

D. Date of the auditor's report and concern contingencies that are not reflected in the financial statements.

Answer (C) is correct. *(CPA, adapted)*

**REQUIRED:** The definition of subsequent events.

**DISCUSSION:** Subsequent events are those that occur subsequent to the balance sheet date, but prior to the issuance of the financial statements, that have a material effect on the financial statements and therefore require adjustment or disclosure in the statements (AU 560). If the balance sheet date is 12/31/X0, and the financial statements are issued on 3/1/X1, the subsequent events period is from 12/31/X0 to 3/1/X1.

**183.** Two types of subsequent events require consideration by management and evaluation by the auditor. One type consists of those events that provide additional evidence with respect to conditions that existed at the date of the balance sheet and affect the estimates inherent in the process of preparing financial statements. The financial statements should be adjusted for any changes in estimates resulting from the use of such evidence. The second type of subsequent event consists of those events that provide evidence with respect to conditions that did not exist at the date of the balance sheet but arose subsequent to that date. These events

A. Are also used in adjusting the financial statements.

B. Should not be considered for any purposes.

C. Should ordinarily be disclosed in the auditor's report.

D. May require disclosure in notes to the financial statements.

Answer (D) is correct. *(Publisher)*

**REQUIRED:** The extent to which subsequent events relevant to conditions arising after the balance sheet date should be reflected in the statements or in the audit report.

**DISCUSSION:** These events should not result in adjustment of the financial statements, although they may require disclosure to keep the financial statements from being misleading. Disclosure may be made in the notes and occasionally by presentation of pro forma data giving effect to the subsequent event as if it had occurred at the balance sheet date. If the event has a sufficiently material impact, the auditor may wish to refer to it in an explanatory paragraph in the report (AU 560).

Answer (A) is incorrect because only the subsequent events that provide additional evidence of conditions existing at year-end (first type) should result in adjustment. Answer (B) is incorrect because subsequent events that provide evidence with respect to conditions that did not exist at the balance sheet date (second type) should be disclosed. Answer (C) is incorrect because the second type of subsequent event is only occasionally noted in the audit report.

**184.** Which of the following procedures will an auditor most likely perform to obtain evidence about the occurrence of subsequent events?

A. Recomputing a sample of large-dollar transactions occurring after year-end for arithmetic accuracy.

B. Investigating changes in equity occurring after year-end.

C. Inquiring of the entity's legal counsel concerning litigation, claims, and assessments arising after year-end.

D. Confirming bank accounts established after year-end.

Answer (C) is correct. *(CPA, adapted)*

**REQUIRED:** The auditing procedure for the subsequent events period.

**DISCUSSION:** Procedures applied after the balance sheet date should include the examination of data to determine that proper cutoffs have been made and to evaluate assets and liabilities as of the balance sheet date. Additional procedures include (1) reading the latest available interim statements; (2) inquiries of and discussion with officers and other executives as to whether substantial contingent liabilities or commitments exist, whether there was any significant change in equities or long-term debt, the current status of items that were accounted for on the basis of tentative, preliminary, or inconclusive data, and whether any adjustments had been made during the period from the balance sheet date to the date of inquiry; (3) reading the available minutes of meetings of shareholders, directors, and other committees; (4) inquiring of the client's legal counsel; (5) obtaining a representation letter; and (6) making additional necessary inquiries (AU 560).

Answer (A) is incorrect because testing arithmetic accuracy does not obtain evidence about the occurrence of a subsequent event. Answer (B) is incorrect because the auditor should inquire of officers and other executives as to significant changes in equity, but an investigation of such changes is less likely than the inquiry of legal counsel. Answer (D) is incorrect because a bank account established after year-end is not an asset that existed at the balance sheet date.

**185.** Some subsequent events provide evidence of conditions not in existence at the balance sheet date. Some of these events are of such a nature that disclosure is required to keep the financial statements from being misleading. Adequate disclosure of these events may include

A. Adjustment of the financial statements.

B. Pro forma financial statement presentation.

C. Notes to the auditor's report.

D. Restatement of prior-period financial statements.

Answer (B) is correct. *(Publisher)*

**REQUIRED:** The proper disclosure of a subsequent event related to a condition not existing at year-end.

**DISCUSSION:** Subsequent events related to conditions that did not exist at the date of the balance sheet should not result in adjustments of the financial statements. These events are usually disclosed in statement notes. Occasionally, such an event may be significant and have such pervasive effects that disclosure can best be made by supplementing the historical statements with pro forma financial data giving effect to the event as if it had occurred on the date of the balance sheet. AU 560 suggests presentation of pro forma statements, usually a balance sheet only, in columnar form on the face of the historical statements. But firms usually incorporate the pro forma balance sheets in notes.

Answer (A) is incorrect because only subsequent events that relate to conditions existing at the balance sheet date require adjustment of the financial statements. Answer (C) is incorrect because notes are attached to financial statements, not auditors' reports. Answer (D) is incorrect because only subsequent events that relate to conditions existing at the balance sheet date require adjustment of the financial statements.

**186.** Subsequent events affecting the realization of assets ordinarily will require adjustment of the financial statements under audit because such events typically represent the

A. Culmination of conditions that existed at the balance sheet date.

B. Final estimates of losses relating to casualties occurring in the subsequent events period.

C. Discovery of new conditions occurring in the subsequent events period.

D. Preliminary estimate of losses relating to new events that occurred subsequent to the balance sheet date.

Answer (A) is correct. *(CPA, adapted)*

**REQUIRED:** The reason subsequent events affecting asset realization require adjustment of the statements.

**DISCUSSION:** All information that becomes available prior to the issuance of the financial statements should be used by management in its evaluation of the conditions on which the estimates underlying the statements were based. The financial statements should be adjusted for events in the subsequent events period that provide additional evidence concerning conditions that existed at the balance sheet date. Subsequent events affecting the realization of assets typically represent the culmination of conditions that existed at year-end (AU 560).

Answer (B) is incorrect because conditions that did not exist at the balance sheet date, if material, require note disclosure or even pro forma presentation but not adjustment of the statements. Answer (C) is incorrect because conditions that did not exist at the balance sheet date, if material, require note disclosure or even pro forma presentation but not adjustment of the statements. Answer (D) is incorrect because conditions that did not exist at the balance sheet date, if material, require note disclosure or even pro forma presentation but not adjustment of the statements.

**187.** Wilson, CPA, completed the field work of the audit of Abco's December 31, 20X0 financial statements on March 6, 20X1. A subsequent event requiring adjustment of the 20X0 financial statements occurred on April 10, 20X1, and came to Wilson's attention on April 24, 20X1. If the adjustment is made without disclosure of the event, Wilson's report ordinarily should be dated

A. March 6, 20X1.

B. April 10, 20X1.

C. April 24, 20X1.

D. Using dual dating.

Answer (A) is correct. *(CPA, adapted)*

**REQUIRED:** The date of the report if the statements are adjusted for a subsequent event without disclosure.

**DISCUSSION:** If a subsequent event requiring adjustment occurs after the date of the report but prior to the issuance of the financial statements, and the event comes to the auditor's attention, the statements should be adjusted. If the statements are not adjusted, the opinion should be qualified. In some cases, a disclaimer of opinion or an adverse opinion may be appropriate. When the adjustment is made without disclosure, the report should usually be dated as of the completion of field work (AU 530).

Answer (B) is incorrect because, when a subsequent event of the type requiring adjustment is not disclosed, the report should usually be dated as of the completion of field work. Answer (C) is incorrect because, when a subsequent event of the type requiring adjustment is not disclosed, the report should usually be dated as of the completion of field work. Answer (D) is incorrect because dual dating is not permitted when the subsequent event is not disclosed.

**188.** Which of the following material events occurring subsequent to the December 31, 20X0 balance sheet date will not ordinarily result in an adjustment of the financial statements before they are issued on March 2, 20X1?

A. Write-off of a receivable from a debtor who had suffered from a deteriorating financial condition for the past 6 years. The debtor filed for bankruptcy on January 23, 20X1.

B. Acquisition of a subsidiary on January 23, 20X1. Negotiations had begun in December of 20X0.

C. Settlement of extended litigation on January 23, 20X1 in excess of the recorded year-end liability.

D. A 3-for-5 reverse stock split consummated on January 23, 20X1.

Answer (B) is correct. *(CPA, adapted)*

**REQUIRED:** The material subsequent event not requiring adjustment of the statements.

**DISCUSSION:** The financial statements should be adjusted for material subsequent events that provide information relative to conditions existing at the balance sheet date. The acquisition of the subsidiary did not occur until after year-end; hence, the purchase required only note disclosure, not adjustment of the statements.

Answer (A) is incorrect because the poor financial condition of the debtor existed at year-end. Answer (C) is incorrect because the litigation was pending at year-end. Answer (D) is incorrect because retroactive effect should be given to stock splits according to SFAS 128, *Earnings per Share.*

**189.** Creditor Co. had a large account receivable that was considered fully collectible at its year end. However, the debtor's plant was destroyed during the subsequent events period. Because the debtor was uninsured, it is unlikely that the account will be paid. What is the effect of this event on the year-end statements?

A. Disclosure by means of supplemental, pro forma financial data.

B. Adjustment of the financial statements.

C. Disclosure in a note to the financial statements.

D. No financial statement disclosure necessary.

Answer (C) is correct. *(Publisher)*

**REQUIRED:** The proper treatment of a debtor's major casualty subsequent to year end.

**DISCUSSION:** A debtor's major casualty subsequent to year-end rendering a major receivable uncollectible is not indicative of conditions existing at the balance sheet date, so adjustment of the financial statements is not appropriate. Because the event could influence the users of the financial statements, disclosure in a note should be made (AU 560).

Answer (A) is incorrect because disclosure by means of supplemental, pro forma financial data would be inappropriate. Answer (B) is incorrect because adjustment of the financial statements would be inappropriate. Answer (D) is incorrect because financial statement disclosure is necessary.

**190.** The U.S. Tax Court ruled in favor of Defendant Co. after year-end but before completion of the audit. Litigation involved deductions claimed on prior years' tax returns. The company had credited accrued taxes payable at year-end for the full amount sought by the IRS. The IRS will not appeal the ruling. What is the effect of this event on the year-end statements?

A. Disclosure by means of supplemental, pro forma financial data.

B. Adjustment of the financial statements.

C. Disclosure in a note to the financial statements.

D. No financial statement disclosure necessary.

Answer (B) is correct. *(Publisher)*

**REQUIRED:** The proper treatment of the settlement of litigation subsequent to year-end.

**DISCUSSION:** The ruling of the Tax Court provides additional evidence with respect to conditions that existed at the date of the financial statements and affects the estimates used in their preparation. Consequently, the settlement in the subsequent events period for an amount different from that recorded requires the client to adjust the statements.

Answer (A) is incorrect because disclosure by means of supplemental, pro forma financial data would be inappropriate. Answer (C) is incorrect because disclosure in a note to the financial statements would be inappropriate. Answer (D) is incorrect because financial statement disclosure is necessary.

**191.** After year-end but before completion of the audit, a major investment adviser issued a pessimistic report on Investee Co.'s long-term prospects. The market price for its common stock subsequently declined significantly. What is the effect of this event on the year-end statements?

A. Disclosure by means of supplemental, pro forma financial data.

B. Adjustment of the financial statements.

C. Disclosure in a note to the financial statements.

D. No financial statement disclosure necessary.

Answer (D) is correct. *(Publisher)*

**REQUIRED:** The proper treatment of a major decline in the price of stock subsequent to year-end.

**DISCUSSION:** The market price of common stock is not a financial event that affects the fairness or interpretation of the financial statements. Accordingly, no disclosure is necessary for changes in the market price of the securities.

Answer (A) is incorrect because disclosure by means of supplemental, pro forma financial data would be inappropriate. Answer (B) is incorrect because adjustment of the financial statements would be inappropriate. Answer (C) is incorrect because disclosure in a note to the financial statements would be inappropriate.

**192.** Advertiser Co.'s directors voted immediately after year-end to double the advertising budget for the coming year and authorized a change in advertising agencies. What is the effect of this event on the year-end statements?

A. Disclosure by means of supplemental, pro forma financial data.

B. Adjustment of the financial statements.

C. Disclosure in a note to the financial statements.

D. No financial statement disclosure necessary.

Answer (D) is correct. *(Publisher)*

**REQUIRED:** The proper treatment of an increase in the advertising budget subsequent to the balance sheet date.

**DISCUSSION:** Changing of budgets and other managerial decisions made by the directors or management are not significant subsequent events. Hence, no financial statement disclosure or adjustment is necessary.

Answer (A) is incorrect because disclosure by means of supplemental, pro forma financial data is inappropriate. Answer (B) is incorrect because adjustment of the financial statements is inappropriate. Answer (C) is incorrect because disclosure in a note to the financial statements is inappropriate.

**193.** Parent Co. sold a major division during the subsequent events period. The new owner assumed the bonded indebtedness associated with this property. What is the effect of this event on the year-end statements?

A. Disclosure by means of supplemental, pro forma financial data.

B. Adjustment of the financial statements.

C. Presentation of a narrative description in a note to the financial statements.

D. No required financial statement disclosure.

Answer (A) is correct. *(Publisher)*

**REQUIRED:** The proper treatment of the sale of a division after the balance sheet date.

**DISCUSSION:** The sale of a major division in the subsequent events period provides evidence of conditions not existing at the balance sheet date and thus does not require adjustment of the statements. Disclosure must be made, however, because the event is of such a nature that nondisclosure would make the statements misleading. The form of the disclosure depends upon the significance of the event. In this case, many accounts are affected, and pro forma statements presented on the face of the historical statements are the best method. However, the pro forma statements are sometimes presented in a note.

Answer (B) is incorrect because adjustment of the financial statements would be inappropriate. Answer (C) is incorrect because a narrative disclosure in a note to the financial statements would be insufficient. Answer (D) is incorrect because financial statement disclosure is necessary.

**194.** If a subsequent event requiring only disclosure occurs after completion of field work but prior to issuance of the financial statements, the auditor should

A. Modify the opinion and dual date the audit report. No additional field work is required.

B. Date the audit report as of the last day of field work and caption the note disclosing the subsequent event as being subsequent to the completion of the field work.

C. Not modify the audit opinion if the event is properly disclosed and date the audit report as of the time of completion of the field work.

D. Either dual date the audit report or date the audit report as of the time of the completion of the extended field work.

Answer (D) is correct. *(Publisher)*

**REQUIRED:** The action when a subsequent event requiring only disclosure occurs after completion of field work but prior to issuance of the financial statements.

**DISCUSSION:** The auditor may use dual dating or date the entire report as of the date of the subsequent event occurring after completion of field work. If the report is dual dated, the auditor's responsibility for events subsequent to the completion of field work is limited to the specific event. If the date of the report is the date of that event, responsibility extends to that date. Accordingly, the auditor should perform the necessary additional subsequent events procedures through the new date of the report (AU 530).

Answer (A) is incorrect because, if the client properly notes or otherwise discloses the item, no opinion modification is necessary. Answer (B) is incorrect because captioning the note is insufficient. Answer (C) is incorrect because the occurrence of the event must be acknowledged in dating the report.

**195.** Toby Hooper, CPA, had drafted an unqualified opinion on the audit of Chem Waste Disposal when she received a letter from the client's independent counsel. The letter indicated that the state Department of Environmental Protection may prohibit Chem Waste from accepting any further waste for processing because of irregularities in its operating practices. Counsel intends to take all appropriate action to keep the firm in business, but the outcome is highly uncertain. Based on this information, Hooper should

A. Express an unqualified opinion with disclosure of the event in a separate explanatory paragraph of her report.

B. Issue a standard report because the event happened after year-end.

C. Express an adverse opinion on the financial statements and disclose all reasons therefore.

D. Add a note to the audit report explaining the event.

Answer (A) is correct. *(Publisher)*

**REQUIRED:** The appropriate action when the CPA has obtained new information affecting the audit report.

**DISCUSSION:** According to AU 341, an evaluation must be made as to whether substantial doubt exists "about the entity's ability to continue as a going concern for a reasonable period of time, not to exceed 1 year beyond the date of the financial statements." If the auditor reaches this conclusion after identifying conditions and events that create such doubt and after evaluating management's plans to mitigate their effects, (s)he should consider the adequacy of disclosure and include an explanatory paragraph (after the opinion paragraph) in the report. This paragraph must use the phrases "substantial doubt" and "going concern." If disclosure is inadequate, the departure from GAAP requires modification of the opinion. If the uncertainty is sufficiently material, a disclaimer may be appropriate.

Answer (B) is incorrect because, if a material uncertainty exists as to whether the client is a going concern, a standard report cannot be issued. Answer (C) is incorrect because grounds do not exist for an opinion that the statements are not fairly presented. Answer (D) is incorrect because a note is not appropriate for an audit report.

**196.** Subsequent to the issuance of the financial statements, the auditor became aware of facts existing at the report date that would have affected the report had the auditor then been aware of such facts. After determining that the information is reliable, the auditor should next

A. Determine whether there are persons relying or likely to rely on the financial statements who would attach importance to the information.

B. Request that management disclose the newly discovered information by issuing revised financial statements.

C. Issue revised pro forma financial statements taking into consideration the newly discovered information.

D. Give public notice that the auditor is no longer associated with financial statements.

Answer (A) is correct. *(CPA, adapted)*

**REQUIRED:** The step performed by an auditor who becomes aware of facts existing at the report date that would have affected the report.

**DISCUSSION:** AU 561, *Subsequent Discovery of Facts Existing at the Date of the Auditor's Report*, states that, if an auditor decides that action should be taken to prevent future reliance on the report, (s)he should advise the client to make appropriate disclosures to persons who are known to be relying or who are likely to rely on the financial statements and the related report.

Answer (B) is incorrect because, although requesting that management issue revised statements is appropriate, it should not be the first step taken by the auditor. Answer (C) is incorrect because management is responsible for the financial statements, not the auditor. Answer (D) is incorrect because the auditor may continue association with the client as long as appropriate measures are taken.

**197.** When a contingency is resolved immediately subsequent to the issuance of financial statements with a report that included a paragraph emphasizing the contingency, the auditor should

A. Insist that the client issue revised financial statements.

B. Inform the audit committee that the report cannot be relied upon.

C. Take no action regarding the event.

D. Inform the appropriate authorities that the report cannot be relied upon.

Answer (C) is correct. *(CPA, adapted)*

**REQUIRED:** The proper auditor action for resolutions of contingencies after the issuance of the audit report.

**DISCUSSION:** After the date of the report, the auditor is under no obligation to make any further or continuing inquiry or perform any other auditing procedures with respect to the audited financial statements covered by the report, unless new information that may affect the report comes to his/her attention. The resolution of a contingency is not deemed to be new information for this purpose (AU 561).

Answer (A) is incorrect because the auditor has no obligation with regard to the resolution of contingencies after the date of the report. Answer (B) is incorrect because the auditor has no obligation with regard to the resolution of contingencies after the date of the report. Answer (D) is incorrect because the auditor has no obligation with regard to the resolution of contingencies after the date of the report.

**198.** When the effect of subsequently discovered facts that existed at the date of the auditor's report can be promptly determined, the client should issue, to those relying on the statements and related auditor's report,

A. Revised statements with the revision described in a note to the statements. The original audit report should accompany the revised statements.

B. Revised statements with the revision described in a note to the statements. No auditor's report should accompany the statements.

C. A narrative explanation of the effect of the subsequent discovery of facts existing at the date of the report.

D. Revised statements and a revised audit report with the revision described in a note to the statements and referred to in the revised report.

Answer (D) is correct. *(Publisher)*

**REQUIRED:** The client action when the effects of subsequently discovered facts existing at the date of the audit report can be readily determined.

**DISCUSSION:** AU 561 states, "If the effect on the financial statements or auditor's report of the subsequently discovered information can promptly be determined, disclosure should consist of issuing, as soon as practicable, revised financial statements and auditor's report. The reasons for the revision usually should be described in a note to the financial statements and referred to in the auditor's report."

Answer (A) is incorrect because the auditor's report, appropriately modified, should be included with the revised financial statements. Answer (B) is incorrect because the auditor's report, appropriately modified, should be included with the revised financial statements. Answer (C) is incorrect because the client will normally include the reason for the change in a note to the revised financial statements.

**199.** The auditor learned of the following situations after the date of the audit report on February 6. Each is important to users of the financial statements. For which one does the auditor have responsibility for disclosure of the newly discovered facts?

A. A major lawsuit against the company, which was the basis for a modified report, was settled on unfavorable terms on March 1.

B. The client undertook merger negotiations on March 16, and concluded a merger agreement on April 1.

C. On February 16, a fire destroyed the principal manufacturing plant.

D. A conflict of interest involving credit officers and a principal company supplier was discovered on March 3.

Answer (D) is correct. *(CPA, adapted)*

**REQUIRED:** The situation for which the auditor has a responsibility for disclosure of newly discovered facts.

**DISCUSSION:** The auditor has a responsibility after the date of the report for events that come to his/her attention for which (s)he would have extended procedures or modified the report. A conflict of interest situation would have been examined by the auditor had (s)he known about it during the audit process. Consequently, the auditor has a responsibility to determine the nature of the event and whether it might affect the fairness of the financial statements and the propriety of the report (AU 561).

Answer (A) is incorrect because the auditor has no responsibility to update the report for resolutions of contingencies that were properly disclosed. Answer (B) is incorrect because the auditor need not apply any other audit procedures or update the report for occurrences after the date of the report.

Answer (C) is incorrect because the auditor need not apply any other audit procedures or update the report for occurrences after the date of the report.

**200.** An auditor has found that the notes to the financial statements do not mention that, 15 days after the balance sheet date, the company issued a substantial amount of debentures. According to the company's attorney, the debenture agreement restricts the payment of future cash dividends. The client has declined to include the matter of the debentures in the notes because the issuance occurred after the balance sheet date. The auditor should

A. Add the note to the financial statements.

B. Provide the missing information in the report and express an adverse opinion.

C. Provide the missing information in the report and express a qualified opinion.

D. Provide the missing information in the report and disclaim an opinion.

Answer (C) is correct. *(Publisher)*
**REQUIRED:** The proper action by an auditor when the client refuses to disclose a material subsequent event.
**DISCUSSION:** A subsequent event not providing evidence as to conditions existing at the balance sheet date does not result in adjustment of the statements. However, it may require disclosure to keep the statements from being misleading. AU 560 cites the sale of a bond issue as an example of a subsequent event requiring disclosure but not adjustment. When such an event occurs between the report date and the issue date of the related financial statements, it should be disclosed in a note or the auditor should modify the opinion (AU 530).
Answer (A) is incorrect because the auditor has no authority to add a note to the financial statements. All assertions therein are the representations of management. Answer (B) is incorrect because the auditor should usually express a qualified opinion if the client refuses to make a necessary disclosure about subsequent events. However, an adverse opinion may be justified in some cases. Answer (D) is incorrect because the auditor should usually express a qualified opinion if the client refuses to make a necessary disclosure about subsequent events. However, an adverse opinion may be justified in some cases

**201.** Soon after the financial statements were issued with Boyd's audit report attached, Boyd learned of certain related-party transactions that occurred during the year under audit. These transactions were not disclosed in the notes to the financial statements. Boyd should

A. Plan to audit the transactions during the next engagement.

B. Recall all copies of the audited financial statements.

C. Determine whether the lack of disclosure would affect the auditor's report.

D. Ask the client to disclose the transactions in subsequent interim statements.

Answer (C) is correct. *(CPA, adapted)*
**REQUIRED:** The step the auditor should take when (s)he becomes aware of previously unknown information.
**DISCUSSION:** An auditor may become aware of information related to the financial statements previously reported on that was not known at the date of the report. If the nature and source of the information are such that (s)he would have investigated it had it been discovered during the audit, the auditor should, as soon as practicable, determine whether (1) the information is reliable and (2) the facts existed at the date of the report. If these criteria are met, the auditor must take appropriate action if (1) the report would have been affected and (2) (s)he believes persons who are currently relying or likely to rely on the statements would consider the information important (AU 561).
Answer (A) is incorrect because the auditor must take more immediate action if the lack of disclosure affects the report. Answer (B) is incorrect because recall of the audited financial statements is not feasible. Answer (D) is incorrect because issuance of revised statements and notice to appropriate parties may be necessary, but only if the auditor has determined that the original statements would be affected by the lack of disclosure.

**202.** Bill Blake, CPA, as a result of newly discovered facts, has concluded that action should be taken to prevent future reliance on the report. He should

A. Advise the client to make appropriate disclosure of the facts to persons who are known to be currently relying on the financial statements.

B. Recall the financial statements.

C. Make appropriate disclosure of the correction in the statements of a subsequent period.

D. Issue a disclaimer of opinion that should usually be followed by revised statements and a qualified opinion.

Answer (A) is correct. *(Publisher)*
**REQUIRED:** The proper action to prevent future reliance on the auditor's report.
**DISCUSSION:** If the auditor has concluded that the report should no longer be relied upon, (s)he should advise the client to make appropriate disclosure of the newly discovered facts. When the client undertakes to make such disclosures, the method used and the disclosure made will depend on the circumstances. If the effect on the financial statements or auditor's report can promptly be determined, however, disclosure should consist of issuing, as soon as practicable, revised financial statements and a revised auditor's report (AU 561).
Answer (B) is incorrect because the client should issue appropriate revised financial statements but need not recall the original statements. Answer (C) is incorrect because the client should make appropriate disclosures to third parties relying upon the financial statements in revised statements for the current period. Answer (D) is incorrect because a disclaimer of opinion should not be issued prior to issuing the appropriate report with the revised financial statements.

**203.** On February 25, the financial statements were issued with an auditor's report expressing an unqualified opinion on the statements for the year ended January 31. On March 2, the CPA learned that on February 11 the entity incurred a material loss on an uncollectible trade receivable as a result of the deteriorating financial condition of the entity's principal customer that led to the customer's bankruptcy. Management then refused to adjust the financial statements for this subsequent event. The CPA determined that the information is reliable and that there are creditors currently relying on the financial statements. The CPA's next course of action most likely is to

A. Notify the entity's creditors that the financial statements and the related auditor's report should no longer be relied on.

B. Notify each member of the entity's board of directors about management's refusal to adjust the financial statements.

C. Issue revised financial statements and distribute them to each creditor known to be relying on the financial statements.

D. Issue a revised auditor's report and distribute it to each creditor known to be relying on the financial statements.

Answer (B) is correct. *(CPA, adapted)*

**REQUIRED:** The actions of an auditor related to an event discovered subsequent to the issue of the financial statements.

**DISCUSSION:** If the auditor decides that action should be taken to prevent future reliance on the report, (s)he should advise the client to make appropriate disclosures to persons who are known to be currently relying or who are likely to rely on the financial statements and the related report. However, if the client fails to take appropriate action, the auditor, who has determined the information's reliability and creditors' reliance on the statements, should notify each member of the board of directors of the refusal. Failing a satisfactory settlement, the auditor should notify the client that the report must no longer be associated with the statements. The auditor also should notify appropriate regulatory agencies and each person known to be relying on the financial statements that the auditor's report should no longer be relied on.

Answer (A) is incorrect because the board of directors should be notified first. Answer (C) is incorrect because the auditor has no authority to revise management's financial statements. Answer (D) is incorrect because the auditor should not revise the report but should notify those relying on the report that it is no longer valid.

**204.** An auditor completed field work for a client on February 15. The related financial statements were issued on March 10. On April 8, the client suffered the loss of a significant portion of its plant facilities by fire. The client requested additional copies of the previously issued report on May 5. Assuming no additional audit work has been or will be performed, the auditor should

A. Disregard the casualty and reissue the original report with no change in date.

B. Have the client disclose the event in a separate note to the statements identified as "Event (Unaudited) Subsequent to the Date of the Report of the Independent Auditor."

C. Use dual dating.

D. Either have the client disclose the event in a separate note to the statements identified as "Event (Unaudited) Subsequent to the Date of the Report of the Independent Auditor" OR use dual dating.

Answer (B) is correct. *(Publisher)*

**REQUIRED:** The treatment in a reissued report of a material event that occurred after the original report date.

**DISCUSSION:** A major casualty occurring after the date of the original report requires disclosure in the financial statements covered by the reissued report. The reissuance of a report for purposes of AU 530 includes furnishing additional copies of a previously issued report. If the auditor performs procedures with respect to the casualty, (s)he may use dual dating. If no audit work is performed relative to this event, it should be marked unaudited in a note to the financial statements captioned as described.

Answer (A) is incorrect because the auditor cannot disregard the casualty. It must be disclosed in the financial statements. Answer (C) is incorrect because dual dating is inappropriate when the subsequent event is unaudited. Answer (D) is incorrect because dual dating is inappropriate when the subsequent event is unaudited.

**205.** Under which of the following circumstances may audited financial statements contain a note disclosing an event occurring after the balance sheet date that is labeled unaudited?

A. When the subsequent event requires adjustment of the financial statements.

B. When the event occurs after completion of field work and before issuance of the related financial statements.

C. When audit procedures with respect to the event were not performed by the auditor.

D. When the event occurs between the date of the auditor's original report and the date of the reissuance of the report.

Answer (D) is correct. *(CPA, adapted)*

**REQUIRED:** The basis for including a note disclosing an unaudited event.

**DISCUSSION:** When an event of the type requiring only disclosure occurs between the date of the independent auditor's original report and the date of the reissuance of such a report, the event may be disclosed in a separate note to the financial statements captioned as follows: "Event (Unaudited) Subsequent to the Date of the Report of the Independent Auditor" (AU 530).

Answer (A) is incorrect because the note may pertain only to an event that requires disclosure but not adjustment. Answer (B) is incorrect because the auditor's report must cover a disclosable event occurring prior to the issuance of the related financial statements. Answer (C) is incorrect because a note disclosing an unaudited event may refer only to an event occurring after the report date that requires disclosure in, but not adjustment of, the statements. The note is not appropriate for any unaudited event occurring after the balance sheet date.

**206.** Karr has audited the financial statements of Lurch Corporation for the year ended December 31, 20X0. Although Karr's field work was completed on February 17, 20X1, Karr's report was dated February 28, 20X1 and was received by the management of Lurch on March 5, 20X1. On April 4, 20X1, the management of Lurch asked that Karr approve inclusion of this report in its annual report to shareholders that will include unaudited financial statements for the first quarter ended March 31, 20X1. Karr approved the inclusion. Under the circumstances, Karr is responsible for inquiring as to events occurring through

A. February 17, 20X1.

B. February 28, 20X1.

C. March 31, 20X1.

D. April 4, 20X1.

Answer (B) is correct. *(CPA, adapted)*

**REQUIRED:** The date through which the auditor assumes responsibility.

**DISCUSSION:** Normally, the date of the completion of field work is the date of the report, and the auditor has no responsibility to make any inquiry or carry out any procedures for the period after the date of the report. An independent auditor may also reissue the report. Use of the original report date in the reissued report removes any implication that records, transactions, or events after that date have been audited or reviewed. The auditor has no responsibility in such cases to make further investigation or inquiry as to events after the original report date (AU 530).

Answer (A) is incorrect because, in this situation, the auditor assumed responsibility up to 2/28/X1, not the date of completion of field work, 2/17/X1. Answer (C) is incorrect because the auditor assumed responsibility for events only up to the date of the report. Answer (D) is incorrect because the auditor assumed responsibility for events only up to the date of the report.

**207.** A registration statement filed with the Securities and Exchange Commission may contain the reports of two or more independent auditors on their audits of the financial statements for different periods. What responsibility does the auditor who has not audited the most recent financial statements have relative to events occurring after the date of his/her report that may affect the financial statements on which (s)he reported?

A. The auditor has responsibility for events up to the subsequent fiscal year-end.

B. The auditor has responsibility for events up to the date of the subsequent audit report.

C. The auditor has responsibility for events up to the effective date of the registration statement.

D. The auditor has no responsibility beyond the date of the original report.

Answer (C) is correct. *(CPA, adapted)*

**REQUIRED:** The responsibility of the predecessor auditor for comparative statements filed with the SEC.

**DISCUSSION:** An auditor of financial statements for a prior period but not for the most recent audited period has a responsibility for events occurring after the date of the prior period financial statements and up to the effective date of the registration statement. The predecessor auditor should (1) read pertinent portions of the prospectus and of the registration statement and (2) obtain a representation letter from the successor auditor regarding whether the audit revealed any matters that might have a material effect on the financial statements reported on by the predecessor. The predecessor auditor should make inquiries and perform other procedures regarding the appropriateness of any adjustment or disclosure affecting the prior-period statements (AU 711).

Answer (A) is incorrect because, although the auditor ordinarily has no responsibility beyond the date of the original report, the filing of a registration statement extends the responsibility to the effective date of the registration statement. Answer (B) is incorrect because, although the auditor ordinarily has no responsibility beyond the date of the original report, the filing of a registration statement extends the responsibility to the effective date of the registration statement. Answer (D) is incorrect because, although the auditor ordinarily has no responsibility beyond the date of the original report, the filing of a registration statement extends the responsibility to the effective date of the registration statement.

**208.** A continuing auditor should update the report on prior financial statements by issuing a report modified for the

A. Resolution of an uncertainty related to and discovered in the current period.

B. Removal in the current period of doubt about the entity's ability to continue as a going concern.

C. Determination in the current period that a substantial doubt exists about the entity's ability to continue as a going concern for a reasonable time.

D. Inconsistency involved in restating prior-period statements to correct an error discovered in the prior years' inventory count.

Answer (B) is correct. *(Publisher)*

**REQUIRED:** The reason a continuing auditor should update the report on prior statements.

**DISCUSSION:** A continuing auditor should update the report on prior-period statements presented comparatively with those of the current period (AU 508). If the auditor determines that, in the current period, a substantial doubt has been removed about the reporting entity's ability to continue as a going concern for a reasonable period, the related explanatory paragraph in the report on the prior-period statements need not be repeated (AU 341).

Answer (A) is incorrect because resolution of an uncertainty discovered in the current period does not affect prior-period statements. Answer (C) is incorrect because determination that a going concern issue exists in the current period typically does not affect prior-period statements. Answer (D) is incorrect because restatement based on correction of an error not involving an accounting principle does not require recognition as to consistency (AU 420).

## 7.12 Other Auditors

**209.** When two or more auditing firms participate in an audit, one firm should be the principal auditor. If the principal auditor makes reference to another auditor in an audit that would otherwise result in an unqualified opinion, the type of audit report issued should be

A. An unqualified opinion.

B. A qualified opinion.

C. An adverse opinion.

D. A disclaimer of opinion.

Answer (A) is correct. *(CMA, adapted)*

**REQUIRED:** The audit opinion expressed when the principal auditor refers to the work of another auditor.

**DISCUSSION:** The principal auditor must decide whether to accept responsibility for the work of the other CPAs. If the principal auditor does not accept responsibility for their work, the division of responsibility should be stated in the report. However, this division of responsibility does not influence the nature of the opinion expressed.

Answer (B) is incorrect because, if the statements are fairly presented, in all material respects, in accordance with GAAP, an unqualified opinion is indicated. Answer (C) is incorrect because, if the statements are fairly presented, in all material respects, in accordance with GAAP, an unqualified opinion is indicated. Answer (D) is incorrect because, if the statements are fairly presented, in all material respects, in accordance with GAAP, an unqualified opinion is indicated.

**210.** Hal Halsey is auditing the consolidated financial statements of Rex, Inc., a publicly held corporation. Lincoln is the auditor who has audited and reported on the financial statements of a wholly owned subsidiary of Rex, Inc. Halsey's first concern with respect to the Rex financial statements is to decide whether he

A. May serve as the principal auditor and report as such on the consolidated financial statements of Rex, Inc.

B. May refer to the work of Lincoln in his report on the consolidated financial statements.

C. Should review the documentation of Lincoln with respect to the audit of the subsidiary's financial statements.

D. Should resign from the engagement because an unqualified opinion cannot be expressed on the consolidated financial statements.

Answer (A) is correct. *(CPA, adapted)*

**REQUIRED:** The first concern of an auditor when a subsidiary has been audited by another auditor.

**DISCUSSION:** The auditor must decide whether his/her participation is sufficient to justify serving as the principal auditor and reporting as such on the financial statements. Thus, the auditor must consider the extent of his/her knowledge of the overall financial statements, the importance of the components (s)he audited in relation to the enterprise as a whole, and the materiality of the portion audited by the other auditor (AU 543).

Answer (B) is incorrect because the decision whether to refer to the other auditor is made only after the decision to serve as the principal auditor. Answer (C) is incorrect because the decision to review the audit documentation of the other auditor is made after the decision to serve as principal auditor. It is a procedure that may be performed when deciding whether to refer to the other auditor's work. Answer (D) is incorrect because performance of part of the audit by another auditor does not preclude expressing an unqualified opinion.

**211.** When a principal auditor decides to refer to another auditor's audit, the principal auditor's report should always indicate clearly, in the introductory, scope, and opinion paragraphs, the

A. Magnitude of the portion of the financial statements examined by the other auditor.

B. Disclaimer of responsibility concerning the portion of the financial statements examined by the other auditor.

C. Name of the other auditor.

D. Division of responsibility.

Answer (D) is correct. *(CPA, adapted)*

**REQUIRED:** The disclosure requirement when reference to another auditor is made.

**DISCUSSION:** The division of responsibility between the portion of the financial statements covered by the principal auditor's own audit and that covered by the other auditor should be clearly defined in the introductory, scope, and opinion paragraphs (AU 543).

Answer (A) is incorrect because the portion of the financial statements audited by the other auditor should be disclosed by stating the dollar amounts of total assets, total revenues, or other appropriate criteria in the introductory paragraph. Answer (B) is incorrect because a division of responsibility, not a disclaimer, is indicated. Answer (C) is incorrect because naming the other auditor is not required; (s)he may be named only if (s)he gives express permission and if his/her report is presented together with that of the principal auditor.

**212.** If the principal auditor decides to refer in the report to the audit made by another auditor,

A. The principal auditor assumes responsibility for the report of the other auditor.

B. The other auditor is relieved of responsibility for his/her report but not his/her work.

C. The other auditor is responsible for both his/her report and his/her work.

D. The other auditor is relieved of responsibility for his/her work but not his/her report.

Answer (C) is correct. *(Publisher)*

**REQUIRED:** The effect of referring to another auditor's audit.

**DISCUSSION:** Whether or not the principal auditor refers in the report to the audit made by the other auditor, the other auditor remains responsible for the performance of his/her work and for his/her report (AU 543).

Answer (A) is incorrect because the principal auditor assumes responsibility for the other auditor's work insofar as it relates to the principal auditor's expression of an opinion on the financial statements taken as a whole only when (s)he does not refer to the work of the other auditor. Answer (B) is incorrect because the other auditor is not relieved of the responsibility for his/her work. Answer (D) is incorrect because the other auditor is not relieved of the responsibility for his/her report.

**213.** Pell, CPA decides to serve as principal auditor in the audit of the financial statements of Tech Consolidated, Inc. Smith, CPA audits one of Tech's subsidiaries. In which situation(s) should Pell refer to Smith's audit?

I. Pell reviews Smith's audit documentation and assumes responsibility for Smith's work but expresses a qualified opinion on Tech's financial statements.

II. Pell is unable to review Smith's audit documentation; however, Pell's inquiries indicate that Smith has an excellent reputation for professional competence and integrity.

A. I only.

B. II only.

C. Both I and II.

D. Neither I nor II.

Answer (B) is correct. *(CPA, adapted)*

**REQUIRED:** The situation in which a principal auditor should refer to another auditor's audit.

**DISCUSSION:** Once the principal auditor becomes satisfied as to the independence and professional reputation of the other auditor, (s)he may decide to refer to the other auditor's audit because it may be impracticable for the principal auditor to review the other auditor's work or to use other procedures that (s)he deems necessary to obtain satisfaction as to the other auditor's audit. Such a reference indicates a division of responsibility between the auditors but does not prohibit an unqualified opinion (AU 543).

Answer (A) is incorrect because, if the principal auditor accepts responsibility for the other auditor's audit, (s)he should not state in the report that another auditor performed part of the audit. Such a reference might lead to misinterpretation of the degree of responsibility assumed. The type of opinion expressed is not relevant to the decision to make reference. Answer (C) is incorrect because, if the principal auditor accepts responsibility for the other auditor's audit, (s)he should not state in the report that another auditor performed part of the audit. Such a reference might lead to misinterpretation of the degree of responsibility assumed. The type of opinion expressed is not relevant to the decision to make reference. Answer (D) is incorrect because the principal auditor may refer to the other auditor's audit when (s)he wishes to divide responsibility.

**214.** An auditor's report contains the following: "We did not audit the financial statements of JK Company, a wholly owned subsidiary, whose statements reflect total assets and revenues constituting 17% and 19%, respectively, of the related consolidated totals. Those statements were audited by other auditors whose report has been furnished to us, and our opinion, insofar as it relates to the amounts included for JK Company, is based solely on the report of the other auditors." These sentences

A. Disclaim an opinion.

B. Qualify the opinion.

C. Divide responsibility.

D. Are an improper form of reporting.

Answer (C) is correct. *(CPA, adapted)*

**REQUIRED:** The effect of the quoted language in an auditor's report.

**DISCUSSION:** The quoted language is part of an introductory paragraph provided as an example in AU 543 of appropriately reporting the decision to refer to the work of another auditor. It meets the requirement that such reference indicate clearly the division of responsibility.

Answer (A) is incorrect because the last sentence refers to the expression of an opinion. Answer (B) is incorrect because the language cited does not preclude an unqualified or an adverse opinion. Answer (D) is incorrect because the wording is standard.

**215.** Regarding the magnitude of financial statements audited by the other auditor relative to the overall statements upon which the principal auditor expresses an opinion,

A. The dollar amounts or percentages of total assets, total revenues, or other appropriate criteria should be disclosed in the principal auditor's report.

B. The dollar amounts and percentages of at least total revenues and total assets must be disclosed in the principal auditor's report.

C. No mention is necessary unless approximately 50% or more of the assets or revenues are audited by the other auditor. Disclosure, if necessary, should be according to the appropriate criteria and reveal the portion of the financial statements audited by the other auditor.

D. No mention is necessary unless the audit report of the other auditor is not presented. Disclosure, if necessary, should be according to the appropriate criteria and reveal the portion of the financial statements audited by the other auditor.

Answer (A) is correct. *(Publisher)*

**REQUIRED:** The true statement about disclosure of the portion of the statements audited by another auditor.

**DISCUSSION:** When the principal auditor decides to refer to the work of another auditor, the report should indicate clearly, in the introductory, scope, and opinion paragraphs, the division of responsibility between that portion of the statements covered by his/her audit and that covered by the other auditor. The introductory paragraph of the report should disclose the magnitude of the portion audited by the other auditor by stating the dollar amounts or the percentages. A representation in the scope paragraph is also made that states, "We believe that our audits and the report of other auditors provide a reasonable basis for our opinion." The opinion paragraph states, "In our opinion, based on our audits, and the report of other auditors" (AU 508).

Answer (B) is incorrect because the magnitude of the other auditor's work may be stated either in dollar amounts or in percentages of total assets, total revenues, or other appropriate criteria. Answer (C) is incorrect because a principal auditor who refers to the audit of another auditor must disclose the portion of the statements audited by the other auditor. Answer (D) is incorrect because a principal auditor who refers to the audit of another auditor must disclose the portion of the statements audited by the other auditor.

**216.** An auditor may issue the standard audit report when the

A. Auditor refers to the findings of a specialist.

B. Financial statements are derived and condensed from complete audited financial statements that are filed with a regulatory agency.

C. Financial statements are prepared on the cash receipts and disbursements basis of accounting.

D. Principal auditor assumes responsibility for the work of another auditor.

Answer (D) is correct. *(CPA, adapted)*

**REQUIRED:** The situation in which an auditor may issue the standard audit report.

**DISCUSSION:** If the principal auditor can become satisfied regarding the independence, professional reputation, and the audit performed by the other auditor, (s)he may be able to express an opinion on the financial statements taken as a whole without referring to the audit of the other auditor. If (s)he assumes responsibility for the work of the other auditor, the report should not state that part of the audit was performed by another auditor. This reference could be misleading about the degree of responsibility assumed. In these circumstances, therefore, a standard report is appropriate (AU 543).

Answer (A) is incorrect because the auditor does not refer to a specialist unless (s)he departs from an unqualified opinion or adds an explanatory paragraph (AU 336). Answer (B) is incorrect because the report on condensed statements indicates that the auditor has audited and expressed an opinion on the complete statements, the date of that report, the type of opinion expressed therein, and "whether, in the auditor's opinion, the information set forth in the condensed financial statements is fairly stated in all material respects in relation to the complete financial statements from which it has been derived" (AU 552, *Reporting on Condensed Financial Statements and Selected Financial Data*). Answer (C) is incorrect because a special report may be appropriate.

**217.** In which of the following situations will a principal auditor be least likely to refer to another auditor who audited a subsidiary of the entity?

A. The other auditor was retained by the principal auditor and the work was performed under the principal auditor's guidance and control.

B. The principal auditor finds it impracticable to review the other auditor's work or otherwise be satisfied as to the other auditor's work.

C. The financial statements audited by the other auditor are material to the consolidated financial statements covered by the principal auditor's opinion.

D. The principal auditor is unable to be satisfied as to the independence and professional reputation of the other auditor.

Answer (A) is correct. *(CPA, adapted)*

**REQUIRED:** The situation in which a principal auditor is least likely to refer to another auditor.

**DISCUSSION:** The principal auditor normally does not refer to another auditor when the other auditor is an associate or correspondent firm whose work is acceptable to the principal auditor or when the other auditor was retained by the principal auditor and the work was performed under the principal auditor's guidance and control (AU 543).

Answer (B) is incorrect because, if the principal finds it impracticable to review the work of the other auditor, it is likely that the other auditor will be mentioned in the principal auditor's report. Answer (C) is incorrect because the more material the items audited by the other auditor, the more likely reference will be made in the principal auditor's report. Answer (D) is incorrect because, when the auditor cannot become satisfied as to the independence and professional reputation of the other auditor, the opinion should be qualified or an opinion should be disclaimed with respect to the financial statements taken as a whole.

**218.** Which of the following procedures will the principal auditor most likely perform after deciding to refer to another CPA who audited a subsidiary of the entity?

A. Review the audit documentation and the audit programs of the other CPA.

B. Visit the other CPA and discuss the results of the other CPA's audit procedures.

C. Make inquiries about the professional reputation and independence of the other CPA.

D. Determine that the other CPA has a sufficient understanding of the subsidiary's internal control.

Answer (C) is correct. *(CPA, adapted)*

**REQUIRED:** The procedure most likely to be performed after deciding to make reference to another auditor.

**DISCUSSION:** When the principal auditor decides to divide reporting responsibility and to make reference to another auditor, (s)he should inquire about the professional reputation and independence of the other auditor to one or more of the following: the AICPA, a state society, a local chapter, or a foreign auditor's corresponding professional organization; other practitioners; credit grantors; or other appropriate sources (AU 543).

Answer (A) is incorrect because, if the principal auditor decides not to divide responsibility and not make reference to the other auditor's audit in the report, (s)he should consider visiting the other auditor and reviewing the audit documentation and audit programs. Answer (B) is incorrect because, if the principal auditor decides not to divide responsibility and not make reference to the other auditor's audit in the report, (s)he should consider visiting the other auditor and reviewing the audit documentation and audit programs. Answer (D) is incorrect because, if the principal auditor decides to make reference to the audit of the other auditor, (s)he does not accept responsibility for the other auditor's work and need not test it.

**219.** Investor Co. has a material investment in Investee Co. that was accounted for by the equity method. Marr and Sons, CPAs, audit Investor but not Investee. Marr and Sons may express an unqualified opinion on Investor's financial statements if it

A. Reviews the audit documentation of Investee's auditor.

B. Obtains Investee's audited financial statements and make inquiries concerning the professional reputation and independence of Investee's auditor.

C. Obtains only Investee's audited financial statements.

D. Obtains only Investee's unaudited financial statements.

Answer (B) is correct. *(Publisher)*

**REQUIRED:** The requirement for the principal auditor to express an unqualified opinion when (s)he has not audited an equity investee.

**DISCUSSION:** With respect to investments accounted for under the equity method, the auditor who uses another auditor's report to report on the client's equity and share of earnings or losses is in the position of a principal auditor. But whether or not the principal auditor wishes to refer to the work of the other auditor, (s)he must make inquiries as to the professional reputation and independence of the other auditor (AU 543). Furthermore, the principal auditor may not express an unqualified opinion when an investment is material unless (s)he has acquired sufficient competent evidence about assertions relevant to the investment. The inability to obtain audited statements of the investee is a common scope limitation that would preclude an unqualified opinion (AU 508).

Answer (A) is incorrect because the principal auditor typically reviews the other auditor's audit documentation only if (s)he decides not to refer to the audit performed by the other auditor. The decision to refer is likely in this case because the investment is material, and Investor's auditor has not audited the investee. Answer (C) is incorrect because the principal auditor must inquire as to the reputation and professional standing of the other auditor as well as obtain audited statements. Answer (D) is incorrect because the principal auditor must inquire as to the reputation and professional standing of the other auditor as well as obtain audited statements.

**220.** Thomas, CPA, has audited the consolidated financial statements of Kass Corporation. Jones, CPA, has audited the financial statements of its sole subsidiary, which is material in relation to the total audited by Thomas. It would be appropriate for Thomas to serve as the principal auditor, but it is impracticable for Thomas to review the work of Jones. Assuming an unqualified opinion is expressed by Jones, Thomas should

A. Refuse to express an opinion on the consolidated financial statements.

B. Express an unqualified opinion on the consolidated financial statements and not refer to the work of Jones.

C. Express an unqualified opinion on the consolidated financial statements and refer to the work of Jones.

D. Express a qualified opinion on the consolidated financial statements as a result of referring to the work of Jones.

Answer (C) is correct. *(CPA, adapted)*

**REQUIRED:** The action by the principal auditor when (s)he cannot review the work of another auditor.

**DISCUSSION:** Once the principal auditor is able to become satisfied as to the independence and professional reputation of the other auditor, (s)he may decide to refer to the other auditor's audit because it may be impracticable for the principal auditor to review the other auditor's work or to use other procedures that (s)he deems necessary to obtain satisfaction as to the other auditor's audit. Such a reference indicates a division of responsibility between the auditors. The reference to the other auditor does not prohibit an unqualified opinion (AU 543).

Answer (A) is incorrect because the principal auditor should not refuse to express an opinion; part of an audit may be made by other independent auditors. Answer (B) is incorrect because the principal auditor must refer to the other auditor unless (s)he takes steps (s)he deems appropriate to become satisfied as to the other auditor's audit. Answer (D) is incorrect because the reference to another auditor is not a qualification.

**221.** When the report of a principal auditor refers to the audit by another auditor, the other auditor may be named if express permission to do so is given and if the

A. Report of the principal auditor names the other auditor in both the introductory and opinion paragraphs.

B. Principal auditor accepts responsibility for the work of the other auditor.

C. Report of the other auditor is presented together with the report of the principal auditor.

D. Other auditor is not an associate or correspondent firm whose work is done at the request of the principal auditor.

Answer (C) is correct. *(CPA, adapted)*

**REQUIRED:** The circumstances in which a principal auditor may name the other auditor.

**DISCUSSION:** The other auditor may be named but only with his/her express permission and provided his/her report is presented together with that of the principal auditor (AU 543).

Answer (A) is incorrect because the principal auditor may divide responsibility but should refer to other auditors in the report instead of naming them unless certain conditions are met. Answer (B) is incorrect because, if the principal auditor accepts responsibility for the work of the other auditor, no mention should be made of the other auditor. Answer (D) is incorrect because the other auditor named by the principal auditor may be an associate or a correspondent firm. However, the principal auditor is more likely not to refer to the other auditor in such a case.

**222.** The principal auditor of consolidated financial statements has become satisfied about the independence and professional reputation of an auditor who has audited a subsidiary included in the consolidated group. The principal auditor has also become satisfied about the audit performed by the other auditor. The report of the other auditor expressed a qualified opinion, but the principal auditor believes the qualification to be immaterial in regard to the consolidated financial statements. Accordingly, the principal auditor

A. May express an unqualified opinion but must include a separate paragraph describing the other auditor's report.

B. Must express a qualified opinion but need not refer to the audit of the other auditor.

C. Must express a qualified opinion and refer to the audit of the other auditor.

D. Need not refer to the audit of the other auditor.

Answer (D) is correct. *(Publisher)*

**REQUIRED:** The recognition given by the principal auditor to an immaterial qualification by another auditor.

**DISCUSSION:** The principal auditor need not refer to the audit of the other auditor if (s)he is willing to accept responsibility for the other auditor's work. Because the qualification stated by the other auditor is immaterial to the consolidated financial statements, it need not cause a qualification of the opinion.

Answer (A) is incorrect because, given that the other auditor's qualification is not material to the consolidated statements, the principal auditor need not refer to the other auditor's audit or qualify the opinion. Answer (B) is incorrect because, given that the other auditor's qualification is not material to the consolidated statements, the principal auditor need not refer to the other auditor's audit or qualify the opinion. Answer (C) is incorrect because, given that the other auditor's qualification is not material to the consolidated statements, the principal auditor need not refer to the other auditor's audit or qualify the opinion.

**223.** AU 543 gives guidance to a principal auditor on making inquiries of the other auditor. It also states that the other auditor remains responsible for the performance of his/her work and report. To fulfill that responsibility, the other auditor

A. May make inquiries of the principal auditor.

B. Must make inquiries of the principal auditor.

C. May not make inquiries of the principal auditor.

D. May make inquiries but only if the principal auditor has initiated the communication.

Answer (A) is correct. *(Publisher)*

**REQUIRED:** The true statement about inquiries made by other auditors of the principal auditor.

**DISCUSSION:** Before issuing the report, the other auditor should consider whether (s)he should inquire of the principal auditor as to matters that may be significant to his/her audit. The other auditor's consideration of whether to make the inquiry may be based on various factors. One such factor might be the existence of unusual or complex transactions or relationships between the component (s)he is auditing and the component the principal auditor is auditing. Another factor to be considered is the knowledge that, in the past, matters relating to his/her audit have arisen that were known to the principal auditor but not to him/her (AU 543).

Answer (B) is incorrect because inquiries by other auditors of principal auditors are allowed but not required. Answer (C) is incorrect because inquiries by other auditors of principal auditors are allowed but not required. Answer (D) is incorrect because inquiries by other auditors of principal auditors are allowed but not required.

# STUDY UNIT EIGHT
# SPECIAL REPORTS AND OTHER REPORTING ISSUES



This Study Unit includes questions on miscellaneous reporting issues. These include special reports, compilations, reviews, reports on internal control, letters to underwriters, and governmental auditing.

**QUESTIONS**

**8.1 Definition and Purpose of Special Reports**

**1.** Auditors may issue a special report for all of the following except an audit of financial presentations

A. That are prepared on a basis of accounting that the entity uses to file its tax return.

B. Of specified elements or accounts.

C. Of an organization that has limited the scope of the audit.

D. To comply with contractual agreements.

Answer (C) is correct. *(Publisher)*

**REQUIRED:** The report not considered a special report.

**DISCUSSION:** Special reports are issued in connection with (1) statements prepared in accordance with a comprehensive basis of accounting other than GAAP; (2) specified elements, accounts, or items of a statement; (3) compliance with aspects of contractual agreements or regulatory requirements related to audited statements; (4) financial presentations to comply with contractual agreements or regulatory provisions; and (5) financial information presented in prescribed forms that require a prescribed form of auditor's report (AU 623, *Special Reports*). A limitation imposed by the client on the scope of the audit is therefore not a proper basis for issuing a special report.

Answer (A) is incorrect because the tax basis is a comprehensive basis other than GAAP. Answer (B) is incorrect because special reports include those on specified elements, accounts, or items. Answer (D) is incorrect because special reports include those on financial presentations to comply with contractual agreements.

**2.** For reporting purposes, the independent auditor should consider each of the following types of financial presentation to be a financial statement, except the statement of

A. Changes in equity.

B. Operations by product lines.

C. Changes in the elements of working capital.

D. Cash receipts and disbursements.

Answer (C) is correct. *(CPA, adapted)*

**REQUIRED:** The presentation not a financial statement.

**DISCUSSION:** AU 623 defines a financial statement as a "presentation of financial data, including accompanying notes, derived from accounting records and intended to communicate an entity's economic resources or obligations at a moment in time or the changes therein for a period of time in accordance with a comprehensive basis of accounting." AU 623 lists ten types of financial statements but excludes the statement of changes in working capital.

Answer (A) is incorrect because statements of changes in equity are financial statements. Answer (B) is incorrect because statements of operations by product lines are financial statements. Answer (D) is incorrect because statements of cash receipts and disbursements are financial statements.

**3.** An auditor's report is designated a special report when it is issued in connection with

A. A review of interim financial information of a publicly held company.

B. Compliance with aspects of regulatory requirements related to audited financial statements.

C. Application of accounting principles to specified transactions.

D. Limited use prospective financial statements such as financial projection.

Answer (B) is correct. *(CPA, adapted)*

**REQUIRED:** The service resulting in a special report.

**DISCUSSION:** Entities may be required by contractual agreements, such as bond indentures, or by regulatory agencies to furnish compliance reports by independent auditors. Reports based upon compliance with aspects of contractual agreements or regulatory provisions should be provided in conjunction with an ordinary audit of financial statements. The report envisioned provides negative assurance that may be given in the report on the financial statements or in a separate report. But this assurance should not extend to any covenants relating to matters that have not been subjected to audit procedures (AU 623).

Answer (A) is incorrect because AU 722, *Interim Financial Information*, applies to reviews of interim financial information. Answer (C) is incorrect because a report on the application of accounting principles is governed by AU 625, *Reports on the Application of Accounting Principles*. Answer (D) is incorrect because AT 301, *Financial Forecasts and Projections*, applies to projections.

**4.** Auditors' reports issued in connection with which of the following are not considered to be special reports?

A. Specified elements, accounts, or items of a financial statement.

B. Compliance with aspects of contractual agreements related to audited financial statements.

C. Financial statements prepared in conformity with the price-level basis of accounting.

D. Compiled financial statements prepared in accordance with appraised liquidation values.

Answer (D) is correct. *(CPA, adapted)*

**REQUIRED:** The improper basis for a special report.

**DISCUSSION:** Special reports relate to (1) statements prepared in accordance with a comprehensive basis of accounting other than GAAP; (2) specified elements, accounts, or items of a statement; (3) compliance with aspects of contractual agreements or regulatory requirements related to audited statements; (4) financial presentations to comply with contractual agreements or regulatory provisions; and (5) financial information presented in prescribed forms (AU 623). Appraised liquidation values are not usually considered a comprehensive basis of accounting other than GAAP.

Answer (A) is incorrect because a special report may be issued on specified elements, accounts, or items of a financial statement. Answer (B) is incorrect because a special report may be issued on compliance with contractual agreements. Answer (C) is incorrect because a special report may be issued on price-level basis financial statements.

**5.** An auditor should provide a list of procedures performed and related findings but should not provide an opinion or negative assurance about fair presentation when (s)he is requested to report on the

A. Compilation of prospective financial statements.

B. Compliance with the provisions of the Foreign Corrupt Practices Act.

C. Results of applying agreed-upon procedures to an account within unaudited financial statements.

D. Audit of historical financial statements.

Answer (C) is correct. *(CPA, adapted)*

**REQUIRED:** The report in which a list of procedures and related findings is provided but an opinion or negative assurance is not.

**DISCUSSION:** An engagement to perform specific agreed-upon procedures on the specific subject matter of specified elements, accounts, or items of a financial statement does not entail performance of an audit. The auditor does not express an opinion or provide negative assurance about fair presentation of the specified elements, accounts, or items. For example, the auditor should not state "nothing came to my attention that caused me to believe that the specified element, account, or item is not fairly stated in accordance with GAAP." Moreover, the absence of an exception should also not be expressed in the form of negative assurance. Instead, the report should be in the form of procedures and findings.

Answer (A) is incorrect because a compilation provides no findings. Answer (B) is incorrect because an auditor should not provide findings about compliance with the FCPA. Such compliance requires a legal determination (AT 501, *Reporting on an Entity's Internal Control over Financial Reporting*). Answer (D) is incorrect because an audit is a form of examination. It is undertaken to afford a reasonable basis for a positive opinion (AT 101, *Attest Engagements*).

**6.** An auditor's report on financial statements prepared in accordance with a comprehensive basis of accounting other than GAAP should include all of the following except

A. Reference to the note to the financial statements that describes the basis of presentation.

B. A statement that the basis of presentation is a comprehensive basis of accounting other than GAAP.

C. An opinion as to whether the basis of accounting used is appropriate under the circumstances.

D. An opinion as to whether the financial statements are presented fairly, in all material respects, in conformity with the other comprehensive basis of accounting.

Answer (C) is correct. *(CPA, adapted)*

**REQUIRED:** The item not in a report on statements prepared on a comprehensive basis other than GAAP.

**DISCUSSION:** In a report on such statements, the independent auditor should include a title with the word independent; a paragraph stating that the statements were audited, that the financial statements are the responsibility of management, and that the auditor is responsible for expressing an opinion thereon; a scope paragraph; a paragraph stating the basis of the presentation, referring to the note describing that basis, and stating that the basis is a comprehensive one other than GAAP; a paragraph expressing or disclaiming an opinion (an explanatory paragraph(s) may be needed); and, in some cases, a paragraph restricting use. The auditor should not express an opinion on the propriety of the basis of accounting used.

Answer (A) is incorrect because the report should refer to the note describing the basis of accounting. Answer (B) is incorrect because the report should state that the basis of accounting is not GAAP. Answer (D) is incorrect because the report should express an opinion.

**7.** Which of the generally accepted auditing standards of reporting normally applies to an auditor's special report on cash-basis statements?

| | Conformity with GAAP | Consistency | Adequacy of Disclosure |
|---|---|---|---|
| A. | No | Yes | Yes |
| B. | Yes | Yes | Yes |
| C. | No | No | Yes |
| D. | No | No | No |

Answer (A) is correct. *(Publisher)*

**REQUIRED:** The GAAS applicable to special reports on cash-basis statements.

**DISCUSSION:** According to AU 623, an auditor should indicate in the report that the financial statements on which (s)he is reporting are prepared on a comprehensive basis of accounting other than GAAP. The cash basis is such a comprehensive basis. The first reporting standard, which is concerned with whether the financial statements are presented in accordance with GAAP, therefore does not apply (AU 150, *Generally Accepted Auditing Standards*). However, the second reporting standard (consistency), the third standard (disclosure), and the fourth (regarding the degree of responsibility taken) are applicable.

**8.** When an auditor reports on financial statements prepared on an entity's income tax basis, the auditor's report should

A. Disclaim an opinion on whether the statements were examined in accordance with generally accepted auditing standards.

B. Not express an opinion on whether the statements are presented in conformity with the other comprehensive basis of accounting (OCBOA) used.

C. Include an explanation of how the results of operations differ from the cash receipts and disbursements basis of accounting.

D. State that the basis of presentation is a comprehensive basis of accounting other than GAAP.

Answer (D) is correct. *(CPA, adapted)*

**REQUIRED:** The content of a report on financial statements prepared on the income tax basis.

**DISCUSSION:** A separate paragraph of the auditor's special report on financial statements prepared on a comprehensive basis of accounting other than GAAP, e.g., the income tax basis, should state the basis of the presentation, refer to a note to the statements explaining the basis chosen, and state that the basis of the presentation is a comprehensive basis other than GAAP. An OCBOA may be the tax basis, the cash basis, the requirements of a regulatory agency, or a definite set of criteria having substantial support and applied to all material financial statement items (AU 623).

Answer (A) is incorrect because the auditor applies GAAS in the engagement. Answer (B) is incorrect because the auditor expresses an opinion on whether the statements are presented in conformity with the OCBOA. Answer (C) is incorrect because a note in the financial statements should explain how the basis of accounting differs from GAAP, but the report need only refer to that note.

**9.** Delta Life Insurance Co. prepares its financial statements on an accounting basis insurance companies use pursuant to the rules of a state insurance commission. If Wall, CPA, Delta's auditor, discovers that the statements are not suitably titled, Wall should

A. Disclose any reservations in an explanatory paragraph and qualify the opinion.

B. Apply to the state insurance commission for an advisory opinion.

C. Issue a special statutory basis report that clearly disclaims any opinion.

D. Explain in the notes to the financial statements the terminology used.

Answer (A) is correct. *(CPA, adapted)*

**REQUIRED:** The proper action when statements prepared on an OCBOA are not suitably titled.

**DISCUSSION:** Terms such as balance sheet, statement of income, or similar unmodified titles are ordinarily understood to apply to statements presented in conformity with GAAP. Consequently, the auditor of statements prepared under an OCBOA should consider whether the statements are suitably titled. If (s)he believes they are not, the auditor should disclose any reservations in an explanatory paragraph and qualify the opinion (AU 623).

Answer (B) is incorrect because AU 623 does not require the auditor to apply to the state insurance commission for an advisory opinion. Answer (C) is incorrect because the opinion should be qualified. Answer (D) is incorrect because the notes are the responsibility of management, not the auditor.

**10.** An auditor is reporting on cash-basis financial statements. These statements are best referred to in the opinion by which of the following descriptions?

A. "Financial position" and "results of operations arising from cash transactions."

B. "Assets and liabilities arising from cash transactions" and "revenue collected and expenses paid."

C. "Balance sheet" and "income statement resulting from cash transactions."

D. "Cash balance sheet" and "statement of cash flows."

Answer (B) is correct. *(CPA, adapted)*

**REQUIRED:** The best description of cash-basis financial statements in an auditor's report.

**DISCUSSION:** Terms such as balance sheet, statement of financial position, statement of operations, income statement, statement of cash flows, and similar unmodified titles suggest that the statements were prepared in conformity with GAAP. According to AU 623, appropriate titles for comparable cash-basis statements are statement of assets and liabilities arising from cash transactions and statement of revenue collected and expenses paid.

Answer (A) is incorrect because terms such as financial position and results of operations imply that the statements were prepared in conformity with GAAP. Answer (C) is incorrect because terms such as balance sheet and income statement imply that the statements were prepared in conformity with GAAP. Answer (D) is incorrect because terms such as balance sheet and statement of cash flows imply that the statements were prepared in conformity with GAAP.

**11.** Which of the following statements is true with respect to an auditor's report expressing an opinion on a specific item on a financial statement?

A. Materiality must be related to the specified item rather than to the financial statements taken as a whole.

B. Such a report can only be issued if the auditor is also engaged to audit the entire set of financial statements.

C. The attention devoted to the specified item is usually less than it would be if the financial statements as a whole were being audited.

D. The auditor who has expressed an adverse opinion on the financial statements as a whole can never express an opinion on a specified item in these financial statements.

Answer (A) is correct. *(CPA, adapted)*

**REQUIRED:** The true statement about expressing an opinion on specified elements of financial statements.

**DISCUSSION:** In an engagement to express an opinion on one or more specified elements, accounts, or items of a financial statement, materiality must be measured in relation to each element, account, or item reported on rather than in relation to their aggregate or to the financial statements as a whole (AU 623).

Answer (B) is incorrect because this form of special report is not contingent upon a complete audit. Answer (C) is incorrect because the attention devoted to the specified item is usually greater (not less). Answer (D) is incorrect because, although piecemeal opinions are prohibited, the auditor is allowed to express an opinion on specific items after expressing an adverse opinion if the specified items do not constitute a major portion of the financial statements.

**12.** Whenever a special report, filed on a printed form designed by authorities, calls upon the independent auditor to make an assertion that the auditor believes is not justified, the auditor should

A. Reword the form or attach a separate report.

B. Submit a standard report with explanations.

C. Submit the form with questionable items clearly omitted.

D. Withdraw from the engagement.

Answer (A) is correct. *(CPA, adapted)*

**REQUIRED:** The auditor action when asked to make an unjustified assertion in a prescribed form.

**DISCUSSION:** Printed forms designed by the agencies or other authorities that they will be filed with often prescribe the wording of the auditor's report. Many are unacceptable to auditors because they conflict with reporting standards. When a report form calls for an unjustified assertion, an auditor should reword the form or attach a separate report (AU 623).

Answer (B) is incorrect because a standard report is not appropriate for a special reporting situation. Answer (C) is incorrect because omission of questionable items does not meet the auditor's reporting responsibility; these items should be resolved. Answer (D) is incorrect because withdrawal from the engagement is an extreme measure unnecessary in most circumstances.

**13.** An auditor may express an opinion on an entity's accounts receivable balance even if the auditor has disclaimed an opinion on the financial statements taken as a whole, provided that the

A. Report on the accounts receivable discloses the reason for the disclaimer of opinion on the financial statements.

B. Distribution of the report on the accounts receivable is restricted to internal use only.

C. Auditor also reports on the current asset portion of the entity's balance sheet.

D. Report on the accounts receivable is presented separately from the disclaimer of opinion on the financial statements.

Answer (D) is correct. *(CPA, adapted)*

**REQUIRED:** The condition for expressing an opinion on an account balance despite disclaiming an opinion on the financial statements as a whole.

**DISCUSSION:** An auditor may be requested to express an opinion on one or more specified elements, accounts, or items of a financial statement. The report should be a special report (AU 623). However, the auditor may not express such an opinion after disclaiming an opinion on the financial statements if such reporting is tantamount to a piecemeal opinion on the financial statements. Nevertheless, an auditor may be able to express an opinion in these circumstances if a major portion of the financial statements is not involved. For example, an auditor who has disclaimed an opinion on the financial statements may be able to express an opinion on the accounts receivable balance. Moreover, the report should be presented separately.

Answer (A) is incorrect because the report on accounts receivable should disclose the departure from the standard report on the financial statements if it is considered relevant, but any reasons for the departure need not be described. Answer (B) is incorrect because the report need not be restricted to internal use unless the presentation does not conform with GAAP or another comprehensive basis of accounting. Answer (C) is incorrect because a report may be presented on one or more specified elements, accounts, or items of a financial statement.

## 8.2 Condensed Statements and Other, Supplementary, and Accompanying Information

**14.** Which of the following best describes "other information" in documents containing audited financial statements?

A. Supplemental information required by GAAP.

B. Information contained in a registration statement filed under the Securities Act of 1933.

C. Information presented in addition to the audited financial statements, such as the president's letter, history of the firm, and explanatory material.

D. Notes to the financial statements.

Answer (C) is correct. *(Publisher)*

**REQUIRED:** The best description of other information.

**DISCUSSION:** An entity may publish various documents that contain information in addition to audited financial statements. This material is defined as other information by AU 550, *Other Information in Documents Containing Audited Financial Statements.*

Answer (A) is incorrect because the auditor's responsibilities regarding supplementary information required by GAAP differ from those regarding other information. Answer (B) is incorrect because AU 550 does not apply to registration statements. Rather, the procedures described in AU 711, *Filings under Federal Securities Statutes*, should be followed. Answer (D) is incorrect because the notes are integral to the statements.

**15.** The other information in a published report containing audited financial statements may be relevant to an independent auditor. With respect to other information,

A. The auditor's responsibility does not extend beyond the financial information identified in the report.

B. The auditor is obligated to perform auditing procedures to corroborate other information contained in a document.

C. The auditor need not be concerned with the other information.

D. The auditor must include the other information in the report.

Answer (A) is correct. *(Publisher)*

**REQUIRED:** The auditor's responsibility for other information.

**DISCUSSION:** AU 550 states that the auditor's responsibility does not extend beyond the financial information identified in his/her report. AU 550 is not applicable, however, to SEC registration statements.

Answer (B) is incorrect because the auditor need not perform auditing procedures to corroborate other information. Answer (C) is incorrect because the auditor should read the other information and consider whether it or its presentation is materially inconsistent with the audited financial statements. Answer (D) is incorrect because such information ordinarily is not included. However, one of the auditor's options when the other information is materially inconsistent with the audited statements and the client does not revise it is to include an explanatory paragraph.

**16.** When audited financial statements are presented in a document containing other information, the auditor

A. Has an obligation to perform auditing procedures to corroborate the other information.

B. Is required to express a qualified opinion if the other information has a material misstatement of fact.

C. Should read the other information to consider whether it is inconsistent with the audited financial statements.

D. Has no responsibility for the other information because it is not part of the basic financial statements.

Answer (C) is correct. *(CPA, adapted)*

**REQUIRED:** The auditor's responsibility for other information.

**DISCUSSION:** AU 550 states that the auditor should read the other information and consider whether it and its manner of presentation are consistent with the financial statements on which (s)he is expressing an opinion or whether it contains a material misstatement. AU 550 is not applicable, however, to registration statements.

Answer (A) is incorrect because the auditor must read but need not corroborate the other information. Answer (B) is incorrect because, if the audited information is presented fairly, the opinion should be unqualified. However, the auditor should request the client to revise other information that is materially misstated. If revision is not made, (s)he should consider modifying the report to include an explanatory paragraph, withholding use of the report, or withdrawing from the engagement. However, if auditing procedures have been applied to the other information in the audit of the basic statements, the auditor may express an opinion on whether it is fairly stated in all material respects in relation to those statements. Answer (D) is incorrect because the auditor should read the other information to consider whether it is inconsistent with the audited financial statements.

**17.** An auditor concludes that there is a material inconsistency in the other information in an annual report to shareholders containing audited financial statements. If the auditor concludes that the financial statements do not require revision, but the client refuses to revise or eliminate the material inconsistency, the auditor may

A. Revise the auditor's report to include a separate explanatory paragraph describing the material inconsistency.

B. Express a qualified opinion after discussing the matter with the client's directors.

C. Consider the matter closed because the other information is not in the audited statements.

D. Disclaim an opinion on the financial statements after explaining the material inconsistency in a separate paragraph.

Answer (A) is correct. *(CPA, adapted)*

**REQUIRED:** The auditor action when the client presents other information with a material inconsistency.

**DISCUSSION:** If the other information contains a material inconsistency, the auditor should determine whether the statements or the report need revision. If they do not, (s)he should request the client to revise the other information. If revision is not made, (s)he should consider revising the report to include an explanatory paragraph, withholding use of the report, or withdrawing from the engagement. The action taken will depend on the circumstances and the significance of the inconsistency.

Answer (B) is incorrect because the opinion is expressed on the financial statements only. The inconsistency in the other information does not affect that opinion. However, if auditing procedures have been applied to the other information in the audit of the basic statements, the auditor may express an opinion on whether the other information is fairly stated in all material respects in relation to the statements. Answer (C) is incorrect because the auditor may not ignore a material inconsistency in other information. Answer (D) is incorrect because the auditor's decision to disclaim an opinion is not affected by the other information.

**18.** The auditor's inquiries of management regarding required supplementary information (RSI) should be directed to the judgments made concerning

A. Relevance and validity.

B. Measurement and presentation.

C. Accuracy and objectivity.

D. Rights and obligations.

Answer (B) is correct. *(CPA, adapted)*

**REQUIRED:** The direction of auditor inquiries about RSI.

**DISCUSSION:** Certain entities may be required by GAAP to present supplementary information. Thus, authoritative guidelines for its measurement and presentation have been established. The auditor should inquire about (1) whether the RSI is within the guidelines, (2) whether methods of measurement or presentation have changed and the reasons for any change, and (3) any significant assumptions or interpretations (AU 558, *Required Supplementary Information*).

Answer (A) is incorrect because the relevance of data is for management to decide. The validity of assertions is a concern in an audit. Answer (C) is incorrect because AU 558 specifically refers to measurement and presentation rather than accuracy and objectivity. Answer (D) is incorrect because an auditor's concern with rights and obligations is appropriate to an audit of basic financial statements.

**19.** What is an auditor's responsibility for required supplementary information (RSI) that is placed outside the basic financial statements?

A. Label the information as unaudited and expand the auditor's report to include a disclaimer on the information.

B. Add an explanatory paragraph to the auditor's report and refer to the information as RSI.

C. Apply limited procedures to the information and report deficiencies in, or the omission of, the information.

D. Audit the RSI in accordance with applicable auditing standards.

Answer (C) is correct. *(CPA, adapted)*

**REQUIRED:** The auditor's responsibility for RSI.

**DISCUSSION:** RSI differs from other information outside the basic statements because GAAP consider it to be an essential part of the financial reporting of certain entities. The auditor at minimum should apply limited procedures and should report deficiencies in, or the omission of, such information. However, an auditor is permitted to express an opinion on the RSI in relation to the basic statements as a whole. In that case, the RSI must have been subjected to the audit procedures performed in the audit of the basic statements (AU 558).

Answer (A) is incorrect because only if the RSI is not presented outside the basic financial statements should it be labeled as unaudited. If the information is presented within the financial statements and is not clearly labeled, the auditor should expand the report to include a disclaimer. Answer (B) is incorrect because an explanatory paragraph should not be added unless (1) the information is omitted, (2) the information departs materially from prescribed guidelines, (3) the prescribed procedures were not completed by the auditor, or (4) there are unresolved substantial doubts about adherence to prescribed guidelines. Answer (D) is incorrect because RSI need not be audited. However, if auditing procedures have been applied to the RSI in the audit of the basic statements, the auditor may express an opinion on whether it is fairly stated in all material respects in relation to those statements.

**20.** If management declines to present supplementary information required by generally accepted accounting principles, the auditor should express

A. An adverse opinion.

B. A qualified opinion with an explanatory paragraph.

C. An unqualified opinion.

D. An unqualified opinion with an additional explanatory paragraph.

Answer (D) is correct. *(CPA, adapted)*

**REQUIRED:** The effect on the opinion of the client's failure to disclose RSI.

**DISCUSSION:** Failure to present supplementary information required by GAAP does not affect the auditor's opinion because such information does not change the standards of financial accounting and reporting that were followed in preparing the financial statements. Instead, the auditor should express an unqualified opinion with an additional explanatory paragraph stating that supplementary information required by accounting principles generally accepted in the U.S. was omitted. The information itself need not be presented by the auditor (AU 558).

Answer (A) is incorrect because the auditor should expand the report but not change the opinion. Answer (B) is incorrect because the auditor should expand the report but not change the opinion. Answer (C) is incorrect because the opinion should include an additional explanatory paragraph.

**21.** If management chooses to place required supplementary information (RSI) in the notes attached to the financial statements, this information should be clearly marked as

A. Unaudited.

B. Supplementary information required by GAAP.

C. Disclosures required by GAAP.

D. Audited financial data required by generally accepted accounting principles.

Answer (A) is correct. *(CPA, adapted)*

**REQUIRED:** The proper marking of RSI.

**DISCUSSION:** RSI should be distinct from the audited statements, but management may choose not to place it outside of the basic financial statements. In that event, unless it is audited as part of those statements, the RSI should be clearly marked as unaudited. If it is not, the report must be expanded to include a disclaimer on the information (AU 558).

Answer (B) is incorrect because, although RSI should be clearly identifiable, much flexibility is allowed regarding presentation. However, it must be clearly marked as unaudited if it appears in the notes. Answer (C) is incorrect because the auditing standards do not prescribe how RSI should be identified, only that it be labeled as unaudited. Answer (D) is incorrect because RSI may not be audited, although the auditor should apply certain limited procedures.

**22.** Which of the following best describes the auditor's reporting responsibility concerning information accompanying the basic financial statements in an auditor-submitted document?

A. The auditor has no reporting responsibility concerning information accompanying the basic financial statements.

B. The auditor should report on the information accompanying the basic financial statements only if the auditor participated in its preparation.

C. The auditor must disclaim an opinion on the information if it is supplementary information required by GAAP.

D. The auditor should report on all the information included in the document.

Answer (D) is correct. *(CPA, adapted)*

**REQUIRED:** The auditor's reporting responsibility for information accompanying the basic financial statements.

**DISCUSSION:** AU 551, *Reporting on Information Accompanying the Basic Financial Statements in Auditor-Submitted Documents*, concerns information presented outside the basic statements and not deemed necessary for their fair presentation in conformity with GAAP, e.g., additional details or explanations of items in or related to the statements, consolidating information, statistical data, historical summaries, etc. However, when an auditor submits a document containing audited financial statements to the client or to others, (s)he must report on all the information included in the document.

Answer (A) is incorrect because the auditor has an unconditional obligation to report on all information in an auditor-submitted document. Answer (B) is incorrect because the auditor has an unconditional obligation to report on all information in an auditor-submitted document. Answer (C) is incorrect because the auditor has three options: (1) disclaim an opinion; (2) express an opinion if the auditor has been engaged to examine the RSI; or (3) express an opinion on whether the RSI is fairly stated in all material respects in relation to the basic statements as a whole, provided that auditing procedures have been applied to the RSI in the audit of those statements.

**23.** Investment and property schedules are presented for purposes of additional analysis in an auditor-submitted document. The schedules are not required parts of the basic financial statements, but accompany the basic financial statements. When reporting on such additional information, the measurement of materiality is the

A. Same as that used in forming an opinion on the basic financial statements as a whole.

B. Lesser of the individual schedule of investments or schedule of property by itself.

C. Greater of the individual schedule of investments or schedule of property by itself.

D. Combined total of both the individual schedules of investments and property as a whole.

Answer (A) is correct. *(CPA, adapted)*

**REQUIRED:** The measure of materiality required for the purpose of reporting on information presented for additional analysis in an auditor-submitted document.

**DISCUSSION:** "When reporting in this manner, the measurement of materiality is the same as that used in forming an opinion on the basic financial statements taken as a whole. Accordingly, the auditor need not apply procedures as extensive as would be necessary to express an opinion on the information taken by itself" (AU 551).

**24.** When financial statements audited by the independent auditor contain notes that are captioned "unaudited" or "not covered by the auditor's report," the auditor

A. May refer to these notes in the auditor's report.

B. Has no responsibility with respect to information contained in these notes.

C. Must refer to these notes in the auditor's report.

D. Is precluded from referring to these notes in the auditor's report.

Answer (A) is correct. *(CPA, adapted)*

**REQUIRED:** The auditor's responsibility when financial statements include notes labeled "unaudited."

**DISCUSSION:** Financial statements sometimes contain unaudited information, such as pro forma calculations or other similar disclosures. If these disclosures are unnecessary to fair presentation of the statements, they may be identified as "unaudited" or "not covered by the auditor's report" (AU 508). If they are properly identified, the auditor is not required by any pronouncement to refer to them in the report. However, a reference to these notes is not expressly prohibited. If the content is inconsistent with the financial statements or otherwise misleading, the auditor should provide an explanation in a separate explanatory paragraph.

Answer (B) is incorrect because the auditor must ascertain that unaudited notes are clearly labeled as unaudited. Answer (C) is incorrect because the auditor may, but is not required to, refer to unaudited notes in the report. Answer (D) is incorrect because the auditor may, but is not required to, refer to unaudited notes in the report.

**25.** According to AU 552, *Reporting on Condensed Financial Statements and Selected Financial Data*, an auditor should

A. Issue the same report on both the condensed statements and the complete statements from which they are derived.

B. Express no opinion on the condensed statements.

C. Not report on selected financial data derived from audited financial statements.

D. Express an opinion as to whether the selected financial data were fairly stated.

Answer (D) is correct. *(Publisher)*

**REQUIRED:** The auditor's obligation regarding condensed statements and selected financial data.

**DISCUSSION:** AU 552 concerns reporting in a client-prepared document on (1) condensed statements derived from audited statements of a public entity required to file complete audited statements with a regulatory agency and (2) selected financial data of a public or nonpublic entity. The auditor's report should indicate that the auditor has expressed an opinion on the complete statements, the type of opinion expressed, and an opinion as to whether the information set forth is fairly stated in all material respects in relation to the complete statements. In the case of condensed statements, the report should also indicate the date of the report on the complete statements.

Answer (A) is incorrect because the report on condensed statements is typically a two-paragraph report. Answer (B) is incorrect because an opinion is expressed stating that the information is fairly stated in all material respects in relation to the complete statements. Answer (C) is incorrect because a report on selected financial data must be presented.

**26.** In the standard report on condensed financial statements that are derived from a public entity's audited financial statements, a CPA should indicate that the

A. Condensed financial statements are prepared in conformity with another comprehensive basis of accounting.

B. CPA has audited and expressed an opinion on the complete financial statements.

C. Condensed financial statements are not fairly presented in all material respects.

D. CPA expresses limited assurance that the financial statements conform with GAAP.

Answer (B) is correct. *(CPA, adapted)*

**REQUIRED:** The indication in a standard report on condensed financial statements.

**DISCUSSION:** The report should state that the auditor has audited and expressed an opinion on the complete statements, the date of that report, the type of opinion expressed, and an opinion as to whether the condensed statements are fairly stated in all material respects in relation to the complete statements (AU 552).

Answer (A) is incorrect because condensed financial statements are prepared from GAAP-based financial statements. Answer (C) is incorrect because condensed financial statements may be fairly presented. Answer (D) is incorrect because the CPA expresses an opinion.

## 8.3 Interim Financial Information

**27.** The objective of a review of interim financial information of a public entity is to provide an accountant with a basis for reporting whether

A. A reasonable basis exists for expressing an updated opinion regarding the financial statements that were previously audited.

B. Material modifications should be made to conform with generally accepted accounting principles.

C. The financial statements are presented fairly in accordance with standards of interim reporting.

D. The financial statements are presented fairly in accordance with generally accepted accounting principles.

Answer (B) is correct. *(CPA, adapted)*

**REQUIRED:** The objective of a review of interim financial information.

**DISCUSSION:** The review provides the accountant with a basis for reporting whether (s)he is aware of material modifications that should be made for such information to conform with GAAP. This objective differs significantly from that of an audit, which is to provide a basis for an opinion (AU 722, *Interim Financial Information*).

Answer (A) is incorrect because the review of interim financial information does not provide a basis for expressing an opinion. Answer (C) is incorrect because reporting on whether the statements are fairly presented is the expression of an opinion. Answer (D) is incorrect because reporting on whether the statements are fairly presented is the expression of an opinion.

**28.** Auditors of public companies are often requested to report on interim financial statements. A review of interim financial information consists primarily of

A. Vouching and tracing.

B. Reconciling and reperforming.

C. Inquiries and analytical procedures.

D. Confirmation and observation.

Answer (C) is correct. *(Publisher)*

**REQUIRED:** The procedures performed in a review of interim financial information.

**DISCUSSION:** Timeliness is an important element of interim reporting. The development of documentation and information underlying the report is necessarily less extensive at interim dates than at year-end. Consequently, a review primarily consists of analytical procedures and inquiries addressed to persons with responsibility for financial and accounting matters. It does not include (1) tests of accounting records or of the effectiveness of controls, (2) obtaining corroborating matter, or (3) other standard audit procedures (AU 722).

Answer (A) is incorrect because vouching and tracing are more extensive procedures than those listed in AU 722. Answer (B) is incorrect because reconciling and reperforming are more extensive procedures than those listed in AU 722. Answer (D) is incorrect because confirmation and observation are more extensive procedures than those listed in AU 722.

**29.** Which of the following statements is not included in an auditor's report on the interim financial statements of a public entity?

A. "We conducted our review in accordance with auditing standards."

B. "A review of interim financial information consists principally of applying analytical procedures and making inquiries of persons responsible for financial and accounting matters."

C. "Based on our review, we are not aware of any material modifications that should be made to the accompanying interim financial information (statements) for it (them) to be in conformity with accounting principles generally accepted in the United States of America."

D. "This (these) interim financial information (statements) is (are) the responsibility of the company's management."

Answer (A) is correct. *(Publisher)*

**REQUIRED:** The statement not in a report on a review of interim financial information.

**DISCUSSION:** The scope of a review of interim financial information is less than the scope of an audit. The accountant's report should therefore include a statement indicating that the review is substantially less in scope than an audit in accordance with auditing standards, the objective of which is an expression of an opinion on the statements as a whole. The report also states that no opinion is expressed and that the review was made in accordance with AICPA standards (AU 722).

Answer (B) is incorrect because a description of the procedures is a proper element of the report. Answer (C) is incorrect because a statement about whether the accountant is aware of any material modifications that should be made is a proper element of the report. Answer (D) is incorrect because a statement that the financial statements are the responsibility of management is a proper element of the report.

**30.** Procedures for a review of interim financial information of a public entity are ordinarily limited to inquiries and analytical procedures concerning significant accounting and disclosure matters relating to the financial information to be reported. The extent to which the procedures are to be applied depends on each of the following considerations except

A. The accountant's time budget allotted for the tests.

B. Conditions indicating the possible inability of the entity to continue as a going concern.

C. Litigation, claims, and assessments.

D. Questions raised in performing other procedures.

Answer (A) is correct. *(Publisher)*

**REQUIRED:** The matter not considered in determining the extent of procedures applied.

**DISCUSSION:** The procedures in a review of interim financial information include (1) analytical procedures, (2) reading the minutes of meetings, (3) reading the interim information, (4) obtaining reports of other accountants who have reviewed interim information of components of the entity, (5) inquiry of members of management with responsibility for financial and accounting matters, (6) reconciling the interim information with the general ledger on other accounting records, and (7) obtaining written representations from management. The accountant extends procedures if (s)he believes that the interim information does not conform with GAAP. However, the accountant's time budget should not be a determining factor.

Answer (B) is incorrect because a review is not intended to identify such conditions. However, if they existed at the date of the previous statements or if the auditor becomes aware of them, (s)he should (1) inquire of management about its plans to deal with the conditions and (2) consider the adequacy of disclosure. Answer (C) is incorrect because an inquiry of the client's lawyer may be appropriate if the accountant learns that the interim financial information may contain a departure from GAAP related to litigation, claims, or assessments. Answer (D) is incorrect because, if the accountant has reason to question whether the interim information conforms with GAAP, (s)he should make additional inquiries or employ other appropriate procedures.

**31.** A clear understanding should be established with a public client regarding the services to be performed in a review of interim financial information. Accordingly, the accountant should document the understanding, which should preferably be in writing. Thus, an engagement letter includes all of the following except

A. A statement that a review is not designed to identify reportable conditions.

B. An explanation that such procedures are substantially less in scope than an audit made in accordance with auditing standards.

C. A statement that management is responsible for correcting material misstatements.

D. The form and content of the documentation that will be maintained by the accountant.

Answer (D) is correct. *(Publisher)*

**REQUIRED:** The topic not included in the understanding with a public client about a review of interim financial information.

**DISCUSSION:** The form and content of the documentation are the responsibility of the accountant and are inappropriate for discussion in an engagement letter. The form or content of the documentation that the accountant should prepare cannot be specified because circumstances differ from one engagement to another. The documentation includes significant findings, facilitates supervision and review, and identifies evidence supporting the conclusion that the interim information reconciled with the accounting records (AU 722).

Answer (A) is incorrect because a review is not designed to provide assurance on internal control or identify reportable conditions. However, any reportable conditions found must be communicated to the audit committee. Answer (B) is incorrect because the accountant must communicate that the scope of the review is less than that of an audit. Answer (C) is incorrect because management is responsible for adjusting the interim financial information and for stating in the representation letter that uncorrected misstatements are not material.

**32.** A modification of the accountant's report on a review of interim financial information of a publicly held company is necessitated by which of the following?

A. A substantial doubt about the entity's ability to continue as a going concern.

B. Lack of consistency.

C. Use of another accountant's report.

D. Inadequate disclosure.

Answer (D) is correct. *(CPA, adapted)*

**REQUIRED:** The reason for modifying a review report on interim financial information.

**DISCUSSION:** Modification of the report on a review of interim financial information is necessary for departures from GAAP, including inadequate disclosure. But many circumstances that preclude the issuance of an unmodified report on audited statements do not cause a modification of a review report (AU 722).

Answer (A) is incorrect because AU 722 specifically states that a substantial doubt about the entity's ability to continue as a going concern is not a cause for modification if appropriately disclosed. Answer (B) is incorrect because AU 722 specifically states that lack of consistency is not a cause for modification if appropriately disclosed. Answer (C) is incorrect because the use of the report of another accountant may result in, but does not require, modification of the report. The accountant may be able to conclude, after considering the guidance in AU 543, *Part of Audit Performed by Other Independent Auditors*, that referring to the other accountant's report is not necessary.

**33.** The SEC requires a registrant to obtain a review by its independent auditors of interim financial statements to be filed on SEC Form 10-Q. In performing this review, the accountant should determine whether matters that should be communicated to the audit committee, as they relate to the interim statements, have been identified. Accordingly, the accountant

A. Rather than management must communicate the process used by management to make sensitive accounting estimates directly to the audit committee.

B. Must communicate such matters prior to the entity's filing or refuse to be associated with the interim financial statements.

C. Should discuss with the audit committee the quality of the entity's accounting principles; the consistency of their application; the clarity and completeness of the statements; and matters affecting the representational faithfulness, verifiability, and neutrality of the information.

D. Ordinarily should limit the discussion of the quality of the entity's accounting principles to the effect of significant events, transactions, and changes in estimates considered in performing the review.

Answer (D) is correct. *(Publisher)*

**REQUIRED:** The communication with the audit committee in connection with a review of interim financial statements of an SEC client.

**DISCUSSION:** Auditors of SEC clients should attempt to discuss with audit committees the matters listed in AU 380, *Communication with Audit Committees*, prior to the filing of Form 10-Q. However, the discussion of judgments about the quality of the accounting principles applied in the entity's interim reporting ordinarily is limited to the effects of significant events, transactions, and changes in estimates considered while performing the review procedures described in AU 722. Such procedures do not provide as much assurance as an audit.

Answer (A) is incorrect because the accountant should communicate the matters described in AU 380 to the audit committee or be satisfied, through discussions with the audit committee, that management has done so. However, material fraud, fraud involving senior management, and reportable conditions must be communicated directly to the audit committee. Answer (B) is incorrect because the accountant should attempt to communicate the identified matters to the audit committee, or at least its chair, and management prior to the filing, but, if the communication cannot be made at that time, the accountant should make it as soon as practicable. Answer (C) is incorrect because these responsibilities for the communication of judgments about the quality of accounting principles are imposed on practitioners in SEC engagements who have performed audits, not reviews.

**34.** Lara Green, CPA, is aware that her name is to be included in the interim report of National Company, a publicly held entity. National's quarterly financial statements are contained in the interim report. Green has not audited or reviewed these interim financial statements. Green should request that

I. Her name not be included in the communication

II. The financial statements be marked as unaudited, with a notation that no opinion is expressed on them

A. I only.

B. II only.

C. Both I and II.

D. Either I or II.

Answer (D) is correct. *(CPA, adapted)*

**REQUIRED:** The request(s) of an accountant who is associated with financial statements of a public entity that (s)he has not audited or reviewed.

**DISCUSSION:** If Green is aware that her name is to be included in a client-prepared written communication of a public company containing financial statements that she has not audited or reviewed, she should request either (1) that her name not be included in the communication or (2) that the financial statements be marked as unaudited and that a notation be included to the effect that she does not express an opinion on them (AU 504, *Association with Financial Statements*).

**35.** A public company includes selected interim financial information in the notes to its annual financial statements. The independent auditor has made a review of the information and is satisfied with its presentation. The note containing the information is marked as unaudited. Under these circumstances, the auditor's report on the annual financial statements

A. Should be modified to refer to the review and the selected interim financial information.

B. Need not be modified to refer to the review but should be modified to refer to the selected financial information.

C. Should be modified to refer to the review but not the selected interim financial information.

D. Need not be modified to refer to the review or the selected interim financial information.

Answer (D) is correct. *(CPA, adapted)*

**REQUIRED:** The effect on the audit report of including interim financial information in a note.

**DISCUSSION:** An auditor normally is not required to modify the report on the audited financial statements to indicate that (s)he had previously performed a review if the information is marked as unaudited (AU 722). If the note is not appropriately marked, the audit report should include a disclaimer on the information. The interim information is not necessary for the fair presentation of the statements in conformity with GAAP. Modification is necessary, however, when quarterly data required by SEC Regulation S-K are omitted or have not been reviewed. Regulation S-K specifies selected quarterly financial data to be reported.

## 8.4 Unaudited Statements, Compilations, and Reviews

**36.** An accountant may compile a nonpublic entity's financial statements that omit all of the disclosures required by GAAP only if the omission is

I. Clearly indicated in the accountant's report

II. Not undertaken with the intention of misleading the financial statement users

A. I only.

B. II only.

C. Both I and II.

D. Either I or II.

Answer (C) is correct. *(CPA, adapted)*

**REQUIRED:** The situation in which an accountant may compile a nonpublic entity's financial statements that omit all of the disclosures required by GAAP.

**DISCUSSION:** An accountant may accept an engagement to compile financial statements that omit substantially all disclosures required by GAAP "provided the omission is clearly indicated in the report and is not, to his/her knowledge, undertaken with the intention of misleading those who might reasonably be expected to use such financial statements" (AR 100, *Compilation and Review of Financial Statements*).

**37.** When an independent CPA assists in preparing the financial statements of a publicly held entity, but has not audited or reviewed them, the CPA should issue a disclaimer of opinion. The CPA has no responsibility to apply any procedures beyond

A. Ascertaining whether the financial statements are in conformity with generally accepted accounting principles.

B. Determining whether management has elected to omit substantially all required disclosures.

C. Documenting that internal control is not being relied on.

D. Reading the financial statements for obvious material misstatements.

Answer (D) is correct. *(CPA, adapted)*

**REQUIRED:** The procedure applied to public-company financial statements that the CPA has assisted in preparing.

**DISCUSSION:** AU 504 states that the accountant has no responsibility to apply any procedures beyond reading the financial statements for obvious material misstatements. Any procedures applied should not be described.

Answer (A) is incorrect because an audit is conducted to ascertain whether the financial statements are in conformity with GAAP. Preparation of the financial statements of a public entity is prohibited if performed during the audit. Answer (B) is incorrect because the disclaimer is modified if the accountant concludes on the basis of facts known to him/her that the unaudited financial statements do not conform with GAAP. Lack of adequate disclosure is a departure from GAAP. Answer (C) is incorrect because the CPA in these circumstances need not consider internal control and therefore has no responsibility for documentation.

**38.** Statements on Standards for Accounting and Review Services (SSARSs) establish standards and procedures for which of the following engagements?

A. Assisting in adjusting the books of account for a partnership.

B. Reviewing interim financial data required to be filed with the SEC.

C. Processing financial data for clients of other accounting firms.

D. Compiling an individual's personal financial statement to be used to obtain a mortgage.

Answer (D) is correct. *(CPA, adapted)*

**REQUIRED:** The accounting service for which SSARSs establish standards or procedures.

**DISCUSSION:** SSARSs apply when the accountant submits unaudited financial statements of a nonpublic entity to the client or a third party. A submission involves presenting to a client or a third party financial statements that the accountant has prepared either manually or through the use of computer software (AR 100). The presentation of information in the form of financial statements that is the representation of management (owners) without undertaking to express any assurance thereon is a compilation. In this case, the nonpublic entity is an individual. AR 100 describes the accountant's procedures and reporting responsibilities relative to this service. (AR 600, *Reporting on Personal Financial Statements Included in Written Personal Financial Plans*, provides an exemption from the SSARSs for personal financial statements under certain conditions.)

Answer (A) is incorrect because assisting in adjusting the books of account does not constitute a submission of financial statements. Answer (B) is incorrect because AU 722 describes the accountant's responsibilities for interim financial information of public companies. Answer (C) is incorrect because processing financial data for clients of other accounting firms does not constitute a submission of financial statements.

**39.** A CPA is required to comply with the provisions of Statements on Standards for Accounting and Review Services (SSARSs) when

| | Assisting in Adjusting the Books of Account | Consulting on Accounting Matters |
|---|---|---|
| A. | Yes | Yes |
| B. | Yes | No |
| C. | No | Yes |
| D. | No | No |

Answer (D) is correct. *(CPA, adapted)*

**REQUIRED:** The circumstances in which a CPA is required to comply with SSARSs.

**DISCUSSION:** SSARSs apply when the accountant submits unaudited financial statements of a nonpublic entity to the client or a third party. A submission involves presenting to a client or a third party financial statements that the accountant has prepared either manually or through the use of computer software (AR 100). Neither assisting in adjusting the books of account nor consulting on accounting matters constitutes a submission of financial statements.

**40.** Statements on Standards for Accounting and Review Services (SSARSs) apply when the accountant has

A. Typed client-prepared financial statements, without modification, as an accommodation to the client.

B. Provided a client with a financial statement format that does not include dollar amounts, to be used by the client in preparing financial statements.

C. Proposed correcting journal entries to be recorded by the client that change client-prepared financial statements.

D. Generated, through the use of computer software, financial statements prepared in accordance with a comprehensive basis of accounting other than GAAP.

Answer (D) is correct. *(CPA, adapted)*

**REQUIRED:** The situation in which SSARSs apply.

**DISCUSSION:** SSARSs apply when the accountant submits unaudited financial statements of a nonpublic entity to the client or a third party. A submission involves presenting to a client or a third party financial statements that the accountant has prepared either manually or through the use of computer software (AR 100). This principle applies whether the financial statements are based on GAAP or on a comprehensive basis of accounting other than GAAP.

Answer (A) is incorrect because typing client-prepared financial statements, without modification, as an accommodation to the client does not constitute preparation of financial statements. Answer (B) is incorrect because, without dollar amounts, the presentation is not a financial statement. Answer (C) is incorrect because journal entries are not a financial statement.

**41.** SSARSs define the compilation and review of financial statements of a nonpublic entity and provide guidance concerning the standards and procedures applicable to such engagements. For the purposes of SSARSs, which of the following is a nonpublic entity?

A. One whose securities trade on a stock exchange or over the counter, including securities quoted only regionally or locally.

B. One that makes a filing with a regulatory agency in preparation for a sale of any class of securities to the public.

C. A subsidiary, corporate joint venture, or other entity controlled by a public entity.

D. A closely held corporation.

Answer (D) is correct. *(Publisher)*

**REQUIRED:** The entity considered a nonpublic entity for purposes of SSARSs.

**DISCUSSION:** A nonpublic entity is one whose shares are not traded in a public market, that has not made a filing with a regulatory body preparatory to public sale of its securities, and that is not controlled by a public entity. For example, a proprietorship, partnership, or closely held corporation might be considered a nonpublic entity.

Answer (A) is incorrect because an entity whose shares are traded is considered to be a public entity for the purposes of SSARSs. Answer (B) is incorrect because an entity that makes a filing with a regulatory agency in preparation for a sale of any class of securities to the public is considered to be a public entity for the purposes of SSARSs. Answer (C) is incorrect because a subsidiary, corporate joint venture, or other entity controlled by a public entity are all considered to be public entities for the purposes of SSARSs.

**42.** A CPA who is not independent may issue a

A. Review report.

B. Comfort letter.

C. Report expressing a qualified opinion.

D. Compilation report.

Answer (D) is correct. *(CPA, adapted)*

**REQUIRED:** The report that a CPA may issue.

**DISCUSSION:** A compilation is the presentation in statement form of information that is the representation of management (owners) without expressing any assurance. A CPA who is not independent may issue a compilation report if (s)he discloses the lack of independence in the report (AR 100).

Answer (A) is incorrect because a CPA may not issue a review report if (s)he is not independent. A review entails the expression of limited assurances based primarily on inquiries and analytical procedures. Answer (B) is incorrect because a letter for underwriters (a comfort letter) cannot be issued by a CPA who lacks independence (AU 634, *Letters for Underwriters and Certain Other Requesting Parties*). Answer (C) is incorrect because auditing standards prohibit a CPA from expressing any opinion when not independent.

**43.** Which of the following representations does an accountant make implicitly when issuing the standard report for the compilation of a nonpublic entity's financial statements?

A. The accountant is independent with respect to the entity.

B. The statements have not been audited.

C. A compilation consists principally of inquiries and analytical procedures.

D. The accountant does not express any assurance on the financial statements.

Answer (A) is correct. *(CPA, adapted)*

**REQUIRED:** The implicit representation in a standard compilation report.

**DISCUSSION:** Although an accountant who lacks independence is not precluded from issuing a compilation report, (s)he should specifically disclose the lack of independence in the report. Thus, the standard report is silent with respect to independence.

Answer (B) is incorrect because a compilation explicitly states that the financial statements have not been audited. Answer (C) is incorrect because a compilation does not include application of inquiry and analytical procedures. Answer (D) is incorrect because a compilation explicitly states that no assurance is expressed.

**44.** When engaged to compile the financial statements of a nonpublic entity, an accountant is required to possess a level of knowledge of the entity's accounting principles and practices. This requirement most likely will include obtaining a general understanding of the

A. Stated qualifications of the entity's accounting personnel.

B. Design of the entity's internal controls placed in operation.

C. Risk factors relating to misstatements arising from illegal acts.

D. Internal control awareness of the entity's senior management.

Answer (A) is correct. *(CPA, adapted)*

**REQUIRED:** The knowledge required to perform a compilation.

**DISCUSSION:** To perform a compilation, the accountant should possess an understanding of the nature of the entity's business, its accounting records, the qualifications of its accounting personnel, and the content and accounting basis of the financial statements.

Answer (B) is incorrect because the consideration of internal control is not necessary to perform compilation services. Answer (C) is incorrect because no assessment of risk or application of auditing procedures is required in a compilation. Answer (D) is incorrect because the consideration of internal control is not necessary to perform compilation services.

**45.** The accountant's knowledge of the accounting principles and practices of the client's industry should enable him/her to compile appropriate financial statements. Also, the accountant should understand the nature of the entity's business, its accounting records, the qualifications of its personnel, the accounting basis of the financial statements, and their content. To acquire such knowledge, the accountant does not normally

A. Consult Audit and Accounting Guides.

B. Read industry publications and consult textbooks and periodicals.

C. Obtain an understanding of internal control and assess control risk.

D. Make inquiries of the entity's personnel.

Answer (C) is correct. *(Publisher)*

**REQUIRED:** The procedure not normally performed.

**DISCUSSION:** The consideration of internal control is not necessary to perform compilation services. No auditing procedures need be applied in a compilation. The financial statements, however, should be read to determine whether they are in an appropriate form and free of obvious material errors, such as clerical mistakes or departures from GAAP, including inadequate disclosure.

Answer (A) is incorrect because AICPA Audit and Accounting Guides are appropriate sources of the knowledge of the accounting principles and practices of the industry required to perform a compilation. Answer (B) is incorrect because industry publications, textbooks, and periodicals are appropriate sources of the knowledge of the accounting principles and practices of the industry required to perform a compilation. Answer (D) is incorrect because inquiries of the entity's personnel are the primary procedures employed to gain an understanding of the client.

**46.** An accountant's compilation report should be dated as of the date of

A. Completion of field work.

B. Completion of the compilation.

C. Transmittal of the compilation report.

D. The latest subsequent event referred to in the notes to the financial statements.

Answer (B) is correct. *(CPA, adapted)*

**REQUIRED:** The date of a compilation report.

**DISCUSSION:** When an accountant has performed a compilation for a nonpublic entity, the date of the report should be the completion date of the compilation (AR 100).

Answer (A) is incorrect because field work is performed in attestation engagements, such as a financial statement audit or a review, not a compilation. Answer (C) is incorrect because the date of the transmittal of the compilation report, which refers to the time of its communication to the user, is not appropriate. Answer (D) is incorrect because the dates of subsequent events may be significant for an audit but not a compilation.

**47.** An accountant has compiled the financial statements of a nonpublic entity in accordance with Statements on Standards for Accounting and Review Services (SSARSs). Do the SSARSs require that the compilation report be printed on the accountant's letterhead and that the report be manually signed by the accountant?

| | Printed on the Accountant's Letterhead | Manually Signed by the Accountant |
|---|---|---|
| A. | Yes | Yes |
| B. | Yes | No |
| C. | No | Yes |
| D. | No | No |

Answer (D) is correct. *(CPA, adapted)*

**REQUIRED:** The requirements of a compilation report.

**DISCUSSION:** The compilation report need not be printed on the accountant's letterhead or manually signed by the accountant. However, the report must be signed in some manner by the accounting firm or the accountant. For example, the signature could be manual, stamped, electronic, or typed.

**48.** Which of the following should not be included in an accountant's standard report based upon the compilation of an entity's financial statements?

A. A statement that a compilation is limited to presenting in the form of financial statements information that is the representation of management.

B. A statement that the compilation was performed in accordance with Statements on Standards for Accounting and Review Services.

C. A statement that the accountant has not audited or reviewed the statements.

D. A statement that the accountant does not express an opinion but provides only limited assurance on the statements.

Answer (D) is correct. *(CPA, adapted)*

**REQUIRED:** The statement not made in the report.

**DISCUSSION:** A compilation report does not express an opinion or any other form of assurance. Any procedures that the accountant may have performed should not be described because readers may be misled into believing that the statements have been subjected to review or audit.

Answer (A) is incorrect because the report should include a statement that a compilation is limited to presenting in the form of financial statements information that is the representation of management. Answer (B) is incorrect because the report should include a statement that the compilation was performed in accordance with SSARSs issued by the AICPA. Answer (C) is incorrect because the report should include a statement that the accountant has not audited or reviewed the statements.

**49.** Each page of the financial statements compiled and reported on by an accountant should include a reference such as

A. See Accompanying Accountant's Notes.

B. Unaudited, See Accountant's Disclaimer.

C. See Accountant's Compilation Report.

D. Subject to Compilation Restrictions.

Answer (C) is correct. *(CPA, adapted)*

**REQUIRED:** The reference on each page.

**DISCUSSION:** Each page of the financial statements compiled and reported on by the accountant should include a reference such as "See Accountant's Compilation Report" (AR 100).

Answer (A) is incorrect because "See Accompanying Accountant's Notes" is not an appropriate reference to be included on each page of compiled financial statements. Answer (B) is incorrect because "Unaudited, See Accountant's Disclaimer" is not an appropriate reference to be included on each page of compiled financial statements. Answer (D) is incorrect because "Subject to Compilation Restrictions" is not an appropriate reference to be included on each page of compiled financial statements.

**50.** In performing a compilation of financial statements of a nonpublic entity, the accountant decides that modification of the standard report is not adequate to indicate deficiencies in the financial statements taken as a whole, and the client is not willing to correct the deficiencies. The accountant should therefore

A. Perform a review of the financial statements.

B. Issue a special report.

C. Withdraw from the engagement.

D. Express an adverse audit opinion.

Answer (C) is correct. *(CPA, adapted)*
**REQUIRED:** The appropriate action.
**DISCUSSION:** If the accountant becomes aware that information supplied by the entity is incorrect, incomplete, or otherwise unsatisfactory, (s)he should request the client to provide additional or revised information. If the client is not willing to correct the deficiencies, the accountant is advised to withdraw from the engagement.
Answer (A) is incorrect because the accountant is under no obligation to upgrade the service to a review. Answer (B) is incorrect because a special report can be issued only in conjunction with auditing services. Answer (D) is incorrect because an opinion may be expressed only after an audit.

**51.** An accountant has been asked to compile and report on the financial statements of a nonpublic company on a prescribed form that omits substantially all the disclosures required by generally accepted accounting principles. If the prescribed form is a standard preprinted form adopted by the company's industry trade association, and is to be transmitted only to such association, the accountant

A. Need not advise the industry trade association of the omission of all disclosures.

B. Should disclose the details of the omissions in separate paragraphs of the compilation report.

C. Is precluded from issuing a compilation report when all disclosures are omitted.

D. Should express limited assurance that the financial statements are free of material misstatements.

Answer (A) is correct. *(CPA, adapted)*
**REQUIRED:** The accountant's responsibility.
**DISCUSSION:** AR 300, *Compilation Reports on Financial Statements Included in Certain Prescribed Forms*, provides for an alternative form of the standard compilation report when a prescribed form or related instructions call for departure from GAAP by specifying a measurement principle not in conformity with GAAP or failing to require disclosures in accordance with GAAP. The presumption is that the information required in a prescribed form is sufficient to meet the needs of the body that designed or adopted the form. In the standard report on statements included in such a form, the accountant should indicate that the statements are in a prescribed form and that they may differ from those presented in accordance with GAAP, but (s)he need not describe the differences.
Answer (B) is incorrect because this disclosure is unnecessary. Answer (C) is incorrect because the report may be issued in these circumstances. Answer (D) is incorrect because a compilation report expresses no assurance.

**52.** When an accountant compiles and reports on a nonpublic entity's financial statements that omit substantially all disclosures required by generally accepted accounting principles, the accountant should indicate in the compilation report that the financial statements are

A. Restricted for internal use only.

B. Not to be given to financial institutions for the purpose of obtaining credit.

C. Compiled in conformity with a comprehensive basis of accounting other than generally accepted accounting principles.

D. Not designed for those who are uninformed about the omitted disclosures.

Answer (D) is correct. *(CPA, adapted)*
**REQUIRED:** The language needed in the report.
**DISCUSSION:** The accountant may not accept the engagement unless two conditions are satisfied: (s)he must modify the standard compilation report to clearly indicate that substantially all disclosures required by GAAP have been omitted, and the omission must not be made to mislead users of the statements. The language given is a quotation from the compilation report when substantially all disclosures are omitted (AR 100).
Answer (A) is incorrect because the accountant need not indicate in the compilation report that the financial statements are restricted for internal use only. Answer (B) is incorrect because the statements may be given to financial institutions for the purpose of obtaining credit. Answer (C) is incorrect because the omission of disclosures required by GAAP does not result in conformity with a comprehensive basis of accounting other than GAAP.

**53.** Miller, CPA, is engaged to compile the financial statements of Web Co., a nonpublic entity, in conformity with the income tax basis of accounting. The statements are expected to be used by third parties. If Web's financial statements do not disclose the basis of accounting used, Miller should

A. Disclose the basis of accounting in the accountant's compilation report.

B. Clearly label each page "Distribution Restricted--Material Modifications Required."

C. Issue a special report describing the effect of the incomplete presentation.

D. Withdraw from the engagement and provide no further services to Web.

Answer (A) is correct. *(CPA, adapted)*

**REQUIRED:** The effect on a compilation report of failure to disclose the basis of accounting used.

**DISCUSSION:** An accountant must provide a report when (s)he (1) is engaged to report on compiled financial statements or (2) submits financial statements reasonably expected to be used by third parties. Although the accountant is not expected to perform any procedures, if (s)he is aware of misapplications of GAAP or an other comprehensive basis of accounting (OCBOA) or the absence of required disclosures, (s)he should disclose that information in the compilation report. When statements are not expected to be used by third parties, the accountant, in lieu of issuing a compilation report, may document an understanding with the entity by use of an engagement letter. However, this engagement letter should contain a statement disclosing departures from GAAP or on OCBOA or the opinion of substantially all disclosures.

Answer (B) is incorrect because each page of the financial statements should contain the statement, "See accountant's compilation report." Answer (C) is incorrect because a special report is issued in conjunction with an audit. Answer (D) is incorrect because the accountant need not withdraw from the engagement.

**54.** When unaudited financial statements of a nonpublic entity are presented in comparative form with audited financial statements in the subsequent year, the unaudited financial statements should be clearly marked to indicate their status, and

I. The report on the unaudited financial statements should be reissued.

II. The report on the audited financial statements should include a separate paragraph describing the responsibility assumed for the unaudited financial statements.

A. I only.

B. II only.

C. Both I and II.

D. Either I or II.

Answer (D) is correct. *(CPA, adapted)*

**REQUIRED:** The appropriate reporting when unaudited financial statements of a nonpublic entity are presented in comparative form with audited financial statements.

**DISCUSSION:** The financial statements that have not been audited should be clearly marked to indicate their status and either (1) the report on the prior period should be reissued or (2) the report on the current period should include as a separate paragraph an appropriate description of the responsibility assumed for the financial statements of the prior period (AU 504).

**55.** An accountant's standard report on a review of the financial statements of a nonpublic entity should state that the accountant

A. Does not express an opinion or any form of limited assurance on the financial statements.

B. Is not aware of any material modifications that should be made to the financial statements for them to conform with GAAP.

C. Obtained reasonable assurance about whether the financial statements are free of material misstatement.

D. Examined evidence, on a test basis, supporting the amounts and disclosures in the financial statements.

Answer (B) is correct. *(CPA, adapted)*

**REQUIRED:** The statement in a standard review report.

**DISCUSSION:** The standard review report states, "Based on my review, I am not aware of any material modifications that should be made to the accompanying financial statements in order for them to be in conformity with generally accepted accounting principles" (AR 100).

Answer (A) is incorrect because a review provides negative assurance. Answer (C) is incorrect because an audit provides reasonable assurance about whether the financial statements are free of material misstatement. Answer (D) is incorrect because an audit entails gathering sufficient competent evidence to support the amounts and disclosures in the financial statements.

**56.** Which of the following procedures is an accountant least likely to perform during an engagement to review the financial statements of a nonpublic entity?

A. Observing the safeguards over access to and use of assets and records.

B. Comparing the financial statements with anticipated results in budgets and forecasts.

C. Inquiring of management about actions taken at the board of directors' meetings.

D. Studying the relationships of financial statement elements expected to conform to predictable patterns.

Answer (A) is correct. *(CPA, adapted)*

**REQUIRED:** The procedure least likely to be performed during a review engagement.

**DISCUSSION:** A review does not contemplate (1) obtaining an understanding of internal control or assessing control risk, (2) testing accounting records or responses to inquiries by obtaining corroborating evidence, or (3) other tests ordinarily performed in an audit (AR 100).

Answer (B) is incorrect because a review contemplates the application of analytical procedures. Comparing financial statements with anticipated results is an analytical procedure. Answer (C) is incorrect because a review encompasses inquiries to management about numerous operating activities. Answer (D) is incorrect because a review contemplates the application of analytical procedures. Studying relationships among the significant financial statement items is an analytical procedure.

**57.** In a review engagement, the accountant should establish an understanding with the client, preferably in writing, regarding the services to be performed. The understanding should include all of the following except a

A. Description of the nature and limitations of the services to be performed.

B. Description of the report the accountant expects to render.

C. Provision that the engagement cannot be relied upon to disclose errors, fraud, or illegal acts.

D. Provision that any errors, fraud, or illegal acts that come to the accountant's attention need not be reported.

Answer (D) is correct. *(Publisher)*

**REQUIRED:** The false statement about the accountant's understanding with the client in a review engagement.

**DISCUSSION:** Although the engagement cannot be relied upon to disclose errors, fraud, or illegal acts, the accountant should indicate to the client that any such acts discovered will be reported to management or the directors unless the acts are clearly inconsequential (AR 100).

Answer (A) is incorrect because a description of the nature and limitations of the services to be performed should be included in the understanding with the client. Answer (B) is incorrect because a description of the report the accountant expects to issue should be included in the understanding with the client. Answer (C) is incorrect because a provision that the engagement cannot be relied upon to disclose errors, fraud, or illegal acts should be included in the understanding with the client.

**58.** Which of the following inquiry or analytical procedures ordinarily is performed in an engagement to review a nonpublic entity's financial statements?

A. Analytical procedures designed to test the accounting records by obtaining corroborating evidential matter.

B. Inquiries concerning the entity's procedures for recording and summarizing transactions.

C. Analytical procedures designed to test management's assertions regarding continued existence.

D. Inquiries of the entity's attorney concerning contingent liabilities.

Answer (B) is correct. *(CPA, adapted)*

**REQUIRED:** The procedure ordinarily performed during a review of a nonpublic entity's financial statements.

**DISCUSSION:** These procedures consist of (1) inquiries about accounting principles and practices and the methods of applying them; (2) inquiries about procedures for recording, classifying, and summarizing transactions, and accumulating information for disclosure; (3) analytical procedures; (4) inquiries about actions at directors' meetings, etc.; (5) reading the statements; (6) obtaining reports from other accountants, if any; and (7) inquiries of responsible persons about preparation of the statements in conformity with GAAP, accounting changes, changes in business activities, subsequent events, and questions arising while applying the foregoing procedures (AR 100).

Answer (A) is incorrect because a review does not require gathering corroborating evidence. Answer (C) is incorrect because a review does not require testing assertions about continued existence. Answer (D) is incorrect because a review does not require making inquiries of the entity's attorney.

**59.** Which of the following procedures should an accountant perform during an engagement to review the GAAP-based financial statements of a nonpublic entity?

A. Communicating reportable conditions discovered during the assessment of control risk.

B. Obtaining written representations from management.

C. Sending bank confirmation letters to the entity's financial institutions.

D. Examining cash disbursements in the subsequent period for unrecorded liabilities.

Answer (B) is correct. *(CPA, adapted)*

**REQUIRED:** The procedure performed in a review.

**DISCUSSION:** Written representations (1) addressed to the accountant, (2) dated no earlier than the report date, and (3) signed by responsible and knowledgeable parties (preferably the CEO and CFO) must be obtained for all statements and periods covered by the report. If the statements are GAAP-based, management must specifically (1) acknowledge its responsibility for, and belief in, the fair presentation of the statements in accordance with GAAP, and (2) state that its responses are full and truthful. Other specific representations concern completeness of information and subsequent events. Additional representations should be made addressing matters specific to the business or industry.

Answer (A) is incorrect because reportable conditions must be communicated in an audit, not a review. Answer (C) is incorrect because confirmations to financial institutions are normally sent in an audit, not a review. Answer (D) is incorrect because tests of details, e.g., tests of subsequent payments, are performed in an audit, not a review.

**60.** A review does not provide assurance that the accountant will become aware of all significant matters that would be disclosed in an audit. However, if the accountant becomes aware that information coming to his/her attention is incorrect, incomplete, or otherwise unsatisfactory, (s)he should

A. Withdraw immediately from the engagement.

B. Perform the additional procedures (s)he deems necessary to achieve limited assurance.

C. Perform a complete audit and issue a standard audit report with appropriate qualifications.

D. Downgrade the engagement to a compilation and issue the appropriate report.

Answer (B) is correct. *(Publisher)*

**REQUIRED:** The accountant's response to unsatisfactory information in a review.

**DISCUSSION:** In a review, the accountant primarily makes inquiries and applies analytical procedures. If information appears unsatisfactory, (s)he should perform the additional procedures deemed necessary to achieve limited assurance that no material modifications need be made to the statements for them to conform with GAAP. These procedures are left to the judgment of the accountant (AR 100).

Answer (A) is incorrect because the accountant should withdraw only after (s)he has concluded that the financial statements are not in conformity with GAAP and that modification of the standard report is inadequate. Answer (C) is incorrect because the accountant cannot decide to perform a complete audit; (s)he must be engaged to do so by the client. Answer (D) is incorrect because unsatisfactory information is not a basis for changing the engagement if the accountant can perform necessary procedures.

**61.** Appendix A of AR 100 lists more than 75 questions that may be appropriate to address to management in a review engagement. Which of the following is true concerning this list?

A. The list is intended to be a checklist or program so that all appropriate questions will be addressed.

B. The questions are all-inclusive and should be applied in every engagement.

C. It may be necessary to make several inquiries to answer one question.

D. The questions cover only general management procedures rather than specific account balances.

Answer (C) is correct. *(Publisher)*

**REQUIRED:** The true statement concerning the inquiries listed in AR 100.

**DISCUSSION:** The inquiries to be made in a review of financial statements are a matter of the accountant's judgment. The accountant may believe it is necessary to make several inquiries to answer one of the questions listed.

Answer (A) is incorrect because AR 100 indicates specifically that the list is not intended to be a program or a checklist. Answer (B) is incorrect because AR 100 indicates specifically that the list is not intended to be all-inclusive. Answer (D) is incorrect because the questions range from general questions concerning procedures for recording, classifying, and summarizing transactions to specific questions concerning the accounts on the income statement and balance sheet.

**62.** Which of the following is never included in an accountant's report based upon a review of the financial statements of a nonpublic entity?

A. A statement that the review was in accordance with GAAS.

B. A statement that all information included in the financial statements is the representation of management.

C. A description of the principal procedures performed and the conclusions based upon the results of the review.

D. A reference to the statements of comprehensive income and retained earnings.

Answer (A) is correct. *(CPA, adapted)*

**REQUIRED:** The statement not included in an accountant's report based upon a review.

**DISCUSSION:** The report should include a statement that the review is substantially less in scope than an audit in accordance with GAAS. GAAS apply to audits, not reviews. A review consists principally of inquiries and analytical procedures applied to financial data (AR 100).

Answer (B) is incorrect because a statement that all information included in the financial statements is the representation of management is included in the standard report. Answer (C) is incorrect because a description of the principle procedures performed and the accountant's conclusions based upon the results of the review are included in the standard report. Answer (D) is incorrect because APB 12 requires disclosure of a change in capital, e.g., in a retained earnings statement, but it does not require such a statement. SFAS 130 requires reporting of all components of comprehensive income but not necessarily in a separate statement. Thus, a review report must refer to the statements of retained earnings and comprehensive income only when they are presented.

**63.** Baker, CPA, was engaged to review the financial statements of Hall Company, a nonpublic entity. Evidence came to Baker's attention that indicated substantial doubt as to Hall's ability to continue as a going concern. The principal conditions and events that caused the substantial doubt have been fully disclosed in the notes to Hall's financial statements. Baker

A. Is not required to modify the accountant's review report.

B. Is not permitted to modify the accountant's review report.

C. Should issue an accountant's compilation report instead of a review report.

D. Should express a qualified opinion in the accountant's review report.

Answer (A) is correct. *(CPA, adapted)*

**REQUIRED:** The reporting responsibility in a review given a substantial doubt about the going concern assumption.

**DISCUSSION:** AR 100 states, "Normally, neither an uncertainty nor an inconsistency in the application of accounting principles would cause the accountant to modify the standard report provided the financial statements appropriately disclose such matters. Nothing in this statement, however, is intended to preclude an accountant from emphasizing in a separate paragraph of the report a matter regarding the financial statements."

Answer (B) is incorrect because an accountant may emphasize a matter in a separate paragraph. Answer (C) is incorrect because, if appropriate procedures have been applied and the accountant has formed a conclusion, a review report may be issued. Answer (D) is incorrect because, unless an audit has been conducted, an opinion may not be expressed.

**64.** An accountant has been engaged to review a nonpublic entity's financial statements that contain several departures from GAAP. If the financial statements are not revised and modification of the standard review report is not adequate to indicate the deficiencies, the accountant should

A. Withdraw from the engagement and provide no further services concerning these financial statements.

B. Inform management that the engagement can proceed only if distribution of the report is restricted to internal use.

C. Determine the effects of the departures from GAAP and issue a special report on the financial statements.

D. Issue a modified review report provided the entity agrees that the financial statements will not be used to obtain credit.

Answer (A) is correct. *(CPA, adapted)*

**REQUIRED:** The effect of uncorrected departures from GAAP when modifying the review report is not adequate.

**DISCUSSION:** If the accountant believes that modification of the standard report is not adequate to indicate the deficiencies in the financial statements taken as a whole, and if the client is unwilling to correct the deficiencies, (s)he should withdraw from the engagement and provide no further services with respect to those financial statements. The accountant may wish to consult with legal counsel in such circumstances. The standards do not provide for an adverse review report (AR 100).

Answer (B) is incorrect because no report should be issued in this situation. Answer (C) is incorrect because a special report is an audit report on financial statements prepared in conformity with another comprehensive basis of accounting; specified elements, accounts, or items of a financial statement; etc. Answer (D) is incorrect because no report should be issued in this situation.

**65.** Each page of a nonpublic entity's financial statements reviewed by an accountant should include the following reference:

A. See Accountant's Review Report.

B. Reviewed, No Accountant's Assurance Expressed.

C. See Accompanying Accountant's Footnotes.

D. Reviewed, No Material Modifications Required.

Answer (A) is correct. *(CPA, adapted)*

**REQUIRED:** The reference on each page of financial statements reviewed by an accountant.

**DISCUSSION:** Each page should include a reference such as "See Accountant's Review Report" (AR 100).

Answer (B) is incorrect because a review report ordinarily expresses limited assurance. Answer (C) is incorrect because footnotes are part of the financial statements, not the accountant's report. Answer (D) is incorrect because the review report states that the accountant is not aware of any modifications that should be made other than those indicated in the report.

**66.** During an engagement to review the financial statements of a nonpublic entity, an accountant becomes aware of a material departure from GAAP. If the accountant decides to modify the standard review report because management will not revise the financial statements, the accountant should

A. Express negative assurance on accounting principles not conforming with GAAP.

B. Disclose the departure from GAAP in a separate paragraph of the report.

C. Express an adverse or a qualified opinion, depending on materiality.

D. Express positive assurance on accounting principles conforming with GAAP.

Answer (B) is correct. *(CPA, adapted)*

**REQUIRED:** The accountant's reporting responsibility in a review engagement given a material departure from GAAP and management's refusal to revise the statements.

**DISCUSSION:** AR 100 states that, if the accountant concludes that a departure from GAAP will result in a modified review report, the report should contain a separate paragraph disclosing the departure, including its effects on the financial statements if they have been determined by management or are known as the result of the accountant's procedures.

Answer (A) is incorrect because the accountant provides negative assurance when no departures from GAAP exist. Answer (C) is incorrect because a review does not result in the expression of any form of positive assurance, including an opinion. Answer (D) is incorrect because a review does not result in the expression of any form of positive assurance, including an opinion.

**67.** An accountant has been asked to issue a review report on the balance sheet of a nonpublic company but not to report on the other basic financial statements. The accountant may not do so

A. Because compliance with this request would result in a violation of the ethical standards of the profession.

B. Because compliance with this request would result in an incomplete review.

C. If the review of the balance sheet discloses material departures from GAAP.

D. If the scope of the inquiry and analytical procedures has been restricted.

Answer (D) is correct. *(CPA, adapted)*

**REQUIRED:** The situation in which an accountant may not issue a review report on a single financial statement.

**DISCUSSION:** "An accountant may be asked to issue a review report on one financial statement, such as the balance sheet, and not on other related financial statements, such as the statements of income, retained earnings, and cash flows. (S)he may do so if the scope of the inquiry and analytical procedures has not been restricted" (AR 100).

Answer (A) is incorrect because the accountant may report on one financial statement. Answer (B) is incorrect because the accountant may report on one financial statement. Answer (C) is incorrect because, if the review discloses material departures from GAAP, the accountant may issue a modified report.

**68.** Davis, CPA, accepted an engagement to audit the financial statements of Tech Resources, a nonpublic entity. Before the completion of the audit, Tech requested Davis to change the engagement to a review of financial statements. Before Davis agrees to change the engagement, Davis is required to consider the

| | Additional Audit Effort Necessary to Complete the Audit | Reason Given for Tech's Request |
|---|---|---|
| A. | No | No |
| B. | Yes | Yes |
| C. | Yes | No |
| D. | No | Yes |

Answer (B) is correct. *(CPA, adapted)*

**REQUIRED:** The matter(s) to be considered before changing an engagement from an audit to a review.

**DISCUSSION:** Before an accountant who was engaged to perform an audit agrees to change the engagement to a compilation or a review, at least the following should be considered: (1) the reason given for the client's request, particularly the implications of a restriction on the scope of the audit, whether imposed by the client or by circumstances; (2) the additional audit effort required to complete the audit; and (3) the estimated additional cost to complete the audit (AR 100).

**69.** An accountant who had begun an audit of the financial statements of a nonpublic entity was asked to change the engagement to a review because of a restriction on the scope of the audit. Given reasonable justification for the change, the accountant's review report should refer to the

| | Scope Limitation That Caused the Changed Engagement | Original Engagement That Was Agreed To |
|---|---|---|
| A. | Yes | No |
| B. | No | Yes |
| C. | No | No |
| D. | Yes | Yes |

Answer (C) is correct. *(CPA, adapted)*

**REQUIRED:** The reference(s) in a review report issued after a change of the engagement.

**DISCUSSION:** An accountant may be asked to change the engagement from a higher to a lower level of service. If the accountant concludes that the change is reasonably justified and if (s)he complies with the standards applicable to the changed engagement, the accountant may issue the appropriate review report. The report on the changed engagement should not mention the original engagement, any auditing procedures performed, or scope limitations that led to the changed engagement.

**70.** During a compilation, the client requests that the accountant test certain cash disbursement transactions. The accountant agrees and performs such procedures. The procedures

A. Are part of an auditing service and change the scope of the engagement to that of an audit in accordance with GAAS.

B. Are part of an accounting service and are not performed for the purpose of conducting an audit in accordance with GAAS.

C. Are not permitted when the purpose of the engagement is to compile financial statements and the work to be performed is not in accordance with GAAS.

D. Would require the accountant to issue a report indicating that the audit was conducted in accordance with GAAS but was limited in scope.

Answer (B) is correct. *(Publisher)*

**REQUIRED:** The true statement about audit procedures performed during an engagement to compile statements.

**DISCUSSION:** Accountants may perform other accounting services in connection with a compilation or review of unaudited financial statements of a nonpublic entity (AR 100). Similarly, an accountant who is associated with statements of a public entity (s)he has not audited or reviewed may have performed some procedures (AU 504).

Answer (A) is incorrect because testing transactions does not convert the engagement to an audit. An audit entails comprehensive procedures to understand internal control and assess control risk, test accounting records, etc. Answer (C) is incorrect because the accountant is allowed to perform additional procedures when compiling statements, but such procedures may not be disclosed in the report. Answer (D) is incorrect because the accountant must prepare a report stating that the statements have not been audited or reviewed.

**71.** When an accountant performs more than one level of service (for example, a compilation and a review, or a compilation and an audit) concerning the financial statements of a nonpublic entity, the accountant ordinarily should issue the report that is appropriate for

A. The lowest level of service rendered.

B. The highest level of service rendered.

C. A compilation engagement.

D. A review engagement.

Answer (B) is correct. *(CPA, adapted)*

**REQUIRED:** The report issued when an accountant performs more than one level of service.

**DISCUSSION:** The report should indicate the degree of responsibility, if any, that the accountant accepts regarding the financial statements. If an accountant performs a compilation or review of the statements of a nonpublic entity, (s)he should report in accordance with the SSARSs. But if more than one service is performed, (s)he "should issue the report that is appropriate for the highest level of service rendered" (AR 100). An exception is permitted, however, if an accountant has both compiled and reviewed the financial statements of a nonpublic entity and if the compilation report for the same period concerns financial statements included in a prescribed form that requires a departure from GAAP (AR 300).

**72.** During the course of an audit of financial statements, the client informs the accountant that (s)he may not correspond with the client's legal counsel. Under these circumstances, the accountant

A. May issue the standard review report with no mention of a scope limitation.

B. Should refuse to issue a review report but would not ordinarily refuse to issue a compilation report.

C. Should ordinarily refuse to issue either a review or a compilation report.

D. Should mention the scope limitation in the review report.

Answer (C) is correct. *(Publisher)*

**REQUIRED:** The effect of a client-imposed scope restriction.

**DISCUSSION:** The accountant must consider that the information affected by the restriction may be incorrect, incomplete, or otherwise unsatisfactory. An accountant who has been engaged to audit the financial statements ordinarily should refuse to issue either a review or a compilation report when not allowed to consult with the client's legal counsel (AR 100).

**73.** A continuing accountant is one who has been engaged to audit, review, or compile and report on the financial statements of the current period and one or more consecutive periods immediately prior to the current period. A continuing accountant who performs the same or a higher level of service with respect to the financial statements of the current period should

A. Update his/her report on the financial statements of a prior period.

B. Disclaim any assurance on the prior periods' statements.

C. Reissue the report on the financial statements of a prior period.

D. Express an adverse opinion with respect to the prior period's financial statements.

Answer (A) is correct. *(Publisher)*

**REQUIRED:** The report by a continuing accountant.

**DISCUSSION:** When a continuing accountant performs the same or a higher level of service, an updated report should be issued that considers information of which (s)he becomes aware during the current engagement and that reexpresses the previous conclusions or, depending on the circumstances, expresses different conclusions on the financial statements of a prior period as of the date of the current report (AR 200, *Reporting on Comparative Financial Statements*).

Answer (B) is incorrect because the previous conclusions should be reexpressed unless circumstances require otherwise. Answer (C) is incorrect because a reissued report results when the continuing accountant performs a lower-level service in the current period. A reissued report bears the same date as the original report but may be revised for the effects of certain events. In that case, the report may be dual dated. Answer (D) is incorrect because opinions do not result from compilations and reviews.

**74.** When the financial statements of a prior period have been compiled or reviewed by a predecessor whose report is not presented, the successor should refer in an additional paragraph of the report on the current-period financial statements to the predecessor's report on the prior-period financial statements. This reference should include the date of the report and all of the following except

A. A statement that the financial statements of the prior period were compiled or reviewed by another accountant.

B. A description of the standard form of disclaimer or limited assurance, as applicable, included in the report.

C. A description of the procedures applied by the other auditor.

D. A description of any modifications of the standard report and of any paragraphs emphasizing a matter.

Answer (C) is correct. *(Publisher)*

**REQUIRED:** The matter in a predecessor's review or compilation report that should not be included in a successor's report.

**DISCUSSION:** The procedures applied by the other auditor should not be described or discussed in the successor's report. Such a description might be misleading to the users of the report.

Answer (A) is incorrect because a statement that the financial statements of the prior period were compiled or reviewed by another accountant should be included in the successor's reference to the predecessor's report when that report is not presented. Answer (B) is incorrect because a description of the standard form of disclaimer or limited assurance, as applicable, should be included in the report. Answer (D) is incorrect because a description of any modifications of the standard report and of any paragraphs emphasizing a matter regarding the financial statements should be included in the report.

**75.** AR 400, *Communications between Predecessor and Successor Accountants*, provides guidance regarding compilations and reviews. A successor accountant

A. Must communicate with the predecessor before accepting the engagement.

B. Must not communicate with the predecessor. Communication would be a breach of confidentiality.

C. Need not communicate with a predecessor but may decide to do so.

D. Must communicate but not until after accepting the engagement.

Answer (C) is correct. *(Publisher)*

**REQUIRED:** The true statement concerning predecessor-successor communication.

**DISCUSSION:** The successor accountant is not required to communicate with the predecessor, but may believe it is beneficial to obtain information from the predecessor prior to accepting the engagement. If the successor decides that communication is useful, (s)he should obtain the consent of the prospective client and ask specific and reasonable questions of the predecessor either orally or in writing. Inquiries might concern (1) the integrity of management, (2) disagreements about accounting principles or similarly significant matters, (3) fraud or illegal acts, and (4) the predecessor's understanding of the reason for changing accountants.

**76.** An accountant who has reviewed statements that did not omit the disclosures required by GAAP may subsequently be requested to compile and report on statements for the same period that do omit substantially all of those disclosures when they are presented in comparative financial statements. In these circumstances, the accountant may report on the comparative compiled financial statements that omit such disclosures if (s)he

A. Does not mention the omissions.

B. Does not mention the prior report.

C. Includes in the report an additional paragraph indicating the nature of the previous service rendered.

D. States in the report that (s)he is not aware of any material modifications that should be made for the financial statements to be in conformity with GAAP.

Answer (C) is correct. *(Publisher)*

**REQUIRED:** The basis for reporting on comparative compiled statements that omit disclosures required by GAAP that appeared in previously reviewed statements.

**DISCUSSION:** The accountant may report on the comparative compiled statements that omit these disclosures if the compilation report includes the date of the previous report and a paragraph that explains the prior service provided (AR 200).

Answer (A) is incorrect because the compilation report must mention the omission of the disclosures. Answer (B) is incorrect because the prior report based upon another accounting service should be referred to and its date given. Answer (D) is incorrect because limited assurance is provided in a report on a review of financial statements, not a compilation.

**77.** Clark, CPA, compiled and properly reported on the financial statements of Green Co., a nonpublic entity, for the year ended March 31, 20X0. These statements omitted substantially all disclosures required by GAAP. Green asked Clark to compile the statements for the year ended March 31, 20X1, and to include all GAAP disclosures for the 20X1 statements only, but otherwise present both years' statements in comparative form. Clark may

A. Not report on the comparative financial statements because the 20X0 statements are not comparable with the 20X1 statements that include the GAAP disclosures.

B. Report on the comparative financial statements provided the 20X0 statements have no obvious material misstatements.

C. Report on the comparative financial statements provided an explanatory paragraph is added to Clark's report on the comparative financial statements.

D. Report on the comparative financial statements provided Clark updates the report on the 20X0 statements.

Answer (A) is correct. *(CPA, adapted)*

**REQUIRED:** The accountant's responsibility when compiled financial statements are presented comparatively but the earlier year's statements omit most disclosures required by GAAP.

**DISCUSSION:** Compiled financial statements that omit substantially all of the disclosures required by GAAP are not comparable to financial statements that include such disclosures. Accordingly, the accountant should not accept an engagement to report on comparative financial statements when statements for one or more, but not all, of the periods presented omit substantially all of the disclosures required by GAAP (AR 200).

**78.** One of the conditions required for an accountant to submit a written personal financial plan containing unaudited financial statements to a client without complying with the requirements of AR 100 is that the

A. Client agrees that the financial statements will not be used to obtain credit.

B. Accountant compiled or reviewed the client's financial statements for the immediate prior year.

C. Engagement letter acknowledges that the financial statements will contain departures from GAAP.

D. Accountant expresses limited assurance that the financial statements are free of any material misstatements.

Answer (A) is correct. *(CPA, adapted)*

**REQUIRED:** The condition for an accountant to submit a written personal financial plan.

**DISCUSSION:** The accountant must have an understanding with the client, preferably written, that the statements "will be used solely to assist the client and the client's advisers to develop the client's personal financial goals and objectives" and that they "will not be used to obtain credit or for any purposes other than developing these goals and objectives." Nothing must come to the accountant's attention during the engagement that indicates a use of the statements that violates the understanding (AR 600).

Answer (B) is incorrect because the accountant need not be a continuing accountant or have audited, reviewed, or compiled the statements. Answer (C) is incorrect because the accountant's report should indicate that the statements may be incomplete or contain a departure from GAAP, but AR 600 establishes no such requirement for the engagement letter. Answer (D) is incorrect because the accountant expresses no assurance on these statements.

## 8.5 Reports on Internal Control

**79.** Public companies (issuers) are required by the PCAOB to obtain an auditor's report attesting to management's assertion that internal control over financial reporting is effective (AS No. 2). Likewise, private companies may retain an auditor to issue a report on management's assertion over internal control in accordance with the AICPA attestation standards (AT 501). Which of the following statements best characterizes the relation between these two standards?

A. The two standards have different purposes as the AICPA standards address only controls relating to the safeguarding of assets while the PCAOB's standards relate more broadly to financial statements.

B. The AICPA standards recognize that the internal controls are the responsibility of the auditor while the PCAOB standards recognize that the internal controls are the responsibility of management.

C. The AICPA standards accept COSO's *Internal Control - Integrated Framework* as suitable and available framework for control while the PCAOB standards do not.

D. Both the AICPA standards and the PCAOB standards require management to provide a written assessment or assertion concerning the effectiveness of controls.

Answer (D) is correct. *(Publisher)*

**REQUIRED:** The representative statement about the AICPA and PCAOB standards on reporting on internal control.

**DISCUSSION:** Both standards require management to assess internal controls over financial reporting and provide a written assessment of the effectiveness of those controls.

Answer (A) is incorrect because both standards define internal control over financial reporting to include the process necessary to properly record the transactions to permit the preparation of financial statements in accordance with GAAP and to detect unauthorized acquisition, use, or disposition of assets that could have a material effect on the financial statements. Answer (B) is incorrect because both standards recognize that management is responsible for internal control over financial reporting. Answer (C) is incorrect because COSO is recognized as a suitable and available framework for both AT 501 and AS No. 2.

**80.** A practitioner may accept an engagement to examine the effectiveness of a private company's internal control over financial reporting in effect

| | As of a Specified Date | During a Specified Period of Time |
|---|---|---|
| A. | Yes | Yes |
| B. | Yes | No |
| C. | No | Yes |
| D. | No | No |

Answer (A) is correct. *(CPA, adapted)*

**REQUIRED:** The applicability of a report on an examination of the effectiveness of internal control.

**DISCUSSION:** The engagement is usually to examine the effectiveness of internal control as of the end of a private company's fiscal year, but the client may choose a different date. Furthermore, a practitioner may be engaged to examine the effectiveness of internal control during a period of time (AT 501).

**81.** Which of the following best describes a CPA's engagement to report on an entity's internal control over financial reporting?

A. An attest engagement that results in issuance of an examination report relating to the effectiveness of internal control.

B. An audit of the financial statement that results in communicating reportable conditions.

C. A prospective engagement to project, for a period of time not to exceed one year, and report on the expected benefits of the entity's internal control.

D. A consulting engagement to provide constructive advice to the entity on its internal control.

Answer (A) is correct. *(CPA, adapted)*

**REQUIRED:** The best description of an engagement to report on an entity's internal control over financial reporting.

**DISCUSSION:** In such an attest engagement, the practitioner issues a report relating to the effectiveness of the entity's internal control over financial reporting. The practitioner, as part of engagement performance, obtains from management a written assertion about such effectiveness. The objective of the engagement to attest to internal control over financial reporting is similar for AT 501 and AS No. 2.

Answer (B) is incorrect because an engagement to report on internal control is a service separate and distinct from a traditional financial statement audit. Answer (C) is incorrect because the opinion expressed should not extend into the future. Answer (D) is incorrect because consulting engagements do not result in the expression of an opinion.

**82.** Which of the following is a true statement concerning an attest engagement to examine an entity's internal control over financial reporting?

A. The practitioner relies on management's assertion about the effectiveness of internal control.

B. The responsible party evaluates the effectiveness of internal control.

C. Management relies on the practitioner's audit in making their assertion about the effectiveness of internal control.

D. Management agrees not to include the practitioner's report in a general-use document.

Answer (B) is correct. *(CPA, adapted)*

**REQUIRED:** The true statement concerning an attest engagement to examine and report on an entity's internal control.

**DISCUSSION:** As part of engagement performance for both AT 501 and AS No. 2, the practitioner must obtain from management a written assertion about internal control effectiveness.

Answer (A) is incorrect because the practitioner gathers evidence to test management's assertion that internal control is effective. Answer (C) is incorrect because the practitioner gathers evidence to test management's assertion that internal control is effective. Answer (D) is incorrect because the report is for general use.

**83.** Snow, CPA, was engaged by Master Co. to examine the effectiveness of Master's internal control over financial reporting under AT 501. Snow's report should state that

A. Because of inherent limitations of internal control, errors or fraud may occur and not be detected.

B. Management's evaluation of the effectiveness of internal control is based on criteria established by the American Institute of Certified Public Accountants.

C. The results of Snow's tests will form the basis for Snow's opinion on the fairness of Master's financial statements in conformity with GAAP.

D. The purpose of the engagement is to enable Snow to plan an audit and determine the nature, timing, and extent of tests to be performed.

Answer (A) is correct. *(CPA, adapted)*

**REQUIRED:** The statement in a CPA's report on an examination of the effectiveness of internal control over financial reporting.

**DISCUSSION:** The independent accountant's report should contain an introductory paragraph describing the subject matter and the responsible party, a scope paragraph describing the standards applied and the nature of the procedures performed, a paragraph describing the inherent limitations of internal control, and an opinion paragraph indicating whether the entity maintained effective internal control in all material respects over financial reporting based on the control criteria.

Answer (B) is incorrect because the CPA's examination is based on attestation standards established by the AICPA. Answer (C) is incorrect because the results of the CPA's tests will form a basis for the opinion either on the fairness of management's assertion about internal control or directly on the effectiveness of internal control. Answer (D) is incorrect because the purpose of the engagement is to enable the CPA to collect sufficient, competent evidential matter to support his/her opinion on whether the entity maintained effective internal control.

**84.** Cain Company's management engaged Bell, CPA, to examine the effectiveness of Cain's internal control over financial reporting under AT 501. Bell's report, which was accompanied by the responsible party's separate report presenting its written assertion about the effectiveness of internal control, described several material weaknesses and potential errors and fraudulent activities that could occur. Subsequently, management included Bell's report in its annual report to the board of directors with a statement that the cost of correcting the weaknesses would exceed the benefits. Bell should

A. Disclaim an opinion as to management's cost-benefit statement.

B. Advise the board that Bell either agrees or disagrees with management's statement.

C. Express an adverse opinion as to management's cost-benefit statement.

D. Advise both management and the board that Bell was withdrawing the opinion.

Answer (A) is correct. *(CPA, adapted)*

**REQUIRED:** The practitioner's action when the report is included in the client's annual report with a statement that the cost of corrective action exceeds the benefits.

**DISCUSSION:** If the assertion accompanying the practitioner's report includes a statement that the cost of corrective action exceeds the benefits of implementing new controls, the practitioner should include as the last paragraph of the report language that disclaims an opinion on the cost-benefit statement.

Answer (B) is incorrect because the practitioner would discuss the matter with management if (s)he believes that the statement is a material misstatement of fact. Answer (C) is incorrect because an adverse opinion should be expressed when the practitioner believes that the internal controls are not effective. Answer (D) is incorrect because, even assuming that the practitioner believes that the statement is a material misstatement, withdrawal of the opinion is not a necessary immediate action.

**85.** For a private company, how do the scope, procedures, and purpose of an engagement to examine the effectiveness of an entity's internal control compare with those for the consideration of internal control in a financial statement audit?

| | Scope | Procedures | Purpose |
|---|---|---|---|
| A. | Similar | Different | Similar |
| B. | Different | Similar | Similar |
| C. | Different | Different | Different |
| D. | Different | Similar | Different |

Answer (D) is correct. *(CPA, adapted)*

**REQUIRED:** The comparison of an engagement to examine a private company's internal control and the understanding of internal control in an audit.

**DISCUSSION:** The purpose of an examination of internal control is to express an opinion on the effectiveness of internal control. The purpose of the consideration of internal control in a financial statement audit is to enable the auditor to plan the audit. The two engagements also differ in scope. In the latter, the auditor is only required to obtain an understanding of internal control and assess control risk. Accordingly, the consideration in an audit is usually more limited than that undertaken to express an opinion. However, the types of procedures typically performed are similar.

**86.** When an independent auditor reports on an examination of the effectiveness of internal control based on criteria established by a regulatory agency, the report should

A. State that the practitioner assumes responsibility for the comprehensiveness of the criteria if they have not been subjected to due process procedures.

B. Modify the inherent limitations paragraph.

C. Limit the use of the report if the criteria have not been subjected to due process procedures.

D. Identify the control criteria in the scope paragraph.

Answer (C) is correct. *(Publisher)*

**REQUIRED:** The true statement about a report on internal control based on established criteria.

**DISCUSSION:** If the control criteria are established by a regulatory agency after following due process procedures, including broad distribution of proposed criteria for public comment, and the criteria are available to users, the standard form of reporting may be used. If the control criteria are not available to users or have not been subjected to due process procedures, and the practitioner determines that they are appropriate only for a limited number of users, the standard report must be modified. The principal modification is a limitation on use stated in a paragraph following the opinion paragraph.

Answer (A) is incorrect because the practitioner assumes no responsibility for the control criteria, but (s)he must report material weaknesses that come to his/her attention even if they are not covered by the criteria. Answer (B) is incorrect because AT 501 lists seven conditions for modification of the standard reports, but none requires omission or amendment of the inherent limitations paragraph. Answer (D) is incorrect because the control criteria are identified in the introductory and opinion paragraphs but not the scope paragraph.

**87.** A practitioner has been engaged to examine the effectiveness of an entity's internal control without performing an audit of the financial statements. The practitioner has obtained from the responsible party a written assertion about the effectiveness of internal control. The assertion is contained in a separate report that will accompany the practitioner's report, and is based on control criteria issued by experts that follow due process procedures. What restrictions, if any, should the practitioner place on the use of this report?

A. This report should be restricted for use by management.

B. This report should be restricted for use by the audit committee.

C. This report should be restricted for use by a specified regulatory agency.

D. The practitioner does not need to place any restrictions on the use of this report.

Answer (D) is correct. *(CPA, adapted)*

**REQUIRED:** The restrictions, if any, on the use of a report on an examination of the effectiveness of internal control.

**DISCUSSION:** An examination of the effectiveness of internal control over financial reporting may be performed if management accepts responsibility for the effectiveness of internal control, the responsible party evaluates effectiveness using suitable criteria, and sufficient evidence exists or can be developed to support the evaluation. As part of engagement performance, the practitioner must obtain from the responsible party a written assertion about effectiveness, contained either in a separate report to accompany the practitioner's report or in a representation letter. Criteria issued by groups of experts that follow due process procedures, including exposure of proposed criteria for public comment, are usually suitable. Moreover, performance of an audit of the financial statements is not a condition for performance of the engagement. Accordingly, no basis for restricting use of the report is presented.

**88.** King Corp. has received a local government grant and asked you, as a CPA, to examine the effectiveness of internal control that is required by the terms of the grant. The governmental agency responsible for the grant has prepared written criteria for such a report that have not been subjected to due process procedures. During your consideration of internal control to prepare the report, you find what you consider to be a material weakness in accounting for the grant. This weakness was not covered by the criteria established by the governmental agency. What action should you take in your report to the governmental agency?

A. Include the weakness in the report even though it is not covered by the agency's criteria.

B. Do not include the weakness in the report because it is outside the criteria established by the agency.

C. Advise King Corp.'s audit committee but do not include the weakness in the report.

D. Include a comment in the report that you do not believe the criteria established by the agency are comprehensive but do not include the weakness in the report.

Answer (A) is correct. *(CPA, adapted)*

**REQUIRED:** The proper action when a material weakness is discovered that was not covered by the applicable criteria established by a governmental agency.

**DISCUSSION:** According to AT 501, a material weakness in this context is "a condition in which the design or operation of one or more of the specific internal control components does not reduce to a relatively low level the risk that misstatements due to error or fraud in amounts that would be material in relation to the applicable grant or program might occur and not be detected on a timely basis by employees in the normal course of performing their assigned functions." A material weakness is also "a condition in which the lack of conformity with the regulatory agency's criteria is material in accordance with any guidelines for determining materiality that are included in such criteria." A practitioner who identifies material weaknesses in internal control that are not covered by the criteria set by the agency should include these material weaknesses in the report. (S)he does not, however, assume responsibility for the comprehensiveness of the agency's criteria.

Answer (B) is incorrect because professional standards require that this weakness be included. Answer (C) is incorrect because, although the CPA should advise King's audit committee about the problem, (s)he should also include it in the report. Answer (D) is incorrect because it is inappropriate to comment about the criteria established by the agency.

**89.** A service organization's internal control may interact with that of the client. The user auditor

A. Is not required to evaluate the service organization's controls.

B. Should obtain absolute assurance that the service organization's internal control will prevent or detect errors or fraud.

C. Should not consider weaknesses in the service organization's internal control to be weaknesses in the client's system.

D. Need not be concerned with the service organization's internal control if the client has effective controls related to service organization processing.

Answer (D) is correct. *(Publisher)*

**REQUIRED:** The true statement about the interaction of controls at the service and client organizations.

**DISCUSSION:** When the client has effective controls related to service organization processing, the user auditor may be able to assess control risk at an acceptably low level and forgo the service auditor's report.

Answer (A) is incorrect because, when controls of the client and service organizations interact, the service organization's controls must be evaluated in conjunction with the client's. Answer (B) is incorrect because reasonable, not absolute, assurance should be obtained that the service organization's controls will prevent or detect errors and fraud. Answer (C) is incorrect because the user auditor should consider the combination of controls at the client and service organizations.

**90.** AU 324, *Service Organizations*, applies to a financial statement audit of an entity that uses services of another organization as part of its information system. For this purpose, the user auditor may need to obtain a service auditor's report. Which of the following is a true statement about a service auditor's report?

A. It provides the user auditor with assurance regarding whether control procedures have been placed in operation at the client organization.

B. It should include an opinion.

C. If it proves to be inappropriate for the user auditor's purposes, (s)he must personally perform procedures at the service organization.

D. A user auditor need not inquire about the service auditor's professional reputation.

Answer (B) is correct. *(Publisher)*

**REQUIRED:** The true statement about a service auditor's report regarding internal control.

**DISCUSSION:** A service auditor's report on controls at the service organization should be helpful in providing a sufficient understanding to plan the audit of the user organization. The service auditor's report may express an opinion on the fairness of the description of the controls placed in operation at the service organization and whether they were suitably designed. If the service auditor has also tested controls, the report may also express an opinion on the operating effectiveness of the controls.

Answer (A) is incorrect because a service auditor's report is helpful to the user auditor in obtaining an understanding of internal control at the service organization, but it does not provide assurance regarding conditions at the client organization. Answer (C) is incorrect because audit procedures at the service organization may be performed by the service auditor on the request of (and under the direction of) the user auditor. Answer (D) is incorrect because the user auditor should inquire about the service auditor's professional reputation.

**91.** Payroll Data Co. (PDC) processes payroll transactions for a retailer. Cook, CPA, is engaged to express an opinion on a description of PDC's internal controls placed in operation as of a specific date. These controls are relevant to the retailer's internal control, so Cook's report may be useful in providing the retailer's independent auditor with information necessary to plan a financial statement audit. Cook's report should

A. Contain a disclaimer of opinion on the operating effectiveness of PDC's controls.

B. State whether PDC's controls were suitably designed to achieve the retailer's objectives.

C. Identify PDC's controls relevant to specific financial statement assertions.

D. Disclose Cook's assessed level of control risk for PDC.

Answer (A) is correct. *(CPA, adapted)*

**REQUIRED:** The components of a service report.

**DISCUSSION:** Service auditors may (1) report on controls placed in operation or (2) report on controls placed in operation and tests of operating effectiveness. The report limited to controls placed in operation should include a disclaimer of an opinion related to operating effectiveness of the controls.

Answer (B) is incorrect because the report should state whether PDC's controls were suitably designed to provide reasonable assurance of achieving the specified control objectives of the service organization. Answer (C) is incorrect because specific controls relevant to specific financial statement assertions need not be identified in the service auditor's report. Answer (D) is incorrect because the assessed level of control risk is not disclosed.

## 8.6 Prospective and Pro Forma Financial Information

**92.** A financial forecast consists of prospective financial statements that present an entity's expected financial position, results of operations, and cash flows. A forecast

A. Is based on the most conservative estimates.

B. Presents estimates given one or more hypothetical assumptions.

C. Unlike a projection, may contain a range.

D. Is based on assumptions reflecting conditions expected to exist and courses of action expected to be taken.

Answer (D) is correct. *(Publisher)*

**REQUIRED:** The true statement about a financial forecast.

**DISCUSSION:** According to AT 301, a financial forecast consists of prospective financial statements "that present, to the best of the responsible party's knowledge and belief, an entity's expected financial position, results of operations, and cash flows." A forecast is based on "the responsible party's assumptions reflecting conditions it expects to exist and the course of action it expects to take."

Answer (A) is incorrect because the information presented is based on expected (most likely) conditions and courses of action. Answer (B) is incorrect because a financial projection (not a forecast) is based on assumptions by the responsible party reflecting expected conditions and courses of action, given one or more hypothetical assumptions (a condition or action not necessarily expected to occur). Answer (C) is incorrect because both forecasts and projections may be stated as point estimates or ranges.

**93.** The AICPA recommends that the format of prospective financial statements be similar to

A. Historical financial statements, such as income statements, balance sheets, and statements of cash flows.

B. Worksheet formats so that adjustments can be readily made.

C. Specialized schedules that do not resemble financial statements.

D. Computer printouts so that the sophisticated nature of forecasting can be demonstrated.

Answer (A) is correct. *(Publisher)*

**REQUIRED:** The recommended format appropriate for prospective financial statements.

**DISCUSSION:** The AICPA states that information in prospective financial statements should be communicated by using the format of historical financial statements that would be issued for the period(s) covered, unless the responsible party and potential users agree on another format. Thus, this information may be put in the form of income statements, balance sheets, and statements of cash flows to facilitate comparisons with prior periods as well as with the actual financial statements for the prospective period (AT 301).

Answer (B) is incorrect because worksheet formats are inappropriate for prospective financial statements. Answer (C) is incorrect because specialized schedules are inappropriate for prospective financial statements. Answer (D) is incorrect because computer printouts are inappropriate for prospective financial statements.

**94.** AT 301 provides for minimum presentation guidelines for prospective financial information that

A. Permit prospective financial statements to be limited to certain minimum items.

B. Apply to pro forma statements.

C. Apply to partial presentations distributed for general use.

D. Require the usual notes associated with historical statements, including summaries of significant accounting policies and assumptions.

Answer (A) is correct. *(Publisher)*

**REQUIRED:** The correct provision of the minimum presentation guidelines.

**DISCUSSION:** Under the guidelines, prospective financial statements may take the form of complete basic statements or be limited to the following minimum items: (1) sales or gross revenues; (2) gross profit or cost of sales; (3) unusual or infrequently occurring items; (4) provision for income taxes; (5) discontinued operations or extraordinary items; (6) income from continuing operations; (7) net income; (8) basic and diluted earnings per share; (9) significant financial changes in position, including significant cash flows (but a cash flow statement is not required); (10) a description of what the responsible party intends the statements to present, a statement that the assumptions are based on the responsible party's judgment when the information was prepared, and a caveat about achievability; (11) summary of significant assumptions; and (12) summary of significant accounting policies.

Answer (B) is incorrect because pro forma statements demonstrate the effect of a consummated or hypothetical transaction or event by showing how it might have affected the historical statements if it had occurred during the period covered by those statements. Answer (C) is incorrect because a presentation is partial if it omits one or more of items (1) through (9) above. A partial presentation is ordinarily not appropriate for general use. The presentation is not deemed to be partial and the provisions of AT 301 still apply if items (10) through (12) are omitted. Answer (D) is incorrect because the details of each statement may be summarized or condensed, and the usual notes need not be included as such.

**95.** Which of the following statements concerning prospective financial statements is true?

A. Only a financial forecast would normally be appropriate for limited use.

B. Only a financial projection would normally be appropriate for general use.

C. Any type of prospective financial statements would normally be appropriate for limited use.

D. Any type of prospective financial statements would normally be appropriate for general use.

Answer (C) is correct. *(CPA, adapted)*

**REQUIRED:** The true statement about prospective financial statements.

**DISCUSSION:** Limited use of prospective financial statements means use by the responsible party and those with whom that party is negotiating directly, for example, in a submission to a regulatory body or in negotiations for a bank loan. These third parties are in a position to communicate directly with the responsible party. Consequently, AT 301 states, "Any type of prospective financial statements that would be useful in the circumstances would normally be appropriate for limited use."

Answer (A) is incorrect because projections as well as forecasts are appropriate for limited use. Answer (B) is incorrect because only a forecast is appropriate for general use.
Answer (D) is incorrect because only a forecast is appropriate for general use.

**96.** A practitioner's compilation report on a financial forecast should include a statement that

A. The forecast should be read only in conjunction with the audited historical financial statements.

B. The accountant expresses only limited assurance on the forecasted statements and their assumptions.

C. There will usually be differences between the forecasted and actual results.

D. The hypothetical assumptions used in the forecast are reasonable in the circumstances.

Answer (C) is correct. *(CPA, adapted)*

**REQUIRED:** The statement included in an accountant's compilation report on a financial forecast.

**DISCUSSION:** The standard report states that a compilation is limited in scope and does not enable the accountant to express an opinion or any other form of assurance. It adds that there will usually be differences between the forecasted and actual results (AT 301).

Answer (A) is incorrect because a forecast may stand alone. Answer (B) is incorrect because a compilation provides no assurance. Answer (D) is incorrect because a financial projection, not a financial forecast, contains hypothetical assumptions.

**97.** The practitioner's standard report on the examination of prospective financial statements should include all of the following except

A. An identification of the prospective financial statements presented and a statement that the examination was made in accordance with AICPA attestation standards.

B. A statement that the practitioner assumes no responsibility to update the report for events and circumstances after the report date.

C. The practitioner's opinion that the statements are in conformity with AICPA presentation guidelines and that the underlying assumptions provide a reasonable basis for the projection given the hypothetical assumptions or a reasonable basis for the forecast.

D. The practitioner's opinion that the prospective results will be attained.

Answer (D) is correct. *(Publisher)*

**REQUIRED:** The inappropriate element in a report on prospective financial statements.

**DISCUSSION:** Whenever a practitioner submits prospective financial statements that (s)he has assembled that reasonably might be expected to be used by a third party or reports on such statements, (s)he should examine, compile, or apply agreed-upon procedures to the statements. An examination is a professional service involving evaluation of the preparation of the statements, of the support underlying the assumptions, and of the presentation of the statements in conformity with AICPA guidelines. It also entails issuance of a report. However, the practitioner should provide a caveat that the prospective results may not be attained (AT 301).

**98.** When a CPA examines a client's projected financial statements, the CPA's report on these statements should

A. Explain the principal differences between historical and projected financial statements.

B. State that the CPA performed procedures to evaluate management's assumptions.

C. Refer to the CPA's auditor's report on the historical financial statements.

D. Include the CPA's opinion on the client's ability to continue as a going concern.

Answer (B) is correct. *(CPA, adapted)*

**REQUIRED:** The true statement concerning the report on projected financial statements.

**DISCUSSION:** AT 301 indicates that as a result of an examination of a client's prospective financial statements, the CPA has a basis for reporting on whether, in his or her opinion, (1) the prospective financial statements conform with AICPA guidelines, and (2) the assumptions provide a reasonable basis for the responsible party's forecast, or they provide a reasonable basis for the responsible party's projection given the hypothetical assumptions. Accordingly, the scope paragraph of the report states that the accountants performed procedures that were considered necessary to evaluate both the assumptions used by management and the preparation and presentation of the forecast (projection).

**99.** When a practitioner examines a financial forecast that fails to disclose several significant assumptions used to prepare the forecast, the practitioner should describe the assumptions in the practitioner's report and express

A. An "except for" qualified opinion.

B. A "subject to" qualified opinion.

C. An unqualified opinion with a separate explanatory paragraph.

D. An adverse opinion.

Answer (D) is correct. *(CPA, adapted)*

**REQUIRED:** The appropriate opinion if a forecast fails to disclose several significant assumptions.

**DISCUSSION:** An examination entails evaluating the preparation of the statements, the support underlying the assumptions, and the presentation of the statements for conformity with AICPA guidelines. It also involves issuance of a report stating the practitioner's opinion on whether (1) the presentation conforms with AICPA guidelines, and (2) the assumptions provide a reasonable basis for the forecast. If assumptions that appear to be significant at the time are not disclosed in the presentation, including the summary of assumptions, the practitioner must express an adverse opinion. Moreover, a practitioner should not examine a presentation that omits all such disclosures.

Answer (A) is incorrect because omission of assumptions that appear significant requires an adverse opinion. Other departures from the presentation guidelines, however, may justify either a qualified or an adverse opinion. Answer (B) is incorrect because the language "subject to" is never permissible. Answer (C) is incorrect because an explanatory paragraph is insufficient when significant assumptions are omitted (AT 301).

**100.** A practitioner's standard report on a compilation of a projection should not include a

A. Statement that a compilation of a projection is limited in scope.

B. Disclaimer of responsibility to update the report for events occurring after the report's date.

C. Statement that the practitioner expresses only limited assurance that the results may be achieved.

D. Separate paragraph that describes the limitations on the presentation's usefulness.

Answer (C) is correct. *(CPA, adapted)*

**REQUIRED:** The item not in a practitioner's standard report on a compilation of a projection.

**DISCUSSION:** Limited assurance (e.g., based on a review) should not be provided by the practitioner based on any prospective financial statement service.

Answer (A) is incorrect because the report should state that a compilation is limited in scope and does not provide any form of assurance. Answer (B) is incorrect because the report should contain a statement that the practitioner assumes no responsibility to update the report for events and circumstances occurring after the report date. Answer (D) is incorrect because, if the practitioner has reservations about the usefulness of the statements (e.g., the statements fail to provide notes), (s)he should so indicate in a separate paragraph.

**101.** The party responsible for assumptions identified in the preparation of prospective financial statements is usually

A. A third-party lending institution.

B. The client's management.

C. The reporting accountant.

D. The client's independent auditor.

Answer (B) is correct. *(CPA, adapted)*

**REQUIRED:** The party responsible for assumptions identified in the preparation of prospective statements.

**DISCUSSION:** Management is usually the responsible party, that is, the person(s) responsible for the assumptions underlying prospective financial statements. However, the responsible party may be a party outside the entity, such as a possible acquirer.

**102.** Which of the following is a prospective financial statement for general use upon which a practitioner may appropriately report?

A. Financial projection.

B. Partial presentation.

C. Pro forma financial statement.

D. Financial forecast.

Answer (D) is correct. *(CPA, adapted)*

**REQUIRED:** The prospective financial statement for general use upon which a practitioner may report.

**DISCUSSION:** Prospective financial statements are for general use if they are for use by persons with whom the responsible party is not negotiating directly, e.g., in an offering statement of the party's securities. Only a report based on an examination or a compilation of a financial forecast is appropriate for general use.

Answer (A) is incorrect because a projection is appropriate only for limited use, i.e., by the responsible party or by those with whom that party is negotiating directly. The reason is that it is based on one or more hypothetical assumptions. Answer (B) is incorrect because a presentation not in compliance with minimum guidelines is not appropriate for general use. Answer (C) is incorrect because pro forma statements are essentially historical, not prospective, statements.

**103.** Given one or more hypothetical assumptions, a responsible party may prepare, to the best of its knowledge and belief, an entity's expected financial position, results of operations, and cash flows. Such prospective financial statements are known as

A. Pro forma financial statements.

B. Financial projections.

C. Partial presentations.

D. Financial forecasts.

Answer (B) is correct. *(CPA, adapted)*

**REQUIRED:** The prospective statements based on one or more hypothetical assumptions.

**DISCUSSION:** Prospective statements include forecasts and projections. The difference between a forecast and a projection is that only the latter is based on one or more hypothetical assumptions, which are conditions or actions not necessarily expected to occur.

Answer (A) is incorrect because pro forma statements are essentially historical, not prospective, statements. Answer (C) is incorrect because partial presentations are not prospective statements. They do not meet the minimum presentation guidelines. Answer (D) is incorrect because forecasts are based on assumptions about conditions the responsible party expects to exist and the course of action it expects to take.

**104.** Accepting an engagement to examine an entity's financial projection will most likely be appropriate if the projection is intended to be used by

A. All employees who work for the entity.

B. Potential shareholders who request a prospectus or a registration statement.

C. A bank with which the entity is negotiating for a loan.

D. All shareholders of record as of the report date.

Answer (C) is correct. *(CPA, adapted)*

**REQUIRED:** The situation in which acceptance of an engagement to examine a projection is appropriate.

**DISCUSSION:** A projection is based on one or more hypothetical assumptions and therefore should be considered for limited use only. Limited use of prospective financial statements means use by the responsible party and those with whom that party is negotiating directly. Examples of appropriate use include negotiations for a bank loan and submission to a regulatory body.

**105.** A practitioner's compilation report on a financial forecast should include a statement that the

A. Compilation does not include evaluation of the support for the assumptions underlying the forecast.

B. Hypothetical assumptions used in the forecast are reasonable.

C. Range of assumptions selected is one in which one end of the range is less likely to occur than the other.

D. Prospective statements are limited to presenting, in the form of a forecast, information that is the practitioner's representation.

Answer (A) is correct. *(CPA, adapted)*

**REQUIRED:** The true statement about a compilation report on a financial forecast.

**DISCUSSION:** A compilation of a financial forecast involves assembling, to the extent necessary, the statements based on the responsible party's assumptions, performing required compilation procedures, and issuing a compilation report. The procedures include reading the statements and considering whether they meet AICPA presentation guidelines and are not obviously inappropriate. The standard report states that a compilation "does not include evaluation of the support for the assumptions."

Answer (B) is incorrect because a projection is based on hypothetical assumptions. Also, a compilation does not enable the practitioner to express an opinion or any other form of assurance. Answer (C) is incorrect because AT 301 states, "When a forecast contains a range, the range is not selected in a biased or misleading manner, for example, a range in which one end is significantly less expected than the other." Answer (D) is incorrect because the responsible party, which is usually management, is responsible for the preparation and presentation of the forecast.

**106.** When third-party use of prospective financial statements is expected, a practitioner may not accept an engagement to

A. Perform a review.

B. Perform a compilation.

C. Perform an examination.

D. Apply agreed-upon procedures.

Answer (A) is correct. *(CPA, adapted)*

**REQUIRED:** The engagement regarding prospective statements that may not be accepted.

**DISCUSSION:** AT 301 does not provide for the review form of engagement with regard to prospective statements.

Answer (B) is incorrect because a compilation may be performed provided the report does not express any form of assurance. Answer (C) is incorrect because an examination report may express an opinion on presentation in conformity with AICPA guidelines and the reasonableness of assumptions. Answer (D) is incorrect because an agreed-upon procedures engagement is permissible, but the report must state that the work performed does not constitute an examination.

**107.** A practitioner may perform an agreed-upon procedures attest engagement regarding prospective financial statements provided that

A. Use of the report is to be restricted to the specified parties.

B. The prospective financial statements are also examined.

C. Responsibility for the sufficiency of the procedures performed is taken by the practitioner.

D. Negative assurance is expressed on the prospective financial statements taken as a whole.

Answer (A) is correct. *(CPA, adapted)*

**REQUIRED:** The condition for performing an agreed-upon procedures attest engagement regarding prospective financial statements.

**DISCUSSION:** AT 301 establishes conditions for performing such an engagement: (1) the practitioner is independent, (2) the specified parties have agreed upon the procedures and take responsibility for their sufficiency, (3) the statements include a summary of significant assumptions, (4) the statements are subject to reasonably consistent evaluation against suitable and available criteria, (5) the practitioner and the specified parties have agreed upon the criteria to be used in determining findings, (6) the procedures are expected to result in reasonably consistent findings using the criteria, (7) use of the report is restricted to the specified parties, (8) evidence is expected to exist providing a reasonable basis for expressing the findings, and (9) the practitioner and the specified parties agree upon materiality limits for reporting.

Answer (B) is incorrect because the practitioner should state that the work performed does not constitute an examination. Answer (C) is incorrect because the specified parties must assume responsibility for the sufficiency of the procedures. Answer (D) is incorrect because the practitioner should not provide negative assurance.

**108.** Which of the following presents what the effects on historical financial data might have been if a consummated transaction had occurred earlier?

A. Prospective financial statements.

B. Pro forma financial information.

C. Interim financial information.

D. A financial projection.

Answer (B) is correct. *(Publisher)*

**REQUIRED:** The presentation that reflects the results of a consummated transaction had it occurred earlier.

**DISCUSSION:** According to AT 401, *Reporting on Pro Forma Financial Information*, pro forma information shows "what the significant effects on historical financial information might have been had a consummated or proposed transaction (or event) occurred at an earlier date." Examples of these transactions include a business combination, disposal of a significant portion of the business, change in the form or status of an entity, change in capitalization, and proposed sale of securities and application of the proceeds.

Answer (A) is incorrect because forecasts are not presentations of historical information. Answer (C) is incorrect because interim financial information states actual results. Answer (D) is incorrect because projections are not presentations of historical information.

**109.** A practitioner may report on an examination of pro forma financial information if the related historical financial statements have been

A. Audited.

B. Audited or reviewed.

C. Audited, reviewed, or compiled.

D. Reviewed or compiled.

Answer (A) is correct. *(Publisher)*

**REQUIRED:** The service(s) on historical statements permitting an examination of pro forma financial information.

**DISCUSSION:** A practitioner may examine or review pro forma financial information if (1) the document includes or incorporates by reference the complete historical statements, (2) the assurance provided is limited to that given on the historical statements, and (3) the reporting practitioner is knowledgeable about the reporting practices of each significant part of the combined entity. Thus, an examination of pro forma information is appropriate only if the historical statements have been audited (AT 401).

Answer (B) is incorrect because, if the historical statements have been reviewed, only a review of the pro forma information is appropriate. Answer (C) is incorrect because a compilation of the historical statements provides no assurance; it does not provide a basis for examining or reviewing the pro forma statements. Answer (D) is incorrect because a compilation of the historical statements provides no assurance; it does not provide a basis for examining or reviewing the pro forma statements.

**110.** The practitioner's report on an examination of pro forma financial information

A. Should have the same date as the related historical financial statements.

B. Should be added to the report on the historical financial statements.

C. Need not mention the report on the historical financial statements.

D. May state an unqualified, qualified, or adverse opinion.

Answer (D) is correct. *(Publisher)*

**REQUIRED:** The true statement about the practitioner's report on an examination of pro forma financial information.

**DISCUSSION:** The report should include an opinion on whether (1) management's assumptions provide a reasonable basis for the significant effects attributable to the transaction or event, (2) the pro forma adjustments give appropriate effect to the assumptions, and (3) the pro forma column reflects the proper application of those adjustments to the historical data. Scope limitations, reservations about the assumptions or the presentation (including inadequate disclosure), and other matters may lead to modification of the opinion, a disclaimer, or withdrawal from the engagement (AT 401).

Answer (A) is incorrect because the report should be dated as of the completion of procedures. Answer (B) is incorrect because the report may appear separately. If it is combined with the report on the historical statements, the combined report may need to be dual-dated. Answer (C) is incorrect because the report should refer to the financial statements and state whether they were audited or reviewed.

**111.** A practitioner's report on a review of pro forma financial information should include a

A. Statement that the entity's internal control was not relied on in the review.

B. Disclaimer of opinion on the financial statements from which the pro forma financial information is derived.

C. Caveat that it is uncertain whether the transaction or event reflected in the pro forma financial information will ever occur.

D. Reference to the financial statements from which the historical financial information is derived.

Answer (D) is correct. *(CPA, adapted)*

**REQUIRED:** The statement that should be included in a review of pro forma financial information.

**DISCUSSION:** A practitioner's report on pro forma information should include a title that includes the word "independent" and (1) an identification of the pro forma information, (2) an identification of the responsible party, (3) a reference to the financial statements from which the historical financial information is derived and a statement as to whether such financial statements were audited or reviewed, (4) a statement that the review was made in accordance with standards established by the AICPA, (5) a caveat that a review is substantially less in scope than an examination and that no opinion is expressed, (6) a separate paragraph explaining the objective of pro forma financial information and its limitations, and (7) the practitioner's conclusion providing negative assurance (AT 401).

Answer (A) is incorrect because the report should not mention internal control. Answer (B) is incorrect because the practitioner should disclaim an opinion on the pro forma financial information. Answer (C) is incorrect because the transaction may already have occurred.

## 8.7 SEC Reporting and Letters for Underwriters and Certain Other Requesting Parties

**112.** The Securities and Exchange Commission has authority to

A. Prescribe specific auditing procedures to detect fraud concerning inventories and accounts receivable of companies engaged in interstate commerce.

B. Deny lack of privity as a defense in third-party actions for gross negligence against the auditors of public companies.

C. Determine accounting principles for the purpose of financial reporting by companies offering securities to the public.

D. Require a change of auditors of governmental entities after a given period of years as a means of ensuring independence.

Answer (C) is correct. *(CPA, adapted)*

**REQUIRED:** The authority of the SEC.

**DISCUSSION:** The SEC has the authority to regulate the form and content of all financial statements, notes, and schedules filed with the SEC, and also the financial reports to shareholders if the company is subject to the Securities Exchange Act of 1934. The SEC has stated that financial statements conforming to FASB standards will be presumed to be in accordance with GAAP. However, the SEC reserves the right to substitute its principles for those of the accounting profession and to require any additional disclosures it deems necessary. The Sarbanes-Oxley Act of 2002 authorized the SEC to recognize as generally accepted any accounting principles established by a standard-setting body that meets the act's criteria.

Answer (A) is incorrect because the SEC may not prescribe specific auditing procedures. The Public Company Accounting Oversight Board (PCAOB), established by the Sarbanes-Oxley Act, must adopt auditing standards related to preparation of audit reports for public companies. Answer (B) is incorrect because the SEC may not deny lack of privity as a defense. Answer (D) is incorrect because the SEC may not require a change of auditors of governmental entities.

**113.** Accountants are often called upon to confer with clients, underwriters, and their respective counsel concerning the accounting and auditing requirements of the Securities Act of 1933 and of the SEC. A service often requested is the issuance of letters for underwriters and certain other requesting parties, commonly called comfort letters. Which of the following statements is true?

A. Comfort letters by the accountant are required under the Securities Act of 1933.

B. Comfort letters should not state that the accountant carried out procedures that (s)he considered necessary in the circumstances.

C. Copies of comfort letters should be filed with the SEC.

D. All of the answers are correct.

Answer (B) is correct. *(Publisher)*
**REQUIRED:** The true statement about comfort letters.
**DISCUSSION:** Much of the uncertainty and consequent risk of misunderstanding with regard to the nature and scope of comfort letters has arisen from the necessary limitations on the comments that accountants are permitted to make with respect to financial information in a registration statement that has not been audited. What constitutes a reasonable investigation of unaudited financial information sufficient for the purposes of an underwriter or other requesting party has never been authoritatively established. Consequently, the underwriter or other party should establish those procedures necessary for his/her purposes. However, the accountants cannot provide any assurance about the sufficiency of those procedures, and they should avoid any implication that they are carrying out such procedures as they consider necessary (AU 634).

Answer (A) is incorrect because comfort letters are not required by the SEC. They are requested by underwriters and certain others. Answer (C) is incorrect because comfort letters need not be filed with the SEC. Answer (D) is incorrect because two statements are false.

**114.** Comfort letters ordinarily are addressed to

A. The Securities and Exchange Commission.

B. The intermediary who negotiated the agreement with the client.

C. Creditor financial institutions.

D. The client's audit committee.

Answer (B) is correct. *(CPA, adapted)*
**REQUIRED:** The addressee of a comfort letter.
**DISCUSSION:** The letter should not be addressed or given to anyone other than the client and the named underwriters, broker-dealer, intermediary, or buyer or seller. "The appropriate addressee is the intermediary who has negotiated the agreement with the client, and with whom the accountants will deal in discussions regarding the letter" (AU 634).

**115.** Underwriters or other requesting parties occasionally request the accountants to repeat in the comfort letter their report on the audited financial statements included in the registration statement. They may also request negative assurance regarding the accountants' report. When these requests are made, the accountants should

A. Honor both requests.

B. Not honor either request.

C. Honor the request to repeat the report, but not provide negative assurance.

D. Provide negative assurance, but not repeat the report.

Answer (B) is correct. *(Publisher)*
**REQUIRED:** The appropriate response to a request to repeat the audit report or to provide negative assurance concerning the report.
**DISCUSSION:** "Because of the special significance of the date of the accountants' report, the accountants should not repeat their opinion." Also, accountants should not provide negative assurance regarding their report. "Because accountants have a statutory responsibility with respect to their opinion as of the effective date of the registration statement, and because the additional significance, if any, of negative assurance is unclear and such assurance may therefore give rise to misunderstanding, accountants should not give such negative assurance" (AU 634).

**116.** Comfort letters ordinarily are signed by the client's

A. Independent accountants.

B. Underwriters of securities.

C. Audit committee.

D. Senior management.

Answer (A) is correct. *(CPA, adapted)*
**REQUIRED:** The persons who sign a comfort letter.
**DISCUSSION:** A common condition of an underwriting agreement in connection with the offering for sale of securities registered with the SEC under the Securities Act of 1933 is that the accountants furnish a comfort letter to the underwriters. Hence, the independent accountants sign the comfort letter.

**117.** When an accountant issues to an underwriter a comfort letter containing comments on data that have not been audited, the underwriter most likely will receive

A. Positive assurance on supplementary disclosures.

B. Negative assurance on capsule information.

C. A disclaimer on prospective financial statements.

D. A limited opinion on pro forma financial statements.

Answer (B) is correct. *(CPA, adapted)*

**REQUIRED:** The most likely assurance, or lack thereof, provided in a comfort letter commenting on unaudited data.

**DISCUSSION:** According to AU 634, capsule information is unaudited summarized interim information for subsequent periods used to supplement the audited financial statements or unaudited condensed interim financial information in a registration statement. The accountant may give negative assurance regarding conformity with GAAP if the capsule information is in accordance with the disclosure requirements of APB 28, *Interim Financial Reporting*, and if the accountants have performed an AU 722 review of the underlying financial statements.

Answer (A) is incorrect because a comfort letter expresses, at most, negative assurance. Answer (C) is incorrect because prospective statements do not appear in a registration statement. Answer (D) is incorrect because a limited opinion is not a permissible form of reporting.

**118.** Which of the following matters is covered in a typical comfort letter?

A. Negative assurance concerning whether the entity's control activities operated as designed during the period audited.

B. An opinion regarding whether the entity complied with laws and regulations under *Government Auditing Standards* and the Single Audit Act.

C. Positive assurance concerning whether unaudited condensed financial information complied with GAAP.

D. An opinion as to whether the audited financial statements comply in form with the accounting requirements of the SEC.

Answer (D) is correct. *(CPA, adapted)*

**REQUIRED:** The item in a typical comfort letter.

**DISCUSSION:** A typical comfort letter expresses an opinion on whether audited financial statements and schedules "included in the registration statement comply as to form in all material respects with the applicable accounting requirements of the Act and the related published rules and regulations" (AU 634). However, the comfort letter does not state or repeat an opinion about the fairness of presentation of the statements.

Answer (A) is incorrect because comfort letters concern financial information contained in registration statements filed with the SEC under the Securities Act of 1933. Answer (B) is incorrect because comfort letters concern financial information contained in registration statements filed with the SEC under the Securities Act of 1933. Answer (C) is incorrect because comfort letters concern financial information contained in registration statements filed with the SEC under the Securities Act of 1933.

**119.** A comfort letter to underwriters or other requesting parties provided by a CPA may use which of the following terms to describe the work performed?

| | Audited | Read | Made General Review |
|---|---|---|---|
| A. | Yes | Yes | Yes |
| B. | No | No | No |
| C. | Yes | No | Yes |
| D. | Yes | Yes | No |

Answer (D) is correct. *(Publisher)*

**REQUIRED:** The terms an accountant may use in a letter for underwriters or other requesting parties.

**DISCUSSION:** The accountant performs a reasonable investigation to provide negative assurance in a comfort letter. "Terms of uncertain meaning (such as general review, limited review, reconcile, check, or test) should not be used in describing the work unless the procedures comprehended by these terms are described in the comfort letter" (AU 634).

**120.** A CPA should not express negative or limited assurance in a standard

A. Compilation report on financial statements of a nonpublic entity.

B. Review report on financial statements of a nonpublic entity.

C. Review report on interim financial statements of a public entity.

D. Comfort letter on financial information included in a registration statement of a public entity.

Answer (A) is correct. *(CPA, adapted)*

**REQUIRED:** The report in which a CPA should not express negative or limited assurance.

**DISCUSSION:** The standard compilation report states that the financial statements have not been audited or reviewed and, accordingly, the accountant does not express an opinion or any other form of assurance (AR 100).

Answer (B) is incorrect because a review report provides limited assurance. Answer (C) is incorrect because a review report provides limited assurance. Answer (D) is incorrect because the standard comfort letter regarding such information may contain negative assurance, which "consists of a statement by accountants that, as a result of specified procedures, nothing came to their attention that caused them to believe that specified matters do not meet a specified standard" (AU 634).

**121.** Which of the following is a true statement about the accountant's responsibility for letters to underwriters and certain other requesting parties?

A. An accountant who states in the letter that (s)he is independent may have an interest of the type requiring disclosure in the prospectus or registration statement.

B. An accountant may comment in the letter on compliance as to form in regard to any information contained in a registration statement.

C. An accountant may issue a draft comfort letter regarding a single shelf registration statement filed to cover delayed offerings of securities over an extended period.

D. Certain reports previously issued by an accountant may be repeated in the letter if they are not included in the registration statement.

Answer (C) is correct. *(Publisher)*

**REQUIRED:** The accountant's responsibility for letters to underwriters and certain other parties.

**DISCUSSION:** A shelf registration statement permits a company to register "a designated amount of securities for continuous or delayed offerings during an extended period." At the date of the registration, an underwriter may not have been chosen but the client or legal counsel for the underwriting group may request a comfort letter. Because only the underwriter can determine the procedures necessary for its purposes, the accountants should not issue a letter addressed to the client, legal counsel, or a nonspecific addressee, but they may issue a draft describing procedures performed and comments based thereon with a statement that the final letter will depend on procedures requested by the underwriter.

Answer (A) is incorrect because Regulation S-X lists the interests that must be disclosed. An accountant with one or more of these interests cannot be independent. Answer (B) is incorrect because an accountant should comment on compliance with SEC rules and regulations as to form only with respect to those requirements that apply to the form and content of financial statements and schedules. Answer (D) is incorrect because certain reports previously issued by an accountant may be attached to, but not repeated in, a letter for underwriters if they are not included in the statement.

**122.** An item typically included in a comfort letter is

A. The independence of the CPA.

B. Permission to distribute the letter to interested parties.

C. Positive assurance about whether the financial statements are fairly presented in conformity with GAAP.

D. Negative assurance about information included in management's discussion and analysis (MD&A).

Answer (A) is correct. *(Publisher)*

**REQUIRED:** The item a CPA would typically refer to when writing a comfort letter.

**DISCUSSION:** The independence of the CPA is a matter customarily addressed in comfort letters. The following example of a statement about independence is given in AU 634: "We are independent CPAs with respect to The Blank Co., Inc., within the meaning of the Act and the applicable published rules and regulations thereunder." The allusion is to the Securities Act of 1933.

Answer (B) is incorrect because the letter should include a statement that the "letter is solely for the information of the addressees and to assist the underwriters." Answer (C) is incorrect because the CPA should not repeat the audit opinion in the comfort letter. Answer (D) is incorrect because, although the accountant may refer to an examination or review of MD&A information, no assurance should be included in the comfort letter. Furthermore, the accountant should not refer to any restricted use report, such as a report on agreed-upon procedures.

**123.** Whenever negative assurance is provided by a CPA, it is based upon

A. An absence of nullifying evidence.

B. A presence of substantiating evidence.

C. An objective audit in accordance with applicable auditing standards.

D. A judgmental determination in accordance with guidelines promulgated by the AICPA.

Answer (A) is correct. *(CPA, adapted)*

**REQUIRED:** The basis upon which a CPA would provide negative assurance.

**DISCUSSION:** "Negative assurance consists of a statement by accountants that, as a result of specified procedures, nothing came to their attention that caused them to believe that specified matters do not meet a specified standard" (AU 634). For example, this phrasing might suggest the absence of evidence that financial statements are not fairly presented.

Answer (B) is incorrect because substantiating evidence would be the basis for positive assurance. Answer (C) is incorrect because negative assurance is provided by the application of procedures substantially more limited than those in an audit in accordance with auditing standards. Answer (D) is incorrect because, although the authority to permit negative assurance rests with the AICPA, the basis for rendering it is the lack of nullifying evidence.

**124.** An independent accountant's report is based on a review of interim financial information. If this report is presented in a registration statement, a prospectus should include a statement clarifying that the

A. Accountant's review report is not a part of the registration statement within the meaning of the Securities Act of 1933.

B. Accountant assumes no responsibility for subsequent events.

C. Accountant's review was performed in accordance with rules and regulations adopted by the Securities and Exchange Commission.

D. Accountant obtained corroborating evidence to determine whether material modifications are needed for such information to conform with GAAP.

Answer (A) is correct. *(CPA, adapted)*

**REQUIRED:** The statement in a review report on interim financial information included in a registration statement.

**DISCUSSION:** According to AU 711, when an independent accountant has reviewed interim information and his/her report is presented or incorporated by reference in a registration statement, the SEC requires that a prospectus containing a statement about the accountant's involvement clarify that the report "is not a 'report' or 'part' of the registration statement within the meaning of sections 7 and 11 of the Securities Act of 1933." The prospectus should state that reliance on the report should be restricted given the limited procedures applied and that the accountant is not subject to the liability provisions of section 11.

Answer (B) is incorrect because the registration statement contains audited financial statements. Thus, procedures should be extended from the date of the audit report to the effective date of the filing. Answer (C) is incorrect because the wording suggested by AU 711 is that "the independent public accountants have reported that they have applied limited procedures in accordance with professional standards for a review of such information." Answer (D) is incorrect because accountants make inquiries and apply analytical procedures to determine whether modifications are needed for financial information to conform with GAAP. They do not collect corroborating evidence in a review.

**125.** When an independent audit report is incorporated by reference in an SEC registration statement, a prospectus that includes a statement about the independent accountant's involvement should refer to the independent accountant as

A. Auditor of the financial reports.

B. Management's designate before the SEC.

C. Certified preparer of the report.

D. Expert in auditing and accounting.

Answer (D) is correct. *(CPA, adapted)*

**REQUIRED:** The reference to an independent accountant in a prospectus.

**DISCUSSION:** In filings under the Securities Act of 1933, the prospectus often states that certain information included in the registration statement is in reliance on the report of a named expert. Accordingly, the prospectus may state that reliance has been placed on the report of the independent public accountant, given on his/her authority as an expert in auditing and accounting (AU 711).

**126.** SEC Form S-3 is an optional, short-form registration statement that relies on the incorporation by reference of periodic reports required by the Securities Exchange Act of 1934. Form S-3 offers substantial savings in filing costs over other forms because minimal disclosures are required in the prospectus. The SEC permits the use of Form S-3 only by those large public firms that have filed periodic reports with the SEC for at least 3 years if the registrant

A. Does not have stock held by nonaffiliates.

B. Does not qualify for Form S-1.

C. Is widely followed and actively traded.

D. Has not had to file Form 8-K during the most recent 2-year period.

Answer (C) is correct. *(CMA, adapted)*

**REQUIRED:** The requirement for use of Form S-3.

**DISCUSSION:** Form S-1 is used for a first registration and for any securities for which no other form is authorized. Form S-2 is used by companies that have filed timely reports for 3 years. Incorporation by reference from the annual shareholders' report of Basic Information Package disclosures is allowed in Form S-2. If a company meets the requirements for use of Form S-2 and a specified amount in value of its stock is held by nonaffiliates (or it meets the requirements for total stock outstanding and for annual trading volume), Form S-3 may be used. It allows most information to be incorporated by reference to other SEC filings.

Answer (A) is incorrect because Form S-3 may not be used unless nonaffiliates hold the company's stock. Answer (B) is incorrect because Form S-1 is used for original filings. Answer (D) is incorrect because not having to file Form 8-K during the most recent 2-year period is not a requirement for use of Form S-3.

**127.** An audit of the financial statements included in Form 10-Q is not required. However, an external auditor's involvement with a Form 10-Q that is being prepared for filing with the SEC most likely consists of

A. A compilation report on the financial statements included in Form 10-Q.

B. A comfort letter that covers sub-period financial data.

C. An opinion on internal controls under which the Form 10-Q data were developed.

D. A review of the interim financial statements included in Form 10-Q.

Answer (D) is correct. *(CMA, adapted)*

**REQUIRED:** The external auditor's most likely involvement with Form 10-Q.

**DISCUSSION:** Form 10-Q is the quarterly report to the SEC. It must be filed for each of the first three quarters of the year within 45 days after the end of the quarter. It need not contain audited financial statements, but it should be prepared in accordance with APB 28. Moreover, the SEC requires a registrant to obtain a review by its independent auditors of interim financial statements reported on Form 10-Q or Form 10-QSB. Some entities also must present certain quarterly supplementary data with the audited annual financial statements (SEC Regulation S-K). The independent accountant who has audited the annual financial statements for the periods for which such data are presented should review the selected quarterly data. A review by an accountant based on inquiries and analytical procedures would permit an expression of negative assurance that no material modifications need to be made to the statements for them to be in conformity with GAAP. A review helps satisfy the SEC requirement of "adequate and accurate disclosure of material facts."

Answer (A) is incorrect because a compilation provides no assurance and would thus not satisfy the SEC requirement stated above. Answer (B) is incorrect because comfort letters are addressed to underwriters, not the SEC. Answer (C) is incorrect because the SEC does not require an external auditor's opinion on internal control.

**128.** Form 10-K is filed with the SEC to update the information a company supplied when filing a registration statement under the Securities Exchange Act of 1934. Form 10-K is a report filed

A. Within 90 days of the end of a company's fiscal year.

B. Within 45 days of the end of each quarter.

C. Within 2 weeks of the end of each month.

D. Within 15 days of significant events.

Answer (A) is correct. *(CMA, adapted)*

**REQUIRED:** The true statement about filing Form 10-K.

**DISCUSSION:** Form 10-K is the annual report to the SEC. It must be filed within 90 days after the corporation's year-end. It must contain audited financial statements and be signed by the principal executive, financial, and accounting officers and by a majority of the board. The content is essentially that in the Basic Information Package.

**129.** Form 8-K must be filed within

A. 90 days after the end of the fiscal year covered by the report.

B. 45 days after the end of each of the first three quarters of each fiscal year.

C. 90 days after the end of an employee stock purchase plan fiscal year.

D. 15 days after significant events.

Answer (D) is correct. *(CMA, adapted)*

**REQUIRED:** The filing deadline for Form 8-K.

**DISCUSSION:** Form 8-K is a current report used to disclose material events affecting a company. It must be filed within 15 days after the occurrence of a material event that is required to be reported (5 business days after a change of external auditors or resignation of a director). An extension may be obtained for filing financial statements and pro forma information required for an acquisition. Material events include changes in control, bankruptcy, acquisition or disposition of significant assets not in the ordinary course of business, a change in the independent auditors, etc.

**130.** In an effort to consolidate the registration process, the SEC has adopted new securities forms. However, these forms do not cover all circumstances. A registrant would use Form S-4 to register securities

A. In connection with mergers and related business-combination transactions.

B. When the registrant does not qualify for Form S-1.

C. When the registrant has not had to file Form 8-K during the most recent 2-year period.

D. Of real estate investment trusts.

Answer (A) is correct. *(CMA, adapted)*

**REQUIRED:** The circumstance under which a registrant would use Form S-4.

**DISCUSSION:** Form S-4 is a simplified form for business combinations, such as mergers. It is part of the integrated disclosure system established to simplify reporting requirements under the Securities Act of 1933 and the Securities Exchange Act of 1934. Thus, Form S-4 may incorporate much information by reference to other reports already filed with the SEC. The integrated disclosure system permits many companies to use the required annual report to shareholders (if prepared in conformity with Regulations S-X and S-K) as the basis for the annual report to the SEC on Form 10-K. Some may even use this report as the basis for registration statements.

## 8.8 Governmental Auditing

**131.** Financial audits of certain governmental entities are required to be performed in accordance with generally accepted government auditing standards (GAGAS) as promulgated in *Government Auditing Standards.* These standards do not require, as part of an auditor's report, the inclusion of

A. A statement as to whether the tests performed provide sufficient evidence to support an opinion on internal control over financial reporting.

B. The reportable conditions, with identification of material weaknesses.

C. Sampling methods used to test the controls designed to detect fraud whether or not material fraud is found.

D. A description of the scope of testing of internal control over financial reporting.

Answer (C) is correct. *(CPA, adapted)*

**REQUIRED:** The item not required by GAGAS to be identified in an audit report.

**DISCUSSION:** The Governmental Accountability Office (GAO) promulgates *Government Auditing Standards* (the Yellow Book). GAGAS apply to financial audits, attestation engagements, and performance audits. They incorporate GAAS for reporting and field work for financial statement audits as well as stating additional standards. GAGAS also incorporate any new AICPA standards relevant to financial statement audits (unless specifically excluded). Furthermore, AICPA standards addressing specific types of financial related audits are included in GAGAS. However, they do not require that the report identify specific sampling techniques used to test the controls. Nevertheless, when presenting material fraud, auditors should follow the report contents standards for performance audits that pertain to, among other things, methodology. Thus, if sampling significantly supports the findings, the auditor should describe the sample design and state why it was chosen.

Answer (A) is incorrect because auditors should state whether tests provided sufficient evidence to support an opinion on internal control over financial reporting and whether such an opinion is being provided. However, an opinion is not required. Answer (B) is incorrect because auditors should report deficiencies considered to be reportable conditions, with identification of those individually or cumulatively deemed to be material weaknesses. Answer (D) is incorrect because the report on the financial statements should describe the scope of testing of compliance with laws and regulations and internal control over financial reporting and present the results of those tests or refer to separate reports containing that information.

**132.** In reporting under *Government Auditing Standards*, an auditor most likely would be required to report a falsification of accounting records directly to a federal inspector general when the falsification is

A. Discovered after the auditor's report has been made available to the federal inspector general and to the public.

B. Reported by the auditor to the audit committee as a significant deficiency in internal control.

C. Voluntarily disclosed to the auditor by low-level personnel as a result of the auditor's inquiries.

D. Communicated by the auditor to the auditee and the auditee fails to make a required report of the matter.

Answer (D) is correct. *(CPA, adapted)*

**REQUIRED:** The time when an auditor is required to report externally under *Government Auditing Standards.*

**DISCUSSION:** Under *Government Auditing Standards*, auditors must report fraud or illegal acts directly to parties outside the auditee (for example, to a federal inspector general or a state attorney general) in two circumstances. These requirements are in addition to any legal requirements for direct reporting. First, if auditors have communicated such fraud or illegal acts to the auditee, and it fails to report them, the auditors should communicate their awareness of that failure to the auditee's governing body. If the auditee does not make the required report as soon as practicable after the auditors' communication with its governing body, the auditors should report the fraud or illegal acts directly to the external party specified in the law or regulation. Second, management is responsible for taking timely and appropriate steps to remedy fraud or illegal acts that auditors report to it. When fraud or an illegal act involves assistance received directly or indirectly from a government agency, auditors may have a duty to report it directly if management fails to take remedial steps. If auditors conclude that such failure is likely to cause them to depart from the standard report or resign from the audit, they should communicate that conclusion to the auditee's governing body. If the auditee does not report the act as soon as practicable to the entity that provided government assistance, the auditors should report directly to that entity.

**133.** An auditor who is engaged to audit the financial statements of a governmental entity should

A. Design the audit to provide reasonable assurance that the statements are free of material misstatements resulting from illegal acts having direct or indirect effects.

B. Obtain an understanding of the possible financial statement effects of laws and regulations having direct and material effects on amounts reported.

C. Assume responsibility for assuring that the entity complies with applicable laws and regulations.

D. Assess control risk with respect to each component of internal control.

Answer (B) is correct. *(Publisher)*

**REQUIRED:** The responsibility of an auditor.

**DISCUSSION:** According to AU 801, *Compliance Auditing Considerations in Audits of Governmental Entities and Recipients of Governmental Financial Assistance*, the auditor must obtain this understanding. The auditor must also assess whether management has identified laws and regulations that might have such effects. Procedures to obtain the understanding and make the assessment may include considering knowledge from prior audits; obtaining written management representations; discussions with the entity's legal counsel, chief financial officer, or grant administrators; and reviewing minutes of the appropriate legislative body.

Answer (A) is incorrect because auditors are primarily concerned with direct and material effects on financial statement amounts. Answer (C) is incorrect because management should assume responsibility for assuring that the entity complies with applicable laws and regulations. Answer (D) is incorrect because control risk should be assessed with respect to financial statement assertions.

**134.** The purpose of governmental effectiveness or program auditing is to determine if the desired results of a program are being achieved. The first step in conducting such an audit is to

A. Evaluate the system used to measure results.

B. Determine the time frame to be audited.

C. Collect quantifiable data on the program's success or failure.

D. Identify the legislative intent of the program being audited.

Answer (D) is correct. *(CIA, adapted)*

**REQUIRED:** The first step in conducting a governmental effectiveness or program audit.

**DISCUSSION:** A program audit of a government program obtains information about the costs, outputs, benefits, and effects of the program. It attempts to measure the accomplishments and relative success of the undertaking. However, this measurement depends on the actual intent of the legislation that established the program.

Answer (A) is incorrect because evaluating the system used to measure results is a subsequent step. Answer (B) is incorrect because determining the time frame to be audited is a subsequent step. Answer (C) is incorrect because collecting quantifiable data on the program's success or failure is a subsequent step.

**135.** Governmental auditing may extend beyond expressions of opinion on the fairness of financial presentation to include

| | Program Audits | Attestation Engagements | Economy and Efficiency Audits |
|---|---|---|---|
| A. | Yes | Yes | No |
| B. | Yes | Yes | Yes |
| C. | No | Yes | Yes |
| D. | Yes | No | Yes |

Answer (B) is correct. *(CPA, adapted)*

**REQUIRED:** The scope of a governmental audit.

**DISCUSSION:** Under *Government Auditing Standards*, an audit may be a financial audit, an attestation engagement, or a performance audit. Financial audits are primarily concerned with whether the financial statements are fairly presented in accordance with GAAP or with a comprehensive basis of accounting other than GAAP. Attestation engagements concern examining, reviewing, or performing agreed-upon procedures on a subject matter or an assertion about a subject matter and reporting on the results. Performance audits include economy and efficiency audits, program audits, internal control audits, and compliance with legal and other requirements.

**136.** An auditor was engaged to conduct a performance audit of a governmental entity in accordance with *Government Auditing Standards*. These standards do not require which of the following to be included in this auditor's report?

A. A statement of the audit objectives and a description of the audit scope.

B. Significant violations of contract provisions and significant abuse discovered during the audit.

C. The pertinent views of the entity's responsible officials concerning the auditor's findings.

D. A concurrent opinion on the financial statements taken as a whole.

Answer (D) is correct. *(CPA, adapted)*

**REQUIRED:** The action not required of an auditor in a performance audit.

**DISCUSSION:** Performance audits may have many objectives, for example, assessing (1) program effectiveness and results, (2) economy and efficiency, (3) internal control, (4) compliance, (5) prospective analyses, (6) guidance, or (7) summary information. However, GAGAS do not require that a financial audit be conducted simultaneously or concurrently with a performance audit.

Answer (A) is incorrect because the reporting standards for performance audits require auditors to report the audit objectives and the audit scope and methodology. Answer (B) is incorrect because the reporting standards for performance audits require auditors to report all significant (1) deficiencies in internal control, (2) violations of contracts and grant agreements, and (3) abuse. All instances of fraud and illegal acts should be reported unless clearly inconsequential. Answer (C) is incorrect because the reporting standards for performance audits require auditors to report the views of responsible officials about auditors' findings, conclusions, and recommendations, as well as corrections planned.

**137.** Because of the pervasive effects of laws and regulations on the financial statements of governmental units, an auditor should consider obtaining written representations from management regarding

A. Completeness of management's identification of laws and regulations that have a direct and material effect on its financial statements.

B. Implementation of controls designed to detect all illegal acts.

C. Expression of both positive and negative assurance to the auditor that the entity complied with all laws and regulations.

D. Employment of internal auditors who can report their findings, opinions, and conclusions objectively.

Answer (A) is correct. *(CPA, adapted)*

**REQUIRED:** The audit procedure that should be considered in a governmental audit.

**DISCUSSION:** The auditor should obtain an understanding of the possible financial statement effects of laws and regulations widely recognized by auditors as having direct and material effects. The auditor should also assess whether management has identified such laws and regulations. Thus, the auditor may consider obtaining written representations from management about the completeness of management's identification (AU 801).

Answer (B) is incorrect because internal control typically safeguards assets and promotes the reliability of financial statements but, given its inherent limitations, cannot be expected to prevent or detect all illegal acts. Answer (C) is incorrect because management does not express assurance, either positive or negative, that it has complied with all laws and regulations in an audit. Answer (D) is incorrect because the entity will decide whether to employ internal auditors.

**138.** The Single Audit Act is intended to be the definitive legislation concerning the audit of federal awards administered by nonfederal entities. Which of the following statements is a false statement about the act?

A. The single audit concept changes the focus from individual grants to grant recipients.

B. The act requires federal auditors to rely on single audit findings, to base any supplemental auditing on them, and to pay any additional auditing costs.

C. The recipient must designate one of the grant providers as a cognizant agency to act as a liaison between the auditee and the federal agencies providing funds.

D. Audit reporting should cover an opinion on the fairness of the financial statements, a report on internal control, and a report on compliance with grant requirements.

Answer (C) is correct. *(Publisher)*

**REQUIRED:** The false statement concerning the act.

**DISCUSSION:** A recipient expending more than $25 million per year in federal awards must have a cognizant agency for audit. The designated agency is the federal awarding agency that provides the predominant amount of direct funding, unless the OMB specifies another cognizant agency or the cognizant agency reassigns cognizance to another federal awarding agency. The cognizant agency overseeing the audit process acts as a liaison among the auditor, the auditee, and the granting agencies. Guidance for the application of the Single Audit Act is provided in OMB Circular A-133, *Audits of States, Local Governments, and Non-Profit Organizations.* Generally accepted governmental auditing standards (GAGAS) and generally accepted auditing standards (GAAS) apply when appropriate.

Answer (A) is incorrect because the single audit concept changes the focus of audits from individual grants to the grant recipients. Answer (B) is incorrect because the act requires federal auditors to rely on single audit findings. Answer (D) is incorrect because the audit report or reports should cover the financial statements, internal control, and compliance with grant requirements.

**139.** When performing an audit of a city that is subject to the requirements of the federal Single Audit Act, an auditor should adhere to

A. Governmental Accounting Standards Board General Standards.

B. Governmental Finance Officers Association Governmental Accounting, Auditing, and Financial Reporting Principles.

C. *Government Auditing Standards.*

D. Securities and Exchange Commission Regulation S-X.

Answer (C) is correct. *(CPA, adapted)*

**REQUIRED:** The standards for an audit of a city.

**DISCUSSION:** The Single Audit Act establishes audit requirements for recipients of federal awards administered by nonfederal entities. The act requires that audits of such entities be in accordance with *Government Auditing Standards* promulgated by the GAO. OMB Circular A-133 and related GAAS are also applicable. The act and the circular also state certain requirements that exceed those of the GAO's Standards.

**140.** In auditing compliance with requirements governing awards under major federal programs performed in accordance with the Single Audit Act, the auditor's consideration of materiality differs from materiality under generally accepted auditing standards. Under the Single Audit Act, materiality for the purpose of reporting an audit finding is

A. Calculated in relation to the financial statements taken as a whole.

B. Determined in relation to a type of compliance requirement for a major program.

C. Decided in conjunction with the auditor's risk assessment.

D. Ignored, because all account balances, regardless of size, are fully tested.

Answer (B) is correct. *(CPA, adapted)*

**REQUIRED:** The materiality determination under the Single Audit Act.

**DISCUSSION:** Under the Single Audit Act, the emphasis of the audit effort is on major programs related to federal awards administered by nonfederal entities. According to OMB Circular A-133, the schedule of findings and questioned costs includes instances of material noncompliance with laws, regulations, contracts, or grant agreements related to a major program. The auditor's determination of whether a noncompliance is material for the purpose of reporting an audit finding is in relation to a type of compliance requirement for a major program or an audit objective identified in the OMB Circular A-133 Compliance Supplement. Examples of types of compliance requirements include activities allowed or unallowed; allowable costs/cost principles; cash management; eligibility; matching, level of effort, and earmarking; and reporting.

Answer (A) is incorrect because, in a for-profit financial statement audit, materiality is related to the financial statements taken as a whole. Answer (C) is incorrect because a risk assessment is performed in planning the audit; however, the decision to report a finding depends on its materiality in relation to a type of compliance requirement for a major program or an audit objective identified in the compliance supplement. Answer (D) is incorrect because materiality must be considered in determining the appropriate tests to be applied.

**141.** Tell, CPA, is auditing the financial statements of Youth Services Co. (YSC), a not-for-profit organization, in accordance with GAGAS as promulgated in *Government Auditing Standards*. Tell's report on YSC's compliance with laws and regulations is required to contain statements of

| | Positive Assurance | Negative Assurance |
|---|---|---|
| A. | Yes | Yes |
| B. | Yes | No |
| C. | No | Yes |
| D. | No | No |

Answer (D) is correct. *(CPA, adapted)*

**REQUIRED:** The assurance, if any, provided regarding compliance in a report on a financial statement audit in accordance with GAGAS.

**DISCUSSION:** An additional reporting standard for financial audits states, in part, that the report should either (1) describe the scope of the auditors' testing of compliance with laws and regulations and present the results of those tests or (2) refer to a separate report containing that information. No statement of assurance is required. However, the auditor should report whether tests provide sufficient evidence to support an opinion on compliance and whether an opinion is provided.

**142.** The financial statement auditor's report on internal control and compliance with laws and regulations in accordance with *Government Auditing Standards* (GAS or the Yellow Book) is required to include

I. The scope of the auditor's testing of internal control.

II. Uncorrected misstatements that were determined by management to be immaterial.

A. I only.

B. II only.

C. Both I and II.

D. Neither I nor II.

Answer (A) is correct. *(CPA, adapted)*

**REQUIRED:** The item(s), if any, included in the report on internal controls and compliance with laws and regulations in accordance with GAS.

**DISCUSSION:** According to an additional GAS reporting standard for financial audits, the report on the financial statements should either (1) describe the scope of the auditors' testing of compliance with laws and regulations, describe the scope of testing of internal control over financial reporting, and present the results of those tests; or (2) refer to separate report(s) containing that information. In presenting the results of the tests, auditors should report fraud, illegal acts, other material noncompliance, and reportable conditions in internal control over financial reporting. In some circumstances, auditors should report fraud and illegal acts directly to parties external to the audited entity.

Answer (B) is incorrect because the auditor's report is not necessarily required to include uncorrected misstatements that were determined by management to be immaterial. However, under the SASs, which are included in GAS unless specifically excluded by the GAO, the auditor should evaluate the effects of uncorrected misstatements. The evaluation includes estimating the total likely misstatements. If the effects of likely misstatements, individually and in the aggregate, are not material, the report is not affected. Answer (C) is incorrect because the auditor's report is not necessarily required to include uncorrected misstatements that were determined by management to be immaterial. However, under the SASs, which are included in GAS unless specifically excluded by the GAO, the auditor should evaluate the effects of uncorrected misstatements. The evaluation includes estimating the total likely misstatements. If the effects of likely misstatements, individually and in the aggregate, are not material, the report is not affected. Answer (D) is incorrect because the scope of the auditor's testing of internal control must be included in the auditor's report.

**143.** In a financial statement audit under *Government Auditing Standards*, procedures have disclosed material instances of noncompliance with regulations. The report should

A. Also disclose immaterial instances of noncompliance.

B. Indicate that the audit was designed to provide reasonable assurance that illegal acts that could result in criminal prosecution would be detected.

C. Be qualified.

D. Place the findings in proper perspective.

Answer (D) is correct. *(Publisher)*

**REQUIRED:** The necessary element of a report on a financial statement audit given material noncompliance with regulations.

**DISCUSSION:** To give the reader a basis for judging the prevalence and consequences of material fraud, illegal acts, or other noncompliance, the instances identified should be related to the universe of the number of cases examined and be quantified in terms of dollar amounts, if appropriate.

Answer (A) is incorrect because instances of immaterial noncompliance need not be disclosed in the report but must be included in a separate communication to the auditee, preferably in writing. Answer (B) is incorrect because the auditor's duty regarding illegal acts by clients as defined by AU 317, *Illegal Acts by Clients*, is to design the audit to consider the possibility of, and to detect, such acts. Answer (C) is incorrect because the report need not express an opinion.

**144.** Reporting on internal control over financial reporting as part of a financial statement audit under generally accepted governmental auditing standards (GAGAS) requires a

A. Written report describing the entity's controls specifically designed to achieve the internal control objectives of safeguarding of assets and compliance with laws and regulations.

B. Written report describing each reportable condition observed, including identification of those considered material weaknesses.

C. Statement of negative assurance that the controls not tested have an immaterial effect on the entity's financial statements.

D. Statement of positive assurance that controls designed to detect material errors and fraud were tested.

Answer (B) is correct. *(CPA, adapted)*

**REQUIRED:** The requirement of GAGAS regarding reports on internal control.

**DISCUSSION:** GAGAS require auditors to identify reportable conditions that are individually or cumulatively material weaknesses.

Answer (A) is incorrect because identification of specific controls in not required under GAGAS. However, under GAGAS, auditors should report the scope of their testing of internal control over financial reporting, including whether the test provided sufficient evidence to support an opinion on internal control. Answer (C) is incorrect because GAGAS do not require expression of any form of assurance on internal control. Answer (D) is incorrect because GAGAS do not require expression of any form of assurance on internal control.

**145.** An auditor most likely would be responsible for assuring that management communicates significant deficiencies in the design of internal control

A. To a court-appointed creditors' committee when the client is operating under Chapter 11 of the Federal Bankruptcy Code.

B. To shareholders with significant influence (more than 20% equity ownership) when the reportable conditions are deemed to be material weaknesses.

C. To the Securities and Exchange Commission when the client is a publicly held entity.

D. To specific legislative and regulatory bodies when reporting under *Government Auditing Standards.*

Answer (D) is correct. *(CPA, adapted)*

**REQUIRED:** The auditor's responsibility for assuring communication of significant deficiencies in internal control outside the audited entity.

**DISCUSSION:** An auditor is required to include reportable conditions in a report prepared under *Government Auditing Standards.* Under an additional reporting standard for financial audits, the report is required to be distributed to the appropriate officials of the organization audited, officials of the organizations requiring or arranging for the audits, other officials who have legal oversight authority or who may be responsible for taking action, and others who may be authorized to receive the report.

Answer (A) is incorrect because management would be responsible for providing audited financial statements to a creditors' committee. Answer (B) is incorrect because the auditor's communication of internal-control-related matters noted in an audit is to the audit committee, management, or others in the organization, not to external parties. Answer (C) is incorrect because management is responsible for providing audited financial information to the SEC.

**146.** An auditor is auditing a nonfederal entity's administration of a federal award pursuant to a major program. The auditor is required to

| | Report Findings Related to Compliance | Express an Opinion on Compliance |
|---|---|---|
| A. | Yes | Yes |
| B. | Yes | No |
| C. | No | Yes |
| D. | No | No |

Answer (B) is correct. *(Publisher)*

**REQUIRED:** The reporting in a compliance audit of a nonfederal entity's administration of a federal award pursuant to a major program.

**DISCUSSION:** Under OMB Circular A-133, after an audit of a nonfederal entity that expends federal awards, the audit report on compliance must include an opinion or a disclaimer of opinion as to whether the auditee complied with laws, regulations, and the provisions of contracts or grants that could have a direct and material effect on each major program. This report should also refer, when applicable, to the separate schedule of findings and questioned costs.

**147.** Under the Single Audit Act, the auditor must report on compliance with laws, regulations, and the provisions of contracts or grant agreements, noncompliance with which could have a material effect on the financial statements. This report must also express or disclaim an opinion on whether the auditee complied with laws, etc., that could have a direct and material effect on each major program. In accordance with the act and OMB Circular A-133, which contains policies, procedures, and guidelines to implement the act, the auditor

A. Is not responsible for identifying major federal programs.

B. Must apply a concept of materiality in the audit of major federal programs that is similar to that in an audit under GAAS.

C. Must determine whether the recipient has engaged in activities to which particular types of compliance requirements apply.

D. Is required to restrict control risk and assess inherent and detection risk.

Answer (C) is correct. *(Publisher)*

**REQUIRED:** The true statement about compliance auditing of major federal financial assistance programs.

**DISCUSSION:** OMB Circular A-133 and the related Compliance Supplement list the types of compliance requirements, e.g., activities allowed or unallowed; allowable costs/cost principles; cash management; eligibility; matching, level of effort, and earmarking; and reporting. The data collection form submitted by the auditee should include, for each federal program, a yes or no statement as to whether there are audit findings for each of the types of compliance requirements and the total of any questioned costs.

Answer (A) is incorrect because the auditor determines whether a federal program is major. The auditor uses a risk-based approach that considers current and prior audit experience, oversight by federal agencies and pass-through entities, and the inherent risk of the program. Most large programs (Type A), except those determined to be low risk, and smaller programs (Type B, i.e., non-Type A programs that meet one of two quantitative thresholds) determined to be high risk are audited as major programs. A federal agency or pass-through entity may also request that a program be audited as a major program. Answer (B) is incorrect because, under the act, the materiality of an instance of noncompliance is in relation to a type of compliance requirement for a major program or an audit objective identified in the OMB Circular A-133 Compliance Supplement. Answer (D) is incorrect because the auditor assesses inherent and control risk and restricts detection risk.

**148.** Which of the following is a documentation requirement that an auditor should follow in a financial statement audit in accordance with *Government Auditing Standards*?

A. The working papers should contain copies of documents examined.

B. The auditor's working papers should contain sufficient information to permit another auditor to ascertain the evidence that supports audit conclusions and judgments.

C. The auditor need not document the basis for assessing control risk for material assertions significantly dependent on computerized systems unless that assessment is below the maximum level.

D. The working papers should contain a caveat that all instances of material errors and fraud may not be identified.

Answer (B) is correct. *(CPA, adapted)*

**REQUIRED:** The documentation requirement under *Government Auditing Standards*.

**DISCUSSION:** *Government Auditing Standards* requires that a record of the auditor's work be retained in the form of working papers. According to the additional working paper standard for financial statement audits, "Working papers should contain sufficient information to enable an experienced auditor having no previous connection with the audit to ascertain from them the evidence that supports the auditors' significant conclusions and judgments." Thus, in an audit in accordance with GAGAS, the working papers not only provide support for the audit report and aid in the conduct and supervision of the audit but also allow for the review of audit quality by providing written documentation of the evidence.

Answer (A) is incorrect because the working papers should document the work performed to support significant conclusions and judgments, including descriptions of transactions and records examined that would enable an experienced auditor to examine the same items. However, the auditors are not required to include copies of documents examined or to list detailed information from those documents. Answer (C) is incorrect because, according to the additional control standard for financial statement audits, planning the audit requires auditors to document in the working papers the basis for assessing control risk at the maximum for assertions that are significantly dependent upon computerized information systems. This standard is intended to heighten awareness of the risks of auditing in a computerized environment. Answer (D) is incorrect because this type of caveat is appropriate for the auditor's report, but it need not be stated in the working papers.

**149.** In accordance with the genera standard on independence stated in *Government Auditing Standards*, an audit organization may perform nonaudit services that do not violate the overarching principles that the standard is based on. Thus, the audit organization most likely may do which of the following without impairing its independence with respect to the audited entity?

A. Perform internal audit services.

B. Prepare tax filings.

C. Operate the audited entity's information technology system.

D. Prepare accounting records.

Answer (B) is correct. *(Publisher)*

**REQUIRED:** The activity most likely to be permissible under the independence standard.

**DISCUSSION:** According to the general standard on independence, "In all matters relating to the audit work, the audit organization and the individual auditor, whether government or public, should be free both in fact and appearance from personal, external, and organizational impairments to independence." The standard is based on two overarching principles: (1) Audit organizations should not provide nonaudit services involving management functions or making management decisions, and (2) audit organizations should not audit their own work or provide nonaudit services when the services are significant or material to the subject matter of the audits. For a nonaudit service that does not violate the principles, certain supplemental safeguards also must be met, for example, (1) personnel who perform nonaudit services must be precluded from performing related audit work, (2) the auditor's work cannot be reduced beyond the level appropriate if the nonaudit work had been performed by an unrelated party, and (3) various documentation and quality assurance requirements are satisfied. These supplemental safeguards do not apply to routine activities. Accordingly, an audit organization may, for example, prepare and draft financial statements if prepared by management, prepare routine tax filings, advise on IT system design, or advise on control self-assessment.

Answer (A) is incorrect because audit organizations may not perform internal audit services unless they reasonably conclude that they will not examine their own work during the audit. Answer (C) is incorrect because prohibited nonaudit services include operating the IT system. Answer (D) is incorrect because prohibited nonaudit services include preparing and maintaining accounting records.

**150.** Which of the following statements represents a quality control requirement under *Government Auditing Standards*?

A. A CPA who conducts government audits is required to undergo an annual external peer review when an appropriate internal quality control system is not in place.

B. A CPA seeking to enter into a contract to perform an audit should provide the CPA's most recent external peer review report to the party contracting for the audit.

C. An external peer review of a CPA's practice should include a review of the working papers of each government audit performed since the prior external peer review.

D. A CPA who conducts government audits may not make the CPA's external peer review report available to the public.

Answer (B) is correct. *(CPA, adapted)*

**REQUIRED:** The quality control requirement under government auditing standards.

**DISCUSSION:** According to a general standard stated in *Government Auditing Standards*, an audit organization conducting an audit in accordance with these standards must have an appropriate internal quality control system in place and undergo an external peer review. For example, a CPA seeking to enter into a contract to perform an audit should provide the CPA's most recent external peer review report to the party contracting for the audit.

Answer (A) is incorrect because organizations conducting audits in accordance with the *Government Auditing Standards* should have an external peer review at least once every 3 years. Answer (C) is incorrect because an external peer review consists of evaluating a sample of audits performed and working papers prepared since the last external peer review. Answer (D) is incorrect because audit organizations should ordinarily make their external peer review reports available to those who request them and to appropriate oversight bodies. It is recommended that the report be made available to the public as well.

## 8.9 Compliance Attestation

**151.** According to AT 601, *Compliance Attestation*,

A. The field work and reporting but not the general attestation standards apply to this type of engagement.

B. The practitioner may accept an engagement to perform an examination of the effectiveness of internal control over compliance or an assertion thereon, but in either case should obtain the assertion in writing.

C. A compliance attest engagement is intended to result in a legal determination of an entity's compliance with specified requirements.

D. An engagement to perform an examination of compliance with specified requirements is restricted to providing assurance concerning the responsible party's written or nonwritten assertion thereon.

Answer (B) is correct. *(Publisher)*

**REQUIRED:** The true statement about compliance attest engagements.

**DISCUSSION:** AT 601 applies to engagements related to an entity's compliance with specified requirements (laws, regulations, rules, contracts, or grants) or the effectiveness of an entity's internal control over compliance with specified requirements. The practitioner may perform agreed-upon procedures to assist users in evaluating either or both of the foregoing subjects (or assertions related thereto). The practitioner may also examine (1) compliance with specified requirements or a written assertion thereon, or (2) the effectiveness of internal control over compliance or a written assertion thereon. As part of the performance of either agreed-upon procedures or an examination engagement, the practitioner obtains the responsible party's written assertion, presented either in a separate report that will accompany the practitioner's report or in a representation letter.

Answer (A) is incorrect because the general attestation standards also apply. Answer (C) is incorrect because a report issued in accordance with AT 601 does not provide a legal determination on compliance with specified requirements, but it may be useful to legal counsel or others in making such determinations. Answer (D) is incorrect because the objective of an engagement to perform an examination of compliance with specified requirements is to express an opinion (1) on an entity's compliance, in all material respects, with specified criteria, or (2) on whether the responsible party's written assertion about such compliance is fairly stated, in all material respects, based on the specified criteria.

**152.** A practitioner may accept a compliance attest engagement to perform

| | Agreed-Upon Procedures | Examination | Review |
|---|---|---|---|
| A. | Yes | Yes | Yes |
| B. | No | Yes | Yes |
| C. | Yes | Yes | No |
| D. | No | No | Yes |

Answer (C) is correct. *(Publisher)*

**REQUIRED:** The type(s) of compliance attest engagements.

**DISCUSSION:** The practitioner may accept an agreed-upon procedures compliance attest engagement as long as the specified users agree upon the procedures to be performed and take responsibility for the sufficiency of such procedures for their purposes. The practitioner may also conduct an examination in which (s)he gathers evidence to support an opinion. Both types of engagements may be performed with respect to compliance with specified requirements (or an assertion thereon) or the effectiveness of internal control over compliance (or an assertion thereon). However, AT 601 does not provide for a review engagement.

**153.** A practitioner's report on agreed-upon procedures related to an entity's compliance with specified requirements should contain

A. A statement of restrictions on the use of the report.

B. An opinion about whether the entity complied, in all material respects, with specified requirements.

C. Negative assurance on compliance.

D. An acknowledgment of responsibility for the sufficiency of the procedures.

Answer (A) is correct. *(CPA, adapted)*

**REQUIRED:** The statement in a report on a compliance attestation engagement to apply agreed-upon procedures.

**DISCUSSION:** The fourth attestation standard of reporting indicates that the report on an attest engagement to apply agreed-upon procedures should contain a statement restricting its use to specified parties (those who have agreed upon such procedures). Nevertheless, if the report is a matter of public record, the practitioner should so indicate.

Answer (B) is incorrect because the report on agreed-upon procedures should be in the form of a summary of procedures and findings, not an opinion. Answer (C) is incorrect because negative assurance is not permitted in reports on applying agreed-upon procedures. Answer (D) is incorrect because the parties who agreed to the procedures are responsible for their sufficiency.

**154.** According to AT 601, a practitioner may examine compliance with specified requirements. The objective is the expression of an opinion on whether the entity complied, or on whether the responsible party's assertion about compliance is fairly stated, in all material respects, based on the specified criteria. For this purpose, the practitioner accumulates sufficient evidence to limit attestation risk to an appropriately low level. Attestation risk is the risk that

A. Material noncompliance with specified requirements could occur, assuming no related controls over compliance exist.

B. Material noncompliance that could occur will not be prevented or detected on a timely basis by the entity's controls.

C. The practitioner may unknowingly fail to modify appropriately the opinion.

D. The practitioner's procedures will lead to the conclusion that material noncompliance does not exist when, in fact, such noncompliance does exist.

Answer (C) is correct. *(Publisher)*

**REQUIRED:** The nature of attestation risk.

**DISCUSSION:** Attestation risk is the risk that the practitioner may unknowingly fail to modify appropriately the opinion. Its components are inherent risk, control risk, and detection risk.

Answer (A) is incorrect because inherent risk is the risk that material noncompliance with specified requirements could occur, assuming no related controls over compliance exist. Answer (B) is incorrect because control risk is the risk that material noncompliance that could occur will not be prevented or detected on a timely basis by the entity's controls. Answer (D) is incorrect because detection risk is the risk that the practitioner's procedures will lead to the conclusion that material noncompliance does not exist when such noncompliance does exist.

## 8.10 Management's Discussion and Analysis

**155.** In accordance with AT 701, *Management's Discussion and Analysis*, the presentation of an MD&A constitutes a written assertion that

A. May be examined but not reviewed.

B. May be examined or reviewed.

C. A practitioner may attest to only if the entity is public.

D. A practitioner may attest to only if the entity is nonpublic.

Answer (B) is correct. *(Publisher)*

**REQUIRED:** The true statement about an attest engagement performed upon the presentation of an MD&A.

**DISCUSSION:** A practitioner may perform an attest engagement regarding an MD&A prepared pursuant to SEC rules and presented in an annual report or other document. This presentation constitutes a written assertion that may be examined or reviewed whether the entity is public or private. However, a report on a review cannot be filed with the SEC.

Answer (A) is incorrect because the MD&A may be reviewed. Answer (C) is incorrect because the entity presenting the MD&A may be public or private. Answer (D) is incorrect because the entity presenting the MD&A may be public or private.

**156.** AT 701, *Management's Discussion and Analysis*, provides guidance for an engagement regarding management's discussion and analysis (MD&A) prepared under the rules and regulations adopted by the SEC. A practitioner who undertakes such an engagement

A. May review but not apply agreed-upon procedures to MD&A.

B. Must comply with the general and reporting but not the field work attestation standards.

C. May perform services regarding MD&A of a public but not a private entity.

D. Must have audited the entity's financial statements for the latest period to which MD&A relates if the service provided is an examination.

Answer (D) is correct. *(Publisher)*

**REQUIRED:** The true statement about an engagement to provide services regarding MD&A.

**DISCUSSION:** A practitioner may examine MD&A if (s)he has performed an audit in accordance with auditing standards of the financial statements for at least the most recent period to which the presentation relates. Furthermore, the financial statements for the other periods covered by the presentation must have been audited by the practitioner or a predecessor auditor. A base knowledge of the entity obtained in this way is necessary to provide knowledge sufficient to evaluate the results of the examination. A practitioner may also review MD&A of a public entity for an annual period if (s)he has audited the statements for the latest annual period and if the other statements covered by the presentation were audited by the practitioner or a predecessor auditor. In addition, a practitioner may review MD&A of a public entity for an interim period if (1) (s)he has reviewed the historical statements for the related comparative interim periods or audited the interim statements and (2) MD&A for the most recent fiscal year has or will be examined or reviewed.

Answer (A) is incorrect because agreed-upon procedures may be performed if the practitioner applies AT 201. Answer (B) is incorrect because the attestation standards for field work must be followed. Answer (C) is incorrect because attest services may be provided regarding an MD&A presentation of a nonpublic entity whose management furnishes a written assertion that it was prepared using the rules and regulations adopted by the SEC.

# STUDY UNIT NINE
# INTERNAL AUDITING



This study unit concerns the following pronouncements of The Institute of Internal Auditors (The IIA):

1. The IIA *Code of Ethics*
2. International Standards for the Professional Practice of Internal Auditing Standards
3. Practice Advisories (PAs)

Other questions unique to internal auditing are also included. The concepts and terminology used are from The IIA's pronouncements and may differ from those found in other authoritative literature. Many citations are to the Standards (including the Glossary), which consist of Attribute, Performance, and Implementation Standards. Other citations are to Practice Advisories (PAs), which provide nonmandatory interpretations of the Standards endorsed by The IIA. Two other acronyms are used in this study unit: IAA (internal audit activity) and CAE (chief audit executive).

Questions from the CIA exam and internal auditing questions from the CMA and CPA exams appear in the study units that cover subject matter common to both external and internal auditing (Study Units 3, 4, 5, and 6).

**QUESTIONS**

**9.1 Introduction to Internal Auditing**

**1.** The proper organizational role of internal auditing is to

A. Assist the external auditor in order to reduce external audit fees.

B. Perform studies to assist in the attainment of more efficient operations.

C. Serve as the investigative arm of the board.

D. Serve as an independent, objective assurance and consulting activity that adds value to operations.

Answer (D) is correct. *(CIA, adapted)*

**REQUIRED:** The role of internal auditing.

**DISCUSSION:** According to the definition of internal auditing, "Internal auditing is an independent, objective assurance and consulting activity designed to add value and improve an organization's operations. It helps an organization accomplish its objectives by bringing a systematic, disciplined approach to evaluate and improve the effectiveness of risk management, control, and governance processes."

Answer (A) is incorrect because reducing external audit fees may be a direct result of internal audit work, but it is not a reason for staffing an internal audit activity. Answer (B) is incorrect because the primary role of internal auditing includes, but is not limited to, assessing the efficiency of operations. Answer (C) is incorrect because internal auditors serve management as well as the board.

**2.** Internal auditing is a dynamic profession. Which of the following best describes the scope of internal auditing as it has developed to date?

A. Internal auditing involves evaluating the effectiveness and efficiency with which resources are employed.

B. Internal auditing involves evaluating compliance with laws, regulations, and contracts.

C. Internal auditing has evolved to verifying the existence of assets and reviewing the means of safeguarding assets.

D. Internal auditing has evolved to evaluating all risk management, control, and governance processes.

Answer (D) is correct. *(CIA, adapted)*

**REQUIRED:** The scope of internal auditing.

**DISCUSSION:** The IAA evaluates and contributes to the improvement of risk management, control, and governance processes using a systematic and disciplined approach (Standard 2100). According to PA 2100-1, internal auditors evaluate the whole management process of planning, organizing, and directing to determine whether reasonable assurance exists that objectives and goals will be achieved. These evaluations, in the aggregate, provide information to appraise the overall management process. All business systems, processes, operations, functions, and activities within the organization are subject to the internal auditors' evaluations. The comprehensive scope of work of internal auditing should provide reasonable assurance that management's:

- Risk management system is effective.
- System of internal control is effective and efficient.
- Governance process is effective by establishing and preserving values, setting goals, monitoring activities and performance, and defining the measures of accountability.

Answer (A) is incorrect because evaluating effectiveness and efficiency is an incomplete description of the scope of work of internal auditing. Answer (B) is incorrect because evaluating compliance is an incomplete description of the scope of work of internal auditing. Answer (C) is incorrect because verifying the existence of assets and reviewing the means of safeguarding assets are not the only functions of internal auditors.

**3.** Of the following, which is the major objective of The Institute of Internal Auditors (The IIA)?

A. Cultivate, promote, and disseminate information concerning internal auditing and related subjects.

B. Oversee the activities of internal auditors.

C. Promulgate standards that must be followed by all corporations.

D. Investigate accusations that Certified Internal Auditors have violated The Institute of Internal Auditors *Code of Ethics*.

Answer (A) is correct. *(CIA, adapted)*

**REQUIRED:** The major objective of The IIA.

**DISCUSSION:** The articles of incorporation of The IIA state its purposes: "To cultivate, promote, and disseminate knowledge and information concerning internal auditing and subjects related thereto; to establish and maintain high standards of integrity, honor, and character among internal auditors; to furnish information regarding internal auditing and the practice and methods thereof to its members, and to other persons interested therein, and to the general public; to cause the publication of articles relating to internal auditing and practices and methods thereof; to establish and maintain a library and reading rooms, meeting rooms and social rooms for the use of its members; to promote social intercourse among its members; and to do any and all things which shall be lawful and appropriate in furtherance of any of the purposes hereinbefore expressed."

Answer (B) is incorrect because The IIA is not a regulatory agency. Answer (C) is incorrect because the Standards are mandatory guidance for individuals and entities that provide internal auditing services, not for corporations, per se. Answer (D) is incorrect because investigating ethics violations is not a major objective.

**4.** A major reason for establishing an internal audit activity is to

A. Relieve overburdened management of the responsibility for establishing effective controls.

B. Safeguard resources entrusted to the organization.

C. Ensure the reliability and integrity of financial and operational information.

D. Evaluate and improve the effectiveness of control processes.

Answer (D) is correct. *(CIA, adapted)*

**REQUIRED:** The major reason for establishing an IAA.

**DISCUSSION:** According to the Glossary, control processes are defined as "The policies, procedures, and activities that are part of a control framework, designed to ensure that risks are contained within the risk tolerances established by the risk management process." Hence, they have a prominent role in internal auditing, which "helps an organization accomplish its objectives by bringing a systematic, disciplined approach to evaluate and improve the effectiveness of risk management, control, and governance processes."

Answer (A) is incorrect because management is responsible for the establishment of internal control. Answer (B) is incorrect because risk management, control, and governance processes ultimately serve to safeguard the organization's resources. Answer (C) is incorrect because the IAA cannot ensure the reliability and integrity of financial and operational information. Its responsibility is to evaluate risk exposures relating to governance, operations, and information systems regarding the reliability and integrity of financial and operational information (Standard 2110.A2). Based on the risk assessment, it then evaluates the adequacy and effectiveness of controls (Standard 2120.A1).

**5.** The most accurate term for the procedures used by the representatives of the organization's stakeholders to provide oversight of processes administered by management is

A. Governance.

B. Control.

C. Risk management.

D. Monitoring.

Answer (A) is correct. *(Publisher)*

**REQUIRED:** The most accurate term for the means of providing oversight of processes administered by management.

**DISCUSSION:** An organization uses various legal forms, structures, strategies, and procedures to ensure that it (1) complies with society's legal and regulatory rules; (2) satisfies the generally accepted business norms, ethical precepts, and social expectations of society; (3) provides overall benefit to society and enhances the interests of the specific stakeholders in both the long and short term; and (4) reports fully and truthfully to its owners, regulators, other stakeholders, and general public to ensure accountability for its decisions, actions, conduct, and performance. The way in which an organization chooses to conduct its affairs to meet those four responsibilities is commonly referred to as its governance process. The organization's governing body (such as a board of directors or trustees or a managing board) and its senior management are accountable for the effectiveness of the governance process (PA 2130-1).

Answer (B) is incorrect because control is any action taken by management, the board, and other parties to manage risk and increase the likelihood that established objectives and goals will be achieved. Management plans, organizes, and directs the performance of sufficient actions to provide reasonable assurance that objectives and goals will be achieved. Answer (C) is incorrect because risk management is "a process to identify, assess, manage, and control potential events or situations, to provide reasonable assurance regarding the achievement of the organization's objectives" (Glossary). Answer (D) is incorrect because monitoring consists of actions taken by management and others to assess the quality of internal control system performance over time. It is not currently defined in the Standards and Glossary.

**6.** Internal auditing is an assurance and consulting activity. An example of an assurance service is a

A. Advisory engagement.

B. Facilitation engagement.

C. Training engagement.

D. Compliance engagement

Answer (D) is correct. *(Publisher)*

**REQUIRED:** The example of an assurance service.

**DISCUSSION:** According to the Glossary, an assurance service is "an objective examination of evidence for the purpose of providing an independent assessment on risk management, control, or governance processes for the organization. Examples may include financial, performance, compliance, system security, and due diligence engagements." Consulting services include "advisory and related client service activities, the nature and scope of which are agreed with the client and which are intended to add value and improve an organization's governance, risk management, and control processes without the auditor assuming responsibility. Examples include counsel, advice, facilitation, and training."

**7.** The work of the internal audit activity includes evaluating and contributing to the improvement of risk management systems. Risk is

I. The negative effect of events certain to occur
II. Measured in terms of impact
III. Measured in terms of likelihood

A. I only.

B. I and II only.

C. II and III only.

D. I, II, and III.

Answer (C) is correct. *(Publisher)*
**REQUIRED:** The nature of risk.
**DISCUSSION:** The IAA should assist the organization by identifying and evaluating significant exposures to risk and contributing to the improvement of risk management and control systems (Standard 2110). Risk is the possibility of an event the occurrence of which could have an effect on the achievement of organizational objectives. It is measured in terms of impact and likelihood (Glossary). Risk involves uncertainty, and the effects of events are not necessarily negative.

**8.** The chief audit executive is best defined as the

A. Inspector general.

B. Person responsible for the internal audit function.

C. Outside provider of internal audit services.

D. Person responsible for overseeing the contract with the outside provider of internal audit services.

Answer (B) is correct. *(Publisher)*
**REQUIRED:** The best definition of the CAE.
**DISCUSSION:** The CAE is the "top position within the organization responsible for internal audit activities. Normally, this would be the internal audit director. When internal auditing services are obtained from outside service providers, the CAE is the person responsible for overseeing the service contract and overall quality assurance, reporting to senior management and the board regarding internal audit activities, and follow-up of engagement results. The term also includes such titles as general auditor, chief internal auditor, and inspector general" (Glossary).

**9.** The actions taken to manage risk and increase the likelihood that established objectives and goals will be achieved are best described as

A. Supervision.

B. Quality assurance.

C. Control.

D. Compliance.

Answer (C) is correct. *(Publisher)*
**REQUIRED:** The term for actions taken to manage risk and increase the likelihood that established objectives and goals will be achieved.
**DISCUSSION:** Control is any action taken by management, the board, and other parties to manage risk and increase the likelihood that established objectives and goals will be achieved. Management plans, organizes, and directs the performance of sufficient actions to provide reasonable assurance that objectives and goals will be achieved.
Answer (A) is incorrect because supervision is just one means of achieving control. Answer (B) is incorrect because quality assurance relates to just one set of objectives and goals. It does not pertain to achievement of all established organizational objectives and goals. Answer (D) is incorrect because compliance is conformity and adherence to policies, plans, procedures, laws, regulations, contracts, or other requirements.

**10.** The purpose of the internal audit activity's evaluation of the effectiveness of existing risk management processes is to determine that

A. Management has planned and designed so as to provide reasonable assurance of achieving objectives and goals.

B. Management directs processes so as to provide reasonable assurance of achieving objectives and goals.

C. The organization's objectives and goals will be achieved efficiently and economically.

D. The organization's objectives and goals will be achieved in an accurate and timely manner and with minimal use of resources.

Answer (B) is correct. *(CIA, adapted)*
**REQUIRED:** The purpose of the evaluation of the effectiveness of risk management processes.
**DISCUSSION:** "Effectiveness of risk management, control, and governance processes is present if management directs processes in such a manner as to provide reasonable assurance that the organization's objectives and goals will be achieved. In addition to accomplishing the objectives and planned activities, management directs by authorizing activities and transactions, monitoring resulting performance, and verifying that the organization's processes are operating as designed" (PA 2100-1).

**11.** Which of the following best describes the internal audit activity's purpose in evaluating the adequacy of risk management, control, and governance processes?

A. To help determine the nature, timing, and extent of tests necessary to achieve engagement objectives.

B. To ensure that material weaknesses in internal control are corrected.

C. To determine whether the risk management, control, and governance processes provide reasonable assurance that the organization's objectives and goals are achieved efficiently and economically.

D. To determine whether the risk management, control, and governance processes ensure that the accounting records are correct and that financial statements are fairly stated.

Answer (C) is correct. *(CIA, adapted)*

**REQUIRED:** The purpose of evaluating the adequacy of risk management, control, and governance processes.

**DISCUSSION:** "Adequacy of risk management, control, and governance processes is present if management has planned and designed them in a manner that provides reasonable assurance that the organization's objectives and goals will be achieved efficiently and economically. Efficient performance accomplishes objectives and goals in an accurate, timely, and economical fashion. Economical performance accomplishes objectives and goals with minimal use of resources (i.e., cost) commensurate with the risk exposure. Reasonable assurance is provided if the most cost-effective measures are taken in the design and implementation stages to reduce risks and restrict expected deviations to a tolerable level. Thus, the design process begins with the establishment of objectives and goals. This is followed by connecting or interrelating concepts, parts, activities, and people in such a manner as to operate together to achieve the established objectives and goals" (PA 2100-1).

Answer (A) is incorrect because the nature, timing, and extent of certain tests must be determined before the adequacy of control processes can be evaluated. Answer (B) is incorrect because internal auditors have no authority to ensure correction of material weaknesses. Answer (D) is incorrect because the scope of internal auditing is much broader than concern for the fairness of financial statements.

**12.** The internal auditors' ultimate responsibility for information security includes

A. Identifying technical aspects, risks, processes, and transactions to be examined.

B. Determining the scope and degree of testing to achieve engagement objectives.

C. Periodically assessing information security practices.

D. Documenting engagement procedures.

Answer (C) is correct. *(Publisher)*

**REQUIRED:** The internal auditors' ultimate responsibility for information security.

**DISCUSSION:** "Internal auditors should periodically assess the organization's information security practices and recommend, as appropriate, enhancements to, or implementation of, new controls and safeguards. Following an assessment, an assurance report should be provided to the board, audit committee, or other appropriate governing body. Such assessments can either be conducted as separate stand-alone engagements or as multiple engagements integrated into other audits or engagements conducted as part of the approved audit plan" (PA 2100-2).

**13.** Risk management is the responsibility of management. The role of the internal audit activity (IAA) in the risk management process may include which of the following?

I. Monitoring activities.
II. Evaluating the risk management process as part of the engagement plan.
III. Participation on oversight committees, monitoring of activities, and status reporting.
IV. Managing and coordinating the process.

A. I only.

B. II only.

C. I, II, and III only.

D. I, II, III, and IV.

Answer (D) is correct. *(Publisher)*

**REQUIRED:** The role of the IAA in the risk management process.

**DISCUSSION:** The IAA evaluates and contributes to the improvement of risk management, control, and governance processes using a systematic and disciplined approach (Standard 2100). The specific role of the IAA in the risk management process depends on management's and the board's expectations of the IAA. The IAA's understanding of these expectations should be codified in the charters of the IAA and the audit committee. Accordingly, this role may evolve over time and may include responsibilities along a continuum that extends from no role to evaluating the risk management process as part of the engagement plan; to active, continuous support and involvement in the risk management process through participation on oversight committees, monitoring activities, status reporting, etc.; to managing and coordinating the process (PA 2100-3).

**14.** If management has not established a risk management process for the organization, the internal auditors should suggest establishment of such a process. The function that the internal auditors preferably should perform in the initial establishment of a risk management process is

A. A proactive role that supplements traditional assurance activities.

B. Assumption of ownership of risks.

C. Responsibility for the management of the risks identified.

D. An oversight role to determine that adequate and effective processes are in place.

Answer (A) is correct. *(Publisher)*

**REQUIRED:** The function that the internal auditors preferably should perform in the initial establishment of a risk management process.

**DISCUSSION:** If requested, internal auditors can play a proactive role in assisting with the initial establishment of a risk management process for the organization. A more proactive role supplements traditional assurance activities with a consultative approach to improving fundamental processes. If such assistance exceeds normal assurance and consulting activities conducted by internal auditors, independence could be impaired. In these situations, internal auditors should comply with the disclosure requirements of the Standards. Additional guidance can also be found in Practice Advisory 1130.A1-2: Internal Audit Responsibility for Other (Non-Audit) Functions (PA 2100-4).

Answer (B) is incorrect because a proactive role in developing and managing a risk management process is not the same as an "ownership of risks" role. In order to avoid an "ownership of risk" role, internal auditors should seek confirmation from management as to its responsibility for identification, mitigation, monitoring, and "ownership" of risks. Internal auditors can facilitate or enable risk management processes, but they should not "own" or be responsible for the management of the risks identified. Answer (C) is incorrect because a proactive role in developing and managing a risk management process is not the same as an "ownership of risks" role. In order to avoid an "ownership of risk" role, internal auditors should seek confirmation from management as to its responsibility for identification, mitigation, monitoring, and "ownership" of risks. Internal auditors can facilitate or enable risk management processes, but they should not "own" or be responsible for the management of the risks identified. Answer (D) is incorrect because boards and audit committees have an oversight role to determine that adequate and effective processes are in place.

**15.** Which of the following is most likely to be an element of an effective regulatory compliance program?

A. The internal audit activity should be assigned overall responsibility for overseeing the program.

B. The program is communicated to employees in a video format on a one-time basis.

C. The organization should use monitoring and auditing systems reasonably designed to detect criminal conduct.

D. The organization should obtain as much information as possible when performing background checks on employees.

Answer (C) is correct. *(Publisher)*

**REQUIRED:** The most likely element of an effective regulatory compliance program.

**DISCUSSION:** The organization should take reasonable steps to achieve compliance with its standards, e.g., by using monitoring and auditing systems reasonably designed to detect criminal conduct by its employees and other agents and by having in place and publicizing a reporting system for employees and other agents to report the criminal conduct of others within the organization without fear of retribution (PA 2100-5).

Answer (A) is incorrect because specific individual(s) within high-level personnel of the organization should be assigned overall responsibility to oversee regulatory compliance with standards and procedures. High-level personnel of the organization means individuals who have substantial control of the organization or who have a substantial role in the making of policy within the organization. Answer (B) is incorrect because the effectiveness of a compliance program will depend upon the ways in which it is communicated to employees. Generally, an interactive format works better than a lecture. Programs communicated in person tend to work better than programs communicated entirely through video or game formats. Programs that are periodically repeated work better than one-time presentations. Answer (D) is incorrect because the organization should use due care not to delegate substantial discretionary authority to individuals the organization knows, or should know through the exercise of due diligence, have a propensity to engage in illegal activities. However, care should be taken to ensure that the organization does not infringe upon employees' and applicants' privacy rights under applicable laws. Many jurisdictions have laws limiting the amount of information an organization can obtain in performing background checks on employees.

**16.** The internal audit activity should assist the organization by identifying and evaluating significant exposures to risk and contributing to the improvement of risk management and control systems. With respect to assessing the adequacy of risk management processes, internal auditors most likely should

A. Recognize that organizations should use similar techniques for managing risk.

B. Become satisfied that the key objectives of risk management processes are being met.

C. Determine the level of risks acceptable to the organization.

D. Treat the evaluation of risk management processes in the same manner as the risk analysis used to plan engagements.

Answer (B) is correct. *(Publisher)*

**REQUIRED:** The responsibility of internal auditors for assessing the adequacy of risk management processes.

**DISCUSSION:** The internal auditors may be charged with the responsibility for providing assurance to management and the board about the adequacy of the organization's risk management processes. This responsibility requires them to formulate an opinion on whether those processes are sufficient to protect the organization's assets, reputation, and ongoing operations. For this purpose, the internal auditors must obtain sufficient information to satisfy themselves that five key objectives of risk management are being met: (1) risks are identified and prioritized; (2) management and the board have determined the level of acceptable risks; (3) risk mitigation activities are designed and implemented to reduce, or manage, risks at acceptable levels; (4) ongoing monitoring is conducted to reassess risk and the effectiveness of risk management controls periodically; and (5) the board and management receive periodic reports concerning the results of risk management processes, and the governance process periodically communicates with stakeholders about risks, risk strategies, and controls (PA 2110-1).

Answer (A) is incorrect because risk management processes vary with the size and complexity of an organization's business activities. Answer (C) is incorrect because management and the board determine the level of acceptable organizational risks. Answer (D) is incorrect because evaluating management's risk processes differs from the internal auditors' risk assessment used to plan an engagement, but information from a comprehensive risk management process is useful in such planning.

**17.** Senior management has requested a compliance audit of the organization's employee benefits package. Which of the following is considered the primary engagement objective by both the chief audit executive and senior management?

A. The level of organizational contributions is adequate to meet the program's demands.

B. Individual programs are operating in accordance with contractual requirements and government regulations.

C. Participation levels support continuation of individual programs.

D. Benefit payments, when appropriate, are accurate and timely.

Answer (B) is correct. *(CIA, adapted)*

**REQUIRED:** The primary engagement objective of a compliance audit of the employee benefits package.

**DISCUSSION:** The IAA evaluates risk exposures related to governance, operations, and information systems regarding, among other things, compliance with laws, regulations, and contracts. Based on the risk assessment, the IAA evaluates the adequacy and effectiveness of controls encompassing governance, operations, and information systems. This evaluation should include, among other things, compliance with laws, regulations, and contracts (Standards 2110.A2 and 2120.A1). Operation in accordance with contracts and regulations takes precedence over all other objectives because it relates to the most basic aspects of the programs.

**18.** Which of the following activities is outside the scope of internal auditing?

A. Assessing an operating department's effectiveness in achieving stated organizational goals.

B. Safeguarding of assets.

C. Evaluating controls over compliance with laws and regulations.

D. Ascertaining the extent to which objectives and goals have been established.

Answer (B) is correct. *(CIA, adapted)*

**REQUIRED:** The activity outside the scope of internal auditing.

**DISCUSSION:** Safeguarding assets is an operational activity and is therefore beyond the scope of the IAA, which evaluates and contributes to the improvement of risk management, control, and governance processes. However, internal auditors should evaluate risk exposures relating to governance, operations, and information systems regarding the safeguarding of assets. Based on the risk assessment, they should evaluate the adequacy and effectiveness of controls encompassing governance, operations, and information systems. This evaluation extends to safeguarding of assets (Standards 2110.A2 and 2120.A1).

Answer (A) is incorrect because internal auditors should ascertain the extent to which results are consistent with established goals and objectives (Standard 2120.A3). Answer (C) is incorrect because evaluating controls over compliance with laws, regulations, and contracts is within the scope of internal auditing (Standard 2120.A1). Answer (D) is incorrect because ascertaining the extent to which operating and program objectives and goals have been established is within the scope of internal auditing (Standard 2120.A2).

**19.** The minimum role of the internal audit activity in the ethical culture of an organization is to

A. Avoid active support of the ethical culture because of possible loss of independence.

B. Evaluate the effectiveness of the organization's ethics-related programs and objectives.

C. Assume accountability for the effectiveness of the governance process.

D. Become the chief ethics officer.

Answer (B) is correct. *(Publisher)*

**REQUIRED:** The minimum role of the internal audit activity in the ethical culture of an organization.

**DISCUSSION:** According to Standard 2130, the IAA should assess and make appropriate recommendations for improving the governance process. Among other objectives, the assessment and recommendations should address the promotion of appropriate ethics and values within the organization. The ethical culture is linked to the governance process. Thus, at a minimum, the IAA periodically should assess the organization's ethical climate and the effectiveness of its processes for achieving the desired level of compliance with its legal, ethical, and societal responsibilities. Furthermore, the IAA "should evaluate the design, implementation, and effectiveness of the organization's ethics-related objectives, programs, and activities" (Standard 2130.A1).

Answer (A) is incorrect because internal auditors should be active ethics advocates. However, assuming the role of, for example, chief ethics officer may, in some circumstances, conflict with the independence attribute. Answer (C) is incorrect because the organization's governing body and its senior management are responsible for the effectiveness of the governance process. Answer (D) is incorrect because the minimum role is to be the assessor of the ethical culture. However, an internal auditor may become chief ethics officer or a member of an ethics council, although the former role may, in some circumstances, conflict with the independence attribute.

## 9.2 Charter, Independence, and Objectivity

**20.** An element of authority that should be included in the charter of the internal audit activity is

A. Identification of the organizational units where engagements are to be performed.

B. Identification of the types of disclosures that should be made to the audit committee.

C. Access to records, personnel, and physical properties relevant to the performance of engagements.

D. Access to the external auditor's engagement records.

Answer (C) is correct. *(CIA, adapted)*

**REQUIRED:** The element of authority that should be included in the charter of the internal audit activity.

**DISCUSSION:** The purpose, authority, and responsibility of the internal audit activity should be defined in a charter, consistent with the Standards, and approved by the board (Standard 1000). The charter should establish the internal audit activity's position within the organization; authorize access to records, personnel, and physical properties relevant to the performance of engagements; and define the scope of internal audit activities (PA 1000-1).

Answer (A) is incorrect because the charter should not specifically identify the subjects of engagements. Answer (B) is incorrect because disclosure to the audit committee is an obligation, not an element of authority. Answer (D) is incorrect because access to the external auditor's engagement records cannot be guaranteed.

**21.** You have been asked to be a member of an external assessment team. In assessing the independence of the internal audit activity (IAA) being reviewed, you should consider all of the following factors except

A. Access to and frequency of communications with the board, audit committee, or other governing authority.

B. The criteria of education and experience considered necessary when filling vacant positions on the internal auditing staff.

C. The degrees to which internal auditors assume operating responsibilities.

D. The scope and depth of objectives for the engagements included in the review.

Answer (B) is correct. *(CIA, adapted)*

**REQUIRED:** The factor not relevant to assessing the independence of the IAA.

**DISCUSSION:** These criteria are related to professional proficiency, not independence. The CAE should establish suitable criteria of education and experience, giving due consideration to scope of work and level of responsibility (PA 1210-1).

Answer (A) is incorrect because independence is achieved through organizational status and objectivity. Organizational status is enhanced by direct communication with the board, audit committee, or other appropriate governing authority (PA 1110-1). Answer (C) is incorrect because assumption of operating duties impairs objectivity and therefore independence. Answer (D) is incorrect because the scope of the IAA's work is a function of its organizational status and therefore its independence.

**22.** Internal auditors may provide consulting services that add value and improve an organization's operations. The performance of these services

A. Impairs internal auditors' objectivity with respect to an assurance service involving the same engagement client.

B. Precludes generation of assurance from a consulting engagement.

C. Should be consistent with the internal audit activity's empowerment reflected in the charter.

D. Imposes no responsibility to communicate information other than to the engagement client.

Answer (C) is correct. *(Publisher)*

**REQUIRED:** The internal auditors' responsibility regarding consulting services.

**DISCUSSION:** According to Standard 1000.C1, the nature of consulting services should be defined in the charter. Internal auditors have traditionally performed many types of consulting services, including the analysis of controls built into developing systems, analysis of security products, serving on task forces to analyze operations and make recommendations, and so forth. The board (or audit committee) should empower the internal audit activity to perform additional services if they do not represent a conflict of interest or detract from its obligations to the committee. That empowerment should be reflected in the internal audit charter (PA 1000.C1-1).

Answer (A) is incorrect because consulting services do not necessarily impair objectivity. Decisions to implement recommendations made as a result of a consulting service should be made by management. Thus, decision-making by management does not impair the internal auditors' objectivity. Answer (B) is incorrect because assurance and consulting services are not mutually exclusive. One type of service may be generated from the other. Answer (D) is incorrect because a primary internal auditing value is to provide assurance to senior management and audit committee directors. Consulting engagements cannot be rendered in a manner that masks information that in the judgment of the chief audit executive (CAE) should be presented to senior executives and board members (PA 1000.C1-1).

**23.** A charter is being drafted for a newly formed internal audit activity (IAA). Which of the following best describes the appropriate organizational status that should be incorporated into the charter?

A. The chief audit executive should report to the chief executive officer but have access to the board of directors.

B. The chief audit executive should be a member of the audit committee of the board of directors.

C. The chief audit executive should be a staff officer reporting to the chief financial officer.

D. The chief audit executive should report to an administrative vice president.

Answer (A) is correct. *(CIA, adapted)*

**REQUIRED:** The appropriate organizational status that should be incorporated into the charter.

**DISCUSSION:** The CAE should be responsible to an individual in the organization with sufficient authority to promote independence and to ensure broad engagement coverage, adequate consideration of engagement communications, and appropriate action on engagement recommendations. The higher the level to which the IAA reports, the more likely that independence will be assured. Ideally, the CAE should report functionally to the audit committee, board of directors, or other appropriate governing authority, and administratively to the CEO (PA 1110-1). Functional reporting means that the governing authority (1) approves the IAA's charter, (2) approves the risk assessment and audit plan, (3) receives communications deemed necessary by the CAE, (4) approves appointment or removal of the CAE, and (5) appropriately inquires of management and the CAE about scope or budgetary limits on the IAA. Administrative reporting addresses (1) budgeting and management accounting, (2) administration of human resources and internal policies and procedures, and (3) internal information flows (PA 1110-2).

Answer (B) is incorrect because placing the CAE in a position of operational control will impair his/her objectivity. Answer (C) is incorrect because this choice limits the influence and independence of the IAA. Answer (D) is incorrect because this choice limits the influence and independence of the IAA.

**24.** In which of the following situations does an internal auditor potentially lack objectivity?

A. An internal auditor reviews the procedures for a new electronic data interchange (EDI) connection to a major customer before it is implemented.

B. A former purchasing assistant performs a review of internal controls over purchasing 4 months after being transferred to the internal auditing department.

C. An internal auditor recommends standards of control and performance measures for a contract with a service organization for the processing of payroll and employee benefits.

D. A payroll accounting employee assists an internal auditor in verifying the physical inventory of small motors.

Answer (B) is correct. *(CIA, adapted)*

**REQUIRED:** The situation in which the internal auditor may lack objectivity.

**DISCUSSION:** Persons transferred to or temporarily engaged by the internal audit activity should not be assigned to engagements involving any activities they previously performed until a reasonable period of time (at least one year) has elapsed. Such assignments are presumed to impair objectivity. Additional consideration is required when such persons are supervising the engagement work and communicating engagement results (PA 1130.A1-1). However, internal auditors may provide consulting services relating to operations for which they had previous responsibilities (Standard 1130.C1), provided that prior disclosure is made to the client of any potential impairments of independence or objectivity (Standard 1130.C2).

Answer (A) is incorrect because objectivity is not adversely affected when the internal auditor recommends standards of control for systems or reviews procedures before they are implemented. Operating, designing, installing, or drafting procedures for systems is presumed to impair objectivity. Answer (C) is incorrect because objectivity is not adversely affected when the internal auditor recommends standards of control for systems or reviews procedures before they are implemented. Operating, designing, installing, or drafting procedures for systems is presumed to impair objectivity. Answer (D) is incorrect because use of staff from other areas to assist the internal auditor does not impair objectivity, especially when the staff is from outside of the area where the engagement is being performed.

**25.** When faced with an imposed scope limitation, the chief audit executive should

A. Refuse to perform the engagement until the scope limitation is removed.

B. Communicate the potential effects of the scope limitation to the audit committee of the board of directors.

C. Increase the frequency of engagements concerning the activity in question.

D. Assign more experienced personnel to the engagement.

Answer (B) is correct. *(CIA, adapted)*

**REQUIRED:** The appropriate response to an imposed scope limitation.

**DISCUSSION:** A scope limitation is a restriction placed upon the IAA that precludes the accomplishment of its objectives and plans. Among other things, a scope limitation may restrict (a) the scope defined in the charter; (b) the IAA's access to records, personnel, and physical properties relevant to the performance of engagements; (c) the approved engagement work schedule; (d) necessary engagement procedures; and (e) the approved staffing plan and financial budget. A scope limitation along with its potential effect should be communicated, preferably in writing, to the board, audit committee, or other appropriate governing authority (PA 1130-1).

Answer (A) is incorrect because the engagement may be conducted under a scope limitation. Answer (C) is incorrect because a scope limitation does not necessarily require more frequent engagements. Answer (D) is incorrect because a scope limitation does not necessarily require more experienced personnel.

**26.** An audit committee of the board of directors of an organization is being established. Which of the following is normally a responsibility of the committee with regard to the internal audit activity (IAA)?

A. Approval of the selection and dismissal of the chief audit executive.

B. Development of the annual engagement work schedule.

C. Approval of engagement work programs.

D. Determination of engagement observations appropriate for specific engagement communications.

Answer (A) is correct. *(CIA, adapted)*

**REQUIRED:** The responsibility of an audit committee.

**DISCUSSION:** Independence is enhanced when the board concurs in the appointment or removal of the CAE (PA 1110-1). The audit committee is a subcommittee of outside directors who are independent of management. The term "board" includes the audit committee.

Answer (B) is incorrect because development of the annual engagement work schedule is an operational function of the CAE and the IAA staff. The annual engagement work schedule, staffing plan, and financial budget are submitted to senior management and the board (PA 2020-1). Answer (C) is incorrect because approval of engagement work programs is a technical responsibility of the IAA staff. Answer (D) is incorrect because the determination of engagement observations appropriate for specific engagement communications is a field operation of the IAA staff.

## 9.3 Standards and Proficiency

**27.** The purposes of the Standards include all of the following except

A. Establishing the basis for the evaluation of internal audit performance.

B. Guiding the ethical conduct of internal auditors.

C. Delineating basic principles that represent the practice of internal auditing as it should be.

D. Fostering improved organizational processes and operations.

Answer (B) is correct. *(CIA, adapted)*

**REQUIRED:** The item not a purpose of the Standards.

**DISCUSSION:** The IIA *Code of Ethics* describes Rules of Conduct that constitute "behavior norms expected of internal auditors. These rules are intended as an aid to interpreting the Principles into practical applications and are intended to guide the ethical conduct of internal auditors" (Introduction). The purposes of the Standards are to:

1. Delineate basic principles that represent the practice of internal auditing as it should be.
2. Provide a framework for performing and promoting a broad range of value-added internal audit activities.
3. Establish the basis for the evaluation of internal audit performance.
4. Foster improved organizational processes and operations.

**28.** Use of outside service providers with expertise in health care benefits is appropriate when the internal audit activity is

A. Evaluating the organization's estimate of its liability for postretirement benefits, which include health care benefits.

B. Comparing the cost of the organization's health care program with other programs offered in the industry.

C. Training its staff to conduct an audit of health care costs in a major division of the organization.

D. All of the answers are correct.

Answer (D) is correct. *(CIA, adapted)*

**REQUIRED:** The reasons for using specialists in health care benefits.

**DISCUSSION:** The internal audit activity should collectively possess or obtain the knowledge, skills, and other competencies needed to perform its responsibilities (Standard 1210). In regard to an assurance engagement, the CAE should obtain competent advice and assistance if the internal audit staff lacks the knowledge, skills, and other competencies needed to perform all or part of the engagement (Standard 1210.A1). In regard to a consulting engagement, the CAE should decline the engagement or obtain competent advice and assistance if the internal audit staff lacks the knowledge, skills, and other competencies needed to perform all or part of the engagement (Standard 1210.C1). Accordingly, if the internal audit staff lacks expertise with regard to health care costs, outside service providers should be employed who can provide the requisite knowledge, skills, and other competencies. These outside service providers can provide assistance in estimating the company's liability for postretirement benefits, in developing a comparative analysis of health care costs, and in training the staff to audit health care costs.

**29.** A chief audit executive has reviewed credentials, checked references, and interviewed a candidate for a staff position. The CAE concludes that the candidate has a thorough understanding of internal auditing techniques, accounting, and finance. However, the candidate has limited knowledge of economics and information technology. Which action is most appropriate?

A. Reject the candidate because of the lack of knowledge required by the Standards.

B. Offer the candidate a position despite lack of knowledge in certain essential areas.

C. Encourage the candidate to obtain additional training in economics and information technology and then reapply.

D. Offer the candidate a position if other staff members possess sufficient knowledge in economics and information technology.

Answer (D) is correct. *(CIA, adapted)*

**REQUIRED:** The proper hiring decision for an IAA.

**DISCUSSION:** The IAA should collectively possess or obtain the knowledge, skills, and other competencies needed to perform its responsibilities (Standard 1210). These attributes include proficiency in applying internal auditing standards, procedures, and techniques. The IAA should have employees or use outside service providers who are qualified in such disciplines as accounting, auditing, economics, finance, statistics, information technology, engineering, taxation, law, environmental affairs, and such other areas as needed to meet the IAA's responsibilities. Each member of the IAA, however, need not be qualified in all of these disciplines (PA 1210.A1-1).

Answer (A) is incorrect because the Standards do not require each internal auditor to possess a knowledge of all relevant subjects. Answer (B) is incorrect because the IAA's needs may be for additional expertise in economics or information technology. Answer (C) is incorrect because encouraging the candidate to obtain additional training does not adequately address the IAA's current needs.

**30.** Proficiency is required of internal auditors with respect to which discipline?

A. Internal auditing procedures and techniques.

B. Accounting principles and techniques.

C. Management principles.

D. Marketing techniques.

Answer (A) is correct. *(CIA, adapted)*

**REQUIRED:** The organizational discipline that matches the skill level described.

**DISCUSSION:** Proficiency in applying internal auditing standards, procedures, and techniques is required in performing engagements. Proficiency means the ability to apply knowledge to situations likely to be encountered and to deal with them without extensive recourse to technical research and assistance (PA 1210-1).

Answer (B) is incorrect because proficiency in accounting principles and techniques is required only of auditors who work extensively with financial records and reports. Answer (C) is incorrect because an internal auditor is required to have an understanding of, not a proficiency in, management principles. Answer (D) is incorrect because internal auditors ordinarily need not be proficient in marketing techniques.

**31.** An understanding is required of internal auditors with respect to which discipline?

A. Internal auditing procedures and techniques.

B. Accounting principles and techniques.

C. Management principles.

D. Marketing techniques.

Answer (C) is correct. *(CIA, adapted)*

**REQUIRED:** The organizational discipline that matches the skill level described.

**DISCUSSION:** An understanding of management principles is required to recognize and evaluate the materiality and significance of deviations from good business practice. An understanding means the ability to apply broad knowledge to situations likely to be encountered, to recognize significant deviations, and to be able to carry out the research necessary to arrive at reasonable solutions (PA 1210-1).

Answer (A) is incorrect because internal auditors must have proficiency in, not an understanding of, internal auditing standards, procedures, and techniques. Answer (B) is incorrect because proficiency in accounting principles and techniques is required only of auditors who work extensively with financial records and reports. Answer (D) is incorrect because internal auditors ordinarily need not be proficient in, or have an understanding or appreciation of, marketing techniques.

**32.** Internal auditors are required to have an appreciation of which discipline?

A. Internal auditing procedures and techniques.

B. Accounting principles and techniques.

C. Management principles.

D. Marketing techniques.

Answer (B) is correct. *(CIA, adapted)*

**REQUIRED:** The organizational discipline that matches the skill level described.

**DISCUSSION:** Internal auditors are required to have an appreciation of the fundamentals of subjects such as accounting, economics, commercial law, taxation, finance, quantitative methods, and information technology. An appreciation means the ability to recognize the existence of problems or potential problems and to determine the further research to be undertaken or the assistance to be obtained. However, proficiency in accounting principles and techniques is required of auditors who work extensively with financial records and reports (PA 1210-1).

Answer (A) is incorrect because proficiency, not an appreciation, is required of internal auditors in applying internal auditing standards, procedures, and techniques. Answer (C) is incorrect because an internal auditor must have an understanding, not an appreciation, of management principles. Answer (D) is incorrect because internal auditors ordinarily need not be proficient in, or have an understanding or appreciation of, marketing techniques.

**33.** Which of the following statements is true with respect to due professional care?

A. An internal auditor should perform detailed tests of all transactions before communicating results.

B. An item should not be mentioned in an engagement communication unless the internal auditor is absolutely certain of the item.

C. An engagement communication should never be viewed as providing an infallible truth about a subject.

D. An internal auditor has no responsibility to recommend improvements.

Answer (C) is correct. *(CIA, adapted)*

**REQUIRED:** The true statement about due professional care.

**DISCUSSION:** Due professional care implies reasonable care and competence, not infallibility or extraordinary performance. Due professional care requires the internal auditor to conduct examinations and verifications to a reasonable extent, but it does not require detailed reviews of all transactions. Accordingly, internal auditors cannot give absolute assurance that noncompliance or irregularities do not exist. Nevertheless, the possibility of material irregularities or noncompliance should be considered whenever an internal auditor undertakes an internal auditing assignment (PA 1220-1).

Answer (A) is incorrect because an internal auditor should conduct reasonable examinations and verifications, but detailed tests of all transactions are not required. Answer (B) is incorrect because absolute assurance need not, and cannot, be given. Answer (D) is incorrect because an internal auditor should recommend improvements to promote compliance with acceptable procedures and practices.

**34.** Assurance engagements should be performed with proficiency and due professional care. Accordingly, the Standards require internal auditors to

I. Consider the probability of significant noncompliance

II. Perform assurance procedures with due professional care so that all significant risks are identified

III. Consider the use of computer-assisted audit tools

A. I and II only.

B. I and III only.

C. II and III only.

D. I, II, and III.

Answer (B) is correct. *(Publisher)*

**REQUIRED:** The responsibilities of internal auditors regarding proficiency and due professional care.

**DISCUSSION:** Standard 1220.A1 states that the exercise of due professional care involves considering the extent of work needed to achieve management's objectives; the relative complexity, materiality, or significance of matters to which assurance procedures are applied; the adequacy and effectiveness of risk management, control, and governance processes; the probability of significant errors, irregularities, or noncompliance; and the cost of assurance in relation to the benefits. Standard 1220.A2 requires internal auditors to consider the use of computer-assisted audit tools and other data analysis techniques. Moreover, Standard 1220.A3 states that the internal auditor should be alert to the significant risks that might affect objectives, operations, or resources. However, assurance procedures alone, even when performed with due professional care, do not guarantee that all significant risks will be identified.

## 9.4 Control

**35.** Control self-assessment is a process that involves employees in assessing the adequacy of controls and identifying opportunities for improvement within an organization. Which of the following are reasons to involve employees in this process?

I. Employees become more motivated to do their jobs right.

II. Employees are objective about their jobs.

III. Employees can provide an independent assessment of internal controls.

IV. Managers want feedback from their employees.

A. I and II.

B. III and IV.

C. I and IV.

D. II and IV.

Answer (C) is correct. *(CIA, adapted)*

**REQUIRED:** The reasons to involve employees in control self-assessment.

**DISCUSSION:** Control self-assessment is consistent with total quality management's continuous improvement of quality in every aspect of organizational activities. For total quality management to be effective, all members of the organization must participate. Employees should be empowered, that is, adequately trained, provided with necessary information and tools, involved in important decisions, and fairly compensated. Participation by employees has a positive effect on motivation because it tends to increase commitment to the job and resulting ego satisfaction. Moreover, full employee participation requires two-way communication and therefore encourages feedback from employees.

Answer (A) is incorrect because employees often lack the perspective to be objective about their jobs or performance. Answer (B) is incorrect because, although employees can be involved in assessing internal controls, their assessments are not independent. Answer (D) is incorrect because employees often lack the perspective to be objective about their jobs or performance.

**36.** Which of the following best defines control?

A. Control is the result of proper planning, organizing, and directing by management.

B. Control refers to statements of what the organization chooses to accomplish.

C. Control is provided when cost-effective measures are taken to restrict deviations to a tolerable level.

D. Control accomplishes objectives and goals in an accurate, timely, and economical fashion.

Answer (A) is correct. *(CIA, adapted)*

**REQUIRED:** The best definition of control.

**DISCUSSION:** According to the Glossary appended to the Standards, a control is "any action taken by management, the board, and other parties to manage risk and increase the likelihood that established objectives and goals will be achieved. Management plans, organizes, and directs the performance of sufficient actions to provide reasonable assurance that objectives and goals will be achieved." Thus, control is the result of proper planning, organizing, and directing by management.

Answer (B) is incorrect because established objectives and goals are what the organization chooses to accomplish. Answer (C) is incorrect because, during the development of risk management, control, and governance processes, reasonable assurance of achieving objectives and goals efficiently and economically is provided when the most cost-effective measures are taken in the design and implementation stages to reduce risks and restrict deviations to a tolerable level (PA 2100-1). Answer (D) is incorrect because efficient performance accomplishes objectives and goals in an accurate, timely, and economical fashion (PA 2100-1).

**37.** The procedure requiring preparation of a prelisting of incoming cash receipts, with copies of the pre-list going to the cashier and to accounting, is an example of which type of control?

A. Preventive.

B. Corrective.

C. Detective.

D. Directive.

Answer (A) is correct. *(CIA, adapted)*

**REQUIRED:** The kind of control exemplified by a pre-list of cash receipts.

**DISCUSSION:** A prelisting of cash receipts in the form of checks is a preventive control. It is intended to deter undesirable events from occurring (PA 2100-1). Because irregularities involving cash are most likely before receipts are recorded, either remittance advices or a prelisting of checks should be prepared in the mailroom so as to establish recorded accountability for cash as soon as possible. A cash register tape is a form of prelisting for cash received over the counter. One copy of a prelisting will go to accounting for posting to the cash receipts journal, and another is sent to the cashier for reconciliation with checks and currency received.

Answer (B) is incorrect because a corrective control rectifies an error or irregularity. Answer (C) is incorrect because a detective control uncovers an error or irregularity that has already occurred. Answer (D) is incorrect because a directive control causes or encourages a desirable event.

**38.** Directors, management, external auditors, and internal auditors all play important roles in creating proper control processes. Senior management is primarily responsible for

A. Establishing and maintaining an organizational culture.

B. Reviewing the reliability and integrity of financial and operational information.

C. Ensuring that external and internal auditors oversee the administration of the system of risk management and control processes.

D. Implementing and monitoring controls designed by the board of directors.

Answer (A) is correct. *(CIA, adapted)*

**REQUIRED:** The best description of senior management's responsibility.

**DISCUSSION:** Management plans, organizes, and directs the performance of sufficient actions to provide reasonable assurance that goals and objectives will be achieved. Management periodically reviews its objectives and goals and modifies its processes to accommodate changes in internal and external conditions. Management also establishes and maintains an organizational culture, including an ethical climate that fosters control (PA 2100-1).

Answer (B) is incorrect because internal auditors are responsible for evaluating the adequacy and effectiveness of controls, including those relating to the reliability and integrity of financial and operational information (Standard 2120.A1). Answer (C) is incorrect because senior management's role is to oversee the establishment, administration, and assessment of the system of risk management and control processes (PA 2120.A1-1). Answer (D) is incorrect because the board has oversight responsibilities but ordinarily does not become involved in the details of operations.

**39.** The chief audit executive's responsibility for assessing and reporting on control processes includes

A. Communicating to senior management and the audit committee an annual judgment about internal control.

B. Overseeing the establishment of internal control processes.

C. Maintaining the organization's governance processes.

D. Arriving at a single assessment based solely on the work of the internal audit activity.

Answer (A) is correct. *(Publisher)*

**REQUIRED:** The CAE's responsibility for assessing and reporting on control processes.

**DISCUSSION:** Senior management and the audit committee normally expect that the CAE will perform sufficient engagement work and gather other available information during the year in order to form a judgment about the adequacy and effectiveness of the control processes. The CAE should communicate that overall judgment about the organization's system of controls to senior management and the audit committee. A growing number of organizations have included a management's report on the system of internal controls in their annual or periodic reports to external stakeholders. The report of the CAE should therefore be presented, usually once a year, to senior management and the audit committee (PA 2120.A1-1).

Answer (B) is incorrect because senior management is responsible for overseeing the establishment of internal control processes. Answer (C) is incorrect because the board is responsible for establishing and maintaining the organization's governance processes. Answer (D) is incorrect because the challenge for the IAA is to evaluate the effectiveness of the organization's system of controls based on the aggregation of many individual assessments. Those assessments are largely gained from internal auditing engagements, management's self assessments, and external auditor's work (PA 2120.A1-1).

**40.** The U.S. Securities and Exchange Commission has adopted rules regarding quarterly reports, disclosures, and certifications. The rules apply to both foreign registrants and U.S. registrants with the SEC. The most likely role of the internal auditors is

A. For the chief audit executive to be a member of the disclosure committee.

B. For the chief audit executive to certify that disclosure controls are effective.

C. To disclose to the external auditors any significant deficiencies in the controls over financial reporting.

D. To disclose to the external auditors any fraud involving management.

Answer (A) is correct. *(Publisher)*

**REQUIRED:** The most likely role of the internal auditors regarding quarterly reports, disclosures, and certifications.

**DISCUSSION:** Under SEC rules adopted to implement the Sarbanes-Oxley Act of 2002, the CEO and CFO of an SEC registrant must certify in quarterly and annual reports that (1) the report does not contain a material false statement or omit a material fact; (2) the financial statements are fairly presented; (3) they are responsible for disclosure controls and procedures; and (4) they have evaluated the effectiveness of internal controls and presented their conclusions about these controls. Internal auditors should promote the establishment of a disclosure committee to coordinate and oversee the process. The committee should be composed of representatives of key areas of the entity. Normally, the committee will include the CAE.

Answer (B) is incorrect because the CEO and CFO are the certifying parties. Answer (C) is incorrect because the CEO and CFO must certify that they have disclosed (1) deficiencies in internal controls, (2) any management fraud, (3) significant changes in internal controls, and (4) corrective actions (PA 2120.A1-3). Answer (D) is incorrect because the CEO and CFO must certify that they have disclosed (1) deficiencies in internal controls, (2) any management fraud, (3) significant changes in internal controls, and (4) corrective actions (PA 2120.A1-3).

**41.** In evaluating the effectiveness and efficiency with which resources are employed, an internal auditor is responsible for

A. Determining the extent to which adequate operating criteria have been established.

B. Verifying the existence of assets.

C. Reviewing the reliability of operating information.

D. Verifying the accuracy of asset valuation.

Answer (A) is correct. *(CIA, adapted)*

**REQUIRED:** The internal auditor's responsibility for evaluating economic and efficient use of resources.

**DISCUSSION:** The internal audit activity evaluates the controls encompassing governance, operations, and information systems. This evaluation includes the effectiveness and efficiency of operations (Standard 2120.A1). Moreover, the internal auditors should "ascertain the extent to which management has established adequate criteria to determine whether objectives and goals have been accomplished" (Standard 2120.A4). They should also "evaluate the established operating targets and expectations and should determine whether those operating standards are acceptable and are being met" (PA 2120.A4-1).

Answer (B) is incorrect because verifying existence relates to the safeguarding of assets. Answer (C) is incorrect because the reliability of operating information concerns the reliability and integrity of information. Answer (D) is incorrect because the accuracy of asset valuation concerns the reliability and integrity of information.

## 9.5 Planning and Supervising the Engagement

**42.** Internal auditors should develop and record a plan for each engagement (Standard 2200). The planning process should include all the following except

A. Establishing engagement objectives and scope of work.

B. Obtaining background information about the activities to be reviewed.

C. Identifying sufficient information to achieve engagement objectives.

D. Determining how, when, and to whom the engagement results will be communicated.

Answer (C) is correct. *(CIA, adapted)*

**REQUIRED:** The item not part of the planning process.

**DISCUSSION:** Planning should include establishing engagement objectives, scope of work, and timing; obtaining background information about the activities to be reviewed; determining the resource allocations necessary to perform the engagement; and informing those in management who need to know about the engagement. It also includes performing, as appropriate, a survey to become familiar with activities, risks, and controls; to identify areas for engagement emphasis; and to invite comments and suggestions from engagement clients. Furthermore, planning extends to developing work programs; determining how, when, and to whom engagement results will be communicated; and obtaining approval of the engagement work program. Identifying sufficient information to achieve engagement objectives is done during field work, not planning.

Answer (A) is incorrect because the planning process includes establishing engagement objectives and scope of work. Answer (B) is incorrect because the planning process includes obtaining background information. Answer (D) is incorrect because the planning process includes determining how, when, and to whom the engagement results will be communicated.

**43.** The scope of an internal auditing engagement is initially defined by the

A. Engagement objectives.

B. Scheduling and time estimates.

C. Preliminary survey.

D. Engagement work program.

Answer (A) is correct. *(CIA, adapted)*

**REQUIRED:** The factor initially defining the scope of an internal auditing engagement.

**DISCUSSION:** According to Standard 2220, "The established scope should be sufficient to satisfy the objectives of the engagement." Moreover, according to PA 2210-1, "Planning should be documented. Engagement objectives and scope of work should be established. Engagement objectives are broad statements developed by internal auditors and define what the engagement is intended to accomplish. Engagement procedures are the means to attain engagement objectives. Engagement objectives and procedures, taken together, define the scope of the internal auditor's work."

Answer (B) is incorrect because the scheduling and time estimates are based on the objectives and scope of the engagement. Answer (C) is incorrect because the preliminary survey is performed before the objectives are determined, but the objectives and procedures define the scope of the engagement. Answer (D) is incorrect because the work program is developed after the preliminary survey and is based on the objectives of the engagement.

**44.** Which of the following activities represents the greatest risk to a post-merger manufacturing organization and is therefore most likely be the subject of an internal auditing engagement?

A. Combining imprest funds.

B. Combining purchasing functions.

C. Combining legal functions.

D. Combining marketing functions.

Answer (B) is correct. *(CIA, adapted)*

**REQUIRED:** The activity representing the greatest risk.

**DISCUSSION:** According to Standard 2210.A1, "Internal auditors should conduct a preliminary assessment of the risks relevant to the activity under review. Engagement objectives should reflect the results of this assessment. In a consulting engagement, the objectives should address risks, controls, and governance processes to the extent agreed upon with the client (Standard 2210.C1). Purchasing functions represent the greatest exposure to loss of the items listed and are therefore most likely to be evaluated. The financial exposure in the purchasing function is ordinarily greater than in, for example, the legal and marketing functions. After a merger, risk is heightened because of the difficulty of combining the disparate systems of the two organizations. Thus, the likelihood of an engagement is increased.

Answer (A) is incorrect because imprest funds are typically immaterial in amount. Answer (C) is incorrect because legal functions do not typically represent a risk of loss as great as the purchasing functions. Answer (D) is incorrect because marketing functions do not typically represent a risk of loss as great as the purchasing functions.

**45.** An outside consultant is developing methods for the management of a city's capital facilities. An appropriate scope of an engagement to evaluate the consultant's product is to

A. Review the consultant's contract to determine its propriety.

B. Establish the parameters of the value of the items being managed and controlled.

C. Determine the adequacy of the risk management and control systems for the management of capital facilities.

D. Review the handling of idle equipment.

Answer (C) is correct. *(CIA, adapted)*

**REQUIRED:** The appropriate scope of an engagement to evaluate a consultant's product.

**DISCUSSION:** According to Standard 2201, "In planning the engagement, internal auditors should consider:

- The objectives of the activity being reviewed and the means by which the activity controls its performance.
- The significant risks to the activity, its objectives, resources, and operations and the means by which the potential impact of risk is kept to an acceptable level.
- The adequacy and effectiveness of the activity's risk management and control systems compared to a relevant control framework or model.
- The opportunities for making significant improvements to the activity's risk management and control systems."

Answer (A) is incorrect because the review of the consultant's contract to determine its propriety is related to the procurement decision. Answer (B) is incorrect because the establishment of parameters for values of items being managed and controlled is a management responsibility. Answer (D) is incorrect because management must determine policies regarding idle equipment. Some equipment may be retained for emergency use.

**46.** Writing an engagement work program occurs at which stage of the engagement?

A. During the planning stage.

B. Subsequent to evaluating risk management and control systems.

C. As the engagement is performed.

D. At the end of each engagement when the standard work program should be revised for the next engagement to ensure coverage of noted problem areas.

Answer (A) is correct. *(CIA, adapted)*

**REQUIRED:** The stage of the engagement during which the work program is written.

**DISCUSSION:** Standard 2200 states, "Internal auditors should develop and record a plan for each engagement, including the scope, objectives, timing, and resource allocations." Thus, Standard 2240 states, "Internal auditors should develop work programs that achieve the engagement objectives. These work programs should be recorded." Furthermore, work programs should be approved prior to their implementation, and any adjustments should be approved promptly (Standard 2240.A1). Accordingly, work programs are prepared during the planning stage.

Answer (B) is incorrect because the work program states the scope, degree, nature, and extent of testing. Hence, it must be written in the planning stage. Answer (C) is incorrect because the internal auditor should write the work program during the planning stage, not as the engagement is performed. However, the work program may be modified during the engagement. Answer (D) is incorrect because, although revising the work program at the end of one engagement for the next engagement is allowed, it should still be written during the planning phase.

**47.** In planning an assurance engagement, a survey could assist with all of the following except

A. Obtaining engagement client comments and suggestions on control problems.

B. Obtaining preliminary information on controls.

C. Identifying areas for engagement emphasis.

D. Evaluating the adequacy and effectiveness of controls.

Answer (D) is correct. *(CIA, adapted)*

**REQUIRED:** The planning item with which a survey would not assist.

**DISCUSSION:** A survey is a process for gathering information, without detailed verification, on the activity being examined. A survey may involve discussions with the client, documenting key control activities, and identifying significant engagement issues (PA 2210.A1-1). A survey does not help in evaluating the adequacy and effectiveness of controls except to the extent the internal auditor gains familiarity with the controls. Evaluation requires testing.

Answer (A) is incorrect because a survey could assist with obtaining client comments and suggestions on control problems. Answer (B) is incorrect because a survey could assist with obtaining preliminary information on controls. Answer (C) is incorrect because a survey could assist with identifying areas for engagement emphasis.

**48.** The best control over the work on which internal auditors' opinions are based is

A. Supervisory review of all engagement work.

B. Preparation of time budgets for internal auditing activities.

C. Preparation of engagement working papers.

D. Staffing of internal audit activities.

Answer (A) is correct. *(CIA, adapted)*

**REQUIRED:** The best control over the work on which internal auditors' opinions are based.

**DISCUSSION:** Engagements should be properly supervised to ensure objectives are achieved, quality is assured, and staff is developed (Standard 2340). Supervision includes (1) ensuring that the auditors assigned possess the requisite knowledge, skills, and other competencies to perform the engagement; (2) providing appropriate instructions during the planning of the engagement and approving the engagement work program; (3) seeing that the approved engagement work program is carried out unless changes are both justified and authorized; (4) determining that engagement working papers adequately support the engagement observations, conclusions, and recommendations; (5) ensuring that engagement communications are accurate, objective, clear, concise, constructive, and timely; (6) ensuring that engagement objectives are met; and (7) providing opportunities for developing internal auditors' knowledge, skills, and other competencies. Hence, supervision is a control that encompasses all aspects of engagements (PA 2340-1).

Answer (B) is incorrect because, although useful, time budgets do not assure the adequacy of work supporting opinions. Answer (C) is incorrect because engagement working papers support the conclusions and engagement results, but supervision is necessary to ensure the adequacy of work. Answer (D) is incorrect because proper staffing is required, but supervision is essential to ensure an adequate basis for opinions.

**49.** Determining that engagement objectives have been met is part of the overall supervision of an engagement and is the ultimate responsibility of the

A. Staff internal auditor.

B. Audit committee.

C. Engagement supervisor.

D. Chief audit executive.

Answer (D) is correct. *(CIA, adapted)*

**REQUIRED:** The person(s) with ultimate responsibility for determining that engagement objectives have been met.

**DISCUSSION:** The CAE is responsible for assuring that appropriate engagement supervision is provided. Supervision is a process that begins with planning and continues through the examination, evaluation, communication, and follow-up phases of the engagement (PA 2340-1).

**50.** Why should organizations require assurance engagement clients to reply promptly and outline the corrective action that has been implemented on reported observations?

A. To remove items from the pending list as soon as possible.

B. To effect savings or to institute compliance as early as possible.

C. To indicate concurrence with the engagement observations.

D. To ensure that the engagement work schedule is kept up to date.

Answer (B) is correct. *(CIA, adapted)*

**REQUIRED:** The reason clients should promptly reply and outline the corrective action that has been implemented on reported observations.

**DISCUSSION:** Communications should be timely to enable prompt corrective action, and they should be distributed to those in a position to take corrective action or to ensure that corrective action is taken (PA 2420-1 and PA 2440-1). Moreover, internal auditors should follow up to ascertain that appropriate action is taken on reported engagement observations and recommendations. The internal auditors should determine that corrective action being taken has the desired results or that senior management or the board has assumed the risk of not taking corrective action (PA 2500.A1-1). Consequently, it follows that the objectives of engagements and the timely reporting of observations and recommendations would be defeated if engagement clients do not promptly implement and report on corrective action.

Answer (A) is incorrect because removing items from the pending list concerns a mechanical and immaterial aspect of the communication process. Answer (C) is incorrect because the client may not concur with the observations and recommendations. This dispute may or may not be considered in closing the engagement. Answer (D) is incorrect because ensuring that the engagement work schedule is kept up to date is an administrative function of the internal audit activity.

**51.** Upon reviewing the final communication of engagement results, senior management decided to assume the risk of not implementing corrective action on certain engagement observations. Which of the following is the best course of action for the chief audit executive?

A. Notify regulatory authorities of management's decision.

B. Perform additional engagement procedures to further identify the policy violations.

C. Conduct a follow-up engagement to determine whether corrective action was taken.

D. Discuss the matter with senior management and possibly the board if the residual risk accepted is excessive.

Answer (D) is correct. *(CIA, adapted)*

**REQUIRED:** The best course of action when management agrees to assume the risk of not implementing corrective action.

**DISCUSSION:** According to Standard 2600, "When the chief audit executive believes that senior management has accepted a level of residual risk that may be unacceptable to the organization, the chief audit executive should discuss the matter with senior management. If the decision regarding residual risk is not resolved, the chief audit executive and senior management should report the matter to the board for resolution."

Answer (A) is incorrect because regulatory authorities do not need to be notified. Management has decided to assume responsibility, and no regulatory violations were mentioned. Answer (B) is incorrect because no further action is required unless the CAE believes that the residual risk assumed is too great. Answer (C) is incorrect because no further action is required unless the CAE believes that the residual risk assumed is too great.

## 9.6 Performing the Engagement

**52.** Engagement information is usually considered relevant when it is

A. Derived through valid statistical sampling.

B. Objective and unbiased.

C. Factual, adequate, and convincing.

D. Consistent with the engagement objectives.

Answer (D) is correct. *(CIA, adapted)*

**REQUIRED:** The circumstance in which information is usually considered relevant.

**DISCUSSION:** Information should be sufficient, reliable, relevant, and useful to provide a sound basis for engagement observations, conclusions, and recommendations. Relevant information supports engagement observations, conclusions, and recommendations and is consistent with the objectives for the engagement (PA 2310-1).

Answer (A) is incorrect because whether sampling is appropriate and the results are valid are issues related to the determination of sufficiency and reliability rather than relevance. Answer (B) is incorrect because objectivity and lack of bias do not assure that information will support observations and recommendations and be consistent with the engagement objectives. Answer (C) is incorrect because sufficient information is factual, adequate, and convincing so that a prudent, informed person would reach the same conclusions as the internal auditor.

**53.** What characteristic of information is satisfied by an original signed document?

A. Sufficiency.

B. Reliability.

C. Relevance.

D. Usefulness.

Answer (B) is correct. *(CIA, adapted)*

**REQUIRED:** The characteristic of information satisfied by an original signed document.

**DISCUSSION:** Reliable information is competent and the best attainable through the use of appropriate engagement techniques (PA 2310-1). An original document is the prime example of such information.

Answer (A) is incorrect because sufficient information is factual, adequate, and convincing. The information contained on the document may be none of those things. Answer (C) is incorrect because relevancy concerns the relationship of the information to some objective of the engagement. No engagement objective is disclosed in the question. Thus, whether the information on the document is relevant to the investigation cannot be determined. Answer (D) is incorrect because usefulness is achieved if the item helps the organization (the internal auditor, in this case) to accomplish predetermined goals. No such goals are specified.

**54.** When sampling methods are used, the concept of sufficiency of information means that the samples selected provide

A. Reasonable assurance that they are representative of the sampled population.

B. The best information that is reasonably obtainable.

C. Reasonable assurance that the information has a logical relationship to the engagement objective.

D. Absolute assurance that a sample is representative of the population.

Answer (A) is correct. *(CIA, adapted)*

**REQUIRED:** The meaning of sufficiency of information when sampling methods are used.

**DISCUSSION:** Information is deemed sufficient if it is factual, adequate, and convincing so that a prudent, informed person would reach the same conclusions as the internal auditor (PA 2310-1). The results of a properly executed statistical sampling procedure are usually sufficient for an internal auditor's purposes. A sample by definition can provide only reasonable assurance. Because of cost-benefit considerations, absolute assurance is seldom possible.

Answer (B) is incorrect because the best reasonably obtainable is reliable information. Answer (C) is incorrect because the logical relationship indicates relevance. Answer (D) is incorrect because cost-benefit considerations usually preclude absolute assurance.

**55.** An inexperienced internal auditor notified the senior internal auditor of a significant variance from the engagement client's budget. The senior auditor told the new internal auditor not to worry because the senior auditor had heard that there had been an unauthorized work stoppage that probably accounted for the difference. Which of the following statements is most appropriate?

A. The new internal auditor should have investigated the matter fully and not bothered the senior.

B. The senior used proper judgment in curtailing what could have been a wasteful investigation.

C. The senior should have halted the engagement until the variance was fully explained.

D. The senior should have aided the new internal auditor in formulating a plan for accumulating appropriate information.

Answer (D) is correct. *(CIA, adapted)*

**REQUIRED:** The senior internal auditor's proper response to a significant budget variance.

**DISCUSSION:** The variance was not adequately investigated or explained. When analytical procedures identify unexpected results or relationships, the internal auditor should examine and evaluate such results or relationships. The examination and evaluation should include inquiries of management and the application of other engagement procedures until the internal auditor is satisfied that the results or relationships are sufficiently explained. Unexplained results or relationships may be indicative of a significant condition such as a potential error, irregularity, or illegal act. Results or relationships that are not sufficiently explained should be communicated to the appropriate levels of management. The internal auditor may recommend appropriate courses of action, depending on the circumstances (PA 2320-1).

Answer (A) is incorrect because the extent of supervision varies with the proficiency and experience of the internal auditor and the complexity of the engagement (PA 2340-1). An inexperienced internal auditor should refer this matter to the senior. Answer (B) is incorrect because the facts given do not support the conclusion that accumulating additional information would be wasteful. Answer (C) is incorrect because the variance needs explanation, but the engagement should continue.

**56.** The internal auditor of an organization with a recently automated human resource system reviews the retirement benefits plan and determines that the pension and medical benefits have been changed several times in the past 10 years. The internal auditor wishes to determine whether further investigation is justified. The most appropriate engagement procedure is to

A. Review the trend of overall retirement expense over the last 10 years. If it has increased, further investigation is needed.

B. Use generalized audit software to take a monetary-unit sample of retirement pay and determine whether each retired employee was paid correctly.

C. Review reasonableness of retirement pay and medical expenses on a per-person basis stratified by which plan was in effect when the employee retired.

D. Use generalized audit software to take an attribute sample of retirement pay and perform detailed testing to determine whether each person chosen was given the proper benefits.

Answer (C) is correct. *(CIA, adapted)*

**REQUIRED:** The most appropriate procedure to determine if further investigation of the retirement benefits plan is needed.

**DISCUSSION:** Analytical procedures provide internal auditors with an efficient and effective means of assessing and evaluating information collected in an engagement. The assessment results from comparing information with expectations identified or developed by the internal auditor. Analytical procedures are useful in identifying, among other things, differences that are not expected, the absence of differences when they are expected, potential errors, potential irregularities or illegal acts, and other unusual or nonrecurring transactions or events (PA 2320-1). Accordingly, significant changes, such as those in pension and medical benefits, require the internal auditor to refine his/her expectations. In these circumstances, the internal auditor must stratify the sample according to the plans in effect when the employees retired and develop a predicted result for each person based on the stratum to which (s)he belongs.

Answer (A) is incorrect because reviewing the trend of overall retirement expense over the last 10 years does not consider the changes in plans or the number of employees retired. Answer (B) is incorrect because the sample should be stratified. The population is not homogeneous. Answer (D) is incorrect because taking an attribute sample of retirement pay does not meet the engagement objective of determining whether further investigation is warranted.

**57.** An internal auditor was evaluating the effectiveness and efficiency of the operation of the motor pool. The engagement work program included the use of analytical procedures to observe the trend of expenses for major overhauls of heavy-wheeled vehicles. This trend showed a substantial increase in the last year of the ratios of amounts spent in relation to (1) the number of vehicles being used, (2) the mileage of the vehicles, (3) the age of the equipment, and (4) environmental conditions. The internal auditor's investigation indicated that two new maintenance firms were being used. The expenditure packages from the maintenance work were complete; however, the billings for the work had an unusual regularity. The identification of the vehicles serviced did not correspond to the vehicle maintenance reports. Possible engagement procedures include

1. Discussing the matter with the superintendent of maintenance and ask for an explanation.
2. Preparing a schedule of the types of maintenance being performed and comparing with manufacturers' maintenance guides.
3. Analyzing vehicles' trip tickets to determine if they contain indications of problems needing attention.
4. Reviewing deadline reports to determine that vehicles were not in service on the dates of maintenance work.
5. Reviewing dispatch schedules to determine whether vehicles were dispatched for use on days the maintenance work was reported as performed.
6. Discussing the matter with plant security.

What priority should the above actions have?

A. 1, 6, and 4.

B. 4, 5, and 6.

C. 6, 5, and 1.

D. 2, 3, and 4.

Answer (B) is correct. *(CIA, adapted)*

**REQUIRED:** The order of priority of procedures performed in evaluating the effectiveness and efficiency of motor pool operations.

**DISCUSSION:** Analytical auditing procedures may be performed using monetary amounts, physical quantities, ratios, or percentages. Specific analytical auditing procedures include, but are not limited to, ratio, trend, and regression analysis; reasonableness tests; period-to-period comparisons; and comparisons with budgets, forecasts, and external economic information. Analytical auditing procedures assist internal auditors in identifying conditions that may require subsequent engagement procedures (PA 2320-1). Thus, substantial increases in maintenance cost ratios indicate a need for a more extensive investigation. Items 4 and 5 could provide information regarding the status of vehicles. If discrepancies are found, the appropriate authorities within the organization should be consulted.

Answer (A) is incorrect because discussing the matter with the superintendent could compromise the investigation if (s)he is engaged in fraudulent activities or tells someone who is. Answer (C) is incorrect because discussing the matter with the superintendent could compromise the investigation if (s)he is engaged in fraudulent activities or tells someone who is. Answer (D) is incorrect because items 2 and 3, although potential indicators of fraud, do not provide conclusive information.

**58.** An adequately documented working paper should

A. Be concise but complete.

B. Follow a unique form and arrangement.

C. Contain examples of all forms and procedures used by the engagement client.

D. Not contain copies of engagement client records.

Answer (A) is correct. *(CIA, adapted)*

**REQUIRED:** The characteristic of an adequately documented working paper.

**DISCUSSION:** Engagement working papers provide the principal support for the engagement communications. They are the documentation of engagement activities. They record the information obtained and the analyses made and should support the bases for the observations and recommendations reported. Clarity, conciseness, and accuracy are desirable qualities of working papers, but completeness and support for conclusions are paramount considerations (PA 2330-1).

Answer (B) is incorrect because working papers should be uniform and consistent. Answer (C) is incorrect because working papers should contain only information related to an engagement objective. Answer (D) is incorrect because copies of engagement client records should be included whenever necessary.

**59.** During an engagement, the internal auditor should consider which of the following factors in determining the extent to which analytical procedures should be used during the engagement?

A. Adequacy of the system of internal control.

B. Significance of the area being examined.

C. Precision with which the results of analytical audit procedures can be predicted.

D. All of the answers are correct.

Answer (D) is correct. *(CIA, adapted)*

**REQUIRED:** The factors to be considered in determining the extent of analytical procedures.

**DISCUSSION:** When determining the extent to which analytical procedures should be used, the internal auditor should consider the significance of the area being examined, the adequacy of the system of internal control, the availability and reliability of financial and nonfinancial information, the precision with which the results of analytical procedures can be predicted, the availability and comparability of information regarding the industry in which the organization operates, and the extent to which other engagement procedures provide support for engagement results (PA 2320-1).

**60.** Use of electronic working papers

A. Does not comply with the Standards for supervisory review.

B. Does not comply with the Standards for documentation criteria.

C. Does not comply with the Standards for retention requirements.

D. Raises unique issues, but is permitted under the Standards.

Answer (D) is correct. *(Publisher)*

**REQUIRED:** The true statement about electronic working papers.

**DISCUSSION:** The Standards apply to engagement records regardless of the form in which they are stored. The Standards encompass the use of traditional hard copy "paper" as well as other forms, such as tape, disk, diskette, films, or other media (PA 2330-1). Some unique issues are raised by the use of electronic working papers:

1. Electronic working papers and reviewer comments should be protected from unauthorized access and change.
2. Information recorded in working papers "scanned in" should have adequate control to ensure their continued integrity.
3. Working paper retention policies should consider changes made in the original operating system, other software, and hardware to ensure the continued retrievability of electronic working papers throughout the retention cycle.

Answer (A) is incorrect because supervisory review may be facilitated by using electronic media. For example, electronic working papers may be viewed from remote sites. Answer (B) is incorrect because unique control issues exist, but electronic working papers permit more extensive documentation. Answer (C) is incorrect because unique control issues exist, but electronic working papers permit more retention of information.

**61.** To control working papers properly, the internal auditor should not

A. Share the results of an engagement with the engagement client.

B. Permit access to external auditors.

C. Permit access to government auditors.

D. Make them available to people who have no authority to use them.

Answer (D) is correct. *(CIA, adapted)*

**REQUIRED:** The practice that does not result in proper control of working papers.

**DISCUSSION:** Engagement working-paper files should ordinarily remain under the control of the internal audit activity and should be accessible only to authorized personnel. Engagement working papers may be shown to other members of the organization and to external auditors subject to the approval of the CAE. Approval for access by parties outside the organization other than the external auditors should be given by senior management or legal counsel, as appropriate (PA 2330.A1-1).

Answer (A) is incorrect because, given the CAE's approval, working papers may be shown to the engagement client and other members of the organization to substantiate or explain engagement observations and recommendations or for other business purposes. Answer (B) is incorrect because, subject to the CAE's approval, external auditors may be given access to avoid duplicate work. Answer (C) is incorrect because, subject to the CAE's approval, government auditors may be given access to avoid duplicate work.

**62.** Which of the following states an inappropriate policy relating to the retention of engagement working papers?

A. Working papers should be disposed of when they have no further use.

B. Working papers prepared for fraud investigators should be retained indefinitely.

C. Working-paper retention schedules should be approved by legal counsel.

D. Working-paper retention schedules should consider legal and contractual requirements.

Answer (B) is correct. *(CIA, adapted)*

**REQUIRED:** The inappropriate policy relating to the retention of engagement working papers.

**DISCUSSION:** The CAE should develop retention requirements for engagement records (working papers) for both assurance and consulting engagements. The retention requirements should be consistent with the organization's guidelines and any pertinent regulatory or other requirements (Standard 2330.A2 and Standard 2330.C1). Although working papers pertaining to fraud investigations might be kept apart from others, no working paper will have to be kept indefinitely.

Answer (A) is incorrect because the duration of retention should be determined by usefulness. Answer (C) is incorrect because approval by legal counsel is appropriate. Answer (D) is incorrect because legal and contractual requirements may determine the retention period.

**63.** Internal audit activity policies should be developed to govern the content of engagement records, the retention period, the handling of external access requests, and the procedures to be followed when legal counsel is involved in an investigation. The most important consideration in the development of these policies is that

A. Records not protected by attorney-client privilege are accessible in criminal proceedings.

B. The work product of the internal auditors is protected from disclosure.

C. Records created with an expectation of confidentiality are protected from disclosure.

D. Documents revealing attorneys' thought processes will be subject to forced disclosure.

Answer (A) is correct. *(Publisher)*

**REQUIRED:** The most important consideration in the development of policies relating to engagement records.

**DISCUSSION:** Access to engagement records by outside parties has been sought in several different types of proceedings, including criminal prosecutions, civil litigation, tax audits, regulatory reviews, government contract reviews, and reviews by self-regulatory organizations. Virtually all of an organization's records that are not protected by the attorney-client privilege are accessible in criminal proceedings. In noncriminal proceedings the issue of access is less clear (PA 2330.A1-2).

Answer (B) is incorrect because, regardless of any expectation of confidentiality, most records not protected by the attorney-client privilege are accessible in criminal proceedings and may be accessible in civil proceedings. An accountant or auditor privilege is ordinarily not recognized. Answer (C) is incorrect because, regardless of any expectation of confidentiality, most records not protected by the attorney-client privilege are accessible in criminal proceedings and may be accessible in civil proceedings. An accountant or auditor privilege is ordinarily not recognized. Answer (D) is incorrect because an attorney-client privilege usually protects documents, revealing an attorney's thought processes and strategies.

**64.** An internal auditing manager is reviewing the engagement working papers prepared by the staff. Which of the following review comments is true?

A. Each working paper should include the actual and the budgeted times related to such engagement work.

B. Including copies of all the forms and directives of the engagement client constitutes over-documentation.

C. Conclusions need not be documented in the working papers when the engagement objectives are achieved.

D. Each working paper should include a statement regarding the engagement client's cooperation.

Answer (B) is correct. *(CIA, adapted)*

**REQUIRED:** The review comment that is true.

**DISCUSSION:** All engagement working papers should be reviewed to ensure that they properly support the engagement communications and that all necessary engagement procedures have been performed (PA 2340-1). However, adequate support includes only those forms and directives that are relevant to the engagement or to the observations. Thus, including copies of all the forms and directives of the client constitutes over-documentation.

Answer (A) is incorrect because actual and budgeted times are documented in the budget section of the working papers and not on each working paper. Answer (C) is incorrect because conclusions should be documented in the working papers whether or not the engagement objectives are achieved. Answer (D) is incorrect because only noncooperation is likely to be documented.

## 9.7 Managing the Internal Audit Activity

**65.** Which of the following factors is not included in determining the engagement work schedule?

A. Engagement work programs.

B. The effectiveness of risk management and control processes.

C. Workload requirements.

D. Issues relating to organizational governance.

Answer (A) is correct. *(CIA, adapted)*

**REQUIRED:** The activity not included in developing the engagement work schedule.

**DISCUSSION:** Engagement work schedules should include (1) what activities are to be performed; (2) when they will be performed; and (3) the estimated time required, taking into account the scope of the engagement work planned and the nature and extent of related work performed by others. Matters to be considered in establishing engagement work schedule priorities should include (1) the dates and results of the last engagement; (2) updated assessments of risks and effectiveness of risk management and control processes; (3) requests by senior management, the audit committee, and the governing body; (4) current issues relating to organizational governance; (5) major changes in the enterprise's business, operations, programs, systems, and controls; (6) opportunities to achieve operating benefits; and (7) changes in and capabilities of the staff. The work schedules should be sufficiently flexible to cover unanticipated demands on the internal audit activity (PA 2010-1). Development of work programs occurs during the planning phase of an individual engagement.

Answer (B) is incorrect because determining an engagement work schedule includes considering the effectiveness of risk management and control processes. Answer (C) is incorrect because determining an engagement work schedule includes considering workload requirements. Answer (D) is incorrect because determining an engagement work schedule includes considering issues relating to organizational governance.

**66.** Which of the following factors serves as a direct input to the internal audit activity's (IAA's) financial budget?

A. Engagement work schedules.

B. Activity reports.

C. Past effectiveness of the internal audit activity in identifying cost savings.

D. Internal auditing activity's charter.

Answer (A) is correct. *(CIA, adapted)*

**REQUIRED:** The direct input to the IAA's financial budget.

**DISCUSSION:** The IAA's planning process involves establishing goals, engagement work schedules, staffing plans and financial budgets, and activity reports. The plans and budgets, including the number of internal auditors and the knowledge, skills, and other competencies required to perform their work, should be determined from engagement work schedules, administrative activities, education and training requirements, and research and development efforts (PA 2030-1).

Answer (B) is incorrect because activity reports compare actual performance with goals and schedules and actual expenditures with financial budgets. Answer (C) is incorrect because past performance is an indicator of the value of internal auditing, but it will not affect the funds committed to current operations. Answer (D) is incorrect because the charter defines the purpose, authority, and responsibility of the IAA.

**67.** The chief audit executive routinely presents an activity report to the board as part of the board meeting agenda each quarter. Senior management has asked to review this presentation before each board meeting so that any issues or questions can be discussed beforehand. The CAE should

A. Provide the activity report to senior management as requested and discuss any issues that may require action to be taken.

B. Withhold disclosure of the activity report to senior management because such matters are the sole province of the board.

C. Disclose to the board only those matters in the activity report that pertain to expenditures and financial budgets of the internal audit activity.

D. Provide information to senior management that pertains only to completed engagements and observations available in published engagement communications.

Answer (A) is correct. *(CIA, adapted)*

**REQUIRED:** The action that should be taken regarding the review of internal auditing reports by senior management.

**DISCUSSION:** The CAE should submit activity reports to senior management and to the board annually or more frequently as necessary. Activity reports should highlight significant engagement observations and recommendations and should inform senior management and the board of any significant deviations from approved engagement work schedules, staffing plans, and financial budgets, and the reasons for them (PA 2060-1).

Answer (B) is incorrect because activity reports should be presented to senior management. Answer (C) is incorrect because the report should not be restricted to expenditures and financial budgets. Information about significant deviations from engagement work schedules and staffing plans should be included. Answer (D) is incorrect because the information need not be limited to completed engagements and observations available in published engagement communications.

**68.** The chief audit executive for an organization has just completed a risk assessment process, identified the areas with the highest risks, and assigned an engagement priority to each. Which of the following conclusions most logically follow(s) from such a risk assessment?

I. Items should be quantified as to risk in the rank order of quantifiable monetary exposure to the organization.

II. The risk priorities should be in order of major control deficiencies.

III. The risk assessment process, though quantified, is the result of professional judgments about both exposures and probability of occurrences.

A. I only.

B. III only.

C. II and III only.

D. I, II, and III.

Answer (B) is correct. *(CIA, adapted)*

**REQUIRED:** The conclusion(s) logically following from a risk assessment process.

**DISCUSSION:** Risk is the possibility of an event's occurrence that will have an impact on the achievement of objectives. According to the Glossary appended to the Standards, risk is measured in terms of impact (exposures) and likelihood (probability). Engagement work schedules should be based on, among other things, an assessment of risk priority and exposure. Prioritizing is needed to make decisions for applying relative resources based on the significance of risk and exposure. A variety of risk models may assist the CAE in prioritizing potential engagement subject areas. Most of these models use risk factors to establish the priority of engagements, for example, monetary materiality, asset liquidity, management competence, quality of internal controls, degree of change or stability, time of last engagement, complexity, or employee and governmental relations (PA 2010-2). Higher priorities are usually assigned to activities with higher risks. However, this process necessarily involves the exercise of professional judgment. Thus, although risk factors may be weighted to determine their relative significance, a ranking based solely on such specific criteria as monetary exposure or control deficiencies is not always indicated.

**69.** Which of the following is most essential for guiding the internal audit staff in maintaining daily compliance with the internal audit activity's (IAA's) standards of performance?

A. Quality program assessments.

B. Position descriptions.

C. Performance appraisals.

D. Policies and procedures.

Answer (D) is correct. *(CIA, adapted)*

**REQUIRED:** The item most essential for guiding the internal audit staff in maintaining daily compliance with the IAA's standards.

**DISCUSSION:** The CAE should establish policies and procedures to guide the IAA (Standard 2040). The form and content of written policies and procedures should be appropriate to the size and structure of the IAA and the complexity of its work. Formal administrative and technical manuals may not be needed by all IAAs. A small IAA may be managed informally. Its staff may be directed and controlled through daily, close supervision and written memoranda. In a large IAA, more formal and comprehensive policies and procedures are essential to guide the staff in the consistent compliance with the IAA's standards of performance (PA 2040-1).

Answer (A) is incorrect because quality program assessments do not provide specific daily guidance to the staff with respect to performance standards. Answer (B) is incorrect because position descriptions do not provide specific daily guidance to the staff with respect to performance standards. Answer (C) is incorrect because performance appraisals do not provide specific daily guidance to the staff with respect to performance standards.

**70.** The chief audit executive is responsible for establishing a program to develop the human resources of the internal audit activity (IAA). This program should include

A. Continuing educational opportunities and performance appraisals.

B. Counseling and an established career path.

C. An established training plan and a charter.

D. Job descriptions and competitive salary increases.

Answer (A) is correct. *(CIA, adapted)*

**REQUIRED:** The CAE's responsibilities for the IAA's human resource development program.

**DISCUSSION:** The CAE should establish a program for selecting and developing the human resources of the IAA. The program should provide for developing written job descriptions for each level of the staff, selecting qualified and competent individuals, training and providing continuing educational opportunities for each internal auditor, appraising each internal auditor's performance at least annually, and providing counsel to internal auditors on their performance and professional development (PA 2030-1).

Answer (B) is incorrect because counseling is an attribute of the program, but an established career path is not. Answer (C) is incorrect because training is part of the development program, but a charter is not specified. Answer (D) is incorrect because written job descriptions are necessary, but salary increases are not.

**71.** Which of the following is a false statement about the relationship between internal auditors and external auditors?

A. Oversight of the work of external auditors is the responsibility of the chief audit executive.

B. Sufficient meetings should be scheduled between internal and external auditors to assure timely and efficient completion of the work.

C. Internal and external auditors may exchange engagement communications and management letters.

D. Internal auditors may provide engagement work programs and working papers to external auditors.

Answer (A) is correct. *(CIA, adapted)*

**REQUIRED:** The false statement about the relationship between internal and external auditors.

**DISCUSSION:** Oversight of the work of the independent outside auditor, including coordination with the internal audit activity, is generally the responsibility of the board. Actual coordination should be the responsibility of the CAE. However, the board in the exercise of its oversight role may request that the CAE assess the performance of the external auditors. Ordinarily, this assessment is made in the context of the CAE's function of coordinating internal and external auditing activities (PA 2050-1). Coordination between internal and external auditors involves, among other things, (1) sufficient meetings to assure coordination of work and efficient and timely completion of activities, and to determine whether observations and recommendations from work performed to date require that the scope of planned work be adjusted; (2) access to each other's work programs and working papers; (3) exchange of internal audit communications and external auditors' management letters; and (4) common understanding of techniques, methods, and terminology.

Questions 72 and 73 are based on the following information. You are the chief audit executive of a parent organization that has foreign subsidiaries. Independent external audits performed for the parent are not conducted by the same firm that conducts the foreign subsidiary audits. Because the internal audit activity occasionally provides direct assistance to both external firms, you have copies of audit programs and selected working papers produced by each firm.

**72.** The foreign subsidiary's auditors want to rely on some of the work performed by the parent organization's audit firm, but they need to review the working papers first. They have asked you for copies of the working papers of the parent organization's audit firm. What is the most appropriate response to the foreign subsidiary's auditors?

A. Provide copies of the working papers without notifying the parent's audit firm.

B. Notify the parent's auditors of the situation and request that they either provide the working papers or authorize you to do so.

C. Provide copies of the working papers and notify the parent's audit firm that you have done so.

D. Refuse to provide the working papers under any circumstances.

Answer (B) is correct. *(CIA, adapted)*

**REQUIRED:** The proper response to a request by one external audit firm for another external audit firm's working papers held by the internal auditors.

**DISCUSSION:** Coordination of internal and external auditing efforts involves access to each other's work programs and working papers. However, such access carries with it the responsibility to respect the confidentiality of those programs and working papers (PA 2050-1). Hence, the internal auditors should seek the approval of the parent's external auditors before granting access to their working papers to the external auditors of the subsidiaries.

Answer (A) is incorrect because the working papers are the property of the parent's external auditors, and their confidentiality should be respected. Answer (C) is incorrect because the external auditors should give prior authorization for the release of their working papers. Answer (D) is incorrect because the internal auditors have the responsibility to ensure proper coordination with external auditors.

**73.** The foreign subsidiary's external audit firm wants to rely on an audit of a function at the parent organization. The audit was conducted by the internal audit activity. To place reliance on the work performed, the foreign subsidiary's auditors have requested copies of the working papers. What is the most appropriate response to the foreign subsidiary's auditors?

A. Provide copies of the working papers.

B. Ask the parent's audit firm if it is appropriate to release the working papers.

C. Ask the board for permission to release the working papers.

D. Refuse to provide the working papers under any circumstances.

Answer (A) is correct. *(CIA, adapted)*

**REQUIRED:** The proper response to a request by external auditors for the internal auditors' working papers.

**DISCUSSION:** Internal and external auditing efforts should be coordinated to ensure adequate coverage and to minimize duplication of effort. Coordination involves access to each other's work programs and working papers. Access to the internal auditors' work programs and working papers should be given to the external auditors in order for them to be satisfied as to the propriety, for external audit purposes, of relying on the internal auditors' work (PA 2050-1).

Answer (B) is incorrect because the working papers are the property of the organization. The responsibility of the CAE is to maintain the security of the working papers and to coordinate efforts with the external auditors. Thus the decision belongs not to the parent's external auditors but to the CAE. Answer (C) is incorrect because access to working papers by external auditors should be subject to the approval of the CAE (PA 2330.A1-1). Answer (D) is incorrect because the CAE should ensure proper coordination with external auditors by, among other things, granting the external auditors access to the internal auditors' working papers.

**74.** A quality assurance and improvement program of an internal audit activity provides reasonable assurance that internal auditing work is performed in accordance with its charter. Which of the following are designed to provide feedback on the effectiveness of an internal audit activity (IAA)?

I. Proper supervision
II. Proper training
III. Internal reviews
IV. External reviews

A. I, II, and III only.

B. II, III, and IV only.

C. I, III, and IV only.

D. I, II, III, and IV.

Answer (C) is correct. *(CIA, adapted)*

**REQUIRED:** The elements designed to provide feedback on the effectiveness of an IAA.

**DISCUSSION:** A quality assurance and improvement program should be designed to provide reasonable assurance to the various stakeholders of the IAA that it (1) performs in accordance with its charter, which should be consistent with the Standards and the Code of Ethics; (2) operates effectively and efficiently; and (3) is perceived by the stakeholders as adding value and improving operations. The program should include appropriate supervision, periodic internal assessment and ongoing monitoring of quality assurance, and periodic external assessments (PA 1300-1).

**75.** Quality program assessments may be performed internally or externally. A distinguishing feature of an external assessment is its objective to

A. Identify tasks that can be performed better.

B. Determine whether internal auditing services meet professional standards.

C. Set forth the recommendations for improvement.

D. Provide independent assurance.

Answer (D) is correct. *(CIA, adapted)*

**REQUIRED:** The distinguishing feature of an external assessment.

**DISCUSSION:** External assessments should be conducted at least once every 5 years by a qualified, independent reviewer or review team from outside the organization (Standard 1312). The individual or organization performing the assessment, the members of the assessment team, and anyone else participating should be free from any obligation to, or interest in, the organization that is the subject of the external assessment or its personnel. Assessments by individuals in another department of the organization or in a related organization are not independent. Moreover, reciprocal peer reviews between two organizations should not be performed (PA 1312-1).

Answer (A) is incorrect because an internal assessment will identify tasks that can be performed better. Answer (B) is incorrect because an internal assessment will determine whether internal auditing services meet professional standards. Answer (C) is incorrect because an internal assessment will set forth recommendations for improvement.

**76.** External assessment of an internal audit activity (IAA) is not likely to evaluate

A. Adherence to the internal audit activity's charter.

B. Compliance with the International Standards for the Professional Practice of Internal Auditing.

C. Detailed cost-benefit analysis of the internal audit activity.

D. The tools and techniques employed by the internal audit activity.

Answer (C) is correct. *(CIA, adapted)*

**REQUIRED:** The purpose not served by external assessment of an IAA.

**DISCUSSION:** The external assessment has a broad scope of coverage that includes (1) compliance with the Standards, the Code of Ethics, and the IAA's charter, plans, policies, procedures, practices, and applicable legislative and regulatory requirements; (2) the expectations of the IAA expressed by the board, executive management, and operational managers; (3) the integration of the IAA into the governance process; (4) the tools and techniques employed by the IAA; (5) the mix of knowledge, experience, and disciplines within the staff, including the staff focus on process improvement; and (6) the determination whether the IAA adds value and improves the organization's operations (PA 1312-1). However, the costs and benefits of internal auditing are neither easily quantifiable nor the subject of an external assessment.

Answer (A) is incorrect because adherence to the IAA's charter is within the broad scope of coverage of the external assessment. Answer (B) is incorrect because compliance with the Standards is within the broad scope of coverage of the external assessment. Answer (D) is incorrect because the tools and techniques of the IAA are within the broad scope of coverage of the external assessment.

**77.** Internal auditors may report that their activities are conducted in accordance with the Standards. They may use this statement only if

A. They demonstrate compliance with the Standards.

B. An independent external assessment of the internal audit activity is conducted annually.

C. Senior management or the board is accountable for implementing a quality assurance and improvement program.

D. External assessments of the internal audit activity are made by the external auditors.

Answer (A) is correct. *(Publisher)*

**REQUIRED:** The condition permitting internal auditors to report that their activities are in accordance with the Standards.

**DISCUSSION:** Internal auditors are encouraged to report that their activities are "conducted in accordance with the *International Standards for the Professional Practice of Internal Auditing*." However, internal auditors may use the statement only if assessments of the quality improvement program demonstrate that the internal audit activity is in compliance with the Standards (Standard 1330).

Answer (B) is incorrect because an independent external assessment of the internal audit activity should be conducted at least once every 5 years (Standard 1312). Answer (C) is incorrect because the CAE must develop and maintain a QA & IP that covers all aspects of the IAA and continuously monitors its effectiveness (Standard 1300). Answer (D) is incorrect because external assessments should be conducted at least once every 5 years by a qualified, independent reviewer or review team from outside the organization (Standard 1312). External auditors need not be the reviewers.

**78.** According to Standard 1340, *Disclosure of Noncompliance*, disclosure should be made to senior management and the board whenever

A. The internal audit activity does not comply with the Standards.

B. The internal auditors do not comply with the Code of Ethics.

C. The internal audit activity does not comply with the Standards, or the internal auditors do not comply with the Code of Ethics.

D. Noncompliance with the Standards or the Code of Ethics affects the overall operation of the internal audit activity.

Answer (D) is correct. *(Publisher)*

**REQUIRED:** The circumstance in which disclosure should be made to senior management and the board.

**DISCUSSION:** Although the internal audit activity should achieve full compliance with the Standards and internal auditors with the Code of Ethics, there may be instances in which full compliance is not achieved. When noncompliance affects the overall scope or operation of the internal audit activity, disclosure should be made to senior management and the board (Standard 1340).

## 9.8 Ethics

**79.** A primary purpose for establishing a code of conduct within a professional organization is to

A. Reduce the likelihood that members of the profession will be sued for substandard work.

B. Ensure that all members of the profession perform at approximately the same level of competence.

C. Promote an ethical culture among professionals who serve others.

D. Require members of the profession to exhibit loyalty in all matters pertaining to the affairs of their organization.

Answer (C) is correct. *(CIA, adapted)*

**REQUIRED:** The primary purpose for establishing a code of conduct within a professional organization.

**DISCUSSION:** The IIA *Code of Ethics* is typical. Its purpose is "to promote an ethical culture in the profession of internal auditing." The definition of internal auditing states that it is "an independent, objective assurance and consulting activity." Moreover, internal auditing is founded on "the trust placed in its objective assurance about risk management, control, and governance." The IIA *Code of Ethics* further emphasizes that it provides guidance to internal auditors "serving others."

Answer (A) is incorrect because, although this result may follow from establishing a code of conduct, it is not the primary purpose. To consider it so would be self-serving. Answer (B) is incorrect because a code of conduct may help to establish minimum standards of competence, but it would be impossible to legislate equality of competence by all members of a profession. Answer (D) is incorrect because, in some situations, responsibility to the public at large may conflict with, and be more important than, loyalty to one's organization.

**80.** The Rules of Conduct set forth in The IIA *Code of Ethics*

A. Describe behavior norms expected of internal auditors.

B. Are guidelines to assist internal auditors in dealing with engagement clients.

C. Are interpreted by the Principles.

D. Apply only to particular conduct specifically mentioned.

Answer (A) is correct. *(CIA, adapted)*

**REQUIRED:** The true statement about The IIA *Code of Ethics.*

**DISCUSSION:** A code of ethics is necessary and appropriate for the profession of internal auditing, founded as it is on the trust placed in its objective assurance about risk management, control, and governance. The Institute's *Code of Ethics* extends beyond the definition of internal auditing to include two essential components: (1) Principles that are relevant to the profession and practice of internal auditing and (2) Rules of Conduct that describe behavior norms expected of internal auditors. These rules are an aid to interpreting the Principles into practical applications and are intended to guide the ethical conduct of internal auditors.

Answer (B) is incorrect because the Rules of Conduct provide guidance to internal auditors in the discharge of their responsibility to all those whom they serve. Engagement clients are not the only parties served by internal auditing. Answer (C) is incorrect because the Rules of Conduct are an aid in interpreting the Principles. Answer (D) is incorrect because the conduct may be unacceptable or discreditable although not mentioned in the Rules of Conduct.

**81.** The *Code of Ethics* requires internal auditors to perform their work with

A. Honesty, diligence, and responsibility.

B. Timeliness, sobriety, and clarity.

C. Knowledge, skills, and competencies.

D. Punctuality, objectivity, and responsibility.

Answer (A) is correct. *(CIA, adapted)*

**REQUIRED:** The qualities internal auditors should exhibit in the performance of their work.

**DISCUSSION:** Four rules are stated under the integrity principle. According to Rule of Conduct 1.1 of The IIA *Code of Ethics*, "Internal auditors shall perform their work with honesty, diligence, and responsibility."

Answer (B) is incorrect because timeliness, sobriety, and clarity are not mentioned in the Code. Answer (C) is incorrect because knowledge, skills, and competencies are mentioned in the Standards. Answer (D) is incorrect because punctuality is not mentioned in the Code.

**82.** Which of the following is permissible under The IIA *Code of Ethics*?

A. Disclosing confidential, engagement-related, information that is potentially damaging to the organization in response to a court order.

B. Using engagement-related information in a decision to buy an ownership interest in the employer organization.

C. Accepting an unexpected gift from an employee whom the internal auditor has praised in a recent engagement communication.

D. Not reporting significant observations and recommendations about illegal activity to the board because management has indicated it will address the issue.

Answer (A) is correct. *(CIA, adapted)*

**REQUIRED:** The action permissible under The IIA *Code of Ethics.*

**DISCUSSION:** Under Rule of Conduct 1.2, "Internal auditors shall observe the law and make disclosures expected by the law and the profession." Thus, the requirement not to use information in any manner detrimental to the legitimate and ethical objectives of the organization (Rule of Conduct 3.2) does not override the legal obligation to respond to a court order.

Answer (B) is incorrect because Rule of Conduct 3.2 prohibits internal auditors from using information for personal gain. Answer (C) is incorrect because Rule of Conduct 2.2 prohibits internal auditors from accepting anything that may impair or be presumed to impair their professional judgment. Answer (D) is incorrect because Rule of Conduct 1.3 prohibits knowingly being a party to any illegal activity. Internal auditors must also disclose all material facts known to them that, if not disclosed, might distort the reporting of activities under review (Rule of Conduct 2.3).

**83.** An internal auditor, working for a chemical manufacturer, discovered that toxic waste was being dumped in violation of the law. Out of loyalty to the organization, no information regarding the dumping was collected. The internal auditor

A. Violated the *Code of Ethics* by knowingly becoming a party to an illegal act.

B. Violated the *Code of Ethics* by failing to protect the well-being of the general public.

C. Did not violate the *Code of Ethics*. Loyalty to the employer in all matters is required.

D. Did not violate the *Code of Ethics*. Conclusive information about wrongdoing was not gathered.

Answer (A) is correct. *(CIA, adapted)*

**REQUIRED:** The ethical implication of failing to gather information about the organization's illegal act.

**DISCUSSION:** Rule of Conduct 1.3 prohibits knowingly being a party to any illegal activity. Internal auditors must also disclose all material facts known to them that, if not disclosed, might distort the reporting of activities under review (Rule of Conduct 2.3). The internal auditor apparently also failed to perform his/her work with diligence (Rule of Conduct 1.1).

Answer (B) is incorrect because The IIA *Code of Ethics* does not impose a duty to the general public. Answer (C) is incorrect because an internal auditor may not use information in any manner detrimental to the legitimate and ethical objectives of the organization (Rule of Conduct 3.2) and must respect and contribute to such objectives (Rule of Conduct 1.4). However, illegal dumping of toxic waste is neither legitimate nor ethical. Answer (D) is incorrect because the internal auditor should have collected and reported such information in accordance with the Standards.

**84.** An internal auditor discovered some material inefficiencies in a purchasing function. The purchasing manager is the internal auditor's next-door neighbor and best friend. In accordance with The IIA *Code of Ethics*, the internal auditor should

A. Objectively include the facts of the case in the engagement communications.

B. Not report the incident because of loyalty to the friend.

C. Include the facts of the case in a special communication submitted only to the friend.

D. Not report the friend unless the activity is illegal.

Answer (A) is correct. *(CIA, adapted)*

**REQUIRED:** The proper internal auditor action given a conflict between professional duty and friendship.

**DISCUSSION:** Under Rule of Conduct 2.3, "Internal auditors shall disclose all material facts known to them that, if not disclosed, may distort the reporting of activities under review." Furthermore, under Rule of Conduct 1.4, "Internal auditors shall respect and contribute to the legitimate and ethical objectives of the organization."

Answer (B) is incorrect because this action is at variance with the internal auditor's duties under the Code. Answer (C) is incorrect because this action is at variance with the internal auditor's duties under the Code. Answer (D) is incorrect because this action is at variance with the internal auditor's duties under the Code.

**85.** The chief audit executive (CAE) has been appointed to a committee to evaluate the appointment of the external auditors. The engagement partner for the external accounting firm wants the CAE to join him for a week of hunting at his private lodge. The CAE should

A. Accept, assuming both their schedules allow it.

B. Refuse on the grounds of conflict of interest.

C. Accept as long as it is not charged to employer time.

D. Ask the comptroller whether accepting the invitation is a violation of the organization's code of ethics.

Answer (B) is correct. *(CIA, adapted)*

**REQUIRED:** The CAE's response to a social invitation by an external auditor who is subject to evaluation by a committee on which the CAE serves.

**DISCUSSION:** Under Rule of Conduct 2.1, "Internal auditors shall not participate in any activity or relationship that may impair or be presumed to impair their unbiased assessment. This participation includes those activities or relationships that may be in conflict with the interests of the organization." Furthermore, under Rule of Conduct 2.2, "Internal auditors shall not accept anything that may impair or be presumed to impair their professional judgment."

**86.** Which of the following concurrent occupations could appear to subvert the ethical behavior of an internal auditor?

A. Internal auditor and a well-known charitable organization's local in-house chairperson.

B. Internal auditor and part-time business insurance broker.

C. Internal auditor and adjunct faculty member of a local business college that educates potential employees.

D. Internal auditor and landlord of multiple housing that publicly advertises for tenants in a local community newspaper listing monthly rental fees.

Answer (B) is correct. *(CIA, adapted)*

**REQUIRED:** The concurrent occupations that could create an ethical issue.

**DISCUSSION:** Under Rule of Conduct 2.1, "Internal auditors shall not participate in any activity or relationship that may impair or be presumed to impair their unbiased assessment. This participation includes those activities or relationships that may be in conflict with the interests of the organization." As a business insurance broker, the internal auditor may lose his/her objectivity because (s)he might benefit from a change in the employer's insurance coverage.

Answer (A) is incorrect because the activities of a charity are unlikely to be contrary to the interests of the organization. Answer (C) is incorrect because teaching is compatible with internal auditing. Answer (D) is incorrect because, although dealing in commercial properties might involve a conflict, renting residential units most likely does not.

**87.** Internal auditors should be prudent in their relationships with persons and organizations external to their employers. Which of the following activities will most likely not adversely affect internal auditors' ethical behavior?

A. Accepting compensation from professional organizations for consulting work.

B. Serving as consultants to competitor organizations.

C. Serving as consultants to suppliers.

D. Discussing engagement plans or results with external parties.

Answer (A) is correct. *(CIA, adapted)*

**REQUIRED:** The external relationship most likely not to involve an ethics violation.

**DISCUSSION:** Professional organizations are unlikely to be employees, clients, customers, suppliers, or business associates of the organization. Hence, the consulting fees are not likely to impair or be presumed to impair the internal auditors' professional judgment (Rule of Conduct 2.2). Moreover, relationships with professional organizations are not likely to create a conflict of interest or impair or be presumed to impair internal auditors' unbiased judgment (Rule of Conduct 2.1). Also, the consulting engagement should not result in the improper use of information (Rule of Conduct 3.2).

Answer (B) is incorrect because this relationship might create a conflict of interest. Answer (C) is incorrect because this relationship might create a conflict of interest. Answer (D) is incorrect because internal auditors should "be prudent in the use and protection of information acquired in the course of their duties" (Rule of Conduct 3.1). Furthermore, such discussion might be "detrimental to the legitimate and ethical objectives of the organization" (Rule of Conduct 3.2).

**88.** During an engagement, an employee with whom you have developed a good working relationship informs you that she has some information about senior management that is damaging to the organization and may concern illegal activities. The employee does not want her name associated with the release of the information. Which of the following actions is considered to be inconsistent with The IIA *Code of Ethics* and the Standards?

A. Assure the employee that you can maintain her anonymity and listen to the information.

B. Suggest that the employee consider talking to legal counsel.

C. Inform the employee that you will attempt to keep the source of the information confidential and will look into the matter further.

D. Inform the employee of other methods of communicating this type of information.

Answer (A) is correct. *(CIA, adapted)*

**REQUIRED:** The action inconsistent with The IIA *Code of Ethics* and the Standards.

**DISCUSSION:** An internal auditor cannot guarantee anonymity. Information communicated to an internal auditor is not subject to a testimonial privilege. Moreover, Rule of Conduct 2.3 states, "Internal auditors shall disclose all material facts known to them that, if not disclosed, may distort the reporting of activities under review." The identity of the informant may be a material fact.

Answer (B) is incorrect because suggesting that the person seek expert legal advice from a qualified individual is appropriate. Answer (C) is incorrect because promising merely to attempt to keep the source of the information confidential is allowable. This promise is not a guarantee of confidentiality. Answer (D) is incorrect because the employee could be directed to other methods of communicating the information in order to maintain her anonymity.

**89.** During the course of an engagement, an internal auditor discovers that a clerk is embezzling funds from the organization. Although this is the first embezzlement ever encountered and the organization has a security department, the internal auditor decides to interrogate the suspect. If the internal auditor is violating The IIA *Code of Ethics*, the rule violated is most likely

A. Failing to exercise due diligence.

B. Lack of loyalty to the organization.

C. Lack of competence in this area.

D. Failing to comply with the law.

Answer (C) is correct. *(CIA, adapted)*

**REQUIRED:** The ethics rule most likely violated.

**DISCUSSION:** Rule of Conduct 4.1 under the competency principle states, "Internal auditors shall engage only in those services for which they have the necessary knowledge, skills, and experience." Internal auditors may not have and are not expected to have knowledge equivalent to that of a person whose primary responsibility is to detect and investigate fraud.

Answer (A) is incorrect because the requirement to perform work with diligence does not override the competency Rules of Conduct or the need to use good judgment. Answer (B) is incorrect because loyalty is better exhibited by consulting professionals and knowing the limits of competence. Answer (D) is incorrect because the internal auditor may violate the suspect's civil rights as a result of inexperience.

**90.** Which situation most likely violates The IIA *Code of Ethics* and the Standards?

A. The chief audit executive (CAE) disagrees with the engagement client about the observations and recommendations in a sensitive area. The CAE discusses the detail of the observations and the proposed recommendations with a fellow CAE from another organization.

B. An organization's charter for the internal audit activity requires the chief audit executive (CAE) to present the yearly engagement work schedule to the board for its approval and suggestions.

C. The engagement manager has removed the most significant observations and recommendations from the final engagement communication. The in-charge internal auditor opposed the removal, explaining that (s)he knows the reported conditions exist. The in-charge internal auditor agrees that, technically, information is not sufficient to support the observations, but management cannot explain the conditions and the observations are the only reasonable conclusions.

D. Because the internal audit activity lacks skill and knowledge in a specialty area, the chief audit executive (CAE) has hired an expert. The engagement manager has been asked to review the expert's approach to the assignment. Although knowledgeable about the area under review, the manager is hesitant to accept the assignment because of lack of expertise.

Answer (A) is correct. *(CIA, adapted)*

**REQUIRED:** The situation most likely to be considered a violation of The IIA *Code of Ethics*.

**DISCUSSION:** According to Rule of Conduct 3.1 of The IIA *Code of Ethics*, "Internal auditors shall be prudent in the use and protection of information acquired in the course of their duties." According to Rule of Conduct 3.2, "Internal auditors shall not use information for any personal gain or in any manner that would be contrary to the law or detrimental to the legitimate and ethical objectives of the organization." Consequently, discussion of sensitive matters with an unauthorized party is the situation most likely to be considered a Code violation. The information conveyed might be used to the detriment of the organization.

Answer (B) is incorrect because approval of the engagement work schedule by the board and senior management is required (Standard 2020). Answer (C) is incorrect because information must be sufficient to achieve engagement objectives (Standard 2300). Answer (D) is incorrect because the Standards allow use of experts when needed.

**91.** In some countries, governmental units have established audit standards. For example, in the United States, the General Accounting Office has developed standards for the conduct of governmental audits, particularly those that relate to compliance with government grants. In performing governmental grant compliance audits, the auditor should

A. Be guided only by the governmental standards.

B. Be guided only by The IIA Standards because they are more encompassing.

C. Be guided by the more general standards that have been issued by the public accounting profession.

D. Follow both The IIA Standards and any additional governmental standards.

Answer (D) is correct. *(CIA, adapted)*

**REQUIRED:** The standards an auditor follows when performing governmental grant compliance audits.

**DISCUSSION:** Rule of Conduct 4 2 of The IIA *Code of Ethics* states, "Internal auditors shall perform internal auditing services in accordance with the Standards for the *Professional Practice of Internal Auditing*." Furthermore, an internal auditor is legally obligated to adhere to governmental standards when performing governmental grant compliance audits.

**92.** Which of the following most likely constitutes a violation of The IIA's *Code of Ethics*?

A. Janice has accepted an assignment to perform an engagement at the electronics manufacturing division. Janice has recently joined the internal audit activity. But she was senior auditor for the external audit of that division and has audited many electronics organizations during the past 2 years.

B. George has been assigned to perform an engagement at the warehousing function 6 months from now. George has no expertise in that area but accepted the assignment anyway. He has signed up for continuing professional education courses in warehousing that will be completed before his assignment begins.

C. Jane is content with her career as an internal auditor and has come to look at it as a regular 9-to-5 job. She has not engaged in continuing professional education or other activities to improve her effectiveness during the last 3 years. However, she feels she is performing the same quality work she always has.

D. John discovered an internal financial fraud during the year. The books were adjusted to properly reflect the loss associated with the fraud. John discussed the fraud with the external auditor when the external auditor reviewed working papers detailing the incident.

Answer (C) is correct. *(CIA, adapted)*

**REQUIRED:** The violation of The IIA's *Code of Ethics*.

**DISCUSSION:** Rule of Conduct 4.3 states, "Internal auditors shall continually improve their proficiency and the effectiveness and quality of their services."

Answer (A) is incorrect because no professional conflict of interest exists per se, especially given that the internal auditor was previously in public accounting. However, the internal auditor should be aware of potential conflicts. Answer (B) is incorrect because, according to Rule of Conduct 4.1, "Internal auditors shall engage only in those services for which they have the necessary knowledge, skills, and experience." Thus, George may perform this service if he has the necessary knowledge, etc. Answer (D) is incorrect because the information was disclosed as part of the normal process of cooperation between the internal and external auditor. Because the books were adjusted, the external auditor was expected to inquire as to the nature of the adjustment.

## 9.9 Fraud

**93.** After noting some red flags, an internal auditor has an increased awareness that fraud may be present. Which of the following best describes the internal auditor's responsibility?

A. Expand activities to determine whether an investigation is warranted.

B. Report the possibility of fraud to senior management and the board and ask them how they would like to proceed.

C. Consult with external legal counsel to determine the course of action to be taken, including the approval of the proposed engagement work program to make sure it is acceptable on legal grounds.

D. Report the matter to the audit committee and request funding for outside service providers to help investigate the possible fraud.

Answer (A) is correct. *(CIA, adapted)*

**REQUIRED:** The internal auditor's responsibility after noting some fraud indicators.

**DISCUSSION:** An internal auditor's responsibilities for detecting fraud include evaluating fraud indicators and deciding whether any additional action is necessary or whether an investigation should be recommended (PA 1210.A2-1).

Answer (B) is incorrect because the internal auditor should notify the appropriate authorities within the organization only if (s)he has determined that the indicators of fraud are sufficient to recommend an investigation. Answer (C) is incorrect because the internal auditor does not have the authority to consult with external legal counsel. Answer (D) is incorrect because the internal auditor should notify the appropriate authorities within the organization only if (s)he has determined that the indicators of fraud are sufficient to recommend an investigation.

**94.** In the course of their work, internal auditors must be alert for fraud and other forms of white-collar crime. The important characteristic that distinguishes fraud from other varieties of white-collar crime is that

A. Fraud encompasses an array of irregularities and illegal acts that involve intentional deception.

B. Unlike other white-collar crimes, fraud is always perpetrated against an outside party.

C. White-collar crime is usually perpetrated for the benefit of an organization, whereas fraud benefits an individual.

D. White-collar crime is usually perpetrated by outsiders to the detriment of an organization, whereas fraud is perpetrated by insiders to benefit the organization.

Answer (A) is correct. *(CIA, adapted)*

**REQUIRED:** The trait distinguishing fraud from other white-collar crimes.

**DISCUSSION:** Fraud encompasses an array of irregularities and illegal acts characterized by intentional deception. It can be perpetrated for the benefit of or to the detriment of the organization and by persons outside as well as inside the organization (PA 1210.A2-1).

Answer (B) is incorrect because fraud may be perpetrated to the detriment of the organization. Answer (C) is incorrect because fraud may be perpetrated for the organization's benefit or for otherwise unselfish reasons. Answer (D) is incorrect because fraud may be perpetrated to the detriment of the organization.

**95.** The internal audit activity's responsibility for deterring fraud is to

A. Establish internal control.

B. Maintain internal control.

C. Evaluate the system of internal control.

D. Exercise operating authority over fraud prevention activities.

Answer (C) is correct. *(Publisher)*

**REQUIRED:** The internal audit activity's responsibility for deterring fraud.

**DISCUSSION:** The principal mechanism for deterring fraud is control, and management has the primary responsibility for establishing and maintaining control. Internal auditors are responsible for assisting in the deterrence of fraud by examining and evaluating the adequacy and the effectiveness of the system of internal control (PA 1210.A2-1).

Answer (A) is incorrect because management has the primary responsibility for establishing internal control. Answer (B) is incorrect because management has the primary responsibility for maintaining internal control. Answer (D) is incorrect because internal auditors should not assume operating responsibilities.

**96.** An internal auditor who suspects fraud should

A. Determine that a loss has been incurred.

B. Interview those who have been involved in the control of assets.

C. Identify the employees who could be implicated in the case.

D. Recommend whatever investigation is considered necessary under the circumstances.

Answer (D) is correct. *(CIA, adapted)*

**REQUIRED:** The action to be taken by an internal auditor who suspects fraud.

**DISCUSSION:** When an internal auditor suspects wrongdoing, the appropriate authorities within the organization should be informed. The internal auditor may recommend whatever investigation is considered necessary in the circumstances. Thereafter, the auditor should follow up to see that the internal auditing activity's responsibilities have been met (PA 1210.A2-1).

Answer (A) is incorrect because determining the loss could alert the perpetrator of the fraud. The perpetrator could then destroy or compromise evidence. Answer (B) is incorrect because interviewing those who have been involved in the control of assets is part of the fraud investigation. Answer (C) is incorrect because identifying the employees who could be implicated in the case is part of the fraud investigation.

**97.** The internal auditors' responsibility for the prevention of fraud includes all of the following except

A. Determining whether the organizational environment fosters control consciousness.

B. Ensuring that fraud will not occur.

C. Being aware of activities in which fraud is likely to occur.

D. Evaluating the effectiveness of actions taken by management to deter fraud.

Answer (B) is correct. *(CIA, adapted)*

**REQUIRED:** The item not part of the internal auditors' responsibility for the prevention of fraud.

**DISCUSSION:** Control is the principal mechanism for the deterrence of fraud. Internal auditors are responsible for assisting in the deterrence of fraud by examining and evaluating the adequacy and the effectiveness of the system of internal control, commensurate with the extent of the potential exposure/risk in the various segments of the organization's operations. However, management is responsible for establishing and maintaining internal control (PA 1210.A2-1). Moreover, due professional care requires the conduct of examinations and verifications to a reasonable extent but does not require detailed reviews of all transactions. Thus, the internal auditors cannot give absolute assurance that noncompliance or irregularities do not exist (PA 1220-1).

Answer (A) is incorrect because internal auditing is responsible for evaluating the organization's control consciousness. Answer (C) is incorrect because the internal auditor should have sufficient knowledge of fraud indicators and be alert to opportunities that could allow fraud. Answer (D) is incorrect because deterrence of fraud is the responsibility of management; evaluating the effectiveness of management efforts is the responsibility of internal auditing.

**98.** During an engagement to review payments under a construction contract with a local firm, the internal auditor found a recurring monthly reimbursement for rent at a local apartment complex. Each reimbursement was authorized by the same project engineer. The internal auditor found no provision for payment of temporary living expenses in the construction contract. Discussion with the project engineer could not resolve the matter. The internal auditor should

A. Inform the chief audit executive.

B. Call the engineer into a private meeting to confront the situation.

C. Complete the engagement as scheduled, noting the recurring reimbursement in the working papers.

D. Wait until the engineer is surrounded by plenty of witnesses and then inquire about the payments.

Answer (A) is correct. *(CIA, adapted)*

**REQUIRED:** The action the internal auditor should take when fraud is suspected.

**DISCUSSION:** When fraud is suspected, the internal auditor should inform the appropriate authorities within the organization. The CAE should then determine the course of action to take. The CAE is responsible for reporting immediately any incident of significant fraud to senior management or the board (PA 1210.A2-1).

Answer (B) is incorrect because the project engineer has already been asked about the facts and did not resolve the issue. Answer (C) is incorrect because the unexplained payment may be an indication of fraud. Answer (D) is incorrect because raising this issue in public may expose the internal auditor to liability for defamation.

**99.** The chief audit executive uncovers a significant fraudulent activity that appears to involve the executive vice president to whom the CAE reports. Which of the following best describes how the CAE should proceed?

A. Conduct an investigation to ascertain whether the executive vice president is involved in the fraudulent activity.

B. Interview the executive vice president to obtain essential evidence.

C. Notify regulatory authorities and police.

D. Report the facts to the chief executive officer and the audit committee.

Answer (D) is correct. *(CIA, adapted)*

**REQUIRED:** The appropriate action when suspected fraudulent activity involves the CAE's superior.

**DISCUSSION:** The internal auditor should inform the appropriate authorities within the organization when wrongdoing is suspected, recommend any necessary investigation, and follow up to see that internal audit activity's responsibilities have been met (PA 1210.A2-1). When the CAE's superior is suspected of involvement in fraudulent activities, the appropriate authority within the organization is a level of management higher than the level of fraudulent activity, i.e., the chief executive officer and the audit committee.

Answer (A) is incorrect because management must determine whether an investigation will be carried out. Answer (B) is incorrect because the internal auditor should avoid confronting persons suspected of theft or fraud until the appropriate authorities within the organization have been notified and have determined the appropriate action. Answer (C) is incorrect because the internal auditor's ethical obligations normally do not include reporting fraudulent activity to outside authorities unless senior management does not take appropriate action.

**100.** A significant employee fraud took place shortly after an internal auditing engagement. The internal auditor may not have properly fulfilled the responsibility for the deterrence of fraud by failing to note and report that

A. Policies, practices, and procedures to monitor activities and safeguard assets were less extensive in low-risk areas than in high-risk areas.

B. A system of control that depended upon separation of duties could be circumvented by collusion among three employees.

C. There were no written policies describing prohibited activities and the action required whenever violations are discovered.

D. Divisional employees had not been properly trained to distinguish between bona fide signatures and cleverly forged ones on authorization forms.

Answer (C) is correct. *(CIA, adapted)*

**REQUIRED:** The respect in which the internal auditor may not have properly fulfilled the responsibility for the deterrence of fraud.

**DISCUSSION:** Internal auditors are responsible for assisting in the deterrence of fraud by examining and evaluating the adequacy and the effectiveness of the system of internal control, commensurate with the extent of the potential exposure/risk in the various segments of the organization's operations. In carrying out this responsibility, internal auditors should, for example, determine whether written policies (e.g., a code of conduct) exist that describe prohibited activities and the action required whenever violations are discovered (PA 1210.A2-1).

Answer (A) is incorrect because for cost-benefit reasons, control policies, practices, and procedures should be more extensive in high-risk areas. Answer (B) is incorrect because even the best system of control can often be circumvented by collusion. Answer (D) is incorrect because forgery, like collusion, can circumvent even an effective control.

**101.** An internal auditor has detected probable employee fraud and is preparing a preliminary report for management. This report should include

A. A statement that an engagement conducted with due professional care cannot provide absolute assurance that irregularities have not occurred.

B. The internal auditor's conclusion as to whether sufficient information exists to conduct a full investigation.

C. The results of a polygraph test administered to the suspected perpetrator(s) of the fraud.

D. A list of proposed engagement tests to help disclose the existence of similar frauds in the future.

Answer (B) is correct. *(CIA, adapted)*

**REQUIRED:** The content of a preliminary report on probable employee fraud.

**DISCUSSION:** A preliminary or final report may be desirable at the conclusion of the detection phase. The report should include the internal auditor's conclusion as to whether sufficient information exists to conduct a full investigation. It should also summarize observations and recommendations that serve as the basis for such a decision (PA 1210.A2-1).

Answer (A) is incorrect because a report on fraud that has been detected should not include this language. Answer (C) is incorrect because the investigation should follow the preliminary report. Answer (D) is incorrect because a report to operating management would not include such details.

**102.** If there is fraud in the marketing department, which of the following is beyond the scope of the internal auditor's responsibility?

A. Informing the wrongdoer of his/her legal rights.

B. Determining the effects of the wrongdoing.

C. Discussing the wrongdoing with an appropriate level of management.

D. Including the wrongdoing in a report that will go to the audit committee.

Answer (A) is correct. *(CIA, adapted)*

**REQUIRED:** The action beyond the scope of the internal auditor's responsibility regarding fraud.

**DISCUSSION:** The internal auditor is responsible for having sufficient knowledge to be able to identify indicators that fraud might have been committed. In the investigation of fraud, the internal auditor should assess the probable level and the extent of complicity in the fraud and should design procedures to identify the perpetrators, the extent of the fraud, the techniques used, and the cause. When the internal auditor suspects wrongdoing, (s)he should inform the appropriate authorities within the organization. Reporting of fraud includes various oral or written, interim, or final communications to management. Furthermore, the CAE must report immediately any significant fraud to senior management and the board (PA 1210.A2-1). However, the criminal investigation is the responsibility of external authorities. The internal auditor does not have the responsibility or the right to inform the wrongdoer of his/her legal rights.

Answer (B) is incorrect because determining the effects of the wrongdoing is a responsibility of the internal auditor. Answer (C) is incorrect because discussing the wrongdoing with the appropriate authorities is a responsibility of the internal auditor. Answer (D) is incorrect because including the wrong doing in a report to the audit committee is a responsibility of the internal auditor.

**103.** When conducting fraud investigations, internal auditors should

A. Clearly indicate the extent of the internal auditors' knowledge of the fraud when questioning suspects.

B. Assign personnel to the investigation in accordance with the engagement schedule established at the beginning of the fiscal year.

C. Perform its investigation independent of lawyers, security personnel, and specialists from outside the organization who are involved in the investigation.

D. Assess the probable level of, and the extent of complicity in, the fraud within the organization.

Answer (D) is correct. *(CIA, adapted)*

**REQUIRED:** The role of the internal auditors in fraud investigations.

**DISCUSSION:** When conducting fraud investigations, internal auditors should assess the probable level of, and the extent of complicity in, the fraud within the organization. This can be critical to ensuring that the internal auditor avoids providing information to, or obtaining misleading information from, persons who may be involved (PA 1210.A2-1).

Answer (A) is incorrect because, by always giving the impression that additional evidence is in reserve, the internal auditors are more apt to obtain complete and truthful answers. Answer (B) is incorrect because fraud investigations usually occur unexpectedly and cannot be scheduled in advance. Also, the fraud investigation must be conducted by individuals having the appropriate expertise, even if another engagement must be delayed. Answer (C) is incorrect because the internal auditors should coordinate their activities with the other investigators mentioned.

**104.** Internal auditors are responsible for reporting fraud to senior management and the board when

A. The incidence of significant fraud has been established to a reasonable certainty.

B. Suspicious activities have been reported to the internal auditors.

C. Irregular transactions have been identified and are under investigation.

D. The review of all suspected fraud-related transactions is complete.

Answer (A) is correct. *(CIA, adapted)*

**REQUIRED:** The responsibility of internal auditors for reporting fraud to senior management and the board.

**DISCUSSION:** Sufficient investigation should take place to establish reasonable certainty that a fraud has occurred before any reporting is done. When the incidence of significant fraud has been established to a reasonable certainty, senior management and the board should be notified immediately (PA 1210.A2-1).

Answer (B) is incorrect because no reporting is required merely because suspicious acts have been reported. Answer (C) is incorrect because irregular transactions under investigation would not require reporting until the investigation determines with reasonable certainty that a significant fraud has occurred. Answer (D) is incorrect because reporting should occur when the incidence of significant fraud has been established to a reasonable certainty.

**105.** A fraud report is required

A. At the conclusion of the detection phase.

B. At the conclusion of the investigation phase.

C. At the conclusion of both the detection and the investigation phases.

D. Neither at the conclusion of the detection phase nor at the conclusion of the investigation phase.

Answer (B) is correct. *(CIA, adapted)*

**REQUIRED:** The situation in which a fraud report is required.

**DISCUSSION:** A written report or other formal communication should be issued at the conclusion of the investigation phase. It should include all observations, conclusions, recommendations, and corrective action taken (PA 1210.A2-1).

Answer (A) is incorrect because a fraud report may be desirable, but is not required, at the conclusion of the detection phase. Answer (C) is incorrect because a fraud report may be desirable, but is not required, at the conclusion of the detection phase. Answer (D) is incorrect because a fraud report is required at the end of the investigation phase.

**106.** Which of the following is the proper listing of information that must be included in a fraud report at the conclusion of an investigation?

A. Purpose, scope, results, and, when appropriate, an expression of the internal auditor's overall opinion.

B. Criteria, condition, cause, and effect.

C. Background, observations, and recommendations.

D. Observations, conclusions, recommendations, and corrective action.

Answer (D) is correct. *(CIA, adapted)*

**REQUIRED:** The proper listing of information that must be included in a fraud report.

**DISCUSSION:** A written report or other formal communication should be issued at the conclusion of the investigation phase. It should include all observations, conclusions, recommendations, and corrective action taken (PA 1210.A2-1).

Answer (A) is incorrect because the purpose, scope, and results are included in every final engagement communication. Results include conclusions (opinions) (PA 2410-1). This definition does not include corrective action. Answer (B) is incorrect because criteria, condition, cause, and effect are the attributes of observations and recommendations. A fraud report includes more than observations and recommendations. Answer (C) is incorrect because background is recommended, but not required, for inclusion in a final engagement communication. Furthermore, conclusions and corrective action are omitted.

**107.** An internal auditor finds that senior management has given tacit approval to activities that have resulted in prematurely recognizing revenue for goods that were not shipped. A preliminary investigation corroborates the internal auditor's initial observations. As part of the annual financial statement audit, the internal auditor coordinates work with the external auditor, who has asked to review the engagement working papers related to sales activities. Assuming the amounts could be material to the financial statements, the internal auditor should report the observations to

A. The internal legal counsel to gain an assessment as to whether the action might constitute a fraud.

B. The audit committee because it is a significant accounting matter that should be addressed before the year-end audit report is issued.

C. The external auditor as part of the process of sharing working papers.

D. All of the answers are correct.

Answer (D) is correct. *(CIA, adapted)*

**REQUIRED:** The recipient(s) of a report on an irregularity by senior management.

**DISCUSSION:** Because the internal auditor is not trained in the law, internal legal counsel should be consulted to provide expert advice about the matter. Given that senior management is involved, the audit committee must be informed about significant fraud. Furthermore, coordination of internal and external audit efforts should extend to sharing of programs, working papers, and reports.

## 9.10 Communicating Results

**108.** Which of the following is not included in the statement of scope in an engagement final communication?

A. Period covered by the engagement.

B. Engagement objectives.

C. Activities not reviewed.

D. Nature and extent of the work performed.

Answer (B) is correct. *(CIA, adapted)*

**REQUIRED:** The item not included in the statement of scope in an engagement final communication.

**DISCUSSION:** Scope statements should identify the activities reviewed and include, when appropriate, supportive information such as the time period reviewed. Related activities not reviewed should be identified if necessary to delineate the boundaries of the engagement. The nature and extent of engagement work performed also should be described. A purpose statement describes the engagement objectives (PA 2410-1).

**109.** Which one of the following elements of an assurance engagement is not always required?

A. A statement that describes the engagement objectives.

B. A statement that identifies the activities reviewed.

C. Pertinent statements of fact.

D. An evaluation of the impact of the observations and recommendations on the activities reviewed.

Answer (D) is correct. *(CIA, adapted)*

**REQUIRED:** The element of an engagement final communication not always required.

**DISCUSSION:** A statement of conclusions (opinion) evaluates the impact of engagement observations and recommendations on the activities reviewed (PA 2410-1). A final communication of engagement results contains the internal auditor's overall opinion or conclusions only when appropriate (Standard 2410.A1).

Answer (A) is incorrect because statements of the purpose, scope, and results are required. The description of the engagement objectives is in the statement of purpose. Answer (B) is incorrect because statements of the purpose, scope, and results are required. Identification of the activities reviewed is in the statement of scope. Answer (C) is incorrect because statements of the purpose, scope, and results are required. Results include observations, conclusions, recommendations, and action plans. Observations are pertinent statements of fact.

**110.** Which of the following best defines an internal auditor's opinion expressed following an assurance engagement?

A. A summary of the significant engagement observations.

B. The internal auditor's professional judgment about the situation that was reviewed.

C. Conclusions that must be included in the final engagement communication.

D. Recommendations for corrective action.

Answer (B) is correct. *(CIA, adapted)*

**REQUIRED:** The best definition of an internal auditor's opinion.

**DISCUSSION:** Conclusions (opinions) are the internal auditor's evaluations of the effects of the observations and recommendations on the activities reviewed. They usually put the observations and recommendations in perspective based upon their overall implications. Engagement conclusions, if included in the final engagement communication, should be clearly identified as such. Conclusions may encompass the entire scope of an engagement or specific aspects. They may cover, but are not limited to, whether operating or program objectives and goals conform with those of the organization, whether the organization's objectives and goals are being met, and whether the activity under review is functioning as intended (PA 2410-1).

Answer (A) is incorrect because the summary of significant observations and recommendations is not an opinion. An opinion is the internal auditor's professional judgment about the situation under review. Answer (C) is incorrect because the Standards do not require the inclusion of opinions. However, the opinion is a desirable component of the final engagement communication. Answer (D) is incorrect because recommendations for corrective action are separate from the opinion. The opinion is the internal auditor's professional judgment.

**111.** A final communication issued by an internal auditor following an assurance engagement should contain an expression of opinion when

A. The area of the engagement is the financial statements.

B. The internal auditors' work is to be used by external auditors.

C. A full-scope engagement has been conducted in an area.

D. An opinion will improve communications with the readers of the communication.

Answer (D) is correct. *(CIA, adapted)*

**REQUIRED:** The circumstances in which an engagement final communication issued by an internal auditor should contain an expression of opinion.

**DISCUSSION:** A statement of conclusions (opinion) evaluates the impact of engagement observations and recommendations on the activities reviewed (PA 2410-1). A final communication of engagement results contains the internal auditor's overall opinion or conclusions only when appropriate (Standard 2410.A1). The criterion of appropriateness is improvement in communications.

Answer (A) is incorrect because the area of the engagement is irrelevant to decisions about whether an overall opinion is appropriate. Answer (B) is incorrect because whether the internal auditors' work is to be used by external auditors is irrelevant. The external auditors cannot depend on an overall opinion but must examine details and form their own opinion. Answer (C) is incorrect because an overall opinion is not mandatory.

**112.** The internal audit activity for a chain of retail stores recently concluded an engagement to evaluate sales adjustments in all stores in the Southeast region. The engagement revealed that several stores are costing the organization substantial sums in duplicate credits to customers' charge accounts. The final engagement communication, published 8 weeks after the engagement was concluded, incorporated the internal auditors' recommendations to store management that should prevent duplicate credits to customers' accounts. Which of the following standards has been disregarded in the above case?

A. The follow-up actions were not adequate.

B. The internal auditors should have implemented appropriate corrective action as soon as the duplicate credits were discovered.

C. Internal auditor recommendations should not be included in the final engagement communication.

D. The final engagement communication was not timely.

Answer (D) is correct. *(CIA, adapted)*

**REQUIRED:** The standard that was disregarded.

**DISCUSSION:** Communications should be accurate, objective, clear, concise, constructive, complete, and timely (Standard 2420). "Timely communications are well-timed, opportune, and expedient for careful consideration by those who may act on the recommendations." The timing should be set "without undue delay and with a degree of urgency and so as to enable prompt effective action" (PA 2420-1). The report, which was not published until 8 weeks after the engagement was concluded, was not issued in a timely fashion, given the significance of the observations and the need for prompt, effective action.

Answer (A) is incorrect because information is not sufficient to evaluate the effectiveness of follow-up. Answer (B) is incorrect because internal auditors may properly make recommendations for potential improvements but should not implement corrective action. Answer (C) is incorrect because internal auditor recommendations are part of the results of the engagement. Final engagement communications should at least include the purpose, scope, and results of the engagement (PA 2410-1).

**113.** The internal auditor completed work on a segment of the engagement work program. As a result, the internal auditor determined that a modification of the organization's distribution procedures is required. The engagement client agreed and has implemented revised procedures. The internal auditor should

A. Research the problem and recommend in the final engagement communication measures that should be taken.

B. Jointly develop and communicate an appropriate recommendation.

C. Communicate the problem and assume that management will take appropriate action.

D. Indicate in the final engagement communication that the client determined and implemented corrective action.

Answer (D) is correct. *(CIA, adapted)*

**REQUIRED:** The action an internal auditor should take when an engagement client has implemented changes.

**DISCUSSION:** Engagement communications may include recommendations for potential improvements and acknowledge satisfactory performance and corrective action. Furthermore, information about engagement client accomplishments may be necessary to represent the existing conditions fairly and to provide a proper perspective and appropriate balance to the final engagement communication (PA 2410-1).

**114.** A recommendation in a final engagement communication should address what attribute?

A. Cause.

B. Statement of condition.

C. Criteria.

D. Effect.

Answer (A) is correct. *(CIA, adapted)*

**REQUIRED:** The attribute of a recommendation.

**DISCUSSION:** Recommendations are based on observations and conclusions. They call for action to correct existing conditions or improve operations. Engagement observations and recommendations should be based on four attributes. Criteria are the standards, measures, or expectations used in making an evaluation or verification (what should exist). Condition is defined as the factual evidence that the internal auditor found in the course of the examination (what does exist). If actual and expected conditions differ, the cause is the reason for the difference between the expected and actual conditions (why the difference exists). The effect is the risk or exposure the organization or others encounter because the condition is not the same as the criteria (the impact of the difference) (PA 2410-1). Thus, a recommendation addresses the cause attribute because it states the necessary corrective action.

Answer (B) is incorrect because the condition attribute simply describes "what is" to serve as a basis for comparison with given criteria. Answer (C) is incorrect because criteria describe "what should be" and are compared with the statement of condition. Answer (D) is incorrect because the effect attribute addresses the importance of an observation.

**115.** An internal auditor has just completed an engagement and is in the process of preparing the final engagement communication. The observations in the final engagement communication should include

A. Statements of opinion about the cause of an observation.

B. Pertinent factual statements concerning the control weaknesses uncovered during the course of the engagement.

C. Statements of both fact and opinion developed during the course of the engagement.

D. Statements concerning potential future events that may be helpful to the engagement client.

Answer (B) is correct. *(CIA, adapted)*

**REQUIRED:** The information included in a final engagement communication.

**DISCUSSION:** Observations are pertinent statements of fact. They should be based on a comparison of what should exist with what does exist. If there is a difference, observations should state the reasons and the resulting effects (PA 2410-1).

Answer (A) is incorrect because observations must be statements of fact rather than statements of opinion. Opinions are the internal auditor's evaluations of the effects of observations and recommendations on the activities reviewed. Answer (C) is incorrect because observations must be statements of fact rather than statements of opinion. Opinions are the internal auditor's evaluations of the effects of observations and recommendations on the activities reviewed. Answer (D) is incorrect because observations concern current, not future, factual conditions or events.

**116.** Which of the following is false with respect to the use of interim engagement communications? Interim engagement communications

A. Are used to communicate information that requires immediate attention.

B. Are used to communicate a change in engagement scope for the activity under review.

C. Keep management informed of engagement progress when engagements extend over a long period of time.

D. Eliminate the need for issuing final engagement communications.

Answer (D) is correct. *(CIA, adapted)*

**REQUIRED:** The false statement about interim engagement communications.

**DISCUSSION:** Interim engagement communications may be written or oral and may be transmitted formally or informally. They are used to communicate information that requires immediate attention, to communicate a change in engagement scope for the activity under review, or to keep management informed of engagement progress when engagements extend over a long period. The use of interim engagement communications does not diminish or eliminate the need for final engagement communications (PA 2410-1).

**117.** A final engagement communication should be reviewed and approved by the

A. Engagement client or the person to whom the client reports.

B. Internal-auditor-in-charge.

C. Chief audit executive or designee.

D. Chief financial officer.

Answer (C) is correct. *(CIA, adapted)*

**REQUIRED:** The person who should review and approve a final engagement communication.

**DISCUSSION:** The CAE or a designee should review and approve and may sign the final engagement communication before issuance and should decide to whom it will be distributed. If specific circumstances warrant, consideration should be given to having the internal-auditor-in-charge, supervisor, or lead internal auditor sign the communication as a representative of the CAE (PA 2440-1).

Answer (A) is incorrect because final engagement communications should be reviewed and approved by the CAE or a designee. Answer (B) is incorrect because the internal-auditor-in-charge should not approve final engagement communications unless designated by the CAE. Answer (D) is incorrect because engagement communications should be reviewed and approved by the CAE or a designee prior to distribution.

**118.** One purpose of the exit interview is for the internal auditor to

A. Require corrective action.

B. Review and verify the appropriateness of the engagement communication based upon client input.

C. Review the performance of internal auditors assigned to the engagement.

D. Present the final engagement communication to management.

Answer (B) is correct. *(CIA, adapted)*

**REQUIRED:** The purpose of the exit interview.

**DISCUSSION:** The internal auditor should discuss conclusions and recommendations at appropriate levels of management before issuing final engagement communications. Furthermore, discussion of conclusions and recommendations is usually accomplished during the course of the engagement or at postengagement meetings (exit interviews). Another technique is the review of draft engagement conclusions, observations, and recommendations by management of the activity reviewed. These discussions and reviews help ensure that there have been no misunderstandings or misinterpretations of fact by providing the opportunity for the engagement client to clarify specific items and to express views of the observations, conclusions, and recommendations (PA 2440-1).

Answer (A) is incorrect because the internal auditor cannot require corrective action. Only management can. Answer (C) is incorrect because internal auditor performance is reviewed in private with the individual employee, not at the exit interview. Answer (D) is incorrect because the exit interview is normally based on draft communications. The final engagement communication is subject to modification based on the results of the exit interview.

**119.** An internal auditor has completed an engagement to review an organization's activities and is ready to issue a final engagement communication. However, the engagement client disagrees with the internal auditor's conclusions. The internal auditor should

A. Withhold the issuance of the final engagement communication until agreement on the issues is obtained.

B. Perform more work, with the engagement client's concurrence, to resolve areas of disagreement. Delay the issuance of the final engagement communication until agreement is reached.

C. Issue the final engagement communication and indicate that the engagement client has provided a scope limitation that has led to a difference as to the conclusions.

D. Issue the final engagement communication and state both the internal auditor and engagement client positions and the reasons for the disagreement.

Answer (D) is correct. *(CIA, adapted)*

**REQUIRED:** The action to be taken when an engagement client disagrees with an internal auditor's conclusions before the final report is issued.

**DISCUSSION:** As part of the internal auditor's discussions with the engagement client, the internal auditor should try to obtain agreement on the results of the engagement and on a plan of action to improve operations, as needed. If the internal auditor and engagement client disagree about the engagement results, the final engagement communication may state both positions and the reasons for the disagreement. The engagement client's written comments may be included as an appendix to the final engagement communication. Alternatively, the engagement client's views may be presented in the body of the final engagement communication or in a cover letter (PA 2410-1).

Answer (A) is incorrect because, if the engagement is complete, the final engagement communication should be issued in a timely manner. Moreover, agreement with the engagement client is not mandatory. Answer (B) is incorrect because, if the internal auditor is satisfied with the conclusions drawn from the engagement, there is no reason to perform more work. Answer (C) is incorrect because the disagreement on conclusions is not a scope limitation.

**120.** Internal auditors should communicate engagement results promptly but should be careful about communicating matters with legal ramifications. Thus, the roles of the internal audit activity and legal counsel should be defined and policies should be established regarding methods of communication. These measures should address how internal auditors' communications may appropriately be shielded from discovery during legal proceedings. Communications are most likely to be protected when they

A. Consist of documents delivered to an attorney before the attorney-client relationship came into existence.

B. Are created for self-evaluation after the events resulting in a private litigant's claim.

C. Are made to an attorney whether or not in confidence.

D. Are part of the internal auditors' work product and are sought by a government agency.

Answer (B) is correct. *(Publisher)*

**REQUIRED:** The communications most likely to be protected from discovery during legal proceedings.

**DISCUSSION:** Some courts have recognized a qualified privilege that shields self-critical material, such as the internal auditors' work-product, from discovery. In general, the recognition of this privilege is premised on the belief that the confidentiality of the reviews in the instances involved outweighs the valued public interests. It allows individuals or businesses to assess candidly their compliance with regulatory and legal requirements without creating evidence that may be used against them by their opponents in future litigation. In general, three requirements must usually be met for the privilege to apply: the information subject to the privilege must result from a self-critical analysis undertaken by the party asserting the privilege, the public must have a strong interest in preserving the free flow of the information contained in the critical analysis, and the information must be of the type whose flow would be curtailed if discovery were allowed. Moreover, the justification for the privilege is said to be at its strongest when the analysis follows the events resulting in the plaintiff's claim. The self-evaluative privilege is also more likely to be recognized when documents are sought by a private party rather than by a government agency (PA 2400-1).

Answer (A) is incorrect because documents delivered to an attorney are protected neither by the attorney-client privilege nor by the work-product doctrine if no attorney-client relationship exists. Answer (C) is incorrect because an attorney-client privilege does not exist unless the communication was made in confidence. Answer (D) is incorrect because the work-product doctrine applies to documents only if they are prepared by an agent of the attorney, the self-evaluative privilege is less likely to apply when the documents are sought by a government agency, and the attorney-client privilege applies only to communications in confidence between an attorney and client.

**121.** Communication skills are important to internal auditors. The internal auditor should be able to convey effectively all of the following to the engagement client except

A. The engagement objectives for a specific engagement client.

B. The evaluations based on a preliminary survey of an engagement client.

C. The risk assessment used in selecting the area for engagement investigation.

D. Recommendations that are generated in relationship to a specific engagement client.

Answer (C) is correct. *(CIA, adapted)*

**REQUIRED:** The matter that an internal auditor need not convey to the engagement client.

**DISCUSSION:** Internal auditors should be skilled in oral and written communications so that they can clearly and effectively convey such matters as engagement objectives, evaluations, conclusions, and recommendations (PA 1210-1). However, the internal auditor's risk assessment is not specifically mentioned in Practice Advisory 1210-1 with respect to communication skills.

**122.** When a final engagement communication contains a significant error, the Standards require the chief audit executive to

A. Issue a written report to individuals who can ensure that engagement results are given due consideration.

B. Issue a written report to individuals who received the original communication.

C. Communicate corrected information to all individuals who received the original communication.

D. Communicate corrected information to all those who might have relied on the original communication.

Answer (C) is correct. *(Publisher)*

**REQUIRED:** The duty of the CAE when a final engagement communication contains a significant error.

**DISCUSSION:** If a final engagement communication contains a significant error or omission, the CAE should communicate corrected information to all parties who received the original communication (Standard 2421). Hence, the Standards do not require a written report.

**123.** The final communication of engagement results must contain

A. The reasons for any noncompliance with the Standards.

B. Background information and summaries.

C. Engagement client accomplishments.

D. The engagement client's views about engagement conclusions and recommendations.

Answer (A) is correct. *(Publisher)*

**REQUIRED:** The information that must be included in the final communication of engagement results.

**DISCUSSION:** When noncompliance with the Standards affects a specific engagement, communication of the results should disclose the Standard(s) with which full compliance was not achieved, reason(s) for noncompliance, and the impact of noncompliance on the engagement (Standard 2430).

Answer (B) is incorrect because communications should include the engagement's objectives and scope as well as applicable conclusions, recommendations, and action plans. Background information and summaries may be included (PA 2410-1). Answer (C) is incorrect because communications should include the engagement's objectives and scope as well as applicable conclusions, recommendations, and action plans. Engagement client accomplishments may be included (PA 2410-1). Answer (D) is incorrect because communications should include the engagement's objectives and scope as well as applicable conclusions, recommendations, and action plans. The engagement client's views about engagement conclusions and recommendations may be included (PA 2410-1).

**124.** The chief audit executive should disseminate results to the appropriate parties (Standard 2440). Disseminating information outside the organization

A. Is prohibited by the Standards.

B. Requires the elimination of references to the Standards.

C. Requires that an engagement performed to generate such information be conducted in accordance with the Standards.

D. Is permissible only if a new engagement is performed.

Answer (C) is correct. *(Publisher)*

**REQUIRED:** The true statement about disseminating information outside the organization.

**DISCUSSION:** Engagements performed to generate internal auditing reports or communications to be disseminated outside the organization should be conducted in accordance with applicable Standards and include reference to such Standards in the report or other communication (PA 2440-2).

Answer (A) is incorrect because the Standards permit dissemination of information outside the organization. Answer (B) is incorrect because the report or other communication should refer to applicable Standards. Answer (D) is incorrect because, in certain situations, it may be possible to revise an existing report or information to make it suitable for dissemination outside the organization. In other situations, it may be possible to generate a new report based on work previously conducted.

**125.** Exit interviews serve to ensure the accuracy of the information used by an internal auditor. A secondary purpose of an exit interview is to

A. Get immediate action on a recommendation.

B. Improve relations with the engagement clients.

C. Agree to the appropriate distribution of the final engagement communication.

D. Brief senior management on the results of the engagement.

Answer (B) is correct. *(CIA, adapted)*

**REQUIRED:** The secondary purpose of an exit interview.

**DISCUSSION:** The internal auditor should discuss conclusions and recommendations at appropriate levels of management before issuing final engagement communications. Discussion with the engagement client not only provides a quality control review but is also a courtesy that enhances the internal auditor-client relationship. In addition, the exit interview is an important aspect of the participative approach to internal auditing because it involves the client in the engagement process as well as in any recommended changes arising from the engagement. People are more likely to accept changes if they have participated in the decisions and in the methods used to implement changes. Moreover, the participative approach tends to engender feelings of mutual liking and trust that contribute to amicable relationships, which produce a more favorable environment for the engagement effort.

Answer (A) is incorrect because an interim engagement communication would have been used to obtain immediate action on a recommendation. Answer (C) is incorrect because the distribution of communications is not a secondary purpose of an exit interview. Answer (D) is incorrect because senior management ordinarily should be given a summary of the results.

# APPENDIX A
# CHAPTER CROSS-REFERENCES TO AUDITING TEXTBOOKS

The next section contains the tables of contents of current auditing textbooks with cross-references to the related subunits or study units in this study manual. The books are listed in alphabetical order by the first author. As you study a particular study unit in your auditing textbook, you can easily determine which subunit(s) to study in this manual. You should review all questions in the subunit.

Professors, students, and accounting practitioners should all note that, even though new editions of the texts listed below may be published as you use this book, the new tables of contents usually will be very similar, if not the same. Thus, this edition of *Auditing & Systems Exam Questions and Explanations* will remain current and useful.

**AUDITING TEXTBOOKS**

Arens, Elder, and Beasley, *Auditing and Assurance Services: An Integrated Approach*, First Edition, Prentice Hall, Inc., 2003.

Arens, Elder, and Beasley, *Essentials of Auditing and Assurance Services: An Integrated Approach*, Eleventh Edition, Prentice Hall, Inc., 2006.

Boynton and Johnson, *Modern Auditing: Assurance Services and the Integrity of Financial Reporting*, Eighth Edition, John Wiley & Sons, Inc., 2006.

Guy, Carmichael, and Whittington, *Audit Sampling: An Introduction*, Fifth Edition, John Wiley & Sons, Inc., 2001.

Kinney, *Information Quality Assurance and Internal Control for Management Decision Making*, First Edition, McGraw-Hill, Inc., 2000.

Knechel, *Auditing: Assurance and Risk*, Second Edition, South-Western, 2001.

Konrath, *Auditing: A Risk Analysis Approach*, Fifth Edition, South-Western, 2002.

Louwers, Ramsey, Sinason, and Strawser, *Auditing and Assurance Services*, First Edition, McGraw-Hill, Inc., 2005.

Messier, Glover, and Prawitt, *Auditing & Assurance Services: A Systematic Approach*, Fourth Edition, McGraw-Hill, Inc., 2006

O'Reilly, McDonnell, Winograd, Gerson, and Jaenicke, *Montgomery's Auditing*, Twelfth Edition, John Wiley & Sons, Inc., 1998 (2001 supplement).

Ricchiute, *Auditing*, Eighth Edition, South-Western, 2006.

Rittenberg and Schwieger, *Auditing: Concepts for a Changing Environment*, Fifth Edition, South-Western, 2005.

Sawyer, Dittenhofer, and Scheiner, *Sawyer's Internal Auditing*, Fifth Edition, The Institute of Internal Auditors, Inc., 2003.

Strawser and Strawser, *Auditing Theory and Practice*, Eighth Edition, Dame, 1999.

Whittington and Pany, *Principles of Auditing and Other Assurance Services*, Fourteenth Edition, McGraw-Hill, Inc., 2003.

## SYSTEMS TEXTBOOKS

Study Unit 5, Information Systems, covers the material in systems textbooks.

## CHAPTER CROSS-REFERENCES TO AUDITING TEXTBOOKS

Professors, students, and accounting practitioners should all note that even though new editions of the texts listed below may be published as you use this book, the new tables of contents usually will be very similar, if not the same. Thus, this edition of *Auditing & Systems Exam Questions and Explanations* will remain current and useful.

**Arens, Elder, and Beasley, *Auditing and Assurance Services: An Integrated Approach*, Eleventh Edition, Prentice Hall, Inc., 2006.**

Part I: The Auditing Profession
- Chapter 1 - The Demand for Audit and Other Assurance Services - 1.1
- Chapter 2 - The CPA Profession - 1.1-1.10
- Chapter 3 - Audit Reports - SU 7
- Chapter 4 - Professional Ethics - 1.5-1.8, 9.2
- Chapter 5 - Legal Liability - 1.9, 2.3, 2.4

Part II: The Audit Process
- Chapter 6 - Audit Responsibilities and Objectives - SU 1, SU 2
- Chapter 7 - Audit Evidence - 2.2, 4.1, 4.2, 5.12
- Chapter 8 - Audit Planning and Analytical Procedures - SU 2, 4.2
- Chapter 9 - Materiality and Risk - 2.2-2.4
- Chapter 10 - Internal Control and Control Risk - 3.1-3.5
- Chapter 11 - Fraud Detection - 2.3, 2.4
- Chapter 12 - The Impact of Information Technology on the Audit Process - SU 5
- Chapter 13 - Overall Audit Plan and Audit Program - SU 2, 3.1-3.5, 4.1, 4.2

Part III: Application of the Audit Process to the Sales and Collection Cycle
- Chapter 14 - Audit of the Sales and Collection Cycle: Tests of Controls and Substantive Tests of Transactions - 3.6, 4.3
- Chapter 15 - Audit Sampling for Tests of Controls and Substantive Tests of Transactions - SU 6
- Chapter 16 - Completing the Tests in the Sales and Collection Cycle: Accounts Receivable - 4.3
- Chapter 17 - Audit Sampling for Tests of Details of Balances - SU 6

Part IV: Application of the Audit Process to Other Cycles
- Chapter 18 - Audit of the Payroll and Personnel Cycle - 3.8, 4.11
- Chapter 19 - Audit of the Acquisition and Payment Cycle: Tests of Controls, Substantive Tests of Transactions, and Accounts Payable - 3.7, 4.4
- Chapter 20 - Completing the Tests in the Acquisition and Payment Cycle - 3.11, 4.7, 4.8
- Chapter 21 - Audit of the Inventory and Warehousing Cycle - 3.10, 4.6
- Chapter 22 - Audit of the Capital Acquisition and Repayment Cycle - 3.9, 4.9, 4.10
- Chapter 23 - Audit of Cash Balances - 3.6, 3.7, 4.5

Part V: Completing the Audit
- Chapter 24 - Completing the Audit - 3.12-3.14, 4.12-4.17

Part VI: Other Assurance and Non-Assurance Services
- Chapter 25 - Other Audit, Attestation Services, and Compilation Engagements - 1.11-1.15, 8.1-8.7, 8.8, 8.10
- Chapter 26 - Internal and Government Financial Auditing and Operational Auditing - 8.8, SU 9

**Arens, Elder, and Beasley, *Essentials of Auditing and Assurance Services: An Integrated Approach*, First Edition, Prentice Hall, Inc., 2003.**

Part I: The Auditing Profession
- Chapter 1 - Assurance Services and the CPA Profession - 1.1-1.10
- Chapter 2 - Audit Reports - SU 7
- Chapter 3 - Professional Ethics - 1.5-1.8, 9.2
- Chapter 4 - Legal Liability - 1.9, 2.3, 2.4

Part II: The Audit Process
- Chapter 5 - Audit Responsibilities and Objectives - SU 1, SU 2
- Chapter 6 - Audit Evidence - 2.2, 4.1, 4.2, 5.12
- Chapter 7 - Audit Planning and Analytical Procedures - SU 2, 4.2
- Chapter 8 - Materiality and Risk - 2.2-2.4
- Chapter 9 - Internal Control and Control Risk - 3.1-3.5
- Chapter 10 - Overall Audit Plan and Audit Program - SU 2, 3.1-3.5, 4.1, 4.2

Part III: Application of the Audit Process to the Sales and Collection Cycle
- Chapter 11 - Audit of the Sales and Collection Cycle: Tests of Controls and Substantive Tests of Transactions - 3.6, 4.3
- Chapter 12 - Completing the Tests in the Sales and Collection Cycle: Accounts Receivable - 4.3
- Chapter 13 - Audit Sampling for Tests of Details of Balances - SU 6

Part IV: Application of the Audit Process to Other Cycles
- Chapter 14 - Audit of the Acquisition and Payment Cycle: Tests of Controls, Substantive Tests of Transactions, and Accounts Payable - 3.7, 4.4
- Chapter 15 - Audit of the Inventory and Warehousing Cycle - 3.10, 4.6
- Chapter 16 - Audit of Cash Balances - 3.6, 3.7, 4.5

Part V: Completing the Audit
- Chapter 17 - Completing the Audit - 3.12-3.14, 4.12-4.17

**Boynton and Johnson, *Modern Auditing: Assurance Services and the Integrity of Financial Reporting*, Eighth Edition, John Wiley & Sons, Inc., 2006.**

Part I: The Auditing Environment - What Can the Public Expect from Auditors
- Chapter 1 - Auditing and the Public Accounting Profession - Integrity of Financial Reporting - 1.1, 1.10-1.14
- Chapter 2 - Auditor Responsibilities and Reports - 1.4, SU 7
- Chapter 3 - Professional Ethics - 1.5-1.8
- Chapter 4 - Auditor's Legal Liability - 1.9

Part II: The Decision Making of Audit Planning
- Chapter 5 - Overview of the Financial Statement Audit - SU 2
- Chapter 6 - Audit Evidence - 2.2, 2.5, 4.1, 4.2
- Chapter 7 - Accepting the Engagement and Planning the Audit - 2.1, 2.2
- Chapter 8 - Materiality Decisions and Performing Analytical Procedures - 2.3, 4.2
- Chapter 9 - Audit Risk: Including the Risk of Fraud - 2.3, 2.4
- Chapter 10 - Understanding Internal Control - 3.1-3.4

Part III: The Decision Making of Collecting and Evaluating Evidence
- Chapter 11 - Audit Procedures in Response to Assessed Risks: Tests of Controls - 2.3, 3.5
- Chapter 12 - Audit Procedures in Response to Assessed Risks: Substantive Tests - 2.3, SU 4
- Chapter 13 - Audit Sampling - SU 6

Part IV: Auditing the Transaction Cycles and Completing the Audit
- Chapter 14 - Auditing the Revenue Cycle - 3.6, 4.3
- Chapter 15 - Auditing the Expenditure Cycle - 3.7, 4.4
- Chapter 16 - Auditing the Production and Personnel Services Cycles - 3.8, 3.10, 3.11, 4.6, 4.7, 4.11
- Chapter 17 - Auditing the Investing and Financing Cycles - 3.9, 4.9, 4.10
- Chapter 18 - Auditing Investments and Cash Balances - 3.6, 3.7, 4.3-4.5
- Chapter 19 - Completing the Audit/Postaudit Responsibilities - 3.12, 4.12-4.17

Part V: Other Attest and Assurance Services
- Chapter 20 - Attest and Assurances Services and Related Reports - 1.8, 1.11-1.15, SU 8
- Chapter 21 - Internal, Operation and Governmental Auditing - 8.8, SU 9

**Guy, Carmichael, and Whittington, *Audit Sampling: An Introduction*, Fifth Edition, John Wiley & Sons, Inc., 2001.**

Chapter 1 - Overview of Audit Sampling - 6.1-6.3
Chapter 2 - Selecting a Representative Sample - 6.4
Chapter 3 - Attribute Sampling - 6.5
Chapter 4 - Using Variable Sampling for Accounting Estimation - 6.6
Chapter 5 - Using Variable Sampling for Audit Hypothesis Testing - 6.6
Chapter 6 - Probability-Proportional-to-Size Sampling - 6.7
Chapter 7 - Nonstatistical Audit Sampling - SU 6

**Kinney, *Information Quality Assurance and Internal Control for Management Decision Making*, First Edition, McGraw-Hill, Inc., 2000.**

Chapter 1 - Introduction and Overview - 1.1
Section I - Informing Yourself
Chapter 2 - Business Measurement Systems: Information Relevance - 1.1
Chapter 3 - Business Measurement Systems: Information Reliability and Risk Assessment - 2.3, 3.1
Chapter 4 - Internal Control over Transactions - 2.4, 3.1-3.3
Chapter 5 - Analytical Monitoring: Business Operations Analysis and Account Modeling Procedures - 4.1, 4.2
Chapter 6 - Detailed Monitoring: Tests of Controls, Transactions, and Balances - 3.5, 5.11, 5.12, 6.1
Section II - Informing Others
Chapter 7 - Informing Outsiders: Management Assertions and Independent Certification - 7.1-7.4
Chapter 8 - Financial Statement Audits, Adjustments, and Disclosures - 2.3, SU 4
Chapter 9 - Auditors' Reports and Their Interpretation - SU 7
Chapter 10 - Other Certification, Investigation, and Origination Assurance Services - 1.11-1.14, 8.1-8.6, 8.9, 8.10
Section III - Public Disclosure Laws and Regulations
Chapter 11 - Regulatory Reporting and Disclosure from Management's Perspective - 3.11, 8.7
Chapter 12 - Legal and Ethical Responsibilities in Public Reporting - 1.2-1.10

**Knechel, *Auditing: Assurance and Risk*, Second Edition, South-Western, 2001.**

Chapter 1 - An Introduction to Auditing and Assurance - 1.1
Chapter 2 - The Role of Auditing and Assurance in a Market Economy - 1.1
Chapter 3 - An Overview of Financial Statement Audits - 4.1-4.2
Chapter 4 - Client Acceptance and Initial Engagement Planning - 2.1-2.3
Chapter 5 - Understanding the Client's Business: Strategic Analysis - 4.2
Chapter 6 - Understanding the Client's Business: Management and Strategic Risks - 2.3
Chapter 7 - Process Analysis and Risk Assessment - 3.1-3.5
Chapter 8 - Evaluating Internal Process Controls - SU 3
Chapter 9 - Business Measurement and Analytical Evidence - N/A
Chapter 10 - Planning the Audit of Financial Statement Assertions - 2.2, 4.1
Chapter 11 - Auditing Marketing, Sales and Distribution Management - 3.6, 3.10, 4.3-4.6
Chapter 12 - Auditing Supply Chain and Production Management Processes - 3.7, 3.10, 4.5-4.11
Chapter 13 - Auditing Resource Management Processes - 4.6-4.11
Chapter 14 - Completing the Audit and Reporting - 3.12, 4.12-4.17, SU 7
Chapter 15 - Auditor Decision Making: Judgment, Ethics, and Legal Liability - 1.2-1.10
Chapter 16 - Statistical Evidence for Auditing - SU 6
Chapter 17 - Assurance Services Beyond the Financial Statement Audit - 1.11-1.14, SU 8

**Konrath, *Auditing: A Risk-Analysis Approach*, Fifth Edition, South-Western, 2002.**

Chapter 1 - Auditing, Attestation, and Assurance - 1.1-1.3
Chapter 2 - Defining Professional Responsibility: Quality Standards and Ethics - 1.5-1.10, 9.12
Chapter 3 - Maintaining Professional Responsibility: Regulation and Legal Liability - 1.9, 2.3, 2.4
Chapter 4 - Audit Evidence and Audit Programs - 2.2-2.5, 3.4, 3.5, 3.14, SU 4, SU 6, 9.8
Chapter 5 - Audit Planning: Assessment of Inherent Risk and Materiality - 2.3, 3.2
Chapter 6 - Internal Control: Concepts - 3.1-3.4
Chapter 7 - Audit Planning: Assessment of Control Risk - 2.3, 3.2-3.5
Chapter 8 - Internal Control and Computer Based Information Systems (CBIS) - 5.1-5.13
Chapter 9 - Statistical Sampling for Testing Control Procedures - 3.5, 6.1-6.5
Chapter 10 - Statistical Sampling for Substantive Testing - 6.1-6.4, 6.6
Chapter 11 - Substantive Audit Testing: Revenue Cycle - 3.6, 4.3, 4.5
Chapter 12 - Substantive Audit Testing: Expenditure Cycle - 3.7, 4.4, 4.5
Chapter 13 - Substantive Audit Testing: Financing and Investing Cycle and Completing the Audit - 3.9, 4.9, 4.10
Chapter 14 - Audit Reports - 1.4, SU 7
Chapter 15 - Other Assurance Services - 1.8, 1.11-1.15, SU 8, 9.10
Chapter 16 - Operational and Governmental Compliance Auditing - 8.5, 8.8, 8.9, SU 9

**Louwers, Ramsay, Sinason, and Strawser, *Auditing and Assurance Services*, First Edition, McGraw-Hill, Inc., 2005.**

Part I: Auditing and Assurance Services in the 21st Century
Chapter 1 - Auditing and Assurance Services - 1.1-1.4
Chapter 2 - Professional Standards - 1.2-1.8, 1.13, 1.14
Chapter 3 - Management Fraud and Audit Risk - 2.3, 2.4, 4.1, 4.2
Chapter 4 - Engagement Planning - 2.1, 2.2, 2.5, 3.13, 3.14, 4.14
Chapter 5 - Internal Control Evaluation: Assessing Control Risk - 3.1-3.5, 3.12, 3.15
Part II: Performing the Financial Audit
Chapter 6 - Employee Fraud and the Audit of Cash - 3.6, 4.5, 4.17
Chapter 7 - Revenue and Collection Cycle - 3.6, 4.3
Chapter 8 - Acquisition and Expenditure Cycle - 3.7, 4.4
Chapter 9 - Production and Payroll Cycle - 3.8, 3.10, 4.6, 4.11
Chapter 10 - Finance and Investment Cycle - 3.9, 3.11, 4.7-4.10, 4.16
Chapter 11 - Completing the Audit - 4.12, 4.13, 4.15
Chapter 12 - Reports on Audited Financial Statements - SU 7
Part III: Other Topics
Chapter A - Assurance and Other Public Accounting Services - 1.11-1.15, 8.1-8.7, 8.9, 8.10
Chapter B - Professional Ethics - 1.5-1.8, 1.10
Chapter C - Legal Liability - 1.9
Chapter D - Internal, Governmental, and Fraud Audits - 8.8, 9.1-9.10
Chapter E - Overview of Sampling - 6.1-6.4, 6.8
Chapter F - Attribute Sampling - 6.5
Chapter G - Variables Sampling - 6.6, 6.7
Chapter H - Information Systems Auditing - SU 5

**Messier, Glover, and Prawitt, *Auditing & Assurance Services: A Systematic Approach*, Fourth Edition, McGraw-Hill, Inc., 2006.**

Part I: Introduction to Financial Statement Auditing
- Chapter 1 - An Introduction to Assurance and Financial Statement Auditing - 1.1, 1.11-1.15
- Chapter 2 - The Financial Statement Auditing Environment - 1.1

Part II: Basic Auditing Concepts: Risk Management, Materiality, and Evidence
- Chapter 3 - Risk Assessment and Materiality - 2.3
- Chapter 4 - Audit Evidence and Audit Documentation - 2.5, SU 4

Part III: Planning the Audit and Understanding Internal Control
- Chapter 5 - Audit Planning and Types of Audit Tests - 2.2, 3.5, 4.2-4.16
- Chapter 6 - Internal Control in a Financial Statement Audit - SU 3
- Chapter 7 - Auditing Internal Control over Financial Reporting in Conjunction with an Audit of Financial Statements - SU 3

Part IV: Statistical and Nonstatistical Sampling Tools for Auditing
- Chapter 8 - Audit Sampling: An Overview and Application to Tests of Control - 3.5, 6.1-6.6
- Chapter 9 - Audit Sampling: An Application to Substantive Tests of Account Balances - SU 6

Part V: Auditing Business Processes
- Chapter 10 - Auditing the Revenue Process - 3.6, 4.3
- Chapter 11 - Auditing the Purchasing Process - 3.7, 4.4
- Chapter 12 - Auditing the Human Resource Management Process - 3.8, 4.11
- Chapter 13 - Auditing the Inventory Management Process - 3.10, 4.6
- Chapter 14 - Financing Process: Auditing Prepaid Expenses and Property, Plant, and Equipment - 3.11, 4.7, 4.8
- Chapter 15 - Financing Process: Auditing Long-Term Liabilities and Stockholders' Equity - 3.9, 4.9, 4.10
- Chapter 16 - Financing Process: Auditing Cash and Investments - 3.6, 3.7, 4.5, 4.8

Part VI: Completing the Audit and Reporting Responsibilities
- Chapter 17 - Completing the Engagement - 3.12, 4.12-4.16
- Chapter 18 - Reports on Audited Financial Statements and on Internal Control over Financial Reporting - SU 7, SU 8

Part VII: Professional Responsibilities
- Chapter 19 - Professional Conduct, Independence, and Quality Control - 1.5-1.8, 1.10
- Chapter 20 - Legal Liability - 1.9

Part VIII: Assurance, Attestation, and Internal Auditing Services
- Chapter 21 - Assurance, Attestation, and Internal Auditing Services - 1.11-1.15

**O'Reilly, McDonnell, Winograd, Gerson, and Jaenicke, *Montgomery's Auditing*, Twelfth Edition. John Wiley & Sons, Inc., 1998 (2001 supplement).**

Part I: The Audit Environment
- Chapter 1 - An Overview of Auditing - 1.1
- Chapter 2 - Organization and Structure of the Auditing Profession - 1.1, 1.10-1.15
- Chapter 3 - Auditing Standards and Professional Conduct - 1.2-1.8
- Chapter 4 - Auditor's Professional Responsibility - 1.9, 2.3, 2.4, 3.12
- Chapter 5 - Auditor's Legal Liability - 1.9

Part II: Theory and Concepts
- Chapter 6 - The Audit Process - 2.1, 2.2, 4.1
- Chapter 7 - Engagement Planning and Management - 2.1, 2.5, 3.13, 4.14
- Chapter 8 - Obtaining Information About the Entity - 2.3
- Chapter 9 - Overview of Internal Control - 2.4, 3.1, 3.2
- Chapter 10 - Understanding Entity-Level Controls - 3.1-3.4, 3.14
- Chapter 11 - Understanding Activity-Level Controls - 3.1-3.4, 3.14
- Chapter 12 - Assessing Control Risk and Developing the Audit Strategy - 3.5, 3.14
- Chapter 13 - Auditing the Revenue Cycle - 3.6
- Chapter 14 - Auditing the Purchasing Cycle - 3.7
- Chapter 15 - Substantive Tests - 2.2, 4.1, 4.2
- Chapter 16 - The Use of Audit Sampling - SU 6

Part III: Auditing Specific Accounts
- Chapter 17 - Auditing Cash and Cash Equivalents - 3.6, 3.7, 4.5
- Chapter 18 - Auditing Accounts Receivable and Related Revenue Cycle Accounts - 3.6, 4.3
- Chapter 19 - Auditing Inventories and Cost of Sales - 3.10, 4.6
- Chapter 20 - Audit Prepayments and Accruals - 3.8, 4.10, 4.11
- Chapter 21 - Auditing Investment in Debt and Equity Securities and Related Income - 3.9, 4.8
- Chapter 22 - Auditing Property, Plant, and Equipment, and Intangible Assets and Deferred Charges - 3.11, 4.7, 4.8
- Chapter 23 - Auditing Accounts Payable and Related Purchasing Cycle Accounts - 3.7, 4.4
- Chapter 24 - Auditing Income Taxes - N/A
- Chapter 25 - Auditing Debt and Equity - 4.9, 4.10
- Chapter 26 - Auditing Financial Statement Disclosures - 4.15, 4.16, 7.10

Part IV: Completing the Work and Reporting the Results
- Chapter 27 - Completing the Audit - 4.2, 4.12-4.17
- Chapter 28 - Reporting on Audited Financial Statements - SU 7
- Chapter 29 - Other Reporting Situations Related to Audits - 8.1, 8.2
- Chapter 30 - Reporting on Nonaudit Services - 8.3, 8.4, 8.6, 8.7
- Chapter 31 - Attestation Engagements - 1.13, 8.5, 8.9, 8.10
- Chapter 32 - Compliance Auditing - 8.8

Part V: Auditing Specialized Industries - covered in various chapters
- Chapter 33 - Auditing Banks and Savings Institutions
- Chapter 34 - Auditing Employee Benefit Plans
- Chapter 35 - Auditing Engineering and Construction Companies
- Chapter 36 - Auditing Gas, Electric, and Telecommunications Companies
- Chapter 37 - Auditing Government Contractors
- Chapter 38 - Auditing Governmental Units
- Chapter 39 - Auditing Health Care Organizations
- Chapter 40 - Auditing High Technology Companies
- Chapter 41 - Auditing Insurance Companies
- Chapter 42 - Auditing Investment Companies
- Chapter 43 - Auditing Lodging Companies
- Chapter 44 - Auditing Mining Companies
- Chapter 45 - Auditing Not-for-Profit Organizations
- Chapter 46 - Auditing Oil and Gas Producing Activities
- Chapter 47 - Auditing Real Estate Companies
- Chapter 48 - Auditing Retail Companies
- Chapter 49 - Auditing Securities and Commodities Broker-Dealers

**Ricchiute, *Auditing*, Eighth Edition, South-Western, 2006.**

Part One: Responsibilities and Reporting
- Chapter 1 - An Introduction to Audit and Other Assurance Services - 1.1
- Chapter 2 - Standards, Materiality, and Risk - 1.2-1.4, 2.2-2.4
- Chapter 3 - Audit Reports - 1.4, SU 7, SU 8, 9.10
- Chapter 4 - Professional Ethics - 1.5-1.8, 1.10, 9.12
- Chapter 5 - Legal Liability - 1.9, 2.3, 2.4

Part Two: The Audit Process and Internal Control
- Chapter 6 - Evidence - SU 4, 9.8
- Chapter 7 - The Audit Process and Detecting Fraud - SU 2
- Chapter 8 - Internal Control - SU 3, 5.1-5.13

Part Three: Auditing the Revenue/Receipt and the Expenditure/Disbursement Cycle
- Chapter 9 - Audit Sampling - SU 6
- Chapter 10 - Sales and Cash Receipts Transactions - 3.6, 6.5
- Chapter 11 - Accounts Receivable and Cash Balances - 4.3, 4.5
- Chapter 12 - Purchases and Cash Disbursements Transactions - 3.7, 6.5
- Chapter 13 - Accounts Payable, Prepaids, and Accrued Liabilities - 4.4, 4.5

Part Four: Auditing Other Cycles and Completing an Audit
- Chapter 14 - Personnel and Payroll - 3.8, 4.11, 6.5, 6.6
- Chapter 15 - Inventory and Fixed Assets - 3.10, 3.11, 4.6, 4.7, 6.5, 6.6
- Chapter 16 - Investments, Debt, and Equity - 3.9, 4.9, 4.10, 6.5, 6.6
- Chapter 17 - Completing an Engagement - 3.12, 4.12-4.16, SU 7

Part Five: Assurance and Attestation Services, Compliance and Internal Auditing
- Chapter 18 - Other Assurance and Attestation Services - 1.12-1.15, 8.9
- Chapter 19 - Compliance and Internal Auditing - 8.5, 8.8, 8.9, SU 9

**Rittenberg and Schwieger, *Auditing: Concepts for a Changing Environment*, Fifth Edition, South-Western, 2005.**

- Chapter 1 - Importance of Auditing - 1.1, 1.13, 1.14
- Chapter 2 - Corporate Governance: Enhancing the Audit Function - 1.2-1.8
- Chapter 3 - Ethics: Understanding and Meeting Ethical Expectations - 1.2-1.8
- Chapter 4 - Audit Risk and Business Risk - 2.3, 2.4
- Chapter 5 - Internal Control over Financial Reporting - SU 3
- Chapter 6 - Computerized Systems: Risks, Controls, and Opportunities - SU 5
- Chapter 7 - Audit Evidence: A Framework for Directly Testing Account Balances and Transactions - SU 2, 4.1, 4.2
- Chapter 8 - Auditing for Fraud - 2.3, 2.4
- Chapter 9 - Audit Sampling - SU 6
- Chapter 10 - Auditing Revenue and Related Accounts - 3.6, 4.3
- Chapter 11 - Audit of Acquisition Cycle and Inventory - 3.7, 3.10, 4.4, 4.6, 4.11
- Chapter 12 - Audit of Cash and Other Liquid Assets - 3.9, 4.5, 4.8
- Chapter 13 - Audit of Fixed Assets and Related Expense Accounts - 4.7, 4.8
- Chapter 14 - Audit of Acquisitions, Related Entity Transactions, Long-Term Liabilities, and Equity - 4.9, 4.10
- Chapter 15 - Completing the Audit - 3.12, 4.12-4.16
- Chapter 16 - Communicating Audit and Attestation Results - 3.12, SU 7
- Chapter 17 - Professional Liability - 1.9, 2.3, 2.4
- Chapter 18 - Internal Auditing and Outsourcing - 8.8, 8.9, SU 9

**Sawyer, Dittenhofer, and Scheiner, *Sawyer's Internal Auditing*, Fifth Edition, The Institute of Internal Auditors, Inc., 2003.**

Part 1: Introduction to Internal Auditing
- Chapter 1 - The Nature of Internal Auditing - 9.1
- Chapter 2 - Control - 9.5

Part 2: Techniques of Internal Auditing
- Chapter 3 - Risk Assessment - 2.3, 3.2
- Chapter 4 - Preliminary Surveys - 9.7
- Chapter 5 - Audit Programs - 9.7
- Chapter 6 - Field Work - I - 9.8
- Chapter 7 - Field Work - II - 9.8
- Chapter 8 - Audit Findings - 2.4
- Chapter 9 - Working Papers - 2.5, 9.6
- Chapter 10 - Control Self-assessment - 9.4

Part 3: Sampling and Analytical Methods
- Chapter 11 - Sampling - SU 6
- Chapter 12 - Analytical and Quantitative Methods - 9.8

Part 4: Data Processing
- Chapter 13 - Information Systems Auditing - I - SU 5
- Chapter 14 - Information Systems Auditing - II - SU 5
- Chapter 15 - Information Systems Auditing - III - SU 5
- Chapter 16 - Using Personal Computers in Auditing - SU 5

Part 5: Reporting
- Chapter 17 - Reports - 8.5, 9.10
- Chapter 18 - Audit Report Reviews and Replies - 3.12
- Chapter 19 - Reports to Executive Management and the Board - 3.12

Part 6: Administration
- Chapter 20 - Establishing the Auditing Activity - 9.7
- Chapter 21 - Selecting and Developing the Staff - 9.7
- Chapter 22 - Preparing Long-Range Schedules - 9.7
- Chapter 23 - Controlling Audit Projects - 9.4, 9.7
- Chapter 24 - Quality Assurance - 9.6, 9.7

Part 7: Other Matters Relating to Internal Auditing
- Chapter 25 - Principles of Management - 9.7, 9.11
- Chapter 26 - Environmental Auditing - 9.1
- Chapter 27 - Employee and Management Fraud - 2.4
- Chapter 28 - Dealing with People - 9.10
- Chapter 29 - Relationships with External Auditors - 3.13
- Chapter 30 - Relationships with Boards of Directors and Audit Committees - 9.10
- Chapter 31 - Standards for the Professional Practice of Internal Auditing and Code of Ethics - 9.2, 9.3

**Strawser and Strawser, *Auditing Theory and Practice*, Eighth Edition, Dame, 1999.**

Part I: The Auditing Environment
- Chapter 1 - The CPA and the Auditing Environment - 1.1-1.9
- Chapter 2 - The Code of Professional Conduct - 1.5-1.8, 9.12
- Chapter 3 - Auditors' Legal Liability - 1.9, 2.3, 2.4

Part II: The Audit Process
- Chapter 4 - Audit Planning - SU 2
- Chapter 5 - Internal Control and the Assessment of Control Risk - 3.1-3.5
- Chapter 6 - Substantive Testing and Control of Detection Risk - SU 4
- Chapter 7 - Introduction to Sampling and Attribute Sampling - 6.1-6.5
- Chapter 8 - Variables Estimation Sampling - 6.6
- Chapter 9 - Computer Controls and Audit Techniques - SU 5

Part III: Audit Procedures
- Chapter 10 - The Revenue Cycle - 3.6
- Chapter 11 - The Revenue Cycle: Substantive Tests - 4.1-4.3, 4.5
- Chapter 12 - The Purchases and Disbursements Cycle - 3.7
- Chapter 13 - The Purchases and Disbursements Cycle: Substantive Tests - 4.4, 4.5
- Chapter 14 - The Conversion Cycle - 4.6-4.11
- Chapter 15 - The Investing and Financing Cycle - 4.9

Part IV: Auditors' Communications
- Chapter 16 - Completing the Audit Examination - 4.12-4.17
- Chapter 17 - The Auditor's Report - SU 7
- Chapter 18 - Reporting: Other Information and Special Reports - 8.1-8.7

Part V: Other Types of Auditing
- Chapter 19 - Other Accountant Engagements and Reports - 1.11-1.15, 8.8-8.10
- Chapter 20 - Compliance, Internal, and Operational Auditing - 8.5, 8.8, 8.9, SU 9

**Whittington and Pany, *Principles of Auditing and Other Assurance Services*, Fourteenth Edition, McGraw-Hill, Inc., 2003.**

- Chapter 1 - The Role of the Public Accountant in the American Economy - 1.1
- Chapter 2 - Professional Standards - 1.2-1.4, 1.10
- Chapter 3 - Professional Ethics - 1.5-1.8, 9.12
- Chapter 4 - Legal Liability of CPAs - 1.9, 2.3, 2.4
- Chapter 5 - Audit Evidence and Documentation - 4.1
- Chapter 6 - Planning the Audit; Designing Audit Programs - 2.1-2.4
- Chapter 7 - Internal Control - 3.1-3.4
- Chapter 8 - Consideration of Internal Control in a Computer Environment - SU 5
- Chapter 9 - Audit Sampling - SU 6
- Chapter 10 - Cash and Financial Instruments - 3.6, 3.7, 3.9, 4.3-4.5, 4.8
- Chapter 11 - Accounts Receivable, Notes Receivable, and Revenue - 3.6, 4.3
- Chapter 12 - Inventories and Cost of Goods Sold - 3.10, 4.6
- Chapter 13 - Property, Plant, and Equipment: Depreciation and Depletion - 3.11, 4.7
- Chapter 14 - Accounts Payable and Other Liabilities - 3.7, 4.4
- Chapter 15 - Debt and Equity Capital - 4.9, 4.10, 4.13
- Chapter 16 - Auditing Operations and Completing the Audit - 3.12, 4.12-4.16
- Chapter 17 - Auditors' Reports - 1.4, SU 7, SU 8, 9.10
- Chapter 18 - Special Reports and Accounting and Review Services - 8.1, 8.4
- Chapter 19 - Other Assurance Services - 1.11-1.15, 8.2, 8.3, 8.5-8.7, 8.10
- Chapter 20 - Internal, Operational, and Compliance Auditing - 8.5, 8.8, 8.9, SU 9

# INDEX

**CPA**

**COMPLETE GLEIM CPA SYSTEM with REVIEW ONLINE**

All 4 parts, including books*, software, audio cds, Review Online, plus bonus book bag. ☐ $924.95

Also available by exam part @ $256.95 (does not include book bag).

*Fifth book: *CPA Review: A System for Success*

$________

**CMA/CFM**

**COMPLETE GLEIM CMA/CFM SYSTEM with ONLINE COURSE for the UNCHANGED EXAM**

Includes: books, software, audio cds, and Online Course, plus bonus book bag.

☐ CMA $681.95 ☐ CFM $681.95 ☐ CMA/CFM $855.95

Also available by exam part @ $198.95 (does not include book bag).

**COMPLETE GLEIM CMA SYSTEM with ONLINE COURSE for the "REORGANIZED" EXAM**

Includes: books, software, audio cds, and Online Course, plus bonus book bag.

☐ CMA $739.95 ☐ CMA/CFM $913.95

Also available by exam part @ $213.95 (does not include book bag).

$________

**CIA**

**COMPLETE GLEIM CIA SYSTEM with ONLINE COURSE**

Includes: books, software, audio cds, and Online Course, plus bonus book bag. ☐ $824.95

Also available by exam part @ $224.95 (does not include book bag).

**GLEIM CIA SET**

All 4 parts, including books, software, audio cds, plus bonus book bag. ☐ $483.80

Also available by exam part @ $120.95 (does not include book bag).

$________

**EA**

**GLEIM EA REVIEW SYSTEM**

Includes: books and software. ☐ $279.80

Also available by exam part @ $69.95 (does not include book bag).

$________

**EQE**

**"THE GLEIM SERIES" EXAM QUESTIONS AND EXPLANATIONS**

Includes: 5 books and EQE Test Prep software. ☐ $112.25

Also available by part @ $29.95.

**CPE**

**GLEIM CPE**

Includes book and service. ☐ Financial Acctg ☐ Auditing ☐ Federal Tax ☐ $200 each

For our Online CPE courses and course catalogue, please visit www.gleim.com/CPE

$________

Contact
**GLEIM PUBLICATIONS**
for further assistance:

**www.gleim.com**
**(800) 874-5346**
**sales@gleim.com**

**SUBTOTAL** $________

Complete your order on the next page

# GLEIM PUBLICATIONS, INC.

## P. O. Box 12848 Gainesville, FL 32604

TOLL FREE: (800) 874-5346
LOCAL: (352) 375-0772
FAX: (888) 375-6940 (toll free)
INTERNET: www.gleim.com
E-MAIL: sales@gleim.com

Customer service is available (Eastern Time):
8:00 a.m. - 7:00 p.m., Mon. - Fri.
9:00 a.m. - 2:00 p.m., Saturday
Please have your credit card ready,
or save time by ordering online!

**SUBTOTAL** (from previous page) $ ________
Add applicable sales tax for shipments within Florida. ________
Shipping (nonrefundable) 15.00
**TOTAL** $ ________

Fax or write for prices/instructions on shipments outside the 48 contiguous states, or simply order online.

NAME (please print) ________________________________

ADDRESS ________________________________ Apt. ________
(street address required for UPS)

CITY ________________________ STATE ________ ZIP ________

_____ MC/VISA/DISC _____ Check/M.O. Daytime Telephone ( ) ________________

Credit Card No. ________ - ________ - ________ - ________

Exp. ____ / ____ Signature ________________________________
Month / Year

E-mail address ________________________________

1. We process and ship orders daily, within one business day over 98.8% of the time. Call by 3:00 pm for same-day service.
2. Please PHOTOCOPY this order form for others.
3. No CODs. Orders from individuals must be prepaid.
4. Gleim Publications, Inc. guarantees the immediate refund of all resalable texts and unopened software and audios if returned within 30 days. Applies only to items purchased direct from Gleim Publications, Inc. Our shipping charge is nonrefundable.
5. Components of specially priced package deals are nonrefundable.

Prices subject to change without notice.

For updates and other important information, visit our website.

GLEIM KNOWLEDGE TRANSFER SYSTEMS®

**www.gleim.com**

Please forward your suggestions, corrections, and comments concerning typograph cal errors, etc., to **Irvin N. Gleim • c/o Gleim Publications, Inc. • P.O. Box 12848 • University Station • Gainesville, Florida • 32604.** Please include your name and address so we can properly thank you for your interest.

1. ______________________________

2. ______________________________

3. ______________________________

4. ______________________________

5. ______________________________

6. ______________________________

7. ______________________________

8. ______________________________

9. ______________________________

10. ______________________________

11. ______________________________

12. ______________________________

13. ______________________________

14. ______________________________

15. ______________________________

16. ______________________________

17. ______________________________

18. ______________________________

Remember, for superior service: Mail, e-mail, or fax questions about our books or software.
Telephone questions about orders, prices, shipments, or payments.

Name: ______________________________

Address: ______________________________

City/State/Zip: ______________________________

Telephone: Home: __________ Work: __________ Fax: __________

E-mail: ______________________________